T0305107

Harvard Studies in Business History XLI

Published with the support of the Harvard Business School
Edited by Alfred D. Chandler, Jr.
Isidor Straus Professor of Business History
Graduate School of Business Administration
George F. Baker Foundation
Harvard University

The History of Foreign Investment in the United States to 1914

Mira Wilkins

Harvard University Press

Cambridge, Massachusetts

London, England

1989

This book is printed on acid-free paper, and its binding materials
have been chosen for strength and durability.

Library of Congress Cataloging-in-Publication Data

Wilkins, Mira.
  The history of foreign investment in the United States to 1914 /
  Mira Wilkins.
    p.   cm.—(Harvard studies in business history ; 41)
  Bibliography: p.
  Includes index.
  ISBN 0-674-39666-9
  1. Investments, Foreign—United States—History—19th century.
  2. Investments, Foreign—United States—History—20th century.
  I. Title.   II. Series.
HG4910.W427   1989   88-19129
332.6'73'0973—dc19   CIP

Editor's Introduction

In the introduction to Mira Wilkins's *The Maturing of Multinational Enterprise: American Business Abroad from 1914 to 1970*, I emphasized that the book is "central to the understanding of the development of modern, large-scale enterprise and its changing role in the international economy." That book and its predecessor, *The Emergence of Multinational Enterprise: American Business Abroad from the Colonial Era to 1914*, have become the standard works on the history of American multinationals. This new book will certainly be the standard work on the history of foreign multinationals in the United States, and indeed on the history of all foreign investment in the United States. The book reviews the history of foreign direct investments made in American factories, sales offices, land, mines, and banking, from the founding of the Colonies until World War I; in addition, it tells the story of foreign portfolio investment, namely investments by foreigners that did not carry control, such as investments in securities of government bodies and of railroad and other companies.

From the Revolution until the last quarter of the nineteenth century, there was much more portfolio than direct foreign investment in the United States. Until 1875, portfolio investment was also much stronger in government than in corporate securities. Foreigners helped to finance the Revolution and then the early national government, including funding the Louisiana Purchase. Next came investments in state and city governments for internal improvements, such as canals, river navigation, and railroads. Foreign investors acquired U.S. federal government securities in the 1850s, 1860s, and early 1870s. There was a very large foreign loan to the Confederacy. Foreign investors were active buyers of state securities during Reconstruction. All this changed after the mid-1870s. Part of the reason lay in state government defaults. More important, once the massive expansion of American railroads took off after 1875, the amounts invested in private securities quickly outpaced those in public ones.

While foreign portfolio investment in the United States continued to exceed foreign direct investment, the latter became increasingly more significant. The new role of foreign direct investment reflected the speeding up after 1875 of a profound transformation in the economies of western Europe and the United States, from rural, agrarian, and commercial to urban and industrial. Just as the new American industrial enterprises began to move abroad in the late nineteenth century, so, too, did those of Britain, Germany, France, and some of the smaller nations of western Europe begin to invest in the United States, first in marketing establishments, then in factories and mines. The patterns of this direct investment reflected the strengths of the investing companies. The direct investments made by German managerial enterprises were more profitable than those made by personally run British companies. And those firms, mostly British ones, that made direct investments without first building up a viable enterprise at home almost always failed.

The data presented here on both direct and portfolio investment are rich in their breadth of coverage and depth of detail. The book provides new information on the changing ways of finance and the changing forms of financial institutions, on the transfer of technology and the rise and development of new industries, and on the birth of a wide variety of modern business practices and procedures.

The book does much more than just describe. It evaluates judiciously the impact of multifaceted investments on the countries whose citizens put their money into American government and corporate securities and whose businessmen and industrialists invested in facilities and personnel in the United States. It also considers the profound effect that investment had on the economic growth and wealth of the United States as a nation and on the different sectors and industries of its economy. The book looks into the ever-changing attitudes and relationships between those making investments and those using them. Such descriptions and analyses make this study one of the most important yet written on international enterprise and international investment. It will be of enormous value to historians and economists of many different schools and subdisciplines.

In addition, the history told here has relevance for today. From the beginning of its history to World War I the United States was a debtor nation, and from the Civil War until 1914 it was by far the largest debtor nation in the world. Then it became the world's largest creditor nation. Suddenly in the 1980s the country found itself back in the situation where it had been before 1914. Although the economic complexities facing the country and the foreign investors differ from those of the pre-1914 era, the long history of the nation as a debtor can provide significant clues and insights for policymakers not only in the United States but also in the creditor nations, particularly Japan.

Alfred D. Chandler, Jr.

Preface

This is the first book devoted exclusively to the history of foreign investment in America. It covers the years from the colonial era to 1914, when the country was a debtor in international accounts, owing more than it was owed. A second volume will turn to foreign investment after 1914. Once again, America in 1985 became a debtor nation in world accounts. Because of the country's international status, this work is not merely past history, but assumes a current interest.

The book has been very difficult to write because of the paradox of abundance and shortage: although vast quantities of relevant data are available, bearing witness to the subject's significance, I have nonetheless had to fill immense gaps. The writing of this work has been an exercise in discovery. I have had to put together pieces in a puzzle. My approach has been open minded, seeking out published and unpublished information, going to archives, calling on numerous specialists for aid, selecting and evaluating everything with the goal of deciphering and understanding a story that has never been fully told. When published materials have been available, I have used them. When they have been absent, I have gone in many cases to the primary sources. I began this study over a dozen years ago and finally feel reasonably confident that the contours of what I am describing and analyzing are correct and that for the first time readers will be able to obtain a complete picture of the path of foreign investment in the United States in the years before 1914.

I have confined my research to long-term, nonresident investment from abroad and its impact. I have excluded short-term commercial credits (unless they were transformed into long-term stakes), foreign holdings of U.S. treasury notes, and foreign bank deposits. I have considered both foreign portfolio and direct long-term investments. A foreign investment is a nonresident, out-of-country claim on American assets. With a foreign portfolio investment, the investor is engaged in finance—that is, in a loan or an equity investment where the recipient controls the use of the capital. By contrast, a foreign direct investment involves the investors in both ownership and control—or the potentials for control. A direct investment can be in securities or in real assets; it matters not. What characterizes a direct investment is the potential for management and control. Today's multinational enterprises make direct investments. My definitions are not unique; they correspond with those of the U.S. Department of Commerce. I have been concerned herein with the changing *level* over time of foreign portfolio and direct investments rather than with monitoring annual capital *flows*.

I began my research as a student of foreign direct investment and realized that I had to enlarge the canvas. In a systematic manner I have inquired the following of the period 1607 to 1914: How much investment in America came from abroad? How much was portfolio investment? How much was direct investment? In what nations did the foreign investors reside? To what extent did the capital come from foreign governments and to what extent from the private sector—from firms and individuals? How did such investors make American investments, and why? What were the information flows that help to explain the nature and pace of the investments? In what economic activities did foreign firms and individuals invest in the United States? How much investment went into government finance, and how much to the private sector? Which industries were most attractive to investors from abroad? In what cities and regions in America did foreign investors place their monies, and why? How much and what kind of influence did the foreign investors actually have once the investment was made? How were foreign investments managed? What were the reactions to the foreign investments? How did the answers to these questions alter over the years? Were there patterns? Where did foreign investments in America fit in the general worldwide international-investments panorama? Finally, and most important, how significant were the foreign investments in America's overall development?

The first part of this book reviews the years from 1607 to 1875. Each chapter covers the spectrum of foreign investments. Then, as the sheer quantity of such investments rose, I decided in the second part to divide my materials by industry: after an overview chapter (Chapter 5), I make these divisions for the years 1875–1914.

In the colonial era, direct investments from overseas predominated. From 1776 to 1914, although foreign portfolio investments exceeded direct investments, the latter became substantial after 1875 and had a major impact (accordingly, I have devoted special attention to foreign direct investments in the chapters covering the years 1875–1914). Virtually all investment from overseas in the colonial era (except some by the early chartered companies) was in the private sector. From 1776 to 1875, public sector foreign borrowings (federal, state, and local) seem to have been preeminent. From 1875 to 1914, the private sector in America once more was the principal place for both portfolio and direct investments from abroad. These and other shifts in the patterns of foreign investment will emerge in this volume.

The results of my research should demonstrate conclusively that American economic historians must consider foreign investments (that is, obligations to out-of-country investors) and that foreign direct investments, which have often been shortchanged in the literature of U.S. economic history, cannot be neglected. My research reveals facets of U.S. (and other nations') economic history that are little known; much will also be familiar, but viewed now in a new context.

I hope the reader will enjoy this volume and obtain from it an overall, intelligible grasp of the extent and significance of foreign investment in the pre–World War I American economy. The process of unraveling the story and accumulating the evidence has ultimately been satisfying. The book should interest specialists in U.S., British, and continental European economic and business history. Indeed, I trust that students of modern economic and business history, economic development, international finance, and multinational corporations, and, more generally, economists, historians, and political scientists, as well as others concerned with the functioning of the world economy, will find herein much that is new, useful, and thought provoking.

Today, with the universal recognition of America's deep involvement in the world economy, with international debt and the role of multinational enterprise widely discussed, and with foreign portfolio and direct investments in the United States mounting rapidly, this study of America's past experience as a debtor nation—and certainly in 1875–1914 the world's largest debtor nation—not only fills a lacuna in the academic literature but should also be both topical and pertinent.

Mira Wilkins

Acknowledgments

I am happy to have had the help and assistance of many wonderful friends, without whom this book would have been impossible. Among these, Alfred D. Chandler, Jr., stands out. At each stage he encouraged the book's development by offering an intellectual challenge, reading the typescript with care and attention, permitting me to benefit from his work in progress, and directing me to materials that I had neglected. Lou Wells read the first rendition of the manuscript and made extremely perceptive comments; he was a splendid critic. Likewise, I want to thank John Dunning for his wise advice and support. He gave me access to his files on British manufacturing companies in America, and I have learned from his formidable knowledge of multinational enterprise. I truly appreciated his invitation to the University of Reading, where, in a lecture, I tested before a perceptive audience some preliminary findings. My studies of foreign direct investment have long been greatly influenced by the work of Ray Vernon, to whom I owe a profound debt.

My appreciation is extended to the John Simon Guggenheim Foundation, which gave me funds for a wonderful sabbatical year devoted to searches of foreign archives. Likewise, the Florida International University Foundation contributed most welcome monies for my research efforts.

Over the years I have called on many researchers for aid. Some were old friends (or became good, new friends); others were men whose scholarship I admired but whom I never met. These individuals gave advice generously. In England, Les Hannah at the Business History Unit, London School of Economics, provided me an office and shared his insights into the history of British business. Also in England, Geoff Jones has broken new ground on the history of British multinationals, and his work has been immensely useful to me. Vince Carosso, Larry McFarlane, and Ed Perkins read versions of some chapters in this volume, offering keen insights in their areas of expertise. I particularly wish to thank the following scholars for their assistance: Tetsuo Abo, Bernard Alford, Robert Aliber, Franklin Brooks, Stuart Bruchey, Sir Alec Cairncross, Rondo Cameron, Fred Carstensen, Mark Casson, Pierre Cayez, Stanley Chapman, Roy Church, Tony Corley, Phil Cottrell, Don Davis, Richard Davis, Patrick Fridenson, Gene Gressley, Charles Harvey, Jean-François Hennart, Peter Hertner, René Higonnet, Anthony Howe, J. B. K. Hunter, David Jeremy, Charles Jones, Charles Kindleberger, Frank King, Jim Laux, Maurice Lévy-Leboyer, Jonathan Liebenau, Doniver Lund, Ra Lundström, Donald Marchand, Albro Martin, John McKay, Richard Morris, Keiichiro Nakagawa, Irene Neu, Steve Nicholas, Christopher Platt, Bill Reader, Robert V. Roosa, Ruth Roosa, S. B. Saul, Harm Schröter, Barry Supple, Alastair Sweeney, Dick Sylla, Alice Teichova, Patricia Thane, Richard Tilly, Geoffrey Tweedale, Hiroaki Yamazaki, Stephen Young, Tsunehiko Yui, and Charles Wilson. In addition, from a distance my work has been greatly influenced by that of Kenneth Arrow, Michael Edelstein, Douglass C. North, and Oliver E. Williamson. My colleagues at Florida International University, including Robert Cruz, Amitava Dutt, Panos Liossatos, Jim Mau, James Melton, Howard Rock, Jorge Salazar-Carrillo, Carlos Sevilla, Phil Shepherd, and Maria Willumsen, have in various ways advanced this endeavor.

My debts to numerous librarians and archivists are immense. I especially want to thank Ginny Wheeler and Linda Norvesh, in the Interlibrary Loan Department, and Hortensia Rodriguez, the Government Documents librarian, at Florida International University Library. Without Interlibrary Loan this book could never have been written. Ginny and Linda were extraordinarily patient with my seemingly endless flood of requests and persistent in locating the most obscure books, articles, and microfilms.

My thanks also go to Yvonne Clarke, Gershon Knight, and Simone Mace at the Rothschild Archive in London and John Orbell at Baring's; my good friend Marianne Burge, a partner in Price Waterhouse in New York, opened doors for me, and I was privileged to use the Price Waterhouse, London, archival records. John Barrett in that firm's archives was most helpful. A. F. Peters at Shell, in London, allowed me access to Shell records. J. D. Keir of Unilever permitted me to delve into that firm's extensive archives; Maureen Staniforth was of assistance there. Russell Williams provided data on Eberhard Faber. John Steinway sent materials from the Steinway papers, while

Sir Titus Salt's grandson, Denys Salt, offered information on his grandfather's U.S. activities. Likewise, B. F. Howard (Lord Strathcona's great-grandson) made fine suggestions. Richmond Williams sent me material from the Du Pont archives. Numerous other companies and individuals gave me access to archives and unpublished company histories; I am very appreciative. The best archives in the world are the public archives in Ottawa, open twenty-four hours a day, seven days a week—a researcher's paradise.

I uncovered invaluable materials on foreign manufacturers in America in town libraries. I appreciate the aid of town librarians in Bay City, Michigan; Fulton, New York; Pawtucket, Rhode Island; and Milltown, New Jersey. These towns hosted subsidiaries of United Alkali, Nestlé, J. & P. Coats, and Michelin.

My sincere thanks go to Karen Hill and Patti Clifford, who for more than three years remained cheerful as they deciphered my handwriting, toiled over my manuscript, and tolerated my incessant revisions. Karen and Patti took immense pride in their work. At the penultimate stages, however, they were replaced by Sandie Bergeson, who has done just splendidly. The word-processing skill of each of these women was indispensable.

Last, and most important, putting up with my moods, my travels, and my frequent overcommitment to this book, has been my husband, George Simmons. He has lived with this creation from its inception—that is, for more than a dozen years. Without his moral support and his confidence in me, this manuscript could never have been completed. I have deeply cherished his role in the emergence of this tome.

Contents

Contents

Tables

Figures

PART I

A Developing Country: 1607–1874

1.

The Earliest Investments:
1607–1776

The first of the long-term overseas investments in what became the United States were made in the seventeenth century by large chartered trading companies, but by the mid-eighteenth century the age of these corporations was past; investments in trade were by merchant houses. In the colonial era America's shipping was dominated by nonresident owners, or alternatively by Britishers temporarily living in this country. Land was, likewise, an important sector for nonresident investments from abroad. Also attractive to overseas capital was mining and manufacturing—principally iron related. All the investments (1607–1776) were direct ones, with overseas owners expecting to exercise control over their assets in America. With the exception of the chartered companies (which, along with their trading and other functions, had a political role), investment from abroad went into private rather than "public" sector endeavors. This chapter surveys the changing investments from abroad during colonial times and attempts, at the end, to summarize the extent of such investments in 1776, on the eve of the Declaration of Independence.[1]

The Virginia Company

On April 10, 1606, two companies were organized in London and chartered by King James I. One was the London Company, soon to be called the Virginia Company, which established the first permanent English settlement in America, in Jamestown, Virginia. The other was the Plymouth Company. British stockholders in these companies hoped their enterprises would discover gold and silver mines and obtain profitable trade. Each company planned to start colonies and saw in colonization a method by which riches would come from the new world to the old. The Spaniards had found wealth across the Atlantic; why not the British? The charter to the two companies stipulated that one-fifth of all gold and silver extracted in America was to be reserved for the Crown.[2]

Before 1606 the British Crown had chartered the great trading firms: the Muscovy Company (1555), the Eastland Company (1579), the Levant Company (1592), and the East India Company (1600). Each obtained exclusive trading privileges in a defined region. The London and Plymouth companies of 1606 had similar exclusive rights.[3]

The London Company was owned by London "knights, gentlemen, merchants, and other adventurers,"[4] who expected a return on their investment. Initially it was administered by a Royal Council, appointed by the King. Its "employees" (some 145 men), under the direction of Captain Christopher Newport, left England on December 20, 1606, sailing on ships leased from the Muscovy Company. On May 24, 1607, the vessels landed in Virginia, at a site the settlers named Jamestown. For several years Jamestown was a "fortified trading post." No gold or silver was found.[5]

From 1607 to its demise in 1623, the Virginia Company was reorganized several times.[6] From 1609 to 1619 it was headed by Sir Thomas Smith, who resided in London. Smith was probably the leading British businessman of his time and an active participant in the Muscovy, the Levant, and the East India companies.[7] As treasurer (that is, a chief officer) of the Virginia Company, he presided over a London Council that chose and gave instructions to the "Governor" of the colony, who lived in Virginia.

In 1612 the Crown broadened the Virginia Company's charter. A "Court" made up of shareholders was established to manage corporate affairs.[8] On instructions from London, the colonists in Jamestown concentrated on agriculture to sustain the Virginia Company's existence and, more important, to provide a source of revenue for what was after all a profit-seeking venture. It has been suggested that the early trading companies differed from modern multinational enterprises in that they did not produce the goods they traded, and therefore their circulating capital far exceeded their fixed capital. This distinction is, however, inappropriate when we consider the Virginia Company, for its colony did produce.[9] Moreover, there is evidence that its fixed capital after 1613 began to exceed circulating capital (that is, capital invested in commodities intended for sale).

The Virginia Company did not find a suitable revenue-producing crop until 1613, when John Rolfe imported tobacco seed from the West Indies, crossed it with local Indian-grown tobacco, and exported the output. At this point certain wealthy London stockholders in the

Virginia Company formed the "Magazine."[10] Headquartered in England, this joint-stock company sold food, clothing, and provisions to the colonists; in return, it received from the Virginia Company a monopoly of selling Virginia tobacco in England. The Virginia Company was the principal "Adventurer" (stockholder) in the Magazine. The Magazine sent its first ships to Virginia in 1616.[11]

The Magazine was not the only subsidiary company established with specified functions relating to the new colony. Subordinate joint-stock societies proliferated in England in 1617–1619 to settle particular "Plantations." Each provided its own financial and other resources and obtained a "patent" from the Virginia Company; each directed its new world enterprise from England; each was a miniature of the Virginia Company (there appears to have been some interlocking stock ownership).

By 1618 the Magazine was under attack in London and in Virginia for its exorbitant prices, and the Virginia Company limited the Magazine's profit on sales to 25 percent! To ensure enforcement, the Court in London instructed the Governor of the Virginia Company to receive and to check invoices covering all sales of the Magazine. The Magazine's monopoly of the tobacco trade was, however, soon compromised by the new joint-stock societies that were permitted by the Virginia Company to send their crop directly to their own offices in England, although each could deal with the Magazine if it wished.[12]

By 1619 some British stockholders in the Virginia Company were accusing the Magazine of siphoning off funds that should legitimately have been the Virginia Company's. Almost nothing remained of an estimated £66,666 to £80,000 invested in the Virginia Company.[13] Sir Thomas Smith, who participated in the Magazine (among his many interests), was forced from the leadership of the Virginia Company because of "apparent misprosperinge of the plantation, and the foulness of the Accounts here [in London]."[14] The Court elected Sir Edwin Sandys as treasurer of the Virginia Company.[15] The Magazine was dissolved in January 1620, and trade was freed.[16] Although a new Magazine was organized in 1620, it lacked the importance of its predecessor and seems to have had no monopoly privileges.

Under Sir Edwin Sandys' management, the Virginia Colony elected a legislative assembly, attracted new settlers, and tried to become self-sufficient in food. Sir Edwin Sandys raised additional money. The Virginia Company spent £5,000 to establish an iron industry on the James River.[17] In 1621, despite King James I's dislike of tobacco, the Virginia Company convinced the British Parliament not to prohibit tobacco imports into Britain, lest the colony (and, of course, the company) be ruined.[18]

Sir Edwin Sandys' ambitious plans for the colony were thwarted in 1622, when Indians killed one-third of the settlers and destroyed the iron works. By 1622 the Virginia Company was bankrupt: many of its shareholders refused to pay installments due on their stock subscriptions, and profits were nonexistent. The company was, moreover, torn asunder with internal management dissension. The King in 1622 barred the entry of Spanish tobacco into England to aid the Virginia Colony and the Virginia Company. The assistance was inadequate.[19] In 1623 the Crown took over the company (the modern-day equivalent of a receivership).

James I directed the Attorney General to enter suit against the Virginia Company, declaring that its objects had not been fulfilled. The Attorney General accused the company of spreading false information about the colony through letters, books, and "cozening ballads" and, as a consequence, of having led hundreds of the King's subjects to their death. In 1624 the Virginia Company was dissolved; Virginia became a Crown colony.[20]

The Virginia Company—the first foreign direct investment in America* and the country's first business enterprise—was in existence eighteen years. One historian, William Stith, writing in 1747, estimates that private individuals invested over £100,000.[21] Another, Charles Andrews, explains the Virginia Company's demise as

due to its lack of success as a colonizing and profit-making agency. Unlike its models, the older joint-stock companies, which found their markets and sources in the eastern world already prepared and immediately available for profit, the Virginia Company had first to create its colony in America before any adequate profit from it could be expected. It fell in its effort to accomplish this result and lost its Charter before it could bring into existence a working agricultural and industrial community such as it needed in order to return to its subscribers any earnings on their investments.[22]

The Plymouth Company and Its Successors

In 1606, at the same time the London (the Virginia) Company was formed, merchants from Plymouth, Bristol, and Exeter, England, organized its twin, the Plymouth Company (see Figure 1.1), which made a futile attempt to establish a trading post at Sagadahoc at the mouth of the Kennebec River in 1607; it employed Captain John Smith of the Virginia Company to explore the American coast. It did little else and by 1620 was moribund. While plans were made to reorganize

---

* Henceforth I will use the word *America* to refer to the territory that became the United States.

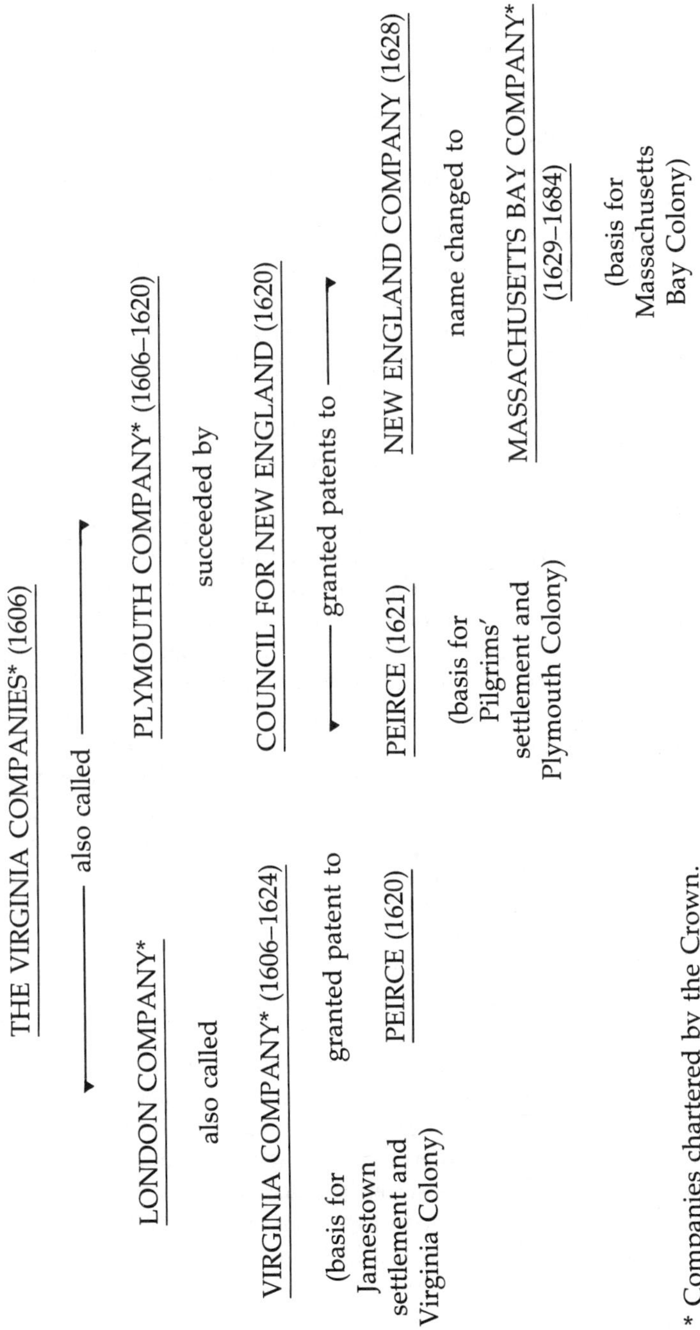

THE VIRGINIA COMPANIES* (1606)

———— also called ————▶

LONDON COMPANY*

also called

VIRGINIA COMPANY* (1606–1624)

granted patent to

PEIRCE (1620)

(basis for Jamestown settlement and Virginia Colony)

PLYMOUTH COMPANY* (1606–1620)

succeeded by

COUNCIL FOR NEW ENGLAND (1620)

———— granted patents to ————▶

PEIRCE (1621)

(basis for Pilgrims' settlement and Plymouth Colony)

NEW ENGLAND COMPANY (1628)

name changed to

MASSACHUSETTS BAY COMPANY* (1629–1684)

(basis for Massachusetts Bay Colony)

* Companies chartered by the Crown.

Figure 1.1. The early companies.

this company under a new charter, the Pilgrims joined with British stockholders in an unincorporated joint-stock venture, obtaining for "John Peirce and his Associates" a patent from the Virginia Company. The Pilgrims settled in a town they named Plymouth, in New England. In 1621 Peirce got a second patent, this one from the successor to the Plymouth Company, the newly established Council for New England.[23] This Peirce patent became the basis of the Pilgrims' rights to settle and to found the Plymouth Colony.

The British partners of the Pilgrims lost money, obtaining no return on their investment that had provided the immigrants with ships and supplies. In 1626 the Pilgrims agreed to buy out the British shareholders for £1,800, to be paid at the rate of £200 a year for nine years. Management of the unincorporated company was no longer split between England and America, having shifted to the new world. Not until 1648 did the Pilgrims finally pay off the £1,800. The business had become Americanized.[24]

Meanwhile, in 1628 the Council for New England granted a patent to the New England Company, another unincorporated joint-stock company, which had mobilized £2,915 from ninety British shareholders. The New England Company sent ships, men, provisions, and tools to settlers who, in 1627, had gone to what became Salem, Massachusetts, to fish and to trade with the Indians and had founded a prosperous, deeply religious community. On March 4, 1629, the Crown granted a charter that changed the New England Company into the Massachusetts Bay Company.[25] Some of the same British stockholders who had been partners with the Pilgrims invested in this company. All the stockholders were Puritans, and wealthy. The Massachusetts Bay Company was an incorporated trading company, established to inaugurate a profit-making, but also a religious, colony. It was anticipated that the corporate headquarters of the Massachusetts Bay Company would remain in England, as had been the case with all the earlier *chartered* companies, from the East India Company to the Virginia Company. But in August 1629, when many of its founders decided to migrate to America, they wished to carry with them the corporate charter, and the stockholders voted for the transfer of the headquarters from London to Boston. In October 1629 they elected John Winthrop Governor. Like the Pilgrims, the Puritans transferred their governance across the Atlantic.

To direct the commercial side of the Massachusetts Bay Company, a subordinate firm was organized in London in December 1629—to traffic in the furs and other commodities from Massachusetts. Little is known of this venture, except that it continued to do business at least until 1638. It did not have a monopoly of trade, and soon the private

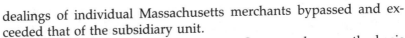

dealings of individual Massachusetts merchants bypassed and exceeded that of the subsidiary unit.

The charter of the Massachusetts Bay Company became the basis for the establishment of a self-governing colony in America, and the company itself became a thoroughly political organization. On July 23, 1637, Charles I decided to take the government of the colony into his own hands, as his father, James I, had done thirteen years before with the Virginia Colony. Governor John Winthrop responded on behalf of the Massachusetts General Court, refusing to return the charter, that is, to relinquish sovereignty.

The British Civil War intervened. By 1652 the Massachusetts Bay Company had been transformed into an independent Commonwealth. In 1691 Massachusetts was in the hands of the King—as a royal province. That year, Massachusetts annexed the Plymouth Colony. By then all overseas direct investment aspects of the Massachusetts Bay Company had long ceased to exist; no shareholders in Britain expected a return on investment.[26]

Dutch and Swedish Chartered Companies

Private Dutch and Swedish investors also used trading companies as agencies of trade and colonization in what became the original thirteen colonies. In the mid-seventeenth century, Amsterdam was the commercial center of the world, an entrepôt where goods from foreign lands were received, warehoused, and then reshipped. The historian Carlo Cipolla has described the Dutch economy of that era as "the most dynamic, the best developed, and the most competitive in Europe."[27] In 1602 the Dutch East India Company had been organized to trade in the East. In 1621 the Dutch West India Company was formed. At origin, each of these Dutch companies had capital far in excess of any of its British counterparts.[28] These were private trading enterprises, undertaking business on behalf of private Dutch merchants. Even before the formation of the Dutch West India Company, Dutch traders had bought furs from North American Indians, and in 1615 one firm, the New Netherland Company, had established a trading post at Fort Nassau, in what is now upstate New York.[29]

More than the seventeenth-century British trading companies, the Dutch West India Company had from its start a political mandate on behalf of the Sovereign; the Dutch government saw the company as a strategic force in challenging Spain's new world trade and granted the Dutch West India Company a monopoly of Dutch commerce with North and South America and West Africa. In these regions the company was permitted to engage in war, to maintain naval and military forces, and to undertake administrative functions. Whereas the British trading companies were totally privately financed, the Dutch state contributed a million of the over 7 million guilders of the capital of the Dutch West India Company, and the Dutch government encouraged wary Dutch merchants to provide the balance.[30] The Dutch state had a representative on the central coordinating body of the company.[31] Nonetheless, as in the case of the British trading companies, the private individuals participating did seek profit.

In 1624 the Dutch West India Company opened a trading post at Fort Orange (now Albany, New York) and two years later one at New Amsterdam (now New York City). It took over the earlier Dutch outpost at Fort Nassau, "a cannon shot away" from Fort Orange. These three "trading posts" were "New Netherland" in 1626. New Netherland was the only territory within the limits of the Dutch West India Company's charter outside the influence of the Spanish Crown.[32]

Initially the Dutch West India Company did not intend to colonize New Netherland; rather, it planned only enough agriculture to sustain its employees, who took part in the fur trade.[33] Several of the shareholders, including Kiliaen Van Rensselaer, an Amsterdam jeweler, persuaded the company in 1629 to issue a "Charter of Privileges to Patroons." A "patroon" would bring fifty persons to New Netherland and, in exchange, receive from the company land with fifteen miles of river frontage, fishing and hunting rights, and a limited role in the fur trade. Trade in fur was allowed only "where the [Dutch West India] Company has no agent." All traded fur was subject to an export duty—payable to the company—of one guilder for each beaver or otter pelt. The patroon obtained the right to tithes from his tenants and rights over grinding grain. The Dutch West India Company had a monopoly of the overseas carrying trade of the patroonships (all exports and imports were carried on company ships); it also had the potential for taxing the patroons. Patroonships were granted along the Hudson and Delaware rivers; the earliest ones were established by men already associated with the Dutch West India Company. Of the seven actually created, only Van Rensselaer's proved successful. In 1638–39, the Dutch West India Company opened trade to and from New Netherland to all inhabitants of the home country, that is, the United Province, but duties had to be paid to the company and transatlantic shipments still had to be made on company ships (or on private ships, with a company supercargo on board).[34]

In 1638 the Swedish West India Company set up Fort Christina in "New Sweden" (where Wilmington, Delaware, is today). The Swedish company transported to America about 200 to 300 Swedes and

Finns, who carried across the Atlantic the idea of the log cabin. Swedish traders—desirous of exclusive trade—banned employees of the Dutch West India Company from the Delaware Bay. In response, Peter Stuyvesant, the Governor of the Dutch West India Company in New Netherland, invaded and in 1655 annexed New Sweden.[35]

The Dutch West India Company's presence persisted barely nine more years. In August 1664 Richard Nicholls, representing the Duke of York and British King Charles II, sailed into the harbor at the mouth of the Hudson. Stuyvesant surrendered. By the end of October 1664, the English had control over the key forts in New Netherland and renamed the formerly Dutch province New York (New Amsterdam became New York City; Fort Orange became Albany).

Meanwhile, by 1628 the Dutch West India Company had established a handful of outposts in Guiana (in South America) and in 1634 had captured from Spain the islands of Curaçao, Aruba, and Bonaire off the coast of Venezuela. From 1637 to 1645, the company had sizable interests in Brazil. It maintained slave-trading posts on the west coast of Africa. But by 1674 the Dutch West India Company was bankrupt; that year a new company replaced it, which in turn was dissolved in 1730.

The French Chartered Company

In 1712 the French Crown granted Antoine Crozat a fifteen-year monopoly of Louisiana trade; in exchange this Frenchman was required to settle the region. Prior to this, individual French merchants in the seventeenth century had traded in North America. By the 1670s Robert Cavalier de La Salle had established French trading posts on the Illinois River and along the Mississippi to the Ohio River; in 1682, having reached the mouth of the Mississippi, La Salle claimed the Louisiana area for France. Crozat held the first monopoly in this trade granted by the French Crown. According to the historian W. J. Eccles, "Crozat concerned himself only in reaping swift and substantial profits with minimum investment"; yet by 1717 his losses proved more than his gain, and Crozat sold his franchise to John Law, who was adviser to the Regent, the duc d'Orléans (the latter virtually served as King during the minority of Louis XV). Law organized the famous Company of the West, commonly known as the Mississippi Company.

The Mississippi Company acquired from Crozat exclusive rights to trade with Louisiana, to mine there, and to settle the region. In 1718 it received from the French Crown a marketing monopoly for Canadian beaver. It founded New Orleans that year. The Mississippi Company's shares sold well in France, and flush with monies, its sponsors purchased the French tobacco monopoly (1718); in 1719 they changed the company's name to Compagnie des Indes, acquiring in the process five huge French trading firms with worldwide business.

In January 1720 John Law became the French Finance Minister; he merged the French government bank (opened in 1716 and modeled after the Bank of England) with his Compagnie des Indes. The price of the stock of the Compagnie des Indes soared as speculators rushed to buy the shares, until in July 1720 the bubble burst. In December John Law fled France into exile. The activities of the Companie des Indes in Louisiana, nonetheless, remained under its governance until 1731, when the territory reverted to the French Crown. Thereafter, French merchants in this region were independent of any giant trading company.[36]

The Chartered Companies' Investments

The British, Dutch, Swedish, and French trading companies are all examples of early foreign direct investment in America. The investments carried with them management and control. They were relatively large-scale businesses. Each had, at origin, monopoly privileges. All were privately owned (only the Dutch West India Company had any government equity participation). Each, however, was expected to serve a public purpose, providing the Crown with revenues and extending national influence. In each case profitable trade was anticipated.

These companies' American investments illustrate several important themes. Foreign enterprise in America:

1. Did not always achieve its goals (the Virginia Company did not find gold or silver);

2. Did not always prove profitable (neither the Virginia Company nor the Plymouth Company was profitable; nor was the Dutch West India Company from New Netherland;[37] there is no evidence the Swedish West India Company was profitable; the Compagnie des Indes never made profits in Louisiana);

3. Did not always have a long history (the Plymouth Company failed in its first effort to establish a trading post; the Swedish West India Company lasted only seventeen years in America; the Virginia Company existed for eighteen years);

4. Often became "domesticated," taking on a different form.

The last point requires special attention, for the reader will see its frequent repetition. In many cases businesses crossed the Atlantic and stayed, severing their managerial, financial, technological, and other cords with companies in the former mother nation. America as host to the overseas enterprise became a home country: nonresidents became resident investors. The "headquarters" was transferred over the water and established in America. The timing of this "domestication" process would vary. The exact point when domestication occurred is, on occasion, imprecise. The phenomenon is beyond dispute.

Thus the Virginia and Massachusetts companies brought British business to America, left enduring settlements, and had a profound impact on the course of American history; yet, at a certain point, they ceased to represent investment from abroad. The "foreign" became "domestic." In time the successors of these firms owed allegiance not to companies headquartered abroad nor to individual overseas owners, who contemplated private profit, but rather, as colonies, to the Crown. The original private, economic rationale had been transformed in these cases into a political association. The Swedish West India Company did not create a long-lasting colony, but it did introduce a technology of log construction in America that proved appropriate in a timber-rich land. The French community in Louisiana survived the end of the Compagnie des Indes' sovereignty; Frenchmen became residents.

While the process of business headquarters' crossing the Atlantic was similar to "domestication" of other overseas investments that occurred in subsequent years, distinctive about these early stakes was that the trading companies—in the British and French cases—became the foundation for the extension of European sovereignty to the new world; what followed the trading company was political authority from abroad. The Compagnie des Indes, whose business activities persisted to 1731, was the last of this set of chartered companies in America. Later, in other parts of the world—in India and Africa, for example—the path of trading companies' setting the stage for the extension of political sovereignty would be repeated.

The Merchant Investor

After the heyday of the large chartered companies in America (and while some still remained), individuals and family trading houses set up outposts in this country and developed sizable businesses. These had no monopoly privileges and no charter from the Monarch. Overseas trade continued of paramount importance to the economic life in the new world. In 1776 Adam Smith, in his *Wealth of Nations*, reported:

The greater part both of the exportation and coasting trade of America is carried on by the capitals of merchants who reside in Great Britain. Even the stores and warehouses from which goods are retailed in some provinces, particularly in Virginia and Maryland, belong many of them to merchants who reside in the mother country, and afford one of the few instances of the retail trade of a society being carried on by the capitals of those who are not resident members of it.

Outside New England a high percentage of the vessels that traveled between American colonial and British ports in the eighteenth century were owned by Britishers, who either resided in Great Britain or were temporarily resident in the colonies. Table 1.1 reflects these ownership relations. The reader should add the numbers in the two columns headed "Great Britain" and "British merchants temporarily resident in colonies" to determine overseas ownership percentages. Presumably, most of the British shipowners were also engaged in trade. Although these figures would suggest that the trade of North Carolina, South Carolina, and Georgia was as much dominated from abroad as that from Virginia and Maryland, the *size* of that trade was substantially smaller.

With the movement of settlement into the interior of Virginia and Maryland in the eighteenth century, according to the economic historian Stuart Bruchey, "there arose a method of direct purchase of the tobacco by resident representatives of English or Scottish firms who established warehouses at convenient locations or dealt with planters

Table 1.1. Ownership of vessels clearing American colonial ports, trading between British and American colonial ports, 1770 (in percentages)

| Colonies from which vessel cleared | Residence of vessel's owners | | | |
	Great Britain	British merchants temporarily resident in colonies	American residents	Total
N. Carolina, S. Carolina, and Georgia	62.5	25.0	12.5	100
Virginia and Maryland	75.0	12.5	12.5	100
New York	37.5	37.5	25.0	100
Pennsylvania	25.0	37.5	37.5	100
New England	12.5	12.5	75.0	100

Source: John J. McCusker and Russell R. Menard, *The Economy of British America, 1607–1789* (Chapel Hill: University of North Carolina Press, 1985), p. 192.

at their wharves." Tobacco planters in Virginia and Maryland relied on the British merchants for shipping, insurance, and final sale of tobacco. Most of the great merchants who handled Charleston's overseas trade in the eighteenth century were Englishmen or Scots.

Virginia planters, in particular, ordered goods from London and paid with IOU notes. The historian Allan Nevins later wrote that they "let their debts run up to ruinous sums." Nevins continued, "Many debts had become hereditary from father to son, so that as Jefferson (himself a debtor) expressed it, 'the planters were a species of property annexed to certain mercantile houses in London.' " An important Glasgow (Scotland) mercantile firm—John Glassford and Co.—formed several partnerships and established a chain of stores in Virginia and Maryland, with a supervisory office in Norfolk, Virginia. By 1774 the Scottish interests of William Cunninghame and his partners operated seven stores in Maryland and fourteen in Virginia. Another Scottish house, Spiers and French & Co., also had a number of stores. The stores were designed principally to purchase tobacco, but they also retailed imported goods from Europe and from the West Indies. Cunninghame participated in several interrelated partnerships with some partners resident in Virginia and Maryland. Goods were shipped on the firms' account and at their risk. As of 1776 the Cunninghame interests claimed an investment of £135,563, of which £95,200 was outstanding debts owed the firms. All these Scottish businesses were managed from abroad.

Jefferson estimated that the debts of Virginians to the British at the end of the Revolution (debts incurred before the war) were in the range of 10 million to 15 million dollars. He believed that the debts of Virginians to British trading houses were almost as large as those of all other Americans combined (and added, to show the dimensions of the indebtedness, that the total amount equaled twenty to thirty times as much as all the money in circulation in Virginia in 1786)! Since the trade obligations had been carried from father to son, they had in effect become long-term investments by British merchants in America.[38]

Dutch traders, although not as significant as those from Britain, also had interests in colonial America. The New York merchants Charles Crommelin (in the late seventeenth century) and Jacob Le Roy (in the eighteenth century), for example, had close associations with Dutch houses. Despite British colonial restrictions, these firms flourished. French traders increased their business in eighteenth-century Louisiana. When, in November 1762, the French Crown ceded Louisiana to Spain, French merchants were well established in the region. Under Spanish rule they maintained their commerce. In

1764 French traders founded St. Louis on the west bank of the Mississippi.[39] In short, by the time of the American Revolution, traders from Europe in this country, like their many American counterparts, were individuals and family houses, not large corporations.[40] British capital was preeminent in shipping. By 1776 the amount of trade was greater than in earlier times.

Land

Overseas land holdings before independence were sizable. Many had involved no capital flows to America. Nonetheless, the numerous land grants from British monarchs were long-term investments in that they represented nonresident, out-of-country claims on American assets. Thus, for example, Sir George Carteret and Lord John Berkeley had obtained land that constituted the Province of New Jersey. Lord Baltimore received the proprietorship of Maryland. The historian Samuel Eliot Morison tells us that "few lords [sic] proprietors ever visited Maryland, but the entire line derived a handsome revenue from the Province." The Penn family were proprietors in Pennsylvania up to the Revolution.[41]

Many Britishers were land speculators who never visted the colonies. Dr. Daniel Cox, in the late seventeenth century, for instance, traded in American land. He was represented on this side of the Atlantic by a "deputy" and then later (after 1701–02) by his son, who did settle. In one transaction (1692), Cox sold land in New Jersey for £9,800 to a group of forty-eight investors, mainly London merchants. Edwin Perkins has suggested that in the seventeenth century, when British shippers/merchants received "headrights"—that is, the basis for establishing a claim on land in exchange for immigrants brought to America—logically this would have put land into nonresident British hands (without capital flows). Professor Russell R. Menard writes me, however, that the shippers typically sold these headrights to residents rather than using them to establish a claim to land. I found no indication that this process was significant as a genesis for the existing nonresident ownership of land at the time of the Revolution.[42]

Representatives of the British Crown, in America for temporary stays, frequently did acquire land—especially after the middle of the eighteenth century, as the population in the colonies grew and as land values seemed bound to increase. Thus John Earl of Dunmore, when Governor of New York in 1769 and of Virginia from 1770 to 1776, obtained vast acreage in both colonies, along with slaves, buildings, a grist mill, horses, hogs, sheep, and cattle. He had what he called a "Palace" at Williamsburg, yet he had no intention of settling (that is, of remaining) in America. Other British governors who obtained large land holdings included Sir James Wright (Governor of Georgia) and Thomas Boone (Governor of New Jersey and then of South Carolina). Boone returned to England in 1764, retaining in South Carolina several rice plantations, with Negroes, cattle, horses, and so forth; an agent in the colony administered his properties.[43] In North Carolina, James Iredell arrived in 1768 to serve as "deputy for his principal London patron, who owned large tracts of North Carolina land." With sizable nonresident British ownership in that colony, its legislature in 1773 clarified that North Carolina property of persons who had never resided in the colony was nonetheless still attachable for debt.[44]

The long roster of Englishmen who owned American lands in the colonial period included Lord Eglington, Lord Dartmouth, Lord Holland, Lord Stirling, Lord Egmont, Lord Adam Gordon, Lord Temple, Charles Townshend, George Grenville, Thomas Pitt, and Sir Jeffrey Amherst.[45] The Duke of Bedford was offered, for instance, a share in the Ohio Company (a land-holding company) for his assistance in London in enlarging the size of the company's land grant.[46] Peter Hasenclever, whose name the reader will encounter in relation to other investments in the colonies, made a number of land purchases in America, generally in association with British investors.[47]

On occasion, British merchants obtained land in lieu of cash payments. This probably was the reason the economist C. K. Hobson concluded (in 1914) that, at the time of the American Revolution, considerable "investments" had been made by British "merchants in tobacco and other plantations."[48] His statement should be viewed with caution and contrasted with the contemporary one of Adam Smith, who in 1776 had noted that societies of merchants in London and other trading towns frequently purchased "waste lands" in the West Indian sugar colonies "to improve and cultivate with profit by means of factors and agents." Smith wrote that there were no similar attempts by British capital to improve and to cultivate the corn provinces of North America; and, of Virginia and Maryland, Smith insisted, "I have never even heard of any tobacco plantation that was improved and cultivated by the capital of merchants who resided in Great Britain." Smith attributed the differences in experience between these two sets of colonies to the greater profits gained by planters in the West Indies.[49] Hobson's and Smith's statements can be reconciled only if Hobson's is recognized as a reference to *trade* debts that could be called tantamount to involvement in tobacco plantations (as Jefferson asserted), whereas Smith's reference is to the actual transfer of capital and personnel with the intent to develop and to cultivate tobacco. The distinction is important, and the evidence supports Smith's view. I can find no "considerable" investments made by British merchants directly in tobacco plantations, although there were obviously the large trade debts.[50] Of the land in America owned in 1776 by nonresident Britishers, much of it was by titled and well-connected men for speculative purposes, rather than by merchants for cultivation of the products in which they traded. "Speculators," however, often—through their representatives—did cultivate, arrange settlement, and improve their land, seeking to increase its worth.

Land speculation in America in the colonial period was sufficiently large to become important in British politics. Those Britishers with substantial interests in the colonies *east* of the Appalachian Mountains hoped for appreciation in value as the land became populated, and they believed development would be retarded were the fertile western territories opened to settlement. Accordingly, they opposed the westward movement. Other Britishers hoped to profit from "western" lands and sought new land grants from the British Crown.[51]

Many of the nonresident British owners (or their children) eventually settled on this side of the Atlantic and became Americans. What was once "investment from abroad" thus became domestic. There was no ongoing out-of-country claim on American assets. At the same time, some American residents returned to Great Britain to become nonresident investors. As noted, other Britishers never came to America, obtaining title to land (by grants from the Crown, purchase, or inheritance) that they never saw and dispatching deputies (including family members) to administer their holdings. In short, at the time of the Revolution, substantial landholdings of Britishers who lived in the mother country existed, along with those holdings of Britishers who saw their stay in America (in service of their Monarch or otherwise) as temporary and their home as England. There was no basic difference between these two types of holdings. Claims after the Revolution suggest that such landholdings, plus the improvements upon them (clearing, cultivation, building), were sizable.[52]

Mining and Manufacturing

In the British colonies in America, investment from overseas also went into mining and manufacturing. The abortive effort of the Virginia Company to inaugurate an iron works in Jamestown in the 1620s was followed more than two decades later by the activities of the "Company of Undertakers for the Iron Works in New England."

Two settlers, Thomas Dexter and Captain Robert Bridges, had discovered deposits of bog iron in what is now Saugus, Massachusetts. Bridges, apparently accompanied by John Winthrop, Jr. (son of the Massachusetts Governor), took ore specimens to the mother country, where the colonies interested eleven Englishmen in advancing £1,000 to finance an iron works. In the summer of 1643 Winthrop returned to New England with these funds, skilled workmen, and materials.

In March 1644 the newly formed Company of Undertakers for the Iron Works obtained from the General Court of the Massachusetts Bay Company "the sole priviledge in our jurisdiction" for twenty-one years to erect iron works.[53] This company, financed by the English monies, was to set up furnaces and forges. Its market was to be mainly within the colony, but it was also granted the right "to transport what the inhabitants [of the Massachusetts Bay Colony] neede not." It received "free liberty" to sell any surpluses "to other parts or places of the world . . . for their [the company's] best advantage," as long as the customer was not in a place "in actuall hostility with us." The company was to be free of taxation for any funds employed in the venture. In November 1644 the General Court specified that the bar iron produced should be sold at not more than £20 a ton.

In 1645 the English investors sent Richard Leader "a perfect Accountant," with "skill in mynes and tyrall of metalls," to run the new works, located at Braintree, Massachusetts. Leader was appointed to serve seven years at a salary of £100 a year. When the ore ran out at Braintree, the company built a furnace, forge, and rolling and slitting mill at Lynn. That plant would supply bar iron, rod iron, and cast and hollow ware to the colonists, but the latter had no means of paying, except in beaver, wheat, and wampum—and only the beaver could be sold in England. The English owners became dissatisfied with the returns on their investment. In 1650 they dispatched from England a manager to replace Leader. Meanwhile the number of Englishmen investing had increased. Over time, the British owners claimed they spent £15,000.

The works at Lynn have been described as equal in size and technology to contemporary units in Great Britain and on the Continent, yet costs were higher.[54] The output does not ever appear to have become competitive with goods made in the mother country, and no evidence exists that any of the production was exported to England. Throughout, the business was a financial disaster, and from 1653 it came to be plagued by lawsuits over financial irregularities. Ownership control may have passed to the American side of the Atlantic, because of debts the company incurred in the colony; the historian E. N. Hartley writes of the "obscure" ownership structure after 1654.

Production nonetheless continued until 1671, after which the plant operated only sporadically; by 1688 it was completely abandoned. The British owners seem to have lost their entire investment. They had failed to recognize the difficulties of operating over distance in a less-developed land and of effectively delegating managerial responsibilities. On the other hand, the workmen trained at this plant assisted in the start of many iron works in the colonies. Thus, for example, Henry and James Leonard, whose names are importantly associated with the history of the American iron industry, had their first experience at this venture.[55] If the British investors lost, the American colonies did not.

In the eighteenth century, iron works in the colonies became more common. The first successful iron furnace in Virginia was started in 1714 by Governor Alexander Spotswood; it was partly British financed.[56] Governor Spotswood wrote in 1710, when the works were being planned, that they were justified because Great Britain was "obliged to import great quantitys [sic] of Iron from foreign parts, which if this succeeds may be supply'd from hence."[57] In the early eighteenth century, England was an importer of iron, mainly from Sweden. The timber shortage in England had meant the absence of fuel for iron production there (coal use was not yet technologically viable). British manufacturers transformed imported iron into fabricated products.

Much more important than Spotswood's venture was the British stake in the Principio Company. According to the historian Earl Chapin May, in 1715 British ironmasters took the initiative, hoping to find better-quality iron than was imported from Sweden; they dispatched an English ironmaster, Joseph Farmer, to the new world. America, with rich timberlands for fuel and possible iron resources, seemed a promising source of supply. Farmer's backers came to include the ironmasters Joshua Gee of Shrewsbury and the Russells and the Chetwynds of Birmingham, along with John Wightwick of London. Farmer chose a site in Maryland and obtained from his British associates both financial and managerial aid (the latter in the form of three Englishmen), along with twenty indentured workmen; in 1718 the first iron produced in Maryland arrived in England; it may have been a consequence of Farmer's efforts.[58]

In 1720 the Principio Company was formed in England to continue what Farmer, who would return to England, had begun. In 1723 the British owners sent the ironmaster John England across the Atlantic to develop and to administer the Maryland properties.[59] England, who had a minority interest in the business, was a salaried employee. He managed a company town that had its own agriculture, a company store (selling goods imported from England), and also the iron works that exported to the parent enterprise in Britain.

In 1724 William Chetwynd—one of the major shareholders—wrote John England for information on "what quantity you think may be sold in a year upon your Continent, either in Maryland, Pennsylvania [*sic*], Virginia or elsewhere." Chetwynd also wanted to know what "you would be paid in."[60] The works in Maryland began to produce a differentiated, trademarked product: exported iron was stamped "Principio 1724."

The Principio Company—with its headquarters in London— expanded into Virginia in 1725, buying properties from Augustine Washington (George's father) and, in turn, giving the older Washington a small minority interest in the business. From Great Britain the owners sent additional skilled men to aid John England, and the shareholder William Russell proposed to send his son to Maryland to look at the accounts: "John England is in no way capable of accounts more than a mechanick is of Logic," he wrote his partner, William Chetwynd, in February 1725.[61]

That year Chetwynd instructed John England that although the company was not interested in expansion into the "Jerseys," he and his brother were:

We would have you begin these works as soon as possible even whilest you're building the Virginia works . . . We think it a place extremely well chosen of [*sic*] with mine and other conveniences as well as lying in a good Country and near a good market so that I am of the mind that it may be as proffitable [*sic*] a work as can be met with anywhere on the Continent.

Chetwynd was apparently looking to a local market in the proposed Jersey expansion. His letter to John England continued, dealing with the Principio Company in general and urging John England "to send us the surplus of the pigs [pig iron] as soon as you can." Chetwynd told England that he could count on a "constant supply of all Cargoes you write for and whatever bills you draw shall be punctually paid. And you have full power to buy at any time 40 or 50 Blacks or what number you think proper." Chetwynd closed his September 19, 1725, letter with the complaint that some of his colleagues were "Penny wise and Pound Foolish."[62]

From Chetwynd, England got directions and information on purchasing "seasoned blacks" rather than "raw ones," on raising output, on sending monthly accounts, on the relations between the partners in Britain, and on iron shipments to Bristol and London.[63] In 1727 the principal partners in the Principio Company in Britain set down "Orders and Regulations for the Better Manageing and Carrying on the Companys Affairs," which stipulated that the books be kept in London and that there be regular meetings of the partners to review the accounts. A clerk was appointed to keep the records.[64]

When John England died in 1734, the Principio Company was the largest iron maker in the colonies. England left an ongoing enterprise in America; the business was, however, directed by the Russells, ironmasters in Birmingham, England, who exercised what has been called by the historian Earl Chapin May "remote control of Principio affairs."[65] The pig and bar iron produced in Maryland and Virginia was exported to England. The Principio Company appears to have sold iron to its investors, to iron merchants, and also directly to such large enterprises as the Crowley Iron Works in Newcastle.[66]

One of the partners in the Principio Company, Joshua Gee, was the author of the frequently reprinted book *The Trade and Navigation of Great Britain Considered* (first edition London, 1729), in which he dealt with British imports of iron from the American colonies and advocated the encouragement of production there and the elimination of all English duties on pig and bar iron. It was better to import iron from the colonies than from Sweden, Gee believed. In his plea, Gee noted that "what is made in the Plantations [the colonies] is and must be made by Men of Estates in this Kingdom, and the Profits accruing to our Mother Country almost the same as if the Iron Mine was dug out of the Earth here, and made into Bars."[67]

In 1750 the British Parliament passed the Iron Act. While it prohibited the colonists from constructing rolling, slitting, or planning mills or steel furnaces and from making wrought iron or finished products, the law also met Gee's wishes and permitted pig and bar iron to enter England duty free, thus encouraging the output of the raw material in the colonies.[68] By 1752 the Principio Company owned four furnaces, two forges, and 30,000 acres in Maryland and Virginia.[69] It served colonial and mother-country markets.

In 1764 twenty-three-year-old Thomas Russell II was dispatched by the English owners of the Principio Company to reorganize the colonial enterprise because the investors had become dissatisfied with the quality of the output. Remember that the investors were customers of the American works. Thomas Russell II was the son and grandson of the Russells who had visited America (probably in 1720) to help Joseph Farmer start up the Principio enterprise, the Russells who ran the business from Birmingham after John England's death, and the very same Russells whose plant in Birmingham, England, used the American iron. Young Russell went back to England in 1769 to aid his brother at the Birmingham works only to return and to settle in the colonies in 1771; he married into a Maryland family. When the Revolution occurred, this manager (minority owner) of the Principio iron enterprise was a committed patriot.[70] The controlling ownership of the Principio Company, however, remained in Britain.

Meanwhile, in 1732 five wealthy individuals in Maryland had created a partnership called the Baltimore Company to develop iron works. As ironmaster they hired Stephen Onion, who had been sent to America in 1720 by the British to assist Joseph Farmer at the Principio venture. The American-financed Baltimore Company depended on exports to England, where the firm was judged by how its product compared with that of the much larger and more important British-owned Principio Company. The partners in the Baltimore Company marketed individually, but at least one used John Price of the Principio Company in London as a principal London agent in the 1750s.[71]

In 1745 James Russell of Maryland (no relation to the Russells of Birmingham, as far as I can gather) established the White Marsh Furnace and the Long Calne Forge (otherwise known as the Nottingham Iron Works) in Maryland. James Russell was in copartnership with several London merchants, and this enterprise was said to be very extensive, worth about £30,000 at the time of the Revolution. In 1772 Thomas Russell II was inquiring of his partners in England on the price of and demand for James Russell's bar iron.[72]

Then in the 1760s Peter Hasenclever (1716–1793) made large investments in iron manufacturing in New York and New Jersey. Hasenclever's ventures were truly multinational. He was a German who in 1748–49 had established a commercial house in Cadiz, Spain.[73] His family's Westphalian trading firm (from Remscheid) traced its origins back to 1632;[74] it was active in Paris and Amsterdam.[75] In London, in 1763, Hasenclever was a founding partner of the mercantile house Hasenclever, Seton, & Crofts. Charles Crofts had been associated with a firm in Amsterdam.[76]

In 1764 Hasenclever collected funds from a group of Englishmen and sailed for America, arriving that June. He purchased an existing (but dilapidated) iron plant, the Ringwood Iron Works.[77] At the end of September, his cousin had sent to America, from Germany, 535 experienced German miners and ironmasters, along with their wives and children. By November Hasenclever was ready to manufacture iron; he was buying forest lands and iron mines and generally expanding his business.[78] His company in the colonies was the American Iron Company, or more simply, the American Company. In June 1766 Hasenclever advertised that a number of miners, who were "still engaged by contract for 3 years and 4 months, who have been brought into this country from Europe at a very great expense," had run away. The men were arrested shortly thereafter and returned to work.[79]

By 1768 Hasenclever had, in New Jersey and New York, iron mines, six blast furnaces, seven forges, a stamping mill, dams for power, roads and bridges, as well as sales outlets. His was the largest industrial enterprise in the British colonies (overnight, of far greater significance than the Principio Company).[80] The historian Victor S. Clark later described the works as "essentially European in its business character," a European enclave in America that did not represent "a stage in the indigenous development of industrial organization." In five years Hasenclever spent £55,000 (about $250,000); when he failed to get further funding from his English sponsors, he left the colonies (in 1769).[81]

Before he returned to England, Hasenclever had expressed his disenchantment over the possibilities of industry in America: "This country is not yet ripe for manufactures," he wrote on January 6, 1768. "Labor is too high—too much land to be settled."[82] These comments related to proposed textile manufacture. As for the iron industry, Hasenclever penned a long and pathetic letter to the New York Governor, Sir Henry Moore, on May 11, 1768, telling of his personal problems, his sacrifice of "the greatest part of my fortune to advance the enterprise," his accomplishments, and how he had been treated with "ignominy and ingratitude" by the English investors. Hasenclever asked Sir Henry to appoint merchants to examine his books. He complained that "the method which my Copartners have taken to carry on the Iron works, is the strangest I ever have heard of. They Protest my Bills and do not send a Letter of Credit to their new manager [Jeston Humfray]." Hasenclever, however, had assured New York merchants that the new manager's bills would be honored. "Should he not be able to negotiate a certain sum of money, I am afraid," Hasenclever wrote, "of very disagreeable Consequences, & that the works, which are now in their Orient, will soon run to their occident." His company, he boasted, "will cause an annually [sic] Circulation of £30,000 to £35,000, maintain alone hundreds of poor People, which if the works were to discontinue would will [sic] be put to great Distress, besides it affords a Considerable remittance for great Britain."[83]

Jeston Humfray had become manager of the American Iron Company in 1767. Humfray was soon replaced by J. J. Faesch and then in 1771 by Robert Erskine, sent over from England by the British owners.[84] The latter concluded that, with the absence of profits as well as the disturbed political situation between Britain and its colonies, no further investments should be made, and in 1772 Erskine decided to sell the properties, planning to return the proceeds to the English investors. He found no buyer, so he kept the works functioning until the outbreak of the Revolution, at which point Erskine sided with the colonists![85]

While the bulk of the eighteenth-century overseas investment in mining and manufacturing appears to have been iron related, in about 1700 copper ores were discovered at Simsbury (East Granby), Connecticut. A mining company was formed in Connecticut in 1707 and obtained capital in London and Amsterdam. The mine was worked for about sixty years; by the time of the Revolution, it was exhausted.[86]

Clark's *History of Manufactures in the United States* refers to colonial production financed by German money. Hasenclever was, of course, German, but aside from his personal money, his financing was British. As another "German" example, Clark points to Baron Heinrich Wilhelm Stiegel's glass and iron works in Pennsylvania, which used monies the Baron brought to America from Germany.[87] Here is a case of a "domesticated" investment, for there is no evidence that Baron Stiegel remitted profits to Germany or that he retained his German residence. He emigrated and became an American; there remained no foreign claim on assets.[88] In short, I cannot identify any *nonresident* German investments in colonial mining or manufacturing.[89]

Hasenclever was not only involved in iron making; he also participated in building another colonial industry. In the seventeenth and early eighteenth centuries, textile bleachers in England imported potash from Russia and the Baltic. Since the price was high and the supply irregular, in 1751 Parliament passed an "Act for encouraging the making of Pott Ashes and pearl Ashes in the British Plantations in America." The response was not immediate, but during the 1760s British imports of potash from America climbed.[90] The rise appears to have been directly associated with Hasenclever's activities. His correspondence indicated that in 1765 and 1766 he took part in this industry and in the export of both potash and pearl ash.[91] In 1752 Britain imported no potash or pearl ash from North America. By 1767, 53 percent of such imports came from North America, and by 1770 American potash "dominated the British market."[92]

Investments from Abroad in 1776

In conclusion, on the eve of the Revolution business in America was financed both locally and from abroad, essentially from the mother country. Although colonial merchants (especially those from New England, Philadelphia, and New York) flourished and even had their own overseas trading outlets,[93] British mercantile houses remained important. Shipping outside New England was dominated by non-resident or temporarily resident British owners. Firms with Dutch connections existed, British navigation laws notwithstanding. In the interior, French traders were significant. Absentee land ownership by Britishers was substantial. Large-scale activities in mining and manufacturing had received funds and technology from Britain, but by 1776 most infant industries in America were small scale and domestic.[94] Of the five principal British investments in operating iron works in the colonial era, the seventeenth-century Company of Undertakers for Iron Works was long defunct, its plant abandoned; the Spotswood furnace (1714) had no continuing British investments; by contrast, British investments persisted in the Principio Company (formed in 1720) and in the Nottingham Iron Works (established in 1745); but the newer Hasenclever venture, the American Iron Company (begun in 1764), had become for all practical purposes the property of its American resident manager. The eighteenth-century British-financed iron works in America exported the bulk of their output to Great Britain.

During the Revolution assets of those loyal to the British cause were confiscated. For the sequestors, little distinction was made between the holdings of "resident" Loyalists and "nonresident" British subjects.[95] After the peace (1783) former owners sought restitution; I studied the claims records, seeking to estimate the size and characteristics of nonresident British investment in America in 1776.[96] In 1783 the British government formed a commission to evaluate claims made by American Loyalists and British subjects of losses of *real and personal* properties. After seven years, and consideration of 5,072 claims, amounting to £8 million,[97] the commission recommended compensation payments of almost £3.3 million. Included among the claimants were "Loyalists resident in Britain," "British proprietors," and the largest single claimant, the Penn family.

The Loyalists resident in Britain were owners of American properties who either before or during the Revolution were or had become residents in the United Kingdom. Their thirty-one claims amounted to £342,189, of which the commission allowed £140,927.[98] These claims were clearly "foreign" investment. Four investors in the Principio Company, resident in England, were in this category. Although their claim was £66,604, they were awarded a mere £12,500.[99] This was not a "company" claim, but a claim made by the investors in the company. Far larger awards went to two "proprietors," resident in Great Britain; they received £290,000, the bulk of which went to the estate of Henry Harford, a "proprietor of Maryland." The Penn family that lived in England eventually claimed £947,817 and was allowed £500,000.[100] In short, the giant claims and awards related to land holdings.[101] Of the £3.3 million in claims awarded, roughly one-third, or £1.1 million, appears to have been to British residents. The other two-thirds went mainly to those who fought for and gave support to the British side in America. Some of these claimants remained in North America (some went to Canada); others in time moved to England.

This British commission did *not* reimburse firms or individuals for losses associated with *commercial* debts. Thus in 1790–91, in a separate submission, British merchants made claims on their government for trade debts owed them by U.S. citizens; these obligations totaled almost £5 million, which included interest accrued since 1776. After subtracting such interest, the economic historians J. F. Shepherd and Gary M. Walton believed the resulting £2.5 million greatly exaggerated the extent of British financing of U.S. trade in 1776.[102] On the other hand, more recent, and to me more convincing, research by the economic historian Jacob Price disputes Shepherd and Walton's use of balance-of-payments data to determine the scope of trade financing and finds that the British debt claims (which Price calculated to be £2.9 million, as of 1776) were not out of line with the reality.[103]

This evidence notwithstanding, it is clear that we do not know the level of overseas investment in America on the eve of the Revolution, nor how realistic the British claims were, nor exactly how much of the loss claims allowed for real and personal property actually did, in fact, represent nonresident investment.[104] I can conclude, however, that what long-term investment from abroad existed—in trade, land, iron works, and perhaps potash manufacture—was a consequence of either trade financing or direct investment, that is, stakes carrying with them control over properties in the colonies. Excluding the trade financing (the commercial debt), my estimate, based on my review of the "allowed-claims" data, is that the long-term foreign investments (all of which were foreign *direct* investments) as of 1776 came to roughly £1.1 million. If I use Alice Hanson Jones's figure of £110 million as the aggregate physical wealth of the thirteen colonies,[105] foreign (British nonresident) investment would equal a trivial 1 percent of colonial wealth. Even if I add to this figure £2.9 million (assuming— as we obviously should not—that all the "claimed" commercial debt was long term), the figure still comes to less than 4 percent of "colonial domestic wealth." The percentages—if accurate—are extraordinarily small. Out-of-country investments in America, *after* political independence, would rise in percentage as well as in absolute terms.[106]

2.

Political Independence/ Economic Dependence: 1776–1803

With the Revolution came political independence but, paradoxically, more economic dependence. The Revolution and the creation of completely indigenous American governing institutions meant new public finance requirements: the nation would also need banks, insurance, and transportation enterprises. America borrowed abroad to assist in paying the high costs of the Revolution and then to satisfy the awesome requirements of the new nation. A type of foreign investment—up to this point virtually unknown in America— emerged: foreign portfolio investments.

During the Revolution, from 1776 to 1783, while British properties were being confiscated, Americans sought loans from France, Spain, and Holland to help in the fight for independence. Obligations to foreign investors continued to mount from 1783 to 1789— albeit slowly—as the newly independent nation charted its future course. With the Constitution and the foundation of a new federal government (1789), with the funding of national and state debts to assure public credit (1790), and with the purchase of the Louisiana Territory (1803), America became increasingly reliant on foreign finance.

In the decades after the Declaration of Independence (1776), the nation had political independence. The country, however, looked to Europe for imports of many manufactured goods and for export markets for its tobacco and then raw cotton. The use of foreign capital was part of this broader economic dependence. The amounts invested from abroad were far greater than in the colonial era, because domestic needs rose. The amounts were greater in both absolute and relative terms.

1776–1783

With the Revolution, naturally there was an abrupt end of British financial flows for public purposes. Colonial governments in America had been financed through local revenues, printed currency, and direct infusions from the British state.[1] Administering the colonies did mean British monies came to America, but not as "foreign investment," since after the spending there was no claim on assets by private or public investors; no bonds were issued to finance colonial governments; no "foreign" public debt was incurred.

With independence, matters changed; the Continental Congress had to raise money to finance the Revolution.[2] It looked to Europe, especially to France[3] and then to Holland.[4] In the *Wealth of Nations* (1776) Adam Smith wrote, "The mercantile capital of Holland is so great that it is, as it were, continually overflowing, sometimes into public funds of foreign countries, sometimes into loans to private traders and adventurers of foreign capital."[5]

The French provided loans to the revolutionaries against their common enemy, Great Britain. The Spanish, also for political reasons, made (small) American loans. On December 20, 1780, Great Britain declared war on the Netherlands, and in 1781 the first Dutch loan went to America, guaranteed by the French Court. In September 1782 the American Congress approved the floating of a $10 million (25 million florins) issue in Holland. When in 1783 the Peace Treaty between America and Britain ended the war, the funds from this last flotation had not yet been received. At that time America had outstanding revolutionary war debts of $4.4 million (French loans), $1.8 million (the 1781 Dutch loan), and $0.2 million (two Spanish loans).[6] In addition, individual states had borrowed overseas (Virginia and North Carolina, for example, from the French—apparently for trade financing).[7] Proceeds from the French loans had been used in 1781 by the American government to pay $254,000 for 633 shares in the new Bank of North America, in Philadelphia, the country's first real bank.[8] Thus, during the revolutionary years, the nation and the various states borrowed abroad.

At the same time, existing British properties were "Americanized." On November 27, 1777, Congress suggested that the states seize the possessions of men who had forfeited "the right to protection," sell these, and invest the proceeds in loan certificates issued by the Continental Congress. Individual states enacted confiscation laws, authorizing the takeover of British holdings.[9] British-owned land was expropriated and resold by the states to Americans.[10] In a similar manner, British stakes in iron manufacturing ended. Maryland gave one of the forges of the Principio Company to a partner, Thomas Russell, who lived in this country and sided with the revolutionaries; the state sold off the rest for $240,000.[11] The British-owned Nottingham Iron Works in Maryland was also confiscated and sold to an American. The Principio iron works manufactured cannons and cannon balls, and the Nottingham Iron Works cast cannon balls for the American cause during the war.[12] The manager of the American Iron Company, Robert Erskine, was a patriot; divorced from its British owners' control by the wartime conditions, this company similarly produced to fill American revolutionaries' needs. In this instance, New Jersey lawmakers concluded that the investment was inseparable from Erskine's "personal" properties, and through a convoluted process the once British-owned company became American.[13] The process of Americanization was repeated state by state: British holdings became American. After the Revolution the properties would not be returned.[14] (In Chapter 1 I used the "claims data" of the postrevolutionary years to attempt to determine the extent of nonresident British investment in 1776.)

Before the Peace Treaty was signed in 1783, merchant houses from the European continent, especially those from France, saw fresh prospects in America. In 1778 the United States and France signed a Treaty of Amity and Commerce, giving Frenchmen the right to bequest and to inherit real property in America; subjects of the French King would not be treated as "aliens" in the United States with respect to their real property.[15] This was an important guarantee that their property rights would be secure; problems of "alien property rights" would be a perennial concern of foreign investors in future years. Six French firms set up commercial outlets in Baltimore during or directly after the Revolution.[16] One French and one Hamburg trading company opened in Philadelphia.[17] Two Belgian houses—Prager, Liebaert & Co. and de Surmont—started mercantile establishments in Philadelphia and Charleston, respectively.[18] These new mercantile establishments notwithstanding, from 1776 to 1783, when America and Great Britain were at war, by far the largest new foreign investments were in loans (totaling $6.4 million) to finance the Revolution, with Frenchmen the major lenders. The amount borrowed appears to have been larger than the value of the confiscated British properties— resulting in a rise in America's out-of-country obligations.

1783–1789

In 1783, when the Peace Treaty was being negotiated, Benjamin Franklin pointed out that the states, not the national government, had confiscated the British properties.[19] Thus, in the treaty, Congress would only promise to "earnestly recommend to the Legislatures of the respective states to provide for the restitution of all estates, rights and properties which have been confiscated, belonging to real British subjects" (article 5) and that "no future confiscations" would be made against persons because of their revolutionary roles (article 6).[20] The treaty sought to reassure British property owners. Few, however, were satisfied: there was, as noted, no restitution (nor would there ever be); still wary, in the years 1783 to 1789, Britishers did not resume their prerevolutionary primary place as overseas investors in this country.[21]

Now when America looked to foreign sources for the national financing that it still required, the French, because of their own domestic political disarray, could no longer contribute. After 1783 the French stopped new lending to America. Accordingly, the country turned increasingly to Holland, and obligations to the Dutch multiplied, with $3.6 million in proceeds from the loans of 1782, 1784, 1787, and 1788.[22] The Dutch replaced the French to rank first as America's largest creditor.[23]

In these years, as in 1776–1783, it was public finance that attracted the most foreign capital. Table 2.1, prepared from data in Alexander Hamilton's *Report on Public Credit* (1790), indicates that the country's total federal debt as of December 31, 1789, had reached $54 million. The accumulated "foreign" debt of $11.7 million (principal and accrued interest) represented 21.6 percent of the public national debt at that time.[24] The foreign debt comprised monies actually raised in Europe. This debt was denominated in foreign currencies. On American books it was listed in both dollars and the foreign currency. In addition, as indicated in the notes to Table 2.1, a portion of America's "domestic" public debt had drifted abroad. This was denominated in dollars. In November 1788 the domestic debt held in Holland and, to a far lesser extent, in England came to an estimated $2,768,840.[25] (It was nonetheless still called the domestic debt, to differentiate it from the foreign debt.) As trade had resumed, American merchants often paid European exporters in securities representing American government obligations; hence the transfer of the domestic debt overseas. When it seemed likely that America would honor her debts, foreign merchants became more willing to accept this form of payment. At the same time, foreign speculators (principally Dutch and British) purchased American debt securities, which raised the amount of the domestic debt owned in Europe to roughly $4 million in 1789. If I add this $4 million to the loans actually negotiated abroad (the "foreign loans"), America's public debt held outside the country reached not

Table 2.1.   America's public debt, December 31, 1789 (in U.S. dollars)

Total federal debt (principal and interest)		54,124,464.56
Foreign debt as a percentage of total federal debt		21.6%
Foreign debt (principal and interest) to France, Spain, and Holland		11,710,378.62
France[a]	4,444,443.90	
Spain	174,011.00	
Holland[a]	5,451,852.10	
Total principal	10,070,307.00	
Arrears interest	1,640,071.62	
Domestic debt (principal and interest)		42,414,085.94[b]
Total state debts (principal and interest)	25,000,000.00[c]	
Known foreign debt, Virginia (principal and interest)	136,087.00	
Known foreign debt, South Carolina (principal and interest)	496,328.00	

Source: Alexander Hamilton, "Report on Public Credit" (1790), in U.S. Congress, *American State Papers on Finance* (Washington, D.C., 1832), I, 22, 26, 28, 29.

[a] In the published accounts, the 1781 Dutch loan of $1.85 million was included with "French debts," since it was raised by France in Holland and was guaranteed by the French Court (*American State Papers on Finance*, I, 26, 482). Were I to have followed *that* pattern in Table 2.1, the foreign debt to France would read $6.3 million instead of $4.4 million and that to Holland would be $3.6 million instead of $5.45 million. (Even when America paid no interest on this loan, France fulfilled its obligation to the Dutch money lenders. See P. J. van Winter, *American Finance and Dutch Investment*, New York: Arno Press, 1977, I, 260 n. 31.)

[b] In November 1788 the New York merchant William Duer, who was secretary to the Board of Treasury, discovered that a total of $2,768,840 of the American *domestic* debt was entered against the names of foreigners, of which $2,501,177 was in Dutch hands. Estimates push the *domestic* debt held abroad to $4 million in 1789 (Van Winter, *American Finance and Dutch Investments*, I, 240–241, 354–357; II, appendixes 3 and 4). If we were to include this $4 million, some 29 percent of the American debt was held abroad.

[c] On foreign speculation in state paper, see van Winter, *American Finance and Dutch Investment*, I, 358–359, 383 n. 143.

22 percent, but roughly $15.7 million, or 29 percent of the total U.S. federal government obligations at the end of 1789.[26] In 1789 federal government debt was by far the most important component in the overall foreign investment. State debts, which had risen between 1783 and 1789 and some of which were held abroad, are also included in Table 2.1. The table, however, is deficient in that it contains only

those known foreign state debts, as listed in the appendix to Hamilton's *Report on Public Credit*.[27]

In the years 1783–1789, European investors obtained equity interests in some American businesses. Shares in the country's first bank, founded in 1781, the Bank of North America, were, for example, purchased by Dutchmen (1783–1789); by 1786, 13 percent of its stock was held abroad.[28] Bremen merchants financed the activities of their countryman Johann Friedrich Amelung, who migrated to New Bremen (Fredericktown), Maryland, brought in about 100 skilled workers from Bohemia and Thuringia, and between 1784 and 1794 manufactured glass; his Maryland glassworks then failed for lack of sufficient capital, since the Bremen merchants offered Amelung no subsequent financing.[29]

Much more important, merchant firms from across the Atlantic opened more offices in America, even while some of those established earlier did not survive.[30] After 1783, gradually, as Anglo-American trade revived, British commercial houses joined continental European firms in sending representatives to American cities. British and French transatlantic packet service began.[31] The interruption in British-American commerce appears to have been of much shorter duration than that of British-American investment relationships.

Dutch and other European land speculation took place.[32] Land in the colonial era had tempted mainly Britishers; now the Dutch became especially interested. In 1789 four Dutch banking firms (Stadnitski & Son, van Staphorst, P. & C. van Eeghen, and ten Cate & Vollenhoven) dispatched Théophile Cazenove to the United States to oversee their growing and various American investments in land and public debt, and to a lesser extent other securities.[33]

On the eve of the establishment of America's new national government in 1789, foreign investments were mounting. To recapitulate, by that year about 29 percent of the public national debt was held abroad ($15.7 million). There were no public loans from the British (since Americans had fought against them), but a small amount of the domestic debt had been acquired by Britons. While the French had stopped new lending to America, the American government retained an outstanding debt to France. Spain, likewise, had ended its lending, and the small debt to that country had been in part repaid. Miscellaneous other investments by Europeans existed, including more than $600,000 in state debts. Of all the overseas investors, the Dutch, with their good-sized holdings of U.S. public debt securities and smaller interests in the stock of the Bank of North America and in land, were unquestionably preeminent. In the late eighteenth century, since the Dutch were the world's greatest lenders, their role in financing the new Republic was hardly remarkable. Total long-term foreign investment in the United States in 1789 was roughly $17 million to $18 million.[34]

1789–1803: An Overview

With the ratification of the Constitution and the establishment of the new federal government, the British grew less wary of American investments. Until 1794 the Dutch added to their commitments; then, with the Napoleonic wars and the French occupation of Amsterdam (1795–1799), temporarily the Dutch curtailed (but did not halt) their U.S. involvements. Although the U.S. federal debt to Dutch investors continued and other stakes remained, and although Dutch bankers retained interests in the country, in the late 1790s and early 1800s the Dutch would pass their first-place position in U.S. investments to the British.

As British interests in the United States rose in absolute terms and vis-à-vis those of the Dutch, important interconnections existed. Hope & Co. was a great eighteenth-century Amsterdam banking house. In 1794, when the French advanced onto Dutch soil, the Hope family moved to London. The Hopes and the British House of Baring had had commercial associations dating back before 1770, and in 1794 Francis Baring's son, Alexander (aged twenty), was employed as "principal assistant in Mr. Hope's [Amsterdam] accounting house."[35] In future years Alexander Baring would bring the Hope family into numerous U.S. ventures. The London merchant Francis Baring had traded with American firms in the colonial era and in 1783 had resumed such business. The Barings would have long and significant relations with America and make and arrange large foreign investments in this country.[36]

Between 1789 and 1803, America hosted foreign portfolio investments in (1) obligations of the federal and state governments and (2) securities of American corporations. Portfolio and direct investments arose in connection with trade and trade financing. There were also some foreign direct investments in land and other enterprises. Despite (and in part because of) the chaos of the Napoleonic wars, European investors looked to America. By far the largest foreign interests were in government securities.

On August 4, 1790, Congress required that provision be made "for fulfilling the engagements of the United States, in respect to their Foreign debt, and for funding their Domestic debt." This commitment to uphold public credit made it much easier for the new Republic to borrow abroad. In this Funding Act of 1790, for that reason, highest priorities were given to interest payments on the existing foreign debt.[37]

In the early 1790s the United States successfully floated new loans in Amsterdam and one in Antwerp.[38] By 1793 the previously incurred Spanish debt, and by the end of 1795 the French obligations, were repaid. America liquidated its debts to Spain and France with the monies borrowed in the Netherlands.[39] By the close of 1795, the "foreign debt" of the United States was held exclusively in Amsterdam and Antwerp. The phrase "foreign debt"—to repeat—covered only those monies exclusively raised abroad; the foreign debt totaled $11,939,000 as of January 1, 1796.[40]

From 1796, accounts presented in the *American State Papers on Finance*, volume I, show that the foreign debt dropped steadily, so that by January 1, 1804, it was a mere $5.7 million, and by 1810 it was extinguished completely.[41] The report is, however, misleading,[42] for at the same time more of the "domestic debt" went overseas.[43] Instead of declining, the U.S. government's obligations to foreigners rose. In 1791 the London stockbrokers Bird, Savage & Bird placed several million dollars of the U.S. domestic debt in Britain. The Bird firm became general agent for the U.S. government in London. Especially in anticipation of, and then after, the Jay Treaty of 1794, which settled outstanding disputes and provided for U.S. payment to the British of Americans' prewar commercial debts, British and other foreign investors felt comfortable in acquiring U.S. government securities.[44] When in February 1803 Bird, Savage & Bird failed, the House of Baring was appointed the official agent of the U.S. government in London.[45]

Adam Seybert's *Statistical Annals* (1818) provided a fine presentation of the progress of the public debt and the creation of the different issues.[46] The first section of Table 2.2 is from this work and gives the public debt of the United States before the Louisiana Purchase (1803) that was owned by creditors outside the United States—$32.1 million total; this figure excluded the remaining "foreign debt," which was always kept separate in the accounts.[47]

France had acquired the Louisiana Territory from Spain in a secret treaty of October 1, 1800. For the Louisiana Purchase in 1803, the United States agreed to pay the government of France $15 million—$3.75 million to be represented by American mercantile claims on the French government, which had been taken over by the United States (this figure was carried as "American claims" on U.S. accounts) and the remaining $11.25 million to be paid in "stock" at 6 percent.[48] The Louisiana 6 percent stock was issued, following an act of Congress

Table 2.2. U.S. domestic debt held by foreigners before and after the Louisiana Purchase (in millions of U.S. dollars)

Domestic debt, June 30, 1803 (before Louisiana Purchase)	
Total domestic debt	70.0
Held by English investors	15.9
Held by Dutch investors	13.7
Held by other foreigners	2.5
Total in foreign hands	32.1
Percentage held abroad	46%
Domestic debt, Dec. 1, 1803 (after Louisiana Purchase)	
Total domestic debt	81.0
Total in foreign hands	43.0
Percentage held abroad	53%

Source: Calculations based on data in Adam Seybert, *Statistical Annals* (Philadelphia: Thomas Dobson, 1818), pp. 736, 751, and Timothy Pitkin, *A Statistical View of the Commerce of the United States* (1816; rpt. New York: Augustus M. Kelley, 1967), p. 287.

passed November 10, 1803.[49] It was made payable to the assignees of the French government—the British and the Dutch houses, Francis Baring & Co. and Hope & Co. The interest on $6.25 million was payable in London and on $5 million in Amsterdam. The $11.25 million represented foreign obligations of the United States, not to the French, but to the British and Dutch financial institutions.[50]

In 1802, with temporary peace, the House of Hope had returned from London to Amsterdam. Instead of old Henry Hope being in charge, however, Alexander Baring's brother-in-law, Pierre C. Labouchere, became head of Hope & Co. The capital for Hope & Co. came from the Hope family, who continued to reside in England. The House of Baring and Hope & Co. maintained their cordial relations.[51]

By December 1, 1803, the U.S. public debt (again excluding the "foreign debt") stood at about $81 million, and of this foreigners held roughly 53 percent (see Table 2.2). Table 2.2 indicates the importance of British capital, the rise in the debt after the Louisiana Purchase, and the resulting growth of America's foreign obligations from 46 to 53 percent of the domestic debt. If I add the remaining "foreign debt" of about $5.7 million, the percentage of the total U.S. public debt owned abroad in December 1803 rises to 56 percent, or about $48.7 million.[52] The total was much greater than in 1783 or 1789, and, of course, before the Revolution there had been no public debt.

Unfortunately, comparable data for 1803 on state debts are not available. There had been foreign speculation in state paper early in 1790. Dutch investors, counting on federal assumption of state debts, acquired Massachusetts, South Carolina, Pennsylvania, New York, Virginia, and Maryland obligations. Practically all of this debt was assumed by the federal government with the August 1790 legislation. In the 1790s, states borrowed abroad for state projects, and Dutch investors lent to Massachusetts, South Carolina, and Pennsylvania. Undoubtedly there were also some English purchases of state securities.[53] No figures, however, exist on state debts held abroad in 1803. The amount was certainly much less than the $48.7 million of the federal debt held by foreign investors.[54]

1790–1803: Corporate Securities

As of late 1803, Samuel Blodget—writing in 1806—estimated that of the $48.4 million in corporate stock outstanding in this country (stock in state banks, the Bank of the United States, insurance companies, canals, and turnpikes) almost $16 million, or 33 percent, was held in foreign lands![55] Table 2.3 reveals the distribution. America was not yet a "corporate society." Nonetheless, corporations were participating in large-scale economic activity, especially in banking. That America could draw on capital from abroad for major ventures helped to provide a needed infrastructure for economic development.

Most of this investment appears to have been of a portfolio nature

Table 2.3. Corporate stock held by foreigners, 1803

Type	Total stock outstanding (in millions of U.S. dollars)	Held by foreigners (in millions of U.S. dollars)				Held by all foreigners (in percentages)
		English	Dutch	Others	Total	
State banks	26.00	5.00	3.00	1.00	9.00	35%
Bank of the U.S.	10.00	4.00	2.00	0.20	6.20	62
Insurance companies	9.00	0.50	—	—	0.50	6
Turnpikes and canals	3.40	0.10	0.08	—	0.18	5
Total	48.40	9.60	5.08	1.20	15.88	33

Source: Samuel Blodget, *Economica: A Statistical Manual for the United States of America* (1806; rpt. New York: Augustus M. Kelley, 1964), p. 198.

with no intention of control. Of the "corporate stocks," the $9 million in foreign investments in state banks represented the largest in dollar totals. The Bank of North America in Philadelphia (founded in 1781) attracted many foreign investors. In the early 1790s, Dutch investors bought stock in the Bank of New York (founded in 1784) and the Bank of Maryland (founded in 1790).[56] British investments in state banks rose to exceed those of the Dutch (by 1803, $5 million versus $3 million).

No single corporation would obtain more foreign capital in this period than the Bank of the United States. It was America's largest business enterprise. By 1803, headquartered in Philadelphia, it had branches in New York, Boston, Baltimore, Charleston, Norfolk, and Washington, D.C. When in 1791 the Bank of the United States was founded, as the historian Bray Hammond explains, "in effect the Treasury drew for $2,000,000 on the United States commissioners engaged in selling government securities in Amsterdam, deposited the drafts with the Bank, and then drew against the deposit to pay for the stock." Technically, this meant that the stock purchase by the U.S. government in the first Bank of the United States was financed by Dutch funds.[57]

At the start, in 1791, the Bank of the United States had a capital of $10 million, divided into 25,000 shares. The U.S. government subscribed for 5,000 shares with the $2 million. Alexander Hamilton had considered using the Bank of North America as the national bank instead of forming a new firm. An objection was that the charter of the Bank of North America had no guards against the influence of foreigners, no prohibitions against their becoming directors or their voting by proxy.[58] Thus, in the Act of Incorporation of the Bank of the United States, February 25, 1791, there was the explicit statement that "none but a stockholder, being a citizen of the United States, shall be eligible as a director." Only stockholders actually resident in the United States could vote by proxy.[59] Initially the stock ownership was American.

Gradually, however, foreign investors had acquired shares in the Bank of the United States. Nothing in the charter prohibited their doing so. By 1793 Dutch and British interests in the bank had become so important (and the directors of the bank so eager to make its shares marketable in Europe) that the dividend was made payable in Amsterdam and London as well as in Philadelphia.[60] Between 1796 and 1802 the U.S. government sold its 5,000 shares in the bank. Of these, in 1802 Alexander Baring acquired 2,200. The U.S. government sold Baring the shares, after the firm had offered to act as the financial intermediary in remitting on the Dutch debt.[61] By 1803 the Bank of the United States stock held abroad (now principally in England) reached 62 percent, or $6.2 million![62] Despite this formidable sum, no evidence exists that any British or Dutch group *controlled* the Bank of the United States, nor that British or Dutch stockholders participated in any manner in its management; under its charter there could be no British or Dutch directors, nor could any foreign resident vote his shares by proxy. Nonetheless, the amount was impressive.[63]

As for other corporate ventures, the foreign interests were relatively small. The Dutch were not at all involved in U.S. insurance companies, whereas the British had about a half-million dollars invested in such enterprises.[64] Dutch capital in the early canal and navigation companies—the Connecticut Canal Company, the James River Company, the Lock Navigation Company of New York State, the Potomac Canal Company, and the Santee Canal Company—was apparently all in the form of portfolio investments, made by Théophile Cazenove on behalf of his principals.[65] British investment in such "transportation" enterprises was only slightly higher than that of the Dutch ($100,000 versus $80,000).

In sum, of the total U.S. corporate stock held abroad ($15.88 million) in 1803, 60 percent was in British hands, and roughly 32 percent was owned by Dutch investors. As with the public debt, so too with these other investments, the British had assumed preeminence. The corporate foreign investments were overwhelmingly in banking. They were not floated abroad, nor were they marketed on foreign stock exchanges. They had moved into European hands in two fundamental ways. One was through purchases made in the United States by representatives of foreign investors, such as Cazenove. (It also seems that visitors and, more important, immigrants may have acquired securities on behalf of family members in Europe; likewise, American merchants with international connections were intermediaries. The U.S. government had sold to the Barings its shares in the Bank of the United States.) The second way was specifically through trade-related transactions, that is, as payments for goods purchased abroad. This was especially important in the British case. Note that all these investments were in American corporations (*incorporated in the United States*); the companies were not set up abroad to do business in America. The individual foreign owners held American corporate securities. It is remarkable, given the still immature international securities markets, that in 1803 so large a percentage (33 percent) of American corporate securities was held overseas.

1790–1803: Trade-Related Investments

Foreign investment can be trade related. Because my concern is with long-term interests, I need to pay attention to trade and trade financing only when they become the basis for more permanent stakes: that is, when (1) the foreign business to control the trading activity made U.S. investments in representation; (2) through defaults, or for other reasons, a foreign house became an investor in producing the American products whose export it had been financing; (3) the seller of goods (or the financier of the goods sold) acquired American securities or property instead of cash payments and thus became a long-term investor; and (4) the foreign enterprise, because of its knowledge of U.S. conditions, decided to make other long-term investments.

In the 1790s British merchants reestablished prerevolutionary trading connections and opened new outlets in America. In 1792 William Heth in Virginia wrote to Secretary of the Treasury Alexander Hamilton: "The trade of this state is carried on chiefly with foreign [British] capital. Those engaged in it [the trade], hardly deserve the name of merchants, being factors, agents, and Shop-keepers of the Merchants and Manufacturers of Great Britain—and their business to dispose of the goods of that, for the produce of this country, and remit it to the order of their principals with whom the profits of the trade of *course* centre."[66]

The passage does not reveal whether the "factors, agents, and Shop-keepers" were salaried, or partners in the British firms, or financially independent units that acted for British houses on a purely commission basis. The distinction becomes important in understanding the rise of foreign direct investments. Generally, in the early stages of the business growth, resources are small. A company in the home country appointed independent agents abroad to serve on its behalf (such agents could be of the home, host, or a third-country nationality). The independent "agent" was not an extension of the home-nation business. By contrast, and by definition, a multinational enterprise—making a foreign direct investment—has not only ownership but also control over the business abroad. What determines whether the factor, agent, or shopkeeper represents a foreign direct investment is the relationship to the parent company. If the business is owned or controlled, or if the man who runs it is salaried or a partner, then we have the extension of the parent firm.

This distinction seems clear-cut; reality was not that simple. Confusion manifested itself in the following ways: (1) If an agent was dependent on a British business for its goods, for its markets, for its financing, even if it was American-run and the ownership was American, is it not odd to call it independent? In terms of foreign direct investment, however, such an "agent" was "independent." (2) If a Britisher went to America to serve as "agent" for a British company, was this a foreign direct investment? If the Britisher went to America on his own (not financed by a parent firm or by any other British company) and settled in America, to the extent that he carried resources with him, this was a British foreign investment that became (once he became a resident) domesticated, Americanized. If the Briton went to America and his activities were financed by a British-headquartered firm (his passage and salary paid, his ties to the company acknowledged), then this was a foreign direct investment of the British firm that sent him to America. (3) If an American-run enterprise acted for a British trading firm; if all the U.S. principals were born on this side of the Atlantic, but the capital for the warehouses, inventory, and the like was British; and if British partners had interests in the profit of the U.S. trading firm, this would be a British direct investment. The British partners linked the transatlantic houses. (4) Finally, suppose a member of the family of a British trading or (later) manufacturing company traveled to America to represent the family firm. The immigrant set up a business that soon became self-sustaining and independent. It represented other British and American houses, as well as the family one. Was this a foreign direct investment of the British family firm? By my definition, the answer is yes. The outlet in America was established to serve the family firm in the home country, and as long as the member of the family acted as part of a family concern, this would be a direct investment. In time, such investments often lost their character as foreign direct investments, and relations with the initial parent were severed. Regrettably, the commonly used words *factor, agent,* and *shopkeeper* fail to reveal whether there was or was not a foreign direct investment. In short, in early America, just as in the colonial era, sometimes the factors, agents, and shopkeepers were members of the family, partners in, or employees of a British trading firm. Then, as noted, their operations represented foreign direct investments. Sometimes they were Americans, in debt to the British, but independent of British "direct" investments. The exact ratios are unknown. This discussion is applicable not only to British but also to continental European houses.

Likewise, I do not know the extent to which, through defaults, Britishers who financed the U.S. tobacco or cotton trade became investors in American cultivation. Apparently this occurred. More important, often Americans paid for imports with securities, thus transforming the European exporters into long-term foreign investors. U.S. federal government debt served this purpose. Likewise, studies show that a large portion of the stock of the first Bank of the United States went to Europe to discharge indebtedness.[67] In addition, European merchants involved in trade financing (the House of

Baring is a superb example) participated in non–trade-related U.S. investments, especially in land.[68]

The vast bulk of the long-term foreign investment that emerged from international trade was British. Most came as a consequence of transatlantic commerce. In these years, however, Russian, French, and Spanish, as well as English, traders also established outposts— that is, investments—as they took part in America's domestic fur trade and in the China trade.[69] Dutch, Belgian, and German merchants participated in transatlantic commerce.

1790–1803: Direct Investments in Land and Other Activities

Of the foreign direct investments, the ones in land were the most significant. American "land salesmen" spread throughout Europe, visiting London, Paris, Alsace, the Rhine, and Belgium. In 1791, through one of his land salesmen, Robert Morris sold about 1.3 million acres in New York State to a group headed by Sir William Pulteney (price, £75,000, or about $350,000). The British investors appointed an agent, Charles Williamson, who forecast that with development the investors would "reap an advantage fifty times their outlay!" Williamson spent the investors' monies on roads, towns, stores, theaters, taverns, sawmills, potasheries, distilleries, model farms, and dwellings—all the while seeking to sell off land to settlers. By 1800 an additional $1 million (beyond the land purchase price) had been spent, but revenues from land sales had only reached a mere $147,974. In 1801 Pulteney replaced Williamson, employing a New York lawyer, Robert Troup, to act on his behalf.[70]

Robert Morris also sold land to a Dutch group, which acquired from him, as well as from others, a formidable amount of acreage. In 1792 a combination of Dutch bankers (and speculators) that became known as the Holland Land Company started to buy this land and in a few years had obtained title to over 5 million acres in central and western New York and northern and western Pennsylvania. Théophile Cazenove, their U.S. representative, explained to his principals that before they invested, they should be prepared to provide active and intelligent supervision of their land business.[71] He would do that on their behalf.[72]

In 1790 a Dutch trading firm in the United States had sent maple sugar to Holland as a possible raw material for Van Beeftingh & Boon's sugar refinery in Rotterdam. Van Beeftingh & Boon dispatched Gerrit Boon to the United States to consider the matter, and in 1792 Boon acquired, for $54,489, more than 29,000 acres on a tributary of the Mohawk River, in upstate New York. He supervised the development of the property. By 1794 he had built a sawmill, an inn, a barn, and some log cabins and introduced equipment to obtain the sap; then he gave up. Very little sugar had been exported, and Boon concluded the venture would never be profitable. The Dutch Company decided to sell the land to settlers, and this land became part of the properties associated with the Holland Land Company.[73]

In 1796 Alexander Baring bought on behalf of the House of Baring over a million acres in Maine (price $401,000). He brought the Hope family into this purchase. The Hope & Co. historian writes: "Year after year, the reports from Hope's agent in Maine, John Richards, echoed the disconsolate theme of drudgery in getting colonization under way and of scarcity of settlers who, moreover, were not an asset but a liability from the financial point of view. The only redeeming feature in the situation was perhaps that it helped to focus Hope's attention on America."[74] Frenchmen also participated in buying land.[75]

Enterprising Americans sought European monies. Tench Coxe wrote the son-in-law of John Adams, on April 12, 1792, that "if your friends in Europe have a mind to go into this thing," Coxe would buy the land, be their agent, and take a 5 percent commission payable in land.[76] In 1796 Gouverneur Morris was resident in Paris "as the representative of a number of rich American landowners and speculators," seeking, albeit with little success, money for American land purchases.[77]

That same year, Robert Morris published in London a Prospectus of the North American Land Company and attempted to excite British investors over this enterprise, described as owning 5.9 million acres in Pennsylvania, Virginia, North Carolina, South Carolina, Georgia, and Kentucky! The North American Land Company appears to have existed for more than seventy-five years (because of lengthy litigation) and seems to have attracted some British investment.[78] In the 1790s and early 1800s, many American states restricted alien land ownership, but the rules could be, and were, circumvented—for example, by the title's being held in the name of an American citizen or company, or by the passage of special acts by state legislatures that granted a particular alien owner legal title.[79]

While practically all the foreign investment in canals, navigation companies, and turnpikes was of a portfolio nature, sometimes sufficient capital came from Europe to provide the investors with at least the potential for control, and it is control, as indicated, that is crucial to a definition of foreign direct investment. For instance, in the 1790s a London investor, Hodgson Atkinson, furnished most of the capital for internal improvements of the Connecticut River at Bellows Falls, Vermont.[80]

It has generally been believed that European investors in the United States (1790–1803) did not participate in manufacturing. The Dutch portfolio interest of $20,000 in 1791 in the ambitious Society for Establishing Useful Manufactures, in Paterson, New Jersey, is frequently cited as the exception.[81] In *American Business History*, Herman E. Krooss and Charles Gilbert state that the interests of British merchant bankers in American government bonds, banks, and insurance companies released "other [domestic] capital funds for manufacturing enterprises."[82] I do not disagree with this generalization. Nonetheless, foreign direct investments in manufacturing did exist, albeit few. One of the major corporations in the United States today—Du Pont—was founded in 1801 by foreign investors. At origin, the Du Pont Company used French management, capital, machinery, and workmen.[83]

1776–1803: Attitudes toward Foreign Investment

In the new nation, attitudes toward foreign investment were far from uniform. During the Revolution, as British holdings were being confiscated, Americans solicited French, Spanish, and Dutch loans. On July 29, 1782, the Superintendent of Finance, Robert Morris, made a report on public credit in which he strongly favored foreign borrowing and countered the arguments of opponents.[84] With peace in 1783, American merchants and bankers sought overseas money, including British funds. Agrarian interests used British financing of their imports and exports, while, coincidentally, they lashed out at the financial power of large banks and the "foreign elements." They blamed the Bank of North America for admitting "foreigners to investment in America" and feared that the bank's "great dividends" would encourage rich foreigners to buy its stock, "until finally the whole capital of the institution would be owned abroad and the country substantially drained of specie by the exportation of dividend in coin."[85]

After the ratification of the Constitution, one of the first acts of the new Congress in 1789 was to impose differential tonnage duties, giving preference to U.S.–built and U.S.–owned ships.[86] This was followed by a Registration Act, requiring American-owned ships to be registered to qualify for the lower fees. Only ships wholly owned by American citizens could be so documented (registered). Thus began the U.S. practice of treating American-owned and foreign-owned shipping differently.[87] When in 1790 Secretary of the Treasury Alexander Hamilton presented his *Report on Public Credit,* agrarian groups predicted dire consequences, as money passed to Holland and England to service the U.S. debt.[88] When the Bank of the United States was established in 1791, as noted, there were legislative provisions to avoid foreign control. Yet, critics notwithstanding, there continued to be strong supporters of foreign investment.

Many businessmen and statesmen applauded the ongoing foreign purchases of Bank of North America stock "as bringing specie to America and numerous friends abroad. As long as the principal remained here, there should be no worry about dividend payment."[89] Hamilton's funding of the national and state debts was designed to secure public credit and thus to make it possible to raise further foreign monies. Swiss-born Albert Gallatin—Jefferson's Secretary of the Treasury—had no hesitancy in arranging foreign financing of the Louisiana Purchase. No prohibitions against foreign portfolio investments in the Bank of the United States existed (only those over foreign control). In his *Report on Manufactures* (1791), Hamilton had written:

It is not impossible that there may be persons disposed to look with a jealous eye on the introduction of foreign Capital, as if it were an instrument to deprive our own citizens of the profits of our own industry; But, perhaps, there never could be a more unreasonable jealousy. Instead of being viewed as a rival, it ought to be Considered as a most valuable auxiliary, conducing to put in Motion a greater Quantity of productive labour, and a greater portion of useful enterprise, than could exist without it. It is at least evident, that in a Country situated like the United States, with an infinite fund of resources yet to be unfolded, every farthing of foreign capital, which is laid out in internal ameliorations, and in industrious establishments, of a Permanent nature, is a precious acquisition.[90]

Hamilton—who more than any single individual shaped America's early economic policy—felt foreign capital could and should be attracted.[91] The nation's first naturalization law of 1790 made citizenship readily available. Immigrants would arrive, providing a bridge for foreign investment by representing and by giving information to potential overseas investors.

In the years 1791–1803, worries about foreign investments in the United States persisted, always coexisting with the favorable reactions. There were those in America who feared "the allodial and feudal tendency of the land monopolizing systems of Mr. Barings and Pultneys [*sic*]."[92] As noted, a large number of states had constitutional provisions and alien land laws (based on English common law) barring or restricting nonresident foreign investments in land. States wanted settlement, not large-scale absentee foreign ownership.[93] Yet American "land salesmen" sought out foreign investors.

Many Americans denounced the Jay Treaty of 1794, which provided for compensation by the United States to British creditors for prerevolutionary *commercial* debts,[94] but responsible treatment of this debt would encourage more foreign investment. The Jay Treaty (article 9) guaranteed the rights of British subjects to hold land acquired before 1794, as if they were native Americans, and to deed this land to their heirs.[95]

In 1795 sponsors of a venture concerned with navigation of the Schuylkill and Susquehanna rivers felt it was "bad policy" to permit Europeans to control two-thirds of the stock in their company, "although one-third might be prudently vested in this way." Foreign capital might help "ensure the speedy and complete success of the work."[96] The idea of "joint-ventures" with control by nationals of the recipient country is by no means unique to post–World War II less-developed nations.

Throughout this book we will find American ambivalence toward foreign investments. Some of the particular concerns of this era persisted—especially those over foreign ownership of (and control over) shipping, banks, and land. The intensity of the concerns fluctuated; likewise, the ways in which the concerns became translated into public policy changed. Nonetheless, the pattern of ambivalence remained.

1776–1803: The Foreign Investments

Two novel aspects in the path of overseas investments in the United States emerge in the years 1776–1803. First, and most significant, is the new importance of government borrowing. The Revolution, Hamilton's funding of the national and state debts, and the purchase of the Louisiana Territory all relied on foreign finance—and that each was successfully concluded was in no small part due to the contribution from abroad. The importance of French loans in the revolutionary years has long been accepted. Likewise, as the historian James Riley has recently argued, Hamilton's fiscal program could not have succeeded "on the strength of American resources alone"; foreign finance was required, and the Dutch role was vital.[97] Many years ago J. E. Winston, in his article "How the Louisiana Purchase Was Financed," concluded that it would have been impossible to float a loan domestically to pay for the acquisition; American banking at that time was incapable of handling the financing. The contribution of the British and the Dutch merchant bankers was crucial.[98]

Although foreign investors would in subsequent years continue to participate in U.S. public finance, two features related to investments in this sector in this era do *not* repeat themselves in subsequent American history (at least in the period covered by this volume—that is, to 1914). One is the role of foreign governments. The French state was directly involved, and when it did not make loans from French government funds, it guaranteed Dutch credit. The motive was political. The other investment-related feature is that the "foreign loans" of the revolutionary and postrevolutionary years were the only federal government borrowings in the years discussed in this book that were denominated in foreign currencies and taken up exclusively in overseas markets. American debt would continue to be sold and held abroad (informally moving there through purchases or in payment of trade debts, or formally being placed there—as in the case of the dollar-denominated Louisiana 6 percent stock); from 1795 to 1914, however, never again would new American federal debt be denominated in anything but dollars. If these two features—government lenders with political motivations and foreign-currency–denominated national government borrowings—were special to the revolutionary and postrevolutionary era, foreign investors remained involved in American public finance, and in subsequent chapters we will see the changing circumstances. In short, in this period American government borrowing for the first time took on a primary role.

The second novel aspect of foreign investment in the years 1776–1803—unique as compared with colonial times—related to the foreign investments in U.S. banks, insurance, and canal, navigation, and turnpike corporations. These portfolio investments by individuals and merchant banks assisted in providing infrastructure for the new nation. In colonial America there had been no chartered American banks, no commercial banking. From the 1780s to 1803, with the state banks and the Bank of the United States, America began to establish its own rudimentary financial institutions; the foreign investments helped. For many subsequent years banks would continue as an important sector attracting investment from abroad. The new foreign investments in canals, albeit still very small, were harbingers of subsequent giant stakes in future transportation-related enterprises.

Less novel in 1776–1803 were the direct investments in land and the far smaller ones in manufacturing. These resembled what had existed in colonial times, although gone were the days of land grants from the Crown. The role of Americans in promoting the sale of land in this country had taken on a new flamboyance. In the future, with similar gusto, Americans would try to attract foreign investments to many sectors. In manufacturing, the industrial composition of the relatively few investments had altered: in the colonial era there had been the iron works; now there were Amelung's glassworks (1784–1794) and Du Pont's gunpowder establishment (founded in 1801), plus the saw-mills and other small manufactories related to land development.

So too, the trading relationships—the mercantile interconnections—do not seem materially different from those of the last years of the colonial era. There were, however, more nationalities participating. The principal qualitative difference, as compared with earlier years, that I can discern is that now American *securities* (representing the public debt and corporate ventures) were used as a means of payment for trade obligations—and thus, in a formal sense, trade debts became long-term American obligations to the holders of those securities.

It is clear that by 1803 there were surprisingly large foreign invest-ments in America in crucial sectors. To repeat, at the end of 1803, about 56 percent of the federal debt (a sum of $48.7 million) was held abroad, a formidable amount. This was the largest single sector for foreign investment. Sixty-two percent of the capital of America's largest and most important business enterprise, the Bank of the United States, was in Europeans' hands. Thirty-five percent of state bank shares was held by British, Dutch, and other foreign investors. Fully 33 percent of *all* corporate stock outstanding was foreign owned. The corporate entities provided basic infrastructure. Investments from abroad were in banking, insurance, transportation, trade, land, and (to a far lesser extent) manufacturing.

The description of America's foreign obligations provides a snap-shot of a new nation with new needs that required aid from the "capital-rich" countries of the old world. Within the United States, the ambivalence characteristic of debtor nations existed. Already there were policies that differentiated domestic from foreign investments. Some Americans thought the foreign contribution desirable and es-sential. Others believed it dangerous. No one saw it as negligible or unimportant. European (including British) claims on American assets were far greater in 1803 than in 1776, or 1783, or 1789. With political independence, economic dependence—to finance the vitality of the new nation—had increased. Long-term foreign investment in the United States in December 1803 totaled in excess of $65 million and probably more than $70 million.[99]

3.

A Half-Century of Development: 1803–1853

The next fifty years of foreign investment in the United States were marked by dramatic change.[1] First, foreign investment in the federal debt declined in relative importance. Second, individual American states turned in a significant manner to Britain and, to a lesser extent, to the European continent for funding. Third, foreign investment in trade, banking, land, and particularly transportation assumed new roles.

The half-century saw discontinuities caused by the resumption of the Napoleonic wars in Europe and the War of 1812; the rise of Britain as a major creditor nation after 1815; the attractiveness of investment in the United States in the 1830s; American defaults of the early 1840s, with the consequent near evaporation of overseas investors' interest; and then the new European stakes in the late 1840s and 1850s, lured by gold in California and by the railroads.

From 1803 to 1807 the development of the United States remained closely associated with the international economy; this trade and investment intimacy was interrupted by the Embargo, the Non-Intercourse Act, and the War of 1812. Douglass C. North has argued that the "vicissitudes of the cotton trade—the speculative expansion of 1818, the radical decline in prices in the 1820's and the boom in the 1830's—were the most important influence upon the varying rates of growth of the [U.S.] economy during the period [1815–1843]." Sizable foreign investment came with the cotton boom of the 1830s and in turn had linkage effects throughout the American economy. By the 1840s and early 1850s, domestic commerce began to take on a new preeminence—although the value of America's international trade greatly expanded.[2] The cutback in foreign investment in the 1840s proved a temporary phenomenon; by the early 1850s new foreign

Table 3.1. American securities held abroad, 1789–1853—long-term investments only (in millions of U.S. dollars)

Date	Government			Banks				Transportation		Other sectors				
	Total	Federal	State	County, city	First U.S. bank	Second U.S. bank	Other banks*	Turnpike, canal, navigation	Railroads	Insurance	Mining	Manufacturing	Utilities	Other
1789[a]	17.0–18.0	15.7	0.6											
1795[b]		20.3												
1801[b]		33.0												
1803, June[c]		38.0												
1803, Dec.[c]	65.0–70.0	48.7				6.2[d]	9.0[d]	0.18[d]	0.5[d]					
1811						7.0[e]								
1818	35.0–50.0[f]	25.4[g]												
1820						3.0[h]								
1821	30.0[i]**													
1822[j]	31.0	24.0	2.0			3.0	2.0		k					
1824	38.0[l]**	25.8[m]												
1825			2.5[n]											
1828		19.1[m]				4.0[h]								

Year													
1831													8.0[h]
1832													8.4[o]
1833	50.0[p]		p			15.0[p]							
1835, Jan.		0.0[q]											
1836			50.0[r]										
1838[s]	110.0		65.0		1.5	20.0	4.8[t]	2.0[t]		2.5[t]				14.2[t]
1840	200.0[u]												
1841						28.0[v]							
1842				100.0–150.0[w]										
1843													
1847													
1853[x]	222.2	27.0	111.0		21.5		6.7	2.5	52.1	0.4	0.7	0.1	0.1

* After 1836, Bank of the United States (of Pennsylvania).

** For England only.

a Dec. 31, 1789; see Chapter 2. Total includes some investments in land.

b Ralph Hidy, The House of Baring (Cambridge, Mass.: Harvard University Press, 1949), pp. 34–35.

c See Chapter 2. Total includes some investments in land.

d Includes domestic debt held abroad as well as "foreign" debt. Total for Dec. 1803 includes some investments in land.

e Samuel Blodget, Economica: A Statistical Manual for the United States of America (1806; rpt. New York: Augustus M. Kelley, 1964), p. 198.

f J. F. Holdsworth and Davis R. Dewey, The First and Second Banks of the United States, 61st Cong., 2nd sess., 1910, S. Doc. 571, p. 109.

g Paul D. Dickens, "The Transition Period in American International Financing: 1897 to 1914," Ph.D. diss., George Washington University, 1933, p. 757. See Table 3.2 for more details.

h Adam Seybert, Statistical Annals (Philadelphia: Thomas Dobson, 1818), p. 757.

Table 3.1 (Cont.)

h Leland H. Jenks, *The Migration of British Capital to 1875* (New York: Barnes & Noble, 1973), p. 66.

i *Niles' Weekly Register*, 20 (June 30, 1821): 273.

j Herman E. Krooss and Martin Blyn, *A History of Financial Intermediaries* (New York: Random House, 1971), p. 55.

k Included with "Other banks."

l *Niles' Weekly Register*, 16 (June 12, 1824): 248.

m Walter Buckingham Smith, *Economic Aspects of the Second Bank of the United States* (Cambridge, Mass.: Harvard University Press, 1953), p. 68, based on data in Baring Papers, Public Archives, Ottawa.

n Harry N. Scheiber, Harold G. Vatter, and Harold U. Faulkner, *American Economic History* (New York: Harper & Row, 1976), p. 149. This is *only* for New York state bonds to finance the Erie Canal.

o Figure given in Andrew Jackson's veto message of July 10, 1832.

p *Niles' Weekly Register*, 45 (Nov. 16, 1833): 178. No total was given on state securities, except it was indicated that $9.3 million out of $16.5 million Pennsylvania stock was held abroad.

q No federal debt.

r Speech of Daniel Webster in U.S. Senate, May 31, 1836, in Daniel Webster, *Works*, 8th ed. (Boston: Little, Brown, 1854), IV, 261.

s James Garland, as cited in *Niles' National Register*, 44 (July 21, 1838): 322.

t Garland's $4.8 million figure for "Other banks" has to be low; it includes only "Mississippi bank stock," "Tennessee bank stock," and bonds of the Farmers' Loan and Trust Company. Garland included Louisiana bank stock with that state's bonds. The "Other" category probably contains some bank stocks. The $2 million under "Transportation" includes both canals and railroads. The $2.5 million under "Insurance" represents investments in New York Life Insurance and Trust Company and American Life Insurance and Trust Company. These firms were more like "banks" than like "insurance companies" (see text of this chapter).

u G. S. Callender, "The Early Transportation and Banking Enterprises of the States in Relation to the Growth of Corporations," *Quarterly Journal of Economics*, 17 (Nov. 1902): 144, citing a Van Buren message of 1840. See also speech of Daniel Webster, March 30, 1840, in Webster, *Works*, IV, 555, citing the same Van Buren address.

v Callender, "Early Transportation and Banking Enterprises," p. 144. The figure $28 million is often repeated. If, however, the shares are listed at par (that is, $19.8 million) and foreign debt is taken as the explicit balance sheet liabilities ($16.8 million; see text below), the obligation reaches $36.6 million. For these data, see U.S. House, 29th Cong., 1st sess., 1846, Exec. Doc. 226, pp. 442, 469.

w U.S. House, 27th Cong., 3rd sess, 1843, H. Rept. 296, pp. 7, 151.

x U.S. Senate, *Report of the Secretary of Treasury . . . [on] the Amount of American Securities Held in Europe*, 33rd Cong., 1st sess., 1854, Exec. Doc. 42, p. 53, in *Foreign Investments in the United States*, ed. Mira Wilkins (New York: Arno Press, 1977).

investment supported the development of U.S. domestic commerce.

Distances shrank. In 1805 the merchant Vincent Nolte crossed the Atlantic in a "rapid" trip of forty-two days; the same journey in 1815 took him fifty-seven days. By 1838 his trip—now by steam—lasted "only" eighteen days. By 1853 travel across the Atlantic was typically about nine or ten days. After 1818 regular, scheduled North Atlantic service connected New York and Boston with London and Liverpool; by 1838 there was regular transatlantic steamship service. Lower-cost, faster transportation meant rising immigration, providing yet closer international connections.[3]

At the same time, America expanded geographically. In 1803, with the Louisiana Purchase, the nation had obtained a vast region to the west of the Mississippi River. The country added East and West Florida (1819), admitted Texas as a state (1845), acquired and admitted the Oregon Territory (1846–1848), and filled out the West with a large acquisition from Mexico that included California and much of the Southwest (1848); the United States rounded out the new territory with the Gadsden Purchase (1853). This formidable new frontier influenced foreign investors' plans by offering unprecedented opportunities. Total foreign investments in the United States rose—ebbs and flows notwithstanding. See Table 3.1.[4]

Federal, State, and Municipal Obligations: 1803–1838

Never again was the portion of the U.S. federal debt held abroad as high as the 56 percent level at the close of 1803, and in the years 1803–1853, even in absolute terms, the federal debt held abroad never reached its 1803 peak.[5] The total U.S. federal debt declined from $86.7 million on December 1, 1803, to $45.2 million on January 1, 1812, only to soar during the War of 1812, reaching $119.6 million (September 30, 1815).[6] From 1807, and especially with the War of 1812, Britishers sold some of their U.S. debt holdings; domestic funds substituted.[7] From 1815 to the mid-1830s, the U.S. public debt was steadily reduced.[8] After 1815 British investors, however, acquired American paper, and such British investments rose in the 1820s. Table 3.2 indicates that in 1818 some 26 percent of the $99 million federal government debt was held abroad. The British—with holdings of $12.3 million—were the largest foreign investors; the Dutch—with interests of $11.1 million—were in a close second place.[9] Between 1825 and 1827, of the federal debt falling due, one-third was payable overseas.[10] By 1828 British investment far exceeded that of the Dutch, and foreign investment represented about 33 percent of the national debt (see Table 3.2). In January 1835 the national government's debt—foreign and domestic—was liquidated, for the first and only time in U.S. history.[11] Contemporaries marveled at the good faith of the U.S. government— and told British investors that even during the War of 1812, "the interest on the portion of the debt inscribed in the names of British subjects was regularly paid to their agents in America." The investors "ultimately realised [their dividends] at a very favourable rate of exchange."[12] As noted in Chapter 2, after the early so-called foreign loans were liquidated, all U.S. federal government debt was denominated in dollars.

While the U.S. federal government was satisfying its creditors and paying off its obligations, *state* governments raised their borrowings. It is not known exactly when foreign holdings in state securities exceeded those in federal government bonds—probably in the early 1830s.[13] G. S. Callender has pointed out that in eliminating its national debt, the United States lost little, if any, foreign capital.[14] In fact, far more was attracted. By 1838 state debts outstanding came to $172 million, a larger debt than the federal government had ever owed! As we will see, the foreign investment component of that debt came to at least $65 million—a larger foreign obligation than had ever been assumed by the *federal* government.[15]

States fronted for private banks and canal and railroad companies, substituting the stronger credit of a sovereign entity for the inability

Table 3.2. Public (federal) debt of the United States held by foreigners, 1803–1853 (in millions of U.S. dollars)

	1803	1818	1824	1828	1835	1853
Total public debt	86.7	99.02	83.80	58.40	0	58.2
In foreign hands	48.7	25.44	25.75	19.10	0	27.0
Held by British investors	a	12.30	a	14.15	0	a
Held by Dutch investors	a	11.08	a	2.16	0	a
Held by other foreign investors	a	2.06	a	2.80	0	a
Percentage of debt held abroad	56%	26%	31%	33%	0	46%

Sources: 1803 (Dec.): Chapter 2; 1818 (Jan 1): Adam Seybert, *Statistical Annals* (Philadelphia: Thomas Dobson, 1818), p. 757; 1824 and 1828 (U.S. debt): Paul Studenski and Herman E. Krooss, *Financial History of the United States* (New York: McGraw-Hill, 1963), p. 93; 1824 and 1828 (foreign-held debt): Walter Buckingham Smith, *Economic Aspects of the Second Bank of the United States* (Cambridge, Mass.: Harvard University Press, 1953), p. 68 (based on data in Baring Papers, Public Archives, Ottawa); 1835 (Jan.): see Chapter 3; 1853 (June 30): U.S. Senate, *Report of the Secretary of the Treasury . . . [on] the Amount of American Securities Held in Europe*, 33rd Cong., 1st sess., 1854, Exec. Doc. 42, p. 3, in *Foreign Investments in the United States*, ed. Mira Wilkins (New York: Arno Press, 1977).
    a Not available.

of an unknown enterprise to borrow. State bonds would be sold and proceeds passed to the bank, canal, or railroad; the state government would then take the firm's stocks or bonds as security. U.S. banks and merchants bought the state securities, which they could resell in Europe or use as collateral for borrowings in the United States and Europe.[16]

According to the historian Leland Jenks, the first American state securities quoted in London were in 1817—New York 6 percents. Then came a progression: 1824, Pennsylvania, Virginia, and Louisiana; 1828, Ohio; 1830, Maryland; 1831, Mississippi; 1833, Indiana and Alabama—and so forth. Securities of municipalities also moved overseas: a Washington, D.C., loan was quoted in Amsterdam in 1830; Philadelphia and Baltimore securities appeared in London in 1832; New Orleans bonds were also available in England.[17] Nonetheless, state borrowings were far more extensive than those of municipalities.[18]

Most American state loans went through merchant bankers. Most were *not* publicly issued. Few were actively traded until 1837–38. The securities drifted to London as a cover for mercantile credit in much the same manner as federal securities had at an earlier date. By the 1830s Europeans were prepared to acquire American state government securities for the following reasons:

1. *Apparent safety of the investment.* These were government bonds. The U.S. federal government showed itself responsible in paying off its debts. Presumably, state governments were equally trustworthy. British and Dutch investors, wary of investments in individual companies in the United States about which they had little information, preferred the state bonds and let the state governments, in turn, select and finance private enterprise. The guaranty of the state made the securities "palatable."[19] Safety was especially important as British investors turned away from risky South American ventures (during the 1820s there had been numerous defaults on British-held South American bonds).[20]

2. *Prosperity in America.* Investors sought to take advantage of the splendid opportunities. The completion of the Erie Canal in 1825 cast an aura of success on state projects. For the New York state-financed Erie Canal, subscriptions on the first loans had been taken up almost entirely in the state. As progress was made on the canal, the bonds had become attractive in London. The larger issues of later years were absorbed across the Atlantic, so that by 1829 more than one-half of New York's outstanding Erie Canal debt was held abroad.[21] Investors felt secure in the knowledge that state monies were used for productive purposes that would provide revenues for payment of the debts.

Northern states' debts were mainly for canals—and later for railroads. Southern states' debts were more often associated with new banks. Such state-backed banking institutions in the South seemed bound to flourish with the expansion of cotton cultivation. The entire Mississippi debt, for example, was for banking purposes.[22] Callender notes that Englishmen (individuals and merchant bankers) were in these cases investing in aiding their country's own cotton textile industry.[23]

3. *High interest rates.* States offered better returns than European investors could get at home.

4. *Prompt interest payments.* Initially, states were excellent in making payments (often they used other borrowings to do so).

5. *"Imponderables,"* as Leland Jenks called them. Kinship, common language, and familiar legal traditions made American securities especially attractive to the British.

6. *Capital availability,* particularly in England and Holland, for investment abroad.

7. *Ease of investment.* Several states issued bonds denominated in pounds with interest payable in London; they appointed bankers in London to pay out the interest. Dutch bankers developed methods whereby even if securities were denominated in dollars, interest was paid to the Dutch investors in guilders.

8. *Financial intermediaries' promotion of the securities.* As noted, state securities "came to London in blocks as cover for drawing credits."[24] Without the financial intermediaries, it is doubtful that state securities would have become so popular abroad. Thus we must consider these channels for investment.

Overend, Gurney & Co. was an important conduit. Even more prominent was Baring Brothers & Co.[25] In Holland, from about 1836, Dutch banking houses came to handle U.S. state securities. The Rothschilds in England, and to a lesser extent on the Continent, were significant—as was the banker Samuel Jones Loyd (later Lord Overstone).[26] In London, Palmer, MacKillop & Dent, an old East India house, floated sterling loans for Florida Territory and South Carolina. S. V. S. Wilder was the New York correspondent of the French firm Hottinguer & Co., another seller of state securities.[27] The so-called three Ws—the London firms of Thomas Wilson & Co., George Wildes & Co., and Wiggin & Co.—had by the mid-1830s embarked on a speculative spree in American state bonds. The three Ws would suspend payments in 1837.[28] Huth & Co. and McCalmont & Co., both of London, were also active.[29] After we look at the three leading foreign merchant bankers handling the intermediation of American state securities in the late 1830s—the Barings, Hope & Co., and the Rothschilds—I will then mention the key American firms involved.[30]

In 1803 the Barings, as indicated in Chapter 2, had been appointed general agents for the U.S. federal government; over the years the firm enlarged its participation in American business.[31] As noted, the Barings owned securities of the first Bank of the United States. From 1810, Prime, Ward & Sands and its successors were the principal Baring correspondents in New York.[32] During the War of 1812, Baring Brothers & Co. continued to help maintain the credit of the United States, but the house refused to sell new federal issues in London.[33] After the war, the Barings became associated with the new Second Bank of the United States, a connection that would, over time, become intimate.[34] In 1829 Thomas Wren Ward of Boston became the Barings' U.S. representative—to act as if he were a partner and to bind the firm; after 1832, Ward was on a salary.[35] The Barings also had correspondents in New Orleans and Baltimore. Until 1830, in Britain, Alexander Baring (1774–1848; as of 1835, Baron Ashburton) led the firm; then Joshua Bates (1788–1864), an American partner in London, became its main U.S. specialist. Bates became a partner in 1828.[36] With a Louisiana loan in 1828, the name of Baring Brothers was for the first time publicly linked with an American state government issue.[37] In the 1830s the House of Baring had become an important marketer in Britain of American state and state-backed securities.

Alexander Baring's brother-in-law, Pierre C. Labouchere, headed the Amsterdam firm of Hope & Co. from 1802 to 1811.[38] Recall that Baring & Co. and Hope & Co. had in 1803 cooperated in arranging the marketing of U.S. federal government securities to pay for the Louisiana Purchase. In 1805 Hope & Co. had participated in the first "official" administrative office for American securities in Holland.[39] Over the years the Dutch firm kept its close relationship with the Barings, and in 1815 Alexander Baring had become a partner in Hope & Co. (to the extent of one-third interest); that year, Labouchere resumed active management.[40] In 1816 the Dutch government had introduced control over and special duties on foreign loans, a law rigidly enforced up to 1824.[41] There seems to have been something of a hiatus in Dutch involvements in American business in the 1820s and even in the early 1830s.[42] By the late 1830s, however, Hope & Co., which continued its connections with the Barings, became very active. Hope & Co. had clients throughout Europe that it now introduced to American state securities. In 1838 Hope & Co. wrote Baring Brothers that if a state security was payable in New York or London, "this is not altogether inadmissable, having through our Bureau of Administration the means of making it payable here."[43] The Dutch firm came to market bonds of Pennsylvania, Ohio, Indiana, Illinois, and Louisiana, as well as municipal securities of New York City, Boston, and Mobile, Alabama.[44]

Meanwhile, by the mid-1820s, as Ralph Hidy wrote, in Great Britain Alexander Baring "was forced to share with Nathan Rothschild his reputation as the leading spokesman among financiers for conservative investment and marketing policies."[45] The London Rothschild house had been established by Nathan Mayer Rothschild (1777–1836); the firm was called N. M. Rothschild until the founder's death, and thereafter N. M. Rothschild & Sons. The Paris Rothschild house was led by Nathan Rothschild's brother James de Rothschild (1792–1868).[46] In 1821 the Rothschilds' first American agents, Robert and Isaac Phillips in Philadelphia, had been appointed.[47] A dozen years later (in 1833), Robert Phillips introduced the New York firm of J. L. & S. Joseph & Co. to N. M. Rothschild.[48] In 1834 Nathan Rothschild began to buy and to sell American state government securities.[49] That year, the firm R. & I. Phillips, acting for both the British and the French Rothschilds, arranged for N. M. Rothschild, London, to become the financial agent of the U.S. federal government (as of January 1, 1835), replacing Baring Brothers.[50] By the fall of 1835, the Rothschild London house had become actively involved in marketing American state government securities.[51] Then, in the Panic of 1837, both of its U.S. agents, R. & I. Phillips and J. L. & S. Joseph & Co., failed.[52] Indeed, a young man sent by the Rothschilds, August Belmont, arrived in New York in the midst of the Panic.[53] His first letter to the London Rothschilds (written in German) told of the bankruptcies (Joseph had been one of the first to suspend payments—their failure being to the tune of about $6–$8 million); the size of Joseph's business reflects the importance of that Rothschild agent. Belmont asked the London and also the Paris Rothschilds for instructions and for full authority,[54] which he received, and he became—and remained until his death (in 1890), when his son took over—the Rothschild representative in New York.[55] His most recent biographer says his initial salary was $10,000 a year.[56]

Not all the financial intermediaries for American state securities abroad were European. The Second Bank of the United States, the Morris Canal and Banking Company, and George Peabody (an American in London) were among the American concerns and individuals in the 1830s moving state bonds outside the country. It should be noted, however, that there were large European investments in the first two of these firms, and that Peabody—although an American—

had become resident in London. State governments, in addition, authorized individuals to market their issues overseas. In England, the *Circular to Bankers* (a weekly publication of country banks) endorsed the securities.[57] Thus by the 1830s abundant information existed in Britain and on the Continent on how to buy American state bonds; there were, however, inadequate data on their merits.

Most American state securities marketed abroad in the 1830s were initially sold in England, but by 1838 the Dutch and, to a lesser extent, the French, Germans, Swiss, and Portuguese had become buyers.[58] Representative James Garland told the U.S. Congress in July 1838 that of all the state securities outstanding, at least $65 million were held abroad, principally in England. This would represent about 38 percent of state securities outstanding.[59]

Trade-Related Investments: 1803–1838

While the foreign monies flowed into state securities and merchant bankers facilitated this process, investments from abroad in trade and trade financing also accelerated. National and state securities, as noted, often had gone to Europe for payments on trade debts.

By the time of the outbreak of the War of 1812, commercial houses in Manchester, England, had representatives in America to buy cotton and do business on their own account.[60] London and Birmingham merchants were selling goods in America—and a few had salaried "agents" in New York.[61] Liverpool firms were represented—as buyers and sellers. After the War of 1812, many more British merchants and some manufacturers opened outlets in U.S. port cities—in New York, Philadelphia, Boston, Charleston, Baltimore, and New Orleans. By 1821 New Orleans had entered its "golden period of commerce." That city became second only to New York in trade, and this was reflected in the presence of British merchants.[62]

In the 1820s James Finlay & Co. of London, Glasgow, and Liverpool had "branches" in New York, Charleston, and New Orleans.[63] In 1820 the firm of John Clark, Jr. & Co., founded in Glasgow (Scotland) three years earlier, opened a New York "agency" to sell cotton thread. For the first time, cotton thread was sold in the United States on wooden spools.[64] In this decade "agents" of Sheffield and Birmingham hardware manufacturers and Staffordshire potters, as well as cotton and woolen salesmen from the north of England, were well established in New York.[65] A Baring partner counted thirty-five "agents" from different parts of Europe in New York City in 1828.[66]

In Boston Thomas Wren Ward, acting for Baring Brothers, granted a rising volume of commercial credits during the 1830s.[67] Late in 1831 the Barings had opened an office in Liverpool and in the early 1830s were participating in trade in and financing of America's cotton exports.[68] Liverpool was crucial in Anglo-American commerce.[69] In the 1830s the Barings also took orders for British iron rails.[70] In 1833 the London firms of Thomas Wilson & Co., Georges Wildes & Co., and Wiggin & Co. had appointed agents in Boston for consignments, credits, and securities.[71] In 1836 the already-wealthy Briton James Morrison—involved in Morrison, Cryder & Co.—appointed one of the Alsops as his agent in Philadelphia and Francis J. Oliver in Boston. Morrison reportedly provided £1 million for Oliver's business. The Morrison, Cryder & Co. firm was in the front rank of Anglo-American merchant bankers.[72] I have noted the Rothschild presence through agents in New York and Philadelphia. That house also had a correspondent in Baltimore.[73] By the mid-1830s the Paris firm of F. de Lizardi & Co. had set up offices in London and New Orleans.[74]

In February 1837 Benjamin Ingham of Ingham, Stephens & Co., a firm of British merchants in Sicily—which had long traded with the United States and had had a Boston agent as early as 1809—started his association with Barclay & Livingston, New York. The Barclays were British businessmen; Schuyler Livingston was a New York merchant. Ingham became a giant foreign investor in America, reinvesting his earnings from trade; Livingston served as his investment adviser.[75] In 1837 Philip Speyer arrived in New York and established himself as a dealer in foreign exchange and an importer of European merchandise. He represented his family firm, Lazard Speyer-Ellissen, in Frankfurt. This was the start of an important German-American house.[76]

By the mid-1830s, with the boom in the United States, it became common for British and occasionally continental European firms to have correspondents, agents, partly salaried representatives, or partners in the United States. A few of these foreign firms were manufacturers; most were merchants. The amount of credit extended to Americans on commercial account in 1836 has been estimated at £20 million.[77] The line between importer and exporter and merchant banker often became invisible.[78]

Meanwhile, in the 1820s and 1830s, the Hudson's Bay Company—chartered in England in 1670—provided stiff competition to American fur traders in frontier regions. This corporate trade-related business over borders was very different from that of the merchants or merchant banking houses. "Wherever the Hudson's Bay Company plants its iron footsteps, there American trade is sure to decline" was the view of *Hunt's Merchant Magazine* (1840).[79] Hudson's Bay Company's "splendid" organization—its "management of a hierarchy of officials with posts in charge of salaried agents who were supplied with merchandise from a central warehouse"—gave it advantage even over John J. Astor's huge American Fur Company, much less over independent American traders.[80] The American Fur Company retreated from the western field in 1834[81] and went bankrupt in 1842.[82] The Hudson's Bay Company survived and still flourishes today.

Foreign Interests in American Financial and Insurance Firms: 1803–1838

Foreign interests in American financial institutions were closely associated with the other overseas investments in the United States. I noted in Chapter 2 the important foreign investments in American banking. In 1803, 62 percent of the stock in the Bank of the United States was foreign owned; by 1811, when this country was about to go to war with Britain, fully 70 percent of the stockholders in that bank were foreign, principally British. Under its charter, these investors had no directors on the board nor any voting power.[83] Nonetheless, in large part owing to fears of foreign influence, Congress did not recharter the bank.[84]

With the war over, in 1816 Congress established the Second Bank of the United States. Like its predecessor, it had a twenty-year charter containing provisions to assure that foreign investors could not vote their shares.[85] British investors were not deterred by these stipulations. They lost nothing when Congress failed to renew the charter of the first Bank of the United States. They wanted returns on investment, not control. Accordingly, in 1817 and 1818 they lent funds to the new bank. By July 1818 the Second Bank of the United States owed Baring, Thomas Wilson & Co., and Hope & Co., as well as other European firms, $1.76 million.[86] Some of the loans of 1817 and 1818 became the basis for subsequent foreign investment in bank stock. By 1820 English holdings in such equity totaled nearly $3 million; by 1828 the sum was up to $4 million, and by 1831 to $8 million.[87] In his veto message of July 10, 1832, President Andrew Jackson declared that as of January 1, 1832, of the $28 million of private stock of the Second Bank of the United States, $8,405,500 (or 30 percent) was held abroad, mainly in Great Britain.[88] The foreign ownership percentage was substantially less than had been the case with the first Bank of the United States (albeit the dollar sums were greater). As noted earlier, Baring Brothers & Co., the bank's correspondents in London, maintained a tight association with the institution, as it had with the first bank.[89]

The bank was America's largest business enterprise. Its main office was in Philadelphia; it had branches throughout the country. It was far larger, far more important, than the first bank had been. Andrew Jackson's 1832 veto, however, closed off the possibility of the federal government's rechartering the Second Bank of the United States. Jackson's attacks on the bank include a sharp denunciation of the foreign investors. Jackson was particularly hostile to the Barings, who remained loyal to the bank.[90] When the bank's federal mandate expired in 1836, the Bank of the United States was chartered by Pennsylvania and continued to operate. Like its predecessor, the Bank of the United States (of Pennsylvania) had a capital of $35 million. At this point, it became *more* dependent on foreign investors; the percentage of its shares held abroad rose. By 1838 foreign investors were said to own $20 million in the stock of the bank.[91]

Meanwhile, other American banks sought money abroad, for example, the Bank of New York (1823).[92] Banks were very attractive to foreign investors. The Barings bought shares in the New York Bank of Commerce. In December 1833 Prime, Ward & King—New York correspondents of the Barings—forwarded for sale, in London, shares of the Bank of Louisiana and the Louisiana State Bank.[93] The British Rothschilds acquired "Louisiana Bank," Commercial Bank of Albany, and Merchants' Bank of Baltimore shares in 1834–35. In 1837 they bought Union Bank of Florida 8 percent bonds.[94]

In 1833–1835 the Manhattan Bank—one of the banks to which the U.S. government had transferred its deposits after Jackson's veto of the charter of the Second Bank of the United States—was reported as having the Marquis of Carmarthen as a "heavy stockholder."[95] Foreign investors owned substantial stock of the New Orleans Canal and Banking Company (the Canal Bank);[96] the Girard Bank, Philadelphia (27 percent);[97] the Schuylkill Bank (also in Pennsylvania);[98] and the Commercial Bank of Vicksburg (Mississippi).[99] Stock was sold abroad in the Union Bank of Tennessee and the Planters' Bank of Mississippi.[100] Dutch investors owned stocks or bonds in the Merchants' Bank of New York, the Phenix Bank of New York, the Citizens' Bank of Louisiana, the Bank of Pensacola (Florida), and the Union Bank of Florida.[101] Foreign interests in banks seem related to associated state (and municipal) securities and to merchants' trade relations.

According to a Louisiana state government report of December 23, 1837, exceptional as a systematic tally of foreign investment, of that state's sixteen banks, with $39.9 million in paid-up capital, fully twelve attracted capital from abroad, and 52 percent of the total invested, or $20.7 million, came from Europe! (This report included European monies—at least $14.8 million—acquired through the sale of *state* or state-guaranteed bonds.)[102] While the evidence is not conclusive, I believe that although I am able to trace British and Dutch investments in many states (New York, Pennsylvania, Maryland, Mississippi, Tennessee) and at least one territory (Florida did not become a state until 1845) in no single state was foreign capital as significant in banking as in Louisiana.

An additional group of financial institutions attracted foreign investments. The New York Life Insurance and Trust Company (NYLTC) began in business in 1830. It made long-term investments out of its capital ($1 million) and its deposits. Its portfolio was primarily real estate mortgages. In 1834 Baring Brothers held 1,500 shares and was by far the largest single stockholder. NYLTC that year obtained deposits of over $1 million from abroad.[103] When in the early 1830s the New York legislature passed a law requiring the Holland Land Company to pay a tax on debts owed them by New York farmers, the Dutch-owned firm responded by pushing collections and hiking its interest rates; farmer hostility to the foreign company mounted. Ultimately, the New York Life Insurance and Trust Company acquired the mortgage claims on the Dutch land, which it paid for with 4½ percent certificates; the Dutch sold these in London in 1836.[104] Isaac Bronson, an American banker, and his associates "used funds of the New York Life Insurance and Trust Company and other banks . . . to buy a third of a million acres in eight states and territories."[105]

Another trust company, the American Life Insurance and Trust Company, raised monies abroad through the sale of stock and by obtaining deposits.[106] Foreign investors also acquired sizable holdings in the Farmers' Loan and Trust Company.[107] So too, the North American Trust and Banking Company had British investors—with about half of its $2 million capital held in England in 1838.[108] Britishers, in addition, obtained interests in the Ohio Life Insurance and Trust Company.[109]

In 1836 a report of a special committee of the New Jersey legislature on the incorporation of a new trust company noted that an advantage of the trust companies was

the inducement held out by them to the investment of foreign capital. In Europe, interest is so low at this time, not more than three to four per cent in Holland, and some other countries of great wealth upon the continent, that

European capitalists seek, and gladly embrace an opportunity for safe investment in this country, upon an interest of five or at most six per cent. These trust companies are a great inducement to send their capital to this country to be managed, as trustees for the employment of it.[110]

In 1837 a Scottish emigrant, George Smith, formed in Chicago the Illinois Investment Company to intermediate monies from Scotland to the American Midwest. When, two years later, he began issuing circulating certificates of deposit as currency, he did so through the Wisconsin Marine and Fire Insurance Company, which had a capitalization of $225,000; half of the stock was held by Scottish investors. Likewise, Smith started the Michigan, the Aberdeen North American, and the North of Scotland North American companies. By 1840 his five companies were reported to have raised some £380,000 (more than $1.8 million) for transmission from Scotland to the American Midwest.[111] Such banking–trust company–insurance company combinations seem to have been an important feature of the financial intermediation of foreign monies in the 1830s.[112]

Meanwhile, British-headquartered insurance companies had entered the American market. The innovator had been Phoenix Assurance Company, which had opened a New York fire and marine agency in June 1804; in Philadelphia, Charleston, and New Orleans in 1805; and in Baltimore, Boston, Savannah, Norfolk, and Middletown, Connecticut, in 1806. Its Philadelphia agency had closed in 1810; the New York one was shut down by the New York state legislature in 1814 (in the midst of the War of 1812). By 1815, however, five Phoenix agencies remained: the Charleston one, which soon "dwindled away," closing in 1822; the Boston one, which lasted until 1824 (scared off by a high Massachusetts tax); and the New Orleans, Savannah, and Norfolk agencies, which continued during the 1830s. Phoenix's "sister" firm, Pelican Life, had an agency in New York from 1806 or 1807 to 1814 and one in Philadelphia from 1807 to 1810. Israel Whelan—Phoenix's and Pelican's Philadelphia agent—has been described as the first life insurance agent in America. These agencies were to sell insurance and do not appear to have been major financial intermediaries.[113]

As early as 1818, the Bank of Montreal (founded in 1817) had appointed a New York agent, Prime, Ward & Sands. The bank's first U.S. profits came from its dealings in specie and foreign exchange (both English and American).[114] As a by-product of its exchange transactions, Bank of Montreal notes circulated in New England and New York.[115] The Bank of Montreal, from its origin, served as a conduit for the shipment of specie to and from the United States.[116] Senior bank officials traveled regularly from Montreal to New York.[117]

In the 1830s its New York agent, however, did not involve the Canadian bank in substantial U.S. investment.[118] In 1832 the Bank of Nova Scotia (chartered that year) appointed an agent in New York,[119] and in 1836 the newly organized Bank of British North America arranged for Prime, Ward & King to become the BBNA's New York agent.[120]

Despite these involvements, the typical, and by far the largest, foreign investors in or through U.S. financial institutions in the 1830s were not the direct participants in individual banks (aside from the Bank of the United States) or in trust companies, or foreign insurance companies or banks with "agencies," but rather they were the holders of state securities related to financing new banks in Louisiana, Alabama, Mississippi, Florida Territory, Arkansas, Indiana, Illinois, Kentucky, and Missouri.[121] In Louisiana, in particular, in 1837, the important foreign holdings of state bonds and state-guaranteed bonds represented more than 70 percent of the foreign investments in the state's banking institutions.[122]

Foreign Investments in Land, Transportation, and Other Activities: 1803–1838

British investors owned land in Maine, Pennsylvania, Virginia, and undoubtedly elsewhere.[123] One Britisher bought 20,000 acres in Wisconsin in the 1830s.[124] The Holland Land Company, a Dutch firm, retained its upstate New York land into the mid-1830s, but then—as noted—transferred its interests to the New York Life Insurance and Trust Company.[125] The life insurance and trust companies used monies from abroad for investments in land. Some foreign investors took advantage of the 1830s land boom to dispose of acreage acquired earlier. Accordingly, in 1835 the Barings and Hope & Co. *sold* the Maine land they had purchased in 1796.[126]

European investments were made in canal companies: the Morris Canal and Banking Company (Dutch, British, and Spanish investors) and the Delaware and Raritan Canal Company.[127] In the 1830s railroads began to attract foreign investment. By 1838 the Camden and Amboy, the Philadelphia and Reading, the Wilmington and Raleigh, and the Harrisburg and Lancaster railroads had foreign bondholders.[128] In 1837 Wilhem Willink issued fl million bonds in the Batavia-Buffalo Railroad Association and fl million bonds in the Tonawanda Railroad.[129] British ironmasters started to receive American railroad securities (usually mortgage bonds) in payment for iron rails, a practice that, as I will show, became commonplace in the 1850s.[130] The pioneer of "American Rails" on the London Stock

Exchange was the Camden and Amboy Railroad, which appeared on the "Official List" in March 1838.[131]

Just as in banking, so too in transportation developments, in the 1830s the typical pattern was for state governments to sell their own securities abroad to finance canals, railroads, and turnpikes; far more foreign monies went into transportation via the state government route than directly. There was no lack of government intervention in the movement of capital; state governments (and on occasion cities and counties as well) were the major conduit in the 1830s for bringing foreign capital into internal improvements.[132] All of this was portfolio investment.

The securities of a few U.S. mining companies were sold in England in the 1830s: Union Gold Mining Company; Pennsylvania Bituminous Coal, Land and Timber Company; Hazelton (Pennsylvania) Coal Company; and Lehigh Coal and Mining Company.[133] The historian Dorothy Adler suggests the 1830s short-lived British stakes in coal deposits were direct ones.[134] This does seem the case when, in 1835, English businessmen invested in coal mines in Maryland, including the George's Creek Coal and Iron Company,[135] and when, in 1840, a group of Englishmen organized the Chesterfield Coal and Iron Mining Company, acquiring Maidenhead Pits, a coal mine in eastern Virginia.[136] Such interests were clearly isolated ones—of little consequence.

As foreign capital entered the United States in the 1830s, one can note its total absence in the manufacturing sector. Earlier foreign-owned manufactories—the Du Pont Company, for example—had become domestic, since the du Ponts settled in this country and the stock held abroad had been returned to Americans. Most American industry in the 1830s did not require large amounts of capital; U.S. resources were adequate. Moreover, relatively low tariffs meant foreign manufacturers could and did reach U.S. markets through exports;[137] as noted, some British manufacturers had opened *sales* outlets in the United States.

The Collapse of the 1830s Boom

The mid-1830s saw U.S. economic expansion encouraged by the foreign capital that went into state securities, trade-related investments, and other activities. Land speculation (domestic and foreign), along with new financial institutions (domestic and at times foreign financed) fueled inflation and, in general, new prosperity. Imports of Mexican silver expanded the money supply.[138]

The boom did not last. On July 11, 1836, the Jackson administration issued the Specie Circular. Designed to curb speculative excesses, it required that specie (gold or silver) be used to purchase public lands. The supply of specie was inadequate. In England, the Bank of England worried that gold would cross the Atlantic. In August 1836 it imposed restrictive measures.[139]

By early 1837 the American economy was in the doldrums; trade was down, businesses failing. It was in this context that the three English firms—Thomas Wilson & Co., Georges Wildes & Co., and Timothy Wiggin & Co.—suspended payments and the Rothschild agents had failed.[140] Baring Brothers & Co. curtailed its activities and weathered the crisis.[141]

The Specie Circular and the Panic of 1837 seem not to have had long-run negative effects on the Rothschild business in America, the failures of R. & I. Phillips and J. L. & S. Joseph & Co. notwithstanding. Indeed, in early 1838 August Belmont was writing to the Paris Rothschilds about new cotton business, Bank of Arkansas business, and purchases of Missouri securities.[142] In April of that year, James de Rothschild wrote Belmont from Paris, "We are happy to see that since your return you have concluded considerable business for our account."[143]

The Bank of the United States (now rechartered in Pennsylvania) suspended specie payments in the Panic of 1837 (in May) but in August 1838 resumed them.[144] It actively marketed state securities in England. The Specie Circular had been repealed in May 1838.[145] In 1838 states issued new bonds. That year and into early 1839, the credit of the states remained sound on the London market; promotions of the still well respected Bank of the United States added credence to the issues.[146] Recovery seemed apparent.

During 1838 and early 1839, not only state and municipal securities and Bank of the United States (of Pennsylvania) stock, but also stocks and bonds of other American state banks, trust companies, and insurance companies, as well as railroads, flooded European, especially British, markets.[147] In February 1838 the Massachusetts legislature created $2.1 million in 5 percent sterling bonds, assigning them to the Western Railroad Corporation of Massachusetts. Baring Brothers & Co. sold them on consignment. The proceeds were used to pay for rails purchased in England.[148] Baring and Hope & Co. in November 1838 purchased $1 million in South Carolina bonds.[149] And so it went. By December 1838 "the influx of both good and bad American securities . . . estimated by the Barings and others at more than £6,000,000 hung over the [London money] market like a Damoclean sword."[150]

In early 1839 intelligent English observers expressed caution over some of the securities. Alexander Trotter wrote, "The United States of

America, in point of national credit, have long held a high place in public estimation." On the other hand, the credit of the federal government was not identical with that of the separate states.[151] Trotter had no fear over the debts of the northern states, where the people "inspire confidence." By contrast, the South had the "moral degradation which the system of slavery stamps both on master and slave, . . . the enervating climate, and the carelessness which often accompanies the uncertainty of life in the unhealthy marshes." These factors, Trotter warned, led to "reckless habits" and to loosened "moral restraints"; investors should remember this in deciding on the trustworthiness of individual states. Trotter believed that whereas the southern states were "richer," the northern ones possessed the "elements of a more enduring prosperity."[152]

By the summer of 1839, according to one estimate, there were nearly $100 million of American stocks and bonds for sale in the London money market.[153] In October 1839 the Bank of the United States (of Pennsylvania) for a second time suspended specie payments. That month, an informed contemporary (Elisha Riggs) estimated that three-fourths of its stock was held in Europe.[154] Some of the stock had drifted into the hands of British nobility. Numbered among the 1,390 foreign holders of its stock (of which 1,185 were British) were two earls, two marquises, eight counts and countesses, two lords, and twenty-eight knights, barons and baronets![155] The suspension of the Bank of the United States was followed by that of other banks and a general trade recession in the United States.[156]

In October 1839, in response to a plea from Louis McLane, president of the Baltimore and Ohio Railroad Company, Baring Brothers agreed to advance the railroad monies needed to buy iron so the firm could continue construction toward the banks of the Ohio River. The security for the loan was £720,000 in Maryland bonds, which had been assigned to the company by the state. The Barings at the same time acquired from the Chesapeake and Ohio Canal Company some £640,000 (nominal value) of Maryland securities; thus the firm ended up controlling almost all the unsold Maryland bonds of both the Baltimore and Ohio Railroad and the Chesapeake and Ohio Canal Company.[157]

As the Bank of the United States—and its new London agent (Samuel Jaudon)—became overextended, European bankers required collateral in the bank's own securities and more often in state securities.[158] Denison & Co., London; the Rothschilds, London; and Hope & Co., Amsterdam, came to the bank's rescue after it suspended specie payments in October 1839. In return, the bank pledged with these three houses $12.2 million in Pennsylvania, Mississippi,

Michigan, Indiana, Maryland, and Illinois securities.[159] Hottinguer & Co. (which had long acted as Paris correspondent of the bank)[160] required from the bank guarantees in state stock.[161] Even earlier, in May of 1839, Samuel Jaudon had deposited state stock (value of about $1 million) with Baring Brothers & Co.[162] What this meant was that in 1839 and early 1840, more American state securities were transferred into European bankers' hands, often specifically to cover the heavy Bank of the United States borrowings.

On October 16, 1839, Daniel Webster, replying to an inquiry of Baring Brothers, wrote a reassuring letter about American state debts; the letter was widely circulated and reprinted.[163] Europeans expected the Crisis of 1839 to be as short-lived as that of 1837. But by the fall of 1839, informed British investors were very nervous. "I wish that I had a less stake in them [American securities]," the banker Samuel Jones Loyd wrote the Bank of England director, G. W. Norman. When Jaudon, representing the Bank of the United States, came seeking funds, Loyd had turned him down. Loyd worried about state securities. Pennsylvania, he noted, had "relied upon the support of the Bank [of the United States] for the means of carrying on their public works." If the latter were suspended, and therefore unproductive, "whence then is the dividend upon the stock to come?"[164] And in December Loyd wrote of Jaudon's activities: "What consummate impudence! Borrow more English money to pay debt in America."[165]

Until about June 1840, the Barings managed to dispose of *some* of their existing American holdings (four Paris firms helped out).[166] For the most part, American securities were heavily discounted or even went unsold in London. In November 1840 Erastus Corning had traveled to England, carrying $60,000 in New York state bonds issued to aid the Auburn and Rochester railway. He hoped to sell the bonds or exchange them for railroad iron. His timing was terrible. Iron-masters refused to have "anything whatsoever to do with bonds or stocks of the U.S." Nonetheless, eventually he disposed of the bonds—in January and April 1841—at 85 and 81 (here and subsequently bond prices are quoted as a percent of par, as is conventional). Corning arranged shipment of 1,100 tons of iron to the United States.[167]

In January 1841 the Bank of the United States resumed specie payments, only to suspend them for a third and final time on February 5, 1841. Its books show that by then 197,551 of its 350,000 shares (or 56 percent of its equity) were held abroad. In addition, its balance sheet (as of March 1, 1841) gave as liabilities $13 million in "loans" and "bonds" in Europe, plus $3.77 million for "J. Morrison & Son's account." (J. Morrison & Son was the successor to Morrison, Cryder

& Co.; in the last months of the Bank of the United States, it had become the bank's London agent, and James Morrison had made this large loan.)[168] "It is a bad, very bad business," wrote Loyd on March 6, 1841, on the affairs of the Bank of the United States.[169]

Although the London market was the key source of funds for American states, some states had sought continental investors. A number of state governments, for example, had borrowed in Paris in 1838–1841.[170] In 1838–39 Hope & Co., Amsterdam, had become particularly active in state securities. The image of the Dutch buyer in the secondary literature suggests a seeking after bargains; and in 1839 Hope & Co. was indeed inquiring about "good and cheap American investment."[171] By May 1839 Hope & Co. expressed awe of all the state securities, and the firm wrote, "It is a general complaint that there come over too many of these securities."[172] Not until 1838–1841 were purchasers on the European continent heavily involved in American state securities, and even then, their participation remained far less than that of the British.[173] Nonetheless, every major European financial center had private banking houses that dealt in these securities.[174]

By the spring of 1841, British and European investors lost confidence. Since the states had depended on the Bank of the United States for loans to meet interest payments, since most states could no longer borrow abroad to pay the interest, and since the returns on the underlying investments were virtually nonexistent, in 1841 and 1842 eight American states and one territory stopped interest payments: Mississippi, Arkansas, Indiana, Illinois, Maryland, Michigan, Pennsylvania, and Louisiana, as well as Florida Territory.[175] The Bank of the United States had its new charter in Pennsylvania and had been particularly engaged in intermediating Pennsylvania state securities. Some $24 million of Pennsylvania bonds were held abroad, and Britishers denounced the state as "profligate."[176] Mississippi repudiated a $5 million bond issue of 1838, her Governor asserting that the state would not have the Rothschilds "make serfs of our children."[177] For 1842, Representative William Cost Johnson made calculations "supposing" state securities held in foreign countries to be $150 million! He assumed that the "greater part" of the state bonds outstanding was held in Europe. Far more state securities were owned abroad in 1842 than in 1838.[178]

Even before the states had defaulted, European investors had hoped wistfully that the U.S. federal government would take responsibility for the state debts; they retained that hope. After all, Washington had done so when Alexander Hamilton was Secretary of the

Treasury. As states reneged on their obligations, rumors spread of war with Great Britain unless the federal government funded the debts of the individual states.[179] Congress did nothing, nor did Downing Street, which informed British investors that their loans were their own responsibility.[180]

In such disrepute was American credit by 1841–42 that even the Barings turned down issues of the *federal* government.[181] So did the Rothschilds: "You may tell your government," lectured the Paris Rothschild (Baron James de Rothschild) to an American in January 1842, "that you have seen the man who is at the head of the finances of Europe, and that he has told you that they [the U.S. Treasury] cannot borrow a dollar, not a dollar."[182] Recall that the Rothschilds had been involved in the futile effort to bail out the Bank of the United States and, in exchange, had taken as collateral state securities (its share had a face value of $5 million)![183]

No distinction was made in England (or on the Continent) between different types of American securities; the United States was branded a "nation of swindlers."[184] Americans abroad faced "mortification, obloquy and disgrace" because of their countrymen's behavior.[185] The Canon of St. Paul's, the Reverend Sydney Smith, who had himself bought the presumably "safe" Pennsylvania securities, lashed out at the "drab-coloured men of Pennsylvania" who should not "think of the flesh . . . but of that sin which hurled you from the heaven of Character." Americans "seize with loud acclamations on the money bags of Jones Loyd, Rothschild, and Baring," the Reverend continued, "but they do not give back the pittance of the widow, and the bread of the child."[186]

Thus, amidst the denunciations, in the 1840s the flow of foreign money to the United States virtually evaporated. As Leland Jenks put it, "Investors . . . dumped their . . . American loans upon the speculative dust-heap with the mortgages upon Colombia and dishonored bonds of Spain."[187] The British government did not help. Lord Palmerston, in March 1847, issued a circular indicating that a British subject rendered himself liable to punishment under British law forbidding slave trade "either by receiving and becoming owner of slaves in payment of Debts due him; or by selling such slaves, and exchanging them for the money in lieu of which they were received."[188] And in another circular to consuls abroad, Palmerston in January 1848 wrote, "It has hitherto been thought by the successive Governments of Great Britain undesirable that British subjects should invest their capital in loans to foreign Governments instead of employing it in profitable undertakings at home." He believed the losses of imprudent investors should "prove a salutary warning to others."[189] By contrast, Baring Brothers exerted "much effort" to try to encourage state governments to act responsibly.[190]

The economic historian Douglass C. North has written: "If foreign investment had sustained the [U.S.] boom of the 1830's, the lack of it helped to extend the depressed years of the 1840's . . . The dependence of western expansion upon foreign capital was reflected in almost a cessation of internal improvement."[191] Foreign investors wrote off or divested themselves of existing holdings. By 1843 a number of the trust companies that had attracted foreign investment to America were no longer in existence.[192] Between 1843 and 1848, Barings sold one-third of its portfolio of American securities, for a total of about £60,000. The sales were in the United States, where prices were higher than in Britain. The Barings disposed of federal government paper and state securities, as well as shares in the New York Bank of Commerce. The firm sold on its own account and also sold securities held by its clients.[193] Railroad promoters in Florida and Mississippi found in 1847 that the Barings and Hope & Co. were deaf to their proposals.[194]

The 1840s

The bleak picture of an America with virtually nonexistent credit, foreign divestments, and stagnation should not, however, be overdrawn.[195] Between 1840 and 1849, 5,000 miles of railroad track were laid, more than double that of the previous decade.[196] Statistics show a rise in value added by industry.[197] The territorial acquisitions of the 1840s meant new opportunities.

In 1839 Andrew Coats (brother of James and Peter) of the Scottish firm of J. & P. Coats had come to America, where he would remain for twenty-one years, guiding and managing a thriving thread sales business for the Scottish enterprise. Even before he arrived, in the mid-1830s at least 60 percent of the Coats company's output was exported to the United States, where it had not been sold under the Coats name; Andrew Coats built up a sales network and arranged for the marketing of thread under the Coats name and label.[198] In 1840 a young German, Ernest Leopold Schlesinger Benzon, became the New York agent for and then a partner in the British firm Naylor, Vickers & Co., developing the large U.S. trade of that business in steel bars and sheets from Sheffield, England, for tool manufacture.[199] Both these sales activities were harbingers for future Coats and Vickers business in America.

The Philadelphia and Reading Railroad floated in London issues of

$2 million and $1.5 million in 1843 and 1844, respectively.[200] Likewise, the Illinois and Michigan Canal Company raised money in Britain in the mid-1840s.[201] Britishers even made a few direct investments in the 1840s in U.S. manufacturing. The first heavy rails made in the United States were rolled in 1844 at the Mount Savage Iron Works in Maryland, two years after the U.S. Congress passed a tariff on rails; the firm, the Maryland and New York Iron and Coal Company, was largely British owned. Its output started "U.S." competition with British imports for the American rail market. (In the late 1840s, the Mount Savage works was sold to American investors; a U.S. Treasury report showed the works to be 27 percent owned abroad in 1853.)[202] One or two British packing houses were reported to have opened in Cincinnati in 1842, planning to take advantage of the *lower* British tariffs and to export meat to the United Kingdom.[203] I know nothing of their subsequent history.

A number of Britishers persevered. James Morrison, for example, had—as noted—made large loans to the Bank of the United States, but he had ample security. Morrison's son, Charles, wrote from America on December 5, 1842, to his father that the latter had "immense" investments in that country "reckoned by hundreds of thousands [of pounds]." In June 1843 the Morrisons made a final settlement with the liquidators of the defunct Bank of the United States. James Morrison's biographer suggests that from 1844 onward, he raised his interests in America.[204]

A survey conducted in 1848 identified 134 British mercantile houses in the United States (see Table 3.3). The principal ones were in New York and Philadelphia. The fifteen "hardware" importers located in Philadelphia included the leading Sheffield steel producers, several of which had long been in America and which would, years later, establish manufacturing subsidiaries in this country.[205] Meanwhile, in 1846 a federal court case had determined that a foreign company had equality with domestic enterprise in the protection of trademarks: "An alien gets the right of protection from his obedience, industry, and care while here, and the usefulness of his capital and skills employed here, *when he resides abroad.*"[206]

By 1847 Michigan and Indiana had reached compromises with their debtors; Pennsylvania, Illinois, Maryland, and Louisiana had resumed interest payments. Ohio bonds that had fallen as low as 56 had rebounded to 90. Only Mississippi, Florida, and Arkansas still remained in default.[207] That year (1847) the British Cunard Company built wharves at Jersey City, and the next year established regular service to New York.[208] Meanwhile, in 1846, to take advantage of the new U.S. mail contracts, Edward Mills (an American) had formed the

Table 3.3. British mercantile houses in the United States, 1848

	Boston	New York	Philadelphia	Baltimore	Alexandria	Charleston	Savannah	Mobile	New Orleans	U.S., Total
Merchant	1	3					5			9
Importer		10							1	11
Importer and general commission merchant									3	3
General commission merchant		5	5	2	1				18	31
Shipping and commission merchants								13	1	14
Broker		2								2
Exchange dealer and banker									1	1
Banker		2								2
Importer, hardware	1	2	15			2				20
Importer, iron		1								1
Importer, railroad iron		1								1
Dry goods merchant		1				4				5
Importer, dry goods		3	10							13
Importer, lace		1	2							3
Importer, wine		1								1
Wine merchant		1								1
Provision merchant				1						1
Dealer, cotton						1				1
Dealer, rice						9				9
Cotton spinner				1						1
Steamship agent		1								1
Insurance agent		3								3
Total	2	37	34	2	1	16	5	13	24	134

Source: Based on returns from British Consular Representatives in the United States, 1848–49, in FO 83/111, Public Record Office, London.

Note: Either trade in Philadelphia tended to be more specialized than in New York—or the reporter (the consul) was more specific. I would guess *both* were true. The importers of "hardware" in Philadelphia represented Sheffield and Birmingham firms. Since different consuls did the reporting, there was no uniformity. One cannot conclude that the functions of British mercantile houses in Mobile and New Orleans were very different from one another, since the differences might be one of local definition.

Ocean Steam Navigation Company. He failed to raise adequate capital, and the Senate of Bremen, with the assistance of several German states that wanted direct mail service and steamship facilities for emigrants, provided $286,000 "through American business firms to the capital stock of $534,000" of the Ocean Steam Navigation Company, which came to be largely under German control. The Bremen service began in June 1847.[209]

Then came the 1848 revolutions on the European continent, and Frenchmen and Germans became important purchasers of American securities. Unrest in Europe stimulated capital flight. Moreover, on January 24, 1848 (just before peace came in America's conflict with Mexico), gold was discovered in California. The news excited European attention not only to the West but also to the United States in general.[210] Thus the combination of the 1848 revolutions and the gold discoveries (push-and-pull effects) meant renewed foreign investments in the United States. Much of it was portfolio investment. "California societies" multiplied in France.[211] One estimate put German acquisitions of American securities, largely railroad bonds and shares, at $42 million in the three years between 1848 and 1851.[212] A single German investor from Bremen was said to have bought forty different U.S. securities before 1852![213] Temporarily, investments in the United States from the European continent seemed to soar above those from England.

In 1843 the Barings had once more become the financial agent of the U.S. federal government in London—a position that house had held from 1803 to 1835, only to be replaced by and now to replace the Rothschilds. (The Barings would remain in this role until 1867.)[214] The U.S. public debt had begun to rise after 1836—at first very slowly. When the U.S. government borrowed in 1847–48 to pay for the Mexican War and continued to borrow to pay the Mexican "indemnity," Baring Brothers marketed the securities on the Continent, providing added opportunities for the flight capital.[215] From Paris, Baron James de Rothschild, on February 22, 1848, at the beginning of the French Revolution, wrote his nephews in London, "I think we should purchase some American Treasury bonds, since America is still the most secure country for investment capital."[216] This was the man who six years earlier had scorned U.S. government bonds.[217]

Cautiously, Britishers also once again began to buy American securities.[218] The Rothschilds in England participated in the marketing of U.S. government bonds.[219] In May 1849 the state of Pennsylvania 5 percent stock sold at 80 (compared with 32½ in 1839).[220] By the end of the 1840s—and certainly by the early 1850s—a dramatic turnaround was evident. America's credit-worthiness was restored.

Once more, in the 1850s foreign individuals and firms would make sizable investments—still mainly portfolio ones—in the United States.[221] The lean years were over.

Foreign Investments in America in 1853

Table 3.4 indicates the level of foreign investments in the United States in 1853, as determined by a U.S. Treasury Department survey. According to the Treasury Department estimate, by June 1853 the

Table 3.4. Foreign investments in the United States, June 1853

Type of security[a]	Value held by foreigners (in millions of U.S. dollars)	% of total securities outstanding held by foreigners
U.S. government stocks	27.0	46
State stock	111.0[b]	58[b]
113 cities and towns (bonds)	16.5	21
347 counties	5.0	36
985 banks (stock)	6.7	3
75 insurance companies (stock)	0.4	3
244 railroad companies (stock)	8.2	3
244 railroad companies (bonds)	43.9	26
16 canal and navigation companies (stock)	0.5	2
16 canal and navigation companies (bonds)	2.0	9
15 miscellaneous companies (stock)	0.8	5
15 miscellaneous companies (bonds)	0.3	11
Total	222.2[c]	19

Source: U.S. Senate, *Report of the Secretary of the Treasury . . . [on] the Amount of American Securities Held in Europe,* 33rd Cong., 1st sess., 1854, Exec. Doc. 42, p. 53, in *Foreign Investments in the United States,* ed. Mira Wilkins (New York: Arno Press, 1977). The numbers of cities, towns, counties, and firms listed in the first column are those suveyed by the U.S. Treasury Department, not the number that attracted foreign investment.

[a] Based on returns to the Treasury Department.

[b] This was Winslow, Lanier & Co.'s figure. A Treasury estimate was lower—$72.9 million, or 38 percent of the total. The Treasury Department report printed both figures.

[c] Slightly off because of rounding.

U.S. federal government stock outstanding was over $58 million, of which $27 million (or 46 percent) was in the hands of foreign investors. The percentage was less than 56 percent owned abroad a half-century earlier, but still substantial.[222]

Much more important were the holdings in state securities. Some state government securities had again become salable overseas;[223] George Peabody & Co. managed to place a "fair quantity" of Virginia bonds in England.[224] In 1853 state securities represented, as they had since the 1830s, by far the largest single category of holdings of foreign investors. The U.S. Treasury found some 38 percent of state debts in 1853 held outside the United States. The banking firm Winslow, Lanier & Co., New York, believed this estimate was highly conservative and put state debts owned abroad in 1853 at 58 percent of the total, including all the defaulted Mississippi debt; three-quarters of the Georgia, Indiana, and Illinois debts; more than two-thirds of the Michigan and the still-in-default Arkansas debts; two-thirds of the Ohio debt; more than one-half of the Tennessee and North Carolina debt; and one-half of the Kentucky debt. It found that Dutch investors had large interests in Michigan and Mississippi securities.[225] Treasury estimates of state debt in foreign hands revealed 98 percent for the debt of Alabama, 83 percent for Louisiana, 66 percent for Pennsylvania, 63 percent for Massachusetts, and 55 percent for Maryland![226]

Of the debt of cities, towns, and counties, the U.S. Treasury identified 23 percent as owned by foreign investors in 1853, including more than half of the bonds outstanding for Boston and Cincinnati.[227]

When the U.S. Treasury Department scrutinized the ownership of 985 U.S. banks, as of June 1853, it discovered only 9 that were more than 10 percent owned by foreign investors.[228] (See Table 3.5.) Although the investors were not specified, recall that the Dutch were involved in the Merchants' Bank of New York, and the Barings had marketed the Louisiana State Bank and the Bank of Louisiana stock in London. The British Rothschilds were still holders of New Orleans Canal and Banking Company stock. Only 3 Louisiana banks were included in the 985—with foreign ownership averaging 28 percent. The high foreign percentage in the Bank of Mobile was associated with the cotton trade, as were the other southern bank stock holdings. The Girard Bank is not on the list; I assume the foreign investors sold out when no dividends were forthcoming during most of the 1840s. Indeed, no Pennsylvania bank is included. The Treasury study found miscellaneous small stock holdings in other banks by residents of England, France, Canada, Cuba, Egypt, and the East Indies, none

Table 3.5. U.S. banks owned by foreign investors, 1853

Bank	Location	Capital paid in (in millions of dollars)	Percentage foreign-owned
Merchants' Bank	New York, N.Y.	1.49	10.9
America Bank	New York, N.Y.	2.00	11.8
Merchants' Bank	Baltimore, Md.	1.50	18.9
Bank of Washington	Washington, D.C.	0.20	11.2
Bank of Mobile	Mobile, Ala.	1.50	40.3
Louisiana State Bank	New Orleans, La.	1.99	30.4
Canal and Banking Company	New Orleans, La.	3.16	26.5
Bank of Louisiana	New Orleans, La.	3.99	27.6
Planters' Bank	Nashville, Tenn.	2.25	14.2

Source: U.S. Senate, *Report of the Secretary of the Treasury . . . [on] the Amount of American Securities Held in Europe,* 33rd Cong., 1st sess., 1854, Exec. Doc. 42, pp. 12–31, in *Foreign Investments in the United States,* ed. Mira Wilkins (New York: Arno Press, 1977).

sufficient to exercise control.[229] From this point on, foreign stakes in American state banks in the East and South became relatively less significant as domestic banks proliferated.

A handful of British insurance companies had by 1853 started U.S. agencies and branch offices. The innovator, Phoenix Assurance Company, had closed its New Orleans agency in 1843, albeit its agencies in Savannah and Norfolk (opened in 1806) still existed. Whereas between 1826 and 1845, the U.S. share of the Phoenix parent company's premiums from overseas had been 9.3 percent, from 1846 to 1855 they were a mere 5.3 percent. Much more important, in 1848 the Liverpool & London (as of 1864 the Liverpool & London & Globe) appointed a New York agent and in 1851 set up a New York branch with agencies in other American cities. The Royal Insurance Company (another Liverpool enterprise) inaugurated a New York branch in 1851, and it likewise appointed agents elsewhere in the United States. These direct investments differed from (and were not included in) the small portfolio holdings in insurance in 1853 documented by the U.S. Treasury Department (see Table 3.4). The Liverpool & London & Globe and the Royal Insurance Company would have long histories in the United States and become significant providers of fire insurance coverage in this country.[230]

In 1848–1853 German, French, Swiss, and then British monies

poured into U.S. railroad securities.[231] This great interest in U.S. railroads was a new and important development. In 1852 N. M. Rothschild & Sons, London, made its very first investments in U.S. railroad bonds, in the New York and Erie and in the Pennsylvania Railroad.[232] That same year Baring—which had had earlier interests in American railroads—engaged W. H. Swift in the United States to provide advice; for many years Swift would pen lengthy reports on railroad securities to his London employer. Thomas Baring visited the United States on a tour of inspection (late summer and fall of 1852).[233] The first public issues of American railroad bonds were made in London in 1852. In the spring of 1852, a British syndicate led by Devaux & Co. completed plans to float in London a £1 million loan for the Illinois Central.[234] George Peabody & Co. now became very significant in handling American railroads, and in April 1853 this American house in London floated a new issue of Ohio and Mississippi Railroad bonds.[235]

British investments in railroads were frequently "tied ones."[236] Thus in 1849 the Barings arranged for the Baltimore and Ohio Railroad to purchase 22,000 tons of rails, making arrangements similar to those of earlier years. Half the payment to the English ironmasters was in 6 percent bonds of the railroad, maturing in six to ten years.[237] Rails purchased by U.S. companies in exchange for the securities of the road typically carried an inflated price.[238] Nonetheless, the initiative for the transaction would come from the U.S. railway manager rather than the British exporters, because the buyer of the rails preferred to pay in securities instead of cash. When Sir John Josiah Guest of the Dowlais mill in South Wales turned down U.S. railway bonds as payment for his iron, he found his exports curtailed.[239] British iron maker William Crawshay held £249,099 of American railway mortgage bonds in 1853.[240]

Rapidly rising foreign acquisitions of the U.S. railway stocks and bonds in the early 1850s—through securities purchases and commercial transactions—were likened by contemporaries to the surge in the sale of state government securities in the 1830s.[241] Of the 244 railroads canvassed by the U.S. Secretary of the Treasury in 1853, 76 were found to have attracted foreign investors. Foreign ownership came to $52.1 million—in bonds and stock.[242] Table 3.6 lists a half-dozen U.S. railroads more than 10 percent owned by such investors in June 1853. In addition, the U.S. Treasury Department noted that of the 140,000 shares ($100 each) of Illinois Central stock issued (not paid in) as of June 30, 1853, 28,330 shares (or 20 percent) were issued to investors abroad.[243] Table 3.6 reveals that foreign bond holdings (measured by percentage held abroad) were always in excess of the equity interest.

Table 3.6. U.S. railroads more than 10 percent owned by foreign investors, 1853

Railroad	Capital paid in (in millions of dollars)	Held by foreigners (in millions of dollars)	Held by foreigners (in percentages)	Bonds outstanding (in millions of dollars)	Bonds held by foreigners (in millions of dollars)	Bonds held by foreigners (in percentages)
Atlantic and St. Lawrence (Me.)	$1.8	$0.2	11%	$1.0	$0.2	20%
Western (Mass.)	5.2	0.8	15	4.0	3.2	80
Philadelphia and Reading (Pa.)	7.3	2.0	27	9.4	6.0	64
Madison and Indianapolis (Ind.)	1.6	0.2	12	0.6	0.4	75
Cleveland, Columbus and Cincinnati (Ohio)	3.7	0.5	13	0.1	0.1	75
Erie and Kalamazoo (Mich.)	0.3	0.1	33	0.3	0.2	83

Source: U.S. Senate, *Report of the Secretary of the Treasury . . . [on] the Amount of American Securities Held in Europe,* 33rd Cong., 1st sess., 1854, Exec. Doc. 42, pp. 36–47, in *Foreign Investments in the United States,* ed. Mira Wilkins (New York: Arno Press, 1977). Percentages were calculated before rounding.

Bonds were judged safer. See also Table 3.4, which shows that, of 244 railroads on which the U.S. Treasury Department collected information, the total value of bonds held abroad surpassed that of stock in a ratio of over five to one ($43.9 million compared with $8.2 million). Many railroads not included in Table 3.6 (since more than 90 percent of the equity was held in the United States) had a substantial portion of their bonds in foreign hands. For example, in 1853, $7 million of the $19.2 million in bonds outstanding of the New York and Erie Railroad were owned abroad; even more impressive, the Pennsylvania Railroad had $2.5 million of its $3 million in bonds outstanding in foreign ownership. Frenchmen and Germans had acquired all the outstanding bonds ($500,000) of the Alabama and Tennessee River Railroad; the equity was entirely American.[244] Although the foreign investments were sizable, the managements of the railroads were American.

As noted, after gold was discovered in California, the "rush" began. In 1849–50 alone, some eighty-three "California societies" with a capital of 333 million francs sprang up to capture the monies of Frenchmen. The London firm John Taylor & Sons dispatched a mining engineer to evaluate properties in California in 1850. From October 1851 to January 1853, for which dates we have information, thirty-two mining companies were formed in Britain to take up claims in the United States, practically all of them in California; they raised £2,440,000 in capital. None of the French firms nor any of these thirty-two British ones proved of consequence in terms of gold output or profits to the owners.[245] These investments were *not* included in the U.S. Treasury Department survey of 1853.

In May 1848 Baron James de Rothschild resolved to send his twenty-one-year-old son, Alphonse, to the United States, hoping to keep him safe from the revolutionary fervor. It seemed the Rothschilds would replace August Belmont, the firm's agent, and establish a "House of Rothschild" in America. This plan was not executed.[246] Instead, Benjamin Davidson, a relative (by marriage), opened in 1849 a new Rothschild agency in San Francisco, on behalf of the London and Paris Rothschilds. Davidson sold imported merchandise and bought gold.[247] In 1849 Godeffroy, Sillem & Co. became the San Francisco representative of J. C. Godeffroy & Co., Hamburg, Germany, and Ward & Price of New York. Its initial business was as a commission merchant; in 1850 Godeffroy, Sillem & Co. moved into banking, and in the early 1850s the firm advertised that it had money to lend and was willing to discount promissory notes (its California business apparently did not survive the 1850s).[248] By contrast, the Rothschild's West Coast agency flourished.[249] In 1849 the French Lazard brothers started a firm in California, exporting gold and silver.[250] The gold rush extended foreign investors' interest across the continent.[251] By 1853 California was of great interest to foreign investors.

Absent from Table 3.4 is a category devoted to manufacturing. Heinrich Steinway began manufacturing pianos *in Germany* in 1836. In 1849–50 he and four of his sons, including Charles Steinway, immigrated to the United States. In 1853 they started to produce pianos in New York. Theodore, the eldest of Heinrich's sons, remained behind in charge of the Germany factory. Was the New York venture a "foreign investment"? Who knows. The immigrants had the skills and could manufacture the carefully made product in America. In 1865 Theodore Steinway sold the original German business and also migrated to this country.[252] Long before that (if there was foreign investment), the New York Steinway company seems to have become totally independent of its German origins; it was an American enterprise.

In an entirely different industry, and not associated with immigration, John H. Turnbull of John H. Turnbull & Co., Glasgow (an iron and copper works that had "a profitable sideline in the distillation of wood") came to the United States in 1849 "to scout the possibility of making pyroligneous acid" from American hardwood to be converted into acetate of lime for shipment to Scotland. In 1850, a few miles south of Binghamton, New York, Turnbull & Co., using Scottish workers and equipment, started the first hardwood distillation firm in the United States. The operation (conducted in great secrecy so as not to give out the technology) was a branch of the Glasgow business; it exported most of its acetate output. This was a direct investment to use American resources.[253]

The 1853 Treasury Department survey, likewise, did not include foreign investments in land and real estate or in mortgages. Investments from abroad in American land increased. In 1850 William Scully, a landowner in Ireland, visited Illinois and made his first purchases of land there (by the 1880s Scully's landholdings would become a cause célèbre, as I will show).[254] Some foreign investments in land and real estate came about through defaults on mortgages and trade debts. In the 1840s, for example, the Bank of Montreal had financed Canadian merchants who bought grain in Illinois. The loans were personally secured. When the merchants could not pay, the bank found itself in the early 1850s with a number of properties in Michigan and in Chicago "acquired through possession of hypothecated mortgages."[255]

In short, foreign investments in the United States in 1853 covered a wide range of economic endeavors, with the heaviest existing involvements clearly the portfolio ones in public sector securities, that is, in state government bonds. The new 1848–1853 investments in railroad securities were nonetheless significant and important harbingers for the future.

Reactions

In the fifty years from 1803 to 1853, American reactions to foreign investment remained ambivalent. Men such as Albert Gallatin (1761–1849) and especially Daniel Webster (1782–1852) became the successors to Alexander Hamilton in their favorable views toward foreign money. In an address to the U.S. Senate (1832), Webster noted: "From the commencement of the [U.S.] government, it has been thought desirable to invite . . . the introduction of foreign capital. Our stocks have been open to foreign subscriptions; and the State banks, in like manner, are free to foreign ownership. Whatever State has created a debt has been willing that foreigners should become purchasers, and desirous of it." In the same speech, Webster insisted that there were no dangers in foreign ownership of the Second Bank of the United States: "All the advantages would be on our side. The bank would still be our institution, subject to our own laws."[256] For Webster, foreign investors provided capital needed by the new nation.

As Webster pointed out, state governments had indeed sought monies abroad and continued to do so. In Boston, New York, and Philadelphia, merchants and bankers—associated with international trade and maintaining transatlantic connections—wanted to attract foreign capital to supplement U.S. resources. They helped direct foreign monies into American investments. *The American Railroad Journal* could declare (in July 1852): "We have labored for years to bring our railroad securities to the favorable notice of foreign capitalists, for the reason that we need their money to assist in developing our resources . . . [and] to lessen . . . our rates of interest, which are much too high."[257]

Yet, coincidentally, many reservations existed. In 1821 *Niles' Weekly Register* was complaining of the drain on the American economy in paying interest on American securities held abroad: "In the present state of things when capital is so abundant in the United States, [remitting these interest payments is] a dead loss."[258] Similarly, a committee of the New York state legislature warned (in 1833) that if the interest rate paid foreign capital was too high, foreign capital would "ultimately prove an injurious drain on the country."[259]

In 1817, after the War of 1812 was over, Congress had inaugurated a "navigation monopoly" for American shipping in the coastwise trade to prevent this branch of U.S. transportation from falling into the hands of foreign shippers. The controls persisted, and from that point only ships built and owned in the United State could engage in *coastwise* trade.[260]

Certain states retained earlier laws disqualifying aliens from acquiring, holding, or bequeathing land to their heirs. In 1830 a U.S. Supreme Court decision upheld a Maryland law restricting alien land ownership.[261] In the mid-1830s, the Holland Land Company apparently decided to liquidate its upstate New York investments because of hostile state legislation.[262]

Regulations governing federal land sales initially had had no requirements of citizenship or residence, yet with the influx of foreign investment in the 1830s, critics had asked whether foreign owners should be allowed to acquire low-priced public land. Beginning with the Preemption Act of 1841, laws on federal land sales sought explicitly to encourage settlement and normally contained a clause that the government's sale of such land would be to U.S. citizens or to persons who had declared their intention of becoming citizens.[263] There was in the federal laws nothing, however, that said U.S. purchasers could not sell or transfer this land to a foreign investor.

Within the country, a deep-seated populist, principally agrarian, sentiment swelled against great wealth, domestic and foreign. Concentrated wealth was perceived as undemocratic. Andrew Jackson was not satisfied with the controls on the voting power of foreign holders of the Second Bank of the United States shares. As I have indicated, Jackson attacked foreign interests in the bank: "Should the stock of the bank principally pass into the hands of the subjects of a foreign country, and we should unfortunately become involved in a war with that country, what would be our condition?" Jackson answered his own question: "All its [the bank's] operations within [our country] would be in the aid of the hostile fleets and armies without. Controlling our currency, receiving our public moneys, and holding thousands of our citizens in dependence, it would be far more formidable and dangerous than the naval and military power of the enemy. If we must have a bank . . . it should be *purely American.*"[264] National security was at risk.

Niles' Weekly Register remarked on the paradox whereby U.S. government deposits were removed from the Second Bank of the United States and transferred to other banks, one of which, the Manhattan, was foreign owned "AND IN THIS BANK THE FOREIGN STOCKHOLDERS VOTE!" In a subsequent article, the same weekly declared, "We have no horror of FOREIGN CAPITAL—if subjected to *American management.*"[265]

In the election of 1840, Democrats had fanned the flames of antiforeign sentiment, labeling rich foreign bankers as irresponsible advocates of the assumption of state debts by the U.S. federal government and as meddlers in American politics.[266] Mississippi, which had once feted European buyers of its securities, defiantly refused payment of its debt and condemned "foreign" interference; its governor declared in January 1842 the "sacred truth that the toiling million never shall be burthened with taxes to support the idle few."[267] Americans resented international bankers' intrusion in U.S. affairs (especially demands for payments of debts in default) in much the same way as Latin Americans in recent years have rejected what they interpret as the intervention of U.S. bankers in their political life. Americans were concerned with "dependency."

The so-called locofoco movement of the late 1830s and 1840s defended debtors and denounced domestic and foreign creditors. When Americans wanted to disassociate themselves from European investors, they counted the holdings of earls, counts, and lords, so alien to American democracy. The Locofocos pointed with scorn to the members of British nobility who owned securities of the Bank of the United States.[268]

In California, as foreign investors sought gold, the question arose as to how foreign miners on public lands should be treated. Should the privilege of working our mines be restricted to American citizens (including those who had declared their intention to become Americans)? California imposed special taxes on foreign miners.[269]

Populist views echoed in U.S. rhetoric, opposing wealth, privilege, and absentee ownership and upholding the American over the alien. Nonetheless, other Americans continued to seek out capital from abroad. The level of foreign capital invested in the United States in 1853—America's long-term international indebtedness—was much greater than in 1803, greater even than in the boom years of the 1830s, and in fact, greater than ever before in American history.[270] Foreign investment—ups and downs and criticisms notwithstanding—was keeping pace, or nearly keeping pace, with the growth in size of the American economy.

1803–1853: The Foreign Investments

From 1803 there had been some growth in foreign investment, which was interrupted by the War of 1812, but then slowly resumed until the 1830s, when foreign investment soared, assisting that decade's buoyant prosperity. Capital imports were cut back substantially in the 1840s, to revive in the late 1840s and 1850s.

The fifty years from 1803 to 1853 witnessed variations in the composition of foreign investment in the United States, in both the public and the private sectors. As noted, in 1803 the U.S. federal debt held abroad was 56 percent; in 1835 it was zero (there was no federal debt); in 1853 it was back up to 46 percent—lower than in 1803, but still a significant percentage. The state debt held abroad (small in 1803) had grown dramatically in the 1830s, especially at the decade's end. Then, for the first time, in 1841–42 Americans defaulted on many of their loans; eight states and one territory stopped paying interest on their bonds. In the 1840s, attempts were made to resume interest payments; and by 1853 most states were once again fulfilling their obligations (although not Mississippi, Arkansas, or Florida). According to the New York banking house Winslow, Lanier & Co., state debts owned abroad in 1853 were 58 percent of the total state debts. In both dollar and percentage terms, state debts had become the most important sector for foreign investment—far larger in dollar and percentage terms than in 1803 (and there were, of course, more states; at year-end 1803 the nation had seventeen states compared with thirty-one at year-end 1853). Some local governments—counties, cities, and towns—sought foreign monies in the 1830s. Although less important debtors than the state and federal governments, these borrowers contributed to the sizable public sector foreign obligations of America. In 1853, as in 1803, the public sector in the United States had the largest debt to foreign investors.

Private sector obligations also changed; this was true of both foreign portfolio and direct investments. First, in terms of portfolio investments, in 1803 fully 35 percent of the stock of state banks and 62 percent of the stock of the first Bank of the United States were owned abroad. The War of 1812 saw the end of the Bank of the United States, and at the war's conclusion, the establishment of the Second Bank of the United States. In the 1820s and particularly in the 1830s, much of the foreign investment in state banks went through *state government* channels. By contrast, the Second Bank of the United States (before, but especially after, it became a state-chartered bank in 1836) received a formidable amount of foreign participation. In 1841, when the bank suspended payments for the last time, some 56 percent of its stock was reported to be held abroad; it also had other major foreign liabilities. In 1803, as noted, 35 percent of state bank securities was held abroad; I have no comparable figures for the late 1830s, but the evidence suggests that even including the Bank of the United States (of Pennsylvania) and the substantial involvement in Louisiana banking, the figure was probably lower than 35 percent, because of the large number of new domestically financed banks. By 1853, of 985 banks surveyed, the percentage of shares foreign owned was a mere 3 percent. The drop in foreign holdings of American bank securities was dramatic.

Again in terms of portfolio investments, in 1803 foreign investors had relatively small interests in American transportation companies; in the 1820s and especially the 1830s, most foreign investment in transportation went primarily through investments in state securities. Major canal projects obtained foreign finance. The 1830s were the first decade of American railroads, and slowly foreign investors became involved. That interest in railroads cooled in the 1840s, but by 1853 American railroads offered a new set of investment opportunities for foreign savings. This was the start of what would become truly giant foreign investments in U.S. rails.

As in 1803, so too in 1853 merchant banks abroad were prominent in the transfer of American securities into foreign hands. The House of Baring, London, and Hope & Co., Amsterdam, were significant in 1853 as in 1803. Newly important, however, were the Rothschilds in London and, to a lesser extent, in Paris. In America, new financial intermediaries were formed in the 1830s that acted to bring foreign monies to this nation. Some of these firms were short-lived; others survived—aided by well-established European connections. American financial intermediaries complemented those in Europe.

Foreign direct investment also existed, and here too were some novel features. Despite the publicity over such investments, new ones in land appear to have been relatively less important than they had been before 1803. The best of American businessmen were no longer canvassing Europe to sell their country's land. (Land, to repeat, is considered a foreign direct investment because the foreign owner controls the property.)

Foreign direct investments in trade outlets persisted and increased, with more merchants and, to some extent, foreign manufacturers having American representation. There were direct entries of companies that would later have major stakes in the United States: the Hudson's Bay Company (to engage in the fur trade in the West) and J. & P. Coats (which had sold in America for years and which after 1839 had Andrew Coats in this country, supervising and establishing a sales organization). J. & P. Coats would later emerge as an important multinational enterprise; it might be designated the pioneer British manufacturing company in America. Definitions are difficult. A number of other British manufacturers had earlier direct representation in the United States, but there seems to have been a discontinuity with their later multinational growth. In the case of the Coats firm, the sales network that Andrew Coats established could be and was used by the company when, after the Civil War, it started to manufacture in the United States.[271]

As for foreign direct investments in manufacturing, 1803 to 1853, these were few and far between; only one was motivated by U.S. tariffs—the short-lived British stake in rolling the first heavy iron rails made in America, at Mount Savage Iron Works in Maryland in 1844. There were several foreign direct investments in manufacturing to supply the British market, but none was of great consequence.

Far more important as foreign direct investments were the British-headquartered insurance companies: the Liverpool & London (later the Liverpool & London & Globe) and the Royal Insurance Company, both of which inaugurated their U.S. branches in 1851. These companies had their head offices and main operations in the United Kingdom and extended their business into America.

In these years we begin to see firms (other than those engaged solely in trade) with operations in their home country that moved their business over borders into the United States with direct representation here (and in other foreign countries as well)—firms that would continue into the twentieth century. The institutional form was something new and not yet well defined. Transportation and communication were not adequate for effective coordination and control. Nonetheless, there is a big divide between what was now taking shape and the direct investments from overseas in the colonial era by, for example, the Principio Company. In the case of the Principio Company, the headquarters, first in London and then apparently in Birmingham, had one or two regular employees. In Birmingham, England, owners of the Principio Company had their own plants, but there was no backward integration, no extension of any single iron-manufacturing firm. By contrast, with J. & P. Coats and the British insurance companies, British companies operating at home actually extended themselves internationally. In my research on American business abroad, I identified Singer as the first modern American multinational, noting its initial moves overseas in the 1850s.[272] Perhaps Coats can be called the first modern British multinational, and if so, its initial expansion abroad preceded that of Singer.

Another key change in the pattern of foreign investment in America 1803–1853—direct and portfolio—was its spread westward. New territories and the lure of gold pushed investment to the Pacific. California became a focus of interest. This geographical expansion reflected what was happening in the nation as a whole.

Between 1803 and 1853, the nationality composition of foreign investors in America also altered. The U.S. Treasury report's 1853 information is not divided by nationalities; the report contains only miscellaneous references to the home countries of foreign investors in the United States. Nonetheless, the overall distribution seems clear. In 1853 the British first place was undisputed.[273] Dutch investors were still important in 1853, but in relative terms far less so than in 1803. Since 1848 German stakes in railroad securities had grown. The German interests became increasingly associated with the new German immigration. French investment in the United States in 1853 appears to have been lower than the Dutch or German; the French, moreover, lost substantial sums with the fraudulent "California societies." Some Swiss monies entered. Other nationalities were also present, to a much smaller extent.

In sum, then, in the years 1803–1853, foreign investments in the United States had grown from an estimated $65–$70 million to at least $222.2 million. The bulk of the new foreign investment was of a portfolio nature and went into *government* securities. Much of the government borrowing was, in turn, devoted to aiding banks and transportation projects. Portfolio and direct investments from abroad also went directly into the private sector; here too, foreign portfolio investments exceeded foreign direct ones. There were major portfolio investments in the first and second Banks of the United States. By 1848–1853, railroad investments were mounting rapidly. Foreign direct investments did not constitute, in dollar terms, a significant sum relative to the total long-term foreign investments in the United States. Investments spanned the country from New York to California, from New Orleans to Cincinnati. The British were the principal investors from abroad. The sizable foreign investments in America encountered an ambivalence, as in past years and—as we will see—in future ones.

4.

The Perilous Decades
at Mid-Century:
1854–1874

During the mid-1850s—until the Panic of 1857—foreign investment in the United States rose.[1] The dampening effects of the 1857 Panic were short-lived; but with the outbreak of the Civil War in 1861, as one commentator wrote, "the distrust felt by nearly all foreigners in the future of the United States was so great that the larger portion of American securities—national, state and corporate—held in foreign countries, were returned for sale at almost any sacrifice; and to such an extent was this the case that the country in 1863 may be said to have exhibited a clean national ledger in respect to foreign indebtedness."[2] This statement was an exaggeration.[3]

After 1863 investors from abroad resumed their interest in American opportunities. Writing of 1865–1873, the economist Matthew Simon stated that a "central feature of the international transactions of the United States . . . was the almost continuous inflow of foreign capital in great volume."[4] By 1869 the foreign capital invested in the United States had reached a new peak, estimated at $1.4 billion.[5] The data of the economist Jeffrey G. Williamson indicate that in that exceptional year, net capital imports totaled 27 percent of U.S. net capital formation.[6] Between 1869 and 1873 the climb in foreign investment continued, despite a number of defaults on state government and railroad bonds.[7] The Panic of 1873 represented only a temporary setback. Table 4.1 traces, as best I can establish, the growth of foreign investments in U.S. securities, 1853–1874. It probably understates the amount of foreign investment in U.S. railroads. It includes some direct investments from abroad. It is very rough and should be viewed with caution.

The rise of foreign investment in the 1850s and particularly in the post–Civil War years was aided by new transportation and communi-

Table 4.1. Estimates of long-term foreign investment in the United States, 1853–1874 (in millions of U.S. dollars)[a]

Date	Total	Government			Private sector							
		Federal	State	County/city	Banks	Canals	Railroads	Insurance	Mining	Manufacturing	Utilities	Other
1853[b]	222.2	27.0	111.0	21.5	6.7	2.5	52.1[c][d]	0.4	0.7	0.1	0.1	
1854												
1856[e]	241.0	15.0	111.0	21.5	6.7	2.5	82.9	0.4	f	f	f	1.0
1859		40.0[g]										
1861, Jan.	444.0[h]						100.0[i]					
1863	200.0[j]											
1864, March		150.0[k]										
1865, March		320.0[l]										
1865, June	m	m										
1866[n]	600.0	350.0	← 150.0 →		o	o	100.0	o	o	o	o	
1867		486.0[p]										
1868[q]	938.0	700.0	60.0	f	f	7	150.0	f	f	f	f	21.0
1869[r]	1,390.5	1,000.0	100.0	7.5	f	5	243.0	f	10.0			25.0[s]
1871		845.0[t]										
1872	1,500.0[u]											
1873	1,500.0[u]	w										
1874	1,500.0[v]	92.9[x]					390.0[y]					

Table 4.1. (*Cont.*)

[a] In this table I have excluded (or put in the notes) estimates that seem counter to other information. I have chosen what I believe to be the best (most reliable) figures, but all these figures must be accepted with the greatest caution; authors were not precise on whether their estimates reflected par value, purchase price, or current price of securities. Although I have sought to cite the most knowledgeable, plausible sources, the figures are highly vulnerable. When estimates were expressed in pounds, I have translated them into dollars at the rate £1 = $4.86.

[b] U.S. Senate, *Report of the Secretary of the Treasury . . . [on] the Amount of American Securities Held in Europe*, 33rd Cong., 1st sess., 1854. Exec. Doc. 42, in *Foreign Investments in the United States*, ed. Mira Wilkins (New York: Arno Press, 1977). I have used Winslow, Lanier, & Co. on state figures.

[c] Another estimate, for Nov. 1853, was $70 million. Cited in Ralph Hidy, *House of Baring* (Cambridge, Mass.: Harvard University Press, 1949), p. 429.

[d] The editor of *American Railroad Journal* estimated that $150 million in foreign capital had been invested in U.S. railroads as of Sept. 1854; see Alfred D. Chandler, *Henry Varnum Poor* (Cambridge, Mass.: Harvard University Press, 1956), p. 312n. Although the 1853 Treasury estimate may have been low, this $150 million figure seems high. I have omitted it from the table because the series would give the wrong impression. There is no indication of a sharp rise in European investment in the United States in the years 1853–1854, followed by a fall.

[e] U.S. Secretary of the Treasury, *Annual Report, 1856*, p. 426. The returns are incomplete. I have adjusted the state government figures to coincide with the 1853 manipulation, by adding $38 million to the state securities figure and to the total. The $241 million total seems to me far too low.

[f] Included under "Other."

[g] Unofficial data from *Philadelphia Ledger* (1859), republished in *Bankers' Magazine*, London, 20 (Jan. 1860): 51. I think this number is too high; see text.

[h] *Hunt's Merchant Magazine*, 59 (Oct. 1868): 242ff. This may be high. Compare the 1861 figure with A. Dudley Mann, Washington, to Baring Brothers & Co., Jan. 15, 1861, Baring Papers, Public Archives, Ottawa, vol. 97, p. 054635, wherein there is an estimate of $200 million "of the securities of this country of all kinds" owned in Europe. Mann's rough estimate seems to me too low. John J. Madden, *British Investment in the United States, 1860–1880* (New York: Garland, 1985), pp. 78–79 (tables 14–15), put the total owned in Britain and on the European continent at $239 million (nominal value) in 1860, presumably at year-end.

[i] British only. Dorothy Adler, *British Investment in American Railways, 1834–1898* (Charlottesville: University Press of Virginia, 1970), p. 24. My estimate might double this for worldwide investment in U.S. railroads. See text below. C. K. Hobson, *Export of Capital* (London: Constable, 1914), p. 128, giving no source cites an estimate of £80,000,000 of U.S. railroad stock being held in England in 1857 (that would be about $390 million). I believe he is in error—see text. Madden, *British Investment*, pp. 78–79, put as of 1860 British investments in U.S. rails at $97 million and European continental ownership at $34 million—nominal values. He is probably low on the continental investments. Madden also cites an estimate by Ward, Campbell to Barings, March 22, 24, 1859, that puts foreign investment in U.S. rails at $200 million (p. 403, table 26). The amount may have dropped in 1859–1860, but the drop he suggests is too extreme. (The Barings thought British investment in U.S. rails early in 1859 had reached $600 million; see Madden, *British Investment*, p. 25.)

[j] Charles J. Bullock, John H. Williams, and Rufus S. Tucker, "The Balance of Trade of the United States," *Review of Economic Statistics*, 1 (July 1919): 223. As noted in text, the *Report of the Special Commissioner of the Revenue* (1869), p. xxvi, in *Foreign Investments in the United States*, ed. Mira Wilkins (New York: Arno Press, 1977), put this figure at 0. Obviously, that was an exaggeration. Madden accepted the $200 million figure (*British Investment*, p. 388, table 24, and p. 382). He estimated the breakdown as follows: federal government holdings, $58 million; state and municipal, $39 million; railroad bonds and shares, $92 million; other, $5 million; total, $194 million (see pp. 78–79, tables 14–15). I do not have full confidence in these figures and thus have not included them in Table 4.1.

[k] Ellis P. Oberholtzer, *Jay Cooke* (1907; rpt. New York: Burt Franklin, 1970), I, 309, citing John Sherman's estimate of $150 to $200 million.

[l] Oberholtzer, *Jay Cooke*, I, 514, citing a letter of March 30, 1865, of Frederick Kuhne, of Knauth, Nachod, & Kuhne.

[m] *Hunt's Merchant Magazine*, 52 (June 1865): 421–422, estimated that some $500 million to $800 million of "U.S. bonds" and added sums of U.S. stocks of various enterprises were held by Europeans.

[n] U.S. Secretary of the Treasury, *Annual Report, 1866*, p. 12. These figures seem conservative, especially the one on railroads.

[o] Included in railroad figure.

[p] *Economist*, 25 (March 9, 1867): 33.

[q] *Hunt's Merchant Magazine*, 59 (Oct. 1868): 242ff.

[r] *Report of the Special Commissioner of the Revenue* (1869), pp. xxvii–xxviii. Madden, *British Investment*, p. 391, thought the compiler of these statistics (David A. Wells) had reason to inflate his totals, in the absence of any accurate evidence. Wells wanted to justify a return to low tariffs and the gold standard. The argument ran that a high tariff and an inconvertible currency produced a high-cost economy, which curbed exports and made foreign borrowing necessary to finance imports. The large foreign indebtedness of America was used as proof of this contention. Madden may be right, but I do not find Wells's estimates extraordinarily high.

[s] Real estate mortgages, etc.

[t] Robert L. Nash, ed., *Fenn's Compendium*, 12th ed. (London, 1876), p. 470, and London *Times*, March 27, 1871. According to *Banker's Magazine*, New York, 33 (Jan. 1879): 525, the U.S. Treasury estimated that between $800 million and $1,000 million in U.S. government bonds were held abroad in 1871.

[u] Bullock, Williams, and Tucker, "Balance of Trade," p. 225. I think they failed to realize the rise in investment during the years 1872–1873, presuming the 1872 estimate reflected the 1873 figures as well.

[v] The estimate is my own and very rough. Madden, *British Investment*, pp. 78–79 (tables 14–15), 388 (table 24), gave two estimates—one of $1,667 million and the other of $1,462 million. (The first estimate seems to include and the other to exclude railroad shares, but railroad shares cannot account for the difference.) The estimates are altogether too precise.

[w] While contemporary figures are not available for 1873–1874, there is no evidence of a sharp drop in investment. Indeed, there were the giant refunding issues in London of 1871 and 1873 (see Table 4.6), and the qualitative evidence would indicate a continuing and, in fact, rising investment. Madden's year-end figures (in millions) for U.S. federal debt held abroad were: 1871, $562; 1872, $627; 1873; $643; 1874, $633. Elsewhere in the book (pp. 388, 401) he puts U.S. federal bonds held abroad at $700 million, 1873–1874. I think he was probably low in his estimates. Matthew Simon, *Cyclical Fluctuations and the International Capital Movements* (New York: Arno Press, 1978), p. 151, believed that from July 1870 to Sept. 1873, there was a reduction in the "volume of the European-held [U.S. government] debt," but on his uncertainty, see pp. 153–156.

[x] *Commercial and Financial Chronicle*, 19 (Nov. 14, 1874): 493. Of this $92.9 million, $54.2 million were said to be in default—that is, 58 percent.

[y] As of Dec. 1874 and in reference to bonds only; *Banker's Magazine*, New York, 30 (May 1876): 845. Of this figure an estimated $148 million (38 percent) were in default. An alternative estimate of $375 million was in *Commercial and Financial Chronicle*, 19 (Oct. 10, 1874): 343. It too was for bonds only, with an estimated $150 million or 40 percent in default. This figure seems low. Madden, *British Investment*, pp. 78–79, puts the nominal value of British and continental holdings of U.S. railroad bonds and shares at $894 million (£184 million), of which $141 million was in railroad shares.

cation links, which were in turn often assisted by the infusion of monies from abroad. Steamships provided regularly scheduled transatlantic service that improved in the 1850s. The ships—often British owned—connected with American railroad routes. The railroads were built, aided by foreign finance. Telegraph lines, introduced in the late 1840s, began to crisscross the nation, and in 1856 an American, Cyrus Field, sought U.S. capital for a transatlantic cable; when his countrymen showed no interest, Field got funding in England for his Atlantic Telegraph Company, Ltd. The cable—which revolutionized international communication—eventually became a success in 1866.[8] Meanwhile, in 1861 the telegraph (mainly American financed) had become transcontinental,[9] and in 1869 so had the railroad; by then, railroads were absorbing unprecedented amounts of foreign capital. Steamships, cables, telegraph lines, and railways tied the United States with the world economy in a new and unparalleled manner, and as this occurred, once the Civil War was over, the way was open for major foreign investments. It was all a reinforcing process, with the new foreign investments creating an infrastructure that then encouraged more foreign interest.

The 1850s

From 1853 to 1861, foreign savings flowed into American federal, state, and local government securities, railroad bonds and shares, and, to a lesser extent, other sectors. In sequence, we will look at the pre–Civil War foreign holdings in government bonds, railroad securities (and the way these sizable new stakes arose), and then banks, mining, trade, insurance, and land.

The national debt of the United States shrunk in 1853–1857 and rose again before 1860 to above the 1853 level.[10] Estimates on the amount of federal debt owned abroad reveal a decline in the dollar amount of U.S. government securities held outside the country from $27 million (1853) to $15 million (1856).[11] With the Crimean War (1854–1855) and higher interest rates in Europe, many American federal government securities were repatriated.[12] After 1853 Baring Brothers turned away from marketing U.S. government issues.[13] The Panic of 1857 was a deterrent to new investment from abroad—although with lower tariff revenues, the U.S. Treasury had had to turn to borrowings.[14] An article in the *Philadelphia Ledger*, republished in *Bankers' Magazine*, London, and in *Hunt's Merchant Magazine* in January 1860,[15] provided unofficial information from a writer with access "to the books of the Sub-Treasury" in New York, where interest on seven-eighths of the public debt was said to be paid. The unidentified author estimated that roughly two-thirds of the U.S. public debt was held abroad—a proportion that seems too high, considering the fact that nothing I can find in the U.S. Treasury *Annual Reports,* or in the large secondary literature on the U.S. debt, or in bankers' archives indicates that any major portion of the new issues or of older ones went abroad in 1857–1859. In July 1859 the U.S. debt had risen to $58.8 million, which would mean just under $40 million was in foreign hands (if the two-thirds figure is correct); this seems too sharp a rise from the $15 million 1856 figure to have escaped substantial public comment.[16] What was, however, most interesting about the *Philadelphia Ledger* article was the inclusion of the names of U.S. foreign creditors. The London and Paris Rothschilds and Baring Brothers were listed.[17] The largest foreign creditor (to the extent of $350,000) was Lord Overstone (Samuel Jones Loyd). A leading London banker (his firm was Jones Loyd & Co.), Lord Overstone had been instrumental in the passage of the British Bank Act of 1844 and was a prominent member of the so-called currency school in British banking thought. I have noted his earlier American investments.[18] Reported holders of the U.S. debt also included Lord Elgin ($17,000), Lord Macauley ($30,000), two relatives of the King of Naples ($125,000), the Russian Alexander Herzen ($80,000), and the Frenchman Count Alexis de Tocqueville (no amount given).[19] In short, while it seems likely the article exaggerated the foreign percentage of holdings of U.S. federal government securities, it did reveal a broad interest in such paper.

Although the overall debts of American state governments increased from $192.5 million in 1853 to $257.4 million in 1860[20] and remained much larger than the federal government debt, new European purchases of state bonds were not substantial.[21] New York and Virginia, which did sell bonds abroad, were exceptional.[22] In about 1855 a member of the Geneva firm of Lombard, Odier & Cie. visited the United States, acquired some county bonds, and returned to place these in Switzerland.[23] There also appear to have been sizable sales abroad (especially in Germany) of securities of American cities.[24]

In Chapter 3 I cited the U.S. Treasury Department estimate of $52 million in railroad bonds and stocks held abroad in June 1853. Dorothy Adler, an expert on British investment in American railroads, thought this figure was low.[25] Baring's American agent put the total of "foreign railroad loans" at $70 million in November 1853.[26] By 1856 the U.S. Secretary of the Treasury believed foreign investment in U.S. railroads was equal to $82.9 million.[27] C. K. Hobson cites an estimate out of line with the others of £80 million (or about $390 million) of U.S. railroad securities held in England in 1857.[28] Adler's guess was that by the start of the Civil War in 1861, British holdings in American railway securities came to $100 million.[29] If one adds to the British figures continental European interests (those of Germans, Dutch, Swiss, and French especially), plus Canadian ones, along with those of a wide range of other miscellaneous investors, the sum would be far greater possibly as much as double. All these estimates are crude, owing to (1) the large amount of trading in securities, (2) the existence of nominee accounts and bearer bonds that the Treasury Department survey would not have included as "foreign," and (3) the absence of any regular reporting system.

Between 1853 and 1860, Americans added 16,786 miles of railroad track.[30] The expansion required vast amounts of capital. British firms issued circulars drawing attention to the splendid returns on U.S. railroads. In 1856, for example, they noted that home investments brought 5 percent, while American railroads provided "a minimum return of 10 percent."[31] The London *Times* warned British investors to be cautious, but they were not.[32]

Certain American railroads became especially successful in attracting money from abroad. In its original 1852 financing, the Illinois Central—as noted in Chapter 3—had looked to Europe for capital.[33] When in 1854 Robert Schuyler (who had resigned from the presidency of the Illinois Central in 1853) was involved in a fraud related to New York and New Haven Railroad stock, many Americans made faulty assumptions and sold their Illinois Central holdings. The price of shares and bonds plummeted. By August 1854 the bonds had fallen from $100 par value to $62. Britishers and other Europeans bought both shares and bonds. By February 1856 European investors were estimated to have acquired over 40,000 shares; six months later they held 80,000 shares—or about 60 percent of the stock; they also owned $12 million in bonds of this single railroad.[34]

Then in 1857 Illinois Central bonds fell to a new nadir of $50. A British protective committee was formed and sent representatives to America to investigate the railroad's management and its accounting system. The president of the Illinois Central, William Osborn (an American), found British criticisms often frivolous and lacking in understanding of the difference between a railroad in a frontier region (Illinois) and one in a built-up area (Great Britain), but Osborn accepted some of the Britishers' suggestions because a majority of the shares was after all in their hands. By 1858 the London *Times* estimated that two-thirds of the shareholders in the Illinois Central were English.[35] Despite the high percentage, this was basically portfolio investment.

In other American railroads, British interests similarly soared. By 1857 so large were such holdings in the Philadelphia and Reading that its London banker, McCalmont Brothers, installed the president of that railroad.[36] In 1858 the Duke of Brunswick owned $500,000 of second-mortgage Northern Cross Rail Road bonds. The sum was sufficient that he had "the power to dictate the course that should be pursued [in the railroad reorganization]." Samuel G. Ward, Baring's Boston representative, noted the importance of large investors' having a man in the United States to act on their behalf.[37] (The size of the Duke of Brunswick's investment should be compared with the reported stake of Lord Overstone of $350,000 in U.S. government securities.)

In 1860, when the Marietta and Cincinnati Railway was in difficulty, a London Committee was formed to protect the British bondholders; representatives from that committee joined the road's board of directors.[38] Early in 1861 Benjamin Ingham, a British winegrower and merchant who lived in Sicily, possessed 4,500 shares of New York Central stock (or 1.9 percent of the shares outstanding in 1861). From 1853 to 1861 he was the single largest shareholder in that railroad. His personal holdings in this road alone in 1860 were reported to be worth $640,600. Ingham also had other American railroad investments, including those in the Michigan Central Railroad. In December 1859 that railroad suggested to Ingham that he might care to lend the road $500,000, for three years at a "rather high rate of interest." There is no evidence as to whether he agreed.[39]

In the 1850s bonds of the Erie Railroad, and in 1860 of the Atlantic and Great Western, were sold in London and on the Continent in sizable quantities.[40] During the decade, much more frequently than in the past, U.S. railway securities moved to Britain to pay for the large quantity of imported iron rails. British manufacturers that received the bonds in payment either kept them as investments or had a broker or merchant banker resell them in England or on the Continent.[41] Thus there came to be a market abroad in U.S. railroad securities. In 1856 the Michigan Central and the New York Central sent a man to London to open an office to handle security transfers, so important did these lines judge the British holdings.[42]

While the securities of many U.S. railways were purchased or otherwise acquired by residents of foreign countries, before the Civil War the stock of only seven were listed on the London Exchange: the Erie, the Illinois Central, the Michigan Southern and Northern Indiana, the Michigan Central, the New York Central, the Pennsylvania, and the Philadelphia and Reading.[43]

In the 1850s some U.S. railroad bonds were denominated in sterling, so as to be more attractive to British investors. Dollar bonds were also sold overseas. Arrangements were made for dividends on stock and interest on bonds to be paid in London in pounds, often at a specified rate of 1£ = \$4.44. Techniques developed earlier in the handling of American state government securities were now transferred to railroad security placements.

The Illinois Central was the pioneer American railroad on the Amsterdam exchange in 1856.[44] British ironmasters, who received railroad securities in exchange for iron rails, would, as noted, frequently sell their securities on the Continent. In the 1850s, for the first time, German investors in Frankfurt became greatly interested in U.S. railroad issues, yet only the Erie and the Galena and Chicago were listed on the Frankfurt Bourse.[45]

Frenchmen also purchased American railroad bonds and, to a far lesser extent, shares through American brokers, through London, or through other means. The securities were not, however, listed on the Paris Bourse; Rondo Cameron notes the absence of any records on the types or amounts purchased. Yet by 1856 such securities were held in sufficient quantities in France for a Paris broker to specialize in the payment of coupons on American railroad bonds.[46] Likewise, the Swiss were buyers of American railroad bonds.[47] A different type of foreign investment in American railroads was that of British-financed Canadian railroad lines, which began to cross over the border into the United States.[48]

Export-import companies engaged in merchant banking aided American railroads in raising capital by acting as intermediaries. These houses understood foreign exchange transactions. As railroad securities became available and negotiable, such New York firms specialized in transferring these securities outside the country. Thus, for example, Louis von Hoffman & Co., New York, had overlapping partners with a German firm of that name. H. Gelpcke & Co., New York, appears to have been connected with the Berlin house of Breest & Gelpcke. Adrian and John Iselin from Switzerland had close contacts with Geneva and Basle bankers. John Munroe & Co. had "banks" in New York and Paris. Such houses helped channel European savings into U.S. railroad securities. So did Winslow, Lanier & Co., New York.[49]

Likewise, New York firms such as De Coppet & Co., Marie & Kanz, and Cammann & Co. mailed weekly railway share and bond lists to their foreign customers. In London, Baring Brothers, Robert Benson, and E. F. Satterthwaite circularized their clients with information on American railway securities available there.[50] In 1854 Junius S. Morgan joined the American banking firm of George Peabody & Co. in London; his son, J. P. Morgan (aged twenty), became a junior clerk with Duncan, Sherman & Co., Peabody & Co.'s "agency" in New York. All these firms marketed U.S. railway securities in Europe.[51]

British investors in American railroads and associated banking houses encouraged emigration to the United States. They were said to have "selfish" reasons: more settlement, more railroad traffic, and higher returns on their railroad investments.[52]

Banking firms on the European continent similarly participated in selling American railroad securities. Philip Speyer of Lazard Speyer-Ellissen, Frankfurt, had—as noted in Chapter 3—arrived in New York in 1837. With his brother, Gustavus, in 1845 the two Germans had formed Philip Speyer & Co. (the name changed to Speyer & Co. in 1878).[53] In 1854 the Darmstädter Bank (founded the year before) opened a New York bank, G. vom Baur & Co. The Darmstädter Bank appears to have become interested in American railroads at this time.[54]

In the 1850s foreign investment in American banking itself took on new forms. There were (1) private banking ties, (2) Canadian bank agencies, and (3) residues of earlier interests in state banks. The private banking links included those discussed above in the context of selling railroad securities abroad. The Darmstädter Bank's New York bank, G. vom Baur & Co., for example, appears to have been designed to aid German export trade, as well as to facilitate the sale of American securities in Germany.[55] On the West Coast, an 1856 San Francisco directory indicated that Henry Hentsch was engaged in assaying and banking; undoubtedly his California banking activities were associated with the Hentsch family house in Geneva, Switzerland.[56]

Canadian banks for the first time opened their own New York "agencies"—the Bank of British North America in the mid-1850s and the Bank of Montreal in 1859.[57] A historian of U.S. banking, Bray Hammond, describes the Bank of Montreal "by about 1857 or a little later" as larger than any American bank "and probably the largest and most powerful transactor in the New York money market, where it maintained and employed immense sums." Hammond continued: "This raised the criticism that the bank, by taking Canada's precious funds abroad to deal with foreigners in Wall Street, was neglecting the domestic borrowers and the Provinces' interest. It was sacrificing Canada to the United States."[58] The Bank of Montreal was probably not yet of that importance, although its own historian ranks it as one of the three leading banks in North America.[59] He does not place it in first place in North America until after the Civil War.[60] He notes that in Canada in 1859, the bank was prohibited by law from charging more than 6 percent on ninety-day loans.[61] There were no such restrictions in the United States. The main business of its New York office was short-term loans—and even more important, instruments of foreign exchange.[62] For the half-year ending April 30, 1860, its new New York office had profits of $18,020, or 6 percent of the Bank of Montreal's net profit for that period.[63] When the office made loans, the names of the borrowers had to be submitted to Montreal for approval.[64] Unlike the European banking houses with contacts in New York, no evidence exists that, in the pre–Civil War years, the Canadian banks were involved in American railway securities.

As for foreign holdings in American state banks, they probably dropped during the 1850s. Where I have good data (in the case of Louisiana), this was certainly true. Recall that in 1837 foreign owners of Louisiana bank stock held 52 percent of the total capital of all Louisiana banks. Twenty years later the figure was a mere 13 percent. The total capital in Louisiana banks (and the number of banks) had been reduced, but the foreign pullback had been even greater.[65] In the 1850s state bank stocks were no longer attractive to foreign investors.

California mining ventures still glittered, tarnished to be sure. At the start of 1853, at least twenty California gold-quartz mining companies were selling shares on the London market (about 2 million shares, representing $10 million). Few "returned anything but disappointment to the British shareholders."[66] In 1854 the Paris police investigated how French citizens "had been duped by individuals who offered shares for the exploitation of California gold mines."[67] Nonetheless, as each successive tale of American precious metal discoveries reached European ears, investors succumbed to temptation. Thus in 1858–59 reports of gold in the hills of Colorado lured a stream of miners and promoters to Pike's Peak. In 1859 silver veins in Nevada, the great Comstock Lode, similarly enticed new foreign investors.[68]

In the southeastern corner of Tennessee, in a section called Ducktown, copper discoveries brought capital from Britain.[69] In 1854 the New York and London Mining Company, an English-owned firm, was formed to buy the Hancock copper mine along with 160 acres (the price: $85,000).[70] The enterprise dispatched miners and mechanics from Cornwall to develop the property. It shipped machinery from Britain, including a large engine that arrived at Cleveland, Tennessee, but proved too large to be transported to Ducktown, given the existing transportation facilities. A historian of the region comments, "This was a fair example of the lack of information which London officials seemed to possess of conditions in far-off Tennessee."[71] In May 1859 the U.S.-owned Baltimore Copper Smelting Company took over the mine to satisfy a debt of roughly $12,000; thus ended the British ownership.[72]

In the Midwest, Canadian trading houses opened outlets (about fourteen in 1857) in Chicago. A reciprocity treaty between the United States and Canada (1854–1865) encouraged the Canadians' entry.[73] As in earlier years, so too in the 1850s, many British exporters to the United States appointed agents and opened offices in New York. Rathbone & Company, one of the greatest of the Liverpool mercantile firms, with offices in Shanghai, Canton, and London, had a flourishing New York business, managed by Henry Gair and William Lidderdale.[74] After long years of trading relationships, according to one historian, "the ties between Liverpool and New York were as close as those between Liverpool and London."[75]

In the 1850s British manufacturers enlarged their U.S. exports. Some developed sizable investments in inventories on this side of the Atlantic. Thus Naylor, Vickers & Co.—which had had a representative in New York since 1840—by 1857 had four-fifths of its assets (presumably in inventories) in the United States, which was that firm's largest market for "bells, cogwheels, railway crossings, and rings for rolling into railway tires."[76] Similarly, but in an entirely different industry, the two leading British biscuit makers, Huntley & Palmers and Peek, Frean & Co., exported their fancy biscuits to the United States; no tariff blocked the import. An American historian records that these two firms established "agencies" in every large city in the country, as far west as California.[77] In yet another industry, George A. Clark crossed the ocean in 1856 to represent his family's Scottish sewing thread company (he would form George A. Clark & Brother in 1863).[78]

Other new foreign interests in the 1850s included those in insurance (the British-owned Northern Assurance Company was established in 1854)[79] and those in land (in 1857, the Dubuque and Pacific Railroad sold some 500,000 acres in England).[80]

Overall, the inflow of foreign capital into America between 1854 and 1860 appears to have been large, the 1857 Panic a mere blip in the growth of American prosperity. Abroad, immense interest prevailed in U.S. opportunities. Individual investors' holdings remained substantial. As of June 30, 1857, an investment roster of the London merchant-banker James Morrison indicated that he held £807,000 (roughly $4 million) in "stocks, shares and mortgages in America." Morrison ranked with Benjamin Ingham as one of the largest individual foreign investors in the United States. When Henry Varnum Poor, editor of the *American Railroad Journal*, traveled to England in 1858, he found avid listeners to his views in James Wilson, editor of the *Economist*, and Marmaduke Sampson, financial editor of the London *Times*, as well as in bankers and brokers such as Robert Benson,

Thomas Smith, Henry Thomas Hope, and William Lance.[81] In 1860, especially, British investments multiplied in railroads and mining. In 1859–60, according to Douglass North's calculations, U.S. net outflow for interest and dividends paid abroad reached new peaks.[82] Such returns on European investments helped make American securities very attractive.[83] A Swiss bank historian described pre–Civil War America as that "much lauded country of profitable investments."[84] One estimate suggests that foreign investment in American securities rose from $222 million in 1853 to $444 million before war began in 1861.[85] While the new interests in railroads increased rapidly, it seems likely that, based on the level of foreign investments, those in American government securities (federal, state, county, city) still exceeded those in railroads.[86]

The Civil War Years

The Confederate States of America was organized on February 8, 1861; Lincoln was inaugurated on March 4; and on April 12 the first shots of the Civil War were fired against Fort Sumter. With the Civil War, Europeans dumped American securities, postponed planned investments, and remitted home monies on deposit in the United States.[87] Many Britishers sympathized with the South. U.S. 6 percents fell to as low as 40 percent of par. Yet, at the same time, certain London and Frankfurt houses bought and would make "vast fortunes" when bond prices rose.[88] War meant huge public expenditures, and the U.S. federal debt would soar. In July 1861 Congress authorized a loan of $270 million, of which $100 million "might be sold in Europe."[89] The Rothschild representative in the United States, August Belmont, crossed the Atlantic in mid-July to determine whether it could be placed there. After lengthy discussions with British, French, and German bankers, Belmont reported that prospects were "not at all propitious." The initial military failures of Union armies led him to conclude in October 1861 that there was not the slightest chance of negotiating an American loan abroad.[90] Yet another difficulty existed. On July 15, 1861, Congress passed legislation authorizing U.S. treasury notes (inconvertible paper) as valid in discharge of debts. Later, the U.S. Minister to the Hague would write: "The act making Government paper legal tender raised a general distrust in commercial and financial circles in Europe, which a promise to pay the interest on Government bonds in coin failed to allay. It was argued that the temper which prompted the greater assault on capital would not stick at the less when necessity prompted."[91]

S. P. Chase, U.S. Secretary of the Treasury, in his year-end *Annual*

Report of 1861, wrote: "It affords just occasion of gratulation that, under the most embarrassing of circumstances of shaken credit and immense demands, loans have been effected at home, without resort to any foreign market, to the amount of one hundred and ninety-seven millions of dollars."[92] He added, with a touch of wishful thinking, at least at that point in time, "The wealth and power of the country, manifested in the suppression of the rebellion, will demonstrate the absolute safety of investments in United States stocks, and foreign capitalists, restricted to the lower interests and the inferior security of public debts in other countries, will be attracted by the superior advantages offered by the loans of the Union."[93]

A Confederacy loan, issued in London in 1863 and marketed in London and Paris, was oversubscribed.[94] North Carolina and Massachusetts raised money in London in 1863 and 1865, respectively (see Table 4.2). But for the most part, government financing on both sides of the U.S. Civil War came from domestic sources. This was especially true in the case of the victors.

In March 1863 Jay Cooke, who was subscription agent for the U.S. government, wrote:

I have not the remotest doubt that the holders of foreign capital will, when they see it for their interest and not before, take hold of our government securities. I am equally sanguine that they will have to pay dearly for them. I for one hope that they will never invest a dollar in this country. We are free from foreign debt now. I count it as one of the many blessings to offset the miseries of this war. I do not think it for the interest of our country that our debt should go abroad. Let us hold it here. We are able to do so and had

Table 4.2. Foreign "government" loans issued in London, 1861–1865 (details on American securities only)

Year	Borrower	Issue amount (in millions of pounds)	Issue price (%)	Interest rate (%)	Issue house
1863	Confederacy	3.0	90	7	J. H. Schroeder & Co., E. Erlanger
1863	North Carolina	0.3	par	7	Manchester & County Bank
1865	Massachusetts	0.4	—	—	Baring

Foreign government loans issued in London, 1861–1865: £67.5 million
American issues in London, 1861–1865: £3.7 million
American issues as percentage of worldwide total: 5.5%

Source: Based on Leland H. Jenks, *Migration of British Capital to 1875* (New York: Barnes & Noble, 1973), pp. 421–422, 425.

better not put a whip into the hands of foreigners to punish us whenever they see fit to go to war with us. I am against any foreign negotiations [to sell American bonds abroad].[95]

Others disagreed with Cooke and thought money should be raised abroad; some Union bonds were placed in Europe, but not many. John Sherman, then Senator from Ohio, stated in March 1864, "I doubt now whether of the $1,500,000,000 of our indebtedness, $200,000,000, or even $150,000,000 is held abroad."[96] One hundred and fifty million would mean about 10 percent of the national debt, a minimal percentage compared with pre–Civil War years. In 1864, however, U.S. bonds began to be desired in Europe, especially by the Germans and the Dutch.[97]

Writing in December 1864, U.S. Secretary of the Treasury W. P. Fessenden reported:

Our bonds have already, to a considerable amount, been sought abroad, and to the extent the home market has been relieved and strengthened. Communication with Europe is now so easy and regular, intelligence is transmitted so rapidly, business facilities are so abundant, that foreign markets are almost at our doors . . . To effect a foreign loan would not . . . add much, if at all, to the whole amount of sales, unless stimulated by efforts and inducements, which our financial condition has not, as yet, called for.

He concluded with pride, "This nation has been able, thus far, to conduct a domestic war of unparalleled magnitude and cost without appealing for aid to any foreign people."[98] One estimate revealed that by March 1865 about $250 million in Union loans had drifted to Germany and Holland, while "there can hardly be less than $320 million in Europe as a whole."[99]

With the Civil War, foreign investors became equally uncertain about American railroad securities. The historian Harry Pierce writes that most sterling bondholders held on to their railway securities, whereas British investors in dollar bonds—fearing foreign exchange losses— sold heavily in 1861–1863. In net, British holders of common stock— denominated in dollars—were also sellers.[100] British ownership of common shares in the Philadelphia and Reading Railroad, for example, which totaled 87,974 in January 1861, fell to 84,619 by January 1863.[101] At the same time, some overseas investors purchased U.S. railroad securities at the bargain prices, which kept the amount held abroad high. The British bookseller W. H. Smith and the Scottish thread manufacturer Sir Peter Coats were reported to have profited greatly "from their courageous purchase of American Railroad securities during the early years of the Civil War."[102] The historian of the British stockbroker

Foster & Braithwaite found that the latter's activities on their own account in American railroads continued all during the war.[103]

After 1863, with northern victories, U.S. railroads were once again popular abroad. By 1865 U.S. railway securities issued in London represented roughly one-third of all railway securities issued in that market that year (see Table 4.3). A security that was issued in London did not necessarily mean British subscribers; other nationalities bought in London.[104]

Renewed confidence was, however, apparent. For instance, the board minutes of the Illinois Central Railroad record that by June 1864 over three-quarters of its stock was in foreign hands, a larger percentage than before the war.[105] In January 1865, 119,461 shares of the common stock of the Philadelphia and Reading Railroad were held in England (compared with 87,974 in January 1861).[106] Harry Pierce concluded that in 1865 foreign investment in the common stock of the New York Central and the Pennsylvania railroads was only slightly less than in 1861.[107]

In the early 1860s Thomas Kennard, of a Liverpool banking family, became chief engineer of the Atlantic and Great Western Railroad; the famous British railroad contractor Sir Morton Peto became involved.[108] The railroad route went through the new Pennsylvania oil fields, which made it especially attractive, and construction proceeded during the Civil War.[109] When in 1865 a "Board of Control" (a British management board) of the Atlantic and Great Western was organized, its members included Sir Morton Peto, Joseph Robinson (deputy chairman of the Ebbw Vale Company, Ltd.; Ebbw Vale Com-

Table 4.3. Securities of American railroads issued in London, 1861–1865

Year	Issues of American railroads (in millions of pounds)	Issues of railroads worldwide (in millions of pounds)	American railroads as % of worldwide total
1861	0.0	3.7	0.0
1862	0.0	3.5	0.0
1863	0.2	4.6	4.3
1864	1.3	4.9	26.5
1865	2.7	8.2	32.9
Total	4.2	24.9	16.9

Source: Based on Leland H. Jenks, *Migration of British Capital to 1875* (New York: Barnes & Noble, 1973), p. 426.

pany had obtained an interest in the railroad in exchange for its sale of iron rails—paid for at $40 a ton with bonds at 50),[110] and S. Goodson, M.P., and W. Fenton (respectively, chairman and deputy chairman of the Eastern Railway of Great Britain).[111] By war's end about $50 million of foreign—mainly British—money had been invested in this one railroad. The economist Cleona Lewis classified it as a foreign direct investment involving both foreign ownership and foreign control.[112]

During the Civil War, California attracted substantial American and foreign investment.[113] The new silver mines in Nevada increased the importance of San Francisco as a financial center.[114] The London and Paris Rothschilds had had a San Francisco agency since 1849;[115] by 1863 this agency was described as doing "the largest banking business in San Francisco."[116]

Table 4.4 reveals five British entries into San Francisco banking, 1863–1865.[117] These new banks purchased and shipped gold and silver bullion, discounted bills, issued letters of credit, and sold sterling and other foreign exchange. They often shipped bullion to Far Eastern markets.[118] One, the Bank of British Columbia, also opened a branch in Portland, Oregon, in 1865.[119]

In the Midwest, the Bank of Montreal started a Chicago "agency" in September 1861 "to accommodate the large and valuable trade"

Table 4.4. New British banks in San Francisco, 1863–1865

Bank, headquarters	Date English company established, capital	Date established in San Francisco
Commercial Bank of India, Bombay	1845, £500,000	Dec. 1863
Bank of British North America, London	1836 (Royal Charter 1840), £1,000,000	June 1864
Bank of British Columbia, London	1862, £2,000,000 authorized (£250,000 offered to public)	Aug. 1864
British and California Banking Company, London	1864, £1,000,000	Oct. 1864
London and San Francisco Bank, Ltd., London	1865, £1,000,000 (only £200,000 paid in)	1865

Source: Ira B. Cross, *Financing an Empire: History of Banking in California* (Chicago: S. J. Clarke, 1927), 256–258; Victor Ross, *A History of the Canadian Bank of Commerce* (Toronto: Oxford University Press, 192? I, 22, 255, 302.

Note: All these banks were organized as English companies.

between that city and Montreal. The agency advertised that it would do a general banking business, buy and sell "eastern and sterling exchange," discount produce bills based on shipments, receive deposits, and collect commercial paper.[120] It prospered. The Bank of Montreal, with the Merchants Savings, Loan and Trust Company of Chicago, offered the only "substantial sources of funds available for the accommodation of business" in the windy city during the war years.[121] In New York, the Bank of Montreal's office remained in business; that bank's historian takes issue with earlier polemicists who found that the New York facility reaped enormous profits in the wartime environment.[122]

The U.S. Congress, during the war years, passed national banking legislation, which said nothing about national banks accepting foreign drafts or bills of exchange. In subsequent years U.S. courts held that a national bank could not accept drafts arising from international transactions.[123] As one banking historian has put it, "The acceptance privilege is one of the most important powers possessed by a bank doing foreign business."[124] As a result of the law and interpretations of it (and possibly for other reasons as well), American national banks—the largest of U.S. commercial banks—showed little interest in international business.[125] In the main, they did not handle foreign exchange. Private banks and foreign bank agencies filled the gap; the Bank of Montreal played an important role and would continue to do so.[126]

Between 1863 and the spring of 1865, with the drift abroad of U.S. federal government securities, the renewed foreign interest in railway issues, mining prospects in the West, the banking requirements of the nation, and the generally favorable outlook for Northern armies, it appears that by the time of Lee's surrender at Appomattox (April 1865), foreign investment in the United States was back to its pre–Civil War level.

The Setting: 1865–1874

Once the war was concluded, Europeans looked toward America. In June 1865 a commentator estimated that some $500 million to $800 million of "U.S. bonds" were held in Europe and, in addition, a large amount of foreign capital was being invested in U.S. railway, bank, canal, insurance, telegraph, steamship, and manufacturing and mining stock. He added, "It is utterly impossible to say what the aggregate is." Much of the new investment was made by Germans and Dutchmen. By this time the U.S. federal debt had reached almost $2.8 billion.[127]

British hesitancy to invest in America was in large part a result of the uneasy political relations between the two English-speaking countries. On February 12, 1865, Queen Victoria had recorded in her diary that as soon as the American Civil War was over, victorious Union armies might push into Canada, thrusting Great Britain into war. A year later, in March 1866, fears had not subsided. Lord Overstone, who monitored carefully events across the Atlantic, predicted, "A war with the United States is inevitable and not distant." Now the concern was that the Irish-American society, the Fenians, bent on Irish independence, would, to make trouble, stimulate a U.S. invasion of Canada—and that Northerners, resentful of British aid to the Confederacy and angry that Confederate cruisers had been built in British shipyards and that the British refused to arbitrate the "Alabama claims," would take the occasion to do what they wanted to do anyway, that is, acquire Canada.[128] To the extent that potential British investors believed war imminent, U.S. investment carried high risk. Nonetheless, some continued.

British investors, for example, remained confident about the potentials for a transatlantic cable. Thomas Brassey, a major railroad contractor, and John Pender, later known as the "cable king," were important investors who, even after the August 1865 failure in laying the cable, were prepared to support the venture. In March 1866 a new firm, Anglo-American Telegraph Company, Ltd., was organized, and finally, on July 27, 1866, it succeeded in laying the cable.[129]

British investors also bought certain railroad securities. In this regard, Charles Francis Adams concluded (1869):

Shrewd as the British capitalist proverbially is, his judgment in regard to American investments has been singularly fallible. When our national bonds went a begging at a discount of sixty per cent, he transmitted them to Germany and refused to touch them himself. At the very same time, a class of railroad securities—such as those of . . . [the] Erie Railway, or to cite a yet stronger case those of the Atlantic & Great Western road—was gradually absorbed in London as an honest investment long after these securities had "gone into the street" in America. It was this strange fatuity which did much to bring on the crash of May, 1866.[130]

In May 1866 the British discount house Overend, Gurney & Co. collapsed. This house was ranked second only to the Bank of England as the backbone in British credit. Founded in 1807, it had been associated with American trade at least as early as the 1830s, aiding the Barings, discounting bills received by Anglo-American merchant bankers, lending funds to the Bank of the United States (after it received a state charter in 1836), negotiating with American state governments on behalf of British bondholders (in the early 1840s), and competing with the Barings in exchange and acceptance operations. So extensive had its international business become that when it failed, the British Foreign Secretary sent assurances to the nation's embassies around the world that the finances of Great Britain remained sound. Overend, Gurney's collapse—the Panic of 1866—brought down other British firms as well (including some with U.S. investments), with a result, according to the historian Leland Jenks, of creating "concentric waves from Hong Kong to Buffalo."[131] Its demise had the immediate effect of containing all British capital outflow.[132]

German and Dutch investment in America, however, continued to rise. In December 1866 the banker Gerson von Bleichroeder made his first major investment for Bismarck in U.S. 6 percent bonds. The German Rothschilds became heavy buyers of American securities.[133] In March 1867 the London *Economist* noted that about £100 million of U.S. government securities were held in Europe, primarily by German and Dutch investors.[134] An American Consul in Frankfurt lectured Germans on the marvelous potential of the U.S. economy, predicting the resumption of gold payments and regaling his listeners with tales of prospects for extraordinary profit. He pointed out that 6 percent U.S bonds sold at 40 in Frankfurt, which meant a 15 percent yield on the purchase price. One German recollected, "There was hardly an investor in South Germany, who did not buy United States bonds." Germans, "waiting for the amelioration of the dollar, made large fortunes." This commentator even suggested that the foundation for subsequent German business development lay in the "profits made in American securities." Success with American bonds educated Germans for future international investments.[135]

Despite general British "indifference," in 1868 in England what has been called the first genuine British financial trust of any importance—the Foreign and Colonial Government Trust—was founded. Among its first investments were U.S. 5 percent "Ten-Forties."[136] Likewise, some of the established group of "bill drawers," dealers in foreign exchange, in New York, seem to have participated in intermediating U.S. government securities to Great Britain.[137]

A careful writer in *Hunt's Merchant Magazine*, in October 1868, estimated that $700 million of U.S. government bonds were foreign-owned (see Table 4.5).[138] The next year (1869), David Wells, Commissioner of Revenue, determined that investors abroad owned roughly $1 billion worth of U.S. government securities (at par), which had been purchased at greatly reduced prices.[139] Since the total U.S.

Table 4.5. European holdings in the United States, 1866–1874 (in millions of dollars)

	1866	1868	1869	1874
U.S. government bonds	350	700	1,000.0	c
State bonds⎫	150	60	100.0	93
County/city⎭		a	7.5	c
Railway stocks and bonds	100	150	243.0	390
Other securities	b	28	40.0	c
Total	600	938	1,390.5	1,500

Source: 1866: U.S. Secretary of the Treasury, *Annual Report, 1866,* p. 12; 1868: *Hunt's Merchant Magazine,* 69 (Oct. 1868): 242ff.; 1869: *Report of the Special Commissioner of the Revenue* (1869), pp. xxvii–xxviii, in *Foreign Investment in the United States,* ed. Mira Wilkins (New York: Arno Press, 1977); 1874: Table 4.1; 1869 and 1874 figures include some non-European foreign investments.

[a] Not included.
[b] Included with railroads.
[c] Not available.

debt was $2.2 billion that year, this would mean some 45 percent was held outside the country. Treasury Secretary Hugh McCulloch expressed concern, believing that the debt of the United States should be a "home" one.[140] McCulloch was influenced by Jay Cooke, who had repeatedly stressed the unadvisability of having U.S. debt in the hands of Europeans. Cooke wrote, "If it is held by our own people there is no annual loss of wealth from the collection and payment of interest."[141]

By 1868–69, foreign bankers were engaging in arbitrage transactions, purchasing and selling U.S. government bonds between New York and London. So eager was the Rothschild representative, August Belmont, to encourage such transactions that he agreed to reduce his commission from ¼ to ⅛.[142] Obviously, arbitrage dealings wreak havoc with attempts to determine the level of long-term investment.

In the spring of 1869 the amount of U.S. government bonds (and other securities) sent abroad had been great.[143] The rising price of gold—pushed up by Jay Gould and Jim Fisk's attempted corner—made American securities, including U.S. bonds, temporarily more attractive to foreign investors. After the "Gold Panic," the price of U.S. bonds fell slightly.[144] The gold manipulations had the effect of shaking the confidence of German investors.[145]

In 1870 an American Consul in Amsterdam estimated that some

$300 million of U.S. government bonds were held in Holland, roughly one-third of all such bonds that were held abroad. Some had been purchased at as low as 36.[146] By this time, Swiss and, to a lesser extent, French bankers had also become active in selling U.S. bonds to their customers.[147] When, in the summer and fall of 1870, Germans dumped some of their still-large holdings of American bonds (to finance the war with France), British investors became less cautious.[148] By January 1, 1871, the estimated American government bonds held in Europe were $845 million (down from the $1 billion in 1869, no doubt because of the German and French bond sales).[149]

When in May 1871 the United States and Britain agreed to submit to arbitration outstanding controversies, boundary disputes, the fisheries question, and, most important, the Alabama claims,[150] this cleared the way for major British investments in the United States. After the French war indemnity was paid to Germany, Germans once again came to be important investors in the United States.[151] In 1871 and 1873 two huge U.S. government refunding issues were offered in London (see Table 4.6).[152] Then on July 28, 1874, the U.S. Secretary of the Treasury (B. H. Bristow) entered into a contract with August Belmont & Co., New York (on behalf of N. M. Rothschild & Sons, London), and J. & W. Seligman & Co., New York, for "negotiation" of 5 percent U.S. bonds. The main portion of the bonds subscribed was sold in Europe.[153] Americans remained dependent on European money markets; the earlier reservations of McCulloch and Cooke were forgotten.[154] Tables 4.1 and 4.5 suggest that of all sectors, foreign investment in U.S. federal government bonds was the largest in 1865–1874.[155] Not since the 1820s (or possibly the early 1830s) had the federal government been the single largest attracter of foreign investment.

State securities in lesser amounts were also sold abroad. In the years 1866–1874, security issues of Massachusetts, Alabama, and Louisiana were placed in London (see Table 4.6). Other American state government bonds drifted overseas.[156] With the exception of Mississippi (the bonds of which are still in default today), all the defaults of the early 1840s had been resolved, Arkansas settling as late as 1869 and Florida in 1871.[157] In 1870 Georgia bonds were admitted to dealings on the London, Berlin and Frankfurt exchanges.[158] Arkansas floated loans in Amsterdam.[159] Southern states contracted huge debts during Reconstruction.[160] Northerners and carpetbaggers had no qualms about European borrowings. Under these conditions many southern states overextended, and by 1873 Alabama, Arkansas, Florida, Georgia, Louisiana, North Carolina, Tennessee, Virginia, and West Virginia were in default.[161] South Carolina joined the list in

Table 4.6. Some American federal, state, and municipal securities issued in Lond[?] 1866–1874

Year	Borrower	Issue amount (in millions of pounds)	Issue price (%)	Interest rate (%)	Issue house
1866	Massachusetts	0.4	—	—	Baring
1867	Massachusetts	0.4	77	5	Baring
1868	Massachusetts	0.6	—	5	Baring
1869	Alabama	1.0	81	8	Schroeder
1870	Alabama	0.4	94½	8	Schroeder
1870	Massachusetts	0.6	87	5	Baring
1871	Louisiana	0.4	84⅜	8	Robinson & Flem[?]
1871	Massachusetts	0.6	91	5	Baring
1871	United States	40.0	102⅜	5	[a]
1872	Massachusetts	0.4	93	5	McCalmont Broth[?]
1872	New York City	3.1	92	6	Rothschild
1872	Several American cities	1.5	—	—	Baring, Seligman
1873	Massachusetts	0.1	91½	5	Baring
1873	United States	60.0	102⅜	5	Baring, Rothschil[?] and others
1874	Several American cities	0.7	—	—	Morgan & Co.

Source: Based on Leland H. Jenks, *Migration of British Capital to 1875* (New York: Barnes & Noble, (19[?] pp. 421–422, and other data. Jules Ayer, *A Century of Finance, 1804 to 1904: The London House of Rothsc[?]* (London: n.p., 1905), pp. 54–55, on New York City loan. The original list for the 1871 U.S. loan is give[?] Geo. S. Boutwell, Secretary of the Treasury, to Baring Brothers, Feb. 28, 1871, Baring Papers, Pu[?] Archives, Ottawa, vol. 23, p. 011916. Ibid., p. 011917, explains that "I [Boutwell] have also designated Germany and Switzerland, Messrs. M. A. de Rothschild & Sons at Frankfort; for France, Messrs Rothschild Bros. and Drexel, Harjes & Co. at Paris; for Holland, Messrs. Hope & Co. and Messrs Bec[?] & Fuld [the Rothschild agent there]; and for Frankfort, Messrs. Seligman & Stettheimer."

[a] The original group appointed included Baring Brothers; N. M. Rothschild & Sons; Morton, Rose & C[?] Jay Cooke, McCulloch & Co.; and J. S. Morgan & Co.

1874.[162] Foreign investors in the 1870s expressed the same outrage as in the early 1840s. Southerners did not care, nor did they ever pay.[163]

Table 4.7 indicates the state government securities positively known to be held abroad in 1869. It puts the total at $45.7 million. Other estimates for that year suggest a figure in excess of $100 million. The amount held abroad rose sharply between 1869 and 1873, before the new round of defaults turned European investors away from the issues of most American state governments—and certainly those in the American South. In November 1874 the *Commercial and Financial Chronicle* estimated that $92.9 million in state bonds were

Table 4.7. State securities positively known to state authorities to be held abroad, 1869 (in millions of U.S. dollars)

State	Amount
Alabama	1.48
Georgia	0.07
Illinois	1.40
Louisiana	5.24
Massachusetts	12.28
Michigan	0.80
Missouri	1.50
New York	2.44
Ohio	3.50
Pennsylvania	9.46
Virginia	7.52
Total	45.69

Source: Report of the Special Commissioner of the Revenue, (1869), p. xxvii, in Foreign Investments in the United States, ed. Mira Wilkins (New York: Arno Press, 1977).

held abroad (about one-quarter of the total), and that of that $92.9 million, $54.2 million (or 58 percent) were in default.[164]

New York City, Boston, and St. Louis borrowed in London in 1872–1874 to finance street improvements, lighting, and water systems.[165] By 1872 the Frankfurt Bourse listed eighteen bonds of American cities.[166] The securities of the municipalities proved to be superior investments to the state (at least the southern state) issues.

Railroads: 1865–1874

While new foreign investments were being made in federal, state, and city bonds, there were also large new capital flows from abroad into American railroads. The Civil War had seen a slowdown in the laying of new tracks, as well as destruction of southern rail lines. To make up for this and to rebuild southern lines, U.S. railroad construction accelerated rapidly. Whereas only 819 miles of track were built in 1865, thereafter the totals increased annually, reaching 7,439 miles in 1872 alone; in the decade 1865–1874, 38,893 miles of railroads were put in place, compared with 20,348 miles in the decade before the Civil War.[167] Accordingly, large amounts of capital were required.

Late in 1865 the British railroad contractor Sir Morton Peto, on behalf of the Atlantic and Great Western Railroad, arranged an American junket for prospective British investors. By the spring of 1866, it had become apparent that all was not well with the financial condition of this British-owned and controlled railroad; Sir Morton Peto's own business failed in the wake of the Overend, Gurney crisis.[168] In March 1867, at the general meeting of the Atlantic and Great Western Railroad, held in London, the security holders formed a committee of investigation that included British members of Parliament (Sir William Russell, Thomas Cave, and J. Fildes), the ironmaster Crawshay Bailey (who had sold rails to the venture in exchange for bonds), and, on the nomination of the General Exchange Committee for Public Stocks of Amsterdam, F. W. Oewel. Oewel, of Wertheim & Gompertz, would become a familiar figure in representing Dutch investors in America.[169] The London members of the committee appointed a receiver for the railroad.

When in July 1867 the Atlantic and Great Western came out of the receivership, it was again under the control of a London-based board of directors, made up mainly of the members of the investigation committee. Some seventeen London banks and finance companies had lent money to the Atlantic and Great Western.[170] Its condition led them to difficulties and, in several cases, to liquidation.[171]

The troubles of the Atlantic and Great Western added to the Britishers' caution that I have already noted. On December 17, 1867, August Belmont, in New York, wrote N. M. Rothschild & Sons, London: "I am very sorry you do not think favorably of the 1st Mortgage Bonds of the Union Pacific Road. They are safe beyond a doubt and of a very different character from the Bonds of the Atlantic and Great Western, which never stood in good credit here and which owe their success in London to the management of Sir Peto [sic] and Mr. James McHenry, the latter a very clever but most visionary financier."[172]

In December 1868 Jay Gould's Erie Railroad leased the Atlantic and Great Western line. The Erie had at that time numerous British shareholders and bondholders. The relations of the Erie and the Atlantic and Great Western became complicated, with British owners of the securities in both railroads vying for nonexistent profits. The British had their first unpleasant encounter with the wily Jay Gould.[173]

In March 1872, after three and a half years of Gould control, the Erie Railroad was a "physical wreck"; British investors (including the banking house of Bishoffsheim & Goldschmidt) removed Gould from the railroad's presidency. In his "downfall" (in which Gould was rumored to have made a fortune), European ownership of the Erie stock increased from around 60 percent to almost 100 percent, with British, German, and Dutch buyers. Erie bonds also continued to be held abroad. The lease of the Atlantic and Great Western to the Erie, which had been voided and reinstated, was for a third time restored in June 1874, but before the end of 1874, the Atlantic and Great Western was once more in receivership—and in 1875 so was the Erie, at which time the Erie had more than 3,000 foreign shareholders. In neither of these railroads did foreign shareholders receive returns.[174]

Despite poor experiences with the Atlantic and Great Western and the Erie and despite the conservatism of the Rothschilds, U.S. railroad issues were sold abroad, reaching each year an ever wider clientele—first on the Continent and then in Britain. Foreign stockholders in the Illinois Central received 10 percent annual dividends in 1865–1873,[175] which helped to give American railroads a better name. James Lanier, a New York banker, marketed literally dozens of new issues in Amsterdam and Frankfurt in 1868–1870.[176] As one writer put it, westerners believed "no inducements were too large with which to tempt foreign capital."[177] Especially after 1871, U.S. "rails" became a standard in the portfolio of British investors. In March 1873 the Foreign and Colonial Government Trust formed a new trust, the American Investment Trust, designed to invest in American railroad bonds. Newly established Scottish investment trusts bought U.S. railroad bonds.[178]

As Table 4.8 indicates, between 1870 and 1874, 65 to 74 percent of all railway securities issued in London were for U.S. railroads; even more important, 38 to 55 percent of all securities of private companies operating abroad issued in London were for American "rails."[179] These figures show issues; not all the securities were actually sold; those sold were rarely sold at par. Likewise, not all monies were "called" (that is, called in for collection). Nonetheless, the amounts were very large.[180]

Issues were denominated in both pounds and dollars. McCalmont Brothers offered a $10 million issue of Philadelphia and Reading bonds in 1872.[181] Foster & Braithwaite, a London stockbroker, was associated with a £2 million Pennsylvania 6 percent issue in 1874, a depression year.[182] The size of these particular railroad issues was unprecedented for private companies. The Barings maintained their pre–Civil War involvement with the financing of the Baltimore and Ohio and of the Eastern Railroad in Massachusetts and became newly interested in the Louisville and Nashville (and through it the South and North Alabama Railroad) and the St. Louis and Iron Mountain Railroad.[183]

Private sales supplemented those of merchant bankers. Andrew

Table 4.8. Securities of U.S. railways issued in London, 1866–1874

Year	Securities of U.S. railways issued in London (in millions of pounds)	As percentage of railroad securities issued in London	As percentage of securities of all private companies operating abroad issued in London
1866	2.0	48%	18%
1867	1.0	28	15
1868	1.6	20	16
1869	1.8	30	20
1870	3.9	74	40
1871	6.1	65	40
1872	12.0	69	38
1873	14.3	69	48
1874	14.3	70	55

Source: Based on Leland H. Jenks, *Migration of British Capital to 1875* (New York: Barnes & Noble, 1973), p. 426.

Carnegie, for example, sold railway bonds in Europe. In 1872, on behalf of the Davenport and St. Paul Railroad, he convinced Sulzbach Brothers of Frankfurt to take $3 million in first-mortgage bonds and accept an option on $3 million more. (Carnegie invested his commission from this sale in the famous Edgar Thomson Steel Works.)[184] In Germany there were private sales of bonds of the Oregon and California Railroad Company and of the Kansas Pacific.[185] James Speyer, whose uncle Philip Speyer represented Lazard Speyer-Ellissen of Frankfurt, recalled many years later that after the Civil War, "our firm sold millions of dollars of American railroad securities in Germany, Holland, Switzerland, and all over Europe."[186] Whereas the British had initially been wary of the western railroads, the Germans were less so.

When in May 1869 Jay Cooke agreed to handle the sale of $100 million of 7.3 percent Northern Pacific bonds, while he looked for American sales, his first thought had been of Europe. Cooke knew— his biographer tells us—that "since the building of the Erie Canal, no great American transportation concern had been established without European help." In an attempt to sell the railroad bonds, Jay Cooke's associates tried without success to have the London Rothschilds; Bischoffsheim & Goldschmidt, London; and the Darmstädter Bank market blocks of stock. Even $5 million was too much! Cooke opened his own London house (January 1, 1871)—Jay Cooke,

McCulloch & Co.—headed by the former U.S. Secretary of the Treasury, "to conduct an exchange business, issue commercial and travelers' credits, loan money on government and other bonds, cash coupons for United States, State and railroad bonds, purchase railroad iron . . . and negotiate the sale of railroad and other securities." Most of all, Cooke wanted the firm to push Northern Pacific bonds. In 1872 he was urging on his London partners $10 million of bonds—in the spring—and $10 million for fall. The sums were unrealistic for a road that had no near prospects of significant revenues; his London house could not begin to meet Cooke's wishes, and it was unsuccessful in placing the Northern Pacific bonds, despite the attractive interest rate. In 1873 the Northern Pacific reached Bismarck, North Dakota. That the town was named after the German Chancellor may well have been a bid to attract German capital (and German immigrants).[187]

In April 1872 the German-born American Henry Villard, who, much later, would do very well in selling Northern Pacific securities in Germany, convinced Jacob Stern and the Frankfurt Vereinsbank to buy Wisconsin Central bonds.[188] Americans found in the early 1870s that they could not market railway bonds in France, since in 1869 the Paris banking house Paradis acquired about $5 million of fraudulent bonds of the Memphis, El Paso and Pacific; after major French losses, the fraud was discovered and French investors shied away from the U.S. railway issues.[189]

Not so with the Dutch: A Dutch newspaper in 1873 noted that in the preceding few years, some sixty different American railway securities had been introduced on the Amsterdam market.[190] When the First Division of the St. Paul and Pacific, for example, floated $11 million in bonds, most of the purchasers were Dutchmen, attracted by the high-interest security. Moreover, the underwriter held back enough of the proceeds of the loan from the railroad to guarantee that the Dutch bondholders would get their interest for three years.[191] The Dutch invested in other railways in Minnesota; by 1874 Dutch residents were serving on the boards of directors of the Chicago, Milwaukee and St. Paul as well as the Chicago and North Western.[192] Table 4.9 reveals the importance of U.S. railways on the Dutch market. By 1875 fully 26 percent of all securities and 57 percent of all railways quoted in Amsterdam were U.S. rails.

The Denver and Rio Grande Railway was the inspiration of an American and his English associate, William A. Bell. The two planned new towns in Colorado—Colorado Springs and Pueblo. British interest in Colorado would be in land, in mines, and later in cattle, as well as in railroads. In the early 1870s the securities of the Denver and Rio

Table 4.9. Securities on the Amsterdam Exchange, 1855–1875

	(A)	(B)	(C)	(D)	(E)	(F)	(G)	(H)
		U.S. securities quoted		All railroad securities quoted (U.S. and non-U.S.)		U.S. railroad securities quoted		
Year	Total number of securities quoted (U.S. and non-U.S.)	Number	As percentage of total (B/A)	Number	As percentage of total (D/A)	Number	As percentage of total securities (F/A)	As percentage of railroad securities (F/D)
1855	87	7	8%	4	5%	0	0%	0%
1865	116	14	12	24	21	8	7	33
1875	238	78	33	110	46	63	26	57

Source: Based on K. D. Bosch, *Nederlandse Beleggingen in de Verenigde Staten* (Amsterdam: Uitgeversmaatschappij Elsevier, 1948), p. 139.

Grande were sold in Amsterdam and London.[193] The railroad bought iron rails from Britain and Belgium, paying for them with first-mortgage bonds.[194]

By 1873 some $11 million of bonds in the Oregon and California Railroad Company had passed to Germans and Englishmen, with the largest amount in German hands. In the spring of 1873, the German holders of these bonds dispatched Paul Reinganum, of the Frankfurt Committee for the Protection of Bondholders, to Oregon to investigate. On receipt of a negative report from Reinganum, the committee deputized Henry Villard to arrange protection for the bondholders. In 1874 Villard saw to it that German bondholders had the right to nominate three members of the board of directors of the Oregon and California Railroad and be represented in Oregon by a resident financial agent. Subsequently the Germans raised their interest in the venture.[195]

The Illinois Central remained popular in Europe. In 1873 roughly 78.6 percent of its shares were held abroad.[196] To attract capital from Europe, Alabama endorsed and issued bonds directly to numerous railroad companies, including the Alabama and Chattanooga Railroad (1869–70). English, French, German, and Dutch investors bought these securities.[197]

And so it went. As the popularity of American railroad securities mounted abroad and European markets became flooded with these securities, U.S. and foreign banking firms developed connections in London, Frankfurt, and Paris to facilitate the overseas sales.[198] The Seligmans opened London, Frankfurt, and Paris houses. I have noted Jay Cooke's new London establishment and the Speyer family's international alliances (this German firm had opened a London house in 1862). J. P. Morgan, who had started his career acting on behalf of George Peabody & Co., London, continued in the post–Civil War period his association with its successor, his father's London firm, J. S. Morgan & Co. (formed in 1864). Dabney, Morgan & Co. (founded in 1863) and its successor, Drexel, Morgan & Co., New York (established in 1871), worked closely with Drexel, Harjes & Co., Paris (established in 1868), and J. S. Morgan & Co., London. Morton, Bliss & Co., New York, was connected with Morton, Rose & Co., London; and Henry Clews & Co., New York, with Clews, Habicht & Co., London. Knauth, Nachod & Kuhne, New York and Leipzig, described itself as bankers, while John Munroe & Co., New York, continued to be associated with Munroe & Co., Paris.[199]

A New York broker, James B. Hodgskin, testified in January 1870 that "I frequently may buy over a million of bonds at one time for one large house which exports the bonds to Europe." Although he never identified the house, he listed as his major clients Duncan, Sherman & Co.; F. Schuchardt & Sons; Howland & Aspinwall; the Bank of British North America; J. & W. Seligman & Co.; Grinnell, Minturn & Co.; and Fabbri & Chauncey—all American firms (except the Bank of British North America) and all experts in intermediating American securities abroad.[200]

German-American financial relationships became much closer. In 1867 M. M. Warburg of Hamburg developed ties with the newly formed Kuhn, Loeb & Co., New York.[201] The Darmstädter Bank retained its interest in G. vom Baur & Co., New York, and the Deutsche Bank in October 1872 secured a "silent partnership" in Knoblauch & Lichtenstein, also in New York.[202] In 1848 Lazarus Hallgarten had immigrated from Frankfurt to New York and in 1850 had opened a small office to deal in foreign exchange. After 1865 his firm (the name Hallgarten & Co. was adopted on January 1, 1867) developed into a general stock-and-bond brokerage house. Lazarus Hallgarten maintained his contacts in Europe, and in the post–Civil War years Hallgarten & Co. was an important channel for the monies that flowed from Germany into American railroads.[203]

In 1869 and 1870 Dutch bankers organized "trusts" or holding companies for American securities, typically for railroad issues. Kerkhoven & Co. and Boissevain Brothers administered the Vereenigde Amerikaansche Fondsen, founded in 1869, and in 1870 Wertheim & Gompertz, Westendorp & Co., and F. W. Oewel started the Vereenigd Bezit van Amerikaansche Hypothecaire Spoorwegobligatiën (Holding Company for American Railway Mortgage Bonds). Hope & Co. had its Gemeenschappelijk Bezit to hold American securities.[204]

On the whole, the expanding network of financial intermediaries was successful in forwarding and placing American railroad securities in Europe. Although Cooke failed to market the Northern Pacific bonds abroad and Belmont could not interest the Rothschilds in the Union Pacific, an immense amount of money did come to America.[205] Western railroads were particularly expensive to build and created special problems for investors. Until a railroad was completed, revenues would be virtually nonexistent. A foreign investor, interested in steady returns, did not like the long waiting period.

Nonetheless, Joseph Schumpeter—surely exaggerating—suggested in his Business Cycles that it was "primarily English (and other European) capital which took the responsibility for a great part of the [roughly] 2 billions which are said to have been expended on American railroads from 1867 to 1873." Schumpeter added, referring to the array of banking houses, "A very efficient machinery for pressing European capital into service had by that time replaced the individual efforts of earlier times."[206] *Replaced* is the wrong word, for there were still the individual efforts (note the role of Andrew Carnegie, for example).

Foreign holders of American securities (represented by banking houses or by protective committees established by these houses) investigated American railroads, conducted audits,[207] and on occasion directly intervened in management. A Scottish judge some years later (after the failure of the City of Glasgow Bank) noted, "It strikes one that a Scotch Bank buying and working a railroad in America is about as startling a thing as we can well conceive." Yet from 1859 to 1868, G. A. Thomson, a London stockbroker acting for the City of Glasgow Bank, directed the Western Union Railroad (and its predecessors) that ran from Racine, Wisconsin, to the Mississippi River. The bank had approximately $5 million invested in this road![208]

At the start of the 1870s, a number of American railway securities went into default (see Table 4.10). European investors experienced heavy losses. Early in 1873—before the American crisis of that year—at least $28.2 million of defaulted American railroad securities were already held on the Continent.[209] On the eve of the Panic of 1873, more than $100 million in American railway bonds were being pushed—unsuccessfully—into European markets.[210]

In May 1873 the Vienna stock market had collapsed; the crisis spread to Germany, and then, with the American Panic in September, German, Austrian, Dutch, and French investors all sold. Some securities were returned to New York, but many were picked up in London. According to Dorothy Adler, after 1873 Germany ceased to be a significant market for American railroad securities; she should have added—at least for a while.[211] By December 1874 some $390 million of American railroad bonds were said to be held abroad, of which $148 million (or about 38 percent) were in default. *Banker's Magazine* believed that "a considerable aggregate" of the defaulting bonds were held in Holland, Germany, and France.[212] The *Commercial and Financial Chronicle* concluded that foreigners, particularly those on the European continent, had been unfortunate in their choices of American railroads.[213]

By 1874 defaults had made the British nervous. In 1868 a group of investors had formed in London a private organization to protect holders of foreign securities and to negotiate on their behalf in cases of default by foreign governments and foreign private companies. In 1873 this organization was incorporated and named the Corporation of Foreign Bondholders of Great Britain. Almost at once, the council of this corporation concerned itself with American state government and railroad bond defaults.[214]

Table 4.10. American railway securities, publicly issued in London in default in early 1870s

Date of default	Railway	Year issued
Before 1873	Alabama and Chattanooga	1869
	Alabama bonds (in aid of Alabama and Chattanooga)	1870
	Des Moines Valley	1870
	Georgia bonds (in aid of railways)	1871
	Plymouth, Kankakee and Pacific	1872
1873	St. Paul and Pacific	Various years, starting in 18
	Chesapeake and Ohio	1868
	St. Joseph and Denver	1870
	Chicago, Danville and Vincennes	1870
	Oregon and California	1871
	Burlington, Cedar Rapids and Northern	1872
	Illinois, Missouri and Texas	1873
1874	Atlantic and Great Western	Various years, starting in 18
	Indianapolis, Bloomington and Western	1870
	Atlantic, Mississippi and Ohio	1871
	Northern Pacific	1872
	Gilman, Clinton and Springfield	1872
	Cairo and Vincennes	1872
	Arkansas Central	1872
	New York, Boston and Montreal	1873
	Geneva and Ithaca	1874

Source: Based on Dorothy Adler, *British Investment in American Railways, 1834–1898* (Charlottes: University Press of Virginia, 1970), p. 78.

In response to the American railroad defaults, British, Dutch, and German owners of the securities dispatched more men to the United States, placing them or men of their choice on the boards of directors of American railroad companies, as they had done after the Panic of 1857.[215] The Council of the Foreign Bondholders bargained on behalf of the investors. The latter did not want to control day-by-day management of the railroad, but rather to secure expected financial returns and to safeguard their holdings. The investors' efforts to influence overall managerial policies often proved fruitless, but by the mid-1870s they were clearly seeking more than ever before to have such influence.[216] The foreign lenders' role was hampered by distance and unfamiliarity with American conditions, as well as by the independence of U.S. railway speculators, promoters, and managers.[217] Yet the situation—the sheer size of the investment— was different from that two decades earlier; investors jarred by the railroad defaults paid far greater attention to the way the railroads were run. When the *Commercial and Financial Chronicle* reported in October 1874 that progress toward the settlement of railroad defaults had been "rapid and satisfactory,"[218] foreign investors were not sure this was an honest appraisal.

Land and Land Mortgages: 1865–1874

Land and land mortgages in the post–Civil War years attracted foreign investors. The new land investments were large—bringing to the forefront interests in land reminiscent of that of a much earlier era. John Collinson, who has been described as a British "engineer" but seems more a promoter, had been involved in 1868 in the negotiation in London of bonds for the West Wisconsin Railroad. Later he participated in placing bonds abroad for the Atlantic, Mississippi, and Ohio Railroad (summer of 1871).[219] In between, Collinson and his British friends became engaged in a spectacular venture. On April 30, 1869, they purchased for $1.35 million the so-called Maxwell land grant in New Mexico—"2,000,000 acres of land more or less." Because they were uncertain whether territorial laws authorized foreigners to hold real estate, they incorporated in the territory, the Maxwell Land Grant and Railway Company (May 12, 1869); capital, $5 million. Collinson himself owned over 35,000 of the 50,000 shares issued. He then sought to raise monies to pay for the land acquired, which was done by marketing 7 percent bonds in Great Britain and Holland. A Dutch engineer came to appraise the properties and wrote a glowing report. Since the bonds were offered at 72, Dutchmen, who always loved a bargain, bought many of them. Far more bonds were sold in Holland than in Britain. By 1870 the new company had yearly interest obligations of about $250,000 on the bonds sold abroad. Its plan—like that of land investors of years past—was to obtain revenues through land sales. What the bondholders did not know was that the company had no clear title to the land. Squatters settled on Maxwell land, resisting eviction. No railway went any where near the vast acreage. Although there had been gold discoveries, the principal mine shut down in 1872. By June 1872 the company was in default on interest payments. When matters had not improved in 1873, the Dutch bondholders dispatched a delegation to New Mexico to investigate. The visitors were appalled by what they found, but this did not end the Dutch role.[220] As in the old Holland Land Company, Dutch investors held on to their interests for many years.

John Collinson was far from alone in peddling American land abroad. The historian Herbert O. Brayer documents the activities of the London solicitor and promoter William Blackmore, who first participated in western land speculation in 1868. Blackmore agreed to sell in Europe the Sangre de Cristo grant (located in New Mexico and Colorado); arranged the incorporation in London of the Colorado Freehold Land and Emigration Company, Ltd., to buy the northern half of the grant; and in 1870 formed the United States Freehold Land and Emigration Company (which became Dutch financed) to develop the southern half. Between 1871 and 1874 Blackmore made annual trips to the American West, buying land; in England and Holland he sought monies to pay for and to develop the huge properties that he acquired.[221]

In the early 1870s many British travelers considered opportunities in U.S. land, returning home with encouraging reports. Among the "propositions" offered in the United Kingdom were (in April 1874) the shares of the South Carolina Rice Plantation Trust. In this case, however, "the fact of the unsatisfactory conduct of the State toward its creditors, becoming generally known to the investing public appears to have frustrated any attempt to raise money."[222] British investors, slowly, were starting to pick and choose among offerings.

Many land sales abroad were associated with American railroad construction. Railroads had "Land Departments," which sought settlers. Sometimes, however, they looked to European investors to aid in the land development process. Often foreign land sales and railroad financing were linked.[223]

During the Civil War, jute and linen had been shipped from Dundee, Scotland, to the United States; because ready payment was not available (the dollar was depreciating in value), exporters had taken mortgages in land as security, and U.S. land mortgages had become familiar in Dundee.[224] In 1873 in that city, Robert Fleming founded the Scottish American Investment Trust, and in Edinburgh William J. Menzies established the Scottish American Investment Company, Ltd. These "trusts" became significant in American railroad bond holdings and U.S. land mortgages. Fleming first visited the United States in 1870 on behalf of Edward Baxter (a Dundee linen textile and jute manufacturer with "large interests in American securities"). He returned from his trip to America convinced that the country was a fine field for the investment of British capital.[225] Sir David Baxter (a founder of the Baxter firm in Dundee) died in 1872, the wealthiest man in Britain to die that year.[226] It seems that part of his estate became the basis for Fleming's early investment activities.[227] Menzies also became convinced of America's great potential after his visits.[228]

In 1873 the Oregon and Washington Trust Investment Company was formed in Dundee to invest in U.S. land mortgages; its president was the Earl of Airlie. William Reid, a Glasgow-born solicitor who had been U.S. Consul in Dundee, had published that year a pamphlet, "Oregon and Washington Considered as a Field for Labor and Capital"; 30,000 copies were circulated in Scotland, and in 1893 a historian of the state of Oregon would write, "The influence they exerted upon the development of this portion of the Union is almost beyond calculation." In 1874 Reid migrated to Oregon to represent the Oregon and Washington Trust Investment Company. That year William Mackenzie was appointed secretary of the trust in Scotland and began his "brilliant career in investment trust finance."[229]

That same year, 1874, two Chicagoans, Henry I. Sheldon and Daniel H. Hale, convinced a group of Edinburgh and Dundee investors to join with them in forming the Scottish American Mortgage Company, Ltd., with an authorized capital of £1 million to be used in making loans on first mortgages on land and real estate in Chicago and in Illinois, in general. The firm had one managing director in Edinburgh and one (Sheldon) in Chicago.[230]

Meanwhile, in New York in 1871 the United States Mortgage Company had been incorporated; about 80 percent of its stock was owned in Europe, while nine of its twenty-one directors resided abroad (in Paris, Rome, Vienna, and Brighton). It sought to intermediate funds between Europe and the United States, to bring foreign money into western American mortgages.[231] Louis Frémy, governor of the Crédit Foncier de France, was active in its formation.[232] Crédit Foncier de France, involved in mortgage lending at home, was the model for the new American enterprise.[233]

So too, the Equitable Trust Company, New York, was taking mortgages in Chicago and other western cities at 10 percent and pooling and reselling them with their guarantee at 7 percent; by early 1874 Equitable Trust Company bonds were held to "a great extent" in Great Britain and on the Continent.[234] In short, by 1874 U.S. land and mortgages on land and real estate were becoming well known to European investors.

Mining and Oil: 1865–1874

In 1865–1874 foreign investments also mounted in mining in the American South and West. British investors, in 1860, had formed the Great Kanawha Company to exploit 85,000 acres of coal, iron, and timberland in western Virginia. The plans, shelved during the war, were revived in its aftermath.[235] In 1865 the economist W. S. Jevons published *The Coal Question*, forecasting a sharp rise in the price of British coal because of diminishing returns. Many of the British investments in American railroads appear to have been made in response to the possibilities of expensive coal. The Pennsylvania, the Philadelphia and Reading, the Erie, and the Baltimore and Ohio railroads all bought large amounts of coal lands; these were the very same railroads attracting sizable British investment, which monies were in fact used to buy the coal lands. Whether British portfolio investors actually envisaged Britain as a coal importer is unclear. Nonetheless, rising coal prices would make their investments more valuable.[236]

At its quarterly meeting in February 1866, the American Iron and Steel Association passed a resolution welcoming "the unrestricted emigration from all the world of skilled and unskilled labor, and of *manufacturing capital and experience*" (my italics).[237] By 1873 the *Commercial and Financial Chronicle* was commenting on how English capitalists were making "liberal investments" in coal and iron lands in Virginia and West Virginia, adding that prominent, wealthy British ironmasters had organized stock companies to purchase and to build works in the United States. The author forecast a large movement of foreign capital to this country based on U.S. mineral wealth.[238] If American coal was relatively cheap, American iron production would be competitive. By contrast, the first report of the Council of the Corporation of Foreign Bondholders (February 25, 1874) revealed that the council was discouraging British investment in Virginia coal and iron until "the public engagements" of the state had been met. "No private investment can be safe," declared the council, "where the obligations of justice, morality, and law are set at defiance by the community."[239] Recall that Virginia had defaulted on state debts.

Some ninety-four companies, representing an authorized capital of about $90 million, were registered in Great Britain between 1870 and 1873 to mine and to mill ores in the American West. On the basis of the number of British companies, Nevada was the favored field, with California, Colorado, and Utah following. On the basis of capitalization, California and Utah ranked in first and second place.[240] In Nevada, Adolph Sutro planned a major tunnel from Carson Valley to the Comstock Lode. When funds were not available in the West, he obtained them from New York and London.[241] The new mining followed on (or sometimes anticipated) the openings of areas by the railroads.[242]

Press reports on British investments in California gold mining were numerous in the early 1870s.[243] An Englishman wrote of Nevada in 1872 that its mines were "more British than American."[244] In 1870 the "Terrible" mine near Georgetown, Colorado, had been acquired by a British firm (the Colorado Terrible Lode Mining Company), the first major transfer of a Colorado silver mine to a British concern.[245]

The Dutch invested in mining in Utah.[246] So did the British. British investors organized in 1871 the Emma Silver Mining Company, Ltd.; its capital was £1 million.[247] The company obtained an endorsement from the U.S. Minister to Great Britain, General Robert Cummings Schenck. Its board of directors included three British members of Parliament. It advertised its Utah mine as the new "Potosi," after the famous Bolivian silver deposits.[248] To sell the stock, the promoters dramatically understated present liabilities and future costs. By 1873–74 this venture had proved a major fiasco.[249]

More modest but more successful was the British-managed Richmond Mining Company, formed in 1873 as a subsidiary of the Richmond Consolidated Mining Company, Ltd. (organized in 1871), to mine silver in Nevada; it survived a quarter of a century.[250] In London in 1871, *Mining World* warned British directors of American mining companies to provide "careful supervision of the local management."[251] Management at a distance proved difficult, but the British did send experts. Many of the mining investments were clearly direct investments.[252]

The promotion in Britain of the mining companies set the stage for the subsequent similar enterprises (in mining and other sectors as well). These companies were direct investments in that a firm *owned* by foreign capital extended into the United States. Yet these companies had special characteristics. U.S. owners of the mining properties would associate themselves with promoters (American or British) who would organize a British company—a so-called syndicate—that would contract to buy the properties at three to four times the American book value. The British company would then be offered in London. If the sum was raised, the properties were purchased; if not, they reverted to the vendors.[253] Bolder promoters made the purchases and were stuck with the properties—and the obligations—if the issue failed. Promoters of the mining companies frequently exaggerated, deleted qualifying statements from reports of mining engineers, found corrupt or naive mining engineers "to verify" the value of a mine, manipulated the market value of the shares, and, in the process, made handsome profits.[254] Unlike the American railroads, where the incorporation was practically always in the United States (although bonds might be denominated in sterling), these mining companies were incorporated in London (sometimes they had a U.S. operating subsidiary and sometimes not; if not, the London company itself operated in the West).[255] The London company had a board of directors that met periodically (depending on the enterprise). Securities were denominated in pounds in an attempt to create a known, liquid investment vehicle for the British owner.

Conservative Britons had deep (and legitimate) doubts about these proliferating mining companies. When Andrew Carnegie was asked in December 1871 to sell bonds for a Utah mine, he wrote: "It would not do for me to try London on any mining scheme. I must stick to my role of first class steady-going security man—very adverse to anything speculative or 'too good.' Among the class I have been dealing with you frighten if anything much beyond six percent is talked of."[256] In the category of promotions, in 1865 the English Petroleum and Mining Company—with a capital of £50,000—was set up in Britain to drill for oil in Pennsylvania; its subsequent history is obscure. It appears, however, to have been the first British enterprise in the American oil industry.[257]

A U.S. federal mining law passed on July 26, 1866, stated: "The mineral lands of the public domain . . . are hereby declared to be free and open to exploration by all citizens of the United States and those who have declared their intention to become citizens, subject to such regulations as may be prescribed by law, and subject also to the local customs or rules of miners in the several mining districts."[258] The press in the West liked the law and believed that "Eastern and European capital will flow into California and Nevada in large sums under the new system."[259] There was no thought that the phrase about "citizens" would bar foreign capital. Presumably, American citizens would set up companies that would attract such money from abroad. The phrase on citizens (or a variant thereof) was by this time standard in legislation dealing with federal land. It was, as noted earlier, in the 1841 Preemption Act, and also in the 1862 Homestead Act.[260] It had not deterred foreign investment in land.

The 1866 mining law related only to vein mines; a July 9, 1870, law covered placer mines.[261] On May 10, 1872, a general mining act reiterated the statement about citizens included in the 1866 act and added that "proof of citizenship" in the case of an individual consisted of his own affidavit, and in the case of a group of unincorporated persons, an affidavit by their authorized agent, "made on his own knowledge or upon information and belief." As for a corporation organized under the laws of the United States or any state or territory, proof was simply the filing of a copy of its charter or certificate of incorporation. The law did not deal with ownership of the company. It stated that nothing in the legislation would be construed to impair the rights of existing property owners.[262] Nonetheless, apparently concern existed in Britain over this 1872 legislation.[263]

The three mining laws did not retard foreign investment. If a foreign investor could not obtain a mining claim from the U.S. government, he or his company could purchase the mining "patent" from an American citizen who had acquired it from the U.S. government. Likewise, the foreign investor could form an incorporated company in the United States that could get the patent directly.[264] In the South, land was not U.S. government owned, so the rules were not applicable. Thus, the mining laws notwithstanding, British-owned companies multiplied. Far more a deterrent to investment was the expanding list of bankruptcies, the exposures of the fraudulent property descriptions, and the drastic fall in the value of such company shares after the Panic of 1873.[265]

In sum, in 1865–1874, and especially in the early 1870s, many new foreign investments were made in mining. One set was linked with British expectations of rising coal prices. Another set was in "promotions"—companies floated in England to develop American mines. Whereas the investments in public securities and most of the investments in American railroads were portfolio ones (as were many of those associated with coal mining), in that the British-incorporated mining companies intended to control their own activities in the United States, this set consisted of direct investments.

Manufacturing: 1865–1874

In the post–Civil War years the first surge of foreign direct investments in American manufacturing took place. Most of the new stakes were motivated by the high tariffs imposed during the Civil War; also, the depreciated dollar raised the price of U.S. imports. Thus British investments were made, for example, in spinning and spooling cotton and linen thread.

Manufacturers of cotton thread from Paisley, Scotland, that had long exported to and had had direct sales representation in the United States decided to produce in this country. In 1860 George A. Clark had begun—on behalf of the Paisley, Scotland, firm J. & J. Clark (as of 1879 Clark & Co.)—spooling imported hank thread. These limited operations were expanded in 1865, when he founded the Passaic

Thread Co., renamed that year the Clark Thread Company. It built a mill in Newark, New Jersey, for spinning and spooling. George A. Clark & Brother remained as the sales company.

In 1869 J. & P. Coats, also of Paisley, followed its competitor. Like Clark, its exports were negatively affected by U.S. tariffs and the value of the dollar. In November 1868 Hezekiah Conant—an American who had patented an automatic machine for winding spool cotton—organized the Conant Thread Company in Pawtucket, Rhode Island. In 1864 Conant had visited Scotland and seen the works of J. & P. Coats. In May 1869 he again traveled to Paisley and there "effected a combination with J. & P. Coats." From the latter he obtained a "large" amount of capital and proceeded to expand his small Pawtucket factory. In 1869 Coats's records indicate that the Scottish firm had £21,000 invested in the Conant Thread Company. Conant that year started to manufacture Coats's six-cord spool cotton. By 1874 Conant had built Mill No. 2 (1870), a bleachery (1871), and a large spinning mill (Mill No. 3, 1873). Coats's investment rose. Prior to the completion of the spinning mill, the yarn for spooling had been imported from Scotland. By mid-May 1873, for the first time, the managers in Pawtucket could receive cotton in the bale and transform it into finished thread. The machinery in these new Conant Thread Company mills was in large part of British manufacture; skilled and unskilled workers were imported from Scotland. James Coats (son of Peter Coats of J. & P. Coats) was president of the Conant Thread Company. Hezekiah Conant was treasurer and manager. James Coats (1834–1913) had arrived in America in 1856; he was at that time a junior partner in J. & P. Coats, Paisley; when his uncle Andrew Coats had returned to Scotland in 1860, James Coats had become the overall supervisor of the American business. He married into the Auchincloss family (Auchincloss was Coats's chief selling "agent" in the United States).

Still a third Scottish cotton threadmaker, John Clark, Jr. & Co., Glasgow, built a mill in East Newark, New Jersey, in the early 1870s. It sold a thread named after the location of the parent company's "Mile End" mill.[266]

In linen thread, in about 1864–65, three Barbour brothers, who had migrated to the United States from Lisburn, in northern Ireland, started a factory in Paterson, New Jersey. Their other brothers (there were seventeen siblings) remained in the old country, where the eldest ran the Lisburn plant; the American and British linen thread works were closely associated through the family ties.[267]

John L. Haynes, secretary of the National Association of Wool Manufacturers, declared (in 1870): "Let us keep up the walls about our continent . . . If we want the fabrics of Europe, let us not import them; but bring, by the attractions of our protective system, her capital and establishments, her skill and her workmen to our own land."[268] Haynes hoped many British firms would either migrate to America or invest in this country, retaining their home operations.

Like the threadmakers, Sheffield, England, hardware and crucible steel producers, among them the W. & S. Butcher Steel Works, had long exported to the United States. In 1865 the seventy-four-year-old William Butcher had crossed the Atlantic to help recruit workmen for the Pennsylvania Steel Company in Harrisburg; in 1867 Pennsylvania Steel rolled the first commercial steel rails produced in the United States from its new Bessemer steel mill. That same year, along with a Philadelphia iron merchant (Philip S. Justice), Butcher started the William Butcher Steel Works, in Norristown, near Philadelphia, to manufacture cast steel railway tires and other products. Circumventing tariffs was probably a crucial consideration. Whether Butcher or his Sheffield firm had an interest in Pennsylvania Steel or in Butcher Steel is unclear, although it seems likely that there was one in the latter (which was, incidentally, the predecessor of Midvale Steel Company). Soon Butcher left this enterprise to lease a crucible steel site at the Freedom Iron Works at Burnham, near Lewistown, Pennsylvania (later, as Standard Steel, this works came to be owned by Baldwin Locomotive Company). Butcher's brother, Samuel, died in 1869, and that year or the next, Butcher returned to Sheffield, to die there in December 1870. The deaths ended the Butcher family's British firm, as well as any financial interest it or the brothers may have had in William Butcher's American endeavors.[269] Butcher's ventures— temporary family involvements—were the first of a sequence of major Sheffielders' activities in U.S. manufacturing.

Dye and coal tar products seem also to have attracted foreign investment to America. Thomas and Charles Holliday, sons of Read Holliday (an early English coal tar distiller) arrived in the United States in 1864. The Holliday brothers started to produce aniline oil and then magenta at a factory in Brooklyn, New York, which was soon fabricating other colors that were, according to the historian Williams Haynes, "similar to those made in the affiliated English plant." This U.S. company, run by the two immigrants, the first to synthesize dyes in America, never became an influential enterprise in the new industry.[270]

On the other hand, Bayer did become important. In 1860 (the same year Read Holliday had begun to make aniline dyes in England), Friedrich Bayer had built the first German aniline works, which, after the U.S. Civil War, had started to export to America. A number of authors state that Bayer established a dyestuff factory in Albany, New York, in 1865.[271] More likely, Bayer opened a sales office in New York in that year. The chemical industry historian Williams Haynes, writing of Bayer in the United States, notes that in 1868, following on the Hollidays' Brooklyn venture, Arthur Bott, a German-American cardboard manufacturer, had organized with U.S. financial backing the "first American-owned" dye company in Albany, New York—the Albany Aniline & Chemical Works—which made magenta, Hofmann's violet, and possibly some other colors. When in 1871 Bott withdrew, Haynes writes that Bott sold his interest in this venture to Friedrich Bayer, but American individuals still retained control.[272] From Bayer's German plant, Herman Preiss arrived in Albany, and using German technology he produced there high-quality magenta from imported aniline oil and arsenic acid.[273] The imports apparently came from Bayer's German plant. By the early 1870s the German Bayer certainly had U.S. investments in manufacturing.

In October 1865 Alfred Nobel (1833–1896) took out a U.S. patent for nitroglycerine. In 1866 the Swedish inventor of dynamite visited the United States and, with American partners, formed the United States Blasting Oil Company (in New York); he "surrendered" his patent to this firm. In the next two years Alfred Nobel participated in the organization of the Giant Powder Company in San Francisco, for the California market, and the Atlantic Giant Powder Company, for the eastern United States. These two companies took over the rights of the United States Blasting Oil Company. Alfred Nobel had stock in both. Initially, at least, Nobel seems to have intended a direct investment role but no management function even comparable to Bayer.[274]

Meanwhile, another multiunit facility in a completely different industry came into being in the United States. In 1849 Eberhard Faber (1822–1879), the youngest of the three sons of a German pencil manufacturer, had migrated to the United States. In Stein (near Nuremberg), Eberhard's two brothers ran A. W. Faber, the world's most important lead pencil factory (established in 1761). Eberhard Faber opened a branch to sell imported pencils and stationery in America and a depot for red cedar, a wood used in the German works. In 1857 Eberhard Faber had become an American citizen. In the 1850s he put the first eraser on the pencil and manufactured it at a factory he had started in Newark, New Jersey; this plant also made rubber bands; it would serve the American market. Before the Civil War, Faber had built a cedar mill at Cedar Key in Florida, where the wood was prepared for export. Finally, in 1861, with the growing U.S. market and high duties imposed on imports, Eberhard Faber had begun the manufacture of pencils at a factory in New York City (on 42nd Street, where the United Nations is now located); there he made pencils for the American market. His was the first successful pencil-making works in the United States. When the factory burned down in 1872, Eberhard Faber at once built a new plant in Brooklyn, New York. A contemporary newspaper account of this "branch factory" described the difficulties that Eberhard Faber had to overcome when in 1861 he had first embarked on manufacturing:

The cost of labor is so much higher in this country than in Europe, that machinery had to be devised and constructed to automatically perform the work, which is done so cheaply by hand labor in the old country. In fact, the whole process of necessary machinery was invented . . . and Mr. Faber had the satisfaction of knowing that he could not only make pencils in this country cheaper, but also of a much better and more uniform finish than any before produced.

The same article (undated, but from the context probably written about 1872–73) notes that the parent firm of A. W. Faber had its principal manufactory in Stein, Germany; in addition, it had a large slate factory at Geroldsgrun (Bavaria), branches in Paris and London, an agency in Vienna, as well as the large American business. A. W. Faber was a family affair; Eberhard Faber's brothers ran the Stein works.[275]

These British, Swedish, and German direct investments in manufacturing (with the exception of the origins of Faber's Cedar Key mill) were to serve the U.S. market. They were investments whereby a family firm or an individual inventor (in the case of Nobel) moved into international business; in the Nobel case there was a licensed patent in return for stock, but not for controlling stock. From the beginning, the investments were multinational-enterprise type of stakes in U.S. manufacturing. Often the manufacturing facility in the United States had been motivated by the existence of the U.S. tariff. With Nobel's investment, the nature of the product was what warranted production near the market. In all cases, the parent firm or innovator (in the case of Nobel) had unique goods; the firm had an "advantage."

There were also some (fewer) foreign direct investments in manufacturing for export from the United States. Faber's Cedar Key mill originally fit in that category. Another example was the Glasgow Port Washington Iron and Coal Company, Ltd., which built two blast furnaces in Ohio and began pig iron production in 1872. It purchased 900 acres in Ohio to provide its resources. All its management came from Scotland. At least as late as the early 1880s, it was still operating.

Its founders intended exports to Britain, since they believed America's low-cost and abundant raw materials would make the output competitive. The company was British financed.[276] In Chicago the Liverpool provision merchant firm of John Morrell & Co. opened a new hog-packing plant in 1871 to supply its British trade.[277]

Portfolio investments from abroad in U.S. manufacturing were few and exceptional. The Manchester, England, promoter David Chadwick, who converted a large number of British iron, steel, and coal enterprises into limited liability companies and whose firm served as an agent for American railroad securities, did issue four hundred $1,000 bonds for the Joliet Iron & Steel Company of Chicago in 1874. The Joliet Company had one of the first Bessemer plants in the United States. In 1874 Andrew Carnegie raised money in London for his own steel works.[278]

Insurance, Banking, and Trading Houses: 1865–1875

Foreign enterprise also provided services—in insurance, banking, and trade. As urbanization occurred in post–Civil War America, construction was rapid and often slipshod; wood was abundant and widely used, and fires common. When insurance from domestic firms was not readily available, Britishers met the need. The sizable Liverpool & London & Globe and the Royal, both of which had been in the United States for a number of years, opened new outlets in additional states.[279] They were joined by the North British & Mercantile Insurance Company, Ltd. (1866), the Queen's Office (1866), the Imperial Office (1868), the Commercial Union (1869), and others—a literal "American invasion by British insurers." In 1872 the London Assurance Corporation appointed a New York agent.[280] In 1874 the Western Assurance Company and the British American Assurance Company, both of Toronto, Canada, entered the United States.[281] Some German insurers also ventured into this country: in 1871, General Marine Insurance Company, Dresden, marine insurance only, and in 1873, the Hamburg-Bremen Fire Insurance Company, Hamburg.[282] The main emphasis of the foreign enterprises was on fire insurance.

After the devastating Chicago fire of October 1871, six British insurers paid out £1,182,521, most by the Liverpool & London & Globe and the North British firms. This sum was approximately 6 percent of the total adjusted losses incurred during the conflagration. Then came the Boston fire of November 1872, and an additional £972,231 was paid out by the foreign insurance offices, covering 7.7 percent of the insured property destroyed.[283] The British firms paid their Chicago and Boston fire claims, which was more than could be said for many American carriers. In the end, the losses notwithstanding, the fires "proved . . . to be good advertising" for the U.K. insurers, bringing them more access to American business" because of their demonstrated reliability.[284]

Of the five British banks opened in California in 1863–1865 (see Table 4.4), two failed in 1866, brought down in the wake of the collapse of Overend, Gurney in England;[285] the other three—branches of the Bank of British North America, the Bank of British Columbia, and the London and San Francisco Bank—persisted.[286] In particular, the Bank of British Columbia prospered. It has been described as one of the three outstanding banks in the state of California in the post–Civil War years.[287] Its American profits, from both its San Francisco and its Portland, Oregon, branches, often surpassed those from Canada.[288] Its U.S. and its Canadian businesses were both run from London.[289]

The London and San Francisco Bank, Ltd., which started in 1865 with a paid-up capital of £200,000, was owned by a prominent group of English and German banking companies and a "Manila firm."[290] It opened branches in Portland, Oregon, and in Tacoma and Seattle Washington.[291] Its first New York agent was Dabney, Morgan, and Co. It had a London headquarters, and in that city J. P. Morgan's father, J. S. Morgan, served as the bank's agent.[292] In the late 1860s the London and San Francisco Bank joined others in selling U.S. railway bonds in England and Germany;[293] in 1871 it placed in London a £500,000 bond issue of the Omaha Bridge Company (guaranteed by the Union Pacific).[294] By the early 1870s the bank was marketing in London and Frankfurt bonds of the Oregon and California Railroad.[295]

In 1873 the Anglo-Californian Bank opened, founded by the Seligman family (of New York and London) and the Sassoons (of London and Bombay). Before the Civil War the Seligmans had begun a gold shipment business in California, which the new and soon-to-be-highly-successful bank took over.[296] That same year (1873), the Swiss-American Bank (incorporated in Geneva, Switzerland) inaugurated a San Francisco branch, acquiring the long-established assaying and banking activities of Henry Hentsch and Francis Berton.[297]

On the East Coast of the United States, transatlantic and U.S.-Canadian banking associations continued. Earlier, when I discussed the transfers of European monies into American railroads, I noted the growth of activities by European houses in New York City. The Canadian-American banking relations were more tied to international trade and foreign exchange than to securities intermediation. In May 1872 the Canadian Bank of Commerce (founded in 1867) opened a

New York "branch,"[298] joining the Bank of British North America and the Bank of Montreal in that city. In particular, the Bank of Montreal grew in importance. By the end of 1868, the Bank of Montreal's New York agency had assets of $8.85 million.[299] That bank's Chicago branch had survived the Civil War, joined in the founding of the Chicago Clearing House in 1865, closed temporarily in 1867, and then reopened in 1871 as grain shipments via the St. Lawrence rose.[300] In 1871 the Chicago branch was active in bringing English capital into the city.[301] According to its own historian, by 1873 the Bank of Montreal was larger than any other bank on the American continent.[302]

Canadian banks in the early 1870s played a highly significant role in U.S. banking. The historian of the Canadian Bank of Commerce describes its functions as buying a large proportion of the bills drawn on U.S. exports and arranging for American importers to pay for foreign merchandise. Letters of credit issued by the Canadian Bank of Commerce, for example, covered a wide range of items in international trade.[303] The Canadian banks—with their New York offices— obtained by 1874 a large share of the sterling exchange business.[304]

Foreign interests in American banks—remnants of times far past—still persisted to a small extent. In 1874 Hope & Co., Amsterdam, held $4.3 million in bonds of the Citizens' Bank, New Orleans, a continuation of investments made in the 1830s.[305] Other banking connections, associated with trade and railroad developments, existed in the American South.

Many investments in the United States continued to be made by British trading firms. One firm deserves special mention because of its later importance. Balfour, Williamson & Co., formed in Liverpool in 1851, had set up an overseas house in Valparaiso, Chile, the next year. In 1869 the Liverpool firm opened in San Francisco (under the style Balfour, Guthrie, & Co.) to handle California wheat and other produce exports and also to import merchandise for sale in California.[306] Horace Greeley, the editor of the *New York Tribune* and a believer in protectionist policies, claimed that in the late 1860s, "foreign houses . . . their recognized agencies in New York City, or . . . those affiliated with foreign houses" had provided three-quarters of the funding of the Free Trade League.[307] Trading firms did not approve America's move to protection.

1854–1874: The Foreign Investments

In this chapter I have traced the growing foreign investments of the 1850s, which were temporarily curbed by the Civil War. In the 1850s state government securities were most likely still the largest sector for foreign investment, although interests in railroads mounted rapidly—and by 1860 *may* have equaled or even exceeded those holdings in all public sector (federal, state, and local government) securities. The bulk of investment was clearly of a portfolio nature.

The war interrupted the rise in foreign investment, but it also created a huge national debt for the victors; while war financing was basically done at home, the federal debt could be bought abroad at bargain rates, far below par. Thus, as a gamble, the holdings of Europeans began to increase, especially after 1863. In the immediate postwar years and probably until 1875, the public sector in America attracted the most foreign monies. Federal debt held abroad was supplemented by the sale in Europe of new state debts, and then in the 1870s defaults on many of those state debts again—as in the early 1840s—eliminated enthusiasm for such investments, this time once and for all.

Meanwhile, the Civil War slowdown in railroad building was replaced by a postwar surge in new construction. To finance this activity, Americans turned to Europe. Huge amounts of monies poured into railroads—albeit apparently not enough to offset the still-giant federal government debt held abroad.

A detailed estimate of foreign investment in the United States in 1869 is given in Table 4.11; I do not have comparable detailed data for 1874. Unquestionably foreign stakes rose in the early 1870s (see Tables 4.1 and 4.5). The financial crisis of 1873 was precipitated that

Table 4.11. Long-term foreign investments in the United States, 1869 (in millions of dollars)

Federal securities held abroad	1,000.0
State bonds	100.0
Municipal bonds	7.5
Railway bonds	130.0
Railway shares	113.0
Canal bonds	5.0
Mining bonds and shares	10.0
Real estate mortgages, etc.	25.0
Total	1,390.5

Source: *Report of the Special Commissioner of the Revenue* (1869), p. xxvii, in *Foreign Investments in the United States*, ed. Mira Wilkins (New York: Arno Press, 1977).

Note: In addition, there were $50 million "temporarily invested" plus $25 million "Cuban moneys temporarily transferred in consequence of the revolution."

September by the insolvency of Jay Cooke—the banking house that had sold Union bonds during the Civil War, participated in the refunding of the U.S. debt in 1871, and was in 1873 seeking to sell Northern Pacific securities in Europe. Cooke had hoped to finance the construction of the Northern Pacific Railroad with monies from Britain and Germany, but failed to raise the required sums. The historians Paul Studenski and Herman Krooss have attributed Cooke's bankruptcy, along with the subsequent Panic of 1873 in the United States, to a cessation of U.S. capital imports in the middle of that year.[308] The *Nation*, September 25, 1873, reported that the English market was closed to American railroad securities "under the repeated influence of repeated cases of American rascality such as the Emma Mine . . . and Fremont's swindling Texas enterprise [the Memphis, El Paso and Pacific], and the defaults made by several new roads in payment of their coupons."[309] "American rascality" was clear when, at one point (in 1870), a representative of the English Erie shareholders referred to Jay Gould's actions in the American courts as "an outrage on private rights perpetrated in the name of the law, such as has no parallel in modern times in any civilized country in the world."[310]

These difficulties notwithstanding, in 1874 U.S. railway securities continued to be offered in large quantities on the London and Amsterdam markets (see Tables 4.8 and 4.9); there were some buyers. Securities held as collateral were placed on the market when loan defaults occurred, which raised the number of American securities available abroad.[311] U.S. federal government credit—as the Secretary of the Treasury stated in December 1873—remained high.[312] The new English and Scottish investment trusts weathered the 1873 crisis; indeed, for the Scottish American Investment Company, Ltd., which bought high-grade U.S. railroad securities at bargain prices, the 1873 crisis seemed "evidently sent providentially for the Company's interests," or so its secretary wrote.[313] The 1872 mining legislation in Washington did not imperil foreign investments in mining. European manufacturers looked to the large American market to sell and—occasionally—to manufacture their wares. Americans with good British connections could still finance their ventures in London.[314] Having proved themselves reliable after the 1871 Chicago and 1872 Boston fires, British fire insurance offices had a promising future. Indeed, during the years after the Civil War, Americans had been eager to capture European savings for U.S. development; and Europeans had made heavy investments—primarily but not exclusively portfolio investments. If public sector investments still held first place, it would not be for long.

PART II

The World's Greatest Debtor Nation: 1875–1914

5.

The Setting

From 1875 to 1914 the U.S. economy was transformed. In 1879 about 53 percent of value added by U.S. output was from agriculture; by 1909, 62 percent was from industry.[1] The United States had a population of less than 40 million in 1870 and of 92 million in 1910.[2] Growth in production was impressive (see Table 5.1). In 1870–1875 Great Britain was the preeminent industrial giant of the world, with just under one-third of the world's manufacturing. By 1914 the United States held the lead, with more than one-third of the world's industrial output (see Table 5.2).

Communication and transportation across the Atlantic became cheap, readily available, and fast. The price of a twenty-word cable from New York to London had been $100 in 1866. In 1912 it was $5. That year the transmission of a message between those two cities took three minutes.[3] Transatlantic steamship fares fell in this period. Numerous ships steamed along regularly scheduled routes, and by the early twentieth century a journey could be made from Britain to the United States in six days.[4] The expanding railroad network opened

Table 5.1. Long-term rates of growth, 1870/71–1913 (percent per annum)

Country	Total output	Output per man-hour	Industrial output
United States	4.3	2.3	4.7
Germany	2.9	2.1	4.1
United Kingdom	2.2	1.5	2.1

Source: Adapted from Derek H. Aldcroft, ed., *The Development of British Industry and Foreign Competition, 1875–1914* (London: George Allen & Unwin, 1968), p. 13.

Table 5.2. Percentage distribution of world manufacturing production by country, 1870–1913

Country	1870	1913
United States	23.3	35.8
United Kingdom	31.8	14.0
All other countries	44.9	50.2
Total	100.0	100.0

Source: League of Nations, *Industrialization and Foreign Trade* (1945; rpt. New York: Garland, 1983), p. 13.

the American Far West and South to visitors. Tourists and businessmen, books, pamphlets, magazines, and newspapers provided Europeans with a wealth of data about the new world.[5] Moderately priced, convenient, and relatively rapid transportation, plus the flow of knowledge, fostered the migration of people and of capital.[6] Immigrants, in turn, aided in the nation's development, and they wrote home about their experiences in America. Capital markets in the United States became more integrated. The cost of information declined as travelers and settlers offered reliable and regular news; foreign investors perceived and took advantage of the opportunities.[7]

The value of U.S. merchandise exports soared from $513 million in 1875 to $2.4 billion in 1914 while, high tariffs notwithstanding, the value of U.S. merchandise imports rose from $533 million in 1875 to $1.9 billion in 1914. Behind American tariff walls, U.S. industry and domestic commerce expanded. Import substitution was evident (imports had represented 14 percent of domestic consumption of manufactured goods in 1869; by 1909 that figure was down to 5.9 percent).[8]

U.S. prices dropped in the last quarter of the nineteenth century; the word *depression* was used, but real incomes rose. When the price trend reversed itself in the closing few years of the nineteenth century and in the early twentieth, U.S. real income continued an upward path.[9] In the late 1880s, American businesses had often sought agreements and amalgamations in response to declining prices. The Sherman Antitrust Act of 1890 banned collusive accords. Mergers accelerated, especially in the late 1890s and at the turn of the century, after American courts confirmed the illegality of restraint-of-trade agreements. Rising prices in the years 1897–1903 now came to facilitate combination because new security issues became more salable with the expectations of yet higher prices.

American businesses grew larger in the last decades of the nineteenth century and in the early twentieth, extending themselves through internal growth in addition to mergers. The huge domestic market, increasingly connected by the new railroad network, encouraged the rise of giant enterprise. As companies spread their operations over the immense American geographical expanse and adopted technologies appropriate for large-scale production, their need for capital became more substantial. The corporate form was becoming the typical legal structure for manufacturing as well as for infrastructure projects, aiding in the mobilization of monies and in the development of managerial organizations.

Volume output for the domestic market meant that American businesses required managerial, clerical, marketing, and other nonproduction personnel. Specialized functions emerged within these enterprises. Organizational innovations lowered intrafirm transaction costs. The newly developing big businesses created a demand for financial and other services.[10]

Major change occurred in "professional finance." The word *syndicate* came into frequent use, acquiring three related meanings: (1) a group of bankers who underwrote or placed a security issue, or both; (2) a group of promoters (or a promoter and his associates) who formed a new single company to acquire existing businesses (the securities of the new company, the "syndicate," would then be sold to the public); and (3) a group of promoters, individuals, and possibly bankers who acted in concert and raised money (sometimes for one company, sometimes for several companies, some of which might be new enterprises, but not necessarily). What all these syndicates shared was the gathering together of vast amounts of capital, at home and abroad. The word *trust* was often employed in this era—in the context of "giant companies," "investment trusts," and "trust companies." The term suggested—in a derogatory, neutral, or favorable manner—investors' pooling their monies in or leaving their assets with institutions (corporate or otherwise) for specialized handling.[11]

During the Civil War, the "greenback" had—as we have seen—become legal tender. In 1875 America passed legislation mandating a return to the gold standard, which was achieved in January 1879; the Gold Standard Act of 1900 ratified the monetary standard that existed after 1879. Despite calls for bimetalism among populist leaders and despite some talk of returning to an unbacked currency, in the years 1879–1914 American obligations were pledged in gold. This was important in aiding the formation of domestic capital markets.

A British visitor returned from the United States in 1890 to report: "In America . . . you have the most stable and conservative form of government in the world . . . if our investing public make mistakes in American investments, they have simply themselves to blame. . . . There is no possibility of repudiation. There is no fear of foreign wars. It, therefore, all comes down to a question of efficient management and careful selection."[12] A historian described the changes in this country as follows: "The land that had idealized yeomen farmers and rugged individualists was becoming a land of corporate organization, bureaucratic systematizers, and associational activities."[13]

Foreign investment was important in the transformation of American life. From 1875 to 1914 foreign investments in the United States, encouraged by the growth and promise, multiplied to meet the new needs. As America became the world's greatest industrial power, the country's exports rose and its own businesses also expanded internationally.[14] Its domestic financial institutions grew to serve more of its national requirements. The country nonetheless remained a debtor in world accounts; that is, more foreign capital was invested in America than this country invested abroad. In fact, the United States became the greatest debtor nation ever in history, a magnet attracting unprecedented amounts of both foreign portfolio and direct investments (see Table 5.3).[15]

An Overview of Foreign Investment in the United States: 1875–1914

The large number of estimates notwithstanding, no one knows how much money was invested in the United States from abroad in the years 1875–1914.[16] For many years more attention was paid to determining the quantities of portfolio rather than of direct investments.[17] Both coexisted and on occasion were comingled.[18]

In the open international capital markets of 1875–1914, the level of portfolio investments in the United States fluctuated daily, even hourly. After 1879 America was on the gold standard, and rates of exchange varied only slightly. Foreign investors bought and sold American securities in Europe, Canada, and in the United States; they bought and sold American securities denominated in foreign currencies (pounds, florins, and francs) and in dollars. They bought and sold bearer bonds. They bought and sold securities publicly traded and privately placed. Securities at maturity came up for refunding or redemption. Substitution of one type of security for another was common. The plethora of transactions resulted in changes in long-term foreign claims on American assets (that is, foreign investment in the United States). The highly liquid portfolio investments were made or "unmade" by both foreign individuals and firms. Investors considered interest rates, appreciation potential, and risk. Investments

Table 5.3. A 1914 balance sheet

Principal lenders[a]		Principal borrowers[a]	
Country	Level (in billions of U.S. dollars)	Country	Level (in billions of U.S. dollars)
United Kingdom	18.0	UNITED STATES	7.1
France	9.0	Russia	3.8
Germany	7.3	Canada	3.7
United States	3.5	Argentina	3.0
Netherlands	2.0	Austria-Hungary	2.5
Belgium	1.5	Spain	2.5
Switzerland	1.5	Brazil	2.2
		Mexico	2.0
		India and Ceylon	2.0
		South Africa	1.7
		Australia	1.7
		China	1.6
Other[b]	2.2	Other[c]	11.2
Total	45.0	Total	45.0

Source: These are rough estimates, as of July 1, 1914, prepared by Mira Wilkins, based on compilations of data by the United Nations, Arthur Lewis, William Woodruff, Herbert Feis, Douglass North, Rondo Cameron, Raymond Goldsmith, F. Bartsche (via György Kövér), Olga Crisp, Mira Wilkins, and others. All figures are "gross."

[a] No country is itemized separately that had long-term foreign credits or debts of less than $1.5 billion.

[b] Japan and Russia (especially in China), Portugal (especially in Brazil), Sweden (especially in Russia), Canada (especially in the United States and the Caribbean), for example.

[c] Includes residual *not* separately itemized: $4.7 billion for the rest of Europe, including the Ottoman Empire; $2.3 billion for the rest of Asia; $1.8 billion for the rest of Latin America, including the Caribbean; $2.3 billion for all of Africa, except South Africa; and $.1 billion for the rest of Oceania.

were in negotiable securities. When refunding or redemption of bonds occurred, investors could remain in the new securities or reinvest in other U.S. ones, or they could move their monies elsewhere.[19]

It has long been accepted that in the late nineteenth and early twentieth centuries, the value of foreign portfolio investment far exceeded that of foreign direct investment in the United States. My research confirms this.[20] It also demonstrates that the owners of such securities were not as passive as most scholars have assumed and that many such investments in the United States carried with them—or their owners tried to introduce—at the very least, influence, and on occasion, when things went wrong, financial management and an attempt at control. The latter were not (as I will show) the motives behind these investments, but rather the outcome of the sizable participation.

A multitude of foreign direct investments were made in the United States, where from the start the investor (typically a company) intended to control and to manage the business. In these instances the investor had no inclination to send capital to America without monitoring its use.[21] Such investments were stimulated by the search for raw materials or markets, or both. In the case of these direct investments (as with the portfolio ones), exits as well as entries occurred. Direct investments—those with the intent from origin of carrying management and control—were far more extensive than most scholars have recognized.[22]

Table 5.4 offers estimates of the level of long-term foreign investment in the United States. It shows a rise in such stakes from approximately $1.5 billion in 1875 to about $7 billion on July 1, 1914, that is, before war broke out in Europe. These figures (and all the ones that follow) are crude.[23] Between 1875 and 1914, while there were government attempts to ascertain how much of the U.S. public debt was held abroad, no U.S. census covered all foreign investment in this nation; there was no study in any way comparable in scope to the 1853 and 1869 investigations cited in Chapter 4. Nathaniel T. Bacon's figures for 1899 stand alone as a contemporary scholarly approximation of the overall foreign investments in the United States.[24] Bacon, in conducting his research, had no official authority; his resulting text was peppered with appropriate qualifications. Bacon and George Paish (another contemporary whose numbers are often cited) developed their overall statistics on foreign investments in the United States principally through discussions with informed bankers.[25] This meant, by the very nature of their sources, that both shortchanged direct investments, because many of the direct investors had little to do with bankers.

After 1914 capable scholars have attempted to construct series on foreign investments in the United States for the earlier time. Their reconstructions (like my summary in Table 5.4) are far from satisfactory, resting as they do on a large number of unknowns.[26] In short, the totals presented in Table 5.4 are inadequate, albeit they seem to be the best available. Except for the estimates for July 1, 1914, prepared by Cleona Lewis, the figures exclude most of the many foreign investments that did not leave a trace in the securities market. I would

Table 5.4. Estimates of the level of long-term foreign investments in the United States, 1875–1914 (in millions of U.S. dollars)[a]

Date	Total	Government Federal	Government State/ county/ city	Private sector Railroads	Insurance	Mining	Manufacturing	Other
1875	1,500[b]							
1876	1,500[c]	600[d]	97[e]	390[f]				
1878, April	975[g]	500[h]						
1878, Dec.		200[i]						
1880, Dec.	1,249[j]	249[k]	97[l]	899[l]				
1881		150[m]						
1882						30[n]		
1883	2,000[o]	100[p]						
1885	1,900[q]							46[r]
1889	3,000[s]						20[t]	
1890–91								u
1894	v							
1895	2,500[w]							
1896	2,600[x]							
1897	3,000[y]							
1899	3,145[z]	10[aa]	aa					
1907	6,000[bb]							
1908	6,000[cc]							
1912	dd							
1914, July 1	7,090[ee]			4,170[ff]				2,920[gg]

[a] I have omitted from the table estimates that refer to investments by only one nationality and ones that do not seem plausible. Sometimes I have inserted alternative estimates in the notes. Initially, I had planned to specify whether the estimates given in the tables were at par or market, but in most cases the data are too crude to allow such precision. I have tried to omit from the estimates all short-term obligations. When the estimates were expressed in pounds, I have translated the figures into dollars at the rate £1 = $4.86.

[b] Estimate made by A. J. Warner, as of year-end 1875, in *Banker's Magazine*, New York, 33 (Jan. 1879): 256. It is probably a reasonable "ballpark figure." It seems that in the years 1873–1876, while there were trades and changes, the total amount of foreign investment in the United States remained roughly the same (see Table 4.1). Warner's 1875 estimate was identical with that made for 1873 by Charles J. Bullock, John H. Williams, and Rufus S. Tucker, "The Balance of Trade of the United States," *Review of Economic Statistics*, 1 (July 1919): 225. The statistician Ernest Seyd gave a larger estimate for 1875 in his "The Fall of the Price of Silver, Its Consequences, and Their Possible Avoidance," *Journal of the Society of the Arts*, 24 (March 10, 1876): 311. Seyd's figures were rough, and there were errors in his totals. He believed U.S. international indebtedness in 1875 (at year-end) equaled £450 million, or $2,190 million. His subtotals equal £470 million. He allocated £210 million ($1,020 million) to American federal and state debts held in Europe, £150 million ($730 million) to railways, other public works, and mines—bonds and shares—owned in Europe (of which £100 was attributable to railroad bonds); £20 million ($97 million) represented foreign holdings of

American land and mortgages; £40 million ($195 million) was "the active capital" of "European capitalists" involved in the export and import trade of the United States, while £50 million ($243 million) was an international obligation "required for recovery of specie payment." This last £50 million can be seen as a short-term debt; the £40 million should also be subtracted as short term. The rest would seem to be long-term investment, which after subtracting the £90 million, would come to £380 million ($1,847 million—a figure not too far out of line with Warner's $1,500 million estimate). Seyd, however, believed he was underestimating. John J. Madden, *British Investment in the United States, 1860–1880* (1958; rpt. New York: Garland, 1985), p. 388 (table 24), estimated that total American securities abroad, as of Dec. 31, 1875, came to $1,489 million. He thought his figures were within 15 percent of accuracy, assumed all America's international indebtedness was to England and the European continent, and in table 24 excluded railway shares because "it was impossible to allocate on an annual basis" (p. 382). Madden accepted the $1,500 million figure (p. 401). He put the federal debt held abroad in *1875* as $633 million (p. 3), but put the 1874 figure at $633 million and the *1875* one at $623 million (p. 388).

  [c] My own ballpark estimate. Madden, *British Investment*, p. 388 (table 24) and pp. 78–79 (tables 15–16) gave different figures: $1,440 million and $1,657 million.

  [d] *Economist*, 33 (Oct. 9, 1880): 1171 (quoting a speech of the U.S. Secretary of the Treasury on Aug. 26, 1876). Madden, *British Investment*, pp. 388, 78–79, put the figure at $570 million for Britain and the Continent.

  [e] Madden, *British Investment*, pp. 78–79 (nominal value of U.S. state, county, and city securities held in Europe).

  [f] This figure has to be low. *Banker's Magazine*, New York, 30 (May 1876): 845, indicated that the amount of U.S. railroad bonds held abroad was the same as in Dec. 1874 (see Table 4.1), but that now the amount in default had risen to $253 million, or 65 percent of the total. Madden, *British Investment*, pp. 78–79, estimated that "the nominal value" of American railroad bonds held in Britain and on the European continent was $797 million; he added $141 million to include "the nominal value" of railroad shares. His total came to $938 million. He thought the figure was up from $894 million in 1874. The huge discrepancy lies in part in how quickly one omits securities in default and also in Madden's use of "nominal" values, which undoubtedly inflates this figure. His estimate for Britain alone in 1876 was $559 million. Dorothy Adler, *British Investment in American Railways* (Charlottesville: University Press of Virginia, 1970), p. 166, also thought *Banker's Magazine* underestimated; she set the British investment in U.S. rails in 1876 at $486 million. See also note b above for Seyd's estimate for 1875 and Chapter 4 on the large post–Civil War interest in American railroads.

  [g] There were many estimates made in April 1878. I have included the one made by Edward Young, as of April 1878, given in *Banker's Magazine*, New York, 33 (Jan. 1879): 527 (Young was Chief of the U.S. Bureau of Statistics). Other estimates for April 1878 are those of John A. Stewart, president of U.S. Trust Co. ($1 billion), and George Bliss of Morton, Bliss ($950 million). See U.S. Congress, House of Representatives, Committee on Banking and Commerce, *Resumption of Specie Payment, Hearings*, 45th Cong., 2nd sess., 1878, Misc. Doc. 62, pp. 112, 215. Because of foreign concerns over the Bland-Allison Act, the total was lower than in 1876–77, since securities had been returned to the United States (see ibid., pp. 112, 158).

  [h] John A. Stewart estimated that the amount of U.S. federal government bonds held abroad was probably not over $500 million (*Resumption of Specie Payment, Hearings*, p. 112).

  [i] U.S. Secretary of the Treasury, *Annual Report, 1878*, p. xviii.

  [j] Madden, *British Investment*, pp. 78–79 (tables 15–16), for nominal value of British and continental holdings (£257 million). On p. 388 (table 24), he put the total at $1,043 million (excluding railroad shares). His figures are much too precise.

  [k] U.S. Census Office, *Report on Valuation, Taxation and Public Indebtedness of the United States—Tenth Census* (Washington, D.C., 1884), pp. 490, 518 (registered and coupon bonds). This seems a very good source. The figure was based on verified foreign investment; it might

well have excluded certain investments that it did not verify.

^l Madden, *British Investment*, pp. 78–79 (tables 15–16), for nominal value of British and continental holdings. Note that his figure on railroads is down from his $938 million total for 1876 (see note f above). I do not share Madden's view that between 1876 and 1880 there was a decline in foreign investment in U.S. railroads, although I do believe that because of the way my table is constructed, the apparent rise may be deceptive. (As pointed out in note f, I believe the $390 million figure was low.)

^m August Belmont to Thomas Bayard, Jan. 28, 1881, cited in David Black, *The King of Fifth Avenue* (New York: Dial Press, 1981), p. 587. Compare this with what the *Economist* called a low estimate of $50 million (*Economist*, 39, Jan. 29, 1881: 126).

ⁿ Estimate of American assets of foreign insurance companies in New York state only. *Commercial and Financial Chronicle*, 22 (Feb. 4, 1882): 128.

^o Bullock, Williams, and Tucker, "The Balance of Trade," p. 225.

^p For an intelligent tabulation—calculated on the basis of U.S. Treasury records—which says government debt held abroad does not exceed $100 million, see *Banker's Magazine*, New York, 38 (Jan. 1884): 577. Its figures would indicate possibly an even lower number.

^q Bullock, Williams, and Tucker, "The Balance of Trade," p. 226.

^r Turrentine Jackson, *The Enterprising Scot* (Edinburgh: Edinburgh University Press, 1968), p. 100. British investment in U.S. cattle ranches, plus $1 million, which is my own estimate of Dutch stakes.

^s Bullock, Williams, and Tucker, "The Balance of Trade," p. 226. For 1889, ex-Congressman John Davis (Kansas) estimated that of the $6 billion in U.S. mortgages, $3 billion were held abroad. See John Davis, "Alien Landlordism in America," in *The Land Question from Various Points of View*, ed. C. F. Taylor (Philadelphia: C. F. Taylor, [1898]), p. 56. Davis' obviously exaggerated figure equals the entire foreign holdings in America as later estimated by Bullock, Williams, and Tucker.

^t In the "territories" only. See U.S. Senate, 50th Cong., 2nd sess., 1889, S. Rept. 2690, p. 1.

^u My text below indicates that in 1890–91 in meat- and brewery-related manufacturing operations alone there was in the United States some $170 million in foreign investment.

^v W. H. Harvey, *Coin's Financial School* (Chicago: Coin, 1894), p. 139, put American securities held in Europe in 1894 at more than $5 billion. This is an obvious exaggeration.

^w A. S. Heidelbach's estimate of $2.4 billion for 1895 was included in *Commercial and Financial Chronicle*, 60 (March 30, April 6, April 13, 1895): 542, 585, 630. It was for the "entire European investments" made in the United States in the prior fifteen years "in securities, property, mortgages and temporary loans (productive and unproductive)." This was *not* an estimate of the level of long-term foreign investment in the United States (see pp. 585, 630). Heidelbach also estimated that America's annual charges maturing against this country in favor of Europe "for dividends and interest upon American securities held abroad, [at] minimum [were] . . . $75,000,000" and "for profits of foreign corporations doing business here [in the United States] and of non-residents, derived from real estate investments, partnership profits &c. about . . . $75,000,000" (p. 543). If Europeans received 6 percent on their long-term investment in the United States, the total in 1895 would be $2.5 billion; at 5 percent the figure would equal $3 billion. I do not think a figure of $2.4 to $2.5 billion is unreasonable for the level of foreign investment in the United States. The $2.5 billion is my own estimate.

^x Bullock, Williams, and Tucker, "The Balance of Trade," p. 230. The historian Henry Adams in a letter of July 31, 1896, wrote "the smallest estimate" of European capital in the United States was £600,000,000 (or about $2.9 billion); Henry Adams, *Letters*, ed. Worthington Ford, 2 vols. (Boston: Houghton Mifflin, 1930, 1938), II, 110. Adams, however, included both long-term and short-term stakes and suggested that the bulk of European capital in the United States was money "on call," presumably meaning liquid portfolio stakes that could be quickly withdrawn. Long-term as well as short-term monies placed in American traded securities were, however, equally liquid. The $2.6 billion is my own estimate.

^y This is my own rough estimate. Georges Martin of the Paris Statistical Society put the figure

for "the different kinds of investments, such as loans, railroad stocks, banks, mines, and other joint-stock enterprises," held by Europeans in the United States, at $2,805 million; presented in Michael G. Mulhall, *The Dictionary of Statistics*, 4th ed. (1899; Detroit: Gale Research, 1969), p. 653. Cleona Lewis, *America's Stake in International Investments* (Washington, D.C.: Brookings Institution, 1938), p. 442, put the 1897 figure at $3,145 million. This was Bacon's 1899 estimate. Émile Becque, *L'internationalisation des capitaux* (Montpellier: Imprimerie Générale du Midi, 1912), p. 77, gives the debt of the United States to Europeans (including investments in securities and enterprises) in 1897 as $5 billion.

z Nathaniel T. Bacon, "American International Indebtedness," *Yale Review*, 9 (Nov. 1900): 276. Bacon's estimate was $3.33 billion, but this included $185 million in U.S. insurance on the lives of foreigners. I subtracted this $185 million (as did Lewis when she gave her 1897 figure). Bacon's estimates for Germany and Holland were specified to be at market, not par. In his other estimates he seems to have sought market values. While my figures as given in Table 5.4 suggest a rise in foreign investment in the United States between 1897 and 1899, and while Cleona Lewis obviously thought there was no difference between 1897 and 1899 in the level of foreign investment, the figures of Becque, *L'internationalisation des capitaux*, p. 77, suggest a decline: 1897, $5 billion; 1898, $4.8 billion; 1899, $4.4 billion; 1900, $4.3 billion; and then an upward turn: 1901, $4.35 billion; 1902, $4.65 billion. All of this goes to show how difficult it is to measure the level of foreign investment. Becque does not indicate the source of his information.

aa Bacon, "American International Indebtedness," pp. 269, 271–272 (federal, state, county, and city).

bb Charles F. Speare, "Selling American Bonds in Europe," *Annals of the American Academy of Political and Social Sciences*, 30 (1907): 293. Europe only. Securities only.

cc U.S. Senate, National Monetary Commission, *Trade Balances of the United States* (by George Paish), 61st Cong., 2nd sess., 1910, S. Doc. 579, pp. 174–175. Publicly issued securities only; direct investments excluded. Europe only. Figures are for 1908.

dd Raymond Goldsmith, *A Study of Savings in the United States* (Princeton, N.J.: Princeton University Press, 1955), I, 1089, made the following estimates for foreign assets in the United States—total long-term claims: 1900, $3,001 million; 1912, $5,218 million; 1914, $4,863 million. While his 1900 figures seem reasonable (that is, very close to Bacon's 1899 estimate), I am convinced that his 1912 and 1914 figures are low. Recently he has given higher figures for 1914.

ee Lewis, *America's Stake*, p. 546. Securities were calculated at par. When Lewis calculated common stock at market, she arrived at a figure of $3,933 million for railroad investments, $2,817 million for other investments, reaching a total of $6,750 million (pp. 558, 546). I believe her figures to be convincing. Market is obviously preferable to par in establishing the level; I included the higher figure, because I have identified other stakes that Lewis was not aware of and I believe these offset the discrepancy between market and par, making the roughly $7 billion figure an appropriate one. This figure is higher than others that have been presented. Paul Dickens, "The Transition Period in American International Financing: 1897 to 1914," Ph.D. diss., George Washington University, 1933, put the Dec. 1914 total at $3.9 billion. (The general assumption has been that the Dec. 1914 figure would be lower than the July 1, 1914, one because of divestments as a consequence of the outbreak of war in Europe, yet his figure seems to be very low.) Earlier, Bullock, Williams, and Tucker, "The Balance of Trade," p. 230, put the July 1914 figure at about $4.5 billion. Goldsmith, *Study of Savings*, I, 1089, as indicated above, thought the 1914 figure was $4,863 million, and for July 1, 1914, he sets the figure at $5 billion (p. 1090). By contrast, *Bradstreet's*, Oct. 24, 1914, p. 690 (which excluded direct investment), came close to Lewis' "securities" estimate. Likewise, Harvey E. Fisk, *The Inter-Ally Debts* (New York: Bankers Trust Co., 1924), p. 312, found a $6 billion to $7 billion figure reasonable for foreign investment in the United States before the outbreak of World War I. I have gone over these estimates carefully and am convinced that a July 1, 1914, figure in the range of $7 billion is appropriate.

ff Lewis, *America's Stake*, p. 546, and see note ee above.

gg Ibid., of which $1,710 million was in securities (at par) and $1,210 million in foreign-controlled enterprises. Includes some municipals.

have liked to be able throughout to separate the portfolio and direct investments. To do so, however, would be a disservice, implying a certainty that is belied by the crudeness of the data.[27]

The growth of foreign investments in the United States in 1875–1914 was very uneven. Periods passed when the flow of foreign capital to the United States seemed arrested. The late 1870s saw foreign capital outflow from the country; America appears to have been a net exporter of capital. Figure 5.1, based on balance-of-pay-

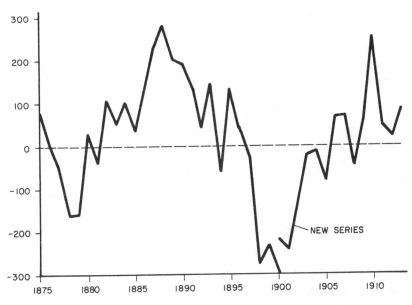

Figure 5.1. U.S. and foreign capital, net flows, 1875–1913. Source: U.S. Department of Commerce, Bureau of the Census, *Historical Statistics of the United States* (Washington, D.C., 1960), 564–565. Figures are given in millions of U.S. dollars; minus (−) figures indicate an outflow of capital; figures after 1900 are from a different series.

ments data, contains *net* estimates, including U.S. investment abroad as well as the movement of foreign capital.[28] It shows the high volatility in the capital flows. This was a function of interest rates, risk perception, and general economic conditions. High interest rates relative to those in Europe made U.S. investments attractive; yet whenever foreign investors in U.S. securities took seriously American silver advocates, they feared currency depreciation and held back or divested. Gold clauses in securities were reassuring, but every sage investor knew such clauses could be disavowed. High securities prices in the United States, at the turn of the century, meant large repatriations of dollar securities that were held abroad. Not only was the interest rate impact a factor, but also investors sought capital gains when the opportunities were presented. Once again the United States was temporarily a net exporter of capital. The crises of the mid-1870s, 1884, late 1890, 1893, and 1907 made foreign investors nervous and resulted in divestments, not because of potentials for gains, but rather because of fears of losses. Throughout, sales of foreign investors' assets were accompanied by new entries; different buyers and sellers had varying expectations. Most important, the level of long-term foreign investment cannot (and should not) be calculated as an accumulation of flows. I have not done so in Table 5.4. Values changed; gains and losses in assets occurred; earnings were reinvested. Despite the volatility in capital flows, despite the years of capital exports, as Table 5.4 indicates—based on other materials—the level of foreign investment in the United States rose in the period 1875–1914. America was a net debtor nation throughout (as measured by the level of foreign investment).

Many authors have argued that in America's early history the nation was more dependent on foreign capital than in the forty years before World War I. Cleona Lewis, for example, estimated that whereas in 1869 America's obligations to foreigners represented about 5 percent of national wealth, in 1914 they equaled roughly 4 percent of national wealth.[29]

From a different vantage point, but by way of confirmation, Margaret Myers wrote:

The half century after the Civil War was notable in the [U.S.] securities market chiefly because it marked the gradual diminishing of foreign domination in that field. In the antebellum period the United States, like every other new country, needed more capital than its own savings could provide and had to depend upon the importation of capital from older nations. In the years between 1863 and 1913 this dependence became gradually less.[30]

Statistics provided by Simon Kuznets and Jeffrey Williamson on the role of foreign investment in U.S. capital formation after 1869 lend support to such an interpretation.[31] In a far more sweeping statement, Douglass C. North, Terry Anderson, and Peter Hill, in the 1983 edition of their American economic history textbook, concluded, "Foreign capital was important in the 1830s, but thereafter its proportion of capital formation dwindled."[32]

Because in certain years between 1875 and 1914 the United States was a capital exporter, because many statements (such as those cited above) have been made on the declining *relative* importance of foreign investment in the United States, and because much of contemporary popular discussion was immensely impressed with America's *growing* stature in the world economy, recently many economic historians, when writing of 1875–1914, have either neglected foreign investment in this country or found its role in this period to be insignificant.[33] They are wrong. Foreign investment in the United States in these years, as I will show, did matter.[34]

Those who have ignored or minimized the importance of foreign investment in America in the period 1875–1914 are not impressed with the rising size of such investments. They point to the ratios. It is indeed true that "foreign obligations" of the United States in 1875–1914 never reached the level of 56 percent or 46 percent of the national debt as in 1803 and 1853, respectively, or even the level of 45 percent of the national debt as in 1869. They did not approach the level of 33 percent of all corporate stock as in 1803, nor that of 38 percent or (more plausibly) 58 percent of state debt as in 1853. Likewise, it is unlikely that in any single year the net capital inflow ever again—at least in the pre–World War I years—amounted to 27 percent of net capital formation (as in 1869—if this figure is correct), although Jeffrey Williamson found that capital inflows reached 26 percent of U.S. net capital formation in the atypical year of 1888.[35] There is, however, no evidence whatsoever to support the proposition that from the 1830s to 1914 the role of foreign investment in U.S. capital formation steadily dwindled.[36] In the chapters that follow I will demonstrate that the contribution of foreign investment remained important throughout the nineteenth and into the twentieth centuries in selected sectors and should definitely be included in studies of the American economy.[37]

The significance of the growing and large foreign obligations of the United States becomes most evident when data are disaggregated. The country, for example, used foreign monies and foreign bankers' aid in the process of resuming specie payments in 1879, as will be evident. The resumption was crucial to the course of U.S. economic history in subsequent years.[38] Capital from Britain and the European continent materially assisted and hastened the growth and completion of the American railroad system.[39] British investors participated in the founding of the iron and steel industry in the American South and had interests in a number of innovative steel firms in this nation. Investors from abroad played a substantial role in the mining, processing, and exporting of America's minerals; they opened foreign markets to that output. By 1914 one of "America's" largest oil companies was foreign owned. Many of the giant cattle ranches of the West were controlled by foreign investors. In 1890 *Banker's Magazine*,

New York, reported that Englishmen were " 'gobbling up' the leading manufactories in almost every profitable branch of industry in the
United States."[40] This was an exaggeration, but at that time foreign-
owned enterprises were for a brief period among the leaders in U.S.
meat packing and flour production, and large amounts of British
monies were being invested in American breweries. In other manufacturing activities, from thread to chemicals, by the early twentieth
century foreign direct investments assumed a surprisingly important
position. Foreign-owned businesses provided mortgage monies as
well as fire insurance and accounting services. The contributions in
railroads were fundamentally those of portfolio investors; in the other
activities there was sizable foreign direct investment.

The above sampling offers a preview, and in subsequent chapters I
will greatly enlarge the canvas. This preface should suggest, however, that the foreign investments were far from trivial. Moreover,
even though the portfolio investments from abroad were in value
larger than the direct ones, the latter may have had far greater overall
economic consequences. The years 1875–1914 were in fact the first age
of significant direct investments by foreign multinational enterprises
in America. Such interests—as will become clear—tended to be concentrated in industries other than the ones in which U.S. multinationals excelled.

Direct investment in manufacturing in America by companies from
Europe was not unique to the years 1875–1914. In the colonial period,
the Principio Company was a long-lived British direct investment that
involved iron manufacture. Du Pont began as a foreign direct investment, albeit the foreign direct investment aspect was soon replaced,
as the firm became totally American. I have reported on some miscellaneous foreign direct investments in manufacturing in the 1840s
and 1850s. Likewise, in the immediate post–Civil War years, a number of European companies began to manufacture in the United
States. Nonetheless, the late nineteenth and early twentieth centuries
can be legitimately identified as the time when multinational manufacturing enterprises from abroad proliferated in the United States.

No state or territory was untouched by the growing foreign investment. Measured by value, the Midwest, West, and South appear to
have received a disproportionate share of the total amounts, but the
East was also host to important out-of-country investors.[41] The region
to which the foreign investment went varied substantially by industry. Moreover, individual foreign-owned companies frequently had
stakes in more than one city, county, state, or region. Just as American enterprise at home was becoming national, so too the foreign
investors often developed multioffice, multiproduction-unit, multi-

functional, and multistate (or multiterritory) businesses in the United States. This was obviously the case with foreign-financed railroads that were interstate, but it was also true of foreign investors in land, mines, manufacturing, and an array of services.

Indeed, as will become evident, in 1875–1914, as the level of foreign investment rose, its reach became wider and more pervasive than in any prior era. Perhaps it is in part because of their neglect of foreign direct investment that many economists have shortchanged the role of foreign investment in the United States in 1875–1914.[42] There is no question that the rise in the level of foreign capital invested in the United States was significant. The long-term foreign investment estimate of roughly $7 billion for July 1, 1914, that I believe to be legitimate was in a country that had a gross national product that year of only $36.4 billion.[43] In subsequent chapters I will document the extent and nature of the foreign capital's involvements and will demonstrate that its influence on U.S. economic development in this period was far greater and far more important than American economic historians have recognized.

British Investment in America: 1875–1914

The leading capital exporter in the world in the years 1875–1914 continued to be the United Kingdom.[44] As Michael Edelstein has put it, "based on historical patterns British capital exports moved to unprecedented levels in the late nineteenth and early twentieth centuries." This is evident no matter what measure is used.[45] Table 5.5 shows Britain's premier position in 1914 vis-à-vis other European capital exporters. Figure 5.2 gives two estimates of annual capital outflow from the United Kingdom.[46] Table 5.6 offers figures that suggest almost a tripling of British overseas investment between 1880 and 1913. By 1913–14 British investment abroad may have equaled one-fourth of its national wealth (see Table 5.7).[47] All these numbers are approximations. Some think they exaggerate.[48] No one, however, disputes that Britain led the rest of the world in international stakes.

Robert Gilpin differentiated British nineteenth-century foreign investments from U.S. twentieth-century ones by investor (in the first case, banks, individuals, the bond market; in the second case, corporations) and by type of investment (portfolio and loans versus direct investment).[49] The distinction is far too extreme.[50] British overseas investors in 1875–1914 included corporations as well as banks and individuals; they invested in shares as well as in bonds; they made direct as well as portfolio investments. In the past, inadequate attention was paid to British foreign direct investment.[51] Numerous British

Table 5.5. European foreign investments worldwide, 1913–14 (in billions of U.S. dollars)

Country	U.N. estimates	Alternative estimates
Great Britain	18.0	18.3–20.0[a]
France	9.0	8.6–9.0
Germany	5.8[7.3][b]	4.6–8.6
Netherlands, Belgium, Switzerland	5.5	4.3–5.5

Source: United Nations, *International Capital Movements during the Interwar Period* (Lake Success, N.Y.: United Nations, 1949), p. 2. Alternative estimates are summarized in W. S. Woytinski and E. S. Woytinski, *World Commerce and Governments* (New York: Twentieth Century Fund, 1955), p. 191; William Woodruff, *The Impact of Western Man* (New York: St. Martin's Press, 1967), pp. 150–154; S. B. Saul, *Studies in British Overseas Trade, 1870–1914* (Liverpool: Liverpool University Press, 1960), p. 66; Eugene Staley, *War and the Private Investor* (Garden City, N.Y.: Doubleday, 1935), pp. 523–534; Staley gives the Dutch investment at $2 billion, the Belgian at $1 billion, and the Swiss at $1.3 billion, but acknowledges the figures are "guesswork" (p. 532). *Except* in the German case, the principal variations (alternative estimates) seem to relate to the exchange rate chosen to translate the foreign currency into dollars and the rounding of numbers.
   [a] I have excluded D. C. M. Platt's recent $15.2 billion estimate (in *Britain's Investment Overseas on the Eve of the First World War*, New York: St. Martin's Press, 1986, p. 60). Platt makes the point that the $18–20 billion figure is the one first set forth in George Paish's Feb. 14, 1914, *Statist* article (reprinted in *British Overseas Investment, 1907–1948*, ed. Mira Wilkins, New York: Arno Press, 1977).
   [b] In the German case, the literature in some instances seems to have confused "gross" and "net" foreign investments. The British and French figures are definitely "gross" ones—that is, the compilers have not subtracted foreign investments in Britain and France. The German alternative estimates of $4.6 billion to $5.8 billion were in some writers' minds net of foreign investment in Germany. The $7.3 to $8.6 billion estimates were obviously gross ones. I have accordingly put in brackets on the table what I believe is the most appropriate "gross" figure.

corporations were newly formed to do business outside the country and to manage that business from Britain.[52] Likewise, many British industrial and service enterprises expanded outside the island nation.[53] The development in Great Britain of limited liability companies, the merger movement there, and the growth in size of British firms in many industries were reflected in British business investments abroad. In 1913–14, according to British Inland Revenue Department figures, the "identifiable income" from abroad from direct foreign investments actually exceeded that from portfolio ones.[54]

London was the undisputed money market center of the world. There existed an unparalleled infrastructure of international banking services. In the early 1870s, much of British lending had been to governments; by 1914, much of it was to private borrowers.[55] Between 1875 and 1914, British capital tended toward the newer areas of the globe—the United States, Canada, Australia, South Africa, and

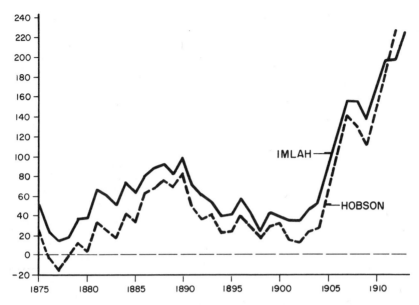

Figure 5.2. Export of capital from the United Kingdom: estimates of C. K. Hobson and A. H. Imlah. Sources: C. K. Hobson, *The Export of Capital* (London: Constable, 1914), 226, and Albert H. Imlah, *Economic Elements in the Pax Britannica* (Cambridge, Mass.: Harvard University Press, 1958), 73–75 (balance on current account). Values are in millions of pounds sterling; minus (−) values indicate capital inflow.

Argentina. Michael Edelstein writes, "Except for the United States, British investment in particular countries or colonies [in these years] tended to be concentrated in short periods of time. . . The U.S. import of British capital was also variable but it was continuous."[56] Although estimates differ, it seems that from 1875 to 1914, at minimum about one-fifth of the U.K. capital abroad was invested in the United States, which was for all the forty pre–World War I years the single overseas country with the greatest British investment.[57] Row 1 in Table 5.8 provides alternative estimates on the rise of British long-term investment in the United States, 1899–1914. British investment in America in 1876 has been estimated at slightly more than $1.1 billion; by July 1, 1914, the figure was in excess of $4 billion. These figures are approximations and controversial.[58]

British money came to the United States mainly from Scotland and England (with very little from Wales and Ireland). In 1884, for example, an editor from Dundee, Scotland, noted that residents of that city had spent on "financial recreations" in foreign lands the savings of at

Table 5.6. British overseas investments worldwide, 1880–1913

Year	Estimates of level (in billions of U.S. dollars)
1880	6.3
1885	6.3
1895	7.8
1905	9.8
1909	11.3
1913	18.3

Source: Royal Institute of International Affairs, *The Problem of Foreign Investment* (London: Royal Institute of International Affairs, 1937), p. 115. Figures are translated into dollars at the rate £1 = $4.86.

Table 5.7. European foreign investments as a percentage of national wealth, 1913–14

Country	Percentage
Great Britain	25
France	15
Germany	8–12
Netherlands	17.5

Source: Carl Iverson, *Aspects of the Theory of International Capital Movements* (Copenhagen: Levin & Munksgaard, 1936), pp. 331–332.
Note: Figures are approximations.

least twenty years. Nine of Dundee's ten principal companies carried on their business in America! Edinburgh investors had special American associations. Liverpool continued its unique relationship with the United States, rooted in trade but now transformed into international investment ties. Other areas of northern England had pockets of British investors in transatlantic enterprise.[59] American securities and U.S. economic conditions were, of course, well known in London.[60] In addition, profits made by British investors in numerous third countries were on occasion recycled through Britain into American investments. Thus, for example, British-headquartered investment trusts, trading companies, investment groups, and some banks that made their principal overseas investments in Asia, Latin America, or South Africa often had U.S. interests as well.

In the case of portfolio investments in the United States, British investors (individuals or firms) did not expect or want to participate

Table 5.8. Estimates of long-term foreign investments in the United States, by nationality, 1899, 1907, 1908, and July 1, 1914 (in millions of U.S. dollars)

Nationality	1899[a]	1907[b]	1908[c]	1914[d]	1914[e]	1914[f]
British	2,500	4,000	3,500	4,000	4,250	4,250[g]
French	50[h]	300	630	1,000[i]	410	480[j]
German	200	1,000	1,000	1,250	950	1,100[k]
Dutch	240	600	750	650	635	650[l]
Swiss	75[h]	100	[m]	[n]	[n]	70[o]
Belgian	20	—	[m]	[n]	[n]	30[p]
Other Europeans	15	—	130	[n]	150[q]	180[r]
Canadian	[n]	—	—	[n]	275	275[s]
Japanese	[n]	—	—	[n]	[n]	25[t]
All others	45	—	—	100	420	30[u]
Total	3,145	6,000[b]	6,000[c]	7,000[d]	7,090[e]	7,100[v]

[a] Nathaniel Bacon, "American International Indebtedness," *Yale Review*, 9 (Nov. 1900): 268–279.

[b] Charles F. Speare, "Selling American Bonds in Europe," *Annals of the American Academy of Political and Social Sciences*, 30 (1907): 269–293. Speare was financial editor of the *New York Evening Mail*. His gross estimate for total European investment was $6 to $6.5 billion. This was only for securities and only for Europe.

[c] U.S. Senate, National Monetary Commission, *Trade Balances of the United States* (by George Paish), 61st Cong., 2nd sess., 1910, S. Doc. 579, pp. 174–175. Publicly issued securities only. No figures given for any countries outside Europe.

[d] Harvey E. Fisk, *The Inter-Ally Debts* (New York: Bankers Trust Co., 1924), p. 312. Fisk estimates "at least" $6 billion and "possibly" $7 billion total. His breakdown is based on the $7 billion figure. These are gross approximations. His own evidence would indicate that his French figure is very much out of line. Compare it with p. 286, where he has $1.2 billion French investment in "America" and with his earlier commentary (p. 285) that most of the French investment in "America" was in South America. Herbert Feis, *Europe: The World's Banker* (New Haven: Yale University Press, 1930), p. 51, gave the $1.2 billion figure for French investment in Latin America. (French investment in the United States, Canada, *and* Australia, Feis believed, was one-third that amount.) The year that Harvey Fisk published these estimates, 1924, he was writing to Julius Klein, Director of the Bureau of Foreign and Domestic Commerce, May 9, 1924, that $6 billion was a better estimate for foreign investment in the United States in 1914 than the $4.5 billion favored by Klein. See data in Record Group 151, 620 General/1919–1925, National Archives, Washington, D.C. See also note e below.

[e] Cleona Lewis, *America's Stake in International Investments* (Washington, D.C.: Brookings Institution, 1938), p. 546. Lewis' estimates were very carefully made. They explicitly included direct and portfolio investments. They were at par value, and were all long-term investments. Lewis also gave totals (but not breakdowns by nationality) "with common stock at market." These came to $6,750 million, rather than $7,090 million. Even so, her figures were higher than the estimates made by her predecessors (except for Fisk). I am much more satisfied with her figures, for example, than with the estimate of Charles J. Bullock, John H. Williams, and Rufus S. Tucker, "The Balance of Trade of the United States," *Review of Economic Statistics*, 1 (July 1919): 230, of $4.5 billion (which was the one Klein was using, see note d above). Lewis' work supersedes completely that of Paul Dickens, "The Transition Period in American International Financing: 1897 to 1914," Ph.D. diss., George Washington

University, 1933, p. 129. Dickens thought the 1914 total was $3.9 billion, of which $2.5 billion was from "England," $200 million from France, $400 million from Germany, $325 million from Holland, $150 million from Switzerland, $60 million from Belgium, $90 million from Canada, and $175 million from the rest of the world.

   [f] These are my estimates, which take into account all the others, plus my own research as presented in this volume. They are at market, not par, and include direct as well as portfolio investments. Each estimate is individually explained.

   [g] My British figure is the same as Lewis', but I arrived at this figure in a slightly different manner from the way that she did. (My figure is at market, and hers was at par; since market was below par, I am suggesting a larger investment than Lewis did.)

   [h] Bacon, "American International Indebtedness," p. 273, noted that French investors were included in the Swiss (as well as the French) totals, since many French residents used Geneva banking houses to make U.S. investments.

   [i] Seems very likely to be in error (see note d above).

   [j] My French estimate is higher than Lewis', since I know of more investments than she did and I include transactions that went through Switzerland, Belgium, and London. It is higher than, but takes into account, the 1913 estimates of Maurice Lévy-Leboyer, in La position internationale de la France (Paris: Editions de l'Ecole des Hautes Etudes in Science Sociales, 1977), p. 25, of $386 million (translated at 1 fr. = $.193). Lévy-Leboyer's estimate was based on a 1913 estimate by Alfred Neymarck, which dealt with securities and not direct investment and one by Herbert Feis, in Europe: The World's Banker, p. 51, which gives the same $386 million (2 billion francs) figure as the 1914 French investment in the "United States, Canada, and Australia." My estimate is down from Paish's 1908 one, since Paish's figures were very crude and his French estimate seemed out of keeping with the estimate of Speare a year earlier. Yet, in 1910, Georges Aubert, La finance Américaine (Paris: Ernest Flammarion, 1910), p. 191, suggested that while there was no precise figure for French fortunes placed in the United States, his estimate was 3 to 4 billion francs (or $579 to $772 million at 1 fr. = $.193). Writing in 1916 about the geographical distribution of French foreign investment before the war, Yves Guyot (editor of Journal des économistes, Paris) stated, "It has been said that French investments in the United States amounted to 5 billion [francs; at 1 fr. = $.193, thus $965 million] . . . the figure is exaggerated"; Yves Guyot, "The Amount, Direction and Nature of French Investments," The Annals, 68 (Nov. 1916): 52. Lévy-Leboyer gives the following figures for French investment in the United States: 1896, $96 million; 1902, $116 million; 1913, $386 million. The Federal Reserve Bulletin, 7 (Oct. 1922): 1181, put French holdings of American securities, "prewar" at about $500 million.

   [k] Based on my own research, I am convinced Lewis' German estimate was low. I chose a figure midway between Lewis' and Fisk's.

   [l] Fisk thought his own Dutch estimate was possibly low; I think it is sensible. Paish's 1908 estimate may have been high.

   [m] Included in "Other Europeans."

   [n] Included in "All others."

   [o] My Swiss estimate was less than Speare's of 1907 and less than Bacon's of 1899, because I added French investments made through Switzerland to the French total.

   [p] My Belgian estimate is based on the 1899 estimate of Bacon and the extraordinarily high estimate of Dickens (see note e above). It seems to reflect what I know of Belgian investments. Jacob Viner, "Political Aspects of International Finance," Journal of Business, 1 (April 1928): 160, writes that before 1914 French investors bought securities on the Brussels Bourse to evade the French securities tax. I have accordingly reduced the Belgian figure and added to the French one.

   [q] Includes Austria-Hungary, Turkey, and Bulgaria.

   [r] My "Other Europeans" estimate includes Austria-Hungary, Bulgaria, and Turkey (as does Lewis'), but also Russian, Spanish, Italian, Swedish, and other Scandinavian interests that she included under "All others." As of Dec. 31, 1913 (based on data collected from Best's

Insurance Reports, 1914), "admitted" assets of U.S. fire and marine insurance companies from these "other European" countries alone came to $27 million (of which less than $4 million came from the first two named countries and none from Turkey).

ˢ Lewis' estimate for Canadian investments in the United States seems plausible.

ᵗ The Bank of Japan estimated that in 1914, Japanese investment in business enterprises in the United States (including Hawaii) came to $24.6 million; unpublished estimate, cited in Harold G. Moulton, *Japan* (Washington, D.C.: Brookings Institution, 1931), p. 391.

ᵘ My figure is far smaller than Lewis' because of my additions to the Swiss, Belgian, "Other Europeans" (see especially note r above), and Japanese totals. I have attempted to break the numbers down by nationality with more precision than Lewis. My "All others" figure (which includes all nationalities outside Europe, Canada, and Japan) was very difficult to determine and highly miscellaneous. A British resident in India or South Africa or Australia, who acquired his holdings before he went overseas, may improperly push up that total. (If Britain remained "home" for him, his stakes should be included as "British.") I am aware of some Chinese and New Zealand investments that fit into the "All others" category. Likewise, there was a Mexican railroad (Lewis put the investment at $3.2 million), some investments by wealthy Latin Americans, and some investments by Americans temporarily living in Latin America (a group I have tried to exclude from my calculations).

ᵛ Note that my total for 1914 is in the same range as those of Lewis and Fisk. I have not included in this table the lower estimates of others, which seemed to me unacceptable.

in management; its delegation was a given—by definition. Yet at times intervention became necessary, to salvage a return. At the other pole, British direct investors (individuals and, far more important, firms)—again by definition—desired to, planned to, and did take part in administering American business. Long distance implies a delegation of authority, but they wanted a controlled delegation. Just as the general literature on British overseas investments has in years past shortchanged direct investment, so too, specifically, has the vast literature on British investment in America.[61]

Literally thousands of companies were set up in Great Britain to do business in the United States. Such companies were usually "bilateral," headquartered in Great Britain and carrying on operations only in the United States. They came into being mainly because promoters recognized that British investors desired higher profits than could be obtained at home, and the investors did not trust unsupervised American management to act on their behalf. The investors wanted direct knowledge from trustworthy Britons about the business in which they were investing. Typically, a company would be floated in England or Scotland to start or, often, to take over a U.S. company (or companies). The board of directors would contain well-known men. I discussed this pattern of investment in America in Chapter 4, with respect to the 1870–1873 mining companies. The British companies made direct investments in the United States; they expected to exercise control from the British headquarters.[62] Whereas what has been thought of as the typical case of multinational enterprise (foreign direct investment, as usually defined) involved an extension of a company into areas related to its operational competence at home (sometimes called internalization of foreign operations), these "free-standing" companies[63] did not involve any operational internalization, for there was no evolution of an existing firm in Britain (the British company was newly created to raise money, to act as owner, and to maintain control). Such a company might act as a holding company or it might operate directly in America. Organization in the United Kingdom had the advantage in obtaining money there: the investor in the company's securities had liquidity; he was making a "British investment."[64]

These numerous free-standing companies provided a frame, so that "disembodied" capital would not flow without supervision. Although, as noted, these companies were usually bilateral (U.K.–U.S.), they might be associated in very loose clusters with other companies that operated outside the United Kingdom and the United States. Indeed, a network of British service sector multinationals (banks, trading companies, accounting firms, and mining engineers) offered, to varying extents, managerial and professional services for these enterprises. Often, however, for the British investments in the United States, this approach proved unsatisfactory, and the absence of internalization of operations may in part explain why so many of the free-standing companies were short-lived. The unity, the evolution from a base that produced goods and services—the essence of the successful multinational-enterprise-type structure—was absent. Ownership had no continuity of internal enterprise experience to project on, to evaluate, and to enrich the business in America. The "home office"—as a home office—was virtually nonexistent. Members of the board of directors were part time; they had other responsibilities. Although in some cases the foreign investor was "lucky" and a free-standing company did well, more often this was not the case. Likewise, although in some instances the service sector supervision proved adequate, under the more usual circumstances in the United States it was not. The heyday of the British-incorporated company in America was 1870 to 1900. In the 1890s and in the early twentieth century, for reasons that ranged from U.S. nationalism to cost cutting, to British tax considerations, to corporate failure, many free-standing companies, especially those only partly owned by British capital (and the rest by Americans), moved to eliminate what was an essentially superfluous British corporate structure. Yet the free-standing ventures cannot be ignored; they were "direct" investments, British companies with intent to control investments abroad.[65]

In contrast and in addition, other British companies invested in the

United States as part of the expansion of a home enterprise that was growing internationally, in what became the more standard way of modern multinationals. This form of British business in America assumed new significance in the years 1875–1914. Because of the needs of free-standing companies, because of British industrial enterprises' lack of experience with large-scale managerial operations at home, and because of Britain's position as a capital exporter and as a large participant in international trade, service sector multinationals played very important roles in British multinational-enterprise expansion in this period in America. Even when the free-standing company in America declined in relative importance, service sector multinationals continued, providing services to other British multinationals and to American businesses.[66]

Just as America ranked in first place among the recipients of British capital—either as portfolio or as direct (free-standing or multinational-enterprise-type) investment—throughout the years 1875–1914, so too, to reverse the coin, British capital was by far the largest of all the foreign stakes in the United States.[67] Table 5.8 indicated its preeminence. There have been attempts to divide this British investment by sector. Table 5.9 gives Matthew Simon's distribution data on *new* British portfolio (only) investment in the United States, by sector—expressed as a percentage of total calls on new issues (Simon equated new issues and portfolio investment)—for the periods 1865–1914 and 1909–1913. I have adjusted Simon's figures based on his data to include "government" issues. Table 5.10 gives John J. Madden's figures on the "nominal" dollar values on British holdings of American securities in 1876; Table 5.11 shows George Paish's figures by sector (in dollar values) of the level of British investments in the United States in 1910. Table 5.12 has Cleona Lewis' estimates of the level of such portfolio and direct investments on July 1, 1914. Madden's figures show the 1876 British involvement with government securities. All four tables, however (especially Tables 5.9, 5.11, and 5.12), support the established view that British investment in the United States was heavily concentrated in railways. Nonetheless, British monies, both portfolio and direct investment, penetrated numerous other parts of the American economy.

British-incorporated companies did business in America (directly or as holding companies) in land development, cattle, mining, manufacturing (from steel to breweries), finance, and public utilities. British multinational enterprises invested in branded consumer goods (grocery products, textiles, and medicines) and in producer goods (textile machinery, chemicals, transportation equipment, and wireless apparatus). Some products—for example, rayon and wireless

Table 5.9. Sectoral composition of new British portfolio investments in the United States, 1865–1914, 1909–1913 (as percentages of total calls on new issues)

Sector	1865–1914[a]	1909–1913
"Government"	6.0	0.0[b]
Agriculture	0.8	0.5
Mining	5.7	4.9
Manufacturing	7.4	11.1
Transportation	61.8	62.7
Utilities	7.3	12.0
Finance, real estate	5.9	4.1
Trade	0.6	1.2
Public works	3.6	3.5
Miscellaneous	0.8	0.0
Total	100.0 %[c]	100.0 %

Source: Matthew Simon, "The Enterprise and Industrial Composition of New British Portfolio Foreign Investment," *Journal of Developmental Studies,* 3 (April 1967): 283, 284, 287, 289. Note that Simon used the term *portfolio* investment to refer to securities that were issued on British money markets. This included "free-standing" companies—which in my text I have called "direct" investments.

[a] I recalculated Simon's figures to include American government issues (federal, state, and municipal).

[b] Before "rounding," Simon included some "investments" in municipal bonds, 1909–1913.

[c] Total does not reach 100 percent because of rounding.

Table 5.10. Estimated nominal value of British holdings of American securities by type, 1876 (in millions of U.S. dollars and percentages)

Sector	Millions of dollars	Percentage
Federal government	447	39
State and municipal governments	78	7
Railways	559	49
Other	53	5
Total	1,137	100

Source: John J. Madden, *British Investment in the United States* (New York: Garland, 1985), p. 78 (table 14). I have translated pounds into dollars at the rate £1 = $4.86.

Table 5.11. Level of British investments in the United States by sector, 1910 (in millions of U.S. dollars and percentages)

Sector	Millions of dollars	Percentage
Government (U.S. federal government)	—	0.0
Municipals	38.4	1.1
Railways	2,849.1	85.2
Mines	105.1	3.1
Coal, iron, and steel	1.7	0.1
Oil	17.4	0.5
Breweries and distilleries	55.9	1.7
Motor traction and manufacturing	1.9	0.1
Other commercial and industrial companies	76.4	2.3
Finance, land, and investment companies	152.8	4.6
Banks	4.5	0.1
Telegraphs and telephones	21.1	0.6
Gas and water	5.5	0.2
Tramways	14.3	0.4
Total	3,344.1	100.0

Source: George Paish, "Great Britain's Capital Investment in Individual Colonial and Foreign Countries," *Journal of the Royal Statistical Society,* 74 (Jan. 1911): 176; reprinted in *British Overseas Investments, 1907–1948,* ed. Mira Wilkins (New York: Arno Press, 1977). The 1910 year is given on p. 167. I have translated pounds into dollars at the rate £1 = $4.86.

Table 5.12. Level of British investments in the United States by sector at par value, July 1, 1914

Sector	Millions of U.S. dollars	Percentage
Railways	2,800	65.9
Other American securities	850	20.0
Direct investments in controlled enterprises	600	14.1
Total	4,250	100.0

Source: Cleona Lewis, *America's Stake in International Investments* (Washington, D.C.: Brookings Institution, 1938), p. 546.

equipment—were "high-technology" ones. There were, in addition, British direct investments in oil. In the service industries, important British multinational-enterprise-type investments existed. Most of these direct investments are not appropriately reflected in the statistics of Simon, Madden, or Paish, as given in Tables 5.9–5.11. Since much of the investment came after 1876, Madden's exclusion introduces the least distortion.[68] My text will reveal substantial concern in the United Kingdom over the management and control of British investments in the United States.

Important additions to the British total investment in the United States, not reflected in any of these figures, came as a result of the move to London in the 1890s by the American-born William Waldorf Astor (1848–1919), when his vast holdings in New York real estate became "British" investments in America. Similarly, "when [Consuelo] Vanderbilt married the Duke of Marlborough she added [to British overseas investments] the market price of her railroad stock."[69]

Why of all nationalities did British investment in the United States remain so outstanding? The obvious reasons, applying to both portfolio and direct investment, can be stated quickly: British capital availability, well-developed capital markets, industrial maturity, and a closeness fostered by trade[70] as well as by the shared traditions of language, culture, and heritage. Was the absence of opportunity in the United Kingdom important? This would seem demonstrated by the inverse relationship of British capital outflows to the British building cycle and British capital formation, well documented by both A. K. Cairncross and Brinley Thomas.[71] Yet for many British companies, the large U.S. market, made increasingly inaccessible by protectionism and at the same time more tempting by innovations in transportation and communication, seems to have prompted investments motivated more by defending and augmenting sales of goods in the United States than by specific conditions in Great Britain. It can, of course, be argued that British enterprises had enlarged their exports in the first place to expand beyond their relatively limited domestic market. Because of familiarity and common background, because of the large U.S.–U.K. trade, and because the United States was the growth nation of this era, it does not seem surprising that British investment—portfolio and direct—would be extensive. In addition, because America was rich in resources, British investors sought opportunities where land was cheap and raw materials were abundant; this was true of both portfolio and direct investors. Interest rates were typically higher in the United States than in the United Kingdom, a very important consideration for the purely financial stakes. Also, when Americans desired foreign capital, the first place they went to find it was to Great Britain. Push and pull—U.K. capital availability to take advantage of opportunities, entrepreneurial trafficking of information across the Atlantic, and U.S. needs—combined to raise the level of British portfolio and direct investment in the United States.[72]

French, German, Dutch, Canadian, and Other Investments in America: 1875–1914

Second only to Britain as a worldwide capital exporter in 1914 was France (see Table 5.5). With estimated foreign investments of $9 billion in 1914, French stakes abroad were heavily concentrated in Europe; in 1914 Russia was the single country attracting the most French foreign investment.[73] The reasons lay both in economic promise and in political associations. There were important French influences in nineteenth- and early-twentieth-century Russia. About 15 percent of French national wealth was invested abroad in 1913–14.[74] Table 5.8 provided some rough figures on French investment in the United States.[75] My own estimate for July 1, 1914, is about $480 million, part of which went through Swiss intermediaries, some very small part through Belgium, and some through London. This amounts to a little over 5 percent of the total French foreign investment.[76]

By 1914 French investments in the United States were principally portfolio ones in railroads, although they were also in other securities. At the same time, there were a surprising number of direct investments in land, mining, oil, manufacturing (woolen yarn, silk, automobiles, rubber tires, consumer chemicals, and aluminum), insurance, and banking. Table 5.13 contains Cleona Lewis' estimates on

Table 5.13. Level of French investments in the United States by sector, at par value, July 1, 1914

Sector	Millions of U.S. dollars
Railways	290
Other American securities	75
Direct investments in controlled enterprises	45
Total	410

Source: Cleona Lewis, *America's Stake in International Investments* (Washington, D.C.: Brookings Institution, 1938), p. 546.

the distribution, which I believe understate the amounts.[77] In the early twentieth century, strikes against the Rothschild oil properties in Russia occurred, and the French became nervous about their huge commitments in that country.[78] In 1907 an American financial writer reported that socialism in Russia had its terrors for French business- men and predicted—as a by-product—promising prospects for U.S. sales of railway bonds in France. Similarly, in 1911 American bankers sought out new French investment.[79] Just as "British" investment in America was increased by Americans resident there, so too Ameri- cans domiciled in Paris raised the amount of "French" investment in the United States.[80] Yet, if Herbert Feis's figures are accepted, French investments in Russia in 1914, as in 1900, represented roughly one- quarter of the total French foreign investment; the numbers fail to support any indication of a switch to U.S. stakes.[81]

In short, the geographical distribution of French investment abroad differed from that of the British.[82] Feis explains the relatively low French investment in the United States in 1914 as a result of "the tax arrangements and various legal requirements" that re- duced the number of U.S. securities listed on the Paris Bourse.[83] The economist Harry White concluded more generally that because revenues on foreign securities were taxed at a higher rate than domestic income, considerable incentive existed in France to dis- guise foreign investment.[84] Close relationships between Geneva and Lyon (associated with a shared Protestant outlook) meant that Geneva bankers often represented French investors, especially those from Lyon. Accordingly, the figures on French foreign invest- ment in the United States must be viewed with those on Swiss in- vestment abroad.[85] Likewise, Brussels was used by French banks— to avoid taxes.[86] So too I found that companies set up in London to do business in the United States could be in large (or small) part French owned.[87] Nonetheless, although French investors could and did buy U.S. securities and make U.S. investments through Gene- va—and through Basle, Zurich, Brussels, and London—this was not as convenient as undertaking the transactions at home, and when tax evasion was the motive, there were always attendant risks. Thus the fewer available securities and the need to use third- country investment routes does appear as one reason why French investment in the United States was less than that of the other principal capital exporters.

In my view, a much more important explanation lies in the smaller (compared with most other major capital exporters) French trade with America, the lower French immigration to the United States over the years, and the fewer French visitors to America, all of which meant

more constricted Franco-American information flows and consequently more limited and less convenient institutional conduits for
the investments. Most significant, along the same line of argument,
whereas Britain shared with the United States a common language
and heritage, France did not.[88]

Far more crucial than the French as investors in the United States
were the Germans. Residents in Germany have been variously estimated as having between $4.6 billion and $8.6 billion invested abroad
in 1913–14 (see Table 5.5); $7.3 billion seems the best choice.[89] Ger-
man foreign investment has been calculated at between 8 percent and
12 percent of national wealth (in 1913–14).[90] Although Europe and the
Middle East figured prominently in attracting German capital, in 1914
no single foreign country appears to have had more German investment than the United States[91] and, remember, America was a magnet
for numerous German immigrants. The connection is vital. By July 1,
1914, the level of German investment in the United States was $950
million to $1,250 million (see Table 5.8).[92] Approximately 15 to 16
percent of total German foreign investment seems to have been invested in the United States.[93] Table 5.14 (based on Bacon's and Lewis'
figures) provides very rough estimates on German interests in the
United States in 1899 and 1914, by sector.

In the chapters that follow, I will present new, rich material on
German investment in the United States. I found in the archives of
the Alien Property Custodian in Washington extensive information
on such investments, particularly on direct investments. Published
data by the Alien Property Custodian were also helpful.[94] The Alien
Property Custodian in 1919 described German investment in

Table 5.14. Level of German investments in the United States by sector,
1899 and July 1, 1914 (in millions of U.S. dollars)

Sector	1899	July 1, 1914
Railways	103	300
Other American securities	97	350
Direct investments in controlled enterprises	a	300
Total	200	950

Source: 1899: Nathaniel T. Bacon, "American International Indebtedness," *Yale Review,* 9
(Nov. 1900): 269; at market value. Dietrich G. Buss, *Henry Villard* (1976 diss. New York: Arno
Press, 1978), pp. 186–187, thinks these figures are low. 1914: Cleona Lewis, *America's Stake in
International Investments* (Washington, D.C.: Brookings Institution, 1938), p. 546; at par value.
ª Not included by Bacon.

pre–World War I America as being of two types: (1) investments by German individuals of small sums in real estate, mortgages, and industrial and transportation securities (portfolio investments); and (2) investments that "sought dominance and frequently secured control of great industrial and commercial establishments in the United States." The Alien Property Custodian felt that these latter investments (foreign direct investments) were by far the more important ones—"Germany's great industrial army on American soil."[95]

German banks in Berlin and Frankfurt were active in pushing American bonds. Obtaining a listing on the Berlin Bourse was expensive, but by 1907 about thirty American bonds and several U.S. stocks were so listed.[96] The business investments—direct investments—of the Germans for the most part bypassed the securities markets. They were part and parcel of a vigorous international expansion of German enterprises.[97] German investments were much larger than those of the French in the United States, principally because of information flows. Many Germans had come to the United States after the 1848 revolution. Many more followed. German immigrants returned to their native land for visits and wrote home describing opportunities. Germans knew about America. They had countrymen in this nation, whom they trusted. In 1884–85 German immigration to the United States was more than nine times the immigration from the Netherlands, Belgium, Luxembourg, Switzerland, and France combined. Indeed, every year from 1875 to 1914, German immigration to the United States greatly exceeded the immigration from these combined northwestern European nations.[98] What mattered was not merely the numbers but also the middle-class character of these immigrants. Germans who came to this country acted as intermediaries for German investors and as their partners. German immigrants (and the firms founded by them) associated with German bankers. Family members and friends on both sides of the Atlantic frequently joined in business. Joint-ventures were the norm. German direct investments in American manufacturing were made in textiles, prepared foods, ethical drugs, and automobiles (consumer products), but the Germans were even more strongly represented in metallurgical, chemical, electrical and nonelectrical machinery, and instrument industries (producer goods).[99]

A large number of the goods sold or produced, or both, in the United States by subsidiaries of German companies were invented in Germany and patented in the United States by the parent firm. They represented new technology. World War I investigations showed that before the war the "usual course" pursued by a German enterprise in establishing a business in this country was to incorporate an American company, the stock of which the enemy [the Germans] controlled, and to issue a license to the American company under patents owned by the enemy. In this way the enemy was enabled to control the American corporation, not only through his stock ownership but also through his ownership of the patents, and was enabled to collect a large part of the profits of the American corporation under the guise of royalties for the use of the patents, rather than as dividends upon its stock.[100]

The dual means of control meant that the German investor could lose stock ownership or lower it, but could still retain control (or so the investigators thought; this was often not true—indeed rarely so); it also meant that the foreign investor could "evade payment of income taxes by taking his profits under the guise of royalties, thus largely decreasing the apparent earnings of the American corporation."[101] America had introduced a federal corporate excise (income) tax in 1909. The study found, in addition, that the trademark property of German firms was substantial, particularly in the drug industry.[102] German-trademarked goods covered the gambit from Henckels' "twins" on cutlery, pocket knives, and scissors to "Jaeger" underwear.[103]

By 1914 Dutch investments worldwide were smaller than those of the major European powers (Great Britain, France, and Germany).[104] Dutch foreign investment in 1913–14, however, approximated 17.5 percent of the nation's wealth.[105] Opportunities in Holland were limited. Dutch investments in the United States appear to have been greater than those of the French. As of July 1, 1914, they probably equaled between $635 million and $650 million (see Table 5.8).[106] Table 5.15 provides one set of estimates by sector. Unlike the German

Table 5.15. Level of Dutch investments in the United States by sector, 1899 and July 1, 1914 (in millions of U.S. dollars)

Sector	1899	July 1, 1914
Railways	214	300
Other American securities	27	200
Direct investments in controlled enterprises	a	135
Total	241	635

Source: 1899: Nathaniel T. Bacon, "American International Indebtedness," *Yale Review,* 9 (Nov. 1900): 269; at market value. In Table 5.8 herein the 1899 Dutch total is given as $240 million—as in Bacon's own rounding (p. 276). 1914: Cleona Lewis, *America's Stake in International Investments* (Washington, D.C.: Brookings Institution, 1938), p. 546; at par value.
a Not specified by Bacon.

investments, in this instance immigration does not help to explain the substantial interests. Rather, the reason lies in the historical background. Since the revolutionary period, as I have shown, the Dutch had made major investments in America. The close Anglo-Dutch connections resulted in some coincidence between the British and Dutch investment patterns. Because Dutch financial houses were intimately linked with British ones, the rise of British investment in the United States was often accompanied by a comparable and associated Dutch expansion. Frequently, in fact, when British intermediaries could not sell American securities in Britain, they disposed of them in Holland. The Dutch appear to have been more adventurous than the British investors, more ready to buy low in expectation of future gain. They seem to have been prepared to take more risks than their British counterparts. By 1909 some 60 American stocks and over 100 American bonds were listed on the Amsterdam exchange,[107] far more than on the French or German bourses. U.S. railroad securities remained attractive to the Dutch, and after 1900 a number of American industrial corporations were listed in Amsterdam; Dutch interest in the industrials mounted rapidly.[108] Dutch holdings in U.S. land continued, and there were new entries in the mineral industries, particularly in oil.

One estimate states that in both 1890 and 1913, about one-third of the foreign portfolio of Dutch investors was American.[109] If this is true (and it seems plausible),[110] in 1913 the U.S. proportion was higher than the U.S. share of either British or German investments, much less French ones.[111] In 1914, as in the case of British and German investors, the United States ranked first among the individual foreign countries in which the Dutch had made investments. While Dutch portfolio investments surpassed direct ones in the United States, both coexisted. The Dutch remained significant investors in America.[112]

In addition, the United States attracted the interests, in lesser amounts, of the Swiss, Belgians, Italians, Austrians, Swedes, Bulgarians, Spaniards, Russians, Danes, and other Europeans.[113] Many of their holdings were in securities that did not carry control, but the interests of Nestlé, Solvay, Fiat, Hermann Schmidtmann, de Laval, and the "Bulgaria," First Bulgarian Insurance Co., were multinational-enterprise-type involvements.[114]

Canada was a debtor nation in world accounts.[115] Nonetheless, its geographical position—its long frontier with the United States—meant that there would be not only U.S. investments in Canada, but also Canadian investments in the United States.[116] Canadians bought U.S. securities; individual Canadians made significant U.S. investments, and Canadian firms made direct investments across the border. Table 5.16 gives Cleona Lewis' estimates, by sector. The table is not reliable, because frequently the "Canadian" investments prove, in fact, to be U.K. investments, if one looks at beneficial ownership. British-owned or controlled companies in Canada spilled over into the United States. When studying Canadian enterprise in the United States, one finds that the financial trail often goes back to London. This was true of such diverse businesses as Hudson's Bay Company, the Canadian Pacific Railway, and the Electric Reduction Company, Ltd. Likewise, a number of Canadian residents who made their money in Canada and invested in the United States retired to Great Britain; such a "Canadian" investor in the United States would accordingly become a British investor in the United States, with his change in residence.[117] In this era Canadians had their principal interests in the United States in connecting railroad lines (British-financed ventures) and in traded securities.[118] Canadians played a role in public utilities in Toledo, Ohio; Detroit; and Minneapolis.[119] The major Canadian banks were present in New York and other U.S. cities. Likewise, a number of Canadian insurance firms crossed the border. Only a few Canadian industrial firms did so. At the start of the twentieth century, Canada had an economic boom; to a large extent the "idle resources" of earlier years that had drifted into U.S. investments were redirected by Canadians back to their own country.[120]

Nathaniel Bacon wrote of the flight of capital from Cuba in 1899: "Owing to the danger to property in Cuba during the various revolutions in that unhappy land, many wealthy Cubans invested large sums in our securities."[121] By 1913 the National Bank of Cuba (which

Table 5.16.   Level of "Canadian" investments in the United States, by sector at par value, July 1, 1914

Sector	Millions of U.S. dollars
Railroad securities	48
Other U.S. securities	95
Direct investments by "Canadian" railways	82
Other direct investments	50
Total	275

Source: Cleona Lewis, *America's Stake in International Investments* (Washington, D.C.: Brookings Institution, 1938), p. 546.

seems to have been U.S. controlled) had a New York agency.[122] There was some Mexican investment in the United States by 1914, mainly as a consequence of the nationalization of formerly American- and British-owned Mexican railways.[123]

Japan—another debtor nation in world accounts—had begun to have foreign investments, principally in China. The Bank of Japan calculated that as of July 1914 Japanese foreign investments equaled 461 million yen (or about $227 million dollars, at 0.4925 yen to the dollar). Of this amount, it estimated that Japanese investment in business enterprises in the United States (including Hawaii) had reached 50 million yen, or $24.6 million.[124] The United States was second only to China as a place for Japanese overseas investment. Japanese interests in the United States were all direct investments—basically in trade, banking, insurance, and shipping.[125]

In determining foreign investment in the United States, I have tried to correct for foreign investments in companies *incorporated* in the United States that operated abroad. Already in this period, especially in the early twentieth century as American money markets began to take on an international dimension, there were the beginnings of such enterprises. Thus the U.S.-headquartered Cuban-American Sugar Company, with business in Cuba, listed its bonds on the London and Amsterdam exchanges.[126] The Lake Superior Corporation, organized in New Jersey in 1904, seems to have operated in Canada; certain of its securities were listed on the London stock exchange.[127] So, too, the American Congo Company, with a rubber concession in the Belgian Congo, had been incorporated in New York in 1906; 100 percent of its common shares and 50 percent of its preferred shares were owned by the Belgian government; it can hardly be called a Belgian investment in America.[128] Such "American" multinational businesses raised capital abroad for their own international investments.[129]

Some Significant Aspects of Foreign Portfolio Investment Growth: 1875–1914

Long-term foreign portfolio investments—principally in public finance and, more important, in railroads—involved money markets and financial intermediaries (at home and abroad). Such investments were liquid—and often volatile. The bulk was in fixed-income securities; some were, however, in corporate shares. They were closely associated with immigration.

As I have stated many times, my study is on *nonresident* investment. Once an immigrant became an American resident, he was not a foreign investor. Yet, as Brinley Thomas found, "each inflow of labour in America, accompanied by a rise in the import of capital, transforms the production functions, inducing a widespread adoption of automatic machines, interchangeable parts, standardized output and dilution of labour." Thomas argued that in the years 1881–1888 and 1903–1913, when there was a formidable U.S. inward migration, there was also a coincident upswing in capital imports.[130]

In a much more specific manner, immigrants from capital-exporting countries had a vital place in relation to portfolio investment from abroad.[131] Immigrants told people back home about opportunities for investment. It became common practice for foreign investors in the late nineteenth and early twentieth centuries not only to obtain information from knowledgeable immigrants of their own nationality but also to have these individuals represent them in America. Scots and Germans, in particular, who came to America often did not carry capital but attracted monies from the old country. That foreign investors had men in the United States whom they knew personally and trusted reduced uncertainty and encouraged more investment. As Douglass C. North put it (in a totally different context), "honesty, integrity, and good performance are values to the parties engaged in contracting."[132] They could be expected from compatriots.

Some Significant Aspects of Foreign Direct Investment Growth: 1875–1914

No evidence exists that over the years foreign portfolio and direct investments followed similar, much less identical, patterns, albeit at times they went in tandem. Foreign direct investments typically involved more than the transfer of capital. By definition, as indicated, they carried the attempt at management and control. They often included technology transfer, trademarks, a range of relations with immigrants, and, most important in this context, they always faced matters associated with business organization.

The argument has repeatedly been made that if a company had a technological edge, it would be more prone to make foreign direct investments.[133] I hypothesized that there would thus be a connection between foreign patents taken out in the United States and foreign direct investment. Patents have been used as a measure of technological advantage, although they are a far from perfect proxy.

Table 5.17 shows the patents issued to foreign inventors by the U.S. Patent Office at roughly five-year intervals, 1885–1914.[134] Of all the foreign inventors, those from England, Germany, Canada, and France stood out. The first-place role of England through 1895 seems

Table 5.17. Foreign holders of U.S. patents

Year	U.S. patents granted to citizens of foreign countries					Patents issued to U.S. citizens	Patents gra foreign citi as % those gra
	Total	England	Germany	Canada	France		
1885	1,549	549	298	284	138	22,535	6.4
1890	2,105	721	452	371	178	24,103	8.0
1895	2,049	614	539	302	202	19,949	9.3
1900	3,483	987	1,070	367	341	22,935	13.2
1905	3,292	770	987	413	303	26,978	10.9
1910	3,719	894	1,083	534	315	32,059	10.3
1914	4,595	1,033	1,475	667	379	37,009	11.0

Source: *Reports of the U.S. Commissioner of Patents.*

to be reflected in the foreign direct investment pattern. The Patent Office reports refer to "England" and not "Britain"; I do not know the level of Scottish patents; they may well have been classified under "England."[135] The rise of important German direct investment is mirrored in Germany's lead in patents granted after 1900.

Jonathan Liebenau has pointed out that although British exports exceeded German exports to the United States, German patents came to surpass those of the British because German products by their very nature required more patent protection. Many German firms had high-technology goods, and the patent system became a significant part of their "market tactics."[136] I will show that some large German investments in America were in sales networks rather than in fabrication; nothing in U.S. patent law obligated manufacture to retain a patent. Thus manufacture had to be based on other rationales (tariffs or cost considerations, for example) or to take place when competitors emerged after the patent had expired.

The number of Canadian and French patents was far smaller than that of English or German patents, and this is evident in the foreign direct investment pattern. Yet Canada's third place pressed me to ask why the ranking was even that high. My initial assumption was that some British patents were classified as Canadian. Further research, however, led me to accept the view of Keith Pavitt and Luc Soete that the reason for the relatively large number of patents (the third-place position) lay in Canada's geographical proximity to the United States, which meant that—unlike European inventors—Canadian inventors routinely took out U.S. patents.[137] They did not necessarily follow up their patenting behavior with foreign direct investments.

Regrettably, Patent Office records in Washington cannot easily be used to divide nationalities by industry classifications. The Alien Property Custodian materials do reveal, however, a great number of German patents in the chemical and electrical industries—and offer an excellent source for lists of German patents.[138]

U.S. Patent Office statistics were based on the inventor and his residence (city and country).[139] While the "assignee" was listed on the patent application, the statistics prepared for the annual reports of the Patent Office did not provide this information, which makes it extremely difficult to employ the already-assembled patent statistics in this period to study the technology transfers associated with foreign direct investment.[140]

There seems no question that foreign direct investors in the United States served as conduits for technology transfer to America. This was true in numerous industries, from rayon to chemicals to magnetos. Frequently patents were or had been involved. One should recognize, however, that companies could have a technological advantage, and no patents need be issued. There existed cases in which direct investments were made *to obtain* U.S. technology, but these were rare.

Many foreign direct investments in the United States in the years 1875–1914 were by companies, especially British and German ones, with trademarked, highly advertised products. Managers of such enterprises were deeply concerned with imitators. The advantage of a foreign multinational enterprise in the United States often lay in its brand name, which denoted to the buyer a reputation and a consistent quality. Such names are as relevant as new technology in understanding the growth of foreign multinationals in America. Brand names were particularly significant in food products, soaps, patent medicines, and pharmaceuticals, but also in apparel, thread, cutlery, and gasoline, as well as in automobiles, tires, machinery, and instruments. I know of no scholarly study dealing with the period 1875–1914 that offers original research on trademarks and brand and company names. Most trademarks were registered either in Washington or in particular states, or both. Scattered data in company files on these registrations sometimes provide an indication of when companies began to show an interest in the U.S. market.[141]

The literature on the theory of foreign direct investment customarily discusses the relationship between foreign direct investment and licensing; usually the licensing of intangible assets (patents and trademarks) is studied as an alternative to investment.[142] In 1875–1914 there were many licensing accords whereby the foreign firm (or inventor) retained no equity interest in the U.S. enterprise. I found, however, that the more typical arrangement was one of complementarity. Licensing of a patent or a trademark went with a foreign direct investment in a joint-venture. Licensing of independent U.S. firms or licensing accompanied by a small minority interest seems to have been the chosen route when one or both of the following conditions held: (1) The foreign enterprise was not prepared to make a large U.S. commitment, but because of tariffs or for some other reason, it could not continue to export; the foreign firm sometimes wanted a return on its intangible assets and had no inclination to export.[143] (2) An American enterprise took the initiative and desired the license (often an American firm would seek a license for a highly specialized process; the rest of the U.S. enterprise's technology would be American). Frequently scholars confuse a *license* (whereby the ownership of the patent or trademark remained abroad and the U.S. company paid a royalty) and a *sale* of the patent or trademark rights (whereby the U.S. firm became the owner and in exchange for the receipt of the intangible asset might pay either in securities of the U.S. enterprise, creating a minority foreign investment, or in cash and often—especially in the case of patents—with a royalty on future product sales). Both are called licensing in the general literature, albeit with the sale, the ownership of the intangible asset (the patent or trademark) came to be held by the U.S. user. Both were common, and both might be accompanied by investment; parental control was always more difficult with the sale.

Immigrants were as important vis-à-vis foreign direct investments as vis-à-vis foreign portfolio ones, but in a slightly different manner. Immigrants often served not merely as intermediaries of capital but also in an ongoing role as agents, licensees, partners, or employees of foreign multinational enterprises. Foreign direct investors hired in managerial (and nonmanagerial) positions immigrants with whom they had no difficulty communicating. The language of the French-owned woolen yarn mills in Rhode Island was, for example, French. Immigrants to the United States served an added function in relation to foreign direct investment. They offered a market for products they knew at home. They did not have to be "reeducated" on the worth of a particular good. Foreign direct investors found the specialized immigrant markets easy to penetrate, and a number catered to such groups.

Why were foreign direct investments made in America? In many instances (in iron, copper, salt, oil, tobacco, explosives, harvesters, and electrical equipment, for example), particular foreign direct investment decisions can be viewed as reactions to "threats" (or potential ones): an American company was exporting (or Europeans anticipated U.S. exports) or an American company had made a "menacing" direct investment abroad. A European or Canadian (in the case of harvesters) company responded with a counterthrust, an investment—or the announcement of an investment—in the United States. The response could be an aggressive entry into U.S. business to meet a U.S. firm on its own territory (Royal Dutch-Shell in 1912); a "counterthreat" to be resolved in a division-of-market arrangement and no investments in manufacturing (in explosives in 1896–97); or an attempt to stop or to control potential U.S. exports (the German-controlled Edison General Electric's purchase of Sprague Electric in 1889). Thus "threatened" foreign companies would react to American moves, but with diverse outcomes. Although there were numerous cases of threats and responses, the pattern was very far from a universal explanation of the motivations of foreign direct investors, and I have found that many more foreign direct investments were made and grew without this motivation than with it. For threat and counterthreat, moreover, there had to be a possibility of American business competition across borders. Frequently, where foreign direct investment in the United States existed, there was no such threat (in cotton and linen thread, rayon, and aspirins, for example).[144]

Many foreign direct investments were influenced by the height of U.S. tariffs. Tariffs had an important impact on the decisions of foreign companies to manufacture in the United States rather than to try to continue exporting to America. In 1875–1914, in the main, American law provided protection for domestic industries. Yet tariffs by themselves were insufficient as "causal" factors for all foreign direct investment. Many foreign enterprises did not jump tariff barriers and make investments behind them. In addition, there arose a plethora of investments by free-standing companies and other foreign direct investments in supply-related endeavors, and still others in services, where tariffs were not germane to foreign investment strategies.

Some foreign direct investors in the United States started new enterprises in cattle raising, mining, manufacturing, or banking. Others in the same sectors "took over" existing American businesses (both healthy and weak ones). Free-standing direct investors tended toward takeovers, albeit there were some new activities. Foreign enterprises expanding in the United States from a domestic base usually started new businesses in this country, although here too there were takeovers. A single foreign company might follow both paths: it might start new economic activitiy *and* also take over one or more competitors, suppliers, or other related businesses. In every case managerial coordination posed problems (with acquisitions there was the added uncertainty that the existing American management would not conform to the new owner's wishes).

Some foreign direct investors held a 100 percent interest in their business in the United States. Joint-ventures, however, between capital from abroad and that of U.S. residents became very common in these years. Sometimes, as indicated, a British or a continental European firm obtained an equity in an American company in exchange for a license to use the parent's technology or trademark (ownership of the intangible asset could be vested in the U.S. or foreign firm). As noted, immigrants were often participants in joint-ventures with foreign direct investors. Many of the free-standing companies were in part owned by the American "vendors"—that is, Americans whose companies had been taken over. Foreign direct investment in America ranged from 100 percent to minority interests.[145]

Typically, scholars consider foreign direct investments of enterprises that used the corporate form. In 1875–1914 the development of large-scale corporations did facilitate business growth both domestically and internationally. Sometimes a foreign corporation did business in the United States directly; more frequently a subsidiary or affiliate was set up in an American state to undertake operations. Coincidentally, with the spread of the corporate form, there persisted the use of partnerships in international business, and the number and variety of foreign direct investments in the United States utilizing that seemingly inappropriate structure came as a surprise. Often a British or German partnership would be established and then a separate American one, with partners sometimes identical and sometimes overlapping (if the latter, possibly with U.S. partners—often resident immigrants—included). Partnerships in international business were sustained over decades, the partners changing as deaths, retirements, and personal quarrels occurred. Partnerships were sometimes combined with corporate investments, the partners having controlling interests in one or more corporations. In relation to foreign direct investment in the United States, I have found—as will be evident later—partnerships (as parents, as the U.S. operating entity, or as both) in trade, manufacturing, banking, land holdings, accounting, and other sectors.

There does not seem to be a difference between "older" and "newer" industries in the use of this legal form. What did seem to make a difference was (1) the amount of capital employed and (2) whether outside capital (beyond that of family and close friends) was required. If the capital requirement was great or the public's capital was desired, the partnership form was not suitable. What was fundamental to the partnership were "family" and friendships that provided cohesion to the firm. Loyalty and confidence among family members (some of whom migrated to America) could substitute for formal corporate hierarchies, creating an ease in intrafirm coordination. When corporations were employed by a family or by family groups (for the reasons indicated above), they sometimes left traces in the securities market; frequently they did not. To understand foreign investment in the United States, administrative organization has to be studied along with the legal structure. Direct investors used a variety of legal forms.[146]

Almost by definition, a business that makes foreign direct investments tends to be larger than a solely domestic one: we are talking about interactions over geographical distance, but size was far less important than innovative behavior. For a foreign direct investor, it took something extra to invest over boundaries, and in the case of the foreign direct investment, that "advantage," that "something extra," not only had to be there at origin but also had to persist if the investment was to succeed. The U.S. market was unique in its dimensions. Many foreign firms (with experiences in smaller markets) found it necessary to have more than one plant, office, or agency in the United States. They could not easily replicate home practices. Some adapted. Many failed to succeed, ultimately withdrawing. Much depend on the nature of competition from domestic companies and on the strength and persistence of the foreign firm's advantages.

At the same time, and under related circumstances, European companies often took part in anticompetitive agreements.[147] Sometimes such agreements arose out of "threats" and "counterthreats"; frequently they came in lean times; on occasion they were based on aggressive behavior; more typically they were defensive solutions. The "treaties" joined otherwise-independent firms and sought to stabilize (or to raise) prices, to divide markets, to set production levels, or a combination thereof. Some of these associations achieved their goals, others did not. Arrangements tended to be short-lived and subject to frequent renegotiation. Some had governmental sponsorship, especially those of the Germans. Most accords involving Americans were between private companies and operated without any government's knowledge, much less its assent. Such agreements had various (and far from uniform) impacts on foreign firms as they planned and did business in America.

European "sellers' cartels" invested in marketing in the United States—the German potash cartel, for example. Its unity gave the Europeans a competitive advantage and was the basis for aggressive expansion rather than for retreat. Frequently European businessmen urged American enterprises in which they had investments—from railroads to meat-packing concerns—to cooperate with rivals, assuming that the recommended price fixing would bring higher dividends to the investors. In some industries agreements temporarily divided world markets, and when the arrangements broke down, the door to foreign investment in the United States opened—in aluminum and oil, for instance. Division of markets might mean that a large U.S. company would act for its European counterpart in America, keeping the European firm at bay; this occurred in matches and condensed milk. Foreign investors sometimes did not actively compete with one another within the United States—in thread in the early twentieth century, for example. Frequently intercontinental pacts and foreign direct investment went together. In numerous chemical products, from rayon to alkalies, agreements accompanied foreign direct investment in the United States and set the rules of the game. In the chemical and electrical industries, territorial accords were normally associated with patents; in other industries they were not. Some agreements stopped sizable foreign direct investments in America—for example, in explosives (as noted) and cigarette manufacture for the U.S. market. European cartels had an impact on America's export trade, lowering the prices received by U.S. raw material producers—in copper, for one. Some U.S. manufacturers agreed not to export at all, or only to neighboring or specified countries. In short, collusive accords differed in nature and in impact.[148]

Because of the propensity of many European businessmen toward a "negotiated environment,"[149] negotiated between and among enterprises to avoid uncertainty (and designed to raise profits), European business in the United States frequently ran afoul of America's growing body of antitrust law. Foreign investors often could not understand why American businessmen or managers hesitated to join with them in increasing prices or dividing markets. They viewed with disbelief the attitudes of American government policymakers toward cooperation between otherwise independent firms. As I write of foreign businesses in the United States in these years, I will consider the role of restraint-of-trade agreements.

Sectors Attracting Foreign Investment in the United States

The rise of foreign investment in the United States was, as noted earlier, selective. Certain sectors were, and others were not, attractive to foreign investors. Because the sums had by 1875–1914 become so great, I will discuss the investments by sector, always differentiating the purely portfolio interests from those that carried with them (or sought to carry with them) management and control.

U.S. federal government securities were of interest to foreign investors during the early years of this period; yet the totals for such securities held in Britain were by 1910 so negligible that the editor of the *Statist*, George Paish, excluded them when tabulating British stakes in the United States in that year (see Table 5.11). Even earlier a pall had fallen on state government securities. The southern states' defaults of the mid-1870s had finally signaled to foreign investors that such issues were not secure. Some issues of American municipalities, however, continued to be held and marketed abroad.[150] In the concluding section of this chapter, I will consider briefly the foreign investments in American national, state, and local government paper —all of which were, of course, portfolio investments.

Far larger were the foreign stakes in the private sector in America. Chapter 6 covers the huge and important investments in railroads and the related ones in land. As railroads crossed the country, mines and oil properties were developed by foreign owners. Chapters 7 and 8 turn to foreign interests in mining, looking at precious metals as well as other minerals, including oil; the two chapters also examine investments in the processing and marketing of such minerals. Chapter 9 surveys the multitude of foreign investments in food, drink, tobacco, and grocery products. It deals with foreign investments in U.S. cattle ranches and in the processing, manufacturing, and marketing of products such as meat, flour, beer, canned milk, chocolates, and soap. Chapter 10 focuses on foreign investment in textiles and leather goods, including cotton plantations and apparel. Chapters 7 through 10 treat raw materials, manufacturing, and marketing; at times I provide information on key inputs (chemicals for the textile and leather goods industries, for example). As will be clear, the data themselves led me to these vertical classificatory clusters. I felt that to adopt rigidly the standard industrial classifications (SIC codes) would result in a sacrifice of understanding; instead, I followed the investors.

In Chapter 11 I do rely on a standard category when I consider the numerous and highly significant foreign direct investments in the U.S. chemical industry. Chapter 12 is devoted to investments in manufacturing not covered elsewhere—those in harvesters, automobiles, rubber tires, nonelectrical and electrical machinery, and other goods. Foreign investments were also made in a variety of service activities, comprising financial, commercial, and communication services, as well as insurance, accounting, and construction. Chapters 13–15 pay attention to these and added service sector investments. Finally, in Chapter 16 I review the U.S. and non-U.S. reactions to the formidable foreign investment in America, 1875–1914.

Chapters 6 through 15, in short, turn to the sizable foreign portfolio and direct investments in the many branches of the private sector in this country in the years 1875–1914. For now, however, I will briefly review the quite separate foreign interests in American public finance.

The Public Sector

U.S. public finance in the four years 1875–1879 was greatly assisted by access to European capital markets. As noted in Chapter 4, on July 28, 1874, the Secretary of the Treasury (B. H. Bristow) entered into a contract with Messrs. August Belmont & Co., New York, on behalf of Messrs. N. M. Rothschild & Sons, London, and associates, and Messrs. J. & W. Seligman & Co., New York, for the "negotiation" of $45 million of 5 percent U.S. bonds. The bankers had the option of the balance of the loan ($122,688,550). The understanding was that the main portion of these bonds, for refunding the national debt, would be sold in Europe.[151] The contract was renewed on January 29, 1875, and Drexel, Morgan & Co. was added to the group.[152] Despite the defaults of state governments and railroads, the Council of the Corporation of Foreign Bondholders declared in February 1875 that "the credit of the United States Government has been maintained on the highest standard."[153] In 1875 the U.S. Congress passed legislation to return America to the gold standard in 1879.

On August 24, 1876, the U.S. Secretary of the Treasury (Lot M. Morrill) made a contract with the same group of bankers that his predecessor had used (and also Morton, Bliss & Co.) for negotiation of 4 percent bonds and redemption of an equivalent amount of 6 percents.[154] Early in June 1877 John Sherman, the new Secretary of the Treasury, arranged for the sale abroad of 4 percent U.S. bonds.[155] The next year, however, Sherman could report that the U.S. market was absorbing these U.S. government securities; in December 1878 he believed that not more than $200 million of U.S. bonds were held outside the country.[156] In January 1879 the United States resumed specie payments.[157] The sale abroad of U.S. securities had at critical junctures assisted the process.[158]

In the refunding and in the resumption of specie payments, a significant role was played by August Belmont and the London Rothschilds.[159] Thus in April 1877 Secretary Sherman was writing to N. M. Rothschild & Sons, London, that "the operations of the [banking] syndicate have become so important" that he was sending Charles F. Conant to London to assume the general management and supervision of U.S. government business there.[160] Conant sent Sherman regular, comprehensive reports from London on the market for U.S. securities.[161] In all these transactions in the late 1870s, Baring

Brothers was not in any way involved;[162] the bankers' syndicate for U.S. securities was led by the Rothschilds. As Sherman wrote, "The leading motive for employing the syndicate was because of their foreign alliances."[163]

It was not all easy. At one point (May 1877), Sherman learned that the Dutch, who had held large amounts of 6 percent called loans, instead of exchanging them for 4 percents had sold them and invested in Russian stock. The Dutch had bought this U.S. paper at 60 percent of par and sold at par, thus obtaining a handsome return.[164] Europeans were upset when in February 1878 Congress overrode the President's veto of the Bland-Allison bill, which made silver dollars legal tender. The arrangements with the syndicate were canceled, only to be reinstated in April 1878.[165] In 1879 the U.S. Treasury was again arranging with the bankers to market U.S. bonds in Europe.[166]

In June 1880, with the tenth census of the United States, an attempt was made to determine ownership of the national debt. Of the registered bonds, on which quarterly or semiannual interest was paid, a mere $28 million were held by foreign owners. By contrast, of the "coupon bonds," interest on at least $221 million was paid at the subtreasury in New York and was sent through New York banking houses to foreign bondholders. This meant at minimum some $249 million of U.S. bonds were owned abroad.[167]

In 1881 a London agency of the U.S. Treasury was temporarily reestablished to exchange the 6 percent bonds (the loans of July and August 1861 and the loan of 1863) that were redeemable on June 30, 1881. This London agency issued about $44.5 million of the so-called continued bonds—at 3½ percent per annum.[168] Early in 1881 August Belmont estimated that only $150 million of our national debt was still held abroad.[169] Three years later an informed estimate put the figure at less than $100 million.[170] During the 1880s the U.S. government's debt was steadily reduced; the interest rate on the debt was low. Accordingly, the role of European capital markets in U.S. federal government finance became relatively unimportant.

When in November 1890 the Baring Crisis occurred, Britishers sold U.S. government securities.[171] In 1893 the further sale by European investors of many American securities (government and other issues) put pressure on Treasury gold; during 1893, $72.3 million in gold was exported, the largest amount to that date. Attempts made to replenish American gold reserves in 1894 proved inadequate. August Belmont & Co. (on behalf of themselves and N. M. Rothschild & Sons, London) and J. P. Morgan & Co. (on behalf of themselves and J. S. Morgan & Co., London) in January and February 1895 offered to assist the U.S. Treasury. Under an agreement of February 8, 1895, between the U.S. Secretary of the Treasury and the four banking houses, the latter agreed to sell and deliver to the United States 3.5 million ounces of gold coin of the United States, payable in U.S. thirty-year bonds.[172] On February 27, 1895, August Belmont wrote Lord Rothschild, "I congratulate your Lordship and your House most sincerely upon the success of the loan on your side."[173] In the summer of 1895, J. P. Morgan, acting for the syndicate, traveled to London to arrange the sale of $101,970,000 of American bonds to protect U.S. gold reserves. Less than one-third of the securities that the syndicate was marketing were U.S. government paper (most of the remainder were railway issues).[174] Included among the U.S. government securities were the newly issued thirty-year 4 percents.[175]

Late in January 1895, Baron Alphonse de Rothschild, Paris, had written his cousins in London, "The loan may be but a palliative rather than an expedient, a factitious way to refill the Treasury's chests to be emptied next day much like the feat of circus acrobats entering by one and leaving by another door."[176] Nonetheless, the British and French Rothschilds participated with J. P. Morgan and J. S. Morgan & Co. in trying to curb the outflow of Treasury gold.[177]

Baron Alphonse de Rothschild was right; the American gold outflow soon resumed. In late December 1895, President Grover Cleveland decided to make another bond sale abroad to obtain gold. At the same time, the long-dormant dispute between Venezuela and Great Britain over the Venezuelan–British Guiana border captured the headlines. Cleveland demanded that the matter be submitted to arbitration and invoked the Monroe doctrine.

In this context, August Belmont & Co. asked the British Rothschilds whether they wished to participate in the placing of the new U.S. bonds. Their answer was an unequivocal no.[178] Many European (especially British) investors, frightened by Cleveland's "pugnacious" attitude in the Venezuelan dispute, were selling their American holdings.[179] Early in 1896 the U.S. Treasury decided to bypass J. P. Morgan's proposed syndicate and to offer the bonds for public subscription in the United States rather than try to market them in Europe.[180]

In 1899, with the Boer War and with high interest rates in Britain, the few Britishers who still held U.S. government bonds dumped them.[181] Nathaniel Bacon, writing in 1900, found that some Dutch, German, and Swiss investors retained U.S. government bonds—U.S. 4 percents.[182] In 1907 Charles F. Speare, financial editor of the *New York Evening Mail*, marveled that the U.S. 4 percents of 1907, just redeemed, had been originally placed abroad in the late 1870s by the

Rothschilds in Holland and Germany and had been held for all that time—some thirty years![183]

In 1909 George Paish wrote that British income from U.S. government bonds was too small to include in his study of income from foreign investments.[184] In a tally of British foreign investment outflow, July 1, 1908 to June 30, 1909, he documented no purchases of U.S. federal issues. When in 1911 Paish presented his findings to the Royal Statistical Society, he calculated British investments in the United States for 1910—and, as noted earlier, included zero for U.S. government holdings.[185] In sum, by the twentieth century most Europeans had no interest in U.S. federal government bonds. There were minor German purchases of U.S. government 3 percent fifty-year Panama Canal bonds, but this was exceptional.[186]

Defaults on American *state* bonds in the 1870s for all practical purposes ended their sale abroad. As noted in Chapter 4, at the end of 1874 some 58 percent of state bonds held abroad were in default.[187] The Council of the Corporation of Foreign Bondholders reported regularly on the "impaired credit" of the southern states.[188] The council was outspoken in seeking recovery of defaulted state debts, but it had little success.[189] The Barings floated a small issue for Massachusetts in 1875 and subsequently did not handle any American state, county, or city issues.[190] Writing of British investments in the United States in 1893, the British economist R. H. Inglis Palgrave did not mention state bonds. He did discuss British interests in U.S. "municipal bonds," which he noted were small—since "if the municipality is little known it is distrusted. If it is widely known and well established, the rate of interest paid is not sufficient to attract the British investor."[191] In 1899–1900 Nathaniel Bacon found that "on almost all of our [America's] State, county, municipal bonds there is so high a special value at home for savings banks that only two States, six cities, and one county in the United States had securities on the London list [the London Stock Exchange]."[192]

Nonetheless, in 1878 a Baltimore paper had reported that "one of the largest coteries of American residents in Paris consisted of sellers of American municipal bonds."[193] Bacon—as of the fall of 1899—discovered that Dutch investors held about $5 million in U.S., state, county, and municipal bonds, and he estimated that this sum was about three times that held in England.[194] He noted that Alabama 4 percents were quoted on the Frankfurt exchange. He also verified that about $1 million to $2 million of American county and city bonds were held in Germany and found bonds of two counties and nine cities quoted on the Frankfurt lists.[195] Swiss investors, Bacon wrote, had once been very active in American county issues, but not in 1899.[196] Bacon said nothing about French investors in these securities. In 1913 the London *Economist* stated that tenders were asked for the purchase of $11 million 4 percent bonds of Louisiana and that the Council of the Corporation of Foreign Bondholders was warning investors against them as a consequence "of Louisiana defaults."[197]

Between 1907 and August 1914, New York City raised an estimated $61.6 million in London and an additional $17.5 million in Paris. Its obligations were listed in Amsterdam in 1910. Germans also bought New York City securities. New York was the only U.S. city to offer its securities on a regular basis in Europe.[198] Paish, writing of British foreign investment outflow July 1, 1908–June 30, 1909, found in that year only £338,200 ($1.6 million) in acquisitions of American municipals. This represented a small proportion (2.5 percent) of the total new British investment in the United States that year.[199]

In 1911, when Paish addressed the Royal Statistical Society in London, he was asked how he handled the British investments "in certain States [that] had absolutely repudiated their engagements, e.g., Louisiana, Mississippi, West Virginia, and other states which were almost hopelessly and fraudulently bankrupt."[200] He indicated that in determining British investment, he had excluded money lent to the defaulting states.[201] Indeed, his tabulation lists nothing for any U.S. state.[202] He included among British investments in the United States a mere $38.4 million for municipals.[203]

There were, however, other foreign purchasers of American government issues: by 1914 a number of foreign insurance companies had established themselves in the United States.[204] To do business on a regular basis in this country, *their U.S. branch assets* had to include a portfolio of American securities. Many of these foreign firms acquired U.S. municipals (some had state securities and a few held U.S. government bonds).[205] Their holdings represented a foreign claim on assets in the United States and thus were "foreign investments."

In short, by 1914 in the United States, the domestic capital market (including foreign insurance companies located here) acquired U.S. federal, state, and local government issues. New York City excepted, in the early twentieth century local governments did not typically go abroad for funds. There was little interest in Europe in American government securities. If one looks solely at "public" finance, those who point to the insignificance of foreign money in the United States in 1914 are right. A study of foreign investment in the United States in the late nineteenth and early twentieth centuries must include government securities but must look far beyond them. Whereas before the mid-1870s, throughout our history as a nation, it seems that either federal or state government securities had been the largest single attraction for foreign investors,[206] in the years 1875–1914 this was no longer the case. The private sector took top priority. The vast bulk of foreign investment in the United States now went from private sector investors abroad into private sector activities in America—and it is to those stakes in the private sector that we must therefore devote our main attention.

6.

Railroads and Land

By far the largest single sector to attract foreign investment in America (1875–1914) was the railroad.[1] The investment from abroad was awesome, far greater than in prior years. Railroads were capital intensive and required more funding than Americans could supply. Europeans had invested in American railroads since the 1830s, but much more monies were called for by the post-1875 railroads because of the longer distances: at the start of 1875, 72,385 miles of track were in operation; the comparable figure on June 30, 1914, was 387,208 miles.[2] To build this mileage meant that the sums invested from abroad in American railroads, 1875–1914, substantially surpassed the totals of times past.[3]

For Europeans who sought investment opportunities, American railroads seemed to offer excellent returns. Information in Europe on U.S. "rails" was now abundant.[4] American railroad managers, who found East Coast capital markets inadequate, continued to seek and to obtain capital from Britain and the European continent. It became increasingly easier to do so as the channels for capital movements became more developed. There was not a prominent American railroad leader who did not desire and expect foreign monies.

Albro Martin has written, "No other single factor contributed so much to the settlement of the North American continent, to the rapid development of its natural and human resources, and to the transformation of the material and cultural aspects of American life as the maturing railroad system."[5] Railroads stimulated domestic and foreign investments in many other sectors. As the railroads opened the country, foreign investments were made in land, mining, and cattle ranches. Railroads created the potential for national markets.[6] The sizable, albeit short-lived, foreign investments in the predecessor of

General Electric were directly related to the activities of Henry Villard, whose initial entré to German capital was through railroad securities. American investment banking and its integration with international banking was intimately associated with railway finance. By 1875 railroads required the "professionalization of capital mobilization."[7]

François Caron has explained that the French saver who had bought government bonds in the early nineteenth century looked to fixed-income railroad securities at the end of the century.[8] This French domestic pattern was replicated internationally. British and continental European investors and financial intermediaries in the late nineteenth century bought and offered railroad bonds, including those of U.S. railroads, to provide that desired "guaranteed income."[9] Foreign investors who had once owned U.S. government bonds reinvested in U.S. railway securities when the bonds matured or were refunded (in the 1870s and 1880s).[10] As in earlier years, the bulk of foreign investment in American railroads continued to be in bonds rather than in shares.[11]

In studying foreign investments in American railroads, however, it is desirable to consider both bonds and shares. While throughout the period the former predominated in international investments, there were also substantial stakes in the latter; the ratio between bonds and shares held abroad seems to have varied (unsystematically) in the years 1875–1914.[12] Investors abroad acquired more U.S. railroad bonds than shares because (1) bonds carried a fixed return; (2) bonds could often be purchased at deep discounts and would be redeemed at par (of course, buying below par also provided the investor with a realized interest rate above the stated one); and most important (3) bonds presumably meant less risk than equity holdings, albeit less expected return.[13] Many foreign investors owned railroad mortgage bonds, which represented (or investors thought they represented) a claim on real assets.[14] Many held "gold bonds," with interest and principal payable in gold. For Americans, selling bonds instead of stock meant that they retained control—at least until receivership.

The *Economist* (London) regularly warned investors against U.S. railroad shares, sometimes with snide comments: "As the country fills up the dividends upon American railway shares may become more stable, and these securities may come to possess something more of an investment character."[15] Trusts such as the Scottish American Investment Company, Ltd., bought large quantities of railroad bonds, but for its first decade this company would not buy railroad shares (its historian states that this was an "unquestioned rule" until 1882).[16] Of course, if a railroad went bankrupt (and many did), bondholders as well as shareholders lost, although the former may have recouped more in reorganizations. The *Economist* urged its readers to buy only well-secured bonds and to avoid all "contingent American railroad securities," such as collateral trust mortgage bonds, income bonds, second-mortgage bonds, and debenture bonds.[17] Likewise, the Scottish American Investment Company, Ltd., cautioned that the future revenues of a railroad had to be adequate to service its debts—not a profound warning, but one that was often forgotten.[18]

Although they came to be thought of as conservative investments, there was risk (and speculation) in U.S. railroad bonds. The free-wielding, virtually unregulated course of American railroad finance brought gains to the shrewd, but major losses to the unwary. Defaults, as I will show (and have shown), were commonplace. Bond prices fluctuated. Frequently bonds were issued and traded at well below par. Investors repeatedly ignored warnings and were tempted by bonds that were not well secured. Western railroads, in particular, often lacked revenues to pay interest on their accumulating debt, and their bond prices fell.[19] The value of shares was more unstable than that of bonds.[20] The Dutch, especially, took advantage of the ups and downs, looking for "cheap" securities (bonds and stocks) and anticipating appreciation.[21] Some German investors followed the same path, more with bonds than with shares.[22] The English and French seemed less prone to, but not entirely immune from, such speculative behavior.[23]

In considering pre-1875 investments, I outlined some of the difficulties in determining the size of foreign investments in the railroads based on railroad issues in London and on the Continent.[24] The problems of measurement in the mid-1870s were similar to those in 1914.[25] In 1875–1914, however, far more than in prior years, Europeans increasingly traded in already-issued securities, buying from one another or from Americans. Original subscription prices and market prices were typically different. If these were bearer bonds, as was common, or bonds or shares in "street names," it was virtually impossible to trace the holdings.[26] Also railway securities held as collateral for short-term U.S. financing or for "collateral trust bonds" would be released in London or on the Continent as defaults occurred. When this happened, one type of debt became transformed into another; in the first case, short-term credit became long term. This explains, as I noted earlier, why in crisis times long-term foreign investment often increased rather than decreased (at least temporarily).[27] After railroad reorganizations—which were very frequent—one type of security many times replaced another; the student of foreign investment must be careful to avoid double counting.

It is also difficult to establish the nationality of the railroad security owner. In January 1897 a stock exchange act came into effect in Germany, and consequently Germans often bought and sold American railway securities in London, Paris, New York, Amsterdam, or Basle "to escape the German tax on securities." Although such securities were German owned, they usually remained outside the country, for example, in London branches of German banks.[28] Similarly, many British purchases took place in New York, as a convenience.[29] British merchant bankers would, on occasion, buy U.S. railway securities in New York on joint-account with an American agent. The security, a "foreign investment," would be paid for out of other accounts. The railway security, owned in part by the British merchant bank, might never leave the United States.[30]

U.S. railroad securities were acquired and held by many non-U.S. firms. U.S. branches and affiliates of British, German, Russian, Canadian, and other foreign insurance companies, for instance, bought substantial amounts of U.S. railroad bonds, usually purchasing them on Wall Street.[31] These were long-term foreign investments, claims by foreigners on U.S. railroads, but they are likely to be omitted from the tabulations of foreign investments because the transaction took place in the United States and the owner of record had a U.S. address.

Given these and other complications, one must be very cautious about all statistics presented.[32] Table 6.1 gives Cleona Lewis' $4.17 billion estimate of foreign investment in U.S. railroads on July 1, 1914, by nationality.[33] These calculations were at par, not at market value; par in 1914 was generally higher than market.[34] What Lewis' figures reveal in gross terms is the existence of large investments. What is also clear is that of all the foreign investors, the British, with about $2.8 billion invested in U.S. rails, took the lead. Likewise, of particular interest, if these figures are to be trusted, is the relative importance of railroads in the British and French stakes in the United States versus the German and the Dutch holdings.[35] In absolute terms, German, Dutch, and French investments in American railroads in 1914 were about equal (see Table 6.1).[36]

The Course of Foreign Investment in Railroads

The course of foreign investment in U.S. railroads, 1875–1914, was highly erratic. Booms and busts characterized railroad building in America; rate wars were punctuated by agreements; financial performance was volatile. Many foreign investors retreated after the defaults on principal and interest in 1873 and 1874 (by 1876, an estimated

Table 6.1. Foreign investment in U.S. railroads, July 1, 1914

Nationality	Level (millions of U.S. dollars)[a]	Percentage of nationality's total investment in America
British	2,800	66
German	300	32
Dutch	300	47
French	290	71
Canadian	130	47
Central European	70	47
Mexican	3	[b]
Other nationalities	277	66
Total	4,170	59

Source: Cleona Lewis, *America's Stake in International Investments* (Washington, D.C.: Brookings Institution, 1938), p. 546. See also pp. 532–533, on the way Lewis reached the totals. I have calculated the percentages, based on her figures.

[a] Values at par.

[b] Not available.

65 percent of European holdings of American railroad bonds were in default).[37] Then, in the 1880s foreign investors reentered this market, so that in July 1887 *Banker's Magazine,* New York, reported, "It is very certain that Europe in a quiet way has absorbed a large if not the greater part of the bonds recently issued by our railroad corporations."[38] In November 1890 the House of Baring—an important participant in U.S. railroad finance—was near collapse, associated with problems in Argentina; the Baring Crisis created in Great Britain a need for liquidity; as the economist Charles Kindleberger put it, British investors sold good American railroad securities to help carry bad Latin American loans.[39]

In 1891 the Duke of Marlborough wrote: "We have seen so much ruinous speculation in American railways in England . . . At present the foreign investor is practically powerless. He is absolutely ignorant of the Wall Street intrigues."[40] The Panic of 1893 made European investors even more wary. "Yankee Rails," a "favorite medium of speculation in the [London] Stock Exchange" in the 1870s and 1880s, faced "stagnation" in the 1890s;[41] in the mid-1890s, 60 to 70 percent of the capital stock of American railroads was paying no dividends, and key railroads were in receiverships.[42] Nonetheless, one estimate indicates that in this decade, the ratio of the market value of British holdings in U.S. railways to their total capitalization was 15 to 20 percent,[43] and this ignored the Dutch, German, and other foreign investors. Also, at the same time as the numerous failures occurred, some U.S. railroads in the 1890s were very successful investments.[44]

At the turn of the century, the Boer War pulled monies back to the United Kingdom. Interest rates in Britain had become more attractive. Many Britishers, unhappy with their experiences with U.S. railroads, took advantage of the rising prices of these securities in America to sell; and in the railroad mergers of 1899–1902, Americans repurchased securities once held abroad.[45] Table 6.2 indicates the decline in stock holdings by foreign investors in U.S. railroads from the period 1890–1896 to 1905.[46]

Yet by 1907–08, British as well as other foreign interest in U.S. railroads had once more resumed, with $65 million in U.S. railway securities "subscribed" in London in 1907 and $83 million in 1908.[47] By 1910 the year's figure was $110 million.[48] In January 1911 George Paish could write that in "recent years" U.S. railways had met their interest obligations in full and provided satisfactory dividends.[49] The decade before World War I witnessed a revival of foreign investment in American rails. Britishers bought already-issued securities, as well as new issues.

In this pre–World War I decade, the French especially paid new attention to U.S. railroad securities. In 1906 the Pennsylvania Railroad

Table 6.2. Foreign-owned stock in American railroads, 1890–1896, 1905

	Percentage held abroad	
Railroad	1890–1896[a]	1905
Illinois Central	65	21
Pennsylvania	52	19
Louisville and Nashville	75	7
New York, Ontario and Western	58	12
New York Central and Hudson River	37	9
Reading	52	3
Great Northern	33	2
Baltimore and Ohio	21	17
Chicago, Milwaukee and St. Paul	21	6

Source: William Z. Ripley, *Railroads: Finance and Organization* (New York: Longmans, Green, 1915), p. 5.

[a] Although Ripley does not specify what he means by 1890–1896, he seems to have chosen a percentage that was available to him in one of the years between 1890 and 1896.

marketed a $50 million loan in Paris—payable in francs and listed on the Paris Bourse.[50] The following year in Paris, the New York, New Haven, and Hartford Railroad had an issue of debentures for $28 million,[51] and the St. Louis and San Francisco one for $17 million.[52] In 1910 a major loan for the Chicago, Milwaukee and St. Paul was placed in France.[53] By 1914, in addition, Frenchmen had obtained sizable interests in the Southern Pacific, the Union Pacific, the Central Pacific, and the Chesapeake and Ohio.[54] The French—out of the U.S. railroad securities market for many years because of the Memphis, El Paso and Pacific scandal of 1869 (see Chapter 4)—were now back into U.S. railroads on a large scale.[55]

Huge German investments had been made in U.S. railroads, especially in the Northern Pacific, in the late nineteenth century.[56] Early in 1911, the Prussian government—involved in a dispute with the United States over potash (see Chapter 8)—refused to allow the listing of Chicago, Milwaukee and St. Paul bonds on the Berlin exchange.[57] German buyers bought these bonds in Paris or London. German investment in American railroads continued.

Dutch capital flowed into U.S. railroads, especially into midwestern and southwestern ones. Dutch investors had substantial interests in the Missouri, Kansas and Texas; the Chicago and North Western; the Missouri Pacific; and the Denver and Rio Grande.[58] The Amsterdam correspondent for the *Economist* reported in 1913 that "the amount of the higher priced shares, such as the Southern Pacific, Union Pacific, Atchison, Baltimore, Norfolk, Louisville and Nashville" in Dutch hands had dropped. "But faithful to the system generally followed in their dealings in securities," Dutchmen had "acquired large quantities of low-priced shares, which are considered to have prospects, such as Eries, Southern Railway, Rock Islands, Denvers."[59]

The boom in sales of American railway securities in Europe in the years 1906–1913 collapsed in 1913–14 with scandals relating to the financing of both the New York, New Haven and Hartford and the St. Louis and San Francisco railroads.[60] Frenchmen were particularly hurt in this new round of railway defaults.

Writing of the years before 1914, the Harvard economist William Z. Ripley noted:

It is a deplorable feature of European investment—characteristic of several generations of experience—that interest is persistently manifested in speculative rather than conservative investment properties. Foreigners seem unable to learn the lesson that first-class American railway shares are often preferable to the bonds of second or third rate speculative or heavily overcapitalized enterprises; and that a railway bond . . . should be known by the sort of company it keeps.[61]

Table 6.3. British investments in American railroad securities, 1876–1913 (rough estimates)

Year	Level in millions of U.S. dollars
1876	486
1880	486
1881	778
1885	972
1890	1,458
1895	1,458
1898	1,700
1910	2,850
1913	3,000

Source: For the years 1876–1898 (except 1880): Dorothy Adler, *British Investment in American Railways* (Charlottesville: University Press of Virginia, 1970), pp. 166–168. For the year 1880: Robert Lucas Nash, *A Short Inquiry into the Profitable Nature of Our Investments*, 3d ed. (London: Effingham Wilson, 1881), p. 131. For the years 1910, 1913: George Paish, "Great Britain's Capital Investment in Individual Colonial and Foreign Countries," *Journal of the Royal Statistical Society*, 74 (Jan. 1911); reprinted in *British Overseas Investments, 1907–1948*, ed. Mira Wilkins (New York: Arno Press, 1977). Adler's, Nash's, and Paish's figures are given in pounds, which I have translated into dollars at the rate £1 = \$4.86. For the later years, I have rounded the numbers to avoid misleading precision. Adler's figures are at "market value." Paish's are of "capital publicly subscribed."

It may be that by 1913–14 foreign investments in U.S. railway securities had declined from the 1890s level.[62] I doubt it. Some writers noted the repatriations at the turn of the century but failed to realize the sharp rise in sales of U.S. railway securities in Europe in the years 1907–1913. Some records indicate a substantial increase by 1913–14.[63] Table 6.3, which estimates the growth of British holdings in U.S. railroad securities, suggests a continuous rise.[64]

It has been noted that whereas by the early 1890s *controlling* interest (50 percent or more of stocks, not bonds) in key U.S. railroads was held abroad, this was not the case in 1914. It does seem that the five important railroads known to have more than 50 percent of the voting stock owned abroad in the 1890s (as indicated in Table 6.2)—the Illinois Central; the Pennsylvania; the Louisville and Nashville; the New York, Ontario and Western; and the Reading—were not majority owned by foreign investors in 1914.[65] This does not, however, mean a diminution of total investment; large European purchases of bonds—as I have shown—occurred in the years 1907–1913.

Table 6.4 gives Leland Jenks's very rough estimates of foreign investment in U.S. railway securities (stocks and bonds). His estimate that 30 percent of the nominal value of U.S. railroad securities was held abroad in 1914 seems high. In 1914 railroad capital outstanding in the United States was $20.2 billion.[66] If we use Cleona Lewis' foreign investment figure of $4.17 billion in U.S. railroads, this comes to slightly more than one-fifth of U.S. railroad securities held abroad in 1914. (The denominator here is inflated because it includes those securities nominally outstanding as well as those actually outstanding.) The 30 or 20 percent figures for 1914 are, in sum, crude, but whether we choose the greater or the lesser percentage, each approximation reveals a continued formidable foreign involvement.

Particular Railroads

The path of foreign investment in each U.S. railroad differed. Thus during the entire 1870s less than 5 percent of the New York Central and Hudson River Railroad stock was held in Britain. But when William H. Vanderbilt sold his holdings (late 1879–early 1880), British interests rose to 14 percent of the railroad shares (as of September 30, 1880). By 1895 they reached 37 percent, only to drop to 14 percent in 1900 and to 9 percent in 1914. The 37 percent held in Britain in 1895 was an all-time high for this road. These percentages relate only to U.K. investors, not to those on the Continent, and they do not include bond holdings.[67]

The Pennsylvania Railroad, which had long obtained huge sums in Europe, had its own representative in London in the 1880s.[68] In 1871 a mere 7.3 percent of its stock was held by foreign investors; in 1890 this railroad (which took the lead in system building) had over 50 percent of its stock held abroad. The amount would drop sharply, so that in 1914 about $75 million (par value), or 15 percent of the issued shares of the Pennsylvania Railroad, was owned outside the United

Table 6.4. Foreign investment as a percentage of the nominal value of U.S. railroad securities, 1873, 1890, 1914

Year	Percentage
1873	20
1890	33
1914	30

Source: Leland Jenks, "Railroads as an Economic Force in American Development," *Journal of Economics History,* 4 (May 1944): 9; these are rough estimates.

States.[69] The railroad continued to raise substantial monies on European bond markets.[70]

For decades, stocks and bonds of the Erie Railroad were traded in Europe.[71] When in April 1908 it looked as if the Erie would not meet its obligations (for about the fifth time), E. H. Harriman came to the rescue, and James Stillman offered the backing of the National City Bank, New York, since, as he told a friend, "If Erie defaults no American bonds can be sold in Europe."[72]

Not only, or particularly, eastern lines attracted foreign capital. Midwestern roads also continued to seek financing from abroad. The Illinois Central, 79 percent of whose stock—as we have seen—was in the hands of foreign investors by 1873, remained "largely owned by English and Continental" investors until the turn of the century.[73] In 1900 a Dutch syndicate had held a block of 40,000 shares of this railroad for more than thirty years.[74] As noted, the Chicago and North Western attracted Dutch monies.[75]

Jay Gould wanted foreign capital for the Wabash Railroad in 1880–81. Since Britishers had little sympathy with Gould (recalling his skullduggery with the Erie in the early 1870s), Gould used the good offices in London of another railroad, and the Wabash managed to sell in England a "vast" amount of stock and some $11.5 million in general mortgage bonds; but by 1884 it was in receivership, and Britishers were commenting on how few "frauds on earth [there were] so black as that associated with the name Wabash, and few men . . . so black as Mr. Gould himself, the president of this wretched swindle."[76]

In the Southwest, the Atchison, Topeka and Santa Fe came to have as its largest single stockholder in Britain in the 1880s, Baring Brothers.[77] When the promoter Arthur E. Stilwell sought monies for the Kansas City, Pittsburgh and Gulf Railroad after the crisis of 1893, he turned to Dutch sources.[78]

In the fall of 1883, the Deutsche Bank (Berlin) and Jacob Stern of Frankfurt sold nearly half of an $18 million bond issue for the Northern Pacific in Germany.[79] Henry Villard (president of the Northern Pacific from September 1881 to January 1884)[80] became in 1886 the Deutsche Bank's investment adviser in the United States. In the period 1886–1890, he personally placed $64.3 million of German money into American securities; eleven of the twelve enterprises into which these funds were directed were railroads, and the one most favored (with over $22 million) was the Northern Pacific. In the fall of 1887 Villard was back on its board of directors, now acting for the German bankers.[81]

In 1890 James Hill's new Great Northern (formed in 1889) at once sought financing in London. Hill had long looked abroad to finance his railroad projects. Now Baring Brothers agreed to lead a syndicate to take £6 million of St. Paul, Minneapolis and Manitoba Railroad bonds (an associated company), but with Baring's near collapse in November 1890, only £3 million of the bonds were sold.[82] Hill's friends (including important foreign investors) had adequate resources to persevere.

When the Central Pacific was reorganized in 1899, the Southern Pacific was reported to have purchased a majority of the Central Pacific's stock from a London shareholders' committee.[83] German holdings in Southern Pacific Railroad securities in 1899 were said to have a market value of between $15 million and $17 million.[84] The Southern Pacific was second only to the Northern Pacific in attracting German monies.[85]

Between 1884 and 1891, even though the Union Pacific paid no dividends, its stock held in England had mounted, so that in 1891, 185,220 shares were held there, or about one-third of the total.[86] In January 1913 N. M. Rothschild & Sons, London, was handling dividends on 27,375 shares of Union Pacific.[87] In the early twentieth century, Baring Brothers became involved with Union Pacific issues in London.[88]

So too, foreign capital was employed in not only the American Southwest but also throughout the American South. The Baltimore and Ohio, the Alabama Great Southern, the Norfolk and Western, and the Louisville and Nashville railroads, in particular, obtained substantial British investments.[89] In 1879 only 5,000 shares of the Louisville and Nashville Railroad were held by foreign investors.[90] By contrast, in December 1895, 413,764 shares were held in Europe, compared with 114,236 shares in the United States.[91]

This brief overview suggests only some of the more important involvements. An extraordinary number of railroads attracted foreign capital that went into shares as well as into bonds. Railroads in the East, Midwest, Southwest, West, and South needed financial support from abroad.[92] In the fall of 1914, L. F. Loree began a study of the 144 railroads in the United States that were over 100 miles in length, and as of January 31, 1915, he found that 105 of these had foreign investors of record.[93]

Conduits for Foreign Capital

The conduits for the transfer of foreign capital became increasingly efficient, importantly facilitating the international flows. A special section of the London Stock Exchange was devoted to American rails.[94] By 1887 half of the new railroad securities listed in New York were almost simultaneously listed in London.[95] In 1888 the securities of eighty-two American railroads were quoted on the Official List of the London Exchange.[96] Table 6.5 shows the rise in the nominal (face) value of American railway securities quoted on the London Stock Exchange. The more than twentyfold increase over four decades reflects the larger capitalization and borrowings of American railways, the greater availability of these securities to the British public, and the huge amount of capital demanded. Translated at $4.86, the quoted American railroad securities came to $8.4 billion at the close of 1913,[97] or about 42 percent of the entire nominal capitalization of U.S. railroads.[98] These figures in no way reflect the actual British investment—only the availability of traded securities in the London market. It should be noted that many U.S. railroad securities were also traded on British provincial exchanges. The figures do demonstrate the point made by Dorothy Adler: despite the earlier introduction and circulation of U.S. railroad securities in the United Kingdom, it was not until the 1880s that "American railway securities gained substantial popularity in London."[99]

Why were these securities so popular? Michael Edelstein has prepared a "ranking of the anticipated return on U.K.-held debenture capital 1870–1913"; the attraction of U.S. railroads vis-à-vis "conservative" British securities is evident (see Table 6.6). It is interesting to see how the interest-rate gap narrowed. Edelstein attributes "at least some of this relative [and surely absolute as well] decline in U.S. yields to declining risk premiums."[100] When he compared anticipated and actual returns, he found that "both equity and debenture assets of U.S. railways offered very high risk-adjusted returns, confirming the special desirability of U.S. assets" to the British investor.[101]

Table 6.5. Nominal value of American railway securities quoted on the London Stock Exchange, 1873–1913 (in millions of pounds)

Date	Value
Jan. 1, 1873	82.7
Jan. 1, 1883	307.6
Dec. 28, 1893	743.7
Dec. 31, 1903	1,107.5
Dec. 31, 1913	1,729.6

Source: E. Victor Morgan and W. A. Thomas, *The Stock Exchange: Its History and Functions* (London: Etek Books, 1962), pp. 280–281.

In Amsterdam, U.S. railway issues had long been actively traded. Table 6.7 shows the growth of all listings on the Amsterdam exchange (column A),[102] and the special importance of U.S. railroad securities (columns F, H, and I). From 1875 to 1914 the number of U.S. railroad securities quoted in Amsterdam rose from 63 to 194.[103]

In 1872 thirty-five U.S. railways listed their securities on the Frankfurt Bourse. In 1904 the number was sixty-nine.[104] U.S. rails were listed on the Berlin, Paris, Geneva, Zurich, Basle, Brussels, and Antwerp exchanges. Some American railway bonds were denominated in dollars. Other U.S. railways issued sterling bonds, especially for the British market.[105] Securities offered in London and on the Continent were sold in the national currencies (with bankers arranging the foreign exchange transactions). U.S. railroad securities were available in Europe in a form that encouraged their sale. Thus, for example, the coupons on the $1,000 first-mortgage bonds of the Denver and Rio Grande were payable to the bearer as $35 in New York, £7 4s 5d in London, or 86 florins in Amsterdam.[106] In many cases railroad bond coupons were stamped with a guarantee on the rate of exchange.[107]

Financial houses in Britain and on the Continent saw to it that buyers of railroad securities never worried about foreign exchange or about collecting dividends or interest across borders. Everything could be done at home. Railroads traded in London had London bankers who handled such matters. The process was routine. London stockbrokers sold U.S. rails as readily and as easily as they sold any British security.[108] Similarly, the Dutch administrative offices made the purchase and sale as well as the collection of dividends and interest on American securities as simple for the Dutch investor as dealing in domestic paper.

In these years American railroad men used U.S. and foreign financial intermediaries to assist in raising monies. In Chapter 4 I discussed the rise of new banking houses. By the late 1870s seven international

Table 6.6. Anticipated return on debentures held by U.K. investors, 1870–1913 (in percentages)

Debenture	1870–1879	1880–1889	1890–1893	1900–1913
U.S. rails	6.50	5.20	4.25	3.75
British rails	4.00	3.50	3.00	3.50
British consols	3.25	3.00	2.75	3.00

Source: Based on Michael Edelstein, *Overseas Investment in the Age of High Imperialism* (New York: Columbia University Press, 1982), pp. 94–95. Note that the years specified are not uniform.

Table 6.7. Securities on the Amsterdam Exchange, 1875–1914

	(A)	(B)	(C)	(D)	(E)	(F)	(G)	(H)	(I)
		U.S. securities quoted		All railroad securities quoted (U.S. and non-U.S.)		U.S. railroad securities quoted			
	Total number of securities quoted		As percentage of total		As percentage of total		As percentage of total securities	As percentage of railroad securities	As percentage of U.S. securities
Year	(U.S. and non-U.S.) Number	Number	(B/A)	Number	(D/A)	Number	(F/A)	(F/D)	(F/B)
1875	238	78	33%	110	46%	63	26%	57%	81%
1885	432	106	24	175	40	98	23	56	92
1890	611	141	23	238	39	123	20	52	87
1895	782	173	22	284	36	150	19	53	87
1900	1010	166	16	275	27	147	14	53	88
1905	1253	190	15	306	24	168	13	55	88
1910	1471	254	17	320	22	185	12	58	73
1914	1796	302	17	328	18	194	11	59	64

Source: Based on K. D. Bosch, *Nederlandse Beleggingen in de Verenigde Staten* (Amsterdam: Uitgeversmaatschappij Elsevier, 1948), p. 139.

firms stood out in the negotiation of U.S. railroad securities, although numerous others participated. These acted as managing houses and as group participants. Three of the seven had American headquarters and London houses: Brown Brothers; Morton, Bliss & Co.; and J. & W. Seligman & Co.[109] Four were European based with American associates: J. S. Morgan & Co., London (associated with Drexel, Morgan & Co., New York); Baring Brothers, London (just beginning its close alliance with Kidder, Peabody in Boston); the Rothschilds, London, Paris, and Frankfurt (represented in New York by August Belmont & Co.); and Lazard Speyer-Ellissen, Frankfurt (interconnected with Speyer & Co., New York, and Speyer Brothers, London).[110] Perhaps I should add Hallgarten & Co.—an American house—to this list.[111] As the historian of one of these houses put it, "Just as Morton, Bliss & Company handled securities trading on the New York exchange for Morton, Rose & Company, so the London firm handled trading for the New York firm in London."[112] The cable meant that transactions could be done swiftly in any market.

Whereas in the twenty-five years prior to 1875, established European banking firms had handled American railways (some with caution, others less so), in the period 1875–1914 every major "investment" banker in Europe had an interest in U.S. railroad securities. As Stanley Chapman points out, in Britain merchant banks; joint-stock, international, and imperial banks; discount houses; stockbrokers; and trusts were all involved in American railroad issues.[113] Writing in April 1883, the British economist R.H. Inglis Palgrave commented: "The [American] railway undertakings floated in this country [England] by houses such as Barings, Brown, Shipley, and Company [Brown Brothers' British house], the Rothschilds and firms of a similar character have usually been prosperous. Such houses have reputation to lose and they may be expected to be careful not to imperil it." He continued:

There is considerable moral fibre in the United States, and it would be difficult to find higher examples of business qualities than among its first-rate men. There are many intermediary houses of first rate standing, whether purely American, like Maitland, Phelps and Company; Kuhn, Loeb and Company; or Anglo-American, like Speyer Brothers and Speyer and Company, J. and W. Seligman and Company and Seligman Brothers, J. S. Morgan and Company and Drexel Morgan and Company. It would be extremely easy to multiply these names, but enough has been said to show that there is ample opportunity for transactions [in American railroads] on a satisfactory basis.[114]

Drexel, Morgan & Co. (after 1895, J. P. Morgan & Co.) in New York and J. S. Morgan & Co. (after 1910, Morgan, Grenfell & Co.) in London came to lead in handling U.S. railroad securities.[115] J. P.

Morgan had sold W. H. Vanderbilt's New York Central stock in England in 1879–80 and that railroad's securities abroad in subsequent years. By the late 1880s and especially in the 1890s, he developed a reputation for his skill in reorganizing U.S. railroads and in dealing with foreign bondholders and stockholders in the process.[116]

The International Financial Society, R. Raphael & Sons, Stern Brothers, Robert Benson & Co., and C. J. Hambro & Son were among the numerous London firms that marketed new issues of U.S. railroad securities.[117] In Paris there was the Morgan house of Drexel, Harjes & Co.[118] Munroe & Co., Paris, and John Munroe & Co., New York, also advised Frenchmen on U.S. railroads, as did that bank's knowledgeable partner, Edward Tuck.[119]

Others active in U.S. railroad finance included the Erlangers from Frankfurt and Paris, who had established a London branch in 1870.[120] J. S. Kennedy & Co. and its successor, J. Kennedy Tod & Co., in New York, acted for Dutch bankers in connection with James J. Hill's railroads; that firm also served as the New York agent for the Scottish American Investment Company, Ltd., a trust that was a large investor in U.S. railroads.[121] Winslow, Lanier & Co., an American house, was associated with Glyn, Mills, Currie & Co. (London) and Hottinguer & Co. (Paris).[122] Winslow, Lanier & Co. had long been involved in U.S. railroad finance.

Many Dutch banking institutions had acquired special competence in American railroads. Hope & Co. remained important. So did Wertheim & Gompertz, Adolph Boissevain & Co., and Broes & Gosman. Earlier the Dutch had devised so-called administrative bureaus that greatly facilitated Dutch investment in U.S. railroads.[123] The Boissevain family in Amsterdam and London were connected with Blake Brothers in New York and Boston, which in turn worked closely with the Speyer houses.

By the 1880s the Deutsche Bank, Berlin, and Jacob Stern, Frankfurt, handled large quantities of U.S. railroad securities.[124] The Dresdner Bank and Disconto-Gesellschaft were likewise significant as German "distributing mediums" for American issues.[125] Kuhn, Loeb & Co., founded in New York in 1867, had become an active marketer of U.S. rails abroad by the 1880s.[126] Kuhn, Loeb & Co. and M. M. Warburg & Co., Hamburg, were united in business ventures, as well as through a number of intermarriages.[127] In London Sir Ernest Cassel and in Paris Edouard Noetzlin (of the Banque de Paris et Pays Bas) collaborated with Kuhn, Loeb's senior partner, Jacob Schiff.[128] Kuhn, Loeb also dealt in rail issues jointly with Crédit Suisse in Zurich and the Bankverein in Basle.[129] The latter was a large distributor and subscriber to the best underwritings.[130] Lombard, Odier & Cie. in

Geneva similarly handled U.S. "railroad bonds of the better class."[131] The Boston house of Lee, Higginson & Co.—important in U.S. railroad issues—opened a London house in 1906.[132] And so it went. On the larger issues, syndications became the norm.

In 1912 Frederick A. Cleveland and F. W. Powell, in a book on railroad finance, listed the seven "great" financial interests engaged in U.S. railroad consolidations: (1) J. P. Morgan (with houses in London and Paris); (2) J. J. Hill (with ties with Baring Brothers); (3) Jacob Schiff of Kuhn, Loeb, "representing strong financial interests in Germany" (actually its European contacts were not confined to Germany); (4) W. K. Vanderbilt [133] (allied with Morgan and his international connections); (5) George J. Gould[134] (without banking associations until 1908, when he began to rely on Kuhn, Loeb); (6) W. H. and J. H. Moore (who used Speyer & Co. and its English and German houses); and (7) the Pennsylvania Railroad (H. C. Frick; Cleveland and Powell simply presumed everyone knew about its ability to arrange large bond sales abroad).[135]

By 1913 American and European banking houses had had decades of cooperation in raising the vast sums required for U.S. railroads. By that year the five principal U.S.-headquartered international banking houses were the three New York ones: J. P. Morgan; Kuhn, Loeb; and Speyer; and the two Boston ones: Kidder, Peabody and Lee, Higginson. All were prominent in underwriting and placing U.S. railroad securities at home and abroad, and all did business in close association with bankers in Europe.[136] Briefly below and in more detail in Chapter 13, I will add data on the European-based bankers. I must emphasize, however, that by 1913–14 there was the active role of the U.S.-headquartered investment banks in directing the sales of American railroad securities domestically and in Europe; America had its own banking infrastructure well connected with houses located across the Atlantic.

In London a network of bankers remained highly au courant on U.S. railroads. In 1905 a star-studded "finance" committee was appointed to the King's Hospital Fund to administer a large donation of U.S. railroad securities. The administrators, recommended by the knowledgeable donor of the securities,[137] were:

1. Hugh Colin Smith (1836–1910). Smith had been the governor of the Bank of England, 1897–1899; in 1905 he was a director of the bank and on the important Committee of the Treasury. His son, Vivian Hugh Smith, was a partner in J. S. Morgan & Co. The Bank of England provided accommodations and banking services to the King Edward's Hospital Fund.[138]

2. Lord Rothschild (Nathaniel Mayer Rothschild, 1840–1915). His firm had long participated in American investment, was active in U.S. "rails," and received regular reports and advice from August Belmont & Co., New York, on railroad matters.[139]

3. Lord Revelstoke (John Baring, 1863–1929, the second Lord Revelstoke, as of 1897). The House of Baring had more than a century of experience in Anglo-American business; it had its own adviser (G. S. Morison) to report on individual U.S. railroads.[140] In 1885–86 John Baring had spent several months in the United States. Lord Revelstoke was a director of the Bank of England from 1898 to 1929.[141]

4. Sir Ernest Cassel (1852–1921). A Cologne-born banker, resident in London, and naturalized British subject, Sir Ernest had begun his British banking career in 1870 as a clerk with Bischoffsheim & Goldschmidt, a firm that in the early 1870s was associated with the Atlantic and Great Western and the Erie railroads. Cassel was a close friend of Jacob Schiff of Kuhn, Loeb. In 1884 Cassel had left Bischoffsheim & Goldschmidt to act on his own. (By then he was a wealthy man, having made a personal fortune when he acquired Swedish rights to the Thomas-Gilchrist process in 1882). In 1884, with Kuhn, Loeb, he had participated in the reorganization of the Louisville and Nashville Railroad. By 1910 Sir Ernest Cassel would be described as a representative of "Harriman interests" in London. His international contacts were extensive.[142]

5. Robert Fleming (1845–1933). Fleming was a pioneer in Scottish investment trusts. He was frequently in the United States and from the mid-1870s onward served on numerous U.S. railroad reorganization committees. By 1900 he had moved his residence from Dundee, Scotland, to London, where he became a consultant on U.S. investments, particularly those in U.S. railroads. Like Sir Ernest Cassel, Fleming was an intimate friend of Jacob Schiff. Between 1901 and 1909 Fleming's "participations" in American railway securities came to almost $34 million.[143]

Lord Rothschild, Lord Revelstoke, Sir Ernest Cassel, and Robert Fleming ranked at the pinnacle of the many in Edwardian London who were extraordinarily well versed on U.S. railroad finance. They talked and listened to one another. Hugh Colin Smith knew virtually everyone in London financial circles.

Categories of Foreign Investors in U.S. Railroads

Foreign investors in American railroads in the period 1875–1914 can be divided into three basic categories: (1) individuals; (2) nonrailroad companies, including merchant and commercial banks, trusts, insurance offices, and industrials; and (3) railroad companies.[144] In general, only in the last case were there pyramided (or foreign) boards of directors; in the first two cases, the board of directors and the management of the American railroad were located in the United States.[145]

Foreign individuals (the first category) generally bought—normally through stockbrokers—American railroad securities listed on stock exchanges in London, other British cities, Amsterdam, Paris, Berlin, Frankfurt, elsewhere in Europe, Montreal, Toronto, or New York.[146] These could be new issues or existing ones. Foreign individuals also obtained U.S. railroad securities that were privately placed by banks. They came to own railroad shares and bonds through gifts and legacies (this was often the case with women investors).[147] On occasion, individual investors participated directly in U.S. railroad activities, obtaining their securities as a result of that involvement.[148] Individuals' holdings changed as railroads substituted one security for another (in reorganizations), as bonds matured and were redeemed or refunded, and as sales and purchases were made. Most individual investors were not "speculators," stock traders, or manipulators, because they were not close enough to the American market.[149]

The historian Harry Pierce describes foreign owners of the New York Central and Hudson River Railroad stocks as "just ordinary Englishmen who purchased the securities as long-term investments."[150] A study of the 6,526 stockholders in the Illinois Central in 1900 found that they held 599,948 shares; of these owners, 2,543 (or 39 percent) were resident in Great Britain and held 198,616 shares (or 33 percent of the shares outstanding). The average British holding was 78 shares.[151]

Dutch investors in bonds of the First Division of the St. Paul and Pacific Railroad (some $11 million worth, par value) in 1875 comprised "over 600 individuals, nearly all of whom are persons of moderate circumstances—small farmers and trades people, who believed they were investing their savings in a reliable American enterprise."[152] The Alien Property Custodian (in 1919) noted that many pre–World War I private investments in U.S. rails were of modest proportions, held by individuals living in Germany.[153] Individual Canadians, similarly, invested in U.S. railroad stocks and bonds. The general pattern of these personal investments appears to have been that of widely spread foreign ownership.

When this dispersion existed, the individual foreign stockholder (or bondholder) had no power to influence management, much less to exercise control. Yet, as defaults occurred, these investors—stockholders and bondholders—came to be represented by "protective committees" (frequently as part of a receivership process). The issuing house that had marketed the securities often felt that its name and reputation were at stake and tried to aid the investor to obtain resumption of interest or dividend payments and to push for higher dividends.

The Barings, for example, assisted English bondholders in the Eastern Railroad in Massachusetts. In December 1876 the Baring representative in the United States (S. G. Ward) wrote to Joseph Hickson, general manager of the Grand Trunk, "You may have heard that Messrs. Baring having formerly negotiated Bonds of the Eastern Railroad in Massachusetts which got in trouble last year, very honorably undertook to make good the loss of interest to holders in England, amounting to large sums." Ward added that because the Barings had an interest in the success of the Eastern Railroad, they were concerned with its relations with the Grand Trunk. Hickson replied in a friendly manner.[154] The correspondence also reveals the limits of London's interest. Hickson mentioned casually that he was going to England. Ward did not suggest that he visit the Barings in London.[155]

In 1876 Robert Fleming acted on behalf of the British bondholders in the Erie Railroad and insisted on effective control of the management of that road by the "real owners"—the bondholders.[156] In 1877 the Illinois Central, which had been paying 10 percent (1865–1873) and 8 percent (1874–1876), reduced its annual dividend to 4 percent. European shareholders appointed a committee to investigate and to demand an increase.[157]

Over the years numerous protective committees were organized in England, Holland, and Germany, far more than before 1875. They intervened on many occasions on behalf of individual investors to restructure financially troubled U.S. lines and to raise dividends.[158] There were separate committees for shareholders and bondholders, and even for different classes of bondholders.[159] As Dorothy Adler has noted of the British committees, they did not leave all practical matters to American managers: "When it came to reorganizations, the representatives of the British investors were . . . taking a very active part in the formulation of plans . . . In the 1880's, default was no sooner announced than British representatives were on their way to the United States."[160] English banking houses often took the initiative in forming protective committees and in arranging for the installation of new directors for the U.S. railroads.[161]

In 1884 the English Association of American Bond and Shareholders, Ltd., was formed principally to deal with financial problems related to U.S. railroad securities. It obtained proxies to vote the shares of individual holders. The association became an organizer of protective committees and in time took part in the reorganization of railroads such as the Wabash; the St. Louis and Pacific; the Denver and Rio Grande; the Texas and Pacific; the Cincinnati, Washington and Baltimore; the Ohio and Mississippi; and the Missouri, Kansas and Texas.[162] In 1887 English shareholders formed a committee to represent their interests in the Pennsylvania Railroad Company; they wanted larger dividends.[163] When the Chicago, St. Paul and Kansas City Railway (CSPKC) was in difficulty in the early 1890s, John S. Gilliat, a director and formerly the governor of the Bank of England and managing partner in J. K. Gilliat & Co., was a leading member of the British protective committee sent over for the reorganization.[164] In 1894 William Lidderdale, a director and formerly the governor of the Bank of England, was chairman of the London Finance Committee of the successor to the CSPKC, the Chicago Great Western.[165]

Dutch banking houses normally had ongoing relationships with individual Dutch investors, holding their railroad securities, concentrating ownership and control, and providing representation for them in U.S. railroad reorganizations.[166] Thus a handful of Dutch banking firms acted for the individual Dutch investors in the St. Paul and Pacific Railroad. These Dutch bankers worked through the New York banking house of J. S. Kennedy & Co.[167]

In 1876 H. J. de Marez Oyens of Oyens & Co. was in charge of an "administrative office for American railroad securities in Holland." When Morton, Bliss & Co. and its London house, Morton, Rose & Co., were in that year "rescuing foreign bondholders" in the Gilman, Clinton and Springfield Railroad and bringing that railroad into the Illinois Central, Oyens actively participated.[168] In March 1883 "the Administration of American Railroad Securities" in Amsterdam— holders on behalf of individual Dutch investors of a large block of Louisville and Nashville securities—demanded that a director be elected to that railroad board to represent their interests.[169] W. F. Whitehouse of New York was elected. In 1884 Milton H. Smith, the new president of the Louisville and Nashville Railroad, "dared not act [in his reorganization] without full support from foreign interests." The reference was to both Dutch and British interests. Individual English stockholders had likewise sent a man to act on their behalf.[170] In 1884–85 a representative of Dutch investors, along with those of British securities owners, participated in the reorganization of the New York, Ontario and Western and joined that railroad board.[171] In 1885 the Administratiekantoor van Hubrecht, Van Harencarspel and Vas Visser became concerned with the management of the Florida Central.[172] When the Erie was reorganized after a receivership in 1886, "negotiations . . . [were] conducted direct with Amsterdam."[173]

In the spring of 1888, a Dutch committee installed a new management for the Missouri, Kansas and Texas Railroad.[174]

One English participant in the reorganization of the Denver and Rio Grande (some years later) described procedures. A group of eight had gathered in London: "We chose a chairman. He was a gentleman of high position and much principle. His morality was of great use to us throughout our deliberation. No local interest was represented at our meeting." The group decided that the American president of the railroad had to be removed: "*He* must have nothing more to do with the road, nor would we ever under any circumstances seek *his* advice."

"Put the knife in deep." The phrase was used by one of our numbers who had acquired a semi-professional reputation in such work as ours [Robert Fleming?]. He was from a district in Scotland notorious for much, but especially for a tendency towards investments which yield a high rate of interest and from which is expected the very maximum of security . . . "Put the knife in deep." We who were new to the work wondered what the oracular phrase imported. It was revealed to us that it meant two things—cutting the railroad bonds in half and slicing off some of the branch railroad lines.

This Englishman later felt that to cut off the branch lines was to wound the system and that the British experts who visited the lines made "crude" suggestions and their information was "sadly partial."

We were all capable of managing our own businesses, but none of us had experience of the affairs of which we had assumed control . . . Certainly we managed to cripple the future of the line most successfully . . .

There was a New York committee and a Paris committee [he probably meant an Amsterdam committee, although there could have been a Paris one as well] for foreign bondholders—committees of stockholders, of holders of income bonds, car trusts, and junior securities generally. We gave in to them all, one after another . . . We blustered bravely, but always came to their terms in the end for the sake of peace . . . All this consumed a lot of time and a great deal of money . . .

Thus our line was reorganized . . . The last thing we dealt with was our own remuneration . . . We were accountable to no one, and there was a considerable sum in our hands, the relic of the assessment on the stock. We left the matter to our chairman. He dealt admirably by us, and if talents were never more unwisely exercised they were certainly never more redundantly rewarded.[175]

Other actions of overseas investors' representatives were equally unhelpful. Thus, for example, in 1892, when foreign stockholders were dissatisfied with Gould's leadership of the Union Pacific, an Amsterdam group sought his ouster, but the Gould slate won (by 10,000 votes), because an unidentified London banking house broke ranks and delivered its proxies to an American firm friendly to Gould![176]

In 1893, when the Union Pacific once again went into receivership, A. A. H. Boissevain of Amsterdam was on the reorganization committee; an American lawyer, Victor Morawetz, represented a Dutch committee whose constituents held substantial amounts of seven different issues.[177]

That British, Dutch, or German committees participated in U.S. railroad reorganizations did not necessarily mean the installation of Britishers or Dutchmen or Germans in management or even on the boards. Thus a report for the Amsterdam committee in the reorganization of the Denver and Rio Grande (1885) advocated both a financial and a managerial reorganization: "The custom of appointing most, if not all of the directors out of persons who live thousands of miles away from the property . . . ought to be discontinued," wrote T. H. A. Tromp of the Dutch committee. Tromp argued in favor of the selection of men who lived in "the neighborhood of the property."[178] The Dutch, in fact, typically delegated authority to Americans.

German banks with their own investments in American railroads acted for individual German bondholders when there were defaults and difficulties. With their large holdings in American railroads, Germans formed protective committees and had their own spokesmen. Francis Edwin Hyde argues that the German investors in the Oregon and California Railroad, 1876–1880, for example, exercised substantial, albeit short-lived, influence.[179] In 1889, when the St. Louis, Arkansas and Texas Railroad defaulted, Hallgarten & Co. and Speyer & Co. represented German bondholders. Ultimately an American lawyer went to Germany to negotiate the railroad reorganization.[180] By far the most important German involvements were with the reorganization of the Northern Pacific (discussed further below). In sum, although foreign stockholders and bondholders might have invested modest sums (individually), often protective committees, after there were difficulties, represented them in American matters.[181]

By contrast, some individual foreign investors had personal U.S. railroad holdings that were large enough to give them the possibility of having direct influence on American railroad policies. One such man was George Smith (1808–1899), a Scot who had made his money in real estate and banking in the American Midwest and then took up residence in the London Reform Club in 1861, where he lived for the remainder of his long life. Smith invested much of his own wealth in U.S. railroad securities. After 1866 he did not return to the United States, but he had American representatives watching over his holdings in the Chicago, Milwaukee and St. Paul (in the late nineteenth century, possibly some $20 million in stocks and bonds) and in the

Chicago, Burlington and Quincy. As a consequence of his large interests, he had at least one man on the board of directors of these railroads from the mid-1870s to the time of his death. In 1877 we find him introducing "Alex" Mitchell, president of the Chicago, Milwaukee and St. Paul, to Baring Brothers. His biographer writes of Smith as knowing "as much as anyone could know about the future of American railroad stocks."[182] She tells us that his estate was valued at $52 million, apparently largely invested in U.S. railroad securities. He was one of England's wealthiest men.[183] With the exception of the introduction of Mitchell and some very specific interventions (for example, on the terms of payment on a particular contract),[184] George Smith—his multimillion-dollar holdings notwithstanding—seems to have been simply a distant owner, a collector of dividends and interest. It is hard to perceive his hand in any major decision.

It was a different matter with two other giant individual foreign investors, also Scots by birth. They played important roles. Donald A. Smith (1820–1914),[185] who became Lord Strathcona and Mount Royal, and his cousin George Stephen (1829–1921), who became Lord Mount Stephen, had both separately migrated to Canada at a young age; they did not meet until 1866. In time both men moved back to Britain and each died in England. In August 1901 Lord Strathcona's share holdings—at market value—in the Great Northern Railroad alone (he owned securities of other U.S. railroads as well) came to $9.7 million, while Lord Mount Stephen's shares (held by various trusts) in the same railroad were valued at that time at $9 million.[186]

George Stephen was the president of the Bank of Montreal in the years 1876–1881. He arranged that the bank provide some $700,000 in seed money in 1878–79 that gave James J. Hill his start in railways. Stephen and Donald Smith added their own monies. Stephen was never a passive investor in Hill's railways.[187] Hill's papers contain several hundred letters from Stephen.[188] Stephen knew railways. He was the founding president of the Canadian Pacific Railway (1881–1888); after he left Canada to settle in England (in the 1890s), he continued to support Hill's projects.

On October 18, 1894, Stephen, by now Lord Mount Stephen, cabled Hill from London that he had met with Georg von Siemens, chairman of the Supervisory Board of the Deutsche Bank, who was in the process of trying to salvage the large German investment in the Northern Pacific. Georg von Siemens headed a German bondholders' committee.[189] Lord Mount Stephen recommended the unification of the Northern Pacific and the Great Northern under James Hill.[190] Hill was enthusiastic, having been thinking along the same lines;[191] plans were made and revised; finally in August 1896, at a London meeting,

J. P. Morgan (who was by this time handling the reorganization of the Northern Pacific), James Hill, Lord Mount Stephen, and Deutsche Bank director Arthur von Gwinner agreed that "GN and NP shall form a permanent alliance."[192]

When there was a misunderstanding of the accord, Gaspard Farrer (a partner in H. S. Lefevre & Co. and soon to become a director of Baring Brothers) wrote Lord Mount Stephen (May 1, 1900) to ask von Gwinner whether

> he thinks it reasonable to suppose that Mr. [James J.] Hill, Lord Strathcona, and yourselves would at a critical financial time have subscribed large cash funds and otherwise assisted passively and actively to prevent dismemberment of the Northern Pacific system and to rehabilitate its finance for the sake of that degree of control which the Great Northern today possesses.[193]

This is hardly a record of a correspondence relating to disinterested investors—either British or German.

In 1900, finally, the way was open for Hill to obtain control of the Northern Pacific.[194] Then E. H. Harriman and the Union Pacific, in a dramatic move, sought to capture that prize (May 1901). Hill's London friends—principally Lord Mount Stephen and Lord Strathcona—rallied behind him. As Hill later (December 1901) wrote: "So great was the effort to get this control [by Harriman] that one of my friends in London, who owned two millions of Northern Pacific common, was offered and refused fourteen million dollars for his stock."[195] After 1900–01, as Hill's plans materialized for the new Northern Securities Company (which would be formed in 1901), the Germans moved into a subsidiary role. Lord Mount Stephen, however, followed developments carefully. By 1902 one-fifth of the capital of Northern Securities was owned in Europe.[196] I do not know how much was held by Lord Mount Stephen, but his holdings were substantial. In short, Lord Mount Stephen had a major part in Hill's railroad developments. He gave Hill loyalty and ideas on policy; Hill ran the railroads.[197] In 1908 E. H. Harriman wrote of Lord Mount Stephen, "He is exceptionally endowed with fairmindedness and common sense. Most other foreigners only look to the dividends paid without knowing anything of the difficulties or giving them a thought."[198]

Donald Smith (Lord Strathcona and Mount Royal) was also important.[199] Smith had joined the Hudson's Bay Company (HBC) in Canada at the age of eighteen (in 1838) and had spent the next decades as a fur trader in Labrador, saving and investing his earnings and becoming a wealthy man. His latest biographer, Alastair Sweeny, describes him as "an HBC man to the end."[200] In 1870 Smith became the chief commissioner of the Hudson's Bay Company; that year he met Hill, in whose ventures he involved Stephen.[201] The historian of the Great Northern, Muriel Hidy, notes that Smith had a "vital interest in the completion of rails from Minnesota to St. Boniface" in Manitoba.[202] He backed Hill with his own monies and with the share fund of the HBC traders and factors that he managed.[203] Smith took part (in a subordinate role) with Stephen in the development of the Canadian Pacific, held political office, was a vice president of the Bank of Montreal in 1882–1887, president in 1887–1905, and "honorary president" in 1905–1914; for forty-seven years he was a director of the Bank of Montreal and the controlling shareholder for most of that time.[204] In 1889 Smith was named governor of the Hudson's Bay Company (the senior position) and in 1896 was appointed Canadian High Commissioner in London, a post he held until his death.

While in London, Smith (now Lord Strathcona and Mount Royal) was active in encouraging emigration to the Dominion and served on numerous corporate boards (he was from 1909 to 1914 chairman of the Anglo-Persian Oil Company).[205] Strathcona died in 1914, and his estate showed that he held $6.6 million in Great Northern shares, $3.4 million in Northern Pacific shares, and an additional $2 million in the Southern, the Burlington, the Atchison, Topeka and Santa Fe, the New York Central, and other American railroads.[206] Yet, the next year, James Hill would call him "a strong and able man" who "knew little about and had little to do with railroading."[207] After his initial highly entrepreneurial role in American railroad matters (in the 1870s), Smith seems, in the main, to have deferred to George Stephen, following his cousin's wise advice while at the same time investing his vast personal resources in ways that supported Hill's plans. There is evidence that the hitherto published literature has substantially understated Strathcona's importance. Hill's comments on Lord Strathcona must be taken literally. Clearly Donald Smith did not on a sustained basis participate in railroad management or in strategy determination, but from a financial standpoint his contribution was formidable.[208]

Other individuals in Britain, on the Continent, and in Canada had multimillion-dollar investments in U.S. railroads;[209] none, to my knowledge, had as influential a role as the two cousins.[210] Most individual foreign investors in U.S. railroad securities did look at dividends and interest and, especially in the case of Dutch investors, at capital gains. Most did not expect or desire to be consulted or to exercise influence, much less control, although as I have shown, when satisfactory returns were not forthcoming, they turned to protective committees and to placing their "representatives" on American railroad boards. Lord Mount Stephen and Lord Strathcona were highly atypical, both in the size of their holdings and in their attention to policy in good times as well as bad.

The second of our categories of foreign investors in American railroads is the nonrailroad company. Merchant and investment banks presented railroad securities to the public, held securities on behalf of individual investors, and also owned some on their own account. Sometimes these banks kept securities to maintain a market, sometimes as investments, and sometimes because they could not dispose of an issue. On occasion they held on to the securities because they had loaned money directly to a railroad; the railroad's bonds were collateral for the bank loan.

An 1883 stockholder list for the Atchison, Topeka and Santa Fe showed Baring Brothers as the owner of record of 22,300 shares.[211] A historian of that railroad indicates that in 1888 Baring's holdings were still 22,300 shares.[212] The firm was the largest single shareholder. Over the years the Rothschilds had large interests in U.S. railroads, sometimes on their own account and sometimes on joint-account with August Belmont & Co.[213] The Deutsche Bank, Berlin, was a sizable owner of American rails. Dutch houses held securities, as noted, on behalf of individual investors and on their own account.

Many foreign commercial banks purchased U.S. railroads as investments. The Bank of Montreal had almost $2 million in U.S. railroad bonds in its portfolio, 1889–90.[214] Stephen Randall found that to operate in Puerto Rico the Royal Bank of Canada and the Bank of Nova Scotia were required to deposit American securities as indication of the banks' reliability, and they used U.S. railroad bonds for this purpose.[215] In 1908 the Bank of Nova Scotia owned $3.1 million worth of U.S. railroad bonds (40 percent of its total investment portfolio that year was in U.S. railroad bonds).[216]

Likewise, English and Scottish commercial banks, especially in the early twentieth century, typically owned U.S. railroad bonds. C. A. E. Goodhart provides excellent material on the American railway bonds in the investment portfolios of the Metropolitan Bank of England and Wales and of the Union Bank of London, Ltd., and its successor, the Union Bank of London and Smiths, Ltd. Geoffrey Jones found U.S. railroads included in the 1913–14 investment ledgers of the Imperial Bank of Persia (a British-owned bank).[217] Banks on occasion obtained U.S. railroad securities through defaults. Thus the City of Glasgow Bank had accepted American railway securities as collateral on a domestic loan; when the borrower defaulted, the bank had become a major investor.[218]

Large British stockbrokers, who sometimes acted in bank syndicates, owned U.S. rails on their own account.[219] So, too, British promoters dealt in U.S. rails; H. Osborne O'Hagan's City of London Contract Corporation, for example, participated in the sale of the Chicago, Hammond and Western Railroad to the Chicago Junction Railways and Union Stock Yards Company in 1897;[220] in the process it was owner for a short time.

Even more important, Scottish and English investment trust companies bought and held huge quantities of U.S. railroad securities. For example, in 1913 the Scottish American Investment Company, Ltd., alone had £4.1 million in American investments, in the main U.S. railroad bonds.[221]

British insurance companies were among the large holders of U.S. rails. The Scottish Widow's Fund and Life Assurance Society, for instance, acquired some £1.5 million of American railway gold mortgage bonds in the early 1890s, and the Commercial Union held about £700,000 in American railroad securities in 1900. In 1914 Prudential Assurance Company, Ltd., had major interests in U.S. railway bonds.[222] *Best's Insurance Reports of 1914* contain the stock and bond portfolios of most branches and affiliates of foreign insurance companies in the United States; I counted for that year eighty-nine such U.S. branches and affiliates,[223] which owned (as of December 1913) railroad securities equal to roughly $110 million, market value.[224]

Not only foreign banks, investment trusts, and insurance companies acquired American railroad securities, but British industrial enterprises in the late nineteenth and early twentieth centuries also invested. W. D. & H. O. Wills, leaders in the British tobacco industry, had by the 1880s a portfolio of securities that included the Pennsylvania Railroad and the Indianapolis Railway.[225] The British glassmaker Pilkington had in 1914 an investment portfolio of £342,000, of which £81,000, or fully 24 percent, was represented by nine American railways, with the largest interests in the Buffalo and Lake Huron (£21,000) and the Illinois Central (£15,000).[226]

The "Shell" Transport and Trading Company, Ltd., owned American railway "short notes" and some long-term American railroad bonds. Its railway securities in 1913 included those of the Union Pacific, the Chesapeake and Ohio, the Pennsylvania Railroad, and the New York Central. At year-end 1914—by market value—its £199,397 stake in American railroads came to about 19 percent of "Shell" Transport and Trading's investment portfolio.[227] These were parent company investments, not those of Shell's affiliates in the United States; they had no operating connection with Shell's far larger direct investments in the American oil industry. Similarly, Burmah Oil Company, Ltd., had American railroad securities in its investment portfolio in 1913: bonds of the Kansas City Southern, the Southern Pacific, and the Chesapeake and Ohio. Most of its U.S. holdings were in gold bonds, with coupons of about 4 to 5 percent; U.S. rails represented about 15 percent (£74,258) of the firm's portfolio. Unlike Shell, it had no direct investments in the United States.[228]

So too, in 1914, in the portfolio of the British retailer Home and Colonial Stores (which also had no business operations in America) were securities of the New York, New Haven and Hartford; the Chicago, Milwaukee and St. Paul; the Southern Pacific; and the Baltimore and Ohio.[229] Individually, each of these sample portfolio investments in American railroads of Wills, Pilkington, Shell, Burmah Oil, and Home and Colonial Stores came to little (the amounts for the most part were too small for us to monitor), but when one adds up the thousands of industrial and retailing firms in Britain, such totals accumulate. The evidence suggests that most medium and large companies in Britain that had investment portfolios owned some American railroad securities.[230]

In an earlier era, as I have noted, iron-manufacturing enterprises obtained American railroad bonds in payment for iron rails. In the years 1875–1914, the growth of the domestic American iron and steel industry (able to provide the now-desired steel rails), along with the increasing professionalization of investment banking, meant that this type of commercial transaction declined; the exchange of long-term securities for British exports lost significance as the basis for the giant foreign investments in U.S. railroads.[231]

Did any of these investments in U.S. railroads by nonrailroad companies (including those by financial institutions) carry management and control or influence beyond that of providing capital? Certain banking houses had important influence. Dorothy Adler notes that of all the American railways, the Alabama Great Southern (organized in 1877) "was undoubtedly the most completely British. It was British owned, British managed, and largely British built." John Swann of Emile Erlanger & Co., London, participated in the reorganization of the railway in 1877 and became its manager. (Later Swann would become associated with other railways that had strong British interests; he became a naturalized American.)[232]

An intimate relationship existed between the Philadelphia and Reading and its London bankers, McCalmont Brothers, from the 1850s to the early 1880s. In the late 1870s, when the railroad was in difficulty, McCalmont Brothers, which owned the controlling shares, came to its rescue. In 1882, however, after a quarrel between the railroad president and the London bankers, the latter sold out.[233]

Dorothy Adler wrote that by the 1880s, British banking houses had "built up" a group of operating railroad men in the United States in whom they had confidence. New England–born Frank Bond (who served British interests on the Reading, the Texas and Pacific, the Alabama Great Southern, and the Chicago, Milwaukee and St. Paul), Thomas Fowler (long-time president of the New York, Ontario and Western), and A. B. Stickney (of the Minnesota and Northwestern; the Chicago, St. Paul and Kansas City; and finally the Chicago Great Western).[234] The British influence was strongly that of the banking houses, acting for individual investors (as noted above) or on their own behalf. That these banks had Americans representing them did not negate their influence. Often the bankers engaged Americans. Henry Villard, when president of the then British-controlled Oregon Railway and Navigation Company, wrote a British banker (P. Buchan) on February 3, 1882: "I must not be expected to submit to dictation in the details of management. If I possess the confidence of the stockholders, these [details] must be left to me or otherwise they must find somebody else willing to serve them."[235]

The Baring Archives in London bear witness to an extensive flow of information from the United States to London on railroads in which the Barings had been, were, or might become interested. In the case of the St. Louis and Iron Mountain Railroad, for example, in which the Barings had obtained a large stake (in 1877), Thomas Baring went to the United States, gathered votes, and attempted to change the management.[236]

Likewise, in October 1885 G. S. Morison, Baring's U.S. adviser on railroads, was writing on the Ohio and Mississippi that "the English stockholders" now had a clear majority of the new board of directors.[237] In 1886 Thomas Baring took up residence in the United States, and his letters to his brother Edward C. Baring, the first Lord Revelstoke, provide a fascinating commentary on American railroads: "The Atchison System recommends itself to one—whether one be a traveller only or also a shareholder."[238] On the Baltimore and Ohio: "I agree with you entirely that we had better leave Mr. [Robert] Garrett to get his money from some one else: he is a miserable skunk and dishonest."[239] On the Chicago, Rock Island and Pacific Railway: "The individuals with whom one has to deal . . . are all such infernal rogues."[240] By contrast, he liked the Illinois Central.[241]

When the Atchison, Topeka and Santa Fe was in financial difficulty in 1888–89, Baring Brothers—with Kidder, Peabody—stepped in to reorganize the railroad. George C. Magoun, a Kidder, Peabody partner, became chairman of the board, and Thomas Baring (as of May 1889) became a director of the Atchison. The new management "simplified" and "economized operations."[242] Johnson and Supple's just-quoted comments do not effectively capture what happened. The railroad quickly embarked on an expansion program, arranging to purchase the St. Louis and San Francisco Railroad (the "Frisco") in May 1890 and the Colorado Midland in September 1890. These purchases, with their financing through new issues, meant that the market became flooded with Atchison securities.[243] Baring Brothers, in difficulties, began to sell its Atchison holdings in October. When in 1893 the Atchison, Topeka was once again in trouble, Baring Brothers was not in a position to "save" the railroad; George Magoun died in December, and almost immediately thereafter the road went into receivership.[244]

Protective committees were formed in London and Amsterdam to reorganize the Atchison, Topeka; Robert Fleming arrived from London, and Hope & Co. sent John Luden from Amsterdam to defend, respectively, the British and Dutch interests. Thomas Baring, still on the Atchison, Topeka board, resigned in 1894.[245] In 1895 the railroad was reorganized; $111,486,000 in preferred stock replaced income bonds and went primarily to English holders of income and second-mortgage bonds[246] (the size of the issue indicates the formidable British involvement). Baring Brothers agreed to participate in underwriting the cost of the reorganization.[247] As a majority of bonds were held in Europe, the London and Amsterdam committees controlled the management of the new company.[248] In the process, the railroad cast off the "Frisco" and the Colorado Midland railroads.[249]

British banking houses were similarly involved with the Baltimore and Ohio[250] and the Louisville and Nashville railroads,[251] in each case making decisions on management and dealing with financial reorganizations. This was also true of other American railways.

Likewise, Dutch banking houses continued to participate in American railroad reorganizations. E. H. Harriman's biographer attributes his election as a director of the Illinois Central (in 1883) to the votes of the Boissevain firm. In the 1890s A. A. H. Boissevain took part in the reorganization of Union Pacific (1893) and the Norfolk and Western (1895).[252] Teixeira de Mattos Brothers of Amsterdam played a role in the 1897–1899 readjustment of the debt of the Central Pacific.[253] In 1909 Daniel G. Boissevain, of the younger generation of that family, was in the United States, serving on several U.S. boards of directors on behalf of his family house.[254]

The Deutsche Bank became disenchanted with Henry Villard (its representative in the United States from 1886 to 1890).[255] Villard had directed the bank into its huge involvements in the Northern Pacific Railroad. One railroad analyst argues that the problems that this railroad had in the early 1890s were directly related to events surrounding the Baring Crisis of 1890. The Northern Pacific had made a number of commitments; when, because of the general financial panic, its bonds could be sold only at a great discount, its board had chosen instead to borrow on a short-term basis, hoping to refund later. The rate war between the Great Northern and the Northern Pacific had reduced the latter's revenues. Faced with a mountain of debt and no means of paying, the Northern Pacific had gone into receivership in 1893.[256] At this point the Deutsche Bank became a participant in the reorganization. Edward D. Adams served on the reorganization committee of the Northern Pacific. He replaced Villard as the U.S. representative for the Deutsche Bank. Adams had been a partner in the firm of Winslow, Lanier & Co., and during the 1880s had been active in railroad reorganizations.[257] When in 1896 a voting trust was established for the Northern Pacific, Georg von Siemens served on it, and it was specified that his successors were always to be nominated by the Deutsche Bank.[258] In 1897 Adams became the chairman of the board of the reorganized Northern Pacific.[259]

Georg von Siemens and Arthur von Gwinner of the Deutsche Bank had met with Lord Mount Stephen in London (and James Hill met with von Gwinner) to resolve the outstanding issues and eventually to work on the details for the unification of the Northern Pacific and the Great Northern. The German bankers sought satisfactory financial returns, not control, but if good management could be introduced only with their intervention, they were prepared to intervene.[260]

Dorothy Adler found that British investors "on occasion covertly exercised influence in the settlement of rate wars."[261] As an example, she gives the support of "British holders" of securities of the New York, Ontario and Western to arrangements made by J. P. Morgan in 1885 to curb competition between the Pennsylvania and the New York Central;[262] at that time Jacob Schiff (of Kuhn, Loeb), Sir Ernest Cassel, and Wertheim & Gompertz of Amsterdam were seeking to rescue the New York, Ontario and Western.[263] In general, foreign banking houses (and also U.S. ones, such as Morgan) had little patience with competition. Agreement, cooperation, and, accordingly, stable returns to the investor seemed preferable.

The ability to obtain a foreign loan could make or break a U.S. railroad executive; Charles Francis Adams, Jr., attributed his removal from the presidency of the Union Pacific in 1890 to his failure to arrange financing with the Barings.[264] The Garretts temporarily lost control of the Baltimore and Ohio after a financial crisis caused by Garrett's inability to gain the confidence of foreign banking houses.[265]

J. Laurence Laughlin, writing in 1918, emphasized America's pre–

World War I credit dependence on foreign markets and related a story told him by "the president of a large American railway," who found his request for a $3 million or $4 million loan *in New York* held up because of the Baring Crisis of 1890. A rival road in the West cut rates and took his traffic, "quite against reason and repeated offers to adjust the situation." That road's securities were in the main held in England and were being sold in American money markets "as the best means of realizing cash resources for the Barings." The railroad had to show large receipts while its foreign holdings were marketed in New York. The president's own road consequently did badly, which made the loan to him difficult. Laughlin concluded, "Thus the relation between Argentine *cedulas* [which brought about the Baring Crisis] and railway rates and credit in the Pacific coast territory of our own country was direct and inevitable."[266]

Foreign banking houses aided U.S. railroad mergers. I have noted the Deutsche Bank's role in the merger of the Great Northern and the Northern Pacific. When Collis P. Huntington wanted to combine the Central Pacific and the Southern Pacific in 1897–1899, he required an adjustment of the former's financial condition. Speyer & Co., New York; Speyer Brothers of London; Lazard Speyer-Ellissen of Frankfurt; Teixeira de Mattos Brothers of Amsterdam; and the Deutsche Bank took part in the reorganization of the Central Pacific. The London committee had a role in the transfer of the Central Pacific to the Southern Pacific.[267]

To consider further foreign influence, I went to Thomas Cochran's *Railroad Leaders*. What did railway managers think of the foreign investor's role? On June 12, 1888, Henry Ledyard, president of the Michigan Central, wrote a fellow railway executive:

From what I hear from those having charge of railroad properties, where there is a large foreign holding of stock, it seems impossible to make the foreign stockholder see anything but dividends . . . The foreign investor simply cares for dividends from year to year and cannot understand how in this country where business is not fully developed, improvements must be made out of earnings or the capital account will be so much increased as to render the payments of dividends impossible.[268]

When the Louisville and Nashville Railroad wanted to expand rather than to declare dividends, foreign stockholders objected. To appease the railroad president's wishes and those of the stockholders, the Louisville and Nashville paid out in 1888 what its historian believes may have been the first "stock dividends," an idea suggested by the London stockholders.[269]

Heather Gilbert quotes a letter from Gaspard Farrer, director of

Baring Brothers, which had invested in the Union Pacific, to E. H. Harriman, March 8, 1906: "Today I am writing . . . as one of your 'd——d shareholders'; and a hungry one at that—content with 6%—not a bit! 'L'appétit vient en mangeant.'" Gilbert adds that in August 1906 the Union Pacific dividend was increased from 6 percent to 10 percent.[270]

In short, the major foreign banking houses that invested in and handled American railway securities were not passive. Although they did not want to run the railroads, circumstances required their frequent involvement. It seems that the foreign investment banker's posture in relation to U.S. railroads was very similar to that of American investment bankers. By contrast, foreign commercial banks that simply held U.S. railroads in their portfolio seem to have, in general, played a trivial role. (They sold their securities if they were dissatisfied.)

Investment trust companies typically did not attempt to influence railroad management (they rarely had a large enough interest in any single railroad to do so).[271] Robert Fleming was exceptional and did serve on a number of protective committees.[272] He was also a director of the Norfolk and Western for many years.[273] In 1884, with Sir Ernest Cassel and Jacob Schiff, Fleming took part in the reorganization of the Texas and Pacific;[274] he played a major role in the 1894 reorganization of the Atchison, Topeka and Santa Fe.[275] In 1914 he was a voting trustee of the Chicago Great Western Railroad.[276]

For the Barings, the Rothschilds, the Deutsche Bank, and Fleming, as well as for others who recommended American railroads to British and European investors, it was important that their advice be confirmed by the successful performance of the securities that they endorsed; thus they had a direct interest in the ongoing earnings of these railroads, since their own reputation was at stake.[277]

On the foreign firms—not railway companies—that owned U.S. railroad securities, one can conclude that the banking houses held "related" investments, associated with their issues, their financial returns, and their other business (when they became owners of collateral). More frequently than has generally been recognized, investment banks (including merchant banks) became very much involved in U.S. railroad financial management. British, Dutch, and German passivity is a myth. The banking houses did not want to manage the railways. They wanted knowledge and their own man on the board if their holdings were sizable, and they wanted to change conditions or to intervene only when returns were not satisfactory. They felt keenly that interest on the bonds must be maintained, and dividends must be paid, the higher the better. They saw rate stabilization as contributing to better financial performance. Their men on the boards of directors (and on reorganization and finance committees) were "to protect" their large holdings and to see to it that returns went to security owners. They used their expertise in the financial restructuring of weak railroads. They had influence because their aid was essential to the success of the reorganizations. Their role was no different in these respects from that of U.S. investment bankers.[278]

Many foreign commercial banks bought railroad stocks and bonds for their portfolios. Stockbrokers and promoters temporarily held railway securities. Investment trust companies looked for good securities and a diversified portfolio; they sought high returns and low risk; they did not want management control. Among investment trust company leaders, Robert Fleming was rare as a direct participant in U.S. railroad reorganizations.[279] The primary goal of insurance offices and other businesses in their railroad investments was stable returns, not extension of their own operations. In the case of many foreign commercial banks, stockbrokers, promoters, most investment trust companies, and all the insurance offices, industrials, and retail firms that invested in American railroads, the holdings were not enough to obtain representation on a railroad board; these were pure portfolio investments, bought and sold only on the basis of financial criteria.

The third category of foreign investor was the railroad company. No railroad enterprise operating in England or on the European continent planned or carried out "related" investments in the United States in railroads; that is, none saw trade extending along its rail lines via steamships into the United States as warranting its investing in U.S. railroads.[280] By contrast, Canadian railroads, most of them British financed, did cross the border to complete their systems. Cleona Lewis estimates their direct investments, principally by the Canadian Pacific and the Canadian Grand Trunk, at $82 million in 1914.[281] That year the Canadian Pacific controlled U.S. railroads with a capital stock and funded debt of $53.2 million, while the comparable figure for the Canadian Grand Trunk was $22.9 million.[282] I have some difficulty deciding whether these should be classed as British or Canadian investments, for the financial chain led back to the United Kingdom.[283]

Herbert Marshall, Frank Southard, and Kenneth Taylor have summarized the major extensions by Canadian railroads into the United States. The predecessors of what became the Canadian National—the Central Vermont group, the Grand Trunk group, and the Canadian Northern group—built 1,778 miles of track into Vermont, Maine, and upstate New York and also served Cincinnati,

Detroit, Chicago, and Duluth.[284] The Canadian Pacific Railway had even more mileage in the United States, in excess of 5,000 miles of track. Its first U.S. lines were in northern New England; in 1887 it was planning on entering Chicago; in 1888 it acquired control of the Minneapolis, St. Paul and Sault Ste. Marie (the Soo Line); other U.S. connections followed.[285]

These primarily British-financed and in some instances British-controlled Canadian railroads affected U.S. competition. For example, when in the late 1870s Gustavus F. Swift wanted to use refrigerated railroad cars to ship chilled beef, U.S. railroads opposed the idea, fearing lower income from freight as well as losses on their investments in cattle cars and eastern stockyards (both the New York Central and the Pennsylvania owned stockyards in the East). Swift responded by having his own refrigerator cars built. He would use them on the Canadian, Grand Trunk. This road had not handled much livestock, was not a member of the Trunk Line Association, and had a reputation as a consistent rate cutter. The threat worked, and Swift introduced his innovation.[286]

In 1879 the Grand Trunk had won its battle to get into Chicago, and this, of course, had given Swift his opportunity. Not long after, 40 percent of the receipts of the Grand Trunk came from traffic originating in the windy city. George Stephen was, according to the historian Merrill Denison, closely associated with the Grand Trunk Railroad, and when he was president of the Bank of Montreal (1876–1881), he frequently visited Chicago in connection with Grand Trunk business.[287]

Then came competition from the Canadian Pacific. On January 15, 1887, Henry B. Ledyard, president of the Michigan Central, wrote Cornelius Vanderbilt: "I do not believe it is possible to keep the Canadian Pacific out of Chicago. With the backing of the Canadian Government, they are in the position to build anywhere they want to and the question it seems to me is resolved to this. What arrangement can be made with them that will be fair to all interests involved, and at the same time prevent their further extension westward." Ledyard urged that the New York Central and Boston and Albany interests be brought into the discussions.[288] In 1888 Ledyard was writing to a general freight agent on the Michigan Central (A. Mackay) that the Canadian Pacific would very soon be one of "our most active competitors."[289] The Canadian Pacific aggressively expanded.[290] George Stephen's close association with both the Canadian Pacific (he was president in the years 1881–1888) and James Hill's railroad ventures meant that although the two railroad interests bickered, they seem to have seldom hurt one another—at least while Stephen had influence on the Canadian Pacific. Stephen continued to be a member of the four-man Canadian Pacific executive committee until 1892 and a director of the railroad until 1893.[291] Donald Smith, the other giant Canadian investor in Hill's railroads, was also a member of that same four-man executive committee of the Canadian Pacific. [292] Likewise, while Vanderbilt interests felt challenged by the Grand Trunk, Hill appears to have been relatively unaffected. Can we discern Stephen's influence?[293]

Cleona Lewis includes among the foreign investments in the United States in 1914 a railroad owned by Mexico, valued at $3.2 million.[294] Two principal lines of Mexican railways had crossed the border: (1) the Mexican Central, which was British financed, British incorporated, and British managed, and (2) the Mexican National, incorporated in the United States with both U.S. and British capital.[295] The two systems were acquired by the Mexican government in 1906–07 and absorbed in the National Railways of Mexico.[296] The extensions of these Canadian and Mexican lines over U.S. borders represent multinational-enterprise-type investments in railroads in the United States. These were direct investments.

Conclusions on Foreign Investments in Railroads

The immense quantity of money from abroad—mainly British, German, Dutch, French, and Canadian—had a major impact on the financing of American railroads. It is doubtful that without the foreign capital, the U.S. railroad network could have been completed as swiftly or as effectively. The influence of foreign investors often extended beyond aid to capital formation, affecting management (with the numerous reorganizations) and also competition. With the major exception of the "Canadian" railroads (and the minor one of the Mexican lines), multinational-enterprise-type investment did not exist in railroads.[297] This did not mean, however, an absence of foreign investors' attention to their large investments. The oft-repeated assumption of Leland Jenks, who stressed the vast amount of British capital while noting the small amount of British entrepreneurship, business leadership, and control,[298] must be qualified. I agree with Dorothy Adler, who found an "increase of active British participation in directing American railway affairs" in the last decades of the nineteenth century.[299] That the British, Dutch, and Germans delegated responsibilities to Americans does not demonstrate indifference or lack of influence.

Most important, all foreign investors in American railroads were not identical. To equate, for example, the widow and the orphan who held a few shares with Lord Mount Stephen, or the Bank of Nova Scotia with Baring Brothers, or a New York branch of a German insurance company with Georg von Siemens, or even Robert Waley Cohen of Shell with Robert Fleming, is to err. In each pair, the last-mentioned foreign investor had a direct and consequential impact on American railroad developments, serving or having representation on boards and on protective and reorganization committees, and aiding in the formulation of strategic decisions. Their choices on buying or selling affected security prices. Their assistance was fundamental. The first named in the pairs were, by contrast, "price takers"; their holdings were liquid financial assets—that is, purely portfolio in nature—and whether any one of them bought or sold had little effect on either the railroad or the market for its securities. My research also leads me to join with Dorothy Adler in her conclusion that British participation in running U.S. railroads ranged from 100 percent (as in the Alabama Great Southern —and that was by a banking group) to very little (as in the Pennsylvania and the New York Central).[300]

Foreign investors' primary interest unquestionably centered on the return on their assets. Some buyers of U.S. railroad securities made fortunes;[301] many made more than they would have on comparable home investments;[302] others lost money.[303] Because the goals were financial, European investors expected regular interest payments on their bonds and the principal to be redeemed when due; they clamored for higher dividends. Initially the Dutch and Germans had been more adventurous in investing in "developmental" railroads. By the late nineteenth and early twentieth centuries, the British had become very much involved; by the early twentieth century, western railroads were no longer "developmental"; the frontier was closed, and the railroads served to unify the nation.

Railroad managers knew that the larger the dividend, the more capital would be attracted. This was not always salutary. Albro Martin concluded that Henry Villard, when head of the Northern Pacific and when a director, had been a magician in bringing in German capital, but that this had served to handicap the road, because "the Northern Pacific paid dividends and even interest out of the proceeds of fresh issues of securities, while the crying need for physical improvement was ignored."[304]

Lord Mount Stephen, whose vision and persistent assistance in U.S. railway expansion transcended his concern over immediate financial returns, seems to have been, as E. H. Harriman suggested, exceptional among foreign investors. On the other hand, the financial reorganizations undertaken by British, Dutch, and German bankers usually (but not always) strengthened the affected railway.[305] It should be noted, too, that there was substantial discussion in Britain and on the Continent on the difficulties of long-distance management. A typical comment was that of the Duke of Marlborough (1891): "One great drawback to all English enterprise in America which have purely English management, or are controlled and directed from this side of the water, is the impossibility of making the 'long arm' as efficient as the short one . . . Such management does not wear well in competition with purely American or Anglo American enterprise with the seat of administration in New York."[306]

A distinction should be made, moreover, between the foreign investors' exercise of influence and their exercise of control. The evidence is overwhelming that foreign investors had opportunity to influence and frequently did influence American railroad developments. By influence, I mean the investor had the ability to change outcomes within certain very important limitations and constraints. By contrast, control—the overall ability to formulate the strategies and tactics of a U.S. railroad enterprise—seems to have been exercised, but seldom over long periods. New railroad lines, requiring vast amounts of monies, were more vulnerable to foreign control than those operating lines that needed little new capital and had adequate revenues to pay for that capital.

The United States had railroad executives able to equip and to operate its railroads. From India to Argentina, when Britishers invested in railroads, they supplied on-the-spot management and rolling stock and did assume direct control. In the United States, by contrast, managers and, increasingly, equipment and the rails themselves were American; and Americans made the fundamental operating and strategic decisions.[307] The ongoing problem for foreign investors rested on whom they trusted when they delegated responsibility and on how much influence could be sustained through delegation.[308] Their financial reorganizations and their own directors on the boards were to influence policy to protect their sizable interests.

In short, not only were the foreign investments in American railroads substantial, because of the promise of better returns than were available at home, but British, Dutch, and German banking houses, by their choices and by their abilities to raise (or not to raise) capital, affected the building of the American railroad system. Foreign investors tried to exercise influence in the selection of managements and in the formulation of policies that related to the safeguarding of their interests and the returns on their investment. The construction of the American railroad network depended on capital from abroad—and there were strings attached.

Land

As the railroads penetrated the country and the population moved westward, land values rose. In the late 1870s, and particularly at the start of the 1880s, major new investments in land and land mortgages were made by foreign individuals and companies in the American South and West. These investments were directly and indirectly linked to the expansion of railroads.

Railroads, which had received large land grants, sought foreign buyers for their properties (mainly settlers, but sometimes investors).[309] Thus there are letters in the files of the Northern Pacific, of December 17, 1881, to a Mr. [Richard?] Sykes of Stockport, England, "on your land in the vicinity of the Jamestown Branch," and of May 4, 1882, on "interesting the Duke of Manchester in the lands along the Northern Pacific."[310]

Companies were formed to buy railroad land. The Close brothers (three of whom migrated to America; one stayed in England) bought and sold such lands, organized companies, and attracted British capital.[311] They were associated with the formation of the Iowa Land Company, Ltd., in 1881,[312] and they established the Kansas Land Company (which in 1885 bought 100,000 acres from the Kansas Pacific Railroad) and the Second Kansas Land Company (which in 1886 purchased 150,000 acres from the Atchison, Topeka and Santa Fe). Still another of the Close brothers' companies, the Western Land Company, in 1887 bought 38,000 acres in Iowa from the Chicago, Milwaukee and St. Paul Railroad.[313]

Foreign investors in the Alabama and Chattanooga Railroad became recipients of land, in settlement of railroad bonds in default. In 1880 the Texas and Pacific Railroad had transferred ownership of 640,000 acres of its land (this road had a land grant of almost 5.5 million acres) to the Fidelity Insurance Trust and Safe Deposit Company of Philadelphia, in trust for foreign claimants (that is, foreign investors in the railroad).[314]

Some foreign investors bought land directly. Others purchased or acquired stock in or bonds of U.S. or foreign companies, which in turn held the acreage. In the wake of the Memphis, El Paso and Pacific fraud (see Chapter 4), the French bondholders in that railroad became shareholders in the Franco-Texan Land Company, chartered in Texas, which had 567,000 acres. The firm, formed on July 25, 1876, was an attempt to substitute an interest in a land company for $4.1 million defaulted railway mortgage bonds.[315] J. Fred Rippy estimated that between 1880 and 1890 more than sixty corporations were formed

in the British Isles to hold U.S. land and land mortgages.[316] Britishers
often invested through such British-incorporated land and mortgage
companies (see Chapter 14); there were also French and Dutch chartered land companies.[317] The United States Mortgage Company,
formed in 1871 (see Chapter 4), provided farm mortgages, using
foreign monies.[318]

New farms on the frontier, in turn, meant the emergence of important American mortgage companies, for example, Equitable Mortgage Company of New York, the Jarvis-Conklin Mortgage Trust, the
Lombard Investment Company, and the J. B. Watkins Land Mortgage
Company, all of which sought monies outside the country (primarily
from Britain);[319] land mortgages led the grantor to land holdings if
there were foreclosures.[320]

In 1884 lists were presented to the U.S. House of Representatives
on American land owned by nonresident foreigners. See Table 6.8. I
know of a number of large holdings that were not included. From
these tabulations, in January 1885 a U.S. House Committee on Public
Lands "ascertained that certain noblemen of Europe—principally
Englishmen—have acquired, and now own, in the aggregate, about
21,000,000 acres of land in the United States."[321] (The 21,000,000 acres
identified earlier as "foreign owned" somehow casually became that

Table 6.8. Acres of land purchased by foreigners "within a recent period" of March 27
and June 3, 1884.

Purchaser	Location	Acreage
English syndicate no. 1	Texas	
or "Holland Land Company"	New Mexico	4,500,000
English syndicate no. 3 (XIT Ranch)	Texas	3,000,000
Sir Edward J. Reed and syndicate (Florida Land and		
Mortgage Company)	Florida	2,000,000
J. Philpotts, head English syndicate	Mississippi	1,800,000
Cattle Ranche and Land Company, London (Marquis of		
Tweeddale)	Texas	1,750,000
Phillips, Marshall & Co., London	Mississippi	1,300,000
German syndicate	Unknown	1,100,000
Anglo-American syndicate headed by Mr. Rogers (or		
Rodgers), London	Unknown	750,000
English company headed by Bryan H. Evers, London	Mississippi	700,000
M. Ellerhauser, Halifax, Nova Scotia	West Virginia	600,000
Scotch syndicate	Florida	500,000
Duke of Sutherland	Iowa/Minnesota	425,000
British Land and Mortgage Company	Kansas	320,000

Table 6.8   (*Cont.*)

Purchaser	Location	Acreage
William Whalley, M.P. Peterborough, England	Unknown	310,000
Missouri Land and Livestock Co., Edinburgh	Missouri	300,000
Scotch Land Company, Dundee	Unknown	247,000
Robert Tennant, London	Unknown	230,000
Missouri Land Company, Edinburgh	Missouri	165,000
Scotch syndicate	California	140,000
George and Alexander Grant, London	Kansas	135,000
Lord Dunmore	Montana	120,000
English syndicate (represented by Close Brothers)	Wisconsin	110,000
Benjamin Newgass, Liverpool	Unknown	100,000
Lord Houghton	Florida	60,000
Lord Dunraven (Estes Park Company)	Colorado	60,000
English syndicate	Florida	59,000
A. Boyesen, Danish Consul in Milwaukee	Wisconsin	50,000
English Land Company	Florida	50,000
English Land Company (Benj. Newgass)	Unknown	50,000
"English capitalist"	Arkansas	50,000
Albert Peel, M.P. Leicestershire (probably Albert Pell, who was chairman of the English and Scottish American Mortgage and Investment Company, Ltd)	Unknown	10,000
Sir John Lester Kaye (or Kay), Yorkshire	Unknown	5,000
Total		20,996,000

Source: I have combined two lists, corrected several obvious misspellings, and made some other minor modifications. N. W. Nutting of New York, in a speech to the House of Representatives, March 27, 1884, listed foreign investors with 20,941,666 acres. Charles B. Lore of Delaware, on June 3, 1884, gave the House of Representatives a similar (not identical) list accounting for 20,747,000 acres. Both lists were republished in U.S. House of Representatives, 48th Cong., 2nd sess., 1885, Exec. Doc. 247, p. 46. The reader should be aware of the impreciseness of my combined list; neither original list, for example, gave an "English syndicate no. 2." The 4,500,000 acres was listed on Nutting's roster as "English syndicate no. 1, Texas," and Lore's as "Holland Land Company, New Mexico." This has to be the same 4,500,000 acres—but numerous inquiries on my part to "frontier" historians have failed to identify any such land holding of this size. See my text for an explanation. Each list contained duplications. The 700,000 acres in Mississippi and the Phillips, Marshall & Co. holding of 1,300,000 acres appear to be the same land (see Robert L. Brandfon, *Cotton Kingdom of the New South*, Cambridge, Mass.: Harvard University Press, 1967, pp. 52–59, which in any case, according to Brandfon, was not in British hands by 1884). Cleona Lewis, *America's Stake in International Investments* (Washington, D.C.: Brookings Institution, 1938), pp. 568–569, reprints a list of 26.7 million acres of foreign-owned land, originally published in the *Philadelphia Bulletin*, Dec. 6, 1909, which seems to have been based on these 1884 lists (there are many of the same typographical errors). The *Bulletin* list has additional errors—and included land that I know did not belong to foreign investors in 1909.

of "noblemen" in the House Committee's rendition.)[322] In addition,
the committee noted that the foreign investments in American railroad and land mortgage bonds "covered 100 million acres; with defaults this land might eventually go to the [foreign] bondholder."[323]

In the early 1880s, members of Parliament, earls, dukes, and mar-
quises sat on the board of directors of newly established land companies set up in Britain. They added luster in Britain to the
enterprises and were there to attract British investors; many of these
noblemen traveled to the United States to inspect the properties or
even to stay for a time.[324] Some of the land acquired by foreign
investors contained mineral resources (see Chapters 7 and 8). Many
of the largest land holdings in Texas, New Mexico, Montana, Colorado, Wyoming, and the Dakota Territory were for cattle ranching
(see Chapter 9). Investors had other agricultural properties (corn,
wheat, rice, sugar beet, orange groves, cotton); some owned timberland. Land went to developers ("colonizers"), who planned to sub-
divide the property and to attract immigrants to settle. Other
purchases were sheer speculations. Americans often sought out the
European capital.

The largest holding in Table 6.8, 4,500,000 acres, was referred to on
one list as "English syndicate no. 1, Texas," and on the other as the
"Holland Land Company, New Mexico." I am convinced that this
was one, not two holdings, that the "4" was a typographical error for
"1" (the lists were replete with similar errors), and that the land in
question had to be that of the famous Maxwell Land Grant Company
in New Mexico, whose predecessor was founded by an English syndicate (see Chapter 4), had Englishmen involved, and at one time, in
fact, almost changed its name to the New Holland Land Company. It
involved large Dutch investments. Nowhere else on either list is this
well-known investment included, which would lend support to my
identification. In Chapter 4 I wrote of the origins of the Maxwell Land
Grant and Railroad Company, which by the summer of 1875 was-
bankrupt. Until 1877–1879 the size of the grant was by no means
clear, nor whether the U.S. government would accept its legality. A
survey in 1877, however, charted 1,714,764 acres (nearly 2,680 square
miles), and on May 19, 1879, Secretary of Interior Carl Schurz issued
a patent for that acreage.

When it seemed likely that its land grant would be confirmed,
Frank Remington Sherwin, "former Wall Street operator and London
broker," participated with the Dutch bondholders in reorganizing the
company, so that on April 20, 1880, a new enterprise—the Maxwell
Land Grant Company, incorporated under the laws of the Netherlands—replaced the earlier bankrupt one. It was under Dutch control,

with Sherwin as president. He lived in New Mexico, furnished a house "half in Persian and half in Mexican style," and had an extravagant lifestyle. The Dutch decided Sherwin was stealing from the company, and in 1883 a Dutch stockbroker, Willem Frederik Ziegelaar, accompanied by two Dutch barons, who were investors, went to New Mexico to remove him. After "stormy scenes," they bought Sherwin out. One observer wrote that "Mr. Z[iegelaar] had definitely decided to fight a duel with him if it wasn't settled that evening, just to get him out of the Maxwell so he could not do any more harm." The story of the Maxwell company's attempt to assert its rights to its land (and the "war" with squatters), to develop its resources (coal and gold), to raise cattle, to sell its land, and to try to find sources of income is well told in Jim Berry Pearson's *The Maxwell Land Grant*. By 1914 this was still a huge Dutch investment in New Mexico.[325]

William Scully, an Irishman who began buying Illinois land in 1850, had in the 1870s and early 1880s greatly enlarged his American holdings, purchasing farmland in Illinois, Kansas, Nebraska, and (in the 1890s) Missouri, states in which he had by 1888 acquired 183,000 acres and by 1896 225,000 acres. For the 225,000 acres, he paid about $2.5 million. Although his acreage was far smaller than that of the Maxwell Land Grant Company or that of other foreign investors (see Table 6.8), his ventures attracted extraordinary attention, since from the 1860s onward, Scully—atypically—did not sell but leased his land for cash rents. His income came from his tenants in the United States (and also in Ireland). From 1878 onward he became the target of Populists, who objected to large land ownership by nonresident aliens.[326]

British holdings in the west–north central states received far more contemporary consideration and criticism than their size merited. Larry McFarlane put British ownership of farm acreage in 1890 at 1.8 percent in North Dakota, just over 1 percent in Missouri, 0.6 percent in South Dakota, 0.4 percent in Nebraska, and a mere 0.06 percent in Minnesota.[327] As for Kansas and Iowa, McFarlane concluded that "with the exception of the Scully lands in Kansas, a number of short-lived stock farms in Iowa," and the Kansas land acquired through foreclosures (and then resold), the British in 1890 were not important holders of land in these two states.[328] The 1884 lists (Table 6.8) include the Kansas holdings of the British Land and Mortgage Company and of George and Alexander Grant, as well as the Duke of Sutherland's investment, which I identified as being in Iowa and Minnesota.[329] George Grant, a native of Scotland and "late of Grant & Gask," London, who owned 100,000 acres, had migrated to Kansas in the mid-1870s and thus should be excluded.[330] In any case, all these midwestern holdings do not compare in size to the truly giant ones in Texas and New Mexico, and also in Florida and Mississippi.

In the American South, foreign investors did acquire huge tracts. C. Vann Woodward writes of an English "syndicate" that purchased 2 million acres in Florida in 1881. Sir Edward J. Reed, a British member of Parliament, in 1882 formed the Florida Land and Mortgage Company to hold this property and, hopefully, to sell it off in small parcels at a profit. By May 1888 the company still owned 1.6 million of the original acres.[331] Phillips, Marshall & Co. of London reportedly bought 1.3 million acres in the Yazoo Delta from the state of Mississippi in 1881, 800,000 acres of which was in cotton country and the remainder in pine regions.[332]

In 1882 the North American Land and Timber Company, Ltd. (NALTC), came into being in London, under the chairmanship of a British member of Parliament, H. R. Brand. It raised (mainly in England) some $2.5 million. Along with other companies controlled by the American Jabez B. Watkins, NALTC purchased 1.5 million acres of undeveloped marsh and prairie land on the Louisiana gulf coast between the Texas border and Vermilion Bay, at a cost of between $0.125 and $1.25 an acre. The "Watkins Syndicate" (as the group was called) sought first to reclaim the marshland and then, using new technology, converted this prairie land into a rice-growing area. By 1889 Louisiana had become the largest rice-producing state in the nation.[333] Over time NALTC sold or disposed of its land. On June 30, 1913, it retained a mere 77,111 acres.[334]

There were foreign interests in fruit growing in California. Edwin Waterhouse (of the accounting firm Price, Waterhouse) invested in land irrigation and the cultivation of oranges in California (through the Riverside Orange Company, Ltd., registered October 11, 1890).[335] California attracted foreign investments in timberland. The California Redwood Company, Ltd., with an authorized capital of £900,000, established in Edinburgh in July 1883, bought 72,000 acres of redwood forest in Humboldt County. About $2.25 million was immediately obtained in Britain for the new venture. Mills were purchased, but the company was liquidated in 1885 when it ran afoul of America's Timber Act of 1878 and was accused of land fraud.[336]

Other regions of the country attracted foreign investment in timber. Investors from Glasgow in 1884, for example, formed the Scottish Carolina Timber and Land Company, with an authorized capital of £40,000. It bought 40,000 acres of pine forest located northwest of Asheville, North Carolina, along the North Carolina–Tennessee border, and planned to cut timber, develop land, raise cattle, and attract Scottish settlers.[337]

While many investments in timberlands were by companies set up exclusively for that purpose,[338] traders also became involved. In 1880 Alexander Mitchell, a Glasgow timber merchant, joined with other Scots and with Cook & Brothers in Montreal and Toronto (Herman Cook was a lumber merchant) to buy timberlands and timber rights in both Canada and the United States (Michigan and Wisconsin).[339] In 1889 the Southern States Land and Timber Company, Ltd., was registered in London to acquire the business of pitch pine timber and lumber manufacture carried on by three companies near Pensacola, Florida.[340]

This survey merely offers a sample. By 1889 the rapid pace of foreign investment in American land was subsiding, in part because the new stakes had generated intense opposition in this country. State and federal legislation passed that reflected American concern that the national heritage was being alienated to foreign, titled, and disinterested absentee owners. In Chapter 16 I document the vitriolic reaction to foreign investors in U.S. land. Here I need only note that in the decade 1885–1895 twelve states, and in 1887 the federal government, passed anti-alien property laws. The investment frenzy also subsided as the huge cattle companies had disappointing financial returns (see Chapter 9). It lapsed in the 1890s with the "terrible shrinkage in the value of farm lands" and consequent losses to landowners.[341] It also slowed as the frontier closed and "cheap" good land that would (or so it was assumed) soar in value was no longer readily available.

In the early twentieth century, some new investments by foreign enterprises and individuals occurred related particularly to mortgage lending, timber, and cotton. Balfour, Guthrie—the California house of the Liverpool firm Balfour, Williamson—invested in agricultural land and land development, the latter as a consequence of foreclosures on properties covered by its mortgages.[342] In 1903 Bryant & May, Britain's leading match company (which in 1903 appears to have been American controlled) issued £100,000 debentures to acquire a one-half interest in 180,000 acres of California pine timberland;[343] the next year Bryant & May issued additional sterling debentures of £150,000 to complete the works on the California lands.[344] In 1908, however, it sold its 50 percent share in the California properties to its joint-venture partner, Diamond Match Company, for $2.16 million, substantially more than its investment, assuming that only the debenture money was invested.[345] In 1911 another (this time definitely) British-owned company integrated backward and acquired Mississippi cotton plantations (see Chapter 10).

Dutch investments in land, while concentrated in the Maxwell

Land Grant Company and its associated companies, were in other enterprises as well.[346] German nonresident land ownership also existed, although most German landowners migrated and settled in this country and thus are outside the scope of my study. The "German syndicate," included in Table 6.8 with 1,100,000 acres, seems to have owned either land obtained when railroad bonds held by Germans went into default or land acquired through railroad land sales. I have no evidence of sustained ownership. By 1914 many of the earlier nonresident British landholdings had been liquidated; the railroads were no longer selling vast acres; the scale of foreign investment in U.S. land had been reduced.

In sum, the expansion of the railroads was accompanied by important foreign investments in U.S. western and southern lands. The 21 million acres publicized as foreign owned in 1884 seemed a specter that terrified many Americans; the possibility that through railroad failures and land-mortgage foreclosures masses of land might pass into alien hands scared the farmer; European corporate holdings in excess of a million acres staggered the imagination; tenant farming with rents sent overseas angered the public; for a while it looked as though our most valued resource, our land, was falling into foreign, principally British, hands. By 1914, however, investment from abroad in land had lost some of its attractions, and the sums invested appear to have been modest in absolute terms—and also relative to the still very formidable foreign stake in American railroads.

7.

Precious Metals and Coal, Iron, Steel

The mineral riches of America attracted foreign investors. The nation had abundant resources—gold and silver, coal and iron, as well as a range of other nonprecious and nonferrous minerals, all of which became newly accessible as the American railroad network was constructed. In this chapter and the next I will consider foreign investments in U.S. mining and associated mineral-based industries. By way of preface, however, a few general statements about foreign investments in American mining are appropriate.

Many of the stakes in mining were by what I have called in Chapter 5 free-standing companies, albeit some of these companies were part of larger groups or linked by the same "managing" engineers. The free-standing company was omnipresent in the first set of ventures I will consider—those in gold and silver. It was also prevalent in coal- and iron-related activities, but less common in most nonprecious and nonferrous metals, although in all facets of the extraction of minerals, there were such firms. Free-standing companies, recall, were those that did not develop directly out of the operations of an existing business enterprise in the source-of-investment country; rather, they were formed independently for the distinct purpose of monitoring a particular business abroad. They sold their securities (shares and sometimes bonds) in the capital-exporting country; the corporations were the conduits for capital movement. Anti-alien legislation notwithstanding, foreign investments in mining and mineral industries grew in the years 1875–1914.

Clark C. Spence uncovered evidence of at least 584 limited liability joint-stock companies with a nominal capital of £81,185,000 (about $395 million) registered in Britain between 1860 and 1914 to engage in mining or milling in the "intermountain West and Southwest."[1]

Spence writes that British capital flowed into the mineral industry of the trans-Mississippi West "in significant amounts."[2] An earlier study by Edward Ashmead identifed 659 companies registered in Britain between 1880 and 1904 for mining in the United States, with a capital of £99,568,738![3] There are no comparable evaluations of the investments from other nations, although my research indicates that in the years 1875–1914, British stakes in U.S. mining exceeded those from the rest of the world.

British enthusiasm for American mines surged—and then at times subsided. The Emma mine fiasco in the early 1870s served (in the mid-1870s) to deter new British entries—or at least created a healthy skepticism.[4] The caution evaporated in the 1880s, when large investments were made. T. A. Rickard, many years later, recalled the manner in which American mining enterprises

were guided in London. It was *opéra bouffe*. In those days [the mid-1880s], it was a common thing for a smart American to obtain an option on a group of claims in Montana or Colorado for, say, $50,000, and then to sell them in London for £50,000 [almost $250,000]. To clinch the absurdity, he, the promoter, would pose as a mining engineer and would be appointed manager of the mine at a good salary, thereby being given the chance to postpone the day of exposure. A mill would be built and the mine would be developed by aid of English capital; then a shilling dividend would be declared, and the shares would go at a premium. What is a dividend? The shilling was a meagre return, not *on*, but *of*, the capital of the mining company. Next year, or the year after, there would be a "reconstruction"; the manager-promoter would resign and disappear, leaving a hole in the ground in the possession of the company.[5]

Rickard's description left out one item: the promoter in the process of selling the shares in London would obtain "vendor shares" in exchange for the properties he transferred to the new, overcapitalized corporation. Once the dividend was declared and the price of the shares went at a premium, the promoter would then sell out his holdings, obtaining the extra profit and leaving the gullible investor on his own.

By 1893 Britishers once again shied away from the American mining stock and other U.S. securities with which they had had bad experiences. We read of U.S. mining companies traded in London in 1893:

New Montana is struggling against lawsuit costs as well as overcapitalization and the fall in price of silver; Yankee Girl is on the point of vanishing altogether; American Belle is in a state of suspense; and New Guston and Maid of Erin are far from prosperous. The Yankee Girl property is being sold by the debenture holders, as the shareholders will not subscribe for a recon-

struction. The La Plata Company has ceased operations at its mine in Colorado, and . . . Mr. Niness has been dispatched to the Mozambique territory
in East Africa to prospect for gold reefs . . . The Golden Leaf Company,
working mines in Montana and New Mexico, has practically ceased work . . .
The New Eberhardt Company closed its Eberhardt mine in Nevada.[6]

This was but a sample of the litany of woes.[7] Spence reports that only
about one in ten of the British companies he studied paid any dividend whatsoever.[8] Among the most profitable British investments
were those in Camp Bird, Ltd. (gold mining), De Lamar Mining
Company, Ltd. (initially gold and silver mining), Richmond Consolidated Mining Company, Ltd. (silver mining), and eventually, the
Arizona Copper Company, Ltd.[9] Despite the less-than-satisfactory
overall performance of most British companies, and despite new
mineral developments in other countries in the decade before World
War I that competed with the United States for attention,[10] German,
French, Belgian, and Dutch as well as British investors were from
1875 to 1914 excited by every new announcement of U.S. mineral
discoveries, and investors remained dreamers about "fabulous" returns.

In this period the investments covered the spectrum from direct to
portfolio stakes, from precious to industrial metals, from mining to
processing, to manufacturing, to trade. Mining companies were registered in London, Edinburgh, Glasgow, or, less likely, Paris (many—
as noted—were what I have called free-standing companies); a company registered in London might have shareholders that were not
necessarily British—that is, they might have been French, German, or
other nationality (sometimes there was partial American ownership,
usually by the seller of the mine).[11] Other companies were incorporated in an American state and owned by foreign residents or for-
eign-registered companies. Some companies were floated abroad,
others not. Some raised money through bond issues. H. Osborne
O'Hagan, an important British promoter, has written of his experiences with one American mining enterprise. Baring Brothers had
been contacted by American bankers who wanted their help in forming an English company "to take over" a property known as the Little
Annie Gold Mine. Baring Brothers asked O'Hagan to handle the
promotion, which he agreed to do if an expert mining engineer of his
choice gave a favorable report on the mine. O'Hagan dispatched
Algernon Moreing of Bewick, Moreing & Co. to the site. Moreing was
honest, and his "unsatisfactory" report halted the flotation.[12] As
noted, other promoters were far less scrupulous, and numerous
fraudulent mining securities were offered in Britain.

The 1892 *Mineral Industry* directory included stock prices for thirty-five U.S. mining companies traded on the London market and another handful (with no duplication) on the "Paris Mining Stock Market."[13] The large number noted by Spence and Ashmead compared with those listed in 1892 reflects the highly transient nature of many of the firms, the existence of numerous investments that bypassed securities markets,[14] and the limited number of companies traded in any one year. Foreign mining companies in America came and went.[15]

Spence found that those enterprises incorporated in Great Britain had boards of directors that met in the United Kingdom to determine broad corporate policies. Most sent an individual (known as an agent, general manager, superintendent, or even managing director) to America with authority to run the mine, hire (and discharge) personnel, and contract debts. Most companies had "managing directors" and other directors headquartered in London, who periodically traveled to America to look into problems.[16] The Emma mine failure of the early 1870s had been blamed on inferior British management; Britishers now sought to do better.[17] When in 1878 the directors of the Eberhardt and Aurora Mining Company, Ltd., contemplated forming a U.S. subsidiary to hold its Nevada properties, its London solicitors warned that control might be very difficult to exercise. In a formulation that expressed British "extraterritorial" prerogative normally associated with less-developed countries, Henry Kimber & Co. wrote, "All questions as to the powers and rights of the shareholders over their property would be determined in America and by American law, in a state [Nevada] in which the legal tribunals can hardly be considered as satisfactorily settled."[18]

Similarly, *Mineral Industry, 1893* reported that the Flagstaff Mining Company, Utah, whose shares had been practically valueless for some time, had been reconstructed: "The English directors and chief shareholders determined to get rid of the managing director at the mine, Professor [Minos Claiborne] Vincent, as they consider that he carried on operations solely for his own benefit, and not for the benefit of the shareholders."[19]

Western mining men (like American railway managers) thought the British too concerned with dividends; companies paid dividends out of borrowed money. Despite their visits to America, directors in England had trouble enforcing policies and finding trustworthy administrators. As one historian put it, "No one seemed to realize that financial reserves had to be established to deal with natural disasters."[20]

In 1886 the Exploration Company, Ltd., was founded in London by two American engineers, Hamilton Smith and Edmund DeCrano.

The capital came from the British Rothschilds. The firm had important mining ventures in the United States. It was not confined to any single mineral. It was associated with British attempts to control their mining properties abroad. One company in which the Exploration Company was interested (and a successful one) had, for example, in its Memorandum of Association the specific statement that the directors "may establish any local board or agency for managing the affairs of the [Tomboy Gold Mines] Company . . . or may appoint any persons to be members of such local board, or managers or agents."[21]

T. A. Rickard, a graduate of the Royal School of Mines, London, served as manager or consulting engineer for a number of British-owned mines in California and Colorado.[22] The Consolidated Gold Fields of South Africa, Ltd., had an American subsidiary, Gold Fields American Development Company, Ltd., that employed the best engineers (often Americans) to find, examine, purchase, and oversee the operation of its U.S. mining properties.[23] In 1909 Guy Wilkinson was the American manager of Gold Fields' interests and seems to have had his head office in California.[24] The Gold Fields group had not only gold-mining properties but also (as will be evident in Chapter 8) other U.S. mining interests.

In 1887, as noted, Congress passed an Alien Property Act.[25] It prohibited the acquisition, and thereafter the ownership, by aliens or by companies more than 20 percent owned by aliens, of land in the territories. It came to affect foreign investors in the Dakotas, Idaho, Montana, New Mexico, Utah, Washington, Wyoming, Oklahoma, and Alaska. Mines were not excluded. North and South Dakota, Montana, and Washington became states in 1889 and thus were no longer subject to this legislation. In 1890 Idaho and Wyoming joined the Union as states, and Utah followed in 1896. Then the federal law was amended in 1897 to exempt mineral lands. The 1887–1897 restrictions appear, on the one hand, to have temporarily slowed foreign mining investment (as well as investment in land) and, on the other hand, to have been often circumvented and not enforced. Clark Spence reported that "British mining companies continued to be formed and to enter into operations in the territories despite the bothersome statute."[26]

There were in all roughly 1,500 to 2,000 mining and mineral-related companies formed to do business in America in the period 1875–1914 and financed by foreign capital. My numbers (which may be conservative) are far in excess of the figure identified by Spence and Ashmead, owing to their many exclusions,[27] but what is significant is not the number of participants but their influence. Here and in the next chapter I will show both the formidable variety of investment patterns and the great importance of foreign stakes in many different American mineral industries. This chapter will cover gold and silver, and coal, iron, and steel. Gold and silver are "monetary" metals and thus are subject to special influences. By 1875 the United States was the world's largest producer of both metals.[28] Coal, iron, and steel provide the foundation for an industrial economy. In 1875 Great Britain still exceeded the United States in coal, iron, and steel production.[29] In Chapter 8 I will discuss nonprecious and nonferrous minerals. My conclusions in Chapter 8 will be for both chapters.

Gold

Precious metals had long lured European investors to America (from the Virginia Company onward). The interest had truly accelerated after 1848, with the gold rush to California. Now each new discovery brought forth waves of additional foreign investments. When after 1850 the United States had become a significant gold producer, California had become the principal gold-producing region in the world.[30] During the 1860s and 1870s, Montana ranked second to California in placer gold. As railroads in the 1880s made accessible the Colorado mines, Colorado replaced California as America's leading gold-producing state.[31]

In Chapter 4 I noted the British investments in California gold mines.[32] In 1883 the Montana Company, Ltd., was "presented" to the British public as about to acquire the Drumlummon Mine at Maryville, Montana, "believed to be one of the Greatest Silver and Gold Mines in the World." This was typical puffery, but in this case, with the aid of British money, gold was indeed mined until 1914, when the mine was exhausted.[33] From 1893 to 1908, mines in the area of Cripple Creek, Teller County, Colorado, supplied most of the gold in the United States. At least seventeen different "Anglo-Colorado" companies, promoted in 1895–1898, used "Cripple Creek" as part of their name.[34] In 1899 Winfield S. Stratton sold his Independence mine in Colorado to the Venture Corporation of London for a reported $10 million (the sale and subsequent London issue became the basis of long litigation). Clark Spence calls Stratton's Independence, Ltd., "one of the largest English firms ever to operate in western [American] mines." By 1908 the British parent had 4,500 shareholders.[35] Camp Bird, Ltd., located in the same part of Colorado and promoted in 1900, with a nominal capital of £1,000,000 ($4.86 million), became a more successful British gold-mining venture, although some Britishers were cautious, having been disappointed with Stratton's Independence mine.[36] By 1911 Camp Bird was raising about $8 million in Paris; it was traded in the "Coulisse."[37]

Alaskan gold discoveries in the Yukon in 1886 and the Klondike in 1896 enticed eastern U.S. and British capital.[38] When in the 1890s gold was discovered in the southern part of British Columbia, Canadians rushed westward and a number of Canadians started prospecting south of the border in Washington.[39] Gold was mined by foreign-owned firms in South Dakota and Nevada (more important in silver than in gold). British companies invested in gold mines in New Mexico.[40] In Arizona, as copper mines were developed, gold was a by-product. So too, by the late 1880s gold was frequently produced as a by-product of copper in Montana and of copper and lead in Utah.[41] The profitable British-owned De Lamar Mining Company, Ltd., in Idaho started in 1891 by purchasing a group of gold and silver mines already in operation.[42] In the American South, in North Carolina, between 1880 and 1900 at least sixteen limited liability companies were incorporated in England to mine gold in that state; by the end of 1910 all but one had been dissolved, closed voluntarily, or had their property seized by creditors.[43]

Although there were hundreds of individually incorporated gold-mining companies, it should be recognized that all such firms were not necessarily independent of one another. "International groups," headquartered in London, were involved in some of the most successful of the entries. The groups included the Rothschilds (through the Exploration Company), Cecil Rhodes's friends (through Consolidated Gold Fields of South Africa), the "Hirsch Syndicate" (through a number of different corporations), and Wernher, Beit & Co., a British firm active in South Africa.

In sum, many foreign (especially British) investments in American mining were attracted by prospects of gold. Since most gold-mining companies had their own refineries at the mine, investment in additional processing was not significant to commercial control. Only when gold was mined as a by-product of silver, copper, or lead output did investment in processing become distinct.[44] There was always a market for the gold produced; British, Canadian, and American banks were active as purchasers and shippers.[45]

As in U.S. mining in general, so too specifically in U.S. gold mining, although some Canadian and continental European (mainly French) investments existed, the British seem to have been the principal foreign participants. Also, as noted, the French and Germans invested in British companies that in turn made the U.S. investments. One estimate suggests that of the gold mined in the United States in 1917, 95 percent was from U.S.-owned mines and 5 percent from mines owned by British companies.[46] In earlier years the percentage of U.S.-mined gold by British-incorporated and British-financed firms would undoubtedly have been far higher. Despite the extraordinary proliferation of gold-mining companies and the use of substantial British capital (as witnessed in the stock registers of companies incorporated in London), the British never dominated U.S. gold mining, and their interests were smaller in 1914 (and even smaller in 1917) than in the 1880s and 1890s. In 1914 American mines produced 2.7 times as much gold as in 1875, but the nation was no longer the world's largest producer; South Africa held first place, with an output almost double that of the second-rank United States.[47] The expansion in U.S. production had been assisted by British capital—and, as we will see, by two other foreign contributions—one British and the other German.

As the world output of gold rose after 1850, countries around the globe adopted the gold standard. In 1879 the United States went onto gold, on a de facto basis. In the 1880s and much of the 1890s, production of goods in America increased more rapidly than that of gold. The money supply—based on gold—could not expand fast enough, and in part for this reason, prices in the country dropped. Every schoolchild has read the speech of William Jennings Bryan in 1896, expressing the discontent and declaring, "You shall not crucify mankind on a cross of gold."[48]

Yet when Bryan's words rang out, two changes were occurring that heralded a substantial growth in the amount of gold available. One was gold discoveries, which led to the rise in output in South Africa and in the Klondike; the second, and possibly more important, change was the use of the cyanide process of gold recovery.[49] The cyanide process was that of MacArthur-Forrest, a British development, introduced into the United States by a British firm. The technology moved quickly into the public domain, so the Scottish patent holder played no role in its subsequent American use. By contrast, a crucial German direct investment in the United States provided much of the cyanide required for U.S. industry. The German investor was the Deutsche Gold-und Silber-Scheideanstalt (DEGUSSA).[50]

DEGUSSA started as the small assaying firm of Ernest Friedrich Roessler, who was master of the Frankfurt (Germany) mint. In 1868 Roessler's two sons took over their father's business, and in 1873 they merged it with another German assaying concern founded many years earlier by Philipp Abraham Cohen. The merged company was Deutsche Gold-und Silber-Scheideanstalt, which diversified its product line and in the late 1880s started to make cyanides.[51]

In 1882, before DEGUSSA began to prepare cyanides, Franz Roessler traveled to America to represent his family firm. Two years later he was joined by another German, Jacob Hasslacher; the pair started a partnership in the United States, with control in the hands of DEGUSSA. In 1889 they formed the corporation Roessler & Hasslacher Chemical Company to replace the partnership; it issued 1,500 shares, with the German DEGUSSA owning 1,325 of them.[52] This U.S. subsidiary of DEGUSSA prospered, advertising and selling cyanide of potassium, hyposulfite of soda, and other chemicals.[53] In 1895 it obtained the American rights to the new Castner process of making metallic sodium, used to produce cyanide.[54] That year the Roessler & Hasslacher Chemical Company, its parent DEGUSSA, and the British firm Aluminium Company, Ltd. (one-third each), formed the Niagara Electro Chemical Company to make metallic sodium at Niagara Falls, New York; the new enterprise would take advantage of the cheap electric power available there.[55] The sodium would be used to make cyanide.[56] The Germans became the sole large U.S. producer of cyanide,[57] which, in turn, revolutionized the gold recovery process in America and, as a consequence, contributed to the dramatic growth of U.S. gold output and to rising American prices. The Roessler & Hasslacher Chemical Company did the marketing of the cyanide in the United States.[58]

Silver

The discovery of the Comstock Lode in Nevada in 1859 had inaugurated large-scale silver mining in the United States. From 1859 to 1902 additional important silver discoveries occurred in the American West.[59] In silver mining as in gold mining, British capital participated. The notorious Emma mine in Utah was in silver.[60] Richmond Consolidated (organized in 1871) was a large and successful British-controlled silver-mining firm in Nevada; by 1893 it had paid out $4.3 million in dividends, but it skipped dividend payments in 1888–1890 and 1892.[61] So, too, the British firm Cortez Mines, Ltd., also in Nevada, started in 1888, had seemed to have high potential; but in the early 1890s the low price of silver forced this firm into bankruptcy and liquidation; it sold its properties to an American enterprise.[62] Many other British companies were floated to mine silver.[63] One mining historian found absentee (in part British) ownership of silver mines in Nevada even greater than absentee ownership (mainly of gold mines) in Colorado.[64] The Société Anonyme des Mines de Lexington, a French-financed firm, mined silver in Montana.[65]

Mineral Industry, 1893 reported:

For the silver mining industry the year 1893 was one which history will rank with 1873. The demonetization of silver, begun in the latter year, was finally completed in 1893 by the repeal of the Sherman law in the United States, which withdrew the last of the great nations of the world from the futile attempt to uphold the price of the metal, while furthermore the Indian mints were closed to the coinage of silver . . . the only countries which are on a silver basis, wholly or partially, are Mexico, some of the South American nations, and the East. The future of the metal now deprived of the cheap coinage demand is extremely gloomy.[66]

By 1893 bankruptcies of silver companies were commonplace. T. A. Rickard writes of the "silver panic of 1893."[67]

Silver came from silver deposits, but in the late nineteenth century, as new technology emerged and as the demand for silver collapsed, more frequently this precious metal was mined as a by-product of copper and lead.[68] Indeed, in 1917, a date for which information is available, only one-third of the U.S. silver output came from silver mines, with the rest coming from lead and copper mines. This meant that silver production became increasingly associated with output of the base metals.[69] Control over the smelting and refining of nonferrous metals became important to the silver trade, and foreign investors did figure prominently in the processing and selling of such metals (see Chapter 8). Merchant banking houses (particularly the Rothschilds) that dealt in gold also had large silver accounts.[70]

British Direct Investments in Coal, Iron, and Steel in the American South

The numerous foreign investments in American coal, iron, iron works, and steel in the late nineteenth and early twentieth centuries were less glamorous and less speculative than those in gold and silver. By 1878, when Britain still held first place in iron and steel output, that nation's ironmasters were already convinced that because of the rising U.S. production and the tariffs protecting it, the British iron and steel industry had "lost" the American market. The British feared, moreover, the anticipated competition from the United States in world trade.[71] In the mid-1870s "the most important man" in the British iron and steel industry, Sir Lowthian Bell, attributed U.S. accomplishments "not to native Americans but to English workers who went there." He added, "It would seem to be only the most ordinary prudence that British capital, which is equally threatened with displacement, should also seek the same proven fields of enterprise and share in the great advantage they assuredly offer."[72] In part, owing to his advice and suggestions, iron and steel developments in the American South came to be profoundly influenced by

British men, money, technology, and enterprise. When one reads of the British iron and steel industry, Birmingham, Cumberland, Middlesbrough,[73] and Sheffield are all there; identical names are encountered in the iron and steel industry of America; and, of course, Cleveland—not only Cleveland, Ohio, but also Cleveland, Tennessee, and Cleveland, Alabama.

The first important entry into this post–Civil War southern industry, albeit ultimately unsuccessful as a *British* venture, began in April 1874, when James Bowron, Sr., traveling on behalf of a group of Quaker ironmasters from the Cleveland district in northern England, arrived in Tennessee, trying to find a suitable place to start an iron and steel enterprise to produce from rich American resources at lower cost than could British industry.[74] An area forty miles south of Chattanooga, in southern Tennessee near the Alabama border, impressed him (see Figure 7.1). After meeting with the president of the Nashville and Chattanooga Railroad and obtaining his commitment for a railroad link, and after communicating with Thomas Whitwell (Bowron's principal sponsor and the founder of the Thornaby Iron Works in Stockton, England), the Englishman bought a farm to be used as a site for a new town, South Pittsburg. He also acquired contiguous coal and iron ore lands covering 163,000 acres.[75] The Southern States Coal, Iron and Land Company, Ltd., incorporated in England in 1875, would hold these properties.[76] Table 7.1 indicates some of the directors of this new company; note that all the men were identified with comparable businesses in Britain. These were not token directors. Instead, they planned to use their own expertise in developing the American enterprise.

This new project was formidable. Then almost sixty (born in 1816), but vigorous, Bowron remained in America to found the town of South Pittsburg, to import machinery, and to recruit men from Britain.[77] In 1877 Thomas Whitwell visited and found progress evident but production not yet begun.[78] That summer, thirty-three-year-old James Bowron, Jr., at Whitwell's request, severed his "mercantile business" connections in England and Spain and, with his family and a small contingent of industrial workers, went to Tennessee to assist his father.[79] The elder Bowron died late that summer of 1877; the directors cabled his son to assume management. For young Bowron, the new assignment was overwhelming: "I had it all to learn," he recollected.[80]

The next summer (on August 5, 1878), Whitwell was killed in a gas explosion at his Thornaby iron works. Whitwell, a distinguished engineer and metallurgist and innovator in blast furnace construction,[81] had been the genius behind the American plans. His

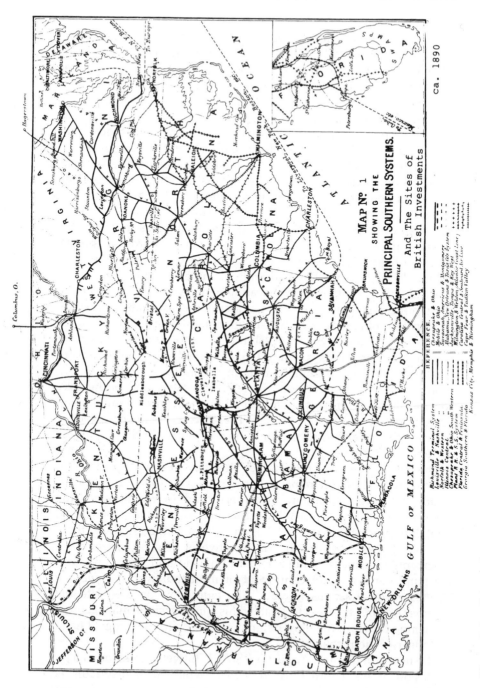

Figure 7.1.   Principal southern railroad systems and the sites of British investments, ca. 1890.

Table 7.1. Directors of Southern States Coal, Iron and Land Company, Ltd.

Name	British affiliation or occupation
Thomas Whitwell	William Whitwell and Co. (the Thornaby Iron Works), Stockton-on-Tees
Henry Fell Pease, J.P.	Coal owner, Darlington
William Barrett	Norton Iron Company, Ltd., Stockton-on-Tees
Henry Barrett	Iron and brass founder, London
Joshua Stagg Byers	Stockton Iron Furnace Company, Stockton-on-Tees
William Henry Hewlett	Wigan Coal and Iron Company, Ltd., Wigan

Source: Dorothy Adler, *British Investment in American Railways, 1834–1898* (Charlottesville: University Press of Virginia, 1970), p. 124n, and Ethel Armes, *The Story of Coal and Iron in Alabama* (1910; rpt. New York: Arno Press, 1973), 385.

death meant for South Pittsburg "practically dislocation of the home office."[82] Young Bowron proposed selling out to the existing Tennessee Coal, Iron and Railroad Company, but the English directors said no, so their investment rose and the initial furnace finally went into blast in 1879, five years after the project was started. C. Vann Woodward has called it the first furnace in Tennessee.[83]

Revenues were unimpressive. Iron works in Tennessee (and in Alabama) faced small nearby markets and high transportation costs elsewhere. A British expert reported in 1883 that the men who went into the iron business with the hope of making iron cheaper than in England had lost their money. "The great drawback . . . to Southern iron making is the cost of getting it to the great centers of industry [American or British] where it is worked up into a thousand shapes and forms."[84]

By that time (1883), the English Quakers had sold their property. On February 1, 1882, the Tennessee Coal, Iron and Railroad Company acquired the Southern States Coal, Iron and Land Company, Ltd., for $700,000 of its own stock and $700,000 of its own bonds. The capital of the Tennessee company was raised to $3 million. It became the largest coal and iron producer in that state. James Bowron was employed by this company and eventually became a vice president.[85] The Southern States enterprise had lasted less than eight years. It was a direct investment, introducing from Britain management, capital, technology, and control. It had been closely associated with several ongoing British enterprises. The initiative had come from England, not from an American (or British) "promoter."

The discouraging experiences of this company did not deter other

British investors. In 1885 David Roberts, a representative of a phosphate-mining concern headquartered in Charleston, South Carolina, arrived in Alabama, where he acquired an option on 30,000 acres of coal lands, located some thirteen miles south of Birmingham. By 1885 Birmingham, Alabama, with its nearby iron and coal riches, seemed destined to become a major center of iron and steel manufacture. Roberts obtained financial support from his Charleston business associates and also from a British group that included F. F. Gordon, C. C. Wyllie, E. H. Watt, Dilwynne [sic] Parrish, and Alfred Parrish.[86] In 1886 Roberts formed the DeBardeleben Coal and Iron Company, capitalized at $2 million (Colonel Henry F. DeBardeleben, who had owned the acquired coal lands, was important in the development of the Birmingham region and became president of the new company; Roberts was vice president and general manager); the lands were purchased for $1 million. The new company planned a city (called Bessemer), complete with a steel plant.[87] In 1887 DeBardeleben and Roberts raised the company's capital to $13 million ($3 million in bonds).[88] I do not know how much the British investors were asked to contribute either in 1886 or in 1887. The DeBardeleben company seems to have been American run. It became an active rival of the Tennessee Coal, Iron and Railroad Company, which finally in 1891 absorbed its competitor—the stockholders of the DeBardeleben company, exchanging their $10 million in stock for $8 million of the Tennessee company's securities.[89] By 1892 the capital of the Tennessee company had reached $20 million.[90] Other southern companies were merged into the Tennessee Coal, Iron and Railroad Company; it became fully integrated and dominated the coal, iron, and steel output of the Tennessee-Alabama area. The center of its activity was Birmingham. By 1907, when the Tennessee company was acquired by United States Steel Corporation, its capital was in excess of $30 million.[91] Some of the sizable foreign *portfolio* investments in United States Steel Corporation in 1914 were undoubtedly an outcome of the Southern States–DeBardeleben–Tennessee Coal–U.S. Steel merger sequence that in each case involved securities issued to the vendors.

Meanwhile, in 1882 the Alabama Coal, Iron, Land and Colonization Company (ACILCC) had been formed; it operated on land that British investors had received in exchange for defaulted Alabama state government bonds. Its British owners—including the banking house Emile Erlanger & Co.—were the identical group involved in the Alabama Great Southern Railroad. The ACILCC proved profitable, apparently through land sales rather than through coal and iron mining, its name notwithstanding.[92] Another company, the Northern Alabama Development Company, connected with the Birmingham, Sheffield, and Tennessee River Railway Company (a British-controlled railroad), had as its object in 1890 to purchase and to develop coal and iron ore properties in northern Alabama. The Tennessee Coal, Iron and Railroad Company agreed to buy its output.[93]

Dorothy Adler discovered large British interests in coal and iron in many parts of the South, frequently linked with British railway involvements. In Virginia and West Virginia,[94] for example, British investors expanded their earlier interests in the Kanawha coalfields.[95] British monies financed the Flat Top Coal Company, formed to develop coal lands along the line of the Norfolk and Western Railroad,[96] a railroad in which there was substantial British investment. In 1889 Vivian Gray & Co., a London banking house, associated since 1883 with the Norfolk and Western Railroad, invited subscriptions to the Virginia Development Company (capital, $5 million), with "mining and manufacturing" planned near the Norfolk and Western.[97] In 1883 what was called the largest furnace in the United States went on blast in Rockbridge County, Virginia; it was owned by another British company.[98]

By far the most substantial British entry in the American South was that of the American Association, Ltd., London, formed on January 11, 1887. It was a typical free-standing company, set up by promoters. It acquired 60,000 acres of mineral land in Kentucky, Tennessee, and Virginia and founded the new industrial town of Middlesborough (later renamed Middlesboro), Kentucky (see Figure 7.1). By 1890 the ubiquitous British director Dillwyn Parrish was on its board. The managing director was Jacob Higson of Manchester, England, and associated with him were Edgar and Frank Watts of Watts, Ward & Co., of Cardiff, Wales. Edgar Watts was a mining engineer. A cluster of companies was organized, including the Watts Steel and Iron Syndicate, Ltd. (capital, £250,000), which in time would build four iron furnaces and a steel plant.[99] All the companies were floated in London. *Banker's Magazine* (August 1889) wrote of the "very heavy" British investment and expenditures of $4 million by the American Association, Ltd., "in developing an iron, steel, and railroad center, and $6 million additional have been subscribed for the further prosecution of the work."[100] In May 1889 Middlesborough, Kentucky, had 50 inhabitants. Four months later the Louisville and Nashville Railroad's extension reached the town; by August 1890 the population was 6,200 and soon thereafter 15,000.[101] After a visit in 1891, the Duke of Marlborough described Middlesborough as "an English town in the Southern States, built and run with English money."[102]

The Baring Crisis, however, made Britishers wary of all American securities, and with the depression of 1893, British investors literally lost interest. The bubble burst. By October 1893 the American Association, Ltd., had failed.[103] The promoters-investors had not thought through their ambitious plan. There was no "operating" parent to the American Association, Ltd., no effective administrative structure. In 1899 the Virginia Iron, Coal and Coke Company acquired the furnaces and the steel plant. The historian Victor Clark would later—in an understatement—refer to this once-huge British investment as "ill-considered."[104] The historian of the Louisville and Nashville Railroad writes that Middlesboro—contrary to its founders' expectations— never became "a second Birmingham"[105] (Alabama or England). The reason was that the plans exceeded the Britishers' ability to pursue them. No effective ongoing managerial organization was established to run this formidable enterprise.

Farther south, in southeastern Tennessee, the British-owned Duck-town Sulphur, Copper and Iron Company, Ltd., was organized in 1891 and was based in Isabella, Tennessee, in an area that had attracted some pre–Civil War British monies (see Chapter 4). This company proved more important in copper than in iron.[106] Early in 1893, in northeastern Tennessee near the Virginia border at Shady Valley, just east of Bristol, Tennessee, an English syndicate headed by Sir Walter Oliver was said to have purchased for about $600,000 some 62,000 acres of land rich in iron and manganese; there is no indication that this was ever developed.[107]

In short, in the 1870s, 1880s, and early 1890s, substantial British capital came into coal, iron, and steel developments in the American South. By the mid-1890s, however, British direct investment in this region was past history. That the direct investment was short-lived does not make it less important. It helped set the foundations for the industrialization of the new American South.

British Direct Investments in Coal, Iron, and Steel in the American West, Midwest, and East

British stakes in the U.S. coal, iron, and steel industry were not confined to the South; they were also in the West, Midwest, and East. In the West, British companies mined in coal in New Mexico, Utah, Wyoming, and Washington, often to supply railroads. Thus the White Oak Coal Mines in New Mexico attracted "foreign capitalists" and sold its output to the Kansas City, El Paso and Mexican Railroad, while the Rocky Mountain Coal and Iron Company in Wyoming, in which British capital was invested, had the Central Pacific Railroad as its customer.[108] In 1879 the Central Pacific Coal and Coke, Ltd., invited British applications for £150,000 first mortgage 8 percent debentures. Its prospectus described its coalfields as comprising 10,760 acres of freehold land in the "richest mining districts" of the United States.[109] These "promotions" in London seem to have been linked and perhaps to have been "free riders" on the sales of American railroad securities.

In 1886 Peter Kirk had traveled to the American West Coast to sell steel rails to the Seattle, Lake Shore and Eastern Railway. His trip became the basis for a more ambitious venture than he had intended. Kirk and his brother-in-law, Charles Valentine, in 1873 had founded Kirk & Valentine in Cumberland, England; its successor company (which Valentine appears to have led) was, in 1881, the Moss Bay Hematite Iron and Steel Company, Ltd. According to one source, in 1886 Kirk sold his interest in the British Moss Bay company and emigrated to the state of Washington, inaugurating there an integrated iron and steel enterprise. Kirk retained his British contacts, and in anticipation of his change from rails salesman to steel producer, he shipped samples of iron ore from the American Pacific Coast back home to Cumberland for testing. In 1888 Kirk participated in the formation of several companies in the United States, including the Moss Bay Iron and Steel Company of America (capital, $5 million) to make steel rails, a land development firm, an iron-ore-mining enterprise, and a coal-mining concern. Kirk and the American Moss Bay's management believed the new plant in Washington would produce steel rails to sell at half the price then prevailing in the Far West.

It seems unlikely that Moss Bay Iron and Steel Company of America (MBISA) was controlled by Moss Bay Hematite Iron and Steel Company, Ltd., although there were overlapping associations, and in 1888 the British enterprise proposed to the Liverpool-headquartered trading company, Balfour, Williamson (or to its California house, Balfour, Guthrie) cooperation in the development of coal- and iron-ore-*mining* properties in the Cascade Mountains in Washington to supply MBISA. Balfour, Williamson was at that time importing coal from Australia to the Pacific Coast and faced high U.S. duties; independently of Kirk's plans, it liked the idea of obtaining local sources for its own existing markets. Presumably the coal mine would produce more coal than Kirk required. Thus Charles Valentine of the British Moss Bay company went into two joint-ventures with Balfour, Guthrie to develop the Washington coal and iron mines. Balfour, Guthrie put up 38 percent of the capital of the Durham Coal Mine and the Cle Elum Iron Ore Properties.

By the autumn of 1888, coal was being mined, a new town had been established, and the Moss Bay Iron and Steel Company of America had ordered its machinery from Britain. Then in 1890 MBISA had a liquidity crisis. It was dissolved, and in May the new Great Western, Iron and Steel Company was formed to replace it. The financing of this more modest manufacturing enterprise (capital, $1 million) appears to have been entirely American, albeit the coal-mining company continued to be British owned. Peter Kirk and W. W. Williams of the original "English group" were listed as stockholders in the Great Western (Kirk, recall, had migrated to America). In 1891 construction of the steel mill at the new town of Kirkland began, but even before the mill opened, the Great Western company was bankrupt. A historian (in 1962) called the entire project "the last major effort of private capital to erect an integrated iron and steel mill on the West Coast." Only the British-owned coal-mining operations continued— and with far from satisfactory results.[110]

The Otis Steel Company, Ltd (capital, £600,000), was floated in London in 1889 to acquire and to carry on as a going concern the business and works of the existing Otis Steel and Iron Company of Cleveland, Ohio, formed in 1873.[111] The newly constituted British company paid $4.5 million for the Ohio firm.[112] The latter's plant had begun operation in October 1875 and pioneered in the United States in the exclusive production of open hearth steel.[113] Its output had a "high reputation."[114] The chairman of the board of the new Otis Steel Co., Ltd., London, was Josiah Timmis Smith,[115] who had been general manager from 1860 to 1886 of the Barrow Hematite Steel Company, Ltd., located in northwestern England, a company that had been an innovator in open hearth steel production in England starting in 1867.[116] Charles A. Otis was retained to manage the Otis Steel works in Ohio.[117] This was in keeping with the pattern of many free-standing companies of the late 1880s. Often such enterprises were unsuccessful. In this case, however, under British ownership the Otis firm expanded; its *American* management was good; in 1913 it built a new plant on a 342-acre tract in Cleveland, which became the base of its main activity.[118] It seems, however, to have resumed as an Ohio incorporated company in 1911, the British investors becoming stockholders (portfolio investors) in the U.S. business. While the new company still had a London director (in 1914, J. E. Touche), it was clearly run from Cleveland; British direct investment had become portfolio interests.[119]

Important and totally different British investors were the Sheffield crucible steel manufacturers. Unlike the Otis Steel Company, Ltd., which was a free-standing type of investment (set up by "promoters"), the Sheffield steelmakers had been exporters to the United States for many years; some had been selling in the U.S. market since the 1820s. Faced with American tariffs and, even more important, the rise of U.S. output behind those tariff walls, they resolved to manufacture in this country and continue to sell through the sales channels long used for imports. In 1876 Sanderson Brothers, one of the largest crucible steelmakers in Sheffield, bought from Sweet's Manufacturing Company its "Geddes Steel Works" in Syracuse, New York. A new corporation, which Sanderson Brothers controlled—Sanderson Brothers Steel Company (capital, $450,000)—was formed. William Sweet was retained as general manager; Sweet apparently held a minority interest in the business, which he sold to the English shareholders when he resigned six years later.[120]

Sanderson Brothers Steel Company, Syracuse, at origin had the "exclusive right" to use the Sanderson "name, trade marks, patents . . . and all confidential information of whatever kind employed in the Sheffield process of steel manufacture." Its parent provided capital and skilled workers trained in Sheffield. The Syracuse firm used Swedish iron (as did the parent), and the parent envisaged that the subsidiary would produce "the identical uniform qualities and tempers of steel hitherto supplied from Sheffield [England]." Soon it was manufacturing the highest grades of tool steel, and by 1881 it employed about 250 men and had revenues of almost $800,000.

Geoffrey Tweedale (the foremost authority on the Sheffield steel companies' subsidiaries in America) found, however, that the Sanderson Syracuse venture did not meet its parent's expectations, and "the Sheffield methods were gradually abandoned." Yet output grew from 3,000 tons (1882) to 5,000 tons (1892) to 7,000 tons (1901), and the firm took new paths in the late 1890s, developing chromium-tungsten steels.

In 1900 the Crucible Steel Company of America was organized (capital, $50 million); it combined thirteen of the principal plants in the country that made crucible steel—including Sanderson's Syracuse works. The new giant made about 95 percent of the nation's crucible steel and at once was the world's largest producer. Its first president was Charles Herbert Halcomb, son of the managing director of Sanderson Brothers, Sheffield. At age twenty-two (in 1881), Halcomb had joined the Syracuse works; thus he had been nineteen years in America. While it is unlikely that Sanderson Brothers, Sheffield, retained any interest in Crucible Steel when the Syracuse company was acquired by that big business, nonetheless Halcomb and other metallurgists trained at Sanderson Brothers (in Sheffield and Syracuse) continued to have an important influence on the development of tool steel manufacture in America.[121]

Meanwhile, a second well-known Sheffield steelmaker, Thomas

Firth & Sons, Ltd., which, like Sanderson, had for many years exported to the United States, found that by 1895 its "American business had attained such proportions that the opportunity to establish
manufacture on the spot was taken after mature consideration." The
British company in 1896 purchased a controlling interest in the Wheeling Sterling Steel Company, an enterprise that already had a "high
reputation" for its crucible cast steel and armor-piercing shell. Firth
renamed its acquisition Firth Sterling Steel Company and expanded
production. Firth Sterling's capital in 1897 was $800,000. The works
produced all brands of "Sterling" steel and added Firth tool steel,
made in the same fashion as at Sheffield. When the Crucible Steel
Company was formed in 1900, it did not acquire this facility. In 1908
the second electric furnace introduced in the United States to make
steel was installed at the Firth Sterling's McKeesport, Pennsylvania,
plant (McKeesport is just south of Pittsburgh). In sum, the company
appears to have been a relatively small but innovative venture.[122]

A third Sheffield steelmaker, William Jessop & Sons, fearful that
the competition from Crucible Steel Company (protected by the high
U.S. tariffs) would reduce its exports, determined in 1901 to build a
crucible steel works in Washington, Pennsylvania, some twenty-five
miles south of Pittsburgh. There its new factory was constructed on
"American lines." It made no attempt to replicate Sheffield methods,
adopting instead the latest U.S. labor-saving technology. Jessop's
Steel Company—as this new enterprise was called—made saw steel
that it sold to American manufacturers. It filled a highly specialized
niche in the U.S. market.[123]

A fourth Sheffield company to invest in America was Edgar Allen
& Co., which in 1910 organized the Edgar Allen Manganese Steel
Company. The latter took over a plant of the American Brake Shoe
and Foundry Company, in Chicago Heights, Illinois, and also acquired the small steel-casting foundry of the Tropenas Steel Company
of New Castle, Delaware. The British role in manganese steel was at
the frontier of knowledge.[124]

All of these four Sheffield producers—Sanderson Brothers, Firth,
Jessop, and Allen—invested to serve the U.S. market; most introduced new technology. None went through British or American capital markets in their entry into the United States. All made
multinational-enterprise-type investments. This was also true of still
a fifth Sheffield steelmaker, Vickers, which made U.S. investments in
this same period but not in steel making (see Chapter 12 on Vickers'
involvements). These entries are not surprising. All were in specialized branches of steel production, where the British had long excelled
and had long exported their products. All filled a special segment of

the American market, where these firms' excellence gave them a particular advantage.[125]

In another market niche, British investors also perceived opportunities. In the United States, when bicycles witnessed a brief but dramatic boom in the 1890s,[126] their construction created a demand for a lightweight tubular material that American bicycle makers had initially imported. In 1891, using British technology (though apparently not British capital), Shelby Steel Tube Company, Shelby, Ohio, became America's first commercially successful producer of seamless tubing.[127] Like the tube companies in Britain (other than the affiliate of the German Mannesmann), Shelby Steel used hollow billets imported from Sweden that had been pierced on a press.[128] In about 1891–92 Samuel Snell came from Birmingham, England, to the United States to be an agent for Hudson's tubing (Hudson & Co., Ltd.) and for Thomas Warwick & Sons, Ltd. In 1896 Snell started the American Weldless Steel Tube Company in Toledo, Ohio, to produce tubes; Edward Warwick of Thomas Warwick & Sons became its general manager.[129] In 1897 the *New York Times* would call the works of the American Weldless Steel Tube Company an "English plant."[130]

Meanwhile, in 1895, employing the new and superior patent of Ralph C. Stiefel (a Swiss engineer who migrated to the United States), the Ellwood Weldless Tube Company, Ellwood City, Pennsylvania, became the first company in America to pierce tubes.[131] Its innovations in piercing (and the protection granted by the 1897 Dingley Tariff) meant that imports of tubes to the United States fell sharply. It was American-owned.

In the summer of 1897, the British public was offered shares in Tubes (America), Ltd., a new company with its principal directors from Tubes, Ltd., a British enterprise in the same industry. The prospectus indicated that Tubes (America), Ltd., would merge the Ellwood Weldless Tube Company (which had the important Stiefel patent), the American Weldless Steel Tube Company of Toledo, Ohio, and another, smaller U.S. tube-making concern.[132] Tubes (America), Ltd., never carried out this plan, because at a critical point the president of Shelby Steel arrived in England to announce his intention to invade that market. The British tubemakers rapidly retreated from their projected full-scale entry into investment in the United States and instead, in 1897, a number of producers of seamless steel tubing (including the Ellwood firm and American Weldless Steel Tube) combined into a reorganized, larger Shelby Steel Tube Company (capital, $5 million) with plants in Ohio, Indiana, and Pennsylvania.[133] Historians have reported (probably incorrectly) that the new Shelby company was majority owned by Englishmen.[134] In 1898–99, the Shelby Steel Tube Company expanded, acquiring additional competitors and obtaining a virtual U.S. monopoly in manufacturing tubing for bicycles. Its capital was raised to $15 million. Then with the advent of the automobile, the bicycle boom collapsed; Shelby Steel Tube diversified into making other products but was not competitive in the new fields, and finally in 1901, with the formation of the United States Steel Corporation, Shelby Steel became a subsidiary of the steel giant.[135]

Closely associated with the developments in iron and steel were those in tinplate. Indeed, tinplate production is considered part of the iron and steel industry. The United States had been a large importer of tinplate from Wales, before the McKinley tariff of 1890 raised duties. With the high tariff, some Welsh manufacturers appointed resident agents in the United States and others opened branch offices for direct shipment of their wares, in a "forelorn and belated attempt" to prevent the complete loss of their U.S. market. Still other Welsh producers—for instance, John Rogers of E. Morewood & Co., Llanelly, and William Edwards of the Duffryn Works, Morriston—set up so-called tinhouses in America, "located near the tide-water," where they coated black steel plates imported from the parent plant.[136] The Morewood company expanded, completing four large iron buildings in Gas City, Indiana, for tinplate manufacture.[137] By late 1893 Rogers was in the United States. He decided to concentrate his U.S. business at Gas City and soon was making tinplate and terne plates at the new works there. Initially the plant used foreign and American black plate, but when the company completed its rolling mill, it planned to produce its own black plate.[138]

The Wilson tariff of 1894 retained duties on tinplate and increased them on imports of black steel plate, thus ending once and for all the import of black plate and the building of tinhouses without rolling mills.[139] The Morewood company already had its U.S. rolling mill. What happened to this Welsh-controlled enterprise in the United States is not clear. Between 1894 and 1898, however, the American tinplate industry grew rapidly, adopting new technology. In 1898 the American Tin Plate Company was formed and became the principal producer in the U.S. industry, with more than 90 percent of the output. In the United Kingdom, by 1898 E. Morewood & Co., once one of the largest and most technologically innovative of the Welsh tinmakers, was bankrupt, a casualty in an industry that saw seventy-seven out of ninety-one firms fail in the years 1890–1899 because of the evaporation of their U.S. export trade. Although Edwards' firm in Morriston did survive in Wales, I find no evidence that it persisted in its U.S. investment. By the turn of the century, a new, strong American tinplate industry had emerged; in 1901 the American Tin Plate Company was absorbed by the United States Steel Corporation.[140]

All of the British investments (or plans for them) in coal, iron, and steel that I have described in this chapter were, to be sure, small relative to the overall size of the rapidly expanding American iron and steel industry; yet clearly there was an important British role in this sector—from Southern States' new venture of the 1870s to that of the crucible steel producers including the Thomas Firth takeover in the 1890s, to the Edgar Allen entry into manganese steel making in 1910, to the defensive forays of the tinplate producers. In general, where the British participated, British iron-and-steel men, technology, and machinery were employed; practically all the investments had some direct association with existing British companies. These enterprises are of substantial interest. When the majority were inaugurated, Britain had leadership in the world iron and steel industry. By 1914 America had clear superiority. Some of the ties with existing British companies had been tenuous, and the deaths of Bowron and Whitwell and the formidable and continued capital needs of both the American Association, Ltd., and Moss Bay of America resulted in the end of British involvement in these cases.[141] Yet in 1914 British direct investments remained, and some in flourishing enterprises. In the main, the successful ones—principally those in crucible steel—were extensions of existing British companies into America first through sales and then into manufacturing, rather than those enterprises that emerged out of attempts to develop "cheap" U.S. raw materials. Also important was whether an effective management organization had been acquired or introduced. If not, there was no success.

From a regional standpoint, the British impact was probably greatest on the new iron and steel industry of the American South. There British capital had assisted in building the first furnace in Tennessee and in the development of the new industry located near and in Birmingham, Alabama. Where British investment *and control* did last, in the cases of the Firth company, the Jessop works, and the Allen plants, the stakes were in highly innovative companies of relatively modest scale. They garnered a specialized and limited market. Facilities were in the Pittsburgh area, in Chicago, and in New Castle (Delaware). British direct investment helped in the creation of the American iron and steel industry. In addition, as a consequence of the earlier direct investments, British portfolio ones continued in evidence.[142]

German, French, and Other Foreign Direct Investments in Coal, Iron, and Steel

Some pre–World War I German investments in U.S. coal existed, related, however, to activities other than iron and steel. Thus the German-controlled American Metal Company owned 100 percent of the American Zinc & Chemical Company (incorporated in 1913). American Zinc was located in the new town of Langeloth, Pennsylvania, at a place chosen because "of its proximity to a source of fuel for its furnaces, coal mines."[143] It owned coal-mining rights over an area of 2,450 acres of the Pittsburgh and Rooster veins, with estimated coal reserves of 18 million tons.[144] The German-controlled Elly Coal Company, organized in August 1913 (capital, $2 million), held title to 30,000 acres of undeveloped coal lands near Girard, Illinois, south of Springfield.[145] The Lehigh Coke Company—established by a syndicate represented by the Deutsche Bank—was another pre–World War I German investment in America.[146]

In 1893 Friedrich Alfred Krupp visited Pittsburgh en route to the Chicago World's Fair, where there was a Krupp exhibit.[147] In 1900 the Krupp company (of Essen, Germany) had an American representative, Captain A. E. Piorkowski.[148] "Kruppized" armor plate was made by Bethlehem Steel,[149] possibly under license. Aside from the American representative, I have not identified any other U.S. presence by the huge German steelmaker.[150]

J. A. Henckels of Solingen, Germany, an important producer of specialty steels—scissors, shears, razors, pocket knives, table knives and forks, and so forth—which competed with Sheffielders in world markets, was represented in the United States from 1883 by an exclusive agent; in January 1909 the firm established J.A. Henckels, New York, a sales company, under the leadership of Hermann Kind. This American firm was 50 percent owned by the German parent and 50 percent by Americans from the replaced agency.[151]

More significant, in seamless tubing Germans attempted to enter into American manufacturing. Here the Germans were far superior to the British in technology. In 1885 Max and Reinhard Mannesmann of Remscheid, Germany, had invented and patented a process to make seamless steel tubing; the brothers decided to build tube mills at home and abroad.[152] In Wales in 1887, they acquired an existing company and built a tube plant that exported to the United States,[153] but it met stiff competition in America as U.S. tube output (especially that of the Shelby Steel's works) rose. In the summer of 1893, the Mannesmanns resolved to produce in the United States; and in the fall of 1894, they announced a joint-venture with Colonel A. A. Pope (a leading U.S. bicycle maker); it never materialized.[154] Then in 1896, the same year that the British-owned American Weldless Steel Tube Company was formed, the far larger German-owned Mannesmann Cycle Tube Company was organized. It built a plant near Adams, Massachusetts; but soon it faced financial difficulties and was reorganized in March 1897 as the Mannesmann Cycle Tube Works. Once again, the Mannesmanns found success elusive; the factory closed in 1898.[155] The German Mannesmann firm's attempted entries in the years 1893–1898 indicate how difficult it was—even with a high-technology product—to penetrate the U.S. market when Americans (in this case, with the competing Stiefel patent—the Ellwood company) were in production. Unlike the Sheffield steel producers, there proved to be no special market niche that the Mannesmanns could fill far better than their American competition; and, of course, the decline of the bicycle trade sharply reduced the demand for the Mannesmanns' offering.

A number of other German firms did produce and/or sell a variety of specialized iron and steel products in America; Becker Steel Company of America (owned by Stahlwerk-Becker, A. G., Willich, Germany) was in this category. Most of the output of such companies was "machinery and equipment," and I will consider such enterprises in Chapter 12.

French investors were less in evidence. French technology was employed in the American steel industry—the Héroult electric furnace, for example.[156] For the early Héroult furnaces, electrodes were imported from Sweden. In 1910 Paul Héroult organized the Electrode Company of America at Niagara Falls, New York, to manufacture that product.[157] I have no idea how it was financed or whether there was a French investment.

Dutch investments existed in coal mining in New Mexico, associated with the development of the resources of the Maxwell Land Grant Company; the coal was sold to the Atchison, Topeka and Santa Fe.[158] Otherwise, there were no Dutch stakes in coal, iron, and steel (except for the portfolio ones in the largest U.S. iron and steel companies).

As for Canadian interests, Cleona Lewis believed that the Canadian firm, Dominion Foundries and Steel, Ltd., and the Canada Foundries and Forgings, Ltd., had U.S. branches or subsidiaries by 1914; I have found no information on their pre–World War I location or on their business (undoubtedly sales).[159] For a short period in the 1890s, the Canadian Pacific controlled the Duluth and Winnipeg Railroad, with its valuable iron ore deposits on the Mesabi Range; James J. Hill acquired the railroad and its iron properties in 1897 (Hill's British supporters shared in his iron ore investments).[160] Cleona Lewis reported that the Sterling Coal Company, Ltd. (capital, $2 million in 1914), was Canadian owned.[161]

Cartels in Steel

America once had been a large importer of iron and then of steel rails from Britain. In the late nineteenth century, U.S. industry came to supply its own giant domestic requirements; in 1893, for the first time, U.S. exports of iron and steel products exceeded imports.[162] In 1900 English manufacturers of rails were disturbed when Carnegie Steel Company made a large sale to the British enterprise, the Great Eastern Railway Company.[163] In 1901 the giant United States Steel Corporation was formed. Meanwhile, the German steel industry also expanded. In November 1904 an international steel rail agreement was made by German, British, Belgian, French, and probably U.S. producers. The "North American rail market south of the Great Lakes" (that is, the United States and Mexico) was for Americans, whereas the Canadian and South American markets were assigned "collectively" to companies based in Germany, England, France, Belgium, and the United States; in all other markets the Europeans were to be free from American competition.[164] For some additional steel products—pipes, for example—U.S. manufacturers apparently took part in international agreements.[165] Such arrangements probably inhibited German, French, and Belgian producers from investing in the U.S. steel industry, yet even without these accords, it seems unlikely that more entries would have occurred, considering the growing competitive strength of the Americans.

Foreign Direct and Portfolio Investments in Coal, Iron, and Steel

While most of the nineteenth-century and some of the early-twentieth-century foreign investments in the United States in coal, iron, and steel were direct investments, carrying with them (or attempting to carry with them) management and control, there also came to be some exceptionally large foreign portfolio interests in iron and steel. As of June 1, 1914, according to its corporate records, $122.4 million of the common shares and $27.5 million of the preferred shares of the United States Steel Corporation were held outside the nation, mainly by British, Dutch, German, French, Swiss, and Canadian investors.[166] This huge amount was far more than can be accounted for by the Tennessee-Alabama and other predecessor-company British investments of earlier years.[167] Bethlehem Steel also issued bonds that traded in London and Amsterdam, and in 1912 it had raised some $7.2 million abroad.[168] In 1914 Otis Steel had important British portfolio investors.

In short, in the late nineteenth and early twentieth centuries, there had been both foreign direct and portfolio interests in the American coal, iron, and steel industries. The total amounts invested were substantial.[169] The foreign participation was much larger than is usually recognized; and more often than has been previously realized, the initial investments had carried with them an attempt to exercise management. In various facets of the industry, as import substitution took place, foreign investors had played a catalytic role. Tariffs had been important in encouraging new investment from abroad—and from at home. In the early twentieth century international cartels may have reduced the incentives for some potential foreign investors to enter. Far more significant, the growth and continuing existence of a strong and formidable American-owned industry—albeit stimulated by foreign entries—appears to have discouraged subsequent foreign direct investments. Except for Balfour, Williamson and some others in coal mining and the makers of crucible steel, in 1914 there was little lasting foreign direct investment in coal, iron, and steel. The $150 million in stock of the United States Steel Corporation held abroad —portfolio investment—seems awesome, until one recalls that this was America's first billion-dollar enterprise. The foreign investors' contribution notwithstanding, there is no question that by 1914 the U.S. iron and steel industry—the world's greatest—was under domestic control.

8.

Other Minerals: Copper to Oil

In nonprecious, nonferrous minerals from copper, lead, and zinc to phosphates, potash, and pyrites, to salt, to borax and radium, to alumina and aluminum, and to oil, foreign enterprises planned for and in a number of cases made sizable investments. Some stakes were in mining. Often, however, they were in processing (smelting and refining). Sometimes they were in "manufacturing"—the making of fertilizers, for example. Free-standing firms were present, as were vertically integrated multinationals. In addition, there were large portfolio investments from abroad, primarily by individual investors. Little uniformity prevailed in the entry patterns, and the story of the foreign role in these mineral industries is a tangled one. The principal actors include foreign trading companies and merchant bankers, along with industrial firms. Foreign direct investment and portfolio ones coexisted.

Copper, Lead, and Zinc

Copper, lead, and zinc can be considered separately if, for example, the mine was primarily a copper one. The three minerals were, however, sometimes found in the same mine; smelting and refining companies often handled all three; but each had different end uses. There was a formidable complexity in the industrial organization of the mining, processing, and trading of these minerals.

Foreign investors participated in the U.S. mining of copper, lead, and zinc; over time they became more significant in processing and trade. British, French, German, and some Dutch interests existed. America in 1883 became the world's largest copper producer, when U.S. copper output exceeded that of Chile. The copper production

met rising domestic and international demand, principally from the
new electrical industry. Foreign investments in U.S. copper mining,
smelting, and refining had not propelled America into first place in
the world's industry, for such stakes were minimal at the start of the
1880s. Two German immigrants, the Lewisohn brothers, participated
in the formation of the Montana Copper Company in 1880 and sold its
securities abroad; the Scottish-controlled Arizona Copper Company,
Ltd., a free-standing company, had been organized in Edinburgh in
1882; and that appears to have been the extent of the early 1880s
foreign involvements—that is, they were small.[1]

This would change as foreign investors obtained an equity interest
in the Anaconda company. In 1881 an American, Marcus Daly, convinced three fellow countrymen, James B. Haggin, Lloyd Tevis, and
George Hearst, to buy the Anaconda Silver Mining Company, with its
small silver mine in Montana. The price was $30,000.[2] That company
found copper and in the early 1880s used Balfour, Guthrie, the California house of the Liverpool firm Balfour, Williamson, as its shipping
agent and broker. From Butte, Montana, Balfour, Guthrie shipped
Anaconda's copper matte to Swansea, in Wales, for refining. In 1884
Anaconda's owners "offered the mine" to Balfour, Guthrie for
$1,250,000. Balfour, Williamson considered and rejected the
proposition.[3] That same year, a representative of the Paris Rothschilds sought to convince his principals (and also the Rio Tinto Company, a British-incorporated copper-mining company in Spain that
was associated with Rothschild interests) to purchase the Anaconda
mine, but as that man would later recall, he had met with incredulity
and scorn. In 1884 the Anaconda mine was still "unknown."[4]

Anaconda's output and overseas sales grew, and by 1885–1887
European mine owners (including the Rothschilds) became nervous,
for the large U.S. exports were depressing world copper prices. At the
end of September 1887, M. Secretan, the chief executive of Europe's
largest copper consumer, the Société Industrielle et Commerciale de
Métaux (SICM)—acting through that company and with the support
of Baring Brothers, the French Rothschilds, and the Comptoir d'Escompte de Paris—started to buy both copper-mining securities and,
more important, copper itself, on a formidable scale. By year-end
1887, Secretan's group controlled the leading Spanish copper mines,
and by the middle of 1888 Secretan had contracted for three-quarters
of the world's copper output! His copper inventories rose. In February 1889 the French Rothschilds canceled their contract with
Secretan.[5] The crash came in March. The bankers called their loans.
Secretan dumped mining securities and physical holdings of copper.
The manager of the Comptoir d'Escompte committed suicide.

Secretan had failed to corner the copper market and to raise world-wide copper prices.[6]

According to one account, as an aftermath of the Secretan disaster Anaconda had incurred a debt to the Rothschilds, and the loan carried an option to buy the mine, an option that was declined at the time.[7] Another commentator (Thomas R. Navin) reports that when George Hearst died in 1891, his widow wanted to liquidate some of her inheritance and tried to sell the Hearst holdings to the London Rothschilds, whom the Hearst lawyers had met at the time of the Secretan Syndicate. Navin believed the London Rothschilds were given an option to handle the stock, which they did not exercise at the time.[8] I have found nothing in the Rothschild Archives in Paris or in London to substantiate either version. In 1891 American and European copper producers desired to stabilize prices and had little success.[9] Correspondence in the August Belmont Papers makes it clear that in the fall of 1891, the London Rothschilds did have "an option on the Anaconda Mine." On September 15, 1891, the Rothschild's American agent, August Belmont, wrote Lord Rothschild that he (Belmont) and Jacob Schiff (of Kuhn, Loeb) were sorry to hear the decision of "the London interests in the Anaconda purchase." Belmont and Schiff "feared that the end of a good piece of business has been reached." The British banker Ernest Cassel, who knew "all the circumstances," concluded, "We are all very much better off in not pursuing this matter any further."[10]

Yet the matter was far from closed. The next year, 1892, the Paris Rothschilds began negotiations to buy the Anaconda mine,[11] and with it, its new smelter and brand new electrolytic refinery. The electrolytic refinery was the first of its kind in the American West. Anaconda was by this time a large integrated enterprise.

In July 1894, when these discussions had still not been concluded, Lord Rothschild, writing from London, informed his American agent, August Belmont, "We are most anxious to see an understanding brought about between American and European mines, as soon as possible."[12] None was reached.[13] The price of copper rose in August 1895,[14] and in September the Rothschilds and the "Explorations" (a reference to the Exploration Company, Ltd., the British Rothschild company) finally became truly intent on purchasing shares of Anaconda.[15] In mid-October 1895 the Rothschilds bought one-quarter of the stock in Anaconda—for $7.5 million,[16] an interest they turned over to the Exploration Company, Ltd., London.[17] Through their investment in Anaconda and in other mines (outside the United States), by the late 1890s the Rothchilds appear to have "controlled"— that is, to have had power over the sale of—about 40 percent of the world's copper.[18] In the 1890s Anaconda was the premier copper producer in the world, with, as noted, its own smelting and refining facilities.

It has been implied that the Rothschilds were active in marketing Anaconda securities and that their investment was of a portfolio nature.[19] This is wrong. Both the British and the French Rothschilds had long participated in the copper trade and in the 1890s had a number of investments in copper mining—in the giant Rio Tinto mine (Spain) and the Boleo mine (Mexico).[20] They were active in lead and nickel trade and mining as well. Their metals trade was an integral part of their business.[21] Theirs was the most significant European investment in American copper mining.

Meanwhile, other foreign investments in U.S. copper mining rose. By 1899 foreign-controlled American copper-mining output came to more than 25 percent of the total! Anaconda alone, at that time, produced 17 percent of U.S. copper. The Mountain Copper Company of California mined about 4 percent and was under Scottish control, as was the Arizona Copper Company, with roughly 3 percent of American output.[22] In addition, there was the British-controlled Ray Copper Mines, Ltd., near Kelvin, Arizona, which was (at this time) far less important.[23] Also British owned was the Ducktown Sulphur, Copper and Iron Company, Ltd., in Tennessee, formed in 1891 (for which I do not have 1899 production figures; it was not one of the great copper mines). Europeans had shares (extent unknown) in the Boston & Montana Consolidated Copper & Silver Mining Company, which in 1899 did represent fully 11 percent of U.S. copper production.[24] I have not included this production in my 25 percent figure, because I have no evidence (nor do I believe) that the Boston & Montana was "controlled" from abroad. In 1898 the Boston Consolidated Copper and Gold Mining Company, Ltd. (capital, £500,000), had been floated in London to mine copper, gold, and silver in Utah; it would later become a giant copper producer.[25] In short, by the waning years of the nineteenth century, major European investment existed in American copper mining, both direct and portfolio investments.[26]

The Rothschild role in Anaconda was brief. In 1896–1898 the Paris house began to hear reports that the mine's future was limited.[27] When in 1899 Amalgamated Copper Company was organized and acquired the majority of the stock in Anaconda Copper Company, the latter reverted to American control.[28] The Exploration Company, Ltd., resigned the European Agency for Anaconda in November 1899. The Rothschild's main interest in "controlling" Anaconda was—as noted—to market its output in Europe in a manner that would not upset copper prices. When H. H. Rogers and William Rockefeller formed the Amalgamated Copper Company, the first thing they did was to have Lewisohn Brothers take over the European marketing.[29]

At origin, in 1899 Amalgamated acquired not only Anaconda but also properties in which Lewisohn Brothers was interested; at least one of the properties—the Boston & Montana Consolidated Copper & Silver Mining Company, which earlier had absorbed the Montana Copper Company—had attracted European investment.[30] The initial capital of Amalgamated was $75 million. While about $9.7 million of the issue was sold in London and Amsterdam,[31] this stock was widely distributed. The banking house of J. Henry Schroeder received subscriptions in London.[32] The Rothschilds appear to have had no role whatsoever.

From its start, Amalgamated Copper was the world's largest copper company. During the early years of the twentieth century, U.S. copper companies, including Amalgamated and its subsidiary, Anaconda, expanded into international investments.[33] When copper prices were low in 1902, a news report indicated that "the Rothschilds are perfectly agreeable to any combination promising success."[34] The Rothschilds retained their sizable interests in the Rio Tinto mines in Spain, the only significant rival of U.S. copper producers in the pre–World War I years.[35] From what I can establish, however, after 1899 they had no direct stake in U.S. copper mining.

Thus by 1914 there were fewer British direct investments in U.S. copper mining than in 1899. British investors remained in control of Arizona Copper Company,[36] Mountain Copper Company in California, and the Ducktown company.[37] Together these three firms represented roughly 2½ percent of U.S. copper-mining output.[38] In addition, British, French, and possibly other European investors held a considerable minority interest in the Utah Copper Company, which in 1910 had acquired the Boston Consolidated Copper and Gold Mining Company, Ltd. In 1910 owners of the latter ("mainly Europeans") obtained 310,000 shares of Utah Copper Company. Utah Copper proved highly profitable.[39] When in September 1915 a group of unspecified French bankers sold 100,000 shares in Utah Copper (representing 6.1 percent of the 1,624,490 shares outstanding), they received $6.6 million.[40] In 1912 the promising Ray Consolidated Copper Company—the successor to the unsuccessful Ray Copper Mines, Ltd.— seems to have raised $4 million in a Paris flotation.[41] In 1914 the French had no controlling interest in any American copper mine, but obviously they had important portfolio investments. The French (and the British) Rothschilds continued to play a key role in the world copper trade. To this roster of foreign copper mining interests in 1914 in the United States, one must add the widely held European—purely portfolio holdings—in the giant Amalgamated Copper Company.[42] In conclusion, in 1914 substantial portfolio interests by Europeans in U.S. copper mining prevailed, but the *control* over 25 percent of U.S. copper output that existed in 1899 was now reduced to less than 3 percent.

This, however, is not the end of the story. As American copper production had mounted from the 1880s onward, so had the country's smelting and refining capacity. Initially, as indicated, Anaconda's copper had been processed in Wales; sizable domestic output had resulted in *U.S.* smelting and refining. When foreign-owned mining companies in America—such as Anaconda—had integrated into processing, foreign investors were ipso facto involved in smelting and refining. This had, of course, been the case when the Rothschilds had interests in Anaconda (1895–1899). The historian Thomas Navin reports that British capital in the 1880s backed the New Jersey Extraction Company at Elizabethport, an early and not entirely satisfactory electrolytic refinery; this was an exceptional British free-standing investment in refining.[43] Preferred stock of the U.S.-controlled American Smelting and Refining Company (ASARCO) and the associated American Smelters Securities Company was also sold abroad, resulting in purely portfolio investments.[44]

In addition to these foreign interests in processing, three highly significant German-controlled firms processed and sold U.S. copper, as well as lead and zinc. While these German activities in the United States were separate from the direct and portfolio British and French interests I have just discussed, the German metal traders worldwide were closely allied with the other European leaders in the copper business. Thus, although I find no evidence that the Germans cooperated with the French Rothschilds in American business, the Paris Rothschilds were associated with the parents of the German companies that were present in America.[45] The expanding German electrical industry was a large user of copper, and German copper imports soared in the late nineteenth and early twentieth centuries.[46]

None of the German enterprises was important in U.S. mining; all began in trade and integrated backward into processing. The German direct involvement in the U.S. metals trade began in 1880, when the Ladenburg family of Frankfurt, who were related by marriage to the Merton family of Frankfurt and London, opened a private banking house in New York—Ladenburg, Thalmann & Co.—which had a small metals department. In 1887 American Metal Company was formed and took over that department. At origin, American Metal was owned by three German-controlled firms that were intimately linked through both family and business: Ladenburg, Thalmann & Co., New York; Henry Merton & Co., London; and Metallgesell-schaft, Frankfurt.[47] American Metal Company would trade not only in copper but also in lead, zinc, and other metals. (As noted, lead and zinc were often found in nature with copper, and thus the businesses were connected.)

Before the end of 1887, Ladenburg, Thalmann & Co. had sold its holdings in the new company—American Metal Company—to the other two co-owners. One of these, Metallgesellschaft, handled American Metal's trade on the European continent, while the other, Henry R. Merton & Co., was responsible for American Metal Company's commerce in the British Isles and most of the rest of the British Empire. Whenever American Metal Company planned a new project, it acted only after consultation and agreement with its two parent firms. American Metal Company, in its daily market operations, "kept in hourly touch" with these houses in Frankfurt and London.[48] The group came to participate in a significant portion of the international metal trade. When in 1889–90 the Secretan Syndicate sought to dispose of its copper inventories, it had turned to Metallgesellschaft.[49] American Metal Company imported *into* the United States, mainly from Latin America and Canada, copper-bearing materials for treatment in the new American custom smelters and refineries, and it sent U.S. copper abroad for sale in British and European continental markets. In 1892 it opened an office in St. Louis, Missouri.[50]

As the Michigan, Arizona, and Montana copper regions came into production, and as Americans adopted new technology in smelting and refining and broke the monopoly held since the early 1800s by the smelters of Swansea in Wales, the owners of American Metal Company decided that that firm would trade in metals and in addition would have to engage in the treatment of ores, minerals, and metals.[51] In 1891, the same year that Anaconda started its first major refinery, American Metal Company participated in organizing the Balbach Smelting & Refining Company, in Newark, New Jersey, which smelted and refined copper and lead. The new facility received technical assistance from Frankfurt. It pioneered in successful electrolytic refining. By 1913 American Metal Company owned one-third of the Balbach firm and marketed its entire output.[52]

Sometime in the early 1890s American Metal Company acquired a substantial interest in the Nichols Copper Company at Laurel Hill in Long Island, with its much larger refinery than Balbach's. In 1896 American Metal Company made agreements with the Orford Copper Company, the Société le Nickel (a Rothschild company), and the Canadian Copper Company that involved American Metal in the nickel business.[53] American Metal's interests became even broader. In 1912, when a French enterprise planned an aluminum plant in North Carolina (see below), according to American Metal's company history it acquired a 25 percent interest.[54]

In addition, by 1913 American Metal Company owned 65 percent of the stock in the Ohio and Colorado Smelting & Refining Co., with a lead smelter in Salida, Colorado.[55] American Metal had obtained control of various zinc smelters in Oklahoma and Kansas.[56] In 1913 it organized the American Zinc & Chemical Company, making major investments in this new enterprise.[57] Likewise, almost from its start American Metal Company had been an investor in important Mexican mines and smelters.[58]

American Metal Company, in short, had virtually no mining properties in the United States (only coal mines owned in conjunction with its American Zinc & Chemical Company's Pennsylvania venture).[59] It had by 1914, however, through its various joint-ventures, become a significant factor in America's new smelting, refining, and processing industries, as well as in America's international trade in metals. Throughout, it remained German controlled. In 1914, 66.6 percent of the 35,000 shares outstanding of American Metal Company were held by its two parent firms.[60] Its capital stock in 1887 had been a mere $200,000; by 1899 it was up to $1 million; in 1906 it reached $3 million; and by 1914 it was $3.5 million.[61] The returns on its investments were substantial (see Table 8.1). As Harold Hochschild (son of American Metal's first manager, Berthold Hochschild) would put it, "The Metallgesellschaft–Henry R. Merton & Company, Limited–American Metal Company group business was founded on its internationalism and on a continuing and close personal relation between the leaders of the three companies."[62]

Table 8.1. American Metal Company performance, 1909–1914

Year ending July 1	Capital stock outstanding	Total sales	Net earnings
1909	$3,120,000	$64,274,041	$ 854,720
1910	3,500,000	84,402,083	685,335
1911	3,500,000	68,519,484	842,781
1912	3,500,000	57,060,048	1,365,816
1913	3,500,000	79,243,603	1,001,895
1914	3,500,000	68,835,489	1,088,771

Source: Alien Property Custodian, *Report, 1918–1919,* p. 84.

Two other German enterprises likewise became prominent in the pre–World War I U.S. nonferrous metal trades. One firm was Aron Hirsch & Sohn of Halberstadt, Germany, which started a U.S. subsidiary—L. Vogelstein & Co.—in 1897.[63] Its president, Ludwig Vogelstein (1871–1934),[64] became a naturalized American, but the German parent house did not give up its interest.[65] Like American Metal Company, L. Vogelstein & Co. began as a trading firm. In July 1901, however, Ludwig Vogelstein made an agreement with J. R. De Lamar for the construction of an electrolytic copper refinery at Chrome, New Jersey, 75 percent financed by De Lamar and 25 percent by L. Vogelstein & Co. The latter, in return for its contribution of funds, received the sole selling agency for the copper business of this refinery and a guaranteed 1 percent commission on copper sales. The refinery began operations in 1902 under the name De Lamar's Copper Refining Company.[66]

In 1905 L. Vogelstein & Co. acquired De Lamar's interest in the refining company, part of which Vogelstein sold to a company that came to be called the United States Smelting, Refining and Mining Company (USSRMC), incorporated in Maine on January 10, 1906.[67] USSRMC immediately expanded the output of the Chrome, New Jersey, copper refinery and that year opened America's first electrolytic lead refinery, located near Chicago, in Grasselli, Indiana.[68]

Meanwhile, in November 1903 the United States Metals Refining Company was incorporated (in New Jersey). At some point it became the owner of the Chrome electrolytic copper refinery and the Grasselli electrolytic lead refinery; it in turn came to be owned one-third by L. Vogelstein & Co. and two-thirds by the United States Smelting, Refining and Mining Company.[69] L. Vogelstein & Co. had an exclusive contract for the output of the copper refinery for a ten-year period, beginning January 1, 1906,[70] and seems also to have had a similiar arrangement on the lead sales. Likewise, L. Vogelstein & Co. appears to have had a stake in and an exclusive sales contract with Bunker Hill & Sullivan Mining & Concentrating Company (with a lead smelter in San Francisco and a refinery in Sweeny, Idaho),[71] as well as with the multiplant American Zinc, Lead & Smelting Company.[72]

The third German participant in the American metal trades started its U.S. business as late as 1906, when Beer, Sondheimer & Co., of Frankfurt, opened a New York branch.[73] The branch traded mainly in zinc, making contracts for the total output of a number of zinc ore producers in Idaho, Montana, Washington, and Colorado; in 1907 it obtained a controlling interest in the National Zinc Company (with a zinc smelter at Bartlesville, Oklahoma); that year it leased another zinc smelter, in Springfield, Illinois, and an acid plant in Argentine, Kansas. By 1908 it was investing in copper mining in Cuba and taking a long-term lease on a copper smelter in West Norfolk, Virginia, which it operated under the name Norfolk Smelting Company. In 1911 it contracted for copper ore and copper concentrates from U.S. producers.[74] By 1913 Beer, Sondheimer & Co. had become involved in the principal minerals separation company in the United States, which held key patents covering a flotation process for extracting metals.

The flotation process, developed in England, had been patented in the United States; in 1903 a British company, Minerals Separation, Ltd., was organized to hold the patents. In 1910 this firm had conveyed the U.S. patents to a new English corporation, Minerals Separation American Syndicate (Ltd.), designed to use the patents in the United States; the syndicate made a contract with the Beer, Sondheimer & Co. U.S. branch to represent it. Then in 1913 still a third British company was set up—Minerals Separation American Syndicate (1913), Ltd.—in which Beer, Sondheimer & Co. was a stockholder. This new company was authorized to grant licenses to U.S. companies to utilize the flotation process, which became important in American mining.[75] By 1914 the minerals-separating process had been introduced around the world; in the United States the "British" firm was in litigation against U.S. mining companies for patent infringement.[76] In short, in its eight years of existence before 1914, the American branch of Beer, Sondheimer & Co., representing all of its German parent's U.S. interests, had become a significant trader in zinc, controlled several zinc and copper smelters in the United States, and was playing a major role in the transmission of the new minerals separation technology.

The German metal "trio," Metallgesellschaft, Aron Hirsch & Sohn, and Beer, Sondheimer & Co.—parents respectively of American Metal Company, L. Vogelstein & Co., and Beer, Sondheimer & Co. (U.S.)—were in every sense multinational enterprises, with more than 245 affiliates located around the world, participating in mining, processing, and trading in metals.[77] Their American involvements constituted a crucial part of their international business.

The Germans had a profound impact on the world copper markets; American Metal Company and L. Vogelstein & Co. ranked among the six major "U.S." copper exporters.[78] The Germans had an even greater impact on the world lead trade. When in 1909 the International Lead Convention was formed, Metallgesellschaft was its exclusive agent. American Metal Company joined this group, which regulated output and fixed world prices.[79] The French Rothschilds were also involved.[80] As for zinc, in 1909 the German Zinc Syndicate included all three German metal traders, and in 1911 (with the formation of the International Zinc Syndicate) they in turn joined with all the major European producers. With an eye to holding up world prices, the zinc traders' agreement provided for the limitation of the output of zinc smelters as inventories rose.[81] By controlling supplies, the syndicate controlled the world price of zinc. The German trio dominated the American zinc market.[82] The German role in world metal markets was greatly enhanced by the German firms' direct investments in the American Metal Company, L. Vogelstein & Co., and the Beer, Sondheimer & Co. branch; these stakes secured for their owners a position in the United States, the world's largest mineral-producing nation.

Other significant traders and treaters of metals in America, the Guggenheims and the Lewisohns, in particular, were of German heritage. These families, however, established their headquarters in the United States and became American; while they looked to European money markets (and kept European contacts), their enterprises were based in the United States and were not controlled from abroad; thus I have excluded from "German firms" in the United States those of the Guggenheims and Lewisohns (albeit I do note their use of foreign capital).[83] In vivid contrast, the German metal trio had German head offices and a U.S. business that was organized, coordinated, and to a large extent controlled from the European side of the Atlantic. These were foreign direct investments in the United States.

In sum, by 1914 the German influence, through direct investments in the U.S. metals trade, was "potent" and growing.[84] In markets abroad, the German firms were significant sellers of copper and alleged to control "completely" the lead and zinc markets of the world.[85] Since the United States was a large producer of all three of these minerals, the German traders had extended into the United States; they had integrated backward and invested in processing to obtain security of supply. Their investments in smelters and refineries were usually not 100 percent interests, but they were enough to guarantee information and a steady, secure output. The British and the French Rothschilds, with their interests in Anaconda in 1895–1899, seem to have made a foray in the same direction—yet they retreated. I suggested earlier that the reason lay in reports that Anaconda's resources were near exhaustion.

At the 1914 hearings on the Clayton Antitrust Act, John D. Ryan of Amalgamated Copper told a congressional committee that the United States produced 75 percent of world copper and sold 55 percent of that amount in an unmanufactured form to the rest of the world:

When we sell that copper in Europe—to Germany, England, and France—we have to sell it to combined buyers. Repeatedly and regularly the dealers or consumers of Europe have combined to force the American manufacturers of copper to unload, especially at times when business conditions were not good and when a surplus was accumulating. At those times they have almost named their own price, and the result has been that on a business of $850,000,000 in raw copper in 14 years from 1901 to 1913 inclusive $450,000,000 of it was done with foreign countries, mostly in Europe, at a sacrifice of half a cent a pound as against the price secured in the sale of the product to domestic manufacturers.

Ryan urged that the Clayton Act be written in such a way that "producers of copper in this country can protect themselves against the combined buying power of European countries."[86]

To conclude, by 1914, in copper, lead, and zinc, foreign enterprise in America was significant, especially in international trade. The direct British-French role in copper exports (with the Secretan Syndicate) and in mine ownership in the late 1890s, particularly, was reduced by 1914, although British and French portfolio interests remained substantial and the (British and French) Rothschilds still had a major influence on the metals trade abroad. The truly important position of the British in American copper mining in 1895–1899 had been short-lived. By contrast, the German role that started modestly with the small 1880 metals trade department of a private bank had grown dramatically—accompanying the rise and requirements of German industrialization—so that by the outbreak of World War I in Europe in the summer of 1914, three German-controlled businesses in America were key participants in U.S. smelting, refining, and trading in the three principal nonferrous metals. Their processing and commercial stakes were adequate. The Germans had no need to integrate backward into large investments in the U.S. mining of these minerals.[87]

Fertilizers and Some Ingredients: Phosphates, Potash, and Pyrites

In several minerals employed in the preparation of fertilizers, and in one instance in a fertilizer company, foreign investors were important. This was the case in phosphates, a vital ingredient in fertilizers. In the early twentieth century the United States ranked as the world's largest producer of natural phosphates, with an output in 1913 equal to 44.4 percent of global production.[88]

The first foreign investors in U.S. phosphates were British, attracted in the 1870s and 1880s to the new South Carolina phosphate industry.[89] In 1890 the London & Colonial Finance Corporation, Ltd., purchased phosphate-rich land in South Carolina.[90] That same year, the Florida Phosphate Company, Ltd., was floated in London to acquire and to work the newly discovered phosphate deposits in Florida.[91] A contemporary British source described Florida Phosphate Company, Ltd., in 1892 as among the largest (if not the largest) land pebble companies in Florida. It used new technology (a dipper dredge) that proved low cost and efficient. Its Florida headquarters was at Phosphoria, in Polk County.[92] All of these investments appear to have been made by free-standing companies.

France had phosphate mines, but as that nation's reserves dwindled, French output fell in the late nineteenth and early twentieth centuries.[93] Germany had no phosphate deposits of commercial value.[94] Thus, in the late nineteenth and early twentieth centuries, as France and Germany became large importers, French and German companies invested in phosphate mining in Florida. They exported the output and transformed it into fertilizer in Europe.[95] There does not appear to have been vertical integration. Foreign brokers seem to have handled the export sales of these firms as well as those of American producers.[96]

When phosphates were discovered in North Africa (especially in Tunis),[97] the French in 1909–1913 turned away from the United States to obtain their imports from the geographically nearer source. One French firm, Compagnie Générale des Phosphates de la Floride, sold its Florida properties in 1913 for $1 million to the Coronet Phosphate Company of New York,[98] and before World War I, French investment in U.S. phosphate mining had begun to decline.[99] By contrast, the German mining stakes remained large. A sizable percentage of phosphate rock exported from the Florida deposits went to Germany;[100] the Germans in this case were participants in the mining as well as in the trade.

In 1914 some 46 percent of U.S. phosphate output had come to be mined by three U.S.-based fertilizer companies, namely, the American Agricultural Chemical Company, the Virginia-Carolina Chemical Company, and the International Agricultural Corporation (I.A.C.).[101] From its start in 1909, the I.A.C. attracted Austrian investment, associated with I.A.C.'s potash requirements. (Potash, used in making fertilizer, was available only in Germany.)[102] The story of I.A.C.'s formation in 1909 and the activities of its principal foreign investor merit attention.[103]

In the early twentieth century, control over the output and the price of potash was maintained by the German Potash Syndicate, a voluntary association of German potash mine owners that dated back to the 1880s and that was periodically re-formed. The head of this potash cartel was appointed by the Prussian government. In 1905 a wealthy Austrian, Hermann Schmidtmann, acquired the new Sollstedt mine in Prussia, with 50 million tons of potash reserves.[104] Schmidtmann also held controlling interest in the Aschersleben enterprise, one of the oldest of the German Potash Syndicate members, which had an exceptionally large mine in Prussia. While Aschersleben was in the syndicate, the Sollstedt firm refused to join.

In 1905 Hermann Schmidtmann set out to break the Prussian cartel. About the middle of that year, his twenty-five-year-old son, Waldemar Schmidtmann,[105] traveled to the United States to make contracts with American buyers on behalf of the new Sollstedt venture. The contracts were below syndicate prices. At that time, American Agricultural Chemical Company and Virginia-Carolina Chemical Company, the two giants in the U.S. industry, were obtaining volume discounts from the syndicate. Schmidtmann approached the smaller, independent U.S. fertilizer producers and guaranteed that his prices would never exceed those granted by the syndicate to the two American leaders.

Naturally, the Prussians were alarmed, and under German pressure, on May 10, 1907, the Sollstedt company capitulated and joined the Potash Syndicate. This did not mean, however, that the Schmidtmanns had been tamed. The syndicate agreement ran until June 30, 1909. In the wee hours of the morning of July 1, before the syndicate could be re-formed, Hermann Schmidtmann made new American contracts for his potash output.[106]

Two weeks before, on June 14, 1909, his son helped to organize an American firm, the International Agricultural Corporation, which acquired the Tennessee phosphate properties of Thomas C. Meadows (an American).[107] I.A.C. became, at origin, the third giant U.S. fertilizer company. Waldemar Schmidtmann was its first president; Meadows became a vice president.[108] The new enterprise attracted American capital.[109] Shortly after its formation, I.A.C. bought 100 percent of the capital stock of Kaliwerke Sollstedt Gewerkschaft, which owned the German Sollstedt potash mine, and agreed to pay $4 million to the sellers.[110] Prior to July 1909, 75 percent of the Sollstedt firm had been owned by Hermann Schmidtmann and 25 percent by Kaliwerke Aschersleben Gesellschaft, a German corporation controlled by Hermann Schmidtmann.[111] In payment for the Sollstedt stock, the former owners received shares in I.A.C. valued at $4 million.[112] When the German Potash Syndicate was reconstituted in July 1909, both the Sollstedt and Aschersleben enterprises stayed outside.

In March 1910 International Agricultural Corporation represented

Kaliwerke Aschersleben in the new electrochemical industry in the Niagara Falls area. That German-based, Austrian-controlled potash firm had obtained control over the existing business of Roberts Chemical—through a mortgage given the latter in exchange for its potash imports. A new German-owned firm, Niagara Alkali Company, took over the assets of Roberts Chemical.[113]

The Schmidtmanns expanded their potash exports to the United States and acted as participants in I.A.C., to the dismay of the Prussian mine owners. By offering potash at $20 a ton, well below the syndicate price, the Sollstedt and Aschersleben mines captured contracts for fully 80 percent of the U.S. potash requirements! The Sollstedt works in Germany raised its output nearly fivefold to supply the U.S. trade.[114] Then in May 1910 the German Reichstag passed a law mandating a compulsory potash cartel,[115] which made production allocations and imposed penalties for "excess" output. Overnight American buyers saw their contract price raised to $42 a ton (with the penalty tax of $22 added to the earlier $20 price). The German Potash Syndicate had established an American subsidiary, German Kali Works, incorporated in the state of New York in 1909 to sell potash in this country. They now offered it at $35.75 a ton.[116]

After immense confusion and negotiations, late in October 1911 Sollstedt and Ascherleben gave in and agreed to join the cartel.[117] I.A.C. realized that with the 1910 German law, ownership of a potash mine in Prussia no longer offered it any advantage; thus it sold to Kaliwerke Aschersleben one-half of its Sollstedt company shares. It gave Aschersleben an option to purchase the other 50 percent.[118] In December 1913 Waldemar Schmidtmann resigned as president of I.A.C. (he remained a director); an American replaced him.[119] These transactions notwithstanding, Hermann Schmidtmann–related interests retained their holdings ($4 million par value) in I.A.C. stock.[120]

I.A.C. expanded its mining of phosphates in Tennessee and into Florida and invested in acidulating and fertilizer plants.[121] In 1914 it was an important enterprise, with a New York headquarters in lower Manhattan. Its capital stock outstanding was $7,303,500 common and $13,055,500 preferred; and according to a later report of the Alien Property Custodian, the "enemy" interest (predominantly the Schmidtmann holdings) in I.A.C. represented 23.27 percent of the capital stock.[122]

Meanwhile, when the May 1910 German potash law passed, American buyers of potash had faced the high compulsory German cartel price; thus new interest arose in this country in developing a domestic source of this vital raw material. As early as 1898, Americans had known of potash in the Searles Lake brines in California, but while cheap potash from Germany remained available, there had been no incentive to develop the resources. Now, with the high price, investors staked out claims. One entry was the California Trona Company (with claims to 26,000 acres); since 1909 this company had been controlled by interests associated with the Consolidated Gold Fields of South Africa, Ltd. (Cecil Rhodes's company). In June 1913 the California Trona Company was taken over by the new American Trona Corporation (capital, $12,500,000), whose control remained with the Gold Fields group. American Trona completed a potash-processing facility in 1914, although it would take time before commercial production began.[123]

In short, by 1914 there had been British investments in South Carolina and Florida phosphates; there were German and French interests in phosphate mining in Florida. Most important, however, was the 23.27 percent, primarily the Austrian Schmidtmann stake in International Agricultural Corporation, with its highly significant phosphate-mining properties in both Florida and Tennessee. The motive for the foreign investment in I.A.C. had related not to phosphates, but to the potash business. The May 1910 German legislation establishing a compulsory potash cartel, a response to the Schmidtmanns' maneuvers, in turn stimulated British investments in mining and extracting potash from California brine; in 1914 these stakes were still small, and America remained an importer of German-mined potash.

The United States also imported pyrites, which were, like phosphates and potash, inputs for fertilizer production. In 1873 the Rio Tinto Company had started to mine copper ores in Spain,[124] and by the mid-1880s Rio Tinto had become associated with Rothschild interests.[125] In 1891 Rio Tinto granted to the American firm Pennsylvania Salt Manufacturing Company the exclusive right to sell Rio Tinto cupreous pyrites in the United States.[126] Eleven years later (in 1902), Rio Tinto, seeking to market "washed pyrites," set up its own sales branch in the United States, under the supervision of an American chemical engineer, fertilizer specialist, and businessman, A. D. Ledoux. The Pennsylvania Salt Manufacturing Company remained a customer for the pyrites.[127] In 1911 the Rio Tinto Company organized the Pyrites Company, Ltd., in Britain, as a sales subsidiary for the U.S. market; A. D. Ledoux was its first president.[128] The Pyrites Company, Ltd., sold to fertilizer companies, particularly the Virginia-Carolina Chemical Company and the smaller Davison Chemical Company of Delaware.[129] Those two firms were prepared to purchase sizable amounts of cupreous pyrites only if the Pyrites Company, Ltd., disposed of the by-product, cinders. Accordingly, in 1913 the

Pyrites Company, Ltd., began to build two plants, one near Wilmington, Delaware, close to the Davison Chemical Company facilities, and the second—a huge installation—at Roanoke, Virginia, adjacent to the Virginia-Carolina Chemical Company works. These new plants treated the cinder from the imported pyrites used by the fertilizer companies and profitably employed the cinder "as a source of iron."[130] Thus by 1914 the British-incorporated Rio Tinto Company (a Rothschild-dominated enterprise with its main operations in Spain) had a sales subsidiary and two treatment plants in the United States. Rio Tinto's investment in America was based on its desire to sell pyrite in the U.S. market. In sum, the foreign businesses in fertilizer-related activities followed a variety of different patterns. Like the Schmidtmann's investments in I.A.C., Rio Tinto's interests in America were designed to market European output in this country.

Salt

England was a large producer and exporter of salt. In 1888 sixty-four English firms joined in forming the Salt Union, Ltd., constituting about 90 percent of production.[131] This British combination almost at once (in 1889) made plans to consolidate American salt interests. Accordingly, the directors of the Salt Union dispatched a member of the board, James Stubbs, to America to look into the possibilities "of harmonizing the operations of the two great salt-producing countries of the world." Stubbs died on his way back to Britain, but Thomas Ward, J. P. (who had accompanied him), reported on the desire in the United States to form a company to stop the ruinous competition. Arrangements would be made with the Salt Union, Ltd., so that English salt would not push down American prices. The plan was that a new company (North American Salt Company) would be floated in London; it would own seven-eighths of the entire salt output of the United States and Canada. Its London advisory board would consist of Lord Thurlow, chairman of the Salt Union, Ltd., Joseph Verdin, managing director of the Salt Union, Ltd., and two other individuals, both directors of the British Salt Union. A prospectus was issued for North American Salt Company; evaluations of the U.S. properties were made by Price, Waterhouse in New York; the company was formed. Apparently the flotation failed.[132] When, a decade later, in 1899, the National Salt Company of New Jersey attempted to achieve the identical goal of unifying American producers and eliminating competition, there was no discussion of the earlier failure and no indication of British involvement.[133]

Borax and Radium

Borax and radium were minerals used for medicinal purposes. Borax had further uses—in food preservation, for example. It was the only U.S. mineral resource that in 1914 was virtually entirely in foreign hands, that is, under British control. British investors had not, however, been the innovators in the American borax industry, and in fact they did not make their investments until after the major U.S. mines had been opened.[134]

In 1896 an American, Francis Marion Smith, who had developed and controlled the mines and supplies of U.S. borax and in 1890 founded the Pacific Coast Borax Company, was in England, in search of markets and monies to aid his mining venture. There he arranged "an amalgamation" of his business with that of Redwood and Sons, an English food-preservative manufacturer, with plans to establish its own borax refinery. For Redwood and Sons, this U.S. merger would be backward integration to secure a source of supply. It was an obviously complementary relationship, satisfying the needs of both Smith and Richard C. Baker (of Redwood). The Pacific Borax and Redwood's Chemical Works, Ltd. (PBRC), was, accordingly, formed in June 1896 and acquired all the borax properties of the Pacific Coast Borax Company (which remained in existence). Smith obtained about three-quarters of the shares of the new London firm. The two joint–managing directors were Smith, who ran the American operations, and Baker, who from London handled corporate finance, the British and other international business, and acquisitions for PBRC. In 1899 Baker set up a new parent firm, Borax Consolidated, Ltd. (BCL), also headquartered in England, which at origin merged a dozen enterprises, including not only the U.S. interests (the holdings in the mines and processing plants of the PBRC), but also three leading borax-mining companies in Chile and two in Peru, as well as the major British and French borax buyers and processors. Borax Consolidated, Ltd., had a capital of £1,400,000 (roughly $7 million), made up of £600,000 in voting ordinary shares and £800,000 of preferred ones; there was in addition a further £1 million in first-mortgage debentures. Although Baker took the initiative in organizing this multinational enterprise, Smith remained by far the largest shareholder. In 1901 Smith suggested a move of BCL's headquarters to New York; Baker demurred, and Smith dropped the idea. Smith ran the American side of the enterprise with considerable autonomy (albeit monitored by British auditors); Baker made annual trips across the Atlantic and managed Borax Consolidated, Ltd., the parent company. In the United States the business was fully integrated—from mine to consumer products. It advertised widely, promoting borax as good for digestion and for curing epilepsy and bunions, as a bath powder, as a whitener for clothes—and for many other uses.

Meanwhile, Smith was not content to devote himself to these activities; his personal speculations mounted, and in 1913 the California business community "was rocked" by Smith's financial collapse. Baker then acquired Smith's entire holdings in BCL for $4 million, and the securities were placed with the British public. In the spring of 1914 Baker told Smith that under British law a person who became insolvent could not continue to hold a company directorship. Smith was out of the picture. Borax Consolidated, Ltd., under Baker's leadership thus obtained full control of the American business and embarked on further expansion in the United States. Borax Consolidated dominated the U.S. and the world borax industry.[135]

In 1909 the International Vanadium Company in Liverpool, England, formed an American subsidiary, the General Vanadium Company, which began to mine carnotite ores, containing vanadium, uranium, and radium in Colorado the next year. By 1913 General Vanadium ranked as one of the two largest U.S. producers of carnotite ores (the other was Standard Chemical Company of Pittsburgh). General Vanadium exported much of its output, and in 1914 its parent firm started to build a plant in Liverpool to process the ore. In 1914 scientists thought radium was a cure for certain forms of cancer, and concern rose in the U.S. Congress over foreign ownership and export of the carnotite ores.[136] Borax and radium were exceptional as minerals for medicinal purposes.

Aluminum

Aluminum—a new industry—would also bring foreign investment to America. A plant in France, using the Deville process, had made the world's first aluminum in 1855, which it sold for $90 a pound; France monopolized output until in 1882 production started in England. By 1887–88 the British firm Aluminium Company, Ltd., also employing the Deville technique, had lowered the cost and could sell its product at a profit at $5 a pound. Then, in 1888–89 in the United States, the Cowles Company and the Pittsburgh Reduction Company (with the new Hall process) could market aluminum at a profit at $2 a pound. In Europe the Héroult method, similar to Hall's, proved to yield an equally high-volume, low-cost product. By 1891–92, when the output by the new methods had driven the price to 50 cents a pound, producers using either Hall or Héroult patents could still make a profit.[137] The Deville technology had become obsolete.

In 1892 the largest aluminum maker in the world was Aluminium Industrie, A.G. (A.I.A.G.), at Neuhausen, Switzerland, which was formed in 1888 and started commercial production in 1889, with Héroult's process. A.I.A.G. was organized by Swiss and German interests.[138] It soon invested in Germany and Austria as well as in Switzerland.[139] By 1893 Pittsburgh Reduction Company (formed in 1888 and renamed Aluminum Company of America—Alcoa—in 1907) had become the sole producer in the United States. Pittsburgh Reduction Company exported, built a plant in France 1891–92 (which was unsuccessful), made a short-lived market-sharing agreement with A.I.A.G. (1895–96), and invested in Canada (successfully); in 1901 its Canadian subsidiary concluded an agreement with the Swiss, two French, and one British aluminum enterprise[140] wherein each national group reserved its home market exclusively for domestic producers. The United States was "a closed market" to all but the American firm. In 1906 and 1908, new international agreements confirmed the division of markets.[141]

In December 1911 A. V. Davis, president of Alcoa, visited Europe, where he learned that a French aluminum group "had decided" to build an aluminum plant in the United States.[142] At this time the U.S. Justice Department was scrutinizing Alcoa's lone position in the U.S. aluminum industry. On June 7, 1912, Alcoa signed a consent decree, which (among other things) prohibited it from making any agreement to restrict exports or imports into the United States and voided the restrictive covenants of the 1908 international accord. Before Alcoa had signed the decree, in February 1912 Davis wrote J. A. Fowler, assistant to the attorney general, explaining that the English and German aluminum companies had expressed some dissatisfaction that the French producers were planning a U.S. investment by themselves. "It was suggested" that the new venture be undertaken by all producers outside the United States; Alcoa noted that this group would include its wholly owned Canadian subsidiary, Northern Aluminum Company; Davis asked the Justice Department whether it had any objection to this.[143] I have not found the Justice Department's reply.[144]

In its June 22, 1912, issue, the *Engineering and Mining Journal* announced the "formation" of the Southern Aluminium Company.[145] Its president was Adrien Badin, managing director of l'Aluminium Français.[146] Southern Aluminium was under French management.[147] Paul Héroult himself would do the original engineering work.[148] Historians have described Southern Aluminium as a French venture.[149] Most did not realize that the German-controlled American Metal Company and its parent, Metallgesellschaft, were also involved.[150] But what could be more logical, since participating in the organization of l'Aluminium Français (in France) in 1911 was none other than Metallgesellschaft. (Metallgesellschaft became the German representative of l'Aluminium Français.)[151] Apparently Alcoa's Canadian subsidiary, Northern Aluminum Company, did not obtain an interest in Southern Aluminium. In 1915 Southern Aluminium's attorney would describe the enterprise as 90 percent French owned and 10 percent German.[152]

Southern Aluminium Company's initial capital was $6.4 million.[153] It purchased 3,000 acres in Whitney, North Carolina, began to build a dam on the Yadkin River to provide water power, and started construction of an aluminum plant, which, when completed in 1915, was projected to employ between 1,200 and 1,500 men.[154] The original plan was that the alumina (produced with the new Serpek technique) required for this plant would be supplied by a proposed joint-venture company in the United States consisting of Alcoa; its Canadian subsidiary, Northern Aluminum; and the new Southern Aluminium.[155]

Southern Aluminium Company's major multimillion-dollar venture received substantial press attention. Probably its entry occurred because Alcoa, under antitrust pressures, did not feel that 1912 was the appropriate time to insist that the Europeans stay out of America.[156] The French also planned to introduce a new technology—the Serpek technique—in alumina production, and Alcoa would share in this. The planned joint-enterprise to supply alumina seemed to guarantee that Southern Aluminium would not be totally independent.[157] When war broke out in Europe in 1914, Southern Aluminium's ambitious facility was still under construction.[158]

Oil

Last but not least, foreign investment mounted in the U.S. oil industry. In the nineteenth and early twentieth centuries, the United States was the world's major producer and exporter of oil.[159] Although there were some nineteenth-century foreign investments in U.S. oil production, they seem minimal.[160] In the main, before 1900, when Europeans invested in oil resources, they turned eastward. Beginning in 1874 the Swedish Nobels invested in Russian oil.[161] In 1886 Burmah Oil Company was formed to produce in Burma.[162] In 1890 the Royal Dutch Company had its origins in developing existing oil properties in the Netherlands East Indies.[163]

In the nineteenth century, French, British, and German firms traded in oil. In 1866 the Paris Rothschilds began to participate in oil distribution; by the early 1880s they were refining U.S. oil imported into Europe; and in 1883 they invested in Russian oil production. The Rothschilds spent nearly $10 million to complete the railroad from Baku to Batum, which began to make Russian oil competitive with U.S. output in west European markets.[164] The predecessor to Shell, M. Samuel & Co., was a merchant house established in the 1830s to traffic with the Orient; it began to sell Russian oil in the Far East in the 1890s. In 1895–96 M. Samuel & Co. made its first entry into oil production, in Dutch Borneo.[165] Before the turn of the century, the Deutsche Bank had become an importer of oil into Germany and invested in producing oil in Rumania.[166] Thus there was no absence of European interest in the international oil industry.

The minimal European investment in American oil in the late nineteenth century was probably in part at least a consequence of the importance of Standard Oil, which dominated the purchase and refining of American crude oil and exported and invested in marketing worldwide.[167] In the early years of the twentieth century, with new oil finds in America and rising demand for oil, competition increased in the United States. European investors then participated. The context for the initial large European investment was first and foremost the new American oil discoveries, in which they actually took part. The entry was also influenced by the growth of the U.S. automobile industry, which provided new markets. As I will show, the most important of all the foreign investors in the American oil industry was by 1914 starting to help meet U.S. gasoline requirements.

In 1899 Balfour, Guthrie & Co., the San Francisco house of the Liverpool firm Balfour, Williamson & Co., had invested in California oil but found only dry holes. Undeterred, in 1901 Balfour, Williamson & Co. organized the California Oilfields, Ltd., a public corporation in which it held control. The new company acquired oil lands in the Coalinga field in California. Its initial capital was £250,000. This British investment was a true bonanza; production rose rapidly, and by 1904 California Oilfields, Ltd., accounted for fully 11 percent of California oil output. California Oilfields, Ltd., sold its crude oil to the predecessor of Standard Oil of California and then to the company itself, which accordingly expanded its refinery capacity to use the growing supply. Balfour, Williamson & Co.'s investments in California oil were not related to the automobile industry; its motives lay in its recognition that one product of the newly developing industry, fuel oil, was a threat to its existing coal import trade.[168] This was the first successful British investment in American oil.

In 1901 Englishmen flocked to Texas to gather information on oil.[169] That year the Texas Oilfields, Ltd., was formed in Britain to purchase oil lands near Beaumont, Texas. It issued in London $1,054,410 in common stock (denominated in sterling).[170] Onetime Texas Governor James Stephen Hogg bought land at Spindletop and participated in the formation of the Hogg-Swayne Syndicate;[171] in February 1902 Hogg visited England to raise money; there he found men "well posted as to the quality and quantity of Texas oil."[172] A plan was drafted for a new English company to buy out the Hogg-Swayne Syndicate's properties for $6 million (part in cash and part in stock).[173] This did not occur, and on Hogg's return to the United States, the Hogg-Swayne Syndicate was transformed (on April 7, 1902) into the Texas Company (later known as Texaco).[174] In the summer of 1902 a representative of that company was in England seeking capital, but to no avail.[175] There were no important British successes in Texas oil production.

An English syndicate reported it was obtaining output from the Shannon pool in Wyoming in 1902, and beginning in 1905, sizable Belgian, French, and Dutch investments were made in oil properties and later in the most important refining company in Wyoming.[176] Meanwhile, in 1906 the Glenn pool discovery in Oklahoma excited attention,[177] and in 1907–08 two Dutchmen, who had done well as independent producers in Sumatra (joined by another of their countrymen), organized the Oklahoma Petroleum Company (headquartered at the Hague), and a year later (in 1909) the Union Petroleum Company and the Tulsa Petroleum Company.[178] This Dutch group sold out in 1911 to a Paris firm, the Union des Pétroles d'Oklahoma.[179] In 1912 the latter was France's largest oil company; one author ranked it fifty-eighth in assets among French concerns traded on the Paris Bourse.[180] Also investing in oil in Oklahoma in 1914 were Alexander Mackay (a Scot who was active in the Matador Land and Cattle Company) and R. Leicester Harmsworth, a brother of Lord Northcliffe of newspaper fame.[181]

Farther west, by 1913 the British shipping magnate Andrew Weir (later Lord Inverforth) was on the board of General Petroleum Company, and in October 1913 the press reported that Weir and his associates would take over that company and the Union Oil Company, then under option to General Petroleum.[182] In January 1914 the Weir "syndicate," which was said already to control General Petroleum, was maneuvering for Union Oil, which in turn controlled the Independent Producers' Agency, comprising 175 different companies.[183] On March 13, 1914, General Petroleum Company, Ltd., was registered in London to acquire its American namesake. Some weeks later the Western Ocean Syndicate (Weir and associates) obtained a controlling position in Union Oil, and later, in July 1914, they formed the British Union Oil Company, Ltd., in London, to hold their interest in Union Oil and to provide it with over $12 million in cash. With General Petroleum and Union Oil in Weir's hands, his group would reign over about one-third of California oil production. When World War I broke out in Europe, this outcome seemed likely. That it never came to pass is part of a later tale.[184]

The archives of S. Pearson and Son reveal that, beginning in 1901, this British construction firm was offered many U.S. oil properties— in Texas (1901), in Nebraska and Texas (1907), and in Oklahoma, Wyoming, and Texas (1908)—all of which the company declined, most without even investigating. The proposals were brought to the firm's attention by individuals and companies, both American and British.[185] S. Pearson and Son did, however, become a large investor in Mexican oil (with the Mexican Eagle Oil Company, Ltd.—the "Aguila" Company). It sold its Mexican crude oil to Standard Oil of New Jersey,[186] and by 1913 it had established a New York office of its Anglo Mexican Petroleum Products Company, Ltd. (AMPPC), incorporated in England on July 24, 1912. The New York office supervised the establishment of bunkering stations for its Mexican oil, handled on a c.i.f. (cost, insurance, freight) basis crude and fuel oil sales in the United States, and purchased materials for "Aguila" in this country. A director of the British AMPPC, Herbert Carr, ran the New York office.[187]

Of the numerous early-twentieth-century foreign entries into the U.S. oil industry, the most significant and enduring was that by the Royal Dutch-Shell group, which by 1914 was the only foreign investor involved in all facets of the American oil business, the only one fully integrated, which operated on a national scale in the United States.[188] During much of the 1890s Shell's predecessor (M. Samuel & Co.), the Royal Dutch Company, and Standard Oil of New York had competed in east Asian markets. In 1897 the "Shell" Transport and Trading Company was organized in Great Britain. That year, in the Far East, the British Shell had formed an uneasy coalition with Royal Dutch, a cooperative relationship that became formal in 1902–03 when the British and Dutch firms, joined by the Paris Rothschilds, organized the Asiatic Petroleum Company to sell oil from Japan to South Africa.[189] In 1907 Shell and Royal Dutch merged their worldwide business, on the basis of 60 percent of profits to Royal Dutch, 40 percent to Shell. Royal Dutch-Shell now looked worldwide for both markets and sources of oil supply.

Meanwhile, in 1905 Standard Oil of New York and Asiatic Petroleum Company had agreed to quotas in the far eastern oil trade, an accord that Standard Oil of New York violated in August 1910, when it lowered prices, seeking larger sales. At the same time, in 1910 Standard Oil of California, which had been purchasing Asiatic Petroleum's surplus gasoline (for which there was no demand in the Far East) told Royal Dutch–Shell's chief executive, Henri Deterding, that the product was no longer required. Standard Oil of California had its own refinery to produce gasoline and was purchasing and expected to purchase large amounts of crude oil from two companies owned by Balfour, Williamson—the California Oilfields, Ltd., and the Lobitos Oilfields, Ltd. (in Peru).[190]

With the new circumstances existing in 1910, Deterding responded, telling Walter Teagle of Standard Oil of New Jersey—the principal company in the Standard Oil group—that no understanding could be reached for Eastern markets without a settlement in Europe,[191] and to make his point, Royal Dutch-Shell entered the *European* kerosene markets with oil from Rumania, offering a challenge to Standard Oil. Far more important, early in 1911 Deterding announced that he would invade Standard Oil's home territory, the United States. His company would sell its own "surplus" Sumatra gasoline on the American West Coast, the output that Standard Oil of California refused to buy.[192]

Deterding had long considered selling in America, the world's largest national market. As early as June 1909 the Asiatic Petroleum Company, Ltd., had registered in Washington, D.C., the mark: "Shell" Petroleum Spirits for Automobiles.[193] Likewise, Deterding—whose group had purchased crude oil in America[194]—had been tempted by prospects of U.S. investments in production. In 1909 the Dutch investors in Oklahoma (interests to which I referred earlier) had approached Royal Dutch-Shell for financial help; Deterding had been sufficiently interested to contemplate a pipeline to the Gulf of Mexico, a refinery there, and "an all embracing business"; he had, in fact, dispatched a man to investigate, who scotched the idea of an investment, believing that the oil output of the particular oil property in Oklahoma would soon decline.[195] Royal Dutch had received other offers, since the company seemed a potential buyer. Increasingly, in 1909 Deterding had considered a "well-to-wick" (crude oil to lamp oil) business in America.[196] He apparently had thought of gasoline sales as well, since that was the mark registered in Washington that year.

In the spring of 1910, according to the historian F. C. Gerretson, the Banque Franco-Américaine had suggested to Deterding a joint venture in purchasing the Barnsdall oil holdings, covering 1.1 million acres in Oklahoma, Illinois, and Indiana.[197] As Deterding evaluated this proposition, Walter Teagle of Standard Oil of New Jersey opened negotiations with him designed to stabilize world markets; Deterding terminated his talks with the Barnsdall interests. Gerretson writes,

"The entry of Royal Dutch into America was still more in the nature of a threat than a firm decision; in his heart Deterding still preferred a new division of the market on the old basis," that is, an agreement with Standard Oil.[198]

In May 1911 the U.S. Supreme Court ordered the dissolution of Standard Oil. Under such conditions, Teagle-Deterding negotiations were clearly inappropriate. That summer of 1911, Royal Dutch's J. C. van Eck and F. P. S. Harris (the London manager of Asiatic's gasoline department) selected locations for ocean terminals in Seattle, Portland, Vancouver, and San Francisco.[199] These terminals would store Sumatra gasoline for sale on the American West Coast. In June 1911 Asiatic Petroleum Company, Ltd., registered the "Shell" trademark in California.[200]

Still, the Royal Dutch-Shell plans proceeded casually, despite "fierce" competition[201] from Standard Oil companies, until Standard Oil of New Jersey, thwarted in its expansion at home by the antitrust action, resolved to invest in an oil concession in Sumatra. This stab into the heart of Royal Dutch Company territory apparently galvanized Deterding into rapid action.[202] When on April 11, 1912, Standard Oil of New Jersey formed the Nederlandsche Koloniale Petroleum Maatschappij to seek oil in the Netherlands East Indies, immediately (April 12)—according to Gerretson—at a Royal Dutch Company board of directors meeting, Deterding explained the crisis, outlined the measures required, obtained the board's approval, returned to London, and proceeded to act.[203]

On two separate fronts, Deterding made decisions: First, he would sell Sumatra gasoline on the American West Coast. Second, he would produce in America's midcontinental fields. The two strategies developed together. In April 1912 the group sent an American, Donnell G. Fisher, to Seattle to direct Shell's sales efforts on the West Coast. Fisher rented office space and expedited the construction of Shell's Seattle terminal.[204] On September 3, 1912, the group organized the American Gasoline Company (in New York) to sell gasoline ("Shell Motor Spirit") on the Pacific Coast. After Shell's ocean terminal north of Seattle was completed, on September 16 a Shell tanker brought in a cargo of more than one million gallons of Sumatra gasoline.[205]

Meanwhile, in June 1912 Deterding had formed the 's-Gravenhage Association, with a capital of £1 million in ordinary shares and £1,000 in deferred shares, a company in which the Royal Dutch-Shell group owned 51 percent of the shares and the rest was held by the group's "financial friends," chiefly London and Paris banking houses, including the Paris Rothschilds, which had the largest minority share (9.4 percent). In July Shell personnel arrived in Tulsa, Oklahoma, to purchase properties in that state to be held by the newly formed Roxana Petroleum Company, which in turn (through a New York company) came to be owned by the 's-Gravenhage Association. Deterding's representatives acquired six companies, producing 2,900 barrels (not the 15,000 output that Deterding desired).[206] Nonetheless, with the West Coast marketing and the Oklahoma acquisitions, Deterding could write in December 1912, "We *are* now in America."[207]

Later Deterding would recall: "When our business grew to such international dimensions, we obviously had to dig ourselves in as traders on American soil; otherwise we would have lost our foothold everywhere else. Until we started trading in America, our American competitors controlled world prices . . . So to put an end to this state of things, I decided that we must take America . . . into our general working plan."[208]

From this point onward, Royal Dutch-Shell's U.S. expansion was vigorous. Standard Oil companies—fettered by the antitrust action—did little as Deterding's invasion mounted. The firm installed a marketing representative in New York.[209] In February 1913 Deterding dispatched to America from London the geologist B. H. van der Linden, who had just returned from the Netherlands East Indies. His assignment was to seek out producing properties in California. Deterding was convinced that U.S. Pacific Coast markets could not continue to be served by imports from the Netherlands East Indies. On August 6 Shell men in California received a cable from the London home office to communicate with Balfour, Guthrie & Co. of San Francisco, representative of the British Balfour, Williamson & Co., which owned controlling interest in the successful California Oilfields, Ltd.[210]

At an August 8, 1913, board of directors meeting of the "Shell" Transport and Trading Company, the directors heard Robert Waley Cohen (who was then second only to Deterding in the group) describe the properties of California Oilfields, Ltd. An investment in this firm, Waley Cohen reported, would be expected to yield a profit of 57 percent per annum on Shell shares. Thus, other considerations aside, the purchase was "attractive on its merits," but Waley Cohen added that California Oilfield's output had supplied "half the total quantity of bulk kerosene shipped by the Standard Oil Co. to compete with us in the East." The acquisition would, accordingly, have a favorable impact on Far Eastern markets. The board authorized Deterding and Marcus Samuel to pursue negotiations leading to the purchase. At the same August 8, 1913 meeting, the commitment to American business was further affirmed, when after a detailed presentation by Waley Cohen, the board resolved that Deterding and

Samuel act for the "Shell" Transport and Trading Company in negotiations (that included the Royal Dutch Company) to buy out the
minority interest (49 percent) in the 's-Gravenhage Association, the
holding company for the group's Oklahoma producing enterprises.[211]
Van der Linden cabled a favorable report on the California properties
from a geologist's view. Deterding acquired them for the group on
August 11, 1913.[212] He also obtained for the group the 100 percent
interest in the 's-Gravenhage Association.[213]

In October 1913 Sir Marcus Samuel, as chairman of the board of the
"Shell" Transport and Trading Company, described the group's California oilfields as comprising 7,040 acres, of which 4,960 were oil-
bearing lands. "There are 115 wells producing and 17 being
drilled."[214] For the next decade and a half, Shell's California oil output would be greater than that from its midcontinental fields.[215]
Balfour, Williamson had had reservations about selling this valuable
California property;[216] Shell's offer, however, appeared good to that
firm. Most important, California Oilfields' three-year sales contract
with Standard Oil of California was up for renewal in August 1913;
Balfour, Williamson and its principal customer were "far apart" on
the price of crude.[217] Deterding's timing proved excellent.[218]

In 1913–14 Deterding sought to acquire Gulf Oil Corporation and
with it a significant position in Texas (these negotiations did not
accomplish their purpose).[219] The Royal Dutch-Shell group, however,
continued its expansion in Oklahoma. In California it made an offer
(which came to naught) for General Petroleum Company.[220] It did
add to its existing oil lands in that state.[221] It began to build a pipeline,
and at Martinez on San Francisco Bay, it started to construct a giant
modern refinery.[222] In 1914 the group changed the name of its California marketing company from American Gasoline Company to the
Shell Company of California, Inc.[223] Early in 1914 Donnell Fisher, its
marketing manager, acquired the first curbside gasoline pump for use
in the Northwest.[224]

By 1914 the U.S. direct investments of the Royal Dutch-Shell group
(which had been zero in January 1912) were in excess of $17.7
million.[225] The company produced oil in California and Oklahoma; by
my count it owned three small refineries in California and had a major
one under construction there;[226] it was laying a $3 million pipeline in
that state; it had developed marketing outlets on the West Coast. It
had a New York office. Its U.S. crude oil production of roughly 5
million barrels in 1914 already represented almost 2 percent of all U.S.
output.[227] While there remained other foreign investors in the American oil industry in 1914 (a number of purely British firms, the important Weir interests in California, the French company in

Oklahoma, a Dutch-French group as well as the French-Belgian-Dutch group in Wyoming, and the Pearsons in marketing),[228] Royal Dutch-Shell was the only one with important multistate operations. It had made multinational-enterprise-type investments. Deterding from London made the strategic decisions; experts were sent from Britain and Holland; the U.S. business was an integrated part of Royal Dutch-Shell's worldwide operations. Both its genesis and its growth were associated with Deterding's global plans. By the time of the outbreak of World War I in Europe, Royal Dutch-Shell had set the foundations for its successful future in the U.S. market. Shell had become a significant "American" oil company. In 1914 it had the greatest direct investment of any single foreign industrial enterprise in the United States.[229]

Minerals and Mineral-Based Industries

In the years 1875–1914, a large number of foreign direct investors in the United States—from Britain, Germany, France, Austria, Belgium, and Holland—participated in extracting, recovering, processing, transforming, and exporting American minerals. The Alien Property Act of 1887 represented no long-run material obstacle. Throughout the entire period U.S. developments continued to attract foreign capital, skills, technology, and business organization in many different branches of the mineral industries. American railroads opened up vast quantities of resources that, for the first time in these years, could be moved into domestic and world trade. Population growth along with new industries in Europe *and* America created unprecedented demands on the mineral industries. Foreign direct investors with special knowledge of markets overseas were important in spurring U.S. exports. America's rich resources drew in investors from abroad. Sometimes the foreign direct investors helped to start up mineral developments (in gold and silver and in phosphates, for example); often they entered after such development was well under way (in copper, borax, and oil, for instance).

London was the center of mining finance, and many free-standing mining companies were floated there. Far fewer such companies took part in processing and primary mineral manufacture. None was in the mineral trades. All free-standing companies in the mineral industries were not alike, although all were based on their founders' (and investors') desire to take advantage of opportunities for profit. They included (1) companies that U.S. and British promoters arranged to float in London to put their hands on British and other foreign monies (these abounded in gold and silver mining especially); (2) companies set up in London by individuals in the same industry in Britain, but not directly integrated through regular intracompany trade with the firms of their founders (this was the case with the Southern States Coal, Iron and Land Company, for example); (3) companies established by promoters to raise extra capital, but which had on their initial boards men with more than token knowledge of the business (Otis Steel Company, Ltd., for instance); (4) companies formed as adjuncts to railroad finance (the coal companies that would sell to American railroads); and (5) entities loosely coupled to one another but that bore a strong resemblance in their groupings to the institutional structure of a multinational enterprise (gold-mining companies that were floated in London, for instance, with participants who carefully investigated the prospects, used reliable mining engineers, and had representation in the United States; there were networks of merchant bankers in London closely allied with metal traders, or metal traders themselves, who made "related mining investments" in what seemed, to the casual observer, to be otherwise independent companies). Some free-standing companies set up in England or Scotland were identified with British investment trust companies (the American Association, Ltd., Otis Steel, and Arizona Copper Company, for instance). Some free-standing companies may have served— or may even have been established—to provide markets for machinery produced in the United Kingdom by their founders or directors (Thomas Whitwell seems to have sold blast furnace stoves to the Southern States Coal, Iron and Land Company; Edgar Watts' Cardiff company had a contract with the American Association, Ltd., to build its U.S. plant). More investigation is required to define the exact nature of some of the free-standing companies in the U.S. phosphate and oil industries; in these, interlocking principals with other free-standing companies, however, have been identified.

I have called the British-incorporated free-standing companies foreign *direct* investment because the stated purpose for forming such companies in Great Britain was to exercise control. A large number of the free-standing companies in the mineral industries proved to be short-lived, since they were overcapitalized and sometimes shams (from the very beginning) and since their founders' profits came from their establishment rather than from their operations. Many had brief lives because the absence of a full-time staff at the home office frequently meant the inability to manage effectively what took place across the Atlantic Ocean, desires notwithstanding. Mine management firms were employed to cope with this administrative deficiency and to provide trustworthy information to investors. In fact, the most successful of the free-standing companies seem to have been parts of clusters—associated with experienced groups, with interlocking participants. Such arrangements helped them to cope with management problems. The British and French Rothschilds appear in numerous contexts, from precious metals to copper to oil, their role in U.S. mineral industries mirroring their worldwide involvements. They had contacts with the best mining engineers. Never did they have 100 percent ownership of a gold mine, copper property, or oil-producing venture. Rather, they (or the Exploration Company, Ltd.) invested in production with an eye to the latter's impact on world metal or oil markets, or to assist associated firms. The Rothschilds played a role in free-standing companies set up in Britain and also in American-incorporated units.[230]

Foreign-headquartered multinational enterprises in the U.S. mineral industries included such different firms as the Consolidated Gold Fields of South Africa, Ltd.; Deutsche Gold-und Silber-Scheideanstalt (DEGUSSA); Balfour, Williamson; Sanderson Brothers; Thomas Firth & Sons, Ltd.; William Jessop & Sons; Edgar Allen & Co.; Tubes, Ltd.; E. Morewood & Co.; the Duffryn Works; Mannesmann; Metallgesellschaft; Aron Hirsch & Sohn; Beer, Sondheimer & Co.; Schmidtmann's companies; Rio Tinto Company; the Salt Union, Ltd.; Borax Consolidated, Ltd.; International Vanadium Company; l'Aluminium Français; S. Pearson and Son; and Royal Dutch-Shell. Several of these made American plans that did not materialize or made brief investments that can be designated as failures. Others, however, proved highly successful, and many of these became involved in more than a single mine or a single processing unit. Some became multiplant, multistate or multiterritory operations of formidable dimensions. All of those that were successful had some special advantage, talent, or market niche.

The German metal traders, in particular, in copper, lead, and zinc had such multiplant, multistate facilities. They were significant in world mineral markets—their advantage lying in the experience and contacts of their parents. They made important investments in backward integration into U.S. smelting and refining. Frequently their interests were less than 100 percent in smelters and refineries, but there was overall management of the cluster of affiliates.

While the German metal traders (and other trading firms, such as Balfour, Williamson, in mining and oil production) integrated backward, rarely was there backward vertical integration by European *manufacturers* to serve their needs at home.[231] Thus no foreign steel company invested in U.S. iron ore for its own use in England, France, or Germany; no foreign electrical firm owned American copper mines; no foreign electric storage battery enterprise acquired U. S. lead mines; and no British, French, or German fertilizer manufacturer (to my knowledge) invested in South Carolina or Florida phosphate mining.

The few cases of backward integration by European manufacturers were (1) Redwood and Sons (later Borax Consolidated) in borax, and in that situation there was effectively a partnership with an American producer (with the original initiative taken by the latter);[232] (2) International Vanadium Company, which built its British plant *after* it had begun to mine carnotite ores in the United States; and (3) Royal Dutch-Shell, which did *not* invest in American crude oil production for sale to its refineries abroad.

How is this overall absence of investment by foreign manufacturers in U.S. raw materials extraction for their own use abroad to be explained? Different reasons appear appropriate in different industries; the reasons seem to include those related to alternative raw material availability, transportation costs, costs of investment in an unfamiliar activity, and differences in scale economies between the mine and the manufacturing process. Thus, while American minerals were exported, while foreign-owned trading houses participated in a highly significant manner, and while the German traders had sizable investments in American smelters and refineries, European *manufacturers* (Borax Consolidated excepted) did not integrate backward to invest in obtaining their home raw material needs.

By contrast, foreign manufacturers (and also foreign mining companies) did invest in America in the mineral industries *to sell* in the United States either their home- or U.S.-produced output, or both. Interestingly, iron- and steel-manufacturing firms (or their principals) in the United Kingdom appear to have invested or participated in the formation of free-standing companies (not to get raw materials, but—as indicated above—to market their machinery). This insight represents an unexpected, although thoroughly plausible, form of vertical integration (forward rather than backward).

Desire to sell their home or foreign output in the United States was clearly the case (with no free-standing companies involved) when the Welsh tinplate makers invested in tinhouses in America, when the Schmidtmanns helped to form International Agricultural Corporation, when Rio Tinto Company built plants in Delaware and Virginia to treat the cinder from the imported pyrites, when S. Pearson and Son opened an office in New York, and when Royal Dutch-Shell constructed terminals on the West Coast to sell Sumatra gasoline. Likewise, with the aim of reaching American customers, DEGUSSA invested at Niagara Falls, and the Sheffield crucible-steel makers built and acquired plants in this country. Indeed, numerous foreign enterprises, mining companies as well as manufacturers, invested in selling, further processing of their output, or manufacturing in America to capture more of the U.S. market.

Free international trade in minerals did not exist. In copper, lead, zinc, potash, aluminum, and oil, cartel agreements (and the process of making or "unmaking" them) shaped the course of foreign investment as well as that of commerce. In no instance, however, was competition totally absent. Antitrust action in aluminum and oil, in fact, cleared the way for sizable foreign direct investments in the United States, even though the ones in aluminum would prove of limited duration.

In the mineral industries, in many cases, the foreign direct investments were in industries in which there was no U.S. direct investment abroad (in crucible steel, tinplate, phosphates, and salt, for example). On the other hand, in copper, aluminum, and oil there were U.S. direct investments in foreign countries. Nonetheless, in each of these industries there was a marked asymmetry in the patterns of cross investment.[233]

To conclude, foreign direct investment assisted in the development of America's mineral resources—gold, silver, coal, iron, copper, lead, zinc, phosphates, borax, carnotite ore, and oil. The stakes were in mining, processing, manufacturing, and trade. Technological advances introduced by the foreign direct investors included a new process of gold recovery (the MacArthur-Forrest process), production of cyanide for that process, machinery for southern iron and steel works, crucible-steel-manufacturing know-how, possibly tinplate technology (although this is less clear), electrolytic refining methods, flotation process technology, and dipper dredges (used in phosphate mining). Had the Serpek technique to make alumina worked, it would have been a major case of technological transfer by foreign direct investors. Foreign direct investors played a central role in U.S. exports of copper, lead, and zinc. For foreign direct investment to persist, investors needed some kind of advantage; generally, capital was not enough. The foreign direct investors that remained in America in 1914—among them DEGUSSA, the crucible-steel makers, American Metal Company, Borax Consolidated, and Royal Dutch-Shell—provided careful management for their large U.S. interests.

In addition to the foreign direct investments in America's mineral industries, portfolio interests from abroad became substantial. Portfolio investments resulted from two routes. First, direct investments turned into portfolio ones—in the case of United States Steel Corporation (where direct investments in the predecessor companies became portfolio interests) and in the case of Otis Steel (where the dissolution of the parent British free-standing company left British investors as portfolio investors in an American concern). The second path, probably more important, was the sale of newly issued and existing American securities abroad—both of companies and of their successor companies (when there were mergers). Such sales of securities accounted for most of the portfolio interests in United States Steel Corporation, Bethlehem Steel, Amalgamated Copper, American Smelting and Refining—and a whole range of lesser firms such as Utah Copper and Ray Consolidated Copper. Indeed, in dollar value, portfolio investments in 1914 may well have surpassed direct ones in America's mineral industries. Measured by impact—that is, by the development of new properties, new markets, and new technologies—the direct investments, however, were far more significant.

I am not rewriting U.S. economic history. I do not dispute the view that by the start of World War I America's mineral industries (or at least, mining industries) were basically in U.S. hands. Foreign trade in key minerals was more strongly affected, and the role of foreign investment in mineral-related industries in these years was clearly substantial. In the process of the development of America's abundant natural resources in the period 1875–1914, foreign capital, technologies, managerial skills, and particularly international marketing talents were used. The history of America's mineral industries cannot be written without constant references to the participation by European business.

9.

Food, Drink, Tobacco, and Grocery Products

Foreign direct investments in food, drink, tobacco, and grocery products were numerous. Major investments—primarily British— were made in cattle raising; in East Coast beef slaughtering, exporting, and selling abroad; and in midwestern meat packing of hogs and beef, as well as in the Union Stock Yards. British investors produced in America everything from rice to fruit, but most notable were their involvements in the grain trade (more than in wheat production) and particularly in flour mills. British companies took over and merged many American breweries, while other alcoholic beverages attracted some, albeit far less, attention. British, Swiss, and German enterprises offered branded food and drink products—from condensed milk to baby food to chocolates, from dog biscuits to coffee, tea, and carbonated soft drinks; such businesses had sales outlets and factories in America. British tobacco companies also invested in the United States. So did British soapmakers and other producers of nonfood grocery products. The methods used by foreign firms to distribute their branded goods in this country were not identical— and although they might involve foreign direct investments, this was not inevitable.

In these products the three types of foreign direct investors, not unlike those encountered earlier, were (1) individuals, (2) free-standing companies (similar to many of the mining enterprises discussed in Chapters 7 and 8), and (3) companies operating abroad that extended their business into America, as in the modern multinational enterprise. In the first case, individuals would form partnerships with Americans or send their own representatives to the United States. In the second, very common case, promoters combined with business-men to raise capital on foreign (mainly British) money markets; these

British companies made the direct investments in America. Sometimes, as these companies were dissolved, the foreign direct investments in America made by British companies were transformed into
portfolio ones of the individuals who had once had interests in the
British firms. In the third case, an existing company (typically headquartered in Britain or on the European continent, and in one rare
instance in Japan) reached out either for sources of supply or, more
often, for American markets, and in the process made investments in
the United States. Foreign direct investments in food, drink, tobacco,
and grocery products were sizable, whereas foreign portfolio ones
were minimal; thus this chapter will deal almost exclusively with the
foreign direct investments.

The Cattle Companies

As the railroads and the mining frontier pushed westward, so too it
became possible to raise cattle on the vast open spaces. Range cattle
in the Great Plains was a post–Civil War development; foreign investors were important participants. The pioneer major foreign investment in American cattle ranches was in the JA Ranch, in Texas. The
investor, John G. Adair of Scotch-Irish background, was a large land-
holder in Rathdair, Ireland. He had made his first trip to the United
States in 1866 and had that year set up (under the charge of an agent)
a "brokerage" office in New York. He borrowed money in Britain at
4 percent and then lent it in the United States at 10 percent. He
married an American in 1869, and the couple lived part of the time in
the United States and part in Ireland. "Home" seems to have been
Ireland, and in an 1882 contract Adair was described as "of Ireland."

In 1874 Adair went on a hunting trip to the American West, a
fashionable activity for wealthy Britishers. In 1875 he moved his
brokerage office (which really seems to have been a loan office) to
Denver, Colorado. He saw the potential for financing cattle raising,
and on June 18, 1877, he joined in a partnership with an American,
Charles Goodnight. By 1885 Goodnight had acquired on his and
Adair's behalf more than 1,335,000 acres in the Texas Panhandle and
100,000 head of cattle; the venture from the start proved extremely
profitable.[1]

Meanwhile, in the late 1870s, with rising U.S. exports of cattle
(livestock) and dressed beef (refrigerated meat), English and Scottish
stock raisers became concerned and investigated the potential
competition.[2] Their studies (along with those of others), made in the
late 1870s, concluded that low-cost land in the United States, far
cheaper than in Britain, offered prospects for extraordinary profits in

cattle raising. Here were excellent opportunities for English and Scottish capital. Some reports suggested that investors could get free land, or at least that their cattle would have "free range" over the plains.[3]

After 1879, stimulated by the imports of cattle and beef and even more by the anticipation of great profits, English and Scottish stock raisers, joined by many other British investors, took part in cattle companies that made huge investments in U.S. cattle raising.[4] Frequently investors were encouraged by the activities of American entrepreneurs who, like Goodnight, sought out British capital. Unlike Adair's partnership arrangement, however, most of these post-1879 ventures in raising cattle were carried forth by companies chartered in Great Britain. Table 9.1 reveals the proliferation of British cattle companies.[5]

The Earl of Airlie, the first chairman of the board of the Prairie Cattle Company, Ltd., had raised one of the finest herds in Scotland.[6] His name on the board of this company would encourage British investors.[7] Promoters of the cattle companies—Americans and Britons—praised them as producers of 25 to 50 percent annual profits. Who could resist?[8] The opportunities had the glitter of gold and silver mines. Those who knew of Adair's success envisaged equal gain. American promoters, traveling to the United Kingdom, touting the properties, were very important in the intermediation of monies.

All the companies listed in Table 9.1 were registered in England or in Scotland. The table excludes direct acquisitions of ranches by individual British and French investors.[9] Likewise, it does not include American-incorporated cattle companies that sought money in London.[10] The table presents only the initial acreage obtained; some ranches grew much larger over time. In Chapter 6 I discussed a variety of British stakes in land; those in cattle ranches were by far the largest.[11]

In 1880 there were 800,000 range cattle in Texas and 250,000 in Wyoming; by 1883 the figures soared to over 5 million in Texas and roughly 1 million in Wyoming. Foreign investors were in great part responsible.[12] Major cattle ranches in Texas, Wyoming, Colorado, and New Mexico came to be owned by British companies. The Dakotas and Montana also attracted foreign monies. British investors, in particular, impressed New Yorkers and Chicagoans, much less westerners, by the formidable amount of financial resources at their command and their grand acquisitions.

Methods of financing the ventures varied from the sale of common stock in the British companies set up to own the properties (Espuela Land and Cattle Company, Ltd.) to the sale of fixed-interest bonds

(Capitol Freehold Land and Investment Company, Ltd.). Sometimes there was a public issue abroad; at other times a group of British investors acted together to form a British company with no outside participation. The Scottish American Mortgage Company, Edinburgh, was an intermediary in financing the famous Prairie Cattle Company and other cattle companies as well. The British cattle companies were free-standing enterprises, not subsidiaries of other British firms, although many were closely associated with Scottish investment trusts and mortgage companies.

Robert Fleming, the Scot discussed in Chapters 4 and 6, took part in the important Matador Land and Cattle Company. William J. Menzies' Scottish American Investment Company group, of Edinburgh, had a number of cattle company interests (see Table 9.1). William Mackenzie of Dundee figured importantly in cattle ranches (through his involvement with the Dundee Mortgage and then the Alliance Trust Company). Several cattle companies involved James W. Barclay, member of Parliament from Forfar, Scotland (see Table 9.1), who was a close friend of William Mackenzie and Lord Airlie.[13] Sir John Pender (1815–1896), who had other U.S. businesses, invested in the Dakotas.[14]

One careful student of these interests—W. Turrentine Jackson—estimated that British stakes in American cattle ranches approached $45 million in the 1880s, with the principal investments being made in the first part of the decade.[15] Cattle breeds improved as imported British pedigree animals raised the quality of American stock.[16] Foreign investment carried the expertise of the Scottish stock raisers to America. "Artificial watering facilities, barbed wire fencing, and permanent ranges owned in fee" became the norm. Ranges became ranches.[17]

Many British-owned cattle ranches hired American managers. In some cases—for example, the huge XIT Ranch in Texas—the British directors "had almost nothing to do with its [the ranch's] operations." The American managing director of XIT made annual reports to the British board, giving the "conditions of the ranch, number of cattle, sales, and values," and that was it.[18] By contrast, other ranches were under conscientious British management. The Matador Land and Cattle Company, which started in Texas in 1882, began after an American had traveled to Dundee to seek out investors. The American became the manager of the ranch as well as a director of the newly organized Scottish company, but most important, the Scots sent William Fife Sommerville, a Dundee merchant with "some experience in the cattle business in northern Britain," to serve as assistant manager. Sommerville, who became manager (from 1885 to his death in 1890),

Table 9.1. British companies' acquisitions of cattle ranches in the American West, 1879–1889

Date of prospectus	Company, location, organizer	Capital at origin (in pounds)	Territories and /or states in which business done	Acreage owned (if known)	Comments
1879	Anglo-American Cattle Co., Ltd., London	70,000	Wyoming and Dakota Territory	Unknown	By 1882 dropped from Stock Exchange list
	Colorado Ranche Co., Ltd., London (James W. Barclay, Scottish M.P., founder)	25,000	Colorado	10,000	Associated with Colorado Mortgage and Investment Co., Ltd. (in land and mining); in difficulty, 1884–1886
1880	*Prairie Cattle Co., Ltd., Edinburgh enterprise "with large overtones of Dundee control" (Earl of Airlie first chmn.)	200,000	New Mexico, Colorado, Texas	2,240,000 (by 1883 "control over")	Associated with Scottish American Mortgage Co.; liquidated Dec. 1914
1881	*Texas Land and Cattle Co., Ltd., London (Dundee monies)	240,000	Texas	236,000	Sold off land and herd 1901–1906
1882	Arkansas Valley Land and Cattle Co., Ltd. (a Barclay co.)	250,000	Colorado	Enclosed over 1,000,000 acres by 1884	Decided to go out of business 1890
	California Pastoral and Agricultural Co., Ltd. (Scottish-Amer. Investment Co. group)	250,000	California	94,000	Sold ranch 1911
	Cattle Ranche and Land Co., Ltd., London (chief promoter Rufus Hatch; Dundee investors)	200,000	Texas	1,280,000	Did not survive beyond 1893
	*Hansford Land and Cattle Co., Ltd., Dundee	210,000	Texas, New Mexico	14,000	Finally liquidated in 1912

Company	Capital (£)	Location	Acres	Remarks
*Matador Land and Cattle Co., Ltd., Dundee	400,000	Texas	303,260 (but a "range of 1,800,000" secured)	Continued after World War II
Maxwell Cattle Co., Ltd. (London board included Duke of Manchester and Earl of Rosslyn)	200,000 (1st-mortgage bonds)	Colorado, New Mexico	1,750,000	Went out of business in 1886; bondholders lost £200,000; share capital held privately (not listed in London directories); large Dutch interests; part of larger Maxwell Land Grant, which absorbed it about 1886
Missouri Land and Livestock Co., Ltd., Edinburgh	100,000	Missouri	475,000	Became in 1883 a colonizing and lead and zinc exploration co.; eventually sold off land
Powder River Cattle Co., Ltd. (Board included Duke of Manchester, Earl of Wharncliffe, and Lord Henry Nevill)	300,000	Wyoming		Went into voluntary liquidation in 1886; £200,000 loss
Western American Cattle Co., Ltd. (Scottish-Amer. Investment Co. group)	220,000	Dakota Territory		
Western Land and Cattle Co., Ltd., London	115,000	Texas, Kansas		Wound up in 1892
*Wyoming Cattle Ranche Co., Ltd.	200,000	Wyoming	Over 2,560,000	Went out of business in 1886; £100,000 loss
1883				
Dakota Stock and Grazing Co., Ltd., London	250,000	Dakota Territory	400,000	By 1884 practically defunct; wound up in 1886; £70,000 loss
Deer Trail Land and Cattle Co., Ltd., London	400,000	Colorado	10,000 (much more contracted)	No capital forthcoming; project terminated before it started
Kansas and New Mexico Cattle and Land Co., Ltd., London	150,000	Kansas	1,000	No public funds solicited

Table 9.1 (*Cont.*)

Date of prospectus	Company, location, organizer	Capital at origin (in pounds)	Territories and/or states in which business done	Acreage owned (if known)	Comments
1883	Nevada Land and Cattle Co., Ltd., London	300,000	Nevada	30,000	No public funds solicited; went into receivership in 1892
	New United States Cattle Ranche Co., Ltd., London	250,000	Kansas	30,000	
	Rocking Chair Ranche, Ltd., London (Lord Tweedmouth)	150,000	Texas	150,400	"A major financial disaster"
	Sand Creek Land and Cattle Co., Ltd., London	100,000	Wyoming	150,000	
	*Swan Land and Cattle Co., Ltd., Edinburgh	600,000	Wyoming	520,966 (1885)	Introduced sheep in 1905
	Union Land and Cattle Co., Ltd., London	350,000	Texas		Never appeared on London lists
	*Western Ranches Co., Ltd., Edinburgh (Scottish-Amer. Investment Co. group.)	112,000	Dakota Territory, Wyoming, Montana	70,000	A successful company in 1890s; reorganized as Western Ranches and Investment Co., Ltd., in 1910; liquidated, 1919–21
1884	*American Pastoral Co., Ltd., London (a Barclay co.)	400,000	Texas	204,000	Settlers as well as cattle planned; sold LX Ranch at outbreak of World War I
	Carrizoro Cattle Ranch Co., Ltd.	80,000	New Mexico		
	Cattle Ranche and Freehold Land Co., Ltd.	100,000	Texas	17,000	Never did what was intended
	*Espuela Land and Cattle Co., Ltd., London	500,000	Texas	494,500	Sold ranch 1907

Year	Company	Acres / Location	Capital	Remarks
	Montana Sheep and Cattle Co., Ltd.	8,000 Montana		Lost £22,000 by 1890; soon "folded"
1885	*Capitol Freehold Land and Investment Co., Ltd., London (Earl of Aberdeen, Lord Thurlow, Marquis of Tweeddale, chmn.)	3,000,000 Texas	3,000,000	Trustees of this company owned the famous XIT ranch; in 1909 the directors completed the bond redemption, and the British company went out of existence
	Cedar Valley Land and Cattle Co., Ltd., London	150,000 Texas	75,000	Cushioned collapse of cattle operation with land sales; sold herd in 1893
	Chalk Butts Ranche and Cattle Co., Ltd.	a Montana		Soon "folded"
	Chama Cattle Co., Ltd., London	a New Mexico		Stillborn
	Cresswell Ranche and Cattle Co., Ltd., Edinburgh	320,000 Texas	189,000	Ceased ranching in 1890s
1886	Deervale Ranche Co., Ltd.	a Texas		Soon folded
	International Cattle Co.	a Texas		Was the reorganized Powder River Co.
1887	Wyoming Hereford Cattle and Land Association, Ltd., London	150,000 Wyoming	86,879	
	Denver Ranching Co., Ltd.	10,000 Colorado	259,000	
	Rio Arriba Land and Cattle Co., Ltd., London	160,000 New Mexico	270,000	
1889	Cattle Ranche Co., Ltd.	80,000 Texas		Formed to take over Cattle Ranche and Land Co., Ltd., properties (see 1882)

Source: See text and notes of chapter for the various sources.
* Indicates the most important companies.
a Not available.

took directions from the Scottish board. He sent detailed weekly, or more often twice-weekly, reports to Dundee. When the American ranch superintendent objected to the foreign interference, Alexander Mackay, the Matador company's secretary in Scotland, scolded: "You must try to put yourself in the position of the Board placed thousands of miles away from a property the management of which they are responsible, and to recognize that the very fullest information must be continually sent to enable them to have, as it were, the ranch and its working under their own eyes . . . The Managers will tell you *when* and *what* to drive, but *how* to drive is your business."[19] To be certain the board's wishes were carried out, Mackay made annual visits to the property, some lasting about a month; he was usually accompanied by a British director.[20] In 1890 the Matador company hired the Scottish-born former manager of Prairie Cattle Company (as noted, another Scottish cattle company in America). When the new manager was reprimanded for being tardy in sending information to the Scottish board, he explained that the Prairie owners did not require regular reports. Mackay countered, "We write a good deal," and added that the board in Dundee required the data, since it met once a week.[21] The first resident manager of the Espuela Land and Cattle Company, Ltd., was an American; the next two were Scots.[22]

With the cattle ranches, the degree of control from the British Isles varied sharply from one British-owned company to another, with the lack of supervision over the immense (3-million-acre) XIT Ranch in Texas at one extreme, and the careful direction of the Matador venture at the other pole. On the whole, Scottish investors seemed more prone to monitor carefully their investments than did their English counterparts (which was true of the Scottish mining and mortgage companies as well).

British investors in the corporate cattle ranches did not make the fabulous profits they had expected. As early as 1884, they began to realize that "their rush to organize cattle companies had been ill-advised."[23] Cattle prices were lower than the investors anticipated. Some companies sold off young animals to make their profit-and-loss statement palatable, thus reducing their sources of future income.[24] Then came the harsh winter of 1886–87, which decimated herds, pushing a number of these enterprises into bankruptcy.[25] When in March 1887 the U.S. Congress passed legislation on alien land ownership in the territories, this further discouraged new investment (Colorado enacted an alien property law the same year). By 1890 contemporaries were commenting on the "loss and disaster which have overtaken English investment in ranching and cattle breeding in the west."[26] One scholar estimated that in the years 1885–1895, the losses to the English-financed enterprises ran to about $10 million, while the Scottish-owned ventures lost about $7 million to $8 million. The Scots seem to have lost less because they paid more attention to management.[27]

Certain cattle companies, however, persevered and recouped their losses in the twentieth century, mainly by selling off land. A very few persisted as British-owned cattle ranches.[28] Some British managers left for other parts of the world. "Dick" Walsh, who managed the JA Ranch after 1887, eventually moved to ranching in Rhodesia, and Murdo Mackenzie of the Matador Land and Cattle Company went to Brazil in 1911 to manage a giant ranch there.[29] Thus in 1914 some British investment in western cattle ranches remained, but the stakes were far less than in the early 1880s. The reason lay mainly in the losses to investors in the mid-1880s and the 1890s as well.

U.S. exports of cattle and chilled meat to Britain in the late 1870s had prompted British *interest* in investment in American cattle ranches. Subsequently, the role of U.S. exports became almost irrelevant to the foreign investment decisions in cattle raising and to the strategies of investors. Cattle ranches were a romance, the investments an episode, a fad. As with gold and silver mines, many investors had been deceived. Nonetheless, the investments had been large and had had a major impact on cattle raising in the West. British cattle companies in America (like their U.S. counterparts) never integrated forward, despite charters that would have permitted at least some of them to do so and despite the desires of some to break what they saw as the Chicago packers' control over price.[30] From their earliest investments onward, British ranch owners sold their cattle in America, primarily to commission livestock brokers;[31] accordingly, U.S. prices for cattle shaped their plans. When we consider participants in the export trade, we must turn to a different set of foreign investors.

East Coast Slaughtering, Exporting, and Selling Abroad

The first *domestic* commerce within the United States in "fresh beef" involved the shipping of livestock: cattle were sent by rail from the West, slaughtered in the East, and then the meat was sold in eastern markets. The export of live cattle and of dressed beef from the United States to Britain began at about the same time (ca. 1868–69) and was, in effect, an extension of domestic commerce. As noted, these exports rose sharply in the late 1870s. By then, the leading cattle shipper and exporter, who handled both live cattle and dressed-beef exports, was Timothy C. Eastman (1821–1893), of New York.[32] He shipped livestock east and then abroad; he also slaughtered in New York, selling in the East and exporting as well. His business would, in time, become British owned.

In 1875 Eastman sent the first refrigerated beef shipped *in quantity* to Britain.[33] In October of that year, amid great fanfare, he forwarded to Queen Victoria a gift of American chilled beef.[34] He built refrigerator units in ships and also at his "killing yard" in New York.[35] Early in 1877 the Scottish firm John Bell & Sons (which some four years earlier had transported live cattle from the United States to Britain) became the Glasgow agent for Eastman's dressed beef.[36] Henry (later Sir Henry) Bell and his brother James (later Sir James), the sons of John Bell, had become interested in mechanical refrigeration and had formed a partnership with J. J. Coleman (Bell-Coleman Mechanical Refrigeration Company), which took out patents in 1877 in refrigeration. With innovations in refrigeration, in 1878 the dollar value of American dressed-beef exports to Britain actually (and atypically) exceeded that of U.S. live-cattle exports.[37] In the spring of 1879, the first Bell-Coleman mechanical refrigeration machine was fitted on a ship.[38] All during the 1880s, however, the dollar value of U.S. cattle-on-the-hoof exports to Britain each year surpassed that of the dressed meat;[39] the key constraint in shipping dressed beef was refrigeration—and refrigeration technology was still in its infancy.

The continuing coexistence of the live cattle and "dead" (dressed) meat trade appears to have been a result of British preference. As late as the 1880s and early 1890s, many Britishers still believed that chilled or frozen meat was inferior to that "brought it on the hoof."[40] Dead meat was cheaper (and had a poor-people's market); its position expanded as refrigeration techniques improved, especially in the 1890s.

Meanwhile, it was the Bell brothers in the United Kingdom who took the lead in selling refrigerated meat. They not only introduced refrigeration on ships but in 1879 started to open retail meat shops (butcher shops) in Great Britain. Soon their firm was selling imported frozen and chilled beef on a retail level in their own numerous British meat shops. As the Bells' British retail business expanded, the company continued to serve as agent in Britain for Eastman.[41] In 1888 John Bell and Sons registered as a limited liability company, with all the shares held by the members of the firm or its managers; less than a year later, in January 1889, the Bell brothers organized in Great Britain Eastmans, Ltd., with a capital of £900,000. It merged the New York cattle and beef business of Timothy C. and Joseph Eastman (probably Timothy's son) with the trading organization of John Bell and Sons, Ltd., of London and Glasgow. By that time the Bell firm had some 330 retail meat shops in Great Britain.[42] The investment in the United States of Eastmans, Ltd.—the purchase of the Eastman business—was reported to total over $5 million.[43] Whereas Swift, Armour, and Hammond were by this time exporting chilled beef to Britain, none of these companies had integrated into retail selling in Great Britain.

Although the Eastman name was used for this new British company, no Eastman was listed as a director. Among the first directors were Lord Grenville, Henry Bell, and James Bell.[44] Yet Joseph Eastman was left in charge of the American business and owned a "large block of the English company's securities."[45] At origin, Eastmans, Ltd., was a British–controlled integrated enterprise, with the "great abbatoir establishment"[46] in New York, the transatlantic trading and shipping business in cattle and chilled beef, and the cold-storage facilities and retail outlets for fresh meat in the United Kingdom. While Eastmans, Ltd., was set up coincidentally with many British free-standing firms, its principal directors were full-time managers. The Bells were investing in America to supply their British stores.

No sooner was Eastmans, Ltd., formed than the new British owners were unhappy with Joseph Eastman, who wanted to ship "too much": "He is stubborn and seems to be determined to injure the other shippers of dressed meat." The American was difficult to control.[47] Then in 1891–1894, Eastmans, Ltd., met with heavy losses in the U.S. cattle and beef shipments.[48]

During the 1890s, with improved refrigeration, shipments of chilled and even frozen beef became the method of choice. Why ship cattle when there were major economies in shipping refrigerated meat? The United States was by far the largest source of dressed (refrigerated) beef imports into the United Kingdom, but in the 1890s British beef imports from South America (mainly Argentina) had begun to climb. In 1899 Henry Bell of Eastmans, Ltd., became chairman of the board of the River Plate Fresh Meat Company, which slaughtered, froze, shipped, and marketed Argentine beef in Britain.[49] The next year, 1900, Eastmans, Ltd., disposed of its U.S. business (the former properties of Timothy C. and Joseph Eastman).[50] In 1912 Eastmans, Ltd., had cold storage depots and over 1,400 shops in Great Britain; it was a large buyer of New Zealand lamb and mutton and handled frozen and chilled beef from all parts of the world. In that year it had no investments in meat packing in the United States.[51] America was no longer competitive as a source of supply for British markets. Even the American packers were investing in Argentina for the British market.[52]

Midwestern Meat Packing

The first category of foreign direct investments in meat was in cattle raising; the second was by Eastmans, Ltd., in an integrated East Coast slaughtering and British selling enterprise; and the third group was in meat packing in the American Midwest. Foreign stakes in Midwest meat packing were first in hogs and then in beef.

Meat packing in the American Midwest—in Cincinnati and then Chicago—had begun in hogs. Although there was no significant foreign investment in hog raising, there were important involvements in pork packing. As noted in Chapter 4, in 1871 the Liverpool provision merchant house of John Morrell & Co. invested in a Chicago hog-packing establishment to serve the British trade. In 1877 John Morrell & Co. leased a pork-packing plant in Ottumwa, Iowa, and the next year purchased sixty-one acres in Ottumwa to build its own facility. Its output was in large part for export.[53]

All during the 1880s, the dollar value of U.S. exports to the United Kingdom of bacon and ham exceeded the combined dollar value of U.S. exports of cattle and dressed beef to that destination.[54] The Morrell firm (as of 1880, John Morrell & Co., Ltd., in both the United Kingdom and the United States) was a significant contributor to these U.S. bacon and ham exports. In 1888 John Morrell & Co., Ltd., closed its Chicago plant and concentrated its production in Ottumwa, Iowa. By 1889 its Iowa enterprise had 500 employees and sold ham, bacon, and sausages carrying brand names. When the Iowa plant burned in 1893, John Morrell & Co., Ltd., replaced it with a larger, more modern one. In 1893 the firm acquired its first refrigerator cars, twenty-five in all. This number was small compared with that of the giants—Swift, Armour, Morris, and Hammond.

Nonetheless, Morrell was a multinational-enterprise-type activity, with the U.S. and English businesses coordinated from Great Britain, albeit much of the financing of the American operations apparently came from U.S. domestic banks. Morrell & Co., Ltd., sold in the United States as well as abroad and developed an American whole-saling network, with branch offices in key U.S. cities. In 1904 the Ottumwa plant had 1,150 employees. In 1909 the firm acquired an additional packing plant at Sioux Falls, South Dakota. That year, owing to British tax laws, a separate American company was established to buy and to run the U.S. business. When this new firm was formed, the U.S. properties of Morrell were valued in excess of $1 million. The reorganization notwithstanding, the company's historian writes, "The English business still maintained a semblance of control over its more lusty American youngster."

Prior to 1909, the slaughtering of cattle was only a minor part of the U.S. business of Morrell (it remained primarily a pork packer), but that year the company built a new "beef house" in Ottumwa, and beef became important in the enterprise's output. The Morrell never became involved in lamb or mutton. Indeed, its new attention to beef coincided with its greater concern with American *domestic* sales; over time, the U.S. market grew relatively more significant in its corporate strategy.[55] Morrell & Co. was the only British investment in U.S. meat packing that persisted for the entire period of 1875–1914. It was, however, far from the only one in midwestern meat packing—pork or beef.

Another British investor was Thomas J. Lipton. Lipton was born in Glasgow in 1850; he had as a teenager visited the United States, staying for four years and taking various jobs, from one on a Virginia tobacco plantation to another in a New York City grocery store. After the young man returned to Glasgow in 1869, Lipton worked in his parents' shop and in 1871 opened his own store in that city, where he sold Irish bacon; when he could not get enough of the product, he began to import American bacon and hams. Soon he was starting other shops in Scotland and England.[56]

In August 1880 Lipton made his second trip to America, where he organized a "buying agency" to purchase the bacon and ham for sale in his British stores. The historian Peter Mathias believes that "almost certainly" on this 1880 trip Lipton acquired a Chicago hog-packing plant, with a daily capacity of some 300–400 hogs. Thus he joined Morrell & Co., Ltd., in that city. Lipton would export his output to Britain and sell it through his own British retail sales network.[57]

By the mid-1880s Lipton was boasting that he was "the largest retail provision dealer in the world." With his British sales expanding, he required added imports from America; thus in November 1886, in South Omaha, Nebraska, he started a Lipton Packing Company plant, with a capacity of 2,000 hogs a day. He hired some 400 people. Lipton now sold his output in the United States as well as abroad.[58]

According to Mathias, Lipton's U.S. business "rapidly assum[ed] a life of its own independent of the demand from Lipton's shops which first brought it into existence." Lipton opened a New York depot and also pursued a West Coast trade from the Nebraska facility. For the American market, he developed a distinct "processing technique and separate brands." He formed the Johnstone Packing Company (Johnstone was his middle name) for his U.S. trade, while the Lipton Packing Company cured meat for British consumption.[59]

Within a year from the inauguration of the South Omaha plant, Lipton discovered that the bacon from Nebraska hogs was "a trifle too fat" for British taste; accordingly, when in 1887 Philip Armour and his partner Michael Cudahy offered Lipton $70,000 for the new facility, the Scot sold it (this meat-packing plant came to be owned by the American firm Armour Cudahy Packing Company).[60] Lipton, still committed to U.S. business, now bought a larger factory in Chicago, located in the Union Stock Yards, where he could process between 2,000 and 4,000 hogs daily. He expanded his production to include lard and sausage making. By the late 1880s Lipton's sales from this plant were divided approximately evenly between the British and American markets.[61] Lipton established a fleet of refrigerator cars, with the word *Lipton* painted on them in bold letters; they went all over the United States as advertisements. He never opened retail stores in America to sell his pork products. He went through American retail channels, confining his U.S. marketing to the wholesale trade.[62]

In Britain in 1898, Lipton formed a limited liability company but decided to exclude his sizable U.S. business.[63] By that time, his activities in America also included tea sales, promoted from his Chicago headquarters.[64] Whereas his tea sales would subsequently expand (as would his wholesale network promoting tea, as I will indicate later), his meat-packing operations ended in 1902 when Lipton sold, for $250,000, his Chicago plant to Armour, his friend and neighbor in the Union Stock Yards.[65]

In short, for about twenty-two years (1880–1902) Lipton took part in hog packing in the United States; he never participated in the fresh beef industry (nor in lamb or mutton); all his U.S. investments in meat packing related to hogs.

Morrell & Co. and Lipton were not atypical in their lack of interest in American lamb or mutton. American meatpackers were not particularly active in these meats either—which was to be expected, as Americans had never developed a taste (in terms of mass markets) for lamb or mutton. I have no evidence of foreign investment in packing lamb or mutton in the United States. Britishers (and the French) made some U.S. investments in sheep raising, which appear to have been related more to wool than to meat.[66]

By contrast, by the early 1890s British investors were—like their American competitors—taking part in *midwestern* beef packing on a formidable scale. In Britain, bacon, hams, and "tinned" meat were sold in grocery stores, whereas chilled meat often (as noted in the case of the Bells) sold in chain butcher shops. The British marketing structure for the meats was different.[67] In the U.S. industry, however, the same meatpackers handled (at different plants) both pork and beef. British investors that acquired U.S. companies followed the

American pattern and continued to process both meats. As I have shown, Morrell & Co. in time would adopt the U.S. procedures, adding beef to its output.

Between 1890 and 1892, five important British corporations were organized to own U.S. midwestern meat-packing establishments; all were floated in London (the date in parentheses is that of the British registration): (1) G. H. Hammond Company, Ltd. (March 3, 1890); (2) Chicago Packing and Provision Company, Ltd. (July 8, 1890); (3) Fowler Brothers, Ltd. (September 8, 1890); (4) George Fowler, Son & Co., Ltd. (July 11, 1891); and (5) International Packing and Provision Company, Ltd. (May 21, 1892).[68]

The first was the largest of the group (although the capitalization figures do not reflect this).[69] George H. Hammond, a New Englander by birth, had settled in Detroit in the 1860s, opened a slaughterhouse there, become involved in the wholesale and retail meat trade, transported refrigerated beef to New England as early as 1869, built a packing plant across the Illinois state line in Indiana (a short distance from the Chicago Union Stock Yards), and formed the George H. Hammond Company (1873). He took part with the other large American meatpackers in a price-fixing division-of-market pool (in about 1885) and opened an additional packing plant in Omaha, Nebraska (1885–86). By the time of his death in 1886, Hammond ranked with Swift, Armour, and Morris as one of the "big four" in American meat packing.[70] By 1889 the Hammond enterprise had "plants and agencies at Chicago, Hammond [Indiana], Detroit, Boston, New York, London, and Liverpool."[71]

That year, when Britishers were evaluating a number of U.S. industrial properties for their investment potential, the Hammond enterprise was available and attractive. H. Osborne O'Hagan, the British promoter who had presented Eastmans, Ltd., in London in 1889, assisted in the transfer of the Hammond business to British hands.[72] Although the takeover was to be effective July 1, 1889,[73] Hammond Company securities were not offered to the British public until 1890, timed right after the first Eastmans, Ltd., dividend.[74]

George H. Hammond's company was known in London as the "Ham & Beef Company." In 1889–90 O'Hagan acquired all the shares in the American company, which he resold to the newly incorporated English concern, G. H. Hammond Company, Ltd. (capital, £940,000 in shares and £340,000 in mortgage debentures).[75] When in 1890 Joseph Eastman was shipping without control, an American law firm proposed that the Hammond company discipline him.[76] The Hammond company, like its major U.S. competitors, exported chilled beef, but under British ownership it paid more attention to hog packing and to the export of bacon and ham. British direction appears to have made no difference in Hammond's relations with the other big packers; the company continued to participate in pools in the United States with Armour, Swift, and Morris in 1891, 1893–1896, and 1898–1901.[77] In 1898 the Hammond company formed an affiliated firm, the Hammond Packing Company (Illinois), with a slaughter-house in St. Joseph, Missouri, and a capital of $1.7 million. By 1901 the British-controlled Hammond group owned 1,195 refrigerator cars (an investment of $620,136), a large number of branch houses (valued at $1,553,964), and three major slaughterhouses, in Hammond, Indiana, South Omaha, Nebraska, and St. Joseph, Missouri (worth, in total, $2,528,152). It was a multimillion-dollar, multiplant, vertically integrated firm.[78]

The other four 1890–1892 promotions in Britain involved two pairs of "independent" meatpackers. The first set included the Chicago Packing and Provision Company, Ltd. (capital, £400,000), which ac-quired the bacon and ham business of a Chicago company of the same name and that of H. Botsford & Co. Two years later an associated group, the International Packing and Provision Company, Ltd. (IPPC), merged the Chicago businesses of International Packing, T. E. Wells, Allerton Packing, John Cudahy, John C. Hately, Hately Broth-ers, and Jones & Stiles Packing. The president of IPPC was H. Bots-ford, and T. E. Wells, S. W. Allerton, J. Cudahy, J. C. Hately, and J. Stiles (all of Chicago) joined Botsford and six Britishers as directors of this enterprise. IPPC had an authorized (and obviously inflated) cap-ital of £1.7 million plus $2.5 million in first-mortgage bonds.[79] In February 1894 W. J. Caesar (Price, Waterhouse's representative in Chicago) wrote his home office in London that he had learned that the Chicago Packing and Provision Company was to be reorganized as an American company because the American shareholders ob-jected to the expense of English management, "and this if true would also mean the International Packing & Provision Co." "As to audits in these companies, there can be no doubt what would take place under American control." Caesar meant that there would be no audits.[80] On January 21, 1896, a liquidator for IPPC was appointed; by 1901 Chi-cago Packing and Provision Company, Ltd., was also in liquidation. These firms returned to American control.[81]

The second set of 1890–1892 promotions involved Liverpool-based entrepreneurs. Securities of Fowler Brothers, Ltd., were presented to the British public in 1890. Its share capital was £1,151,000; it merged a number of firms engaged in "curing, packing and distributing American provisions": Fowler Brothers, Ltd., Liverpool; Fowler Brothers, New York; the Anderson Fowler Company, New York; the

Anglo-American Refrigerator Car Company, Indiana; and the Anglo-American Provision Company, Chicago, including that company's interest in the Omaha Packing Company in Nebraska. One-third of the debentures, preference, and ordinary shares were taken by the sellers of the amalgamated businesses, and the rest were offered to the public in London.[82] George Fowler, Son & Co. Ltd.—like Fowler Brothers, Ltd.—had its head office in Liverpool. Although the names of the two firms are similar and writers refer to them as "associated" companies, at formation they had no directors in common nor did they share a common Liverpool address. George Fowler, Son & Co., Ltd., was registered on July 11, 1891. Its capital was £240,000, and it acquired the works and businesses of George Fowler & Co. of Liverpool and George Fowler & Son of Kansas City, the trade consisting of the "preparation for both the English market and American markets of hogs and cattle and products of those animals."[83] These, then, were the five principal British promotions involving midwestern meatpackers (the Hammond interests, the two independent groups, and the Fowler companies).

Meanwhile, an even more impressive midwestern U.S. property had moved into the hands of British investors. In July 1890 the chairman of the Scottish American Mortgage Company told his shareholders that the Union Stock Yards in Chicago had been sold to a London company for $19 million![84] The Union Stock Yards, which covered 300 acres and had facilities for loading 500 railroad cars at a time, had been established by nine railroads in 1865. It was the world's largest stockyards.[85] Armour and Lipton, among others, had packing plants within the yards.

The story behind this transaction is best told in O'Hagan's *Leaves from My Life* and Robert T. Swaine's *The Cravath Firm.*[86] O'Hagan, who had floated Eastmans, Ltd., and the G. H. Hammond Co., Ltd., controlled a firm called the City of London Contract Corporation.[87] Probably early in 1890 O'Hagan was asked by a "friend" of the Bostonian Frederick H. Prince to "put together" a company to raise capital to buy the Chicago yards. In June 1890 Prince and the City of London Corporation purchased controlling interest in an Illinois company (the Union Stock Yards and Transit Company).[88] They sold their interest to a new New Jersey–incorporated company established in 1890, the Chicago Junction Railways and Union Stock Yards Company;[89] $6.5 million in common shares and $6.5 million in preferred shares, plus $3.5 million in bonds of this New Jersey enterprise, were offered at par in New York, Boston, London, and Amsterdam (Blake, Boissevain & Co. handled the London offering and Adolph Boissevain & Co., the one in Amsterdam). The funds raised were in part to pay Prince for his holdings and in part to repay the City of London Contract Corporation.

No sooner was the issue floated than the Baring Crisis (November 1890) discouraged British purchases of all American securities. Moreover, even earlier the London *Economist* had reported conflicts over who would manage the new firm.[90] The common shares were a drug on the market; only about 40 percent were sold, and then mainly to Americans.[91] When Chicagoans looked at the board of directors of the New Jersey company, they discovered that four of the ten directors lived in London[92] and five were easterners, leaving only one from Chicago.[93] The major Chicago meatpackers were incensed, for they had been totally ignored in the reorganization and resented the presence of easterners and railroadmen (far more, it seems, than the London role); they threatened to start a rival yard.[94] The price of the common shares plummeted, and O'Hagan acquired stock to stop the rout.[95]

O'Hagan tells a fascinating story of Gustavus Swift and Philip Armour's visit to London (undoubtedly in 1891) and the month of daily negotiations between O'Hagan and the two U.S. industry leaders. Eventually, in 1892, the American meatpackers obtained $3 million in new 5 percent income bonds (ranking after the debentures and preference shares), as well as representation on the board of the Chicago Junction Railways and Union Stock Yards Company.[96] Then there were problems with the independent packers (including some that were British owned).[97] Once this litigation was settled, the stockyards prospered; Chicagoans invested, and the British holdings in the New Jersey company drifted back to the United States.[98] By the mid-1890s foreign money—which had been the catalyst in the reorganization—no longer had any significance.

In fact, with the exception of Morrell & Co., all the British interests associated with meat packing in the Midwest proved short-lived.[99] In 1902 most of the remaining British investors sold their American plants, marketing facilities, and sales outlets in Great Britain to the major U.S. meatpackers.[100] The latter planned a giant merger,[101] and in anticipation, in June 1902, the U.S. plants and properties controlled by George Fowler, Son & Co., Ltd., and Fowler Brothers, Ltd., were acquired by Armour and Swift (the officers of Armour bought the Omaha Packing Company from Fowler Brothers, Ltd., at a price said to be $2.5 million; five other Fowler group companies were purchased by Swift for more than $6.2 million).[102] That same month, the officers of Armour bought for $4.4 million the stock of G. H. Hammond Company, Ltd., and its affiliated Hammond Packing Company.[103]

When the merger planned by the U.S. packers did not occur,

Armour and Swift, in 1903, placed their new acquisitions from Hammond and the Fowler group (including Fowler Packing, Omaha Packing, and Anglo-American Provision) under a holding company, the National Packing Company, that came to be owned by Armour, Swift, and Morris. The authorized capital of National Packing Company was $15 million.[104]

In short, in 1900–1902 a British exodus occurred from U.S. investment in meat packing: the British sales of their Hammond and Fowler interests, as well as the divestments of Eastmans, Ltd., and Lipton and the liquidation of the Chicago Packing and Provision Company, all fall within those years. The British meat-packing investment sold in those three years alone seems to have totaled about $18 million to $20 million.[105] The retreat was associated with consolidation in U.S. meat packing[106] and also—probably as important—with the development in the United Kingdom of alternative sources of beef supplies: Argentina, Australia, and New Zealand. U.S. exports of dressed beef to Britain (measured by weight) peaked in 1901, and in 1905 South American beef imports into the United Kingdom surpassed those from the United States.[107] Similarly, U.S. bacon imports to the United Kingdom (measured by weight) reached their highest point in 1901; by 1910 Denmark had passed the United States as the principal provider of British bacon.[108] Growing population and rising real incomes in America meant that domestic demand absorbed much of the U.S. meat output. As indicated, U.S. meatpackers invested in Argentina—to supply British markets. It was symbolic that when the Union Cold Storage Company of Liverpool was formed in 1897 and developed a worldwide business, which by 1914 stretched from Buenos Aires to Hankow, it had no U.S. interests.[109] The divestments, moreover, should be seen in the context of the more general British pullback from U.S. investments at the turn of the century that I have already noted. After years of low prices and low (or nonexistent) profits in the 1890s, when Britishers were offered high prices for their American assets, the temptation to sell was often irresistible. Whereas in some other sectors British monies reentered, this was not the case in meat packing. Only Morrell & Co. endured, and by 1914 a large part of its business was in serving the U.S. market.

In sum, for a short interlude in the late nineteenth century, the British had major investments in American "meat industries"—in U.S. cattle ranches (roughly from 1879 to 1900), eastern slaughtering and the cattle and dressed-meat export trade from New York (1889–1900), midwestern hog packing (1878–1902), midwestern beef (1889–1902), and the Chicago stockyards (for a brief but indeterminate time after 1890). In the early 1890s these investments may have exceeded

$80 million.[110] Most carried with them management and control, which was exercised to varying extents. Many took the form of free-standing companies, albeit some, such as Eastmans, Ltd., which merged the Bell and Eastman business, were clearly promotions but seem more in the pattern of the multinational enterprise than that of the typical free-standing firm. After Eastmans, Ltd., retreated from American business, it maintained operations and its headquarters in Britain. By contrast, the British Hammond was a typical free-standing firm. It had no "operating" parent. When its American properties were acquired by Armour, the latter also obtained the *subordinate* British sales outlets; the ex-British parent company was dissolved. Likewise, when, for example, the British companies that united the Chicago independents were liquidated, there remained no headquarters in Britain. Some British shareholders may have become portfolio investors in the American businesses.

Certain British investments in cattle ranches persisted. Morrell & Co.—not a free-standing company—continued as an important independent packer. Lipton stayed in the United States as a seller of tea. By 1914, however, the era of large British involvements in American meat packing and meat exports was past history. All the investments discussed in detail were British. There were, in addition, some Dutch stakes (in the Maxwell Cattle Company, Ltd.) and some French interests in cattle raising.[111] I can find no other significant continental European investments in stock raising or meat packing, although in the early twentieth century European capital did go (on a portfolio basis) into financing key American meatpackers.[112]

Foreign Investments in Food Production, the Grain Trade, and Flour Making

There were a number of foreign stakes in U.S. agriculture, in raising food and also in processing agricultural and (on rare occasions) fish products. I mentioned in Chapter 6 the British investments in rice output in Louisiana. On the Pacific Coast, Balfour, Guthrie, the U.S. house of Balfour, Williamson, a Liverpool trading firm, owned vineyards, farmed fruitlands, had an equity holding in an enterprise that dried and packed its own prunes, took part in the raisin trade, and even had an interest in the Alaska Packers Association, for which Balfour, Guthrie exported a large quantity of canned salmon.[113] In the 1890s the manager of John Walker & Co., sugar refiners at Greenock, Scotland (near Glasgow), organized a "syndicate" (with American participation) that invested £7,000 in the Washington State Sugar Company, Ltd., to acquire leases to 3,000 acres in Spokane County,

Washington, to grow sugar beet and to buy a sugar refinery in Waverly, Washington. The company apparently spent most of its resources combating restrictions on alien business activities imposed by the state of Washington, and never succeeded.[114]

While there were foreign investments in wheat growing—in Iowa, Kansas, and elsewhere in the Plains states, as well as on the West Coast[115]—there were also important foreign stakes in the wheat and flour trade. The best work on the trading companies in grain is that by Morton Rothstein, who shows the role of William Rathbone & Co., David Bingham, the Patterson Brothers, and the Ralli Brothers (an Anglo-Greek firm); all these had New York offices by the late 1870s. By the 1880s Louis Dreyfus et Cie. was active in the New York market. On the American West Coast a different group of merchant traders and shippers participated in the wheat trade.[116] As large importers of wheat and flour, the British were particularly prominent in related investments that included not only those in wheat growing and trade but also those in railroads, mortgages to farmers, and trade financing.

The British Land and Mortgage Company of America, Ltd., had in the mid-1880s a wheat farm, a grain elevator, and a flour mill in Kansas—a short-lived venture.[117] There were some unsuccessful Scottish interests in Oregon flour mills for flour export in the mid-1880s.[118] By 1889 Balfour, Guthrie, which was a large grain exporter, had one-third ownership ($100,000) of a flour mill in Stockton, California.[119] It was 1889–90 when British investors were taking special interest in American meat packing and in the Chicago stockyards that they also made major investments in grain storage and flour milling.

In 1889 Douglas Gordon McRae, editor of the London *Financial Times*, visited Chicago, seeking to place English capital in midwestern industrial enterprises. He contacted Levy Mayer, a Chicago attorney, who arranged that a new British company, the Chicago and North-West Granaries Company, Ltd., would acquire the capital stock of both the Star Elevator Company of Minneapolis and G. W. van Dusen & Co. of Rochester, Minnesota, encompassing a chain of grain elevators in the Northwest. Van Dusen was an important grain dealer in Minnesota, Dakota, and Montana.[120] The *Northwestern Miller* commented that the London board of the new company consisted of one Lord and two members of Parliament.[121] About the same time, the City of Chicago Grain Elevator Line came into existence, and a British company (the City of Chicago Grain Elevators, Ltd.) acquired it.[122] The purchase was made, contemporaries said, to "free the British of the grip Americans had over the grain trade."[123] In addition, in

1889–90 British investors were reported to have bought up a number of St. Louis flour mills.[124]

Of most consequence, in 1889 a British group obtained control of the Pillsbury mills, the principal U.S. flour producer.[125] Charles A. and his uncle John S. Pillsbury were both born in New Hampshire. As young adults they had moved to Minneapolis, where by 1872 Charles Pillsbury had organized C. A. Pillsbury and Co., a family partnership that bought and built mills, innovated in mill design, created a system of terminal elevators, and sold "Pillsbury Best" flour, which by the mid-1880s had obtained "an international reputation."[126] As flour prices fell in the mid-1880s, Minneapolis flour millers contemplated mergers to curb competition and to stabilize prices. With a similar goal, in 1889 a British "syndicate" purchased the three mills of C. A. Pillsbury and Co. and two mills of one of its competitors (the Washburn Mill Company), giving the new venture a total of 14,500 barrels of capacity. The Britishers added two water power companies and the Minneapolis and Northern Elevator Company, which meant that they had control over the water power of St. Anthony Falls, a large terminal elevator capacity, and a line of country elevators in northern Minnesota and North Dakota. The British owners formed Pillsbury-Washburn Flour Mills Company, Ltd., with a capital of £1 million (plus £635,000 of mortgage debentures); the company was chartered in England in 1889. The purchase price for all the American properties was $6,250,000, partly in cash and partly in securities of the new enterprise.[127]

Charles A. Pillsbury was appointed managing director, and the Pillsbury family held "considerable" stock in the new British company. On formation, Pillsbury-Washburn Flour Mills Company, Ltd., was the largest milling enterprise in the world.[128] Charles, his uncle John S. Pillsbury, and W. D. Washburn formed an "American Committee of Management."[129] A British board of directors expected reports from America.

Dorothy Adler attributed the establishment of the Pillsbury-Washburn Flour Mills Company, Ltd., directly to British interests in U.S. railways and specifically to the new system of British-controlled roads that carried grain and flour east—"the Minneapolis, Sault Ste. Marie and Atlantic (later the Minneapolis, St. Paul and Sault Ste. Marie), running from Minneapolis to the Canadian border at the Sault Ste. Marie, the Canadian Pacific, and the New York, Ontario, and Western."[130] The *New York Commercial Bulletin* predicted the result would be more flour and lower wheat exports.[131] The British directors of the large enterprise were participants in banking, trade, and shipping.[132] British director Sydney T. Klein, for example, was a "flour merchant."[133] According to Morton Rothstein, William Klein & Sons (which had both continental and British offices) was Pillsbury-Washburn's chief agent in the United Kingdom.[134] Pillsbury-Washburn Flour Mills Company, Ltd., had a London head office, which would have "expenses" of about £3,300 per annum[135] but did not carry on any vertically integrated operations in connection with the overseas trade of the Minneapolis mills.[136]

The 1889 promotion of Pillsbury-Washburn Flour Mills Company, Ltd., in London did not go well. The underwriters were left with shares that they deposited in the hands of various British trust companies.[137] The merger did have an immediate impact in the United States. In response, the American-financed Northwestern Consolidated Milling Company was organized to unite six independent Minneapolis mills, with a total capacity of 11,400 barrels.[138]

Under British ownership, Pillsbury-Washburn faltered.[139] One writer has described Charles Pillsbury as not as efficient a manager as he had been an entrepreneur.[140] By contrast, the historian of the Pillsbury company found no change in the way the business was run before and after the takeover.[141] In 1894 the *Northwestern Miller* suggested, however, that during the first two years of British ownership, when the company "was handled according to American ideas," it paid dividends; but "since that time, the wishes of the English interests have been dominant. Thus, if the dividends are not satisfactory, the British themselves, and not the Americans are responsible for it . . . an American mill partially controlled abroad is actually handicapped."[142] Most important, low prices in the 1890s meant low profits.

Then Charles A. Pillsbury's health deteriorated; he died in 1899. His uncle, John S., also active in the business, died late in 1901. Prior to the 1889 merger, over the years 1882–1888, despite millers' complaints about "bad times," the constituent firms in Pillsbury-Washburn had averaged $800,000 in profits per annum. For nine years through 1898, after the amalgamation, profits averaged only $412,000 per annum, and dividends were frequently passed.[143]

In 1898 a New York promoter, Thomas McIntyre, began to acquire flour mills around the nation, and in February 1899 he formed the United States Flour Milling Company and sought control over the major companies in the industry, including Pillsbury-Washburn, Washburn-Crosby, and Northwestern Consolidated. It seemed likely that the dissatisfied English shareholders would acquiesce in U.S. Flour Milling Company's absorbing Pillsbury-Washburn, but this did not occur, because members of the Pillsbury family made sufficient purchases of the securities of the *parent* British company to thwart

McIntyre's plans. (Northwestern Consolidated did become part of U.S. Flour Milling Company, which in February 1900 went into receivership, to reemerge as the Standard Milling Company.)[144]

Aloof from the McIntyre's combination, the Pillsbury-Washburn Flour Mills Company, Ltd., failed to improve its performance, and in the early years of the twentieth century the company lost large sums on wheat speculation, cut its flour grades, and let its properties deteriorate, until finally, in August 1908, Minneapolis banks refused to grant it credit, forcing the British firm into receivership. The existing English stockholders had no desire to send good money after bad; the Pillsbury family saw no reason to have a British company parent. Faced with a no-win proposition, the English stockholders accepted a plan—offered by the Pillsbury family and a receiver from Minneapolis (A. C. Loring)—whereby a new American incorporated and controlled *operating* company, the Pillsbury Flour Mills Company, would be formed and would obtain a twenty-year lease on the properties in return for a minimum rental and division of its profits. Loring became president of Pillsbury Flour Mills. The old British corporation remained in existence—a mere shell, with income-earning properties but no operations.[145]

Correspondence in the Minnesota Historical Society, supplemented by Gaspard Farrer's London letters, casts considerable light on the relations between the British parent and the Minneapolis operations after Charles A. Pillsbury's death. A 1901 letter from John S. Pillsbury (Charles A.'s uncle) to the London board chairman, R. H. Glyn, indicates that that year John S. Pillsbury had wanted the business transferred to (incorporated in) the United States. Glyn objected, and Pillsbury did not pursue the matter, noting: "We have no reason whatever to complain of the treatment and action received at the hands of the English Company. Their movements and general conduct of the company have been all we could ask."[146]

Minneapolis managers would send brief reports to London. Frank Spencer, who became the London secretary of Pillsbury-Washburn Flour Mills Company, Ltd., in 1889 and later "managing director" (while still residing in London), wrote in 1907 that flour profits were "under one continual cloud, and for the life of me I cannot understand how it is that an intelligent body of men, as the Minneapolis Millers undoubtedly are, cannot combine to fix prices so that every barrel sold would leave a profit to the miller."[147]

In this 1907 letter Spencer commented on "certain large balances" and felt the directors should be informed. Often, Spencer complained, "being so far away from the business it is impossible to keep in close touch with everything that is going on." He thought the Americans sent to London only the "very scantiest description."[148] When the directors in London asked for added information, Spencer justified the request: "We are the men who stand to be shot at in the event of anything going wrong." He felt the London directors could not use "the excuse" that they left everything to the American committee of management.[149]

When in July 1908 the Pillsbury-Washburn company was "hard up for money," the news was a surprise to the London board. "We could only surmise that the lowness of cash was accounted for by careful finance," Spencer wrote.[150] On July 27, 1908, Spencer learned by cable "of the discovery of over $1,000,000 indebtedness greater than supposed"; Alfred Pillsbury and a company lawyer, Ralph Whelan, were en route to London "to report to the Board." Spencer (nominally "managing director") added, "We are entirely in the dark."[151] By August 13, 1908, Spencer was writing, "It looks to me as if we all [in London] have been thoroughly deceived and the Balance Sheets for years have been incorrect and misleading."[152] And, he lamented, "we had no say as to who should be appointed receivers."[153]

The London friends of James J. Hill, including Lord Mount Stephen, had all invested in Pillsbury-Washburn Flour Mills Company, Ltd., and in the fall of 1908, as the revelations of abuses unfolded, Baring Brothers' director, Gaspard Farrer, began to seek independent information to evaluate the scheme for reorganization. He was aware of the "large amount of English money" invested. In a private letter, he wrote of Pillsbury-Washburn that "its management has hitherto been little short of a scandal."[154]

In July 1910, British managing director Frank Spencer's "agreement" with Pillsbury-Washburn Flour Mills Company, Ltd., expired, and after twenty years with the company, he "said goodbye to the old ruined concern."[155] At his fellow British director, Sydney T. Klein—who was the largest individual British stockholder in the Pillsbury-Washburn Company[156]—Spencer took a parting shot: "He [Klein] is a shareholder in the operating Coy—buys their flour & has a boy in the Minneapolis office so that his interest is easily traced."[157] In short, after 1910 (or more accurately after 1899 and the McIntyre threat), the British owners and the London directors had lost control over Pillsbury. Long-distance "direction," or the lack of it, had resulted in failure.[158]

The 1889 British ventures in grain elevators were likewise ill fated. In 1894 the City of Chicago Grain Elevator Company, Ltd., was acquired by an American company, the Chicago Railway Terminal Company, and shed its British parent, the American shareholders objecting "to the expense of British management."[159] The Chicago and North-West Granaries Company, Ltd., went into liquidation in 1910.[160]

By contrast, the trading firm Balfour, Guthrie, with its direct management over its enterprises, moved into new activities related to the grain trade, investing in warehouses and elevators on the Pacific Coast. "They have discarded all middlemen and now have eighty grain warehouses and elevators up and down wheat country," an observer would write of this firm in 1903. In 1910 Balfour, Guthrie built a large flour mill in Portland, Oregon (Crown Mills).[161] All its investments carried careful management and were an integral part of its international business. Apparently, throughout the years under consideration, foreign firms—with Balfour, Guthrie the most prominent—dominated the wheat and flour trade of the Pacific Coast. "They influenced the nature of the grading system, of contract forms, and of handling methods."[162]

In short, while foreign—principally British—investors were involved in raising various food products, the greatest involvements were in the grain trade, grain elevators, and flour milling. The investments in Pillsbury-Washburn, albeit not profitable to the investors, were significant ones. Balfour, Guthrie stands out as a principal company in the West Coast grain and flour business.

Alcoholic Beverages

Like meat packing, grain elevators, and flour milling, American breweries also attracted major attention of British investors in the years 1888–1891. Unlike meat and flour (or cattle and wheat, for that matter), Britain was *not* an importer of beer. In the late nineteenth and early twentieth centuries, British breweries ranked among that nation's largest enterprises.[163] Investments in U.S. beer making were part of a merry round of promotions, with the British intoxicated by the prospects of profits. The brewery investments were totally unrelated to international trade. Yet many of the same individuals involved in other U.S. stakes participated in the brewery endeavors.[164]

In 1886 the shares of Arthur Guinness (Dublin) had been floated in London by Baring Brothers. In 1887 the London and Westminster Bank offered Samuel Allsopps and Sons, Ltd., another British brewery. British brewery mergers and subsequent flotations became the norm.[165] Some of the Britishers in domestic brewery finance turned to the same type of American activities.[166] American writers on the U.S. brewery combinations of 1888–1891 put them in the context of the Standard Oil Trust (1882), the Cotton Oil Trust (1884), and the Sugar Trust (1887).[167] Both events in Britain and the United States were relevant.

The first British group to buy and to consolidate American breweries was the New York Breweries Company, Ltd., in 1888.[168] Another set of Britishers brought J. F. Betz and Son in Philadelphia. The
two 1888 entries were separate, but American journalists saw them as
the start of a huge "beer trust."[169] British promoters visited Frederick
Pabst, who owned an important Milwaukee brewery, to try to convince him to merge with Schlitz and with Blatz.[170] Their U.S. representative wrote Pabst of the advantages of such a consolidation,
emphasizing the worldwide advertising that would be achieved by
bringing "the company out in London." The venture "would be
second only to the 'Guinness,' " which had an "increase in sales and
profits of 30 percent within a year of reorganization."[171]

British promoters approached American brewers with attractive
offers of cash, shares in a new company, and debentures. The pattern
was similar to that of Fowler Brothers, Pillsbury-Washburn, and many
other contemporary industrial flotations. It followed a procedure used
earlier with the American mining company promotions in the United
Kingdom. The promoter O'Hagan (who put together Eastmans, Ltd.,
and G. H. Hammond, Ltd.) writes of nine brewery amalgamations in
the United States in which he personally participated.[172] Levy Mayer,
a Chicago attorney who had helped structure the International Packing and Provision Company, Ltd., and the Chicago and North-West
Granaries Company, Ltd., was also instrumental in interesting English capital in Chicago breweries.[173]

In 1888–1891 twenty-four English "syndicates" acquired about
eighty American breweries and two malt houses! Their reported investment approximated $90 million. The investments in U.S. brew-
eries were larger, in total, than those in cattle ranching and meat
packing, or in granaries, grain elevators, and flour mills. The breweries bought by the British companies were located throughout the
United States, from Boston to San Francisco (see Table 9.2). The new
enterprises were multiplant establishments.

The largest was the St. Louis Breweries Company, formed in 1889
(initial capital, £2,850,000); it united seventeen breweries in St. Louis
and one in East St. Louis, including Miller Brothers Brewing Company.
Another formidable British-promoted merger (in 1890) was the Mil-
waukee and Chicago Breweries, Ltd. (capital, £2,271,000), with five
Chicago breweries. In 1891 it acquired V. Blatz of Milwaukee. Valentine
Blatz became its president.[174] The board of the Milwaukee and Chicago
Breweries, Ltd., had several British brewers, among them Edward
Thomas Helme, chairman of the sizable Ind., Coope & Co.[175]

Whereas Blatz sold his firm to a British company, Pabst and Schlitz
did not.[176] Likewise, in St. Louis the British acquired Miller Brothers

Table 9.2. "Syndicate" breweries, April 1891

Company	Capital (in pounds)
Baltimore Breweries Company	190,000
Bauernschmidt and Marr Brewing Company	
Bartholomay Brewing Company	970,000
Bartholomay Brewing Company; Rochester Brewing Company; Genesee Brewing Company; the malthouses of E. B. Parsons and J. N. Oothout	
Betz, J. F., and Son	550,000
J. F. Betz and Son, Philadelphia	
Chicago Breweries Company	1,000,000
McAvoy Brewing Company; Wacker and Birk Brewing and Malting Company	
Cincinnati Breweries	230,000
Jung Brewing Company, Cincinnati; Crescent Brewing Company, Aurora	
City of Baltimore United Breweries Company	335,000
John Bauernschmidt; William Miller and Company; H. Strauss Brothers Company	
City of Chicago Brewing and Malting Company	1,900,000
Conrad Seipp West Side Brewing Company; F. J. Dewes; malthouses of George Bullen and Company and L. C. Huck	
Denver United Breweries Company	600,000
Ph. Zang Brewing Company; Denver Brewing Company	
Detroit Breweries	160,000
Charles Endriss; Jacob Mann; Bavarian Brewing Company; A. Goebel and Company	
Emerald and Phoenix Brewing Company	470,000
T. C. Lyman and Company, New York; F. J. Kastner, Newark	
Hills Union Brewery Company	115,000
William Hill, Newark	
Illinois United Breweries	300,000
Gipp's Brewing Company; Union Brewing Company; Gus Leisy Brewing Company; J. Kollmer and Company; Edwin Porter, Joliet; Markert and Company, Wilmington	
Indianapolis Breweries Company	430,000
C. F. Schmidt; Pihieber Brewing Company; C. Maus	
Jones, Frank, Brewing Company	1,300,000
Frank Jones, Portsmouth, New Hampshire; Jones, Cook and Company, Boston	

Table 9.2   (*Cont.*)

Company	Capital (in pounds)
Milwaukee and Chicago Breweries	2,271,000
M. Brand Brewing Company; Bartholmae and Leicht Brewing Company; Ernest Brothers Brewing Company; Bartholmae and Roesing Brewing Company; K. G. Schmidt Brewing Company, Chicago; V. Blatz of Milwaukee	
New England Breweries Company	610,000
John Roessle; Haffenreffer and Company; Suffolk Brewing Company, Boston; Stanley and Company, Lawrence	
New York Breweries Company	930,000
H. Clausen and Son Brewing Company; Flanagan, Nay and Company	
St. Louis Breweries Company	2,850,000
Anthony and Kuhn Brewing Company; Bremen Brewery Company; Brinkwirth-Nolker Brewing Company; Cherokee Brewery Company; Excelsior Brewery Company; Green Tree Brewery Company; A. Griesedieck Brewing Company; H. Grone Brewery Company; Hyde Park Brewery Company; Klausmann Brewery Company; Liberty Brewing Company; Miller Brothers Brewing Company; Schilling and Schneider; Joseph Schnaider; Charles G. Stifel's; Wainwright Brewery Company; Jul. Winkelmeyer Brewing Company Assoc.,—all of St. Louis; and Heims Brewery Company of East St. Louis	
San Francisco Breweries Company	1,500,000
Wieland Brewery Company; United States Brewery; Chicago Brewery Company; Willows Brewing Company; South San Francisco Brewing Company; Pacific Brewery—all of San Francisco; Fredericksburg Brewery, San Jose; Oakland Brewery, Oakland; Brooklyn Brewery, East Oakland; Hofburg Breweries, West Berkeley	
Schoenhofen, Peter, Brewing Company	617,000
P. Schoenhofen Brewing Company	
Springfield Breweries Company	135,000
Schneider Brothers; Vorce and Blee, Springfield, Ohio	
United States Brewing Company	1,100,000
Albany Brewing Company, Albany, New York; G. Krueger Brewing Company; P. Hauck and Company; Mrs. C. Trefz—all of Newark; and A. Huepfel's Sons, New York	
Voight Brewery Company	200,000
E. W. Voight, Detroit	
Washington Brewery Company	161,000
Albert Cary, Washington	

Source: Western Brewer, 16 (April 15, 1891): 878, and Thomas C. Cochran, *The Pabst Brewing Company* (New York: New York University Press, 1948), pp. 405–406.

and others but failed to take over Anheuser Busch, although they offered Busch $8 million.[177] In 1892 the two British brewery enterprises in Chicago decided to buy or lease "saloons which shall be controlled exclusively by these companies."[178] They were following British brewery industry practice, with so-called tied houses.[179]

Erastus Wiman, writing in 1889, noted that the British had carefully investigated the acquired breweries, secured the continuance of the services of the seller and his staff, and kept the U.S. companies' former owners involved with minority stock holdings.[180] The British parent companies, Wiman wrote, were "officered by men of prominence and position, whose presence in a board of directors is a guarantee to capitalists that thorough investigation has taken place, and that the business will be honestly and efficiently administered."[181] As in the case of other promotions, London directors were chosen because they had titles, prestige, and connections.[182]

Even from the start, some observers had doubts. A New York correspondent to the British *Economist* wrote (1889):

It would perhaps be well for intending investors in these securities to inquire why these breweries have been sold—why they are marketed at a distance, instead of at home . . . and why their sale or management is placed under the charge of reputable English firms, who are not in a position, not possessed of the experience, to judge intelligently regarding what they have to sell or supervise?

The writer warned that the brewery companies were overcapitalized.[183] Despite the presence of prominent brewers on the boards, these British companies were free-standing enterprises, not part of any British breweries' multinational expansion.

The New York *Nation* in 1889 noted that a document published by the Church Temperance Society had disclosed that most of the beer saloons in New York were "held under Chattel mortgage by the brewers," and one brewer owned nearly 200 saloons. The *Nation's* writer continued:

Of course the strictest attention is needed to secure the proper returns from each saloon. Now, fancy all the brewers consolidated and the management of these and their outlying dependencies, the saloons, put under a single management responsible to a board of some kind sitting in London. What would probably be the end of such speculation? We have heard of cheating in Western mines owned by foreigners, when there was only one thing and not more than half-a-dozen people to be watched. Who will watch the breweries and saloon-keepers in a dozen American cities and render faithful accounts weekly or monthly to a confiding syndicate in Lombard Street?[184]

British management over their American breweries varied. The English companies sent representatives from Britain to the Bartholomay (Rochester), the St. Louis, and the San Francisco breweries; these men made their homes in these cities and participated directly in local management, keeping the London office informed. In 1890 the British owners in St. Louis dismissed the former owner-managers, a path that *Banker's Magazine*, New York, diagnosed as "suicidal." No similar interventions existed with the Chicago breweries, but the British accounting firm Price, Waterhouse's Chicago office, in addition to its audit function, provided advisory services to the Chicago brewers' *London* office, Price, Waterhouse's Chicago branch manager offered opinions on operating and financial, as well as accounting, policies.[185]

Prestigious board members and attempts at direction from Britain notwithstanding, contemporaries with reservations about the U.S. brewery securities were right. Most British investors in U.S. breweries came to be highly dissatisfied. Not only were there the problems of long-distance management, but in the 1890s, with falling prices, British-owned breweries in the United States participated in a "number of disagreeable and unprofitable 'price wars.' " U.S.-owned companies joined forces against their British rivals. Thus a group of small brewers in St. Louis, backed by Anheuser Busch and Lemp, formed an association to fight their British competitors.[186] The historian Thomas Cochran notes that the British companies had to compete against the strongest American firms.[187]

Britisher Russell Monro, O'Hagan's U.S. representative,[188] who was deeply involved in the American brewery investments and their management, wrote his friend and accountant, J. Gurney Fowler of Price, Waterhouse, in August 1894 on the plight of these British breweries that Monro insisted was the result of the temporary depression. Monro argued that the breweries were splendid, "sound concerns," which "will come out all right in the long run."[189] It was a cry in the dark.

Poor returns persisted, but so did the British involvements; Nathaniel Bacon, writing of foreign investment in the United States in 1900, made special note of the large brewery interests.[190] Cleona Lewis identified twenty-three "British breweries and liquor companies" operating in the United States in 1899, with a nominal capital of about $75 million.[191] John Vaizey, a historian of the British brewing industry, writes that at the end of 1908, British investors were disenchanted with both British and American brewery shares; the British-owned American breweries, "whose shares had been issued from 1888 to 1890 [,] had paid out 'little or nothing in dividends to their shareholders.' "[192] The *Economist* in 1908 commented on the "scandalous overcapitalization of most of the [British-owned American] breweries."[193]

George Paish estimated the level of British investments in U.S. breweries and distilleries in 1910 at $55.9 million.[194] Cleona Lewis' estimate was similar. She located in financial manuals sixteen British brewing companies and one liquor company in the United States in 1914 (down from the twenty-three total in 1899); their nominal capital was roughly $58 million (compared with $75 million in 1899).[195] In short, in 1914, although the British retained sizable interests in U.S. breweries, their role was less important than in earlier years. In their investments, the British never added anything truly distinctive to American brewery technology, distribution, or management. Their sole contribution seems to have been to accelerate consolidation.[196]

Nonresident German stakes in U.S. breweries were few. German immigrants did invest in brewing in the United States, but those were not, by our definition, foreign investment. Pabst was 13 percent German owned in 1914, apparently portfolio interests.[197] United States Brewing Company, Newark, New Jersey, established during the 1888–1890 period by a London syndicate, had by 1914 become 61 percent German owned;[198] the principal interest in it—and in three other brewery companies in Newark—was by Gotfried Krueger, an American citizen who resided in Germany in 1914.[199] Peter Schoenhofen Brewing Company, Chicago, was 63 percent German owned by 1914.[200]

In other alcoholic beverages, foreign investors also participated. In 1889 a free-standing British company purchased a group of Kentucky distilleries (bourbon producers).[201] British makers of Scotch exported to the United States, finding the market promising. In 1902 James Buchanan opened a branch office in New York (it was short-lived). By 1910 John Dewar had a New York office. John Haig & Co., Ltd., began in 1912–1914 to develop the U.S. trade, appointing American agents. Haig & Haig (a different company) in 1897 gave an agent the exclusive rights to sell its "Pinch" in the United States; and by 1912–13, Haig & Haig had a booming business in this country. Thus, while British producers of Scotch did not open or acquire distilleries in the United States, they did not ignore this market.[202] Likewise, the Canadian firm Hiram Walker & Sons, Ltd., which manufactured "Canadian Club Whiskey" in Walkerville, Ontario, just across the river from Detroit, developed a large U.S. business, all the while fending off imitators of its bottles, labels, and brand name.[203] The French had trading firms that sold French champagne in America. German merchants with U.S. outlets imported wine and liquor.[204] All these interests in alcoholic beverages were small compared with the heavy British investments in the breweries.

In conclusion, British brewery companies in America had encouraged mergers. Since combinations were the norm in America at this time, the British role was probably not decisive. Whereas the British takeover of Hammond had temporarily given the foreign owners a position among the "big four" in U.S. meat packing, and the acquisition of Pillsbury and part of Washburn had put the British, again temporarily, at the pinnacle in the U.S. flour-milling industry, overseas investors failed to acquire any one of the American big three in beer (Schlitz, Pabst, and Anheuser Busch), although they did take over Miller and Blatz, two important brewers. That the British did not buy out the industry leaders in brewing in the United States was not from want of trying. Substantial British monies were invested in American breweries; British companies ranked in the top six among American brewers. By contrast, the foreign investments in other alcoholic beverages were, in total, insignificant.

Condensed Milk, Baby Food, Chocolates, and Other Candies

Other branded food and drink products made in the United States by Swiss, German, and British companies included condensed milk, baby food, chocolates, and toffees. The Swiss interests involved a complex and different story from much of what we have considered thus far in the food and beverages industries; their entry was very much in keeping with what today is identified with the growth and operations of multinational industrial enterprises. Swiss firms produced in America condensed milk, baby food, and chocolates. German companies did not make or sell condensed milk or baby food, but one had an important role in chocolate making. British firms tried to introduce chocolates and did make toffees. Here, too, in the case of the German and British enterprises, the pattern was that of manufacturers' expanding from a base at home into foreign countries (including the United States).

In 1882 the Anglo-Swiss Condensed Milk Company of Cham, Switzerland, decided to manufacture condensed milk in the United States in order to bypass the high U.S. import duties that were reducing its exports. Anglo-Swiss had been organized to do business in Switzerland in 1866 by two American brothers, Charles and George Page; it was apparently initially financed by British and Swiss capital and, in time, became a completely European enterprise. Its headquarters was in Cham, where in 1867 it had started to produce condensed milk; by the end of the 1870s, it manufactured in England and Bavaria as well. George Page acquired for Anglo-Swiss its first U.S. factory in 1882 at Middletown, New York, entering into direct competition with the American leader, Borden. Borden counterattacked with "low-price fighting brands." Anglo-Swiss lost money; but undeterred, it enlarged its output, building and buying additional American facilities so that by 1900 it was a multiplant venture in the United States, with five manufacturing plants in this country. By then, however, Borden's competition had proved too intense, and in 1902 Anglo-Swiss sold its U.S. assets to Borden for $2 million; its American employees joined Borden. At the same time, on February 15, 1902, the two firms entered into an agreement that gave Borden exclusive rights to U.S. and Canadian markets; in return, Borden would withdraw from all other markets around the world.[205]

Meanwhile, in Switzerland, at Vevey (some 120 miles from Anglo-Swiss's headquarters at Cham), Henri Nestlé began in 1867 to produce a "milk food" for babies. Vevey had long been an important center for Swiss chocolates, and Nestlé's factory was located near Daniel Peter's chocolate plant. In 1875 an employee of Peter's mixed Nestlé's milk with Peter's chocolate; the result was a "milk chocolate" that Peter started to manufacture and to market. In 1878 the Nestlé company produced condensed milk for the first time (the year before, Anglo-Swiss had developed a baby food based on condensed milk, bringing it into direct rivalry with Nestlé, which had responded by moving into Anglo-Swiss's market and canning condensed milk).[206]

Nestlé's operations spread outside Switzerland, but not until 1900 did the firm decide to build a factory in the United States. It did so at Fulton, New York, where, with "rich meadow land and large herds of cattle," there were excellent supplies of fresh milk. According to its 1901 publicity, Nestlé required "the purest and richest milk." Its new American business advertised "Nestlé's Food for Infants" and "Nestlé's Condensed Milk." The company's Fulton plant was described as modern "with every attention paid to automatic, labor saving machinery, to insure the perfect product."[207]

In 1905 the Swiss parent enterprises of Anglo-Swiss and Nestlé merged to form the Nestlé & Anglo-Swiss Condensed Milk Company.[208] Since Anglo-Swiss had in 1902 ceded to Borden exclusive rights to the U.S. market and Nestlé had no such arrangement, before the merger in Switzerland could be consummated, negotiations with Borden were essential. Accordingly, Nestlé agreed in 1905 to withdraw from the U.S. and Canadian condensed milk trade (Borden got the exclusive right to the brand "Nestlé Condensed Milk" in the United States and Canada). Nestlé could stay in the baby food business, but it contracted to pay Borden a one-cent-per-can royalty on all baby food that it sold in the United States and Canada.[209] That year the newly merged Swiss firm established the Nestlé's Food Company of New York, with a capital of $250,000, to make Nestlé baby food and sell it in the United States.[210] A city of Fulton guide in 1913 described the Nestlé Food Company as a manufacturer of "Nestlé's Food for Infants, Children and Invalids." Unlike the 1901 publicity, there was no mention of condensed milk.[211]

That same 1913 Fulton guide reported that in 1907, in the city of Fulton, the Peter, Cailler, Kohler Swiss Chocolate Company had begun to manufacture chocolate, including "Nestlé's milk chocolate." The chocolate company's president (in 1913) was C. A. Corliss of New York.[212] This was another Swiss investment in America. The background is complicated. In January 1904, in Switzerland, Peter and Kohler had merged their chocolate business,[213] and in July 1904 (before the Anglo-Swiss Nestlé merger), Nestlé had promised to contribute capital to the new Peter & Kohler, which would manufacture a Nestlé brand of milk chocolate.[214]

Nestlé would market the new firm's chocolates.[215] In 1905 Thomas W. Lamont (later a partner of J. P. Morgan's) tasted Peter's chocolate in Switzerland.[216] Roughly a decade earlier, in 1894, Lamont had become involved in Cushman Brothers Company, which acted as a sales agent for manufacturers.[217] When Cushman Brothers was near bankruptcy in 1898, Lamont reorganized it.[218] By 1900 it specialized in branded food products, including Wesson cooking oil and salad oil.[219] Lamont's papers do not reveal when Lamont, Corliss & Co. was organized (his autobiography says 1898); certainly by 1904 Lamont, Corliss & Co. (Charles A. Corliss was Thomas Lamont's brother-in-law) had replaced Cushman Brothers.[220] The secretary of Lamont, Corliss & Co., New York, on April 4, 1905, described his firm to "August Roussy, c/o Henry Nestlé, Vevey, Switzerland," as follows:

We act as sole and exclusive representatives of a few Manufacturers of high class food products. The territory which we cover for them embraces the United States of America and Canada. Our headquarters are in this city, where we occupy entirely a seven-story building, and we have well equipped branch offices in all the cities indicated upon our letter-head as above [Boston, Philadelphia, Washington, Buffalo, Pittsburgh, Chicago, Minneapolis, St. Louis, Montreal, San Francisco; London, England]. From New York, and from our various branches as headquarters we cover the trade throughout the country, having no less than 70 selling representatives, and in this way forming a fairly complete network throughout the entire country.

Our system of business relieves the Manufacturer entirely of all the detail connected with the developing and up-building of his trade in the American market. We are supposed to be "experts" in the work of establishing trade-marked food products upon this market, and are pleased to have anyone, who is contemplating business with us, enquire in regard to our methods from those Manufacturers whom we are already representing, such as the Cream of Wheat Co.; E. McIlhenny's Son (Tabasco Sauce); The Mackintosh Toffee Co., Ltd., etc. We accept the representation of no Manufacturer unless said Manufacturer agrees to back our efforts to a liberal and reasonable extent with proper advertising. By making this provision a condition of our representation, we are enabled to reduce to a minimum the chances for failure . . .

We are accustomed to discount at a reasonable per centum our entire purchases from the Manufacturers that we represent; such purchases being invariably subject to a selling commission covering our own very heavy expenses of selling.[221]

The letter continued, giving the officers of the company and emphasizing that the firm's financial connections "are of the strongest."[222] Lamont obtained for Lamont, Corliss & Co. the exclusive North American rights for the chocolates of Peter & Kohler.[223]

Two years later (in 1907), Peter & Kohler began to manufacture chocolates at Fulton, New York.[224] In 1909 it seems that Peter & Kohler (Switzerland) obtained a 37 percent interest in Lamont, Corliss & Co.; the Peter & Kohler American business was merged with Lamont, Corliss;[225] C. A. Corliss became president of the Swiss chocolate company's U.S. enterprise, in effect creating a vertically integrated American business.[226] In Switzerland in 1911, Cailler amalgamated with Peter & Kohler, and the Swiss and the American operations both became Peter, Cailler, Kohler Swiss Chocolates.[227] Lamont, Corliss decided (in 1912) to employ "special chocolate salesmen."[228] In 1913 the Peter, Cailler, Kohler Swiss Chocolate Company was increasing the weight of its chocolate packages in America "so as to bring them approximately to the weight of Hershey," since the latter was "walking away" with the "milk chocolate business."[229] The Swiss chocolates—made in America—were by this time said to be "known and obtainable in every city and town in the country and on nearly every train and passenger steamboat that travels to and from within the broad limits of the North American continent."[230]

In sum, in 1914 no Swiss investment remained in the production of condensed milk in the United States; Borden was supreme, with Carnation and Helvetia Milk Condensing Company, later renamed Pet Milk (making "evaporated milk"—a process of preserving milk without sugar), its two major competitors. But the Nestlé & Anglo-Swiss Condensed Milk Company, through its own U.S. subsidiary, the Nestlé Food Company, produced and marketed baby food (paying a royalty on each can to Borden); and through its Swiss connections with Peter, Cailler, Kohler Swiss Chocolate Company (Nestlé owned a 39 percent interest in that Swiss firm in 1911),[231] Nestlé was engaged in manufacturing chocolates in the United States. Both the baby food and the chocolates were made in Fulton, New York, for sale in the United States. Peter, Cailler, Kohler Swiss Chocolate Company made Peter's Milk Chocolate, Cailler's Milk Chocolate, Nestlé's Milk Chocolate, Kohler's Chocolate (without milk), and Peter's Bon-Bons, which were sold in this country by Lamont, Corliss & Co., in which the Swiss chocolate firm had a 37 percent interest.[232] The complexities of the corporate structure aside, Nestlé had started its long history in America.

Nestlé was not the only foreign investor in chocolates—or in candy, for that matter. For many years Gebrueder Stollwerck, A.G., Cologne, had sold its trademarked chocolates in the United States through agents. In about 1904 that German enterprise had acquired some forty-three acres in Stamford, Connecticut, and over a two-year period (1905–1907) it built an American factory to manufacture its chocolate products. The new plant was equipped, in the main, with German-made machinery. As business grew, the firm in 1909 enlarged its manufacturing facilities. Stollwerck Brothers, Inc., opened its own sales offices in New York, Boston, Chicago, and San Francisco. By 1914 the capital of this American manufacturing and sales subsidiary was $1.25 million.[233] The historian Bruno Kuske described it as having the second largest chocolate factory in the United States (after Walter Baker in Boston). It apparently made "cooking" chocolates, as well as chocolate candy.[234]

The British also tried to appeal to Americans' love of chocolate. Cadbury Brothers, which made its first cocoa and chocolate products in Britain in 1831, set up an American "agency" in 1882 that sold Cadbury Cocoa and Chocolates to shops in New York City and Philadelphia. But, unlike the Swiss and unlike Stollwerck, Cadbury did not manufacture in the United States. The firm's historian notes that this country "always proved a somewhat disappointing field for the sale of Cadbury products."[235] Tastes seemed different.[236]

Another British candymaker did attempt to produce here. In 1890 John Mackintosh had started to make toffee in a retail store in Halifax, Yorkshire. He built his first British toffee works in 1894, advertising lavishly. In 1903, on his first visit to the United States, he made a contract with the U.S. advertising agency J. Walter Thompson. In 1904 he returned to America. On one of these trips (probably the first), he arranged to have Lamont, Corliss & Co. act as his wholesale distributor (this was before that firm had made its contract with the Swiss). On the 1904 visit, Mackintosh decided to manufacture in

America and purchased a factory in the seaside resort town of Asbury Park, New Jersey, a facility that he staffed in part with employees from his British plant.

Mackintosh plunged into the U.S. business, opening retail shops in a number of American cities, handing out free samples, and continuing to advertise; yet his business failed to prosper. While the Swiss and German chocolate makers did well, toffee was new to Americans, and Mackintosh sold it unpackaged in broken slabs. In the summer heat it became soft and sticky. In 1907 or 1908, Mackintosh decided to shut down his U.S. factory. His son later recalled, "It was not until we had learned how to wrap and package the product in modern form that we achieved any success in the American market"; he added, "In his American adventure Father had lost almost all the money he had made in England and the firm at home found finances somewhat strained."[237] What is important is that Mackintosh—like the chocolate makers, a manufacturer of a trademarked, advertised product that did not ship well (that is, it was not easy to export)—tried to compete in the United States.

To conclude, in 1914 Nestlé was in America, making baby food and chocolates. Stollwerck was an important chocolate maker in this country. In chocolates and toffee, Swiss, German, and British-owned firms had invested in America to manufacture for the U.S. market. Their experiences were diverse; only the Swiss and the Germans were successful. Cadbury never seems to have had the courage to pursue American business in an ambitious fashion, while Mackintosh's failure lay in the firm's not adopting modern packaging.

Other Brand-Name Foods and Nonalcoholic Beverages

Numerous "branded" British food products were sold in U.S. groceries and through American mail-order houses—for example, Spratt's Dog Cakes; Colman's Mustard; Lea & Perrins Worcestershire Sauce; Crosse & Blackwell's India Soy Sauce, Bengal Club Chutney, and English pickles; Peek, Frean Biscuits; Huntley & Palmers Biscuits; and Liebig's Extract of Beef.[238] Of these, only Spratt's dog biscuits were made in this country, by a subsidiary of a British firm. In 1886 Spratt's Patent, Ltd., established a U.S. company and started to manufacture its branded dog biscuits in the United States.[239] As for the other products, British companies typically had agents or a representative in America.[240] The Swiss and Germans introduced Maggi seasonings and Loriot peppermints.[241]

There was even one Japanese branded food product made in the United States—through a direct investment. The Japanese maker of soy sauce, Kikkoman, had established its own product image at home and abroad and registered its trademark in 1879 in California and in 1906 in Washington, D.C., for the United States as a whole. In 1892 in Denver, Colorado, the Kikkoman firm built a small factory that produced soy sauce in the United States to cater to Japanese immigrants.[242] Unquestionably, however, more British branded food products were introduced into the United States than those of any other nationality.[243]

A few German investments in the United States were in coffee-related products. Kaffee Handels, A.G., founded in 1907 by the son of an affluent Bremen coffee merchant, Ludwig Roselius, established a multinational business that included Kaffee-Patent, A.G., which owned 50 percent of Kaffee Hag Corporation (formed in March 1914). Kaffee Hag Corporation marketed in the United States a caffeine-free coffee, then called DeKofa, which many years later came to be sold under the name Sanka.[244] In 1909 Ludwig Roselius discussed the possibility of doing business with Lamont, Corliss & Co. regarding "the Caffeine-Freed proposition."[245] Apparently nothing came of the discussions, and the genesis of Kaffee Hag Corporation occurred when the president of New York City Car Advertising Company (a railway car advertising firm) saw the success of the caffeine-free coffee in Germany. This U.S. firm came to own the other 50 percent of Kaffee Hag in the United States, in consideration of its providing $500,000 worth of advertising.[246]

Heinrich Franck Söhne of Ludwigsburg, Germany, had branches throughout Europe and one in the United States. In Europe this German firm handled a variety of food products, but its U.S. business was confined to raising, curing (at a factory in Flushing, New York), and marketing chicory to be used as "an adulterant of" or substitute for coffee. It provided chicory seed from German growers to U.S. farmers near Bay City, Michigan, who raised the crop under contract. This company did mainly German-language advertising in the United States, selling to that special group of immigrants. It had a trade-marked product, "Franck's Feinster Cichorien-Extract." It called attention to its brand, warning against imitations. Emil Seelig was another "manufacturer" of chicory (50 percent German owned).[247]

Lipton's Tea Company packed and blended tea in the United States, as noted earlier. Thomas J. Lipton sought "to teach" Americans to drink tea. In 1890 he began to promote his branded, prepackaged black Ceylon tea in this country. In two years he had added to his meat distribution system and established a network of agents to seek hotel and restaurant sales. His headquarters was in Chicago, center of his meat-packing interests. Lipton contemplated opening retail shops

to sell tea (and did try and fail with four of them). Instead, he
assumed direct control of the wholesale trade in his tea, pursuing
extensive advertising campaigns. He set up an American marketing
company, which imported, packed, and distributed branded teas,
coffees, and, on occasion, other food products.[248] As indicated, when
in 1898 Lipton, Ltd., was established in London, it did not acquire
any of Lipton's American assets.[249] By 1914 Lipton's U.S. tea business
was a great success. By then, Lipton's head U.S. office and main
"factory" (that is, tea packing and blending facility) were on Franklin
Street in downtown New York.[250] The firm remained British owned,
with Lipton himself apparently the principal owner.

Meanwhile, in 1888 an employee of Joseph Tetley & Co. had visited
the United States and had appointed an agent. Tetley's teas—like
Lipton's—were widely advertised and became well known in the
United States. That company decided in 1913 to incorporate a U.S.
subsidiary, Tetley Tea Company, Inc.[251]

In 1884 Schweppes had set up a bottling plant in Brooklyn, New
York, which was unsuccessful and closed in 1892. The firm for the
eight years sold mineral water. Its historian does not explain the
reason for the failure.[252] By 1892 there were many carbonated soft-
drink producers and soda fountains in America. Schweppes apparently had no special advantage.[253] Other British nonalcoholic
beverages available to the American consumer included Epps' Cocoa
and Fry's Homeopathic Cocoa. These were imported—and do not
appear to have been even packed in the United States.[254]

Branded food products from abroad that were sold in the U.S.
market seem to have been mainly specialty items. It is of interest how
many branded nonalcoholic "drink" products there were—but coffee,
tea, and cocoa would have to be imported anyway. Possibly this gave
the German or British investor a certain advantage (or at least no
disadvantage vis-à-vis U.S. competitors).[255]

Tobacco

In 1901 the giant American Tobacco Company acquired Ogden, Ltd.,
one of Britain's leading cigarette producers. In response to this American "invasion," thirteen British firms formed the large Imperial Tobacco Company, which resolved to counterattack and to manufacture
in the United States. It did not do so, choosing instead in 1902 to
divide world markets with American Tobacco; thereafter its interests
in the United States were to be limited to obtaining leaf tobacco.[256] At
the same time, in 1902, British-American Tobacco Company (BAT)
was incorporated in England, owned two-thirds by American To-

bacco and one-third by Imperial; it was to pursue international business. After a 1911 U.S. Supreme Court decision, American Tobacco distributed its shares in BAT to its stockholders. Thus BAT remained American owned, and its interests in "certain producing companies in the United States" were not foreign investments, since the beneficial ownership (and the management) of BAT in London was American.[257]

As for Imperial Tobacco, its predecessor companies had long been concerned that American Tobacco might "corner" the Virginia tobacco crop.[258] At origin, Imperial had set up a central leaf-buying committee and opened an office in Richmond, Virginia. It bought its raw material more cheaply than through middlemen. One of the British firms that Imperial had acquired (William Clarke & Sons) already had a processing plant in Kentucky to handle its "Dark Western" tobacco requirements. Under the 1902 division-of-markets agreement, Imperial Tobacco was allowed to continue to invest in obtaining leaf tobacco in the United States, for *export* to the United Kingdom. In February 1902 it incorporated the Imperial Tobacco Company of Kentucky, which "annexed" William Clarke's local subsidiary and it existing facility. In 1904 Imperial constructed an office building in Richmond, Virginia, from which it coordinated its U.S. leaf tobacco operations, "based now on half a dozen processing plants." Four years later (in 1908), it bought Fallon & Martin of Durham, North Carolina, and some other processing plants.[259] These investments were all to supply tobacco for its British factories.[260] Its purchases were often large enough to make it vulnerable to the charge that it was pushing down prices.

Similarly, albeit on a smaller scale, Gallaher's, an independent British cigarette manufacturer, had a manager in Virginia and North Carolina to purchase "Dark Western" tobacco; Tom Gallaher often visited America. Like Imperial Tobacco, Gallaher's interests in the United States involved backward integration to buy tobacco.[261]

The only foreign-owned stake in cigarettes to serve the U.S. market in the decade before World War I that I have identified was the business of Philip Morris. *Burdett's Official Intelligence, 1891,* London, describes Philip Morris & Co., Ltd., London, as tobacco manufacturers and dealers and cigar importers.[262] Apparently the "'tobacconist" Philip Morris had opened a shop on London's Bond Street in 1847. In 1854 he saw an officer home from the Crimean War smoke tobacco wrapped in paper; he decided to make hand-rolled smoke-cured, Turkish-tobacco cigarettes. He seemed to have been one of the earliest British cigarette makers and may have even coined the word, *cigarette.*[263] At some point, Philip Morris & Co., Ltd., appointed a

U.S. agent and in 1902 organized the Philip Morris Corporation in New York; this firm was reincorporated in 1909 as Philip Morris & Co., Ltd., a New York corporation. I know little of its activities, save that they appear to have been designed for the U.S. market. In time, of course, Philip Morris would become an important *U.S.-based* tobacco company. By then, it had shed its British ownership ties. It became a leader in the U.S. industry. All that happened much later.[264]

Soap and Other Nonfood Grocery Products

Many products manufactured and distributed by foreign investors in the United States were sold in American-owned grocery stores, including Lipton's bacon and Lipton's tea, Pillsbury's "Best" flour, the trademarked beers, Nestlé's Food for Infants, Stollwerck's chocolates, Kaffee Hag's decaffeinated coffee, and Tetley's tea. These trademarked consumer goods involved advertising, special packaging, and often pictorial or at least colorful wrappings or labels. Among these grocery products offered by British investors in the United States were Lever Brothers' soaps.[265]

In 1888 (while his new factory at Port Sunlight in England was still under construction), the founder of Lever Brothers, William Hesketh Lever, visited America to arrange for a sales agency to handle his exports.[266] Subsequently, Lever would make many transatlantic trips. In 1894 he bought a cottonseed oil mill in Vicksburg, Mississippi, to supply Port Sunlight, an exceptional (for Lever) supply-related U.S. investment.[267] The following year, Lever opened a sales office in New York to encourage soap exports from Britain.[268] American tariffs on soaps had been lowered, and sales expansion seemed promising.[269] The tariff reduction was temporary, and with duties once again up in 1897 and freight rates high, Lever decided to manufacture in the United States to reach the American market.[270] In 1897 he bought controlling interest in the Curtis Davis Company of Boston/Cambridge and at the same time obtained the rights to its Welcome soap.[271] Two years later, in 1899, Lever acquired Benjamin Brooke & Co., Philadelphia, with its well-known Monkey Brand scouring soap.[272] By the turn of the century, Lever had three U.S. factories: one at Vicksburg, Mississippi, the second in Cambridge, Massachusetts (called the Boston Works), and the third in Philadelphia (the Philadelphia Works). In addition, the New York office still existed.

Lever's sales in America were modest. By 1902 he was bothered by the "happy-go-lucky" way in which his Philadelphia Works was run. "They had simply got into a routine of the manufacture of Monkey Brand which moved along automatically and when they came to make Laundry Soap, both Sunlight and Lifebuoy, requiring constant vigilance, they were not equal to the strain."[273] In 1903 Lever was losing money in his U.S. business.[274] By April of that year he arranged to purchase the minority shareholders' interests in Lever Brothers Ltd., Boston Works (the successor to the Curtis Davis Company).[275] "Having done this," he wrote, "I have decided to close the Philadelphia works and transfer the manufacture of Sunlight, Lifebuoy and Monkey Brand to Boston. We have just completed the extension of the Boston Works, so that Boston is now in a position to take care of this extra output. This change will effect a saving of about $30,000 a year in working expenses."[276] The wholly owned American Lever subsidiary in 1903 was named Lever Brothers Company.

In 1904 Lever was at Vicksburg, Mississippi, arranging to sell the cottonseed oil mill.[277] Several years later, he explained that although the original intent of this facility had been to supply the Port Sunlight factory in Britain, the American market "being so much better than the English market, the price was really higher in America; therefore we sold the oil made at Vicksburg and rebought in its place, in Liverpool, oil crushed at Hull from Egyptian seed." This state of affairs continued for six years, when Lever decided that "as we were Soapmakers and only oil makers in order to find oil for soap making," it would be wise to sell the mill.[278] By 1905 Lever was again making small profits in America.[279] In 1906 Lux Flakes—which had been sold in England for a half-dozen years—was introduced in the United States.[280]

Lever personally followed every detail of the American business, from the wrapping of soap to freight charges, to the texture of the product ("I am going into the question of brittle Monkey Brand . . . upon my return to Port Sunlight"), to broken cases, to salaries of salesmen.[281] The brittle-soap problems, he wrote the Cambridge management, "arise from your not working at the right temperature."[282]

In the early years Lever dispatched Englishmen to run the U.S. business. Yet from America Lever obtained a new soap, Monkey Brand, which came to be manufactured in England. On buying Benjamin Brooke & Co., he also obtained Sidney Gross, who joined the British board of Lever Brothers, Ltd., and remained with the parent company in England until 1910.[283] Lever and Gross wrote often, discussing advertising and marketing. Lever informed Gross of his interest in the colored illustrations for Fry's chocolates, and suggested the possibility of his company doing something similar.[284] He discussed the advertising of Huntley & Palmers Biscuits, Epps' Cocoa, Cadbury chocolates, as well as Peek, Frean Biscuits.[285]

In 1903 Lever provided a letter of introduction to his Boston Works for Ludwig Stollwerck, director of Stollwerck Brothers, chocolate manufacturers of Cologne.[286] The Stollwerck firm, as I have indicated, would subsequently make sizable investments in the United States; Ludwig Stollwerck was a partner of Lever's in Sunlight Seifenfabrik of Mannheim. Apparently there were similarities in marketing packaged branded chocolates and packaged branded soap.

By 1909 Lever was dissatisfied with the progress made in soap sales in the United States. Tastes were different. The British Sunlight soap was not popular, and American consumers apparently disliked the smell of Lifebuoy. Lux Flakes did reasonably well, considering that it had just been introduced. That year, 1909, Francis A. Countway, an American who had come to Lever Brothers Company from the Curtis Davis company in 1897, reorganized the U.S. selling organization of Lever Brothers and appointed Lamont, Corliss & Co. its sole selling agent outside New England. Recall that Lamont, Corliss & Co. had represented Mackintosh, Ltd., and the Swiss chocolate makers and had considered taking on a German caffeine-free coffee product.[287] Lamont, Corliss' wholesaling network could provide better services for jobbers and retailers nationwide than the Lever subsidiary could on its own—at least at this stage. The Lever Boston Works supervised, however, nearby New England sales itself, covering that region with its own salesmen.[288]

Initially the relationship between the Lever enterprise and Lamont, Corliss & Co. was uneasy. C. A. Corliss wanted to retain the line ("They pay us about $25,000 a year gross"), but he wrote in 1912, "These people are old-fashioned type of manufacturers. They come at us with a club every few weeks. It does no good to argue with them and show them where they are wrong."[289] That year, 1912, Countway—newly appointed general manager of the American Lever Brothers—decided to stop marketing Sunlight soap in the United States and to concentrate on Welcome, Lifebuoy, and Lux Flakes.[290]

Countway proved to be a remarkable salesman, and as he assumed increasing importance in the management of Lever's U.S. subsidiary, its sales would rise. Some seven years later Lever, discussing a problem of his Canadian subsidiary, compared its operation with the American one and reflected: "It is only since we have had Mr. Countway that there has been any genius introduced into our American business . . . I am strongly of the opinion . . . that it is genius that we want in Canada, and not resin in Sunlight soap."[291]

Apparently, as early as 1905 Lever Brothers Company in the United States engaged the services of J. Walter Thompson. Later, this American advertising agency would contribute to Lever's spectacular success.[292] Indeed, while the existing Lamont, Corliss & Co. papers provide no evidence, it seems likely that Lamont, Corliss did become, in time, far happier with the Lever account. Lamont, Corliss & Co.'s established organization presumably did for Lever Brothers what it had done earlier for the food companies.

Brunner, Mond and Company—the Belgian Solvay's affiliate in England—supplied Lever Brothers in Britain with alkali.[293] In 1911 Brunner, Mond bought control of two large British soap manufacturers, Crosfield's and Gossage's, but two years later Brunner, Mond promised the British Lever company not to expand further in the soap business. The "Lever family" of companies—except those in Europe and North America—agreed to purchase all their alkali from Brunner's; in Europe and North America they "should give preference to Brunner Mond and their allies, in return for which Brunner's promised to 'use their influence to secure for Lever Brothers and their Associated Companies preferential treatment.' "[294] Thus Lever's British accord extended across the Atlantic, and Lever Brothers Company in the United States was affected.

Meanwhile, Crosfield's had purchased a patent taken out by a German chemist for converting certain oils into hard fats by the hydrogenation process and had licensed Lever's competitor in the United States, Procter & Gamble.[295] In May 1914 Lever Brothers Company and Procter & Gamble made an agreement in the United States whereby a new hydrogenation company was to be established to hold hydrogenation patents belonging to both parties.[296] This was not the start of cooperation between the two rivals. They remained highly competitive. I note it simply to show the impact of the international investment connections.

In 1914 Lever's manufacturing in America was concentrated in a single factory in Cambridge, Massachusetts. Lever's U.S. company had a capital stock of $3.75 million, but only 148 people were employed at the Cambridge factory and office. Sales—at a new high in 1914—came to a mere $912,320. In New England marketing was done by the American subsidiary; Lamont, Corliss & Co. continued to handle the rest of the United States. While Lever's U.S. business remained small, the foundations had been laid for future expansion.[297]

In 1892 the British firm Reckitt and Sons, Ltd., opened a New York branch to sell its trademarked products, including Robin Starch and Paris Blue. In 1904 this firm bought a factory in New Brunswick, New Jersey, to make Blue (a whitening agent). In 1908 it formed a subsidiary, Reckitt (U.S.A.), Ltd., to conduct its American business.[298] Like Lever Brothers Company in the United States, it manufactured and sold laundry products.

An added British product must be included—Pears' Soap—which was widely and exquisitely advertised in the United States. From 1884 to 1920 the distribution of Pears' Soap was by Walter Janviers of New York.[299] Although the product was sold in drug stores rather than in groceries,[300] it had many similarities to the grocery store goods.[301] The British Pears' company appears to have owned warehouse space in Brooklyn in 1888.[302] In 1889, when the promotion of Nairn Linoleum began in California, a W. & J. Sloane director promised that "Nairn Linoleum will soon be as familiar a household word on the coast as Pears' Soap."[303] In 1903 an American advertising man declared that "as a result of advertising, Pears' soap is better known than England itself."[304] In 1911 Thomas J. Barratt, chairman and managing director of A. & F. Pears, Ltd., visited the United States to look at sites for American manufacturing. The U.S. duty was 50 percent; soapmakers in this country were copying the British product; but when U.S. tariffs were reduced in 1913, the British Pears company suspended its negotiations for the planned American factory, and its U.S. customers continued to be supplied through imports.[305] Pears seemed to have found in Walter Janviers a devoted and totally satisfactory independent agent to handle its U.S. marketing. The advertising was brilliant, and Pears' "space buyer" (that is, buyer of advertising space) did follow Pears to the United States—see Chapter 15.

Another branded good, matches, was wrapped, labeled, advertised, and trademarked. Beginning in 1904, the American company Diamond Match served as sales agent in the United States for Jonkopings & Vulcans Tandsticksfabriks, A. B., Sweden's leading producer (formed in 1903). In 1910 Jonkopings & Vulcans considered opening a U.S. factory—but other international priorities took precedent. In 1913 AB Forenade Svenska Tandsticksfabriker merged all the Swedish factories that were independent of Jonkopings & Vulcans and began to export to the United States. Diamond Match "demanded" that Forenade's sales company in New York (Stromborg Export and Import Company) cease competition.[306] Before World War I, Diamond Match successfully controlled imports.

Distribution of Trademarked Grocery Products

The methods of distribution of foreign branded consumer products do not fit neatly into a simple schemata. Some foreign firms had no foreign direct investments and used nonexclusive independent sales agents. For example, Loriot peppermints used Lamont, Corliss & Co.;[307] some licensed their "agent" to manufacture in the United

States as well as to distribute (Lea & Perrins);[308] and one used as a distributor the major U.S. manufacturer in the industry (Jonkopings & Vulcans).[309] Some, for short periods, joined in using a single, partly salaried distributor (Huntley & Palmers; Rowntree).[310] Some had "hybrid" relations with their distributors, jointly owning with their distributor a factory in the United States and also having partial, minority ownership of the nonexclusive distributor (Peter's chocolates); one manufactured and used its own salesmen in a region near its factory and an independent nonexclusive wholesaler for the rest of the country (Lever Brothers); another produced and also handled its own national wholesaling (Stollwerck chocolates). Only a few opened retail shops (Mackintosh and Lipton), and these were soon closed. Some foreign firms in the United States became successful manufacturers or packers (breaking down bulk); some became successful wholesalers on their own account or in joint-ventures; none became a successful retailer. The specific form of entry into distribution (at the above level of detail) did not predict success or failure of these firms in the United States in subsequent years.

The Food, Drink, Tobacco, and Grocery Products

In sum, in a wide variety of food, drink, tobacco, and grocery goods, there were foreign direct investments, principally from Great Britain, but some important ones from Germany and Switzerland as well (French, Dutch, and Canadian interests were of far less consequence). Some significant investments were stimulated by British needs for food imports (thus the genesis of investments in cattle ranches and meat packing, as well as in grain and flour). Yet potential profits to investors rather than import requirements per se were clearly paramount in motivating the largest British investments in these sectors as well as in American breweries where there was no connection with international trade. In 1880–1883 the vogue in Britain had been U.S. cattle company promotions. In 1888–1890 the new attention was given to American meat packing, granaries, flour mills, and brewery promotions. In all these investments, the British expected some role in management. However, with one prominent exception—Eastmans, Ltd.—the rash of floated companies were free-standing ones, with no integrated operations by a parent firm in the United Kingdom (although some of the acquired meatpackers had or subsequently developed sales branches in England). By contrast, neither Morrell & Co. nor Lipton raised outside monies in British capital markets for their American ventures. Each had business in Britain associated with its U.S. investments; each invested in America to supply its British operations. With few exceptions (Matador Land and Cattle and Morrell & Co., the most notable), British investors in cattle companies and meat packing—whether of the free-standing variety or of the usually defined multinational-enterprise sort—disposed of their U.S. interests when alternative sources of supply became available or when sizable profits were not forthcoming, or for both reasons.

Balfour, Williamson—the Liverpool-headquartered trading firm—through its California house, Balfour, Guthrie, made a number of managed supply-oriented investments in trade and in food production. Imperial Tobacco's investments in the United States were supply related, serving that company's British factories. So too, W. H. Lever's first U.S. participation in manufacturing was to provide his English plant with cottonseed oil. Imperial Tobacco's and Lever's investments were of a multinational-enterprise character—involving backward vertical integration by industrial enterprises to the processing stage (but not to agriculture itself). Lever sold the cottonseed oil factory when his Sunlight works could purchase more cheaply elsewhere. Imperial Tobacco kept its investments because tobacco leaf from the United States was essential to its United Kingdom business. As I review the "supply-oriented" stakes by foreign investors in U.S. food and tobacco, determinants of success or failure related to business conditions and managerial responses; alien-property legislation had no material impact.

The largest amount of foreign direct investment in the United States in food, drink, and grocery products was to serve American markets. This came to be true of most of the free-standing corporations—their genesis notwithstanding. As for the breweries, U.S. sales had been, of course, the goal in the first place. Likewise, Lipton (before its withdrawal from meat packing) and Morrell & Co.—neither of which was U.S. "market oriented" in its initial strategy—both developed a substantial U.S. trade in meat products. Foreign entries in branded grocery goods were made by European companies to reach U.S. customers and were part of the international expansion of the parent firm's operations. From the start this was true of the Swiss in condensed milk and baby food; Swiss, German, and British firms in candies (including chocolates) and in other branded foods; German businesses in coffee-related goods; British ones in tea, bottled mineral water, and other branded nonfood grocery products; and the Swedish matchmakers. Sometimes the multinational extension did not involve investment and was confined to appointing a sales agent (as in the case of Jonkopings & Vulcans); sometimes a sales branch was opened; some purveyors of branded food products licensed U.S. companies to produce in America. A number of Swiss, German, and

British enterprises manufactured in the United States to provide products for the American consumers and acted as we have come to expect multinational firms to behave (Nestlé, Stollwerck, and Lever are good examples).

Most of the market-oriented European direct investors did not achieve startling success. Enterprises that developed from a business abroad tended to have a lower mortality rate than the free-standing ones. Yet if business conditions dictated, market-oriented stakes of multinational enterprises would be disposed of or reduced (Anglo-Swiss sold out; Mackintosh closed down, as did Schweppes; Lever sold his Philadelphia plant). There was, in short, no more necessary permanence than in the supply-related investments. Here as in the case of the supply-related investments, alien-property legislation had little impact (the only instance in which there was a clear obstacle in such laws was that of beet-sugar growing and refining in the state of Washington; I am assuming, perhaps incorrectly, that this was a market-oriented investment). Some companies, however, with their specialized, differentiated trademarked products, persevered to become, in time, highly successful.

An interesting feature of these food, drink, tobacco, and grocery product investments is the mixture of supply- and market-related operations, of success and failure. The cattle companies, stimulated by supply-related considerations, eventually marketed their output in the United States (and not abroad); the meat-packing facilities, in the main, fit the same pattern; I have seen no evidence that flour exports rose after Pillsbury became British owned. From the beginning, the brewery, distillery, and condensed-milk investments were to provide for the American market. Imperial Tobacco had threatened to invade the U.S. market, but its successful investments were supply related. Lever's first investment was supply related; its subsequent ones, market related. The same was true of Lipton. Supply-related entries often led to market-related ones. Far less frequently, market-related plans would lead to supply-oriented ones (the case of Imperial Tobacco seems atypical). Ultimately, as indicated, market-related investments predominated.

For market-related businesses, the importance of the trademarked, branded, highly advertised product stands out. There were numerous such British products.[311] Yet sizable expenditures on advertising did not by definition mean direct investments in manufacturing (Pears' Soap is a good case in point). Nor did the mere presence of a trademarked product (popular at home) guarantee success; neither Cadbury chocolates nor Mackintosh toffees pleased American consumers. Tariffs often served to motivate manufacture behind the barrier, but tariffs did not compel manufacture. Many companies failed to respond to the curtailment of their exports. There was nothing inevitable in the expansion process. Certain products by their very nature need to be made near the customer. Chocolates, for example, get stale. Decisions to manufacture in America might lie the nature of the product (and be unrelated to tariffs); yet here again there was no inevitability. Whereas Swiss and German chocolate companies manufactured in the United States, no British chocolate company did. An occasional firm licensed its agent to produce a branded product (Lea & Perrins Worcestershire Sauce is an example), a compromise approach—usually a result of an American company's initiative.

The U.S. market was large and very special. Many foreign firms found they could not compete. The failure rate (or pattern of retreat) is impressive. As British-owned companies, Pillsbury dropped from its first place in American flour milling[312] and Hammond lost its front rank in the top four in beef production. In these instances, absentee ownership and economically meaningless transatlantic hierarchy could not maintain the superiority. An office in Britain, staffed with one full-time man at most and part-time directors with other business interests, was not conducive to prosperous enterprise in America. Yet, as indicated, multinational organization also did not assure success. Anglo-Swiss, after a vast expansion, exited, accepting a division-of-market arrangement with Borden; only after its merger with Nestlé did Anglo-Swiss reenter the United States.

The impacts of the substantial foreign investments in food, drink, tobacco, and grocery products were not uniform. Capital for new economic activity was provided. U.S. livestock production grew, and quality improved. The investors in cattle raising increased the amount of fencing, thereby accelerating the transformation from range to ranch. Their investments had major consequences. Otherwise, it does not seem that foreign companies had profound effects on the *total* output or on the quality of most food products or on tobacco. I doubt, for example, that America made more or better flour and beer because of the British entries, albeit British business probably did augment bacon and ham, grain, and leaf tobacco exports.

British promotions served to encourage mergers in meat packing, flour, and brewing, but, as noted earlier, amalgamations were the norm in late-nineteenth-century America, and it is unclear whether a British catalyst was required. That many of the foreign-owned firms were multiplant operations was not unique to foreign-owned enterprises. The short-lived, spectacular British financing of the Chicago stockyards seems to have had the sole effect of assisting in changing the U.S. ownership of the yards.

One of the key contributions of the foreign investors covered in this chapter was their introduction of a large number of highly advertised new "brand names"—new consumer products—that have subsequently (if not before 1914) become household words in America: Nestlé chocolates, Lux Flakes, Lipton's Tea, Tetley's Tea, Philip Morris cigarettes. Before 1914, probably only Lipton's Tea and possibly Tetley's Tea were household names nationwide, although Nestlé's chocolates were widely sold.

What is crucial is that the "successful" foreign firms (those that ultimately persisted as foreign controlled and in the long run brought good profits to their owners) were always characterized by integration with a parent organization and attention to management; those that sold in the American market also presented distinctive and widely advertised trademarked products.

Writing in 1914, C. K. Hobson found that British capital was flowing less into the United States "and more to Canada and Argentina, which are now two of the chief sources of food supply for Great Britain." He believed that British investments in American foodstuffs had been curtailed because the "law of diminishing returns" had come to apply to U.S. agriculture. Canada and Argentina remained virgin territories.[313] Nonetheless, firms such as Balfour, Williamson continued to make agricultural investments in the United States. Hobson's comments are also inapplicable to British investors in beer and in grocery products from tea to soap (not foodstuffs for export) and to the Swiss and German interests in chocolates (again, not foodstuffs for export). In 1914 the financial commitments of multinational companies in producing and marketing such consumer goods in the United States were still small when compared with the earlier formidable stakes in cattle, meat, flour, and beer; nevertheless, beer excepted, the investments of the early twentieth century represented modern multinational enterprise.[314]

10.

Textiles, Apparel, Leather Goods and Related Products

Most economic historians view the American textile industry of 1875–1914 as technologically mature, which was certainly the case in cottons and in many woolen products. Specialized segments of the textile industry, however, were characterized by novelty. Woolen *worsted* yarn and cloth, the developing silk manufacture, better-quality laces, a newly and fully internationalized cotton and linen thread business, the first of the synthetic fabrics, innovations in chemicals for dyes and bleaches, and improved textile machinery provided a dynamism that was in the main absent in the older, more traditional branches of this industry.

In this chapter I consider the sizable number of foreign investments (practically all direct investments) in the U.S. textile industry, from cotton plantations to cotton, woolen, and silk manufacture and "textile finishing," to thread, to rayon, to apparel. I include the small interests in the leather industry. In addition, I review briefly foreign involvements in dyes and alkalies, inputs required in textile production, and European stakes in machinery manufacturing in the United States to supply this nation's textile makers. The extent of foreign direct investment in U.S. textiles came as a surprise.[1] In my conclusion I will try to explain the reasons for this major role and suggest what the involvements tell us about foreign investments (particularly direct investments) in the United States and how they compare with the others already studied.

The Raw Materials

Most cotton plantations in the United States were American owned and managed, although the raw cotton trade was—as it had been for many years—often British financed, and planters had in these years, as in times past, debts to British trading and financial houses.[2] In the 1880s and 1890s, as British mortgage companies extended loans to farmers, cotton plantations occasionally came into their hands through payment delinquencies. One case on which I have documentation was that of the Ashley Company, Ltd., which in 1894 operated a group of cotton plantations in Madison Parish, Louisiana, acquired through foreclosure. It apparently then mortgaged these properties. Scottish mortgage companies late in 1894 organized the Deltic Investment Company, Ltd., to keep the Ashley firm solvent. The Scots acquired the mortgages of the Ashley Company for $569,000, employed men to manage the plantations, determined the extent of cultivation, and arranged to market the crop. They encouraged immigration to Louisiana. Six years later, in 1900, the Scots decided to stop direct cultivation and to lease the properties to tenants. By 1906 the Scottish owners were encouraging *Italian* families to migrate to Louisiana to work the land; the next year (1907) Deltic Investment Company, Ltd., began to sell off its properties while leasing the remainder. Then came the boll weevil, decimating the cotton crop, and in 1913 Deltic was financing its tenants on a crop-sharing basis. Its cotton plantations were never profitable to the Scottish investors.[3]

A different type of foreign direct investment in U.S. cotton plantations was that of the Fine Cotton Spinners' and Doublers' Association, a firm that had been formed in May 1898 to merge thirty-one English companies involved in spinning fine (Sea Island) cotton or in doubling yarns from this and other staples of cotton. The process was done in Britain, mainly in Lancashire. In 1911, in what has been described as the "biggest sale" ever seen in the Yazoo Delta (in Mississippi), the association purchased approximately 38,000 acres of cotton-growing lands for about $2 million to $3 million and organized two operating plantations. These were leased to the newly formed Mississippi Delta Planting Company, whose capital stock was 100 percent owned by the Fine Cotton Spinners' and Doublers' Association. (In 1919 the Mississippi enterprise, still British owned, assumed the name Delta and Pine Land Company.)[4]

The cotton grown in Mississippi on the association's plantations was to be exported to Britain. According to one historian, the investment was "warranted only by the recurring difficulties in securing the requisite supplies of long stapled cotton for spinning superfine yarn."[5] A student of the Delta region, Robert Brandfon, explains that in 1909–10, with small crops, the price of fine cotton fibers had soared. For the British there were additional problems, since their supplies of Egyptian long-fiber cotton had been disappointing. At an international congress in 1910, a report had revealed that the Yazoo Delta region could become an excellent source for the special fibers needed for fine spinning. Thus in 1911 the direct investment had been made.[6] It was an exceptional case of backward vertical integration; most foreign spinners did not own their own cotton plantations. Moreover, Brandfon writes that "the English fine cotton spinners did not use a pound of their Delta cotton," for the fibers proved not to be competitive with the long ones from Egypt and with those that could be purchased elsewhere in the American South. The cotton was, accordingly, sold on the open market. The Fine Cotton Spinners' and Doublers' Association, however, did not dispose of its Mississippi plantations when it found that the output was unsuitable for its particular needs; rather, it kept the subsidiary because it was profitable.[7]

As for wool, some British investments existed in raising sheep.[8] The investments were small and miscellaneous and appear to have had no impact on multinational-enterprise behavior, the price of raw wool, or the nature of American sheep raising. Whereas in cotton, with the Fine Cotton Spinners' and Doublers' Association's investment, a large British enterprise did invest to obtain its raw material, there was nothing comparable in raw wool procurement in the United States.[9]

Textile Manufacture

Foreign direct investments in U.S. textile manufacturing were all to serve the American market. They were by British, German, French, and Swiss firms. They were in cotton, woolens, woolen floor coverings, other floor coverings, silk making, lace, embroidery, and mercerizing and dyeing cloth. I will survey each nationality's investments in turn.

Although the U.S. tariff legislation of 1883, in general, had temporarily lowered duties, it increased them on the better qualities of cotton fabric.[10] As a result, "several" Lancashire firms were reported to have started cotton cloth manufacturing in the United States, to produce for the U.S. trade behind the tariff wall.[11] These unidentified companies do not seem to have had a major role in the large U.S. cotton cloth industry.[12]

John P. Dixon, speaking of the British cotton industry in 1905, reported that U.S. tariffs "have compelled many of our good English firms who were doing business [that is, exporting] to open works in America," but the example he offered was odd: A Manchester producer with practically a monopoly of the book-binding cloth trade in the United Kingdom and the United States, when it found itself shut out of America, "in self-defiance . . . opened works there." Since the mill had started in America, this firm's production in England had been reduced, yet "they have secured the same monopoly there that they had before with 'made in America' cloth." Dixon did not identify the company by name.[13] Could it be the Winterbottom Book Cloth Company, Ltd., which, when registered in England (November 26, 1891) as a limited liability company, consolidated the businesses of seven British companies and the Interlaken Mills, in Providence, Rhode Island, that it had purchased in 1883?[14] Note that book-binding cloth is a differentiated, specialized product, not a run-of-the-mill cotton textile.

Another firm, also with a highly specialized cotton product, J. & J. Cash, Ltd., of Coventry, England, had exported woven labels and name tapes to the United States. It had had a sales office in New York since 1875, and in 1906 started to manufacture in South Norwalk, Connecticut. Many years later its management explained its decision to manufacture in the United States in terms of the need to respond quickly to seasonal demand.[15] In short, the cotton textile lines of British firms in America that I can identify comprised specialized products, not ordinary yard goods.[16]

Faced with tariffs, some British woolen cloth makers, likewise, invested in the United States, including Sir Titus Salt, Bart., Sons & Co., Ltd., of Saltaire. Sir Titus Salt's great-grandson indicates that the Saltaire firm established Salt's Textile Company in 1891 in Bridgeport, Connecticut, to produce plush, used in making breeches for men. It manufactured there until 1939.[17]

At a 1905 hearing on tariffs held in England, a Bradford woolen textile manufacturer (J. K. Empsall) testified: "We have one house which is leaving us now for America . . . they have shipped their looms to America . . . They are keeping on their factory here but they have reduced it [production]."[18] Another manufacturer (W. H. Mitchell) from Burley-in-Wharfedale, Yorkshire, perhaps referring to the same company, reported that "a large firm who have made goods for America for very many years in Bradford, Messrs. Benn & Co., and who have been a most successful firm have just transferred a large part of their mills to America, and are going to employ 1,000 work people there, simply on account of the duties."[19] In a similar vein, Alfred Sykes of Huddersfield added that one of his companies had started a branch plant in America because "the duties are so high."[20]

British carpet makers also began manufacturing in the United States. One investor was T. F. Firth & Sons of Heckmondwike, Yorkshire.[21] In Cornwall, New York (a town on the west bank of the

Hudson River, south of Beacon), its subsidiary, Firth Carpet Company, built a plant and initiated production in 1884. The new venture prospered; its properties were valued at $1 million by 1900.[22] A 1905 report on the British carpet industry indicated that an unidentified British carpet manufacturer (which must have been T. F. Firth & Sons) had begun manufacturing in America in 1884: "We spin and manufacture ourselves in America, and manufacture exactly the same goods as we do here, only not the same colors, as there is a difference in taste," this producer testified.[23] Another unidentified maker of carpets in Britain reported that until 1874 the United States was its chief market. "Since then we have started works in America and have a large manufactory for spinning worsted, and printing and weaving carpets in that country."[24]

G. Marchetti, of John Crossley & Sons, Ltd., Halifax, an important British carpet producer, indicated in 1905 that his firm had opened manufacturing plants in Russia and Austria and would probably do so elsewhere on the Continent. "We have now an offer to go to the United States, where actually a combination of gentlemen have offered half of the capital." Earlier this company had had a large U.S. trade, but with the tariffs, Marchetti declared, "we cannot possibly fight."[25] In 1911 John Crossley & Sons, Ltd., acquired land at Easton, Pennsylvania; the firm, however, postponed building the factory because of difficulties in raising adequate capital;[26] this is a rare example of capital constraints on manufacturing expansion. Normally, foreign companies either had adequate resources or little trouble in finding the capital.

In a different type of floor covering, the "great linoleum firm of Nairns of Kirkcaldy [Scotland] set up factories in America, France, and Germany in the late nineteenth century to manufacture linoleum."[27] Linoleum was made of jute or burlap and thus can be classified as a branch of the textile industry. Like the carpet producers, Nairn had long exported to the United States. Its American agent (and key customer) was W. & J. Sloane of New York, which at that time specialized in "floor coverings of all kinds."[28] The size of the U.S. market and the W. & J. Sloane requirements meant that the demand existed, and when in the summer of 1886 Michael Baker Nairn visited New York, he sought and found a suitable location for a linoleum factory across the Hudson River at Kearny, New Jersey, and arranged for the formation of Nairn Linoleum Company (capital, $300,000; incorporated in New Jersey). From Scotland Nairn dispatched Peter Campbell, who had shown "ability" and "initiative" within Nairn's home enterprise, to manage the American facility. Nairn and several of his partners were on the board of directors, as

were two members of the Sloane family. I do not know whether
W. & J. Sloane acquired an interest in the manufacturing venture; it
would not be out of keeping; the Sloane firm did remain the sole
selling agent in the United States for Nairn products.[29] The Nairn
investment was motivated not by high tariffs but by the potential
market. Nonetheless, five months before the factory opened (while
part was still under construction), John Sloane wrote his Congressman, advocating the introduction of duties on linoleum; once in
production in New Jersey, Nairn did not wish to face competition
from imports. The business grew, and by 1909 the American subsidiary's capital was raised to $2 million and plans were made to open
marketing outlets in cities where W. & J. Sloan were unrepresented.[30]

The *Stock Exchange Official Intelligence for 1914* indicates that the
Greenwich Inland Linoleum (Frederick Walton's New Patents) Company, Ltd., formed in 1895, held 2,493 shares of $20 in the Greenwich
Linoleum Company, U.S.A., which were in 1914 valued at £10,246. I
know nothing else of this investment.[31] I include it only to indicate
that Nairn was not alone in U.S. investments in linoleum.

In addition, British companies invested in the new silk-making
industry in the United States.[32] Silk production in the late nineteenth
and early twentieth centuries grew dramatically in America. Beginning in 1891, Salt's Textile Company in Connecticut made silk plushes
(plush can be made of silk, cotton, wool, or other material, or two of
these materials combined).[33] Some English and Scottish firms seem to
have owned lace and lace-curtain mills in Pennsylvania, Connecticut,
and New York, set up in response to the 1890 McKinley tariff.[34] A
Belfast firm, York Street Flax Spinning Company, Ltd., started at least
one factory in New York for stitching and hemming Irish linens, also
because of the high duties.[35]

In "textile finishing," in about 1901, the British Cotton and Wool
Dyers' Association acquired a subsidiary in the United States doing a
"good mercerising trade."[36] The giant Calico Printers' Association
sent two representatives to the United States in 1904 to look into the
possibility of setting up works in America, but apparently decided
against it.[37] In dyeing textiles, the chairman of the very important
British enterprise, the Bradford Dyers' Association, Ltd. (formed in
1898), told its shareholders in 1913 that in the late autumn of 1912, the
company had begun operations at "our American works at Bradford,
R.I." "A large part" of the capital addition of £208,608 for the parent,
Bradford Dyers' Association, Ltd., "was related to the building of the
new American works."[38] Discussing 1913, the chairman of Bradford
Dyers' noted the delay in getting "works of magnitude," such as
theirs in America, into full production. "You will appreciate," he told

the parent company's shareholders, "how exceptionally difficult it is to establish such a complex business as ours in a strange land." Problems existed for the Bradford firm in obtaining efficient labor. Once immigrants to America had been from northern Europe; now immigration, the company's chairman complained, "consists in the main of the inert and far less intelligent people of Southern Europe and the West of Asia [sic]." These people the Bradford management found to be "extremely migratory in character." In response, the company felt it necessary to build "a large number" of houses "to attract the more staid, active and intelligent help, as we require family men . . . and not an endless stream of transient and almost unteachable labour." Then there were uncertainties over the lowering of the tariff in 1913. And to make matters worse, a clothing trades strike occurred in New York that year. Nonetheless, by the start of 1914 the Bradford Dyers' chairman was optimistic,[39] only to face new problems when Britain entered World War I.[40]

In short, a number of British textile enterprises contemplated and many made direct investments in manufacturing in the United States. Among the largest entries were those of Sir Titus Salt, Bart., Sons & Co., Ltd., Saltaire; T. F. Firth & Sons, Heckmondwike; and Bradford Dyers' Association, Ltd., Bradford. None of these investors created "new issues" on the London market for their American investments.

German investors had no interest in manufacturing cotton textiles in America, but it was otherwise with woolen, silk, and lace products. Prior to 1890, German woolen and worsted mill owners had exported to the United States. In anticipation of the passage of the McKinley tariff of 1890, Stoehr & Co. (spinners of Leipzig, Germany) decided that to maintain its U.S. market, it ought to manufacture in this country. Thus Stoehr & Co. founded the Botany Worsted Company (capital stock, $3.6 million) and began to produce in 1890 in Passaic, New Jersey. This venture proved highly successful, and other prominent German woolens makers followed the leader into U.S. investments. Within the next two decades, German businesses had established five additional large mills in Passaic (New Jersey Worsted Spinning Company, Passaic Worsted Spinning Company, Gera Mills, Garfield Mills, and Forstmann & Huffmann Company).

In no case was the German stake 100 percent (71 percent for Botany; 75, 71, 89, 47, and 31 percent for the other five). The mills, however, were very much German enterprises, with German executives, technicians, and foremen. They used imported spinning machinery and maintained close associations with their German parent companies. In the words of one historian, the Forstmann & Huffmann factory in New Jersey (opened in 1903) was "as near a replica as possible of their

German establishment." The managers of these firms were strong advocates of high U.S. tariffs. With these German-owned works providing the core, Passaic, New Jersey, became, by the time of World War I, the center in the United States for the manufacture of fine worsted yarns and high-quality dress goods. By 1914 the large, modern German mills in Passaic employed about 15,000 people.[41] That year Massachusetts was first in the United States in wool and worsted manufacture, and then came Pennsylvania, Rhode Island, New York, and New Jersey. In the two and a half decades prior to 1914, New Jersey had moved from thirtieth to fifth in rank, owing to these new German-owned facilities.[42] German direct investments in the wool and worsted dress goods industry seem to have far exceeded those of the British in woolen goods. The Germans clearly had a technological advantage in this industry.[43]

Other German concerns took active part in the silk and velvet trade and manufacture. The huge Susquehanna Silk Mills, owned by the firm H. E. Schniewind, Elberfeld, Germany, and managed by Henry Schniewind, Jr., operated a chain of silk-weaving factories in Pennsylvania and one in Marion, Ohio. It also had a dyeing and finishing works in Sunbury, Pennsylvania. Its multiplant American business, which had started modestly in 1896 (capital, $150,000), by October 1914 had a capital of $3.5 million. It had about 4,300 employees.[44] Other partly German-owned silkmakers in the United States included R. & H. Simon and Audiger & Meyer Company.[45]

German firms built lace-manufacturing plants in America. Alb. & E. Henkels, a partnership from Langerfeld, Germany, was one of the largest lace producers in the world; its U.S. affiliate, International Textile Company, Inc., formed in July 1909, opened a factory in Bridgeport, Connecticut, that made various types of laces; in addition, the firm constructed a second mill at York, Pennsylvania, specializing in narrow fabrics.[46] The Dresdner Gardinen und Spitzen Manufactur, A.G., Dresden, was the principal owner of the Dresden Lace Works, Inc., incorporated in 1910 under Connecticut law, with an authorized capital of $225,000. Its plant at Norwalk, Connecticut, made "art linen" and Cluny lace (sold primarily to American corset manufacturers).[47] American La Dentelle (Inc.), 25 percent German owned, was another producer of Cluny lace in the United States.[48]

Although I know of no French investments in cotton textiles in the United States,[49] three French-owned woolen yarn mills were set up in Woonsocket, Rhode Island, in response to the Dingley tariff of 1897. The investors were from northwestern France, near the Belgian border—the center of French wool textile production (the neighboring cities of Roubaix and Tourcoing). The first investment, the Lafayette Worsted Company (capital, $300,000), was established in 1899. Its parent company was Auguste Lepoutre & Cie., Roubaix. The second followed in 1907, the French Worsted Company (capital, $400,000). Its French parent was C. Tiberghien and Sons, Tourcoing, which had other international business (plants in Austria and Czechoslovakia) before it built its U.S. mill. The third entry was the Jules Desurmont Worsted Company, 1910 (capital, $500,000). Jules Desurmont et Fils of Tourcoing was the parent.[50]

The French firms chose Woonsocket, Rhode Island, for their investments because of its existing French-speaking population, who were already skilled textile workers. A historian of Woonsocket explained, "These workers could easily be trained by cadres from France in the techniques of French process yarn production." The first firm to enter, that of Auguste Lepoutre, had made the choice of Woonsocket (which proved to be a good one) by sheer accident. Auguste Lepoutre—visiting the United States—met a French-speaking priest on a train in Vermont. The priest had recommended the Rhode Island town. The other French businessman had followed their compatriot.[51]

The new mills in Woonsocket were operated by French citizens; the language of the mills was French; and the yarn was spun by the so-called French process. Before these facilities were built, most wool in the United States had been spun by the Bradford, or English, system. French-spun yarn "revolutionized the woolen and worsted industry in the United States . . . The yarn was used at first primarily for high quality women's wear, but gradually became the yarn of choice for almost all woolen or worsted cloth produced in this country."[52]

These French mills undertook all phases of spinning the yarn, to preserve the high quality of the product: they purchased their own supply of raw wool; employed wool sorters to grade it; and cleaned, scoured, and combed the wool to produce "wool tops" that were finally spun into yarn. Two owned dye houses. While the "French yarn" was pure wool, the firms also manufactured a blended wool and cotton fiber product called merino yarn. These French-owned companies grew rapidly and prospered. Their output was sold nationwide in America.[53]

Other Frenchmen invested in the U.S. silk industry.[54] Here the French investment came from an entirely different region in France. French silk cloth, made in Lyon, had for many years been exported to the United States, so that in 1875 French silk goods had ranked first in U.S. silk cloth consumption. Thereafter, Frenchmen watched the rise of American output, which replaced the French imports.[55] In 1898 Leopold Duplan of Lyon founded the Duplan Silk Company. Its plant was in Hazelton, Pennsylvania. Duplan then returned to France, where he established in 1906 Alliance Textile with a large factory in Vizille, some eighty miles southwest of Lyon. Six years later (1912), he left this firm to start Tissages de Vizille, another French giant. The French historian Michel Laferrère writes that Tissages de Vizille, from its origin, participated in manufacturing in the United States through the Duplan Silk Company. In 1914 Jean L. Duplan ran the U.S. business.[56]

The Lyon firm J. B. Martin, a specialist in velours and plushes, established a U.S. subsidiary in 1898 and two years later began production in Norwich, Connecticut. In 1909 this French enterprise formed the J. B. Martin Company in Portland, Maine, which purchased J. B. Martin (Connecticut). The new company had a capital of $380,000. Professor Pierre Cayez writes me that its corporate meetings were held in Portland or in Lyon. All its officers were French residents. Its plant remained in Norwich, Connecticut. Likewise, before 1914 a Lyon silk dyer, Edmond Gillet, participated in the establishment of a U.S. "branch," the United Piece Dye Works, located in Lodi, New Jersey.[57]

Writing in 1917, the Frenchman J.-L. Duplan commented that although the Lyon silk firms had led in developing Russian silk works and had factories in many other countries, he believed the French had only a "weak" role in assisting in the expansion of American silk output. Ironically, he pointed out, Germans from Elberfeld (in a reference to what must be the investment of H. E. Schniewind) had interests in the United States, not in a "German" industry, but in one in which the French had excelled. Duplan chided his countrymen for not assuming a more prominent position in this American industry. Instead, others (immigrants, American-born entrepreneurs, and German foreign investors) had appropriated French talents, including foremen, and captured what once had been and still could be French customers.[58] What Duplan reported was not that French foreign direct investments were absent (the Duplan Silk Company and others existed), but that considering France's significant role in silk and Lyon's one-time (now lost) leadership through exports in the U.S. market, the activities should have been far larger.

Swiss investors were also present in the American textile industry in an important role. The 1901 annual report of the Silk Association of America described Robert Schwarzenbach of Zurich as the largest silk manufacturer in the world, employing over 15,000 operatives in his establishments in Switzerland, France, Germany, Italy, and America. The same report listed as a Silk Association member Schwarzenbach, Huber, & Co., of 472 Broome Street in New York. Jacques Huber was this subsidiary's chief executive. The American mills were in West Hoboken, New Jersey. By 1905 they were described as ranking among the "foremost" ones in this new U.S. industry.[59]

A history of the Swiss Bank Corporation reveals that Arnold B. Heine & Cie. (later Stickereiwerke Arbon, A.G.), embroidery manufacturers in Arbon, Switzerland, had a "branch" in New York in 1912. Its functions (sales or manufacturing) are unknown.[60] The Swiss author Julius Landmann would later write that the embroidery industry in the United States was developed with both Swiss capital and Swiss machinery.[61]

In 1905 the British Tariff Commission (a private, protectionist group) studied the "transfer" of British textile firms to the United States. A number of owners had closed their plants in Britain and migrated across the Atlantic. Others, because of U.S. duties, particularly the McKinley (1890) and the Dingley (1897) tariffs, had opened "branch" factories in America. They had done so since they could no longer maintain or expand existing markets in America through exports.[62] Indeed, it seems that primarily because of the U.S. tariffs, the British-, German-, French-, and Swiss-headquartered enterprises had made a number of U.S. investments in manufacturing; all were direct investments, carrying with them management and control.

In addition, there were other rumored British free-standing investments in American textiles that never came to pass.[63] And then there were some portfolio interests. In 1899 nine U.S. yarn mills had combined into the New England Cotton Yarn Company, which that year raised roughly $5 million in London, selling first-mortgage bond and cumulative preferred shares.[64] Far more European money was in the U.S. textile industry in the form of direct investments than as portfolio investments, and the impact of the direct investments, stimulated in the main by tariffs, was much greater than that of the portfolio stakes.

The European investments in the American textile industry—in which a parent firm or foreign residents retained an interest in the business—must be distinguished from an earlier wave of "immigrant proprietors."[65] The historian Philip Scranton found that in 1882, from a sample of 284 Philadelphia textile manufacturers that employed over fifty workers, 27 percent of the mill owners were English born, 18 percent Irish born, 3 percent Scottish born, and 8 percent German born—that is, fully 56 percent of the owners of the major Philadelphia textile mills (cotton, wool, and mixed goods; carpet; silk; hosiery and knit goods; dyeing and finishing; and spinning mills) were British or German born.[66] Scranton did not explore the ties of these owners with firms in their homeland. Probably in some instances associations persisted; clearly, in the main, these basically single-owner establishments were separate from companies abroad, and no foreign direct investment was involved.[67]

Thread Manufacture

Of all the many direct investments from overseas in the American textile industry, one set stands out in size, market dominance, and long-term role: the British investments in cotton and linen thread production and distribution (no continental European investors took part in this business activity).

The U.S. census of 1890 called the "sewing-cotton" (the cotton thread) industry one of the most important branches of American cotton manufacturing.[68] Less than a decade after that census was taken, virtually every major maker of thread in the United States was British owned, that is, owned by nonresident British companies. It was not always that way. Foreign investments in America in *marketing* cotton thread had begun before the Civil War, and not long after the war's end, two Scottish firms had started to manufacture in Newark, New Jersey (J. & J. Clark; after 1879, Clark & Co.), and in Pawtucket, Rhode Island (J. & P. Coats). At that time many American manufacturers existed.

The lead company in the Scottish and the American thread industry came to be J. & P. Coats. This enterprise, headquartered in Paisley, near Glasgow, had been founded in 1826.[69] By 1900 it was Britain's largest industrial enterprise.[70] Even before the Scottish thread industry had used the automatic spooling machine (invented in 1858) and the ring doubling frame (employed from 1867), the Scots—including Coats—had obtained world leadership in cotton thread making.[71] By the late nineteenth century, cotton thread had become the most capital intensive[72] and also the most profitable branch of the British cotton textile industry; members of the Coats family ranked prominently among British millionaires.[73] Coats and other sewing-cotton companies advertised extensively and marketed branded, labeled products. Coats, in particular, had steadfastly fought imitators, going to court against trademark infringers. With such industry characteristics, it is not odd to find sewing-cotton firms participating in international and particularly U.S. investments.

I noted in Chapter 4 the start of Coats's manufacturing facilities in Pawtucket, Rhode Island (1869), and the even earlier manufacturing plant of J. & J. Clark (a Scottish rival of J. & P. Coats) in Newark, New Jersey (1865); they were joined in the early 1870s by John Clark, Jr. & Co., which had begun to manufacture in East Newark (that is Kearny,

New Jersey). All three firms expanded their U.S. output behind American tariff walls. Coats in Pawtucket—operating under the name Conant Thread Company—built Mill No. 4 in 1876 and a dye house in 1877. By 1878 it employed about 1,500 workers, and its properties were said to be worth "several millions."[74] According to the Coats historian J. B. K. Hunter, Coats's profits from its American business in the 1870s equaled over 90 percent of the Scottish firm's total profits![75] In 1881 Coats opened Mill No. 5 at Pawtucket. Coats's records in Scotland indicate that in 1876 its investment in Conant Thread Company stood at £359,773, and in 1882 it reached £566,343. This U.S. investment represented more than 30 percent of the Scottish firm's total capital in 1882. The Conant Thread Company was "almost 100 percent" owned by J. & P. Coats.[76] The thread was marketed under the Coats name, even though the Pawtucket mills operated until 1893 under the style of their American founder, Conant Thread Company. After 1893, however, the production activities were "conducted as one of the branches of J. & P. Coats (Limited)," but still under the presidency of James Coats and the "executive" direction of the American Hezekiah Conant. The Conant Thread Company remained in existence, leasing its mills to "J. & P. Coats, Ltd., Pawtucket Branch" (this was on legal advice to make the Coats trademark position in the United States more secure). Conant died in 1902; Alfred M. Coats (son of James) took over as general manager. Not until 1913 did J. & P. Coats (R.I.) Inc. become the corporate name for the *manufacturing* operations.[77] By the 1880s Coats was doing extensive advertising in America, distributing photographs, picture cards, paper dolls, jingle books, calendars, and fancy thread boxes. In 1891 the Coats Thread Company was formed to handle the *marketing* of Coats thread.[78]

Meanwhile, the Clark Thread Company in Newark expanded its business. When George A. Clark died in 1873, his brother William Clark assumed the management of the mills and of George A. Clark & Brother, the sales firm. At origin, Clark Thread Company had only tenuous ties with J. & J. Clark in Paisley, but subsequent to George A. Clark's death, the Scottish firm (after 1879, Clark & Co.) raised its participation in the American manufacturing enterprise and by the late 1870s had majority ownership of the Clark Thread Company. In 1883 John Clark, senior partner in Clark & Co., became president of Clark Thread Company, Newark.[79] In the 1880s Clark's "O.N.T." thread (Our New Thread) was advertised in national periodicals in America.[80]

Still a third Scottish producer, John Clark, Jr. & Co., Glasgow, in 1883 through its U.S. subsidiary, Clark Mile-End Spool Cotton Company, enlarged its mills at Kearny, New Jersey (near Newark).[81] In Scotland, Clark & Co. in 1884 absorbed John Clark, Jr. & Co.[82] A fourth Scottish enterprise, Kerr & Co., in 1881 had set up a smaller thread factory in Fall River, Massachusetts.[83] According to Hunter, the English firm James Chadwick & Co. had an American mill from 1883 at Bridgeport, Connecticut, and a larger one in Jersey City, New Jersey, from 1893.[84] During the 1880s and early 1890s in the U.S. market, Coats, Clark, Kerr, and Chadwick competed with numerous American threadmakers and some British exporters.[85] As sewing machine sales had expanded, so did the market for thread on spools.[86]

In Britain in 1890, J. & P. Coats became for the first time a limited liability company; in 1895 J. & P. Coats, Ltd., acquired Kerr & Co., of Paisley, Scotland, and in 1896 Clark & Co., also of Paisley, as well as two English businesses, James Chadwick & Co. of Bolton and Jonas Brook & Co. of Meltham, near Huddersfield. As noted, by 1896 Coats, Clark, Kerr, and Chadwick all had manufacturing plants in the United States. Jonas Brook exported to America and had no mills in this country.[87] With the merger, in 1896 J. & P. Coats, Ltd., had seventeen production centers (in Scotland, England, the United States, Canada, Russia, Austria-Hungary, and Spain); sixty branch houses; and 150 depots.[88] It was a giant multinational enterprise (with over 21,000 employees worldwide)—and in the United States it was a multiplant business, employing more than 6,000 people in production and distribution. Its works at Pawtucket, Rhode Island, alone had over 2,000 employees (in 1897), and the capital invested there was in excess of $4 million.[89]

Outside the Coats group in 1896 were some twenty threadmakers in the United Kingdom, about forty on the European continent, and two large and many small ones in the United States. In Britain, in response to the 1895–96 merger, fourteen firms joined in establishing the English Sewing Cotton Company, Ltd., in 1897.[90] Although this enterprise was organized as a reaction to the Coats combination, it was never entirely independent of J. & P. Coats, Ltd., for at the start the latter acquired £200,000 of the ordinary shares of English Sewing Cotton Company, Ltd.[91] After a reorganization of English Sewing Cotton Company, Ltd., in 1902, J. & P. Coats's British sales company (the Central Agency, Ltd.) came to handle the marketing for English Sewing Cotton Company.[92]

Just as English Sewing Cotton had been formed in Britain in 1897 as a response to the 1895–96 acquisitions of J. & P. Coats, Ltd., in the United Kingdom, so too in America the British Coats merger had ramifications. On March 10, 1898, the American Thread Company was incorporated in New Jersey, a combination of thirteen New England firms (two in Rhode Island, two in Connecticut, one in New York, one in New Hampshire, and seven in Massachusetts).[93] The largest enterprise included in American Thread Company was the Willimantic Linen Company, the earliest U.S.-owned threadmaker.[94] The first president of American Thread Company was Lyman R. Hopkins, who had been about forty years with his own U.S.-owned Merrick Thread Company, which he brought into the new giant corporation.[95] American Thread Company came into being as a response to "ruinous competition" in the U.S. thread industry. In 1898, outside American Thread Company were most of the U.S. mills in the J. & P. Coats group. Indeed, in 1901 Hopkins testified that American Thread's chief competitor was "the immense Coats concern, a foreign company." He explained that Coats manufactured in the United States: "Yes, it is all made here, and the Clark's, which is now with Coats." Hopkins continued: "At present, the companies which manufacture—the Chadwick's, the Brook's—which were foreign concerns, have amalgamated with the Coats Company. They made thread over there, and these threads were sent here at one time . . . Since they amalgamated these threads are put here by the Coats Company."[96]

The American Thread Company merger in 1898 had been arranged by an American attorney, John Dos Passos (father of the novelist). Dos Passos was an expert in creating big corporations, having participated in the organization of, among others, the sugar trust.[97] Early in 1898 Dos Passos had visited with the different heads of the various American thread firms and "got them to agree" on a price for which they would dispose of their stock. Then, according to Hopkins, Dos Passos had traveled to England "and saw parties there that represented English Sewing Cotton Company . . . and got them interested in the project." The new English Sewing Company, Ltd., had combined the independent companies not in the Coats group in Britain. Why not do the same in the United States? Representatives of English Sewing Cotton Company, Ltd., crossed the Atlantic, investigated the proposition, and agreed to provide the needed money to pay for the stock so as to make it possible to merge the U.S. thread firms (the ex-owners would be paid in cash and in bonds of the new American Thread Company). "In the final wind-up of the thing," John Dos Passos acted in the United States on behalf of English Sewing Cotton Company.[98]

At origin, in 1898, American Thread Company had a capital of $12 million—$6 million in common shares (all of which were issued) and $6 million in preferred shares (by 1901, $4,890,475 were outstanding); its bonded debt was $6 million.[99] Its American president, Lyman

Hopkins, told the U.S. Industrial Commission, "When it was decided to consummate the new American Thread Company [in 1898], a prospectus was issued in England and this country and a large majority of the preferred stock was subscribed for mostly in England; some here, and the bonds were nearly all taken in this country." J. & P. Coats, Ltd., reserved for itself $500,000 worth of the preferred stock.[100]

Bonds, of course, had no voting power; neither did the preferred stock. "The voting power is all done by the common stock," Hopkins informed the commission, and English Sewing Cotton Company, Ltd. (under the arrangements proposed by John Dos Passos), obtained nearly all the common stock of American Thread Company, thus assuming control.[101] In short, in 1898 not only was the Coats group of mills British owned, but so was the separate, new American Thread Company.

To make matters more complicated, in 1899 American Thread Company bought 125,000 shares of its parent, English Sewing Cotton Company.[102] The control, however, was clearly east to west, and three managing directors of English Sewing Cotton Company held seats on the American Thread Company board of directors.[103] In addition, the December 1898 prospectus for the American Thread Company revealed that James Kerr, of R. & J. P. Kerr, Paisley, Scotland, was a director; Kerr's U.S. subsidiary, the Kerr Thread Company of Fall River, Massachusetts (also represented on the American Thread board), was one of the firms acquired by American Thread Company. Recall that the parent Scottish firm had been purchased by J. & P. Coats, Ltd., in 1895. There was thus a Trojan—Coats—horse within the American Thread Company camp; Coats did not have to rely on its holdings of nonvoting preferred stock in American Thread or on its holdings of ordinary stock in English Sewing Cotton Company for information about "the competition." Hopkins did not tell the U.S. Industrial Commission anything about Kerr's role, nor did any one on the commission ask. Just as English Sewing Cotton Company was not independent of Coats, so English Sewing Cotton Company's U.S. subsidiary, American Thread Company, was not completely independent of the American Coats group.

Did American Thread Company and the Coats group compete in the U.S. market? Hopkins explained to the Industrial Commission in 1901 that there was no "absolute agreement. They [the Coats mills] do not quarrel as they used to, but they are under us in prices on some things and we are under them on some things," Hopkins continued. "We are not fighting to-day as we used to, but their men go to our people [customers] to try and sell." When asked whether the U.S.

market share held by American Thread Company and the Coats combination of U.S. mills was over 70 percent, Hopkins replied, "Somewhere about that, I could not tell exactly."[104] The two closely interrelated British-controlled groups—subsidiaries of English Sewing Cotton Company, Ltd., and J. & P. Coats, Ltd.—may have had far more than 70 percent of the American sewing-cotton market.[105] At the turn of the century, at a very minimum, two-thirds of the American cotton thread market was controlled from the United Kingdom; 80 to 90 percent would probably be more accurate.

In 1901 no foreign cotton thread was imported into the United States, and no U.S. cotton thread maker exported. J. & P. Coats, Ltd., served its foreign markets from Paisley, Scotland, not from the United States.[106] Coats's U.K. sales subsidiary came to handle English Sewing Cotton's export trade, none of which went to America.[107] Wages in the thread industry in the United States were roughly double those in the United Kingdom. The British companies had decided to manufacture across the Atlantic, because of the steep protective duties. The output was not competitive in world markets. It was strictly for domestic sales.[108] By 1912 in Britain, the English Sewing Company's management would comment on how—especially in the last five years—its firm had benefited "by reason of friendly relations that have existed between its great rival J. & P. Coats Limited and itself."[109] The close connections between the two firms had its echo in America.

In the United States, American Thread Company, soon after the merger, united all the sales offices of its constituent firms in various cities. An American Thread Company unit called the Thread Agency seems to have handled the marketing for the many mills. The company closed the less-profitable mills, and its remaining ones became more specialized. It rationalized all its activities; in January 1903 the separate constituent companies were dissolved and their properties merged.[110]

Meanwhile, in 1891, as noted, the Coats Thread Company had been organized to market Coats products in the United States; in 1898 the name of this subsidiary was changed to the Spool Cotton Company, which on January 1, 1899, took over the sales of the three brands of the Coats and Clark enterprises in the United States: Coats Cotton Spool, Clark's O.N.T., and Mile End (Mile End was where the original John Clark, Jr. & Co. mill had been built in Glasgow in 1817). Darning, crochet, and embroidery cottons as well as sewing threads were produced at Clark's Newark mills from about 1870 onward and at Coats's Pawtucket mills after 1894.[111] In the early twentieth-century—as in the late nineteenth—Coats's mills at Pawtucket, Rhode

Island, were "as large as those at Paisley"; in 1910 J. & P. Coats had at Pawtucket alone at least 2,500 employees.[112]

The U.S. government on March 3, 1913, filed suit against the American Thread group and the "Spools Cotton" (or Coats) group, alleging restraint of trade in violation of section 1 of the Sherman Antitrust Act. The defendants were charged with having interfered with interstate commerce in thread by agreeing to fix prices, restrict output, divide territories, and otherwise cooperate by means of interlocking directorates and stockholdings. A little over a year later, on June 2, 1914, the suit ended with a ten-page final decree entered into in the U.S. District Court of New Jersey.[113]

The defendants in the antitrust suit were, in the first group, the American Thread Company, the Thread Agency, the English Sewing Cotton Company, Ltd., and their agents; in the second group, the Spool Cotton Company, J. & P. Coats, Ltd., the Clark Thread Company, the Clark Mile-End Spool Cotton Company, George A. Clark & Brother, J. & P. Coats (R.I.) Inc., James Chadwick and Brother, Ltd., Jonas Brook & Brothers, Ltd., and their agents. These two groups were found to have formed an illegal combination, which the court ordered dissolved. Interlocking directorates and officerships as well as stock or security holdings between the two groups were prohibited. "If ever and so long" as one or more of the defendants in the first group had any of the same officers, directors, or controlling stockholders as in the second group, both groups were forbidden to engage in interstate commerce within the United States or in the foreign sewing-thread trade of the United States. Likewise, both groups were enjoined from participating in interstate commerce within the United States as long as they were parties to agreements fixing prices, restricting output, or dividing territories "without or within" the United States. The decree contained specific prohibitions against predatory sales practices, including ones against the use of "flying squadrons," defined as a special sales force to handle so-called fighting brands—brands offered to customers at cut-rate prices (lower than those asked by the seller for the same thread under different trade names).[114]

The dissolution decree aimed at separating the two British-American groups but in no way altered the financial relationships between the English Sewing Cotton Company, Ltd., and its U.S. subsidiary, the American Thread Company, nor those between J. & P. Coats, Ltd., and its U.S. subsidiaries. A U.S. Federal Trade Commission report in 1916 (two years after the decree) indicated that at that time English Sewing Cotton Company, Ltd., owned all the common shares of American Thread Company.[115] By then, American

Thread's dividends equaled roughly one-half of its English parent's net profits.[116] In Britain, Coats continued to handle the worldwide marketing of English Sewing Cotton Company's products (outside the United States).[117] J. & P. Coats, Ltd., retained its interests in its New Jersey and Rhode Island mills and its American sales organization.

Thus in 1914 a U.S. antitrust action had modified the structure of British ownership in the American cotton thread industry with an eye to reviving competition. Henceforth, in the United States, the interests of English Sewing Cotton Company, Ltd., and of J. & P. Coats, Ltd., diverged, although both British companies maintained their large U.S. stakes.[118] While the American antitrust action extended over borders to attempt to influence these foreign investors in the United States, it did not cause them to reduce their substantial investments; British interests continued to hold the commanding position in the American cotton thread industry.

Britishers also invested in linen thread in America. In Britain the linen thread industry had come to be led by three family groups: the Barbours (whose original enterprise was founded by a Scot, who had migrated to northern Ireland), the Knoxes, and the Finlaysons. Each of these families had mills in Britain and by the 1880s in the United States: the Barbours in Lisburn, west of Belfast, northern Ireland, and in Paterson, New Jersey; the Knoxes in Kilbirnie, near Paisley, Scotland, and in Baltimore, Maryland; and the Finlaysons in Johnstone, near Paisley, and in North Grafton, Massachusetts.[119] Some, if not all, of their American mills were built in response to the U.S. tariff.[120] The largest and most important of these works was in Paterson where, under the management of three Barbour brothers, the firm produced and marketed through a nationwide sales organization.[121] As noted in Chapter 4, the Paterson venture had been started about 1864–65.[122] The other family mills in America had followed (Finlayson, Bousfield & Co. entered in 1881).[123]

By 1898 competition in both the U.S. and the British linen thread industry had grown intense, and Colonel William Barbour in America proposed to the Marshall mills of Newark (another Scottish firm)[124] and the Finlayson mills that they join forces. Then he headed for Britain to obtain the support of the Barbour and the Knox families. From the colonel's initiative there came into being in 1898 the Linen Thread Company, Ltd., which amalgamated William Barbour & Sons, Ltd., Hilden, northern Ireland; the Barbour Flax Spinning Company, Paterson, New Jersey; Barbour Brothers, New York; Marshall Thread Company, Newark, New Jersey; Finlayson, Bousfield & Co., Ltd., Johnstone, Scotland, and North Grafton, Massachusetts; and W. & J.

Knox, Ltd., of Kilbirnie.[125] The Linen Thread Company, Ltd., had a capital of £2 million.[126] At origin, it was the largest manufacturer of flax thread in the United States and probably in the world. Its output went mainly to the boot and shoe industry and to the carpet trade.[127]

Sir Thomas Glen-Coats of J. & P. Coats, Ltd., was on the board of directors of the new Linen Thread Company, Ltd.[128] The U.S. Justice Department did not concern itself with linen thread when it investigated restraint of trade in cotton thread.[129] Coats was thus represented in the United States in both industries. Likewise, and as an indication of the significance of J. & P. Coats, Ltd., around the turn of the century that Scottish firm acquired 200,000 shares of the Fine Cotton Spinners' & Doublers' Association; the latter, British firm acquired cotton plantations in Mississippi in 1911.[130] In addition, wealthy members of the Coats family (including J. & P. Coats's chief executive, Archibald Coats), attracted by the potentials of the United States, made investments in timberlands and mining in the American Midwest and West. These investments seem to have been unrelated to the thread business (and simply personal speculations of family members). They did not prove profitable.[131] By contrast, where the firm had knowledge—in the thread industry—it did well.

In short, British capital played the leading role in the American thread business. With the successful investments of J. & P. Coats, Ltd., English Sewing Cotton Company, Ltd., and Linen Thread Company, Ltd., in the early twentieth century British enterprise dominated both the American cotton and linen thread industries.

Rayon

Even more impressive, another branch of the American textile industry, rayon production, was by 1914 the exclusive preserve of British capital. Rayon was the world's first synthetic fabric. The father of this new industry was Count Hilaire de Chardonnet, who obtained his original French patent on November 11, 1884. At his birthplace in Besançon, France, Chardonnet opened the world's first "artificial silk" factory; it used the so-called nitrocellulose process.[132] In Britain not long thereafter, a second method of making rayon was developed, the "viscose process," and was patented in 1892 by Charles F. Cross and E. F. Bevan. In 1902 C. F. Topham's discovery of the centrifugal spinning pot solved critical manufacturing bottlenecks related to this process. In 1904 the British firm Samuel Courtauld & Co., predecessor to Courtaulds, Ltd. (Courtaulds, Ltd., was incorporated in 1913), took over the British patents of Cross and Bevan, established a plant at Coventry (1905), worked out important technical problems, made viscose yarn, and began to export its output.[133] On the European continent other firms started to employ the viscose method, and in 1906 Courtauld and the French, Swiss, Belgian, and Italian producers of viscose yarn agreed to avoid competition in one another's territories, to share technical know-how, and to benefit mutually from the sales of patent rights in nations where companies were not yet organized.[134]

Meanwhile, a Philadelphia lawyer, Silas W. Pettit, had in 1904 acquired the U.S. viscose patents, which were then being worked in the United States by the unsuccessful General Artificial Silk Company, a business that Pettit continued as the Genasco Company.[135] The latter's plant at Lansdowne, Pennsylvania, in 1904–1907, remained "experimental,"[136] so much so that in May 1907 Pettit sought technical advice from the thriving Courtauld enterprise in England as well as from the Société Française de la Viscose in France. These two companies (both parties to the European cooperative agreement of 1906) brought Pettit's request to their associates and started conversations with an eye to introducing the American firm into their market- and technology-sharing accord. In August 1908 Courtauld got from Pettit a license to import into the United States in exchange for a fee paid to him (since Pettit held the U.S. viscose yarn patent).[137]

As the lengthy discussions on Genasco's entry into the international agreement proceeded, Pettit died in November 1908, and Samuel A. Savage, Courtauld's U.S. representative, later claimed that he had persuaded the British firm to buy from Pettit's son the father's business, including the American patent rights to the viscose process.[138] Almost coincidentally, the Payne-Aldrich Tariff Act of 1909 imposed a high tariff on artificial silk imported into the United States. Clearly, Courtauld would not be able to remain competitive with exports. Thus, for $150,000, Courtauld acquired the U.S. viscose patent rights and decided to manufacture in America (behind the U.S. tariff wall).[139]

On behalf of Courtauld, H. G. Tetley inspected the existing factory in Lansdowne, Pennsylvania, and found it "pretty well useless."[140] Following Tetley's recommendation, Samuel Courtauld & Co. resolved to build a new works and in 1910 formed a U.S. subsidiary, the American Viscose Company.[141] This company was the true pioneer in rayon production in the United States. At Marcus Hook, Pennsylvania, it erected a modern viscose yarn plant, using all the best improvements in the process; production started in October 1911. Courtauld's initial investment was $837,000, which the British company subsequently increased. In 1914 in Britain, Courtaulds, Ltd., formed Lustre Fibres, Ltd., whose New York branch did the U.S.

marketing for the American Viscose Company. In November 1913 there had been antitrust concerns over Courtauld's U.S. representative's doing the marketing for the American Viscose Company; accordingly, this new marketing structure was adopted; this seems to have been a "legal" rather than an operating change.[142] Chapter 11 reveals similar concerns by German chemical companies.

From its start, the American Viscose Company "enjoyed a complete monopoly in the production of viscose rayon in the United States by virtue of its exclusive rights to the Cross and Bevan and Topham patents."[143] The company was extremely profitable. After less than three years of manufacturing, by mid-1914 the American business was already contributing 13.5 percent of its British parent's gross income, and in 1916 it would provide fully 53.7 percent of Courtaulds' gross income.[144]

Apparel

There were virtually no nonresident foreign direct (or portfolio) investments in the American cotton, woolen, linen, or silk apparel industry. In fact, the only foreign direct investment that I can verify was the ownership by Wilhelm Benger Soehne—a Stuttgart, Germany, partnership—of Dr. Jaeger's Sanitary Woolen System Company, incorporated in New York in April 1887 to manufacture and to sell Dr. Jaeger's Sanitary Woolen System goods. Beginning in 1890 Wilhelm Benger Soehne took out U.S. trademark applications for woolen underwear. In the 1890s Jaeger Underwear was advertising in national periodicals in the United States. Thus this company, while an exceptional apparel maker, was manufacturing a trademarked, widely advertised, specialized product.[145] There may have been other foreign direct investors in apparel production in the United States, but none of significance.

Leather Goods

More important, foreign direct investments did exist in leather goods. In 1863 Alfred Booth & Co., a newly established Liverpool, England, trading firm, decided to specialize in selling in the United States "light leathers" for gloves, handbags, and boots. The enterprise started exporting British sheepskins (some tanned, others not) to America. Soon its U.S. imports broadened and came from many countries; they included goat and kangaroo skins. In 1877 the firm acquired an interest in a Gloversville (Fulton County), New York, tannery, in the heart of America's glove-making industry. The factory had been purchasing the imported skins and had an unpaid debt to Alfred Booth & Co. Nine years later, in 1886, Alfred Booth & Co. completed its acquisition of this works.[146] By 1890 Alfred Booth and its New York house (Booth & Co.) were "middlemen in pickled pelts, specializing in raw material for the Boston market, with a subsidiary interest in a small factory at Gloversville."[147] The firm also had a steamship line that carried its product.[148]

At Booth's Gloversville tannery, the American Augustus Schultz (a chemist employed by a New York firm of aniline dyers) carried on his first experiments in the 1880s in developing a permanent tannage using chrome salts, a process that he patented in 1884. The chrome tanning method, used for light and then heavy leathers, revolutionized the industry in the 1890s: "more progress in the art of leather manufacturing" was made in this decade than in any other one in history.[149] As the industry changed, so too did Booth's business. In Philadelphia, leather tanners—including J. P. Mathieu & Co.—adopted the new tanning process. Booth supplied Brazilian goatskins to Mathieu, in whose factory the skins were chrome tanned and glazed for a fixed charge. The resulting kid leather was then marketed by Booth & Co. under the trade name Surpass. In 1894 Booth's Gloversville factory began chrome tanning on a regular basis on goat and kangaroo skins.[150] By 1901 the Gloversville plant gave up making glove leather to specialize in kid and kangaroo shoe leathers.[151]

Meanwhile, in 1893 the huge United States Leather Company had been formed (capital, $80 million), merging the principal American tanning plants that made sole leather for shoes. The new combination did not involve foreign investment, nor did it include light leather manufacture of "uppers" in which Booth & Co. specialized.[152] By the late 1890s, according to the Booth historian, Surpass leather (produced in Philadelphia) ranked among the best of American manufactured kid.[153] In 1898 Booth & Co. invested in Wolf Process Leather, a company making an enameled kid (a type of patent leather) from skins tanned by Mathieu. The product proved unsatisfactory, and in 1904 Booth & Co. withdrew its interest in this firm.[154] In 1899 the American Hide and Leather Company (capital, about $35 million) was formed, the second large American-owned consolidation in the U.S. leather industry. It manufactured about three-quarters of the "upper" leathers produced in the United States.[155] Booth's Gloversville's factory output of uppers was dwarfed by this U.S.-owned giant.

In December 1904, for the first time, Booth & Co. and J. P. Mathieu & Co. integrated their operations, pooling profits from manufacturing and selling; in 1906 they organized Surpass Leather Company to produce and to market. The majority of the shares in the new company were held by Booth & Co., and arrangements were made "for the gradual liquidation of the holdings of J. P. Mathieu and Company."[156] In its first full year, 1907, Surpass Leather Company's revenues from the sale of tanned skins were $5.6 million, and between 1908 and 1913 its annual revenues ranged between $5 million and $6 million.[157] Surpass Leather tanned and dressed skins imported from South America (mainly Brazil), Spain, the Middle East, China, and India, with the last country representing about half its output.[158] The goatskins entered the United States duty free.[159] Before World War I, Surpass Leather Company tanned about one-eighth of the 240 million square feet of kid leather annual production in the entire United States.[160] Booth & Co.'s purchases of skins on behalf of its subsidiary were large enough to affect the price of these imports.[161] In 1912 and 1913 Booth & Co. acquired interests in two additional American manufacturers, the Gardiner-Lucas Glue and Gelatine Corporation and the Densten Felt and Hair Corporation, both of which had been customers for the by-products of Booth's factories in Gloversville and Philadelphia.[162] Booth & Co. developed a sales organization in the United States for Surpass leather and even exported its output to Europe.[163]

In 1890 Booth & Co. had been principally merchants; in 1914 this British house in America was, first and foremost, a manufacturer, with its imports into the United States—acquired through its trading expertise—providing the raw material for its U.S. factories.[164] It was a multinational firm in the United States, with four manufacturing plants. If we view the U.S. leather industry as a whole, its impact was negligible, unless we consider its stimulus to Schultz's research on chrome tanning.[165] Its output was small compared with that of the industry giants, United States Leather Company and the American Hide and Leather Company. Only in the specialized kid leather branch of the industry was this British business "large" and important, and in this special niche, based on its imports of goatskins, it did have significance in the United States.

Chemicals for the Textile and Leather Goods Industries

The influence of the European chemical industry on the pre–World War I American textile and leather goods industries extended beyond the activities of Courtaulds and of Schultz in Booth's Gloversville tannery. In Chapter 4 I noted the early investments in aniline manufacture by the Holliday brothers in Brooklyn, New York, and by Bayer in Albany, New York. The colors made at these plants appear to have been sold to the textile industry. From 1864 to 1883 the dye industry was protected; but in 1883 the U.S. tariff on crucial dyestuffs was removed. At that time foreign direct investments in the U.S. chemical industry involved some dyes for textiles. In 1914, however, when spinning and weaving factories in the United States accounted for half the dyestuffs consumed in the United States, with the absence of protection most of these dyestuffs were imported.[166]

German industry excelled in dye manufacture. German companies took out numerous U.S. patents and made foreign direct investments in selling their output in the United States. No alizarin, anthracene colors, or synthetic indigo was made in the United States in 1914. These essential dyes, used by American textile makers, were imported from Germany and sold by the branch houses of German firms.[167] Charlotte Erickson writes that in the early nineteenth century the dyeing of textile fabrics in the United States had required the importation of skilled labor from Europe, but by the 1890s it had "ceased to be a highly skilled occupation chiefly because of the large amount of information which came to be furnished by producers of dye colors to those who used them."[168] She does not note, however, that it was German companies that provided this know-how and allowed the substitution of unskilled for skilled workers. In 1908, when U.S. hearings were held on protective tariffs on dyes (and an attempt was made to develop an indigenous American dyestuffs industry), U.S. textile manufacturers opposed protection, and the drafters of the Payne-Aldrich tariff of 1909 were responsive to the needs of the textile producers for low-priced inputs.[169]

The German Friedrich Bayer & Co. had entered the American market first through exports. The firm had sent representatives to America, invested in the Albany Aniline & Chemical Works (see Chapter 4), but then withdrew from this manufacturing venture about 1881. In 1882 it invested anew in the Hudson River Aniline Color Works which built a plant in Rensselaer, New York. Initially this Rensselaer factory produced colors for the leather, not the textile, trades. Bayer imported from Germany the dyes sold to the textile mills. Indeed, and interestingly, an American joint-owner of the Hudson River company (Albany department store owner Louis Waldman) left the partnership when Bayer refused to produce in the United States textile dyes that it was importing from Germany. In the early twentieth century, Bayer may have made some dyes for textiles, but the main ones were still imported.[170]

Heavy chemicals that went into textile production included soda ash and caustic soda.[171] Well into the 1890s, Leblanc soda and bleaching powder, imported from Britain, dominated the U.S. market.[172] In the early 1890s United Alkali Company exported to the United States, as did Brunner, Mond—a producer under the newer Solvay process. Then, primarily because of the U.S. tariff, an indigenous industry developed, assisted by foreign innovations and investments.

The most important foreign investment in alkalies was the large Belgian and British interest in the Solvay Process Company; formed in 1881, this firm was part of an international network of Solvay companies that included Solvay & Cie. in Belgium and Brunner, Mond in Britain. Solvay Process Company was the first producer in America of soda ash (1884) and caustic soda (1889). Its American founder, Rowland Hazard, a textile manufacturer from Rhode Island, knew the importance of alkalies to his business.[173]

In 1896 Mathieson Alkali Works (said to be in part owned by the British Castner-Kellner Alkali Company, Ltd.)[174] started to produce bleaching powder in Virginia. Next, the Mathieson company became the pioneer U.S. producer of alkalis for industrial use at Niagara Falls (in 1898). In 1900 it organized the Castner Electrolytic Alkali Company, which served as the "American representative" of the Castner-Kellner Alkali Company, Ltd. By 1907 Castner Electrolytic Alkali Company was the largest manufacturer of alkali and chlorine in the Niagara Falls area.[175] Germans participated in 1910 in the Niagara Alkali Company, at Niagara Falls; Niagara Alkali produced solid and liquid chlorine.[176]

A U.S. affiliate (Goldschmidt Detinning Company) of Th. Goldschmidt, Essen, Germany, opened a plant in Carteret, New Jersey, in 1910 to meet American Can Company's "detinning" requirements. The process used yielded tin tetrachloride that was sold to the U.S. silk-dyeing industry and supplied the latter's entire needs for this input used in the "weighting of silk." At its peak period of use, "as much as 98 percent of the fabric weight was tin, with only 2 per cent the actual silk!"[177]

Bayer's Rensselaer plant was not the only foreign-owned chemical facility that served the leather trades. Between 1903 and 1907 a young German chemist, Otto Rohm, developed a synthetic (Oropon) to replace natural (dog or bird) dung used in leather tanning. In 1907 Rohm formed a partnership with Otto Haas to manufacture and to sell Oropon in Germany. Two years later Haas traveled to the United States, where he established Rohm & Haas Company, an American branch of the German partnership. At first it imported its unique product. Manufacturing came with the growth of sales; initially the U.S. company only mixed imported ingredients; then in 1914 Haas opened a "full factory" in Chicago, a center of American leather tanning. Rohm & Haas sold to all the major tanners—of hides as well as of sheep, pig, and goat skins.[178]

Also providing inputs for leather tanners was the British-owned Forestal Land, Timber, and Railways Company, the dominant enterprise in producing quebracho extract in Argentina and in the export of quebracho logs from that country. The quebracho extract was employed in leather tanning. In 1914 the British firm bought the factory and real estate of the New York Tanning Extract Company, which had a large extract works in Brooklyn, New York. The Forestal Company had an almost complete monopoly of the manufacture of quebracho extract worldwide.[179]

The next chapter offers details on the highly significant foreign investments in the American chemical industry. What is relevant here (and the reason for this discussion) is that requirements of the U.S. textile and leather goods industries provided important markets for the foreign-owned chemical concerns. The latter played a role in the modernization of the U.S. textile and leather industries.

Textile Industry Machinery

In the second half of the 1870s, about one-quarter of the textile machinery in U.S. cotton mills was British made, imported from the United Kingdom. Behind high tariff walls American companies were, however, undertaking import substitution, making what had been imported. The Wilson-Gorman Tariff Act of 1894, which *lowered* the duty on imported textile machinery from 45 percent to 35 percent ad valorem, did not promise much relief to sellers of British equipment.

Between 1884 and 1894, the Englishman Charles E. Riley had endeavored to market within the United States textile machinery produced by Howard & Bullough, Accrington, England. Customers liked the equipment, but Riley realized that because of the tariff and the U.S. domestic industry, in order to maintain sales, much less expand them, Howard & Bullough would have to manufacture on this side of the Atlantic. The salesman convinced his British employer, and in 1894 Howard & Bullough American Machine Company, Ltd., was organized. It had a British charter; its capital was supplied from Britain; its output would be all British designed. Riley became its chief executive.

The Howard & Bullough American Machine Company, Ltd., was the first significant textile machinery firm in America started in over two decades and the first British direct investment in textile equipment manufacturing that I have been able to verify. In April 1894 *Fibre and Fabric* had reported that the company had been "looking over the ground" at Lowell, Providence, Fall River, and Pawtucket (centers of the American textile industry) for a site to locate an $80,000 plant. The town of Attleboro, Massachusetts, near the Rhode Island border, offered twenty-five acres and a tax exemption of ten years (said to be worth about $60,000) to lure the manufacturer. By June 1894 the British firm had accepted that town's proposal and had factory construction under way. The new company began operation with a smaller plant than its two principal American competitors (Lowell Machine Shop and Whitin Machine Works), but it offered a full line of machinery to equip a cotton-spinning mill. In the United States, only the Lowell Machine Shop could do this. Moreover, already the British products had an international reputation. For its U.S. rivals, according to the historian of one of them, Howard & Bullough's plans for U.S. manufacture were "probably the most unnerving bit of news the textile machinery industry had heard for a generation."[180]

When economic conditions in the card-making business turned down in 1896, the card-building members of the American Cotton Machinery Builders Association met in Boston, seeking to stabilize the market. They did not invite Riley, since he was not welcomed to an association that was primarily devoted to keeping British machinery out of the United States! The Boston meeting resulted in a "voluntary code of competitive ethics," which set minimum prices for cards and associated machinery. Even though not a participant, the Americans expected Howard & Bullough American Machine Company, Ltd., to comply with their rules. That firm, however, evaded the agreement by maintaining its price on card machinery while practically "giving away" pickers. (It sold the two products as a package, but priced them separately; the buyer, of course, cared only about the total cost.) Finally, on July 1, 1898, the American card builders "forced" the British company to agree to hold to the minimum prices on pickers as well as on cards.[181] When in March 1905 the leading U.S. textile machinery makers joined in buying the shares of Lowell Machine Shop, Howard & Bullough American Machine Company participated.[182] By then, the British-owned company had become an integral part of the "American" textile machinery industry.

In 1911 Riley suggested to Howard & Bullough in England that the U.S. business should be incorporated in America rather than in the United Kingdom, arguing that its British charter prejudiced American mill owners against the company. Accordingly, a new firm was incorporated in Maine, as the H & B American Machine Company; it was 60 percent owned by its British parent.[183] The other 40 percent seems to have been held by Riley. The firm raised an additional $1.17 million by selling cumulative preferred shares on the London market in February 1912.[184] The newly "Americanized" (at least by place of incorporation, if not ownership) firm still made the British type of machinery designed by its British parent.

Like its U.S. competitors, H & B American Machine Company specialized in cotton preparation equipment. The wool machinery industry in America was small, and apparently worsted spinning and specialized weaving equipment continued to be imported in large part from Britain and Germany.[185] I can find no evidence of foreign investment in producing equipment for the wool textile industry. Foreign investors in the woolen industry used imported machinery.[186]

By contrast, the manufacture in the United States of knitting machines and their needles came to be dominated by German direct investors; the U.S. Alien Property Custodian wrote in 1919 of the pre–World War I years that this was "one of the most important German-controlled industries" in America. For many years German firms had exported these machines and their needles to the United States. Then, apparently because of the high tariffs, German enterprises became U.S. producers. Thus Grosser Knitting Machine Company, New York, 100 percent owned by Paul Grosser of Germany, first acted as a sales outlet; by the early twentieth century it had started to manufacture in the New York area. By 1914 Ernest Beckert of Chemnitz, Germany, owned three U.S. companies that made knitting needles: the Currier Knitting Machine Company, Manchester, New Hampshire; the Beckert Knitting & Supply Company; and the C. Walker Jones Company, Inc., the last two of Philadelphia.[187] The American knit-goods industry in the twenty-five years before World War I expanded almost fourfold.[188] German machinery—made in America—assisted this progress.

The Foreign Impact

Although there were cases of foreign direct investments in obtaining raw materials for export, this is not what stands out. Rather, it is in other facets of the American textile industry that foreign companies made significant investments. In the late nineteenth and early twentieth centuries, there were virtually no U.S. businesses abroad in the textile industry, as such.[189] Yet in this period British, German, French, and Swiss enterprises were very visible in American textile production, and a number of the participants had multinational manufacturing operations (that is, plants in their home nation, in the United States, and in other European countries). Thus C. Tiberghien and Sons, Tourcoing, France, had mills in Austria and Czechoslovakia, as well as in France and the United States. So did some silkmakers and the thread companies. Certain British textile firms (John Crossley & Sons, for example) had factories in Europe, but not in the United States.[190] What existed was not "bilateral" arrangements or free-standing companies of the sort we so frequently found in U.S. mining, food production, and breweries. Likewise, foreign portfolio investments in textiles were inconsequential. Foreign direct investment of the modern multinational enterprise variety was what prevailed.

Why were there such large European direct investments in American textiles? What characterized these investors? In most cases the European companies in this industry had some advantage over their U.S. rivals, or the foreign investor moved into a specialized niche that for some reason had not attracted American capital, or both. Sometimes they were in facets of the industry in which there was concentration. The advantage could be in technology or in the nature of the product itself. The specialized niche could also be in the production method or in the market segment. The concentration would be in a subindustry.

In cotton goods, for example, it was the book-binding-cloth maker and the woven-name-tape producer rather than the yard goods manufacturer that entered. In woolen products the foreign investor, whether British, German, or French, appears to have specialized in quality rather than in the mass production of goods. The French process of woolen yarn making was especially innovative. The British carpet industry (and certainly the British linoleum producer) seemed to offer goods not readily available in America, at least in terms of quality. As for the silk industry in this period, it was a new one in the United States, and the technology and experience first developed in Europe could be transferred with the foreign direct investments. There was no reason why Americans should have any advantage in this luxury industry. Lace and embroidery involved specialized, detailed work and were not the kinds of industries in which Americans excelled. Dyeing textiles was a highly labor-intensive activity requiring great skill, and although it was taught to Americans, the latter needed instructors; once more, foreign investors could satisfy a need not quickly filled in America, where skilled labor was relatively high priced.

As I went through the list of foreign companies that made investments in cotton goods, woolen and worsted products, carpets and other floor coverings, silk, lace, and embroidery, what seemed clear was that the foreign investor tended toward "top-of-the-line" merchandise. Some of what was marketed (Nairn Linoleum is an excellent example) was advertised and branded. The manufacture of many of the products required special know-how. Often the entries involved new methods and new goods.

The Scottish cotton thread firms had worldwide advantage, based on both technology and marketing expertise. They exported first, established sales organizations in America, and manufactured after a high tariff decimated their exports. Their investments grew over time, owing to skillful advertising and the establishment and maintenance of leadership. Changes in the industrial structure in Britain had their parallels in America: mergers there were duplicated in mergers here. Thread was a branded, highly advertised, differentiated product. In many ways it seems more like chocolates, soap, and matches (other businesses that, as noted, had international direct investments) than like an ordinary textile.[191] But this is my very point—it was not "standard" run-of-the-mill textiles that were part of this documented foreign direct investment process, but rather unique goods that required special handling and marketing attention.[192] In thread, British direct investors replaced American businesses in the U.S. market; no American thread companies expanded internationally.

The same was true in rayon. No U.S. business engaged in rayon production abroad, but as indicated, a British company came to have a monopoly position in this industry in the American market in the years 1911–1914. In part, British supremacy here was the result of patents (yet other processes existed—internationally—covered by other patents, so patents cannot be seen as the sole basis for exclusion of Americans' entry). Of key importance, the expertise was held abroad. In this case a British investor bought an American company (which had a "pretty well useless" factory and which, much more important, held the U.S. patents). Courtaulds, on the basis of its skills and know-how, proved highly successful in the United States.

Normally, and correctly, economic historians consider the American textile industry to lack concentration.[193] Yet if one considers subcategories within the industry, an element of concentration emerges, and interestingly, often (but not always) that was where I found the large and significant role of foreign direct investments. Thus in cotton thread, where there came to be that concentration, British firms by 1914, through their American investments, controlled at least two-thirds of the American market. Likewise, in linen thread the amount seems to have been comparable. In rayon, a British investor held 100 percent of the American market.

In apparel, an industry of many producers, foreign investments were negligible, with the exception of one highly advertised branded product. In the leather goods industry, which came to be dominated by two U.S. giants yet still had a large number of small producers, a British trading firm filled the needs of a highly specialized segment of the industry (kid leather goods).

German companies—primarily through direct investments in sales organizations—controlled the distribution of imported dyes sold to the textile industry. In alkalies and bleaches, used by the textile industry, British, Belgian, and German foreign direct investments in manufacturing were evident. The reasons for the heavy European involvements in these chemical products will be considered in Chapter 11. German and British investments in chemicals and quebracho extracts for the leather trade also existed.

In making machinery for cotton-spinning mills, a subsidiary of a British firm ranked as one of the major producers. This company had an international reputation and had sold in the United States for a number of years before it started to manufacture. German machinery and needles—made by German-owned companies in the United States—dominated the knit-goods industry. German producers of this machinery had, likewise, sold in the United States through exports before they embarked on manufacturing in this country. Germans excelled in the specialized machinery industries.

In the case of many of the European investments—in most of the cotton products, the woolen and worsted dress goods, woolen yarn, carpets, silk goods, embroidered goods, cotton and linen thread, rayon, alkalies, cotton preparation equipment, and knit-goods machinery—tariffs had been crucial to the investors' decision to shift from export to manufacture on the American side of the Atlantic. The principal U.S. tariffs that affected the influx of foreign investment into manufacturing textiles and related products were those of 1883, 1890, 1897, and 1909. The several British-owned thread mills originally established because of the tariffs of the 1860s were atypical.

By contrast, Booth & Co.'s expansion in the United States seems to have been a natural evolution to gain control over price and quality and was unaffected by tariffs. Likewise, on occasion, a market for a trademarked good made by a patented process seemed sufficient to warrant U.S. manufacture without special protection (Rohm & Haas is a good example). Nairn started without protection, but requested it. Textile makers, seeking cheap dyes, were successful in supporting *low* tariffs on dyestuffs, and few basic dyes were made in America.[194]

The duties designed to assist U.S. industry gave foreign-owned businesses the option of vaulting tariff barriers and investing in manufacturing in the United States. The investment process was often associated with a rising U.S. industry *behind* the tariff walls, and the consequent further reduction in European export markets.

Sometimes on their own initiative and sometimes stimulated by Americans, many European firms accepted the challenge. New foreign-owned manufacturing facilities were established in Rhode Island, Connecticut, Pennsylvania, New Jersey, New York, and Massachusetts—centers of the American textile industries. Some ventures involved takeovers of existing viable American firms (by American Thread Company–English Sewing Cotton Company, Ltd.); others were takeovers of barely functioning U.S. operations (American Viscose–Courtauld). Most of the new entries built new factories and transferred technologically advanced methods.

European investors in manufacturing in the textile industry in America sold goods to other producers and end-products to consumers. Because European textile exports to America had once been large, because Europeans had advantages, because the American producer and consumer markets offered immense potential, the foreign involvements in manufacturing rose.[195] They were in many different facets of the pre–World War I U.S. textile industry. As I wrote this chapter, I kept finding additional investments. The extent of the participation and the frequent multiplant enterprises, as noted, initially came as a surprise. Yet my analysis reveals that the successful participants in America were those with specialized technical know-how, patents (on occasion), trademarked products, and/or a particular market niche that Americans had neglected; often they were in subindustries in which there came to be a high degree of concentration. The investments were made by European companies that had advantages vis-à-vis American firms. All things considered, the surprise evaporates, as these are the very characteristics of foreign direct investments that students of multinational enterprise have come to expect.

11.

The Chemical Industry

Foreign direct investment had more impact on the pre–World War I American chemical industry than on any other U.S. industry. Non-U.S. multinational enterprises were ubiquitous actors, either threatening investment or, more frequently, actually investing. Foreign portfolio holdings were negligible. In the context of mineral industries, I have already touched (in Chapters 7 and 8) on the U.S. chemical activities of the German DEGUSSA and its joint-venture with the British firm Aluminium Company, Ltd., in manufacturing cyanide used in gold recovery;[1] the German role in introducing the flotation process to separate metals; the Austrian Schmidtmann's investment in International Agricultural Corporation; the stakes of Borax Consolidated, Ltd.;[2] and German, British, and French interests in electrolytic processes applied to metallurgy.[3] In Chapter 9 I considered Lever Brothers' soap as a grocery product; it can, alternatively, be classified as a consumer chemical.[4] Courtaulds' innovations in rayon manufacture in America involved chemical processes; I included this firm's investments under the rubric "textiles" in Chapter 10. The names of Bayer, Solvay, Rohm & Haas, Th. Goldschmidt, and others appeared in that chapter because they participated in U.S. sales and preparation of chemicals used by American textile and leather producers.

These prior inclusions notwithstanding, the significant story of foreign direct investments in the distribution and production of chemicals in the United States cannot be subsumed under other topics. In the period 1875–1914, in no other industry were Europeans so far in advance of Americans; in no other single industry was the foreign technological contribution so dramatic. The worldwide chemical industry of 1875–1914 comprised tens of thousands of new products, from explosives to colors, to medicines, to flavors, to heavy chemicals. Here I consider the foreign investments in the United States in such goods and give an overview of the transatlantic interactions. Except when absolutely essential, I will not duplicate information presented earlier.

In the years 1875–1914, Germany, England, and Switzerland were centers of innovative chemical research; likewise, Belgium and France attained significance in branches of this industry. As companies in Europe were formed, took out or obtained patents, produced, expanded, and exported, they appointed agents or sales representatives in the large U.S. market. Over time, nonexclusive independent sales agents became exclusive and came to be owned and controlled by the European enterprise (Herman Metz's business for Hoechst, for instance).[5] Often, sales representatives of German firms traveled from Europe to America, settled, and became American citizens. Some established their own businesses (A. Klipstein & Co. and Seydel Chemical had such origins);[6] when they became independent, they were no longer foreign direct investments.

Many German firms based abroad set up sales branches or subsidiaries and next undertook partial and then full manufacturing in the United States (Heyden Chemical and Merck & Co. are excellent examples).[7] Sometimes Americans took the initiative and desired to produce under the patents and using the processes of foreign chemical firms; foreign investment followed (the Solvay Process Company fits this description).[8]

The chemical industry employed patents extensively, and a large percentage of the foreign patents registered in the United States related to chemical processes and products. During World War I, the Alien Property Custodian confiscated about 5,700 German patents, principally associated with chemicals.[9] British, French, Swiss, Belgian, and Swedish inventions in this industry were also patented in the United States. When U.S. companies obtained rights under the foreign-held patents, sometimes, in exchange, they gave a European business an interest in the U.S. enterprise (Aluminium Company's stake in Niagara Electro Chemical Company came about in this fashion, as did Th. Goldschmidt's investment in Goldschmidt Detinning Company).[10] Under U.S. law, a patent did not have to be worked to be upheld. On occasion, patents became tools of European chemical companies to preclude American manufacture. They were sometimes utilized to commandeer and to safeguard markets. In addition, and of great importance, foreign chemical companies registered their numerous trademarks in the United States.[11] These too gave the corporations advantage in the marketplace.

In the nineteenth century, European education in the chemical industries was superior to that in the United States. The sales agents, managers, and chemists for U.S. firms and foreign branches and subsidiaries might be Americans who were schooled abroad, but quite often they were Germans, Britishers, or Frenchmen who had graduated from European (mainly German) universities and then migrated to America. One commentator would describe pre–World War I America as "flooded with German chemists; and those who were not German by origin, were mostly German, directly or indirectly, by training."[12]

In the late nineteenth and early twentieth centuries, as German businesses became highly aggressive in export markets,[13] this was especially true in the chemical industry. Agents and sales representatives promoted the German chemical products in America.[14] If U.S. tariffs impeded German exports, to defend the market the exporter invested in manufacturing inside the tariff walls (Bayer in pharmaceuticals, for example).

In the rivalry, one possible route was an agreement to divide markets. Such accords were intimately associated with the other approaches. Foreign chemical companies that had exported to the United States or even those that manufactured in this country found that the delineation of "territories" created order and stability and relieved them of some of the difficulties of trying to manage large-scale operations over distance. If, for competitive reasons, a foreign patent had to be worked in the United States, then the market of the U.S. factory should be prescribed. Such international agreements in chemicals went with or without (1) licensing arrangements (but often with them); (2) foreign investments (but if foreign investment existed, it would normally be in a minority; 100 percent control meant no need for formal market-sharing accords); and (3) technical assistance (it was not uncommon for Americans to obtain chemists from foreign firms, either on loan for short periods or on a regular basis). While the private "treaties" could be part of the foreign firm's attempt to penetrate the U.S. market, they were also directly linked with the wishes of foreign enterprises to stop U.S. companies from expanding abroad; they were frequently an aspect of a larger worldwide agreement. I noted earlier Courtauld's international associations and will herein show other intercontinental territorial arrangements.[15] Between 1905 and 1914 and even more between 1910 and 1914, as public attention was paid in the United States to antitrust matters, some corporate relationships were restructured and pacts revised, and a number of American-owned firms hesitated to regulate trade as desired by their European brethren.

Historians of the U.S. chemical industry often write vaguely of the "connections" between American and European business. Their obscurity is rooted in the complexities (and frequently changing character) of the interactions. To summarize, the "connections" related to the following considerations:

1. *Trade.* European firms exported and the U.S. ones marketed the former's end-products; European firms exported intermediate products to U.S. enterprises, which used or resold the import.

2. *Personnel.* American firms grew as a consequence of employees coming from Europe (often, but not always, from the parent firms of the European investors); sometimes the men involved were members of the same extended family grouping as in the European business.

3. *Investment.* European companies or their principals owned an interest in U.S. firms, from 100 percent to a small minority; the investment could be forward vertical integration (into sales or further processing) or horizontal (into manufacturing the same products that were made abroad), or more likely both.

4. *Patents, Technical Know-how, and Trademarks.* The European enterprises' intangible assets (patents, technical know-how, and trademarks) were used by U.S. licensing or acquisition; sometimes separate companies were established to do the licensing.

5. *Market sharing.* European businesses had agreements dividing market territories with American ones.

"Connections" at any particular time might involve one, some, or simultaneously all of these braided links. At another time, companies altered the relationships. Clusters of companies existed with different functions and different associations with a foreign parent or parents. Nothing was static about the chemical industry of this period. Alliances, business functions, and markets of companies in one year might differ from those in the next.

The five types of interactions presented above, the fact that they were seldom tidy, and the explosion of technology in the chemical industry in this era makes it little wonder that most historians are vague on the interconnections. In what follows, I will try to penetrate the fog and to document as precisely as possible the role of foreign chemical enterprises in America's chemical industries.

Explosives

Du Pont, formed in the early nineteenth century as a French direct investment, had rapidly become American. Its 1875–1914 international business was in no way related to its foreign origins. Toward the end of the nineteenth century, Du Pont, an explosives maker, found the need to come to terms with a new and competitive product, dynamite. In Chapter 4 I pointed out that the Swede Alfred Nobel (1833–1896) in October 1865 had taken out a U.S. patent for nitroglycerine and in 1866 had established his first company in America. Nobel also started factories in Sweden, Germany, Finland, Norway, Bohemia, and Scotland.[16] He preferred local manufacture to export because of the nature of the product (it did not travel well). After 1866 Nobel never again visited America. His concern with the U.S. companies proved sporadic (he never attempted to provide management), and in time he sold his shares in them (the last of his shares were disposed of in 1885). Nobel continued to get royalties based on his patents, but in 1889 he remarked that these could be "seen only under a microscope."[17]

Meanwhile, in 1871 in Scotland, Alfred Nobel had formed the British Dynamite Company, in which he held half the common stock.[18] In 1877 this company was reorganized and its name changed to Nobel's Explosives Company, Ltd.[19] Even earlier, in 1865, Nobel had started Alfred Nobel & Co. in Germany, known after 1876 as Dynamit, A.G. (or DAG).[20] Alfred Nobel licensed new works in France (1871), Spain (1872), Switzerland, Italy, Portugal, and Hungary (1873).[21]

In September 1884 DAG signed a "price convention" with its major German rivals; in October of that year it entered into the "First International Convention" involving Scottish, European, and Latin American dynamite manufacturers. November 1885 saw a profit-pooling agreement that brought it into a "German Union" with its principal German competitors.[22] In 1886 Nobel companies took part in a "Second International Convention"[23] and a series of "Trust Agreements"; Agreement No. 2 established an English company, registered in London, called the Nobel-Dynamite Trust Company, Ltd., to hold the shares of the Nobel's Explosives Company, Ltd., and the "German Union" companies.[24]

A few weeks after the formation of the Nobel-Dynamite Trust Company, Ltd., its Scottish subsidiary, Nobel's Explosives Company, acquired (in December 1886) 59 percent of the $100,000 capital of a new American firm, Standard Explosives Company of New York, which built a factory at Tom's River, New Jersey, about sixty-five miles from New York City.[25] American makers of dynamite were alarmed at this invasion from abroad. In October 1887 six U.S. producers (including Repauno, which had been formed by Lammot du Pont) cabled Nobel's Explosives, "We insist upon remaining unmolested in the United States and if so will not interfere with you in Europe."[26]

In April 1888 the general manager of Nobel's Explosives, Thomas Johnston, arrived in the United States, voicing optimism about the outlook for Standard Explosives.[27] By December, however, Nobel's Explosives had decided not to compete in America. It sold its shares in Standard Explosives to Americans, and along with all the Nobel-Dynamite Trust companies, it signed a market-sharing and price-fixing agreement with the six principal California and eastern seaboard dynamite makers. In exchange for the withdrawal of the Nobel's Explosives group from the United States and its promise not to return, the Americans agreed to keep out of Europe, Africa, Australia, and colonial Asia. "Equal-rights territories" were designated as Latin America and the Caribbean, Korea, Japan, and China. This 1888 pact lasted until 1893, when it was apparently not renewed.[28]

Then in 1896 an American firm, Aetna Powder Company, exported dynamite to South Africa, to a country the Nobel-Dynamite Trust Company, Ltd., believed to be "British territory." Nobel-Dynamite announced in 1897 that it would build factories in New Jersey and enter the U.S. market, and Rheinisch-Westfälische Sprengstoff (a subsidiary of Nobel-Dynamite) acquired about 600 acres near Jamesburg, New Jersey, for a new plant.

Once more threatened, Du Pont, along with Aetna Powder Company, Laflin and Rand, American Powder Mills, and other U.S. producers of explosives, pledged to their British and German rivals (October 26, 1897) "to avoid anything being done which would affect injuriously the common interest." The Europeans agreed not to complete the works at Jamesburg and to leave to the Americans the U.S. market for a wide range of explosives. The Europeans also bound themselves not to build factories in the future in the United States. The American group promised not to compete in the European producers' "territory." The world was again divided, and the European investors were out of the United States. This 1897 agreement was far broader than the 1888 one, including the manufacture and sale of black power and the new smokeless power, as well as dynamite.[29]

In 1906 Du Pont became nervous that perhaps the 1897 accord might be a violation of U.S. antitrust laws, and in 1907 the company signed a revised agreement with the Anglo-German producers, which it hoped would not be vulnerable under U.S. law. Then in 1911 Du Pont was found by a U.S. court to be in a "combination in restraint of interstate commerce." The district court decree of June 13, 1912, did not challenge the 1907 arrangements with the Europeans, but Du Pont decided in 1913 it would be prudent to abrogate that pact.[30]

In its place a new one was negotiated in 1914, with international cross-licensing of patents and of secret processes. Du Pont believed that by tying the agreement strictly to technology interchanges, markets could continue to be delineated without attracting the opprobrium of U.S. antitrust authorities. The Europeans felt their technology was superior to that of the Americans.[31] It was certainly different. Henry de Mosenthal of Nobel-Dynamite Trust Company, Ltd., remarked that, for a man familiar with European methods, to go through a Du Pont plant "was like going into a wholesale clothing factory when you have been accustomed to work with a West End tailor."[32] With the outbreak of war, the ratification of the 1914 technology-exchange contract was delayed (and the Germans excluded).[33]

The result of this sequence of agreements was that the Americans had succeeded in keeping the British and German Nobel companies at bay. Despite the three attempted entries by European explosive producers into U.S. manufacturing (1866, 1886, and 1897), they made no lasting investments in this country. One historian summed up the 1897–1914 interactions as follows: "transatlantic co-operation in the affairs of the explosives industry worked very smoothly."[34]

Dyestuffs

In the dyestuffs industry, international business relationships were entirely different. The German role was pervasive. There were not mere probes but important, influential foreign entries. German companies dominated world dyestuff output and distribution, and the superiority extended into the United States. Synthetic dyestuffs was a new, technologically advanced industry. By 1914 the largest German manufacturer was Farben Fabriken vorm. Friedrich Bayer & Co., at Leverkusen. Bayer had had a sales office or sales agent in New York City at least as early as the start of the 1870s, and probably as early as 1865;[35] over time, the German firm developed a formidable American sales network, with branch offices in Boston, Providence, Philadelphia, Chicago, San Francisco, and Toronto (Canada).[36] The marketing of dyestuffs required specialized knowledge, experience, and continuing customer service. Because of the complexity of the product, managers of the German Bayer wanted control over the selling; they needed close contacts with their American buyers.

Bayer's first investment in U.S. manufacturing was in the Albany Aniline & Chemical Works, probably in 1871 (see Chapter 4). Herman Preiss, a foreman from Bayer's German operation, had in the 1870s been dispatched from the home plant to supervise production at the Albany factory.[37] Bayer had only a minority interest in Albany Aniline; when the son of the controlling U.S. stockholder sought to determine strategy, Bayer sold out; Herman Preiss and others of the

Bayer group started in 1882 the Hudson River Aniline Color Works, which built a plant in Rensselaer, New York, near Albany. The main source of financing for this new facility came from Louis Waldman, an Albany department store owner. Thus, as in the case of Albany Aniline, here too the German Bayer initially had a minority holding. Through E. Sehlbach, then its U.S. representative, the German Bayer Company invested a mere $10,000 (the capitalization of the 1903 successor company to Hudson River Aniline Color Works was only $41,000). The new Hudson River company produced soluble blues, alkali blues, Bismarck browns, and fuchsin crystals, which were sold to the leather trade.[38] Bayer continued to export from Germany most of the dyes required by the many other industries. In 1898 Waldman—objecting to Bayer's insistence on confining production to dyes for the leather trade—left to start a competing company; Bayer became 100 percent owner of the Hudson River firm.[39]

In 1903 the industrial chemist Carl Duisberg (who had joined the German Bayer Company in 1884), accompanied by Friedrich Bayer, Jr., traveled to the United States to enlarge the capacity of the Rensselaer plant and to start there, for the first time, the manufacture of Bayer's pharmaceuticals. The Germans decided to produce drugs in the United States because of the high tariffs (up to 100 percent). Also, Bayer's U.S. patents on phenacetin (a predecessor of aspirin) had expired; competition might move into Bayer's markets were it not manufacturing in the United States. Accordingly, in 1905 the Rensselaer plant began to make and indeed to specialize in medicines, phenacetin first and then aspirin.[40] At Rensselaer, Bayer developed a substantial aspirin output, installing machinery of special design;[41] the company did not, however, produce adequate supplies and hence supplemented its U.S.-manufactured products with imports from Germany.[42]

By 1913 the Hudson River Aniline Color Works had become a "paper" (a shell) company; the properties at Rensselaer were sold to two new German-controlled firms, Bayer Company, Inc., New York, and Synthetic Patents Company, Inc.[43] The German-owned Bayer was by then the third-largest dyestuff producer in the United States, manufacturing at the Rensselaer plant roughly 17 percent of the very small U.S. output.[44] It was not in colors but in aspirins that its producing role had become most significant. Likewise, by 1914 Bayer held roughly 1,200 U.S. patents.[45] Its active head in the United States was (and had been for many years) Anthony Gref, "a skilled and shrewd patent attorney, whose chief occupation was to protect patent and trademark rights on dyes and drugs."[46] Bayer's American sales organization was huge. The German company had a multimillion-dollar-business investment in this country. It marketed a range of intermediates (mostly imported) and consumer products (aspirins).[47] Not all its goods were coal-tar based. In the early twentieth century Bayer, for example, imported Heroine (a trademarked pharmaceutical), which it advertised worldwide as a substitute for morphine.[48] Aspirins began to be sold over-the-counter before 1914. When the product was first introduced in Germany in 1898, Bayer had circularized some 30,000 doctors, providing samples to many of them.[49] Its first marketing and advertising in the United States had been through doctors—as was Bayer's usual procedure.[50]

When World War I broke out in 1914, the United States had only seven dyestuff plants; the leading three were Bayer and two U.S.-owned firms (Schoellkopf and Heller & Merz), all of which relied on intermediates imported from Germany.[51] The seven facilities all together employed 528 people and manufactured 3,000 tons a year valued at a mere $2.5 million.[52] As the historian L. F. Haber has put it, "for all practical purposes, the United States was wholly dependent on imports."[53] Another estimate indicated that in 1914 roughly nine-tenths of U.S. domestic consumption of dyes was imported.[54] Perhaps the best description of the American industry was provided in an August 1914 statement by Herman A. Metz, the representative of the German Hoechst in the United States:

Practically seventy-five percent of the dye-stuffs, outside of dye woods, that are consumed in the entire world are manufactured in Germany in five or six plants located chiefly along the Rhine and the Main. Countries like Russia, France and England, and even the United States to a small extent, have established plants for manufacturing colors, and are now depending entirely upon Germany for their own material from which they carry on the further operations. Every cotton, woolen and silk mill, as well as every leather manufacturer, paper mill, printers ink and paint manufacturer, is dependent upon the products of these German concerns, whether he makes white or colored goods, because chemicals are used for sizing and finishing as well as dyeing. There is not over sixty days supply of textile chemicals and dyes in the United States, carried in stock by the various importers or agents of German concerns.[55]

In short, in 1913–14 practically all the technologically advanced synthetic dyestuffs came from Germany. German output in 1913 was 135,000 tons; German consumption, 20,000 tons (U.S. consumption was roughly 26,000 tons).[56] America was also dependent on imports of certain pharmaceuticals made by the German dyestuff producers. Yet this dependence on imports must not lead us to ignore the formidable *marketing* organization that the German makers had in the United States. Not only Bayer but all the other leading German chemical companies had important investments in *selling* their products in pre–World War I America. In addition to Bayer, represented in the United States were Badische Anilin und Soda Fabrik, Ludwigshafen on the Rhine (*Badische*, now often known as BASF); Aktien-Gesellschaft für Anilin-Fabrikation, Berlin (*AGFA*); Farbwerke vorm. Meister Lucius & Brüning, Hoechst am Main (*Hoechst*); Leopold Cassella, G.m.b.H., Frankfurt (*Cassella*); Kalle & Co., A.G., Biebrich (*Kalle*); Chemische Fabrik Griesheim Elektron, Frankfurt (*Griesheim*); and Chemische Fabriken vormals Weiler-ter-Meer, Verdingen (*Weiler-ter-Meer*). The last firm was closely associated with the Swiss J. R. Geigy & Co. All were makers of dyestuffs. The first five and Bayer were typically referred to as the big six in German chemicals.[57]

Badische obtained a U.S. patent for alizarin in 1869;[58] by 1914 it held about 500 U.S. patents.[59] In 1860 the fourteen-year-old Adolf Kuttroff arrived in America. Seven years later he was naturalized, and in 1870 he began business in New York, importing fuchsin and other dyes manufactured by A. Poirrier of France and by Badische.[60] Through a succession of partnerships and incorporated units, in association with various members of the Pickhardt family, Kuttroff ran the Badische business in America for more than forty-five years.[61] In 1907 the Badische Company, incorporated in New York, was formed;[62] its stock was "technically" owned by Adolf Kuttroff, Carl Pickhardt, and their employees. World War I investigations found the "ostensible ownership was not genuine" and that the German Badische firm had 100 percent control over the New York sales outlet. The latter even referred to the German Badische parent questions on the salaries of the New York staff as well as numerous other similar matters.[63] The name of the German enterprise was used for the "American" company because of its international reputation.

AGFA in Germany made cotton dyes, a few pharmaceutical specialties, and, most important, photochemicals (developers and fixers, dry plates, and film).[64] It was initially represented in America by Henry A. Gould & Co., next by New York and Boston Dyewood Company, and then it organized a sales unit, the Berlin Aniline Works, incorporated in New York on March 31, 1899. By 1901 the New York office supervised sales offices in Chicago, Charlotte, Cincinnati, Boston, and Philadelphia.[65]

Hoechst's interests in the United States came to be directed by the energetic New York–born Herman A. Metz, who in 1882 (at the age of fifteen) had joined an American dyestuff-importing firm (P. Schulze-Berge) as an office boy. Hoechst at that time was represented in the United States by the agency Lutz & Movius and then by J. Movius & Son, whose manager was Victor Koechl. In about 1884

Koechl joined P. Schulze-Berge, which was renamed P. Schulze-Berge & Koechl; several years later this firm merged with J. Movius & Son, becoming P. Schulze-Berge and Movius; it took over the Hoechst agency, importing antipyrin (used as a sedative), the first of the important coal tar medicinal products. Initially Schulze-Berge and Movius continued to serve as an agent for other European firms as well.[66]

In time, both Schulze-Berge and Movius left the agency, and Victor Koechl & Co. was formed,[67] with Herman Metz as vice president and treasurer. Metz eventually bought out Koechl and became president; later Metz recalled that he divided the concern, continuing Victor Koechl & Co. in the pharmaceutical business and organizing H. A. Metz & Co. for dyestuff imports.[68] Metz also set up the Consolidated Color & Chemical Company,[69] with a factory in Newark, New Jersey, which in 1914 produced about 2 to 3 percent of U.S. dyestuffs.[70]

By a series of agreements, the German Hoechst obtained an interest in and then control over Metz's business.[71] The German parent received 50 percent of H. A. Metz & Co.'s profits on its color business and 75 percent of Herman Metz's profits on the pharmaceutical trade. The latter became particularly significant after Hoechst had developed the manufacture of the antisyphilitic compound Salvarsan (commercial production in Germany in 1910) and the pain-killer Novocaine.[72] Salvarsan—invented by Paul Ehrlich and often called the Magic Bullet—provided the only-known effective cure for syphilis, then a pervasive and devastating disease.[73] Salvarsan and Novocaine both became important trademarks. In 1914 these pharmaceuticals were still imported into the United States.

As a precaution over possible German overcharges, Herman Metz received a percentage of the German parent company's profits on the sale of all Hoechst products to H. A. Metz & Co.[74] In 1912 Farbwerke Hoechst Company was formed, with a capital stock of $200,000 and an address in downtown New York City; it was the successor to H. A. Metz & Co. The name was changed so that the value "of the goodwill might be firmly fixed in the German name."[75] That year Metz was elected a U.S. Congressman from Brooklyn.[76]

In 1912–13 Metz, who remained identified with Hoechst, told the latter that a German equity-controlled company in the United States might be considered as acting in restraint of trade under the Sherman Antitrust Act. He believed that if the German house sold its products through an apparently independent American corporation, it would not be vulnerable. On the basis of these assumptions, in 1913 Metz acquired the stock of the New York Hoechst Company,[77] but the Germans continued in control. The distribution of profits remained

on the same basis. Should Metz die or retire, it was understood that
the stock of the New York company would be reacquired by the
German parent. Later the Alien Property Custodian determined that
even though Metz "held" the stock, the company was in fact 99
percent "owned" from Germany.[78]

Metz's 1914 letterhead identified him as president of Farbwerke
Hoechst Company, with branches in New York, Boston, Philadelphia, Providence, Chicago, Charlotte, Atlanta, San Francisco, Newark, Montreal, Toronto, and Hamburg. The letterhead also showed
him to be president of Consolidated Color & Chemical Company
(Newark, New Jersey), Victor Koechl & Co. (New York), Ettrick Mills
(Worcester, Massachusetts), Stoneville Company (Auburn, Massachusetts), and Textilleather Company (New York–Newark).[79] The
last three were small manufacturing companies, buyers of dyestuffs.
They seem to have been owned by Metz—with no German parent.[80]

Leopold Cassella was in 1914 represented in the United States by
Cassella Color Company, incorporated in New York in 1901[81] and, on
the surface, wholly owned by two American-born men, William J.
Matheson and Robert Shaw. The Alien Property Custodian determined, however, that control (57 percent) rested with the German
parent: just as Metz, as a formality, had acquired the stock of Farbwerke Hoechst Company in 1913, so too, and for the same antitrust
reasons, that year Matheson and Shaw had become the "sole" owners of Cassella Color Company. Prior to 1913 the latter had been 57
percent owned by the German house; before and after 1913 profits
were distributed 57 percent to Cassella in Germany and 43 percent to
the Americans.[82] At least since the early 1880s Matheson had represented Cassella in the United States.[83] The German Cassella, like
Bayer, Hoechst, and to a lesser extent AGFA, had moved into pharmaceuticals and proprietary drugs as well as colors, and its American
house became an outlet for such products.[84] By 1914 the Cassella
Color Company had branches in New York, Boston, Philadelphia,
Atlanta, and Montreal.[85]

In 1896 and probably earlier, the German Kalle & Co. had a New
York outlet of the same name with a German-trained color chemist on
its staff. In 1913 Kalle Color & Chemical Company was formed, incorporated in New York.[86] Griesheim Elektron had as its representatives in the United States Geisenheimer & Co. and A. Klipstein, both
of which seem to have been American controlled agencies but were
dependent on Griesheim for their business.[87] Weiler-ter-Meer's affiliate in the United States before World War I was Geigy-Ter-Meer
Company, in which its ownership was 20 percent. The remainder of
the stock was held by the Swiss Geigy Company; Geigy-Ter-Meer

Company invested in minor manufacturing in the United States in 1903.[88]

In sum, then, beginning in the 1870s but more significantly from the 1880s and 1890s, all the leading German dyestuff companies appointed agents and then developed sales affiliates in the United States. Initially the "agents" had bought goods outright and sold on their own account. Over time, goods were consigned, and the Germans took over the "agents"—"one by one."[89] Between 1899 and 1913 most of the German firms adopted the parent company's name in America to take advantage of the latter's international reputation. All advertised.

Although Bayer and several other German dyestuff companies made direct investments in manufacturing in America, their advantage in the U.S. market was achieved primarily through (1) their extensive nationwide sales organizations staffed by well-trained, experienced specialists, (2) their patents, (3) their trademarked drugs, (4) their parent's name and goodwill, (5) their unique goods without substitutes in the United States, and (6) their export to the United States of both intermediates and end-products. The German presence, and impact, was immense. The investments introduced German output—from colors to medicines—to U.S. customers.[90]

Drugs

In 1903–04 in Germany, Carl Duisberg had combined Bayer, Badische, and AGFA into a loose confederation; at that time he had hoped to include other German manufacturers of pharmaceuticals. In 1905 in Germany, the latter, comprising E. Merck, J. D. Riedel, Knoll & Co., and two more German makers of medicines, formed a group called Pharma, A.G.[91] Like the dyestuff firms, Merck, Riedel, and Knoll had U.S. interests before 1914, with Merck's by far the most outstanding of the trio.

E. Merck of Darmstadt had its beginnings in an apothecary shop in the 1820s. In 1887 a German-born, long-time Merck employee, Theodore Weicker, went to the United States to represent the Darmstadt firm. In 1891, with a capital of $200,000 received from E. Merck, Weicker started the American Merck & Co., with headquarters in lower Manhattan.[92] That year George Merck, the twenty-three-year-old son of the then head of E. Merck (and grandson of the founder), joined Weicker in New York. At first this subsidiary imported products from its parent, but in 1899 Merck & Co. purchased 150 acres in Rahway, New Jersey, and built a factory to manufacture morphine, codeine, and cocaine for sale in the United States. Soon other products were added. In 1906 the U.S. firm bought the manufacturing business of Herf & Frerichs, which became Merck's St. Louis branch.[93] In 1910 Charles Darius of Merck & Co. testified in Washington, opposing a proposed tax on the import of coca leaves because such a tax "is equivalent to a reduction of the protection of the American manufacturer of something like 10 to 12 cents per ounce of cocaine produced in this country."[94] Merck & Co. represented itself as an "American" manufacturer and took advantage of the protection provided. Like other foreign-owned enterprises, once it had begun production in the United States, Merck wanted protection. By 1914 Merck & Co. had a large and profitable business in a number of medicinal products.[95] George Merck himself became an American citizen and ran this flourishing firm. Most of the drugs sold by Merck & Co. in the United States were by 1914 manufactured at its plant in Rahway rather than imported.[96]

George Merck would later explain that the company was "always" treated "as a family affair." On the death of the German founder, E. Merck, his estate had passed to his three sons, Carl, George, and Wilhelm; when they in turn died, their interests went to their children. George Merck's father (Wilhelm) had died in 1901, and George had succeeded to one-half of the holdings that stood to the credit of his father on the books of E. Merck, Darmstadt, Germany. He could draw on that at any time. When in 1908 a corporation was formed in the United States, Merck & Co. (to replace the earlier unincorporated company), the financial resources were drawn in part from E. Merck in Germany and in part from the U.S. firm's accumulated profits. Over the years George Merck remitted profits to Germany, where they were pooled with E. Merck's other income. Roughly once a year, George Merck visited Darmstadt. As for the U.S. business, he claimed (in 1918) that "'for many years" he had run it "in his absolute discretion without interference by E. Merck of Darmstadt, and E. Merck had no voice in its management or control whatsoever." Clearly, the international business was a family affair. George Merck ran the American side. After the United States went to war with Germany, he deposited with the Alien Property Custodian 80 percent of the shares in Merck & Co., representing "enemy ownership," because were the partnership *in Darmstadt* dissolved, he would have been entitled to a 20 percent distribution. He saw this as representing his equity in the American Merck & Co.[97]

Riedel & Co. owned 80 percent of a distributor in New York.[98] The firm had trademarked medicines such as Bornyval, Salipyrin, and Euscopol.[99] Knoll apparently had some operations in the United States, probably sales, established in 1907.[100] It had a number of U.S.

patents, one of which (in 1909) was for digitalis extract.[101] Riedel and Knoll were small in the United States (and in Germany) compared with Merck.

Schering, A.G., whose predecessor dated back to 1851 in Germany, sent members of the family to New York and in the late 1870s participated in founding Schering & Glatz, which seems to have handled imports from the parent. Schering, A.G., took out American patents covering its research in synthesizing camphor. Although Schering & Glatz still existed in 1914, it is doubtful that it was German owned at that time.[102]

Not only did German companies sell and, in the case of Bayer and Merck, manufacture drugs in the United States, but so too Swiss enterprises invested in America in this branch of the chemical industry. In 1905 the Swiss F. Hoffmann–La Roche & Co., Ltd., formed Hoffmann LaRoche Chemical Works, Inc., which started business in downtown New York as an importer.[103]

Sometime between 1914 and 1915, an American producer of pharmaceuticals complained, "We see no reason why French pharmaceuticals should be permitted to come into this country in great volume, as they now do, with no restrictions, and also to be manufactured here, and at the same time, permit France to exclude our preparations."[104] This statement was probably made in connection with pre–World War I conditions, but it is somewhat mysterious, since there is no evidence of large imports of French pharmaceutical products, and I have only a few clues on which French company or companies were producing pharmaceuticals in the United States.[105]

A better record exists of British companies' investments in both selling and manufacturing medicines in the United States. The British Burroughs, Wellcome (founded in London in 1880 by two Americans)[106] had long had an independent sales agent in New York. It opened a New York branch in 1906, which undertook light manufacturing; two years later it started a separate manufacturing laboratory in New York.[107] In 1913 Burroughs, Wellcome products in the United States included a range of Tabloid ethical (science-based) medicines marketed through doctors, as well as Kepler Cod Liver Oil and Kepler Extract of Malt, Toilet Lanoline, Hazeline Snow, saccharin, and artificial eardrums, plus tonics and laxatives with such extraordinary names as Tabloid Livingstone Rouser and Tabloid Forced March.[108]

When in 1889 there had been the flood of British promotions of American breweries and other industrials, an American, H. H. Warner, who sold Safe cures and Log Cabin remedies in the United States, Canada, England, Germany, Austria-Hungary, and Australia, resolved to tap the London capital market for his British and American business. Warner went to the British promoter H. Osborne O'Hagan, who decided that Warner's company might be at "the top of its prosperity" and declined to handle the flotation. Other Britishers were less reserved, and in November 1889 H. H. Warner and Co., Ltd., was presented to the British public; the new firm would acquire Warner's ongoing patent medicine business. Warner embarrassed the British speculators, making a fortune in the transaction; but by 1893 Warner was insolvent. The British company remained—and eventually (by 1908) leased the Rochester, New York, plant to Americans.[109]

The economic historian T. A. B. Corley has helped me decipher the role of Beecham in America. Thomas Beecham manufactured pills in England "for bilious and nervous disorder, wind and pain of the stomach, headaches, giddiness." He advertised widely, and customers liked his products. In 1888 Beecham's "acquired" offices and warehouse facilities in Brooklyn, New York, part of a premises owned by another important British advertiser, Pears' Soap. That year Beecham's sent out 7,000 letters in the United States and Canada promoting its pills. It distributed photographs of U.S. presidential candidates, on the backs of which were advertisements for Beecham's pills. Because Americans wanted their pills sweet, Beecham sugar-coated them for U.S. consumers. In about two years, 1890–91, with sales rising, founder Thomas Beecham's son, Joseph Beecham (1848–1916), told an American reporter that machinery was being installed in Brooklyn to meet promptly the growing demand. From that point onward, Beecham's pills sold in America were American made.[110] Their popularity was such that Joseph Beecham had to run down counterfeiters and infringers on his trademark.[111] He made regular trips to the United States, reputedly taking some sixty trips—if so, almost rivaling the record of another inveterate British investor-traveler, Robert Fleming.[112] In 1911 Beecham's purchased a new factory building, and output in Brooklyn mounted.[113]

Professor Alfred D. Chandler has pointed out to me that the promotion of "consumer chemicals," such as Beecham's pills, was in keeping with that of British "grocery" products. In each case there was special packaging, a brand name, and a commitment to advertising. Indeed, Chandler classified soap (which I included in Chapter 9 as a grocery product) as a consumer chemical. The goods were similar.[114] By contrast, most German medicines—from Salvarsan to Codeine—were marketed by the producer through doctors and hospitals.[115] The Swiss Hoffmann–La Roche & Co. sold through the same channels as the Germans. Burroughs, Wellcome had a line of ethical drugs distributed through professionals, but its patent medicines were retailed without prescription.

The medicines all had trade names. As early as 1912, the American Pharmaceutical Association provided a forum for a debate over the coined trade name in physicians' prescriptions versus the true chemical name. That year Anthony Gref (of Bayer) and Herman Metz (of Hoechst) were the principal advocates of "a crusade to arrest and convict druggists selling substitutes for advertised branded chemicals."[116] Clearly, in remedies—from the "miracle" medications (such as Salvarsan)[117] to the nostrums—European companies were present in America, but they were far more significant (that is, they captured a larger portion of the total market and set an example to be copied) in ethical drugs than in the household cures, where American competitors proliferated.[118]

Fine Chemicals

Foreign companies sold and produced in the United States various "fine chemicals," a term that covered everything from the coal tar medicinals (that I have already discussed) to aromatics. In this category—making flavors and scents—were Fritzsche Brothers, Fries Brothers, and Maywood Chemical Works, each of which had German connections. Fritzsche Brothers was established in New York in 1871 as a sales branch of the Leipzig firm Schimmel & Co.[119] At the turn of the century Dr. Harold H. Fries became the U.S. sales representatives for his German uncle. Both Fritzsche Brothers and Fries Brothers moved from selling to manufacturing in the United States. In the early twentieth century Fritzsche Brothers made "fruit esters," while Fries Brothers manufactured vanillin, saccharin, and other similar products in New Jersey. Fries Brothers had French ownership (by Société Chimiques des Usines du Rhône), as well as the German ties.[120] In addition, the German-owned Maywood Chemical Works produced vanillin in America before 1910.[121] Some of the output of these firms seems to have been trademarked and to be "consumer chemicals" (saccharin was sometimes classified as a "medicine").

The largest of the foreign-owned fine-chemical manufacturers in the United States was clearly Heyden Chemical Works, legally a wholly owned subsidiary of the German enterprise Chemische Fabrik von Heyden, administratively a branch office. Like many such businesses, it had started as an importer of its parent's products. In the 1890s it registered in the United States a number of trademarks, including Sucrol, Alcose, Zuckerin, and Heyden-Sugar. In 1900 it purchased from Fritzsche Brothers a factory in Garfield, New Jersey (Fritzsche Brothers moved to Clifton, New Jersey, where it resumed manufacture). Heyden Chemical Works made salicylic acid (an intermediate for medicines, dyes, and aromatics) and saccharin.[122] In 1902, as a response to pressure from the German sugar beet interests, a German law prohibited domestic manufacture of saccharin; German makers of the sweetener established factories in Switzerland and the United States.[123] Heyden Chemical Works (and Fries Brothers too) apparently began U.S. production of saccharin almost immediately after the German ban.

Perhaps an equally significant reason for German investment in the U.S. production of saccharin was the start of this country of such manufacture by a new American firm, Monsanto, formed in November 1901. German makers of Monsanto's intermediates tried to stop Monsanto by curtailing supplies. Monsanto then turned to the Swiss company Chemische Fabrik vorm. Sandoz for know-how and also for imported intermediates. According to a Monsanto history, at this point the Germans inaugurated the manufacture of saccharin in New Jersey and dropped the price sharply. For Monsanto, it seemed a "losing fight," with bankruptcy imminent. Only after Monsanto diversified and introduced other products such as caffeine, vanillin, and phenacetin did its survival prospects improve.[124] When saccharin output was forbidden in Germany, one German firm, Fahlberg, List & Co., was exempted and allowed to continue to produce there for medicinal purposes.[125] This company had a 100 percent–owned U.S. subsidiary, which also came to make the sweetener in the United States.[126] Almost overnight America had a number of saccharin producers.

Also in fine chemicals was the largest manufacturer of synthetic perfumes in America before World War I, the Haarmann–de Laire–Schaefer Company, which was jointly owned by the German firm Haarmann & Reimer and the French de Laire interests. It sold trademarked products.[127] In 1914 Antoine Chiris, of Grasse (the perfume center of France), who had for many years been represented in the United States by a sales agent, decided to make aromatic chemicals in America; the House of Chiris bought thirteen acres in Delawanna, New Jersey, and started to build a factory—which would open in November 1914.[128] In short, in a range of fine chemicals, from flavors to sweeteners to perfumes, foreign enterprise made important direct investments in the United States.

Heavy Chemicals

According to L. F. Haber, the premier U.S. enterprise in heavy chemicals was the General Chemical Company, organized in 1899 as a merger of twelve producers of sulfuric acid. Just as in England, where the formation of the giant United Alkali Company (in 1891) had been the response by Leblanc producers to the "menace of ruinous competition from the new Solvay process," so too in the United States "the ominous competition of the Badische contact process forced a number of American sulfuric acid makers to join forces more or less unwillingly." Initially, General Chemical tried to circumvent Badische patents; whereupon Badische brought an infringement suit, which was settled out of court. In 1906 General Chemical secured a license from Badische for its contact acid process. The American sulfuric acid industry "grew up." Whereas General Chemical was from its origins American owned and remained so, a number of other enterprises in this country's heavy chemical industry were foreign owned, with British, Belgian, and German companies well represented. One—the British-owned Ducktown Sulphur, Copper and Iron Company, Ltd.— was an innovator in sulfuric acid production. The others made a range of products not in General Chemical's repertory.[129]

Ducktown Sulphur, Copper and Iron Company, Ltd., mined and smelted in eastern Tennessee. Its smelter (along with that of the American-owned Tennessee Copper Company) emitted sulfurous fumes that killed the vegetation in neighboring areas. Protests were intense from Georgia farmers, who brought the companies to court in 1905. In response the two firms—with the Ducktown one in the lead—constructed in 1908 the largest sulfuric acid unit in the world (see Chapter 8, note 37). New technology was used. What had once been a waste and a pollutant was salvaged and became a commercial product.[130]

The growth of other facets of American heavy-chemical production was truly rapid and dramatic. In *Mineral Industry, 1892* Francis Wyatt, commenting on the backward position of America in dyestuffs, stated more broadly, "The American chemical industry is of proportions so insignificant as to be almost a negligible factor, and gives us no voice in fixing the market values of either alkali, soda salts, [or] bleaching compounds." Wyatt concluded that "the American chemical trade has grown to be the prop and mainstay of the United Alkali Company of Great Britain!"[131] A decade later these quoted remarks would be overtaken by extraordinary developments. Not only had General Chemical emerged as a giant enterprise but also, stimulated by foreign investment, numerous products in the heavy-chemical industry had come to be made in the United States. In 1914 the statement that the American chemical trade was in any way beholden to United Alkali Company in Great Britain would have been bizarre—so much had times changed.

The United Alkali Company, Ltd., had been promoted in 1890 and registered in February 1891 in Great Britain; at origin, it was the world's largest chemical firm, with forty-eight British factories. Most of the facilities it merged employed the Leblanc process of making alkalies, a process that contemporaries realized was "not destined to rule much longer."[132] The modern alkali industry had dated from the late-eighteenth-century discovery by the French chemist Nicholas Leblanc of a method of making soda ash by treating common salt with sulfuric acid and heating the product with limestone and coal. The process—used at most of the United Alkali Company factories—had remained unchallenged until 1863, when Ernest Solvay, son of a Belgian salt refiner, developed an ammonia soda process and formed Solvay & Cie. By the 1870s Solvay's method was achieving acclaim, and the Belgian had licensed companies in France and England to manufacture under his direction. Alkalies were essential not only in textile production but also in the glass, paper, soap, and other industries. Solvay's ammonia soda process was a modern continuous-flow operation, which provided the Leblanc batch-process producers with stiff competition.[133]

In the United States, as noted in Chapter 10, Rowland Hazard (1829–1898), a Rhode Island textile manufacturer, recognizing the importance of alkalies, had decided to finance an ammonia soda plant if he could acquire the American rights to Solvay's method. Hazard visited Ernest Solvay in Belgium, obtained his agreement, and in 1881 incorporated the Solvay Process Company in New York.[134] Solvay Process became the pioneer producer of alkalies in America. Solvay & Cie., in Belgium, according to its established practice, did not charge the U.S. firm royalties, but instead acquired almost half the voting stock of the new enterprise.[135] Solvay & Cie. required its American affiliate to submit to Brussels every month a detailed tabulation on all its operations, presented on large, standardized report forms. Other Solvay & Cie. foreign affiliates followed the same procedure.[136] Thus, from its origins, Solvay Process Company was part of a multinational enterprise, headquartered in Brussels.

Solvay Process in 1881 had a capital of $300,000. Rowland Hazard was president.[137] William Cogswell, who had earlier operated a mine for Hazard in Missouri, became the general manager.[138] The new company built its plant near Syracuse, New York. The construction was supervised by Belgian and French engineers, and all the plans came from Solvay & Cie. in Brussels.[139] Four Americans traveled to Solvay & Cie.'s Dombâsle (France) works for training.[140]

Solvay Process Company selected Syracuse, New York, as a site for its new facility because of nearby large deposits of limestone and salt brine springs as well as abundant water from Lake Onondaga. Finally, in January 1884 Solvay Process produced its first soda ash.[141] That year its capital was raised to $500,000.[142] During the 1880s its plant was enlarged and new products added: bicarbonate of soda (1888), caustic soda (1889), and a dense soda for the glass industry (1890).[143] In all of these developments, Solvay Process shared freely in the innovations of Solvay units abroad. An American Solvay engineer described the interactions: "Because of the very liberal policy of the interchange of ideas . . . all the Solvay plants [worldwide] cooperated toward this perfection [of the processes] and one could say that the engineering skill of the entire world was utilized in bringing each piece of apparatus used in the process to a state of efficiency and perfection that benefitted the whole industry."[144]

Because Solvay Process Company was at origin the sole producer of alkalies in the United States, its earliest competition came from imports. Yet annually U.S. imports of caustic soda and other products fell as Solvay Process Company's Syracuse plant raised its output. In 1894 Solvay Process added to its product line sodium sesquicarbonate, which sold as Solvay Snowflake Crystals (an early detergent); in 1895, precipitated hydrated calcium sulfate for the paper industry; and in 1897, calcium chloride.[145] As production rose, costs declined. In 1895 Solvay Process built a second plant in Detroit to produce soda ash (production began in 1897).[146] Even before the Detroit works started, despite some new rival producers, Solvay Process remained the largest manufacturer of soda ash in the United States. In 1896 it employed 3,000 men.[147] In 1900 Solvay Process Company's share in the American soda ash market was 90 percent.[148] By 1905 its Syracuse facility was the biggest soda factory in the world.[149] Solvay Process Company's capital by 1911 had been increased to $10 million.[150]

Meanwhile, to obtain ammonia, in 1892 Solvay Process had built a by-product coke oven in Syracuse; again it was the pioneer in America, "saving vast quantities of materials previously wasted in beehive coke ovens, resulting in many new and important products and providing a foundation for the organic chemical industry." The first such oven had gone into production in Europe in 1882.[151] The Americans used the European technology, and in 1895 Solvay Process spun off a new firm, Semet-Solvay Company, to construct and to operate by-product coke plants. It is not clear how Semet-Solvay was owned, but the Belgian Solvay & Cie. may have had an interest in this new venture.[152] One writer calls Semet-Solvay a "subsidiary" of Solvay Process.[153] By 1914 Semet-Solvay had constructed over 1,000 ovens in the United States. It became the first company in this country to produce pure grades of benzene, toluene, and solvent naphtha. In 1900 it had built a plant at Syracuse to obtain benzene and toluene from crude light oils recovered from coke-oven gas. In 1910, with the General Chemical and Barrett companies as its partners, it organized Benzol Products Company to manufacture aniline oil and aniline salt at Frankford, Pennsylvania.[154]

Between 1900 and 1914, Solvay Process Company met competition from new U.S. producers. Its U.S. success had encouraged others to enter the industry, and its share of the U.S. market in soda ash declined from 90 percent (1900) to 46 percent (1914).[155] Nonetheless, in 1914 both Solvay Process Company and its spin-off, Semet-Solvay Company, were clearly still giants and very much in the vanguard of the American chemical industry. Both were innovators in the creation of American production. Their international connections were vital in their development.

Before Solvay Process had been formed in 1881, Solvay & Cie.'s British affiliate, Brunner, Mond, had assumed that it would market in England and the United States, leaving the Continent to other Solvay companies.[156] Accordingly, Brunner, Mond had watched the plans for Solvay Process with apprehension. In the mid-1880s Brunner, Mond had larger sales (exports) in the United States than in the United Kingdom. In 1885 it made a written agreement with the Belgian Solvay Company (Solvay & Cie.) that the United Kingdom and North America were the British firm's territory.[157] In 1886 Brunner, Mond held with its exports 37 percent of the U.S. alkali market. This was before United Alkali Company was formed, but the latter's predecessor companies (the Leblanc makers) captured even more—48½ percent. In that year the fledgling Solvay Process Company's sales based on U.S. output had constituted a mere 14 percent of the total; nonetheless, as this firm's output expanded, obviously its market share would grow.[158] In 1887 Brunner, Mond acquired $200,000 (par value) of the shares of Solvay Process. I have not determined whether these shares were a new issue or from whom they were acquired. They represented, however, a recognition in Brussels by Solvay & Cie. that Brunner, Mond would be giving up part of the American trade to Solvay Process.[159] At that time, Brunner, Mond signed an agreement with the Hazard family that gave the latter a permanent, irrevocable proxy for the voting rights conferred by Brunner, Mond's stock holdings.[160] In 1887 the Belgian Solvay & Cie. remained a major shareholder in Solvay Process Company.[161]

After 1887, by a series of agreements, the British Brunner, Mond reluctantly but steadily relinquished its American business to Solvay Process Company, relying, as the former's historian would write, for its U.S. profits on its share holdings rather than on exports from the

United Kingdom.[162] For a while, to be sure, Brunner, Mond had sought to continue to export to the United States, sharing the U.S. alkali market with its British competitors and Solvay Process,[163] but by the start of 1889, John Brunner wrote to Ludwig Mond that "any increase of sales by the Solvay Process Co. of alkali in any shape comes into competition with us."[164] Then, with the McKinley tariff (1890) and even more the Dingley tariff (1897), the duties on alkalies became so high as to make British output no longer competitive.[165] Brunner, Mond saw the handwriting on the wall, and in October 1895 Solvay Process Company became the agent for Brunner, Mond in the United States. Solvay Process confined its sales to the United States and did not sell in the "territory" of other companies in the Solvay group.[166]

During the period 1900–1913, as Solvay Process Company's market share in the United States declined because of the competition from a number of new U.S. producers, its "European masters" grew uneasy.[167] By 1913 five firms in the United States made ammonia soda; Solvay Process was still the largest. [168] Semet-Solvay ranked supreme in American industry in its field.[169] Rough calculations, based on data in W. J. Reader's history of Imperial Chemical Industries (I.C.I.) and on other information from the I.C.I. archives provided me by Reader, indicate that of the 137,309 shares of Solvay Process stock outstanding in 1914, Brunner, Mond & Co. owned 23,886 shares and Brunner, Mond "individuals" held 438 shares, totaling 24,324 for the British group, or 17.7 percent. Solvay & Cie., Brussels, had 63,000 shares, or 45.9 percent. The bulk of the remainder was in the hands of Americans, the Hazard family and William B. Cogswell.[170]

In modern terms, Solvay Process Company would be called a joint-venture. It was majority owned abroad, but since the Hazard family voted the Brunner, Mond stock, "control" was in American hands. The initiative to establish this enterprise had come from the United States. The international interchange of technological information proved formidable. An engineer explained that every month each Solvay plant "exhibited" to each of the other plants (in Belgium, England, France, Russia, and so on), its basic technical operating data for the preceding thirty days. Each technical staff had the latest operating data from every other plant in the system, presented on the standard form. Annually an international committee of the principal Solvay engineers met in Brussels to discuss mutual problems. Visits between factories were encouraged, and research results provided to all Solvay plants. Everyone knew everyone else. The main office of

Solvay & Cie. in Brussels served as a clearing house.[171] To repeat, Solvay Process Company was part of a multinational enterprise, with Solvay & Cie. at the center.

By 1914 the American-owned Michigan Alkali[172] at Wyandotte, Michigan, had become Solvay Process Company's principal competitor in the United States.[173] Michigan Alkali was founded in the 1890s by J. B. Ford, an innovator in the American plate-glass industry, who recognized the need to supply his glass works with soda ash. Ford hired men trained at the Brunner, Mond ammonia soda plant in England to run his business.[174] Michigan Alkali had the audacity to export caustic soda, which upset British producers.[175]

A second U.S. competitor of Solvay Process was the Mathieson Alkali Works,[176] established in 1892 to produce caustic soda and soda ash at Saltville, Virginia. Its founders were Americans who, like Michigan Alkali, used British talents, bringing in Thomas T. Mathieson, son of Neil Mathieson, to run the plant. Neil Mathieson & Co., Ltd., had been an important British producer of ammonia soda; its factory at Widnes (in Britain) had in 1892 just been sold to United Alkali Company, Ltd. Accordingly, the new American enterprise was able to acquire the Mathieson name.[177] In 1894 Mathieson Alkali Works obtained U.S. rights to Hamilton Y. Castner's electrolytic cell for the production of caustic soda and chlorine. In the winter of 1896, the firm opened a new plant at Saltville, Virginia, where the first bleaching powder was made in the United States by this process.[178] The historian of Imperial Chemical Industries writes that the British firm Castner-Kellner Alkali Company, Ltd., had shareholdings in the Mathieson Alkali Works.[179] I do not know the extent of the British investment or when it originated.[180]

Mathieson Alkali Works built in 1896–97 (started up in 1898) a new electrochemical facility at Niagara Falls to take advantage of the cheap power there; it dismantled its Virginia bleaching-powder plant, transferring that production to Niagara Falls.[181] In 1900, for the operations at Niagara Falls, Mathieson Alkali Works organized the Castner Electrolytic Alkali Company (which two years later would be described as "the American representative of the Castner-Kellner Co. of England").[182] The enterprise was one of the first five in the new U.S. electrochemical industry of the Niagara Falls area. It was, however, not alone in this innovating group in attracting foreign capital. Two more of the original five entries into the Niagara Falls area involved foreign investment: one was the Niagara Electro Chemical Company and the other was Oldbury Electro-Chemical Company.[183]

Niagara Electro Chemical Company (formed in 1895) had its origins in using Castner's technology in producing sodium as a reducing agent to obtain aluminum. As noted in Chapter 7, Deutsche Gold-und Silber-Scheideanstalt (DEGUSSA); its American subsidiary, the Roessler & Hasslacher Chemical Company; and the British firm Aluminium Company, Ltd. (after 1900, Castner-Kellner Alkali Company, Ltd.), formed Niagara Electro Chemical Company, which manufactured metallic sodium and cyanides that were key to the gold recovery process. Later Niagara Electro Chemical would also produce hydrogen peroxides and peroborates.[184] Niagara Electro Chemical was part of a German group in the United States that included the Roessler & Hasslacher Chemical Company (in 1914, about 75 percent owned by DEGUSSA).[185] The Roessler & Hasslacher Chemical Company marketed DEGUSSA's products in the United States, represented DEGUSSA in the Niagara Electro Chemical Company, and also had its own facilities; in addition, it held a sizable interest in the Perth Amboy Chemical Works, incorporated in 1903, with a capital of $400,000 to manufacture formaldehyde and wood distillation products. Of 4,000 shares in this firm, Roessler & Hasslacher owned 1,960, and a similar amount was held by a German company, Holzverkohlungs Industrie, A.G. (which was closely associated with DEGUSSA); the casting vote, residing in the remaining 80 shares (owned by DEGUSSA), was given to Roessler & Hasslacher.[186] In 1914 Roessler & Hasslacher had a capital of $1.3 million. With its various involvements, it had become a leader in the new American electrochemical industry.[187] The Perth Amboy Works, the Roessler & Hasslacher Chemical Company, and the Niagara Electro Chemical Company were managed as a unit.[188]

Oldbury Electro-Chemical Company, incorporated in November 1896 and a subsidiary of the British enterprise Albright & Wilson, Ltd., was another of the five innovators in the electrochemical industry at Niagara Falls (though with a more limited product line). Albright & Wilson, Ltd.'s, senior executives made annual trips to America to check on its subsidiary's progress. In September 1897 Oldbury Electro-Chemical Company began to produce white phosphorus at Niagara Falls by the electric furnace method. Its initial market was the U.S. match industry. For many years Albright & Wilson had exported to the United States. It had decided to manufacture, because of the growing protectionist sentiment in America. In 1900 the company bought three U.S. competitors (Allen, Moro-Phillips, and Rancocas) and shut them down. At its own Niagara Falls plant, it added new products—chlorates, potassium perchlorate, sesquisulfide, and red phosphorus. With cheap power its costs were considerably under those of its British parent.[189]

Also in the new electrochemical industry and in response to the Dingley tariff, between 1898 and 1910 additional foreign-controlled companies started to produce in the United States.[190] In 1898 the giant United Alkali Company set up a U.S. manufacturing subsidiary. From its origin in 1890–91, United Alkali had paid special attention to the American market, appointing exclusive agents in 1891 to sell its bleaching powder and in 1892 to sell caustic soda.[191] It met both U.S. competition and high tariff barriers. Owing to the duty on potassium chlorate, United Alkali resolved to build a chlorate plant in this country. It sent a "scouting party" to the Midwest and acquired a property in Detroit. Then, after further investigation, it chose Bay City, Michigan, 108 miles north of Detroit, as its production site: there were a good brine bed and nearby coal supplies, and wages were lower than in Detroit. United Alkali formed North American Chemical Company in April 1898, and work on its new plant started that month. (Construction costs came to about $1.25 million.) Production of potassium chlorate began at Bay City in November 1898. The principal sales were to the American match industry. By 1904 the firm had also begun to produce sodium chlorate. The subsidiary offered competition to Oldbury Electro-Chemical as well as to several American firms.[192]

Another foreign entry into heavy chemicals in 1898 was a branch plant of the English-owned and incorporated, but Canadian-based, Electric Reduction Company, Ltd. (E.R.C.). Its principal plant was located in Canada. It started to manufacture at Ogdensburg, New York, hypophosphites of lime, potash, and soda from imported white phosphorus because of the U.S. tariff on hypophosphite. A year later (1899), however, E.R.C. decided to remove the facility to Canada, since high manufacturing costs at Ogdensburg offset the advantage of being inside the U.S. tariff wall.[193]

Although most foreign investors in the chemical industry started new operations, some took over and operated existing facilities. In 1900 two Americans had established Roberts Chemical Company to produce at Niagara Falls by electrolytic processes chlorine and caustic potash from imported muriate of potash. The potash had to be purchased from Germany; in 1910 (as noted in Chapter 8) its Austrian-controlled (Hermann Schmidtmann group) German supplier gained control over Roberts Chemical Company through a mortgage given by the latter in order to secure its raw material. The new owner—Kaliwerke Aschersleben—was represented in the United States by International Agricultural Corporation (I.A.C.). I.A.C. organized the German-owned (beneficially Austrian-owned) Niagara Alkali Company on March 11, 1910, to acquire the assets of Roberts Chemical. Niagara Alkali became the largest manufacturer of caustic potash in the United States; it continued to rely on German raw materials for its production. The firm also produced chlorine gas, the raw material for liquid chlorine.[194] By 1911 it was producing both solid and liquid chlorine.[195]

Likewise, in heavy chemicals, the Goldschmidt Detinning Company had begun to manufacture in the United States. Formed in 1908, it was a joint-venture between Th. Goldschmidt, Essen, Germany, and the American Can Company. In exchange for its chlorine detinning technology, Th. Goldschmidt obtained $1 million in common shares (that is, a one-third stake in the $3 million capital) of the new detinning company.[196] Goldschmidt's detinning process required liquid chlorine, and in October 1909 this firm at its own new works in Wyandotte, Michigan, had been the first to produce liquid chlorine in the United States. Wyandotte was chosen for the site of the new plant because Goldschmidt Detinning needed to purchase gaseous chlorine from the Pennsylvania Salt Manufacturing Company's facility in that city. Goldschmidt Detinning's chlorine liquefaction plant was designed by and used the equipment of Badische Aniline und Soda Fabrik, for which the latter was paid with $100,000 preferred and $50,000 common shares in the Goldschmidt Detinning Company. Goldschmidt Detinning's new metal scrap plant was at Chrome (later renamed Carteret), New Jersey. This factory made the first anhydrous tin tetrachloride produced in the United States, which, as noted in Chapter 10, found a ready market with silk dyers; the New Jersey plant commenced production in January 1910. The Goldschmidt firm opened still a third plant (in 1912) in East Chicago, Indiana, which used another new process—an alkaline detinning one.[197] This multiplant firm was, in short, an innovator in the American chemical (as well as metals) industry.

In 1908 the American law firm Cravath, Henderson & de Gersdorff organized the German-American Coke & Gas Company on behalf of the Oberschlesische Kokswerke und Chemische Fabriken, A.G., "to manufacture coke and gas and deal in its by-products."[198] The German parent had a capital of about $8.5 million and employed 2,200 workers in four tar-distillation and roofing-paper factories.[199] It was among the top fifty companies in Germany—ranked by assets.[200] I know nothing about the activities of its American subsidiary.[201]

In short, the foreign presence in the United States in heavy chemicals (including electrochemical processes) comprised the Belgian Solvay & Cie., the British producers (Castner-Kellner Alkali; Brunner, Mond; United Alkali; Albright & Wilson); the Germans (the DEGUSSA group and Th. Goldschmidt), and the Austrian Schmidtmann's potash-related venture. Badische had a number of licensing arrangements, at least one involving minority shareholdings. In 1899 only 3

percent of the chemicals made in America were by electrical processes. By 1914 the figure was 15 percent.[202] Foreign investments,
technology, personnel, and business operations had a formidable
impact on this transformation. Hamilton Castner was an American,
but his know-how came to the United States via British firms. Other
contributors to U.S. developments in heavy chemicals were primarily
German, Belgian, and British. A completely new American-based
heavy-chemical industry had been created.[203]

This industry came to be criss-crossed with a net of business agreements defining markets and relating to patent use. United Alkali;
Brunner, Mond; and Solvay were associated by interconnections that
embraced their U.S. subsidiaries. Castner-Kellner Alkali was linked in
another series of accords with United Alkali; Brunner, Mond; Solvay;
and DEGUSSA that likewise enveloped the U.S. affiliates. Worldwide
market- and technology-sharing pacts were the norm.[204] Occasionally
a U.S. company broke ranks. In 1910 John Brock of United Alkali
visited America on behalf of the English Caustic Soda Makers Association, hoping to find a way to curb U.S. soda exports (as noted
earlier, Michigan Alkali—an American-owned enterprise—was exporting). Brock got nowhere. He learned that with the U.S. Justice
Department's antitrust investigations, it was an inappropriate time
for Americans to make such an agreement.[205]

From a virtually nonexistent heavy-chemical industry at the start of
the 1890s, import substitution had taken place on a grand scale by the
early 1900s, so much so that American-owned companies had even
begun to export. Stimulated by foreign investment, by 1900 and even
more so by 1914, America had a viable heavy-chemical industry. By
far the largest and most successful of all the foreign investments in
heavy chemicals was that in Solvay Process Company—but it was by
no means alone.

Other Chemicals

In other facets of industrial chemicals, foreign direct investments also
existed. For example, in 1895 Dr. Carl von Linde, of Munich, had
made the first successful commercial machine for liquefying air. Earlier he had set up the German firm Gesellschaft für Lindes Eismachinen. In 1886 Brin Oxygen Company had been formed in England; its
name was changed in 1906 to British Oxygen Company, Ltd.; Carl
von Linde became a director, and the German Linde company came
to own 25 percent of the British firm's shares. In 1906 Carl von Linde
traveled to the United States and, with a group from Cleveland, Ohio,
associated with National Carbon Company, organized the Linde Air

Products Company. The latter hired the Britisher Cecil Lightfoot (whose father, T. B. Lightfoot, was a director and important investor in British Oxygen Company) to install the first Linde equipment in Buffalo. Other installations followed. It seems likely that Carl von Linde, or his German company, held a minority interest in Linde Air Products Company (which would—subsequent to our period—become part of Union Carbide).[206]

A British company, International Paints, was reported to have opened a Brooklyn, New York, plant in 1901. Likewise, in 1913 Hugh and J. C. Rollin, partners in the Hedworth Barium Company, Ltd., of England (the world's largest manufacturer of barium peroxide), organized the Rollin Chemical Company, which built a plant in Charlestown, West Virginia.[207] There were other such miscellaneous foreign-owned chemical companies as well.

Some Generalizations

To conclude, by 1914 few branches of the U.S. chemical industry were untouched by foreign direct investment. No other American industry was as influenced by European business enterprises. All the principal German chemical companies were present in the United States, as were most of the leading British and Belgian firms in this industry. Swiss and French chemical concerns were also in evidence, in far lesser roles. In explosives, the investments by Swedes, Britishers, and Germans had been abortive thrusts, and U.S. corporations remained supreme. In dyestuffs and drugs, it was otherwise. German marketers of dyestuffs dominated the American trade. In medicines, Bayer and Merck ranked as key manufacturers in the United States. Hoechst had patents and trademarks on Salvarsan and Novocaine, scientifically advanced pharmaceuticals on the research frontier. These German firms were in first place in their particular product lines. Burroughs, Wellcome and Beecham's were well established in America in the drug business, albeit they had many American competitors. In fine chemicals, a panorama of producers from abroad marketed and manufactured in the United States, with the German Heyden Chemical Works among the most significant. A new U.S. industry had emerged in heavy chemicals: Solvay Process Company was the giant in U.S.-made soda products. General Chemical, the largest enterprise in heavy chemicals, was American, but it employed Badische patents, licensed by representatives of the foreign investor. Of the totally new electrochemical industry in Niagara Falls, three of the initial five innovating entries were investors from abroad (from Germany and Britain). The first liquid chlorine made in the United States was produced by an affiliate of a German firm. A German scientist participated in the development of oxygen production in America; his technical assistance appears to have been accompanied by direct investment. Across the board, the impacts—especially those of the German firms—were formidable.

Despite the German enterprises' clear preeminence, the role of other nationalities should not be ignored. British companies were present in various capacities. The Belgian Solvay & Cie. was key. The Swiss J. R. Geigy had investments. French firms were involved, for example, in electrochemical processes (in aluminum and alumina), in flavors (Société Chimiques des Usines du Rhône), and in perfumes (de Laire). The aluminum and alumina venture (discussed in detail in Chapter 8) was, to be sure, short-lived—and the French fine-chemicals makers were on the periphery of the basic American chemical industry; nonetheless, the French did have stakes.

Clearly the impacts of the European investors were various, and it is necessary to ask why it was that in the important sector, dyestuffs, Americans remained dependent on German imports (albeit sold directly to American producers by subsidiaries or affiliates of German firms), whereas in an equally significant branch of the chemical industry, alkalies, American and foreign investors together substituted U.S. manufacture for the products previously imported. Both aspects of the chemical industry attracted foreign investment, but the investors followed different paths in the years 1875–1914.

In this case the principal reason for the divergence seems to lie in the specific attributes of these facets of the chemical industry. As one economist wrote, dyestuff production involved "processes [which] are painfully detailed and elaborate, highly trained and highly paid labor being applied slowly and carefully to a variety of products."[208] Dyestuffs required an understanding of chemistry that was much more complex than in the field of alkalies. Research and development were critical. Writing shortly after World War I broke out in Europe, Arthur D. Little (a chemist, trained at MIT, and founder of Arthur D. Little, Inc.) discussed the unattractiveness of the dyestuff industry to U.S. businessmen and explained that (1) the revenues of Sears, Roebuck alone were greater than the total sales of all the German dye companies put together, and Sears, Roebuck's last special dividend had been twice that of the German dyemakers' total dividends for 1913, and (2) in 1913 "the Ford Motor Company, with one standardized product, did a greater annual business than all the German chemical plants with their 1,200 products and earned four times their combined dividends while paying three times their wages."[209] With these industry characteristics, when dyestuff imports were readily available, there was little incentive for U.S. import substitution. More-over, and equally important, U.S. buyers of dyestuffs successfully opposed high American tariffs, fearing a rise in the price of this essential, because dyestuff makers in this country were not viewed as competitive.[210]

By contrast, the alkali industry was energy intensive. Production was appropriate in America, with its abundant natural resources and cheap sources of power. Americans (either domestic or foreign inves-tors) could produce alkalies at a far lower cost than they would pay for the imported product. Perhaps, too, the initiative of Rowland Hazard, an American textile manufacturer turned alkali producer, offered an important stimulus for the new U.S. alkali industry.[211] Tariffs—advocated by textile makers who envisaged the lower Amer-ican costs once U.S. production developed—safeguarded the infant industry's survival. New firms entered, protected by the duties im-posed.

Williams Haynes suggests, along the same line, that shipping ex-penses may have been another consideration. Dyestuffs had a much lower weight-to-value ratio than alkalies. Not only was U.S. alkali production lower in cost than that of enterprises abroad (because of available raw materials and cheap energy), but also the high raw material content of imported alkalies bore the added brunt of steep transportation charges.[212]

Both dyestuffs and alkalies were important inputs for American industry. Both involved patented products and processes and high technology. Later explanations of why U.S. dyestuff manufacture did not develop to any great extent in the pre–World War I years have frequently looked at the so-called anticompetitive tactics of German firms, which were said through their "ruthless" marketing strategy (including control over patents, dumping, systematic price cutting, full-line forcing, bribery, and dishonest and deceptive labeling) to have suppressed American efforts to develop manufacturing. It has even been proposed that there was a plot between the German gov-ernment and that nation's dyestuff companies to keep America mil-itarily defenseless![213]

How do we evaluate these arguments? German patents, it is true, did preclude U.S. production of similar products *without a license*, but licensing was an available option.[214] I find it hard "to blame" German predatory trade practices for the absence of a sizable American dye-stuff industry in this period. Had Americans found it profitable to manufacture dyestuffs on a large scale before 1914, they would have entered this industry, getting licenses (as they did in other branches of the chemical industry), forming joint-ventures, demanding and obtaining high protective tariffs, and designing around patents.[215] Patents did not bar the rise of a domestic alkali and bleaching-powder industry. Purchasing agents and dyers who took bribes would have been discharged. The crucial point neglected by such critics is that imports of dyestuffs from Germany could and did in the pre–1914 years offer U.S. industries low-priced and excellent-quality supplies. As noted, transportation costs on dyestuffs were not high relative to their price. American customers liked the low-cost German dye-stuffs—"dumping" or not. Germans had expertise and produced what was wanted. The labels were not deceptive; trademarks identi-fied companies with international reputations. I find it easy to reject the argument of a German government plot to destroy U.S. military potential; a U.S. explosives industry existed and was not suppressed.

It has also been proposed that Americans, overwhelmed by the superiority of the Germans, did not have the capability or knowledge to make dyestuffs. This does not seem valid. Technical know-how moved easily internationally. As F. W. Taussig later put it, "not lack of aptitude for chemical industries as such, not great scarcity of trained chemists or lack of ability on their [Americans'] part, but the character of the dyestuffs part of the [chemical] industry mainly ex-plains the pre-War situation."[216] The later rapid development of this industry under World War I conditions provides support for Taus-sig's argument. Americans were not competitive in price or in quality with the giant German works of Bayer, Badische, and Hoechst. Al-though the German factories were large, they were not characterized by "mass production," which was Americans' forte. German inves-tors, as long as they could continue to export, had no motivation to develop comparable dyestuff plants in America. By contrast, alkalies were a mass production industry.

The same point can be made vis-à-vis the general electrochemical developments, which relied on cheap power resources and econo-mies of scale. Americans (and foreign investors)—especially with the cheap power at Niagara Falls—could carry forth such operations at low cost. Tariffs gave the new industry its chance. Foreign investors were innovators in American electrochemical production. In short, in the late nineteenth and early twentieth centuries, a U.S. chemical industry emerged; the explosives, alkalies, and electrochemical branches of this industry developed rapidly in a robust manner; dyestuff manufacture did not—because of the nature of this part of the chemical industry and because of the relative German and Amer-ican advantages in production.

My text has neglected the numerous U.S. chemical companies founded by European immigrants and the presence of immigrant managers in existing firms. It has also not included details on the complex transatlantic licensing and cross-licensing that did not involve foreign investments but restricted markets. So too it has not emphasized the urgent attempts by many American-owned ventures to liberate themselves from dependency; the early history of Dow Chemical Company (incorporated in 1897) was, for example, one of frequent combat with foreign competition.[217] Monsanto, as I did note, tried desperately to steer a distinct course as it met fierce German rivalry.

Rather, I have sought to show the ubiquitous and vital contribution of European direct investment in supplying America's chemical needs and, in certain branches, in stimulating U.S. output and providing the first U.S. output of high-technology products. In chemicals, in general, perhaps because this was a modern science-based industry where the Germans in particular had major strength, foreign direct investment was highly significant. I have identified more than fifty chemical enterprises involving foreign direct investment in the United States before 1914. Investments from Europe in chemicals were—as I have shown—part of the expansion of multinational enterprise. The big six dyestuffs manufacturers, as well as Merck, Heyden, DEGUSSA, and Th. Goldschmidt from Germany; Geigy from Switzerland; Solvay from Belgium; and Courtaulds; Brunner, Mond; Burroughs, Wellcome; Beecham's; Albright & Wilson; and United Alkali from Britain introduced into America not just capital but men, skills, scientific knowledge, technical ability, marketing experience, patents, processes, trademarks, and goods, along with multinational business organization. This was far more than simply "finance." Unlike the American railroads or many mining company promoters, who went to Europe to raise money, in these cases the initiative frequently (albeit not always, as in the important case of the Solvay company) came from abroad. Foreign firms extended their operations over borders. Unlike the cattle companies and breweries, and like many of the branded food and thread companies, these were not free-standing enterprises.[218] These European-headquartered chemical companies successfully entered the United States to sell through owned distribution channels; if it was impossible for them to maintain their markets through exports alone, typically they manufactured in the United States. The role of the European chemical concerns was critical in the creation of the modern American chemical industry.

12.

Other Manufacturing

Foreign companies invested in the United States in making and selling farm equipment; automobiles; rubber tires; rubber (and rubberlike) goods other than tires; nonelectrical machinery and equipment, and instruments; electrical machinery and equipment; civilian and military transportation equipment; and a range of other products. Herein I cover a wide variety of foreign manufacturing enterprises in the United States and consider investments not discussed earlier. Foreign investors in these "other manufacturing" activities made direct investments. Unlike in the case of textiles or chemicals, many of the firms discussed here were in industries in which American businesses were very active abroad. Nonetheless, the foreign direct investors either found some special niche in the U.S. market or, alternatively, the investments were short-lived. Toward the end of this chapter, I discuss foreign portfolio investments in these sectors.

Farm Equipment

In farm equipment, where Americans excelled, foreign direct investment in the United States was limited to one Canadian firm, Massey-Harris Harvester Company, the Dominion's most important farm equipment manufacturer.[1] Massey-Harris was a large exporter; in 1900 some 40 percent of its output went abroad, but *not* south of the border to the United States, because a high tariff protected American producers from foreign competition.[2] Massey-Harris' first U.S. investment was in 1906, in a 21,000-acre tract of timber in Arkansas, designed to assist the company when Ontario's stands of high-grade hardwood would be exhausted. Wood was needed in its farm implement construction.[3]

416

In 1902 the just-formed giant International Harvester had begun to erect a plant in Canada, where its manufacturing of harvesting and tillage implements started in 1904.[4] At that time, the competition notwithstanding, apparently Massey-Harris had no thoughts of countering with its own U.S. factory. Yet in 1905–1909, when International Harvester moved to build or to buy plants in Europe,[5] Massey-Harris saw its large export markets threatened and did contemplate following suit there; it decided not to do so. Nonetheless, the Canadian manufacturer watched closely the activities of International Harvester, and in 1906, when it seemed that Canadian tariffs might be lowered (and U.S.-made farm equipment could then flood Dominion markets), Massey-Harris had explored the possibility of constructing a factory in Niagara Falls, New York, to serve both U.S. and Canadian customers.[6] When the Canadian tariff of 1907 retained protection for national industry, such a venture seemed unnecessary. In 1910, as talk of "reciprocity" (a reduction in both U.S. and Canadian tariffs) persisted, Massey-Harris executives were once more considering a U.S. factory so as "to remain in a position to meet lower American manufacturing costs, freight differentials and other [U.S.] competitive advantages." Massey-Harris worried that with reciprocity, American farm equipment would have an advantage in the Canadian market. The Canadian firm wanted a low-cost American base from which to compete.[7]

Accordingly, on November 14, 1910, the shareholders of Massey-Haris met and authorized a stock issue of $1 million to finance the purchase of the Johnston Harvester Company, one of the oldest and largest independent farm-implement makers in the United States with factories in Batavia, New York. Before the end of 1910, Massey-Harris had acquired control of that company (roughly 11,000 of the approximately 15,000 shares outstanding). The Johnston Company did an annual business of about $2.5 million, two-thirds in the United States and the balance in Europe. It had approximately 1,300 employees. This was Massey-Harris' first farm-implement–manufacturing facility outside Canada; it complemented the Canadian enterprise's existing factories, adding needed extra capacity, while at the same time it represented Massey-Harris' first serious attempt at entry into the U.S. market.[8]

In 1910 Massey-Harris also acquired the Deyo-Macey Company of Binghamton, New York, and, using the latter's equipment, began production of stationary gasoline engines,[9] apparently selling the output in Canada.[10] Two years later (in 1912) it decided to manufacture such engines in the Dominion and made plans to dismantle the Binghamton facility and transfer the machinery to Toronto.[11]

Meanwhile, Massey-Harris' acquisition of the Johnston Harvester plant in Batavia (far more important than the Deyo-Macey venture) received substantial press coverage in Canada, where Conservatives labeled it an example of what would happen were Canada to lower its barriers to trade (the nation's firms would leave). Thus, whereas Americans ratified the reciprocity treaty in 1911, Canada rejected the treaty and Canadian tariffs remained.[12]

In 1913 U.S. duties on agricultural equipment were removed. Aside from some transportation-cost savings, the Johnston plant turned out to have none of the predicted cost advantages over Massey-Harris' Canadian factories *in* the U.S. market, and because of Canadian tariffs it could not supplement Massey-Harris' output and sell to the Canadian farmer! Nonetheless, as noted, the new acquisition did give the Canadian firm its initial sales in the United States; having made the commitment, Massey-Harris remained in the U.S. market and, in fact, expanded its operations in Batavia, New York, doubling the capacity of the malleable foundry there and bringing the labor force up to about 2,500 men. To finance the growth, it raised the capital of the Johnston Company from $1,500,000 to $1,750,000. In 1910–1914 the venture proved profitable.[13] The Massey-Harris investment in Johnston Harvester was probably the largest Canadian direct investment *in manufacturing* in the United States in the pre–World War I years.[14]

Bicycles and Automobiles

Very minor British stakes existed in the U.S. bicycle industry. In 1896 a British enterprise took over the American firm Crawford Bicycle Company.[15] Likewise, in the 1890s, as noted in Chapter 7, British investors and a German one (Mannesmann) had short-lived interests in making seamless steel tubes used in bicycle construction.[16] Foreign direct investments in U.S. car production were more important.

In the early twentieth century, at the same time as U.S. automobile output grew rapidly and as American automobile makers started to invest abroad, foreign direct investments came into the United States from France, Germany, and Italy. In 1900 the United States was a net importer of passenger cars, mainly from France. To sell their products, a dozen French manufacturers had agencies in New York by 1904;[17] in 1906 Renault opened a sales branch in that city.[18] Wealthy Americans admired and purchased the hand-crafted luxury European models, since the early American-built cars seemed, and were, inferior. Yet behind a 45 percent tariff, spurred by rising domestic competition and the vast home market potential, American passenger-car makers raised their output and, as important, improved the quality of domestic units. By 1907, measured by both quantity and dollar value, the United States had become a net exporter of automobiles.[19]

When their imports from Europe faced the high duties and competing U.S. car production, some foreign companies responded. As early as 1901–02, a French car, C.G.V. (Charron, Girardot and Voight), was manufactured at the plant of the Rome Locomotive Company, in Rome, New York; the four-cylinder U.S.-made C.G.V. sold for $5,000.[20] In 1905 the American Locomotive Company purchased a license to build Berliet automobiles in the United States; between 1905 and 1908 it produced a car known as the American Berliet and then in 1909–1913 as the Alco. The Berliet firm received 500,000 francs, which it invested in its Lyon, France, factory. I have no evidence that Berliet maintained any interest in American Locomotive.[21]

Meanwhile, and much more significant, the foundations for the manufacture in the United States of the "Mercedes" were being created. In 1888 the American piano maker William Steinway had visited Stuttgart, Germany,[22] and in October of that year Gottlieb Daimler authorized Steinway to form the Daimler Motor Company, to be incorporated in New York.[23] Only a few years before, in 1885, Daimler had developed gasoline engines and started to use them experimentally in motor boats, motorcycles, and automobiles; in 1887 Daimler had licensed Panhard & Levassor in France to produce these motors. Under his 1888 arrangements with Steinway, Daimler would receive sixty-six shares of the capital stock in the new American firm Daimler Motor Company (apparently a minority interest); William Steinway would be the principal owner. In the United States Steinway was deputized to act for the German inventor, who agreed to transfer to the New York company "all letter patents granted to me by the United States of America Patent Office prior to the date of this agreement [October 6, 1888], and any reissues, renewals of such patents or letter patents granted me by the United States, thereafter."[24]

Subsequently, on January 26, 1889, the Daimler Motor Company came into being with an authorized capital of $200,000.[25] Initially it sold imported motors for boats and stationary engines. Then in 1891 William Steinway arranged for the National Machine Company in Hartford, Connecticut, to produce the Daimler motors.[26] Soon Steinway suggested that manufacture take place at a proposed Daimler Motor Company plant, to be located near the Steinway piano factory in Steinway, Long Island; sometime in the early 1890s, two blocks from the piano works, the new Daimler Motor Company facility began production.[27] The latter also had a New York City showroom.

An advertisement in the *American Art Journal* of April 2, 1892, read: "Daimler Motor Company—manufacturers of Daimler Motor Launches and Gas Engines, 111 E. 14th Street, New York, next door to Steinway Hall."[28]

In 1893 Karl Benz installed a representative in New York,[29] and that year an enthusiastic Gottlieb Daimler visited America, bubbling with plans for further business expansion. The Panic of 1893 intervened. William Steinway died in 1896. After his death the Daimler Manufacturing Company was organized (in 1898).[30] The "parent" company was Daimler Motoren Gesellschaft of Untertuerkheim, Germany,[31] although there appears to have been a Steinway family interest in this American subsidiary.[32] Gottlieb Daimler died in 1900.

In its early years, the Daimler Manufacturing Company made motors and delivery trucks at the Long Island factory and imported from Europe Daimler, Mercedes, and Panhard & Levassor automobiles.[33] Then in 1905 the Daimler Manufacturing Company built its first "American Mercedes," a "faithful reproduction in materials, workmanship and design of the foreign car." The U.S.-made Mercedes sold at $7,500, compared with $10,500 for the imported one.[34] Because of the high U.S. tariff, in 1905 the Germans had finally begun automobile manufacture in Long Island.

Italian cars also came to be made in America. In 1906 Giovanni Agnelli (head of Fiat) visited the United States and opened a sales branch in New York City;[35] three years later, in 1910, the Fiat Company, which produced luxury cars in Turin, Italy, started to manufacture automobiles in the United States, in Poughkeepsie, New York.[36] By 1913 a catalog description of the Panhard & Levassor company indicated that it had works in Paris, Reims, and New York.[37] Other French enterprises may also have manufactured in the United States before World War I. The U.S. tariff made imports uncompetitive.

In 1913 the Daimler Manufacturing Company's Long Island factory burned, and for three reasons it was not rebuilt: (1) the outbreak of war in Europe in 1914; (2) the rise between 1905 and 1913 of a highly developed and fully competitive U.S. domestic industry; and (3) the apparent failure of the U.S.-made Mercedes to achieve the high quality of its German counterpart.

The United States in 1913 lowered its import duties on automobiles priced under $2,000 from 45 to 30 percent. This had no influence on the decision not to rebuild the Mercedes factory, because that expensive car would still be subject to the 45 percent levy. Indeed, all the European models were high priced. If foreign automobile makers were to reach the American consumer, they had to manufacture within the country. In 1914 French cars were made in America, and the Fiat Motor Company factory at Poughkeepsie was still in operation. That year U.S. automobile sales totaled 548,139 units, and America imported a mere 708 cars.[38]

No record exists (or can be reconstructed) of how many French, German, or Italian cars were made in the United States between 1900 and 1914. In each case (Berliet excepted), the European manufacturer seems to have had, at minimum, a minority interest in the U.S. producing venture. Undoubtedly the total U.S. output of these foreign automobiles was tiny vis-à-vis that of American automobiles. In the early years of the U.S. automobile industry, numerous companies competed, many with very small scale production and short lives. What is important is that with the high tariff, the growing demand, and the emergence of the American industry, European leaders crossed the Atlantic to substitute U.S. manufacture for exports. As noted, without exception these companies made luxury models in the United States, as at home. By contrast, in 1914 U.S. automobile producers offered both expensive and low-priced units, and Ford had begun to specialize in the mass-produced, cheap car. No European maker sold anything comparable. In August 1914 an American consumer could buy a Model T Ford Roadster for a mere $440.[39] The market it reached was entirely different from the elite one supplied by the Europeans. In essence, by 1914 the foreign direct investors' role in the U.S. automobile industry was minuscule.

Rubber Tire Manufacture

Europeans undertook rubber tire manufacturing in America—and bicycle tires provided the original impetus for the investments. Within a month of the 1889 formation in Dublin of the Pneumatic Tyre and Booth's Cycle Agency, Ltd. (the predecessor of Dunlop Rubber Company), that firm resolved to establish branches and agents worldwide. In 1889 it shipped its first pneumatic-tired bicycles to the United States, and its representatives visited America.[40] In 1891 Harvey du Cros, Sr., on behalf of the firm, licensed Alfred Featherstone of Chicago to make Dunlop bicycle tires in the United States, a licensee that was replaced in 1893, when du Cros's son, Harvey, Jr., arranged for the organization and incorporation in New Jersey of a subsidiary of the British firm, the American Dunlop Tire Company; it produced Dunlop bicycle tires in New York.[41] In 1899 Richard Garland, then the manager of the Canadian branch of the Dunlop firm, on behalf of some Toronto "capitalists" purchased the Dunlop rights in the United States,[42] which the group sold in 1900 to the Rubber Goods Manufacturing Company, a firm that by 1905 was controlled by the United States Rubber Company.[43]

When in 1900 the Rubber Goods Manufacturing Company acquired the entire capital stock of American Dunlop Tire Company, along with all its patents and contracts, the American Dunlop Tire Company was, according to the historian Victor S. Clark, "the most important maker of bicycle and vehicle tires in America."[44] The Rubber Goods Manufacturing Company also purchased the Hartford Rubber Works, and by 1903 this subsidiary was making and marketing a straight-side tire under the Hartford-Dunlop name.[45] At some point subsequent to 1903, the tire was marketed under the name of Dunlop.[46]

As the passenger-car industry emerged in the United States and in Europe, the owners of the British Dunlop regretted their sale of the U.S. rights. At home, in Great Britain, Dunlop now produced automobile as well as bicycle tires and saw the potential for a sizable expansion in worldwide demand. In 1909 Harvey and William du Cros (sons of Harvey, Sr.) and L. M. Bergin—all of the British Dunlop company—went to America, hoping to reacquire from the United States Rubber Company the right to manufacture and to trade in America under the Dunlop name. Bergin later recalled, "I failed to get the use of the Dunlop name from them, but got a raising of the embargo on trading there as far as tyres were concerned—but still without the right to use the name 'Dunlop.' " Thus stymied, the British Dunlop did nothing.[47]

In March 1913 the United States Tire Company (a subsidiary of the United States Rubber Company) placed a full-page advertisement in the popular *Saturday Evening Post* for the "Genuine Dunlop Straight-Side Tire." The advertisement stated that for ten years the firm had been making and selling this tire. "Notwithstanding the fact that it has never been advertised, our Dunlop sales during this time have shown constant growth. Last year alone, this increase amounted to over 600 percent." The advertisement said nothing about the existence of a British Dunlop company and admonished, "Remember, the Genuine Dunlop straight-side Tire is made only by the United States Tire Company."[48] The British must have been perturbed; in 1914 the management of the British Dunlop resumed its efforts to recapture the U.S. rights to the Dunlop name.[49] The largest tire manufacturer in the United States was the United States Rubber Company,[50] and it retained the use of the Dunlop name in America (later—outside our period—the British Dunlop would reacquire rights to its own name).[51]

Meanwhile, Michelin—Dunlop's most important European rival—was expanding internationally. Michelin's first factory in France had been built in 1832. It began to produce pneumatic tires in that country in 1891[52] and started a factory in London in 1904; in Turin, Italy (to serve Fiat) in 1906; and in Milltown, New Jersey, U.S.A., in 1907.[53] Undoubtedly its entry into U.S. production (along with the expanding demands for tires) had stimulated Dunlop's management's attempts to reenter the U.S. market. Also, as noted, in 1906 Agnelli had established a Fiat sales branch in New York; probably Fiat's and Michelin's U.S. endeavors were interconnected, since they clearly were associated in European business.

Michelin bought the plant and machinery of the A & V Tire Company in Milltown, New Jersey. Its new venture was capitalized at $3 million. At once it started to construct eight new buildings at Milltown, based on the plans of the company's branch factory in Turin, Italy.[54] In August 1912 Marcel Michelin, a nephew of the parent company's chief executive, Edouard Michelin, called on the American expert on scientific management Frederick Winslow Taylor, who was in Plymouth, Massachusetts, for the summer holidays. Because his wife was ill (and he could not leave her), Taylor asked his colleague H. K. Hathaway to show Marcel Michelin a number of shops run under the Taylor system. Hathaway, in his travels with Marcel Michelin, also visited the Michelin works at Milltown.[55] As for Marcel Michelin, he was impressed with the American factories he saw and wrote Taylor, "I realize what an enormous advantage can be obtained by working in accord with such a method." He continued this September 11, 1912, letter: "I am going back to France now, and am quite prepared to discuss, with my uncle, the way in which we will apply your method to our particular branch of industry."[56]

As a follow-up, on September 28, 1912, Hathaway dispatched to Marcel Michelin a twelve-page report, recommending the course to pursue should the company decide to use "Scientific Management" in the management of "your works." He wrote:

Mr. Taylor is of the opinion that in undertaking the introduction of Scientific Management in your works the best course to follow would be to first do so in your American plant at Milltown, N.J., sending over to this country at least two first class men to assist, under the direction of a competent consulting engineer, in the development of the system, and in that way secure the thorough training that would enable them to introduce the system into your works at Clermont [France].[57]

Hathaway then mapped out a three-year program.[58]

The Frederick W. Taylor Papers contain no indication as to whether the procedures were adopted; they do, however, reveal that in the 1920s the Michelin Company *in France* was enthusiastic about scientific management. What is important is that by 1912 Michelin had a large manufacturing plant in the United States, was producing automobile tires, and had branch sales offices for its output in sixteen American cities, from New York to Seattle, from Detroit to New Orleans.[59] A member of the Michelin family, J. H. Michelin, was in charge in this country.[60] The firm remained a manufacturer in Milltown, New Jersey, until 1930.[61]

When one recognizes the presence of the French and Italian automobile makers in the pre-1914 U.S. market, the Michelin entry is less surprising than it seemed at first blush. The venture seems to have been more successful than that of the automobile firms. With Southern Aluminium, the Michelin Company ranked as a major French direct investment in America; unlike Southern Aluminum, this was not a short-lived involvement. By 1914, since the United States was the center of the world's automobile industry, it is little wonder that the two leaders in European tire making wanted to sell and to manufacture here. Michelin's pre–World War I multinational expansion was far more impressive than that of any other American (or European) rubber tire producer.[62]

Other Rubber and Rubberlike Goods

Foreign companies made rubber goods other than tires in the United States. In January 1891, at the time when British companies were "taking over" many American industrials,[63] the New York Belting and Packing Company, Ltd., London, was organized and its securities offered to the British public. The new enterprise bought an existing American one, which had been started in 1846 by John Cheever and Henry Durant[64] and included a factory in Sandy Hook, Connecticut (licensed under Charles Goodyear's original rubber patents), that made transmission belting, rubber packings, sheet rubber goods, hose, and waterproof rubber blankets. In 1869 part of the manufacturing of this business had been moved to Passaic, New Jersey. By 1891, when the British takeover occurred, the U.S. company had three large factories: two in Connecticut and the one in New Jersey.

In January 1891 the prospectus of the New York Belting and Packing Company, Ltd., was presented to the British public. Its predecessor's founder, John Cheever, was listed as a director. Another director was Samuel Pope, who was coincidentally chairman of the English Association of American Bond and Shareholders. The offering came shortly after the Baring Crisis. I know nothing of its success (or failure), but in 1892 August Belmont (the Rothschilds' representative in the United States) approached Charles R. Flint, a U.S. promoter who had that year put together the United States Rubber Company; Belmont suggested a consolidation of manufacturers of *mechanical rubber goods* to include New York Belting and Packing Company, Ltd., which he described as principally British owned. Accordingly, that year (1892) the Mechanical Rubber Company, with its headquarters in Passaic, New Jersey, came into being; it bought the New York Belting company, along with several other American firms. At this point ownership clearly passed back to the United States. When in 1899 the Rubber Goods Manufacturing Company was formed (the firm that acquired American Dunlop in 1900), it obtained the stock of the Mechanical Rubber Company. As noted earlier, the Rubber Goods Manufacturing Company would in turn be acquired by the United States Rubber Company.[65]

Another British entry in rubber-type goods production was R. & J. Dick Company, a Scottish enterprise involved in shoe manufacture, making uppers of leather and soles and heels from guttapercha (a rubberlike gum). R. & J. Dick in Britain had introduced in 1885 a "driving belt" made from balata, like guttapercha a vegetable gum. This belt compared favorably with those made of leather, having "exceptional tensile strength, pliability and frictioning." R. & J. Dick had exported the belt, and in 1909 the company opened a sales branch in the United States. Since imitators in the United Kingdom and others producing behind the U.S. tariff competed with their own, brands of balata belting, R. & J. Dick's management decided that to be competitive, the firm would have to make the belts in America. Accordingly, it built a factory in Passaic (completed in 1911) that produced the Dickbelt, a replica of the one it made in Scotland. The firm's first U.S. manager was J. F. Linn, who for many years had been at the London offices of R. & J. Dick.[66] Yet a third British-owned belting company in the United States was British Belting and Asbestos, Ltd., of Cleckheaton, Yorkshire, which set up a U.S. subsidiary in the late nineteenth century and began production, probably in Paterson, New Jersey, in 1904, making belting and brake linings.[67]

Nonelectrical Equipment and Machinery, and Instruments

Numerous German direct investments were undertaken in the United States in facilities to manufacture nonelectrical equipment and machinery, and various instruments, including welding apparatus (Atlantic Welding Corporation), refractories and gas retorts (Didier-March Company),[68] gaskets (Goetze Gasket and Packing Company), chocolate- and cocoa-producing machinery (J. M. Lehmann Company), "gas air" mixing machines (Selas Company), brewing equipment (Simon, Buhler & Bauman), and engineering instruments (Schaeffer & Budenberg Manufacturing Company). The *Alien Property Custodian Report, 1918–1919* contains a long list of machinery and instruments companies, mostly small direct investments, controlled by German capital.[69] No other nationality had nearly as many investments in these industries.

Several German machinery makers were especially important and thus deserve attention. In 1914 Orenstein & Koppel–Arthur Koppel, A.G., Berlin, was a giant German enterprise with worldwide business, ranking among the top twenty industrials in Germany in 1913.[70] The historian Jürgen Kocka describes German machinery manufacturers as making equipment, usually to customer specification. "Their competitive strength lay in technical virtuosity."[71] Orenstein & Koppel fits that description. It manufactured in the United States a wide range of light railway equipment and some other industrial machinery. It began business in 1897 in a town thirty-five miles from Pittsburgh that it named Koppel, Pennsylvania. In 1909 it obtained authority from the state of Pennsylvania to conduct business under the name of Orenstein–Arthur Koppel Company. It organized a collection of subsidiary companies, built a number of factories in Koppel, and owned over 650 acres; in its company town it produced for industrial customers, such as Westinghouse, U.S. Steel, and Du Pont. The enterprise opened branch offices in Pittsburgh, New York, Chicago, and San Francisco. This German-owned American manufacturer did not depend on any German inputs. Moreover, it exported from Pennsylvania to the multinational enterprise's markets in the West Indies and South America.[72]

U.S. Steel in 1906 learned that Dr. Heinrich Koppers of Essen, Germany, had invented a new, efficient coke oven. At the invitation of U.S. Steel, Koppers came to the United States in 1907 and established a branch of his German firm. In 1912 H. Koppers Company was formed and continued building in this country coke ovens for American steel companies. The Koppers firm would in time become an important competitor of Semet-Solvay (see Chapter 11)—but that came later, after 1914.[73]

Meanwhile, in 1872 the German firm Gasmotorenfabrik Deutz, with Gottlieb Daimler as works director, constructed a factory in Deutz, Germany, to manufacture the Otto engine. In 1875 that company developed its first gasoline engine. Gasmotorenfabrik Deutz started a branch in Philadelphia in 1875 to build and sell stationary gas engines.[74] In 1914 Germans owned a majority interest in the Locomotive Superheater Company, which produced patented superheaters for locomotives that were used on practically all the heavy hauling locomotives in America.[75] Another German machinery manufacturer was the Schutte & Koerting Company of Philadelphia, owned by Ernest Koerting of Hanover, Germany, whom the Alien Property Custodian later (and with obvious exaggeration) described as the Andrew "Carnegie of Germany." Koerting's son-in-law, Adelbert A. Fischer, had come to the United States in 1904 to start this factory. The firm owned and controlled the exclusive rights to patents covering automatic ejector and injector boiler valves, used in most American warships.[76]

In 1911 the Norma Company of America was incorporated in New York. Norma Compagnie, GmbH, of Cannstadt, Stuttgart, Germany, owned all the 1,000 shares (original capital, $100,000); it paid cash for 10 shares and transferred patents and trademarks for the remaining 990 shares. In November 1912 the German Norma company lent $200,000 to the U.S. business, which began to manufacture bearings in 1913. The U.S. firm used German-made equipment to do so. Norma Bearings were precision ball bearings employed in high-speed machines.[77] Stahlwerk-Becker Aktien Gesellschaft, Willich, Germany, established Becker Steel Company in the United States, which marketed (and may have manufactured under the parent company's patents) twist drills, boring and reaming tools, and ball bearings.[78]

Yet another German machinery manufacturer in the United States was Gebrueder Stollwerck, Cologne. I have already noted its American chocolate business. This chocolate maker had also become involved in Germany in producing automatic vending machines and then the machinery for automatic restaurants—"automats," as they were called in the United States and Germany. The firm's German automatic vending machine company was Deutsche Automatengesellschaft Stollwerck & Co., formed in 1894. Before 1894, however, the Stollwercks had started to sell the machinery in the United States—machines that dispensed not only chocolates but chewing gum as well. The Stollwercks manufactured the custom-made machines in Brooklyn. In 1911 a new enterprise—Autosales Gum and Chocolate Company—was organized in New York "for the purpose of amalgamating vending, manufacturing and operating the leading chewing gum and chiclet concerns." This company acquired the automatic vending machine "plants . . . and patents" in the United States of Deutsche Automatengesellschaft, Gebrueder Stollwerck, A.G., and three members of the Stollwerck family. It is unclear how this new venture was owned; according to a history of the German Stollwerck enterprise, the latter was a founder. The Autosales Gum and Chocolate Company had assets of $10.4 million (as of April 30, 1914). Its output represents the sort of specialized machinery making in which the Germans excelled.[79]

Kny-Scheerer Corporation (100 percent German owned) ranked as the largest seller and manufacturer of surgical instruments in the United States and had sizable exports. The U.S. firm was owned by Aktien Gesellschaft für Fein Mechanik (A.G.F.M.), which in 1896 had acquired the business from Richard Kny, employing the latter to manage the American subsidiary.[80]

When the Germans found their markets in the United States blocked by high tariffs and U.S. competition, frequently they vaulted the tariff barriers and invested. The British were often less aggressive, a phenomenon widely noted by contemporaries. Thus the Weir factory in the United Kingdom had had large sales in the United States and considered establishing a U.S. factory to bypass the 30 percent duty. An American firm, Worthington Pump, was supplying its U.S. shipbuilder customers; Weir directors discussed the loss of their market, but they did nothing. They did not meet the U.S. competition with a U.S. works. Lethargy appears to have been the explanation.[81]

In 1890 the Blake and Knowles Steam Pump Works, Ltd., was registered in England to acquire the entire capital of George F. Blake Manufacturing Company and Knowles Steam Pump Works, with three American plants. Its capital was £300,000. This appears to have been a free-standing firm—similar to ones discussed earlier.[82] In 1899 the newly formed International Steam Pump Company (ISPC) merged the Blake and Knowles Steam Pump Works, East Cambridge, Massachusetts, with a group of companies (including Worthington's enterprise) that together represented a great part of the American steam pump industry. Interest on ISPC's bonds was paid in London, Paris, and Amsterdam.[83] The European interest had become a portfolio one. E. Green & Son, Wakefield, England, manufactured an economizer to save on heat in boilers. In 1913 it employed 1,000 people at its British plant and was reported to have "branch factories" in the United States. These would be direct investments.[84]

The British had miscellaneous stakes in railroad equipment. British capital participated in making rolling stock in the United States, initially for the Atlantic and Great Western Railroad.[85] In 1889, according to the *American Iron and Steel Association Bulletin*, "English capitalists" bought "the vast car-wheel works and boiler and locomotive plants owned by John Bass, at Fort Wayne, St. Louis, and Chicago." The *Bulletin* reported that Bass had "done all the wheel and boiler work for several western railroads." His foundry and engine shops at Fort Wayne, Indiana, were described as a showcase, visited annually by "hundreds of tourists"; his plant was said to be the largest producer of railroad car wheels in the world. The *Bulletin* also added that Bass had major interests in iron and coal mines in Alabama that had been included in the English purchase.[86] I know nothing more on this.

The above notwithstanding, the scholar must look hard to uncover truly aggressive British companies in America in the engineering industries. One case, that of Howard & Bullough in textile machinery, was described in Chapter 10. Another important participant, albeit short-lived as a direct investment (as was frequently true of the British involvements), had an atypical genesis. On January 7, 1890, Fraser & Chalmers, Ltd., was registered in London to acquire an American company of that name and to erect a works *in England*.[87] Many years earlier (about 1849), two Scots, David R. Fraser (a mechanic and millwright) and Tom Chalmers (a foundryman), had emigrated to the United States, where in 1872 in Chicago they had organized Fraser & Chalmers to produce mining machinery. From its Chicago factory, Fraser & Chalmers supplied U.S. mining enterprises and by the 1880s had developed exports.[88]

With the expansion of diamond (and gold) mining in South Africa, the British Rothschilds and Wernher, Beit & Co. wanted to manufacture mining equipment in the United Kingdom for South Africa.[89] They contacted Fraser & Chalmers in Chicago, which was shipping to South Africa, and the result was the formation of Fraser & Chalmers, Ltd., London. Its initial board included E. G. DeCrano (of Exploration Company, Ltd., Rothschild interests), Robert English (a director of De Beers), and Julius Charles Wernher (later Sir Julius, of Wernher, Beit & Co.). Both the founders of the American business, Fraser and Chalmers, as well as Chalmers' son (William J.), joined the board of the new British parent company; Julius Wernher was chairman. Although shares were offered to the British public, the main interests in Fraser & Chalmers, Ltd., were retained by Wernher, Alfred Beit, and their nominees (who really held control); Rothschild nominees; Fraser; the Chalmers (father and son); and certain Frenchmen involved in South African diamonds.[90] Fraser & Chalmers, Ltd., acted as sales agent abroad for its Chicago Works while the new English factory (at Erith) was under construction. On its completion, the Chicago and Erith plants complemented each other in international business.[91]

In 1901 Edwin Reynolds of Edward P. Allis Company, Milwaukee, met with William J. Chalmers, by then president of the American subsidiary of Fraser & Chalmers, Ltd. The two men arranged a merger that year of Allis, the American Fraser & Chalmers, and two other smaller companies. The new Allis-Chalmers Company emerged. According to the latter's historian, William J. Chalmers had been eager to promote the merger because of the "poor business prospects" of the Chicago Works and its "serious financial difficulties";[92] this explanation is in sharp contrast with the report of the annual meeting (December 11, 1900) of the British parent, Fraser & Chalmers, Ltd., which indicated "satisfactory" progress in Chicago.[93]

When in 1901 Allis-Chalmers was formed and acquired the Chicago plant of Fraser & Chalmers, the latter's British parent obtained a "considerable amount" of stock in the new U.S. venture,[94] but not a controlling interest. In December 1905 Sir Julius Wernher reported at Fraser & Chalmers, Ltd.'s, annual meeting in London that the firm had two sources of revenue: (1) from "the American Company [Allis-Chalmers], in which we have a large preference shareholding" and (2) from "our works at Erith and the trades connected with it." Sir Julius reported to his shareholders that the Allis-Chalmers Company was doing badly: "We have very little control of the American business."[95] When the U.S. merger had occurred in 1901, William J. Chalmers had become a vice president of Allis-Chalmers, but his new American business associates came to dislike him, and, effective December 1, 1905, he resigned; the Milwaukee men assumed complete control.[96]

In November 1906 Allis-Chalmers arranged a $5 million short-term loan through the Deutsche Bank, and the latter's U.S. representative (Edward D. Adams) became chairman of the board of Allis-Chalmers Company.[97] After 1907 the financial condition of Allis-Chalmers weakened,[98] and finally in March 1912 it was reorganized and a receiver appointed that April.[99] Fraser & Chalmers, Ltd., opposed the reorganization and initiated legal proceedings that were apparently unsuccessful. Accordingly, the British parent reduced its holdings of Allis-Chalmers preference shares from 6,500 to 4,500, selling 2,000 shares.[100] It is unclear when Fraser & Chalmers, Ltd., sold the rest of its holdings, but it appears to have done so. In any case, as far as management was concerned, the British parent had for all practical purposes "disposed of its American business in 1901."[101] By 1914, if it retained any interest in Allis-Chalmers, the amount was small. Nonetheless, a 1953 typescript history of the American firm refers to the "friendly relations" between the two companies, presumably subsequent to the 1912 litigation.[102] The principal achievement of the investment by Fraser & Chalmers, Ltd., in the United States had been the transfer of American mining-equipment technology to the Erith works in England. The Deutsche Bank role in relation to Allis-

Chalmers is more obscure; it may well have been a purely financial one.

Cleona Lewis found that Claudius Ash, Sons & Co., Ltd., British merchants and manufacturers of dental materials, instruments, and appliances, had some kind of U.S. operations before 1914. I have been unable to identify these activities.[103] This would be a rare British investment in precision instruments.

In nonelectrical machinery and equipment, at least four important Swedish direct investments in American manufacturing existed. In no other industry were the Swedes more important. One stake was that of AB Gasaccumulator, which made lighthouse beacons (using acetylene gas). It established a U.S. manufacturing subsidiary in 1907, with a head office in Philadelphia. The automatic beacon was invented by a Swede, Gustaf Dalén, and was a unique product.

Two U.S. investments by Swedes involved companies associated with the prolific Swedish inventor Gustaf de Laval. De Laval Angturbin AB—founded in 1893—began, through its U.S. subsidiary (the De Laval Steam Turbine Company), to make steam turbines in Trenton, New Jersey, in 1901. Initially the turbines were installed in water-power plants, factories, and dairies. Around 1909 the development of reversible steam turbines made them applicable to ship propulsion.

Even earlier, in 1879, Gustaf de Laval had developed and patented a cream separator; he exported this product to the United States; and in 1883 he started a sales company in New York, maintaining a minority interest. In 1889 his Swedish firm—AB Separator—acquired a patent from a German engineer for "Alfa" separators. The very next year, AB Separator (later renamed Alfa-Laval) purchased all the shares of its American sales company and made plans to manufacture Alfa separators in Poughkeepsie, New York, where production began in 1892; by 1900 this American operation employed 1,000 workers. By about 1910 the subsidiary provided its Swedish parent with roughly 75 percent of the latter's profits (a temporary phenomenon, but an indicator of its significance). With the Alfa patent, the company had a major advantage and came to capture some 70 percent of the U.S. separator market in the dairy states and about 50 percent of the entire U.S. separator market. When in the early twentieth century its patent expired, the firm retained its first place in the American separator market, although by 1914, owing to new competition from both American and other Swedish producers, its market share dropped to 30 percent.

This brings us to a fourth Swedish investment in the United States.

It involved the prominent Wallenberg banking family in the cream separator industry in America. A member of that family (Gustaf Wallenberg) traveled to the United States, noting the success of Laval's Poughkeepsie venture. Accordingly, with the expiration of the Alfa patent, Gustaf Wallenberg formed a new American cream separator company, Empire Cream Separator Company (its exact date of origin is not known). In Sweden the Wallenbergs (the Stockholms Enskilda Bank) invested and arranged to dispatch Swedish personnel and machinery to the United States for the new business. At some point, probably in 1913, AB Baltic (founded in Sweden in 1904 and a competitor of Laval's in dairy equipment) acquired the Empire Cream Separator Company and its U.S. factory in Bloomfield, New Jersey. In 1913 the Swedish-owned Empire Cream Separator Company held about 7 percent of the total U.S. separator market, compared with the Laval subsidiary's 30 percent.[104]

In addition to these four Swedish-owned manufacturing facilities, AB Lux (founded in 1901 in Sweden to produce a kerosene lamp for outdoor lighting, used mainly in railroad yards) had a U.S. subsidiary, 1910–1920, which may have done some manufacturing in this country.[105] Also, in 1913 a syndicate, led by Marcus Wallenberg, Sr., of Stockholms Enskilda Bank (and including National City Bank and Brown Brothers, New York), provided financing for the new Swedish-controlled McIntosh & Seymour Corporation, which planned to manufacture and to sell reversible diesel engines patented by AB Diesels Motorer (the Wallenbergs had an interest in this Swedish company). McIntosh & Seymour Corporation held diesel patents for the Western Hemisphere plus all U.S. colonies and "interest spheres." Whether manufacture began before July 1914 is uncertain.[106]

Meanwhile, in 1911 Adolphus Busch (the American beermaker), who many years earlier had acquired Rudolf Diesel's original patents for America, went into a joint-venture with Sulzer Brothers of Winterthur, Switzerland, forming the Busch-Sulzer Brothers Diesel Engine Company, which built a new factory in St. Louis (where Busch's brewery was located) and made engines "patterned after the already proved Sulzer Brothers 'K' series." Sulzer Brothers apparently had an equity interest in this company (Robert Sulzer was on the board of directors); Busch, however, retained control.[107]

Despite these Swedish and Swiss investments and the handful of British ones, the Germans clearly led in direct investments in the United States in machinery and equipment, and instruments. The German leadership is not surprising. The Germans invested in those industrial activities in which they excelled—those requiring specialized technology (often patented) and a high degree of precision. Often they appear to have jumped the U.S. tariff barriers. Actually, two of the Swedish investments in the United States (in Alfa separators and diesel motors) and the Swiss one in diesel engines were based on German inventions.[108] Interestingly, however, absent from American investments were such prominent German machinery and equipment makers as Borsig (producers of locomotives), Humboldt, Maschinenfabrik-Augsburg-Nurnberg (M.A.N.), and many others. These had no special advantage in the United States.[109]

Electrical Equipment

Electrical as well as nonelectrical machinery and equipment attracted foreign direct investment in the United States. I have already noted (Chapter 11) certain foreign involvements in electrochemical enterprises. In the U.S. electrical industry (electrochemical industry included), high-technology, innovative German enterprises stand out as investors.

By the 1880s the electrical industry in Germany was dominated by two groups. The first, Siemens & Halske, founded in 1847, became involved in the installation of telegraph lines and the manufacture of cables and other equipment; later it moved into more branches of the electrical industry. The second, and newer, giant was started by Emil Rathenau and American Edison interests. Rathenau saw the Edison lamp at the Paris exposition of 1881 and wanted to introduce it into Europe. When in 1883 it appeared that Siemens & Halske would sue for patent infringement, the two German firms arrived at an understanding. Henceforth they remained distinct, but generally friendly.[110]

In 1883 Rathenau formed Deutsche Edison Gesellschaft to exploit Edison electric light patents in Germany.[111] Four years later, in 1887, his company's name was changed to Allgemeine Elektrizitäts Gesellschaft (A.E.G.). The chairman of the board of A.E.G. was Georg von Siemens, director of the Deutsche Bank and a cousin of Werner von Siemens, the chief executive of Siemens & Halske. As a result of the 1883 accord, A.E.G. and Siemens & Halske together owned Edison's German patents. The largest shareholder in A.E.G. at origin was Siemens & Halske. A.E.G. in 1887 was totally independent of American Edison interests.[112]

Meanwhile, a German immigrant to the United States, Henry Villard, set the stage for huge German investments in America. We encountered Villard in Chapter 4, as a representative of German bondholders, and in Chapter 6, in his role in steering German savings into the Northern Pacific and other railroads. According to his biographer, Dietrich G. Buss, from 1879 Villard had been closely associated with Thomas Edison.[113] After Villard had resigned from the presidency of the Northern Pacific in January 1884, he traveled to Germany, ostensibly to market Edison generating plants.[114] Instead, using Edison's name for entry, he met Werner von Siemens of Siemens & Halske and Emil Rathenau of Deutsche Edison Gesellschaft, and at the same time renewed his earlier acquaintance with Georg von Siemens of the Deutsche Bank.[115] Villard assisted in the negotiations that led in 1887 to the transformation of Deutsche Edison into A.E.G.[116]

Before that, however, in 1886 Villard returned to the United States as the representative of the Deutsche Bank and with the authority from Siemens & Halske to handle "exclusive production rights" for Siemens' armored cables and couplings.[117] With high U.S. duties, Villard suggested that Siemens & Halske manufacture their cables in the United States, and in April 1887 he tried to arrange for a U.S. factory to work the Siemens patents.[118] Villard thought the cable making would be undertaken by an Edison company, under license.[119] In the spring of 1888 Villard was back in Berlin to report to Siemens & Halske; what evolved was a radically different strategy. Villard proposed that he, using German monies, obtain control over the entire Edison business in the United States![120] He met with his friends at Deutsche Bank and at Siemens & Halske, as well as with Emil Rathenau at Allgemeine Elektrizitäts Gesellschaft, and obtained their support.[121]

By the late 1880s the German electrical industry was flourishing. It was therefore not out of keeping that Siemens & Halske, A.E.G., and the Deutsche Bank reacted favorably to Villard's plan. Villard then went to Edison, who—according to Buss—agreed, because "he chafed under the lack of working capital."[122] In April 1889 a new company, Edison General Electric Company, was incorporated in the United States. Under Villard's arrangements, Edison and Werner von Siemens would cooperate and exchange research as well as manufacturing know-how. "The new company will also hold licenses for all the valuable patents owned by Siemens & Halske in this country."[123]

In the Villard Papers, Buss uncovered evidence that Siemens & Halske invested $4 million in stock; A.E.G., $3.8 million; and the Deutsche Bank, $500,000—or a total of $8.3 million out of the $12 million capital of the new firm.[124] This was a formidable sum for a foreign industrial investment in 1889. The German investments were made on April 26, 1889,[125] that is, at the time of the establishment of the new Edison General Electric Company, which was, in short, at origin German controlled—by the two principal German electrical companies. The new enterprise had no foreign investments of its own. Edison, who had built up an international business, had lost control over his foreign activities and now, more than ever before, over his domestic ones as well.[126] Henry Villard (as representative of the Germans and the entrepreneur in this scheme) became the founding president of Edison General Electric Company.[127]

In April–May 1889 Villard proposed merging Sprague Electric Railway & Motor Company (formed in 1884) into Edison General Electric.[128] Frank Sprague had invented a streetcar motor, and his company had successfully installed a streetcar line in Richmond, Virginia. Siemens & Halske feared Sprague's competition in the *European* traction markets. Thus, acting in the interests of Siemens & Halske, Villard arranged to have Edison General Electric (Edison G.E.) acquire the potential rival,[129] and in 1889 Edison G.E. absorbed Sprague.[130] Edison G.E. was a giant business with some 6,000 employees (by 1890–91).[131] It was a German direct investment.

In 1890 the plans for Siemens & Halske's new U.S. cable factory (which had started the whole sequence that resulted in the large German investment) took form. On February 18, 1890, Siemens & Halske licensed its affiliate, Edison General Electric, to use its lead cable patent. The licensing agreement provided details on the construction, maintenance, and bookkeeping for a new factory, the designs for which were to be prepared by Siemens & Halske in Berlin. Edison G.E. agreed to pay for the machinery and equipment and the salary of a plant manager ($10,000 a year). Siemens & Halske was guaranteed 20 percent of the factory's net profits and was given free access to the factory's books.[132] The new facility was built in 1891 at the Edison works in Schenectady, New York.[133]

Villard's next step was to combine Edison General Electric with its most important American rival, Thomson-Houston; he intended to maintain control. To accomplish his goal he required additional funds, but his German backers were by this time unhappy with him (for reasons related to railroad matters). Villard went to J. P. Morgan for financing, and Morgan "turned the tables" on him and at the time of the merger obtained Villard's resignation![134] Edison G.E. and Thomson-Houston merged in 1892; and the General Electric Company was formed, headed by Charles A. Coffin, the former chief executive of Thomson-Houston. General Electric's capital at origin was $35 million.[135] Before the merger and reorganization (probably in 1891), the German investors had withdrawn completely, according to Matthew Josephson, at "a handsome profit of about 200 per cent."[136] Thus ended a major, albeit short-lived (roughly two years), German direct investment in America. The cable factory became part of General Electric's assets. A.E.G., which as I noted had been born as the "Edison" company in Germany, retained its close association with General Electric—directly, however, rather than through any Deutsche Bank connections. From its origin General Electric itself was American owned and controlled.

In the winter of 1891–92, apparently coincident with the Germans' withdrawal from Edison General Electric, Arnold von Siemens (Werner's son) traveled to America to study the possibility of "the exploitation of certain [Siemens] patents."[137] In 1892 von Siemens formed a new company, Siemens & Halske Electric Company of America. Although its initial management would be German, American joint-venture partners were at once included, and the president of the new affiliate was an American, O. W. Meysenburg.[138] Alfred Berliner from the Siemens & Halske's Berlin works became the factory manager. Siemens & Halske Electric Company of America built a plant in Chicago. Meysenburg, however, discharged Berliner, who would, incidentally, later rise to become the chairman of the board of management of the Siemens-Schuckert Werke in Germany.

In 1893 Wilhelm von Siemens (Werner's second son) visited Chicago for the World's Exposition and to inspect the firm's new Chicago works. He discovered that the affiliate "had assumed obligations which were far beyond its modest capital resources of half a million dollars." Wilhelm von Siemens and his American partners agreed to double the capital—to "overcome this post-natal crisis."[139] Siemens & Halske of America became particularly successful in making lighting equipment and selling it to breweries and other enterprises operated by German-born (immigrant) businessmen. The company expanded.[140]

Then in July 1894 its Chicago factory burned. Six months later Meysenburg arrived in Berlin with the proposal that Siemens & Halske of America buy the Grant Locomotive Works, in whose facilities the firm had taken temporary shelter. Meysenburg also suggested that the company build locomotives and that its capital be raised again, now from $1 million to $2 million. The Germans, busy at home and uncertain about the U.S. economy in the aftermath of the Panic of 1893, decided not to add to their investments. Accordingly, the American partners' share in the business rose and, as a historian of the House of Siemens wrote, "the American branch slipped out of the control of the Berlin Company."[141] In 1897 the capital of Siemens & Halske of America was again increased when the U.S. firm acquired the Pennsylvania Iron Works, "thereby being completely alienated from its original purpose." Siemens & Halske (Berlin) began to withdraw.[142]

On May 4, 1899, the Chicago attorney Levy Mayer announced that the Electric Vehicle Company had completed the purchase of the Siemens & Halske Electric Company of America. He reported that the American Siemens company had bought and enlarged the old Grant locomotive works in Chicago "a few years ago," that its plant covered seven acres, and that it had facilities for the employment of 2,000 men; Isaac L. Rice, president of the Electric Storage Battery Company and the Electric Vehicle Company, had been elected president of the American Siemens Company.[143]

In April 1900 (according to John Moody), General Electric acquired all the stock of the Siemens & Halske Company of America.[144] As the Germans had withdrawn, Siemens & Halske of America's competitive position had worsened.[145] In 1900 Siemens & Halske of America signed an adverse contract with the machinists' union. Testimony before the U.S. Industrial Commission on the Chicago Labor Dispute of 1900 revealed that as a result of the agreement the firm would not be competitive with eastern manufacturers.[146]

In 1903 Siemens & Halske, Berlin, desired to cancel its patent agreement with its former affiliate, Siemens & Halske of America, and to eliminate its name from that company. The earlier accord with the American firm meant that the Berlin firm could not manufacture under its own name, or manufacture at all, in America. In 1904, with new arrangements, it could manufacture in the United States under *another* name; it was also free to sell in America under its own name goods imported from Germany.[147] The German Siemens company historian believes the Berlin enterprise lost out because its U.S. affiliate's direction had been placed in the hands of a "foreigner" (an American) who went his own way. The historian thought Siemens should have insisted on its own management.[148] Having lost control, Siemens & Halske finally cut its ties completely. In sum, in the early twentieth century the two major German electrical firms, Siemens & Halske and A.E.G., both of which had briefly had significant direct investments in the United States, no longer held them.

In 1903 General Electric and A.E.G. agreed that A.E.G. would have much of Europe, Turkey, and Asiatic Russia as its exclusive territory, while General Electric would have the United States and Canada as its market area. This agreement was part of a set of international accords made by General Electric[149] that effectively insulated the basic U.S. electrical equipment market from foreign competition. After its abortive investment in Chicago, Siemens & Halske apparently turned its back on the U.S. market, at least for most of its products. I do not believe it was a coincidence that in 1903 Siemens & Halske, Berlin, sought to cancel its arrangements with its former affiliate, and A.E.G. made an international agreement with General Electric. In Germany, since Siemens and A.E.G. cooperated, the G.E.-A.E.G. pact undoubtedly influenced Siemens' role. Symbolic of relations between the two German giants, in 1903 Siemens & Halske and A.E.G., together in Germany, were founding the important Telefunken company.[150]

Siemens & Halske and its associated firm, Siemens-Schuckert, had a U.S. representative, Dr. Karl Georg Frank, who, when Telefunken built a wireless station in Sayville, Long Island (see Chapter 14), disbursed salary payments to Telefunken engineers.[151] Telefunken in America was, however, a mere shadow of the earlier, substantial German involvements. In 1912 an agreement including General Electric, A.E.G., and Siemens was drafted, covering patent exchanges, but the draft was never signed, apparently because Siemens wanted to bring in Westinghouse, whereas A.E.G. thought that such an inclusion would strengthen Westinghouse, which it opposed.[152]

Westinghouse Electric Company was by 1900 second only to General Electric in the American electrical industry. Early in its history it had embarked on extensive business abroad. In the summer of 1907, however, Westinghouse had faced difficulties and had required financial assistance; it sold in Paris and London some $2.7 million in ten-year collateral notes. No evidence indicates that the funds came from any existing European electrical companies.[153] There was *no* foreign direct investment in the Westinghouse company.

Foreign direct investments were present in highly specialized branches of the U.S. electrical industry—out of the general basic electrical equipment field. Robert Bosch of Stuttgart had invented and obtained patents on a magneto used for automobile ignitions.[154] In the early twentieth century, American companies imported Bosch's magneto; with the tariff, in 1906 Bosch recognized that production in the United States was desirable.[155] That year he formed Robert Bosch, New York, Inc. (soon renamed the Bosch Magneto Company). At origin, its capital was $25,000.[156] The year 1906 coincided with the time when the Daimler Manufacturing Company started to make the American Mercedes in the United States. Bosch's new enterprise was initially for sales only. In 1910 it began to manufacture.[157] By the summer of 1914, the Bosch Magneto Company had a combined capital and surplus that exceeded $6.5 million, a modern factory in Springfield, Massachusetts, and "branches" in Detroit, Chicago, and San Francisco. Its main office and its sales department were headquartered in New York City. In addition, it had agencies and supply depots in more than 100 U.S. cities. It produced the best-quality magneto in America and owned approximately 130 patents. It also acquired in 1912 controlling interest in the Boonton Rubber Manufacturing Company (of Boonton, New Jersey), America's largest maker of molded insulation, a product essential to the magneto industry. In May 1914 Bosch Magneto Company purchased for $750,000 in cash the Rushmore Dynamo Works at Plainfield, New Jersey (a plant it shut down and dismantled). In 1912 Bosch Magneto Company owned 900 out of 2,000 shares outstanding in a rival (also German-controlled) magneto firm, the Eisemann Magneto Company, founded by Ernst Eisemann & Co., GmbH, of Stuttgart. The Bosch company was the largest single shareholder in that firm. Together, by 1914 the two German companies, Bosch Magneto and Eisemann Magneto, produced more than half the magnetos made in the United States, dominating this important specialized industry.[158]

Another maker of electrical equipment in the United States was the Marconi Wireless Telegraph Company of America, incorporated in 1899 and controlled by British capital. It used the inventions in radio-telegraphy of the Italian inventor Guglielmo Marconi. Because the bulk of its investments related to communications, I will discuss them in Chapter 14 and merely note here that at least as early as 1905 Marconi of America was manufacturing in the United States apparatus related to radio communication. It came to make vacuum tubes and wireless equipment for installation on merchant ships at a plant in New Jersey.[159] Telefunken may have done some minor manufacturing for its new installation at Sayville, Long Island.[160] Of far less importance, a German-controlled firm, Submarine Wireless Company, also made wireless equipment (for submarines) in the United States.[161]

In an entirely different branch of the electrical industry, the Gramophone Company (set up in Britain in 1898) made a comprehensive agreement in 1901 with the Victor Company (organized that year in the United States). The accord stipulated that (1) the U.S. firm would supply the Gramophone Company with products under specified terms; (2) world markets would be divided, so there would be no competition; and (3) the British enterprise would provide 50 percent of the cost (up to $10,000) for an experimental laboratory in the United States, to be managed by Victor. The last provision meant that the Gramophone Company made a small investment in the United States, in exchange for which it appears to have obtained access to research results generated in America. It had no equity interest in the new facility. Gramophone Company's contribution was associated with the division-of-market relationships. Its stake posed no threat to

Victor.[162] Likewise, and possibly slightly more important, in 1912 Pathe Freres Phonograph Company was organized. It built a modern plant in Brooklyn to manufacture phonographs and records. It was an affiliate of Compagnie Générale des Etablissements Pathé Frères.[163]

In yet another line of electrical products, the Swedish L. M. Ericsson tried to enter the U.S. telephone equipment market. Ericsson had exported to the United States; he started a sales office in New York in 1902 and then a subsidiary, L. M. Ericsson Telephone Manufacturing Company (1904). The firm began to manufacture telephone equipment in 1907 in Buffalo, New York. The U.S.-owned Western Electric had, however, a virtual monopoly of this U.S. market (and a vast international business).[164] When L. M. Ericsson realized it could not compete, it changed the name of its American subsidiary in 1910 to Ericsson Manufacturing Company, stopped producing telephones and began making ignition devices for automobiles.[165]

In 1881 in England, W. O. Callender got patents for an insulated cable, and with his sons—Thomas, William, and James—formed in April 1882 the Callender's Bitumen Telegraph and Waterproof Company (later renamed Callender's Cable and Construction Company). The British firm obtained an American patent, which it sold in 1883 to the newly formed Callender Insulating and Waterproofing Company of the United States, in return for a 100 percent equity interest in the new firm, as well as $400,000 in bonds. The British parent provided the working capital, and W. O. Callender agreed that "he or his son with efficient assistance" would superintend the building and early management of a new factory in East Newark, New Jersey. The factory was built and provided cables for several installations, including, in 1885, the electric lighting of New Brunswick, New Jersey. The subsidiary was not, however, a financial success, and by 1889 it was in liquidation, another fleeting British investment.[166] For a time, in the 1890s, the Okonite Company, important U.S. manufacturers of insulated electrical wire and cable, was also under British control, again for a relatively brief period; by 1914 this firm was totally American.[167]

All these investments from Europe in the U.S. electrical industry were in "high-technology" products. Most (those in magnetos, wireless equipment, and ignition devices were exceptional) were short-lived. A.E.G. and Siemens' huge stake in Edison General Electric Company lasted a mere two years. Some companies (A.E.G., Gramophone Company) accepted divided world markets as a substitute for large investments in the United States. Siemens & Halske let its own American subsidiary slip from its grasp, as (in different industries) had Alfred Nobel, the Dunlop Company, and others. Long-distance management was difficult. Pathe Freres Phonograph Company would later (in 1921) go into receivership. L. M. Ericsson, which had multinational manufacturing operations and a unique product,[168] could not reach American buyers of telephone equipment, because of the entrenched position of Western Electric; instead, it turned to manufacturing ignition devices (until 1920, when it discontinued this operation as well). The Callender venture in the United States was a management failure.

Perhaps of most significance was the inability of the great German electrical companies—Siemens & Halske and A.E.G.—to obtain a strong position in America. This was, of course, in sharp contrast to the penetration of the U.S. market by the major German chemical enterprises. The basic reason for the difference seems to lie in the relative strength of the indigenous American electrical equipment industry compared with that of much of the American chemical industry. The explanation is not in the *German* industry, since the German electrical equipment manufacturers were very active in other foreign markets.[169] A second point is that although the Germans had temporary technological advantages—in cables, for example—these advantages could not be maintained when the firms invested in the United States. Americans from the start had had world leadership in the new electrical industry, and it was relatively simple for U.S. businessmen to do very rapidly practically everything the Germans could. Accordingly, only a few highly specialized segments of the electrical industry were left to foreign investors. By contrast, as I showed earlier, in the case of certain prominent branches of the chemical industry, the Germans had a clear headstart research and development advantage over Americans, which they sustained. A third consideration is that when Siemens & Halske and A.E.G. invested in the important Edison General Electric, the entry was "bank led"; that is, it developed from the very special relationship between Villard and the Deutsche Bank. None of the most fundamental German chemical industry investments had a similar genesis. This, I would suggest, was responsible for the less-viable German stakes in the U.S. electrical industry.

In short, the electrical industry saw substantial international investment and technological interchange. It was a new and dynamic one in the years 1875–1914. The American market was expanding rapidly. The principal contributions, however, were domestic. Only in a few specialized niches—in wireless equipment (still a very small business) and magnetos (more important)—were foreign investors in 1914 in a preeminent role.

Transportation Equipment—Civilian and Military

In transportation equipment, as I have shown, German, French, Italian, Swedish, and British companies made direct investments. Earlier in this chapter I surveyed foreign investments in the bicycle, automobile, and rubber tire industries and looked at various types of electrical and nonelectrical equipment, some of which related to "transportation equipment." To summarize briefly the contributions of these companies to the transportation equipment industry and to include some additional (not mentioned earlier) investments are the dual purposes of this section.

German companies participated in the United States in everything from building automobiles to the manufacture of parts, machinery, equipment, and apparatus for bicycles, automobiles, railroads, ships, and submarines. French firms produced automobiles and rubber tires in the United States. An Italian one made cars in this country. Swedish-owned companies manufactured ignitions, steam turbines, and possibly diesel engines, as well as kerosene lamps for railroad yards, thus providing automobile, ship, and railroad equipment.[170]

British companies made short-lived investments in bicycles and tubing for bicycle construction;[171] Dunlop's initial interest had been in bicycle tires. The British were, however, notably absent in the U.S. automobile and automotive parts industry. Theories that argue that foreign direct investments arise from advantage would predict this absence. The British had no advantage in this sector in the late nineteenth and early twentieth centuries. British capital participated in making railroad equipment. Another British investment in transportation equipment was Marconi's made-in-America wireless apparatus for ships.

One British stake by Vickers, Sons & Maxim, Ltd., was in producing submarines. This investment and another one (planned but not consummated) by Vickers have not been discussed previously and must command our attention here. The predecessors of Vickers, Sons & Maxim, Ltd., had long exported to the United States; before 1897 the firm was basically a steel company, "with one foot in armaments."[172] Thereafter it moved increasingly into armaments and in that context made the two forays, one unsuccessful and the other highly successful, into U.S. investments in transportation equipment.

In joint-ventures or independently, in the late nineteenth century Vickers began to invest internationally in arsenals,[173] and in 1898

Sigmund Loewe of Vickers visited Washington, D.C., proposing to construct in the United States an integrated arsenal capable of delivering "any type of war vessels, built, engineered and fully equipped with ordnance from its own works."[174] Loewe found U.S. government officials receptive, since "England was very far ahead of America."[175]

Vickers considered establishing a company "to appear" as "an American concern," but which would in fact be under Vickers' control.[176] Eventually the plan became known to the public, and in December 1900 the press reacted: "British Gold Seeks Control of U.S. Shipbuilding."[177] Early in 1901, in cooperation with the National Bank of Philadelphia, Vickers still thought it could proceed, and it prepared a prospectus inviting subscriptions to the $15 million authorized capital of a new firm, Cramp, Vickers, Maxim and Midvale Company (a joint-venture between Vickers and William Cramp & Sons of Philadelphia and the Midvale Steel Company).[178] Apparently the prospectus was never made public, perhaps because of the negative reactions to the venture in U.S. newspapers. At one point, in 1901, it seemed that Vickers might acquire 75 percent of the stock of Bethlehem Steel (this too never came to pass).[179] By 1903 Vickers was still hoping to build an integrated ship-building arsenal in the United States, but the project failed to come to fruition.[180] In the early twentieth century, Americans were too nationalistic to have a British-built and British-managed ship-building arsenal.[181]

Meanwhile, Vickers participated in another facet of transportation equipment. Here the initial impetus came from this side of the Atlantic. In 1899 Isaac Rice, an American, had obtained patents for the "Holland submarine," the first operationally viable vessel of its kind. The same Isaac Rice who at that time headed the Electric Vehicle Company, the Electric Storage Battery Company, and Siemens & Halske Electric Company of America, in 1899 also formed the Electric Boat Company to manufacture submarines. He quite naturally believed the U.S. Navy would be his principal customer, but he also wanted to export. In July 1900 he traveled to England to contact the British Admiralty, which sent Rice to meet with Vickers' executives. The British Admiralty required that any vessels it purchased be manufactured at home. On October 27, 1900, Electric Boat Company and Vickers made an agreement under which Rice's firm licensed the British one for twenty-five years to make the submarines in Britain, for sale there, in Europe, and in the British empire. This 1900 agreement did not involve a joint-venture. The American and British companies, while sharing technology, remained independent and distinct. Vickers at once prepared to build submarines in England. By contrast, Electric Boat Company met obstacles in the United States. Theodore Roosevelt told Rice that active presidential support of submarines might mean that the U.S. Congress would not appropriate funds for battleships, Roosevelt's top priority. With few orders, and little interest in Washington, Electric Boat was soon in financial trouble. To aid it, in the spring of 1902 Vickers' directors bought a sizable minority holding—£40,000 worth of the common shares. Vickers did not want its source of technology to go into bankruptcy. Not long thereafter, Vickers' interests raised their investments, and by January 1904 Rice was writing that the latest share arrangements had ensured the British "absolute control" over the Electric Boat Company.

Vickers continued to have more orders from the British Admiralty than its U.S. affiliate had from the American Navy. In the Panic of 1907, Electric Boat had to borrow from its British parent to stay in business. It is not clear how long Vickers (or Vickers' directors) maintained an equity interest in Electric Boat. The historian Clive Trebilcock, when describing the Vickers organization, indicated that in 1914 the latter had a 50 percent stock holding in Electric Boat Company, but he added a question mark.[182] The Vickers' stake was a direct investment, designed to sustain an American enterprise from which it obtained its license and its know-how. The U.S. Navy had no objections to this relationship. Trebilcock writes that in 1907 Electric Boat numbered among its shareholders some of the principal financial houses in the world, including the Rothschilds; Speyers; Ladenburg, Thalmann; and Chaplin, Milne, Grenfell.[183] The investment of a British firm in an American one to obtain U.S. technology was not common, but it was not unprecedented (this had been the motive for the earlier British investment in Fraser & Chalmers and for Gramophone's stake in the U.S. research facility). In short, from railroads to cars, to ships, to submarines, Europeans invested in transportation equipment for civilian and military purposes. The investments covered the spectrum; they were both to reach American markets and, in at least one instance, to obtain American technology.

Other Direct Investments by Foreign Manufacturers

There were numerous other foreign direct investments in manufacturing in the United States that were either too distinctive or not large enough to merit my earlier consideration. A sample from this group shows the wide range.

In lumber and wood products, the pencil maker A. W. Faber of Stein, Germany (after 1900 A. W. Faber-Castell), altered its associations in the United States. In Chapter 4 I documented the origins and growth of Eberhard Faber's important pencil manufacturing. As noted, Eberhard Faber had migrated to the United States, while retaining close relations with the family firm in Stein, near Nuremberg. His eldest daughter, Bertha, married her cousin in Germany, Baron Wilhelm von Faber (1853–1893), who between 1877 and 1893 ran the German A. W. Faber plant. When Eberhard Faber died in 1879, his son, Eberhard Faber II (1859–1946), took over the management of the American company, and between 1879 and 1893 the transatlantic businesses remained part of the same family enterprise.

Baron Wilhelm von Faber had no male heir. When his daughter, Baroness Ottilie, married (1896), her husband headed the *German* business. After 1898 the couple were known as Count and Countess von Faber-Castell, and as noted above, in 1900 the German company was renamed A. W. Faber-Castell.

Baron Wilhelm von Faber's death seems to have coincided with a rift between the German and American sides of the family; for in 1894 A. W. Faber, Stein, severed all connections with the Eberhard Faber business and embarked on a new and separate American undertaking. Thus A. W. Faber, Stein, established a competing pencil factory in Newark, New Jersey, and took the Eberhard Faber enterprise to court over the use of the Faber name. By 1894 and certainly in 1914, the Eberhard Faber business was entirely American; after 1903 it no longer used the name A. W. Faber. (It would *not* be subject to takeover by the Alien Property Custodian during World War I.) By contrast, in 1914 A. W. Faber & Co., a copartnership composed of Count Alexander von Faber-Castell and his wife, Countess Ottilie von Faber-Castell, of Stein, Germany, was manufacturing pencils in Newark. This enterprise was 100 percent German owned and controlled.[184]

At least two British publishing houses were well known in the United States. Oxford University Press opened a New York sales branch in 1896.[185] Much earlier, in the late 1860s, the Macmillan Company, London, sent George Brett to New York "not to print and publish, but with a consignment of English books, and orders to take an office and sell them." Brett founded the American branch of the London house. When in 1890 Brett died, his son replaced him, and the American Macmillan became an "independent" partnership, consisting of members of the London firm with Brett's son, George P., the "resident partner." In 1896 the English Macmillan became a limited company, and its American business then became the Macmillan Company of New York, under the "effective ownership of the British Macmillans." At this point it ceased to be a mere seller of imported

British books and became a publishing firm in its own right. It sold its own as well as British Macmillan titles in the United States at wholesale and on occasion at retail.[186]

Cleona Lewis identified two other British publishers with pre–1914 U.S. operations, Kelly's Directories, Ltd. (the subsidiary of which dated back to 1890 and had an original capital of $100,000), and Raphael Tuck & Sons, Ltd.[187] Sir Arthur Conan Doyle was a director of the Tuck firm.[188] I do not know whether these companies had only sales organizations or were actually involved in publishing in America. Likewise, the Edinburgh publisher Thomas Nelson was reported to have had a branch in New York.[189] Several nonresident German-owned houses (Alpha-Omega Publishing Company, New York, and the Consolidated Newspaper Company, Cleveland) published newspapers for the German immigrant community.[190]

In an entirely different industry, optical glass, German investors were also well represented in America. This was an activity in which Germans excelled. C. P. Goerz American Optical Company was 99 percent German owned (by Optische Anstalt C. P. Goerz, A.G., of Friedenau, Germany); it specialized in photographic and optical goods and operated in the United States under about eighty U.S. patents, all owned by its parent enterprise and covering everything from photographic devices to telescopes for guns and submarines, to a periscope, to distance-measuring instruments.[191] C. P. Goerz-America had a license to these patents that was revocable at the will of its German parent. A later report stated, "The German company was thus placed in a position of being able to at any time revoke the license and shut down American manufacture should the American company get out of control."[192] In short, the German parent could maintain the quality of its product, which for such specialized output was essential.

Even more important in optical glass was Bausch & Lomb Optical Company, founded as a sales agency before the Civil War in the United States by two German immigrants (John Bausch and Henry Lomb). In 1912 the company built a small optical glass furnace and by 1914 was producing "good experimental batches of several types of glass for instruments." Over the years Bausch & Lomb served as sales representative for and maintained close ties with the famous Carl Zeiss Works, in Jena, Germany. The German Zeiss firm owned (in 1914) 25 percent of the equity of Bausch & Lomb, which obtained technological information and patent licenses from the Jena establishment.[193]

At one time America was an importer of cement. In the late nineteenth and early twentieth centuries, the U.S. industry expanded rapidly. In the first decade of the twentieth century, U.S. cement output rose almost twenty-seven-fold; imports fell by about 93 percent.[194] Cement was very costly to ship. In response to the import substitution, two German firms (the Portland-Zement Fabrik, Hemmoor and Oste, and the Alsen'sche Portland Zement Fabriken, Hamburg) built plants in the United States—the first under the style German-American Portland Cement Works, headquartered in Chicago, and the second as Alsen's American Portland Cement Works, with head offices in New York.[195] These subsidiaries neither paid large dividends nor, as a 1916 U.S. Federal Trade Commission report recorded, made "much impression as compared with total American production."[196] In the same industry, on the American West Coast, an English company, Olympic Portland Cement Company, Ltd. (formed in January 1911 and floated in London), built and operated an important cement plant on the shore of Bellingham Bay, in northern Washington. This company was one of the many well-managed projects of the Liverpool firm Balfour, Williamson and its California house, Balfour, Guthrie.[197]

In 1882 the Franco-Texan Land Company had constructed a "plaster of Paris" works, the London Star Plaster Factory, in Fresnay City, Texas, which made plaster of paris, cement, and fertilizer from gypsum. After its French manager was shot to death in a Texas saloon (1883), the factory languished for lack of proper management; it finally was abandoned.[198] The Dutch-controlled Maxwell Land Grant Company, similarly, had an interest in an unprofitable and often-idle cement company in New Mexico (1882–1910).[199] A subsidiary of the Colorado Mortgage and Investment Company, Ltd., made bricks in Colorado.[200] These "building-products" activities were in connection with land development needs.

The German-owned American Refractories Company manufactured fire-clay brick.[201] More important, another German-controlled firm, the German-American Stoneware Works, produced in New Jersey specialized stoneware products. By 1914 it (and its associated firm, Didier-March) had three New Jersey plants, built or bought between 1907 and 1913. The German parent, Deutsche Ton-und Steinzeugwerke of Charlottenburg, Germany, traced its origin back to a pottery works established by Ernst March in 1836.[202]

In yet another industry, piano making, some foreign investments existed. American piano production was dominated by German immigrants and their children. When World War I came, only four of the literally thousands of U.S. piano manufacturers were taken over by the Alien Property Custodian. Of these four, two (Blake Corporation and Sterling Company—respectively, 99 and 57 percent "enemy owned") were later described as being owned "by an officer in the German army." Of the four, Sterling was the only one of any significance. Established in the United States in 1885, its factory produced 4,300 pianos in 1910 (Steinway built only 5,000).[203]

This sampling in no way begins to cover the variety of foreign direct investments. The *Alien Property Custodian Report, 1918–1919* contains everything from German nicotine manufacturers to makers of radium-illuminated watch dials.[204] One major foreign investor was the Canadian S. J. Moore, who before 1914 owned an odd collection of American factories in New York, Massachusetts, and Connecticut involved in printing, manufacturing souvenir silver spoons, making paper boxes, and producing sales books.[205] A British firm, Crittall & Co. of Braintree, Essex—through its affiliate the Fenestra Company—seems to have made, in Detroit, steel sashes for window frames for Ford Motor Company's new Highland Park plant (about 1908), while another British enterprise, Morgan Crucible Company, London, started a U.S. plant in Long Island in 1910 to manufacture carbon brushes.[206] All these were direct investments.

Some Portfolio Investments

There were foreign portfolio investments in many large American companies in the industries covered in this chapter. For example, International Harvester attracted such investments.[207] Likewise, some foreign portfolio interests existed in U.S. automobile companies, particularly Studebaker. The London merchant banker Kleinwort, Sons & Co. participated in the March 1911 reorganization of Studebaker, from which emerged the Studebaker Corporation.[208] The latter's securities were issued in London[209] and Amsterdam[210] in 1911. Dutch investors acquired sizable holdings, and the Dutch Nederlandsch Administratieen Trustkantoor became one of the five largest stockholders in the Studebaker Corporation.[211]

Although I have no evidence of foreign portfolio interests in United States Rubber Company, they undoubtedly existed (probably stemming from the latter's takeover of the Rubber Goods Manufacturing Company, which surely had portfolio foreign investments). Also, in rubber tires, B. F. Goodrich sold an estimated $15 million in preferred and common shares in London in 1912.[212] I have noted the European portfolio interests in International Steam Pump Company. Likewise, I indicated that Westinghouse looked to foreign money markets in the early twentieth century. In 1910 Western Electric offered its gold-backed mortgage bonds abroad.[213] Two years later, in 1912, some $4 million in General Electric fifty-year gold debentures were taken up in London.[214]

Nowhere in this book have I discussed the portfolio investments in the Eastman Kodak enterprise—but it is appropriate to do so here. In 1898 a British-incorporated company, Eastman Kodak Company, Ltd., a typical free-standing firm, acquired its American namesake, which was by that time the world's leading camera and film producer. The prospectus for Kodak, Ltd., contained a list of English, Scottish, French, and German bankers; a member of the British Parliament (Sir James Pender) was chairman, while the prominent Lord Kelvin was vice chairman. The capital was denominated in pound sterling. Kodak, Ltd., designed to raise capital in London for the business (and to provide advertising for its products), had a very short life under British registration and as a British direct investment in America. With the Boer War, a 5 percent English income tax was imposed on its earnings—and since there was no rationale for keeping a London "headquarters" (except to please British providers of capital), the British-registered free-standing company was in 1901 replaced with a New Jersey–incorporated one. The British shareholders had two choices: to take shares in the New Jersey company or to sell out. Many seem to have taken the first path—becoming purely portfolio investors in the American Eastman Kodak.[215] Earlier in this volume we saw the same pattern in the creation of other portfolio investments.

Indeed, in the early twentieth century a number of the larger U.S. corporations in the "other manufacturing" industries discussed in this chapter (just as in many of the industries considered earlier) obtained European portfolio investments. Banking firms, American and European, which had in the late nineteenth century specialized in railroads, at the turn of the century and in the years before World War I arranged for portfolio interests in America's new big businesses—the industrial enterprises. When this occurred, the European investors added to corporate capital resources, but beyond that they were not of great consequence. The foreign direct investments that provided capital and technology as well had much more impact.

An Overview

The foreign companies studied herein had different motives for investing in U.S. manufacture, but in many (not all) cases the high U.S. tariff was basic to the decision. Most of the foreign direct investments discussed in previous chapters were in industries different from the ones in which U.S. business abroad excelled. The principal earlier exceptions were in copper, aluminum, and oil, and in each of these sectors there had been substantial asymmetry in the cross-investment pattern.[216] In this chapter, however, I turned to a number of industries in which American enterprises had significant foreign investments in the pre–World War I years: in farm equipment, automobiles, and electrical and nonelectrical machinery. In every case, however, except that of the Canadian Massey-Harris company, ultimately there was a marked asymmetry in the pre–1914 investment pattern. Thus, in automobiles, Ford invested abroad in manufacturing, assembling and selling a cheap car; European makers of cars in the United States invested in luxury products. Ford's main foreign investments were in Canada and England; no Canadian or British car manufacturer invested in the United States. In nonelectrical machinery, there was a similar lack of congruence in the types of machinery produced by U.S. companies abroad and by foreign enterprises in the United States. Although in electrical equipment there were "cross-investments"—ultimately the successful ones in the United States carved out special niches (from magnetos to wireless equipment) that were entirely different from those of interest to American companies abroad.[217]

Of the foreign direct investors covered in this chapter, some took over existing plants; some built new ones; and some did both. Many had more than one plant and/or sales offices in more than one city. Some operations were very small and others quite substantial. Some firms took the licensing route with or without investments. The variety represented the flexibility of foreign direct investors in attempting to penetrate the U.S. market. With a few exceptions (Massey-Harris' investment in timber stands; the British investment in Fraser & Chalmers), most foreign direct investments were motivated by the desire to reach U.S. customers.

The free-standing company appears in belting and cables and very briefly in cameras and films (the Eastman Kodak case), but otherwise it does not seem as evident as in some industries discussed in earlier chapters.[218] By contrast, Canadian and European firms frequently extended their business over borders in the manner of modern multinational enterprise.

Diversity in success and failure existed. Very frequently investments were short-lived.[219] This was true of the free-standing companies—such as New York Belting and Packing Company, Ltd., and the Okonite Company, Ltd.—but it was also true of many others, including the British stakes in American Dunlop and the Callender's cable factory. It was, in addition, the case with important German investments such as those in Edison General Electric and Siemens & Halske Electric Company of America.

Why were there so many brief entries? Sometimes the reason lay in the neglect of management. Yet even if attention was paid, management was difficult from afar in these industries as in others. Administration over distance required experience that most European firms lacked.[220] The large U.S. market was hard to penetrate; European companies in these industries met competition in the United States from American firms and had no special advantage.

Nonetheless, while many foreign direct investors entered and quickly retreated, some did endure and prove successful. Michelin, for instance, was a sizable producer of tires in New Jersey, serving the growing U.S. demand—its plant well timed to meet an expanding market; it held its own against American competition. The factories of Orenstein & Koppel–Arthur Koppel in Pennsylvania provided high-quality railway equipment and industrial machinery to important U.S. industrial buyers; so did H. Koppers Company, with its coke ovens. The German-owned Kny-Scheerer became the largest manufacturer of surgical instruments in the United States, filling a highly specialized niche. British stakes in Fraser & Chalmers—albeit not lasting as foreign direct investments—facilitated the transfer of mining-machinery technology from the United States to Great Britain. At one point the Swedish enterprise AB Separator (using a German patent) held about 70 percent of the U.S. cream separator market in the dairy states. The German-owned Bosch Magneto Company was the principal firm in America's new magneto industry, one essential to the flourishing U.S. automobile industry. Marconi of America, which was British controlled, was by 1914 the leader in manufacturing apparatus related to radio communication. Another British concern, Vickers, Sons & Maxim, appears to have had a controlling stake in America's foremost submarine builder. Thus many of the companies discussed here were indeed significant in particular subindustries.

Immigrants—especially Germans—played crucial roles in paving the way for some investments (William Steinway acted for Daimler), in providing joint-venture partners (Adolphus Busch with Sulzer Brothers of Switzerland), in representing German firms (John Bausch and Henry Lomb for the Carl Zeiss works), and in offering a market (for Siemens & Halske Electric Company of America). As we have seen, this pattern was not unique to the industries covered in this chapter.

Likewise, family was important. A member of the Michelin family ran that company's American plant. The son-in-law of the German

Ernest Koerting represented him in America. A member of the Wallenberg family started a cream separator company, financed by the family bank. Again, the reader has seen this family role before—from the Frenchmen in the wool mills in Rhode Island to the Mercks in America and Germany.

It should be noted, however, that immigrant and family associations were not a guarantee to prosperity over time. The Steinway connection could not and did not insure the continuation of production of the American Mercedes, nor was the immigrant Henry Villard able to keep his German compatriots involved in Edison General Electric's successor, General Electric. The German "market" notwithstanding, Siemens & Halske did not persist with its U.S. affiliate. So too, "family" was not enough to bind enterprises. W. O. Callender's son proved deficient as manager of the firm's New Jersey factory. The Faber kinship links could not cement through generations the relationship between Eberhard Faber in America and the Faber-Castell works in Stein, Germany. There had to be "advantage" for success.

Retreats and failures there were, but also many new products and processes were introduced from abroad. Immigrants and family connections were in general positive rather than negative influences. Because of the large number of foreign direct investments, they were of much greater consequence than the portfolio ones in these U.S. industries (as in all American manufacturing), albeit in dollar values it seems probable that by 1914 the portfolio interests in these industries exceeded the foreign direct investments. Just as U.S. railroads went abroad for financing, so too did a number of the large manufacturing companies in the industries discussed in this chapter. Yet by the early twentieth century—when these businesses were calling on foreign capital—U.S. capital markets were sufficiently developed so that, for these manufacturers, foreign finance (that is, foreign portfolio investments) served more as a "helping hand" (although a very important one for Westinghouse and Studebaker in particular) rather than as an absolutely essential ingredient in American growth, as in the more general case of railroad finance. Nonetheless, it is evident that in these "other industries" (as in certain large-scale manufacturing activities dealt with in earlier chapters), it was possible for Americans to tap European capital markets and to obtain portfolio investments in U.S.-incorporated manufacturing enterprises. It was, however, the foreign direct investors in "other manufacturing," in the many subindustries, with their transfer of technology as well as of capital, that made the most noteworthy contribution—undoubtedly more substantial than that of the portfolio investors.

13.

Banking Services

The entry and accumulation of foreign capital in the United States involved (and were often assisted by) numerous and diverse "service sector" investments, which offered everything from banking to power and light services. Some investors transferred sizable amounts of capital, sometimes their own and sometimes that of others. They opened new channels of information, acquainting others with opportunities. The names of many of these service sector firms were encountered earlier in this volume. In the next three chapters I consider these foreign enterprises in their own right.

In the service sector, I include banks and banking houses. Other intermediaries of capital and information were stockbrokers, promoters, investment trusts, providers of land and real estate mortgages, traders, shippers, cable companies, and wireless transmitters. A third set comprised participants in advertising; wholesale and retail distribution networks; insurance; accounting; engineering; construction; and power, light, and traction. The banks and banking houses will be the subject of this chapter; the second group will be covered in Chapter 14; and the third in Chapter 15. Conspicuously absent from this highly heterogeneous collection of firms are foreign solicitors and lawyers, whose partnerships did facilitate international business. Linklater's, Freshfield's, and Ashurst's in London, for example, dealt with British investors with American interests and referred their clients to U.S. law firms, but not one of these British law firms extended itself (as a firm) across the Atlantic to the United States. Foreign enterprises in the United States used American, especially New York and Chicago, lawyers. The legal profession had skills, knowledge, and training deeply rooted in a specific locale, advantages not easily transferable internationally.[1]

Within the United States and abroad, many Americans—lawyers, private bankers, promoters, mortgage company organizers (such as John Dos Passos, J. P. Morgan, Henry Villard and Arthur E. Stilwell, and James L. Lombard)—played crucial roles in drawing European monies into the United States.[2] In 1897 the National City Bank, New York, established a Foreign Department that handled foreign exchange, sought accounts from foreigners, and offered a range of commercial services to foreign banks and businesses.[3] In this and the next two chapters, my interest is not in such American individuals or businesses, but rather in the foreign entrepreneurs and, more important, in the foreign-owned and controlled enterprises that were both foreign investors and intermediaries.

Here I turn first to foreign banks. I try to identify the key ones and to decipher their roles and functions as foreign direct investors (that is, as direct participants, with their own personnel in the United States) in offering banking services in this country. I also consider their roles as foreign portfolio (or less often, direct) investors in activities aside from banking and as conduits for other investors' long-term capital contributions.

Foreign Banks and U.S. Commercial Banking

The world's ten greatest banks, measured by deposits at year-end 1913, are listed in Table 13.1. Not one was American. By that time

Table 13.1. Deposits of the world's great banks, year-end 1913 (in millions of pounds)

Bank	Size of deposits
Imperial Bank of Russia	126
Lloyds Bank	104[a]
London City and Midland Bank	94
Crédit Lyonnais	89
London County and Westminster Bank	88
Deutsche Bank	79
Société Générale (Paris)	72
Bank of England	71
National Provincial Bank of England	68
Hongkong and Shanghai Banking Corporation	62

Source: Banker's Magazine, New York, 89 (July 1914); 76.
[a] Including Wilts and Dorset.

some of these ten had or had had a direct U.S. presence, that is, one or more salaried representatives, "agencies,"[4] branches, subsidiaries, or copartnerships. Most had some U.S. business relationships, from correspondent banks to the holding of American securities. Of these leading ten, only one, the Imperial Bank of Russia, had no U.S. interests at all.[5] Only one, the Deutsche Bank, had truly important U.S. stakes, and these were not in American commercial banking—not in the ownership of American national or state banks, and not in banks that held Americans' deposits and made domestic loans.[6] In fact, none of these top ten participated directly in routine domestic commercial banking in the United States.[7]

Part of the reason American domestic banking did not have within its midst these large foreign banks appears to lie in the structure of the U.S. banking system. In the late nineteenth and early twentieth centuries, American railroad, manufacturing, and even insurance enterprises became national organizations (and often international ones); this was not true in commercial banking. While the country had a "national" banking system (under federal legislation), while men such as James Stillman had interests in banks in several states and apparently served on the boards of banks in different states, and while the U.S. correspondent system was extensive,[8] in terms of *operations* (that is, the extension of the firm per se) U.S. banking was not "national." The National Bank Act of 1864 had specified that directors of a national bank be U.S. citizens and resident in the state, territory, or district in which the bank did business.[9] This clause was interpreted to mean that a national bank had a defined place of doing business and could not branch. Nothing in the national banking legislation prevented foreign shareholders in such a bank, but foreign owners could *not* have a director of their own citizenship to represent their interests. This meant that there were two constraints on foreign ownership of American national banks in the federal legislation. One was that a national bank could not grow as a firm beyond a specified and very limited locale,[10] and the other was that, unable to appoint directors of their own nationality, foreign individuals or banks were inhibited in exercising control.[11]

Of still greater significance, America had a "dual" banking system. When the national banking legislation was passed (1863–64) and a tax placed on state bank note issues (1865), many state banks converted into national banks; it was then assumed that state-chartered banking would wither away. Until about 1880 the note-issue privilege of national banks gave federal charters a competitive advantage. After 1880, however, many American bankers turned to state charters, because of lower capital and reserve requirements and fewer restrictions on bank behavior.[12] As they set up additional state-chartered banks, new *state* regulations followed.[13] Thus each state had (and continues to have) its own laws on commercial banking (the taking of deposits and the making of loans). State legislation applied to American and to foreign banks. Any bank from abroad in the United States thus not only faced a federal regulatory regime but would also coincidentally be subject to a different set of regulations in each state in which it desired to transact business.

New York City had become America's financial capital. Banks there were governed by New York state law, which by the early 1880s sharply restricted out-of-state and out-of-country banks. New York City would be the obvious place of entry for a foreign bank, but under New York state law such an institution was not allowed to engage in a "banking business." As the British Consul General in New York City, in an October 27, 1886, letter to the Foreign Office in London, explained: foreign banks in this city "cannot receive deposits, discount notes or Bills, or issue any evidence of debt to be loaned or put in circulation as money." This was the rule on "foreign corporations," although private individuals could, as "private banks," "receive deposits and discount notes or bills."[14] A 1914 New York banking law clearly stated the prohibitions on foreign bank branches. A foreign banking institution could establish an "agency" to do limited business, not including the issue of notes or the receipt of deposits.[15]

Bankers such as Sir Edward H. Holden, chairman of the London City and Midland Bank (the world's third largest bank, measured by deposits), complained in early 1914 that a branch of an English joint-stock bank could not be opened in New York, "because it would not be allowed either to take deposits or to carry on a discount business."[16] At the end of 1913 the London City and Midland Bank had 867 branches.[17] It had established a formidable network of some forty-five correspondent banks in the United States.[18] It may well have desired a New York branch.[19] Sir Edward's complaints were made before the passage of New York's 1914 legislation; the new law did not help. In a similar vein, writing early in 1914, Richard Hauser of the Deutsche Bank noted that under the 1913 U.S. *federal* legislation that established the Federal Reserve System, American national banks could for the first time set up branches abroad. Therefore he felt it was appropriate to urge the repeal of laws such as those existing in the state of New York that barred foreign branch banks.[20] He too was disappointed when the state reaffirmed its prohibitions. Thus New York, the logical place for a foreign bank to have a branch bank, continued to forbid their admission.

By contrast, Illinois law permitted banks from other states and countries;[21] the Bank of Montreal's earlier success in Chicago as a full-service bank stimulated the entry of the Canadian Bank of Commerce (1875), the Bank of British North America (1881), and the Merchants' Bank of Canada (1881).[22] These four Canadian banks accepted deposits in Chicago and provided competition to that city's financial institutions, especially in the financing of the grain trade.[23] Yet the newcomers' activities were short-lived, for with declining profits in financing that trade, the three new arrivals shut their Chicago offices in 1886, leaving once again the Bank of Montreal as the sole foreign-owned bank in that city.[24] In 1891 the Royal Trust Company of Canada (associated with the Bank of Montreal) entered Chicago and was incorporated there in 1893 (under state law) as the Royal Trust Bank; it seems to have done mortgage lending as well as commercial banking; it was, however, absorbed by the Central Trust Company of Illinois in 1909.[25]

Meanwhile, the 1893 Chicago World's Exposition, which attracted visitors from abroad, was the occasion for several foreign banks to open Chicago branches (in 1892–93): the Bank of Nova Scotia, the Crédit Lyonnais, and the Comptoir National d'Escompte, Paris.[26] The tenure of the two French banks proved brief. Crédit Lyonnais seems to have remained open only the one year, 1893, while Comptoir National d'Escompte was in Chicago from 1893 to 1900.[27]

By 1914, in Chicago, the absence of state government rules against them notwithstanding, only two foreign banks remained—the Bank of Montreal and the Bank of Nova Scotia. These did do regular commercial banking business. In 1914 the Bank of Montreal in Chicago had a capital and surplus of $33 million, which meant—measured by that standard—that it was the largest commercial bank in Chicago, slightly larger than its nearest rival, the Continental and Commercial Bank (with a capital and surplus of $32.7 million). The third ranking bank in that city in 1914 was the First National Bank of Chicago, with a capital and surplus of $22.3 million, followed in fourth place by the Bank of Nova Scotia, with a capital and surplus of $17 million.[28]

In summary, in 1914 the Bank of Montreal in Chicago was the largest bank in Illinois, and in fact in the Midwest. It was a member of the Chicago Clearing House. Throughout the years 1875–1914 it played a significant role in financing the region's export trade.[29] The importance of the Canadians (particularly the Bank of Montreal) in providing capital when required was acknowledged in Chicago's banking circles.[30] In all the United States, Chicago was unique in the role of foreign banks in commercial banking during the entire period 1875–1914. State legislation gave the "open door." Interestingly, a Canadian bank, one from a debtor nation in international accounts, not one from a creditor nation of Europe, occupied the preeminent position. All things considered, this was not so odd, as one remembers the economic links and railroad connections between Chicago and Canada; bankers invest to serve their normal customers in trade.[31] It is also not surprising when one recognizes that branch banking was the norm in Canada. Throughout the Dominion the Bank of Montreal had branches and thus had experience in operating outside its headquarters city. No language barriers existed; though based in Montreal, the bank was run by expatriate Scots. These men were themselves very much involved in other U.S. business.

Moving South, before the Civil War foreign bankers had had important business relationships, associated with the cotton trade, in New Orleans. Some investments in that city's commercial banks made in the 1830s persisted fifty years later! Hope & Co., Amsterdam, for example, in the late nineteenth century still held an interest in the Citizens' Bank.[32] By contrast, no evidence suggests that the Barings maintained any of their earlier holdings in Louisiana commercial banking.[33] Likewise, the Civil War and Reconstruction had seen a continuing decline in foreign investment in Louisiana banking. The Canadian Bank of Commerce opened an agency in New Orleans in 1896, but when the state began to impose heavy taxes on it "as a foreign enterprise,"[34] the bank sold its agency in 1901 to the newly established Commercial National Bank of New Orleans, described by the Canadian bank's historian as an "allied institution."[35] Sometime between 1894 and 1897, as part of a broader international expansion, Comptoir National d'Escompte, Paris, set up an agency in New Orleans, which it shut in 1903.[36] By 1902 Hope & Co. was no longer an investor in the Citizens' Bank.[37] A few years into the twentieth century, Louisiana banking was completely American. In 1902 a Louisiana law provided that the banking business in that state could be carried on "only by such incorporated institutions as shall have been organized under the laws of this state and the United States, by individual citizens of the state and by firms domiciled in the state, whose active members shall be citizens of this state."[38]

Foreign investment in land, cattle, and then oil meant an interest by overseas banks in Texas. In 1905 that state forbade "foreign" corporations (except national banks of the United States) from participating in banking in Texas.[39] State laws used the word *foreign* to mean out-of-state, which included out-of-country as well.

Under the laws of the state of Arizona, the Sonora Bank and Trust Company was incorporated on May 25, 1914. Its head office was in Nogales, Arizona. It was controlled by Mexican citizens; in time, it set up branches in Mexico.[40] Nothing in Arizona law barred such a Mexican-controlled institution.

In California out-of-country banks had been significant (as I showed earlier) in the development of that state's banking and finance. Of the fifteen original members of the San Francisco Clearing House Association (1876), six of them—the Bank of British Columbia, the Bank of British North America, Belloc Frères, the London and San Francisco Bank, Ltd., the Swiss-American Bank, and the Anglo-Californian Bank, Ltd.—were known to have important foreign ownership.[41] Davidson & Co., agents for the London Rothschilds, was also a member.[42] In 1877 Lazard Frères joined.[43] The first president of the San Francisco Clearing House Association was the American president of the British-controlled London and San Francisco Bank, Ltd.[44] Table 13.2 lists the most important foreign-owned banks in California in the period 1875–1914 and shows their status as of 1914. Of those in existence in 1875,[45] only three remained in California as foreign owned in 1914: the Hongkong and Shanghai Banking Corporation, the Bank of British Columbia (albeit in 1914 as the Canadian Bank of Commerce), and the Bank of British North America. They were joined by the Yokohama Specie Bank.

The Hongkong and Shanghai Banking Corporation, established in San Francisco in 1875, specialized in foreign exchange transactions and the purchase of silver bullion. China in 1875–1914 was on a silver standard. The Hongkong bank did a large business in San Francisco's Chinatown. The Chinese called the bank *Way Fong*, meaning Rich Exchange. Whenever the bank operated in a Chinese community, its historian writes, it handled "the many thousands of personal remittances of overseas Chinese."[46]

A historian of California banking, Ira Cross, described the San Francisco branch of the Bank of British Columbia (founded in 1864) in its first thirty years as one of the three most outstanding banks in California.[47] The London and San Francisco Bank, Ltd., he characterized as having had a "powerful influence in the development of the agriculture and industries of the Great Northwest."[48] The Bank of British Columbia was acquired in 1901 by the Canadian Bank of Commerce, which became involved in commercial banking in California but was not as significant as had been the Bank of British Columbia in its prime.[49] Likewise, over time the London and San Francisco Bank, Ltd., lost its relative position. Its inability to compete has been explained by its need to obtain approval from its London home office on all large transactions, which put it at a disadvantage vis-à-vis locally managed institutions.[50] In 1905 the American-owned

Table 13.2. Some foreign banks in California, 1875–1914

Financial institution, main locale of business	Place incorporated or headquarters of U.S. business	Date established in San Francisco	Status as of 1914
Anglo-Californian Bank, Ltd., California	London	1873	Merged into Anglo and London Paris National Bank, 1908
Bank of British Columbia, British Columbia/Western North America	London	1864	Acquired by Canadian Bank of Commerce, 1901
Bank of British North America, Canada	London	1864	Still in existence in 1914
Canadian Bank of Commerce, Canada	Toronto	1901	Still in existence in 1914
Hongkong and Shanghai Banking Corporation, Far East	Hong Kong	1875	Still in existence in 1914
Lazard Frères,[a] France/England/U.S.	Paris?	ca. 1849	Branch taken over by London, Paris and American Bank, Ltd., 1884
London, Paris and American Bank, Ltd., California	London	1884	Became U.S.-controlled London, Paris National Bank, 1908
London and San Francisco Bank, Ltd., California	London	1865	Purchased by U.S.-controlled Bank of California, 1905
Swiss-American Bank, California	Geneva	1873	Closed, 1877
Yokohama Specie Bank, international	Yokohama	1899	San Francisco office incorporated under California law Feb. 28, 1910; branch in Los Angeles started Feb. 1913

Source: Ira B. Cross, *Financing an Empire* (Chicago: S. J. Clarke, 1927), vols. 1, 2, and 3. The Hongkong and Shanghai Banking Corporation did not do routine domestic commercial banking (taking deposits and making loans) in California. All the others appear to have done so. According to *Palgrave's Banking Almanac, 1914,* as cited by the U.S. Federal Trade Commission, *Report on Cooperation in Export Trade* (Washington, D.C., 1916), I, 64, the Bank of Taiwan, Ltd., also had a San Francisco "branch" in 1914. I have been unable to verify this.

[a] "Foreign" designation very doubtful; see Chapter 13, note 43.

Bank of California purchased it, along with its branches in Portland, Tacoma, and Seattle; it became "Americanized."[51] The Bank of British North America continued in San Francisco, but not as an especially important bank.

In the summer of 1899 the Yokohama Specie Bank opened a branch in San Francisco, the first Japanese bank in California.[52] This bank "incorporated" its San Francisco office, under state law, on February 28, 1910. It dealt mainly with the foreign exchange business between the United States and Japan; it participated in foreign trade financing. It also served the more general financial needs of the rising Japanese population in San Francisco and nearby areas.[53] It took deposits.[54] In February 1913 it established the Yokohama Specie Bank, Ltd., Los Angeles, as a "branch" of the Yokohama Specie Bank of San Francisco. The Los Angeles branch did commercial banking and also a large business in foreign exchange.[55]

After 1900, Japanese immigrants had poured into California, and between 1903 and 1907 seven "Japanese banks" opened.[56] Whether they, like the Yokohama Specie Bank, were part of a multinational enterprise or (more likely) were established by settlers with no Japanese home office is unclear. In 1907 Theodore Roosevelt negotiated a "gentlemen's agreement" with Japan to stop the immigration.[57] Two years later, when California passed a banking law that sought to place all banks in that state on a sound basis, the regulators subjected the Japanese banks to special scrutiny. Between July 1, 1909, and October 31, 1910, the California Superintendent of Banking closed ten banks (five of them Japanese) and two Los Angeles branches (both Japanese) "because of impairment or absence of capital, or because of bad management." Examiners found that the targeted Japanese banks and their branches had kept records in Japanese and, after preparing translations, discovered the banks had been "looted." Henceforth California law required that bank records be kept in English.[58]

The 1909 California Banking Act prohibited foreign banks from having "branches" in the state—thus the incorporation of the San Francisco "branch" of the Yokohama Specie Bank.[59] The California Bank Superintendent closed the Nippon Savings Bank of Sacramento (chartered in 1907) on October 19, 1909, and then permitted it to reopen as the Nippon Bank of Sacramento on December 7, 1909.[60] By 1910 the Yokohama Specie Bank (which had never been shut) and the Nippon Bank of Sacramento were all that remained of the eight Japanese banks. The Yokohama Specie Bank was clearly a Japanese foreign direct investment; possibly the Nippon Bank was one as well.[61] The Bank of British North America and the Canadian Bank of Commerce survived the 1909 California legislation and continued as commercial banks. The *operations* of the Hongkong and Shanghai Banking Corporation seem to have been unaffected by the new rules.[62]

California law on foreign banking became even more restrictive in 1913. A "branch" of a foreign incorporated bank that operated in California prior to that year could remain in business. It had to meet the requirements of state law, and the capital assigned to it and all the funds and deposits received by it had to be segregated from the general business and assets of the parent corporation, as though it were an independent firm; that is, it could not be a mere "branch." This seems a repetition of the 1909 rules. After 1913, however, a newly established foreign banking corporation could *not* receive deposits in California, although it could be certified by the Superintendent of Banks to pay or to collect bills of exchange, to issue letters of credit, or to have an office (which did not entail doing banking business).[63] In short, unless its entry was prior to 1913, a foreign bank could not do a full banking business in California.

The state of Washington's 1905 legislation allowed foreign banks to do business with certain restrictions: they were barred from taking deposits.[64] The Canadian Bank of Commerce was chartered under state law and allowed to continue to do a general banking business under a "grandfather" clause.[65] In 1899 the Merchants' Bank of Halifax (in 1901 to be renamed the Royal Bank of Canada) had purchased a small private local bank and opened its own branch in the mining community of Republic, Washington, "to serve the needs of prominent Montreal customers who were interested in the considerable prospecting that was going on in that vicinity." The Halifax bank had branches just across the border in British Columbia, where gold mining was booming. Its new Washington branch "made no headway" and was closed in 1904, before the 1905 legislation.[66] Meanwhile, the Bank of Montreal, probably in early 1903, had started a branch in Spokane, Washington; it remained until 1924. Like the Canadian Bank of Commerce, it appears to have been grandfathered in under the 1905 law.[67] Oregon, by contrast, continued to allow foreign banks, and in Portland the Canadian Bank of Commerce did a general banking business.

This, then, constituted practically all the limited amount of commercial banking done by foreign banks in the United States; by 1914 it was Canadian banks in Illinois, California, Washington, and Oregon that were the principal participants.[68] The Mexican-owned bank in Arizona and the Japanese ones in California were atypical. So was the Hongkong and Shanghai Banking Corporation.[69] Americans in 1910 had 7,138 national banks and 17,376 state and private banks.

That year the deposits in these 24,514 commercial banks totaled $12.3 billion.[70] In 1910–1914, in national terms, clearly the role of foreign banks in U.S. commercial banking was not significant.

Foreign Bank Agencies in New York and One Foreign-Owned Trust Company

There were other ways for a foreign bank to enter the United States. America's national banking legislation of 1864–65, as noted in Chapter 4, had not provided a satisfactory basis for the largest American banks to participate in foreign trade financing.[71] Some of that financing was arranged by foreign bank "agencies" that handled the transactions through London, American private houses (such as Brown Brothers) with associated firms in Great Britain, or very exceptionally by state-chartered banks and possibly U.S. trust companies (which also made arrangements through London.)[72] By the early twentieth century, the amount of foreign trade to be financed was not small; America fluctuated in rank—in first or second place—in the value of world exports. Yet to finance much of that trade, American enterprises depended on foreign (mainly British) banking services.[73]

Thus, even if a foreign bank could not undertake a regular banking business in New York, a number of such banks wanted a presence there. Foreign banks could participate in foreign trade financing, in handling foreign exchange, and in serving as conduits of information on what was happening in the world's most important "debtor" nation.

By 1914 twenty foreign (out-of-country) banks had their own "agencies" in New York, licensed to do business under New York state banking law.[74] Table 13.3 gives the twenty, as listed by the New York Superintendent of Banking in his *Report of 1914*. I have added the date the agency was established in New York (when I have been able to determine it) and also the banks' presence in 1914 in other U.S. cities.[75] Note that the list includes ten banks with London headquarters, one of which (the Bank of British North America) operated mainly in Canada. Represented in the London ten were the important "Foreign and Colonial Banks," British banks engaged in trade with Africa, Latin America, and Asia.[76] The list has five banks with Canadian addresses. The remaining five were headquartered in Hong Kong, Naples, Prague, Havana, and Yokohama (the Hongkong and Shanghai Banking Corporation fits properly in the category of British "Foreign and Colonial Banks").[77] The Naples and Prague banks had direct connections with immigration to the United States, in sending immigrant remittances back home. The Havana bank—the National

Table 13.3. "Agencies" of foreign (out-of-country) banks licensed under New York state banking law, 1914

Name and foreign headquarters[a]	Date established in New York	Establishments in other U.S. cities[b]
African Banking Corporation, London	c	None
Anglo South American Bank, London	1907[d]	None
Banco di Napoli, Naples	e	None
Bank of British North America, London	mid-1850s[f]	San Francisco[g]
Bank of British West Africa, London	c	None
Bank of Montreal, Montreal[f]	1818–1841[h]	Chicago, Spokane (Wash.)
Bank of Nova Scotia, Halifax	1859[i]	Chicago, Boston[k]
Bohemia Joint Stock Bank, Prague	[1832][j]	None
Canadian Bank of Commerce, Toronto[l]	c	San Francisco, Seattle, Portland (Ore.)
Chartered Bank of India, Australia, and China, London	1902[m]	None
Colonial Bank, London (operated in the Caribbean)	1890[n]	None
Commercial Bank of Spanish America, London	1912[o]	None
Hongkong and Shanghai Banking Corp., Hong Kong	1879/1880[p]	San Francisco[g]
London and Brazilian Bank, London	q	None
London and River Plate Bank, London	q	None
Merchants' Bank of Canada, Montreal	mid-1870s[r]	None
National Bank of Cuba, Havana	ca. 1901?[s]	None
Royal Bank of Canada, Montreal	1899[t]	None
Standard Bank of South Africa, London	1905[u]	None
Yokohama Specie Bank, Yokohama	1880[v]	San Francisco, Los Angeles

a New York State, Superintendent of Banking, *Annual Report, 1914*, p. 20, for names of banks and headquarters cities. This list included the International Banking Corporation, Bridgeport, Connecticut. It was the only in-country, out-of-state bank included. I have excluded it from the table because it was not an out-of-country bank. The order is alphabetical.

b As of June 1914.

c Unknown.

d David Joslin, *A Century of Banking in Latin America* (London: Oxford University Press, 1963), p. 200.

e Unknown: Luigi de Rosa, *Emigranti, capitali e banche (1896–1906)* (Naples: Edzione del Banco di Napoli, 1980), p. 675, refers to the authorization of an "Inspectorate" (Ispettorato) in New York in 1906; the actual agency was undoubtedly subsequent to that date.

f Data in Bank of Montreal Archives, Public Archives, Ottawa, and Merrill Denison, *Canada's First Bank*, 2 vols. (New York: Dodd, Mead, 1966).

g Ira Cross, *Financing an Empire*, 4 vols. (Chicago: S. J. Clarke, 1927).

h Independent agent.

i Own agency.

j Bank of Nova Scotia, *Bank of Nova Scotia, 1832–1932* (Toronto: privately printed, 1932). p. 43; but in *Banker's Magazine*, New York, 34 (June 1880): 918, no Bank of Nova Scotia agency is listed, and other evidence indicates a discontinuity from the initial 1832 agent. See, for example, D. L. C. Galles, "Bank of Nova Scotia," *Minnesota History*, 42 (Fall 1971): 268, which omits entirely the 1832 New York agent. When, however, in 1911, New York State first required the licensing of agencies of foreign banks, the Bank of Nova Scotia was licensed. New York State, Superintendent of Banking, *Annual Report, 1911*, p. 14.

k Bank of Nova Scotia, *Bank of Nova Scotia, 1832–1932*, pp. 163–164.

l Victor Ross, *A History of the Canadian Bank of Commerce*, 2 vols. (Toronto: Oxford University Press, 1920).

m Compton Mackenzie, *Realms of Silver* (London: Routledge & Kegan Paul, 1954). But according to Leone Levi, "Banking—National and International," *Bankers' Magazine*, London, 41 (March 1881): 191, this bank had a "branch" in the United States in 1881.

n *Banker's Magazine*, New York, 46 (Jan. 1891): 551.

o Joslin, *A Century of Banking*. p. 205.

p Francis A. Lees, *Foreign Banking and Investment in the United States* (New York: John Wiley, 1976). p. 11 (1879): *Banker's Magazine*, New York, 34 (June 1880): 918, notes its presence in New York as of May 1880. According to J. R. Jones, "New York," ca. 1964, in File J4, Archives, Hongkong and Shanghai Banking Corporation, Hong Kong, a decision was made to open the agency at the end of 1879; the "special agent" was sent from England and arrived in New York early in Jan. 1880. In 1881 the Hongkong and Shanghai Banking Corporation indicated that A. M. Townsend was its New York "agents." See *Commercial and Financial Chronicle*, 32 (Jan. 1, 1881): 24.

q The London and Brazilian Bank and the London and Rio Plate Bank, both founded in 1862, very soon thereafter appointed correspondents in New York (Joslin, *A Century of Banking*, pp. 29, 64). Joslin does not indicate when they appointed their own agents in New York.

r Dolores Greenberg, *Financiers and Railroads* (Newark: University of Delaware Press, 1980), p. 35. *Banker's Magazine*, New York, 34 (June 1880): 918, notes its presence in New York as of May 1880.

s See this chapter, note 78.

t Clifford H. Ince, *The Royal Bank of Canada: A Chronology, 1864–1969*, (n.p., n.d.), pp. 15, 111–112.

u J.A. Henry, *The First Hundred Years of Standard Bank* (London: Oxford University Press, 1963). p. 155.

v Mira Wilkins, "American-Japanese Direct Foreign Investment Relationships, 1930–1952," *Business History Review*, 56 (Winter 1982): 507.

Bank of Cuba—was associated with America's important sugar trade.[78] Japan's largest bank, the Yokohama Specie Bank, as noted earlier, financed U.S.-Japanese and probably some U.S.-Chinese trade; its New York office opened in 1880, the very year the bank was founded in Japan.[79] The Yokohama Specie Bank, located at 55 Wall Street, New York, was a long-time member of the Silk Association of America.[80] It was also involved in holding Japanese government monies to pay interest on Japanese borrowings in the United States.[81]

In 1911, for the first time, the New York state banking law had required that these foreign bank agencies be licensed by the Superintendent of Banking, who had to be satisfied that the foreign banks had financial standing such that they "may be safely permitted to conduct business within this state."[82] The banks listed in Table 13.3 were those licensed under this state law. These banks, although they did not participate in branch banking, were important.

Yet the omissions from the list are even more revealing. With the exception of the Hongkong and Shanghai Banking Corporation, none of the world's great banks of deposit (listed in Table 13.1) is included. None of the large British "deposit" banks felt its own "agency" would be an adequate substitute for a "branch." In 1914 London City and Midland's had thirteen correspondent banks in New York City, but not its own agency.[83] Likewise, Lloyds Bank had the Bank of America, American Express, Bankers Trust Company, Bank of British North America, Chase National Bank, A. Iselin & Co., and National City Bank as its New York "agents and correspondents," but no "licensed agency."[84]

The Bank of England is absent from the list. Histories of the bank reveal nothing on its American representation,[85] but as early as 1826 the bank had appointed the New York lawyer R. M. Blatchford as its "financial agent and counsel in the United States." For many years the Bank of England used Blatchford and his successors, directing to the law firm English solicitors and British investors.[86] Many of the governors and directors of the bank knew the United States in an intimate fashion, either having lived in the country or being associated with firms that had substantial U.S. business; many had personal investments in the United States.[87] The Bank of England was well aware of what was happening in America,[88] even though it had no licensed agency in New York.[89]

Likewise, the important British merchant banks with their sizable U.S. involvements did not in 1911–1914 have licensed agencies in New York.[90] Note also that no German, French, Dutch, or Swiss bank appears on the roster.[91] Many, desiring privacy, undoubtedly did not wish to submit to examination by the New York Superintendent of Banking. Yet, as I will show, European (including British) merchant and investment bankers served as conduits for money flows into the United States. Many were in New York in the early twentieth century with representatives and copartnerships, plus a plethora of informal ties, but *no* "regulated" New York "agencies." In short, the lack of a *licensed* New York agency did not mean no U.S. business nor did it necessarily mean no New York or U.S. presence.

Interestingly, French and Dutch financial institutions did have New York agencies in 1880. In April of that year, a bill had passed the New York state legislature to tax foreign bank capital. Affected were four Canadian banks (the Canadian Bank of Commerce, the Bank of Montreal, the Bank of British North America, and the Merchants' Bank of Canada),[92] and also Crédit Lyonnais, the Netherland Trading Society—the Nederlandsche Handel-Maatschappij—and the Hongkong and Shanghai Banking Corporation.[93] The Canadians were irate at the new tax; they called in their loans and invested in sterling exchange, "causing a commotion in the money market."[94] New York's Governor vetoed the bill. One less offensive to the foreign bankers (with a substantially lower tax) was passed and signed in June 1880,[95] but when in 1882 Crédit Lyonnais had closed its New York agency, part of the reason for shutting down, it declared, was the New York tax.[96]

Of the foreign banks with agencies in New York in 1880 and in 1914, the Bank of British North America, London, probably had the longest uninterrupted New York agent or agency (having started in the mid-1850s). It frequently acted as correspondent for other banks. Thus it was a correspondent for London City and Midland's and its predecessor in the years 1893–1907; likewise, it was by 1913–14 one of the agents and correspondents in New York for Lloyds Bank, London.[97]

Of all the banks with licensed agencies, undoubtedly the Bank of Montreal was the most influential in American business. Its Canadian principals—Lord Mount Stephen (George Stephen, president, 1876–1881), his cousin Lord Strathcona and Mount Royal (Donald Smith, vice president, 1882–1887; president, 1887–1905; honorary president, 1905–1913), and R. B. Angus (general manager, 1869–1879; president, 1910–1913)—figured significantly in James Hill's railway projects from the St. Paul and Pacific to the Great Northern. As shown earlier, the bank had provided the seed money to make Hill's projects a success.[98] The Bank of Montreal had had its own agency in New York since 1859 and had long participated in foreign trade financing and in handling U.S., Canadian, and British exchange. In the mid-1870s, for the first time, the Bank of Montreal became involved in investment banking. After 1879 it had a close association with Kuhn, Loeb & Co., which together with the Bank of Montreal offered that year what has been called (aibeit mistakenly) the first foreign loan ever issued in New York. It was for the province of Quebec.[99] Its participation in the opposite flow of funds remained the more typical. In March 1880 the Bank of Montreal extended credit to Kuhn, Loeb & Co.—to a limit of $2 million. By April of that year, its balances due from U.S. banks and agencies exceeded $14.4 million.[100] The Bank of Montreal's general manager (in 1880) believed its New York business was "the safest and most available."[101] Table 13.4 puts the Bank of Montreal figures in context. Well over 50 percent of the Canadian "lending" in the United States (1879–80) was done by the Bank of Montreal. According to the historian R. T. Naylor, Canadian bank loans abroad, virtually all of which were in the United States (*net* of foreign deposits), totaled $23 million in 1900 and $90 million in 1909.[102] Not only did the Bank of Montreal provide seed money for ventures such as Hill's railroads and offer call and short-term bank loans, but it (like other Canadian banks) also acquired U.S. securities as part of its investment portfolio. Thus in 1876 the Bank of Montreal had purchased a "large block" of U.S. government bonds and also Cincinnati municipal bonds.[103] By 1889–90 it owned almost $2 million of U.S. railroad securities.[104] I do not have data on its portfolio for subsequent years, but apparently it continued to hold U.S. securities. In sum, it had both long-term and short-term investments in the United States.

In the early twentieth century, as Canadian demand for capital rose, all the Canadian banks (including the Bank of Montreal) found new opportunities for lending at home, so while their U.S. loan volume appears to have *increased,* the latter became—relative both to their Canadian business and to the total growth of U.S. business— less important. Nonetheless, all these banks, especially the Bank of

Table 13.4. Canadian bank capital employed abroad, 1879 and 1880 (in millions of dollars)[a]

Date	Bank of Montreal	Twenty-four other Canadian banks	Total
Nov. 30, 1879	8.95	8.02	16.97
April 30, 1880	14.42	11.27	25.69

Source: Bank "return" reported in *Banker's Magazine*, New York, 35 (Aug. 1880): 124.
   [a] Identified as balance due from banks and agents outside Canada and Great Britain. This "outside employment" was said to be overwhelmingly in the United States.

Montreal, maintained a significant U.S. presence, and their New York agencies served as their window to American business.

An alternative to having a New York licensed agency, and a way for foreign banks to enter banking in New York City, was for the foreign bank to buy into or to establish a "trust company." I know of only one set of banks that followed this route in the years 1875–1914. (There may have been others.) On May 2, 1912, the Transatlantic Trust Company came into existence in New York, organized by three large Hungarian banks. The new firm served as a "bank" for Hungarian immigrants in America, holding their deposits and remitting their savings to families back home. Its Hungarian owners had a special relationship with the Royal Hungarian Postal Savings Bank, which allowed the new New York "bank" to make money transmissions through the Hungarian postal system. The chief executive of the Transatlantic Trust Company came from Budapest.[105]

Foreign Banks in American Finance

Other European banking houses with no licensed agencies (or trust companies) in New York could, nonetheless, have a prominent role in America's international finance—in the acceptance business, trade financing, and, most important for our purposes, in long-term capital flows, including the origination of issues and participations. Such foreign institutions contributed importantly to America's financial needs.[106] In the late nineteenth and early twentieth centuries, as in earlier years, the "merchant banks" Baring Brothers and the Rothschilds remained significant.[107] Even more outstanding, especially from the 1890s onward, was J. S. Morgan & Co. (after 1910, Morgan, Grenfell & Co.).

J. S. Morgan & Co. had been founded by an American, Junius S. Morgan, who migrated to England and continued the earlier business of George Peabody. Morgan's banking activities were headquartered in London. Since he was American born and as his son, J. P. Morgan, became the preeminent New York banker, a sizable percentage of the transactions in American securities went through J. S. Morgan & Co. and through its successor, Morgan, Grenfell & Co.

Until the mid-1880s (Junius S. Morgan died in 1890), the British house—which had no American-resident partners—was the lead one among the Morgan houses. Vincent Carosso writes that Junius and J. P. Morgan were never partners in the same firm, but father and son worked intimately with one another. In 1890, however, the son became the senior partner in J. S. Morgan & Co., and the activities of the

Morgan houses subsequently became linked through interlocking partners.

In the late 1870s and in 1895 J. S. Morgan & Co. participated in distributing U.S. federal government securities in London. The firm was especially active in American railroad finance, playing a leading role in the Baltimore and Ohio; the New York Central; the Pennsylvania; the Missouri Pacific; the Chicago, Burlington; the Philadelphia and Reading; the Northern Pacific; and many others.

The London Morgan house took part in additional American business, from the London and San Francisco Bank to the Manhattan Elevated Railroad to the Interborough Rapid Transit. From the mid-1880s, the initiative in these transactions emanated from America—rather than from London—as J. P. Morgan took charge. The "headquarters" crossed the Atlantic.[108]

Baring Brothers had been notably absent in the late 1870s when a bankers' syndicate was organized to refund the U.S. debt and to assist in the resumption of specie payments.[109] Yet from the late 1870s, and far more in the 1880s, as Baring Brothers became closely associated with the Boston investment bankers Kidder, Peabody & Co., its U.S. business expanded.[110] In January 1886 Baring Brothers, London, appointed Kidder, Peabody its exclusive U.S. agent;[111] and that year Thomas Baring (1839–1923) became a partner in Kidder, Peabody, joining another Kidder, Peabody partner, George C. Magoun, in the New York office of the Boston house.[112] There was thus no retreat by the Barings from American business.

Baring Brothers participated in U.S. railroad finance—especially in the Eastern Railway of Massachusetts, the St. Louis and Iron Mountain Railroad, and the Atchison, Topeka and Santa Fe.[113] In 1886 it brought out an issue of Illinois Central bonds in London.[114] In May 1889 Kidder, Peabody and Baring Brothers took over the management of the Atchison, Topeka.[115] Baring Brothers was involved in 1887–1889 in financing the Secretan copper corner.[116] In 1890 the house headed a syndicate to place £6 million of St. Paul, Minneapolis and Manitoba bonds in what has been called "one of the largest financings . . . by an American railroad in Europe up to that time."[117]

When in the autumn of 1890 Baring Brothers was near collapse, its Argentine interests were responsible for its troubles, although its U.S. copper involvements may have contributed to the diminution of its resources.[118] After its difficulties in 1890, the Baring house was reorganized as a limited liability company, Baring Brothers & Co., Ltd.; this meant that it had shareholders and directors rather than partners, but no change took place in its operations, which remained as in times past those of a private merchant banking firm.[119]

Baring's financial misfortunes of October–November 1890 had formidable repercussions in the United States (an indication of the firm's importance), affecting the U.S. stock market. As a consequence of its plight, Baring Brothers apparently sold much of its holdings in the Atchison, Topeka and Santa Fe Railroad and disposed of other American securities.[120] Many Britishers followed, selling their American stocks and bonds. Baring's problems meant that it was unable to place more than half the bonds of the St. Paul, Minneapolis and Manitoba Railroad. Other U.S. railroads looked in vain for London financing.[121]

For the first time, in 1891, Baring Brothers organized a New York house with the family name: Baring, Magoun & Co. The Barings contributed $2 million to the new firm, and Kidder, Peabody matched that sum. Cecil Baring joined his uncle, Thomas Baring, as a partner in Baring, Magoun & Co. When Magoun died in 1893, the New York house retained his name, until in 1906 it was restyled Baring & Co.; the Baring then in America was Cecil's brother, Hugo. With Hugo Baring's return to England in 1908, Baring's New York business had a new title, becoming (as it had been 1886–1890) a branch office of Kidder, Peabody, Boston; there was, however, no Baring partner in Kidder, Peabody.[122] In London in the late 1890s and early twentieth century, John Baring (as of 1897, the second Lord Revelstoke) led Baring Brothers & Co., Ltd., and the firm continued to be active in American business.

Baring, Magoun & Co. participated in the reorganization of the Baltimore and Ohio Railroad in 1898.[123] When in May 1901 it appeared that James Hill's control of the Northern Pacific Railroad might be challenged, Gaspard Farrer (of H. S. Lefevre & Co.), who worked with Baring Brothers & Co., Ltd., and became a director in 1902, pledged his and his friends' aid to Hill.[124] In October 1901 Farrer wrote Robert Bacon, care of J. P. Morgan & Co., New York: "Would it be of any advantage to you to have the Chicago, Burlington & Quincy Joint Bonds quoted in London? About $1,000,000 have been placed here within the past few days, to my knowledge, and there appears to be a small demand for a bond paying a clean 4 percent. If you care to send the necessary papers, I would attend to the matter."[125]

Gaspard Farrer's personal circle included Lord Mount Stephen, Lord Strathcona, and James J. Hill.[126] Farrer knew well the prominent New York lawyer John William Sterling, of Shearman & Sterling;[127] Sterling represented both Lord Mount Stephen and Lord Strathcona, after they had moved to England.[128] Sterling, in turn, was a long-time intimate of James Stillman, president of the National City Bank, New York, and of William Rockefeller of Standard Oil of New York. H. H.

Rogers, once of Standard Oil and then president of Amalgamated Copper, used Sterling as his lawyer.[129] In merchant banking, friendships were of vital importance.[130]

The Barings became the banker for the Great Northern in London[131] and then for the Northern Securities Company.[132] After the breakup of Northern Securities, Baring Brothers became bankers for the Union Pacific.[133] In 1905 Baring Brothers and Kidder, Peabody submitted "the winning bid" for $25 million in American Telephone and Telegraph bonds; the Barings in London took $6.5 million.[134] The lawyer Robert T. Swaine writes that the most important utility issue of the early twentieth century was $100 million of American Telephone and Telegraph convertible 4 percent gold bonds in 1906. J. P. Morgan & Co., Kuhn, Loeb & Co., Kidder, Peabody & Co., and Baring Brothers & Co., Ltd., served as managers of the underwriting syndicate.[135]

In short, the Barings' long-time participation in American finance persisted. After 1886 the firm's most important U.S. connections were with Kidder, Peabody, but it also joined with the Morgan houses and Kuhn, Loeb & Co. in American issues. Gaspard Farrer became the most able and trusted colleague of the second Lord Revelstoke.[136] The 1890 Crisis was traumatic, but the house survived and in the years 1891–1914 continued to expedite the transfer of British savings to America.

When in the late 1870s the U.S. Treasury had turned to European markets for funds to assist in "specie resumption" (see Chapter 5), August Belmont & Co., New York, acted on behalf of N. M. Rothschild & Sons, London. The official correspondence on specie resumption and refunding the national debt (August 24, 1876–October 18, 1879) demonstrates the significance of the London Rothschilds.[137] In the contract of June 9, 1877, for example, on behalf of himself and the London Rothschilds, August Belmont took $10,321,500 of the $25 million of U.S. 4 percent bonds—more than twice that of any other single banking house.[138] The size of the loan and its timing vis-à-vis other N. M. Rothschild & Sons' business proved highly advantageous for that firm.[139] In 1881 interest on New York City stock was payable at the New York City Comptroller's office, "except such interest on Gold bonds as is payable abroad and that is payable at Messrs. Rothschild's in London."[140]

When Baron Lionel N. Rothschild, who had led that British house, died on June 3, 1879, the new head was his eldest son, Nathaniel M. Rothschild (1840–1915), who in 1885 became the first Lord Rothschild.[141] Lord Rothschild moved in a select world of British bankers, closely associated with one another.[142] Baron James de Rothschild (1792–1868), who for decades had reigned over the Paris house, had by now been succeeded by his sons, with the eldest, Baron Alphonse de Rothschild (1827–1905), the principal French Rothschild of this new generation. On Alphonse's death, his son, Edouard (born in 1868), assisted by Alphonse's two brothers, Gustave and Edmond, led the French house.[143] The Frankfurt branch of the Rothschilds continued until 1901 and then closed, for want of a male heir.[144] The cousins in N. M. Rothschild & Sons, London, and in Rothschild Frères, Paris—in the new generation of London and Paris Rothschilds—continued the pattern of their parents; that is, each house made independent decisions, while a stream of correspondence kept the family in touch and informed. There does not appear to have been a "hierarchy"—that is, London did not give orders to Paris or vice versa. Both the British and the French branches of the family participated in American business, as in times past.[145]

In the 1870s the British Rothschilds had interests in certain American railways but had not undertaken public issues of these loans on the London market.[146] After Baron Lionel N. Rothschild's death (in 1879), the London Rothschilds became more interested in American railroads—the Pennsylvania, the Illinois Central, the New York Central.[147] The Paris Rothschilds in 1882 invested in the Illinois Central.[148] By the 1880s both the British and the French Rothschilds had become important owners of American railroad securities.[149] At the end of that decade, the Paris Rothschilds were major participants in the Secretan copper syndicate.[150] In 1890 the British Rothschilds were involved in the organization of Fraser & Chalmers, Ltd., London, which acquired an American manufacturing plant.[151] That year Lord Rothschild appeared as a "money subscriber" to the Cataract Construction Company, which was undertaking power developments at Niagara Falls.[152]

The Rothschild name surfaced frequently in the 1890s in a variety of U.S. investments. N. M. Rothschild & Sons, London, became more heavily interested in U.S. railroads, especially the Louisville and Nashville.[153] In 1895 the Rothschilds, with J. P. Morgan, took part in the February contract with the U.S. Treasury to attempt to stem the U.S. gold drain. The "incentive" for the transaction was reported to have come from the London Rothschilds.[154] In the 1890s the Paris Rothschilds remained prominent in the international copper trade.[155] For a short time, 1895–1899, a company financed by N. M. Rothschild & Sons, London, the Exploration Company, Ltd., held a quarter of the shares in Anaconda, America's largest copper producer, and marketed its copper in Europe. The Exploration Company, Ltd., founded in 1886, had other American mining involvements and in the 1890s had a U.S. representative on the Pacific Coast, Captain Thomas

Mein; many of the Exploration Company's U.S. mining interests were in gold (an outcome of the Rothschilds' long involvement in buying and selling that monetary metal).[156] In 1897–1901 the British Rothschilds acted as broker for the Guggenheims for huge silver sales in Europe.[157] The Paris Rothschilds in 1912 aided in financing the entry of Royal Dutch-Shell into oil production in Oklahoma.[158] The London and Paris Rothschilds "rescued" their New York representative, August Belmont, in 1907, when he became overextended in his dealings on the New York subway system.[159]

Throughout, both the London and the Paris Rothschilds retained as American agent the private banking house August Belmont & Co., New York. August Belmont, Sr., had become the Rothschild representative in America in 1837. Over the years the relationships were sporadically stormy, but they persisted.[160] When Belmont died in 1890, his son August (1853–1924), who on his father's death dropped the "Jr.," took charge. Because of his Rothschild connection, his father's reputation, and also in his own right, the younger Belmont became an important individual in American finance; he had been managing August Belmont & Co. (under his father's overall direction) since about 1882.[161] For American businessmen, the name August Belmont was synonymous with Rothschild interests.

The Rothschilds had an agency in California in the years 1849–1880, follo\ _d by a correspondent association with the Bank of California.[162] The London Rothschilds collaborated with Jacob Schiff of Kuhn, Loeb & Co.[163] More important, in 1901 the house made a formal arrangement with Lee, Higginson & Co., Boston. On November 6, 1901, the Boston investment house wrote Lord Rothschild:

> Mr. Higginson has returned to Boston, and we can now, therefore write you our conclusions in regard to the exchange business.
>
> We have decided to undertake this business, at first . . . only to a limited extent, and to see how much it can be developed hereafter.
>
> . . . We sincerely hope that this beginning may result in closer relations, profitable to you and to us.

The rest of this letter contained information about business conditions in the United States.[164] A week later Lee, Higginson wrote that in connection with the exchange business, "we accept the terms you offered our Messrs. Higginson & Lane when they had the pleasure of meeting Lord Rothschild last August." The letter spelled out the commissions and the terms: "Your commission on the larger side of the account to be one-eighth of one percent."[165] In the early years of the twentieth century, N. M. Rothschild & Sons developed a close relationship with Lee, Higginson & Co.[166] Accordingly, the London

Rothschilds' 1913 American accounts show not only accounts with August Belmont, but under the rubric "Lee, Higginson & Co., Boston," there are the headings "General Account," "Our Account," and "Securities Account." Under the latter were investments in bonds of Puget Sound Traction, the city of Omaha, and American Can Company; common shares of U.S. Steel, U.S. Smelting, Refining and Mining (4,000 shares) and Northern Pacific; and preferred shares of American Agricultural Chemical Company (2,000 shares). Only in U.S. Smelting, Refining and Mining and American Agricultural Chemical Company were the London Rothschild interests (as handled by Lee, Higginson) substantial.[167]

The Rothschilds were well informed on what was happening in America. Their correspondence contains detailed information. Lord Rothschild in 1907, for example, wrote his Paris cousins on a range of American matters: "American shares are booming . . . there is a huge American account here" (January 7, 1907); "although Union Pacific have fallen a little, the disclosures [by Harriman] do not seem to have produced the same effect in Wall Street as here" (January 8, 1907); "early this morning we could have lent considerable sums of fresh money on American securities at very high rates, but although we went on with all our old money we declined to lend any more on the American market" (January 14, 1907); "American Railway shares are somewhat under a cloud, but it would be a mistake to be too pessimistic" (January 18, 1907). This small sample from two weeks in January reveals the careful attention.[168] The London Rothschilds expressed dismay at Theodore Roosevelt's hostility to railroad enterprise (March 14, 1907). On March 15, 1907, Lord Rothschild wrote, "Our telegrams from America do not tell us much more than is in the papers and even the best informed like Sir Edgar Speyer can only conjecture, in all probability the sales in New York were occasioned by fears of socialistic legislation or actions on the part of Roosevelt and the various states." Lord Rothschild thought American railways "instead of being overcapitalized are undercapitalized" (April 3, 1907).[169]

In London the Rothschilds followed the course of the 1907 American Panic. In its midst, their correspondence expressed confidence and noted (on October 24, 1907) that in London "all the leading American houses and a great many bargain hunters were considerable buyers of [American] stock all the morning." Lord Rothschild was very impressed with J. P. Morgan's role in the crisis: "Our friend [Morgan] has shown himself on this occasion a greater man than he ever was before" (October 27, 1907). This is a tiny selection from the Rothschild Archives, but it reflects the concern of that house with

American business. These letters of Lord Rothschild in London to his Paris cousins suggest an important French as well as British interest in America: "You no doubt receive almost as many messages from America as we do," Lord Rothschild wrote his Paris cousins on October 24, 1907.[170]

In sum, both the British and the French Rothschilds participated in intermediating monies from Europe to the United States and took part in a number of different American activities. In the years 1880–1914 there was no Rothschild "bank" in the United States, nor was there a Rothschild "copartnership" in any private bank, nor was any member of the family a resident across the Atlantic. Instead, August Belmont & Co. kept both the London and the Paris Rothschild houses abreast of conditions in America, giving advice that was carefully evaluated, sometimes accepted, sometimes rejected. While the Rothschilds acted through the Belmont firm, they also associated with others (as in their dealings with Fraser & Chalmer, with Royal Dutch-Shell in Oklahoma, with Kuhn, Loeb & Co., and in the early twentieth century with Lee, Higginson & Co.). The Rothschilds' role in American finance was noteworthy.[171] A recent study by Stanley D. Chapman suggests that in the years 1870–1914 N. M. Rothschild & Sons—measured by capital—was the most important merchant bank in London.[172] While its American business had its "ups and downs," its extent remained impressive; the Rothschilds by no means neglected America.

The Morgan houses, the Barings, and the Rothschilds were major participants in American finance, but were not alone. Most European bankers involved in U.S. business had some home institutional affiliation; an exception was Ernest Cassel, prominent in his own right, who acted as an individual throughout much of his career and was ubiquitous in American finance.[173] All the principal British merchant banks took part in expediting the flow of British and European capital to the United States, especially into American railroads and then, primarily from 1899 to 1914, into other issues as well.[174] J. Henry Schroeder & Co.—which with E. Erlanger had offered the Confederate loan of 1863—retained its connections in the American South, particularly in Alabama.[175] At the turn of the century, it handled subscriptions for Amalgamated Copper's giant London offering.[176] An issue of Southern Pacific Company bonds had its interest and principal payable at J. Henry Schroeder in London.[177] C. J. Hambro & Son cooperated with the London and New York Morgan houses on American issues. Everard Hambro, its senior partner, was a close friend of J. P. Morgan.[178] Individually as well, C. J. Hambro & Son was involved in American railroad issues.[179]

Bischoffsheim & Goldschmidt—before the mid-1880s—was associated with the Erie and the Atlantic and Great Western.[180] McCalmont Brothers was long identified with the Philadelphia and Reading.[181] J. K. Gilliat & Co. had sizable American business, especially with the Denver and Rio Grande; Maitland and Phelps, New York, had an Englishman, George Coppell, from J. K. Gilliat & Co. as a New York partner.[182] Stern Brothers in London was the British house of the German Jacob S. H. Stern; together and independently they did substantial U.S. business, tied in with the Deutsche Bank.[183] R. Raphael & Sons had Louis von Hoffman as its American agent.[184] Robert Fleming & Co. was another London firm with an important role in American business.[185] Likewise, a sizable portion of the activities of Robert Benson & Co. involved railroads and land financing in America.[186] Kleinwort, Sons & Co. (a firm that many years later would merge with the Benson one to become Kleinwort, Benson) handled American industrials in London—for example, American Smelting and Refining Company and Studebaker Corporation. It had close connections with Goldman, Sachs in New York.[187] E. Erlanger, which had cooperated with Schroeder in the Confederate bond issue, also developed its own extensive business in the American South.[188] Benjamin Newgass, a Liverpool banker turned London banker, likewise had large American interests.[189]

There were merchant houses that are hard to define in terms of nationality. Morton, Rose & Co., for example, was an outgrowth of Morton, Bliss, an American house; Levi Morton was an American;[190] its successor, Chaplin, Milne, Grenfell & Co., however, had no American partner. Whereas Morton, Rose & Co. specialized in American railroads, Chaplin, Milne, Grenfell became particularly involved in mining securities.[191] Then there was Blake, Boissevain & Co.; Stanton Blake and W. B. Blake were Bostonians;[192] the Boissevain family was Dutch (A. A. H. Boissevain was the most important Boissevain of this generation). When Blake, Boissevain & Co., London, went into liquidation, on January 1, 1901, the Swiss Bankverein, which already had substantial American business, took over many of its customers.[193] Lazard Brothers & Co., Ltd.—associated with the New York Lazard Frères and the firm's Paris house—was a participant in American business.[194] Brown, Shipley & Co. and Seligman Brothers were American firms in England. Speyer Brothers, London, is a difficult case; Sir Edgar Speyer was in his own right a significant figure in British and American finance; Speyer Brothers, London, had James Speyer (New

York) as a partner, as well as Eduard Beit von Speyer (Frankfurt). The three Speyer houses each had interlocking partners.[195]

All these houses in England—and many more—facilitated the transfer of long-term British monies to the United States.[196] As noted in Chapter 6, some of these merchant bankers actively intervened in the financial management of U.S. railroads. In a book published in 1915, E. T. Powell wrote, perceptively, that "the investor in foreign bonds trusts the banker rather than the borrower."[197] If an established British banking house or banker underwrote or endorsed an American security, this gave British investors confidence in its soundness.[198] Merchant bankers in England joined with American investment bankers—sometimes those with which they had interlocking partners and sometimes those with which they had had over many years other close associations. The international banking community (and in particular those bankers handling American securities) knew and cooperated with one another. As Vincent Carosso, the historian of American investment banking, writes, "the various investment bankers combined and formed groups, and pooled their underwriting resources."[199]

Commercial banks in the United Kingdom also played a role in U.S. business beyond that of trade financing.[200] Some such as Glyn, Mills served as underwriters of issues of American securities in Britain, retailed the securities for wholesalers (such as J. S. Morgan & Co.), and arranged that payments of principal and interest on bonds could be made at their offices.[201] Parr's Bank—a large British commercial bank—offered Cities Service Company preferred shares to the British public. As compensation for its negotiation of this security, it apparently received common stock.[202] Some commercial banks acted as "depositories" when there were U.S. railroad reorganizations.[203] Some made domestic and foreign short-term loans, taking American securities as collateral, and became owners of the securities with loan defaults.[204] The British Linen Bank made loans directly to American railroads.[205] Prospectuses for new issues printed in the London *Times* (or the *Economist* or elsewhere) for firms in U.S. business always listed British bankers. Thus, for example, in 1891 Lloyds Bank, Ltd., served as "banker" for the Milwaukee and Chicago Breweries, Ltd., while that same year the Manchester and Liverpool District Bank acted in this capacity for the De Lamar Mining Company.[206] In this role the banks often held the firm's British deposits and possibly handled stock transfers.[207] In addition, commercial banks in Great Britain purchased U.S. railroad securities and less often other American securities for their investment portfolios.[208] A French observer (Georges Aubert) in 1910 noted that the London City and Midland

Bank and the Union Bank of London and Smiths had very close connections with "the two largest" New York banks. These British institutions, he wrote, did enormous business that facilitated the commercial exchanges between the United States and the United Kingdom and also the financial transactions that took place on the London Stock Exchange in American securities.[209] All the various connections notwithstanding, clearly the large British merchant banks, much more than the "clearing house" banks, were the principal intermediaries for long-term portfolio investments in the United States.[210]

The years 1875 to 1914 saw the coming of age of the great German universal banks, institutions that were at the same time "deposit banks, credit banks, and financing companies."[211] As the German economy grew, its banks became heavily concentrated. The German private banks, many of which had had U.S. involvements (Bleichroeder, Mendelssohn, Robert Warschauer & Co., Rothschild, Erlanger, and Sulzbach Brothers, for example), yielded to and were dwarfed by the newer giants,[212] which in turn and at once developed important interests in the United States. By 1905 the four largest German banks (measured by capital and reserves) were the Deutsche Bank, the Disconto-Gesellschaft, the Dresdner Bank, and the Darmstädter Bank (the Bank für Handel und Industrie).[213] A fifth large German bank was the Berliner Handels-Gesellschaft.[214] All five financed enterprise in America, as did many smaller German houses. The German banks were international; they brought foreign issues to Germany and assisted German industry abroad.[215] The United States was logically part of their broad multinational business.

Table 13.5 reflects some of the principal allies of the German banks in the United States. With the exception of J. P. Morgan, each of the listed American firms was founded by a man or men who had migrated from Frankfurt (or the vicinity) across the Atlantic and thus had, and retained, close personal connections with the German banking community.[216] Although all the German banks had London establishments, much of their American finance was done directly rather than via London. Nonetheless, often Americans and Germans met in London to conduct business, and it is important to view the relationships as international rather than bilateral.

The largest German bank, the Deutsche Bank, Berlin, had, as noted in Chapter 4, obtained a silent partnership interest in a private New York bank, Knoblauch & Lichtenstein, in 1872. Owing to the speculations of the latter's manager, that venture proved unsuccessful and was liquidated in 1882.[217] Similarly, the Darmstädter Bank withdrew from its "silent" partnership in G. vom Baur & Co., New York (an

Table 13.5. Principal "alliances" between German and American banks in the late nineteenth and early twentieth centuries

Germany	United States (all in New York)
Deutsche Bank in its American transactions often was allied with Jacob S. H. Stern and with Lazard Speyer-Ellissen & Co.	Speyer & Co.
Disconto-Gesellschaft	Kuhn, Loeb & Co., Goldman, Sachs, & Co.
Dresdner Bank connection established in 1905	J. P. Morgan
Darmstädter Bank	Hallgarten & Co.
Berliner Handels-Gesellschaft interest acquired in 1904	Hallgarten & Co.
Lazard Speyer-Ellissen & Co.	Speyer & Co.
Seligman & Stettheimer (to 1900)	J. & W. Seligman
Bleichroeder, S.	Ladenburg, Thalmann & Co.
Warburg (M. M.) & Co.	Kuhn, Loeb & Co.

Source: Paul Emden, *Money Powers of Europe* (New York: Appleton-Century, 1938), pp. 398–399, 223, 239, 244; with modifications and additions. According to Emden (p. 397), Ladenburg, Thalmann & Co., New York, was "for a time" "controlled" by S. Bleichroeder. On Goldman, Sachs, & Co., see Walter E. Sachs "Reminiscences," Oral History Collection, Columbia University, New York, pt. 1, p. 18. Seligman & Stettheimer closed down in 1900.

interest that dated back to 1854); vom Baur & Co. went into liquidation about the end of 1885.[218] In 1904 the Berliner Handels-Gesellschaft had two partners in Hallgarten & Co.[219] The associations listed in Table 13.5 were fundamental to the business relationships in the period 1875–1914. Note that the ties were all with private American banking houses, not with national or state-chartered banks. Note, too, that they were not exclusive and sometimes did and sometimes did not involve interlocking partnerships. Disconto-Gesellschaft worked closely with both Kuhn, Loeb & Co. and Goldman, Sachs & Co. The Dresdner Bank, and others as well, joined in transactions with J. P. Morgan, America's leading banker.[220]

The Deutsche Bank, ranking sixth in the world (in terms of deposits) in 1914, led in its numerous U.S. commitments.[221] Its chief executives, Georg von Siemens (1839–1901) and Arthur von Gwinner (1856–1931), were familiar with America.[222] In the early 1870s the bank had helped finance the Direct United States Cable Company. By 1880–81 the Deutsche Bank was interested in a number of different American railroad bonds. In 1882–83 it was participating in Germany in the financing of the Hamburg-American Line and the North German Lloyd Line, that is, in transatlantic shipping.[223] In 1883 the bank made its first investment in the Northern Pacific.[224] At that time Henry Villard was president of that railroad (he became president in September 1881 and resigned in January 1884). Between 1886 and 1890 Villard, and then between 1893 and 1914 Edward D. Adams, both Americans (the first a German immigrant, the second from an important American family), represented the Deutsche Bank in making sizable investments and in corporate reorganizations in the United States.[225]

The most significant of the Deutsche Bank's U.S. commitments related to the Northern Pacific Railroad.[226] In 1883 the Deutsche Bank had marketed that railroad's bonds in Europe. While Villard was the bank's American representative, the Deutsche Bank acquired and underwrote securities of the Northern Pacific on a grand scale. In 1887 Villard rejoined the board of directors of Northern Pacific, serving on behalf of the Deutsche Bank.[227] Later the Deutsche Bank was highly instrumental in the 1896 reorganization of that railroad, and until the turn of the century it held a significant stake in the Northern Pacific and took part in its financial management.[228] In the late 1890s it was von Gwinner (who joined the board of management of the Deutsche Bank in 1894) who played the key role for the Deutsche Bank, Berlin, in relation to the Northern Pacific.[229] Von Gwinner, after von Siemens' death in 1901, was "primus inter pares, the head, of the Deutsche Bank."[230]

When in 1886 the Deutsche Bank had appointed Villard to act on its behalf in the United States, Georg von Siemens wrote, in his awkward English, to Drexel, Morgan & Co. (September 29), "We would bespeak for him [Villard] as our confidential friend and adviser the goodwill of your firm of which Mr. Morgan kindly gave verbal assurance in advance, and we hope his presence near you will lead to frequent and mutually advantage transactions between our firms."[231] The Deutsche Bank's interests in the Northern Pacific brought it into close contact with J. P. Morgan, and its working relationship with that banking house carried over into other business spheres, other railroads and industrials.[232]

The Deutsche Bank—along with Siemens & Halske and Allgemeine Elektrizitäts Gesellschaft—invested in Edison General Electric Company in 1889; Morgan participated in Edison General Electric Company, and in 1892 in the new General Electric Company (by which time the Germans had withdrawn).[233] In 1893 "some loose ends" from this commitment were still outstanding, and Georg von Siemens traveled to America to straighten them out. Apparently the Deutsche

Bank had become involved with the Cincinnati Light Company, and von Siemens hoped "to shore it up."[234] Meanwhile, in 1890 the Deutsche Bank supplied capital to the Niagara Falls Power Company.[235] The bank also assisted in financing several German direct investments in U.S. mining and manufacturing: Lehigh Coke Company, Botany Worsted Mills Company (through its Leipzig branch), and C. P. Goerz American Optical Company.[236]

Late in December 1895–January 1896, the Deutsche Bank participated with J. P. Morgan in organizing a syndicate to market U.S. federal government bonds in Europe.[237] The bank's involvement in the European petroleum business brought it into contact with foreign investors in the U.S. oil business.[238] In a different industry, in 1906 the bank provided a $5 million short-term loan to Allis-Chalmers Company;[239] the bank's U.S. representative, Edward D. Adams, became chairman of the board of that company.[240]

In its U.S. transactions, the Deutsche Bank often joined with the German Lazard Speyer-Ellissen and the latter's U.S. house, Speyer & Co., and with the Frankfurt firm Jacob S. H. Stern. Arthur von Gwinner married Ann Speyer.[241] Otto Braunfels, a partner in Jacob S. H. Stern, was on the board of the Deutsche Bank and frequently undertook U.S. business on behalf of both firms.[242] In certain syndications, the Deutsche Bank participated with August Belmont & Co. and the London Rothschilds; in addition, the German bank had close ties with Kuhn, Loeb & Co. The biographer of that firm's Jacob Schiff reported that the latter developed "pleasant personal relations" with both Georg von Siemens and Arthur von Gwinner.[243] The Deutsche Bank appears to have had connections with Heidelbach, Ickelheimer & Co. and Müller, Schall & Co., New York.[244] In 1904–1907 the Deutsche Bank helped arrange to have the Central Pacific and the Southern Pacific listed in Berlin and negotiated the sale of their securities.[245] In short, while the largest Deutsche Bank American involvement was with the Northern Pacific Railroad, the bank had multiple U.S. interests.

In a similar fashion, I could outline the U.S. ties and American issues of the Disconto-Gesellschaft, the Dresdner Bank, the Darm-städter Bank (Bank für Handel and Industrie), and the Berliner Handels-Gesellschaft. From railroads to other industries, these banks actively participated in American finance.[246]

So, too, the two largest (measured by deposits in 1913) French banks—Crédit Lyonnais and Société Générale—engaged in American business, although not to the extent of the German banks. The Crédit Lyonnais, as part of its international expansion, had opened a New

York agency in 1879, justified by "l'importance commerciale et finan-cière des États-Unis et leur relations considérable avec la place de Lyon."[247] As noted earlier, Crédit Lyonnais closed this agency in 1882.[248] The bank had been briefly in Chicago during the 1893 World's Fair.[249] It had a role in 1913 in the financing of the giant French aluminum enterprise in North Carolina.[250] Société Générale (Paris) participated in underwriting American securities in France: those of the American Smelter Securities Company and a number of U.S. railroads, including the Pennsylvania; the New York, New Haven; the Chicago, Milwaukee and St. Paul; and the Central Pacific.[251] It seems to have been involved in financing Westinghouse.[252]

The Comptoir d'Escompte de Paris participated (to its misfortune) in the Secretan copper syndicate in 1888–89.[253] Its successor, Comp-toir National d'Escompte, Paris, had a "branch" (or agency) in Chi-cago from 1893 to 1900, and an agency in New Orleans from the mid-1890s to 1903.[254]

Moving to another category of French banks, the largest of the so-called Banques d'Affaires, industrial banks, was the Banque de Paris et des Pays-Bas, established in 1872 by a merger of the Banque de Paris (formed in 1870) and the Banque de Crédit et Dépôt des Pays-Bas.[255] In 1875 its Amsterdam branch had suffered a consider-able loss when it took part with an unidentified New York house (that suspended payments that year) in a syndicate for financing an Amer-ican railroad.[256] Subsequently the Banque de Paris became deeply engaged in sizable international transactions, far greater than any U.S. involvements.[257] It had, however, some American business,[258] and its Edouard Noetzlin was a long-time correspondent of Kuhn, Loeb's Jacob Schiff.[259] In 1883 it had entered into an association with Baring Brothers and Morton, Rose;[260] it appears to have handled in Paris many of the same U.S. securities that these British houses were dealing with in London. Thus it participated in the introduction on the Paris Bourse of the Atchison, Topeka and Santa Fe, as well as the Chicago, Milwaukee and St. Paul, and the Central Pacific.[261] Its par-ticipations and issues included the Union Pacific (in 1897)[262] and American Telephone and Telegraph securities (1906).[263] In March 1907 it sent a representative to America with a plan to establish a French bank in New York[264] (nothing came of the idea).

The Banque de l'Union Parisienne, founded in 1904, another of the large French Banques d'Affaires, presented the securities of the St. Louis and San Francisco Railroad on the Paris Bourse in the early twentieth century.[265] It was the principal organizer of the Société Financière Franco-Américaine.[266] In 1906 or early 1907 the Banque

Franco-Américaine de Paris opened in New York. By 1910 it had an active and prosperous business, apparently placing French capital into industrial activities in the United States.[267]

Like the major British merchant banks and the principal German banks, all the big French banks seem to have participated in U.S. railroad issues. In France in the early twentieth century, these banks offered competition in U.S. business to the long-established private houses, such as Rothschild Frères and Hottinguer & Cie.;[268] in this context I should also include Morgan, Harjes & Co., Lazard Frères, and Munroe & Co.—three American-French houses.[269] The large French banks floated issues and advised investors on their merits. Domestic branches of these banks "gathered savings and in exchange distributed securities issued by their central office." For the leading French banks, the marketing of foreign securities (including American ones) was a substantial source of profits.[270]

Dutch bankers, highly experienced in American finance, handled far more American securities than their French counterparts. The Dutch sent men to sit on U.S. railroad boards and cooperated on a regular basis with American, British, and on occasion German, French, and Swiss investment and merchant bankers. Prominent among the Dutch banking houses in U.S. transactions were the Amsterdamsche Bank (created by the German Darmstädter bank in 1871);[271] Adolph Boissevain & Co.;[272] Broes & Gosman; A. Gansl; Hope & Co.; Hubrecht, van Harencarspel and Vas Visser; Kerkhoven & Co.; Lippmann, Rosenthal & Co.; Nederlandsche Handel-Maatschappij; Oyens & Co.; Teixeira de Mattos; Tutein Nolthenius & De Haan; Wertheim & Gompertz; and Westendorp & Co. In the early twentieth century many of the Dutch houses that once specialized in American railway bonds and shares now marketed the securities of U.S. industrial enterprises as well.[273]

For a time, according to Nathaniel Bacon, the private banking house in Geneva Lombard, Odier & Cie. "had virtually a monopoly" in Switzerland in intermediating monies into U.S. investments, and by the late 1890s, Bacon wrote, one-third of the entire amount of securities of all kinds owned in that Swiss city were American.[274] In the 1840s Alex Lombard had counseled his clients on U.S. state debts. In the mid-1850s his firm had sold American county bonds in Switzerland. Before the end of the Civil War, his house was putting its customers into U.S. government bonds; in 1872 it offered another Swiss bank (the Swiss Bank Corporation) a holding in the Swiss-American Bank (in San Francisco); likewise, in the early 1870s it participated in financing the Nashville and Chattanooga Railroad; by the 1880s and 1890s it specialized in high-quality U.S. railroad bonds.[275]

In those last two decades of the nineteenth century, additional Swiss bankers from Geneva, Basle, and Zurich joined it in negotiating American securities, particularly railroad issues. Like their British, German, French, and Dutch counterparts, the Swiss bankers typically acted in concert with American private banks and often with other European bankers. Frequently Swiss bankers (especially those in Geneva) invested on behalf of Frenchmen.[276] The connections between Geneva and Lyon were intimate.

By 1913 the largest Swiss bank was Schweizerischer Bankverein (the Swiss Bank Corporation) of Basle. It cooperated with Frankfurt institutions, and through them it had developed substantial American business. It opened a London office (Swiss Bankverein) in 1898, which in 1899 joined others in underwriting the Chicago and Alton Railroad stock and Southern Pacific gold bonds. Its historian, Hans Bauer, writes of the Swiss Bank Corporation's loan-issuing activities between 1907 and 1914 that American railroads "were much in favor."[277] The Swiss Bankverein was listed in 1914 as the London agent of the Chicago Junction Railways and Union Stock Yards Company, the firm that owned the Union Stock Yards in Chicago and the railroads connected with it.[278] The Swiss Bank Corporation had links with the "Merton group" of metal traders[279] in London and Frankfurt (that is, Metallgesellschaft), which held controlling interest in the American Metal Company.[280] The Swiss Bank financed domestic industrial concerns, some with investments in America.[281] In 1907 the bank had a sizable loss as a result of an unspecified New York bankruptcy; it accordingly "ceased to grant credits through the mediation of agents and visited customers abroad directly from time to time."[282]

The second largest Swiss bank in 1913 was Crédit Suisse, Zurich. Between 1895 and 1906 it participated in some 250 foreign offerings, of which American railway issues were among the most important.[283]

Banks from other European countries handled U.S. securities or took part in U.S. finance (for example, the Wallenbergs in Sweden),[284] but their role was slight in the overall picture.

Table 13.6 contains estimates based on data compiled by Paul Dickens on the total *nominal* value of foreign underwritings of American securities by class, from 1897 to 1914.[285] The table tells us little about the flow or the level of foreign investment to or in the United States.[286] What it shows is (1) the publicly recorded activity in relation to newly issued American securities abroad and (2) the continuing significance

Table 13.6. Total nominal value of foreign underwriting of American securities by class, 1897–1914 (in millions of dollars)

Year	Govern-ments	Steam railways	Public utilities	Industrials and miscellaneous	British companies	Total of all classes
1897	2.0	21.6	1.9	—	9.4	34.9
1898	0.5	58.5	—	—	12.7	71.7
1899	—	3.5	—	9.7	11.2	24.4
1900	—	4.3	2.5	—	3.0	9.8
1901	—	22.8	—	0.2	4.0	27.0
1902	—	57.0	7.0	—	1.5	65.5
1903	—	101.7	1.5	—	1.7	104.9
1904	—	83.0	20.0	—	0.7	103.7
1905	—	92.8	10.0	1.8	1.1	105.7
1906	—	86.2	25.0	3.0	0.1	114.3
1907	10.0	122.6	70.7	—	7.6	210.9
1908	10.1	89.0	23.0	2.0	0.1	124.2
1909	8.0	104.2	33.2	20.5	—	165.9
1910	24.5	345.9	21.8	7.4	10.1	409.7
1911	5.0	192.0	27.8	20.1	6.4	251.3
1912	15.0	99.2	75.0	59.9	2.4	251.5
1913	5.0	174.9	118.9[a]	20.3	2.7	321.8
1914	30.0	130.9	10.1	0.5	11.5	183.0
Total	110.1	1,790.1	448.4	145.4	86.2	2,580.2

Source: Paul Dickens, "The Transition Period in American Finance," Ph.D. diss., George Washington University, 1933, p. 109. Sterling issues were converted by Dickens at the rate £ 1 = \$4.8665.

[a] By my calculation, based on Dickens, "The Transition," pp. 264–266, much of this figure should have been classified under railroads (some were "electric railroads").

of railroads in the securities offered. Foreign banking houses participated in all these underwritings and in the channeling of at least some portion of this long-term capital into the United States.[287]

The Role of Foreign Banks

In conclusion, when the Federal Reserve System was inaugurated in the United States in 1914, there is no evidence of sizable foreign investments in American commercial banking. Commercial banking in America was not undertaken by branches or subsidiaries of foreign banks; almost all of the numerous American national and state banks were American owned. Unlike U.S. manufacturers and foreign-controlled ones in this country (from J. & P. Coats to Merck) that produced within and sold throughout the nation, no American bank, much less foreign-owned bank, took deposits and made loans through branch offices across the country. By 1914 in only one city, Chicago, were foreign-owned banks of any importance in the domestic market. I have not discussed "savings banks," for with a single exception (in Portland, Oregon), I found little evidence of a foreign investor role in these deposit-taking firms.[288]

By contrast, in the pre–Civil War years foreign investors—including some foreign merchant banks—had owned stock in the first and Second Banks of the United States (albeit nonvoting securities), and thus foreign investors had had sizable investments in American *domestic* banking—on a national scale. Likewise, in Louisiana in the 1830s, they had dominated that state's banking system (as noted, 52 percent of the paid-up capital of Louisiana banks in 1837 came from Europe). So too in California in the early 1870s, foreign-owned banks (in this case foreign direct investors) had been of major consequence; but this was no longer true in 1914. Since the evolution of the banking system in the United States had resulted in banks that did not branch across the country, this probably limited foreign portfolio and direct investments. State laws, in addition, deterred investment from abroad. Much more important, by the late nineteenth and early twentieth centuries, American banks adequately served routine domestic banking requirements. American national and state banks could stand on their own and did not need capital from abroad; foreign banks or foreign-owned banks had no advantage in the purely domestic business.

It was in *international* rather than in national or local transactions that foreign bank "connections" proved vital. There were in 1914 twenty foreign bank agencies in New York. These foreign direct investors (and the agencies can be called foreign direct investments) helped in financing U.S. exports and imports; they handled foreign exchange; they assisted immigrants; they were conduits for information; they were *not*, however, key as intermediaries of foreign capital inflow.

Nevertheless, other foreign banks and banking houses did play a vital role in encouraging the entry of long-term overseas capital into the United States in sectors *other* than banking. While there were some foreign direct investments (the Rothschilds' participation in the metals trade and mining went far beyond finance) and while banks themselves made portfolio investments (that is, held American securities on their own account), foreign banks and banking houses were clearly most important as underwriters and distributors of American securities. They *were* highly significant in the presentation of American securities abroad—in the origination of issues and participations—and in the mobilization of long-term foreign portfolio investments for U.S. requirements. They did collect foreign savings and aided in transferring them to America, but to do this they did not need a major "presence" in the United States.

Some foreign merchant or investment banks or bankers, to be sure, did have close family ties with American private banks (for example, J. S. Morgan with Drexel, Morgan & Co. and Sir Edgar Speyer and Eduard Beit von Speyer with Speyer & Co.). Some had partners in Boston or New York banks with no specific family associations (the Barings in Kidder, Peabody, Boston, 1886–1890; J. K. Gilliat & Co. in Maitland and Phelps, New York in the 1880s; the Deutsche Bank in Knoblauch & Lichtenstein, New York, 1872–1882; the Darmstädter Bank in G. vom Baur & Co., New York, 1854–1885; the Berliner Handels-Gesellschaft in Hallgarten & Co., New York, 1904–1914[?], for instance). Many dealt on a regular basis with an independent New York house (the Rothschilds with August Belmont & Co. is an excellent example; in addition, R. Raphael & Sons with Louis von Hoffman; Disconto-Gesellschaft with Kuhn, Loeb; Banque de Paris et des Pays-Bas, also with Kuhn, Loeb). Some had individuals in the United States who served as their representatives (the Deutsche Bank had Henry Villard, 1886–1890, and Edward D. Adams, 1893–1914). This brief summary samples the complex interrelationships. The form of U.S. representation (the U.S. "presence") of any single foreign bank, banking house, or banker often varied substantially over time (consider the changes in the Baring's U.S. presence between 1875 and 1914, as described in the text). The associations were typically nonexclusive—that is, the "principal" dealt with other U.S. houses (the Rothschilds, for instance, did not work only with August Belmont & Co.), and the "agent" might have ties with various European principals (Kuhn, Loeb acted in concert with many foreign banks and bankers). No matter what the American "connection," be it formal or informal, the foreign banks and banking houses did play a vital role as conduits in the transfer of capital into the United States.

Although the Rothschilds handled U.S. government bonds (in the late 1870s and in 1895) and the Deutsche Bank was ready to do so in 1896, such activities were exceptional. By 1880–1914 government lending was not a key or even an important function of foreign banking houses in the American market.[289] Rather, what occurred was basically the movement of privately held European savings across the Atlantic to finance private business enterprises—railroads and other ones. The vast bulk of the activities of the foreign banking houses involved the placement of nongovernmental American securities that were offered and distributed by the financial intermediaries in the main money markets of Europe. This was the era when many American companies went "public," and as they did so, European banks and banking houses enlarged these corporations' access to capital. The principal financial institutions in Europe participated in American finance.

14.

Financial, Commercial, and Communication Services

Foreign stockbrokers, promoters, investment trusts, and providers of land and real estate mortgages acted as important conduits for overseas investments in the United States. Likewise, foreign traders, shipping concerns, cable companies, and wireless transmitters were both investors in America and "intermediaries." All of these different types of business investors served a dual function in their U.S. involvements. Their first role was as foreign investors. Their second role was as communicators of U.S. investment opportunities to *their* clients, to the users of their services.

Stockbrokers

In Britain a number of large stockbrokers served to channel British savings into U.S. investments during the period 1875–1914. In 1876 Foster & Braithwaite, for example, was involved in a private placement of Pennsylvania Railroad bonds.[1] Others, closely associated with the important London merchant bankers in U.S. transactions, included Borthwick, Wark and E. F. Satterthwaite & Co.[2] The large London stockbroker Vivian, Gray & Co. introduced its customers to the Norfolk and Western Railroad in the 1880s. In addition, Heseltine, Powell & Co., another large stockbroking firm, had put Britishers into the Marietta and Cincinnati Railroad and acted as the representative of the British bondholders. Many Scottish stockbrokers gave advice on U.S. rails and even placed their clients' money in American mortgages.[3] Harry Panmure Gordon, who in 1876 established his own London stockbroking firm (called Panmure Gordon), was known for his ability to place sizable foreign loans. He participated in underwriting the San Francisco Brewery Company in 1890. He visited

America and wrote a book (in 1892) on his travels; in the book he could not resist recommending shares in the Union Stock Yards. None of these (or other) stockbrokers had their own "agencies" or copartnerships in America. All had contacts in the United States.[4] They were intermediaries of monies and sometimes investors (portfolio ones) in their own right, but they were *themselves* local or national rather than international in "operations."[5]

In Holland, Germany, and France, certain stockbrokers specialized in placing American securities. Like their British counterparts, they did not have "agencies" in the United States—albeit some knew America well. Thus Salomon Frederick Van Oss, the author of *American Railroads as Investments* (1893), established his own stockbroker's firm in the Hague soon after the turn of the century and in 1904 started a publication entitled *Van Oss' Effectenboek,* a guide for Dutch investors. Van Oss encouraged the sale of American securities in Holland.[6]

Promoters

Promoters constituted another group of nonbank financial intermediaries. They could be Americans, but there was also a whole coterie of British promoters. British-incorporated firms—mines, cattle companies, breweries, and other industrials—often, as I have shown, purchased American properties. Someone—American or British—had to take the initiative. This was the promoter's role. Sometimes promoters acquired or merged existing companies, and sometimes they started afresh. Thus a promoter might buy a mine or consolidate a group of American firms; he would give the enterprise a new name and then present it to the public in London.[7] Generally a promoter would be less concerned with the ultimate earning power of the venture than with his profits made in acquiring the U.S. assets, "packaging" them (preparing a prospectus attractive to the potential buyers of such securities), and then reselling the "new company."[8]

One such promoter, John R. Whitley of London, for example, would start brand new companies. In 1882 he bought a patent for a wall-decoration product and formed a company in America to exploit it. In 1894 he planned to promote an enterprise to build an ice-skating rink in New York. Whitley had obtained patents for quick-freezing ice surfaces.[9] Established merchant bankers shied away from such speculations.

Herman Krooss and Martin Blyn have described the *American* promoter "as distinct from the investment banker in that he was more an organizer of industrial mergers and distributor of securities than a financier possessing or having ready access to large sums of money." The description applies equally well to most British promoters. Note, however, that in the London market American and British promoters often worked in tandem. Krooss and Blyn point out that the promoter introduced the public to industrial securities before the conservative investment banks would touch such issues; here, too, parallels between the U.S. and British cases exist. They add that, in time, investment bankers did underwrite industrial bonds and preferred stock and that the day of the promoter was short-lived, as he was replaced by the investment bank.[10] A similar pattern seems true in the Anglo-American business. P. L. Cottrell emphasizes that "untried foreign borrowers . . . were not catered for by 'reputable' major merchant banks in London. Their issues were handled instead by 'ad hoc' syndicates." The first-class merchant banks were conservative and biased toward large issues, "which yielded economies of cost."[11] In time, the important merchant banks did come to handle American industrial issues, but only the most "solid" ones. Sometimes, however, in Britain there were close collaborations between promoters and merchant banks. James B. Jefferys makes the point that the promoter was more in evidence for British overseas enterprises than for home ones, since the foreign enterprise had much greater need of his services.[12]

The best known of all the British promoters was H. Osborne O'Hagan. Because of his many activities, he seems to have been more responsible than most, and he continued to be concerned with the enterprises he sponsored. He acted through a company that he controlled, the City of London Contract Corporation (CLCC).[13] Although O'Hagan took part in many U.S. promotions (a great number of them concentrated in the years 1889 and 1890), and although he established a separate company to handle American business—the London and Chicago Contract Corporation, Ltd.[14]—he never visited the United States. He did send representatives; the CLCC's first representative in the United States was Russell H. Monro.[15] O'Hagan made large, short-lived investments in his catalyst role.[16]

Another English firm engaged in American "promotions" had the reassuring name Trustees', Executors' and Securities' Insurance Corporation, Ltd.[17] Formed in 1887 by the so-called Winchester House group[18]—Leopold Salomons, J. Spencer Balfour, and Sir John Pender—it had as its American representative the lawyer Edward C. Henderson. Sir John Pender was deeply involved in cables and had long had U.S. connections.[19] The Trustees', Executors' and Securities' group became for a time ubiquitous in its American business, playing a role in the International Investment Trust; the London and New York Investment Corporation; the United States Debenture Corporation; the American Association, Ltd.; the City of Chicago Grain Elevators, Ltd.; the Frank Jones Brewery, Ltd.; the Southern States Land and Timber Company, Ltd.; and the Cataract Construction Company. Some of these enterprises performed badly; others did better.[20] The Frank Jones Brewery, for example, was described as "overweighted with excessive capital created to pay the heavy underwriting and other commissions shared by those allowed 'inside.'" *Investors' Review*, London, called the "Trustees', Executors' &c's" creation of trust companies "more or less unsubstantial productions of the thimble-rigging order of finance."[21] The *Review*'s comments notwithstanding, in 1892 the market value of Trustees' Executors' securities was in excess of the original value, which was more than could be said for many of the enterprises it promoted;[22] the firm survived, as did the investment trusts with which it was linked.[23]

Then there were firms such as the Mining and Financial Trust Syndicate, Ltd., which floated mining companies—the Elkhorn Mining Company, Ltd. (Montana), 1890, and the DeLamar Mining Company, Ltd. (Idaho), 1891.[24] Indeed, a number of investment trust companies undertook "promotions."

Promoters' charges for setting up a London company to raise money in Great Britain were high. The papers of the American A. L. Barber contain a tabulation (see Table 14.1) of the expenses of an issue of £400,000 of 6 percent debentures for his newly established British-incorporated New Trinidad Lake Asphalt Company, Ltd. (1897). These data reveal the fees of O'Hagan's City of London Contract Corporation, Ltd;[25] they also show the cooperation of various intermediaries in raising monies for American enterprises in London.

Often a promoter saw to it that a company just floated would declare an impressive first dividend (out of the proceeds of the sale of stocks or bonds). This "verified" its "genuineness" and gave the promoter plausibility in his next promotion. More important, it gave the promoter the opportunity to feed his own shares into the market. Then no second dividend would ever be forthcoming! Promoters found prominent men to sit on boards of directors to provide their companies respectability. Promotions were hardly new to the years 1875–1914, but in the last quarter of the nineteenth century they multiplied. Such promotions were basically an Anglo-American phenomenon, albeit there were some similar Franco-American activities.[26] Likewise, promoters in London attracted French, German, and other foreign capital to the British-incorporated American activities.[27]

Table 14.1. Costs of London debenture issue of New Trinidad Lake Asphalt Company, Ltd., 1897 (in pounds)

Total issue of 6% debentures		400,000
Costs		70,000
Underwriting commission 10%	40,000	
City of London Contract Corp., Ltd., and Henry Bell, Esq.	15,000	
Seward, Guthrie & Steele (attorneys in New York)	2,183	
Ashurst, Morris, Crisp (attorneys in London)	1,500	
Expenses of the City of London Contract Corp., Ltd.	1,022	
Accountants, brokers, and miscellaneous expenses	10,295	
Total to the credit of the New Trinidad Company		330,000

Source: Arthur S. Dewing, *Corporate Promotions and Reorganizations* (Cambridge, Mass.: Harvard University Press, 1914), p. 419n.

British Investment Trust Companies

British investment trust companies became in these years important financial intermediaries, siphoning Scottish and English savings into American investment. In a book published in 1930 on pre-1914 times, Herbert Feis noted that these trusts, "grown powerful through a combination of daring faith and careful judgment," played a particularly significant role in American finance, supplying "stability and cool judgment to the movement of investment affairs."[28] Although differently structured financially, the British investment trust companies of this era bore a strong resemblance (from the investors' viewpoint) to the modern mutual fund.

Managers of the investment trust companies used their skills to obtain good financial returns for inexperienced, relatively small investors. These were risk-sharing institutional investments. The British investment trust companies pooled savings of individual investors and spread the investments over many different securities, creating a diversified portfolio.[29] In this section I am going to deal exclusively with the foreign-headquartered investment trust companies.[30] Some of the investment trust companies established in Great Britain in the 1880s were not substantial. Those that weathered the 1890 Baring Crisis and the U.S. Panic of 1893 met Feis's description.[31]

The investment trust company in Great Britain was a new type of financial intermediary, with the first dating from 1868. It catered to the emerging middle class with savings and no knowledge of where to invest. Some investment trust companies specialized by industry; some specialized by geographical area; some were general in nature. In order to obtain higher returns for the investors, many British investment trust companies participated in overseas investments.[32]

In Chapter 4 I discussed some of the early U.S. investments made by such institutions. In the mid-1870s, after the Panic of 1873, Americans temporarily had found it difficult to interest British investors in the United States because of the railroad defaults and because the country had not yet resumed specie payments.[33] A number of British investment trust companies at this time countered the trend, making careful investments and buying at the low prices. The return on U.S. government bonds in 1870–1880 was said to average 7.5 percent, compared with 3.84 percent on British Consols; and on U.S. rails, 9.3 percent, materially higher than British rails.[34] With such incentives the English and Scottish trust companies cautiously and systematically invested in America. When on January 1, 1879, the United States resumed specie payments, the Scottish-American investment trusts in particular obtained sizable exchange profits, since many of their investments were made when the dollar was at a discount of 10 to 16 percent.[35] In the 1880s in Britain, investment trust companies became the vogue, and between 1886 and 1890 more than thirty came into being. Then, in the aftermath of the 1890 Baring Crisis, few new ones were organized, until 1904–1914, when the number formed mounted sharply.[36] Throughout, U.S. investments were important to these institutions.

There were English investment trust companies, most of them headquartered in London, but some in Liverpool, Hull, and other provincial cities. The Scottish ones were principally situated in Dundee and Edinburgh, with a few in Glasgow and Aberdeen.[37] The London trusts often had interlocking directorates,[38] while the Scottish trusts were linked with one another and some with those in London.[39] Some trusts were, or came to be, associated with merchant banking houses.[40] Others seem to have been dominated by an accounting firm.[41] All needed advisers attuned to the investment market. The largest one appears to have been the Alliance Trust Company, Ltd., Dundee, Scotland, formed in 1888, an amalgamation of the Dundee Mortgage and Trust Company and the Dundee Investment Company.[42] Often the successful Dundee investment trust companies served as models for others.[43]

For many reasons (including the long-standing transatlantic connections and the higher interest rates), managers of the British investment trust companies found America particularly attractive. The firms made investments directly in the United States, in American securities traded in London, and in *British* corporations doing business in America. With contacts on Wall Street, managers could buy and sell securities in New York as easily as in Great Britain.

The principals in the major investment companies developed intimate relationships within the United States. Take the United States Trust and Guarantee Corporation, Ltd., London, formed in 1890; in 1911 it became the United States Trust Corporation, Ltd. Its 1890 directors were all British and all had, through their own involvements, knowledge of conditions in the United States.[44] At origin, the directors included Archibald Balfour of Thomson, Bonar & Co.;[45] Bernard T. Bosanquet of Lloyds Bank; Alfred H. Huth, identified as with the Union Bank of Spain and England;[46] and C. Fraser Mackintosh, M.P., of the Anglo-American Land Mortgage and Agency Company. On the American side, there was a seven-man U.S. "Advisory Board," which included members of the Lombard family associated with the Lombard Investment Company[47] and the First National Bank of Kansas City. James Stillman, who in 1891 would become president of the National City Bank in New York, was a member of this board. Sixty Americans from New York, Boston, Philadelphia, Baltimore, and Kansas City were listed in 1890 as "founders," along with fifty-four British individuals and firms. The American founders included several involved in enterprises that had attracted foreign investment—for example, William Barbour (Barbour Brothers, linen thread), George Hotchkiss (Hammond Dressed Beef Company), Thomas Fowler (New York, Ontario and Western Railroad), and R. F. Oakes (Northern Pacific). Also among the founders were American investment bankers with international connections, representatives of John Munroe & Co., August Belmont & Co., J. & W. Seligman, and Morton, Bliss—and commercial bankers, including one from Chase National Bank. Several Standard Oil men, William Rockefeller for one, were among the American participants. The roster of British founders included bankers, an accountant (from Thomas, Wade, Guthrie & Co.),[48] and solicitors. Three of the British directors (Balfour, Bosanquet, and Huth) were also directors of the Imperial and Foreign Investment Agency Corporation, Ltd., another London-headquartered investment trust.[49] All the Britishers and Americans participated in the matching of British financial resources with U.S. opportunities.

I found a large collection of letters documenting the activities and U.S. investments of the United States Trust and Guarantee Corporation, Ltd., 1890–1896. The principal figure in England was Archibald

Balfour. James Stillman became the British firm's investment manager in the United States. He invested for the Britishers in railroad bonds and shares and in Standard Oil shares; but also—quite uniquely—he invested the corporation's monies in small amounts (never more than $5,000, often under $2,000) in shares of local banks around America; each investment he personally evaluated. This British investment trust company had been the creation of the Americans William A. and James L. Lombard, but Stillman very early came to distrust them and eventually saw to it that they were no longer involved. Even so (actually in part as a consequence of getting rid of the Lombards), at the time of the 1893 failure of the Lombard Investment Company, the United States Trust and Guarantee Corporation, Ltd., was the largest shareholder in that company. The trust company had hard times but, as noted, it survived. The British firm in the 1890s used the private bank John Munroe & Co., New York, to hold its securities and to handle payments for stocks and bonds purchased by Stillman for the account of the British enterprise.[50]

Some British investment trust companies underwrote and marketed new American securities issues.[51] Railway Share Investment Trust, Ltd., London, led by Sir Samuel Laing (who was at one time British Finance Minister for India), and its successor, Railway Share Trust and Agency Company, Ltd. (the name changed in 1888), for example, floated American railroad bonds in London.[52] Some investment trust companies, as noted, participated in promotions there. Some of these companies acted to "mop up" unsold issues of American industrial securities. The Colonial Securities Trust, Mercantile Investment and General Trust Company, International Investment Trust, the Industrial and General Trust, and the London and New York Trust Corporation, Ltd., acquired, for instance, Pillsbury-Washburn stock in 1889–1891 that the market had rejected.[53] Many came to have large railroad investments. Ellis T. Powell wrote in 1910, "It is well known that at the time of a comparatively recent great advance in American railroad securities, some of the trusts were found to have enormous holdings, which they sold, in many instances, almost at the top of the advance, with immense benefit to themselves."[54]

It is hard to exaggerate the importance of American investments in the portfolios of these financial intermediaries. "The progress which these concerns [the investment trusts] have made is based on the fact that they have been managed by boards containing men well known by name in Great Britain and men who understand the conditions of success in making investments in the United States," wrote the economist R. H. Inglis Palgrave in 1893.[55]

Merchants' Trust, Ltd., London, was, for example, very much involved in American investments, especially in railroads.[56] After Woodrow Wilson was elected President of the United States in 1912, the chairman of the Merchants' Trust, Ltd., Robert Benson, discussed at the firm's annual meeting (February 28, 1913) the U.S. political and economic outlook as it affected the interests of the firm, indicative of its importance. Robert Benson had long had associations with American business.[57]

While the English investment trust companies were more numerous and in total appear to have placed more monies into American investments, the Scottish trusts proved especially profitable; historians of the Scottish investment trusts suggest they were even more successful than their English counterparts.[58] Dundee's Robert Fleming (founder of the Scottish American Investment Trust) took part in numerous investments trusts. He made 128 trips across the Atlantic between 1870 and 1923.[59] Imagine this in the days of boat travel. In the dreary year of 1894, after the financial crisis of 1893, Fleming's trust companies still paid dividends, but Fleming himself worked hard to realize the profits, crossing the Atlantic seven times in twelve months![60] Fleming participated directly in railroad reorganizations. He knew America, the nation's leading bankers and railroad executives, and its securities. He was a close friend of Jacob Schiff of Kuhn, Loeb & Co.[61] Over time, Fleming transferred his business activities from Dundee (where he had started his career) to London, forming the Investment Trust Corporation, Ltd., London, in March 1888,[62] opening his own London office in 1890[63] or 1900,[64] and finally, in 1909, organizing his London-headquartered Robert Fleming & Co.[65] Fleming served as adviser to numerous Scottish and English trusts. The Fleming companies were from the start involved in stocks and bonds—especially bonds.[66]

Another Scot, William J. Menzies (1834–1904), lawyer and financier, had founded the Scottish American Investment Company, Ltd.,[67] in Edinburgh in 1873 and was long active in U.S. finance. In 1913 the Scottish American Investment Company—which like Fleming's companies concentrated on railroad bonds—had investments of £4.1 million in the United States.[68] Still a third Scot, William Mackenzie, began his career with the Oregon and Washington Trust Investment Company, Ltd. (1873), and in time came to head the giant Alliance Trust Company.[69] One of Mackenzie companies—the Dundee Land Investment Company—acquired in the early 1880s office buildings in Kansas City, downtown Portland, and various real estate properties in the center of Denver.[70] Both Menzies and Mackenzie, like Fleming, were frequent transatlantic travelers.[71] The Mackenzie companies, unlike those of Fleming and Menzies, began principally in the land mortgage business.[72] Other Scots associated with the Scottish American Investment Company and additional U.S. investments included Sir George Warrender, head of a well-known Edinburgh family and a director of the Royal Bank of Scotland, and Thomas Nelson, head of the Edinburgh publishing house Thomas Nelson & Co.[73]

The Scottish investment trusts cooperated closely with U.S. firms. Menzies' Scottish American Investment Company, Ltd., for example, had the shrewd Scot J. S. Kennedy as its first agent in New York. When Kennedy retired in 1884, his nephew John Kennedy Tod became the Scottish trust's New York representative, and on his retirement in 1902, J. P. Morgan & Co. was appointed the New York agent.[74] Menzies believed that "American investments ought to be passed upon by some respectable house in America."[75]

The historian Gene Gressley studied the operations of British-born Francis Smith, who acted in the American Midwest and South on behalf of a number of British investment companies, including the Northern Counties Investment Trust and the Dundee Mortgage and Trust Investment Company. Smith's British clients requested from him up-to-date information on American politics, taxes, alien property laws, and judicial decisions that would affect their investments.[76]

In the 1870s and thereafter, the British investment trusts bought U.S. railway bonds, mainly secured first-mortgage gold-backed bonds.[77] Some bought railway shares, some bought land and real estate, and many held land and real estate mortgages. A few acquired mining securities. In the late 1870s and especially in the 1880s, a number of the Scottish investment trusts (or their managers) became interested in U.S. cattle ranching.[78] Although most of the cattle ranches were not financial successes, the investment trust companies did far better because of their diversified holdings. In the late 1880s some trusts began to buy securities of U.S. industrial enterprises, some incorporated in Britain, some in the United States.[79] Throughout, however, particularly among the most prudent, U.S. railway bonds seem to have been the principal investments.[80] Table 14.2 includes some British investment trusts and shows the approximate percentage of their total investments in 1914 that were in the United States. The list of such institutions with U.S. interests is only a very small sample of the total.[81]

Many years later, when Robert Kindersley began to compile information on British overseas investments, he excluded "financial trust stocks, etc. . . . because their inclusion would lead to double reckoning."[82] John J. Madden, another chronicler of British invest-

Table 14.2.   Representative British investment trust companies: percentage of investments in the United States, ca. 1914

Trust Company	Percentage
American Investment Trust Co., Ltd., London	100
Alliance Trust Co., Ltd., Dundee	83
British Assets Trust, Ltd., Edinburgh	81
Third Scottish American Trust Co., Ltd., Dundee	76
North American Trust Co., Ltd., Dundee	71
Anglo-American Debenture Corp., Ltd., London	60–70
Railway Share Trust and Agency Co., Ltd., London	60–70
Railway Debenture and General Trust Co., Ltd., London	60–70
Second Scottish Northern Investment Trust, Ltd., Aberdeen	60
Merchants' Trust, Ltd., London	51
Scottish Northern Investment Trust, Ltd., Aberdeen	50
Industrial and General Trust, Ltd., London	24

Source: J. C. Gilbert, *A History of Investment Trusts in Dundee* (London: P. S. King, 1939), pp. 94, 80, 104; U.S. Department of Commerce, *British Investment Trusts* (1923), pp. 29–30, reprinted in *European Foreign Investments as Seen by the U.S. Department of Commerce*, ed. Mira Wilkins (New York: Arno Press, 1977); George Glasgow, *The English Investment Trust Companies* (New York: John Wiley, 1931); George Glasgow, *The Scottish Investment Trust Companies* (London: Eyre & Spottiswoode, 1932); Ranald C. Michie, "Crisis and Opportunity: The Formation and Operation of the British Assets Trust, 1897–1914," *Business History*, 25 (July 1983): 141.

ment in the United States, likewise decided to omit American investments by these trusts to avoid double counting, because he assumed their holdings were already "issued" in London and therefore were included in his tabulations.[83] Kindersley's and Madden's point is valid when the investment trusts bought U.S. railroads "issued" and floated or traded in London or securities of British registered companies (the American breweries, Pillsbury-Washburn, or Stratton's Independence, Ltd., for example). Nonetheless, as the historians W. G. Kerr, Ranald C. Michie, W. Turrentine Jackson, and Ronald Weir point out about the Scottish investment trusts and as my research has revealed in relation to some of the English ones, many investments by these trusts in the years 1875–1914 were made not in Britain but directly in the United States.[84] Thus investment statistics based on British stock exchange transactions, railroad issues in London, issues of British publicly registered companies, or registers of British and Scottish companies fail to capture the extent of these holdings.[85] Since the major investment trusts had American agents and representatives, it was easy for them to execute their investments within the United States.[86] Moreover, to the extent that the British investment trust companies participated in American mortgage lending, much of this had to be done directly—although some British investment trusts invested in *companies* that in turn invested in U.S. mortgages.[87]

British Mortgage Lenders

Closely associated with the activities of investment trust companies (and at times indistinguishable from them) were British involvements in U.S. mortgage lending on land and real estate. Many of the Scottish trusts, especially, invested directly in U.S. land and real estate mortgages, which they perceived as an investment "security." As the economist F. Lavington points out, it would be "out of the question for the average investor to attempt to lend against mortgages in real estate in the United States." The experienced trust companies could do just that.[88]

Under American federal banking statutes (until 1913), U.S. national banks were not permitted to make loans backed by land or real estate.[89] In the United States, state banks, trust companies (many of which intermediated foreign monies), mortgage companies (that likewise brought in money from abroad),[90] as well as savings banks and associations and building societies, filled the gap. In addition, foreign investors, through investment, mortgage and land companies organized in their home countries, offered mortgage monies.[91]

Mortgage lending on land and real estate is a very local endeavor. Unlike the acquisition of railroad securities (which was typically done through stockbrokers), mortgage lending brought the creditor into direct contact with the borrowers, and relatively small borrowers at that. In many ways it was not a business in which one would anticipate major foreign involvement. Yet such participation existed, primarily because of the lucrative returns. On the U.S. frontier, the demand for mortgage monies rose as settlement spread westward. In the 1880s Kansas City, Missouri, became the mortgage-granting center of the West.[92] Many of the Scottish investment trusts were in reality mortgage companies or were closely affiliated with mortgage companies.[93] The English became involved in mortgage lending through their own enterprises, and more often than the Scots, they invested through U.S. firms such as the Lombard Investment Company, the J. B. Watkins Land Mortgage Company, the Jarvis-Conklin Mortgage Company, and the Equitable Mortgage Company. Sometimes English trusts and mortgage companies were affiliated with the American ones.[94] An American enterprise could give this credit-granting activity, it was assumed, the careful attention required. A number of foreign enterprises, however, handled mortgage lending directly. In this section I am concerned with the foreign firms that employed American firms as "agents" and also developed their own lending organizations to intermediate foreign savings into land and real estate mortgages in the United States.

British companies providing this type of credit appear to have pursued three basic routes. The first (associated with the investment trust company) perceived the mortgage as a prime security that offered high returns just like an American railroad bond. The second approach concentrated on land development; a company would buy land, sell off parcels, and grant mortgages to the purchasers; the mortgage facilitated land sales. Profits were derived from land development and the subsequent disposal of the land, with improvements, and then also from the complementary mortgage. In the United Kingdom, securities manuals combined "financial, land, and investment companies" under one rubric, reflecting the linkages.[95] The third course grew from already existing trade: land and real estate mortgages became adjuncts to the ongoing commercial operations, a response to customer needs.

Whichever of the three interrelated routes was selected, most (but not all) British mortgage monies went into farm mortgages in the Midwest, West, and South, regions short on capital. Although foreign lending on urban real estate (office buildings and town lots) existed, loans on farmland seem to have been most common.[96] Investors were sensitive to interest rates and, with varying degrees of sophistication, shifted their geographical emphasis from one state to another within the United States to capture the differential.[97] One, highly exaggerated, estimate by a former Congressman from Kansas (John Davis) was that, of the $6 billion in mortgage loans outstanding in the entire United States in 1889, about $3 billion (or 50 percent) came from foreign investors! I include this preposterously high estimate to indicate the visibility of such foreign loans.[98]

I will consider first the mortgage lending done by the investment trusts, that is, by those investors who viewed U.S. land and real estate mortgages as securities with attractive, reliable returns. In this category were the firms organized by the Scots Robert Fleming, William Menzies, and William Mackenzie[99] and scores of others, such as the well-managed Scottish American Mortgage Company, Ltd., of Edinburgh.[100] Holmes Ivory of Edinburgh set up a syndicate to establish the United States Mortgage Company of Scotland, Ltd., in 1884, with a capital of £1 million; an American was appointed to manage the business.[101] Another Scot, James Tait, founded the American Mortgage Company (1877), the Edinburgh American Land Mortgage Company (1878), the Oregon Mortgage Company (1883), and the American Trust and Agency Company, Ltd. (1884; wound up in 1889).[102] The Scot John E. Guild was the first chairman of the Investors' Mortgage Security Company, Ltd. (capital, £1 million), started in 1891, a firm that specialized in U.S. mortgages.[103]

There was also the Union Mortgage and Banking Trust Company, London, with a capital of £2 million, which announced it would lend on first mortgages of improved agricultural property in the United States "so as to combine the advantages of that species of security with the higher yield obtainable in a 'newer' country than Great Britain." The company would obtain money from investors at a "fair" rate of interest in exchange for its own debentures and then invest that pooled money "at a higher rate of interest in small amounts, thus acquiring the guarantee of safety afforded by the law of averages."[104] The Anglo-American Land Mortgage and Agency Company, Ltd., formed in London in 1883, invested in farm loans in Missouri, Nebraska, Kansas, and Iowa.[105] In the 1880s many English companies—with names such as Colonial and U.S. Mortgage Company, Ltd.; United Trust, Ltd.; Canadian and American Mortgage and Trust, Ltd.—joined the Scots in acquiring American farm mortgages, seeing this "paper" as offering fine returns.[106]

All the British mortgage lenders appointed American agents; sometimes these "agents" were U.S. mortgage companies, and sometimes not. The procedure was for the foreign firm to borrow in Britain and lend in the United States, with as much as a six- to seven-point spread (at least in the early 1880s). This meant that the British company borrowed at home at from 3½ to 6 (or 7) percent and lent at 10 to 13 percent,[107] which left adequate profits to be shared with the American agent.[108] William Kerr has described how the Scottish firms did this business. They established regular relationships with American agents and made—through those agents—relatively short-term (three- to five-year) mortgage loans, based on one-third to one-half the property valuation.[109] They provided conservative loan limits to their agents.[110] For the Scots, their home borrowings (debentures issued) were three, five, and seven years,[111] so the maturities of their U.S. lending and their British receipts were reasonably well matched.[112] The Scots appear to have been the innovators in issuing debentures against a portfolio of mortgages—a practice that came to be adopted by U.S. firms.[113]

Writing much later on the differences between Scottish and English *investment trust companies*, George Glasgow noted that one feature of the Scottish trusts was the practice of issuing "terminable debentures, temporary loans and deposits." The English investment trust companies, Glasgow found, confined themselves in the main to the issue of debenture stock. He concluded that hardly any English investment trusts issued terminable debentures, and virtually all Scottish companies did.[114] Although Glasgow did not say so, undoubtedly the close relationship, from their origins, of the Scottish investment trust and the Scottish mortgage-granting firms explained the divergence in practice.[115] The attention to matched maturities was a good prescription. The Scots sent inspectors from Scotland to monitor their American agents; the agents evaluated the properties and executed the loans. The Scots' stakes in U.S. mortgages were clearly direct investments.[116] They were "largely divorced from the London money market."[117]

English mortgage companies as well as Scottish ones participated in furnishing credit to American farmers. Those located outside London, likewise, seem to have been separate from the London money market.[118] McFarlane, who has done superb research on the mortgage enterprises, found that at least in Iowa and Kansas the Scots had entered earlier than the English, and the latter were less aware of alternative possibilities farther west. He found that the Scots tended to have more-diversified investments.[119] The English mortgage companies seem to have been separate from the English investment trust companies.[120]

From the start, many of the *Scottish* investment trust companies and the Scottish mortgage companies shared the same managers and the American connections.[121] If a real estate loan was large, the Scots would syndicate it.[122] McFarlane found that the Scots had a "superior system of business information," yet he also pointed out that in the Midwest, the Scots and the English "nearly always used the same agents" and "occasionally employed the same traveling inspectors."[123] In other parts of the country as well, Scottish and English mortgage-granting institutions engaged identical agents.[124]

In 1882 and 1883 at least nine British (Scottish and English) companies were formed, excluding cattle companies,[125] to buy American land or to handle mortgages, or both. Table 14.3 provides an incomplete list; this group alone involved a capitalization in excess of $23 million.[126] The majority of the companies organized in 1882 and 1883 were involved in "land development." The second route to British mortgage lending in the United States, as indicated above, was the land-development one. Perhaps the most important of these firms was the Texas Land and Mortgage Company, formed in 1882; it bought and sold land, lent money on land mortgages, and acted as "a

Table 14.3. New financial, land, and investment companies engaged in business in the United States, formed in 1882 and 1883

Name, year of incorporation	Headquarters	Capital (in pounds)	Comments
Arizona Trust and Mortgage Co., Ltd., 1883	Edinburgh	300,000	To acquire the obligations of Arizona Copper Co.; W. J. Menzies involved
British Land and Mortgage Co. of America, Ltd., 1883	London	1,000,000	To acquire, develop, and sell lands, to make first-mortgage loans; operations west of Mississippi; C. S. Grenfell, a director
East Florida Land and Produce Co., Ltd., 1883	London	200,000	To acquire and develop land near St. Augustine, Florida
Florida Land and Mortgage Co., Ltd., 1883	London	1,275,000	To acquire properties in Florida
North American Land Association, Ltd.	London	500,000	To purchase land in the United States and British North America; acquired 43,000 acres in North Dakota
Scottish Mortgage and Land Investment Co., of New Mexico, Ltd., 1882	Glasgow	200,000	To invest in mortgages in U.S. real estate, particularly in New Mexico
South Minnesota Land Co., Ltd., 1883	London	250,000	To acquire and resell about 104,415 acres in Minnesota
Texas Land and Mortgage Co., Ltd., 1882	London	500,000	To purchase and develop lands and carry on the loan company in the United States
Western Mortgage and Investment Co. Ltd., 1883	London	500,000	To invest money on the security of property in the United States

Source: Burdett's Official Intelligence for 1884. Cattle companies omitted.

sort of clearing house for British interests in the Southwest." It operated its own office in Dallas.[127]

Many English companies began as land developers and subsequently moved into providing farm loans. Thus Close Brothers Company, London and Chicago, bought land in Iowa and then started to resell it in parcels to immigrants. By the 1890s the Close brothers were heavily involved in making farm loans in Iowa, South Dakota, Nebraska, Kansas, Illinois, and Wisconsin. Their mortgage lending became far more important than their land development activities as a source of profit. There were Close brothers on the spot, and one in Britain.[128]

In 1881 James W. Barclay, member of Parliament for Forfar, Scotland, was chairman of the board of the Colorado Mortgage and Investment Company of London, Ltd.,[129] a company that bought land in New Mexico and participated in land speculation in Colorado.[130] Barclay himself invested in U.S. cattle ranching in the late 1870s and early 1880s.[131]

In 1887 an American, Seaman A. Knapp, traveled to Great Britain to attract capital to Louisiana. He helped to organize the Louisiana and Southern States Real Estate and Mortgage Company, Ltd., Leicester, England. On his return to the United States, he formed a counterpart firm, the Southern Real Estate Loan and Guaranty Company, Ltd., to serve as the "operating agent" for the English enterprise. These companies bought and sold real estate, loaned money on mortgages, laid out and developed two towns in Louisiana, operated twelve large rice farms, purchased timberland, ran sawmills, and produced sugar.[132] On occasion, cattle companies (for example, the Western Ranches, Ltd.) were transformed into mortgage lenders; in 1910 the new Western Ranches and Investment Company, Ltd., which lent money on mortgages, replaced the former cattle company.[133] In short, some Scottish, but even more often English, firms began as land or cattle companies and then moved into mortgage lending to realize better returns on their land investments.

The third route to British mortgage lending in the United States was typified in the behavior of Balfour, Guthrie, in California. This firm—the parent was Balfour, Williamson, in Liverpool—inaugurated its U.S. trading activities as an exporter of grain from the Pacific Coast. It developed regular contacts with farmers, who were "always short of money." The trading firm then made loans, accepting farm mortgages as security. In 1878 it organized the Pacific Loan and Investment Company, Ltd. ("after the model of the Dundee Coy.")[134] and later the Pacific Trust Association, Ltd. In 1886 the Pacific Loan and Investment Company, Ltd., was reconstituted and floated on the

British market as a public company. The British headquarters was in Balfour, Williamson's office in Liverpool. The loan business was run conservatively (first mortgages only—limited to 50 percent of property value); the management was by Balfour, Guthrie.[135] Also in the early 1880s Balfour, Guthrie acted on behalf of the Liverpool Trust and Loan Company (whose principal shareholders were partners in Balfour, Williamson). Stephen Williamson boasted in the early 1880s that this company, lending money through first mortgages, was "getting 9, 10, 11, and 12 percent clear."[136] Note that whatever the path, "investment," "land development," or "trading needs," British companies that granted mortgages in the United States proliferated in the late 1870s and in the 1880s. Through American representatives on the spot, they provided credit to American farmers from Georgia and Alabama in the Southeast to Iowa and Kansas in the Midwest, to Oregon and Washington in the Pacific Northwest.

The rashly high estimate of $3 billion foreign investment in U.S. mortgages made by Congressman Davis for 1889 (and cited earlier) notwithstanding, no one knows how much foreign monies went into American mortgages. William Reid in Portland, Oregon, was said to have made (between May 1874 and June 1885) more than 5,000 loans, amounting to $7,597,741, of which $6 million consisted of Scottish capital.[137] W. G. Kerr's careful study found that in the late 1880s three Scottish mortgage companies in Texas had £1.2 million in mortgages outstanding (or over $5.8 million).[138] McFarlane identified for 1890 some $16.5 million in British mortgage loans in Kansas, Iowa, Nebraska, and the Dakotas.[139] While these three compilations (coming to about $28.5 million) admittedly represent a small part of the total, we are still very distant from Davis' $3 billion figure.[140]

Yet, in the 1880s particularly, there seems no doubt that the demand for monies for farm equipment and farm improvements had frequently led American farmers to mortgage their land. British investors did help fill some of the farmers' needs; and particularly in that decade, mortgage lending on land and real estate had risen rapidly.[141] The presence of British sources of funds seems to have lowered interest rates on the frontier.[142] The British lenders appear to have been the innovators in "debenture companies"—debentures issued against farm mortgages.

Between 1888 and 1894, as drought and other bad weather devastated American crops, farmers defaulted; lenders found no market for the land on which they foreclosed. As a consequence, "most [U.S.] mortgages companies concentrating in loans *in the Plains States* failed."[143] These domestic failures brought in their wake the embarrassment or collapse of several English mortgage companies that had been closely affiliated with the bankrupt American ones.[144] W. Turrentine Jackson estimated that between £7 million and £9 million of English and Scottish money was "tied up" by the failure of four of the largest U.S. mortgage companies in 1893–94.[145]

In 1893 R. H. Inglis Palgrave wrote that mortgages on U.S. real estate were by "no means favorite investments in England at the present time. Agricultural depression had caused many to burn their fingers with advances on land. In the United States the difficulty of finding good mortgages increases." He reported that U.S. real estate mortgages were "less than ever likely to be popular in England."[146] He wrote nothing about Scotland. The historian William Kerr has pointed out that not one of the major Scottish-organized mortgage companies operating in the United States failed.[147]

Another deterrent to new foreign investment after the late 1890s lay in the course of interest rates. Between 1870 and 1896 there was a steady decline in returns from farm mortgages in the Midwest, West, and South as mortgage rates dropped sharply.[148] In 1900 Nathaniel Bacon, in his study of foreign investment in the United States, recorded:

I could find indications of only comparatively small amounts of money lent by English people on real estate mortgages in the United States, except through investment companies. Prior to 1893 there were large investments of this kind, made principally through the Lombard Investment Company and similar corporations, but during the panic of 1893 there was a terrible shrinkage in the value of farm lands, which resulted in bankruptcy for many of these companies, and since then this capital has mostly withdrawn from America.[149]

I think Bacon underestimated the stakes of "English" investors that remained after 1893. Like Palgrave, he totally neglected the sizable Scottish investments in U.S. mortgages.[150] Moreover, after Bacon wrote, especially between 1904 and 1914, new British investments in U.S. mortgages were made.[151]

The foreign direct investments, the directly managed ones, survived the trauma of the 1890s and eventually gave American farm mortgages a decent reputation in Europe. Thus Balfour, Guthrie's Pacific Loan and Investment Company and its Pacific Trust Association, Ltd.'s well-supervised ventures continued to lend in California.[152] Likewise, the major Scottish mortgage companies (as noted) persisted because of their careful attention to the day-by-day changes in the business environment. There existed an infrastructure in America for the investments that succeeded. Balfour, Guthrie offered direct management. Scots in America served the Scottish companies as advisers, agents, and inspectors. The Scottish managers knew American conditions and carefully picked and chose among opportunities to take advantage of the best. The Scottish American Mortgage Company (SAMC) of Edinburgh, for example, used American agents, many of whom were transplanted Scots and thus judged trustworthy. As early as November 1877, SAMC had appointed the Bank of Montreal in Chicago as its "American" banker;[153] the president of the Bank of Montreal at that time was a Scot. Scottish mortgage companies frequently turned to British (often Scottish) insurance offices. British (again often Scottish) accountants helped out, once more typically immigrant Scots. By 1913 SAMC alone had £1,969,478 invested in mortgages on U.S. real estate (its other investments were a mere £134,732).[154]

While in the 1890s many foreign investors had reduced or eliminated their U.S. mortgage lending, clearly, at least among the Scots, many remained.[155] The huge Alliance Trust of Dundee (Mackenzie's company) lowered the mortgage component of its portfolio from 87 percent of its holdings in 1890 to 68 percent in 1900. It continued the cutback until 1905 (to 57 percent); it was down, barely, to 56 percent in 1914. Nonetheless the Alliance Trust's main investments stayed in the United States; in 1914 it had £2,345,182 invested in mortgages, practically all of it in the United States.[156]

The relative newcomer, the Investors' Mortgage Security Company, Ltd., Edinburgh (started in 1891), had £1,250,000 in mortgages and real estate and £680,000 in general investments in 1913. Its mortgages were principally in the United States, although it had some in Canada.[157] Thus the Scottish American Mortgage Company, the Alliance Trust, and the Investors' Mortgage Security Company—probably the three leading Scottish investors in U.S. mortgages—together had in 1913–14 roughly $27 million committed in American mortgages.

To this sum we can add $4 million on loan in 1914 by the Pacific Loan and Investment Company, Ltd. (Balfour, Guthrie's company).[158] Kerr's data reveal that the Texas Land and Mortgage Company, Ltd., had by 1914 almost £800,000 (about $4 million) placed in Texas mortgages (compared with £450,000 in the late 1880s).[159] The Texas Land and Mortgage Company, Ltd., was headquartered in London, but Kerr includes it as a "Scottish firm." The rise in dollar value of its loans outstanding from the 1880s to 1914 does not seem to me substantial after corrections are made for inflation and the boom in Texas property values subsequent to the early-twentieth-century oil discoveries.[160] Nonetheless, the figure confirms that the bulk of British mortgage money had not been withdrawn from America.[161]

In the early 1900s many British participants in mortgage lending in America began to diversify their investments worldwide rather than enlarging their U.S. mortgage lending.[162] Likewise, domestically in America they looked to alternative opportunities. The historian of Balfour, Williamson reported that this house's affiliates in California were (in 1910) devoting less monies to mortgages and more to fixed investment.[163]

For Scottish investment trusts and mortgage companies, mortgage lending in America in the late 1870s and 1880s had been crucial; it remained significant in 1914, but the "craze" of earlier years was muted.[164] By contrast, English monies in land and real estate mortgages in the United States may well have been greater in the 1880s than in 1914.[165] I have not done an analysis by state but would not be surprised if such a study would show a very different regional *distribution* of British mortgage lending in the 1880s than in 1914, with a *relative* decline in midwestern lending vis-à-vis southern and far-western mortgage loans.[166]

Because mortgage lending, properly administered, required an intimate familiarity with on-the-spot conditions, the most successful companies knew not only about mortgage opportunities but about other prospects as well. Thus many of the same firms that provided mortgages sponsored other ventures. I have noted the close associations between the Scottish investment and mortgage companies. Both had connections with cattle companies. Interactions went even further. Thus the directors of the Scottish American Mortgage Company were the entrepreneurs (in 1882) that established the important British-controlled Arizona Copper Company.[167] The links lay in access to information and the knowledge of potentials.[168] In brief, it was not only other businesses that led British firms to move into mortgage lending, but also the awareness derived from mortgage lending that in turn widened the horizons of the foreign investors.

Continental European and Canadian Investment Trusts and Mortgage Companies

Although British nationals are typically and correctly identified with the investment trusts and mortgage companies, these approaches to U.S. lending were not theirs exclusively. Dutch banking houses formed investment companies to hold diversified portfolios of U.S. securities and provided virtually the same services for investors in the Netherlands as the British investment trusts did for their financial counterparts across the Channel. For the most part, like the British, the Dutch investment companies held U.S. railway securities. The investment companies' own securities were then sold to the Dutch public. This gave the ultimate investor liquidity and also securities denominated in a currency (guilders) that he knew. Thus Kerkhoven & Co. and Boissevain Brothers had the Vereenigde Amerikaansche Fondsen; Wertheim & Gompertz, Westendorp & Co., and F. W. Oewell administered Vereenigd Bezit van Amerikaansche Hypothecaire Spoorwegobligatiën; Hope & Co. had Gemeenschappelijk Bezit; and Broes & Gosman founded and directed Vereenigd Bezit van Amerikaansche Fondsen. In 1906 Vermeer & Co. and the Algemeene Trust Mij. established the Syndicaat van Amerikaansche Industrieele Aandeelen to buy preferred stock of American industrials.[169]

The Banque de l'Union Parisienne organized in 1905 the Société Financière Franco-Américaine (S.F.F.A.), with a capital of 50 million francs (just under $10 million)—a holding company for stock in U.S. industrial enterprises, a response to similar requirements of Frenchmen who wished to place some of their capital in American securities but did not know how to select among the vast array of offerings on the New York market. The S.F.F.A. was established in cooperation with Speyer & Co. and Iselin & Co. of New York.[170] The Schweizerischer Bankverein also acquired an interest.[171]

In March 1890 the German-American Trust Company (Deutsch-Amerikanische Treuhand-Gesellschaft), with a capital of 20 million marks (about $5 million), was registered in Berlin (1) to issue its own debentures on the basis of solid American securities to be purchased by it and (2) to represent the interests of holders of securities issued by American enterprises that had become insolvent. Its promoters included Georg von Siemens, Berlin; Otto Braunfels, Frankfurt; the Deutsche Bank, Berlin; and Henry Oswalt and Theodor Stern, Frankfurt. The Deutsche Bank and the Jacob S. H. Stern banking firm held 90 percent of the capital.[172] The venture was not successful.[173] On December 9, 1901, the company was reconstructed as the Deutsche Treuhand-Gesellschaft.[174] A British writer in 1915 concluded that the role of the trust company in Germany was to some extent filled by subsidiary banks (Tochtergesellschaften), which carried on industrial finance by means of capital supplied by the parent company.[175]

The Schweizerischer Bankverein, Basle, participated in a whole coterie of investment companies. Thus in 1904 it acquired the shares of the Zurich-American Trust Company, which conducted business in North American securities. In 1905, as mentioned above, it purchased an interest in the Société Financière Franco-Américaine, Paris.[176] It took part that year in the transactions of the Nordamerikanisches Konsortium der Discontogesellschaft (Berlin). In 1906 it was involved in a "syndicate" for American industrial shares that had been formed by Dutch banks.[177]

The investment trust companies that the Germans, French, Dutch, and Swiss formed were all associated with banks,[178] which was not the case with most British investment trust companies, although some of the latter, as noted, did have ties with British banks and with American banking houses.[179]

Whereas the Scottish investment trust companies had had interests in U.S. mortgages and an association existed between the "investment trust" and the "mortgage company," in the case of continental European investments the typical "investment company" held securities *not* including mortgages. Table 14.4 shows, however, that in the American West and South there were Dutch "mortgage banks." The table gives their date of foundation and other information. A historian of Dutch investment in the United States called the activities of these mortgage banks direct investments. They had f73,137,000 (or $29,254,800) in "mortgage bonds" outstanding as of December 31, 1913.[180]

Some of the activities of these Dutch banks were formidable. They lent on the basis of urban real estate as well as farmlands. In the aftermath of the Panic of 1893, the Northwestern and Pacific Hypotheekbank foreclosed on delinquent loans and acquired a major part (roughly 25 percent) of the best Spokane, Washington, city center properties. The Dutch were secretive about this for fear of a negative antiforeign reaction; they sold the buildings and lots as rapidly as possible. The firm also came to own 78,179 acres in Washington. The bank survived the Panic and continued to lend in Washington— and indeed in 1910 a second Northwestern and Pacific Hypotheekbank was organized (see Table 14.4), which increased the capital available.[181]

In the 1880s Dutch and German monies had been invested in U.S. mortgages through the Lombard Investment Company. When the company was liquidated, an Amsterdam committee was involved. Bacon reported in 1900, however, that there was "almost no German money invested in American real estate or real estate mortgages."[182] This appeared to be true in 1914 as well and is confirmed by data later produced by the Alien Property Custodian.[183] French monies (Louis Frémy and the Crédit Foncier de France) had participated in the United States Mortgage Company, chartered in 1871, which maintained a committee of directors in Paris at least until 1883. I do not know what happened to the French investments.[184] The United States Mortgage Company stopped lending on farmlands and was transformed into a trust company in the early 1890s.[185] In 1910 Georges

Aubert advocated setting up a Crédit Foncier for American real estate lending. No evidence suggests a follow-up on his proposal.[186]

There is nothing to indicate that Canadian financial institutions played a major role in pre-1914 mortgage lending in the United States. Canadian banks were prohibited from engaging in mortgage lending—at home or abroad. The Royal Trust Company of Canada, associated with the Bank of Montreal, did set up business in Chicago in August 1891, with a capital of $500,000. As noted in Chapter 13, it was incorporated in Illinois in 1893 under the name Royal Trust Bank. In 1897 it acquired the Commercial Loan and Trust Company, and in 1909, when its capital was still $500,000, it was absorbed into the Central Trust Company of Illinois.[187] It may have engaged in mortgage lending in the years 1891–1909.

Cleona Lewis estimated the *total* mortgage loans on U.S. real estate, including farmland, by all foreign investors to be more than $200 million to $250 million in 1914, which seems reasonable, although I would put the figure simply in the range of $200 million to $250 million (rather than "more than" that sum).[188] Most of the amount seems to be represented by the Scottish (and to a lesser extent, English) investors; the continental European and Canadian contribution was but a small part of the total.

Trading Companies

Many European investment banks began as merchant banks—and thought of themselves in those terms. Some houses were more traders than bankers but carried on both functions. A good example is the Liverpool firm of Balfour, Williamson & Co., which was active on the west coast of South and North America. Its California house, Balfour, Guthrie & Co. (established in 1869), engaged in trade and shipping (the parent firm actually owned ships); became agents for two British insurance companies; provided insurance itself; made (as noted) mortgage loans; developed wharf and warehouse facilities; invested in a tugboat company (to get lower prices for services it required); provided equity financing for coal, iron ore, and oil production; bought flour mills; farmed fruit land; built a cement plant; had an equity interest in a salmon-canning company; and thus participated in a wide range of diversified activities. It furnished both *capital and management* to enterprises in California, Washington, and Oregon. A number of businesses in which it took part required its raising additional capital in England and going into joint-ventures with Americans. The firm's historian writes that in all these projects, "no matter

Table 14.4. Dutch mortgage banks active in the United States, 1913

Mortgage bank	Head-quarters	U.S. center	Operations in the U.S.	Year of founding	Registered Capital (in florins)		Mortgage bonds outstanding as of Dec. 31, 1913 (in florins)
					Stated	Paid in as of Dec. 31, 1913	
Nederlandsch-Amerikaansche Land Maatschappij	Amsterdam	St. Paul	Minnesota, Iowa, Montana, southern U.S.	1883	f 2,500,000	f 1,532,000	f 11,550,700
1e Northwestern and Pacific Hypotheekbank	Amsterdam	Spokane	Washington, Oregon, Idaho	1889	1,860,000	1,860,000	10,969,000
Nederlandsch-Amerikaansche Hypotheekbank	Uithuizen	St. Paul	Minnesota, Mississippi, Arkansas, Montana, Idaho, Washington, Oregon	1893	4,400,000	1,958,500	25,999,500
Holland-Bank	Amsterdam	Spokane	Washington, Idaho	1896	1,436,400	1,231,200	3,909,200
Internationale Hypotheekbank	Apeldoorn	Spokane	Washington, Idaho, Oregon, Montana, California, Utah, Wyoming, southern U.S.	1909	1,000,000	168,000	4,873,900
2e Northwestern and Pacific Hypotheekbank	Amsterdam	Spokane	Washington, Oregon, Idaho	1910	1,500,000	1,000,000	4,813,500
Holland-Texas Hypotheekbank	Amsterdam	Port Arthur	Texas	1911	1,495,000	1,495,500	500,000
Holland-Washington Hypotheekbank	Amsterdam	Seattle	Washington, Oregon,	1912	1,850,000	805,400	2,754,200
North Pacific Loan and Trust Company	Spokane	Spokane	Idaho	1901	500,000		1,850,000
Hypotheekbank Holland-Amerika	Utrecht	Seattle	Washington, Oregon, Idaho, Georgia, Alabama, Florida, Texas, Arkansas, Mississippi	1912	750,000	246,000	1,808,850

Hypotheekbank voor Amerika	's-Gravenhage	Portland	Oregon, Washington	1912	500,000	50,000	1,509,600
Holland-Noord-Amerika Hypotheekbank	Gorinchem	Seattle	Washington, Idaho, Montana	1912	500,000	100,000	1,357,350
Noord-Amerikaansche Hypotheekbank	Leeuwarden	Bozeman	Washington, Idaho, Oregon, Montana, Georgia, Florida, Alabama, Arkansas	1912	1,476,000	59,000	1,241,200
Total as of Dec. 31, 1913						10,505,600	73,137,000

Source: K. D. Bosch, *Nederlandse Beleggingen in de Verenigde Staten* (Amsterdam: Uitgeversmaatschappij Elsevier, 1948), pp. 440–441.

where the ownership lay, management was always the responsibility of Balfour, Guthrie."[189]

Few trading firms had the breadth of U.S. investment involvements of Balfour, Williamson & Co., but a number existed that combined trade, shipping, and manufacturing (Alfred Booth & Co., for example, participated in international trade, ran shipping lines, and manufactured leather goods in the United States). Rathbone Brothers, originally a Liverpool firm, maintained a New York office (from 1857 to 1863 its branch office had been managed by William Lidderdale, who was governor of the Bank of England during the 1890 Baring Crisis). Rathbone Brothers was active in American railroad issues in London and was involved in U.S. railroad reorganizations and in the grain trade.[190]

Antony Gibbs & Sons, Ltd., traders and bankers, who were (like Balfour, Williamson & Co.) very much engaged in South American business, were also participants in U.S. finance. In 1888 Gibbs & Sons served as issue house in the flotation of United States Brewing Company (capital, £400,000). In the spring of 1889 Pabst and Anheuser-Busch, two of America's leading brewers, rejected an offer of a purchase and subsequent London flotation from Gibbs & Sons. In 1912 Gibbs & Sons opened a branch house in New York, as trade between North and South America made this desirable. The next year it sought a share of the U.S. market for its Chilean nitrates.[191]

The German metal-trading companies, discussed in detail in Chapter 8, were traders that integrated backward and made major investments in U.S. refining, smelting, and other activities. Their role in "finance" was directed toward related operations. For a time the holding company for Metallgesellschaft interests was Metallbank and Metallurgische Gesellschaft, A.G.[192]

The largest Japanese trading company, Mitsui & Co. (started in Japan in 1876), had opened a branch in New York as early as 1879. Its New York office imported raw silk from Japan. When the Japanese government discontinued export subsidies in the early 1880s, Mitsui & Co. closed the New York outlet. Then in 1895 Kenzo Iwahara of Mitsui & Co. left Tokyo for New York to resume business in that city. Since two Japanese competitors were well established, initially Mitsui & Co. had difficulties. Nonetheless, after 1897 Mitsui's U.S.-Japanese business expanded rapidly. In 1898 Mitsui & Co. opened a San Francisco office, which exported wheat and flour, while Mitsui & Co.'s New York office continued to handle imports of Japanese raw silk and exports of U.S. railroad equipment, machinery, and raw cotton. In 1911 Mitsui & Co. established the wholly owned Southern Products Company in Houston, Texas, which moved to Dallas in 1912; this subsidiary was to aid the trading company's important raw cotton exports. Mitsui & Co. came to be responsible for more than 30 percent of the U.S. raw cotton imported into Japan. By 1907 Mitsui & Co. had also become the leader in Japanese raw silk exports. In 1914 its transactions included 33.6 percent of all Japanese silk imports into the United States. Mitsui & Co. had its own fleet of ships, and it chartered vessels from Nippon Yūsen Kaisha (NYK). In 1910 Mitsui & Co.'s New York office had twenty-eight employees; its San Francisco office, a staff of four; and a subbranch of its San Francisco organization in Portland, Oregon, was manned by one individual.[193]

How many other Japanese trading companies had representatives in the United States is uncertain.[194] The historian Nobuo Kawabe found that for the export of raw cotton, the Japan Cotton Trading Company established a subsidiary in Fort Worth, Texas, in 1910, and the Gosho Company formed one in San Antonio, Texas, in 1913.[195] In 1903 a Japanese firm, the Yokohama Silk Trading Company, led in silk exports from Japan, only to be surpassed in 1907 by Mitsui.[196] Williams Haynes, a historian of the U.S. chemical industry, identified Mitsui, Suzuki, Iwai, Miura Shozo, and Kuhara as Japanese trading companies that imported into New York camphor, menthol, pyrethrum (a flower used as an insect repellent), rhubarb root, and other medicinal and aromatic products from Japan and China.[197] Japanese banks—especially the Yokohama Specie Bank—seem to have arranged the financing of much of the U.S. trade with Japan.[198]

Shipping, Cables, Radio, Telephones, and Telegraph

British, German, French, Dutch, and Japanese shipping companies (along with those of other nationalities) had their own representatives in American port cities, some long established, some new to the period 1875–1914. A few companies came to own docks. Throughout the years 1875–1914 the Cunard Line remained the largest British carrier in business with the United States.[199] The two leading German lines—the North German Lloyd and the Hamburg-American—assumed prominence in the early twentieth century[200] and were said by then to own the "largest and best equipped docks for ocean liners not only in the port of New York but in the United States."[201] Compagnie Générale Transatlantique, the principal French firm, and the Holland-America were also important. On the Pacific Coast, Nippon Yūsen Kaisha offered regular service to Seattle, while Tōyō Kisen Kaisha called at San Francisco.[202] No foreign line participated in coastwise trade, because an 1817 U.S. law confined such business to U.S. shipping.[203]

After the death of Frederick Leyland in 1892, John R. Ellerman (1862–1933) had gained control of Frederick Leyland & Co., a British firm that operated a key freight line in the North Atlantic. In 1899 rumors circulated in the United States that Ellerman, through the Leyland company, would buy Atlantic Transport Company, an independent American firm. A Philadelphian, Clement Acton Griscom, head of the International Navigation Company (New Jersey), the most important American firm in North Atlantic shipping (it operated the American and Red Star lines), countered Ellerman's anticipated aggression with his own plan.[204]

Griscom enlisted the cooperation of J. P. Morgan to provide financing, and soon Morgan became deeply involved. That year, 1899, Thomas H. Ismay of Liverpool died. His estate held the largest single block of stock of the White Star Line, which Ismay had founded and which had the world's most prestigious ocean liners. William J. Pirrie (later Lord Pirrie) of the Belfast firm of Harland & Wolff, one of the principal shipbuilders in the world, also had sizable stock holdings in the White Star Line, which was Pirrie's best customer.

In 1902 J. P. Morgan organized the International Mercantile Marine Company (IMM), with an authorized capital of $120 million; it acquired the White Star, the Red Star, the American, the Leyland, the Atlantic Transport, and the Dominion lines, thus merging foreign and domestic shipping lines. IMM had reversed the pattern, acquiring the original aggressor company (Leyland) as well as the original target company (Atlantic Transport), along with Griscom's business (International Navigation) and the White Star Line; in addition, IMM obtained a 25 percent interest in the Holland-America Line.[205] It was a formidable combination.

At the same time, Morgan negotiated a traffic- and profit-pooling arrangement with Albert Ballin of the Hamburg-American Line and Heinrich Weigand of the North German Lloyd Line.[206] Ballin had insisted that the IMM and the German firms acquire an interest in the Holland-America Line to "neutralize" it; so, as a part of the new arrangements, the German shipping lines obtained holdings in the Holland-America.[207] The British saw Morgan's moves as a challenge.[208] Cunard and eight other important British lines stayed outside the giant IMM.[209]

Griscom became IMM's first president. Voting control was in the hands of a five-man trust, including Morgan, his partner Charles Steele, P. A. B. Widener (the financier of Philadelphia streetcar fame), J. Bruce Ismay (son of Thomas H. Ismay), and Pirrie. Ellerman took cash and did not participate. Five of the thirteen directors of IMM were British. Thus initially it looked as though this would be American dominated. There was, however, substantial British influence on the new American corporation, which increased over time. The British companies bought by IMM retained their separate identities, and the majority of *their* directors remained British. Much of the IMM's fleet sailed under a British flag.[210]

In 1903 J. Bruce Ismay replaced Griscom as president of IMM. Contemporaries called this a transfer of IMM to "British control."[211] Under Ismay the firm was not a success; and then, unfortunately, Ismay was a passenger on the White Star liner, the *Titanic*, on its ill-fated 1912 maiden voyage. He survived but, in the ensuing investigation of the disaster, faced disgrace; Ismay as a consequence resigned as president of IMM, to be replaced (as of June 30, 1913) by Harold A. Sanderson, also of the White Star Line, Liverpool, who moved to London on assuming the presidency.[212] IMM never prospered. In September 1914 it suspended interest payments and went into receivership the next year.[213]

The British maintained dominance of the seas.[214] In 1908, 86.5 percent of American imports and 92 percent of American exports moved on foreign flag vessels, roughly half on British flag carriers.[215] Although a foreign "flag" did not necessarily mean foreign ownership or control, in fact foreign ownership was predominant in the shipping engaged in foreign trade that called at American ports.[216]

Before World War I, agreements, "conference" arrangements, and understandings to fix or to regulate rates, to apportion traffic, and to pool earnings had become universal.[217] As a committee representing steamship lines with established services from New York to foreign countries reported, these accords were "the natural outgrowth of intolerable competitive conditions."[218] By 1914 over eighty agreements among companies operating in America's foreign carrying trades set limits on competition, provided rate stability, and did away with facility duplication, creating order in shipping. The accords included almost all the regularly scheduled steamship lines operating on practically all American foreign trade routes.[219] American ocean shipping on a regular basis that was not under foreign ownership or control was committed to full cooperation with the shipping that was.[220] Conferences held abroad frequently determined rates.[221]

Shipping lines carried passengers (who made crucial investment decisions), brought the mails (that provided the basis for the transfer of information), and moved goods (associated not only with trade but also with investment). Under the aegis of the foreign-owned and controlled companies, a vast expansion of shipping services had lowered transportation costs and opened new and unprecedented channels for information, immigration, trade, and investment. Foreign steamship companies handled the bulk of the tonnage for U.S. international trade and most of the carrying capacity of passenger service in the period 1875–1914.[222]

Cable companies, similarly, sped the movement of information, which in turn facilitated foreign investment. Here too foreign—especially British—firms were paramount. The first transatlantic cable service, in 1866, had been financed by foreign capital. By 1883 eight main cables spanned the Atlantic, with £12.8 million invested.[223] The British company Anglo-American Telegraph (capital, £7 million) owned four of the cables. Direct United States Cable Company (capital, £1.3 million) had one. A French company—Compagnie Française du Télégraphe de Paris à New York (capital, £1.68 million)—also operated one. In England Sir John Pender (1815–1896) was the "dominant spirit" in international cables.[224]

J. P. Morgan and J. A. Scrymser in 1896 organized the Pacific Cable Company and sought a U.S. government subsidy, trying in vain to move "into a field already occupied by British companies."[225] In 1900 the Deutsch-Atlantische Telegraphen Gesellschaft laid a submarine cable from Borkum-Emden in Germany to New York, and a second one along the same route in 1904.[226] These German cables barely dented British global supremacy.

Likewise, in the newer field of "wireless telegraphy" the British were preeminent. In 1897 the Wireless Telegraph and Signal Company, Ltd., London, was formed to use Guglielmo Marconi's patents; Marconi was the chief executive.[227] In November 1899 he formed an American affiliate, the Marconi Wireless Telegraph Company of America.[228] (The parent company's name was changed in 1900 to Marconi's Wireless Telegraph Company, Ltd.)[229]

At origin, Marconi of America had an authorized capital of $6.65 million. The capital was lowered in 1910 to $1.66 million (by reducing the nominal value of the shares from $100 to $25). Of this latter sum, roughly 55 percent was owned by the British Marconi company.[230] Marconi of America held exclusive rights to use and to exploit the patents of its British parent.[231] The American subsidiary supplied ships with radio service, erected land stations to communicate with vessels at sea, and by 1905 had started to manufacture ship apparatus (in Roselle Park, New Jersey).[232]

It filed a number of U.S. patent infringement suits, and in March 1912 was suing the bankrupt (but nonetheless important) U.S. firm United Wireless Company.[233] On March 21, 1912, representatives of United Wireless admitted patent infringement, and as a consequence Marconi of America acquired all that firm's patents and assets, obtaining "a practical monopoly" of the supply of apparatus for radio communication in the United States. The acquisition brought with it some 70 shore stations and more than 400 ship installations (in addition to Marconi's own 176 ship installations).[234] In 1912 Marconi of America's principal business related to carrying forth transmissions from ship to ship or ship to shore.

In 1901 Marconi of America had had its initial success with experiments in transatlantic communication.[235] On its wave length, Theodore Roosevelt had sent greetings to King Edward VII in January 1903;[236] but not until 1912, after it acquired the properties of the United Wireless, did Marconi of America start to play a truly dramatic role in *transoceanic* communication.

On March 7, 1912, the British Post Office had signed a tender with the British Marconi for a chain of long-distance wireless stations in the Empire.[237] Two days later Godfrey Isaacs, by then the managing director of British Marconi, left for America, where he would be involved in the takeover of United Wireless and in the ambitious plans to raise the capital of Marconi of America to $10 million to finance the United Wireless acquisition and to provide adequate funding for new American long-distance stations.[238] On March 29, 1912, the English Marconi Company agreed that (subject to a license from the British Postmaster General) it would build in or near London a high-power station, linking the projected U.S. facilities with those installed by the British Marconi Company.[239] Three days later, on April 1, an agreement was made between the British and the American Marconi companies, on the one hand, and Western Union Telegraph Company and North-Western Telegraph Company of Canada, on the other, by which the last two firms agreed to collect and distribute Marconi messages at the same low rates enjoyed by the cable companies.[240] On April 15, 1912, the *Titanic* sank. The tragedy awakened the public to the value of radio communication. Marconi of America—attempting at that time to raise monies for its grand projects—saw its securities soar in price, even before the shareholders had ratified the financial reorganization and the new issue![241]

For the first time, in 1913 Marconi of America started *commercial* transoceanic communication, via Glace Bay, Nova Scotia, and Clifton, Ireland. In July 1914 it was doing the final tests on two new stations at Belmar and New Brunswick, New Jersey. This would provide a direct link between the United States and Wales. It also began construction of other high-powered stations along the Atlantic and Pacific coasts for oceanic radio transmissions.[242] It remained almost completely dependent on its British parent for research and development advances[243] and was in every sense an affiliate of a British multinational.[244] In 1914, 566,826 of its 2 million shares outstanding were owned by Marconi's Wireless Telegraph Company, Ltd., in Britain. It had three London directors, all from the parent company.[245] In the years 1899–1912 it had not paid any dividends; in August 1913 it paid its first one—a mere 2 percent.[246] According to the economic historian Hugh G. J. Aitken, after its absorption of United Wireless (after 1912), Marconi of America had become "unquestionably the dominant firm in the American radio industry."[247]

As the Marconi companies made their plans, German politicians and German businesses became uneasy. Radio seemed to them associated with Britain's domination of the seas.[248] The Germans sought to be competitive, and between 1910 and 1914 German firms undertook and completed the erection of two high-powered wireless stations at Sayville, Long Island, and Tuckerton, New Jersey.[249] The Sayville station was built by the Atlantic Communications Company and used the "Telefunken" system, designed in Germany.[250] Telefunken was the popular name for a joint-venture company of Allgemeine Elektrizitäts Gesellschaft (A.E.G.) and Siemens & Halske.[251] Ninety-seven percent of the stock of Atlantic Communications Company was held in the name of Hans Bredow, manager of a subsidiary of Telefunken, and by another subsidiary of Telefunken.[252] The Germans reportedly spent half a million dollars on the Sayville station.[253] For many years, on an international scale, Marconi and Telefunken had been vigorous competitors, with a rivalry flavored by "vindictive hostility," but in 1912, as the Marconi companies became fully committed to transcontinental radio communication, the British Marconi and the German Telefunken agreed to stop litigation against one another over patents and to exchange them; the agreement covered both firms' global business, including that in the United States.[254]

The Tuckerton, New Jersey, high-powered wireless station was built by Hochfrequenz Maschinen Aktiengesellschaft für Drahtlöse Telegraphie (known as Homag),[255] under contract for a French wireless firm, Compagnie Universelle de Télégraphie et Téléphonie sans Fil (C.U.T.T.). When in 1914 war broke out in Europe, Homag had not yet delivered the just-completed U.S. facility to its French owner. Telefunken (or its parent companies) apparently had "a working understanding" with Homag.[256] In fact, in much of the literature this French company's station is described as having been built by Telefunken.[257] The Alien Property Custodian's *Report, 1918–1919*, insists that the two German-built stations used different systems.[258]

In sum, the British and Germans had become supreme in transoceanic radio communication. No American-controlled companies were involved. This was all very new, and transmissions were not yet reliable;[259] the cable companies retained most of the message-carrying business (and here too the British led).[260] As I have shown, however, the radio companies made agreements that associated them with the telegraph companies on the same terms as had the cable companies. In the field of wireless communication between ships at sea and between ships and shore, the British subsidiary, the Marconi Company of America, in 1914 held a virtual monopoly in the United States.[261] All the activities in shipping, cables, and wireless discussed above were foreign direct investments in crucial sectors.

Foreign portfolio stakes in U.S. domestic telegraphs and telephones existed (George Paish estimated that British holdings in these activities totaled $21 million in 1910, a figure that seems to have been on the very low side).[262] Actually, American telephone and telegraph companies raised substantial capital in London, and their securities were traded on the London Stock Exchange. Issues of American Telephone and Telegraph, Keystone Telegraph, Western Union, and New York Telephone were listed on the Amsterdam exchange and attracted Dutch investment.[263] American Telephone and Telegraph (A.T.T.) was, in addition, a popular stock on the Paris Bourse.[264] In April 1905 H. B. Thayer (vice president of Western Electric Company) had explained in a private letter that A.T.T. required $30 million in fresh capital each year and that the president of A.T.T., Frederick P. Fish, "felt it was worth while to try and draw what he could from outside the country."[265] A.T.T. was successful in obtaining large amounts of European capital.[266] The impressive sums obtained from abroad by the telephone and telegraph companies notwithstanding, judged by overall impact the foreign direct investments were more important.

An Overview

To conclude, many nonbank intermediaries channeled foreign investment into the United States. This was true of foreign stockbrokers and promoters. British investment trusts and mortgage companies with sizable U.S. portfolios were important in the years 1875–1914, directing capital into the U.S. economy. The Dutch had investment companies and mortgage banks that facilitated the transfer of savings from the Netherlands into American projects.

Some large international trading companies, such as Balfour, Williamson especially, and to a much lesser extent Mitsui & Co., participated in diversified American operations. Foreign shipping, cable, and wireless companies towered over American enterprise in international transportation and communication, raising information flows from and capital flows to the United States. A truly significant foreign direct investment in America was that of the British Marconi Company. In 1914 its U.S. affiliate, the Marconi Company of America, was without peer in the new field of radio communication. It carried "high technology" to the United States. Foreign investments in American domestic communication—in American Telephone and Telegraph Company, for instance—were, by contrast, portfolio ones.

In short, the numerous foreign nonbank financial, commercial, and communications intermediaries provided conduits for long-term capital inflows, foreign trade, and information. The foreign investment trust company and mortgage lender offered domestic credit. More important, however, not only did America depend on foreign financing of its international trade (see Chapter 13), but in its international transactions in 1914 the United States had to rely on foreign-owned shipping, foreign-owned cables, and foreign-owned radio communication.

15.

Other Services

Foreign investors furnished other services in addition to the financial, trading, and communications ones. They offered advertising, wholesaling and retailing, insurance, accounting, engineering, construction, and power and light and electric transportation services.[1] In this chapter I will show a mixture of foreign direct and portfolio involvements in providing these services.

Advertising

Since Americans came to excel in advertising, I expected few such businesses from overseas. Nonetheless, at least one existed: T. B. Browne, Ltd. (which began operations in Britain in 1876 and soon thereafter became a space buyer and "agency" for Pears' Soap and other international advertisers), followed Pears' exports to America, opening an office in the United States.[2] Frank Presbrey, writing in 1929 on the history of advertising, concluded, "The English were the first to become international advertisers, and Pears' Soap advertising in the United States exercised an important influence for the beginning of large-scale advertising in America." In the 1880s Pears' Soap innovated in running full-page advertisements in American magazines. According to Presbrey, the English practice of using paintings, either purchased or made especially for the advertiser, was introduced in the United States by Pears' Soap early in the 1890s.[3] This notwithstanding, I found—as anticipated—the foreign role in advertising relatively small when compared with foreign businesses' participation in the distribution of goods. Most frequently, foreign investors used American advertising firms.

Wholesaling and Retailing Services

Participating in U.S. marketing were numerous foreign manufacturing enterprises that sold their products in the United States—goods produced abroad or in this country. I have discussed many of these cases of forward vertical integration in my chapters on the relevant industries. Thus, for example, Lever Brothers' wholesale selling of soap in New England was considered earlier when I covered grocery products. Foreign-owned enterprises in wholesaling in the United States included trading companies that expanded their international trading operations into America and typically sold here goods that they had imported from abroad; I discussed trading companies in Chapter 14.[4] Accordingly, here I want merely to synthesize the materials on foreign manufacturers and trading companies that had their own distribution organizations in America—considering specifically their involvements in wholesale and retail trade. I will also discuss other foreign investments in retailing in America.

In the United States in the years before World War I, many foreign-owned firms had their own men participating (through branches, subsidiaries, and affiliates) in the distribution of branded foods, thread, pencils, books, chemicals, oil products, rubber tires, and specialized machinery. Internalization by a foreign manufacturer of the U.S. wholesaling function was frequent and not confined to any single industry. Nonetheless, highly advertised goods or those that required some sort of specialized treatment or promotion were the most apt to be sold through company-owned channels rather than by an independent wholesaler.[5] Some foreign firms that manufactured in the United States handled their manufacturing and marketing in this country through separate companies, which appear to have corresponded to administrative divisions and not merely to legal requirements. Such separation of foreign-owned manufacturing and selling occurred in a number of different industries and may have replicated practices developed abroad.

When the foreign firms' customers were U.S. producers, frequently American representatives of the foreign enterprises went directly to the buyer rather than utilizing any intervening intermediary. This tended to be the case when the purchasers were relatively few and had special requirements. Thus Japanese trading companies with offices in this country, for example, sold raw silk to the U.S. silk mills. In the case of differentiated goods (dyestuffs or machinery, for instance), the highly trained employees of European manufacturers that had sales branches or subsidiaries in the United States visited and marketed directly to the U.S. textile, glass, chemical, and other factories—explaining at the same time the use of the products and the technical applications.

By contrast, with consumer goods, while foreign manufacturing firms often took part in wholesale distribution, they rarely participated in American retailing and seldom sold to the final user.[6] One conspicuous (and successful) exception was neither a manufacturer nor a trading firm. It was Yamanaka and Co., Osaka, Japan, which around the turn of the century established a New York retail store that sold oriental art and antiques, primarily Chinese works, and catered to New York's new wealthy elite.[7] It filled a highly specialized niche.

Another unique entry into American retailing was the German chocolate maker Gebrüder Stollwerck, whose chocolate and machinery business I have already discussed. Stollwerck made equipment for "automats" ("automatische buffets," or "automatic restaurants") and vending machines. The firm opened automats in the 1880s in New York, Philadelphia, St. Louis, and other American cities. It installed chocolate-vending machines in train stations in New York. The actual ownership of the restaurants and the vending machines is, however, not clear, although the company's historian seems to suggest that at least initially Stollwerck had an ownership interest in the retail sales outlets.[8]

The late nineteenth and early twentieth centuries witnessed a "retailing revolution" in Great Britain, with chain retail stores dotting that country. Was there "horizontal integration"—a comparable set of retail stores in America? Lipton, for example, did—as we noted earlier—contemplate U.S. retail shops and even opened four, but then decided to sell only at the wholesale level its tea (as well as meat) within this country. Lipton's first entry into investment in the United States had been to buy hams for his British stores. Next he had integrated backward in the United States into slaughtering and processing hogs, and forward into wholesaling ham and bacon in America; subsequently, in view of his knowledge of the American market, he sold tea in the United States, first to hotels and restaurants and then to stores.[9]

Other British retailers—like Lipton—had invested in the United States to acquire supplies for their U.K. shops;[10] no British retailing chain in these years made horizontal investments, setting up a parallel retailing organization across the Atlantic. The reasons are clear: it was one matter to sell in many cities and neighborhoods in the relatively small, homogeneous United Kingdom and another to create a chain of stores in the faraway, huge and heterogeneous U.S. market. As Peter Mathias put it, in describing Lipton's decision to confine himself to wholesaling in the United States, "a wholesale trade was managerially safer than large-scale shop management."[11] Accordingly, although British retailers had become an aspect of "big business" in Britain, they could not (and did not) extend themselves in a similar manner into the vast and radically different American market. Interestingly, several of the giant U.S.-owned retailers—A & P, Grand Union, and Krogers (for example)—had their origins in tea retailing; familiar with the home market, they handled the managerial requirements of chain retailing in the United States in these years in a way that British retailers could not.[12] The latter had no advantage.

There were, however, sizable portfolio investments from abroad in U.S. retailers—arranged through American private banks. In the early twentieth century, United Cigar; Sears, Roebuck; Woolworth; and S. S. Kresge raised money in London and on the Continent. The investors were interested in returns and had no intention of exercising managerial perogatives.[13] Note that none of these was a *food*-retailing chain; I can find no evidence of U.S. groceries going abroad for capital.

Insurance Services

Foreign companies provided insurance services at both a wholesale and a retail level in America, and foreign insurance offices became important investors. Foreign companies offered (1) life, (2) fire and marine, and (3) casualty and other insurance. In the first category, U.S. insurance companies were strong and international themselves;[14] aside from a handful of Canadian firms that furnished such coverage to Americans, the foreign role in life insurance was small. The opposite was true in fire and marine insurance, in which foreign enterprises (by this period well established in America) had become highly significant and were selling insurance in the United States on a national scale. As for the third category, "casualty and other," by 1913–14 roughly a dozen foreign firms participated. All these foreign insurance companies not only collected premiums in America (and paid benefits), but they also held sizable U.S. investment portfolios. In this section I will look at these firms in their dual functions—as sellers of insurance services and as purchasers and holders of U.S. financial assets.

In 1875 foreign, and particularly British, insurance offices were no strangers on the American scene. British shipping in the American trade had long been, and continued to be, covered by British marine insurance. As noted earlier, a handful of British fire insurance firms had started doing business in America before the Civil War (one before the War of 1812); more had entered in the immediate aftermath of the Civil War; some had exited; but many remained. As I have also noted, British insurers paid major claims after the great fires of Chicago (1871) and Boston (1872) and as a result gained new respectability.[15] By 1875 British fire insurance companies in America were thus relatively more important than in prior years. They were in fact the giants, the measure and the model for American enterprise. Marquis James, in his history of the Insurance Company of North America (founded in 1792), writes that by 1877 this U.S. concern was able to report "the largest surplus over all liabilities of any American Insurance Company, and *equal to that of any Foreign Company*" (my italics).[16]

Foreign insurers continued to enter the United States with new branches and affiliates and also quite frequently by acquiring existing American companies. Many arrived in the 1880s, 1890s, and early twentieth century. Indeed, every one of the British, German, Canadian, and Swiss branches and affiliates listed in *Best's Insurance Reports* as providing casualty insurance in the United States in 1913 dated its U.S. beginnings after 1881.[17] Likewise, although British companies led the way, insurance firms of many other nationalities joined them in the lucrative U.S. market. In the early 1880s, on average, foreign insurance companies tended to be larger than their American counterparts.[18] In 1914 every state in the United States had licensed foreign insurance companies to do business within its boundaries.[19] The ubiquitous character of the British is evidenced in a Macon, Georgia, directory of 1890, which listed seventeen British insurance companies in that one southern city![20]

Ranking first among the foreign insurers in the United States were the British fire offices. The two largest in this country were headquartered in Liverpool: the Liverpool & London & Globe and the Royal Insurance Company, Ltd.[21] Yet the United States attracted more London insurers than Liverpool ones. Likewise, Edinburgh was the home base of important Scottish insurance offices that marketed fire coverage in America.[22]

In 1881 roughly one-quarter of all American fire insurance was handled by foreign companies, about one-fifth of the total by British firms.[23] For these foreign enterprises, their U.S. premiums added greatly to their worldwide revenues, as the following cases indicate: Sun Insurance Office, a British firm that started its U.S. business as late as 1882 by purchasing the Watertown Company, for example, found that in 1900 its U.S. fire insurance revenues were almost equal to those from the United Kingdom.[24] Royal Exchange Assurance, also a relative newcomer in American insurance, having opened its first

U.S. agency in California in 1891,[25] recorded that from 1902 to 1914 its U.S. fire insurance premiums surpassed those collected in Great Britain. Nine key British insurers in 1905 earned half their £15.6 million *worldwide* premium income from fire coverage in the United States.[26]

Most British firms persevered after the devastating fires that followed the San Francisco earthquake of 1906 and in general managed better than their American counterparts, although for some the substantial losses did pose serious difficulties.[27] Once again, as with the Chicago and Boston fires, that the British houses paid their claims raised their prestige and reputation in the United States.[28]

The major British fire insurance firms in the United States (Liverpool & London & Globe; Royal Insurance Company; and the Commercial Union) had separate U.S. affiliates to provide "casualty and miscellaneous insurance."[29] By far the largest British company in the United States in the casualty business was the independent Employers' Liability Assurance Corporation, Ltd., of London. Organized in Great Britain in 1880, it was said to be the first enterprise to write liability insurance. It entered the United States in 1886, with a branch in Boston. In this country it specialized in liability and compensation insurance and in 1913 collected premiums totaling $6.1 million.[30]

In 1913 alone, thirty-one branches and eleven affiliates of British fire and marine insurance companies collected $68 million in net premiums in the United States.[31] In addition, that year British insurance firms collected some $25 million in premiums covering liability, accident and health, fidelity and surety bonds, workmen's compensation, burglary and theft, and to a far lesser extent, automobile, plate glass, steam boiler, and other miscellaneous coverage.[32]

American and British firms served as agents for the British insurers in various parts of the United States. Thus Balfour, Guthrie—the San Francisco house of the Liverpool trading firm Balfour, Williamson—represented the Caledonian Insurance Company (a Scottish firm) and the British and Foreign Marine Insurance Company.[33] The Caledonian provided fire insurance on grain in transit from farm to ship (Balfour, Guthrie was a large grain exporter).[34]

While throughout the years 1875–1914, the British had the largest insurance presence of all the foreign insurance companies in the United States, firms headquartered in many other nations came to America, and over the period as a whole the relative importance of British offices seems to have diminished. Table 15.1 lists foreign insurance companies in fire and marine insurance in the United States in 1913, by numbers of companies, net premium income, and "admitted assets."

As German immigrants arrived in the United States, German in-

Table 15.1. Foreign insurance companies in fire and marine insurance in the United States, December 31, 1913[a]

Nationality	Total present		Net premium income		"Admitted assets"	
	Number	Percentage of total	In millions of U.S. dollars	In percentages	In millions of U.S. dollars	In percentages
British	42	47%	$ 68	56%	$116	63%
German	13	15	18	15	24	13
Russian	9	10	18	15	19	10
French	9	10	4	3	7	4
Swiss	3	3	3	2	3	2
Bulgarian	2	2	3	3	3	2
Canadian	2	2	3	2	4	2
Swedish	2	2	2	2	3	2
Six others[b]	7	8	2	2	5	3
Total	89	100[c]	121	100	184	100[c]

Source: Tabulation based on data in *Best's Insurance Reports, Fire and Marine, 1914.*

[a] Table includes both branches and affiliates.

[b] Includes those from China (with two branches) and Spain, Holland, New Zealand, Austria, and Japan (one branch each).

[c] Totals are off because of rounding. Percentages were derived before rounding.

surance companies followed—and important German firms headquartered in Berlin, Cologne, Hamburg, Munich, Frankfurt, Mannheim, and elsewhere opened offices in America, usually providing fire insurance.[35] There were nine "Russian" fire insurance companies in the United States in 1913 including one from Warsaw; recall that at that time much of Poland was part of the Russian Empire.[36] The largest Russian company in the United States in 1913 was the Rossia (*sic*) Insurance Company, of St. Petersburg, with a branch in Hartford, Connecticut. It provided fire reinsurance. The branch opened in 1904, and by 1913 its annual net premium income had reached $6.7 million, which ranked it (after the London & Liverpool & Globe, Royal Insurance, and the Commercial Union Group) as the fourth largest foreign insurance company (as measured by net premium income) in the United States.[37] French insurers in America did smaller quantities of business; yet in 1913 nine of them were licensed in the United States to offer fire and marine coverage.[38]

The two Bulgarian companies noted in Table 15.1 both handled fire reinsurance through branches in Hartford. One, the Balkan National Insurance Company of Sofia, had entered the United States in 1910 (it also provided insurance coverage in Bulgaria and Turkey); the other, the "Bulgaria," First Bulgarian Company, of Roustchouk, was admitted to the United States in 1912; it was a truly multinational firm, with business in England, Germany, Belgium, France, Holland, Spain, and Turkey, as well as Bulgaria. What was behind these sizable Bulgarian entries into America is unknown.[39]

The economist Cleona Lewis found that between 1861 and 1914 no fewer than fifty-three foreign insurance companies *closed* their U.S. branches.[40] A number of foreign firms established themselves, collected premiums, defrauded American buyers, and then disappeared! Some operated without registering. In 1914, *Best's Insurance Reports* warned against "unadmitted" foreign companies, those transacting business in the United States without being regularly licensed. American businessmen who could not obtain adequate fire insurance from companies licensed in a state where the insured was located seem to have turned to outside companies for added insurance, often with bad results.[41]

In 1882 the New York state legislature prohibited foreign (out-of-country) companies from exhibiting their foreign accounts (a French company had advertised large assets, only a small part of which were in fact available to cover U.S. losses).[42] As early as 1851 the New York state legislature had passed an act to regulate life and fire insurance companies and to require of them "New York deposits" to demonstrate financial responsibility.[43] From the 1880s onward, state insurance regulations had multiplied to protect customers from unscrupulous sellers. Often foreign enterprises could not gain licenses from state authorities, because of inadequate assets in the United States, and thus retreated.

Some foreign firms would exit from American business for years and then reenter. Some closed branches but started, in their stead, affiliates. At the time of the California fire (1906), many continental European firms folded, failing to pay claims.[44] Some British houses paid but withdrew after the fire and did not resume underwriting in America.[45] Other firms would leave a particular state (such as California after the big fire) but expand in the United States in general.[46]

Despite the closing of the fifty-three branches of foreign insurance firms between 1861 and 1914, in 1914 eighty-nine branches and affiliates of foreign insurance firms were listed in *Best's Insurance Reports* as licensed to do fire and marine business in the United States.[47] Clearly expansion and contraction had coexisted. Indeed, certain British companies held reputations for stability and longevity. Symbolic was the modern eight-story steel frame building on Pine and William

Street in downtown New York, built by the Liverpool & London & Globe in 1881.[48] The annual premiums collected by the eighty-nine branches and affiliates of the foreign fire and marine companies came in 1913 to $121 million (see Table 15.1).[49] In addition, *Best's Insurance Reports, Casualty and Miscellaneous* listed about a dozen branches and affiliates of foreign offices with premiums totaling $27 million in 1913.[50] And to this group we must add the foreign-owned firms present in *Best's Insurance Reports, Life,* which included reports on five Canadian life insurance companies licensed to do business in the United States, the largest of which were Sun Life Assurance Company and Canada Life Assurance Company.[51] Whereas *Best's Insurance Reports, Fire and Marine* and also *Best's Insurance Reports, Casualty and Miscellaneous* paid substantial attention to the foreign insurance companies doing business in the United States, *Best's Insurance Reports, Life* confined itself to U.S. and Canadian firms.[52]

As the foreign insurance companies expanded their marketing in the United States, they also made investments. In 1880 thirteen British insurance offices had U.S. assets of $19 million. That year, the largest U.S. *investors* were Liverpool & London & Globe with $4.4 million; Royal Insurance, $2.7 million; the North British & Mercantile, $1.8 million; the Commercial Union, $1.7 million; and the Queen, $1.5 million.[53]

State laws, as noted, mandated deposits of U.S. securities by the insurance companies as a condition for licensing. Thus Royal Exchange Assurance (REA), when it began to do business in San Francisco in 1891, had to buy and to deposit $250,000 of U.S. 4 percent bonds. By 1909 REA had over $1.75 million in American securities deposited with officials or trustees to comply with local American regulations.[54] As also indicated, state officials wanted a guaranty that the foreign companies had liquid assets in the United States to cover claims.

By year-end 1913, forty-two British branches and affiliates doing fire and marine business in the United States had $116 million in "admitted assets."[55] The growth in assets in the period 1880–1913 had been spectacular. In 1913 the Liverpool & London & Globe's New York branch had admitted assets of more than $14 million; it also had a New York affiliate with another $1 million in assets. Royal Insurance Company's New York branch had over $12.5 million in admitted assets; in addition, its parent company in Great Britain had acquired in 1891 the parent company of Queen Insurance Company, New York, which had an additional $10 million in admitted assets. Apparently Royal and Queen maintained separate corporate structures in the United States (but since they were part of the same organization,

I probably should put their joint-operations in first place). North British & Mercantile had a New York branch with $8.8 million in assets and a New York affiliate with another $2.1 million. The Commercial Union Assurance Company's fire and insurance group included a New York branch with admitted assets of $7.4 million, a California affiliate with $1.1 million in assets, a New York affiliate with another $1.1 million in assets, and the Palatine Insurance Company with $3.2 million in assets.[56]

British casualty insurers had in 1913 assets of about $27 million in the United States, of which roughly $12 million were associated with separate affiliates of the Liverpool & London & Globe, the Royal Insurance Company, and the Commercial Union Assurance Company. In measuring the investments of British insurers, these casualty companies must also be included.[57]

In 1913–14 the British fire and marine companies ranked as the strongest foreign (and U.S.) insurance companies. While British firms represented only 47 percent of the number of foreign fire and marine insurers, they held 63 percent of the *assets* of such firms (see Table 15.1). The percentages were even higher among the casualty companies: British insurers held fully 85 percent of the assets of all foreign firms.[58] Only two foreign, non-British fire and marine insurance companies had admitted assets in the United States of over $5 million, and both were in the fire reinsurance business: the Munich Reinsurance Company ($6.4 million) and the Rossia Insurance Company ($6.7 million).[59]

The investments by foreign insurance companies in the United States seem to fall into three categories: (1) The branches and affiliates of foreign insurance companies that did business in the United States acquired U.S. bonds and stocks—mainly U.S. government (federal, state, or local) or American railroad issues. *Best's Insurance Reports, Fire and Marine, 1914* lists the securities in the portfolios of these branches and affiliates.[60] Most of the investments appear to have been made from premiums collected in the United States. They probably involved little capital inflow from abroad. Nonetheless, these are "foreign" investments, since the ownership was held by the foreign firms in the United States; they represent a claim by foreign enterprises on U.S. assets. Not all of the "admitted assets" were in American stocks and bonds, but such securities constituted a large percentage of the "admitted assets" of the foreign branches and affiliates.

(2) *Parent* insurance companies abroad acquired U.S. securities for their investment portfolios, attracted by high U.S. yields. Lord Roths-

child wrote his cousins in Paris on October 18, 1907, for example, that "North British and Mercantile, so we are told, telegraphed New York today to buy large lines of Atcheson Preference, Union Pacific Preference & Baltimore & Ohio Preference with the money they have at their credit line there."[61] Such securities could be bought in New York or London. The historian R. T. Naylor writes that Canadian life insurance companies (under Canadian law) were "permitted to hold investments in foreign countries in which they had branches to the extent that they were required by law in those countries to deposit securities as a reserve." Naylor notes, however, that Canadian companies invested far in excess of the requirements and "were actively engaged in the export of long-term capital to the U.S. In addition to stock and bond investments, they provided interim financing to American promoters."[62] Later I will show the sizable stakes of the Canadian firm Sun Life, whose interests were clearly well beyond the legal requirements of the midwestern states in which it did business.[63]

(3) Foreign insurance companies that did *not* market insurance in the United States also had American investments. Thus, for example, I have seen no evidence that the Scottish Widow's Fund and Life Assurance Society ever sold insurance in the United States. Yet in the early 1890s it acquired £1.5 million in U.S. railway gold mortgage bonds (as noted in Chapter 6),[64] and in 1896 it engaged a New York law firm to look after its investments in American *real estate* mortgages and in arranging collections on its behalf. In the early twentieth century the law firm continued to handle "many" real estate loans for the Scottish Widow's Fund.[65] Likewise, some of the earliest (pre–World War I) business of the accounting firm Arthur Young & Co. was placing real estate loans for Scottish life insurance companies.[66] Even more important, in the summer of 1915 Prudential Assurance Company, Ltd., held $40 million in American securities![67] These holdings must have existed in 1914. I can find no evidence that this British life insurance company operated, that is, sold insurance, in the United States.[68]

In short, foreign insurance firms, especially those in the fire and marine field, taking advantage of profitable opportunities, did substantial business in the United States. Not only did they provide insurance coverage, but along with other foreign-headquartered insurance offices they were also large investors in American securities, government and railway bonds, mainly the latter; some also owned real estate and some did real estate financing in the United States. One Canadian insurance company made huge investments (as I will show) in American public utilities.

Accounting Firms

Foreign accounting firms had relatively small investments in the United States, yet their presence—as multinational businesses—was nonetheless highly significant. They became the prototypes for comparable American enterprise. In the 1870s several British accounting firms had become involved in American "investigations." A Price Waterhouse history relates that the firm first undertook work in the United States in 1873.[69] Edwin Waterhouse had as a client the Whitwell Iron Works, Stockton, England;[70] when Thomas Whitwell invested in the iron business in Tennessee (see Chapter 7), Price, Waterhouse, London, handled the U.S. audits.[71]

It was not, however, until 1883 that a British accounting firm actually opened an office in America. That year Edwin Guthrie of Thomas, Wade, Guthrie & Co., London and Manchester, was a receiver in the bankruptcy of a British financial concern (name unknown). The latter had properties in the United States. Guthrie crossed the Atlantic to handle his British client's affairs, and when he could not find a suitable American accounting firm to conduct an audit of the properties, he decided to start an accounting practice in New York. With the American John Wylie Barrow, Guthrie organized the first British accounting firm in the United States, Barrow, Wade, Guthrie & Co.[72] Barrow, an actuary, had been in business checking vouchers and certifying the clerical accuracy of monthly statements sent to the home offices of several British fire insurance companies. Thus he already had British connections. He would be the American resident partner.

The British partners in Thomas, Wade, Guthrie & Co. supplied the working capital for the new Barrow, Wade, Guthrie & Co., New York. Barrow died in 1886. Guthrie returned to the United States to install an Englishman (who had just arrived in New York), James T. Anyon, who would run the office in America. Anyon became a partner in 1887.[73] The first British accounting firm with a direct investment in the United States had as an early client in America the New York, Ontario, and Western Railway, which Anyon says was the first American railroad to employ public accountants as auditors and to certify to the correctness of its annual statement.[74] It was a railroad that had attracted substantial British and Dutch investment.[75] Among the other 1880s clients of Barrow, Wade, Guthrie & Co. were the British investors: the Royal Insurance Company of Liverpool; the British and Foreign Marine Insurance Company; the London Assurance Corporation; the Sun Insurance Company; and the York Street Flax Spinning Company.[76] In 1890 both Thomas, Wade, Guthrie *and*

Barrow, Wade, Guthrie were involved in the founding of the United States Trust and Guarantee Corporation, Ltd.[77] By 1890, if not before, Barrow, Wade, Guthrie had opened a Chicago office.[78]

Meanwhile, Price, Waterhouse, London, found in 1887 that its American work had reached sufficient importance to consider its having permanent representation in the United States. As more British capital entered America, Price, Waterhouse had been frequently asked to undertake "investigations" for the investors.[79] Price, Waterhouse handled many inquiries for the promoter H. Osborne O'Hagan. Another British accounting firm, Deloitte, Dever, Griffiths, & Co., also found its U.S. business growing, and by the spring of 1888, when a partner in this firm, John Griffiths, sailed to New York to look into a railroad matter, its historian tells us that the firm had already carried on numerous investigations of businesses in New York, Boston, Brooklyn, Chicago, Denver, "Kentucky" (sic), Minneapolis, and Philadelphia.[80] By 1888–1890 Deloitte seems to have been doing the largest American business of any British accounting firm.[81] Other U.K. accounting houses with U.S. work in the 1880s but no U.S. offices included Hart Brothers, Tibbetts & Co., J. R. Ellerman & Co., and Turquand, Youngs, Bishop, & Clarke.[82] British investors wanted reports from accounting firms that they trusted.

Not until 1890 did Deloitte, Dever, Griffiths & Co. and Price, Waterhouse open their first New York offices. Their immediate reason for doing so lay in the proliferation of London-stimulated U.S. *brewery* amalgamations.[83] Deloitte was involved, among others, in New York Breweries Company, Ltd., and John F. Betz and Son's Brewery, Ltd., two of the earliest promotions. Price, Waterhouse's many brewery accounts included Bartholomay Brewing Company, Milwaukee and Chicago Breweries, Ltd., and San Francisco Breweries, Ltd.[84] At origin, Deloitte's New York staff was larger than that of Price, Waterhouse.[85] Both firms started Chicago offices, Deloitte probably in 1891 and Price, Waterhouse definitely in that year.[86] The entries of these two accounting firms coincided with the surge in new British interest in takeovers of American industrials. The accounting firms followed their customers to the United States. They also handled accounts for corporate reorganizations. In September 1891 and June 1893, respectively, Deloitte, Dever, Griffiths & Co. prepared reports on the financial condition of Westinghouse Electric and Manufacturing Company and National Cordage Company for bankers' reorganization committees.[87]

The archives of Price Waterhouse in London contain rich materials on that firm's activities in the United States. In August 1890 a "Heads of Agreement" was drawn up between Lewis D. Jones (who had been on the London firm's staff since 1877)[88] and Price, Waterhouse. This was turned into a formal agreement dated September 11, 1890. Jones agreed to give his "whole time and energy" to the business of the new "Agency" of Price, Waterhouse to be established in New York. Price, Waterhouse would supply him with working funds and the necessary staff. Jones was not, however, entitled to sign Price, Waterhouse's name to any accounts "unless first specially authorized." The profits of the business in America were to be divided, 20 percent to Jones, 80 percent to Price, Waterhouse, London. Jones was guaranteed a minimum compensation of $4,000 per year.[89]

Among the first projects of Price, Waterhouse's New York office was the examination of a collection of salt works in Warsaw, New York. Its bill was $1,907, which Erastus Wiman, acting for the client, thought outrageous; the firm had major difficulty collecting.[90] The North American Salt Company, Ltd., was floated in London, but apparently the flotation was not successful; the company was stillborn.[91] The role of Price, Waterhouse was to certify the accounts— to reassure British investors.

In the spring of 1891 Jones wrote London on his need for more personnel and of a man he was considering. Price, Waterhouse, London, replied: "So long as our staff in America are Englishmen we do not think our clients will be likely to have the objection, which we have mentioned to you namely the examination of accounts by Americans. At the same time you must be specially careful in engaging men who have been for any length of time in America."[92] Time in America was corrupting.[93]

In 1891 the firm in London sent W. J. Caesar to join Jones in America; Caesar would head the new Chicago office. Price, Waterhouse had important brewery business in Chicago and was also the auditor for G. H. Hammond Company, Ltd., and the Union Stockyards. Because most of the many flotations handled by H. Osborne O'Hagan in London had Price, Waterhouse as the auditor in London, its New York and Chicago offices completed the American investigations.[94] The Chicago office's work involved so much in breweries, stockyards, and meat packing that the staff there referred to themselves as the "beer and beef boys."[95]

When in 1892 Jones and Caesar favored sending out a "circular" to potential American customers, Price, Waterhouse in London opposed the advertising as unprofessional: "You must wait patiently and trust to getting known by degrees for doing good work and not charging exorbitantly. The more acquaintances you can make either in business or socially so much better of course."[96]

About 1892, Hart Brothers, Tibbetts & Co., London, had a New

York office (at 25 Pine Street) and a Denver one as well (it was auditor for Denver United Breweries, Ltd., registered in England in 1889). I know nothing of this firm's subsequent history in the United States.[97] Thus, by the time of the Panic of 1893, I can identify four British accounting firms with eight "branch" offices in America—four in New York, three in Chicago, and one in Denver.

The early 1890s were not prosperous times for these enterprises. The Baring Crisis in November 1890 meant fewer promotions in London and less-successful ones; the British were disenchanted with American securities. The Panic of 1893 further curtailed business, including that of the accountants.[98] Early in 1894 Price, Waterhouse's Jones reported to London that "Deloitte's are materially reducing their staff here in the United States owing to the slackness of business."[99] In January 1894 Jones and Caesar wrote London: "Our experience is that very little American accounting business is done or even understood outside of New York and possibly San Francisco. In Chicago and other large cities it is safe to estimate that over 90 pecent of the accounting business is such as we do viz the examination of the accounts of local industries for English Proprietary companies and that the balance is not of a desirable character." Their letter continued, in New York, "for purely American work our charge of $25 a day is considered too high"; in Chicago, the firm's customers were complaining over the bills. As for future prospects, Jones and Caesar wrote, "we expect nothing from the Railroad Companies as they are generally managed by parties who are not interested in having an independent examination of their accounts unless of course where they desire to raise money in London" And the men added, "This remark applies to the controlling management of most large businesses in this country." Banks were examined by official state examiners, which the accountants believed precluded business there. Jones and Caesar did, however, think there was a possible opening for accountants "who would take up and make a specialty of examining the accounts of Branches of European Insurance Companies and Banking and Commercial Houses doing business in America. There is a very large number of these."[100] But overall, in 1894, after four years of operations in America, Jones and Caesar were discouraged.

Moreover, Caesar had begun feuding with the firm's principal clients in Chicago; Jones therefore proposed that the two accountants switch places. In early 1894 Jones went to Chicago and Caesar to New York.[101] So bad had the outlook for the accounting firms become in early 1894 that Caesar sought another position (he applied to become manager of the U.S. branch of the London Guarantee and Accident

Company, but that British insurance company desired an American manager!).[102]

A new difficulty arose over the question of depreciation. J. Gurney Fowler, a partner in Price, Waterhouse, London, had insisted that the U.S. brewery company accounts include provisions for depreciation. In 1894, with bad times, U.S. shareholders saw their dividends disappear and objected to the depreciation charges. The Britisher Russell Monro, who was active in brewery finance and was O'Hagan's representative in America, wrote Fowler that to pass the preferred dividend "will be the last nail in the coffin of American Breweries."[103] Chicago newspapers called depreciation an invention of those "tiresome" English accountants to rob shareholders. Apparently Price, Waterhouse successfully resisted any reduction in the depreciation figures,[104] and although the breweries continued unprofitable, they did not "die." The dispute added to the general sense of foreboding about the firm's future in America.

Deloitte seems not to have been as scrupulous as Price, Waterhouse in insisting on including depreciation.[105] When the *Miller's Gazette* (London), November 14, 1894, commented on how plant depreciation was entirely overlooked in the balance sheet of Pillsbury-Washburn Flour Mills Company, Ltd. (which Deloitte had certified), the *Northwestern Miller* (Minneapolis) justified the accounting firm's rendition: "In well-conducted American mills there is no depreciation of plant."[106]

In the summer of 1894 Price, Waterhouse's London partners reviewed their New York and Chicago office accounts and were appalled. The partner most responsible for the American business, J. Gurney Fowler, wrote to Jones, "Mr. Waterhouse's principal objection to the Agency is that the balance to your debit appears always to increase and that you never make remittances to reduce the account."[107] Accordingly, Price, Waterhouse decided to revamp its arrangements with its American representatives, seeking to "be free from risk of loss attending establishments of our own at New York and Chicago."[108] Its plan was that Jones and Caesar would start an independent partnership—Jones, Caesar & Co.—to obtain whatever American business they could. This partnership would, in addition, serve as the "Agency" for Price, Waterhouse, London, to be paid on "agency terms." Price, Waterhouse, London, agreed to guaranty the new venture a minimum income for three years.[109]

To the surprise of Price, Waterhouse, London, at once Caesar went after business from other London accountants—Cooper Brothers & Co. and Turquand, Youngs, Bishop & Clarke—writing them, "As you have not been directly connected with American affairs in the same way as those firms who have had offices here, we should not expect much business especially at first."[110] From London, Price, Waterhouse scolded that such a solicitation was "premature"; in a first draft of this letter (a draft that was kept but not mailed), the London firm had added that its fellow British accountants would "not like to be told that their business in America is a small one!"[111]

On January 1, 1895, Jones, Caesar & Co. came into being; it had no London partner. For the next few years the letterhead of Price, Waterhouse in America read: Jones, Caesar & Co., Chartered Accountants, under which was the heading: Agents for Price, Waterhouse & Co. The latter introduced the American partnership to the audit of the Norfolk and Western Railway, its first important railway engagement. Others followed,[112] and slowly revenues in America revived. It became very confusing to sort out "agency" from "partnership" accounts.[113] By the end of 1897 prosperity had returned, and the London firm realized that a relationship that reunited the American and the British enterprises was essential. By then Price, Waterhouse, London, was convinced that in the "best" U.S. commercial circles, there was a new acceptance of the importance of auditing accounts.

Long transatlantic discussions on possible arrangements filled the Price, Waterhouse correspondence. The American partners were concerned about U.S. contract labor laws: the U.S. firm could not bring in "assistants" on contract, whereas Price, Waterhouse, London, could send assistants to America. Caesar wanted a guaranty that the American partners were adequately remunerated, and boasted of the amount of "American" work relative to "Price, Waterhouse–referred" business. Caesar also noted the prejudice in the United States against "foreign business."[114] The state of New York had on April 17, 1896, passed the first legislation in America providing for the issue of a certificate that conferred the title "certified public accountant" (CPA) on qualified persons. In New York the CPA designation would go only to U.S. citizens or to persons who had declared "their intentions to be citizens." This was the start of an accredited accounting profession in the United States.[115] Caesar became a CPA presumably declaring his "intentions" to become a citizen.[116]

By 1897 Jones, Caesar & Co. handled a substantial railroad practice. They undertook a special examination of the Baltimore and Ohio Railroad to determine how the proceeds of certain bond issues had been spent. J. P. Morgan & Co. was involved. By 1897–98 Jones, Caesar was at last making good profits, especially in connection with investigations of the concerns that would merge into American Steel and Wire Company. J. P. Morgan & Co. introduced them to this assignment. After 1897 Caesar and Jones also did investigations for

August Belmont & Co., the Rothschild representative in the United States. In 1898 Price, Waterhouse in America was taking part in Northern Pacific work.[117]

In February or March 1898 Price, Waterhouse, London, and Jones, Caesar & Co. entered into a short-term agreement, pending a far-reaching one, which was drafted in February 1898. The American firm was now doing business in the United States under the styles Jones, Caesar & Co. *and* Price, Waterhouse & Co.[118] Its business surpassed that of Deloitte, the earlier leader. Caesar wrote London in October 1898 that Jones, Caesar & Co. had twice as many employees as Deloitte; "in fact we have the largest office in the country."[119] The same letter rejoiced: "We have just got our first Bank—a Savings Bank."[120]

As deliberations continued on the planned new association between Price, Waterhouse, London, and its American representatives, Caesar wrote London that the name Jones, Caesar & Co. was well known and it was "imperative" that "we should continue practicing in our own names as well as under the Agency." He reported once again on the agitation in New York against employing foreign accountants.[121]

On February 2, 1899, very suddenly Jones died (at the age of forty), and Price, Waterhouse in London postponed entering into the newly proposed agreement with Caesar. The home office felt that the U.S. business needed to be strengthened by "assistance from this side."[122] By contrast, Caesar argued that he could run the practice as the only U.S. partner, conversing by telephone with clients in Chicago, St. Louis, Boston, Baltimore, Rochester, and Washington.[123] London replied that at least one, and maybe more, additional partners were needed to handle the activities in America.

Then in 1900 the forty-one-year-old impetuous Caesar announced that he would retire, and the London firm (not unreluctantly) accepted his resignation. Caesar left an "agency" that was "permanently established at the head of the profession in this country [the United States] and profits . . . last year exceeded $100,000," a new high.[124] "As to getting the business," he wrote, "people now come to us as a matter of course. PW Co being the recognized Railroad Auditors and JC Co the recognized Auditor of large corporations. So firmly is this understood that I believe the same House [a reference to a banking house such as J. P. Morgan] would call in one firm for one class of business and the other for the other class."[125]

With the merger movement in America at the turn of the century, there was more call for accountants. Thomas, Wade, Guthrie & Co; Deloitte (which had by then closed its Chicago office and was confined to New York); and Price, Waterhouse were joined in the United States by George A. Touche & Co.[126] Touche (born in 1861 in Edinburgh) had served his apprenticeship as an accountant under the prominent Scot Alexander T. Niven. As a young man he became involved in investment trusts (at least as early as 1889); by then he was living in London. In 1898 Touche had formed George A. Touche & Co., London. Meanwhile, John B. Niven (son of Alexander), who had apprenticed under his father, had gone to the United States in 1897, where he was employed in the Chicago office of Price, Waterhouse until February 1900, when he left to join George A. Touche in forming Touche, Niven & Co., New York. This firm (now Touche, Ross, Bailey & Smart) represented Touche's first entry into an American accounting practice.[127]

In May 1901 an announcement circulated that "Arthur Lowes Dickinson, M. A. Cambridge, Chartered Accountant," had joined the American Price, Waterhouse. Dickinson became very important in the American accounting profession. He was a giant in the field. An agreement was signed between the English partners and two American partners, Dickinson and Henry Wilmot, that established a new American partnership.[128] For a while this firm used both names, Price, Waterhouse & Co. and Jones, Caesar & Co. (despite the absence of Jones and Caesar).[129] It was under the style Price, Waterhouse & Co. that in 1902 the American partnership was appointed auditors for the nation's largest industrial corporation, United States Steel.[130] By July 1914 the letterhead of the accounting firm read only Price, Waterhouse & Co.[131] In the meantime, the firm flourished.

When Dickinson arrived to assume the post of senior partner in America—in June 1901—Price, Waterhouse and Jones, Caesar, with offices in New York and Chicago, had a large clientele, including breweries, insurance firms, railroads, iron and steel companies, and machinery companies. It was trusted by prominent New York banking firms and lawyers, who were significant in the financial aspects of corporate consolidations and reorganizations.[132] Under Dickinson's able management the firm opened branch offices in St. Louis, Pittsburgh (to handle the important U.S. Steel account), San Francisco, Seattle, Philadelphia, and Boston, as well as in Montreal, Toronto, and Vancouver.[133] All the U.S. partners became certified public accountants.[134] George O. May (1875–1961), who migrated to the United States from England in 1897, became a partner in 1902 and a senior partner in 1911.[135] May became a leader in the accounting profession.[136]

In the same years, Deloitte expanded more modestly in America, with a new branch office in Cincinnati in 1905 and a reopening of its

Chicago office in 1912.[137] Deloitte had the misfortune of having certified the accounts of Pillsbury-Washburn Flour Mills Company, Ltd., over the years, accounts that in 1908 were found to be incorrect and misleading.[138] Deloitte seems to have been dropped by that reorganized company, and John Niven of Touche, Niven & Co. was brought in.[139] In vain, Deloitte urged the receivers of Pillsbury-Washburn to take action against the "fraudulent" parties.[140]

Meanwhile, in 1905 the Armstrong Committee in New York, whose counsel was Charles Evans Hughes, made a major investigation of the life insurance business. Price, Waterhouse & Co. was engaged to examine Equitable Life Assurance Society and New York Life Insurance Company. Deloitte participated, as did the American firm Haskins & Sells, Deloitte's future partner (the firm is now Deloitte, Haskins & Sells).[141]

During a westbound transatlantic voyage in 1911, William B. Peat of the British firm W. B. Peat & Co. (name adopted in 1891) met the Scot James Marwick, who had earlier migrated to America and established in 1897 Marwick, Mitchell & Co. (his partner, Roger Mitchell, was also an immigrant from Scotland). On this trip to New York, Peat (a Scot by birth) and Marwick decided to join forces *in the United States*. They formed a new partnership, Marwick, Mitchell, Peat & Co. (in 1925 it became Peat, Marwick, Mitchell & Co.; in 1950 Barrow, Wade, Guthrie & Co. became part of PMM). On October 1, 1911, the new partnership came into effect, one-fourth owned by Peat. Peat contributed $62,500 to the partnership's capital and provided, in addition, $34,820 to the new firm in payment for the goodwill created and attached to the Marwick, Mitchell name. Peat's cooperation with Marwick and Mitchell gave him an association with a U.S. firm that already had offices in New York; Minneapolis; Chicago; Winnipeg; Toronto; Pittsburgh; Philadelphia; Kansas City; Washington, D.C.; New Orleans; Boston; Milwaukee; and St. Louis. In 1912 it opened offices in Portland, Oregon, and San Francisco.[142]

In 1914 the British firm Whinney, Smith & Whinney (now Ernst & Whinney) set up an office in New York. According to its historian, it did so to assist London City and Midland Bank, London, which was hoping to extend its correspondent relationships in America.[143]

In sum, by 1914 a number of the most prominent English and Scottish accounting firms had established themselves in the United States. They had profound influence on the U.S. accounting profession. Every history of American accounting pays heed to Price, Waterhouse and generally to some of the others, if not to the entire group. One such history states that in the early years American accountants were jealous of their British colleagues, "who seemed to be favored by the bankers, and thus obtained many of the most lucrative engagements." The historian added:

In retrospect, however, the accounting profession clearly gained much from the presence of the English and Scottish chartered accountants. They brought with them a background of discipline, professional training, standards, and professional pride . . . they knew their jobs; they were articulate, and were generally well educated. They were hard workers and astute businessmen. For the most part they were dedicated to high standards.[144]

Whereas most of the men employed by the British accounting firms in America came from the United Kingdom, Price, Waterhouse in 1897 hired its first U.S. college graduate.[145] It was a change from the earlier philosophy that all Americans were "untrustworthy."

In 1907 the Interstate Commerce Commission issued its original accounting standards; in 1909 the U.S. corporate income tax was introduced (known as an excise tax, it was measured by income). Legislation that established the Federal Reserve System was passed in 1913, and that year the states ratified a constitutional amendment allowing an income tax. In 1914 the Federal Trade Commission came into being. These measures all meant a new need in America for independent accountants. Likewise, large publicly traded U.S. corporations wanted outside auditors. British accounting firms in America that relied originally on British approaches and precedents gave direction and guidance to the developing American accounting profession. The Britishers had entered America principally to offer their services to British investors, that is, British-owned companies, but by 1914 the practice of the British accountants included American and British-owned businesses, and most certainly far more of the former than of the latter.

Of today's "Big Eight" accounting firms in the United States, the British side of five (Deloitte, Haskins & Sells; Ernst & Whinney; Peat, Marwick, Mitchell; Price Waterhouse; and Touche Ross) started—as I have shown—their first American offices before World War I. These were direct investments of a multinational enterprise variety. The sixth, Coopers & Lybrand, did U.S. work before 1914, but I have found no evidence of an American office of the British Coopers in the pre–World War I years. The seventh of today's group, Arthur Young, was founded by a Scot who emigrated to the United States in 1890 and opened his American business in 1894. Since he left no British parent firm behind, I have not discussed him in this section, following my rule of excluding immigrant ventures that were not extensions of a business abroad.[146] Only one of today's "Big Eight" (Arthur Andersen) had no British antecedent. Yet Andersen's first position, his "baptism" in accounting in 1908, was in the Chicago office of Price, Waterhouse.[147]

Engineering Services

Just as Britishers did not trust American accountants, so too, at least in much of the nineteenth century, they did not trust American engineers to evaluate their planned investments. Accordingly, there developed a group of "consulting engineers" who looked at new projects and often managed existing ones. Consulting engineers were involved in U.S. mining, construction, and public utility ventures. John Taylor & Sons, a long-established London engineering consulting firm, which had surveyed U.S. gold mining prospects in California in 1850 was, for example, in 1883–1900 frequently called upon to scrutinize mines in America for British investors: four mines in Colorado, three in Idaho, two in Arizona, one in the Dakotas, one in Wyoming, and one in New Mexico in these years.[148] In 1905 John Taylor & Sons was investigating gold mines in Alaska.[149] The house would also act as manager of mines owned by Britishers, for instance, the Silver Peak Mining Company, Colorado (1880); the Broadway Gold Mining Company, Montana (1881); and the Harney Peak (Dakota) Tin Company (1887).[150] It had a vast international business.

Another even more important British firm, Bewick, Moreing & Co., London, was used by H. Osborne O'Hagan and others to report on mining properties.[151] Bewick, Moreing & Co. supervised the operations of several British-owned mines in Nevada and Colorado.[152] In the 1880s and 1890s the firm had branch offices in San Francisco and Salt Lake City.[153] Bewick, Moreing & Co. became deeply involved in mining finance, and by 1901 its senior partner, Charles Algernon Moreing, spent a substantial portion of his time arranging loan flotations, negotiating with stockbrokers, and finding monies for the firm's worldwide ventures. The partnership (for a fee) would provide "offices, facilities for stock transfers and clerical staff for mining companies registered in London."[154]

T. A. Rickard, a graduate of the Royal School of Mines, London, made his first inspection of an American mine in 1886, under the auspices of his uncle, who on behalf of English companies managed several mining properties near Idaho Springs, Colorado. Rickard came from a family of mining engineers. He would eventually become an American.[155] Rickard Brothers (the firm of T. A. Rickard's father) frequently served as "consulting engineers" on American mining projects. In this capacity, the firm had men in America. Unlike Moreing, Rickard disliked the world of "mining finance."[156]

By the early twentieth century, American mining engineers were traveling around the globe (often employed by British companies). London remained, however, the center for the combination of mining engineering, management, and finance. In 1913 A. Chester Beatty (an American by birth and a graduate of the Columbia School of Mines) moved permanently to London.[157] Subsequently he would, as a Britisher, be important in directing capital to American companies, especially to American international business.[158]

British engineers were used in other capacities. Although most of America's vast construction related to U.S. railroads—bridges, roads, and tunnels—was planned (and accomplished) by American engineers, nonetheless, especially in the case of tunnel building, foreign talent was engaged. An American, de Witt Haskin, had begun work on the Hudson Tunnel before 1874, but he lacked sufficient capital, and in the mid-1880s he abandoned the venture. A group of Englishmen—with Sir John Fowler and Sir Benjamin Baker serving as consulting engineers—took up the task. A bond issue was floated in London. On Sir Benjamin's advice, the British construction firm S. Pearson & Son received the contract and began work in November 1889; but in 1891, after the Baring Crisis, when no further monies could be raised in England, S. Pearson & Son gave up.[159] Later the British engineering firm, Thomas Costain & Co., Ltd., would become involved in the Hudson River Tunnel.[160]

British engineers undertook evaluations for potential investors in U.S. public utilities. British investments in the St. Lawrence Power project, for example, were made only after a detailed report was prepared by engineers of the Crown Exploration Company, Ltd., an English promotional organization. The term *exploration company* was often used in the United Kingdom to designate a group of engineers who would look into projects and raise money for them on the British market. The Crown Exploration Company sent British engineers to America in 1896 to prepare a survey; the latter reported favorably on the potentials of the Long Sault Rapids of the St. Lawrence River, near Massena, New York. At one point a U.S. law firm decided that this venture had "too many promoters and too few engineers;" often, in fact, the functions mingled. It appears that some $3 million in British capital went into the St. Lawrence Power project. Eventually (in 1906) the American firm Aluminum Company of America (Alcoa) acquired control of a reorganized company.[161] The paucity of "engineers" notwithstanding, this was a case of British attempts to use their own talent to evaluate American plans. In 1899 Charles Algernon Moreing had become president of the St. Lawrence Power Company![162]

Meanwhile, in 1886 the Niagara River Hydraulic Tunnel, Power and Sewer Company was formed in New York to harness Niagara Falls.[163] It looked abroad for financing, and a tunnel company of the same name was incorporated in London, with an authorized capital of £1 million. The prospectus was printed, but before it was issued, the British promoters retained a New York lawyer, George Bliss, to examine the properties. Bliss found the investment "risky and unwise"; the London group surrendered its options and never floated the company. By mid-1887, with this means of funding out, the Niagara Falls company continued its search for capital.[164]

In 1889 the Niagara Falls company made financing arrangements with a banking group that comprised J. P. Morgan, Brown Brothers, and Winslow, Lanier & Co. Before Winslow, Lanier agreed to participate, it had sent a partner, Edward D. Adams, to investigate. For more than thirty-seven years thereafter, Adams was associated with Niagara power developments. In 1927 (at the age of 81) he wrote a two-volume history of Niagara Power.[165] This was the same Edward Adams who served as Deutsche Bank representative in the United States in the period 1893–1914 (see Chapter 13).

In 1889 the original tunnel company changed its name to the Niagara Falls Power Company; its stock was acquired in 1890 by the Cataract Construction Company (which in turn had been formed in 1889). In 1890 Adams became president of Cataract Construction. Immediately he left for Europe, not to find financing, but to obtain technological information. In London he called on Lord Rothschild (whom he had known for many years) to explain the plans for the utilization of Niagara Falls and the desire of the directors of Cataract Construction Company to learn "the state of the arts they were likely to employ."[166] Rothschild recommended engineers (which he was well equipped to suggest) and then as Adams later recalled, the banker asked:

"I suppose you are not ready with your financial plans?" "Yes," replied President Adams, "they have been adopted to a preliminary extent . . . all previous efforts to utilize Niagara power in an important way have been failures, but we believe that science has so advanced that, with its skillful use, it soon may be possible to harness Niagara upon a commercial basis."

Adams told Rothschild, "We have not come for money, but for advice . . . we wish to begin by investing in the counsel of your scientists and engineers." Lord Rothschild found this request from an American rare and, according to Adams, made an initial subscription of £5,000 "as a result of this interview."[167] There was nothing rare, however, about Adams going to the English Rothschilds for advice about engineers. Richard Davis, in *The English Rothschilds*, notes that as early as the 1840s, when the Rothschilds were heavily involved in financing French railroad construction, "they devoted a good deal of time to sending out engineers." This was very true as well of the Rothschild mining ventures. The Rothschilds clearly had access to and knowledge of the best engineering talent.[168]

There was no public subscription for the Cataract Construction Company, not in the United States nor in Europe, but a number of names mentioned in this book ranked among the original investors: Ernest Cassel, Robert Fleming, Hottinguer & Co. (Paris), Railway Share Trust and Agency Company (London), Trustees, Executors and Securities Insurance Corporation, Ltd. (London), and as noted, Lord Rothschild.[169] Adams writes that "representative foreign capitalists became interested . . . mainly through subscriptions of their New York correspondents."[170] The roster of foreign investors reveals many with U.S. connections that would make it simple for them to participate. Adams had dealt with most of these foreign investors in the 1880s in the financing of railroad reorganizations. That he was going to Lord Rothschild for consulting engineers would make these investors more interested.

Apparently, when Adams sought out the actual technology for harnessing water power, he found Swiss and French expertise more advanced than the British know-how.[171] He visited with scientists and engineers in Switzerland and France. Despite Adams' connections with the Deutsche Bank, there is no indication that he ever turned to Siemens Brothers, London; Siemens & Halske, Berlin; or Allgemeine Elektrizitäts Gesellschaft for technological assistance (although in 1890 Siemens Brothers, London, had presented a project proposal that was not selected).[172] Adams' association with the Deutsche Bank—which came in 1893, after the rejection of the Siemens Brothers project plan—may well have been an important source of information for the *German* electrical industry on U.S. power developments.[173] The principal function of the British consulting engineer was to assure British capital of the soundness of the venture. The Niagara project proved successful. The Cataract Construction Company, having completed its task, was liquidated in 1900; the Niagara Falls Power Company continued as the operating unit.[174]

In short, British "consulting engineers" were called in usually by British investors (or British merchant bankers or promoters) in various capacities to evaluate projects, provide management services, and most particularly to give confidence to the British investors who lacked trust in American reports.[175] When Edward D. Adams—who often dealt with foreign investors—called on Lord Rothschild to ask him to recommend consulting engineers, he was, as noted, also opening the way for foreign capital.

Construction Services

The British construction company S. Pearson & Son, as indicated above, had worked on the Hudson River Tunnel (1889–1891). In 1901 construction was resumed, and the tunnel was finally completed under the supervision of British-born Charles M. Jacobs, who had been involved in tunnel building with James H. Greathead on the City & South London underground (subway). The Pennsylvania Railroad used the tunnel.[176] While work on the Hudson River Tunnel was progressing, in 1902 Weetman Pearson (of S. Pearson & Son) forwarded a formal offer to the Pennsylvania Railroad for a contract on the East River Tunnels. By 1908 four tunnels were joined under the East River; S. Pearson & Son, through a U.S. subsidiary, handled the construction.[177]

Irrigation projects that were capital intensive attracted foreign investment. Temporary wood structures were replaced by "massive headworks of steel and masonry and the employment of the best engineering talent." Elwood Mead writes that many of the "largest and costliest" irrigation canals of the 1880s—built in western states—were constructed with English and Scottish capital.[178] One substantial irrigation venture was undertaken by the San Antonio [Texas] Land and Irrigation Company, Ltd. (incorporated in Canada in 1911, with a head office in Toronto, but apparently financed in London).[179]

With the exception of the tunnel building that required special expertise and the irrigation projects that were associated with British land companies in the West, and with some other exceptions,[180] the British did not participate in a *major* fashion in U.S. construction per se. Typically Americans handled construction.

Power, Light, and Traction Services

It was otherwise with power, light, and traction services—albeit, for the most part, in this case foreign investments were portfolio rather than direct investments. Foreign investment was present in a significant manner. The years 1875–1914 (and especially toward the end of this period) saw a great expansion in power and light facilities and the application of electrical railway systems to urban transport (trolley cars and subways). The investments (domestic and foreign) were giant. Unlike advertising or accounting services, for example, where the investments were fundamentally in professional training, power, light, and traction services required heavy capital expenditures on machinery and equipment.

In many parts of the world, foreign investments in these activities appear to have been related to the sales of power machinery. In Chapter 13 I did note the Deutsche Bank's involvements with the Cincinnati Light Company, which seem to have stemmed from the brief German participation in the Edison General Electric Company. I have, however, been unable to establish a network of European financing of American power companies based on machinery sales.[181] Part of the reason may lie in the 1903 division-of-market arrangements between General Electric and Allgemeine Elektrizitäts Gesellschaft (A.E.G.).[182]

This said, it is clear that there was European finance in the great development of America's power and light and traction facilities—and there was also Canadian participation, as I will show. I have already noted that Edward D. Adams, in connection with the harnessing of water power at Niagara Falls, had gone to England to get advice from Lord Rothschild on engineers and that this huge undertaking had attracted British and French capital.

In his 1927 history of the Niagara power developments, Adams never mentioned that from 1893 to 1914 he represented the Deutsche Bank in the United States, nor did he indicate that the Deutsche Bank was in any way a participant in financing that project. Yet a biographer of Georg von Siemens, head of the Deutsche Bank, noted the bank's involvement in financing the Niagara Falls Power Company.[183] Likewise, several German-owned companies in electrochemical developments (Niagara Electro Chemical Company and Niagara Alkali Company; see Chapter 11) did take advantage of the cheap power generated; they provided revenues for the power company.[184] Foreign capital did contribute to making the power developments at Niagara Falls a success, but it was far from dominant.

Because public utilities required sizable quantities of capital, many looked abroad for financing. In the early twentieth century British, Dutch, and German investors bought securities of American public utilities.[185] Cleona Lewis notes that companies such as St. Lawrence Power (of Massena, New York), American Water Works and Electric, Consolidated Gas Electric Light and Power of Baltimore, Great Western Power, Middle West Utilities, and Mississippi River Power were among the U.S. public utilities listed on one or more European markets in 1914.[186]

Among those companies that turned to British markets for financial assistance was the Brush Electric Light and Power Company of Galveston, Texas. In 1910 the new Cities Service Company (established on September 2, 1910) acquired the already "British"-owned Brush Electric, which it paid for by selling $1.35 million 6 percent cumulative preferred stock and $472,500 common stock to Parr's Bank, London, for $1,350,000. The latter apparently kept the common stock and offered the preferred stock to the British public at $85 a share. The economist Paul Dickens interpreted this transaction as the English simply transferring their interests from one U.S. company to another; the British controlled the first but not the second. As Dickens put it, "Title to and control of the property did change . . . from England to the United States." No international cash transfer was needed; no foreign exchange was involved. In the transaction British interests in American public utilities were, however, enlarged; the investments were now in a bigger company.[187]

When streetcar tracks and then subways were built in New York City, foreign investors took part—making portfolio investments. Robert Fleming helped to arrange the financing of Brooklyn's surface lines from 1897, and August Belmont (the Rothschild representative in New York) was instrumental in the development of the New York subway system.[188] The story of the financing of New York's subways—the machinations of the "traction magnates," including the American Thomas Fortune Ryan—are beyond the scope of my study. What is important is the intimate involvement of Belmont. In 1904 John Moody described the Interborough Rapid Transit Company (the I.R.T.) as under "Belmont control."[189] In May 1907 the I.R.T. issued $10 million in gold notes in London.[190] Late that month Belmont arrived in Britain, "in good spirits." Lord Rothschild wrote his cousins in Paris that Belmont "still thinks very well of his Transit Company, the expenditure he has to incur is for extension of the tramways and he looks forward to the future of that undertaking with unlimited confidence."[191] By August 1907 the mood had changed, although Belmont was still offering assurances.[192] Then came the American Panic of 1907. Belmont had borrowed heavily on Interborough bonds and was personally overextended. He turned to both the British and the French Rothschilds, asking them to allow him to substitute for the Interborough bonds, which he had given as collateral, some of the shares and bonds that he held for Rothschild account, depositing with the latter the Interborough bonds. Lord Rothschild recommended to his Paris cousins that "we can hardly avoid doing it and no doubt our action will be very beneficial to him and to ourselves; it would not only strengthen his position as President of the [Interborough] Company but in all probability it will put him in a very strong position vis-à-vis of Mr. [Thomas Fortune] Ryan."[193] Both Lord Rothschild in London and his cousins in Paris were of "the same mind that something must be done to help Belmont."[194]

The British and the French Rothschilds undertook a very careful appraisal of Belmont's accounts. They sent to New York Lionel Rothschild (1882–1941), Lord Rothschild's nephew, as well as an accountant from London and one from Paris, "to go through Belmont's books and report on the situation."[195] Lord Rothschild was convinced in mid-November 1907 that

if anything should happen to Belmont [that is, if he were to default on his obligations], it would be one of those untoward incidents which if it did not precipitate a fresh crisis [in New York financial markets] would materially affect the present one from passing away . . . and might moreover have a most prejudicial effect on the rehabilitation of the Interborough Railway.[196]

Lord Rothschild likened the situation to the Baring Crisis and "the many anxious months everyone passed through and the time it took to restore confidence."[197] Nonetheless, early in 1908 Lord Rothschild was calling the "Interborough Rapid Transit Ry . . . one of the finest Railway properties in the world and with a little patience must soon assert its prosperity."[198] The subway system raised additional monies in London in 1908 and 1909.[199] Not until 1909 was Belmont finally "out of the woods." On May 22, 1909, Belmont wrote a personal letter to Lord Rothschild on how pleased he was that "it is no longer advisable to have any sort of embargo on any of your securities in our hands for the purpose of possible substitution."[200] In 1914 August Belmont remained as chairman of the board of the Interborough Rapid Transit Company.[201] In helping Belmont, the Rothschilds were in essence helping to develop the New York subway system. This case was atypical. In the main, European involvement in American public utilities tended to go through capital markets. The many U.S. public utilities—power and light and intraurban services—that went to London in the early twentieth century (before World War I) for financing raised substantial sums.[202]

Canadians also participated in U.S. light and power and street railroads; the economist Jacob Viner found that Canadian interests actually controlled certain U.S. public utilities. The Canadian investments were often associated with British ones. Viner reported that Canadian control rested "on ownership of common stock, consisting in large part of promoters' shares, and in most cases representing only a small fraction of the actual capital invested in the undertaking. The financing of these enterprises was done mainly through bond issues in London."[203] Canadians developed specialized experience with utilities finance that they used at home, in the United States, and in Latin America.[204] Thus a giant foreign investment in the American South was that in Alabama Traction, Light and Power Company, Ltd. In 1914 its capital stock was $17,975,000, and its funded debt $13,452,000. Cleona Lewis lists it as Canadian controlled.[205] The company was apparently organized in Canada in 1912, when funds for the Alabama Power Company could not be obtained in that state (or in the United States).[206] The Canadian holding company was in turn largely financed in London.[207]

A different pattern of Canadian investment in U.S. public utilities was evident when the large Canadian firm Sun Life Assurance Company invested. This Canadian financial intermediary made formidable U.S. investments, attracted by the potentially high return. Sun Life had opened its first insurance office in the United States in Detroit in 1895. Some seven years later, in 1902, its management resolved to embark on large-scale investments in U.S. public utilities, and it began to purchase blocks of bonds of a number of firms that would merge and expand under the holding company, the Illinois Traction Company (incorporated in May 1904). Sun Life's investments were made in towns and cities in the central part of southwestern Illinois, in gas companies, electric light companies, street railways, and interurban services. In time, the Illinois Traction Company came to control and operate fifty-five subsidiaries in Illinois, Missouri, Iowa, Kansas, and Nebraska. I do not know the size of Sun Life's investment in 1914, but it was clearly huge. When the insurance company disposed of its holdings in 1922, it received $30.9 million.[208] Other Canadian investments in U.S. public utilities were present in Toledo, Ohio, and Minneapolis, Minnesota.[209] Canadian projects appear to have been very selective; I could not find any evidence, for example, of Canadian participation in the large St. Lawrence Power Company activity or the even larger Niagara Falls Power Company.

The European investments in American public utilities, with some exceptions (as noted), had gone through money markets. Belgian, French, German, and Swiss investors, as well as British ones, acquired stock, but more often bonds, of these companies. Dickens estimated that the nominal value of European acquisitions through "underwritings" of securities of American public utilities (including cable, telephone, and telegraph companies, along with the power, light, and traction companies) totaled $448.4 million in 1897–1914, with the main underwritings concentrated in the years 1904–1913.[210] In no way does this $448.4 million figure reflect the level of foreign investment in 1913–14, since securities were traded. I introduce this figure simply to show that the portfolio investments were large. Canada had major domestic needs for power and light facilities, and in the process of organizing the financing for domestic purposes, her nationals apparently developed expertise that could be used in the United States. Thus Canadians helped in organizing the financing for American utilities. Likewise, Sun Life Assurance Company's important investments were in regions not far from Canada; in a certain sense they were a "spillover" across the American border. Put together, the European and Canadian investments in American power and light and urban transit systems were substantial. The management of these public utilities, however, was American.[211]

The Many Services

In short, in many services—from advertising to distribution, to insurance, to accounting, to engineering, to construction, to public utilities (power and light and interurban and intraurban transit)—foreign investors had a presence that ranged from direct investments to portfolio ones. There were very few direct (and no portfolio) investments in advertising. Some of the investments in distribution were associated with other multinational-enterprise type of activities, but the sizable foreign investments in the large American retailers were all portfolio ones. Foreign insurance companies were direct investors in selling insurance services; their holdings in railroads and other American securities were of a portfolio nature. The accountants and engineers were direct investors; their reports facilitated portfolio capital flows and also direct investments by free-standing companies. The foreign direct investments in construction services were on especially complex projects or on those that were associated with other foreign investments. The large European investments in public utilities were, in the main, portfolio ones; in the case of the New York subway system, however, the Rothschild role was that of protecting the position of an American entrepreneur (August Belmont).[212] The Canadian stakes in U.S. public utilities were of a financial nature, albeit with the use of Canadian expertise in finance.

The services considered in this chapter were clearly diverse, yet all provided benefits for America. We have come full circle in our discussion of 1875–1914 investments—having started with railroads, covering mining and manufacturing, and then returning once more to basic infrastructure contributions. What is remarkable is the combination of multinational-enterprise-type investments in these services (insurance and accounting ones in particular) and portfolio interests (in retailing and public utilities). The foreign investments covered in this chapter rose dramatically in the early years of the twentieth century—before the outbreak of World War I.

16.

The Reactions to Foreign Investment in the United States

The substantial foreign investment in America in 1875–1914 was not ignored by contemporaries. In the United States, as well as in the countries from which the capital came, policies were advocated and sometimes translated into laws, rules, and regulations to promote, to limit, or to stop the investment. Although it is customary to describe these years as ones when international capital movements were generally unrestricted (and this is legitimate in comparison with subsequent decades), nonetheless many government measures affected foreign investors. In this chapter I consider contemporary attitudes (from popular rhetoric to defense of special interests, to journalists' reflections, to serious economic analyses) and seek to determine the extent to which the opinions were translated into public policy. My justification for considering views from such an assorted mélange of individuals and interests and including the economic reactions with the political ones is that (1) the variety of opinions is in itself important; (2) I followed the contemporary evidence to where the comments were made; and (3) public policies arose from just such an admixture of sentiments. Attitudes that were broadly philosophical were interspersed with those founded on a narrow, practical, and pragmatic outlook. Again, the rationale for the inclusion of this medley lies in its very existence.

I have not, in general, divided the material herein by portfolio and direct investments—for reactions to each type covered the gambit; that it, they were positive, mixed, negative, or neutral. Rarely did the opinions divide themselves by portfolio and direct-investment categories, albeit the variations in views, as I will show, did relate to particular interest groups and industries. In the case of European governments I did, however, find—as the reader will learn—some clear de facto policy distinctions between foreign portfolio and direct investments.

The United States: Positive Attitudes and Resulting Government Policies

In the United States many men favored the entry of foreign investment. Thus an investment banker in 1912 declared:

"We might as well face the situation. We cannot supply all the required capital in the United States. We must look to European countries for assistance, and while this demand for capital continues, we should be most careful not to frighten that capital from our shores."[1]

Similarly, the financial editor of the *New York Evening Mail* (1907) wrote: "Without the accumulated and unemployed pound sterling of the Englishman, the francs of the Frenchmen, the Belgians and the Swiss, the guilder of the Dutchman and the marks of the German, the material progress that has been the lot of these United States ever since the close of the Civil War could not continue."[2]

The secretary of the Shreveport, Louisiana, Chamber of Commerce in 1912 requested the U.S. Department of Commerce to use American consuls in foreign countries to answer questions posed by "foreign agriculturalists and businessmen about acquiring land or opening up business enterprises in the United States." He continued, "The millions of foreign capital already invested in America shows that every European business center has a real interest in this country."[3] The San Francisco real estate board, the chambers of commerce, the boards of trade, and the merchants associations united in 1913 to be sure that a California law to restrict resident Japanese ownership of land was framed so as not to curb the very desirable nonresident *European* investment.[4]

American promoters and managers made regular trips to Europe to seek monies they knew were essential to complete the U.S. railroad system. New York bankers routinely called on foreign capital to supplement domestic saving when they financed American railroads.[5] In the Texas Panhandle, from the late 1870s the American rancher Charles Goodnight wanted British direct investment, believing his country required more and cheaper capital.[6]

Western mining interests persistently desired foreign monies.[7] When the U.S. Congress passed a law (in 1887) prohibiting alien land ownership in the territories, a newspaper in New Mexico had a strong retort:

"The unmixed Jackass from Illinois [Rep. Lewis E. Payson], who fathered the alien act in the House of Representatives, probably had as much notion of what he was really doing, as he has of the red spot on the face of Jupiter. The mining industry in the Territories has been largely fostered by foreigners, and hundreds of mines which would have been sold this year will now go without purchasers perhaps for years, because a windy demagogue from Illinois, backed by a sufficient number of similar frauds from elsewhere logrolled through Congress in its closing days a bill of which they knew neither the scope nor effect."[8]

A U.S. Senate Committee observer in 1889 reported that foreign investors in mines in the territories had "facilitated the development of the country, aided in supporting population, enabled farmers to find a market, and all other industries to prosper."[9]

A memorial from the Idaho legislature also looked kindly on foreign investment in mining because such capitalists would take more risks, "for abroad money is more abundant, interest low, and there are few openings for investment." Likewise, Joseph K. Toole, Delegate from the Montana Territory, wrote (January 1, 1888): "Foreign capital has frequently acted as a pioneer in new [mining] districts, and has led United States capital to follow."[10] And in praise of a British mining company in Clifton, Arizona, an American Congressman declared (in 1890) that the foreign investors employed hundreds of American laborers "and have been a blessing."[11]

On the news in 1886 that "a leading steel manufacturer of Sheffield (England)" was about to invest in the United States, inside U.S. tariff walls,[12] *Banker's Magazine*, New York, applauded. The journal argued that there was no reason why many European enterprises "should not be compelled by vigorous tariff regulations" to invest in manufacturing in the United States. "In feeding workmen employed here our farmers have the monopoly of supplying them but in feeding them abroad our agricultural productions are subjected to a competition which is fast becoming ruinous." In short, raising U.S. tariffs would encourage foreign investment in U.S. manufacturing, which would in turn provide jobs for buyers of American farm products; this would lessen farmers dependence on agricultural exports![13]

Quite a different reaction—but similarly friendly—came about when Pillsbury-Washburn Flour Mills, Ltd., was formed in London (1889). The position of the trade journal *Northwestern Miller* was:

"We do not believe that our mills become any the less American from the introduction of foreign capital any more than our railways are the less American because they are built by capital which is largely foreign. Money is cosmopolitan. It talks in all languages. The very number of the holders of the stock is a sufficient guard against the denationalization of the trade. Moreover, we look to see a large increase in capacity . . . The result will be an enormous increase in our milling business, an improvement in our export trade.[14]

When in 1886 the British entrepreneur Thomas Lipton planned a meat packing plant in South Omaha, Nebraska, a hotel manager and a local merchant built the facility free of charge, seeing it as generating new business in the community.[15] Edward D. Adams, president of the company that developed Niagara water power, encouraged foreign businesses to invest in the area, to become users of the low-cost electricity.[16]

Commenting with admiration on the profitability of foreign-owned insurance companies, the *Commercial and Financial Chronicle* in 1882 noted that these firms "have no secret of success, other than lies in the securing of the ablest men and in a better adherence to lines of safety. Their coming is desirable."[17]

It was not often in these years (1875–1914) that Americans called for foreign investment associated with new technology. One instance was in the Dakota Territory, where in 1883 tin had been discovered. American miners had "meager knowledge" of this metal, and managers hoped to obtain in England not only financing but also information on the methods of production and treatment.[18] In another industry, when in 1899 German woolen textile companies were planning major U.S. investments, the American Vice-Consul General (Simon W. Hanauer) at Frankfurt praised the move: "It not only means new capital and skilled labor, whereby the population and national wealth of the United States will be increased, but it strengthens our capacity to compete in the world markets with the country from which this skill and monetary force have been drawn."[19] As noted in Chapter 15, Edward D. Adams had sought European technology—and had gotten both capital and technology.[20]

In sum, constituencies throughout the United States looked with pleasure on the entry of both foreign portfolio and direct investment, especially as a supplement to U.S. capital. No one argued that without the foreign money America could not industrialize. Rather, proponents of investment from abroad believed the additional capital aided and accelerated the process of economic development.

Positive attitudes toward foreign investment were on occasion translated into government policy. Some cities looked abroad for public finance.[21] Muncipalities offered incentives for foreign direct investors to enter (the same incentives that would be offered domestic firms). In 1890, for example, Poughkeepsie, New York, gave AB Separators an industrial site free of charge provided that the Swedish multinational would manufacture its machinery there and hire 200 workers in the next five years. In another case, a town in Massachusetts in 1894 attracted a factory of the British-owned Howard & Bullough American Machine Company, after giving it twenty-five acres and a promise of no taxation for ten years.[22] Likewise, William Watson of Lister & Co. (Manningham Mills), Bradford, England, spinners and makers of silk goods, plushes, and velvets, in 1905 reported an American town's offer of a twenty-five-acre site and local tax exemptions for twenty years, should that firm invest.[23] Towns sought new industry, *irrespective of ownership*, to provide jobs.[24]

So, too, state governments at times tried to lure foreign investments. Some raised money abroad; in 1875–1914 this was not typical.[25] Long past were the years when state goverment securities gave significant direct backing to private enterprises. States (as well as local governments) had in earlier times, as we have seen, provided conduits for foreign savings that went into banks, canals, and railroads.[26] Now the pattern of aid was more that of furnishing an appropriate legal environment.[27] Mining states gave men in Britain authority to witness contracts in real estate transactions.[28] The activities of the "English firm" Moss Bay Iron and Steel Company of America on the Pacific Coast received special treatment from the Washington state legislature to encourage the new industrial activity.[29] When the British company Sun Insurance wanted to do business in New York, it lobbied for (and obtained) a suitable law from that state's government.[30] In 1911, the New York Superintendent of Banks approved new branches abroad for the Equitable Trust Company (New York) in Paris and for the Farmers' Loan and Trust Company (New York) in London and Paris. The branches were expected to increase foreign investments in American securities and, most important, "gain for our institutions a share in the profits of international financial operations."[31] In sum, state governments sometimes took actions to attract and to retain particular businesses and investments from abroad.[32]

The federal government—when it had special needs in the 1870s and in 1895—had looked abroad for financial assistance.[33] Otherwise, as I scrutinized the vast panorama of *federal* government policy making in the period 1875–1914, I uncovered no specific measures designed to bring in more foreign investment. Moreover, in 1875–1879 and again in 1895–96, appeals to foreign lenders to aid in U.S. public finance had *not* involved any special privileges to those investors.[34]

When in 1912 the Shreveport, Louisiana, Chamber of Commerce requested the U.S. Department of Commerce to have American consuls abroad distribute publicity for particular cities in order to attract foreign investment, the Chief of the U.S. Bureau of Foreign and Domestic Commerce liked the idea, but Wilbur J. Carr, Director of the U.S. Consular Service, vetoed the plan, believing the pamphlets of many communities were often "highly colored" and that consular officers could not be asked to vouch for them.[35]

The U.S. Foreign Service was committed to spurring U.S. exports. In 1911 the question arose as to whether official assistance should be offered a foreign-owned firm "located in the United States and engaged in exporting American goods." In this case Carr did promise help "to protect the good name of *bona fide* American goods"; at the same time, he cautioned the foreign-owned trading company that any claims for damages would have to be directed to its own government. In short, the U.S. government would give limited aid to a foreign-owned firm in order to promote American exports.[36]

Sometimes federal government measures had the consequence of aiding foreign investment—almost inadvertently. U.S. tariffs, meant to protect American industry, prompted numerous foreign companies—from French and British textile makers to German and Italian automobile producers—to manufacture in the United States behind the barrier.[37] U.S. patent statutes were valuable for domestic and foreign investors alike. The 1881 trademark law gave protection to marks used in commerce with foreign nations—and helped to define property rights for American enterprise and for business from abroad. Antitrust policies, seeking to increase competition, meant that neither the Aluminum Company of American (Alcoa) nor Standard Oil of New Jersey could prevent foreign enterprises from entering the U.S. home market. While the stake of the French company Southern Aluminium would be short-lived, today Shell Oil remains important. Had it not been for the U.S. Supreme Court decision of 1911 fragmenting Standard Oil of New Jersey, the history of Shell Oil in America would probably have been entirely different.[38] Thus federal government measures did aid foreign investors, but often not intentionally. Indeed, the absence of an active federal government policy to favor foreign investment is in itself significant. Fundamentally, Americans believed they could carry forth the task of development on their own, for the most part with minimal government aid, much less with government-stimulated aid from abroad.[39]

The United States: Mixed Feelings and Resulting Government Policies

Often expressions of welcome to foreign investors were tempered. Americans asked: Were the conditions under which foreign investment was received satisfactory? Would the foreign investment carry with it damaging encumbrances? Thus, although foreign capital was sought by railroad managers, the terms were important. In 1881 John W. Garrett of the Baltimore and Ohio Railroad preferred to wait rather than sell his bonds in Europe below par.[40] Likewise, in September 1884 a group of British and Dutch bankers offered to take $5 million of Louisville and Nashville common stock at 20 cents a share and $1.7 million in 6 percent 10-40 bonds at 60. Despite the railroad's "desperate plight," its board of directors rejected the proposal as too onerous.[41] In both cases, had Americans offered similar terms, the response would probably have been identical.

American railroadmen and mine operators regularly looked abroad for capital, but these same petitioners complained that the investors did not understand that profits had to be reinvested. Foreign investors were accused of having no sense of the vastness of the nation and the needs of western railroads. E. H. Harriman's comments in a private letter in 1908 reflected the general view of American railroadmen: "Most foreigners only look to dividends paid without knowing anything of the difficulties."[42] In mining, foreign owners were similarly seen as calling for immediate returns rather than recognizing the importance of setting aside reserves for emergencies.[43] A Frenchman who attracted French capital to his cattle ranching in the Dakotas had to keep his countrymen at bay—insisting that early payment of dividends would hurt the business.[44]

In their desire for high returns promptly paid, foreign investors were no different from their domestic counterparts in New York, Boston, and Philadelphia. Frequently, however, foreign holders of securities were singled out as particularly lacking in sensitivity and understanding of conditions in the American West.[45]

Banker's Magazine, New York, took the consistent view that foreign investors should not be rewarded with any tax or other advantage. Thus, in its April 1879 issue it stated, "It is not asking too much in the way of favoring the holding by Americans of American securities, that they should be made payable here and in American money, and that foreigners should enjoy no bounties or advantages in competing for them, in the shape of exemption from taxes to which home investors are subjected."[46] Similarly, in 1880 the periodical discussed foreign mortgages: "So long as the number of persons wishing to borrow on American lands is large, and so long as their desire to borrow is eager and urgent, there is nothing to prevent the flow into that business of a good deal of British capital. So far as such a flow reduces the rate of interest on such loans, it is in some aspects not to be depreciated." But, Banker's Magazine expressed a feeling of reluctance that "the freehold property of the United States may be covered with mortgages to British subjects at high rates of interest and to the amount of millions of dollars." Most important, "such a result ought *not* to be facilitated and rendered more probable, by giving to foreign lenders an advantage over home lenders in respect to taxation." "It is certainly proper," the article continued, "that if foreign loan companies plant themselves in this country, or establish agencies here for the purpose of taking mortgages on American freeholds, they shall be made to contribute as much in the way of taxation for all purposes, as American mortgagees are compelled to pay where the circumstances are the same." It added, "Many persons, indeed, would incline to go much further than this, and to maintain that indebtedness of any kind to foreigners is so great an evil, that it ought to be restrained by a differential tax against foreign capital." At this point, in January 1880 *Banker's Magazine* endorsed—albeit cautiously—the foreign investment, insisting, however, on equality of tax treatment.[47]

In the summer of 1880 *Banker's Magazine* was commenting with pleasure on the presence of Canadian capital in the United States: "If common repute is to be relied upon, its employment here has been characterized by great fairness and liberality."[48] Yet, once more, it insisted on no favoritism. Canadian banks should not be specially favored with preferential tax treatment: "New York cannot afford to offer for the use of foreign capital any such bribe as exemption from the same taxation to which domestic capital in the same line is subjected."[49]

In this mixed reaction to foreign investment associated with the terms imposed, the dividend and interest requirements, and equality of treatment, there was in addition the presence of a more amorphous reservation. Clearly, although benefits accrued from foreign investments, the costs might include a London board of directors with little comprehension of U.S. problems. In good times, the fees paid to the Londoners for such an administrative arrangement were accepted by businessmen as a necessary expense related to obtaining capital from abroad; in lean times, the hierarchy seemed superfluous, especially if the prospects of additional foreign monies appeared limited. Thus U.S. managements reorganized companies not to eliminate overseas investors, but to do away with pyramided boards of directors, that is, holding-company structures.[50]

There was also the question, Could "absentee"management ever be efficient? Could a London board possibly be familiar with U.S. problems? This topic came up over and over—from railroad matters to breweries to banking. Americans often wondered, When the British intervened, would their interventions be appropriate? Could they ever understand America?

This was an issue in the numerous financial reorganizations of railroads. When British, German, and Dutch investors—represented by protective committees—wanted to cut costs and restructure railroad debt, American railroad builders often sounded like government officials from today's less-developed countries who have been told by the International Monetary Fund that new monies would not be forthcoming unless reforms were undertaken. Austerity would ruin the country is today's response; restructuring would ruin the railroad, was the comment of yesteryear.[51]

In 1889, when large amounts of British capital were being invested in U.S. industrial enterprises such as breweries, the New York correspondent for the London *Economist* reported that one American reaction was to rejoice, for the new investment would add to the productive capacity of the country and reduce interest rates; protectionism was keeping American money at home and was bringing in British money; then the *Economist's* New York correspondent added, should Americans go to war with Britain, Americans could always take over British properties.[52]

The tempered response to foreign investment was mirrored in legislation that applied evenly to foreign and domestic businesses— controlling abuses of both. Thus in the nineteenth century, many state legislatures passed antitrust laws that affected domestic and foreign investors alike. A state antitrust law in Kentucky, for example, resulted in a suit filed against Imperial Tobacco Company and its Kentucky subsidiary. The courts found the parent and its subsidiary guilty of conspiring to force the price of leaf tobacco below its "fair value." For a time it seemed that Imperial Tobacco's subsidiary might lose its state charter; this did not occur, because the U.S. Supreme Court, in a case involving an American company (*International Harvester Company of America* v. *Commonwealth of Kentucky*, June 8, 1914), ruled the Kentucky antitrust law to be unconstitutional.[53] The Kentucky antitrust law had not been specifically targeted at the foreign investor. Rather, it was designed to make all investors behave appropriately, and it just happened to catch a British business within its reach.

In the late nineteenth century but even more in the early twentieth century, state legislatures undertook to regulate domestic banking and insurance; in the process they also imposed new rules on foreign firms under their jurisdiction. Foreign-owned banks were subjected to examination and regulation,[54] and states paid attention as to whether foreign-owned insurance companies had adequate assets available in this country to pay claims.[55] Many measures sought to protect Americans against the possibility that investors from abroad would fail to meet their obligations.[56] Essentially such state legislation aimed at prudent behavior on the part of both domestic and foreign banks and insurance companies—institutions that handled the public's money. These laws were not attacks on the foreign investor per se.[57]

State governments insisted on their sovereign rights. In April 1882 a Texas judge decreed that the Franco-Texan Land Company, which had been incorporated in Texas but was French owned, had to have its "main office" in the state and that shareholders' meetings (as corporate acts) held in Paris, France, were null and void. The Texas Supreme Court in April 1883 upheld this decision. Texas had similar rules on out-of-state (as well as out-of-country) companies. It was often felt that incorporation in this country shifted "the locus of control from Europe to America," that by requiring incorporation in the United States, foreign-owned firms would chose American managers, who were on the spot and presumably more responsible. Such laws were an attack not on foreign investment but on the control that might go with such investment.[58]

A conditional reaction to foreign investment was in federal reciprocity legislation. Between 1881 and 1906, U.S. law for the registration and protection of trademarks contained a reciprocity clause: privileges comparable to those granted U.S. citizens were extended to nonresident aliens who were citizens or subjects of a country "which by treaty, convention, or law, affords similar privileges to citizens of the United States."[59] Conditions associated with America's "open door policy"—no monopoly privileges—were placed on the *entry* of Compagnie Française du Télégraphe de Paris à New York and the Deutsch-Atlantische Telegraphen Gesellschaft when they gained permission to lay U.S. cables.[60]

Federal antitrust policy (like state policy) was applied to foreign investors, not to reduce their investments, but to end "monopoly" practices. When, in the American Tobacco case (1911), the U.S. Supreme Court broke up the "tobacco trust," the decision affected the British-owned Imperial Tobacco Company and the then American-controlled but London-headquartered British-American Tobacco Company (BAT). The Court voided a 1902 international restraint-of-trade agreement.[61] A permanent injunction prohibited the use by Imperial Tobacco and BAT of the same agent to purchase American leaf tobacco.[62] The British-owned American Thread and Coats enterprises in the United States were likewise subjected to antitrust investigation, culminating in a 1914 decree that left the foreign investment untouched while requiring the U.S. affiliates of English Sewing Cotton (the parent of American Thread) and Coats to operate in this country

independently of each other.[63] The U.S. judicial process in the Tobacco and Thread cases sought to compel investors to conform to
American rules, that is, to compete rather than to collude.

U.S. federal antitrust laws were used by Philadelphia lawyers
against German chemical companies in the United States.[64] Several of
these, and also the British rayon company, revised their corporate
legal structures to meet their U.S. managers' perceptions of American
antitrust requirements.[65] U.S. antitrust policy, however, in the years
1875–1914, never singled out foreign investors as a special class of
offenders. In sum, state and federal laws and policies regulated the
behavior of investors from abroad. The latter—like U.S. investors—
operated under American law, as interpreted by the American
courts.[66]

The United States: Hostile Reactions and Resulting Government Policies

Moving along the spectrum of reactions, coincident with these approving and conditional responses, strong opposition also prevailed
to foreign investment in this country, both portfolio and direct investments. *Banker's Magazine,* New York, which four years earlier had
with reservations welcomed Canadian capital and English and Scottish mortgage companies, petulantly editorialized (in 1884): "It will be
a happy day for us when not a single good American security is
owned abroad and when the United States shall cease to be an ex-
ploiting ground for European bankers and money lenders. The tribute paid to foreigners is . . . odious . . . We have outgrown the
necessity of submitting to the humiliation of going to London, Paris
or Frankfort for capital has become amply abundant for all home
demands."[67] Writing in 1900, a commentator on Wall Street practices,
A. D. Noyes, believed that financing U.S. trade through the sale of
American securities abroad carried great risk; when foreigners sold
these securities, it would cause disruption in American markets.[68] A
general fear was of "gold drain." Foreigners' acquisition of American
securities was threatening because in paying interest and dividends—
and worse still, when securities were "returned to America" (that is,
sold or redeemed)—gold had to be exported.[69] The drain would leave
America prostrate.[70]

In the mid-1880s and into the 1890s, a passionate, hitherto un-
matched fury mounted against foreign investment in the United
States.[71] So extreme did it become that in 1892 a New York law firm
doubted that its client (a foreign investor) could obtain fair treatment
in the Illinois courts, because "of the prejudices of the West against
English capital."[72]

As one historian (Robert Riegel) wrote, eastern control of western railways was bad, but foreign "manipulations" were worse. "The West objected to foreign holdings . . . more than it did to those of the East."[73] Men dependent on railroads to move their commodities to market became the strongest antagonists, concerned lest absentee, particularly foreign, investors lacked interest in the provision of an excellent transportation system but instead were solely preoccupied with money making. Users viewed the railroad as a necessity, a public service, that ought not to contribute "monopoly profits" to foreign owners. Railroad managers were lambasted for "wasting" the public lands granted to them by selling these valuable properties to "foreign syndicates."[74] Charles Francis Adams, who would become president of the Union Pacific and would seek out foreign capital, was in 1875 highly critical of such investors from abroad, arguing that in years 1865–1870 "foreign" capital had flowed into American railroads and the result had been immense waste: "The best and the most preposterous lines were equally built . . . The people of the West eagerly invited foreigners to build their railroads for them." The result had been overcompetition, with no benefits to the users.[75] Adams went so far as to compare British ownership of securities of American railroads with British stock in the East India Company, which obtained its income from "Hindostan." No one in England cared about "the misery their exactions caused."[76]

The Texas Railroad Commission set railroad rates; in 1892 foreign bondholders sued, claiming the too-low rates did not cover even the operating expenses; the bondholders won. The Texas Governor (James Stephen Hogg) was mad, directing his rage against the railroads, their supporters, and their creditors.[77] See Figure 16.1.

Farmers complained of railroads' "watered stock," arguing that high freight charges came from inflated capitalization; "honest" capitalization would lower the burden. Although most farmers did not directly associate the "inflated" capitalization with foreign investment, farmers would often decry (in one breath) "eastern and foreign capital."[78]

Unquestionably the strongest, most emotional invectives against foreign investments related to those in land. On this subject the rhetoric was shrill. Many Americans, recognizing that the nation's land resources were limited, believed "our land" should not be handed over to noblemen in Europe, who lacked understanding of American democracy, who introduced a tenancy system incompatible with American equality, and who as speculators failed to employ the land productively. Land, they insisted, should be held by the farmer, not the distant absentee investor; it should be owned by the tiller, not captured in large tracts by the privileged; it should be the property of

Sing a song of 'lection;
"To beat Hogg" is the cry,
And Cuney's flock of blackbirds
Were baked into a pie.

And when the pie was opened,
Cuney began to sing;
And little Georgie really thought
His little self Our King!

But all true Democrats now know
This pair of schemers sly;
And, on the 8th of November,
Will knock both into "pi."

Clark and the Blackbirds. Texas Farmer, *October 29, 1892.*

Figure 16.1. British interests in America railroads. Source: Robert C. Cotner, *James Stephen Hogg* (Austin: University of Texas Press, 1959), 314. James Stephen Hogg was running for Governor of Texas. N. Wright Cuney was a vote-getter for Hogg's opponent, George W. Clark. The election took place in 1892, with Hogg the winner. As this cartoon shows, Clark was branded as being identified with British money.

the settler rather than of the giant impersonal corporation. "Alien" corporations were fraudulently amassing huge holdings and illegally fencing the public domain.[79] Foreign companies in irrigation withheld water and overcharged for this necessity, or so it was alleged.[80] Protesters equated corporate ownership (foreign and domestic) with "land monopoly,"[81] and monopoly was an affront in a democratic society. Economic and political power clashed with the requirements of the common man, they maintained.

From the East, West, and South came a torrential and almost unceasing flood of resentment: "American soil is for Americans, and should be exclusively owned and controlled by American citizens," read a joint resolution passed by the New Hampshire legislature in 1885.[82] The *New York Times* (January 24, 1885) editorialized against "an evil of considerable magnitude—the acquisition of vast tracts of land in the Territories by English noblemen." The "evil," the New York paper continued, "demands the attention of Congress . . . We believe that the building up of great estates by Englishmen should be prevented."[83]

In the prairie states in 1885–1887, particularly in Illinois, Kansas, and Nebraska, a hue and cry arose against "Scullyism." Irishman William Scully, who lived in England and owned large amounts of land in Ireland as well as in these states, became the epitome of "alien landlordism." His American tenants were said to be in a "state of abolute serfdom under his heartless alien rule."[84] The *Chicago Morning News*, May 5, 1887, saw Scully as a "veritable demon, who grinds and tortures his tenants until they are nothing but miserable, groveling, poverty-stricken slaves."[85]

The purpose of U.S. public lands policy was to settle the country. Instead, many people believed that giant enterprise deterred legitimate settlers. In the early 1880s, as cattle companies enclosed grazing land, special agents of the General Land Office, Department of the Interior, reported on widespread "unauthorized" fencing of public lands. British cattle companies were singled out. For example, the Arkansas Valley Company (Colorado) and Prairie Cattle Company (Colorado)—both Scottish-owned corporations—were each said to have enclosed about a million acres.[86]

This was a typical complaint (January 16, 1884):

Years ago settlers were attracted to Southern Colorado by the advantages that the homestead law affords to actual settlers. They acquired titles to their lands, moved their families, and made improvements. They bought cows, and in time acquired small herds, and it became profitable; other settlers were attracted by their success. All this has stopped, and the actual settlers are in danger of being driven off by men who are not and never have been settlers.

A wealthy cattle company in Scotland, called the Prairie Cattle Company, bought a number of herds, brought other cattle from Texas, and stretched their fences across the country so as to exclude those who had not sold to them from any but a very contracted range . . . They have no pretense of title to any of the lands from which they exclude the settlers.

This Scotch company claim they have obtained patents for a continuous line of lands by which they can and will exclude settlers . . . If they have [obtained patents] it is by fraud on the pre-emption and homestead law, for it is known to the settlers that no settlements have ever been made on most of the country which they claim . . .

In the place of a good population such as you now have in that part of Colorado you will have only the employees of the large capitalists, who live in idleness six months of the year, and, having no hope of bettering their condition by acquiring property there, indulge in dissipation, as the cowboys often do.

The writer urged passage of laws "imposing severe penalties for obstructing settlers in the enjoyment of the public range."[87]

The attacks on foreign investment in land reached through the South as well. Representative William C. Oates of Alabama was an ardent opponent of foreign investment in land.[88] Many Texas residents laughed at the pretensions of British owners. Sir Dudley Coutts Marjoribanks (the first Baron Tweedmouth) had sent his son, Sir Archibald Marjoribanks, to manage the Rocking Chair Ranche, Ltd., in the eastern part of the Texas Panhandle. Texans joked about his English saddle (which the cowboys labeled "peckernecks"), resented his disdain for local customs (he insisted on being called Sir Archibald), and taunted him as he road into town in a scissor-tailed coat. One historian explains that their ridicule "was their retaliation for his [Sir Archibald's] treating cowboys as if they were servants, and the settlers who were venturing into the eastern Panhandle, as if they were peasants." The historian continued, "None of the other British outfits was managed in this snobbish manner, but, to an important extent, the Rockers set the unpopular standard by which all were judged. Moreover the hoss-back opinion of the average cowpoke and settler was strongly against any big company."[89]

When candidate for (in 1890) and then as Texas Governor (1891–1895), James Stephen Hogg excoriated British control over large "estates." "As titles of land are concentrated into the ownership of the few, in that proportion patriotism is destroyed." "Large estates dominated by alien landlords spring up to menace the peace and happiness of the citizen and to perpetuate a system of bondage on the tenants themselves." Texas, its Governor believed, needed to "protect our posterity from becoming tenants and peons of foreign-landlords, who neither understand nor care for the principles of our government."[90]

In New Mexico, settlers who faced eviction by the Maxwell Land Grant Company railed at the "Dutch, English, and American corporate land thieves."[91] There was literally war (that is, fighting) between settlers and company management. The Farmers' Alliance and the Populist movement demanded (1886–1892) that the U.S. Congress "take prompt action to devise some plan to obtain all land now owned by aliens and foreign syndicates." "Alien ownership of land," these farmers' groups believed, "should be prohibited."[92]

Foreign-held land mortgages evoked similar hostility. California Senator Leland Stanford in May 1890 introduced a bill for government loans on land and supported his proposal with the statement, "I believe that its provisions will make us independent of the foreign money lender, and that the many millions now going abroad in the way of interest will be kept at home."[93] Leland Stanford was president of the Central Pacific Railroad (1863–1893) and of the Southern Pacific (1885–1890); both railroads were attracting foreign investment.[94] His statement was designed to appeal to the xenophobia in America.

Farmers' groups were far more vehement than the Senator against foreign money lenders. They opposed Stanford's plan for putting the government in the loan business because they did not like any mortgages.[95] In 1892, in an open letter to their Congressmen, farmers from Kansas denounced foreclosures and the transfer of land "from industrious families to the hands of capitalists, either domestic or foreign."[96] Often critics linked the mortgages provided by foreign lenders with tenant farming, both imposing on free Americans a European peasant "mentality."[97] Americans, they declared, should not be behoven to either moneylenders or landlords, equating the two.[98]

In 1898 an ex-Congressman from Kansas, John Davis, penned a scathing assault on "alien landlordism in America," claiming that in the 1890s the situation had deteriorated. "The imagination can scarcely comprehend the extent of our thraldom—the extent to which we are in the hands of our alien masters." He condemned all landlordism, claiming the alien variety "is two or three grades worse than the domestic." The British through world exploitation (since the seventeenth century), Davis argued, had accumulated surplus monies; British "conquests of the sword and the purse" over the long years were "a black and cruel rehearsal of the murder of nations, filling the world with mourning."[99]

Well into the 1890s, apprehensions over giant foreign land holdings and mortgages on agricultural land were blended with those over absentee ownership and servility. "Royalty," kings and nobility, were old world institutions. Americans should never be treated like inhabitants of Ireland or India.[100] Ours was a country of free and independent people. That the Duke of Sutherland, Lord Tweeddale, Sir John Pender, and the Duke of Manchester, for example, were all investors in American land heightened populist concerns and helped enrich the popular rhetoric against those we had fought in 1776.[101]

While foreign investment in land and the related farm mortgages brought forth anger, rage, and fear, less disfavor prevailed toward the equally large foreign investments in mining.[102] Nonetheless, when in 1890 Congress debated the exemption of mines and mining claims from legislation aimed at prohibiting foreign ownership of agricultural properties, a Congressman from Illinois (Lewis E. Payson)— who was not from a mining district, but from one where there was alarm over foreign ownership of agricultural land—received applause when he exclaimed: "I stand, sir, by the principle—keep every source of wealth the God of nations has blessed us with to be developed by Americans for Americans only!"[103]

In that same 1890 debate, a Representative from Indiana complained that European investors in U.S. mines were "taking the national wealth, raw ores, valuable in themselves, but which would be made still more valuable by their [American workers'] labor, and transporting them [the ores] to Europe, to be there reduced and have the precious metals extracted from the ore by European labor." American mines, he insisted, should be worked by Americans and the output processed in the United States. This would raise the value added in this country, thereby providing employment to American citizens.[104] The increased value of American exports would improve the country's terms of trade.

Americans should get higher prices for their output in any case; mine owners in the United States objected to foreign control over prices; they believed prices were depressed by foreign "cartels" and foreign "sharp-dealing" traders.[105] Likewise, concern existed (in 1914) over the ownership and export of ores containing radium that were being mined by a British company. Was it appropriate that American mines containing radium, believed to be a cancer cure, should be foreign owned and the production shipped abroad?[106] The issue did not involve price but limited resources and, more important, the people's health. Other Americans—fertilizer producers—were disturbed when a German "cartel"—which had a sales outlet in the United States—raised the price of potash *imported* into this country.[107]

In short, a range of concerns existed about exports and imports of mineral products by foreign direct investors.

With the rising and sizable foreign stakes in oil production in California, the *Oil, Paint, and Drug Reporter* (January 3, 1914) saw "an unsettled condition,"[108] while *Mineral Industry, 1914* noted that the oil industry in that state was becoming concentrated in the hands of immense concerns.[109] Scottish-born John Barneson, president of General Petroleum Company in California, called the takeover of that enterprise by Andrew Weir and his associates a raid by "English sharks!"[110] For the first time, in 1913–14 worries surfaced that foreign-owned enterprises would exhaust American oil supplies.[111]

In an address in Boston on "Plutocracy or Nationalism—Which?" the novelist and social critic Edward Bellamy declared:

Our new industrial lords are largely absentees. The British are invading the United States, in these days, with a success brilliantly in contrast with their former failure in that line. It is no wonder in these days, when the political basis of aristocracy is going to pieces, that foreign capitalists should rush into a market where industrial dukedoms, marquisates, and baronies, richer than ever a king distributed to his favorites, are for sale . . .

Are we going to permit the American people to be rounded up, corralled, and branded as the dependents of some hundreds of great American and English families?[112]

The address was made at the point (1889–90) when the American press was running stories about British purchases of American breweries, flour mills, and other industrial activities.[113]

When the British buyers of Hammond's meat-packing enterprise suggested that expense could be reduced by having a proposed English corporation own and operate the U.S. manufacturing facilities, their American law firm (in February 1890) rejected the plan, explaining that "the anti-English feeling which prevails in many States, would, in view of the close competition in this business, injuriously affect the prosperity of the business."[114]

Many Americans felt that the country's "savings" should not leave its shores but be spent at home. If foreign banks were allowed "to take" U.S. deposits, they would do literally that, and the hard-earned money of Americans would be shipped from the country.[115] Foreign control over credit scared Americans. Foreign investors desired "sound money" and high interest rates. Many Americans wanted available and cheap money.[116]

W. H. Harvey's famous bimetallism tract, *Coin's Financial School*

(1894), stated that not less than $5 billion of American securities were held in Europe, mainly in England,[117] an enormous overestimate. The Rothschilds were viewed as an "English Octopus" with a stranglehold on Americans, as well as on other people worldwide (see Figure 16.2). At 4 percent—payable in gold—the nation's foreign obligations meant U.S. interest payments of $200 million annually, but world gold production was valued at about $165 million per year. How would America pay? The book explained that the bankers' answer was, "Sell more bonds in England," but Harvey's protagonist retorted that this would raise America's debt and compound the problem. "We have put our head in the mouth of the English lion, and the question now is how to get it out." What England "failed to do with shot and shell in the eighteenth century, she is doing with the gold standard in the nineteenth century." Bimetalism would assist America in paying its foreign (and domestic) debts. The law allowing "gold to be named" in a bond was "statutory treason." "Our national currency should be as sacred as the flag."[118]

In February 1895, when President Grover Cleveland signed a contract with the Morgan-Rothschild Syndicate (see Chapter 5), silver advocates were distraught. The contract provided that the bankers would supply the Treasury with gold, taking 4 percent U.S. government bonds in exchange. If the United States would issue the bonds with a "gold clause," the bankers would lower the coupon rate from 4 to 3 percent. Cleveland asked Congress for the power to issue "gold bonds"; silver forces responded, accusing the administration of being captured by selfish international financiers, and berated the bankers for offering $16 million (the difference between the interest at 4 and 3 percent) for the right to manage U.S. monetary policies. Four percent bonds were issued.[119]

In 1896 the Democratic Party declared against the gold standard, claiming that it placed the United States in financial servitude to London. The gold standard, it argued, was both un-American and anti-American and would stifle "that spirit and love of liberty which proclaimed our political independence in 1776 and won it in the war of the Revolution."[120] In April 1896 the historian Henry Adams wrote: "America is insolvent. Europe drains us of £25,000,000 a year more than she returns to us, and the wealth of Orion and the Pleiades would not stand forever a drain of £25,000,000 a year." Adams damned "the Jews" on "Lombard Street," "who threaten to withdraw their capital, if there was even a danger of free coinage of silver."[121]

On occasion, foreign investors were censured for depriving Americans of employment. Terence V. Powderly of the Knights of Labor

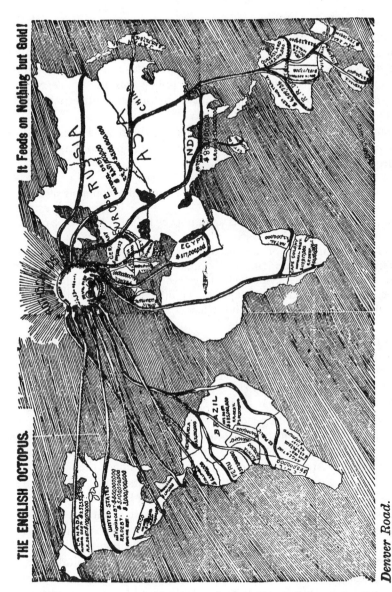

Figure 16.2. "The Devil Fish." Source: William H. Harvey, *Coin's Financial School*, ed. Richard Hofstadter (Cambridge, Mass.: Harvard University Press, 1963), 215. The indistinct U.S. figures appear to read: National debt: $500 million; RR debt: $5.1 billion; Municipal (or possibly Mortgage?) debt: $3 billion.

believed that British investors were prone to violate contract labor laws and bring in cheap labor.[122]

Some American businessmen viewed foreign enterprises in this country as providing unfair competition (their use of "cheap" labor was not the issue; rather, their pricing policy was the concern).[123] Accountants thought it improper that their foreign counterparts obtained "the cream" of the U.S. practice.[124]

Governor James Stephen Hogg of Texas, whom we have already encountered verbally flaying foreign investment in railroads and land, declared (on July 2, 1894):

The American merchant-marine stands by the side of the monopoly of transportation held within the dogmatic, avaricious grasp of England, as a spring sprout by the side of a forest oak, as a minnow by a whale, as a canoe by the "Great Eastern."

. . . The carrying trade [of America] is in the control of England. We make the traffic and Englishmen haul it. We produce the wealth and they get it through the method of transportation taxes. Thus feasting upon the fruit of our labors for these years, the people of that little island have fattened and gradually become our creditors and dictators in finance and commerce.[125]

In 1896 Republican Party planks endorsing high tariffs included the fostering of "our shipping in the foreign-carrying trade, so that American ships, the product of American labor, employed in American ship-yards, sailing under the stars and stripes, and manned, officered and owned by Americans, may regain the carrying of our foreign commerce."[126]

Independent U.S. companies saw foreign control over ocean shipping and cable communication as detrimental.[127] The users of shipping services, American traders, often maintained that "foreign control" over ocean shipping resulted in favoritism to foreign enterprise, delays and irregularities in the transport of U.S. exports, higher freight charges for Americans, and disclosure to their European rivals of America's customers abroad—all of which put this country's merchants at a disadvantage. Foreign control over shipping, they claimed, throttled U.S. export trade.[128] Jay Gould, who did not hesitate to go overseas for capital for his railroads, "thundered against the foreign cable monopoly," insisting that his cable would promote national independence, break the European monopoly, and lower artificially rigged rates.[129]

In the interests of national security, the U.S. Navy feared that foreign investment in this country, with its control of American shipping, wireless communication, and fuel oil supplies would jeopardize the nation's defenses. In 1898 the U.S. War Department was buying projectiles for coastal defense guns, and the American Mannesmann Tube Company (incorporated in New Jersey in 1895 but ultimately German-owned)[130] received the contract. The German subsidiary agreed to manufacture the projectiles in the United States. The U.S. Navy protested, whereas the U.S. War Department justified the contract on the grounds that a new "American" industry would be established and Mannesmann—producing in the United States— could provide rapid delivery. Eventually the contract was annulled, ostensibly for two reasons: Mannesmann's plan to bring in skilled workers seemed in violation of the contract labor law and, most disagreeable, Mannesmann declared that it would exclude U.S. government inspectors from secret phases of the manufacturing process! After the cancellation, the order was split among American companies, and the Mannesmann plant was not built.[131] From the start, the U.S. Navy was the principal opponent of the Mannesmann involvement. Vicker's 1898–1903 proposals to construct American warships in this country also failed to gain approval, undoubtedly owing to hostility from the Navy.[132]

The Navy, moreover, watched uneasily the activities controlled by Marconi Wireless Telegraph Company of America. In 1901, when the Navy planned to end its use of homing pigeons and to substitute wireless communication, its discussions with Marconi of America became strained, for the British firm insisted on leasing equipment, which the Navy wished to buy. The Navy objected to British control over Marconi of America. In 1903 the Navy adopted the competitive German Slaby-Arco system, the one used by the German Navy![133] Equipment had to be imported. The U.S. Navy established its own radio communication facilities, seeking to avoid being at the mercy of foreign (British or German) interests.[134] By the end of 1913, the Navy owned twenty-three radio stations.[135] Yet, in this sphere European technology was supreme, and in many respects the Navy continued to depend on the British-controlled Marconi of America.[136]

From about 1908, as ships came to be oil fueled, the Navy had anxieties over the adequacy of U.S. oil supplies. In September 1909 President William Howard Taft allocated 3 million acres of oil lands in the public domain in California and Wyoming for federal use. When oil prices started to rise (after 1912), the Navy pressed for more reserves.[137] In December 1913 Secretary of the Navy Josephus Daniels noted that "English firms were going into Mexico and elsewhere to supply the demands of the English Navy."[138] Then matters turned more serious: "On account of the increased costs of fuel oil for battleships and the fact that *foreign* corporations are rapidly purchasing reserves of oil in the United States" (my italics), *Mineral Industry*,

1913, published early in 1914, reported that the Secretary of the Navy had recommended to Congress "the policy of producing crude oil from naval reserves and obtaining fuel oil from it."[139] The U.S. Navy had become fully committed to oil-fueled ships,[140] and the issue of "foreign" oil companies' moving into the United States while new provided Secretary Daniels with one more piece of ammunition in his call for more federal government activity in defending America's oil resources.[141] Moreover, as the historian John Ise later noted:

about this time [1914], there was considerable careless talk in England about the necessity of securing some of the world's oil reserves, and about the extent of England's ambitions in this direction; and some of this talk was heard across the Atlantic. In 1914, H. W. A. Deterding, directing head of Royal Dutch-Shell interests, stated that unless unforeseen events occurred, within ten years the Dutch-Shell companies would dominate the fuel oil supply of the world, and that no oil burning vessel could sail the seas without Dutch-Shell oil in its bunkers.[142]

Little wonder the U.S. Navy was uneasy, especially with Royal Dutch-Shell's mounting U.S. investments in 1913–14.[143]

In sum, a broad range of antagonistic, and nervous, feelings in this country existed toward the incoming foreign portfolio and direct investments, much of it targeted specifically against British holdings. The hostility came from populists, who identified foreign investments and investors with monopoly, antidemocratic attitudes, and the gold standard. Yet, not only farmers groups and proponents of bimetalism thought investment from abroad undesirable. U.S. intellectuals, bankers, railroadmen, businessmen, and accountants, on occasion, would articulate in patriotic outbursts their objections—and the U.S. Navy, in particular, expressed alarm about national security. This is not to say that there was a consensus against all foreign investment (as I have shown, in many cases there were favorable responses); what is important, however, is that the negative reactions were not confined to a single interest group. Xenophobia had deeper roots. In America there was a fear of dependence.

In a number of instances the antipathy was translated into legislation at both the state and the federal levels, indicating the importance and the influence of such sentiments. A contemporary author called the "Potter Law" in Wisconsin (passed in 1874 to set low railroad rates) "a practical confiscation of many millions of foreign capital invested in the public improvements of that state." It was repealed in 1876.[144] In 1881 William Mackenzie, chief executive of the Dundee Mortgage and Trust Investment Company and the Dundee Land Investment Company, Ltd. (Scottish-owned companies, both of which had large U.S. investments), complained to the British foreign office about U.S. state legislatures that passed laws against "corporations from other States or Countries." Mackenzie wrote that when he was in Oregon in 1878, he had found that several bills had been introduced "with a view of operating against my own Company to the advantage of local competitors." In October 1880 Lord Airlie noted a bill that was being debated in the Oregon legislature that would impose a license duty of $1,000 a year on foreign corporations. Mackenzie pointed out that although this particular measure had been defeated, "its introduction shadows forth a real danger." Americans, "jealous of foreign Corporations if they are doing a profitable business[,] . . . are very much disposed to handicap them by taxes." The Oregon legislature was in 1881 considering laws "prejudicial" to English insurance companies.[145]

In 1879 Indiana passed a law withdrawing the protection of the courts from nonresident corporations. The Scottish mortgage companies saw it as a "death knell to foreign investment."[146] Their agent convinced them to use the monies invested in Indiana in the American South.[147] State law in this case did not chase foreign investors from America; the latter reallocated the identical funds to another part of the United States.

In 1885–1895 many state legislatures enacted measures to prohibit nonresident alien ownership of land; some laws forbade corporations that were wholly or partly controlled by foreign capital from owning land. Certain states amended their constitutions to ban nonresident foreign (out-of-country) ownership of land. These actions aimed at agricultural land ownership; they often exempted mineral land, urban real estate, and other nonagricultural properties. Sometimes there were exemptions for foreign mortgage lenders. Twelve states—Colorado (repealed 1891), Idaho, Illinois, Indiana, Iowa, Kansas, Minnesota, Missouri, Nebraska, Texas, Washington, and Wisconsin—adopted some form of restrictions on alien land ownership in these years.[148] The laws and constitutional clauses were responses to the intense opposition to foreign (particularly British) nonresident land ownership. The rules were directed at foreign investors and did slow some new investments. Many of the laws were, however, circumvented by foreign investors or were too late (that is, were passed after the investors had already acquired the properties; the laws were not applied retroactively); more often than not, they failed to accomplish their purpose.[149]

At the same time, in the 1880s, 1890s and (in this case) early 1900s, state legislatures tightened their rules on foreign banks, insurance companies, and mortgage lenders; many measures differentiated between domestic and foreign capital and were adverse to the latter. States passed legislation specifically barring out-of-country banks. The state of New York forbade foreign branch banks. This legislation—as I have shown (in Chapter 13)—had a clear impact.[150]

States imposed special regulations on foreign insurance companies. Thus in 1886 a foreign insurance company in New York had to have a paid-up capital of $500,000, whereas $200,000 was the minimum for "home" companies.[151] In 1895 the manager of the Commercial Union, a British insurance company, worried that state legislation might compel "British companies to withdraw altogether from the United States." Its concerns were over the rates allowed by law. Nonetheless it persevered.[152]

In 1890 Samuel Kerr, of the British and American Mortgage Company, mobilized other British and American mortgage companies "to defeat or shelve . . . the usual number of harassing measures" presented to the Texas legislature and aimed at money lenders."[153] When in 1891 the Texas legislature passed a law prohibiting aliens from holding land or buying land at a foreclosure sale, British mortgage lenders were alarmed,[154] but the Texas courts declared the law invalid before the end of the year, and a substitute bill was passed in 1892 that left lenders "not the least hampered."[155]

The state of New York enacted a measure in 1896 requiring all certified public accountants to be American citizens or persons who had declared their intention to be citizens.[156] A number of states taxed or attempted to tax foreign capital differently from that owned by Americans.[157]

It is neither necessary nor possible to review all the laws of each state on foreign investors. What is significant is that state legislatures did pass numerous acts that gave Americans preference over nonresident foreign owners. Some laws clearly deterred, delayed, or prompted divestitures of foreign investment.[158] They affected the legal form used for foreign investment. Investors from abroad successfully fought some laws in American courts and evaded others. Taken as a whole, state statutes (with the important exception of the banking laws) do not seem in the long run to have been a major obstacle to the growth of foreign investment in the United States. In the short run, however, state legislators unquestionably created countless problems for these investors.

Federal laws also discouraged, limited, and even prohibited some foreign investment. Foreign investors believed that legislation prompted by silverite pressure was contrary to their interests. Both the Bland-Allison Act of 1878 and the Sherman Silver Purchases Act of July 1890 resulted in a temporary curtailment of new investment from abroad and repatriation of existing stakes. Their framers were aware that the legislation would discourage foreign investment and did not care.[159] In 1895, on the basis of the silverite appeals, as noted earlier, Congress voted against placing a gold clause in U.S. bonds, which foreign bankers had desired, with the consequence that the U.S. federal government issued 4 rather than 3 percent bonds; the results were more averse to the United States than to the lenders, who received the higher rate and did not lose because the dollar did not fall in value![160]

In 1872 the U.S. Congress had passed a mining act specifying that all valuable mineral deposits and the public lands in which they were found were to be open to exploration and to purchase from the government only "by citizens of the United States and those who have declared their intention to become such." A corporation organized in the United States was seen as a "citizen"; the law did not deal with its ownership. I noted (in Chapter 4) that individual foreign investors could also buy land from those who purchased it from the government; the need for two transactions or the need to organize an American corporation probably raised the price (but not by much) to the foreign investor.[161] On June 3, 1878, Congress enacted a timber law permitting only bona fide U.S. residents to log on public land.[162] The Timber and Stone Act of the same date allowed only U.S. citizens or those declaring their intention to become citizens to purchase 160 acres of public timberland in California, Oregon, Nevada, and the Washington Territory for $2.50 an acre.[163] Litigation under these timber laws affected unfavorably the operations of several foreign-owned enterprises.[164]

Much more important, between 1883 and 1886 eighteen bills were introduced in the U.S. House and Senate to prohibit aliens from acquiring or owning land in the territories or in the United States.[165] In 1885 Congress considered, but did not pass, legislation that would have forbidden American citizens from selling their land "to the lords of Europe, the shieks [sic] of Asia, and all other people who owe no allegiance to the United States."[166] This sweeping xenophobic measure, put forth by Representative William C. Oates of Alabama, would have prevented "persons other than citizens of the United States and such as have legally declared their intention to become citizens" from owning land anywhere in the United States.[167]

In March 1887 Congress approved "an Act to restrict the ownership of real estate in the Territories to American citizens." This law was enacted barely a month after the Interstate Commerce Commission Act and three years before the Sherman Antitrust Act. It reflected the same populist viewpoint. The 1887 Alien Land Act did not affect land within the various states. It confined ownership of real estate (including land) *in the territories* to U.S. citizens or to aliens who declared their intention to become citizens. Under its provisions, no corporation that had more than 20 percent of its stock held by aliens could acquire, hold, or own real estate, nor could any corporation (native or foreign), except those in transportation and communication, own more than 5,000 acres in the territories. This law appears to have been the first federal statute that classified corporations as "aliens," not by their place of incorporation, but by their stock ownership. Existing foreign investors were not affected, unless they desired to expand their holdings.[168] The 1887 act did not exclude mineral lands.[169] The law went far beyond any then existing. Foreign investors were worried.[170] It retarded some new investments.[171] Yet the act was far less injurious than the Oates bill, and British and other foreign investors rapidly became aware of how difficult it would be to enforce. For example, how could the U.S. government know whether more than 20 percent of the stock of an American corporation was owned by aliens? No disclosure of corporate ownership was required.[172] In 1890 Representative Oates reintroduced legislation to prohibit aliens from acquiring land *in any part* of the United States; it never passed.[173]

By 1897 it had become apparent that the federal alien land law of 1887 was a paper tiger. One legal expert wrote, "We are not aware of a single instance where the [U.S.] government has intervened and sought to enforce the forfeiture provided by the act."[174] That year congress specifically exempted mines and mining claims from the law and specifically legalized the alien mortgage business in the territories. The restriction on alien shareholdings in American land-owning corporations was also eliminated.[175] By then the "territories" covered by the act had contracted, as new states had joined the Union.[176] In short, the 1887 law had reflected the widespread hostility toward foreign investment in land. It discouraged some new investment, but the policies implemented under its authority failed totally to live up to its language.

Other federal laws negatively affected foreign investment and investors. In 1885 Congress had forbidden contract labor. Certain British firms in America (in woolen textiles, for example) had contracted labor in Yorkshire for employment in their U.S. mills. As a result of the law, the British firms substituted "tacit wage agreements," which proved "unenforceable and unhonored"; thus "the cost of labor to these British mills in America rose."[177] So, too, the "Capitol Syndicate" in Texas, in which British investment was involved, imported granite cutters from Scotland. The Knights of Labor in 1888 brought suit, claiming that this was contrary to the Contract Labor Act.[178] In

1892 the British-owned John Morrell & Co., Ltd., with a plant in Ottumwa, Iowa, made plans to produce an English pork pie for the American market; it abandoned the idea when the firm learned that to get a "capable bakery man" into the United States, "he must enter as a free man not as a 'bonded pie maker' as the firm desired."[179] In discussing its business arrangements in the United States, Price, Waterhouse took special care not to violate the contract labor law.[180] The law, which treated foreign and domestic business alike, was undoubtedly more onerous to the former than to the latter, since foreign investors were more prone to bring in employees from abroad.[181]

Included among the federal laws adverse to foreign investment were the banking statutes. Under the national banking system, throughout the years 1875–1913 every national bank director had to be a citizen of the United States. The 1913 legislation that established the Federal Reserve System retained the rule, not permitting foreign citizens to be directors of U.S. national banks.[182] Under both systems (pre-1913 and post-1913), foreign individuals and foreign financial institutions could buy shares in U.S. national banks *if* they were prepared to have American citizens as their representatives on the board of directors. That they could not directly control the banks served as a deterrent to investment.

The 1817 law banning foreign carriers from coastwise and inland shipping (see Chapter 3) remained in these years the law of the land; Congress had brought Alaska within the law's scope in 1868 and added Puerto Rico and Hawaii in 1898 and 1899, respectively. One economist concluded that in the absence of this protection, British, Norwegian, and Japanese vessels, as well as those of other nationalities, would have participated in U.S. coastwise trade.[183] In the period 1875–1914, however, most shipping was conducted by companies, and there was no careful scrutiny of the *ownership* of these corporations. Some foreign-controlled firms do seem to have participated. In the early 1880s a "representation was made to the [U.S.] Secretary of Treasury that the shares of a shipping company were held [abroad] in greater proportion than the law allowed," but the U.S. Secretary of the Treasury took no action.[184] Similarly, certain American railroad companies with large foreign ownership had coastwise fleets;[185] no evidence exists that any attempt was made to confront them with their possible violation of the law.

As for national defense, few specific federal restraints on foreign investors were present; the one major exception was the navigation monopoly of coastal trade, which can be seen in national security terms (its original 1817 rationale).[186] The United States failed to create an adequate ship-building industry or an adequate merchant marine engaged in international shipping.[187] Although foreign visitors were not allowed in government arsenals, no law forbad their investing in military production; yet, as I have shown, neither Vickers nor Mannesmann could "work things out." The Navy took the strongest stand of any government department on questions related to foreign investment. It operated its own radio stations and developed its own expertise in wireless; nonetheless, foreign investors were allowed to dominate radio communication.[188] As for oil, President Taft's 1909 withdrawal of public lands for federal use was followed in 1912 by the creation of two naval petroleum reserves at Elk Hills and Buena Vista in California, but no land-leasing rules were adopted before 1914.[189] No restrictions were imposed on U.S. investments by foreign oil companies.

The State Department and Congress did give an implicit green light to antiforeign *state* government laws. Neither was responsive to intermittent diplomatic inquiries from London, requesting the federal government to muzzle state legislators. Secretary of State John Hay replied (in 1899) in a very standard manner to one such request that related to discriminatory taxes against foreign fire insurers: "Legislation such as that enacted by the State of Iowa is beyond the control of the executive branch of the General Government."[190]

In explaining (at a later date) pre–World War I policies of the foreign service, DeWitt C. Poole, who in 1911 was a consular assistant in the U.S. Bureau of Trade Relations in the State Department, recalled that policymakers considered the importance of export promotion as linked with the payment of the nation's foreign debt; U.S. exports would end once and for all the country's disagreeable debtor status.[191]

In sum, many *state* laws passed that were unfavorable to foreign investors; they related to land, mortgage lending, banking, insurance, professional certification, and taxation. Such laws were more extensive and were perceived by most foreign investors to be more threatening as barriers to entry and to remaining in business than the more remote national statutes. Federal laws that seemed to acquiesce to silverite pressures made American securities temporarily less interesting to foreign investors. In land, banking, and coastal shipping, the federal government imposed specific restraints on foreign investment or on foreign investors' control over their holdings. The short-lived restrictions on foreign mining in the territories (part of the federal alien land law, 1887–1897) were exceptional in that they lacked the broad approval present on most of the other "antiforeign" measures. The contract labor law limited some foreign investors' flexibility and raised costs. Federal action thus existed to curb foreign investment. The federal government was never pleased with America's role as a "debtor nation" in world accounts. Views from Washington reflected the national resentment against dependence. The way to cope, however, was principally through export promotion.[192] Federal restrictions on foreign investments were confined to especially sensitive sectors. No attempt was ever made by state or federal authorities to monitor, much less control (or stop), all incoming or existing foreign investment.

The United States: Neutral Reactions and Relevant Government Policies

Along with the coexisting favorable, mixed, and hostile reactions toward foreign investment and investors, many "neutral" views were also present. Thus, although there was substantial effort to attract foreign capital to U.S. railroads, mines, and other activities; although there were mixed reactions when foreign investors sought to demonstrate their presence or to gain special advantage; and although there were years of near hysteria over British investments in U.S. land, much of Americans' social and political commentaries and economic policy making did *not* devote great attention to the sizable influx of monies from abroad.

To be sure, each of the critical economic policy issues in America of the late nineteenth and early twentieth centuries—silver, protectionism, monopoly power—had a dimension associated with foreign investment, but with the possible exception of the mid-1880s years and sporadically in the 1890s, the controversy over foreign investment as such never reached the pitch of that on these other subjects.[193] Thus, while silver advocates vigorously attacked foreign (specifically English) bankers as defenders of gold and dangerous, while they worried about the "drain" to pay interest and dividends abroad, it was, in the main, the U.S. money supply, the desire for lower interest rates, and the declining prices of goods and labor services in the late nineteenth century that most concerned them. Silver advocates wanted an end to gold clauses in bonds rather than explicitly a shutoff of foreign investment. Most farmers opposed the "excessive" profits to "moneylenders" in general rather than to foreign ones in particular. Although foreign creditors—Lombard Street—might be worse, populists condemned domestic ones as well.[194]

Believers in protectionism might claim that U.S. tariff barriers would serve to attract foreign capital or alternatively, and perhaps more frequently, might berate foreign bankers or alien competitors for their endorsement of free trade. These attitudes—approving and disapproving of foreign investors and investment—were in truth peripheral to the basic support for *American* industry by high-tariff proponents.

Likewise, the debates on the rise of big business, "monopoly power," railroad monopoly, land monopoly, trusts, concentration of control over credit, and shipping combinations, along with the discussions of the separation of management and control in giant corporations and absentee ownership, were all inextricably joined with questions related to foreign investment. Foreign investors were affected when the Interstate Commerce Commission was established. When the U.S. Supreme Court ordered the dissolution of Northern Securities Company, this had an impact on foreign investors. Lord Rothschild wrote in March 1907, in the context of Theodore Roosevelt's "hostility" to railroad enterprise, "The demoralization of the American market . . . may be a blessing in disguise," since it would probably prevent socialist legislation and further attacks on the railroads.[195] Foreign investors were the targets of proposals aimed at "land monopoly." The U.S. Supreme Court decision in the Standard Oil case, albeit inadvertently, opened the path for the entry of Royal Dutch-Shell into American business. The effects of U.S. regulatory and antitrust policies on foreign enterprise in the United States were multiple. Yet, taken as a whole, in terms of U.S. policymakers themselves, foreign investment was on the fringe rather than at the core of the major controversies. The distribution of domestic income much more than the "tribute" to the foreign wealthy was behind the assault on big business. In the outcry against monopoly, national rather than international competition was in the spotlight.

On the land issue, where without doubt there was the most fervent antagonism against foreign investors, abuses in the allocation and use of the public domain, along with the diminishing amount of land available as settlement occurred, were most fundamental to the discussions.[196]

In the Pujo Committee Hearings, 1912–13, that committee's counsel, Samuel Untermyer, relentlessly queried key American bankers on the concentration of power over credit. Untermyer was convinced of the presence of a "Money Trust."[197] Many witnesses noted that their banking business was international and testified on foreign participation in American finance.[198] Never, however, did Untermyer pursue a line of questioning focusing on European involvement in American money markets. The omission is extraordinary.[199]

Similarly, in its thorough investigation of ocean shipping, Joshua Alexander's House Committee on Merchant Marine and Shipping, 1913–14, for example, looked at the "combinations" (agreements) among the shippers rather than at the extensive foreign ownership and control of the carrying trades. Indeed, in retrospect it seems astonishing that despite the testimony of witnesses on "the European shipping trust,"[200] and despite the later (1916) Federal Trade Commission findings on foreign control (based on a 1914–1916 investigation),[201] the Alexander committee devoted so little attention to the matter of foreign ownership and control.[202]

Sometimes the apparent U.S. indifference could be explained in light of the foreign investors' intimate identification with the general problems of a particular "industry"—so that the "foreign investor" aspect per se became irrelevant. Thus the interests of *all* owners of railroad securities—American and foreign alike—were in steady, good returns, the higher the better. The Scottish-owned cattle companies desired government-regulated railroad rates as strongly as any American cattle rancher.[203] Foreign investors in manufacturing typically wanted high U.S. tariffs. Foreign bankers were like U.S. ones in favoring the gold standard. Foreign shippers cooperated with their large American counterparts.

In short, it is a distortion, and it is not our intention, to equate American controversies over foreign investment in 1875–1914 with Canadian, Mexican, or Brazilian discussions of 1945–1985. In those nations foreign investment itself was a separate, central issue. As for the United States in 1875–1914, a balanced evaluation must acknowledge that the topic was indeed important. As I have shown, attention was paid to this matter. In fact, much of the rhetoric of this period, with the worries over exploitation, dependence, and sovereignty at bay, anticipated Third World language of the 1970s and 1980s. Yet foreign investment was not *the* or even one of the most burning issues of the late-nineteenth–early-twentieth-century decades, despite the fact that the topic was indirectly associated with all the principal concerns. The absence of treatment of foreign investment in 1875-1914 (or its relegation to a few pages) in standard American economic history textbooks reflects (I believe very much overreflects) the preoccupation of Americans with other subjects and their apparent *relative* indifference to the size, extent, and substantial impact of capital from abroad.[204] In individual years, however, foreign investment in the United States was certainly as much an issue as it has become in this country in 1985–1988.

Abroad: Positive Attitudes and Resulting Government Policies

From the capital-exporting countries came a cacophony of voices on the outflow of their monies to foreign lands, in particular to the

United States, in the period 1875–1914. The range of viewpoints was as broad as that within the United States toward the capital imports. In Europe, especially in Britain, France, and Germany, the capital outflows were, moreover, a *major* matter of debate.[205]

In 1909 the British statistician George Paish declared: "The large sums of capital which Great Britain is now supplying to other lands will ensure greatly increased incomes to her own peoples of all ranks and classes, will widen . . . foreign markets for the goods she manufactures and will greatly assist in providing her dense and constantly growing populations with plentiful supplies of foodstuffs and of raw materials."[206] Paish believed that as Britain had exported capital, the country had grown more prosperous.[207] "By building railways for the world . . . we have enabled the world to increase its production of wealth . . . and to produce those things which this country is specially desirous of purchasing—foodstuffs and raw materials."[208] Prosperity overseas had created purchasing power; other countries could afford to buy British goods.[209] By 1913 Paish was adding to the many benefits of foreign investment the "great income" flowing into Britain.[210] Paish concluded that foreign investment was good for both the capital-exporting and the capital-importing lands.

Paish's views were in keeping with a long tradition of classical economists that looked kindly on the capital outflow.[211] Commentators on Paish's 1909 paper agreed with his positive assessment. Edgar Crammond thought that "one of the most important effects of the investment of capital abroad was the purchasing power it gave to foreign countries . . . in our markets." Foreign investment also "gave a great amount of employment in the city of London and other cities for directors, managers, clerks, solicitors and accountants &c. . . . But it was desirable that the money sent abroad should continue to be controlled by British companies; that was to say, that it should be under the direct control of companies, the head offices of which were situated in this country."[212] In 1911 Crammond wrote that "the investment of British capital has had a beneficial effect upon the shipping, manufacturing, commercial, and financial interests of this country."[213]

John Maynard Keynes, in the *New Quarterly*, February 1910, defended British overseas investments as "developing the purchasing power of our principal customers" and "opening up and supplying with credit and the means of transport our main sources of food and raw materials." The great variety of places from which Britain derived her income increased stability; likewise, the investments abroad provided a great source of wealth that could be drawn on "at need," without disturbing the domestic economy (his example was the repatriation of foreign investment to finance the Boer War). British "expansion abroad," he found, "seems to have been accompanied by, and not to have been at the expense of expansion at home."[214]

Although more reserved, C. K. Hobson in 1914 decided that foreign investment was beneficial to both home and host countries. For the home nation, he believed that foreign investments brought greater returns than domestic ones and "the gains from foreign investments have greatly exceeded the losses."[215] Although foreign investment did raise interest rates at home, this caused more capital to be invested at home than would otherwise have been the case.[216] The overall effect of overseas investment resulted in a rise in national income in Britain.[217] British investment overseas "for the time being," Hobson felt, injured British wage earners by redistributing income in the interest of capital; in the long run, he felt that wage earners would benefit by the overall growth in national income.[218] Hobson, unlike later writers and some of his contemporaries, thought "a boom at home" usually corresponded with "a boom abroad" and that generally the export of capital accompanied high investment at home.[219]

Some Britishers favored investment abroad because they saw no alternatives. Lowthian Bell (later Sir Lowthian), for example, in the 1870s believed that British iron and steel makers should invest in the United States, since British output was no longer competitive.[220] Hyde Clarke, a British economist, suggested that his country's capital *ought* to go where it brought forth the highest returns: "If there be profit obtainable from our business in foreign loans, its abandonment would be a loss and not a benefit to our resources."[221] The higher return to capital would aid the entire British economy.[222]

All these arguments were general, yet Britishers had in mind the large interest in the United States, a country that was viewed as a land of opportunity in which confidence could be placed, "a new country, with a steady form of government, with a good soil, a good climate, and an enterprising race [where] there are so many more openings for the profitable employment of money than in a long-settled country like the United Kingdom." Many a British investor in America—continuing to quote the economist R. H. Inglis Palgrave—was "dazzled by the promise of a distinctly higher rate of return than he [could] obtain in England."[223] Clearly this was true of German, French, and Dutch investors as well.

In Germany, some economists believed that "in order to maintain and strengthen her position in the world markets, Germany will have to increase rather than restrict her foreign financial business."[224] The large German "banks were interested in freedom of opportunity for investments." They had close relations with German industry and often insisted that when foreign loans were made, German industry benefited through orders for their products. The many German firms involved in international business saw their own investments as adding to profits.[225] French banks favored large foreign issues. Articulate Frenchmen criticized their countrymen for not taking advantage of immense and lucrative opportunities in the United States—and thus advocated more foreign investments.[226] Some Frenchmen, including Alfred Neymarck, saw heavy French capital exports as contributing to world peace.[227] Jules Ferry, Prime Minister of France in 1879–1881 and 1883–1885, argued that for rich countries, colonies offered the most profitable and desirable field for investment of capital.[228] Over the years Dutch financial intermediaries, especially those handling U.S. securities, developed experience and became proponents of additional international investments.

On the Continent (as in Britain), advocates of foreign investments favored them for the higher returns and the larger international trade that followed in their wake. French finance was often seen as a "handmaiden of diplomacy"—a reward to those buying French goods.[229] Many saw the investments as enlarging their nation's political influence, identifying foreign investments with "patriotism" and the "flag." Much of the general positive sentiments toward foreign investment that emanated from France and Germany came to be associated with the desirability of the extension of political spheres of influence.[230]

Although British and other European governments had unequal "extraterritorial" treaties with certain less-developed countries and other treaties with developed ones that improved the environment for investment, although governments did actively promote investment abroad for political purposes (the British government invested in the Suez Canal, and the French government, for example, encouraged its nationals to invest in Russia), one looks hard to find actions on the part of any European (or other) government to assist its nationals, or the latter's companies, in investing—much less to spur them to invest—*in the United States.*[231]

The one clear exception would be in ocean shipping, where Cunard—and also the German and the French transatlantic lines—received state support. To be sure, there were numerous diplomatic interventions by European governments on behalf of their nationals who had invested or wished to make investments in the United States, but these interventions appear to have been far from crucial to the enlargement of European stakes in America.[232] Consular services provided information to investors; yet relative to the extensive private information flows, what they revealed on U.S. conditions seems to have been from an overall standpoint of minimal significance.[233] In short, home government promotion of foreign investment in the United States had no fundamental impact that I have been able to discern on the rise of European investment in this country.

Abroad: Mixed Feelings and Resulting Government Policies

Some contemporary economists (C. K. Hobson, for example) recognized that foreign investment was not always desirable.[234] This was true of investments abroad in general and of those in the United States in particular. Intermediaries and investors made choices: certain foreign investments were appropriate, others less so. For each foreign investment in the United States, potential investors evaluated its merits. Some participants in capital exports—intermediaries and investors—felt it wise to clear foreign loans with their governments.

Many of the "mixed" views in Europe toward investments abroad and specifically toward those in the United States related to selection, ability to exercise control, and timing. There were good and bad investments. Good investments could become bad ones. There was a time to invest and a time not to invest. The wise investor had to choose carefully. Robert Lucas Nash, for instance, would write in 1881, "It would be . . . foolish to condemn . . . American Railroad undertakings because Erie or Philadelphia and Reading shares have turned out badly."[235]

Large investors recognized that to obtain returns, not only was selecting important, but a substantial subsequent monitoring of the investment was also needed. Ellis T. Powell, discussing in 1910 how to evaluate investments, urged his readers to look at the seat of operations. In the case of American breweries, he pointed out: "The exigencies of United States law compel these companies to own merely the securities of the American company which is the real and domiciled proprietor of the breweries. In that way, the 'locus' [the seat of operations] is rendered doubly distant from the proprietorship, since the shareholders in England possess only the stock of their own company domiciled here, and this company in turn owns the stock of another company domiciled in a foreign land."[236] This hierarchy of boards—this holding-company structure—meant weak control and was a cause for concern.[237] As we have seen, British investors often employed British accountants and engineers to verify reports on American investments. The attention to the investment seemed a way of reducing risk and gaining good returns.

"Mixed reactions" to foreign investment also related to timing. British bankers would tell their American clients whether this was the opportune moment for a particular issue of securities. Timing was affected not only by the state of money markets but also on occasion by international politics. N. M. Rothschild & Sons cabled its New York agent on December 27, 1895, "We will not take any part either leading or subordinary in an American Bond Syndicate until we are assured both by the American and the English Government that the pending [Venezuela] question is satisfactorily arranged."[238] The suggestion was that the Rothschilds had checked the matter out with the British government, or at least had consulted.

Herbert Feis writes of an informal process whereby the British government gave off-the-record opinions on proposed issues of foreign loans and information on political situations. The Bank of England, Feis suggested, provided "a useful medium between the banks and the government." Moreover, as he stated, "in clubs, country week-ends, shooting parties, Sir Ernest Cassel, Lord Rothschild or Lord Revelstoke could learn the official mind and reveal their own."[239] The most recent historian of the British Rothschilds, Richard Davis, writes that by the last decades of the nineteenth century, the English Rothschilds "had become fully accepted members of that relatively tight little circle [in London] where political questions were canvassed and solutions advanced."[240] What was desirable at one time might not be under different circumstances.

Timing issues could relate to U.S. domestic politics and economics, as well as to international politics. The Dutch banker G. M. Boissevain prefaced an essay on money and banking in the United States (written in November 1908) with the comments, "Now that the election of Mr. TAFT as Mr. ROOSEVELT's successor to the Presidency appears to have removed the apprehensions of Government interference deterimental to the renewed development of commerce and industry, the violent crisis which last year held the United States in its grip . . . may at last be looked upon as surmounted." America was once more a promising place for investors.[241] Roosevelt's attack on giant enterprise in America had been a cause of anxiety.[242]

Another type of "mixed reaction" to foreign investment was provided in the London *Nation*, which editorialized in November 1913 that "a register of all British capital invested abroad [should] be kept in a special department of the Foreign Office or the Board of Trade. Within this register there should be a privileged list of those undertakings which are entitled to some measure of recognition and protection." Only reputable ventures would be supported. "It might prove to be possible to penalize the undesirable undertakings . . . by imposing on their earnings some higher rate of income tax."[243]

Tempered reactions to foreign investment by European governments often involved political goals.[244] In many instances the British government intervened diplomatically on behalf of British investors in the United States, but, as noted, the intervention was halfhearted *because* no commanding political power considerations were in evidence.[245] Likewise, when William Mackenzie (who represented large Scottish investment trust interests in the United States) urged a British treaty with the United States to put British corporations "beyond the reach of prejudicial and hostile legislation" of the U.S. state legislatures, which he sugggested were "often under the control of ignorant or unscrupulous persons," the British government failed to give him strong support.[246]

Sometimes governments sought to protect their own innocent citizens from "unscrupulous" foreigners. This was especially true in France;[247] in 1907 a French law held that an issuing bank was responsible for the accuracy of the sums stated on the prospectus.[248] French investors had had a series of bad experiences with American investments. Such government protection of investors was a "mixed response" to foreign investment.

More often than not, however, in Europe attitudes toward investment abroad were sharply polarized. Some men, as I have shown, thought them highly desirable. Others held the opposite view. Even the mixed reactions can often be seen as representing dichotomies related to good and bad investments, a yes or no decision. Thus I need not linger in the middle ground, but rather will turn to the simultaneous torrent of negative responses to the capital outflow.

Abroad: Hostile Reactions and Resulting Government Policies

As Jacob Viner would later point out, "In all countries which have been great exporters of capital, serious misgivings have been voiced in various influential quarters lest such exports of capital—drain capital." There were fears of "overlending."[249] Foreign investments, many in Europe believed, always carried more risk than domestic ones; money lost abroad brought nothing home. Capital was limited; money and business that went to alien lands represented reduced domestic investment and, accordingly, employment. Interest and dividends accumulated abroad evaded taxation at home.[250] Interest rates went up at home as a result of foreign investment, a rise that critics thought undesirable.[251] Foreign investment, some opponents argued, led to maldistribution of wealth at home (high returns to capital and low ones to labor). It was "unpatriotic" to send monies outside the country when as a consequence there would be less domestic economic activity.[252] Foreign investments, moreover, created competitors abroad who would become competitors at home.

When C. K. Hobson wrote his *Export of Capital* (1914), which I quoted earlier, his introduction tells us that he did so because of the hue and cry that arose "a few years ago" in the United Kingdom over foreign investment, which was regarded as a "portentous phenomenon . . . as a running sore, sapping the life blood of British industry and adding fresh strength to our most formidable rivals and competitors." The matter had been discussed in Parliament, where "speakers lamented the increase of unemployment and stagnation of trade, which they attributed to the unparalleled outflow of capital."[253]

Associated with the negative view toward foreign investment was a prevailing notion (particularly in Britain) that large enterprise was inefficient.[254] With small business, wrote the economist Alfred Marshall, "the master's eye is everywhere; there is no shirking by his foreman or workmen, no divided responsibility, no sending half-understood messages backwards and forwards from one department to another."[255] Big business, and by implication (although not in Marshall) business over borders, had problems of absentee ownership, along with the difficulties of communication over distance.[256] Resources were not well used in international investment.

In Britain particularly, a battle raged between "free traders" and "fair traders," and as D. C. M. Platt has noted, the issue of foreign investment got caught up in the debate over protectionism.[257] Whereas free traders were divided (most believing that foreign investment was good, but others—as we will see—having sharp reservations), most fair traders condemned capital outflows and used such capital exports as an argument in favor of protecting business at home.[258]

Another general concern related to the growth of "finance capital," of "securities," of "paper" that did not reflect production but opened up possibilities of a "South Sea Bubble." In this context the rise of the "international banker" seemed disturbing. Also, concentration in banking—in England, France, and Germany—was by the early twentieth century a major topic of discussion, with a substantial literature attacking this concentration of power. Did large international banks act in the *national* interest?[259]

Negative attitudes toward both portfolio and direct investments abroad were frequently extended, in specifics, to those investments made in the United States. Investment in America was perceived as "speculative." Americans were corrupt and unreliable. State governments had defaulted. Mining company fraud was ubiquitous. Investments were "abetted by unprincipled adventurers."[260] Indeed, even men most committed to and sympathetic toward U. S. investment knew of the disgraces—from the Mississippi pre–Civil War defaults (still a raw issue in 1875–1914) to Virginia's more recent "shameful immorality."[261] Few in England had not heard or read of the Atlantic and Great Western and the Emma mine. Because of investors' losses on the Erie, Jay Gould was a persona non grata with the British.[262] The Dutch took longer to learn than the British and were more bargain oriented, but by 1888 they were not about to repeat their mistake of listening to Gould's promises.[263] In France investors forgot about their grandfathers' and fathers' experiences with American state debts in the 1830s, California societies in 1849–50, and the Memphis, El Paso and Pacific Railroad in 1869, only to be badly burned once more in the "Frisco" railroad debacle of 1913.

Obviously dangers existed in portfolio and direct investments in America. Men who favored U.S. investments and those with mixed feelings believed that risks could be avoided (and excellent profits made). By contrast, critics felt that the pitfalls were part and parcel of the U.S. investment environment. Opponents saw the misrepresentation and fraud as typical of American immorality; tawdry behavior and defaults were considered commonplace, and good opportunities scarce; full and accurate data were available only to "insiders."[264]

The London *Economist*, for instance, often denigrated investments in America.[265] Why were Britishers asked to buy a particular security? Surely Americans had money, but of course Americans knew the security was overpriced. Did railroads presented to the British public actually own the properties and have the advertised potential? Was a mining prospectus truthful?[266] Was the company whose securities the British were being asked to purchase overcapitalized? Was this pure speculation? Was the management honest?[267] How could an investor thousands of miles away know what to do when faced with "Wall Street intrigues."[268] "Of all the Anglo-American mines, and their name is legion, those yielding anything to the shareholders can be counted upon the fingers of one hand," declared the *Economist* in 1889.[269]

In Germany, in response to American railroad defaults, the *Frankfurter Zeitung* proposed in 1884 that "government" (German or American?) supervision of railroad finance be a condition of admittance of American railroad securities to listings on the German stock exchanges, while the *Norddeutsche Zeitung* called for the removal of all U. S. rails from the German exchanges.[270]

In 1908 the London *Economist* conceded that some English companies had obtained good income from various parts of the United States,

but, broadly, it is true that where the British capitalist has advanced money to the American manufacturer the investment has been disappointing and the return quite inadequate. The reason, of course, is that hitherto the good things have not been sent over here. Companies of high standing and assured prospects have been able to raise the funds they need in their own country, as the American financier has naturally been ready to subscribe for all the most promising ventures. He is first on the ground and can take his pick. What is left over may be sent to London.[271]

U.S. proponents of "silver" money got extensive publicity in Britain, and the rhetoric against "sound" money seemed to lend credence to the arguments of those who found fault with American investment. The U.S. Treasury representative in London (Charles Conant) wrote his superiors in Washington in October 1877, "If the views of the extreme advocates of silver money should unfortunately be adopted by Congress, it will certainly ruin our national credit abroad."[272] When William Jennings Bryan's colorful speeches were quoted in Europe, they were represented as symbolic of the perils in America.

Still worse, Americans lived with bankruptcies. The failure rate per 10,000 firms in the years 1875–1914 ranged from a high of 158 (1878) to a low of 63 (1880). In only half of the forty years did the failure rate drop below 100 firms per thousand, and in ten of these years it was above 120 per thousand.[273] When, for example in 1910 Pillsbury-Washburn Flour Mills Company, Ltd., was in receivership, the *Northwestern Miller* contrasted the "American" view with that of the "English." Americans devoted their energies to starting anew. "The English shareholder . . . becomes wildly indignant. Before the collapse, he has been oblivious to conditions. . . . Content to accept formal and perfunctory reports of credulous emissaries he has lived in a fool's paradise. When the downfall comes . . . he howls for revenge." The Minneapolis journal editorialized: "The recent meeting in London [of the shareholders] represented the unprofitable process of threshing out old straw with a great deal of crying over milk hopelessly spilled and irretrievably lost. What is done is done."[274] This very attitude, the British believed, was cavalier and irresponsible. Repeatedly, opponents of foreign investment stressed the dishonesty, the frontier recklessness, and the casual buccaneer behavior of Americans. The latter seemed shameless.[275] "Lysis," a French critic of foreign investment, warned in 1911 that Americans were placing stock—with uncertain dividends—on the French market. Such securities were subject to great manipulations by American financiers— and were a major threat to French savings.[276]

The views on the high risk of investing in America coexisted with the belief in the United Kingdom, and also in Canada, Germany, and France, that such stakes deprived the home nation of capital that could and should be employed domestically. J. Shield Nicholson, a University of Edinburgh political economy professor, in 1901 noted that when Holland became the great lending state of Europe, "its wealth and power steadily diminished."[277] Similarly, he commented:

It is for the interest of the capitalist to obtain a maximum profit, and the place where his capital is employed is to him so far indifferent. But to the labourer and to society at large the place is of vital importance. If capital is devoted to the construction of a railway in America, it may in perpetuity afford a much higher profit than if applied to the construction of a railway in England; but in the one case foreign labour is employed, and in the other English . . . To take an extreme case, it is possible that if all the capital now devoted to manufactures in this country [Great Britain] were sent to the United States it would yield greater returns; but the labourers must in that case either follow it or starve.[278]

Nicholson was convinced that "one of the chief causes of the late depression [in the 1890s] was the enormous transfer of capital from old countries such as England to new countries [such as the United States] for the exploitation of their raw materials and the construction of their railroads."[279]

In 1903 the British economist W. J. Ashley wrote of the "movement of capital" of an "ominous kind—viz., the establishment by English manufacturers of factories within the protected area," behind foreign (including American) tariff walls.[280] Not only did foreign tariffs destroy British jobs by reducing her exports but, Ashley added, jobs themselves were being exported by the building of these plants abroad.[281] Britain was at this time still committed to free trade; Nicholson and Ashley believed in free trade. Most protectionists, however, also argued against foreign investment—insisting that because foreign tariffs were creating jobs overseas, Britain must respond by protecting its own industry. Only with *high* British tariffs could jobs be retained at home.[282]

Cartoons from the *Birmingham Daily Mail* of December 28, 1905, and January 24, 1910, expressed sentiments similar to those of Nicholson and Ashley (see Figure 16.3). They illustrate the views of "The Working Man" when the firm of Albright & Wilson decided to jump the U.S. tariff barrier and to manufacture across the Atlantic. Dividends meant returns to the factory owner but not to employees, who asked, "That's all right for you, Guv'nor, but where do I come in?" Foreign investment redistributed income in a way that benefited capital but not labor—nor the society as a whole—such critics claimed.

Figure 16.3. On Albright & Wilson's American plant. Source: R. E. Threlfall, *The Story of 100 Years of Phosphorous Making, 1851–1951* (Oldbury: Albright & Wilson, 1951), 157, 161. Albright & Wilson, Ltd., kindly provided photographs of these cartoons.

A British Fabian socialist (William Clarke), writing the American Henry Demarest Lloyd in June 1890, commented on the effect of British capital export not on the British workmen but on Americans: "Your 'free' citizens are fast becoming the bond slaves of rich men in London. What would [George] Washington have thought of this kind of 'independence'?"[283]

Another strong critic, not a socialist but one who would influence many socialists, J. A. Hobson, in *Imperialism*, a book published in London in 1902, called foreign investment the "most important economic factor in Imperialism," because "public force [was necessary] to extend the field of . . . private investment." "Financiers" were "economic parasites of imperialism," "parasites upon patriotism." Hobson wrote that the United States was "repaying the capital borrowed from Great Britain and other countries for the early development of their railroads, mines and manufactures, and afterwards becoming themselves a creditor class to foreign countries." He in no way realized the extent of the continuing foreign investment in the United States, nor was it important to him, for there had been no "public force," no "imperialism" to promote this investment! And Hobson would ignore what did not support his case.[284] His critique of foreign investment, which linked it with imperialist endeavors, was totally irrelevant to the investment *in* the United States; I include it only because of its position in the more general debate on foreign investment and its substantial subsequent influence. The opinion was in sharp contrast to that of Neymarck and others, who saw capital exports as contributing to world harmony. The association of capital exports, imperialism, and war resurfaced in many guises in England and on the Continent between 1902 and 1914, challenging the view that an integrated, interdependent world economy was a force for peace.[285]

Canadians expressed concern when the Bank of Montreal invested in the United States. The bank's president had to defend the bank's use of its financial resources south of the border instead of in Canada.[286] Canada was not an important capital-exporting country, yet the worry about "capital drain" nonetheless existed.

An even more negative judgment in Europe on foreign investment and specifically investment in the United States was that of the Austrian Marxist Rudolf Hilferding. Hilferding wrote in 1910:

industry which is menaced by the tariffs of foreign countries now makes use of these tariffs for its own purposes by transferring part of its production [at home] abroad. If this prevents the expansion of the parent concern and excludes the possibility of increasing the rate of profit by reducing costs of production, it is compensated by the increased profit which the same owners of capital receive from the increase in the price of the goods which they now produce abroad.

Hilferding thought the export of capital (direct and portfolio investments) canceled out the falling rate of profit in the domestic market.[287] Although he conceded, as others had before him, that overall the capital export assisted the domestic economy, increased production, and raised employment, more important, he felt that it "inhibits a conscious awareness of the ills of capitalist society and generates an optimistic view of its viability."[288] Later in his argument Hilferding turned to the example of the Scottish investment in thread manufacture in the United States and the consequent employment loss in Britain, "borne by the English [sic] worker and in the last resort the whole nation."[289] While he saw the "export of capital" as a "condition for the rapid expansion of capitalism," he predicted that foreign industry (and his context was American industry) would in time "be strong enough to throw off the yoke of 'English control' and reduce its tribute of interest," at which point the existing temporary benefits to Britain (or the capital exporter in general) would dissipate, and the "ills of the capitalist society" would become apparent.[290] Rivals would be created—to haunt the capital exporters.

In the early twentieth century the large capital outflows from Germany and France provoked immense controversy. The Continent was rife with uneasiness. Rapid German economic growth was viewed as threatening by England and France. There were clashes over colonies. Foreign capital outflows were associated in the minds of many with internationalism, inappropriate political goals, and disturbing economic consequences. Frenchmen worried that French capital was aiding German industry.

German socialists denounced foreign investment "as bringing oppression of weaker races . . . and as certain to involve the country in international conflicts."[291] French socialists also condemned capital outflow.[292] In Britain in the early twentieth century, some critics of foreign investment suggested that capital was being driven abroad by socialistic legislation and confiscatory taxation—another matter, of course![293]

German agrarians denounced foreign investment because as "ardent nationalists" they wanted a strong and self-sufficient Germany, and they objected to foreign investments simply because they were foreign. "Foreign investments represented to them a part of the new era in which industry and capital, both international and too-democratic, were gaining control." The banks, they believed, through their international associations, were breaking down national identities. Moreover, these conservative Germans condemned foreign investment as raising interest rates at home and making agricultural credit more expensive.[294]

While large German landowners denounced the capital outflows as antinationalistic and "too-democratic," the French publicist Lysis also thundered against capital exports, agreeing with the conservatives that the results were antinationalistic but arguing they were in addition *antidemocratic!*[295] Another French writer on capital exports (1912) was equally hostile. Instead of stimulating productive activity in the creditor country (as the "liberal school" maintained), Émile Becque argued that the migration of capital tended to exercise a paralyzing influence at home. Far from prompting merchandise exports to the capital-importing country, he found that the outcome was the development of exports *from* the capital-importing country toward those that furnished the capital. International lending meant neglect of the domestic economy and inevitable difficulties at home as foreign output expanded. Investment abroad was risky because no international law governed its conduct and no satisfactory recourse was available when promises were broken. People bought securities on good faith, and they turned out to be fraudulent. There were defaults (and Becque cited among them those of American southern state governments—Tennessee, West Virginia, Louisiana, Mississippi, Arkansas, Florida). Good information was absent. Becque concluded that the savings of France were being exported and lost, depriving domestic industry of its requirements.[296]

Later, the economic historian Herbert Feis noted that many "industrial employers" in France objected to the capital exports, fearing a rise in interest rates at home[297] and worrying lest investment abroad create or assist competition with French industry.[298] Jacob Viner would write that of all the pre–World War I capital-exporting countries, the opposition to capital exports was strongest in France, "where statesmen, publicists, and manufacturers have looked upon the great outward flow of French savings as a transfer to foreign industry of financial resources which were needed for the development of home industries." Viner added that the opposition became particularly vehement in the years just before the war.[299] In Switzerland, too, foreign investment was subjected to the criticism that capital must be "guided by patriotic considerations and not neglect the country's own needs in favour of others abroad."[300]

In short, in capital-exporting countries major concerns were articulated over investment abroad, with opponents covering a broad range of interests, from liberal professors to financial journalists, from socialists to conservative agrarians to industry leaders. Those hostile to the capital outflow dealt with economic issues such as the effects on home investment, distribution of national income, domestic interest rates, loss of capital, and creation of competition abroad, as well as political questions of "patriotism," nationalism, and international strife. In many instances general criticisms covered specifics related to investments in the United States.[301] Many not favoring capital outflow thought foreign investment served the recipient country at the expense of the source nation. Some, however, ignored the effects on the host country, simply arguing in purely national terms that the export of monies was undesirable. A very few saw it as harmful to both source and recipient country.

Government responses to these negative sentiments varied. The presence of opposition notwithstanding, in Britain it is difficult to uncover any overt British policy or action adverse to U.S. investments—although inaction, neutrality, and indifference (see below) might be so interpreted.[302] Likewise, I identified no Dutch government objections, nor any Swiss rules slowing foreign investment in the United States. By contrast, in Germany and France in the years 1875–1914, succeeding governments did monitor and at times forbid large foreign securities issues and on occasion also imposed special taxes on foreign loans.[303]

In 1887 Bismarck was protesting to the Bleichroeder firm over the outflow of foreign investment.[304] From January 6, 1911 (when the 5 percent bonds of the St. Louis and San Francisco Railroad were listed on the Berlin and Frankfurt exchanges), to the outbreak of World War I, no American railroad bonds were admitted to the German exchanges. In the spring of 1911, the Prussian government forbade the listing of the Chicago, Milwaukee and St. Paul Railroad on the Berlin Bourse, explaining that the German market was not in a position to absorb any more foreign loans. Yet others (not American) were listed, and the historian Walter Herman Carl Laves feels that the real reason related to the potash controversy (see Chapter 8). The German government apparently believed that to stop the Chicago, Milwaukee and St. Paul from a convenient means of raising capital in Germany would give the German government leverage with the U.S. administration on this entirely unrelated matter. Since the German government was, in any case, concerned over the number of foreign securities being floated, the use of this form of economic diplomacy did not seem counterproductive.[305] The German government did not, however, block the export of capital, and any determined German investor (or his representative) could buy the securities of the Chicago, Milwaukee in London. Since all the major German banks had representatives in London, this was no difficult matter.[306]

Similarly, the French government sought to influence its nationals. Joseph Caillaux (French Prime Minister from June 1911 to January 1912 and many times Finance Minister) in 1913 noted, "I have admitted to quotation only those foreign loans which assured France political and economic advantage, and I have considered above all else the needs of the Treasury and its resources."[307] In 1900 Nathaniel Bacon found that the consequences of the "paternal French government endeavors to prevent its lambs from losses through dealing in securities unknown to the powers that be, by prohibiting dealings with them on the Paris Bourse," were twofold: (1) the French were not large investors in the United States, and (2) when the French wanted to invest in the United States, they did so through London, Amsterdam, Brussels, and Geneva, where "brokers . . . wax fat on commissions which would otherwise stay in Paris."[308]

In 1909 the French government refused an official listing on the Paris Bourse to the common stock of United States Steel Corporation, when according to most sources "organized employer groups" pointed out that the steel company was in a "competing" industry.[309] Frenchmen could and did buy the shares in United States Steel Corporation (and other American securities) from bankers or brokers in France or on other stock exchanges.[310]

The German action in relation to the Chicago, Milwaukee and St. Paul and the French one apropos United States Steel were both attempts to encourage the sending of *goods* rather than capital abroad (in the one case, potash; in the other, steel). As for capital exports, the German and French governments had a far more active role than the British by all accounts.

The years 1875–1914 were before the general introduction of foreign exchange controls. No nation—neither France nor Germany—prohibited capital exports. Private individuals and firms made their own decisions as to whether to invest abroad and did so for their own reasons. Financial journals were full of information—of varying degrees of reliability. It is necessary, moreover, in this instance to distinguish government attitudes toward portfolio and direct investments. Pre–World War I government policymakers usually did *not* make the separation in their deliberations.[311] Nonetheless, in point of fact a clear distinction emerges in government *measures*. New securities issues, traded on exchanges, involved "the general public"; this was true of foreign government loans *and* of stocks and bonds of railroads and other enterprises. Securities issues were visible and advertised.[312] By contrast, when a company set up factories outside the country; or a bank established a branch, partnership, or agency abroad; or an insurance office expanded internationally, the decision was made by the heads of the firm.[313] Public discussion of, and specifically opposition to, foreign investment, as I have shown, encompassed both portfolio and direct investments. Yet in the main, European government restrictions—such as determinations on the issues that could be listed on the exchanges—applied only to the portfolio ones. Direct investments, in the sphere of private company decision making, seem to have been beyond the state's reach, even on the Continent. Whereas extensive discussions took place on banks' aiding industry to go overseas and on their international connections, I have not found—at least in relation to those investments in the United States—any home government restrictions on industrial, banking, or insurance *direct* investments.[314]

Abroad: Neutral Attitudes and Relevant Government Policies

This brings me to the "neutral" attitudes in Europe toward foreign investment. Neutrality can be classified in two fashions. The first relates more to direct than to portfolio investments; and the second, to both direct and portfolio investments: (1) Foreign investment was inevitable; thus why protest the already determined? Put another way, foreign investment was part of the normal, natural growth of the firm. And (2) Foreign investment was a matter of importance to the individual investor, not to the nation as a whole.

The first view was held by many foreign direct investors in U.S. manufacturing. A company invested in New York, Pennsylvania, Connecticut, New Jersey, or Rhode Island, not because it was "good" for the firm or for the United Kingdom, Germany, France, Switzerland, or Sweden—or for the United States, for that matter—nor because it was a "patriotic" thing to do, but because the alternative was the loss of a market. With high U.S. tariffs, the enterprise that had exported to America had the options of abandoning the market (and many companies did let their sales wither) or manufacturing behind the U.S. tariff walls.[315] No broad ideological or normative questions of "good" or "bad" were involved, much less discussed. The choices were simple: invest or lose the market.

Similarly, if the market could be reached by a sales organization in the United States, the investment in it was part of the growth of the firm. Again, the United States had developed a mining industry. Smelters and refineries were bound to be built. The wise trader in metals would need to invest in processing. No questions in the investors' mind dealt with "right" or "wrong" vis-à-vis the home economy. Companies sought opportunities where they existed. In the polemical, highly charged world of international politics, it is important to recognize how often businessmen displayed neutrality. Politics and macroeconomic considerations were irrelevant; decisions were made with an eye to an individual firm's benefits.

The second "neutral" view often became the basis for *government policy*, especially in Britain and apparently in Holland. That view was that foreign investment was a matter for the investor and not the state. Despite contemporary uneasiness over the outflow of capital, governments often looked the other way. When Britishers lost money in American investments, usually the Foreign Office seemed indifferent. When anti-British sentiment in the United States on land ownership matters had mounted and Congress passed the Alien Property Act of 1887, the British government collected information but did not seek "to defend" British investments in America in any consequential manner.[316] Charles M. Kennedy in the Commercial Department of the British Foreign Office summed up the prevailing view: "British subjects who invest in foreign countries must take the laws of these countries as they are, and not seek to dictate alterations in them."[317] When in 1889 the Council of Foreign Bondholders, London, wrote a strong letter to U.S. President Benjamin Harrison on those American state debts remaining in default, the Foreign Office even suggested that the letter be toned down.[318]

On August 18, 1910, the United States and Great Britain signed a special agreement for the submission to arbitration of pecuniary claims outstanding between the two countries. British claims did *not* include state debts that were still in default. As Lord Ponsonby would later explain, "His Majesty's Government considered that even if representations were addressed to the Government of the United States the latter would have no power to compel the defaulting states to pay, and there was no reason to suppose that the Federal Government would be disposed to assume any liability in the matter."[319] In short, the British government did nothing.

The "neutrality" of the British government lay in its neither encouraging nor discouraging portfolio or direct investments in the United States.[320] Perhaps its overall neutrality toward the U.S. investments may have made it easier for the British foreign investor, whereas possibly the French and German governments' often more explicitly negative postures made their investors' path marginally more difficult. Yet on the Continent, in most instances, governments were equally passive in relation to U.S investments,[321] and certainly in relation to direct investments in the United States, there appears to have been far more governmental neutrality in France and Germany than has hitherto been recognized.

An Overview

In sum, contemporaries in America and abroad from different walks of life held a wide range of attitudes toward investments in the United States and toward foreign investment in general. On both sides of the Atlantic sharp, acerbic language coexisted with indifference. Proponents and opponents in the years 1875 to 1914 used a variety of economic (and sometimes political) arguments. Those with hostile attitudes, far more than those with favorable ones, tended to appeal more strongly to emotion.[322]

Proponents of foreign investment were often those who personally benefited: financial intermediaries (in the United States and abroad), American and foreign businessmen, U.S. and foreign mining interests, borrowers in America, lenders abroad. From an industry standpoint, in the United States the largest welcome was perhaps accorded to new foreign investments in railroads and even more in mining. The favorable views abroad were less definable by industry designation—tending to cover foreign investments across the spectrum.

Hostility to foreign investment frequently came from those who were hurt, or much more important, from those who *perceived* personal disadvantage: American farmers' organizations, but also German agrarian interests (for different reasons); businessmen in America (who felt an alien role inappropriate and others who saw foreign direct investors as offering unfair competition) and businessmen in Europe (who identified the outflow of funds with higher interest rates at home or new competition from the United States); and labor groups and socialists in America (who sympathized with farmers' causes and objected to "big" business) and the identical parties overseas (who thought the outflow of funds brought the export of jobs). There was antagonism from both borrowers in America (who saw foreign investors as greedy) and borrowers abroad (who connected the outflow of money with rising interest rates in *their* home countries). The panoply of negative responses also was tied to fears of gold drain from America, from the debtor nation (to pay interest and dividends and eventually the principal) and also from the creditor nation (to pay for the capital exports). In addition, many on both sides of the Atlantic resented international investment that by its very existence seemed to diminish national sovereignty in the United States and in the capital-exporting country. From an industry perspective, foreign land ownership attracted by far the greatest antagonism in the United States, while abroad negative attitudes were less industry specific.

Some contemporary economists favored the capital exports, others had serious reservations, and others opposed them. The matter seems to have been far more important to British and continental European economists than to their American counterparts, who were more concerned with the related issues of silver, protectionism, and monopoly power.

It is inappropriate to attempt to detemine where the balance of opinion lay. Clearly no consensus existed—in the United States or abroad. It is the many voices, pro and con, that are of relevance. However, an evaluation of the significance of the jumble of views can be judged by the extent to which they were incorporated into governmental measures.

Governments considered the political consequences of investment. While national governments—and state and local ones within the United States—acted in ways that influenced the capital flows, on the whole this was a period when American and foreign governmental interventions were relatively minimal (at least when compared with times to follow), and this was especially true in relation to the investments in the United States. Some foreign investments entering America were, to be sure, subsidized by muncipalities in this country, and (more important) others were protected by U. S. tariffs, but I searched in vain to find any foreign investments in the United States in 1875–1914 (except those of shipping companies and the tiny investment in a sales subsidiary made by the German potash syndicate) that were *foreign-government* initiated, sponsored, or materially promoted.[323] Likewise, although—in response to public outcry—there were numerous rules and regulations in America and other miscellaneous foreign government curbs that had impacts, the cumulative overall net effects on the growth of foreign investments in the United States were small. American law appears to have been far more important than foreign rules as an influence on the entry of foreign capital. The intense rhetoric that was often hostile and the multiplicity of regulations and restrictions notwithstanding, the easy flow of capital from abroad into America is what stands out rather than the impediments.

Epilogue

This book has documented the growth of both foreign portfolio and direct investments in America from the colonial era to 1914 and the ambivalent reactions to such stakes. It is left for us to sum up the story and to evaluate, from a distance, the consequences of the large foreign participation.

From 1607 to 1914, and especially from 1776 to 1914, long-term obligations of Americans grew in absolute amounts. Tables 3.1, 4.1, and 5.4 have revealed in numerical terms the path of this growth from 1789 to 1914. At the time of independence (1776), America's long-term overseas obligations were a mere £1.1 million.[1] By 1789 the figure for the public debt owned abroad (there was far less foreign investment in the private sector) was in excess of $16 million, with total long-term foreign obligations probably in the range of $17 million to $18 million.[2] In 1914 U.S. long-term foreign obligations—now principally private sector ones—were roughly $7 billion.[3] At the eve of World War I, America was the largest debtor nation in the world. My data indicate that America's long-term foreign obligations were far larger in relative (as well as absolute) terms in 1914 than in 1776.[4]

There were ebbs and flows in foreign investments. In certain periods such investments had greater economic impact than in others. The years 1776–1803, the late 1830s, 1849–1857, the post–Civil War decade, the 1880s, and 1909–1912 stand out as times when the role of foreign capital in America appears particularly outstanding. This volume, in its attempt to provide an overview, has not emphasized the ups and downs as much as the cumulative rise in long-term foreign obligations. In Chapters 1–4 and 16, I have shown the persistent ambivalence in Americans' reactions to the influx and presence of foreign capital. At all times in these pre-1914 years, there were

Americans who welcomed the foreign contribution and those who resented it.

Foreign investment in America not only influenced this country's economic development but also had an impact on the capital-exporting nations. By the late nineteenth and early twentieth centuries, the United States was the largest single national recipient of British, German, and Dutch capital outflows. Thus, very briefly, in this epilogue it is appropriate to consider from a distance the impact on the source nations of their countrymen's U.S. investments. My comments here are designed to be suggestive rather than conclusive, since a full-fledged appraisal is far outside the bounds of this study.[5] Then I want to turn—again as a digest—to the actual costs and benefits of the foreign investments in the United States to this recipient country. Did debtor-nation status *in fact* help or did it hinder America's economic development?

For capital-exporting countries there was never "clear sailing" in American investments. We have learned of losses, bankruptcies, and defaults. From the Virginia Company onward, investors had bad experiences. Short-lived investments, terminated because of bankruptcies or simply lack of success, were frequent, although the only losses through "confiscations" of property (1607–1914) were to the British during the Revolutionary War years. The U.S. federal government never defaulted on its debt, but state governments in the early 1840s and the 1870s did do so. The Mississippi debt (incurred in the 1830s) is still in default. Foreign investors in the 1863 Confederate loan lost their monies.

As we move to the years of 1875–1914 and the rise of truly large-scale foreign investments in the private sector, we can continue to report numerous losses, bankruptcies, and defaults—short-lived ventures that were scams and others that were simply not competitive in the U.S. market, bankruptcies and near bankruptcies, and many railroad-bond defaults. There is no question that substantial savings from abroad evaporated in America, both foreign portfolio and direct investments. Because my book stops in 1914, it does not consider the takeovers by the United States of German assets in America during World War I. Yet in a sense confiscation in future wars was part of the risks of investments abroad.

Losses there were, and would be, but at the same time the opportunities in America were immense; scrutiny of a list of British millionaires reveals an extraordinarily high number who took part (both early and late in their careers) in U.S. investments.[6] Throughout the years 1776–1914, the nominal returns on long-term American investments were higher than those available in Europe.[7] That foreign investors continued to make large investments in America suggests that such a course was perceived as profitable.

What was the actual bottom line? For its creditors were there more failures or more successes in America? The debate—already in existence before 1914—continued. In 1924 John Maynard Keynes wrote an article entitled "Foreign Investment and National Advantage." He divided foreign investments into three categories: (1) those made for "trading, mining and exploitation," which had "generally proved of immense financial benefit" to investor nations; (2) those made to build railroads abroad, which "probably, in their day, redounded to the national advantage,"; and (3) loans to governments and local authorities abroad. The last had "turned out badly on balance"; among the defaults, Keynes cited those of the southern states of the United States. In this article Keynes distinguished between the private benefits to foreign investors and the broader public interest, noting that with two investments of equal risk—the one at home and the one abroad—a loss in either was the same to the private investor, whereas in the case of the domestic investment, the nation as a whole retained "the object of the investment and the fruits of it. With home investment, even if it be ill-advised or extravagantly carried out, at least the country has the improvement for what it is worth . . . A bad foreign investment is wholly engulfed."[8] Such comments notwithstanding, at the end of the 1920s—with the exception of Germans, who still bemoaned their World War I losses in America—most evaluations of investments in the pre-1914 United States from the standpoint of the creditor nation tended to be favorable.[9] And even some Germans who looked back were positive. One Anglo-German banker (Saemy Japhet) went so far as to suggest that the foundations for the great late-nineteenth- and early-twentieth-century German business development were directly attributable to the experiences gained and the profits made by Germans who invested in U.S. government bonds in the post–Civil War years.[10]

In the 1930s, as the woes of creditor nations mounted, scholars relooked at the earlier age and had more reservations about the desirability to the source country of capital exports.[11] In their economic history of Europe (a textbook first published in 1941), Shepard Clough and Charles Cole summarized seven reasons why the "results of foreign investing" in the pre–World War I years were not always what the capital exporters anticipated: (1) "loans did not always cement political alliances"; (2) high interest rates abroad were illusory because of the great number of defaults; (3) in the case of default, capital-exporting countries were left with worthless paper; capital-importing nations, at least, had the railroads, and so forth; (4) foreign investments did increase international trade, but not necessarily the exports of the capital-exporting nation; (5) capital outflows aided the recipient nation, undermining domestic producers in the capital-exporting one (their example was that agriculture in Britain had dropped "to a low level" because British investments in the U.S. railroads had opened up American farming regions, the output of which undersold that of the English farmer); (6) foreign loans went to purchase machinery, adversely affecting the capital-exporting country's consumer goods sectors; because the latter was hurt, this reduced domestic standards; and (7) monies that should have been invested at home contributing to higher wages and raising standards of living instead went abroad.[12] In their commentary, and those of others, increasingly the literature on pre-1914 international investment dealt with portfolio, not direct, investments.[13] The reason lay in the particular problems with portfolio investments in the 1930s—and the more conspicuous nature of such investments.

Both A. K. Cairncross and Brinley Thomas, writing about the pre–World War I years, documented the inverse correlation between British home and foreign investment.[14] Thomas claimed that "when the American system was digesting what it had swallowed, Britain's appetite for home investment would rise and her real income would grow faster than usual, while her exports of men and money became negligible." Then America would be the place for investment, and home investment in Britain would slow down.[15] Scholarly analyses (and less scholarly ones as well) made through the 1950s stressed the high costs to the source countries (England, Germany, and France) of the pre-1914 foreign investment in general, allowing, on occasion, that certain investments in the United States, particularly those of the British, might have paid.[16]

Yet, even as the doubts were expressed, scholars once more returned to the benefits of the foreign investments. Rondo Cameron found that in the years before World War I, the times of unusually large French capital exports coincided with French periods of prosperity and rapid domestic capital formation.[17] The newer general work tends to be even more approving, especially that on the British overseas investment.[18] Michael Edelstein has argued that for the years 1870-1914 and for the United Kingdom, not only were interest rates higher abroad, but also the actual returns on overseas investment (and particularly on stakes in the United States) were in fact greater than for home investment.[19] Foreign investment benefited Britain. Although Edelstein does not dispute "the inverse long-swings" of domestic and foreign investment, he is convinced, and convincing, that the flow of British capital abroad "was not because

new domestic industry was underfunded by institutional immaturity
or inadequacy." Adequate means existed within the British economy
to provide for domestic expansion; capital outflow was not responsible for constraining the growth of new enterprise in Britain in these
years.[20] Edelstein's otherwise superb volume does not, in my view,
come to terms effectively with defaults. Also, he does not deal with
the effects of foreign investment on the decline of British agriculture
(which disturbed Clough and Cole); indeed, few economists have
been worried over the contraction of British agriculture; most saw
(and see) cheaper food imports as enhancing rather than slowing
British economic growth. The arguments of the classical economists
that the small island of Great Britain would gain from importing food
seem difficult to refute.[21]

The latest contribution to the debate on the effects of capital exports
on the British economy, 1870–1914, is the thoughtful essay by Sidney
Pollard, which alas is general rather than specific to British investment in the United States. Pollard points out that by the early 1870s
British returns on overseas investments typically exceeded capital
outflow, with the positive return benefiting Britain. Yet an evaluation
of benefits and costs must take more into account. He suggests that
foreign direct investment was likely to have been "made more ration-
ally" than portfolio investment, but "since it obeyed different criteria,
such as the strategic securing of markets or raw material sources, or
the by-passing of tariff walls, a calculation of how far this corresponded to the national interest is even more difficult." Pollard ex-
plores various topics, looks at the vulnerability of prior studies, and
casts doubt on "simplistic" answers. He concludes that there is no
clear-cut response to the question of whether the benefits to Britain of
the large capital exports exceeded the costs. He does, however, suggest that in the short run there may well have been gains, although
there may have been a sacrifice of the future.[22]

In sum, while over the years a substantial literature has appeared
on both the favorable and the negative features of foreign investment
(and in many cases foreign investment in the United States) with
respect to the source-country economy before 1914, the results still
remain inconclusive. My research adds to these analyses in several
respects. First, on the "political issues": Although there were numerous bilateral diplomatic discussions before 1914 on topics related to
foreign investments, although political considerations on rare occasions took precedent over economic ones in decisions to invest in
America, and although French loans during the American Revolution
certainly cemented political ties between the two countries, what
should impress the reader of this book is how little "political" ques-

tions need figure in a discussion of the pros and cons to the home country of capital exports to America. Political matters from the capital exporters' standpoint seem of little relevance to our discussion.

On economic impacts, my research strongly supports Edelstein's view that capital outflows to America from Britain did not come at the expense of British industry. I found, in fact, that many of the portfolios of British industrial companies came to contain American railroad securities;[23] British industry *itself* invested its surplus in American securities! Likewise, multinational enterprises did not make foreign direct investment at the expense of domestic investments—as I will argue below.

A third new point that emerges from my study relates to the significance of information channels and of managerial influence and control. Crucial to success in American investment—in the case of foreign portfolio as well as direct investments—were experience and knowledge. Losses in the colonial era probably exceeded gains because of the lack of information and the difficulty of administering businesses over long distance with very slow communication. By the nineteenth century information channels improved. Losses at any time came to be more than offset by gains—*if* investors were well informed. There was a "learning by doing," an accumulation of learning experience, a "learning effect." Individuals and financial intermediaries, because of good information and experience, could time their investments to take advantage of opportunities and to buy low and sell high. Such investors did extremely well. The institutional channels to monitor investments, once made, were vital to the realization of returns. In many ways, this explains why British portfolio investors in America tended to be more successful than the French—their sources of information were better developed.[24]

Along the same lines, the principal post-1914 *appraisals* of the pros and cons of pre-1914 capital outflows (Keynes's 1924 article and Pollard's 1985 one were exceptions) have not made the distinction between foreign portfolio and direct investments, or they have dealt exclusively with portfolio stakes.[25] In the years of the largest foreign investments in America, 1875–1914, more foreign direct investments were made than most subsequent commentators have recognized. Numerous foreign investments in the United States carried with them the potentials for direction from abroad. The ability to control, when exercised, reduced (although it did not eliminate) losses.

In the United States two distinct categories of foreign direct investment coexisted. One involved investments that carried the potentials of control but had a fragile, negligible, sometimes virtually nonexistent "home office" organization with little capacity beyond that of raising capital. These companies had no experience in operations at home to project abroad. In the United States these direct investors experienced a high rate of failure and poor performance records. In these cases, none of the key features that we associate with modern multinational enterprise was present; that is, the company investing abroad did not have technology, knowledge, and other company-specific advantages. The promoter often lost interest after the promotion. Included were many of the investments in U.S. mines, cattle ranches, and breweries. This was largely the British way, albeit there were in addition many British direct investments of the second type. The second type of direct investment, akin to today's multinational enterprise, provided the extension into the United States of a company and its operating organizational talents—its own "package" of skills, experience, technology, management, and marketing experience. This clearly became the German way of making foreign direct investments. The home base of multinational firms that successfully invested in the United States seems to have been strengthened, since the stimulant of international expansion extended the firm's organization, offered new challenges, and pressed the enterprise to respond to new demands.[26] Many of these companies proved very profitable, contributing to the parent company's strength. Because a national economy is made up of firms, the latter's increased viability enhances that economy (more profits for national investment, taxation, and distribution to stockholders); although the synchronization is far from perfect, the social benefits seem coincident with the private ones.[27] These direct investments in the United States appear to have had (with some exceptions) a highly favorable impact on the "headquarters country."[28]

In the case of the second type of foreign direct investment in the years 1875–1914, moreover, the decisionmaker was rarely faced with the choice of whether to invest domestically or to invest abroad; my research indicates that if there were opportunities at home, British, German, or other firms always invested there first. The investment in America in a sales network to reach the U.S. market was typically made because of the potential in that market—or if there was an investment in manufacturing, because exports were not feasible. This was not an alternative to domestic projects. As for these multinational enterprises, my findings indicate that no plant was built or acquired by such foreign investors in the United States in the pre–World War I years when a comparable one could have been expanded or built in England, Scotland, Belgium, France, Germany, or elsewhere "at home" to serve as effectively *the U.S. market*. Although it is extremely difficult to evaluate the employment consequences within a home nation of such investments, it does seem evident that since the newly built or acquired American plants were not alternatives to source-country ones, these direct investments cannot be said to "deprive" the home country of employment.[29] As for backward vertical integration by the multinational firm in the United States, these investments were to obtain raw materials not available or not as cheap in the home country. They often lowered the costs of raw materials for European producers.

As noted, both Keynes in his 1924 article and Clough and Cole in their textbook made the point that if Britishers invested in a railroad at home and one abroad and both went bankrupt, in the first case at least the home nation had the railroad (the physical property), whereas when the investment was made abroad both the home nation and the investor lost. This certainly applied to portfolio interests. Yet even when the large German multinational-enterprise-type stakes in the United States were lost during World War I, German firms still retained the managerial know-how, the skills, the knowledge, the technology, and the abilities (the package that went with the direct investments); these intangible "firm-specific" assets that accompanied the multinational-enterprise-type direct investment could serve as a basis for German revival after World War I.[30] In short, if management was intimately associated with the foreign investment, the effects on the source country might well be more positive.

The fourth item that emerges from my research is that in discussing foreign investment's impact on the source nation, it is useful to separate portfolio from direct investments and also to distinguish between the two types of direct investment. The channels of capital export are significant. My evidence confirms Pollard's suggestion that because foreign portfolio and direct investment (and the two types of direct investment) conformed to different institutional patterns, the ways they affected home-nation interests were unlikely to be identical. Although I cannot provide statistics on the relationship between foreign portfolio and direct investment capital outflows, my study reveals the lacuna in the 1870–1914 literature in this regard.

My contribution to the debate of the effects on the source country of the pre-1914 capital outflows is more one of adding new data and new insights than of providing definitive answers. Obviously the experiences with investment in one country—the United States—cannot be said to be typical of all foreign investments. Likewise, clearly there was a wide variety of impacts from individual foreign portfolio and direct investments in the United States at different times on different investors and their home economies; whereas I have found that in general what was good for the investor was good for the home economy, there were some cases in which this was not true. Yet the complexities recognized and acknowledged, I will try to clear up the confusion and concentrate on the "net effects"—glossing over the details and focusing on essentials. Probably, as noted, in the colonial years losses to British long-term investors in America exceeded gains. In 1776–1875, my materials suggest that gains to investor nations from their nationals' U.S. interests may have surpassed losses—but good systematic evidence remains wanting; the more knowledgeable the investor, the better he did. As for the era of the greatest investments, here, too, numerous ambiguities remain, but my research leads me to conclude that the data, in general, point to net benefits of the foreign investment in the United States to all the capital-exporting countries.[31] What is important and of relevance to this study is that by 1875–1914 the investments in the United States were sufficiently large that they had economic impacts on the capital-exporting countries. Investment *in* America was a significant element in the general world-wide international investment panorama.

Whereas numerous articles and monographs have dealt with aspects of foreign investment in the United States before 1914,[32] no analysis has been made—from the vantage point of time—of the overall benefits and costs of foreign investments to the United States in the years before World War I. Rather than reviewing others' work (as I rapidly did on the capital-exporting nations), I will now turn directly to the available evidence, drawing when appropriate on various scholars' scattered conclusions;[33] at the same time, I will take into account contemporary responses to the foreign stakes. I will not set up counterfactuals (alternative development paths), but instead will try to determine on the basis of available information the principal favorable and negative aspects of both foreign portfolio and direct investment.

Obviously the benefits and costs differed by period, because the types and amounts of foreign investments in America changed. As we have seen, in the colonial period direct investors from abroad provided a basis for settlement (with the chartered companies), offered trading and shipping services, and developed major iron works. The costs—remittances of profits overseas—were small (frequently there was no profit to be remitted).

After independence the benefits of the overseas investments—now mainly portfolio investments—were very much in evidence. The Revolution was financed by foreign, principally French, loans; Alexander Hamilton's fiscal program was aided by Dutch finance; the purchase of the Louisiana Territory was made possible by foreign borrowings. On the other hand, Americans seemed "dependent." In 1803 fully 56 percent of the federal debt was held abroad. Sixty-two percent of the capital of America's largest business enterprise, the Bank of the United States, was in foreign hands. Thirty-five percent of state bank shares and 33 percent of all corporate shares were owned by European investors.

The dependency proved not to be oppressive. The percentage of the federal debt held abroad fluctuated over time; but never through their holdings were foreign investors able to control U.S. public policy. Indeed, although there were constant concerns about "dependency," America's federal debt was—after 1795, throughout the period covered by this book—always denominated in dollars. This is very important. In less-developed countries, the national debt has often been stated in the currency of the foreign creditor, which creates by definition an obligation out of the debtor's national monetary authority's control.

Moreover, in America the use of foreign capital to fill domestic banking needs was reduced radically over time. Foreign investment in domestic banking remained important only until the demise of the Second Bank of the United States in the early 1840s; then from a percentage standpoint, the role of foreign investment in this sector declined sharply. American domestic banks multiplied to fill the gap. There was no "crowding out" of domestic investors or domestic institutions, which came to provide capital for this country's routine commercial banking needs.

As U.S. economic development occurred, naturally it was difficult in the early years to attract foreign capital to unknown American companies. Accordingly, states had fronted for private businesses, raised monies abroad, and channeled these foreign savings into American canals, railroads, and banks. Here again, we are talking about portfolio investments, which went into basic infrastructure. The U.S. cotton boom of the 1830s was aided by these investments. By 1841–42 the greater part of America's sizable state debt was held abroad. Then came the era of defaults. Americans could not pay the costs. British bankers seemed ready to intervene, advocating the assumption of state debts by the federal government. America's "independence" seemed imperiled. It was not. The federal government did *not* assume state obligations; Americans and foreign bankers negotiated. Most foreign investors lost money. Americans paid the price of temporarily diminished access to foreign credit. By the late 1840s, however, new foreign investment was entering the country, and in 1853—based on the earlier obligations—some 58 percent of state debt was still held abroad.

Until about 1875, public securities were the largest sector for foreign investment (although the North had not depended on foreign finance to win the Civil War, after victory seemed assured the federal debt had begun to drift abroad). The return to a de facto gold standard after the war (in 1879) was facilitated by foreign investment. New state debts were incurred during Reconstruction; most of these were repudiated in the early 1870s; the costs of the repudiation were once again an inability of southern states to resume foreign borrowing.

Meanwhile, since the start of America's railroad construction in the 1830s, foreign investors had played a role. In the 1850s American railroad bonds often moved abroad in exchange for imported iron rails. The price was high, but it was preferable to paying with specie that was not available. After the Civil War, markets for the securities of American railroads became well developed abroad; America established its own iron and steel industry. The post–Civil War decades saw new monies flowing into U.S. railroad building, no longer linked with rail sales in the United States. In the years 1875 to 1914 unprecedented sums came from Europe to complete the American railroad network—as Europeans bought the securities of American railroads. Although some railroad investments were direct ones, the vast majority were not. American railroads attracted portfolio investments; American managers built the railroad system.

Foreign investments in the private sector far exceeded public sector investments from 1875 to 1914, with railroads luring the most monies. The benefits from this foreign capital were enormous, as railroad lines spread over the vast geographical span of the nation. America's domestic financial resources were inadequate to fill the needs; thus foreign capital supplemented U.S. savings. The availability of the foreign funds helped to bring down interest rates. All the major American railroads looked to foreign finance.

There were, of course, costs in using the foreign capital. Foreigners expected interest on their bonds and dividends on their stock (but so did American investors). Railroad financing in the United States was unquestionably fraught with abuses, yet Americans were as responsible as the foreign promoters and investors (and probably more so). Had foreign *and* U.S. investors looked to long-run rather than short-run returns, Albro Martin might not have concluded (for example) that Henry Villard and the foreign investors he attracted damaged the development of the Northern Pacific.[34] The problems were rectified; the Northern Pacific and other transcontinental railroads were built; and if the process was not as neat, orderly, or efficient as the historian, economist, or for that matter the investor might have liked, to blame the greed of foreign shareholders or bondholders is inappropriate.

Financing growth is not a smooth process anywhere—and was not in the United States. After the Baring Crisis (1890), railroads dependent on London found their sources of funds temporarily cut off, and it hurt; but domestic investment was also periodically curtailed during U.S. business cycles, so this difficulty was not so much a function of dependence on international finance as a characteristic of financial markets. The withdrawal of capital from abroad, though on occasion accenting U.S. downturns, at other times was influenced by conditions exogenous to the U.S. economy (from the Baring Crisis to the need for Boer War financing). Foreign investors, in toto, proved no more fickle than domestic ones. The additions of the foreign investment, however "volatile" the flows, were worthwhile, with benefits sufficient to more than compensate for the frequently erratic course.

Often foreign investors insisted on gold clauses in railroad bonds. They wanted "sound money" in America—and worldwide. The U.S. adherence to a gold standard (after 1879) was, in part, a consequence of America's desire to attract such foreign investment. Until 1898 there was not sufficient gold, and there were hardships in America caused by price declines in the late nineteenth century. Nonetheless, the period was one of real economic growth. The absence of inflation and in fact the presence of deflation helped American exports to become increasingly competitive in world markets. In the late nineteenth century the United States became a significant exporter of manufactured goods, and the U.S. balance of trade in merchandise became (until the 1970s) consistently positive.[35] This meant that adequate gold or foreign exchange was usually available to pay the costs of the foreign investment.

The benefits of the very large foreign portfolio investments were multiple. It is clear that the U.S. railroad system could not have been completed as rapidly had there not been the foreign investment. Linkage effects were formidable. New lands were opened for settlement. Railroads made possible the development of American resources on the frontier, providing the basis for agricultural and mineral sales abroad as well as for the rise in exports of manufactured products. As Ragnar Nurkse has written, the pre–World War I investment of foreign capital led "not only to an enlargement of the export sector itself but also to the building of overhead facilities [especially railroads] essential to the expansion of domestic activities as well."[36]

The portfolio investments from abroad in railroads not only financed the railroad construction, opened new lands, and developed new agriculture and mining areas, but they also had an additional crucial impact on the development of the nation's infrastructure.

American financial intermediaries (especially private banks) cooperated with British merchant banks, Dutch financial houses, and German banks in providing the required capital. In the process, U.S. private banks acquired experience in finance, a professional expertise, which would contribute importantly to the creation of New York City as a financial center.

While the railroad investments—mainly portfolio ones—were of great benefit to America, there were many other foreign investments in this country in the years 1875–1914 that were also of great significance in the nation's economic progress. As the new lands became available for settlement, overseas investors acquired land. In retrospect, it seems apparent that, notwithstanding the contemporary public outcry against alien land ownership, foreign investors were never, as one historian put it, "any great menace to the land poor of the United States."[37] The country did not hand its land to "foreigners." The rhetoric that I reviewed in Chapter 16 must be recognized and dismissed as proceeding from instinct rather than from fact. The foreign investment in American land—direct investment—was sizable, but not relative to the total amount of land, and more important, foreign investors in large part used their land acquisitions for productive purposes; they were not "mere" speculators.

Foreign direct investors became active in developing American mines and introducing new technology in the processing of mineral resources. Foreign direct investors expanded foreign markets for the output of America's mines, as well as for the output of America's farms. Were these "exploitive" stakes? In some sense they probably were. As noted, Americans complained, perhaps with legitimacy, that foreign buyers lowered the price for American copper (for example) in European markets. On the other hand, the foreign traders increased substantially the volume sold abroad, which may well have offset the lower prices. Revenues are based on both price and quantity sold, and if a fall in price serves to raise the volume exported faster than the price declines (that is, if foreign demand is elastic), then revenues will rise. Today, demand for primary products tends to be inelastic. It is not clear that this was the case in 1870–1914. Moreover, while foreign direct investors were important in handling certain exports (from copper to lead to zinc and also from grain to tobacco leaf), Americans also participated. The benefits in enlarging the country's foreign trade seem to have more than counterbalanced any resulting drop in prices for American exports. A major foreign oil company (Royal Dutch-Shell) entered the United States in 1912—as crude oil producer and marketer. This was an investment not for export but for U.S. consumption. The firm became an important one in this country. In 1914 its first significant U.S. refinery was under construction.

If some foreign direct investments served to raise America's international trade in and output of primary products in the years 1875–1914, a large number of foreign direct investments created the basis for import substitution in many industries. Foreign direct investors, for example, were the innovators in the southern iron and steel industry. Although the rewards to the investors were scant, the new industry established was real. The American South benefited.

Tariffs were high from the Civil War to 1913, and behind the tariff walls domestic manufacturing expanded. Foreign direct investors participated in an array of new American industries, introducing and applying advanced technology from abroad. The remarkable aspect of the new entries was their nonobtrusive character. They blended for the most part comfortably into the dynamic, growing economy. They were, however, ubiquitous. From aspirins to alkalies, from rayon to "French process wool," foreign direct investors used new processes and made new products in the United States. They were pioneers in America's nascent chemical industry. Many affiliates of European multinationals not only manufactured but had national sales organizations in America. They were multifunctional enterprises. This was true of Michelin, Hoechst, Orenstein–Arthur Koppel, and numerous others. Many had more than one plant or mill in the United States.

The importance of the foreign direct investors in this country is evident when we realize that in the years 1875–1914 foreign direct investors—albeit for a brief period—ranked first in the new American electrical industry (when Edison General Electric was German controlled), first in American flour production (with Pillsbury-Washburn), first in American mining equipment (with Fraser & Chalmers), in the top four in American meat packing (with Hammond), and at the very pinnacle of America's new radio industry (with Marconi).

Foreign direct investors were, in addition, in first place in American alkali production (Solvay Process Company), rayon production (Courtaulds), thread production (J. & P. Coats), submarine building (Electric Boat), magneto production (Bosch), surgical instruments production (Kny-Scheerer), and cream separator machinery output (AB Separator). They were in the top three in America's small dyestuff production (Bayer); in the leading three in U.S. cotton textile machinery production (Howard & Bullough); and in the top six in American breweries. They were also in front rank in America's ethical drug production, in America's new electrolytic refining, in America's new electrochemical industries, in America's wool and silk production, and in America's chocolate making. From soap to crucible steel to optical products, foreign multinationals were present. This is only a sample. Foreign direct investors were in consumer and producer goods, contributing to America's expanding and extensive industrial output.

Economists have been concerned that foreign capital transfers have led in today's less-developed countries to what has been called "immiserizing growth." The latter occurs under conditions of tariff distortions, in which the inflow of capital from abroad causes immiserization because the country continues to import capital-intensive goods (remaining incompletely specialized), and the country's terms of trade turn against it as export prices drop relative to import prices. "Immiserizing growth" results in declines in welfare because of the deteriorating terms of trade in goods and the loss arising when foreign profits are subtracted in the determination of national income.

Does this apply to the American experience with foreign capital imports in the years 1875–1914? This was a period of tariff distortion, so that condition does hold. What does not fit is that the United States did *not* continue to import capital-intensive goods. Foreign capital created no distortion in the domestic development process and in fact may well have reduced that distortion. Available statistics indicate that America's terms of trade improved in 1869–1913.[38]

American exports rose faster than imports. Foreign direct investors, and domestic ones, took part in import substitution behind the tariff walls.[39] Foreign investment did not "crowd" out domestic industrial investments. While in some industries (thread, for example) there were fewer U.S.-owned plants as a consequence of foreign direct investment,[40] in other industries (alkalies, for instance) foreign direct investment stimulated new U.S. investments—new competitors—in manufacturing. Typically, foreign direct investors, along with domestic ones, raised production in a balanced manner behind American tariff walls. There was real growth, not "immiserizing growth." In addition, and of less importance, not only did America obtain foreign direct investment in the manufacturing sector, but also a number of America's major "industrials" were able to call on foreign money markets to provide for some of their capital needs.

Foreign financial institutions assisted not only in financing U.S. railroads but also in financing American industrials and public utilities. Their direct investments in America were slight compared with their intermediation of portfolio investments. As with railroads, so too with these other securities, especially at the turn of the century and in the early twentieth century, the financing was done in association with New York and Boston banks. That the United States could become in 1919 a leading creditor nation was in no small part due to the learning process and the richness of the experiences gained in *importing* capital in the 1875–1914 period and in prior years. Private American banks acquired sophistication in international finance by cooperating with foreign banking houses in bringing foreign monies to America. The knowledge gained in importing capital came to be used by American financial institutions when they began to lend abroad.

In addition, a number of foreign banks, engaged in financing international commerce, established agencies in New York and aided in the finance of American trade. Likewise, foreign shipping companies and cable companies had direct investments in the United States, once more providing services to American enterprise.

Foreign direct investors in the years 1875–1914 took part in an important fashion in providing Americans with cheaper mortgage monies, better accounting services, and more comprehensive fire and marine insurance. In none of these activities, however, did foreign owners have a monopoly position. In each case American firms sprang up to supplement and to complement the foreign offerings. Often American enterprises were able to copy and replicate the behavior of the foreign firms, which served as models for emerging U.S. businesses.

American economic development was never hampered by the absence of capital; that foreign sources were available assured the nation that capital did not become a constraint on the growth process. By 1914 foreign portfolio and direct investments were present and contributing to the expansion of new economic activity in the industrial East, in the new Niagara Falls power developments, in the Midwest, in the north-central states, in the Southeast, in the Southwest, and in the Far West. No part of the country was excluded. Everywhere, as new development occurred, foreign direct investment in particular participated. The geographical dispersion was impressive.

All of these contributions had costs; the principal ones were that Americans had to pay interest on foreign borrowings and dividends on foreign equity holdings. As in the case of many less-developed countries today, so too U.S. balance-of-payments calculations for the years 1875 to 1914 suggest that the interest and dividends paid to foreigners on their existing investments in this country exceeded new capital inflows.[41] Such calculations (though frequently made in relation to today's less-developed countries) are essentially meaningless. The "tribute" paid abroad (if the figures be accurate), while resented by Americans—who complained vigorously about these costs—did not in fact deprive America of capital. Domestic growth seems to have more than paid for the use of foreign capital. It is not harmful to pay

for foreign investments (and for the accompanying package of business ability when it is foreign *direct* investment) if the benefits exceed
the costs—and this was indeed the case in America as the foreign
investment moved into productive activities. Moreover, in the United
States in this period, rising U.S. exports, as indicated, meant that
interest and dividends could easily be paid out of export earnings,[42]
contemporary anxieties notwithstanding.

With the many roles of foreign investment in America from 1875 to
1914, the question arises, Did foreign investors in this debtor nation
try to dominate America's political life? Did they seek to influence
political decisions to their advantage? Did they act with a flippant
disregard for American law? Frequently today, radical economists
accuse foreign investors of such behavior in less-developed debtor
countries. If there were economic benefits in having foreign investors
present in America, contributing to American economic growth, were
there political costs? Was sovereignty at bay?

Political interventions by foreign investors unquestionably existed.
Britishers made efforts (albeit futile ones) to prevent the passage of
the federal Bland-Allison Act of 1878.[43] Many foreign companies lobbied for low tariffs as they saw their goods excluded. Then once such
a firm made an investment in manufacturing in the United States,
typically it became an advocate of protection, from which it
benefited.[44] English insurance companies spent "a good deal of
money" on the Pacific Coast to counteract the "repugnant" actions of
state legislatures.[45] As noted in Chapter 16, the manager of one
foreign firm even sought (without success) a U.S.-British treaty to
protect foreign direct investors from what he considered the capri-
cious laws passed by state legislatures.[46] Cases existed in which British investors circumvented U.S. law and boasted of it; H. Osborne
O'Hagan wrote that in states with alien land laws that prevented
foreigners from holding real estate, those laws were "got over by
means of a trustee holding the properties."[47]

If, however, I add up the many attempts to influence political
deliberations and evasions of U.S. law, the total seems inconsequential. In the main, American legislation could and did cope with existing or potential (real or imagined)—political and economic—abuses
by foreign investors. Most important foreign investors identified
themselves with their domestic counterparts—and thus presented no
special alien imposition. America's status as an international debtor
never compromised national independence.[48]

Economic benefits were numerous. Political sovereignty was not
sacrificed. Indeed, in evaluating the U.S. experience, I find myself
agreeing with the 1928 comment of Jacob Viner: "From the point of

view of the debtor nation it is difficult to conceive what *economic considerations* of even superficial plausibility could be raised against the free import of capital for *productive purposes.*"[49] In retrospect, the large quantity of contemporary negative responses in America to foreign investment here seems to have been more visceral than rational. The economic benefits far exceeded the costs. The benefits came from both foreign finance (portfolio investments) and foreign direct investments (the presence of foreign-owned and foreign-controlled enterprises).

In fact, America absorbed capital from abroad as no nation had ever done before; foreign portfolio and direct investment entered in unprecedented amounts. It came from Great Britain, Germany, Holland, France, Switzerland, Belgium, and many other countries. By 1875–1914, when the giant influx occurred, the capital went principally into the private sector. European foreign investment in 1913 followed the rule that "to him that hath shall be lent."[50] In no case was this truer than in that of the United States. The country was by far the world's largest debtor nation. In the short term, it benefited. In the long term, the benefits were built upon and retained. Its position as a debtor nation would, in time, provide it the means to become the world's greatest creditor. Foreign capital assisted in the transformation, laying the foundation and helping to create the institutional prerequisites.

Foreign capital opened up American resources—with the huge portfolio investments in railroads and the major direct investments in mining, cattle ranching, and oil wells that followed. Foreign direct investors took part in America's rapid strides in import substitution in a wide range of industrial activities. Foreign multinationals introduced new technology. They offered services from mortgage monies to accounting to fire insurance. Foreign portfolio and direct investors had both an immediate role and a catalytic role in stimulating America's domestic growth. The contributions proved enduring. Foreign portfolio and direct investment had significance in assisting U.S. economic development. The more than $7 billion from abroad invested in the American economy at the eve of the outbreak of war in Europe represented a sum equal to almost 20 percent of the U.S. gross national product in 1914.[51] The benefits derived by the U.S. economy from this sizable foreign investment far surpassed the costs. America in 1875–1914 became the greatest industrial nation in the world. The part played by foreign money and foreign business was material and consequential.

Notes
Bibliography
Index

Notes

1. The Earliest Investments

1. The comprehensive volume by John J. McCusker and Russell R. Menard, *The Economy of British America, 1607–1789* (Chapel Hill: University of North Carolina Press, 1985), 83, notes that "we know almost nothing about long-term investment . . . by British investors in the colonies." The statement is a too-modest one by two well-informed writers. I hope this chapter will contribute to filling the gap.

2. The Crown issued a patent to the two "Virginia Companies," one for the London petitioners and one for the Bristol, Exeter, and Plymouth petitioners. The two were frequently called the "London Company" (or the Virginia Company of London) and the "Plymouth Company" (or the Virginia Company of Plymouth). Later the London Company would be referred to as the Virginia Company. The text of the patent is in William Stith, *History of Virginia*, appendix (1747; rpt. Spartenburg: The Reprint Co., 1965), 1–8.

3. W. R. Scott, *The Constitution and Finance of English, Scottish, and Irish Joint-Stock Companies to 1720*, 3 vols. (Cambridge: Cambridge University Press, 1910–1912). Vols. 1 and 2 are superb on the companies. See also John P. Davis, *Corporations* (1897; rpt. New York: Capricorn, 1961), II, 157–169.

4. The phrase is from the original charter (Stith, *History of Virginia*, appendix). For the actual owners see Theodore K. Rabb, *Enterprise and Empire* (Cambridge, Mass.: Harvard University Press, 1967).

5. I have found particularly useful Charles M. Andrews, *The Colonial Period of American History* (New Haven: Yale University Press, 1934), I, and Wesley Frank Craven, *Dissolution of the Virginia Company* (New York: Oxford University Press, 1932). Wesley Frank Craven, *The Virginia Company of London, 1606–1624* (Williamsburg: Virginia's 350 Anniversary Celebration Corporation, 1957), is a short history. Invaluable are the four volumes of the Virginia Company's published records: Susan Myra Kingsbury, *The Records of the Virginia Company of London*, 4 vols. (Washington, D.C.: Government Printing Office, 1906–1935). The first two volumes contain the Court Records (1619–1624); the last two contain original papers of the company (1607–1626).

6. After 1609 it was known as the Treasurer and Company of Adventurers and Planters of the City of London for the first Colony of Virginia, commonly called the Virginia Company (Stith, *History of Virginia*, appendix, 8–22).

7. Sir Thomas Smith was a founder of the Levant and East India companies and in 1600 was Governor of both. See Davis, *Corporations*, II, 88, 115n, and Rabb, *Enterprise*, 125. He was a member of the Royal Council, which headed the Virginia Company, 1607–1609 (Andrews, *The Colonial Period*, I, 85).

8. Edward D. Neill, *History of the Virginia Company of London* (Albany, N.Y.: Joel Munsell, 1869), 65.

9. Robert E. Tindall, *Multinational Enterprise* (Dobbs Ferry, N.Y.: Oceania, 1975), 4, makes this point. See also Jan de Vries, *The Economy of Europe in an Age of Crisis* (Cambridge: Cambridge University Press, 1975), 132.

10. The Society of Particular Adventurers for Traffique with Virginia.

11. Stith, *History of Virginia*, 171, and Andrews, *The Colonial Period*, I, 127.

12. Andrews, *The Colonial Period*, I, 128–130, 132.

13. Craven, *The Dissolution*, 51; Scott, *Joint-Stock Companies*, II, 257, 258; and Stith, *History of Virginia*, 186. Scott gives Sandys' estimate at £66,666; his own estimate was £67,124. Stith gives the high figure of £80,000. See also Scott, *Joint-Stock Companies*, II, 287, for £80,000 spent during Smith's administration (which includes the Magazine and particular plantations).

14. Craven, *The Dissolution*, 35, 112, 82, and Kingsbury, *Records*, I, 27. By contrast, Scott, *Joint-Stock Companies*, II, 268, sees Sir Thomas Smith as a man of integrity.

15. Kingsbury, *Records*, I, 212.

16. Ibid., 293–294, 303.

17. Craven, *The Dissolution*, 96–104, is excellent on Sir Edwin Sandys' projects.

18. A large number of the shareholders (333) in the Virginia Company sat in the House of Commons. See Rabb, *Enterprise*, 127. King James I had in 1604 issued a pamphlet, *A Counterblaste to Tobacco*, that claimed smoking was a sin. Nonetheless, tobacco was commonly used in Britain by 1614. See B. W. E. Alford, *W. D. and H. O. Wills* (London: Methuen, 1973), 5.

19. Neill, *History*, 323, 394.

20. Andrews, *The Colonial Period*, I, 168–169, 175, 132, 139.

21. Stith, *History of Virginia*, 330. Scott, *Joint-Stock Companies*, II, 286–287, puts the total between £160,000 and £170,000!

22. Andrews, *The Colonial Period*, I, 178. David W. Galenson, "The Rise and Fall of Indentured Servitude in the Americas: An Economic Analysis," *Journal of Economic History*, 44 (March 1984): 2–6, has a fascinating discussion of what he calls the "critical economic problem" facing the early investors in the Virginia Company—that of recruiting and motivating a labor force.

23. The full new name of the successor to the Plymouth Company was the "Council established at Plymouth in the County of Devon, for the Planting. Ruling, Ordering, and Governing of New England in America." It was created by patent, Nov. 3, 1620.

24. Andrews, *The Colonial Period*, I, is excellent on the Plymouth Company and its successors. On Peirce and Associates' first patent, see Kingsbury, *Records*, I, 303. See also Scott, *Joint-Stock Companies*, II, 306–311.

25. The corporate name was the Governor and Company of the Mattachusets Bay in Newe-England (or, more commonly, the Massachusetts Bay Company).

26. On the Massachusetts Bay Company, see Andrews, *The Colonial Period*, I, and Frances Rose-Troup, *The Massachusetts Bay Co.* (New York: Grafton Press, 1930). The original corporate charter was voided in 1684.

27. Carlo Cipolla, *Before the Industrial Revolution* (New York: W. W. Norton, 1976), 247–256.

28. De Vries, *The Economy*, 130–132.

29. Van Cleaf Bachman, *Peltries as Plantations: The Economic Policies of the Dutch West*

India Company in New Netherland, 1623–1639 (Baltimore: Johns Hopkins University Press, 1969), 11–24.

30. De Vries, *The Economy*, 132–134, 137, and C. R. Boxer, *The Dutch Seaborne Empire* (New York: Alfred A. Knopf, 1970), 25, 48–52.

31. Backman, *Peltries*, 27.

32. Ibid., 55.

33. Ibid., 93.

34. Samuel Eliot Morison, *History of the American People* (New York: Oxford University Press, 1965), 75, and Bachman, *Peltries*, 101–119, 151. See also William Chazanof, "Land Speculation in Eighteenth Century New York," in *Business Enterprise in Early New York*, ed. Joseph R. Frese and Jacob Judd (Tarrytown, N.Y.: Sleepy Hollow Restorations, 1979), 56; and best of all, Oliver A. Rink, *Holland on the Hudson* (Ithaca, N.Y.: Cornell University Press, 1986), passim.

35. Morison, *History*, 77, and Bachman, *Peltries*, 117, 163–164.

36. On early French business in America, see W. J. Eccles, *France in America* (New York: Harper & Row, 1972), 87, 89, 161 (quoted passage), 163, 166, 228–229, 246; N. M. Surrey, *Commerce of Louisiana during the French Regime, 1699–1763* (New York: Columbia University Press, 1916); J. Thomas Scharf, *History of Saint Louis City and County* (Philadelphia: Louis H. Everts, 1883), I, 53–54 (on the activities of the Company of the West and its successor in the new world and on the founding of New Orleans, 1718); Shepard B. Clough and Richard T. Rapp, *European Economic History*, 3rd ed. (New York: McGraw-Hill, 1978), 190–191, 199–201; and Shepard B. Clough and Charles W. Cole, *Economic History of Europe* (Boston: D. C. Heath, 1941), 296–299. Apparently there was an attempt to raise silk worms in Louisiana, and mulberry trees were actually planted, but all this came to naught. W. C. Wyckoff, *Silk Manufacture in the United States* (New York: n.p., 1883), 19–20. The company provided currency and the start of a rudimentary banking system. See Stephen A. Caldwell, *A Banking History of Louisiana* (Baton Rouge: Louisiana State University Press, 1935), 21–22.

37. Bachman, *Peltries*, 153, writes that in 1638 the Dutch West India Company's directors were not inclined to abandon New Netherland, although the company had "hitherto experienced losses."

38. Adam Smith, *Wealth of Nations* (1776; rpt. New York: Modern Library, 1937), 347 (quoted passage); McCusker and Menard, *The Economy*, 192; and Stuart Bruchey, *Colonial Merchants* (New York: Harcourt, Brace & World, 1966), 119–122 (the quotation is from p. 119). The best book on mercantile activity in the Chesapeake region is Jacob M. Price, *Capital and Credit in British Overseas Trade: The View from the Chesapeake, 1700–1776* (Cambridge, Mass.: Harvard University Press, 1980). Price gives details on the specific British merchants participating. See also J. H. Soltow, "Scottish Traders in Virginia, 1750–1775," *Economic History Review*, 2nd ser., 12 (Aug. 1959), esp. 85–89, and *Transcripts of Loyalists Claims*, New York Public Library, esp. LIX, 429–463, and XXXVII, 333, 351–355. On Jefferson's estimates see Price, *Capital and Credit*, 5–6, and Allan Nevins, *The American States during and after the Revolution, 1775–1789* (1924; rpt. New York: Angustus M. Kelley, 1969), 337. For additional bibliography on Virginians' debts to the British, see Peter J. Coleman, *Debtors and Creditors in America* (Madison: State Historical Society of Wisconsin, 1974), 199n. Alice Hanson Jones, *Wealth of a Nation to Be* (New York: Columbia University Press, 1980), 112, found in using American probate records that business inventories in the South were far less (one-fifth of those per capita) than in the North. Her explanation related to "factors who as agents of British merchants . . . furnished goods to shopkeepers or retailers on credit terms similar to credits allowed them by their British principals" seems only partially explanatory. Could it be that these business inventories remained the properties of British mer-

chants and thus are not reflected in colonial probate records, and "the credit" represents an "investment" from abroad? Thus the operative explanation lies not in the credit terms, but rather in the ownership of the inventories.

39. Pieter van Winter, *American Finance and Dutch Investment, 1780–1805,* 2 vols. (New York, Arno Press, 1977), 8, and Scharf, *History of Saint Louis,* 61–78.

40. When the British government made an effort to reintroduce vestiges of the old pattern, it proved impossible. As is well known, in May 1773 Parliament gave the East India Company permission to be its own exporter of tea to the American colonies (eliminating middlemen). New England merchants denounced this "illegal monopoly," protesting that the East India Company planned to obtain exclusive rights to *all* colonial commerce, not only tea. The result was the Boston Tea Party (Morison, *History,* 203–204).

41. Ibid., 84, and John Eardley Wilmot, *Historical View of the Commission for Enquiring into the Losses, Services, and Claims of the American Loyalists at the Close of the War Between Great Britain and Her Colonies in 1783* (London: J. Nichols, Son, & Bentley, 1815), 92–93.

42. Jacob E. Cooke, *Tench Coxe and the Early Republic* (Chapel Hill: University of North Carolina Press, 1978), 3–5, 9. (When Coxe's son settled, as did *his* heirs, the overseas investment became American; it was not at origin.) Conversation with Edwin Perkins, March 15, 1986, and Russell R. Menard to Wilkins, April 28, 1986, on headrights.

43. *Loyalist Transcripts,* LVIII, 197–204; XXXIV, 53–87; LIII, 437–474. The Earl of Dunmore claimed ownership of 51,000 acres on Lake Champlain, as well as land in Virginia. Edwin J. Perkins, *The Economy of Colonial America* (New York: Columbia University Press, 1980), 61, describes the Virginia properties of William Fitzhugh, whom he calls a "great planter." How humble they seem when Fitzhugh's 1,000 acres in Virginia are compared with Dunmore's more than 5,500 in that colony, and when Fitzhugh's thirteen-room home is compared with Dunmore's twenty-five-room "palace." Lord Dunmore had a library of 1,300 volumes, three organs, and a harpsichord. Of course, that was in 1776, whereas Fitzhugh's properties are described as of 1686. Nonetheless, the contrast is vivid.

44. Nevins, *American States,* 359, 17.

45. Clarence Walforth Alvord, *The Mississippi Valley in British Politics* (1916; rpt. New York: Russell & Russell, 1959), I, 213.

46. See Shaw Livermore, *Early American Land Comanies* (New York: Commonwealth Fund, 1939), 79, and similarly, Alvord, *The Mississippi Valley,* I, 95, 321, for the American-initiated Mississippi Company, whose representative was to secure the cooperation of "prominent Englishmen," and the Illinois Company, wherein Benjamin Franklin was to add the names of Englishmen likely to aid the undertaking.

47. Sir William Johnson, *Papers* (Albany: University of the State of New York, 1953), XI, 3, 648 (Hasenclever's speculations; Sir William Johnson's land). See also Henry A. Homes, "Notice of Peter Hasenclever," paper read before the Albany Institute, April 7, 1874 (Albany, N.Y.: Joel Munsell, 1875), 6–7.

48. C. K. Hobson, *The Export of Capital* (London: Constable, 1914), 88.

49. Smith, *Wealth of Nations,* 157–158. Might it be also that men in America had the ability and interest in developing these plantations? The comment is associated with the issue of "settlers." Britishers who went to the West Indies often saw Britain as home, whereas those who went to the American colonies frequently remained as settlers, giving up their British residence. This would suggest also that the land obtained by British merchants and shippers as headrights was resold to or became owned by residents in the colonies.

50. John Graham went from England to Georgia in 1753 and embarked in trade in partnership with his brother and John Clarke. The latter resided in London. Graham on his own account became a rice planter. See *Loyalist Transcripts*, XXXIV, 197.

51. Alvord, *The Mississippi Valley*, I, 112–114 and passim.

52. See *Loyalist Transcripts*, hearings in London. Some of the claims were undoubtedly exaggerated, but even taking into account the exaggeration, there were clearly large interests. I cannot give a good figure, but later will discuss some of the largest specific claims. I have made no mention of non-British land investments in the thirteen colonies. These appear to have been negligible, because it is doubtful that non-British investors could by law bequeath American land. Non-British *immigrants* to colonial America sought naturalization to assure their own and their heirs' title to land. See Charles H. Sullivan, "Alien Land Laws: A Re-evaluation," *Temple Law Quarterly*, 36 (1962): 15n, 27–28. I also exclude landholdings of individuals who settled in America.

53. Livermore, *Early Land Comapnies*, 42, makes the point that in terms of business organization, the company's subordinate position vis-à-vis the Massachusetts Bay Company was similar to that of the Magazine vis-à-vis the Virginia Company.

54. Historians write that this was because no expense was spared. It was probably also because the equipment had to be imported, and the lack of market meant overcapacity and thus high unit costs.

55. On this venture, see E. N. Hartley, *Ironworks on the Saugus* (Norman: University of Oklahoma Press, 1957), and Howard Corning, *The First Iron Works in America—1645* (New York: American Iron and Steel Institute, 1928), 1–11. Nathaniel B. Shurtleff, ed., *Records of the Governor and Company of Massachusetts Bay in New England* (Boston: William White, 1853), II, 61–62, 81–82, 103–104, 125–128, has the basic documents. See also James Moore Swank, *History of the Manufacture of Iron in All Ages* (Philadelphia: American Iron and Steel Association, 1892), 108–113, for background.

56. Victor S. Clark, *History of Manufactures in the United States* (Washington, D.C.: Carnegie Institution, 1929), I, 173, and Alexander Spotswood, *Official Letters* (Richmond: Virginia Historical Society, 1832), I, xiii (Spotswood's ties with Robert Cary, merchant in England), 20 (start of iron industry in 1714 with German workers), 20–21, 41 (plans), II, 144 (description of Cary).

57. Especially useful on Spotswood's activity are data from his 1710–1713 correspondence published in the *American Iron and Steel Association Bulletin*, 27 (June 28, 1893): 195.

58. Principio Company records abound. They exist in the New York Public Library—NYPL (1723–1769), the Maryland Historical Society Library—MHSL (1723–1730), the Delaware Historical Society Library—DHSL (1724–1784), and the British Museum—BM, Add Mss 29600, f. 1–46 (1725–1776). Likewise, I have used the *Transcripts of Loyalists Claims*, NYPL. In addition, there exist Michael Warren Robbins, "The Principio Company: Iron Making in Colonial Maryland, 1720–1781," Ph.D. diss., George Washington University, 1972; William G. Whitely [mistake for Henry Whitely, corrected in the third article], "Principio Company," *Pennsylvania Magazine of History and Biography*, 11 (1887): 63–68, 190–198, 288–295; and Earl Chapin May, *Principio to Wheeling, 1715–1945* (New York: Harper & Bros., 1945), 1–53. All three of these authors wrote on the Principio Company from primary data. Although May's book has no footnotes, I have been told that much of what he used was in the Wheeling Steel Company files and was destroyed when Wheeling Steel merged with Pittsburgh Steel (Forrest H. Kirkpatrick, Wheeling, W. Va., to Mira Wilkins, Oct. 20, 1978). I used May, *Principio*, 1–13, as a source for the 1715–1720 background, but with much uneasiness. In their memorials for claims relating to revolutionary losses, the then British owners of the Principio Company pushed back

its origins only to 1720, when Joshua Gee and others entered into articles of part-nership by the name of the Principio Company for the purpose of purchasing lands and erecting iron works for making pig and bar iron. See Memorial of William Pellatt et al., Dec. 29, 1783, and Memorial of May 1786 in *Loyalist Transcripts*, XXXVI, 361, 365. The predecessor company—according to May, *From Principio to Wheeling*, 8—was Farmer & Co. Robbins, "The Principio Company," 190, dates the origins of the venture from 1720 and says nothing about Farmer & Co.; he assumed the iron exported from Maryland in 1718 did not come from the Principio works (ibid., 14). James A. Mulholland, *A History of Metals in Colonial America* (University: University of Alabama Press, 1981), which I read after this chapter had been completed, notes (p. 62) the uneasy political relations between Sweden and England (1714–1718), including the temporary suspension of trade in 1717–18 (p. 62). It is little wonder that British ironmasters were seeking alternative sources of supply.

59. It is correspondence with England that begins the now-existing excellent record collections.

60. William Chetwynd to John England, Feb. 9, 1723 [surely 1724], Principio Papers (PP), NYPL.

61. William Russell, Birmingham, to William Chetwynd, Feb. 27, 1725, BM, Add Mss 29600, f. 1, and ibid., April 17, 1725, Add Mss 29600, f. 3.

62. William Chetwynd to John England, Sept. 19, 1725, MHS, Ms. Coll. 669. On the New Jersey mines of the 1720s, see also J. S. Davis, *Essays in the Earlier History of American Corporations* (Cambridge, Mass.: Harvard University Press, 1917), I, 93. In addition, see William Chetwynd to England, Oct. 5, 1725, BM, Add Mss 29600, f. 5. There is no evidence that England expanded in the "Jerseys"—and it is very clear that the Principio Company itself confined its production to Maryland and Virginia.

63. See, for example, Chetwynd to England, Aug. 19, 1726, BM, Add Mss 29600, f. 6, and Chetwynd to England, Nov. 9, 1726, PP, NYPL.

64. William Chetwynd, John Wightwick, and William Russell, "Orders and Regu-lations for the Better Manageing and Carrying on the Companys Affairs," Jan. 29, 1727, PP, NYPL.

65. May, *Principio to Wheeling*, 43.

66. The Crowley Iron Works imported iron from Sweden and America and man-ufactured anchors, cannons, hoes, spades, axes, hooks, and chains. Arthur Young, *Northern Tour* (1768), III, 9–11, cited in J. L. Hammond and Barbara Hammond, *The Rise of Modern Industry* (New York: Harcourt, Brace, 1926), 135n. See Keach Johnson, "The Baltimore Company Seeks English Markets," in *American Economic History*, ed. Stanley Cobden and Forest G. Hill (Philadelphia: J. B. Lippincott, 1966), 80–81, on Crowley purchases from the Principio Company in the 1730s. There is a history of the Crowley works: M. W. Flinn, *Men of Iron* (Edinburgh: At the University Press, 1962); regrettably, it adds little on the relationship between the Crowleys and the Principio Works, but 1769 accounts of Principio Company, PP, NYPL, do include Crowley & Co. entries, so there seems to have been a long-term relationship. Robbins, "Principio Company," 214, found that the largest purchaser in early 1730 was "Lord Foley, . . . a prominent forgemaster in the West Midlands."

67. Joshua Gee, *The Trade and Navigation of Great Britain Considered* (London, 1729), 68–69. The Gee volume was reprinted in 1730, 1731, 1738, and 1750 (and subsequently). The 1750 text has the exact same passage (p. 73) as quoted from the 1729 edition. Gee actually hoped the colonial iron would supply British export markets, since "what is Sold for Abroad would be remitted Home, and add as much certain Riches to the Nation, as if it was dug out of a Silver Mine in our Plantations, and sent us Home directly" (ibid., 1729 ed., 69). There is, however, no evidence that the Principio Com-

pany exported to the "Coast of Africa, the Mediterranean, Turkey, Italy, Portugal, and even the East-Indies" as Gee had hoped.

68. See Brinley Thomas, "Towards an Energy Interpretation of the Industrial Revolution," *Atlantic Economic Journal*, 8 (March 1980): 4, on British iron imports. Thomas does not note the British attempts to invest in American iron to substitute for the Swedish product. Robbins, "Principio Company," 208–209, says the 1750 act dropped the tariff on pig iron and (for London only) on bar iron; in 1757 the duty-free entry of *bar* iron was permitted at all English ports. The restrictions of the 1750 legislation had no impact on the Principio Company (ibid., 210).

69. Swank, *History of the Manufacture of Iron*, 250–251.

70. May, *Principio to Wheeling*, 46–53. For some of Russell's letters to England (1768–1769 and 1771–1776), see correspondence in BM and NYPL.

71. Aubrey G. Land, "Genesis of a Colonial Fortune: David Dulany of Maryland," in *American Economic History*, ed. Cobden and Hill, 65–66; May, *Principio to Wheeling*, 8; and Robbins, "Principio Company," 275–280 (Stephen Onion). Onion married William Russell's daughter, which made him a brother-in-law to the first Thomas Russell (Johnson, "The Baltimore Company," in *American Economic History*, ed. Cobden and Hill, 72, 79–81, 85, 88).

72. Memorials of John Ewer and Ann Russell, *Loyalist Transcripts*, XXXVI, 447-485, and XXXVII, 311–327, and Thomas Russell II to Principio Company, Dec. 24, 1772, BM, Add Mss 29600, f. 35. See also Robbins, "Principio Company," 33.

73. The best material on Hasenclever is his autobiographical defense. [Peter Hasenclever], *The Remarkable Case of Peter Hasenclever* (London, 1773). There is a 291-page biography of Hasenclever by Rektor Christian Gottlieb Glauber, published in 1794 in Landeshut (Schlesien); I am indebted to Dr. Dascher, Director of Archives, Stiftung Westfälisches Wirtschaftarchiv, for directing my attention to this work. A second biography, by Adolf Hasenclever, *Peter Hasenclever aus Remscheid-Ehringhausen*, was published in Berlin in 1922. The Scottish Record Office, Buccieuch Muniments (G.D. 224), has a 1765 letter from Hasenclever to Charles Townsend, describing his iron manufacturing in America. On Hasenclever see also Clark, *History of Manufactures*, I, 174; Herman Krooss and Charles Gilbert, *American Business History* (Englewood Cliffs, N.J.: Prentice-Hall, 1972), 41; Davis, *Essays*, I, 93; Irene D. Neu, "Hudson Valley Extractive Industries before 1815," in *Business Enterprise in Early New York*, ed. Frese and Judd, 143–149; and Charles S. Boyer, *Early Forges and Furnaces in New Jersey* (Philadelphia: University of Pennsylvania Press, 1963), 12–25. The Shelburne Papers (49:1) at the William L. Clements Library, University of Michigan, Ann Arbor, contain a seventeen-page manuscript, "Thoughts Concerning America," by Peter Hasenclever (n.d. but after 1766). Here he tells of establishing the House in Cadiz in 1748–49.

74. Information from Dr. Dascher, May 2, 1979.

75. S. D. Chapman of the University of Nottingham found information on the business activities of Hasenclever in the Archives Nationales in Paris (A. N. 57, AQ 108, notebook of 1758–1780) and in the Brant Archives in Amsterdam (Brant Archives 1344, letter dated 1763) (letter from S. D. Chapman to Mira Wilkins, May 28, 1979).

76. Boyer, *Early Forges*, 14; *The Remarkable Case*, 2–3; and Glauber, *Peter Hasenclever*, 37.

77. Glauber, *Peter Hasenclever*, 5–6, Boyer, *Early Forges*, 13, 18–19.

78. Boyer, *Early Forges*, 23–24.

79. John Austin Stevens, *Colonial Records of the New York Chamber of Commerce, 1768–1784* (1867; rpt. New York: Burt Franklin, 1971), pt. 2, 137.

80. Clark, *History of Manufactures*, I, 221.

81. Ibid., 174, and Boyer, *Early Forges*, 14. Boyer (p. 15) writes that the London

stockholders discharged Hasenclever, because of the absence of profits. Hasenclever's London firm, Hasenclever, Seton & Crofts, failed, and in 1770 Hasenclever was declared bankrupt (ibid., 14). Actually, Hasenclever went back to England in November 1766 and stayed there until June 1767, whereupon he returned to America. He left the colonies for the last time in 1769.

82. Peter Hasenclever to Sir William Johnson, New York, Jan. 6, 1768, cited in Clark, *History of Manufactures*, I, 217. A burned portion of this letter was published in *The Papers of Sir William Johnson* (1953), XI, 3–5 misdated January 6, 1764. Clark in the 1920s apparently consulted the original before the fire, and his 1768 date is convincing. Hasenclever, "Thoughts Concerning America," puts forth an articulate plea for free trade and expresses the same sentiments that manufacture would not succeed in America because of cheap, good, and "Plenty" land.

83. Peter Hasenclever to Governor Henry Moore, May 11, 1768, BM, Add Mss 22679, ff. 38–41.

84. Boyer, *Early Forges*, 14, and *The Remarkable Case*, passim. Erskine's response to Hasenclever, *The Remarkable Case* (1773), is in a letter to *The New-York Gazette and Weekly Mercury*, Aug. 9, 1773, reprinted in *New Jersey Archives*, 1st ser., XXVIII, 586–592. Letter from Irene Neu to Mira Wilkins, Jan. 29, 1981 (on J.J. Faesch).

85. Boyer, *Early Forges*, 14–15, 21. A biographical sketch on Erskine appears in *New Jersey Archives*, 2nd ser., I, 114.

86. Davis, *Essays*, I, 93.

87. Clark, *History of Manufactures*, I, 144, 147.

88. On Stiegel's works, see ibid., 106, 169, 209; Krooss and Gilbert, *American Business History*, 40, 69; and Albert Bernhardt Faust, *The German Element in America*, 2 vols. (Boston: Houghton Mifflin, 1909), I, 140–143. Faust also writes of many other German immigrants.

89. Governor Spotswood used German miners (*American Iron and Steel Association Bulletin*, 27 [June 28, 1893]: 195), as of course did Hasenclever, but these Germans were not investors.

90. L. Gittins, "Innovations in Textile Bleaching in Britain," *Business History Review*, 53 (Summer 1979): 194–204. Gittins cites the British legislation: 24 George II, c. 51 (1751).

91. Peter Hasenclever to Sir William Johnson, June 5, 1765, *The Papers of Sir William Johnson*, XI, 773, and letters of Hasenclever, Jan. 19, Feb. 26, March 13, March 31, Aug. 11, Aug. 12, Sept. 30, 1766, in ibid., V, 11–14, 41, 74, 137–138, 344, 245, 384. See also Homes, "Notice of Peter Hasenclever," 1–5. On Jan. 12, 1767, Governor Moore wrote the Board of Trade, London, that "this province [New York] is under very great obligation to him [Hasenclever] for the large sums of money he has laid out here in . . . introducing the valuable manufacture of Iron and Pot Ash." Quoted in Stevens, *Colonial Records*, pt. 2, 137.

92. Gittins, "Innovations," 199–200. Gittins' figures show no imports for 1717, 1737, or 1752. On the other hand, Clark, *History of Manufactures*, I, 11, suggests such trade in the seventeenth century!

93. Mira Wilkins, *The Emergence of Multinational Enterprise: American Business Abroad from the Colonial Era to 1914* (Cambridge, Mass.: Harvard University Press, 1970), chap. 1.

94. This is my own conclusion. Victor S. Clark writes, "Until the very end of the colonial period speculative enterprises in America, including the most important manufacturing undertakings, were financed very largely with English or German money, though occasionally wealthy colonists cooperated in these projects" (*History of Manufactures*, I, 144–147). There is a problem here of definition, for if the Britisher or German settled in America, I call that American investment—since there was no ongoing

English or German claim on American assets. Clark, however, counted an immigrant's capital as "foreign investment." Krooss and Gilbert, *American Business History*, 69, conclude that small manufactories were locally financed, "while the larger ones, notably the iron works, had to depend on European capital, mostly English."

95. Nevins, *American States*, 268.

96. Economic historians dealing with colonial America have tried to use balance-of-payments statistics to ascertain long-term obligations. My experience in studying foreign investment—especially foreign direct investment—has been that balance-of-payments reconstructions cannot effectively capture long-term obligations. Balance-of-payments data can, however, be useful on trade financing—if handled with care.

97. Wilmot, *Historical View of the Commission*, 199.

98. Ibid., 188.

99. William Pellatt made the claim in London on behalf of the then British owners of the Principio Company. See *Loyalist Transcripts*, XXXVI, 361–374. On the compensation, see ibid., I, 248 (Pellatt), 154 (Gee), 106 (Calmell), and 314 (Wright). Maryland had received $240,000 when it sold the property in 1782. For the latter, see Clark, *History of Manufactures*, I, 174. Curiously, the ex-owners of the Nottingham Iron Works (whose claim was smaller, £37,521) received more from the claims commission: £18,560. See Ann Russell (widow) and the Ewer family in *Loyalist Transcripts*, XI, 272, 40.

100. Wilmot, *Historical View of the Commission*, 73, 76, 188. Henry Harford had become a proprietor in Maryland, under the will of Frederick late Lord Baltimore. In 1776 Harford was resident in England, had never visited America, and was still a minor. He claimed his loss was £477,850 sterling. See *Loyalist Transcripts*, XXXV, 547–587, and XI, 166. According to these records, the Penn family's huge claim came to £944,817 sterling (ibid., XI, 252). Thomas Penn, living in England in the 1760s, made large land purchases to add to the Penn family holdings. By contrast, John Penn came to America to govern. On the whole, however, the Penn family had its roots in England (Nevins, *American States*, 7, 9).

101. One should compare the giant awards for lost landed properties with the £8,370 awarded the Cunningham trading houses in Virginia and the £3,405 awarded the Glassford enterprises of Virginia and Maryland (*Loyalist Transcripts*, XI, 112, 158).

102. Gary M. Walton and James F. Shepherd, *The Economic Rise of Early America* (Cambridge: Cambridge University Press, 1979), 107. But remember Jefferson's estimate (attributable to 1776) of $10–$15 million commercial debts of Virginians alone—or $20–$30 million for all thirteen colonies! To get the £2.5 million figure, Walton and Shepherd assumed an interest calculated at 5 percent and compounded annually (ibid.).

103. Price, *Capital and Credit*, 8–9, 15, believed merchants did *not* use compound but rather simple interest in preparing debt claims, and thus he sets the total prewar debt (as claimed by British merchants in 1790–91) at £2.9 million rather than £2.5 million.

104. Initially I found myself in difficulty defining nonresident investment. Clearly, an investor-settler who remained in America (despite his "loyalty" to the mother country) must be called an American resident. At the other pole, those who called England "home," even though they may have spent periods as American residents, are English residents, "foreign" investors. But what of the American Loyalist who had his property confiscated and subsequently migrated to England? His initial investment was *domestic*; does his claim filed in England after confiscation represent a claim from abroad? Using the *Loyalist Transcripts*, I have been able to differentiate those *resident* abroad pre-1776 and post-1776, and the intended "residence" or "home" of most investors. After reading McCusker and Menard, *The Economy*, I wondered why I had

not found important claims of losses on shipping. My guess is that ships could be sailed away, and thus their British ownership did not represent an ongoing claim.

105. Jones, *Wealth*, 50. When the research on this chapter was practically completed, I read Alice Jones's erudite work. Would it be possible, I asked myself, to find the percentage of colonial wealth "controlled" from abroad? How dependent were Americans? Jones's work is based on "sample decedents" (p. xxiii). Such estimates would, by definition, exclude property owned in the colonies by men resident in England— *unless* such property represented an obligation of the deceased, and I have argued that the long-term foreign investment (excluding the trade debt that became long-term) was *not* in that form at all. Probate records of deceased American residents cannot—it seems to me—be used to document ownership from abroad. Nonetheless, the estimates do give us a meaningful framework in which to put these allowed foreign "claims" figures.

106. Jones, *Wealth*, 136, notes the need for more research on "foreign balances" in prerevolutionary America. Probate records do give financial liabilities and thus are useful on trade financing. Jones argued that "domestic" financial claims ought to equal "domestic" liabilities. If, as she found, financial liabilities exceeded financial assets, either her sample was not reflecting reality or there had to be a net foreign debt. Her data showed an excess of liabilities of £6 million. This figure is far above the 1776 £2.9 million or £2.5 million trade debt, based on the British merchants' 1790–91 submission to their government (minus the accrued interest), and Walton and Shepherd, as noted, thought the £2.5 million figure high! Jones wondered if short-term foreign debt might distort the data. This is, of course, possible, but defaults after 1776 should include both short- and long-term debts.

However, another (heretical?) thought is that by 1790 many of the pre-1776 debts could have been repaid, so that the £2.5 million or £2.9 million—based on the British merchants' claims—may understate the dependency rather than overstate it. Lending credence to this idea is the resumption of U.S.-British trade by 1790, although not to precolonial levels. Logic dictates that a number of old trade debts would need to be liquidated to make this possible. Likewise, Jones found heavy liabilities on the part of the New England colonies, which she explained in terms of New England/Middle Colonies trade balances, but which also might be explained in terms of short-term trade financing for New England trade with Britain, which debts might well have been paid off by 1790 and not reflected in the 1790–91 submissions.

As must again be noted, none of this discussion relates to overseas residents' long-term investment in colonial land, land improvements (buildings), slaves, iron mining, or manufacturing, which, as far as I can determine, would by definition be totally excluded from colonial probate records. C. H. Feinstein, "Captal Formation in Great Britain," in *Cambridge Economic History of Europe*, ed. Peter Mathias and M. M. Postan (Cambridge: Cambridge University Press, 1978), VII, pt. 1, 71, estimated that British investment abroad (worldwide) equaled £10–£15 million in 1760. The total would have risen by 1776. This crude approximation is given as a context for the equally rough figures I have presented on that nation's investment in America. If all the net liabilities uncovered by Jones were a "foreign debt" (£6 million) and we add my £1.1 million on "other" foreign investments, we come to about £7 million. This figure is not out of line with Feinstein's—if we assume (1) the main British overseas investments would have been in America and the West Indies, and (2) British investments abroad grew between 1760 and 1776. This is all conjecture, but if correct it would raise the degree of American "dependence."

As an aside, some small part of the foreign trade debt—foreign "liabilities"—was undoubtedly not British but Dutch or possibly that of other nationalities. My study is, however, on *long-term* foreign investment. The claim on the £2.5 million or £2.9 million debt would be more legitimately seen as long term (or as having become long term, since it persisted in 1790–91) than any larger figure that would have to be designated as short-term financing. Yet a sizable portion of that £2.5 million or £2.9 million figure *in 1776* would have had to be short-term trade financing.

2. Political Independence/Economic Dependence

1. On colonial finance, see Paul Studenski and Herman E. Krooss, *Financial History of the United States*, 2nd ed. (New York: McGraw-Hill, 1963), 17–24, and E. James Ferguson, *The Power of the Purse* (Chapel Hill: University of North Carolina Press, 1961), chap. 1.

2. A large literature on revolutionary war loans exists. A standard presentation is in Samuel F. Bemis, *A Diplomatic History of the United States* (New York: Henry Holt & Co., 1950), 24. For more details, I recommend the compilation of documents in U.S. Congress, *American State Papers on Finance*, (Washington, D.C., 1832), I; Rafael A. Bayley, *The National Loans of the United States from July 4, 1776 to June 30, 1880* (1881; rpt. New York: Burt Franklin, 1970); Robert R. LaFollette, "The American Revolutionary Debt and Its Liquidation," Ph.D. diss., George Washington University, June 1931; Ferguson, *The Power of the Purse*; Friedrich Edler, *The Dutch Republic and the American Revolution* (Baltimore: Johns Hopkins University Press, 1911), 70–84, 206–216; and Richard B. Morris, ed., *John Jay: The Making of a Revolutionary* (New York: Harper & Row, 1975), I, 716–720, 824, 827. B. U. Ratchford, *American State Debts* (Durham, N.C.: Duke University Press, 1941), 41–42, deals with state debts. I have also referred to Margaret Myers, *The New York Money Market* (New York: Columbia University Press, 1931), 149ff, and Cleona Lewis, *America's Stake in International Investments* (Washington: Brookings Institution, 1938). Robert Morris, *The Papers of Robert Morris, 1781–1784*, 6 vols. (Pittsburgh: University of Pittsburgh Press, 1973–1984), contains invaluable details for 1781–1782, especially on the French loans. See index of each volume under "France."

3. Morris, *Papers*; Bayley, *National Loans*, 5–14; and Myers, *The New York Money Market*, 149–150.

4. Bayley, *National Loans*, 13, 15–28; Edler, *The Dutch Republic*, 71ff; Pieter J. Van Winter, *American Finance and Dutch Investment, 1780–1805*, 2 vols. (New York, Arno Press, 1977), 31–32; J. C. Westerman, *The Netherlands and the United States* (The Hague: Martinus Nijhoff, 1935), 3; James C. Riley, *International Government Finance and the Amsterdam Capital Market, 1740–1815* (Cambridge: Cambridge University Press, 1980), 185–186; and K. D. Bosch, *Nederlandse Beleggingen in de Verenigde Staten* (Amsterdam: Uitgeversmaatschappij Elsevier, 1948), 26–29.

5. Adam Smith, *The Wealth of Nations* (1776; rpt. New York: Modern Library, 1937), 597.

6. Bemis, *Diplomatic History*, 24, gives the French loans as $6,352,500 (including the 1781 Dutch loan). He puts the Spanish loan as $248,098. Other figures are in Lewis, *America's Stake*, 513–514. The 1782 loan is not included, because the proceeds had not yet been received. Actually, only $2 million of the authorized $10 million was issued. La Follette, "American Revolutionary Debt," indicates the United States borrowed, between 1778 and 1783, $6,376,832.93 from France (this includes the 1781 Dutch loan). The United States also got a subsidy from France of $1,633,500. La Follette puts the Spanish subsidy at $638,302 (of which the United States chose to consider $240,982 as a loan). I have included the 1781 loan as Dutch because that is where the money originated. See also Bayley, *National Loans*, 174.

7. Ratchford, *American State Debts*, 41, and Van Winter, *American Finance*, 26. Virginia obtained artillery shipments from the French in 1779—on credit. Maryland negotiated a loan in Holland in 1781–1782, decided the terms were unfavorable, and repaid it instantly. Later it raised another loan from the Dutch to be repaid by annual tobacco shipments. See Allan Nevins, *The American States during and after the Revolution, 1775–1789* (1924; rpt. New York: Augustus M. Kelly, 1969), 506–507.

8. Lawrence Lewis, *A History of the Bank of North America* (Philadelphia: J. B. Lippincott, 1882), 33, 41. In addition, in a crucial period in 1782, French deposits in the Bank were influential in keeping it functioning (Morris, *Papers*, V, 83).

9. By the fall of 1781, every state—except South Carolina—had enacted a confiscation law, and South Carolina also participated in property seizures (Nevins, *American States*, 507–508). New York, for example, passed a Confiscation Act (1779), under which fifty-nine estates owned by "Tories" were taken over and sold, bringing the state $3.6 million in specie (William Chazanof, "Land Speculation in Eighteenth Century New York," in *Business Enterprise in Early New York*, ed. Joseph R. Frese and Jacob Judd [Tarrytown, N.Y.: Sleepy Hollow Press, 1979], 69). These properties were owned by both resident and nonresident Britishers. Thus they cannot serve as a measure of nonresident British investment.

10. The "Memorialists" record the process of confiscation in *Transcripts of Loyalist Claims*, New York Public Library.

11. Maryland, *Revolutionary Laws*, ed. Alexander C. Hanson, May 1781, chap. 33, and Nov. 1782, chap. 2, cited by Victor S. Clark, *History of Manufactures in the United States* (New York: Carnegie Institution, 1929), I, 174. This $240,000 figure can be compared, as I did in Chapter 1, with the paltry £12,500 that the British Claims Commission would later award the British owners of the Principio Company. Part of the difference may lie in the depreciation of American currency.

12. On the Principio Company's war efforts, see Ronald L. Lewis, *Coal, Iron, and Slaves: Industrial Slavery in Maryland and Virginia, 1715–1865* (Westport, Conn.: Greenwood Press, 1979), 13. On the Nottingham Iron Works during the Revolution, see Michael Robbins, "The Principio Company," Ph.D. diss., George Washington University, 1972, 284, 303.

13. According to Charles Boyer, during the revolutionary years, while title to the property was vested in the English stockholders, no record exists to indicate that the New Jersey Commissioners of Forfeited Estates ever attempted to seize the property, probably, Boyer believed, "due to the influence which Erskine had in the community" (Charles S. Boyer, *Early Forges and Furnaces in New Jersey* [Philadelphia: University of Pennsylvania Press, 1963], 21–22). Erskine died on October 2, 1780, and his wife married Robert L. Hooper. On her and her new husband's petition, the New Jersey legislature passed a special Confiscation Act, "under which the property could be seized by the commissioners," but apparently it was not. The widow and Hooper were given the authority to manage Erskine's estate and the company as well, because its accounts were "blended and interwoven" with the personal concerns of Erskine and could not be separated, except to the "detriment" of the deceased estate. In 1783 Hooper wound up the business. See Boyer, *Early Forges*, 16–17, 22, for the subsequent *American* history of the property, which came, in time, to be owned by Abram S. Hewitt. There is no evidence of any reimbursement to the British investors.

14. As noted in Chapter 1, in some cases investors obtained compensation, but there was no restitution of nonresident British-owned investments.

15. 8 U.S. Stats. 18 (1778), Art. 11.

16. Stuart Weems Bruchey, *Robert Oliver: Merchant of Baltimore* (Baltimore: Johns Hopkins University Press, 1956), 34.

17. Van Winter, *American Finance*, 216, 258. The French firm of Hamelin and the Hamburg firm of Sluyter, de Basse & Soyer had financing from Holland.

18. Van Winter, *American Finance*, 177.

19. Richard B. Morris, *The Peacemakers* (New York: Harper & Row, 1965), 277.

20. 8 U.S. Stats., 82–83 (1783), Arts. 5 and 6.

21. Catherine Crary, *The Price of Loyalty* (New York: McGraw-Hill, 1973), 354. *The Loyalist Transcripts* in the New York Public Library reflects the British dissatisfaction. Henry Harford, for example, went to the United States for the first time in 1783. He arrived in Maryland and asked for compensation for his losses. In November 1784—*after* the Peace Treaty—Maryland passed an act by which all confiscated properties remaining unsold were ordered sold! Harford found—despite the Treaty—many of his "manors and reserved lands were . . . sold and the money arising there from applied to the use of the State" (ibid., XXXV, 553–554; see also 573–587). The *Loyalist Transcripts* shows clearly that British residents who sought restoration of their properties were rebuffed.

22. *American State Papers*, I, 26, and Bayley, *National Loans*, 15–22, 174.

23. In Amsterdam the merchant bankers Wilhem & Jan Willink and N. & J. Van Staphorst led in the field of government loans. See Van Winter, *American Finance*, 953; Riley, *International Government Finance*, 187; and Bayley, *National Loans*, 17–22. The Willinks and Van Staphorsts became U.S. financial agents in Holland.

24. See Table 2.1.

25. Van Winter, *American Finance*, 223–233, 240–241, 354–357 and appendixes 3, 5, 6.

26. This percentage is based on my own calculations.

27. South Carolina had begun to borrow from the French in 1784 (Nevins, *American States*, 507).

28. Van Winter, *American Finance*, 105, 126 n.88, 163, 202. The Dutch historian Van Winter attempted to list the holders of shares. The holdings were not sufficient to exercise control (see ibid., 163). According to the bank's historian, the U.S. government sold part of its stock in the Bank of North America to Dutch investors in 1783 (Lewis, *Bank of North America*, 48). By March 1786, of the 2,176 shares outstanding in the bank ($870,400), 285 were owned by foreigners, mainly Dutchman (ibid., 67).

29. Van Winter, *American Finance*, 210n, 215, and Clark, *History of Manufactures*, I, 400.

30. Van Winter, *American Finance*, 177.

31. Ibid., 183, 213. One British house was British managed but also had Dutch shareholders. See Bruchey, *Robert Oliver*, 36, on the packet service. The French line soon proved unsuccessful.

32. See Shaw Livermore, *Early American Land Companies* (New York: Commonwealth Fund, 1939), 138–140, and J. S. Davis, *Essays in the Earlier History of American Corporations* (Cambridge, Mass.: Harvard University Press, 1917), I, 124–173, on the Scioto group and the Ohio Company.

33. Paul D. Evans, *The Holland Land Co.* (Buffalo, N.Y.: Buffalo Historical Society, 1924), 4, and Van Winter, *American Finance*, 349ff. To these important Dutch firms, I should add Wilhem & Jan Willink of Amsterdam, which was not represented by Cazenove, but which participated with the latter's group in various land and other investments (Van Winter, *American Finance*, 953 and passim).

34. In looking at the extent of foreign investment in 1789–90, scholars often cite data included in the U.S. Bureau of the Census, *Historical Statistics of the United States, Colonial Times to 1957* (Washington, D.C., 1960), 566, and republished in the subsequent (1975) edition of this same work. It gives the U.S. "international investment position" ("net liability") figures (1789–1900) derived as accumulated residuals from

current account estimates. The series starts with an estimated $60 million *net* liability in 1789. This includes short-term as well as long-term liabilities. I have not put these figures in my text, because I do not believe they accurately reflect the long-term foreign investment position of the United States in 1789. In all cases I have looked to direct estimates on the level of long-term investments. Likewise, I fully share the reservations expressed in Douglass C. North, "The United States Balance of Payment, 1790–1860," *Trends in the American Economy in the Nineteenth Century*, Studies in Income and Wealth, vol. 24 (Princeton, N.J.: Princeton University Press, 1960), 587, about the figures presented by Worthy P. Sterns, "The International Indebtedness of the United States in 1789," *Journal of Political Economy*, 5 (Dec. 1897): 52. Thus I have excluded Sterns's data. His estimate of U.S. net international liabilities (including short-term trade debt) in 1789 was $82.5 million! The long-term foreign investment in the United States (excluding short-term trade credits) was in 1789 substantially below $60 million, much less $82.5 million; $17–$18 million would probably be closer to the mark. This last estimate is my own, based on documented investments as indicated in my text.

35. Ralph Hidy, *The House of Baring in American Trade and Finance: English Merchant Bankers at Work, 1763–1861* (Cambridge, Mass.: Harvard University Press, 1949), 14. Marten G. Buist, *At Spes non Fractas: Hope & Co., 1770–1815* (The Hague: Martinus Nijhoff, 1974), 40, says the earliest transactions between the Barings and the Hopes took place before 1770; see also Van Winter, *American Finance*, 866–872.

36. Hidy, *House of Baring*, 14, 21–22. Hidy's book is invaluable. For the important Anglo-Dutch relationships, see Charles Wilson, *Anglo-Dutch Commerce and Finance in the Eighteenth Century* (1941; rpt. New York: Arno Press, 1977). Hope & Co. does not, however, appear to have been a participant in the 1781–1789 Dutch investments in America.

37. Studenski and Krooss, *Financial History*, 53.

38. *American State Papers*, I, 181.

39. Ibid.

40. Ibid., 490; see also Riley, *International Government Finance*, 194.

41. *American State Papers*, I, 502; Adam Seybert, *Statistical Annals* (Philadelphia: Thomas Dobson & Son, 1818), 728; and Bayley, *National Loans*, 174–175. The "foreign loans," as noted, were denominated in foreign currency. Interestingly, no foreign exchange loss appears to have resulted from this; in fact, there may have been some gain. See Bayley, *National Loans*, 27–28.

42. Myers, *The New York Money Market*, was among those misled.

43. The "domestic debt" was, of course, denominated in dollars.

44. Leland H. Jenks, *The Migration of British Capital to 1875* (New York: Barnes & Noble, 1973), 65. The domestic debt continued to drift abroad in settlement of trade obligations. The London banking house Smith, Payne & Smiths as early as 1792 acquired from some London silk merchants "American stock," that is, U.S. government securities. The firm bought the securities for £32,295, which was 64 percent of their nominal value (J. A. S. L. Leighton-Boyce, *Smiths the Bankers* [London: National Provincial Bank, Ltd., 1958], 92). In June 1794 Talleyrand, who was then in Philadelphia, recommended to the French Huguenot firm Bourdieu, Chollet, & Bourdieu, London, the purchase of "American funds" (that is, American government securities), because "there is no power whose finances are so prosperous." Talleyrand thought the price would rise—when news came of John Jay's successful London negotiations, which Talleyrand predicted. See Talleyrand's letter of June 10, 1794, published in *Talleyrand in America as a Financial Promoter, 1794–96*, trans. and ed. Hans Huth and Wilma Pugh (New York: Da Capo Press, 1971), 29–30. On Bird, Savage & Bird (1791–1793), see the introduction in ibid., 12–13, and on this firm, see also S. R. Cope,

"Bird, Savage & Bird of London: Merchants and Bankers, 1782–1803," in *Guildhall Studies in London History*, 4 (1981): 202–217.

45. Hidy, *House of Baring*, 32, and Van Winter, *American Finance*, 916. The Barings' first operation on behalf of the U.S. government had been in 1795–96 to raise monies to facilitate negotiations with Barbary (Hidy, *House of Baring*, 31). See ibid., 32, for other particular tasks performed. In 1798 Alexander Baring, son of Francis Baring, married one of William Bingham's daughters. Bingham was well placed, and one historian is convinced that the Bingham connection was an important introduction for Baring & Co. to "the circles concerned with American Government finances" (Buist, *At Spes non Fracta*, 53).

46. Seybert, *Statistical Annals*, 731–736.

47. Compare with ibid., 751.

48. Timothy Pitkin, *A Statistical View of the Commerce of the United States* (1816): rpt. New York: Augustus M. Kelley, 1967), 287; 28th Cong., 1st sess., H. Doc. 15, 502; Bayley, *National Loans*, 45. The $3.75 million went to reimburse U.S. citizens for French "depredations" on their commerce.

49. Pitkin, *A Statistical View*, 287. It was denominated in dollars.

50. Seybert, *Statistical Annals*, 734–735; for the role of Francis Baring & Co. and Hope & Co. in handling the Louisiana 6 percent stock, see Van Winter, *American Finance*, 911–925, and Hidy, *House of Baring*, 33–34. Apparently, Hope & Co. had not participated in the Dutch loans of the 1790s. See Buist, *At Specs non Fracta*, 48. Now, however, according to ibid., 57–60, 188–190, the role of Hope & Co. was crucial. In May 1803—the same month that "Baring and Hope entered into a convention with the French government concerning the terms of payment by the United States for Louisiana"—war broke out between France and England; thus the Dutch Hope & Co. assumed leadership in the new arrangements (ibid., 57). The terms of the loan specified that the annual interest, payable in Europe, was to be paid at the rate of four shillings and six pence for each dollar (or £1 = $4.44), payable in London, and of two and a half guldens for each dollar (1f = $0.40), payable in Amsterdam (Bayley, *National Loans*, 45). As noted, the loan itself was denominated in dollars. The specification of the rate of exchange eliminated exchange uncertainty for all parties. J. E. Winston and R. W. Colomb, "How the Louisiana Purchase Was Financed," *The Louisiana Historical Quarterly*, 12 (April 1929): 189–237, shows the important role of Alexander Baring and his relations with Jefferson's Secretary of the Treasury, Albert Gallatin.

51. Bruchey, *Robert Oliver*, 253, 273; Van Winter, *American Finance*, 915–917; and Buist, *At Specs non Fracta*, 56.

52. The $5.7 million "foreign" debt figure was as of January 1, 1804.

53. Van Winter, *American Finance*, 453; Wilson, *Anglo-Dutch Commerce and Finance*, 191; and Evans, *Holland Land Company*, 3–20.

54. I have searched in vain for figures.

55. Samuel Blodget, *Economica* (1806; rpt. New York: Augustus Kelley, 1964), 198. Blodget gives no source for his figures. They appear reliable.

56. Van Winter, *American Finance*, 441, 602–603, 616, 770. Wilhelm & Jan Willink were particularly interested.

57. Bray Hammond, *Banks and Politics* (Princeton, N.J.: Princeton University Press, 1957), passim, and J. H. Holdsworth, *The First Bank of the United States* (Washington, D.C., 1910), 32–33.

58. See Holdsworth, *The First Bank*, 16. See text of Chapter 2 for the French and then the Dutch contributions to the Bank of North America (founded in 1781).

59. Holdsworth, *The First Bank*, 128.

60. Van Winter, *American Finance*, 441 (on the payments in Amsterdam). The Bank

of the United States announced in June 1793 that British shareholders could obtain their dividends through the House of Baring and through John Henry Cazenove, Nephew & Co. Bird, Savage & Bird had wanted to become the London paying agent but did not get the appointment. Nonetheless, it marketed Bank of the United States stock in Britain (Cope, "Bird, Savage & Bird," 211). John Henry Cazenove, Nephew & Co. was a London stockbroking firm founded by the brother of Théophile Cazenove (Van Winter, *American Finance*, 535 n.132); thus we are talking about Anglo-Dutch connections. Because the securities were used to meet trade debts, it was important that they be accepted. If there was no market and if returns were hard to obtain, merchants would not take the securities.

61. *American State Papers*, I, 473. After Baring did this successfully, the firm in 1803 became the official agent of the U.S. government in London. Thus Baring, at the same time it served the U.S. government owned stock in the first Bank of the United States.

62. Blodget, *Economica*, 198. Of the $10 million outstanding, $4 million was held by English investors, $2 million by Dutch investors, and $200,000 by other foreigners.

63. Were the U.S. Department of Commerce classifying this investment today, it would call it a foreign direct investment (when over 50 percent of the stock is held abroad by unrelated foreigners, an enterprise is designated a foreign direct investment).

64. Herman E. Krooss and Charles Gilbert, *American Business History* (Englewood Cliffs, N.J.: Prentice-Hall, 1972), 111, and Blodget, *Economica*, 198. I have been unable to identify which insurance company or companies the British had invested in as of 1803. But note that insurance companies, like banks, were financial intermediaries, and it is such institutions that attracted these early foreign investors.

65. Van Winter, *American Finance*, chap. 12, and Davis, *Essays*, II, 167–168, 299.

66. Quoted in Stuart Bruchey, *Colonial Merchants* (New York: Harcourt, Brace & World, 1966), 125.

67. Huth and Pugh, *Talleyrand in America, 1794–96*, 10, 103–105; *Banker's Magazine*, New York, 44 (Aug. 1889): 81; and Hammond, *Banks and Politics*, 224. See also this chapter, note 44, on the drift abroad of "American stock" and its acquisition and sale by London silk merchants.

68. The Barings were involved in trade, finance, and land investments.

69. Isaac Lippincott, "A Century and a Half of Fur Trade at St. Louis," *Washington University Studies*, 3, pt. 2, no. 2 (April 1916): 224.

70. See Livermore, *Early Land Companies*, 162, 203. The best account of the Pulteney investment is Paul D. Evans, "The Pulteney Purchase," *New York State Historical Association Quarterly Journal*, 3 (April 1922): 83–95. Williamson often "sold" land and then was never paid. Talleyrand wrote in his notebook that by December 1795 the Pulteney Association had already made sales of $2,467,000. Most of these "sales" were, however, with mortgages (and no money down); the Pulteney group, as Evans pointed out, never got the rewards. On Talleyrand's report, see Huth and Pugh, *Talleyrand in America, 1794–96*, 172–173.

71. Van Winter, *American Finance*, chaps. 13 and 14; Evans, *Holland Land Company*; and Davis, *Essays*, I, 213–253.

72. When in 1798 Sir William Pulteney had his doubts about pouring more money into developing his New York land, Cazenove, who was passing through London on a visit to Amsterdam, reassured the British investor (Evans, "The Pulteney Purchase," 19–92). Cazenove, headquartered in Philadelphia, represented his Dutch principals in America until 1799 (Van Winter, *American Finance*, 907).

73. Van Winter, *American Finance*, 625–628, and Evans, *Holland Land Company*, 14–18, 63–85.

74. Hidy, *House of Baring*, 29; Van Winter; *American Finance*, 869; and Buist, *At Spes*

non Fracta, 53, 552 n.4. Alexander Baring bought the land from William Bingham; two years later Baring married one of Bingham's daughters. The best work on the Baring land purchase and the complicated arrangements is Frederick S. Allis, Jr., ed., *William Bingham's Maine Lands, 1790–1820*, 2 vols. (Boston: Colonial Society of Massachusetts, 1954), esp. I, 342–385, 592–675, and II, passim. Allis' two volumes are also excellent on Americans' attempts to sell land to other Europeans. See, for example, William Bingham to the Dutch bankers, Wilhem & Jan Willink, Dec. 30, 1792, in ibid., I, 234–238, and Bingham's 1793 letters to Théophile Cazenove, in ibid., I, 238–241. See also ibid., I, 280–385, for Major William Jackson's trip to Europe to sell land (1793–1795).

75. The French purchases were not in the "million-acre" category. In 1793 the Chassanis Company was organized in Paris by Pierre Chassanis and his brother-in-law, who, with his father, had been interested in American investments since the Revolution. The company bought 200,000 acres in New York and planned settlement. The venture was not a success, and the project was abandoned in 1797. In February 1797 Robert Morris received from Talleyrand $142,500 for 106,875 acres in Pennsylvania that Talleyrand had sold in France. See Huth and Pugh, *Talleyrand in America, 1794–96*, 88, 22. Jean Samuel Couderc, born in Bordeaux in 1753 but living in Amsterdam after 1774, brought French as well as Dutch monies into U.S. land investments. For the complicated story, see Van Winter, *American Finance*, 814–855. One of the land ventures was not wound up until 1884! For other French land purchases, see B. G. du Pont, *Life of Eleuthère Irénée du Pont, 1799–1802* (Newark: University of Delaware Press, 1924), V, 137, 154, 159–160, and Max Gérard, *Messieurs Hottinguer Banquiers à Paris* (Paris: Hottinguer, 1968), I, 169–176 (on Jean Conrad Hottinguer and the Compagnie Cérès in 1795 and later years).

76. Coxe to William S. Smith, April 12, 1779, in Jacob E. Cooke, *Tench Coxe and the Early Republic* (Chapel Hill: University of North Carolina Press, 1978), 312. This particular land speculation did not materialize.

77. Ibid., 321–322.

78. Livermore, *Early Land Companies*, 168–169; Aaron Morton Sakolski, *Great American Land Bubble* (New York: Harper & Bros., 1932), 50; and Van Winter, *American Finance*, 704–705, 710–711.

79. Du Pont, *Life*, V, 137, 154, 159–160; Sakolski, *Great American Land Bubble*, 79–80; and Huth and Pugh, *Talleyrand in America*, 18. These restrictions were a carryover of British practice. They were a matter of profound concern to sellers of land abroad and, of course, to the buyers. See also, for example, Allis, *Bingham's Maine Lands*, I, 291, 294, 309, 312, 675, and II, 796–797.

80. Davis, *Essays*, II, 169.

81. Van Winter, *American Finance*, 572, and Davis, *Essays*, I.

82. Krooss and Gilbert, *American Business History*, 111.

83. Du Pont, *Life*, V, 196–203; and William S. Dutton, *Du Pont* (New York: Charles Scribner's Sons, 1942), 26–31. As noted, other investments in manufacturing—in saw mills and potasheries, for example—were made in connection with land development projects.

84. *The Papers of Robert Morris*, VI, 40–41, 57–64 (Morris' report).

85. Hammond, *Banks and Politics*, 53, and Lewis, *Bank of North America*, 58.

86. The tonnage duties were six cents per ton on U.S.-built and U.S.-owned vessels, thirty cents per ton on U.S.-built and foreign-owned ships, and fifty cents per ton on foreign-built and foreign-owned ships.

87. On this matter, see Geoffrey Gilbert, "Maritime Enterprise in the New Republic: Investment in Baltimore Shipping, 1789–1793," *Business History Review*, 58 (Spring 1984): 15–16, and Detlev F. Vagts, "The Corporate Alien: Definitional Questions in Federal Restraints on Foreign Enterprise," *Harvard Law Review*, 74 (June 1961): 1489.

88. Van Winter, *American Finance*, 345.

89. Lewis, *Bank of North America*, 59–60.

90. Hamilton, "Report on Manufactures," rpt. in *The Reports of Alexander Hamilton*, ed. Jacob E. Cooke (New York: Harper & Row, 1964), 148.

91. Ibid., 148–149.

92. Blodget, *Economica*, 199.

93. Charles H. Sullivan, "Alien Land Laws," *Temple Law Quarterly*, 26 (1962): 30, and Sakolski, *Great American Land Bubble*, 59–62, 79. So, of course, did Baring and Pulteney, because settlers were to be the source of their revenues.

94. Samuel Flagg Bemis, *Jay's Treaty*, rev. ed. (New Haven: Yale University Press, 1962), passim. Eventually, in 1802, the United States agreed to pay the British government the lump sum of £600,000 sterling, and $2,664,000 was appropriated to fulfill the obligation (ibid., 439).

95. Although the Jay Treaty said nothing about future land titles, it was nonetheless reassuring to property holders.

96. Davis, *Essays*, II, 156.

97. Riley, *International Finance*, 194.

98. Winston and Colomb, "How the Louisiana Purchase Was Financed," 200.

99. The "in excess of $65 million" figure, which is clearly conservative, is my own estimate based on a "domestic" debt held abroad of $43 million plus a "foreign" debt of $5.7 million (or $48.7 million in the U.S. federal debt held abroad), plus $15.88 million of corporate stock held abroad—all of which totals $64.58 million. Foreign investments in state securities, land, and other miscellaneous stakes came to far more than $420,000. Sir William Pulteney and Baring alone had spent three-quarters of a million dollars in original land acquisitions, and Pulteney's group had invested another $1 million on land development by 1800. Then there were the huge investments by the Holland Land Company. Even the $70 million figure may be low. No short-term commercial debts are included in my estimates, because I am looking at long-term investment. My work in this chapter has been influenced by Lewis, *America's Stake*, and even more by North, "The United States Balance of Payments, 1790–1860," 573–627. North (p. 622) thought Lewis' $75 million estimate for 1803 was "reasonable," but that figure included $23 million for short-term debt. Both North's and Lewis' figures on long-term foreign investment for 1803 have to be low, for the reasons indicated above. North did recognize that many stakes had been excluded.

I would like to be able to compare these rough foreign investment figures with ones on national wealth, but cannot find appropriate figures to make meaningful comparisons. Blodget, *Economica*, discusses foreign investment, and on p. 196 he estimates that in 1805 total real and personal property in the United States equaled $2.5 billion, of which $1.7 billion was in land. Blodget never compared his "national wealth" figures with his data on foreign investment. I do not think it appropriate for me to put the two sets of figures together. Were I to do so, $70 million divided by $2.5 billion equals 2.8 percent of national wealth—substantially higher than the 1776 percentages (excluding the trade debt). My 1803 figures exclude all the trade debt (except when it was transformed into long-term securities holdings). I would argue, however, that the foreign investment in government paper and in corporate securities was of far greater significance than these percentage figures imply. In crucial sectors, foreign investment was vital.

3. A Half-Century of Development

1. On the half-century, I have found especially useful Douglass C. North, "The United States Balance of Payments, 1790–1860," *Trends in the American Economy in the*

Nineteenth Century, Studies in Income and Wealth, vol. 24 (Princeton, N.J.: Princeton University Press, 1960), 573–627.

2. Douglass C. North, *The Economic Growth of the United States, 1790–1860* (Englewood Cliffs, N.J.: Prentice-Hall, 1961), 46ff, 67, 71, 76, 79.

3. Vincent Nolte, *Fifty Years in Both Hemispheres or, Reminiscences of the Life of a Former Merchant* (New York: Redfield, 1854), 82, 270, 425, and Mira Wilkins, *The Emergence of Multinational Enterprise: American Business Abroad from the Colonial Era to 1914* (Cambridge, Mass.: Harvard University Press, 1970), 35. N. R. P. Bonsor, *North Atlantic Seaway* (Prescot, Lancashire: T. Stephenson, 1955), 1–11, documents the early steamship sailings. John G. B. Hutchins, *The American Maritime Industries and Public Policy, 1789–1914* (Cambridge, Mass.: Harvard University Press, 1941), 233–235, 260–262, 343.

4. As in the case of all statistics given in this book, I must warn that these are estimates. Purchases of joint account securities (by American agents), for example, on behalf of foreign investors cannot possibly be fully reflected in these figures. Archival data indicate a sizable number of such transactions in this period.

5. In late 1859 an "unofficial" survey estimated that two-thirds of the U.S. government debt was held abroad; I am convinced that this high estimate was mistaken. See Chapter 4.

6. The 1803 figures are for domestic and "foreign" debt; see Chapter 2. On 1812 and 1815 debt, see Paul Studenski and Herman E. Krooss, *Financial History of the United States,* 2nd ed. (New York: McGraw-Hill, 1963), 98.

7. Leland H. Jenks, *The Migration of British Capital to 1875* (New York: Barnes & Noble, 1973), 66, and Ralph Hidy, *The House of Baring* (Cambridge, Mass.: Harvard University Press, 1949), 35.

8. Studenski and Krooss, *Financial History,* 100.

9. Adam Seybert, *Statistical Annals* (Philadelphia: Thomas Dobson, 1818), 757. Taylors & Lloyds (later Lloyds Bank) was among the British investors in U.S. bonds. The bank's historian attributed the 1817 investment to the presence of an "emigrant branch of the Lloyd family" in the United States. See R. S. Sayers, *Lloyds Bank in the History of English Banking* (Oxford: Clarendon Press, 1957), 186.

10. Margaret Myers, *The New York Money Market* (New York: Columbia University Press, 1931), 20, citing the Secretary of the Treasury report, Oct. 15, 1828.

11. Studenski and Krooss, *Financial History,* 100.

12. Alexander Trotter, *Observations on the Financial Position and Credit of Such of the States of the North American Union as Have Contracted Public Debts* (London: Longman, Orme, Brown, Green and Longmans, 1839), 5. Interest on the U.S. debt was on occasion referred to as "dividends."

13. Walter B. Smith, *Economic Aspects of the Second Bank of the United States* (1953; rpt. New York: Greenwood Press, 1969), 67, 89, notes that 1832 was a banner year in the redemption of the federal debt and that after that year state securities in foreign hands rose rapidly. See also ibid., 158–159. In 1829 the total federal debt still exceeded the state debt; see Studenski and Krooss, *Financial History,* 7.

14. G. S. Callender, "The Early Transportation and Banking Enterprises of the States in Relation to the Growth of Corporations," *Quarterly Journal of Economics,* 17 (Nov. 1902): 139.

15. B. U. Ratchford, *American State Debts* (Durham, N.C.: Duke University Press, 1941), 88 (total state debts), and *Niles' National Register,* 44 (July 21, 1838): 322 (foreign holdings).

16. Of the $172 million state debt outstanding in 1838, $54 million was for state bank capital, $60 million for canal construction, and $43 million for railroads (Ratchford, *American State Debts,* 88). See also Smith, *Economic Aspects,* 30.

17. Jenks, *Migration*, 361, 78. By 1834–35, the British Rothschilds owned bonds of the following U.S. cities: Philadelphia, New Orleans, Baltimore, and Wheeling (American Account Book, Rothschild Archives, London [RAL] II/3/0). They also had Philadelphia County bonds. It is impossible to discuss each state or municipal security. Nonetheless, the story of the Washington, D.C., issue in Amsterdam, made on behalf of the Chesapeake and Ohio Canal Company, is too fascinating to omit. In 1828–29 the loan was offered to Baring and to Rothschild in London and to Willink and to Hope in Amsterdam. When they had reservations, Daniel Crommelin & Sons of Amsterdam agreed to market the issue. In 1834 the Chesapeake and Ohio Canal Company went bankrupt. Since in 1828 a federal law had guaranteed the bonds, rather than seeing "the metropolis of the country in the hands of foreign brokers and stockjobbers," in 1836 Congress decided to take the Dutch loan for its own account (Pieter J. Van Winter, *American Finance and Dutch Investment, 1780–1805* [New York: Arno Press, 1977], 973–976). This was an exceptional federal government guarantee. The loan, for Washington, Georgetown, and Alexandria, came to $1.7 million (ibid., 977). The Dutch owners lost nothing.

18. There is a sizable literature on the state debts of this era, including Reginald C. McGrane, *Foreign Bondholders and American State Debts* (New York: Macmillan, 1935); Trotter, *Observations* (1839); William A. Scott, *The Repudiation of State Debts* (New York: Thomas Y. Crowell, 1893); Ratchford, *American State Debts*; and G. S. Callender, "English Capital and American Resources, 1815–1860," Ph.D. diss., Harvard University, 1897. I have also found Jenks, *Migration*, and Hidy, *House of Baring*, useful. Most important, I have delved into the rich primary source material in the N. M. Rothschild & Sons Archives, London—henceforth cited as RAL (Rothschild Archives London)—and in the Baring Papers, Public Archives, Ottawa (henceforth, BAO).

19. McGrane, *Foreign Bondholders*, 11. For example, when the Citizens' Bank of Louisiana issued $12 million in bonds backed by $14.4 million in mortgages, foreign bond houses would not market the issue. Two years later, in January 1836, the state of Louisiana agreed to issue state bonds and take the bank bonds as security. There was no difficulty whatsoever in selling these state bonds abroad. Stephen A. Caldwell, *A Banking History of Louisiana* (Baton Rouge: Louisiana State University Press, 1935), 48.

20. Thomas Raikes, *A Portion of the Journal Kept by Thomas Raikes, Esq. from 1831 to 1847* (London: Longman, Brown, Green, Longmans and Roberts, 1858), I, 30, contains a journal entry for June 23, 1832: "Those who have money at command are buying funds in America or Denmark, which they think least exposed to political change." See also ibid., II, 278, and Sydney Smith, *Letters on American Debts*, 2nd ed. (London: Longman, Brown, Green, and Longmans, 1844), wherein the Reverend Smith explains the assumption of investors that America—a great republic—would be a safe place for investment.

21. Carter Goodrich, *Government Promotion of American Canals and Railroads* (New York: Columbia University Press, 1960), 54. So popular was New York state stock in 1833 that a 5 percent loan for the Chemung Canal sold at $117.61 abroad (*Niles' Weekly Register*, 45 [Nov. 16, 1833]: 179). *Niles' Register* commented, "It surely is a sound policy to export 100 dollars worth of stock that will sell for 115 or 120 dollars in Europe, and to be finally redeemed by 100 only—because that [*sic*] Europeans are content to receive less interest on their capital than money bears, and will command in the United States" (ibid.).

22. Jeffrey G. Williamson, *American Growth and the Balance of Payments* (Chapel Hill: University of North Carolina Press, 1964), 102–103, and Trotter, *Observations*, 305.

23. Callender, "Early Transportation and Banking Enterprises," 143. Williamson, *American Growth*, 42, goes even further, arguing that the inflow of foreign capital in the

1830s was very much a function of the cotton market—and in this decade, it reflected the export of the primary product. In this context, Williamson is, of course, discussing both long-term and short-term foreign finance. See also ibid., 101.

24. Jenks, *Migration*, 78.

25. Hidy, *House of Baring*, passim.

26. Dutch firms included W. & J. Willink, Hope & Co., and Crommelin & Sons (K. D. Bosch, *Nederlandse Beleggingen in de Verenigte Staten* [Amsterdam: Uitgever-smaatschappij Elsevier, 1948], 48–51). An early and large British investor in New York state securities was the well-connected Samuel Jones Loyd (later Lord Overstone), who in 1823 purchased more than £34,000 worth of such securities. See D. J. O'Brien, ed., *Correspondence of Lord Overstone*, 3 vols. (Cambridge: Cambridge University Press, 1971), II, 937 n.5.

27. McGrane, *Foreign Bondholders*, 9, and Jenks, *Migration*, 94. Wilder had become the Hottinguer's New York correspondent in 1811. Max Gérard, *Messieurs Hottinguer, Banquiers à Paris* (Paris, Hottinguer, 1968), I, 213, 434. For Hottinguer's long U.S. involvements, see Julius Landmann, *Leu & Co., 1755–1905* (Zurich: Art. Institut Orell Fusseli, 1905), 118, 378–380, which has an April 14, 1793, report of Hottinguer & Co. on the state of American finance. The firm's founder, a Protestant, Jean Conrad Hottinguer, had migrated from Zurich to Paris in 1784; in 1793 he married an American. He had long-standing ties with Baring Brothers and Hope & Co. See Gérard, *Messieurs Hottinguer*, I; J. S. G. Wilson, *French Banking Structure and Credit Policy* (Cambridge, Mass.: Harvard University Press, 1957), 142; and Anka Muhlstein, *Baron James* (New York: Vendome Press, n.d. [1983]), 50.

28. Hidy, *House of Baring*, 195, and Ratchford, *American State Debts*, 93.

29. Hidy, *House of Baring*, 239. On Frederick Huth & Co., see Joseph Robert Freedman, "A London Merchant Banker in Anglo-American Trade and Finance, 1835–1850," Ph.D. diss., University of London, 1969. Jenks, *Migration*, 361, notes that the extent of the interest of London banking houses in American finance at the end of the 1830s is suggested by the fact that nearly $6 million of the Alabama debt of $11.5 million was "payable in the first instance at one of the following London houses: Reid, Irving & Co., Rothschilds, Gowan & Marx, Magniac, Smiths & Co., Holford & Co., Prescott, Grote & Co., and Denison, Heywood & Co."

30. Brown Brothers and its British house are not included as important in handling state bonds. The firm was very significant in financing Anglo-American trade; it was a large—probably the largest—dealer in sterling exchange, yet it does not seem to have been a principal participant in handling state government securities. See Edwin J. Perkins, *Financing Anglo-American Trade* (Cambridge, Mass.: Harvard University Press, 1975), passim.

31. Hidy, *House of Baring*, 32ff.

32. Prime, Ward & Sands (1810–1826); Prime, Ward, King & Co. (1827–1833); Prime, Ward & King (1833–1846); Prime, Ward & Co. (1847); and James G. King & Sons (1846–1853) successively acted as important New York correspondents for the Barings. I have established the sequence from data in the BAO and from Hidy, *House of Baring*, 49, 351.

33. Ibid., 51–52, and Nolte, *Fifty Years*, 186–187. The British firm was styled Sir Francis Baring & Co. (1800–1806) and after 1806 became Baring Brothers & Co. (Hidy, *House of Baring*, 37–38).

34. Hidy, *House of Baring*, 97–98, 109, 112–120. BAO, vol. 98, contains correspondence from officials of the Second Bank of the United States and its successor.

35. Hidy, *House of Baring*, 98, 101–102. The BAO contains volumes of correspondence from T. W. Ward to Baring Brothers & Co.

36. Hidy, *House of Baring*, 43, 47, 79–83.

37. Ibid., 96.

38. Marten G. Buist, *At Spes non Fracta: Hope & Co., 1770–1815* (The Hague: Martinus Nijhoff, 1974), 65, and Pieter J. Van Winter, *American Finance and Dutch Investment, 1780–1805* (New York: Arno Press, 1977), 1008.

39. The July 1805 prospectus for the Bureau d'Administration et de Direction de Fonds Originaux de l'Amerique had been issued in French and was signed by the administrative office of N. & J. & R. van Staphorst, Ketwich & Vroombergh and W. Borski (on behalf of the administrative office of Hope & Co.). See Bosch, *Nederlandse Beleggingen*, 36–38, 659, and Van Winter, *American Finance*, 896–898. "Administrative offices" of Dutch bankers became the typical media for introducing American securities in the Dutch market. The bureau of administration held securities on behalf of Dutch buyers, paid out dividends and interest in guilders, and returned the principal at maturity in guilders. This device made foreign securities accessible to Dutch buyers. It also had the effect of giving Dutch bankers a concentration of ownership.

40. Buist, *At Spes non Fracta*, 69; Van Winter, *American Finance*, 977, 991; Hidy, *House of Baring*, 53; and Nolte, *Fifty Years*, 262.

41. Van Winter, *American Finance*, 967.

42. Table 3.2 shows the drop of Dutch participation in U.S. federal securities, 1818–1828.

43. Hope & Co. to Baring Brothers & Co., Nov. 30, 1838, BAO, vol. 110, p. 061672.

44. McGrane, *Foreign Bondholders*, 9, and Van Winter, *American Finance*, 978–980. For the firm's initial hesitancy, see Hope & Co. to Baring Brothers & Co., Aug. 16, 1833, BAO, vol. 110, p. 061587. In January 1834 Hope & Co. wrote Baring Brothers & Co. that it preferred Louisiana bonds payable in dollars rather than in sterling, because "in this country we have no confidence in British currency" (ibid., Jan. 10, 1834 [orig. misdated 1833] BAO, vol. 110, p. 061601). Their real preference was for securities that paid in guilders in Amsterdam. But by 1838, as indicated above, Hope & Co. was prepared to take securities payable in New York or London.

45. Hidy, *House of Baring*, 55.

46. Data from the RAL. There were Rothschild houses run by other brothers in Frankfurt, Vienna, and Naples. The firm had agents and correspondents throughout Europe. In relation to the American business, the British and, to a lesser extent, the French Rothschilds ranked supreme.

47. See R. & I. Phillips to N. M. Rothschild, Dec. 4, 1821, RAL XI/38/205A.

48. R. Phillips to N. M. Rothschild, April 13, 1833, RAL XI/38/159A.

49. American Account Book (1831–1839), RAL II/3/0, and J. L. & S. Joseph & Co. correspondence, RAL XI/38/159A.

50. Details are given in RAL T49/1, 2, 6, 7, 11, 12, 14. The correspondence includes a copy of a letter from John Forsyth, Secretary of State, to Baring Brothers & Co., Aug. 6, 1834, RAL T49/11, explaining "that considerations to which it is unnecessary to advert, but which are not founded in any diminuation of the credit of your house have led me with the President's approbation, to transfer the business now transacted by you on behalf of the United States, as their bankers or agents, to N. M. Rothschild Esquire at London after the close of the present year." I located the original letter in BAO, vol. 6, p. 03004. While I do not know for certain the reasons for the shift, a letter in the J. L. & S. Joseph & Co. correspondence, RAL XI/38/159A, provides clues: On Sept. 30, 1833, J. L. & S. Joseph & Co. wrote that the Manhattan Bank, the Bank of America, and the Mechanics Bank were chosen in New York City "for the receipt and deposit of the United States money" and wanted to deal with the Rothschilds in London. The letter continued, "They will no doubt receive an offer from Baring's but

desirous to avoid any connection that may identify them with the Bank of the United States they would prefer going through your house." Hidy, *House of Baring*, 195–196, feels that Baring's relations with the Bank of the United States would have "engendered a feeling of distrust on the part of the Jackson administration." In July 1834 Nicholas Biddle had deducted from the U.S. government's dividends "damages" that the administration had refused to pay on a protested bill. Baring had been involved in the return of the bill. Hidy writes of the wrath of President Jackson (ibid., 196).

51. This is evident from its American Account Book (1831–1839), RAL II/3/0. It would be possible, although tedious—and I have not done so—to use the account book by year to determine the English Rothschild position in these securities at year-end during the 1830s. I was struck by the formidable involvement.

52. J. L. & S. Joseph suspended payments March 17, 1837, and R. & I. Phillips followed less than a week later. See J. L. & S. Joseph & Co. to N. M. Rothschild & Sons, March 19, 1837, and March 23, 1837, RAL XI/38/159B. Thomas Payne Govan, *Nicholas Biddle* (Chicago: University of Chicago Press, 1959), 306–307, notes that early in March 1837, Herman, Briggs & Co., one of the largest mercantile firms in New Orleans, had suspended payments with liabilities of more than $4 million. The Joseph firm was its correspondent in New York, and the Herman, Briggs & Co. failure brought down the New York house.

53. On April 8, 1837, before the Rothschilds had received J. L. & S. Joseph & Co.'s March 19 letter, N. M. Rothschild & Sons had written the Joseph firm that "Mr. Augustus [sic] Belmont, a gentleman in the employ of one of our houses" was planning to visit New York. They requested cooperation with him and "You will please furnish him for our account against receipts with the money he may want for his expenses during his stay in your city, say to the extent of £1000 sterling" (RAL II/10/1).

54. August Belmont, New York, to N. M. Rothschild & Söhne, May 15, 1837, RAL XI/62/OA.

55. Bertrand Gille, *Histoire de la Maison Rothschild* (Geneva: Librarie Droz, 1965), I, 464, II, 580, has some material on August Belmont's start in America. There are two political and social biographies of Belmont: Irving Katz, *August Belmont: A Political Biography* (New York: Columbia University Press, 1968), and David Black, *The King of Fifth Avenue: The Fortunes of August Belmont* (New York: Dial Press, 1981). Neither biographer used the immense Belmont correspondence in the Rothschild Archives, Paris, or that held by N. M. Rothschild & Sons, Ltd., London, RAL XI/62, RAL II/51, and RAL II/10. RAL II/10 contains the London house's letters to Belmont. The Paris Rothschild correspondence is in the National Archives in Paris.

56. Black, *The King*, 25, gives the $10,000-a-year salary, but no source and no indication of which Rothschild house paid the stipend. The first letter of N. M. Rothschild & Sons to August Belmont after London heard the news about J. L. & S. Joseph and R. & I. Phillips was sent April 22, 1837 (in RAL II/10/1, p. 112). It gave August Belmont explicit details on actions to take, such as making sure that Phillips could not collect the dividend "for us" on Philadelphia City stock any more. Belmont was instructed to contact "without delay" the U.S. Bank, the Philadelphia City Bank, the County of Philadelphia Bank, the Pennsylvania Loan Office, and the Virginia Loan Office, canceling Phillips' authority "to collect for us dividends on these various American stocks." The letter gave no salary; initially London did not assume that Belmont would remain in America.

57. Ratchford, *American State Debts*, 92; Jenks, *Migration*, 94; Van Winter, *American Finance*, 973; Muriel Hidy, *George Peabody* (New York: Arno Press, 1978); and Jenks, *Migration*, 80 (on the *Circular to Bankers*).

58. One indication of the distribution pattern is this breakdown (the numbers are in

thousands of U.S. dollars) for Pennsylvania bonds for 1842 (from McGrane, *Foreign Bondholders*, 71): England (20,026); Holland (1,822); France (570); West Indies (563); Switzerland (240); Portugal (231); East India and China (148); Mexico (41); Canada (31); Italy (31); Denmark (6); Spain (5); Halifax, N. S. (3); total (23,736). The total outstanding was $34 million. Yet this list may not reflect the real distribution, for non-British residents often held American securities through British houses. Also, the 1842 data on Pennsylvania may give a mistaken impression of the Dutch role in state securities (Louisiana figures for that year would, for example, reflect a far larger Dutch investment). Likewise, data on Illinois, Ohio, Indiana, and New York state bonds very likely would reveal a somewhat larger French involvement. See Henry Blumenthal, *A Reappraisal of Franco-American Relations, 1830–1871* (Chapel Hill: University of North Carolina Press, 1959), 112, and materials in the BAO. Nonetheless, clearly, British monies were by far the most important. Van Winter, *American Finance*, 990–991, points out that although a great deal of Dutch capital was still going into American securities, the situation was entirely different from that of the late eighteenth century. Then, when "the aid of the Dutch was sought for large-scale American transactions, Amsterdam itself had decided what should be offered to Dutch investors. But now the public [in Holland] was no longer directed by Dutch concerns such as those of Willink and van Staphorst, or of Stadnitski and his business associates, but by the strong English association of Baring and Hope . . . and by new international houses of weight, such as the Rothschilds."

59. *Niles' National Register*, 44 (July 21, 1838): 322; total for 1838 in Ratchford, *American State Debts*, 88.

60. Sydney Norman Buck, *The Development of the Organization of Anglo-American Trade, 1800–1850* (New Haven: Yale University Press, 1925), 40, citing Parliamentary Papers, *Report on Orders in Council 1812*, 355; see also Buck, *Anglo-American Trade*, 42.

61. Buck, *Anglo-American Trade*, 106–107.

62. Caldwell, *A Banking History*, 35.

63. Buck, *Anglo-American Trade*, 42, and S. D. Chapman, "The International Houses: The Continental Contribution to British Commerce, 1800–1860," *Journal of European Economic History*, 6 (Spring 1977): 35.

64. Edward Stanwood, "Cotton Manufacture," in U.S. Department of Interior, Census Office, *Report on Manufacturing Industries in the United States, 11th Census, 1890* (Washington, D.C., 1895), pt. 3, 180.

65. Frank Thistlewaite, *The Anglo-American Connection in the Early Nineteenth Century* (Philadelphia: University of Philadelphia Press, 1959), 12.

66. Hidy, *House of Baring*, 506 n.17.

67. Ibid., 102.

68. Ibid., 107, 174ff, 184ff.

69. Thistlewaite, *Anglo-American Connection*, 12–15, and Aytoun Ellis, *Heir of Adventure: The Story of Brown, Shipley & Co. Merchant Bankers, 1810–1960* (London: Brown, Shipley, 1960), 11–51, 86.

70. Stephen Salsbury, *The State, the Investor, and the Railroad* (Cambridge, Mass.: Harvard University Press, 1967), 107.

71. Hidy, *House of Baring*, 171.

72. Ibid., 195, 526n. I find the £1 million sum cited by Hidy to be extraordinarily large and, indeed, implausible. According to William Ten Eck Hardenbrook, *Financial New York* (New York: privately printed, 1897), 107, Richard Alsop was Morrison, Cryder & Co.'s *New York* agent in 1836. When James Morrison died in England in 1857, he had the largest estate (about £4 million) of any Britisher who died in the United Kingdom in the years 1840–1879 (W. D. Rubinstein, *Men of Property: The Very Wealthy*

since the Industrial Revolution [New Brunswick, N.J.: Rutgers University Press, 1981], 44). For more on Morrison, Cryder, see Stanley Chapman, *The Rise of Merchant Banking* (London: George Allen & Unwin, 1984), 11, 13, 39–41, and Richard Gatty, *Portrait of a Merchant Prince: James Morrison, 1789–1857* (Northallerton, Yorkshire: Pepper Arden, n.d. [1977?]), 157–168. Gatty does not even mention Francis Oliver!

73. Its Baltimore correspondent was J. J. Cohen & Brothers. See Belmont to J. J. Cohen, June 29, 1837, and J. Pennington(?), Baltimore, to Belmont, July 29, 1837, in RAL XI/62/OA.

74. Hidy, *House of Baring*, 195; Stanley D. Chapman, "British Marketing Enterprise: The Changing Roles of Merchants, Manufacturers, and Financiers, 1700–1800," *Business History Review*, 52 (Spring 1979): 205–233; and N. M. Rothschild to August Belmont, April 22, 1837, RAL II/10/1, p. 112 (on Lizardi & Co.'s business).

75. Benjamin Ingham (1784–1861), born in England, went to Sicily in 1806 as a representative of his family firm in Leeds—to sell cloth and woolens. In 1806 he saw the potential of Marsala wine exports. He started to send wine to America. In 1809 he took his only trip to the United States and arranged for Messrs. Greenough to be his Boston agent. The War of 1812 interrupted his trade, but as soon as peace was restored, his exports grew. He dispatched his nephew to Boston, probably in 1828. The latter committed suicide in New York in 1833, and another nephew (Ben Ingham) replaced him and remained in America for two years, thereafter revisiting the country almost every year. It seems that in order to get paid for the exports to America, Benjamin Ingham had to go through London, with a sizable loss in "commissions to middlemen." Thus, to avoid middleman losses, he began making American investments. His trade expanded greatly in the 1830s, and after 1837 Schuyler Livingston (1803–1861) served as Ingham's personal investment counselor and became the architect of the latter's vast wealth. When Benjamin Ingham died on March 4, 1861, in Sicily, his total estate was estimated at nearly £9 million, of which his American assets were listed as $6.5 million!. See Richard Trevelyan, *Princes under the Volcano* (London: Macmillan, 1972), 6, 7, 12, 19, 23, 25, 52–53, 60, 66–68, 76, 88–90, 486n. Irene Neu at Indiana University is the American specialist on Ingham.

76. *New York Times*, Nov. 1, 1941, and U.S. Senate, Committee on Finance, *Sale of Foreign Bonds, Hearings*, 72nd Cong., 1st sess., 1932, pt. 2, 605, on the date of Philip Speyer's arrival and his activities. Lazard Speyer-Ellissen was founded in Frankfurt in 1836 as the successor of an earlier Speyer house. In the late eighteenth century, the Speyers had been the wealthiest Jewish family in Frankfurt, far wealthier than the Rothschilds. See Paul H. Emden, *Money Powers of Europe in the Nineteenth and Twentieth Centuries* (London: Sampson Low, Marston, 1937), 274.

77. Callender, "Early Transportation and Banking Enterprises," 145. This is short-term finance, not long-term investment, but it is important in that it represents the huge volume of business. Some of this "credit" would become long-term, through payments in long-term securities.

78. D. M. Williams, "Liverpool Merchants and the Cotton Trade, 1820–1850," in *Liverpool and Merseyside*, ed. J. P. Harris (London: Frank Cass, 1969), 197. On other British firms involved in U.S. trade and finance, see Hidy, *House of Baring*, 239. W. & J. Brown & Co., an American house in Liverpool, was important in this trade and trade financing. William Brown, born in Ulster, who had migrated to America as a young man (with his father), returned to the United Kingdom, to Liverpool, in 1810, and founded the house that would become Brown, Shipley & Co. His father remained in America—and the "parent" house was American. See Perkins, *Financing Anglo-American Trade*, 19–20.

79. *Hunt's Merchant Magazine*, 3 (1840): 202.

80. Isaac Lippincott, "A Century and a Half of Fur Trade at St. Louis," *Washington University Studies*, 3, pt. 2, no. 2 (April 1916): 234–235.

81. Ibid., 228.

82. Hidy, *House of Baring*, 565.

83. See Chapter 2 on the 1791 charter and 1803 ownership. On the 1811 ownership, see J. F. Holdsworth and Davis R. Dewey, *The First and Second Banks of the United States*, 61st Cong., 2nd sess., 1910, S. Doc. 571, 109.

84. The bank charter was defeated in February 1811. According to Studenski and Krooss, *Financial History*, 73, U.S. specie stock "was seriously reduced by the export of $7 million to pay off foreign stockholders."

85. Bray Hammond, *Banks and Politics* (Princeton, N.J.: Princeton University Press, 1957), 408. On the Second Bank of the United States, see also Ralph C. H. Catterall, *The Second Bank of the United States* (Chicago: University of Chicago Press, 1903); Smith, *Economic Aspects*; and Govan, *Nicholas Biddle*.

86. Hidy, *House of Baring*, 71–72.

87. Jenks, *Migration*, 66.

88. Andrew Jackson's veto message, in Holdsworth and Dewey, *The First and Second Banks*, 302. The total capital was $35 million, of which the government held $7 million. See Hammond, *Banks and Politics*, 408. Thus 24 percent of the total stock was held abroad.

89. The BAO, vol. 98, contains letters from the bank president Nicholas Biddle to Baring Brothers & Co. providing reassurances to British investors (see Dec. 31, 1827, pp. 05480-82; March 19, 1828, p. 054688; April 7, 1830, pp. 054741-43); seeking to continue "the important & confidential connection which has so long and so satisfactorily existed between your respected House and the Bank" (Sept. 20, 1828, pp. 054731-32); arranging for the reimbursement of 3 percent stock of the United States (July 18, 1832, p. 054749; Oct. 31, 1832, p. 054758); and praising Baring for the firm's "zeal to promote the interest of the Bank" (Oct. 15, 1832, p. 054751; Jan. 23, 1834, p. 054765).

90. Jackson's message included in Holdsworth and Dewey, *The First and Second Banks*, 302-303. Jackson made the point that the disenfranchisement of the foreign stockholders meant concentrated control by insiders, because it reduced the number of proxies they needed to collect. On the particular hostility to the Barings, see this chapter, note 50.

91. Rondo Cameron writes that the first foreign joint-stock company to be listed officially with the Paris Bourse was Banca Romana in 1834, followed in 1835 by Banque de Belgique and the Second Bank of the United States (*France and the Economic Development of Europe* [Princeton, N.J.: Princeton University Press, 1961], 82). Note this was after Jackson's veto and one year before the national charter was to expire. Blumenthal says the Bank of the United States was not quoted on the Paris stock exchange until 1836, in which case this would be the Bank of the United States (of Pennsylvania). See *A Reappraisal*, 112; Smith, *Economic Aspects*, 178, 183 ($35 million); and Hardenbrook, *Financial New York*, 190, 173 (rising foreign ownership). In 1824 Pennsylvania had become concerned about foreign ownership of state bank stock and prohibited the transfer of such stock to foreigners; the law was easily evaded and was repealed in 1836 (C. K. Hobson, *Export of Capital* [London: Constable, 1914], 110). The repeal coincided with the Pennsylvania Charter of the Bank of the United States. *Niles' National Register*, 44 (July 21, 1838): 322 ($20 million).

92. Allan Nevins, *History of the Bank of New York and Trust Co., 1784–1934* (New York: privately printed, 1934), 39 (£200,000).

93. Hidy, *House of Baring*, 72, 368, 119. On the Louisiana banks, see Caldwell,

Banking History, 42–43. Both had state as well as private subscriptions and, remember, the Barings were interested in Louisiana *state* securities.

94. American Account Book, RAL II/3/0. They also had Philadelphia City Bank and County of Philadelphia Bank stock. See N. M. Rothschild & Sons to August Belmont, April 22, 1837, RAL II/10/1, p. 112.

95. According to the *New York Evening Star* (as cited in *Niles Weekly Register*, 45 [Nov. 16, 1833]: 178), the Marquis "counts by hundreds of thousands of dollars in it—about, or more than a half million." A later *Niles' Weekly Register*, 48 (May 2, 1835): 145, reported that the most noble Marquis owned the bank, "body and breeches"—"except about a sufficiency to form a board of directors." *Niles' Register* says "Caermarthan," but surely it must be Carmarthen. The Chase Manhattan Bank archivist was unable to locate any mention of the Marquis in the board of directors minutes of the Bank of the Manhattan Company or find any bank records to cast light on this reported investment by the Marquis (Sally Brazil to Mira Wilkins, Dec. 10, 1984).

96. Callender, "Early Transportation and Banking Enterprises," 153. The British Rothschilds acquired stock in the New Orleans Canal and Banking Company in 1833. See J. L. & S. Joseph to N. M. Rothschild, Aug. 23, 1833, RAL XI/38/159A: "We have just completed the purchase of four thousand shares of New Orleans Canal & Banking Co. stock in which you are interested one third, Messrs Jonas Phillips & Son and R. & I. Phillips one third and ourselves the remaining one third." The price was $458,937. See ibid., Aug. 31, 1833, RAL XI/38/159A.

97. *Niles' Weekly Register*, 46 (March 29, 1834): 67.

98. Jenks, *Migration*, 361.

99. Callender, "Early Transportation and Banking Enterprises," 144.

100. Ibid., 153. Both of these banks had private owners along with the state subscription (Trotter, *Observations*, 258, 306).

101. Van Winter, *American Finance*, 978; Bosch, *Nederlandse Beleggingen*, 48; Van Winter, *American Finance*, 968–971; Caldwell, *Banking History*, 48–50 (Citizens' Bank); and George D. Green, *Finance and Economic Development in the Old South: Louisiana Banking, 1804–1861* (Stanford, Calif.: Stanford University Press, 1972), 25 (on Hope & Co.'s involvement in Citizens' Bank, 1835).

102. Caldwell, *Banking History*, 54; $6.9 million came from other states and $12.3 million from Louisiana (much of the latter appears to have been state government subscriptions). Green, *Finance and Economic Development*, 80, lists the twelve banks as follows (in parentheses are the total stock, the foreign stock in millions of U.S. dollars, and the percentage held abroad): (1) Canal (4; 2; 50%) (2) Carrollton (1.9; 0.5; 26%); (3) Citizens' (5.3; 5.3; 100%); (4) City (2; 0.15; 7%); (5) Commercial (3; 0.3; 10%) (6) Consolidated Assoc. (2.5; 2.5; 100%); (7) Gas Light (1.8; 0.04; 2%); (8) Bank of Louisiana (4; 1.6; 40%) (9) Louisiana State (1.9; 1.0; 53%); (10) Mechanics and Traders (2.0; 0.2; 10%) (11) Bank of New Orleans (0.4; 0.1; 25%); and (12) Union Bank (7; 7; 100%). In the case of the Consolidated and the Union Bank, these were state bonds; the Citizens' securities were state-guaranteed bank bonds.

103. John Denis Haeger, *The Investment Frontier: New York Businessmen and the Economic Development of the Old Northwest* (Albany: State University of New York Press, 1981), 18, 22–23, 25. Haeger describes NYLTC as among the first trust institutions in the United States. He says nothing about any insurance functions.

104. Ibid., 32, and Van Winter, *American Finance*, 740–741.

105. Paul Wallace Gates, "The Role of the Land Speculator in Western Development," in *Public Lands*, ed. Vernon Carstensen (Madison: University of Wisconsin Press, 1963), 355.

106. Callender, "Early Transportation and Banking Enterprises," 153n, and *Niles'*
National Register, 44 (July 21, 1838): 322. N. M. Rothschild, in joint account with its
agent, J. L. & S. Joseph, bought 2,000 shares of "American Life and Trust Co." stock
on August 18, 1835, at $50,000 and sold on March 17, 1836, at $57,500, sharing half the
profit with its agent. For the British Rothschilds this in-and-out transaction was atypical. Most of its investments were for longer periods. See American Account Book, RAL
II/3/0. Jenks found American Life Insurance and Trust Company was advertising for
deposit accounts in England in 1836 (Jenks, *Migration*, 361 n.31). These data should be
compared with material in James G. Smith, *The Development of Trust Companies in the
United States* (New York: Henry Holt, 1928), 258–261. Smith discusses the fate of the
petition for incorporation of this firm, 1833–34. He believed the firm was never chartered by the New York legislature. He did not realize that it was set up in Baltimore.
See Edward Ten Broeck Perine, *The Story of the Trust Companies* (New York: G. P.
Putnam's Sons, 1916), 28–29, 70–71.

107. Callender, "Early Transportation and Banking Enterprises," 144, and Van Winter, *American Finance*, 978. See Bosch, *Nederlandse Beleggingen*, 50, on the Dutch investment. The Farmers' Fire Insurance and Loan Company was chartered in New York in
1822. Its name was changed in 1836 to the Farmers' Loan and Trust Company (Smith,
The Development of Trust Companies, 278).

108. Jenks, *Migration*, 361 n.31, says "½ of 10m" in 1838, but this is surely an error.
See Perine, *The Story of the Trust Companies*, 69, for the company's $2 million capital as
of Jan. 1, 1839, and ibid., 77–78, for further British involvement. See also Callender
"Early Transportation and Banking Enterprises," 153n; Fritz Redlich, *The Molding of
American Banking* (New York: Johnson Reprint Corporation, 1968), pt. 2, 342, indicates
that the North American Trust and Banking Company appears to have been established in 1838.

109. Jenks, *Migration*, 361 n.31. The Ohio Life Insurance and Trust Company, incorporated in 1834, apparently never did any insurance business. It was a bank of
deposit and made loans in large volume. See George W. Van Vleck, *The Panic of 1857*
(New York: Columbia University Press, 1943), 65. For details on the OLITC, see
Haeger, *The Investment Frontier*, 39–58.

110. Smith, *The Development of Trust Companies*, 267. The report was on the New
Jersey Trust and Commission Company; there is no evidence that it was ever incorporated. The report continued, "Foreign capital, placed in trust companies in New
York and Philadelphia, is now lent and advanced to our [New Jersey] manufacturers
and agriculturalists, and the whole profit arising from the management of that capital,
is drawn from us to enrich our neighbors" (ibid.).

111. See R. C. Michie, *Money, Mania, and Markets: Investment, Company Formation and
the Stock Exchange in Nineteenth Century Scotland* (Edinburgh: John Donald Publishers,
Ltd., 1981), 61. The Wisconsin Marine and Fire Insurance Company was formed in Feb.
1839. F. Cyril James, *The Growth of Chicago Banks*, 2 vols. (New York: Harper & Bros.,
1938), I, 202, and Alice E. Smith, *George Smith's Money* (Madison: State Historical
Society of Wisconsin, 1966), 29–55n.

112. Smith, *The Development of Trust Companies*, passim.

113. Clive Trebilcock, *Phoenix Assurance and the Development of British Insurance,
1782–1870* (Cambridge: Cambridge University Press, 1985), I, 185, 189–201, 210–215,
218–225, 231–233, 257–260, 297–307, 319, 516. The Phoenix wrote its first American
policy at Charleston in 1785! On Pelican and Whalen in Philadelphia, see also Lester W.
Zartman, ed., *Yale Readings in Insurance: Life Insurance* (New Haven: Yale University
Press, 1909), 83; Herman E. Krooss and Martin R. Blyn, *A History of Financial Intermediaries* (New York: Random House, 1971), 35; and J. Owen Stalson, "The Pioneer in

American Life Insurance Marketing," *Bulletin of the Business Historical Society*, 12 (Nov. 1938): 66. The Pennsylvania legislature prohibited out-of-state life underwriters from doing business in Pennsylvania after March 10, 1810. After the end of the War of 1812, there had been other short-lived British entries into America. See, for instance, William Schooling, *Alliance Assurance, 1824–1924* (London: Alliance Assurance, 1924), 40, on Alliance's brief U.S. investments in 1825.

114. Minutes of Meeting of Directors, Bank of Montreal, Jan. 23, 1818, Resolve Book I, p. 41, Bank of Montreal Records, Public Archives, Ottawa (henceforth, BMAO). As noted earlier, Prime, Ward & Sands was Baring's New York correspondent, and the Bank of Montreal minutes note that "we require of them [Prime, Ward & Sands] a letter of introduction to their correspondents in London, the House of Barings & Co" (ibid.). See also Merrill Denison, *Canada's First Bank: A History of the Bank of Montreal*, 2 vols. (New York: Dodd, Mead, 1966, 1967), I, 125.

115. Ibid., I, 129.

116. Silver that came into the Canadian bank as capital stock or deposits could not be used by the Canadians in trade with the Orient (because of British navigation laws). New York and Boston merchants required the silver for their China trade (ibid., I, 179). Later, as demand for specie in the United States rose, the Bank of Montreal continued to supply it (ibid., I, 257 [referring to 1825]). But it was a two-way street, and for the entire period of 1818–1828, Canadian imports came to exceed greatly exports of specie (ibid., I, 264). In the 1830s, the minute books of the Bank of Montreal monitor the specie imports. For example, July 10, 1835, Resolve Book III, p. 24, BMAO.

117. Denison, *Canada's First Bank*, I, 269.

118. In 1827 Prime, Ward, King & Co.—the successor to Prime, Ward & Sands—became the Bank of Montreal's New York agent.

119. Bank of Nova Scotia, *Bank of Nova Scotia* (Toronto: privately printed, 1932), 43.

120. Denison, *Canada's First Bank*, I, 317. This meant that in the mid-1830s, Prime, Ward & King acted for Baring Brothers, the Bank of Montreal, and the Bank of British North America, and probably others as well.

121. Callender, "Early Transportation and Banking Enterprises," 114. See, for example, the Agreement of Aug. 14, 1832, whereby Baring Brothers & Co. and Prime, Ward, King & Co., New York, agree to purchase $5.5 million of bonds of the state of Louisiana to be issued in favor of the Union Bank of Louisiana (BAO, vol. 24, p. 012061). T. W. Ward wrote Baring Brothers, Sept. 20, 1832 (BAO, vol. 24, p. 012070): "We shall have a variety of Banks and other stocks under state guaranty within a year."

122. Green, *Finance and Economic Development*, 80.

123. Jenks, *Migration*, 66.

124. Sir Charles Augustus Murray. He planned to settle, but changed his mind (Thistlewaite, *The Anglo-American Connection*, 21).

125. Van Winter, *American Finance*, chap. 14.

126. Ibid., 872, and Frederick S. Allis, Jr., ed., *William Bingham's Maine Lands, 1790–1820* (Boston: Colonial Society of Massachusetts, 1954), II, 1254.

127. Callender, "Early Transportation and Banking Enterprises," 153n. The Morris Canal and Banking Company was incorporated in 1824. It had banking and trust powers and, as noted earlier, was an important financial intermediary, bringing in European monies. A historian of American trust companies found that the earliest trust deed by any corporation was dated May 29, 1830, and was entered into by this company and Wilhem Willink, Jr., as trustee. Willink of Amsterdam negotiated a loan of $750,000 in Holland. This corporate fiduciary originated as a "collateral feature" of canal construction. It became a reservoir of long-term credit. See Smith, *The Development of Trust Companies*, 248, 273–274, 281–282. In 1838 the British Rothschilds had

interests in the Morris Canal and Banking Company. The Rothschilds were involved in stock consignments for the Morris Company. See American Account Books (1831–1839), RAL II/3/0. Van Winter, *American Finance*, 971–973, gives details on Willink's role. For Frederick Huth & Co.'s interests in the Morris Canal and Banking Company bonds in 1836–1837, see Freedman, "A London Merchant Banker," 29, 34. At the close of 1837, the Huths sold all their Morris bonds (£25,000) to a Spanish client (Funez y Carillo). On Funez y Carillo, see ibid., 54, and this chapter, note 150.

128. Callender, "Early Transportation and Banking Enterprises," 153n; Van Winter, *American Finance*, 973–978; Jenks, *Migration*, 361 n.31; and Alfred D. Chandler, "Patterns of American Railroad Finance, 1830–50," *Business History Review*, 28 (1954): 250. The British Rothschilds had no American railroad securities in the 1830s—not on their own account, on joint accounts, or on others' accounts. See American Account Books (1831–1839), RAL II/3/0.

129. Bosch, *Nederlandse Beleggingen*, 51, and Van Winter, *American Finance*, 967–968. The issues were associated with the Holland Land Company's properties. There is no evidence that they were picked up by the Dutch public. Indeed, Van Winter (p. 968) believed that it would be another twenty years "before the Dutch began to take a warm interest in American railroads."

130. Dorothy Adler, *British Investment in American Railways* (Charlottesville: University Press of Virginia, 1970), 12, and Harry H. Pierce, "Anglo-American Investors and Investment in the New York Central Railroad," in *An Emerging Independent American Economy, 1815–1875*, ed. Joseph R. Frese and Jacob Judd (Tarrytown, N.Y.: Sleepy Hollow Press, 1980), 128.

131. Charles Duguid, *The Story of the Stock Exchange: Its History and Position* (London: Grant Richards, 1901), 246. These were bonds denominated in pounds sterling (Chandler, "Patterns," 250).

132. Callender, "Early Transportation and Banking Enterprise," 111–162. Jenks, *Migration*, 75, writes that "before 1836 over $90 million had been invested in canals and railroads in the North, of which more than half was a charge on public credit. The bulk of this capital had been procured from England." Douglass C. North, "International Capital Flows and the Development of the American West," *Journal of Economic History*, 16 (Dec. 1956): 495, has mistakenly argued that there was an absence of "government intervention"; undoubtedly, he defined "government" as *federal* government and intervention as regulation. North knew better. Sometimes also securities were issued with the backing of city governments.

133. Jenks, *Migration*, 361 n.31. The Bank of the United States had been involved with the Hazelton Coal Company (Smith, *Economic Aspects*, 116).

134. Adler, *British Investment*, 122.

135. Ronald L. Lewis, *Coal, Iron, and Slaves* (Westport, Conn: Greenwood Press, 1979), 49. British holding in this company in 1853 represented 41.7 percent of the stock and 72.3 percent of the bonds. See U.S. Senate, *Report of the Secretary of the Treasury*, 33rd Cong., 1st sess., 1854, Exec. Doc. 42, 52. Reprinted in *Foreign Investments in the United States*, ed. Mira Wilkins (New York: Arno Press, 1977).

136. Lewis, *Coal, Iron*, 67.

137. As will be evident, foreign direct investments in manufacturing would often later be made to vault high tariff walls.

138. Peter Temin, *The Jacksonian Economy* (New York: W. W. Norton, 1969), 77–82, associates the inflation with the expansion of the money supply based on the growth in the stock of specie, which came from abroad. Changes in the China trade meant this specie remained in the United States (ibid., 82). Temin argues (p. 90) that the land boom retarded inflation. My formulation is more traditional.

139. Hidy, *House of Baring*, 206–207. See S. Jaudon to Baring Brothers, Oct. 15, 1836, BAO, vol. 38, p. 054814, for a reaction.

140. See text and Ratchford, *American State Debts*, 93.

141. Hidy, *House of Baring*, 207–234.

142. Gille, *Maison Rothschild*, I, 284, 268.

143. Ibid., 284. The London Rothschild books also show continued involvement.

144. Temin, *Jacksonian Economy*, 20. When in May 1837 the bank suspended specie payments, it was "a strong, solvent, and liquid institution." It believed, however, that once other banks suspended, it had no choice (Govan, *Nicholas Biddle*, 312). See also Nicholas Biddle to John Quincy Adams, Dec. 10, 1838, published in U.S. House, *Report from the Secretary of the Treasury*, 29th Cong., 1st sess., 1849, Exec. Doc. 226, 405, for Biddle's boasts on how the private engagements of the people of the United States had been met.

145. Hidy, *House of Baring*, 235.

146. Myers, *New York Money Market*, 30.

147. Hidy, *House of Baring*, 237.

148. Ibid., 261.

149. Ibid., 266.

150. Ibid., 267. English financial intermediaries did not confine their sales of American securities to Britishers. Frederick Huth & Co., for example, had a Spanish client, Funez y Carillo, which in 1836 had sold British consols; that year, Huths sought American opportunities for a substantial portion of the £309,605, which the consols had produced. In 1837 and 1838 Huths arranged that a sizable amount of this "recycled" Spanish money went to the Bank of the United States (Freedman, "A London Merchant Banker," 27–28, 43–44, 54; see also ibid., 57–75, for Huth's dealings in American securities in 1838).

151. Trotter, *Observations*, 1–2.

152. Ibid., 362. How right Trotter was. The southern states were the worst offenders in the defaults that followed.

153. Ratchford, *American State Debts*, 94, and Hidy, *George Peabody*, 162–163, for conditions that summer. Take the case of the London merchant bankers, Frederick Huth & Co. It had provided commercial credit to the Bank of the United States and received as a "cover" $2 million in Michigan bonds; in July 1839 it told the Bank of the United States representative that London investors were showing "no interest at all" in these securities. See Andrew T. Murray, *Home from the Hill: A Biography of Frederick Huth* (London: Hamish Hamilton, 1970), 165–166.

154. Hidy, *George Peabody*, 148.

155. U.S. Secretary of Treasury, *Report on Condition of State Banks*, 26th Cong., 1st sess., April 7, 1840, H. Doc. 172, 347, 349. The data on the holdings by nobility are as of January 1, 1840. This report also indicates that as of January 1, 1840, the bank's 1,390 foreign stockholders included 1,185 from Great Britain and Ireland, 59 from Spain, 52 from the West Indies, 36 from France, 26 from Holland, 10 from Germany, and the rest spread out around the world (from Europe, Asia, Canada, and Latin America).

156. Ratchford, *American State Debts*, 94.

157. Hidy, *House of Baring*, 281, and Edward Hungerford, *The Story of the Baltimore and Ohio Railroad, 1827–1927* (New York: G. P. Putnam, 1928), I, 199–200. In April 1840 Maryland made all interest outside the United States payable through Baring (Hidy, *House of Baring*, 293).

158. Data in the BAO, vols. 98 and 110, provide ample support for these generalizations.

159. See list in the BAO, vol. 98, p. 054957. See also Bosch, *Nederlandse Beleggingen,* 49.

160. According to Smith, *Economic Aspects,* 44, Hottinguer & Co. became Paris correspondents for the bank about 1826.

161. Hottinguer & Co., Paris, to Baring Brothers, Sept. 19, 1839, BAO, vol. 110, p. 061350.

162. S. Jaudon to Baring Brothers, Nov. 30, 1839, BAO, vol. 98, p. 054966.

163. Hidy, *House of Baring,* 283–284, 546. For partial reprint and translation into French, see Alex Lombard, *Notice sur la position financière actuelle des états de l'Amérique du Nord* (Geneva: Imprimerie de Ch. Gruaz, 1841), 43–47. Webster was in London on Oct. 16, 1839, the date of his letter. On March 24, 1840, Webster wrote Joshua Bates of Baring Brothers, "As to State Stocks Massths. you know may always be relied on; so I think may N.Y. & Ohio; & I think Pa. will come out alright. I have much confidence, too, in Indiana. As to the rest, I should advise caution; but this I say to yourself only." Quoted in Hidy, *House of Baring,* 284. Baring's sold some of its Maryland bonds (ibid., 281). It returned to America some of its South Carolina bonds that it had not sold (ibid., 283).

164. S. J. Loyd to G. W. Norman, Nov. 11, 1839, *Correspondence of Lord Overstone,* I, 245.

165. Loyd to Norman, Dec. 15, 1839, ibid., I, 247. On Jaudon's pleas and difficulties, see BAO, vol. 98, pp. 054947-94, and vol. 110, pp. 061325-91. As noted, the Rothschilds, Denison & Co., and Hope & Co. did provide assistance.

166. Hidy, *House of Baring,* 289. The Erving-King Papers, folder K30A, New York Historical Society, contain 1840 letters from Prime, Ward & King to Baring Brothers & Co. that reflect the perceptions of Baring's agent. In the BAO, vol. 110, are letters from Hottinguer & Co., Paris, to Baring Brothers, 1839–1840, on a plan for "an administration" in Paris "for American funds" (Nov. 26, 1839, pp. 0161400-02); the plans took shape in March 1840 (see letters, March, 7, 11, 16, 1840, pp. 061428-42). It was this "administration"—made up of Hottinguer & Co. and three other French firms—that acquired the American securities.

167. Quotation is that of William Crawshay, cited in Ann M. Scanlon, "The Building of the New York Central," in *An Emerging Independent American Economy,* ed. Frese and Judd, 112.

168. The shares held abroad are given in U.S.House, *Report from the Secretary of the Treasury on the Returns of the State Banks from 1841 to 1846,* 29th Cong., 1st sess., 1846, Exec. Doc. 226, 469; ibid., 442, for March 1, 1841, bank liabilities. According to Gatty, *Portrait of a Merchant Prince,* 211–212, James Morrison had agreed to become the bank's agent on Jan. 11, 1841. Smith, *Economic Aspects,* 224–226, dates the agency arrangement back to October 1840; I think Gatty is probably right.

169. Loyd to Norman, March 6, 1841, *Correspondence of Lord Overstone,* I, 320. Thomas Raikes entered in his journal, March 25, 1841: "It is said that Lord H—— loses 500,000 *l* by the stoppage of the 'United States' Bank in America. With his immense property, it is a loss that he can hardly feel; but he always had a great dread of revolutions; his expression was frequently that he had secured himself a *clean shirt* and a *valet de chambre* in the funds of every country happen what might. With this view, and supposing a republic least vulnerable to these chances, he made very large investments in American funds" (*Raikes Journal,* II, 275). Was Lord H—— Lord Hertford? See ibid., I, 30, for a suggestion on identification.

170. Cameron, *France,* 84, and Émile Becque, *L'internationalisation des capitaux* (Montpelier: Imperimerie Générale du Midi, 1912), 16. In addition, see Hottinguer & Co.–Baring Brothers & Co. correspondence, BAO, vol. 110. As noted earlier, in the fall of

1838 Hottinguer & Co. required a guarantee in state stock as backing for existing bank credit (Hottinguer & Co. to Baring Brothers & Co., Sept. 19, 1839, p. 061350). When Hottinguer & Co. was planning the "administration" to sell American stocks in France, they begged Baring's "to keep the thing *quite* secret for were it known we should see immediately competition on every side" (ibid., March 7, 1840, p. 061428). In 1835–1839 Count Alexis de Tocqueville had published in France his *Democracy in America*, which had turned new attention in France to America.

171. Hope & Co. to Baring Brothers & Co., Nov. 13, 1838, BAO, vol. 110, p. 061669. The Hope & Co.–Baring Brothers & Co. correspondence shows a sophistication on the part of the Dutch house that seemed absent in the Hottinguer & Co. letters.

172. Hope & Co. to Baring Brothers & Co., May 14, 1839, vol. 110, p. 061700. The Hope & Co. correspondence is very useful—and gossipy. It tells what the Rothschilds and others were doing.

173. Lombard, *Notice sur la position financière actuelle des états de l'Amérique du Nord*, was published in February 1841 by a Geneva banker. It reveals the general interest in Europe in American state debts. Despite the Panics of 1837 and 1839, Lombard saw American prosperity as continuous (p. 17). He concluded with recommendations in favor of New York and Ohio securities (p. 42). La Société Parisienne had recently issued bearer certificates for the bonds of New York and Ohio at a fixed rate of about 5.1 francs per dollar, the certificates being of 1,000 francs for 196 dollars (p. 51). Among the reasons Ohio was particularly attractive, Lombard stated, was the morality of its inhabitants, the many Swiss settlers there, and the fact that the state's settlers were overwhelmingly Protestant (pp. 32–33).

174. See notes above and Vincent P. Carosso, *Investment Banking in America: A History* (Cambridge, Mass.: Harvard University Press, 1970), 9.

175. Ratchford, *American State Debts*, 98.

176. McGrane, *Foreign Bondholders*, chap. 4.

177. Jenks, *Migration*, 368.

178. U.S. House, 27th Cong. 3rd sess., 1843, H. Rept. 296, 7. On p. 151 of the same report, interest payments were worked out "supposing" state bonds held abroad were $100 million. Clearly, no one knew how much was held abroad. The reason more were owned abroad in 1842 than in 1838 were (1) the new issues in 1838, (2) the active role of the Bank of the United States in transferring state securities to Europe, and (3) the promotions of state securities in Europe subsequent to the crisis of 1839.

179. Ratchford, *American State Debts*, 101. See Overend, Gurney & Co. to Colonel William Robinson, Oct. 3, 1842, proposing means by which the federal government could assume state debts. U.S. House, 27th Cong., 3rd sess., 1843, H. Doc. 197, 3–4. Subsequently, the report of Representative William Cost Johnson (Maryland), U.S. House, 27th Cong., 3rd sess., 1843, H. Rept. 296, 8, favored federal assumption of state debts.

180. Jenks, *Migration*, 116. For the British government position toward foreign bondholders, see D. C. M. Platt, *Finance, Trade, and Politics in British Foreign Policy, 1815–1914* (Oxford: Clarendon Press, 1968), 34–36.

181. Hidy, *House of Baring*, 292.

182. Cited in Jenks, *Migration*, 106.

183. Listed in the BAO, vol. 98, p. 054957.

184. Hidy, *House of Baring*, 309, 342–343. On "transatlantic morality," see Murray, *Home from the Hill*, 143, 162–171. Colonel William Robinson was sent by the U.S. Secretary of the Treasury to Europe in 1842 to negotiate a U.S. loan. On his return he wrote, "It seems to me altogether inexplicable, that, while Hamburg and Holland, with a mountain of debt, and even the Pachalic [sic] of Egypt, could fill a loan . . . the

American loan should find no favor." Robinson added that the United States was the only government "on the face of the earth" that had paid off a national debt! See U.S. House, H. Doc. 197, 2.

185. Wilkins, *The Emergence of Multinational Enterprise*, 22.

186. Smith, *Letters*, 17–18, 12–13. Smith's letters were first published in the fall of 1843. In 1843 Charles Dickens' *Martin Chuzzlewit* appeared. Its English hero had a nasty experience with U.S. real estate investments that were misrepresented. The novel's publication coincided with the prevailing mood of distrust of American investments.

187. Jenks, *Migration*, 98.

188. Circular from the Foreign Office, signed by Palmerston, March 19, 1847, FO 83/110, Public Record Office, London (henceforth, PRO). This was not an abstraction. Frederick Huth & Co., London, for example, "found themselves to be the owners" of a Florida plantation with slaves—in exchange for Florida stock. Huth's biographer writes, "They did not keep it very long" (Murray, *Home from the Hill*, 171).

189. Circular from the Foreign Office, signed by Palmerston, Jan. 15, 1848, FO 83/110, PRO. This circular was later quoted in the context of considering U.S. policies toward foreign loans. See unsigned memo, Jan. 12, 1917, RG 59, 811.503/61, National Archives, Washington, D.C. The circular is printed in full in Platt, *Finance, Trade,* 398–399.

190. Hidy, *House of Baring,* 307–341. Substantial material exists in the literature on state debts and in the BAO, for example, on the efforts of foreign bondholders to obtain their just returns. In 1844, for instance, John Horsley Palmer of Palmer, MacKillop, Dent & Co., London, chaired a committee of Indiana bondholders; the committee included the London Rothschilds and Hope & Co. See Haeger, *The Investment Frontier,* 217.

191. North, "International Capital Flows," 503.

192. For example, the American Life Insurance and Trust Company, Baltimore, and the North American Trust and Banking Company, New York. The New York Life Insurance and Trust Company, the Farmers' Loan and Trust Company, and others outside New York survived. See Perine, *The Story of Trust Companies,* 71, 76.

193. Hidy, *House of Baring,* 368–369. North, "Balance of Payments," 586, shows capital outflows in most of the 1840s.

194. McGrane, *Foreign Bondholders,* 268.

195. W. W. Rostow, *The Stages of Economic Growth* (Cambridge: Cambridge University Press, 1960), 38, set the U.S. "take-off" in the years 1843–1860!

196. U.S. Department of Commerce, Bureau of the Census, *Historical Statistics of the United States* (Washington, D.C., 1975), 735.

197. Robert E. Gallman's figures in *The Reinterpretation of American Economic History,* ed. Robert W. Fogel and Stanley L. Engerman (New York: Harper & Row, 1971), 26.

198. J. & P. Coats, "Text of the 150 Year Exhibition," panel 9, Renfrew District Library, Scotland, and Matthew Blair, *The Paisley Thread Industry* (Paisley: Alexander Gardner, 1907), 49. J. B. K. Hunter, the historian of J. & P. Coats, writes (Hunter to Wilkins, April 27, 1986) that Andrew Coats spelled his name "Coates." Andrew Coats built the "selling system" in the United States and appointed "commission agents" to act for the firm. Hugh Auchincloss, a New York merchant, was the chief agent. For interesting data on the Coats business in the United States see *Coats v. Holbrook* (1845), 2 Sand. Ch.R. 586, a New York case, reported in *American Trade Mark Cases,* ed. Rowland Cox (Cincinnati: Robert Clarke, 1871), 20–32.

199. J. D. Scott, *Vickers* (London: Weidenfeld & Nicolson, 1962), 7.

200. Adler, *British Investment,* 15.

201. Some $721,000 between 1843 and 1846 (James, *Chicago Banks,* I, 166–169). For background, see Haeger, *Investment Frontier,* 206–209.

202. Adler, *British Investment*, 28, 123; Jenks, *Migration*, 368 n.1; and U.S. Senate, *Report of the Secretary of the Treasury . . . [on] the Amount of American Securities Held in Europe*, 33rd Cong., 1st sess., 1854, Exec. Doc. 42, 52, in *Foreign Investments of the United States*, ed. Mira Wilkins (New York: Arno Press, 1977); henceforth cited as S. Doc. 42. For the impact of the tariff and the importance of the Mount Savage firm, see W. T. Hogan, *Economic History of the Iron and Steel Industry in the United States*, 5 vols. (Lexington, Mass.: Lexington Books, 1971), I, 38. Hogan knew nothing of the foreign ownership. Henry Thomas Weld (1816–1893), born in London, became a resident of the United States in 1844 as "managing agent and director for the English stockholders" in the Mount Savage rolling mill. The manufacture of the iron rails started under the stimulus of a duty of $25 per ton provided in the tariff of 1842 (*American Iron and Steel Association Bulletin*, 27 [July 26, 1893]: 220). For more data on the Mount Savage works, see Irene D. Neu, *Erastus Corning* (Ithaca, N.Y.: Cornell University Press, 1960), 48–51.

203. London *Times*, Dec. 1, 1842, quoting the *Daily Evening Bulletin*, Boston.

204. Gatty, *Portrait of a Merchant Prince*, 213, 219, 224, 225. The $3.77 million cited earlier in the text (from the Bank of the United States books) is equal to some £750,000 (at a rate of exchange of £1 = $5.00), and £850,000 (at £1 = $4.44).

205. "British Mercantile Houses Abroad," FO 83/111, PRO, London. The British also sought to determine in 1849 the number of mercantile houses established by French citizens in the United States. The Consul in New York replied that it was "impractical to fill in this return." The Consuls in Boston, Charleston, and Savannah listed "none," whereas the Philadelphia Consul identified fifteen French houses, six of which were wine and spirit merchants. The Philadelphia Consul added that all the French merchants in that city imported through New York rather than directly from France. See FO 83/115, PRO, London. Included among the Philadelphia representatives of Sheffield steel producers were those of Sanderson Brothers & Co., Jessop & Sons, W. & S. Butcher, and Naylor & Co. (a predecessor of Vickers). For Sheffield steel exports to the United States, see Geoffrey Tweedale, "Sheffield Steel and America," *Business History*, 25 (Nov. 1983): 225–239, and his dissertation, "Sheffield Steel Industry and Its Allied Trades and the American Market, 1850–1913," London School of Economics, 1983. Some of the Sheffield hardware group had entered the United States not long after the end of the War of 1812. On this list, Andrew Coats's sales business was not included. The cotton spinner in Philadelphia was James Crawford (FO 83/111, PRO).

206. *Taylor* v. *Carpenter* (1846), Fed. Case 13,785 (my italics). Cited in William Marion Gibson, *Aliens and the Law* (Chapel Hill: University of North Carolina Press, 1940), 75.

207. On Ohio bonds, see Adler, *British Investment*, 16, and Alex Lombard, *Notes financières et statistiques sur l'état Ohio* (Geneva, 1847), 4.

208. Robert G. Albion, *The Rise of New York Port, 1815–1860* (Hamden, Conn.: Archon Books, 1961), 20, 43.

209. Hutchins, *The American Maritime Industries*, 352. In 1858 this service was incorporated into that of the North German Lloyd Line (formed in 1857), which had service between New York and Bremen (ibid., 511, 518). This steamship service supplemented the existing German connections by "sail." In 1828 the Bremen firm, H. H. Meier & Co. had established a regular liner service to New York. In 1836 the Hamburg ship broker Robert Miles Sloman inaugurated a packet line to that city. By the beginning of the 1840s, Bremen already had four packet lines, all carrying emigrants. In 1847 there came into being the Hamburg-Amerikanische Packetfahrt A.G. (HAPAG), a sailing packet line to New York. See Lars U. Scholl, "Shipping Business in Germany in the Nineteenth and Twentieth Centuries," in Tsunehiko Yui and Keiichiro Nakagawa, *Business History of Shipping* (Tokyo: University of Tokyo, 1985), 188–190.

210. My colleague René Higonnet directed my attention to Otto Ruhle, *Karl Marx*,

2nd ed. (New York: Viking Press, 1935), 172, which points out how Marx was "taken back" at the discoveries of California gold, believing the prosperity to be generated "had saved European capital"! There was no question about European interest. See BAO, vol. 47, fall 1849, correspondence, for example.

211. Henry Blumenthal, "The California Societies in France, 1849–1855," *Pacific Historical Review*, 25 (Aug. 1956): 251–260.

212. Cleona Lewis, *America's Stake in International Investments* (Washington, D.C.: Brookings Institution, 1938), 45, and Emden, *Money Powers of Europe*, 263.

213. Alfred D. Chandler, Jr., *Henry Varnum Poor* (Cambridge, Mass.: Harvard University Press, 1956), 106. Some of the sizable German investments in American securities, 1848–1852, appear to have been associated with German emigration. Germans would buy the dollar-denominated American securities at home and then bring these securities with them when they emigrated to the United States. This became a way of coping with foreign exchange problems and the transfer of the immigrants' assets. To the extent that this occurred, the German investment became an American one as the traveler crossed the Atlantic. Nowhere have I seen statistics on the proportion of German purchases used for this purpose.

214. Hidy, *House of Baring*, 351. Daniel Webster, Secretary of State, arranged the change. Webster had been a paid consultant of the Barings (ibid., 284). In 1842 Secretary of State Daniel Webster and Lord Ashburton (Alexander Baring)—representing Sir Robert Peel—had successfully negotiated the Webster-Ashburton Treaty, which resolved certain conflicts between the United States and Great Britain and gave the United States 7,000 of the 12,000-square-mile disputed region between Maine and New Brunswick. See Thomas A. Bailey, *A Diplomatic History of the American People*, 6th ed. (New York: Appleton-Century-Crofts, 1958), 211–219. Recall that Alexander Baring in 1796 had introduced the Barings into investment in Maine land. He knew Maine well. For more on the Webster-Ashburton Treaty, see Howard Jones, *To the Webster-Ashburton Treaty* (Chapel Hill: University of North Carolina Press, 1977). In 1842, aside from the controversies over state debts (not considered in the Webster-Ashburton Treaty), there were other causes of friction between Britain and the United States that this treaty resolved.

215. Hidy, *House of Baring*, 373. George Bancroft (U.S. Minister in London) wrote Baring Brothers, Sept. 27, 1848, "I learn from W. W. Corcoran [a Treasury Department agent in this transaction] that he has arranged with your house and that of Overend, Gurney & Co., James Morrison, George Peabody, and Messrs. Dennison [sic] to take three millions of dollars of the six per cent stock of the United States, payable in 1868" (BAO, vol. 97, p. 054155). On George Peabody's role, see Hidy, *George Peabody*, 290–291. Samuel Jones Loyd took part of the $3 million (ibid., 291). BAO, vol. 48, 1850 correspondence contains considerable data on the Mexican indemnity. At the end of the Mexican War, the United States and Mexico had signed the Treaty of Guadalupe-Hidalgo (Feb. 2, 1848), which ceded to the United States territory that included what is now the states of Arizona, New Mexico, California, Nevada, Utah, and Colorado west of the Rockies. For this territory, the United States indemnified Mexico $15 million and assumed the claims of U.S. citizens against Mexico.

216. James de Rothschild to nephews, Feb. 22, 1848, cited in Anka Muhlstein, *Baron James* (New York: Vendome Press, [1983?]), 173, 222n. According to data uncovered by Henry Blumenthal, the French Rothschilds in the summer of 1848 acquired $3 million in U.S. government bonds. *A Reappraisal of Franco-American Relations*, 114–115. These securities were presumably acquired by August Belmont on behalf of the French house. There is no indication of how long they were held. If this be accurate, it is a very large amount for one firm for this period. This coincided with James de Rothschild's dis-

patching his son Alphonse to America. On James de Rothschild's significance in French foreign investments, see Rondo Cameron, "French Foreign Investment, 1850–1880," Ph.D. diss., University of Chicago, 1952, 13.

217. The French Rothschilds also encouraged their friends in France and elsewhere in Europe to invest in American securities. See, for example, Alexander Herzen, *My Past and Thoughts* (Berkeley: University of California, 1982), 399.

218. Samuel Jones Loyd in 1849 purchased £52,675 in U.S. bonds. *The Correspondence of Lord Overstone*, 937 n.5.

219. Hidy, *House of Baring*, 383–384. See Corcoran and Riggs to Baring Brothers & Co., March 16, 1850, BAO, vol. 97, p. 054232, on the Rothschild role. The British Rothschilds' books show at the end of 1852 that they held $223,800 (£53,459 by *their* calculation) in U.S. 6 percent bonds (RAL II/3/5).

220. McGrane, *Foreign Bondholders*, 270.

221. Ralph W. Hidy and Muriel E. Hidy, "Anglo-American Merchant Bankers and the Railroads of the Old Northwest, 1848–1860," *Business History Review*, 34 (Summer 1960): 154. Chandler, *Henry Varnum Poor*, 81–108, is excellent on the renewal of foreign investment, although some houses remained cautious. Mississippi had not resumed payments. In 1852 the British Rothschilds held $1,570,000 in Mississippi bonds; Denison & Co. had $880,000; and Hope & Co. held $628,000 (Hope & Co. to Baring Brothers, March 29, 1852, BAO, vol. 110, p. 062477).

222. S. Doc. 42, 3. The British Rothschild books show a decline in interest in U.S. government securities during 1853—with their holdings at the end of 1853, $137,000 (£33,919 by *their* calculations), compared with $223,800 (£53,459) a year earlier.

223. Hidy, *House of Baring*, 407ff.

224. Hidy, *George Peabody*, 346.

225. S. Doc. 42, 4–7. On Winslow, Lanier & Co. and its expertise, see Chandler, *Henry Varnum Poor*, 88–89. Part of the dispute on size of investment was over how one handled securities in default.

226. S. Doc. 42, 8–10.

227. Ibid.

228. Ibid., 12–31.

229. On the absence of dividends, see Josiah Granville Leach, *The History of the Girard National Bank of Philadelphia, 1832–1902* (1902; rpt. New York: Greenwood Press, 1969), 61. For the basic information, see S. Doc. 42, 12–31. The government report indicated a mere $12,900 in the stock of the Girard Bank was held abroad, about 1 percent of the capital. The Bank of North America, in Philadelphia, had $80,800 of its $1 million capital held abroad, or 8 percent—the most of eight Pennsylvania banks that still had minor foreign investments (ibid., 24). Senate Document 42 is superb on the foreign holdings. There were less than 10 percent foreign holdings in a number of the largest New York City banks. Thus foreign stock holdings in the Bank of Commerce totaled $455,900, and in the Manhattan Bank, $157,700 (ibid., 20). The Citizens' Bank, New Orleans, was not surveyed in this report. It had been in liquidation since October 1842; its charter was renewed in March 1852; Hope & Co. apparently obtained on interest in this rechartered bank, based on its 1830s involvements. See Green, *Finance and Economic Development*, 132, and Chapter 13.

230. Trebilcock, *Phoenix Assurance*, passim; Harold E. Raynes, *History of British Insurance*, rev. ed. (London: Isaac Pitman, 1950), 266–268; and J. Dyer Simpson, *1936 Our Centenary Year* (London: Liverpool & London & Globe, 1936). As noted, the British insurance companies mentioned in my text were not included among the seventy-five U.S. insurance companies surveyed by the U.S. Treasury Department. Of the latter, the foreign stock holdings of $378,178 were spread over thirty companies. In only three

was the percentage of foreign ownership over 10 percent: Knickerbocker, New York (13.5%), Pennsylvania Life, Philadelphia (13.0%); and Merchants', Mobile, Alabama (19.4%) (S. Doc. 42, 32–35).

231. Cameron, *France*, 86; excerpt from *American Railroad Journal*, July 3, 1852, "Negotiation of Railroad Securities at Home and Abroad," reprinted in Alfred D. Chandler, Jr., *The Railroads* (New York: Harcourt, Brace & World, 1965), 60–64; and Chandler, *Henry Varnum Poor*, 97–99, 81–108. Chandler notes that in the early 1850s, Adrian and John Iselin, who were from an old Basle family and whose firm retained close connections with Geneva and Basle bankers, were sending U.S. railway bonds to Switzerland. According to Hans Bauer, *Swiss Bank Corporation, 1872–1972* (Basle: Swiss Bank Corp., 1972), 48, A. Iselin & Co., New York, originated from a firm established in 1803 by Isaac Iselin-Roulet and H. C. de Rham. The former was from Basle and the latter from Yverdon, Switzerland. Charles and Theodore Moran in New York also had ties with Swiss bankers (Chandler, *Henry Varnum Poor*, 94, 97, and Adler, *British Investment*, 17–21). See W. J. Reader, *A House in the City* (London: B. T. Batsford Ltd., 1979), 46–48, for revived British interests in the early 1850s; this history of the stockbroker, Foster & Braithwaite shows their activity in U.S. rails, 1852–1914.

232. American Account Book, 1852–1856, RAL II/3/5. See also Hidy, *George Peabody*, 347–348.

233. Hidy, *House of Baring*, 412–414, and McGrane, *Foreign Bondholders*, 271–274 (on W. H. Swift). See also Hidy and Hidy, "Anglo-Merchant Bankers," 154–164. Henry Varnum Poor urged foreign investors to get careful advice, to know what they were purchasing (Chandler, *Henry Varnum Poor*, 98). Many of Swift's reports are in the BAO. On Thomas Baring's trip, see D. C. M. Platt, *Foreign Finance in Continental Europe and the United States, 1815–1870* (London: George Allen & Unwin, 1984), 158.

234. Adler, *British Investment*, 42 (first public issues), and Paul Wallace Gates, *The Illinois Central and Its Colonization Work* (Cambridge, Mass.: Harvard University Press, 1934), 73.

235. Hidy, *George Peabody*, 349.

236. Even though the loans did not have a formal "tying clause," because the bonds were direct payment for rails one can call these "tied loans."

237. Hidy, *House of Baring*, 410.

238. Ann M. Scanlon, "The Building of the New York Central," 104.

239. Ibid., 102. See also Adler, *British Investment*, 42–43.

240. Alan Birch, *The Economic History of the British Iron and Steel Industry, 1784–1879* (London: Frank Cass, 1967), 220.

241. This point is made in North, "United States Balance of Payments," 586.

242. Based on S. Doc. 42, 36–47, 53. This splendid report lists the railroads by state and gives full details. Of course, *if* the "foreign" holding was in the name of a U.S. firm, it would be excluded from this roster, so the list probably underestimates the actual foreign holdings.

243. Ibid., 46.

244. Ibid., 44. The U.S. Treasury Department study estimated that of the bonds outstanding of 244 railroad companies, 26 percent was held abroad, while only 3 percent of the stock of these same companies was foreign-owned. Emden, *Money Powers of Europe*, 263, notes that of the American railroad bonds that came on the Frankfurt market in the mid-nineteenth century, many had been received by English contractors in payment for work done and materials supplied and then forwarded to the Continent. The Dutch do not appear to have been involved in these early 1850s investments in U.S. railroads. Later they would become very important in U.S. railroad investments.

245. Blumenthal, "California Societies," 255; T. A. Rickard, *Retrospect* (New York: McGraw-Hill, 1937), 9 (John Taylor & Sons); and Jenks, *Migration*, 161, 383.

246. James de Rothschild, Paris, to nephews, May 5, 1848, cited in Muhlstein, *Baron James*, 184–185, 222n. Belmont thought he was being replaced and was prepared to resign (Black, *The King of Fifth Avenue*, 54). See also Gille, *Maison Rothschild*, II, 581–585, on the plans to replace Belmont and establish a Rothschild house in America.

247. Ira B. Cross, *Financing an Empire* (Chicago: S. J. Clarke, 1927), I, 57; Gille, *Maison Rothschild*, II, 552–554, 582–583; and Richard Davis, *The English Rothschilds* (Chapel Hill: University of North Carolina Press, 1983), 31, 131.

248. Cross, *Financing an Empire*, I, 66. See D. K. Fieldhouse, *Economics and Empire* (Ithaca, N.Y.: Cornell University Press, 1973), 234; Eugene Staley, *War and the Private Investor* (Garden City, N.Y.: Doubleday, 1935), 111–127, on the Hamburg firm, which was founded in 1766 and became involved in trade in the Pacific in 1845; and Jeannette Keim, *Forty Years of German-American Political Relations* (Philadelphia: William J. Dornan, 1919), chap. 12, esp. 113 and 144, on Godeffroy in Samoa.

249. It went under a number of different names (Cross, *Financing an Empire*, I, 57). On its later history, see Chapter 4. On Oct. 26, 1849, E. C. Baring (later the first Lord Revelstoke) wrote from Panama to Baring Brothers & Co., London, "Rothschilds have sent an agent to San Francisco, who they say is making a good deal of money." But Baring did not suggest that his house open a San Francisco agency. Indeed, Baring left Panama, not for California, but for Peru (BAO, vol. 17, pp. 008410–3). In February 1852 N. M. Rothschild & Sons acquired the lease of the Royal Mint Refinery. The firm was empowered to refine gold and silver and "to present their bars directly to the Mint and the Bank of England for acceptance at the official rate." Davis, *The English Rothschilds*, 140, explains, "It was this concession which lay behind Rothschild activity in California and other places where the precious ores were discovered."

250. Wilson, *French Banking Structure and Credit Policy*, 145, and Clyde William Phelps, *The Foreign Expansion of American Banks* (New York: Ronald Press, 1927), 10. The founders immigrated, but ties were maintained with the new Paris firm Lazard Frères. See Chapter 13, note 43.

251. Perhaps not for Frenchmen, who lost a lot of money in the California schemes.

252. Cyril Ehrlich, *The Piano* (London: J. M. Dent, 1976), 47–48, 51, and Albert Bernhardt Faust, *The German Element in the United States* (Boston: Houghton Mifflin, 1909), II, 115–116.

253. Williams Haynes, *American Chemical Industry* (New York: Van Nostrand, 1954), I, 378–379. The secrecy was to no avail, and wood distillation plants developed in the United States. What happened to this foreign investment is not clear.

254. By far the best work on Scully is by Homer E. Socolofsky. See his *Landlord William Scully* (Lawrence, Kan.: The Regents Press of Kansas, 1979) and his earlier "William Scully: Ireland and America, 1840–1900," *Agricultural History*, 48 (Jan. 1974): 155–175. See also Paul Wallace Gates, *Frontier Landlords and Pioneer Tenants* (Ithaca, N.Y.: Cornell University Press, 1945), 34–36, and John Davis, "Alien Landlordism in America," in *The Land Question from Various Points of View*, ed. C. F. Taylor (Philadelphia: C. F. Taylor [1898]), 58. The late 1840s had seen massive Irish migration to America because of the potato famine. When Scully first came to America in 1850, he retained his Irish land holdings and soon returned to Ireland to borrow from his brother for further investment. His initial purchases of land were with military land warrants that had been issued to veterans of the Mexican War and were assignable. By 1852 his holdings in Illinois totaled 38,320 acres. On June 7, 1853, he went to the Logan County, Illinois, court house and filed a declaration of intention to become an American citizen. Socolofsky (*Landlord*, 29) believes that this signified he planned "to locate

permanently in Logan County," That he never did so Socolofsky attributes to Scully's wife's illness. Socolofsky is probably correct in saying that Scully intended to emigrate, but there is another possible explanation of his declaration. The 1841 Preemption Act, governing federal land sales, had a clause that sales would be only to U.S. citizens or to those who declared their intention to become citizens. Scully had bought public lands. Perhaps he wanted to assure the titles to his purchases. In any case, he did not settle in Illinois or become a citizen five years after his declaration, and when in the 1880s his name became identified with "alien landlordism," he was in fact a nonresident foreign investor.

255. Denison, *Canada's First Bank*, II, 4.

256. July 11, 1832, speech reprinted in Daniel Webster, *Works*, 8th ed. (Boston: Little, Brown, 1854), III, 427, 428.

257. Chandler, *Railroads*, 61.

258. *Niles' Weekly Register*, 20 (June 30, 1821): 273.

259. Quoted in Smith, *The Development of Trust Companies*, 259.

260. 3 U.S. Stat. 351, and Hutchins, *The American Maritime Industries*, 42, 229, 236, 252, 315, 576. Mercantilist policies had typically protected shipping, and even Adam Smith had allowed that some such protection was legitimate. In 1789 port duties in the United States had discriminated against "foreign ships"; see Chapter 2. The 1817 law, however, contained for the first time an outright prohibition against foreign ships in the U.S. coastwise trade. The navigation monopoly also applied to inland waterways—sounds, lakes, and rivers (Hutchins, *The American Maritime Industries*, 329).

261. See *Spratt v. Spratt*, 7 Law Ed. 897 (1830).

262. Haeger, *The Investment Frontier*, 32.

263. The Preemption Act of 1841, 5 U.S. Stats. 455 (Sept. 4, 1841), read, "Every person . . . being a citizen of the United States, or having filed his declaration to become a citizen . . . who since the first day of June A.D. eighteen hundred and forty, has made or shall hereafter make a settlement in person of public land" could enter 160 acres at the minimum price.

264. Jackson's veto message, reprinted in Holdsworth and Dewey, *The First and Second Banks*, 304. When the first Bank of the United States had been up for recharter, similar comments had been made—although not by the President. In the debate on the first bank, a representative from Kentucky (Mr. Desha) vehemently denounced the bank, declaring he had no doubt that George III was a principal stockholder and that the English monarch saw it as an instrument in effecting his nefarious purposes against the United States! See John Jay Knox, *A History of Banking in the United States* (1903; rpt. New York: Augustus M. Kelley, 1969), 41.

265. *Niles' Weekly Register*, 45 (Nov. 16, 1833): 178, and ibid., 48 (May 2, 1835): 145. The capital letters and the italics were in each case in the original.

266. McGrane, *Foreign Bondholders*, 29; the Barings were singled out for attack (Hidy, *House of Baring*, 284–285). In the summer of 1842, the Democratic newspaper the *Washington Globe* accused Webster of accepting bribes from the Barings and other British bankers to persuade the federal government to take over state debts (Jones, *To the Webster-Ashburton Treaty*, 164). Daniel Meinertzhagen, son-in-law of Frederick Huth, had in 1839 on behalf of the Huth firm concluded an agreement with the Bank of Missouri for the disposal in London of large quantities of Missouri state and bank stock. Meinertzhagen, in a letter to the President of the Bank of Missouri in 1840, expressed optimism for the prospects of the United States, if the Whigs won the presidential election. A Democrat in the bank got hold of the letter, made copies, "and within days people in Missouri, and further afield, were being assailed with blood-

curdling stories of a European bankers' conspiracy to gain control of the government of the United States." The Missouri state legislature, yielding to popular pressure, canceled the agreement with Frederick Huth & Co. (Murray, *Home from the Hill*, 143, 166, 168). See also Freedman, "A London Merchant," 120–121. Senator Thomas H. Benton, Democrat from Missouri, prepared a Senate resolution opposing the assumption by the federal government of any state debts: "That the debts of the States being now chiefly held by foreigners, and constituting a stock in foreign markets now greatly depreciated, any legislative attempt to obtain the assumption or securityship of the United States for their payment . . . must have the effect of enhancing the value of that stock to the amount of a great many millions of dollars, to the enormous and undue advantages of foreign capitalists and of jobbers and gamblers in stock, thereby holding out inducement to foreigners to interfere in our affairs . . . Foreign interference . . . in all ages . . . [has] been the bane and curse of free governments." U.S. Senate, 26th Cong., 1st sess., Feb. 5, 1840, S. Doc. 153, 2.

267. Quoted in M. J. Bonn, *The Crumbling of Empire* (London: George Allen & Unwin, 1938), 168.

268. Jenks, *Migration*, 100, and Hidy, *George Peabody*, 264. Reginald C. McGrane, *The Panic of 1837* (Chicago: University of Chicago Press, 1924), 149–150, describes the Locofoco Party (formed in 1834) as one of mechanics and laborers believing in free trade and equal rights, opposing bank notes and paper money and all forms of exclusive privilege.

269. See the fascinating discussion in Joseph Ellison, "The Mineral Land Question in California," in *Public Lands*, ed. Carstensen, 73–79.

270. See Table 3.1. Indeed, a number of the same investors of the 1830s were back into new investments in the early 1850s.

271. I rejected a number of other possible candidates. Perhaps John Clark, Jr. & Co. (New York agency 1820; the parent company came to be absorbed by Clark & Co. in Scotland in 1884) should be considered the start of J. & P. Coats business in America (Clark & Co. would be absorbed by J. & P. Coats in Scotland in the 1896); my only reason for selecting Andrew Coats's arrival is that I know there was, from that point, continuity with later Coats business. Another possibility is Naylor, Vickers & Co. (representative in the United States in 1840; although Vickers had subsequent investments in the United States, they did not form a pattern of continuously growing enterprise). Some of the other Sheffield steelmakers are real contenders. Their "agency" representation went back to the 1820s. Yet here again, I do not have evidence of the long "continuity" chain of Coats.

272. Wilkins, *The Emergence*, 37–39.

273. Jenks, *Migration*, 413, estimated that in 1854 £59 to £60 million ($222 to $290 million) was invested by Britishers alone in the United States; these figures are in excess of the $222 million total foreign investment in the United States in 1853 identified in the U.S. Treasury report. See Table 3.4. Obviously, one must be wary of all these figures. Chandler, *Henry Varnum Poor*, 97, points out, for example, that many U.S. railroad bonds that reached England in the late 1840s to pay for British iron rails were forwarded to Switzerland or Germany or even returned to New York for sale. Nonetheless, the preeminence of Britain was very much in evidence.

4. The Perilous Decades at Mid-Century

1. Based on Dorothy Adler, *British Investment in American Railways, 1834–1898* (Charlottesville: University Press of Virginia, 1970); Leland H. Jenks, *The Migration of*

British Capital to 1875 (New York: Barnes & Noble, 1973); Margaret Myers, *The New York Money Market* (New York: Columbia University Press, 1931), 36–37; and Douglass C. North, "The United States Balance of Payments, 1790–1860," *Trends in the American Economy in the Nineteenth Century*, Studies in Income and Wealth, vol. 24 (Princeton, N.J.: Princeton University Press, 1960), 586, 626. The rise occurred despite the demands in Europe (1854–1855) for funds to finance the Crimean War.

2. *Report of the Special Commissioner of the Revenue* (1869), xxvi, published in *Foreign Investments in the United States*, ed. Mira Wilkins (New York: Arno Press, 1977).

3. See Adler, *British Investment*, 71, 87, and Harry H. Pierce, "Foreign Investment in American Enterprise," in *Economic Change in the Civil War Era*, ed. David T. Gilchrist and W. David Lewis (Greenville, Del.: Eleutherian Mills-Hagley Foundation, 1965), 51.

4. Matthew Simon, *Cyclical Fluctuations and the International Capital Movements of the United States, 1865–1897* (New York: Arno Press, 1978), 78.

5. *Report of the Special Commissioner*, xxvi.

6. Jeffrey G. Williamson, *American Growth and the Balance of Payments* (Chapel Hill: University of North Carolina Press, 1964), 142. This was the highest in any single year monitored by Williamson, who presented figures for the years 1869–1914. The year 1869 was, of course, that of the "gold panic," when Jay Gould and Jim Fisk (and others) attempted to corner the gold market. See U.S. House, *Gold Panic Investigation*, 41st Cong., 2nd sess., March 1, 1870, H. Rept. 31. Prior to the "gold panic," in the spring of 1869, the amount of American securities sent to Europe had been large. As the price of gold rose with the speculative buying, this effectively devalued the U.S. dollar, making American securities cheaper for foreign buyers.

7. Charles J. Bullock, John H. Williams, and Rufus S. Tucker, "The Balance of Trade of the United States," *Review of Economic Statistics*, 1 (July 1919): 223. In 1958 John J. Madden completed his Cambridge University Ph.D. dissertation on British investments in the United States, 1860–1880. This dissertation—its title notwithstanding—dealt with both British and continental European investments. Aside from the Baring Papers in Ottawa, Madden used no primary sources. Likewise, he was not aware of Matthew Simon's 1955 dissertation at Columbia University, first published in 1978, nor Dorothy Adler's contemporary work on British investments in U.S. railroads. Adler received her Cambridge Ph.D. in 1958. Madden's dissertation has been published as *British Investment in the United States, 1860–1880* (New York: Garland, 1985). It covers this climb in investment.

8. Mira Wilkins, *The Emergence of Multinational Enterprise: American Business Abroad from the Colonial Era to 1914* (Cambridge, Mass.: Harvard University Press, 1970), 21.

9. Alfred D. Chandler, Jr., *The Visible Hand: The Managerial Revolution in American Business* (Cambridge, Mass.: Harvard University Press, 1977), 89.

10. Paul Studenski and Herman E. Krooss, *Financial History of the United States*, 2nd ed. (New York: McGraw-Hill, 1963), 125. At end of fiscal year (July 1) 1853, the U.S. debt was $59.8 million; it fell to $28.7 million in 1857 to rise to $64.8 million in 1860. See also Ellis P. Oberholtzer, *Jay Cooke* (1907; rpt. New York: Burt Franklin, 1970), I, chap. 4, on the rise of debt in 1857–1860.

11. U.S. Senate, *Report of the Secretary of the Treasury . . . [on] the Amount of American Securities Held in Europe*, 33rd Cong., 1st sess., 1854, Exec. Doc. 42, in *Foreign Investments*, ed. Wilkins (henceforth cited as S. Doc. 42, 1854), and U.S. Secretary of the Treasury, *Annual Report, 1856*, 426.

12. Myers, *New York Money Market*, 36.

13. Ralph W. Hidy, *The House of Baring in American Trade and Finance* (Cambridge, Mass.: Harvard University Press, 1949), 430.

14. On the growth and size of the U.S. debt, see Rafael A. Bayley, *The National*

Loans of the United States, 2nd ed. (1881; rpt. New York: Burt Franklin, 1970), 74–76.

15. *Bankers' Magazine,* London, 20 (Jan. 1860): 51, and *Hunt's Merchant Magazine,* 43 (Jan. 1860): 136–137.

16. I have checked a wide variety of sources and find nothing that reveals giant foreign purchases, 1857–1860. S. G. Ward to Baring Brothers & Co., June 29, 1858, Baring Papers, Public Archives, Ottawa, vol. 61, p. 034122, indicates the expectation that the 1858 loan will be taken up in the United States. See also ibid., Aug. 10, 1858, vol. 61, p. 034207. Ralph Hidy (*House of Baring,* 472) tells us that Baring joined with the New York house of Ward, Campbell & Co. in purchasing $150,000 of U.S. bonds in the New York market in 1859; only a small part, however, was sent to England for sale. Because of "the dullness of British demand," Hidy writes, "and the higher prices in America, Baring Brothers & Co. took but very small amounts of new issues of American securities." The American Account Books (1857–1863) of N. M. Rothschild & Sons, Rothschild Archives London II/3/7, reveal no new interest in U.S. government bonds. It is possible that the bonds might have drifted abroad as payments for commercial debts or to cover defaults, but this is not suggested in any of the contemporary literature. A January 1871 estimate prepared by Jay Cooke, McCulloch & Co. showed a high percentage of the 1858 loan held in Europe (see Adler, *British Investment,* 84); I suspect, however, that the 1871 figures reflect a post–Civil War drift of the securities abroad. If the two-thirds percentage given in the *Philadelphia Ledger* is accurate, which I doubt, it would be the highest percentage of the U.S. national debt ever held abroad. The most plausible explanation is that the use of New York subtreasury payments data distorts the amount of U.S. public debt held abroad: For later substantiation of this, see U.S. Census Office, *Report on Valuation, Taxation, and Public Indebtedness, 10th Census* (Washington D.C., 1884), 518.

17. The American Account Books (1857–1863) of N. M. Rothschild & Sons, RAL II/3/7, show *no* U.S. government bond holdings, 1858–1863. Perhaps, since no sums were given in the article, the *Philadelphia Ledger* author just guessed that there should have been British Rothschild holdings.

18. On Lord Overstone, see Jacob Viner, *Studies in the Theory of International Trade* (Clifton, N.J.: Augustus M. Kelley, 1975), 220–235; Jenks, *Migration,* 130–131; T. E. Gregory, *The Westminster Bank through a Century* (London: Westminster Bank, 1936), I, 320–321, and II, 158–186; and best of all, D. J. O'Brien, ed., *Correspondence of Lord Overstone,* 3 vols. (Cambridge: Cambridge University Press, 1971). For Lord Overstone's investments in the United States in the 1820s and 1830s, see Chapter 3.

19. Alexander Herzen, *My Past and Thoughts: The Memoirs of Alexander Herzen* (Berkeley: University of California Press, 1982), 398–399, casts light on his investments. In 1848—while in exile—Herzen, through Baron James de Rothschild, cashed two Moscow savings bonds—and found himself in Paris "with a large sum of money in very troubled times . . . By Rothschild's advice I bought myself some American shares." Baron James de Rothschild was at that time (1848) buying U.S. bonds (see Chapter 3). Undoubtedly, the "American shares" were U.S. federal government bonds. On de Tocqueville's U.S. investments, see Henry Blumenthal, *A Reappraisal of Franco-American Relations, 1830–1871* (Chapel Hill: University of North Carolina Press, 1959), 114. Blumenthal writes that the French nobility bought U.S. securities as protection against upheaval in France (ibid.).

20. B. U. Ratchford, *American State Debts* (Durham, N.C.: Duke University Press, 1941), 127.

21. Ibid., 133. It is important, however, to remember that although there were no new purchases, foreign owners retained securities acquired in earlier years. These appear to have been traded in Europe.

22. Ratchford, *American State Debts*, 133. The Virginia bond issue of 1854 would become a matter of later controversy. See Charles Fenn, *A Compendium of the English and Foreign Funds*, 14th ed. (London: 1889), 652, and Council of the Corporation of Foreign Bondholders, *Annual Report for 1874* and those of succeeding years. For George Peabody's role in marketing Virginia bonds, see Muriel Hidy, *George Peabody* (New York: Arno Press, 1978), 346–347.

23. Nathaniel T. Bacon, "American International Indebtedness," *Yale Review*, 9 (Nov. 1900): 271. Lombard, Odier & Cie had close associations with the Iselin house in New York (the Iselins were of Swiss origin).

24. I was surprised to find the following information "On the Development of Foreign Issues on the Frankfurt Bourse from 1797 to 1860," in Helmut Böhme, *Frankfurt and Hamburg* (Frankfurt: Europaische Verlagsanstalt, 1968), 156–161. These were securities listed for trading purposes, not new issues. Between 1797 and 1848, there were no American securities on the Frankfurt Bourse. In 1849, 6 percent U.S. bonds were listed; there were no new listings in 1850 or 1851; in 1852 St. Louis County and City bonds and Erie Railroad bonds were listed; in 1854 came the literal flood of dollar-denominated securities—twenty-six listings: U.S. federal government 5 percents and U.S. treasury bonds; California, Georgia, Illinois, Indiana, Kentucky, Louisiana, Maryland, Massachusetts, Missouri, North Carolina, Tennessee, and Virginia bonds. Likewise, there were loans to American cities, St. Louis, Chicago, Cincinnati, Covington (Kentucky?), San Francisco, Louisville, New Orleans, Pittsburgh, and Sacramento. Among the cities, "New York" is listed; I presume this was New York City not New York State. The only railroad included in 1854 was the Galena and Chicago. The year 1855 saw three more listings, all of municipals—loans to Milwaukee, Wheeling, and San Francisco; in 1856, new loans for San Francisco and New Orleans; and in 1857–1860, nothing. This German interest in state and city loans is quite remarkable. It does not seem to be adequately reflected in Table 4.1.

25. Adler, *British Investment*, 23.

26. Hidy, *House of Baring*, 429. In September 1854 the editor of the *American Railroad Journal*, who followed such matters closely, estimated that almost $150 million from abroad had been invested in U.S. railroads. See Alfred D. Chandler, Jr., *Henry Varnum Poor* (Cambridge, Mass.: Harvard University Press, 1956), 312n.

27. U.S. Secretary of the Treasury, *Annual Report, 1856*, 426. The report covered 360 railroads.

28. C. K. Hobson, *The Export of Capital* (London: Constable, 1914), 128. Hobson obviously mixed up pounds and dollars.

29. Adler, *British Investment*, 24.

30. U.S. Bureau of the Census, *Historical Statistics of the United States* (Washington, D.C., 1960), 428.

31. See the excellent data in Reginald C. McGrane, *Foreign Bondholders and American State Debts* (New York: Macmillan, 1935), 278–279.

32. Ibid., 279.

33. Paul W. Gates, *The Illinois Central and Its Colonization Work* (1934; rpt. New York: Johnson Reprint Corp., 1968), 66–73, and S. Doc. 42, 1854, 46.

34. Gates, *Illinois Central*, 75–76.

35. Ibid., 79–80; Adler, *British Investment*, 172–173; and Arthur M. Johnson and Barry Supple, *Boston Capitalists and Western Railroads* (Cambridge, Mass.: Harvard University Press, 1967), 143, citing the London *Times*, July 23, 1858. Richard Cobden—Britain's foremost advocate of free trade—was among the investors in the Illinois Central. By 1857 Cobden had 3,000 shares. He visited the United States in the spring of 1859 on behalf of other English shareholders to examine the line and its manage-

ment. See Nicholas C. Edsall, *Richard Cobden*. (Cambridge, Mass.: Harvard University Press, 1986), 316–325, and John Morley, *Life of Richard Cobden* (London: Chapman & Hall, 1883), 443.

36. S. F. van Oss, *American Railroads as Investments* (1893; rpt. New York: Arno Press, 1977), 315. They made a Mr. Cullen president, who speculated too much on his own account; then McCalmont Brothers replaced him with C. E. Smith.

37. The Northern Cross Rail Road was associated with the Chicago, Burlington and Quincy. See S. G. Ward to Baring Brothers, Dec. 27, 1858, BAO, vol. 62, p. 034344, on the size of the Duke's interest; ibid., Dec. 28, 1858, BAO, vol. 62, pp. 034350–53; report on the Northern Cross by W. H. Swift, BAO, vol. 62, pp. 034354–66; Swift to Ward, March 11, 1859, BAO, vol. 62, pp. 034431–35; and Ward to Baring, March 22, 1859, BAO, vol. 62, pp. 034438–40. The Duke of Brunswick apparently had long been an investor in the United States. *Niles' Weekly Register*, 45 (Nov. 16, 1833): 179, listed him as the largest single foreign owner of state of Pennsylvania stock, holding in 1833 $67,500 worth (the roster of foreign owners was incomplete, so others may have owned more).

38. Adler, *British Investment*, 58.

39. Harry H. Pierce, *Railroads of New York* (Cambridge, Mass.: Harvard University Press, 1953), 6, first uncovered Ingham's $640,600 securities ownership. See also Pierce, "Foreign Investment," 49; his "Anglo-American Investors and Investment in the New York Central Railroad," in *An Emerging Independent American Economy, 1815–1875*, ed. Joseph R. Frese and Jacob Judd (Tarrytown, N.Y.: Sleepy Hollow Press, 1980), 154; and Irene Neu, "An English Businessman in Sicily, 1806–1861," *Business History Review*, 31 (Winter 1957): 356. Richard Trevelyan, *Princes under the Volcano* (London: Macmillan, 1972), 7, 90, gives information on Ingham's Michigan Central Railroad interests. As noted in Chapter 3, the New York merchant Schuyler Livingston served as Ingham's investment adviser. Livingston was a close friend of the Albany entrepreneur Erastus Corning (1794–1872), who participated in financing a host of different U.S. ventures and used Ingham's resources.

40. Adler, *British Investment*, 96, 97, 101; Edward Harold Mott, *Between the Ocean and the Lakes: The Story of the Erie* (New York: John S. Collins, 1901), 116, 128, 364; and Jenks, *Migration*, 256–257.

41. Pierce, "Anglo-American," 128, and Ralph W. Hidy and Muriel E. Hidy, "Anglo-American Merchant Bankers and the Railroads of the Old Northwest, 1848–1860," *Business History Review*, 34 (Summer 1960): 154.

42. Pierce, "Foreign Investment," 47; Cleona Lewis, *America's Stake in International Investments* (Washington, D.C.: Brookings Institution, 1938), 36. Pierce says the New York Central's office was established in London in 1857.

43. Pierce, "Foreign Investments," 45–46.

44. Ibid., 56, and K. D. Bosch, *Nederlandse Beleggingen in de Verenigde Staten* (Amsterdam: Uitgeversmaatschappij Elsevier, 1948), 136.

45. Böhme, *Frankfurt and Hamburg*, 156–161.

46. Rondo Cameron, "French Foreign Investment," Ph.D. diss., University of Chicago, 1952, 125.

47. In October 1854 Charles Moran, a New York broker/private banker, and Louis von Hoffman, a New York private banker, were elected directors of the Erie, "in recognition of the interests of foreign creditors of the Company, Moran having placed a large amount of the Company's unsecured, or income, bonds in Switzerland and other parts of Europe" (Mott, *Between the Ocean and the Lakes*, 116). Moran was president of the New York and Erie Railroad, 1857–1859.

48. Herbert Marshall, Frank A. Southard, Jr., and Kenneth W. Taylor, *Canadian-American Industry* (New Haven: Yale University Press, 1936), 188.

49. Chandler, *Visible Hand*, 91; Chandler, *Henry Varnum Poor*, 94, 105, 173, 310–311n, 106; Adler, *British Investment*, 22–23, 49–51; and Charles Kindleberger, *The Formation of Financial Centers* (Princeton, N.J.: International Finance Section, Department of Economics, Princeton University, 1974), 35. Munroe & Co., Paris, began operations in 1851 as successor to the merchandising firm of its founder (Lewis, *America's Stake*, 192). For more on Munroe & Co., see Max Gérard, *Messieurs Hottinguer* (Paris: Hottinguer 1972), II, 671; and on Winslow, Lanier & Co., see Vincent Carosso, *Investment Banking in America* (Cambridge, Mass.: Harvard University Press, 1970), 12.

50. Chandler, *Henry Varnum Poor*, 209. Baring Brothers' Boston agent, Samuel G. Ward, provided the Barings with information on American railroads. See, for example, BAO, vol. 61, pp. 033715–16 (Ward sent to London on Oct. 31, 1857, a letter from Erastus Corning on the New York Central); Ward to Baring Brothers, Dec. 8, 1857, contains advice on Michigan Central securities (ibid., p. 033821).

51. See N. S. B. Gras and Henrietta Larson, *Casebook in American Business History* (New York: Appleton-Century-Crofts, 1939), 546–549, and Hidy, *George Peabody*, 302ff.

52. See the fascinating material in Gates, *Illinois Central*, 224.

53. *New York Times*, Nov. 1, 1941. I do not know that the Speyer house was handling railroad securities at this time, but it seems highly likely. It was still a small firm.

54. J. Riesser, *The German Great Banks and Their Concentration* (1911; rpt. New York: Arno Press, 1977), 61; and Paul Emden, *Money Powers of Europe* (New York: Appleton-Century, 1938), 108, 209. Its main interest, however, must have been in U.S. federal, state, and city bonds. I would guess that this was true of Speyer as well. How else can we account for the coincidental formidable proliferation of such listings on the Frankfurt Bourse? See this chapter note 24.

55. Riesser, *German Great Banks*, 502.

56. Ira B. Cross, *Financing an Empire* (Chicago: S. J. Clarke, 1927), I, 220. On the Hentsch firm in Geneva, see Nicholas Faith, *Safety in Numbers* (New York: Viking Press, 1982), 24, 290. Leroy Armstrong and J. O. Denny, *Financial California* (1916; rpt. New York: Arno Press, 1980), 47, 51, describes Henry Hentsch as the Swiss Consul in San Francisco and indicates his banking business there started in 1855.

57. As noted earlier, in 1818 the Bank of Montreal had appointed a New York agent. Its relationships with Prime, Ward & King terminated in 1841, and it had various firms "looking after its interests"—particularly the Bank of Commerce in New York—in the 1850s. Likewise, the Bank of British North America had used Prime, Ward & King in the late 1830s (see Chapter 3). On BBNA's first New York agency, see Merrill Denison, *Canada's First Bank: A History of the Bank of Montreal*, 2 vols. (New York: Dodd, Mead, 1967), II, 102. On the Bank of Montreal, see ibid., 100–102. See also Bank of Montreal Resolve Book, III, April 2, 1841, 386; ibid., VI, Dec. 3, 1858, p. 42; Dec. 24, 1858, pp. 46–47; and Jan. 21, 1859, p. 51, in the Bank of Montreal Records, Public Archives, Ottawa.

58. Bray Hammond, *Banks and Politics in America from the Revolution to the Civil War* (Princeton, N.J.: Princeton University Press, 1957), 669–670.

59. Denison, *Canada's First Bank*, II, 71. Denison notes that the Bank of Montreal had a capital of $6 million, and New York's Bank of Commerce and Louisiana's Citizens' Bank had capitals of $9 million and $6.7 million, respectively. His figures seem in error for the Citizens' Bank, the capital of which had been sharply reduced (to $1 million) by the late 1850s. See George D. Green, *Finance and Economic Development in the Old South* (Stanford, Calif.: Stanford University Press, 1972), 80–81.

60. Denison, *Canada's First Bank*, II, 181.

61. Ibid., II, 101.

62. Ibid., 103.

63. Ibid.

64. Ibid., 103–104.

65. The foreign ownership of three Louisiana banks dropped in 1853–1857: New Orleans Canal and Banking Company ($840,000; $600,000); Bank of Louisiana ($1,104,600; $914,500); and Louisiana State Bank ($603,800; $547,100). Compare S. Doc. 42, 1854, 27, and Green, *Finance and Economic Development*, 81, which has the 1857 figures for all Louisiana chartered banks. Green details the investments by foreign owners (British, Dutch, French, and German) of $2.2 million in 1857; to this sum he believed $6.7 million of state "property bank bonds" still outstanding should be added. The reduction from the $20.7 million foreign investment in 1837 (of which $14.8 represented state bonds of property banks) arose "not from the sale of stock in surviving banks but from a mixture of default and partial repayment on stocks and bonds of failing banks" (ibid., 81–83).

66. Rodman W. Paul, *California Gold: The Beginning of Mining in the Far West* (Cambridge, Mass.: Harvard University Press, 1947), 146. These figures should be compared with those from Jenks presented in Chapter 3.

67. Henry Blumenthal, "The California Societies in France, 1849–1853," *Pacific Historical Review*, 25 (Aug. 1956): 251.

68. See Rodman W. Paul, *Mining Frontiers of the Far West, 1848–1880* (New York: Holt, Rinehart & Winston, 1963), 38–39, and Herbert O. Brayer, *William Blackmore* (Denver: Bradford Robinson, 1948), I, 173, for the British investments.

69. R. E. Barclay, *Ducktown* (Chapel Hill: University of North Carolina Press, 1946), 48–49.

70. Ibid., 71.

71. Ibid., 72.

72. Ibid.

73. Denison, *Canada's First Bank*, II, 107.

74. A. H. John, *A Liverpool Merchant House* (London: George Allen & Unwin, 1959), 24. Lidderdale later became the governor of the Bank of England.

75. Ibid.

76. J. D. Scott, *Vickers* (London: Weidenfeld & Nicolson, 1962), 7.

77. Chauncey Depew, ed., *1795–1895: One Hundred Years of American Commerce* (New York: D. O. Haynes, 1895), II, 448. See T. A. B. Corley, *Quaker Enterprise in Biscuits: Huntley & Palmers of Reading, 1822–1972* (London: Hutchinson, 1972), 82, for more modest comments on the U.S. business of Huntley & Palmers.

78. J. & P. Coats, "Text of 150 Year Exhibition," panel 18, Renfrew District Library, Scotland. Clark joined his countryman Andrew Coats as a seller of Scottish sewing thread in America. Data on George A. Clark & Brother from J. B. K. Hunter.

79. Lewis, *America's Stake*, 110. It joined other British insurers already in America.

80. Ibid., 81. This was possibly the earliest large sale of land abroad by a railroad. The original contract was for 6 million acres, but the amount actually disposed of was 500,000. See Robert Edgar Riegel, *The Story of the Western Railroads* (Lincoln: University of Nebraska Press, 1926), 282.

81. On James Morrison, see Richard Gatty, *Portrait of a Merchant Prince, James Morrison, 1789–1857* (Northallerton, Yorkshire: Pepper Arden, n.d. [1977?]), 303. At $4.86 = £1, Morrison's holdings came to $3.92 million, a number in the range of the $3.77 million in liabilities of the Bank of the United States to J. Morrison & Son, March 1, 1841 (see chapter 3). Benjamin Ingham had investments in New York, New Jersey, Michigan, and Illinois. One partial list that Trevelyan uncovered (Trevelyan, *Princes under the Volcano*, 90) had forty-seven distinct items as of 1861. On another list, as of

March 1861 Ingham's "American Assets" were given at $6.5 million (ibid., 90). This seems high, considering the returns presented (ibid., 306). Trevelyan reports that after Ingham's death in 1861, the assets depreciated sharply, but what happened to them in the hands of Ingham's heirs is unclear (see ibid., 203, 205–206). If the figures on Ingham's U.S. assets are accurate, by 1857 the latter's were undoubtedly much larger than those of Morrison's. These are, in any case, formidable holdings. On Poor, see Chandler, *Henry Varnum Poor*, 27.

82. North, "The United States Balance of Payments," 573–627, contains no "direct estimates" of U.S. foreign indebtedness in 1858–1860, but his balance-of-payments estimates for 1859 and 1860 (p. 581) show substantial import surpluses and, more important, the highest outflows in recorded U.S. history in payments abroad of interest and dividends ($23.4 million in 1859; $25.1 million in 1860). North makes no comments on the rise. Interest payments can be on short-term as well as long-term debt obligations, so this is not necessarily an indication of a rise in long-term debt.

83. On Jan. 19, 1860, S. G. Ward, Boston, was writing Baring Brothers (BAO, vol. 62, p. 034745), "There has probably never been a time when more advantageous investments might be made in R.R. securities than the present." Yet Baring Brothers did not act to increase its holdings during 1860. Its Washington correspondent, A. Dudley Mann, who had been Assistant Secretary of State under President Pierce, was a close friend of President Buchanan—and when Lincoln was elected, Mann foresaw disaster. By December 1860 he was groaning in letters to the Barings about the bad credit of the U.S. government (Mann to Baring Brothers, Dec. 1, 1860, BAO, vol. 97, p. 054626). Mann believed civil war highly probable (ibid., Jan. 15, 1861, BAO, vol. 97, p. 054635). His comments on Lincoln—"a booby," "his plebian vulgarity," "his utter want of knowledge of the most ordinary proprieties of life" (ibid., Feb. 18, 1861, p. 054654, and Feb. 26, 1861, p. 054658)—must hardly have been reassuring to the London merchant bankers.

84. Hans Bauer, *Swiss Bank Corporation, 1872–1972* (Basle: Swiss Bank Corp., 1972), 39.

85. *Hunt's Merchant Magazine*, 49 (Oct. 1868): 241.

86. This is my own conclusion, yet I remain uncertain. No one knew the size of the foreign investments in U.S. railroads. In early 1859 the Barings thought $600 million of British capital was invested in U.S. railway securities. Ward, Campbell, after checking with brokers in New York, wrote the British banking firm (March 22, 24, 1859) that the total foreign investment in U.S. rails—including state bonds issued for U.S. railroads—did not exceed $200 million, of which some $120 million might be owned in Britain. Quoted in Madden, *British Investment*, 25.

87. All sources discuss the divestments. For example, the Irishman William Scully, who owned 35,000 acres in Illinois that were by his own estimate worth £56,000 and who had U.S. bank deposits, instructed his U.S. representative on May 28, 1861, to remit $7,000, payable in gold (Homer E. Socolofsky, *Landlord William Scully* [Lawrence, Kan.: Regents Press of Kansas, 1979], 33, 42, 37).

88. Emden, *Money Powers*, 264. Lord Overstone wrote G. W. Norman on May 15, 1861: "Our American securities are no doubt in danger" and referred to "my *Federal* misfortune . . . We must hope that all will turn out for the best." On August 13, 1861, he added, "I have determined not to trouble myself about American securities." There is, however, no indication in the published correspondence of his selling the securities or buying more (O'Brien, ed., *Correspondence of Lord Overstone*, II, 953–954, 961).

89. Oberholtzer, *Jay Cooke*, I, 146.

90. Irving Katz, *August Belmont: A Political Biography* (New York: Columbia University Press, 1968), 100–101, and David Black, *The King of Fifth Avenue: The Fortunes of*

August Belmont (New York: Dial Press, 1981), 207–212. Young Salomon de Rothschild (1835–1864) was in the United States in 1859–1861 and was captivated by the American South. He had written home on April 28, 1861, urging the Rothschilds to use their influence to have the Confederacy recognized. He saw the North as totally at fault. See Sigmund Diamond, *A Casual View of America: The Home Letters of Salomon de Rothschild, 1859–1861* (London: Cresset Press, 1962), 123–124. Salomon was a son of James de Rothschild (1792–1868), the famous "Paris Rothschild." August Belmont was a Democrat, a strong supporter of President Buchanan.

91. Leonard H. Courtney, "On the Finances of the United States, 1861–1867," *Journal of the Statistical Society of London*, 31 (June 1868): 173–175. Quotation dated December 17, 1862.

92. U.S. Secretary of the Treasury, *Annual Report, 1861*, 16, presented to Congress, Dec. 9, 1861.

93. Ibid., 16–17.

94. Katz, *August Belmont*, 98; John, *Liverpool Merchant House*, 26; and Jenks, *Migration*, 421. It was also taken up in Liverpool, Amsterdam, and Frankfurt. Stanley Chapman calls the loan to the Confederacy "perhaps the most audaciously successful loan of the century." See his *Rise of Merchant Banking* (London: Allen & Unwin, 1984), 85, for details. John Slidell (the uncle of August Belmont's wife) arranged the Confederacy loan. John Slidell's daughter, Mathilde, married Baron Fréderic Émile d'Erlanger (1832–1911), who was involved in that loan; their son, Baron Émile Beamont d'Erlanger (1866–1939), would become the senior partner in Emile Erlanger & Co., London (based on a family tree in the Belmont Family Papers, Columbia University). On Slidell, see the *Dictionary of National Biography* and on Émile d'Erlanger, see *Who's Who 1915*. The Erlangers would remain involved in U.S. investments.

95. Oberholtzer, *Jay Cooke*, I, 286.

96. Ibid., I, 287, 289, 309.

97. See Lord Overstone to G. W. Norman, Feb. 26, 1864, in *Correspondence of Lord Overstone*, ed. O'Brien, III, 1030.

98. U.S. Secretary of the Treasury, *Annual Report, 1864*, 17.

99. Estimate of Frederick Kuhne of Knauth, Nachod, & Kuhne in Oberholtzer, *Jay Cooke*, I, 514. See also Simon, *Cyclical Fluctuations*, 83–88.

100. Pierce, "Anglo-American Investors," 135.

101. Pierce, "Foreign Investment," 51.

102. Charles Duguid, *The Story of the Stock Exchange* (London: Grant Richards, 1901), 249.

103. W. J. Reader, *A House in the City* (London: B. T. Batsford, 1979), 50. According to 1865–66 data, William Crawshay was the largest holder in Britain of bonds of the Mobile and Ohio Railway Company and the Wilmington and Weldon—bonds that had been provided in payment for rails years before and were still held by Crawshay (John P. Addis, *The Crawshay Dynasty* [Cardiff: University Press, 1957], 157). See also Adler, *British Investment*, 42.

104. D. C. M. Platt, "British Portfolio Investment Overseas before 1870: Some Doubts," *Economic History Review*, 2nd ser., 33 (Feb. 1980): 1–16, makes this point.

105. Gates, *Illinois Central*, 76.

106. Pierce, "Foreign Investment," 51. The rise in this case was owing to stock dividends.

107. Ibid.

108. Adler, *British Investment*, 72.

109. Jenks, *Migration*, 255–258, and Julius Grodinsky, *Jay Gould* (Philadelphia: University of Pennsylvania Press, 1957), 31.

110. Jenks, *Migration*, 257.

111. Adler, *British Investment*, 106 n.77.

112. Lewis, *America's Stake*, 104. There was some Dutch investment, as well. P. L. Cottrell, "Investment Banking in England, 1856–1882," Ph.D. diss., University of Hull, 1974, 345, notes that the bonds of the Atlantic and Great Western were payable in gold—a guarantee to investors against the depreciation of the dollar.

113. Ira B. Cross, *Financing an Empire* (Chicago: S. J. Clarke, 1927), I, 255–256.

114. John Walton Caughey, *California* (New York: Prentice-Hall, 1940), 319.

115. See Chapter 3.

116. Victor Ross, *History of the Canadian Bank of Commerce* (Toronto: Oxford University Press, 1920), I, 300.

117. George J. Goschen, a London merchant banker and at that time a director of the Bank of England, provided the context for this expansion when he wrote in 1865: "Banks abound whose familiar names in every variety suggest . . . the marriage of English capital with foreign demand. There is the Anglo-Austrian Bank, the Anglo-Italian Bank, the Anglo-Egyptian Bank. There is the English and Swedish Bank; there is the British and Californian Bank [*sic*]; there is the London and Hamburg Continental Exchange Bank; there is the London and Brazilian Bank, the London, Buenos Ayres and River Plate Bank, and even a London and South American Bank." See his *Essays and Addresses on Economic Questions (1865–1893)* (1905; rpt. New York: Garland, 1983), 23. His own firm, Frühling & Goschen, was involved in the London and San Francisco Bank.

118. Cross, *Financing an Empire*, I, 255–259, and A. S. J. Baster, *The International Banks* (1935; rpt. New York: Arno Press, 1977), 158.

119. Ross, *Canadian Bank of Commerce*, I, 308.

120. Denison, *Canada's First Bank*, II, 111–115.

121. F. Cyril James, *The Growth of Chicago Banks*, 2 vols. (New York: Harper & Bros., 1938), I, 338. There had earlier been a collapse of incorporated banks in Chicago (ibid., I, 268, 286).

122. Denison, *Canada's First Bank*, II, 124–128.

123. Clyde William Phelps, *The Foreign Expansion of American Banks* (1927; rpt. New York, Arno Press, 1976), 92, writes that national banks could not accept any drafts. But see John A. James, *Money and Capital Markets in Postbellum America* (Princeton, N.J.: Princeton University Press, 1978), 51–58, on bills of exchange and acceptances. James explains the decline in use of acceptances in domestic trade and the divergence from "British practices" as based on domestic considerations. He writes that "two-name paper"—bills of exchange endorsed by the drawer and the "acceptor"—fell from 50 to 20 percent of the total loans and discounts of New York City national banks in 1886–1900, and remained at that level from 1900 to 1913. John James does, however, in a different context note that "it had traditionally been held that what was not specifically authorized by the [National Banking] Act was prohibited" (ibid., 90). Phelps (p. 92) cites court decisions to this effect in his substantiation of his argument that national banks "could not accept drafts drawn upon it." Phelps's principal citation is to *Logan County National Bank* v. *Townsend*, 139 U.S. 67 (a case decided on March 2, 1891). Most historians have put it, as I have, that national banks could not accept drafts arising from *international* transactions.

124. Phelps, *Foreign Expansion*, 92.

125. If John James is right and the law itself was not the deterrent, it seems clear that if national banks were using acceptances less in domestic trade, they would also be less apt to develop experience in international transactions.

126. Denison, *Canada's First Bank*, II, 160.

127. *Hunt's Merchant Magazine,* 52 (June 1865): 422 (quotation); Lewis, *America's Stake,* 54; Adler, *British Investment,* 73; Studenski and Krooss, *Financial History,* 159 (size of debt). Americans were committed to reducing the huge debt.

128. Samuel Flagg Bemis, *A Diplomatic History of the United States,* 3rd ed. (New York: Henry Holt, 1950), 381–382, 406; Samuel Eliot Morison and Henry Steele Commager, *The Growth of the American Republic,* 2 vols. (New York: Oxford University Press, 1937), II, 62–63; and Lord Overstone to G. W. Norman, March 28, 1866, *Correspondence of Lord Overstone,* III, 1108.

129. On the financing in Britain of the transatlantic cable, see Henry M. Field, *The Story of the Atlantic Telegraph* (New York: Charles Scribner's Sons, 1893), and Isabella Field Judson, *Cyrus W. Field: His Life and Work (1819–1892)* (New York: Harper & Bros., 1896). On Thomas Brassey's and John Pender's role, see ibid., 172–173, and on the successful laying of the cable, ibid., 199–206; see also Hugh Barty-King, *Girdle Round the Earth* (London: Heinemann, 1979), 20–23.

130. Charles Francis Adams, Jr., "A Chapter of Erie" (1869), republished in his and Henry Adams, *Chapters of Erie* (1886; rpt. Ithaca, N.Y.: Cornell University Press, 1956), 63.

131. Hidy, *House of Baring,* 120, 183, 202, 313, 394, and Jenks, *Migration,* 21, 246–248, 259–262. See also U.S. House, *Report from the Secretary of the Treasury on the Returns of State Banks, 1841 to 1846,* 29th Cong., 1st sess., 1846, Exec. Doc. 226, 859, wherein in 1841 Overend, Gurney describes itself as a holder of Mississippi bonds.

132. For three months the Bank of England kept its minimum discount rate at 10 percent, which stimulated a recall of British investment from America. See Alexander Dana Noyes, *The Thirty Years of American Finance, 1865–1897* (1900; rpt. New York: Greenwood, 1969), 15.

133. Fritz Stern, *Gold and Iron* (New York: Alfred A. Knopf, 1977), 100.

134. *Economist,* 25 (March 9, 1867): 33. The Nederlandsche Credit- en Deposito-bank of Amsterdam (a French bank in Holland founded in 1863, which came to be known in France as the Banque de Crédit et Dépôt des Pays-Bas and which in 1872 would merge with the Banque de Paris into the Banque de Paris et Pays-Bas) was in the years 1864–1870 negotiating U.S. government bond issues. See Rondo Cameron, *France and the Economic Development of Europe* (Princeton, N.J.: Princeton University Press, 1961), 177–178, 197. D. C. M. Platt, *Foreign Finance in Continental Europe and the United States, 1815–1870* (London: George Allen & Unwin, 1984), 45, 76, citing Charles Jutting to Barings, April 4, 1867, notes that between July 1866 and April 1867, wealthy Russian families (as a hedge against the threatened collapse of the ruble) acquired $3 million of "United States stock."

135. S. Japhet, *Recollections from My Business Life* (London: privately printed, 1931), 13, 32. See also Emden, *Money Powers,* 214, 264. American government bonds that were traded in Europe had differing interest rates and maturities. Thus, for example, the loan of 1858—at 5 percent—was redeemable by the government at any time after Jan. 1, 1874. The loan of 1863 was for 17 years, at 6 percent, redeemable July 1, 1881. The "Ten-Forties" of 1864 were at 5 percent, redeemable after 10 years, and payable in 40 years. The "Five-Twenties" of March and June 1864 were at 6 percent, redeemable after 5 years, and payable in 20 years. The "Five-Twenties" of 1865 were also at 6 percent, redeemable after 5 years, and payable in 20 years. All were denominated in dollars. After 1864 some but not all of the authorizing acts indicated that the interest would be paid "in coin," and the loan itself was payable "in coin." On the maturities and the terms, see Bayley, *National Loans,* 149–150, 160–168.

136. H. Burton and D. C. Corner, *Investment and Unit Trusts in Britain and America* (London: Flex Books, 1968), 15, 18. These bonds had semiannual interest, paid "in

coin," and were ultimately payable in coin. See Bayley, *National Loans,* 164. In short, the buyer did not have to worry about the value of the "greenback."

137. Edwin Perkins, *Financing Anglo-American Trade: The House of Brown, 1800–1880* (Cambridge, Mass.: Harvard University Press, 1975), 209, has a useful 1868 list of some of the major bill drawers in New York: Brown Brothers & Co., on Brown, Shipley & Co., London; Dabney, Morgan & Co., on J. S. Morgan & Co., London; Duncan, Sherman & Co., on the Union Bank, London; Hallgarten & Co., on the Union Bank, London; James G. King & Sons, on Baring Brothers & Co., London; John Munroe & Co., on Munroe & Co., Paris; W. C. Pickersgill & Co., on Fielden Brothers & Co., Liverpool; J. & W. Seligman & Co., on Seligman Brothers, London; Philip Speyer & Co., on Speyer Brothers, London; J. & J. Stuart & Co., on Smith, Payne, & Smiths, London; and Simon de Visser, on Drake, Kleinwort & Cohen, London.

138. *Hunt's Merchant Magazine,* 69 (Oct., 1868): 245, U.S. Secretary of the Treasury, *Annual Report, 1868,* viii, made an estimate of $600 million that December.

139. *Report of the Special Commissioner,* xxvii.

140. U.S. Secretary of the Treasury, *Annual Report, 1869,* viii.

141. Cooke to J. F. D. Lanier, Aug. 19, 1865, cited in Oberholtzer, *Jay Cooke,* I, 657.

142. August Belmont & Co. to N. M. Rothschild & Sons, Dec. 17, 1867, RAL T57/81; August Belmont to N. M. R. & S., Feb. 26, 1869, RAL T58/3; and August Belmont & Co. to N. M. R. & S., Sept. 13, 1881, RAL II/51/OB. There was also an arbitrage business done by lesser houses between Frankfurt and London. See Japhet, *Recollections,* 19, referring to Emil Schwarzchild's business in 1873.

143. U.S. House, *Gold Panic Investigation,* 34.

144. Ibid., 136.

145. Ibid., 334.

146. Bert Forbes, "Investments by Hollanders in America," *Van Norden Magazine,* Oct. 1909 (on microfiche, New York Public Library), 62.

147. Jean Bouvier, *Le Crédit Lyonnais de 1863 à 1882* (Paris: S.E.V.P.E.N., 1961), II, 563–564, is marvelous on Swiss as well as French interests in American securities.

148. Lewis, *America's Stake,* 56.

149. See estimate of Jay Cooke, McCulloch & Co., cited in Adler, *British Investment,* 83.

150. Morison and Commager, *Growth of the American Republic,* 63. The diplomatic negotiations were handled by Sir John Rose—who was important in North American investment banking (Morton, Rose & Co. was the London house of Morton, Bliss & Co.).

151. Sidney J. Chapman, *The History of Trade between the United Kingdom and the United States* (London: Swan Sonnenschein, 1899), 73.

152. On these, see Lewis, *America's Stake,* 55; U.S. Secretary of the Treasury, *Annual Reports;* Bayley, *National Loans,* 94; and Fritz Redlich, *The Molding of American Banking* (New York: Johnson Reprint Co., 1968), pt. 2, 365–367. In Table 4.6, the original list of bankers comes from Geo. S. Boutwell, Secretary of the Treasury, to Baring Brothers, Feb. 28, 1871, BAO, vol. 23, pp. 011916–17. Baring Brothers, the Rothschilds, and Hope & Co. decided not to participate. See Henrietta Larson, *Jay Cooke* (Cambridge, Mass.: Harvard University Press, 1936), 321; Oberholtzer, *Jay Cooke,* 270; and Hope & Co. to Thomas Baring, March 15, 1871, BAO, vol. 111, p. 062870. The loan went badly, and Jay Cooke set up U.S. and European syndicates to handle it (Oberholtzer, *Jay Cooke,* 278–294, Larson, *Jay Cooke,* 318–323). By the end of August 1871, at least $75 million of the $200 million of the 1871 loan had been sold in Europe (Larson, *Jay Cooke,* 322–323). Cooke's European list included R. Raphael & Sons, London; Louis Cohen & Sons, London; Seligman Brothers, London; Seligman & Stettheimer, Frankfurt; Bischoff-

sheim & Goldschmidt, London; Clews, Habicht & Co., London; Behrens & Sons, Hamburg; S. Bleichroeder, Berlin; Lippmann, Rosenthal & Co., Amsterdam; Wertheim & Gompertz, Amsterdam; Emile Erlanger & Co., Frankfurt; Anglo-Hungarian Bank, London; Speyer Brothers, London; L. Speyer-Ellissen, Frankfurt; P. Cazenove & Co., London and Frankfurt; Gerstenberg and friends, London; Samuel Montagu & Sons, London; Oppenheim, Errera & Co., Brussels; Foster & Braithwaite, London; Munroe & Co., Paris; and Jay Cooke, McCulloch & Co., London. The list is given in Linton Wells, "House of Seligman," unpublished manuscript, 1931, 148, copy in New York Historical Society Library, New York. On the 1871 and 1873 loans, see also Bouvier, *Crédit Lyonnais*, II, 567. "Foreign, Colonial, and Commercial Loans," Baring Archives, London (BAL), AC 29, indicates Baring's involvement in both the 1871 and 1873 5 percent funded loans. On the Morgan role, see Lewis Corey, *House of Morgan* (New York: G. Howard Watt, 1930), 115–121.

153. U.S. Secretary of the Treasury, *Annual Report, 1874*, ix. The *Stock Exchange Year Book, 1875* (published in 1874) noted that all quotations of U.S. government securities on the Stock Exchange list were at 4s to the dollar (£1 = \$5.00), whereas the real value was closer to 4s 1d (£1 = \$4.90).

154. McCulloch and Cooke themselves had long forgotten their earlier admonitions. Nonetheless, looking back on that era, *Banker's Magazine*, New York, 33 (April 1879): 746, reviewed the reluctance to seek monies abroad, quoting a March 9, 1870, statement of the late Senator Charles Sumner: "I cannot forget my own country, nor can I forget that great primacy which I hope to see her assume in the money markets of the world. New York is our natural money centre. Why should we revolve about European money centers? Let us keep our own center here at home." In 1870, when the Secretary of the Treasury proposed that to encourage sales abroad, U.S. bonds be made payable in London, Paris, and Berlin, in pounds, francs, and thalers, the U.S. Congress rejected the idea.

155. I feel uneasy about this generalization. Yet I find it difficult to read the figures in Tables 4.1 and 4.5 in any other way or to find any evidence to revise the figures substantially so as to alter this conclusion. To put the numbers in perspective, the U.S. federal funded debt was \$1.1 billion on Aug. 31, 1865; \$2.0 billion on July 1, 1870; and \$1.7 billion on July 1, 1875. (The "gross debt" in those years was \$2.8 billion, \$2.5 billion, and \$2.2 billion.) See Studenski and Krooss, *Financial History*, 174. Williamson, *American Growth*, 125, agrees that in 1865–1869 the largest portion of America's foreign indebtedness was in the form of federal securities. After 1869 he sees a "gradual shift out of federal securities and into railroad issues" (p. 127). See also table 31, ibid., 136, that lends credence to our generalization. Madden, *British Investment*, 388 (table 24), indicates that the level of federal government securities held abroad in 1866–1871 was higher than all "nonfederal" government securities. His figures (pp. 78–79) suggest that by 1874, however, the nominal value of U.S. railroad securities held in Europe exceeded that of American federal government securities. This is possible, but I am not sure that I trust his figures. My text has emphasized the British, Dutch, and German investments, which were clearly the most important, but the French and Swiss interest should not be ignored. Bouvier, *Crédit Lyonnais*, tells of Edouard Kleinmann's trip to the United States, 1870–1871, and Crédit Lyonnais' interest in American business (I, 14, 16; II, 562–568). See Cameron, "French Foreign Investments," 79–80, for French interests in such securities at this time. On the Swiss role, see Bouvier, *Crédit Lyonnais*, II, 562–564.

156. U.S. House, *Gold Panic Investigation*, 34, noted this in 1869.

157. Adler, *British Investment*, 16 ns.77–78. There were some very bad feelings in some of the settlements. Pennsylvania paid off its old loans in "greenbacks," much to the irritation of Britishers. On Jan. 28, 1868, August Belmont & Co. sent to that state

stock for redemption; it added that N. M. Rothschild & Sons continued to hold "about $200,000 more of stock already overdue and becoming due this year." That firm objected to Pennsylvania's paying its debts in depreciated currency. The Treasurer of Pennsylvania curtly retorted that the currency was legal tender: "We are willing to give you the pound of flesh, but not one drop of Christian blood." Belmont came to the Rothschild defense. The London *Times*, Feb. 24, 1868, printed the correspondence, editorializing, "If the agents of British and other foreign creditors were uniformly to make as firm and as able a protest against injustice to their clients [as Belmont has], we should hear less of American repudiation."

158. B. U. Ratchford, *American State Debts* (Durham, N.C.: Duke University Press, 1941), 180; Lewis, *America's Stake*, 57; and Adler, *British Investment*, 78. On the Georgia bonds, see Henry Clews, *Twenty-eight Years in Wall Street* (New York: Irving, 1888), 274, 277.

159. McGrane, *Foreign Bondholders*, 293.

160. On these debts and the sale abroad of Reconstruction bonds, see Ratchford, *American State Debts*, 172–180.

161. Lewis, *America's Stake*, 59. McGrane, *Foreign Bondholders*, 283, notes that the foreign investors had been warned by southern leaders that the people "would never recognize the 'swindling bonds' issued by carpetbag scalawags and negro legislators." On post–Civil War state debts, see ibid., 282–389.

162. Corporation of Foreign Bondholders, *Annual Report for 1874* (1875).

163. All the post–Civil War defaults were by southern states.

164. *Report of Special Commissioner*, xxvii. My Tables 4.1 and 4.5 give $100 million for 1869. Many foreign investors were *not* the investors of record, leaving their stock in the names of American intermediaries. Some of these securities were acquired by foreign investors before the Civil War. Note that in 1869, of the state securities itemized on Table 4.7, over 65 percent of the amount comprised obligations of *northern states*. The 1874 data are from *Commercial and Financial Chronicle*, 19 (Nov. 14, 1874): 493. Alabama's big state bond issue that went into default was in 1870.

165. Lewis, *America's Stake*, 64–65.

166. Émile Becque, *L'internationalisation des capitaux* (Montpellier: Imprimerie Générale du Midi, 1912), 19. See this chapter, note 24, for the popularity of American "municipals" in Germany in the 1850s.

167. U.S. Bureau of the Census, *Historical Statistics of the United States*, 428.

168. Robert Keith Middlemas, *The Master Builders* (London: Hutchinson, 1965), 105–108; when Sir Morton Peto failed, 30,000 men were left unemployed!

169. Brayer, *William Blackmore*, 79.

170. Jenks, *Migration*, 258.

171. Gregory, *History of Westminster Bank*, II, 62–64.

172. RAL, T57/81.

173. An excellent book on Jay Gould is Grodinsky, *Jay Gould*. He describes how Jay Gould used foreign investors' shares (that were in stockbrokers' names) to obtain the votes to make him president of the Erie and how, once president, he bought proxies of foreign investors in the Pittsburgh, Fort Wayne, and Chicago to use to his advantage. For Gould, the Erie, and foreign investors, see ibid., 38–111, esp. 46–47, 50, 61, 64, 67, 71–72, 87, 93–103. Mott, *Between the Ocean and the Lakes*, 176, writes that early in the Gould years (1868–1872), "millions of the overissued stock were purchased by English investors, the low price tempting them." See ibid., 176–185, 192–202, on Gould and the foreign investors in the Erie. The latest biography of Gould is Maury Klein, *The Life and Legend of Jay Gould* (Baltimore: Johns Hopkins University Press, 1986). See pp. 97–98 on Gould's role in disenfranchising most of the Erie's foreign stockholders.

174. Adler, *British Investment*, 103, 105–116; Mott, *Between the Ocean and the Lakes*, 201–208, 218–246; and Jenks, *Migration*, 258–259, 270 (for Bischoffsheim & Goldschmidt's role). *Banker's Magazine*, New York, 44 (Aug. 1889): 81, would refer to the "notorious" experiences of foreign investors in the Atlantic and Great Western and the Erie. See also Grodinsky, *Jay Gould*, 87–88, 93–112; Corey, *House of Morgan*, 111; Cottrell, "Investment Banking," passim; and Klein, *The Life and Legend*, 116–126, 132–133.

175. Lewis, *America's Stake*, 105.

176. Dolores Greenberg, *Financiers and Railroads* (Newark: University of Delaware Press, 1980), 42.

177. Charles Francis Adams, "The Granger Movement," *North American Review*, 120 (April 1875): 397.

178. Burton and Corner, *Investment and Unit Trusts*, 18; J. C. Gilbert, *A History of Investment Trusts in Dundee, 1873–1938* (London: P. S. King, 1939); and Ronald B. Weir, *A History of the Scottish American Investment Company, Ltd., 1873–1973* (Edinburgh: Scottish American Investment Company, 1973).

179. Jenks, *Migration*, 428.

180. Adler, *British Investment*, 203–209, gives a list of American railway securities publicly issued in London in 1865–1874, with the name of the firm marketing the securities, the type of security, the amount, and the issue price. These figures should be compared with the U.S. government refunding issues of 1871 and 1873; see Table 4.6.

181. Adler, *British Investment*, 206.

182. Reader, *House in the City*, 54.

183. Based on data in BAO, vol. 23, pp. 011965–012001; list of "Foreign, Colonial, and Commercial Loans," BAL, AC 29; and data in BAL, HC 5.2.30, pts. 4–8.

184. The BAO contains several letters from Andrew Carnegie to Baring Brothers, attempting to sell them $5 million first mortgage bonds of the Philadelphia and Erie (see Andrew Carnegie to Baring Brothers, Aug. 25, 1871, and Sept. 1, 1871, BAO, vol. 23, pp. 011979–81 and 011983). They turned down the proposal, and he then placed £2.5 million of such bonds elsewhere (ibid., Dec., 8, 1871, BAO, vol. 23, p. 012014). See also Joseph Wall, *Andrew Carnegie* (New York: Oxford University Press, 1970), 280–283, 309. Ibid., 238, says Carnegie placed the $5 million in bonds with Junius S. Morgan. See also James Howard Bridge, *The Inside History of Carnegie Steel Company* (New York: Aldine, 1903), 75. In February 1872 Carnegie wrote Baring Brothers & Co. a long letter on the U.S. and British political scene, dropped names (his close friend talked to the President; he went to a meeting with the President), and concluded the letter hoping Baring Brothers would in the future be interested in Allegheny Valley's bonds (Carnegie to Baring Brothers, Feb. 24, 1872, BAO, vol. 23, pp. 012040–43.)

185. Henry Villard, *Memoirs*, 2 vols. (Boston: Houghton Mifflin, 1904), II, 271–275. Most of some $12 million in Kansas Pacific bonds were held in Germany in 1874 (ibid., 275). See also Dietrich G. Buss, *Henry Villard: A Study of Transatlantic Investment and Interests* (New York: Arno Press, 1978), 35.

186. James Speyer, Testimony before the U.S. Senate, Committee on Finance, *Sale of Foreign Bonds, Hearings*, 72nd Cong., 1st sess., 1932, pt. 2, 609.

187. Larson, *Jay Cooke*, 260–310, 328–406. Quotes are from ibid., 263, 310. See also Oberholtzer, *Jay Cooke*, II, 146–224, 381ff. In the summer of 1871, Cooke feted a delegation of visitors from Europe, who prepared "mixed" reports and then sought to sell the reports to the Northern Pacific and Jay Cooke & Co. for "hush money." In 1872 Jay Cooke, McCulloch & Co. sold Northern Pacific bonds in England in sterling at a price below par in U.S. currency. Cooke was sharply criticized for giving advantages to

foreign over domestic buyers; he rebought the bonds at a loss of £40,000 (ibid., 379–380, and Larson, *Jay Cooke*, 361–362). These were but two of the continuing problems.

188. Buss, *Henry Villard*, 29.

189. Lewis, *America's Stake*, 49–50. Greenberg, *Financiers*, 26, points to the presence in this era of six American banking houses in Paris, all pushing U.S. railroad securities. On other reasons for the reluctance, see Bouvier, *Crédit Lyonnais*, II, 568n. The story of the Memphis, El Paso and Pacific fiasco is wonderfully told in Virginia H. Taylor, *The Franco-Texan Land Company* (Austin: University of Texas Press, 1969), 11–110. According to Taylor, the Memphis, El Paso and Pacific was the first American railroad to be listed on the Paris Bourse. To obtain the French government's permission, the company's representatives (including General John C. Frémont) made fraudulent statements. Only after sizable commitments were made by the railroad to purchase rails and rolling stock from French industrial firms did the French government authorize the sale of the bonds (ibid., 18–19). Apparently Schneider obtained orders, or so we can deduce from ibid., 45. France's defeat in the Franco-Prussian War seems to have also served to curb interest in U.S. investment. See Bouvier, *Crédit Lyonnais*, II, 536–568, for that firm's consideration of U.S. railways along with other U.S. securities.

190. Reported in *Commercial and Financial Chronicle*, 17 (Dec. 6, 1873): 753. See Bosch, *Nederlandse Beleggingen*, 139–168. For the immense Dutch interest in American railroads, 1870–1875, see also Anne T. Ostrye, *Foreign Investment in the American and Canadian West, 1870–1914: An Annotated Bibiliography* (Metuchen, N.J.: Scarecrow Press, 1986), 118–124, items 460–463, 466, 475–530.

191. Albro Martin, *James J. Hill* (New York: Oxford University Press, 1976), 120. The principal Dutch banking house involved was Lippmann, Rosenthal of Amsterdam. See Larson, *Jay Cooke*, 369–370, and Heather Gilbert, *Awakening Continent* (Aberdeen: Aberdeen University Press, 1965), and ibid., 420, for other Dutch bankers involved. The St. Paul and Pacific had various bond issues. The majority of the purchasers were Dutch.

192. Lewis, *America's Stake*, 42.

193. Adler, *British Investment*, 137. The best work on the foreign investment in the Denver and Rio Grande Railway is Brayer, *William Blackmore*, II. The Dutch banking house participating in this railway's construction was Wertheim & Gompertz of Amsterdam.

194. Ibid., II, 61n.

195. Buss, *Villard*, 40–51. Villard also represented the Frankfurt bondholders in the Denver extension of the Kansas Pacific, whose holdings in 1874 totaled about $3.6 million (ibid., 69–70).

196. Lewis, *America's Stake*, 105.

197. McGrane, *Foreign Bondholders*, 287–289. The mortgage bonds of the South and North Alabama Railroad were also endorsed by the State of Alabama. See H. D. Newcomb to Baring Brothers, Nov. 4, 1871, BAO, vol. 23, p. 012000.

198. Dolores Greenberg listed prominent eastern private bankers handling railroad securities in 1873: Drexel, Morgan & Co.; Duncan, Sherman & Co.; John J. Cisco & Co.; Henry Clews & Co.; Clark, Dodge & Co.; Jay Cooke & Co.; Fisk & Hatch; Louis von Hoffman & Co.; August Belmont; M. K. Jessup & Co.; Adrian Iselin & Co.; Kidder, Peabody & Co.; J. S. Kennedy & Co.; Kountze Brothers; J. & W. Seligman & Co.; Winslow, Lanier & Co.; Morton, Bliss & Co. (Greenberg, *Financiers*, 13–14). All these firms were involved in negotiating American railroad securities in Europe.

199. On these connections, see ibid., 26, 42; Emden, *Money Powers*, 271–272 (Speyer's London house was Speyer Brothers); Vincent Carosso, *The Morgans* (Cambridge, Mass.: Harvard University Press, 1987), and Gras and Larson, *Casebook*, 550–551. Levi Parson Morton's partner, Walter Burns, had opened a London office in 1863. In 1869

John Rose replaced Burns in Morton's London partnership. Morton, Bliss, & Co. was formed in the U.S. in 1869, and that year the London house became Morton, Rose & Co. (Greenberg, *Financiers*, 32, 34, 51). For Knauth, Nachod & Kuhne and John Munroe, see *Commercial and Financial Chronicle*, 12 (May 27, 1871): 641. Edward Tuck (1842–1938), who provided the funds for the Tuck School, Dartmouth College, was a partner in the John Munroe Bank, New York and Paris. Letter from Franklin Brooks, July 1, 1982.

200. U.S. House, *Gold Panic Investigation*, 44–45. Hodgskin acted as a commission broker on such transactions. Part of this could be arbitrage transactions.

201. Buss, *Villard*, 172. On the formation of Kuhn, Loeb, see Carosso, *Investment Banking*, 19.

202. Riesser, *German Great Banks*, 435.

203. "History of Hallgarten & Co.," typescript, 1950, provided to me by Jon A. Bulkley, President, Moseley, Hallgarten, Estabrook & Weeden Holding Corp. Indeed, in the year ending June 30, 1865, the immediate predecessor of Hallgarten & Co. (Hallgarten & Herzfeld) was the leading trader on Wall Street, buying and selling some $169 million worth of securities and gold (Edmund Clarence Stedman, *The New York Stock Exchange* [1905; rpt. New York: Greenwood, 1969], 162). Many of these transactions were undoubtedly on behalf of European clients.

204. Bosch, *Nederlandse Beleggingen*, 175.

205. The exact amount will never be known. To prepare a total of the size of each issue advertised in each European market is not an adequate measure, because (1) not all issues were sold; (2) not all sales were fully paid up; (3) most sales were not at par; (4) fees and commissions, discounts, and deposits with foreign intermediaries must be subtracted from funds actually sent to America; (5) listings were often on several exchanges so totals may record the same issue more than once; (6) the breakdown by nationality is obscured when nationalities other than British purchased securities in London; (7) many private sales bypassed securities markets; (8) a British (or other European) investor might buy U.S. railway securities in New York; and (9) after issue, securities were traded—bought *and* sold. While items 1–5 reduce the amount of actual influx of foreign investment, items 7–8 raise the figure. A sharp attrition in the value actually received by the U.S. railroad from the "total" amount issued is well demonstrated in the case of the First Division of the St. Paul and Pacific Railroad. The bond issue was $15 million; $11 million was "floated," of which the Dutch acquired the greatest amount; the railroad netted barely $5 million (Martin, *James J. Hill*, 120). Worst still was the case of the Memphis, El Paso and Pacific. Some $10 million (nominal amount) of bonds were sent abroad for sale; some $4.8 million were actually sold in France; about $4.5 million was "realized"; $900,000 of this sum was paid to French bankers; after expenses and commissions (some paid to Frenchmen, some to Americans), $300,000 went to "railroad construction." French makers of locomotives and rails received $480,000, but when the locomotives arrived in the United States, they were left with customs for want of money to pay the duties. See Taylor, *The Franco-Texan Land Company*, 19–20, 35, 39, 72. As another example, the proceeds from the sale of $2,225,000 first mortgage bonds to cover the initial costs of construction of the Denver and Rio Grande Railway were a mere $1,305,030 (Brayer, *William Blackmore*, II, 66n). These cases notwithstanding, the obligation of the American railroad was not the amount of capital received but the face value of the bonds at maturity. Thus the debt, the level of "foreign investment," was greater than the money that actually reached America.

206. Joseph A. Schumpeter, *Business Cycles* (New York: McGraw-Hill, 1939), I, 335. Pierce, *Railroads of New York* (1953), 134n, believed Schumpeter exaggerated, but in 1953

Pierce's expertise was confined to New York railroads, and the foreign investments were far more extensive. Two contemporary estimates exist, both for railroad bonds only: (1) $375 million (as the level of holdings in 1874) was given in *Commercial and Financial Chronicle*, 19 (Oct. 10, 1874): 363, and (2) $390 million (as the level of holdings in Dec. 1874) was, given in *Banker's Magazine*, New York, 30 (May 1876): 845. Even if we double such figures, we are still far from a large part of $2 billion. Williamson, *American Growth*, 97, writes, "After 1868 the railroads with their phenomenal growth and heavy capital requirements were far and away the chief attraction for foreign long-term capital." This refers to investment flows rather than the level of investment. Lewis Corey, *House of Morgan* (New York: G. Howard Watt, 1930), 86, believed the majority of British investments in American securities (government issues as well as railroad bonds) at this time went through J. S. Morgan & Co., London, and "these investments were large." See ibid., 86–89, for Morgan's involvement in U.S. railroad issues abroad—for example, Erie bonds (1865) and Kansas Pacific bonds (1869). Vincent Carosso's excellent history of the House of Morgan substantiates the very crucial role of J. S. Morgan & Co. in this period. The firm became a major distributor of American railroad securities. It is also important to add German and Dutch and other continental European investment. I do not believe "the majority" went through Morgan. Madden, *British Investment*, 78–79, estimated that "the nominal value" of British and continental European holdings of U.S. railroad stocks and bonds in 1874 equaled $894 million.

207. Pierce, "Foreign Investment," 57–58.

208. See the fascinating account in R. E. Tyson, "Scottish Investment in American Railways: The Case of the City of Glasgow Bank, 1856–1881," in *Studies in Scottish Business History*, ed. Peter L. Payne (London: Frank Cass, 1967), 387–409. The City of Glasgow Bank failed in 1878.

209. Adler, *British Investment*, 76.

210. Simon, *Cyclical Fluctuations*, 169.

211. Charles Kindleberger, *A Financial History of Europe* (London: Allen & Unwin, 1984), 131, 224–225 (on Austrian and German crises and Austrian interests in American railroad securities); Simon, *Cyclical Fluctuations*, 184–185; and Adler, *British Investment*, 77, 79. Adler does not make the qualification, but as I will show, the Germans would return to make large investments in U.S. railroads. Williamson, *American Growth*, 132, suggests that the German and Dutch divestments occurred after 1874, while the British held on longer.

212. *Banker's Magazine*, New York, 30 (May 1876): 848 (estimate for December 1874).

213. *Commercial and Financial Chronicle*, 19 (Oct. 10, 1874): 363, made estimates similar to *Banker's Magazine*. It estimated that $375 million American railroad bonds were held abroad, of which about 40 percent were in default.

214. See First Report of the Council of the Corporation of Foreign Bondholders, Feb. 25, 1874. (I used the set in the London School of Economics library.) This report (p. 52) announced the "advanced state of organization" of an American Council of Foreign Bondholders to deal with all American securities, state and corporate. An early publication of the Corporation of Foreign Bondholders (1875) dealt with bonds of the Alabama and Chattanooga Railroad (British Museum shelf-mark: 8227dd 9).

215. Lewis, *America's Stake*, 43, 47.

216. It was in this context, for example, that Henry Villard in 1874 first became a representative of German investors (Villard, *Memoirs*, II, 271–275; Buss, *Henry Villard*, 42–44).

217. Leland Jenks, "Railroads as an Economic Force in American Development," *Journal of Economic History*, 4 (May 1944): 1–20.

218. *Commercial and Financial Chronicle*, 19 (Oct. 10, 1874): 363.

219. Adler, *British Investment*, 121, describes him as a British engineer. See ibid., 132–135, for his involvement in the West Wisconsin, the Atlantic, Mississippi and Ohio (which became the Norfolk and Western), and the Jacksonville, Pensacola and Mobile (1873).

220. The best work on this subject is Jim Berry Pearson, *The Maxwell Land Grant* (Norman: University of Oklahoma Press, 1961); the specific data in my text draw on ibid., 49–73. The original grant was made to Maxwell's father-in-law and the latter's partner before New Mexico became an American territory. I have also consulted Bosch, *Nederlandse Beleggingen*, 180, 663. This same John Collinson, in this period, "disposed" of $4 million of Florida bonds for $2.8 million in Holland, forming a Dutch syndicate for that purpose. "The story of fraud and corruption" related to the Florida bonds was widely reported in Holland, but at 70 percent of par they seemed a bargain too good to refuse. See Ratchford, *American State Debts*, 180, 173.

221. Brayer, *William Blackmore*, vols. 1 and 2, esp. vol. 1, passim. The second volume of this work is on Blackmore's relations to the Denver and Rio Grande and to land development in Colorado. The "New Mexico Trust Lands" were his project. Overall, Blackmore's ventures in land ended as disasters; he sold New Mexican and Colorado land before it was surveyed, misrepresenting the size of the properties. Virtually no development took place on the properties he controlled. Blackmore committed suicide in 1878, after a decade of involvement in American land speculation.

222. Council of Corporation of Foreign Bondholders, *Annual Report for 1874* (1875), 33.

223. See Gates, *Illinois Central*, esp. chap. 14; Richard C. Overton, *Burlington West: A Colonization History of the Burlington Railroad* (Cambridge, Mass.: Harvard University Press, 1941), 359–369; and Brayer, *William Blackmore*, vol. 2.

224. Gilbert, *Investment Trusts*, 33, and W. H. Marwick, *Economic Developments in Victorian Scotland* (London: George Allen & Unwin, 1936), 113. *Report of Special Commissioner* (1869), xxviii, found that year that "foreigners" had invested $25 million in U.S. "mortgages of real estate, &c."

225. Gilbert, *A History*, 1, 5, 13, and Marwick, *Economic Development*, 19, 83, 93.

226. W. D. Rubinstein, "British Millionaires, 1809–1949," *Bulletin of the Institute of Historical Research* (1974), 208. For relationships of the Baxters, see John Scott and Michael Hughes, *The Anatomy of Scottish Capital* (London: Croom Helm, 1980), 52.

227. Robert Fleming—by then an old man—told a rather imprecise story to Cyrus Adler, the biographer of Jacob Schiff. This is our interpretation meshed with other evidence. See Cyrus Adler, *Jacob H. Schiff* (Garden City, N.Y.: Doubleday, 1928), I, 13.

228. W. Turrentine Jackson, *The Enterprising Scot* (Edinburgh: Edinburgh University Press, 1968), 13. Menzies was in the United States in 1864, 1867, and 1872. The best work on the Scottish American Investment Company, Ltd., is Weir, *A History*. Menzies decided in 1873 that railroad bonds were more suitable than real estate mortgages, because the latter needed far closer supervision and could not be handled from Scotland. Nonetheless, by the late 1870s his company was involved in western real estate mortages (ibid., 9, 12, and Jackson, *Enterprising Scot*, 16).

229. Gilbert, *Investment Trusts*, 33–34. Details on William Reid's career are given in H. K. Hines, *An Illustrated History of the State of Oregon* (Chicago: Lewis, 1893), 310–311.

230. W. G. Kerr, *Scottish Capital on the American Credit Frontier* (Austin: Texas State Historical Association, 1976), 98–100, 103–108, and Jackson, *Enterprising Scot*, 17–19.

231. H. Peers Brewer, "Eastern Money and Western Mortgages in the 1870s," *Business History Reveiw*, 50 (Autumn 1976): 362–363.

232. Cameron, *France and the Economic Development of Europe*, 130–131.

233. J. S. G. Wilson, *French Banking Structure and Credit Policy* (Cambridge, Mass.:

Harvard University Press, 1957), 7, 202, and Ivan Wright, *Farm Mortgage Financing* (New York: McGraw-Hill, 1923), 318.

234. S. G. & G. C. Ward to Baring Bros., Jan. 7 and 9, 1874, in BAL, HC 5.2.30, pt. 8. Note this was not the same company that in 1902 took the name Equitable Trust Company of New York.

235. W. Turrentine Jackson, "British Capital in Northwest Mines," *Pacific Northwest Quarterly,* 47 (July 1956): 75, talks of 1870–1872 as the period of the "first mining mania." See Adler, *British Investment,* 87, on the Great Kanawha Company.

236. Professor Roy Church, University of East Anglia, first pointed out to me the British concerns (which proved temporary) over coal at this time. See Charles P. Kindleberger, *Economic Growth in France and Britain* (1964; rpt. New York: Simon & Schuster, 1969), 30, on the concerns, and Madden, *British Investment,* 221, 318, 334–335, 337, on British investments in "coal roads."

237. *Iron Age,* March 8, 1866, p. 1, quoted in Charlotte Erickson, *American Industry and the European Immigrant* (Cambridge, Mass.: Harvard University Press, 1957), 15.

238. *Commercial and Financial Chronicle,* 17 (Aug. 16, 1873): 209.

239. See *First Annual Report,* 23. The corporation set up a "Virginia Committee" to deal with Virginia defaults; its members visited the United States and met with the U.S. Secretary of the Treasury and with the Governor of Virginia (ibid., 22–24). West Virginia had been carved out of Virginia during the Civil War. The corporation felt it should be responsible for part of Virginia's pre–Civil War bond issue. See ibid., 25.

240. W. Turrentine Jackson, "British Impact on the Utah Mining Industry," *Utah Historical Quarterly,* 31 (1963): 347–375. Many never operated. See *Stock Exchange Year Book, 1875* for details on fourteen of these companies. One should not assume that anything near $90 million was raised, much less reached the United States.

241. Paul, *Mining Frontiers,* 82. The Sutro Tunnel Company had a capital of $12 million. McCalmont Brothers offered the tunnel company's securities in London (Wells, "House of Seligman," 701).

242. Clark C. Spence, *British Investments and the American Mining Frontier, 1860–1901* (Ithaca, N.Y.: Cornell University Press, 1958), 9–10.

243. Paul, *California Gold,* 301–302. Albin Joachim Dahl, "British Investment in California Mining, 1870–1890," Ph.D. diss., University of California, 1961, 130, identified twenty-eight companies registered in Great Britain in 1870–1873 to mine precious metals in California. They had a nominal capital of £4,196,250 ($20.4 million).

244. Jackson, "British Impact," 349.

245. Spence, *British Investments,* 45.

246. Bosch, *Nederlandse Beleggingen,* 202 (in the Winamuck Zilver Mijnen, Ltd., in 1872).

247. Spence, *British Investments,* 53, and *Stock Exchange Year Book, 1875.*

248. Spence, *British Investments,* 141, 146–147. Jay Cooke, McCulloch & Co., London, also participated in endorsing the mine, much to Jay Cooke's dismay. See Oberholtzer, *Jay Cooke,* II, 290.

249. Spence, *British Investments,* chap. 8.

250. Ibid., 196, 255, 98. The initial capital of Richmond Consolidated Mining Company, Ltd., was £270,000 (*Stock Exchange Year Book, 1875*). *Mineral Industry, 1892,* 477, gives the dividend history and minerals produced.

251. Spence, *British Investments,* 114.

252. This point is made by Williamson, *American Growth,* 128.

253. Jackson, "British Impact," 349.

254. See ibid., 349–350, for details. At least some promoters made profits. William

Blackmore, who promoted American mines among his many activities, ended up broke. See Brayer, *William Blackmore,* I, 125, and passim.

255. Spence, *British Investments,* 196.

256. Letter quoted in Wall, *Andrew Carnegie,* 292. This was the time when Carnegie was trying to woo Baring Brothers. See Carnegie to Baring Brothers, Dec. 8, 1871, BAO, vol. 23, p. 0120l4.

257. Lewis, *America's Stake,* 94; other British oil promotions followed, with equally obscure histories. Thus in 1868 "the Anglo-American Oil Company" advertised in England. It included various titled individuals' names on its prospectus, as well as the name of Jay Cooke, who would claim to have nothing to do with the venture (Oberholtzer, *Jay Cooke,* II, 84). It had no connection with its namesake of 1888.

258. 14 U.S. Stat. 251 (July 26, 1866).

259. *San Francisco Bulletin,* July 31, 1866, cited in Joseph Ellison, "The Mineral Land Question in California," in *The Public Lands,* ed. Vernon Carstensen (Madison: University of Wisconsin Press, 1963), 86.

260. See Preemption Act, 5 U.S. Stat. 453 (1841), and Homestead Act, 12 U.S. Stat. 392 (1862).

261. 16 U.S. Stat. 217 (July 9, 1870).

262. 17 U.S. Stat. 91, 94, 96 (May 10, 1872).

263. Spence, *British Investments,* 192–195. Spence did not realize that the phrase about citizenship was in the 1866 as well as the 1872 legislation, a strange oversight in an otherwise excellent book.

264. See ibid., 195ff, and Clark C. Spence, "British Investment and the American Mining Frontier, 1860–1914," *New Mexico Historical Review,* 36 (April 1961): 134, wherein he suggests that to the extent that English investors purchased already patented claims, federal mining laws contributed to raising the price to foreign purchasers.

265. Jackson, "British Impact," 371, notes that £2.12 million in securities (par value) of six large Utah mining companies were issued in London in the early 1870s; by January 1874 their market value had fallen to £425,000. The *Stock Exchange Year Book, 1875* recounts one unfortunate story after another. Take the case of the Eberhardt & Aurora Mining Company, Ltd., established in 1870 to mine in Nevada: It paid a dividend in 1871; a telegram arrived in London saying a great lode had been struck; the shares soared in price. No dividend was paid thereafter.

266. Edward Stanwood, "Cotton Manufacture," in U.S. Department of Interior, Census Office, *Report on Manufacturing Industries in the United States, 11th Census, 1890* (Washington, D.C., 1895), pt. 3, 181; J. & P. Coats, "Text of 150 Year Exhibition," panel 18, Renfrew District Library, Scotland; and Matthew Blair, *The Paisley Thread Industry* (Paisley: Alexander Gardner, 1907), 40–41, 50–51; and Rowland Tappan Berthoff, *British Immigrants in Industrial America* (Cambridge, Mass.: Harvard University Press, 1953), 44. Berthoff dates George Clark's Newark mill from the 1850s. His source is an 1893 newspaper article. The latter may well have confused the sales branch with the manufacturing activity. I have followed the lead of J. B. K. Hunter, the J. & P. Coats historian, in my dates. Charles Batchelor, who became Edison's chief assistant and "most trusted lieutenant," was born in England. In the early 1870s he was sent by an unnamed British engineering firm to help install machinery at the Clark sewing thread mill in Newark. After finishing that task, he was employed by Edison. See Harold C. Passer, *The Electrical Manufacturers, 1875–1900* (Cambridge, Mass.: Harvard University Press, 1953), 96. On the early history of J. & P. Coats's manufacturing operations in Pawtucket, see "Photographs and Brief Description of the Establishments of the Conant Thread Company . . . A souvenir of the visit of Sir Peter Coats during the winter of 1877–1878," 1878, Pawtucket Public Library, Pawtucket, R.I., and Robert Grieve, *An*

Illustrated History of Pawtucket, Central Falls, and Vicinity (Pawtucket, R.I.: Pawtucket Gazette & Chronicle, 1897), 275. I am indebted to Paul Arsenault, Reference Librarian, Pawtucket Public Library, for these references. On the size of Coats's investment, see Sir Alec Cairncross, "The Early Growth of Messrs. J. & P. Coats," unfinished paper (ca. 1956). I have obtained other valuable material on the Coats business from Hunter (J. B. K. Hunter to Wilkins, April 27, 1986). Both J. & P. Coats and Clark Thread sold brand name products. In an 1862 response to a British Parliamentary Committee inquiry, a member of the Coats firm told the following story: A firm of the same name in the United States had imitated their wrappers and thus seriously interfered with their trade. "The Courts stopped the imitation, but could not prevent the use of the name. The name alone, however, was not sufficient, and as soon as the pirates were prevented from imitating the wrappers, their mere use of the name Coats did but little harm." See the discussion in *Journal of the Society of the Arts,* 24 (Nov. 26, 1875): 20. Hunter to Wilkins, April 27, 1986, is my source on the John Clark, Jr. & Co. mill in East Newark.

267. On the founding and the Barbour family, see Linen Thread Co., Ltd., *The Faithful Fibre* (Glasgow: Linen Thread Co., 1956), 25. It gives no date for the Paterson mill. The date comes from Berthoff, *British Immigrants,* 44. *Faithful Fibre* does note that the Paterson mill was "almost" 100 years old.

268. From the *Bulletin of the National Association of Wool Manufacturers,* 2 (1870): 550, as quoted in Erickson, *American Industry,* 209.

269. Geoffrey Tweedale, "Sheffield Steel and America," *Business History,* 25 (Nov. 1983): 229–230, and his "Sheffield Steel Industry and Its Allied Trades and the American Market," Ph.D. diss., London School of Economics, 1983, 220–228. Tweedale records Philip S. Justice's plans to include Butcher, a staff from Sheffield, and machinery from there. Butcher was described as "the first manufacturer who made a solid Cast Steel Tyre in England and has had a very large experience in them, as well as all kinds of Steel." If there was an investment by the Butchers in the William Butcher Steel Works, which seems likely, it was probably not sizable. Apparently the Americans wanted the know-how, not the financing, of the Britishers. (It was at Midvale Steel that, later, Frederick W. Taylor did his experiments on tool steel that had the long-term influence on machine shop practice.) Erickson, *American Industry,* 42, writes of Butcher's role in Pennsylvania Steel in 1865. See also William T. Hogan, *Economic History of the Iron and Steel Industry of the United States,* 5 vols. (Lexington, Mass.: D. C. Heath, 1971), I, 115, on Pennsylvania Steel's Bessemer steel output and its production of steel rails for the Pennsylvania Railroad.

270. The father, Read Holliday, had started making dyes at Huddersfield, England, in 1860. In time Read Holliday & Sons, Ltd., became a large British producer of inorganic acids, intermediates, and a few dyestuffs. Read Holliday's son Robert, who remained in England, died in 1901, and Joseph Turner and Lionel Brook Holliday became joint managers of the British firm. In 1913–1914 Read Holliday & Sons, Ltd., was the only British dyestuff company to have a sales office in Germany. See Williams Haynes, *American Chemical Industry,* 6 vols. (New York: Van Nostrand, 1945–1954), I, 303; L. F. Haber, *The Chemical Industry during the Nineteenth Century* (Oxford: Clarendon Press, 1958), 145; and Haber, *The Chemical Industry, 1900–1930* (Oxford: Clarendon Press, 1971), 148–149. Since the American enterprise (which became in 1916 Holliday-Kemp Company) and the British firm remained under the control of Holliday family members—at least up to World War I—it seems likely that ties were maintained. On the Holliday-Kemp Company (organized in the United States by R. W. Kemp, a grandson of Read Holliday), see Haynes, *American Chemical Industry,* III, 237. See Chapter 11, note 51, for more on Read Holliday & Sons' American business, 1875–1914.

271. On that factory, see U.S. Department of Commerce, *Foreign Direct Investment in the United States*, 9 vols. (Washington, D.C., 1976), V. G-89-93; Christopher Tugendhat, *The Multinationals* (London: Eyre & Spottiswoode, 1971), 12; and Thomas R. Kabisch, *Deutsches Kapital in den USA* (Stuttgart: Klett-Cotta, 1982), 230–231. Despite all these secondary sources, my research makes me doubt the Albany factory was established in 1865.

272. Haynes, *American Chemical Industry*, I, 307–308. Haynes does not mention any manufacturing investment of Bayer in the United States prior to 1871. Haynes's source was "Co. memo to author."

273. It is not clear when Preiss arrived in Albany; in ibid., VI, 174, Haynes writes "in the early 1870s."

274. W. J. Reader, *Imperial Chemical Industries* (London: Oxford University Press, 1970), I, 20.

275. I am indebted to Russell H. Williams of Eberhard Faber, Inc. Wilkes-Barre, Pennsylvania, whose search of that company's records provided the historical data on which I based this account. The impact of the Civil War is very unclear. How did the new New York factory obtain cedar? Mr. Williams sent me a copy of the undated newspaper article; internal evidence indicates it was published in about 1872–73. It is headed "A. W. Faber's Lead Pencils" and provides pictures of both the Stein factory and "A. W. Faber's Branch Lead Pencil and Penholder Manufactory, Brooklyn, N.Y." The quotation is from this article. Because it contains a picture of the Brooklyn factory (built in 1872), the article must be post-1872; it was written when Eberhard Faber was still alive, so it has to be pre-1879. The Eberhard Faber pencil business still flourishes today.

276. Adler, *British Investment*, 125, and Jackson, *The Enterprising Scot*, 9.

277. Lawrence Oakley Cheever, *The House of Morrell* (Cedar Rapids, Iowa: Torch Press, 1948), 45. See Chapter 9 for more on its subsequent U.S. history.

278. P. L. Cottrell, *Industrial Finance, 1830–1914* (London: Methuen, 1980), 113–139. On David Chadwick, see also James B. Jefferys, *Business Organisations in Great Britain, 1856–1914* (1938; rpt. New York: Arno Press, 1977), 79, 82, 108, 298, 306, 313, 317–318, and W. A. Thomas, *The Provincial Stock Exchanges* (London: Frank Cass, 1973), 68, 123. Adler, *British Investment*, III, 204, indicates Chadwick's connection with the Atlantic and Great Western Railroad in 1869 (helping to arrange for payments to unsecured creditors) and his role in 1870 in marketing 8 percent first mortgage bonds ($1,300,000—£178.2.6 per $1,000 issue price) of the Des Moines Valley Railroad. On the Joliet Company, see Victor Clark, *History of Manufactures in the United States* (Washington, D.C.: Carnegie Institution, 1929), II, 236–237; it became part of Illinois Steel Company in 1889. Carnegie had easy entry to J. S. Morgan & Co., London, and a bond issue for $400,000 was "quickly arranged" (Wall, *Carnegie*, 319–320). Perhaps I ought to include in this category the United States Rolling Stock Company. Bischoffsheim & Goldschmidt handled a £1 million stock issue (£20 shares) in 1871. Dorothy Adler calls this an American railway security, but the firm was designed to manufacture railroad equipment. See Adler, *British Investment*, 113, 205.

279. The Liverpool & London & Globe had interrupted its southern business during the Civil War; when the war was over, its activities resumed in New Orleans, an agency was reestablished in Richmond, Virginia, and the company acquired a building in Charleston, South Carolina (J. Dyer Simpson, *1936 Our Centenary Year* [London: Liverpool & London & Globe, 1936], 47).

280. P. G. M. Dickson, *The Sun Insurance Office, 1710–1960* (London: Oxford University Press, 1960), 221–223, and Harold E. Raynes, *A History of British Insurance*, rev. ed.

(London: Isaac Pitman, 1950), 267. In addition, in the early 1870s the Phoenix Assurance Company had agencies in San Francisco, Savannah, and New York, but its business was not large (Clive Trebilcock, *Phoenix Assurance Company* [Cambridge: Cambridge University Press, 1985], I, 320–321).

281. *Best's Insurance Report (Fire and Marine), 1914–1915*, 52, 382. Both Canadian firms were under the same management.

282. *Best's Insurance Report, 1914–1915*.

283. Raynes, *British Insurance*, 274. See also Marquis James, *Biography of a Business, 1792–1942, Insurance Company of North America* (1942; rpt. New York: Arno Press, 1976), 166–167, and Edward Liveing, *A Century of Insurance: The Commercial Union Group of Insurance Companies, 1861–1961* (London: H. F. & G. Witherby, 1961), 33–34.

284. Robert L. Nash, *A Short Inquiry into the Profitable Nature of our Investments*, 3rd ed. (London: Effingham Wilson, 1881), 92.

285. Those two were the Commercial Bank of India and the British and California Banking Company (floated in 1864, with directors representing the London and County Bank, the National Provincial, the City Bank, the London and South American, and the Agra Bank of the East). BCBC had bought an existing San Francisco business (Baster, *International Banks*, 158).

286. Ibid., 157–158. Eventually the Bank of British North America would be acquired by the Bank of Montreal in 1918; the Bank of British Columbia by the Canadian Bank of Commerce in 1901; and the London and San Francisco Bank by the Bank of California in 1905. See Chapter 13.

287. Cross, *Financing an Empire*, I, 259.

288. Ross, *Canadian Bank of Commerce*, I, 251, 315, 321.

289. Ibid., 316.

290. Baster, *International Banks*, 158. According to Baster, the eight key shareholders were (1) Bischoffsheim & Goldschmidt (a house that was active in relation to the Atlantic and Great Western Railroad, the Erie, and other U.S. securities); (2) Frühling & Goschen; (3) Frederick Huth & Co. (this and the preceding firm had partners on the board of the Bank of England; Frederick Huth & Co. in particular had long been active in U.S. business; see Chapter 3); (4) Junius S. Morgan (who had been George Peabody's partner in London and in 1864 had established J. S. Morgan & Co., London); (5) Frederick Rodewald (described by Buss, *Villard*, 40, 57, as "of the London office" of the London and San Francisco Bank; David Joslin, *A Century of Banking in Latin America* [London: Oxford University Press, 1963], 80, says that in 1863 Rodewald had been a founder of the Brazilian and Portuguese Bank and was then a director of the London Joint Stock Bank—a man who had spent many years in Brazil): (6) Stern Brothers (the London house of an important German firm); (7) the International Financial Society (formed in London in May 1863 as a financial company); and (8) the Bank of Saxe Meinigen. To this list, Cottrell, "Investment Banking," 269–270, adds the two private German bankers, May and Sulzbach Brothers. See Cottrell, "Investment Banking," and Jenks, *Migration*, 248, for detailed information on the International Financial Society, Ltd. Its stated purpose was "to assist and take part in financial and industrial undertakings, especially foreign loans and enterprises possessing government guarantees"; its board of directors included J. S. Morgan, Herman Stern (of Stern Brothers), and representatives of Huth and Frühling & Goschen (that is, the same participants as in the London and San Francisco Bank). The "Manila firm," to which Baster referred, has been identified by Cottrell (p. 270) as "Russell and Sturgis," well-known Boston merchants. The Bostonian Russell Sturgis (1805–1887) was at one time a partner in Russell & Sturgis, in Manila; Sturgis migrated to England, where in January 1851 he became a partner in Baring Brothers. In 1873, after the death of Thomas Baring, Sturgis was for

almost a decade the senior partner in Baring Brothers. See Hidy, *House of Baring*, 395.

291. Cross, *Financing an Empire*, I, 258.

292. Buss, *Villard*, 35, 40, 66, 69, 80–83.

293. Ibid., 35, 38.

294. Adler, *British Investment*, 205. S. Japhet repeats a story told him by Carl Pollitz, a Frankfurt broker, who claims that he was traveling to Omaha and was delayed because of the absence of a bridge. He was told there was no bridge, since there was no money. Pollitz and Messrs. Venner & Co. of Chicago founded a company, issued 8 percent Omaha Bridge bonds at 80, which were offered to the public on the Frankfurt Bourse. Union Pacific bought Omaha Bridge Co., and the bonds were paid for at 110. Japhet's comment: "Money was easier to make in those days" (*Recollections*, 33–34). None other than Andrew Carnegie "negotiated" the Omaha Bridge bonds. See Andrew Carnegie to Messrs. Baring, Aug. 25, 1871, BAO, vol. 23, p. 011979.

295. Adler, *British Investment*, 204, and Buss, *Villard*, 35.

296. Baster, *International Banks*, 159; Adler, *British Investment*, 154n; Cross, *Financing an Empire*, I, 268, 389; and ibid., III, 63. Stephen Birmingham, *Our Crowd* (New York: Dell, 1967), 142–146, gives details about the bank. Joseph Seligman—the eldest of eight brothers—who migrated to the United States in 1837 and headed the firm's New York house—wanted the California bank to be "English." Thus his brother Isaac, in London, established the bank and, according to Birmingham, made a public offering in London of £400,000 of bank stock. Isaac monitored the bank's operations carefully. Birmingham says nothing about the Sassoons' role.

297. Cross, *Financing an Empire*, I, 220–221, 389; the Hentsch family bank in Geneva was one of the major private banks there (Faith, *Safety in Numbers*, 24, 287, 289). Hentsch & Cie. was said to cater "to the very cream of French society" (ibid., 290). Apparently Lombard, Odier & Cie., Geneva, was also involved in the Swiss-American Bank. See Bauer, *Swiss Bank Corporation*, 368, who writes that Lombard, Odier & Cie. had offered in 1872 the predecessor of the Swiss Bank Corporation a holding in the Swiss-American Bank, which the latter had turned down.

298. Ross, *Canadian Bank of Commerce*, II, 556, 63–64.

299. Denison, *Canada's First Bank*, II, 160.

300. Ibid., II, 163, 179–180, and James, *Chicago Banks*, II, 1173.

301. Bessie Louis Pierce, *A History of Chicago* (Chicago: University of Chicago Press, 1957), III, 14.

302. Denison, *Canada's First Bank*, II, 181. I think this is correct.

303. Ross, *Canadian Bank of Commerce*, II, 64.

304. Marshall et al., *Canadian-American Industry*, 17, citing the *Monetary Times*, Dec. 4, 1874.

305. Stephen A. Caldwell, *A Banking History of Louisiana* (Baton Rouge: Louisiana State University Press, 1935), 107, 109.

306. Wallis Hunt, *Heirs of Great Adventure* (London: Balfour, Williamson, 1951), 27, 47, 67–75, and Morton Rothstein, "A British Firm on the American West Coast, 1869–1914," *Business History Review*, 37 (Winter 1963): 392–398.

307. Edward P. Crapol, *America for Americans* (Westport, Conn.: Greenwood Press, 1973), 29. The Barings—and those related to them—were said to have contributed over one-quarter of the league's total funding. I have found no evidence of this in the Baring Papers, either in Ottawa or in London.

308. Studenski and Krooss, *Financial History*, 181 n.3. The explanation puts the blame in the wrong place. Cooke, very simply, overextended.

309. Quoted in Taylor, *Franco-Texan Land Company*, 110–111. The Memphis, El Paso and Pacific is not included in Table 4.10, because its bonds were never publicly issued

in London. English investors were, however, aware of the problems of the French bond owners. And then, of course, there were the problems of the Atlantic and Great Western and of the Erie.

310. Grodinsky, *Jay Gould*, 71. On the same events of 1870, see *New York Times*, April 14, 1871, 2, 4. Both Jay Gould and Jim Fisk were accused of having "robbed" the English shareholders.

311. In writing Chapter 3, I was initially mystified why more state securities were available in London in 1838—after the 1837 crisis—than before. The reason lay in part in the release of collateral. The same thing happened with the railroads in 1874.

312. U.S. Secretary of the Treasury, *Annual Report, 1873*, v (the Secretary was William A. Richardson). The *Stock Exchange Year Book, 1875* (published in London in 1874), 22, praised U.S. government finance. The United States had during the Civil War created a huge debt; "the rate of reduction is also equally unprecedented, and is a useful example to all nations."

313. In October 1873. Quoted in Weir, *A History*, 9.

314. Carnegie had no trouble raising money in London for his new steel works (Wall, *Carnegie*, 319–320).

5. The Setting

1. Robert E. Gallman and Edward S. Howle, "Trends in the Structure of the American Economy since 1840," in *The Reinterpretation of American Economic History*, ed. Robert W. Fogel and Stanley L. Engerman (New York: Harper & Row, 1971), 26. These figures are at current prices, with agriculture plus industry equal to 100 percent.

2. U.S. Bureau of the Census, *Historical Statistics of the United States* (Washington, D.C., 1975), pt. 1, 8.

3. Sereno S. Pratt, *The Work of Wall Street* (New York: D. Appleton, 1921), 190–191 (cable costs). R. C. Michie, *Money, Mania, and Markets* (Edinburgh: John Donald, 1981), 258, gives the message transmission time.

4. See N. R. P. Bonsor, *North Atlantic Seaway* (Prescot, Lancashire: T. Stephenson, 1955), on all the transatlantic carriers.

5. Robert G. Athearn, *Westward the Briton* (New York: Charles Scribner's Sons, 1953), studied nearly 300 published books and articles by British travelers to the American West, 1865 to 1900. See also William Kerr, *Scottish Capital on the American Credit Frontier* (Austin: Texas State Historical Association, 1976), 4–5.

6. Brinley Thomas, *International Migration and Economic Development* (1961; rpt. New York: Garland, 1983), 10–11, and his *Migration and Economic Growth*, 2nd ed. (Cambridge: Cambridge University Press, 1973), 233. Thomas shows the relations between migration and capital flows.

7. See John A. James, *Money and Capital Markets in Postbellum America* (Princeton, N.J.: Princeton University Press, 1978), on American capital markets. Alfred D. Chandler has made the point that the shortening of distance in communications is associated with the integration of enterprise.

8. U.S. Bureau of the Census, *Historical Statistics*, pt. 2, 884–885, and Lance E. Davis et al., *American Economic Growth* (New York: Harper & Row, 1972), 572.

9. U.S. Bureau of the Census, *Historical Statistics*, pt. 1, 201, shows price trends based on the Warren-Pearson wholesale price index. Using 1910–1914 as 100, this price index puts 1875 prices at 118. The 1866 figure was 174, so the earlier cited drop in cable prices was far more dramatic than the overall price decline. On the rise in real per capita income, see ibid., 224.

10. Alfred D. Chandler, *The Visible Hand* (Cambridge, Mass.: Harvard University

Press, 1977), and his "Multi-Unit Enterprise," in *Evolution of International Management Structures*, ed. Harold F. Williamson (Newark: University of Delaware Press, 1975).

11. A "trust" with business in the United States could be a formal instrument for combination (as in the Standard Oil Trust) or a word designating "monopolistic arrangements" of big business (the target of "antitrust" actions), a British investment trust company (as in Merchants' Trust), or a banking and fiduciary institution (as in Guaranty Trust Company). In each case the investor put his assets under the charge of (in the trust of) others' management.

12. Duke of Marlborough, "Virginia Mines and American Rails," *Fortnightly Review*, n.s., 49 (June 1891): 792.

13. Ellis Hawley, *The Great War and the Search for a Modern Order* (New York: St. Martin's Press, 1979), 9.

14. Mira Wilkins, *The Emergence of Multinational Enterprise: American Business Abroad from the Colonial Era to 1914* (Cambridge, Mass.: Harvard University Press, 1970).

15. I am uncertain exactly when the United States became the greatest debtor nation in international accounts. This probably was the case in 1875, and even earlier. Existing figures are too imperfect for such a determination. That America was by 1914 the world's largest debtor nation is my own conclusion, based on numerous international comparisons (see Table 5.3). Many American historians write of the growth in the early twentieth century of America as a world power, neglecting to record that before World War I the United States remained a debtor nation in world accounts.

16. There are many estimates. A scholar must consider, for example, the differences between capital flows and level of investments. I have wanted to look at the "level" (the "stock") at particular times. Estimates can vary substantially depending on how the compiler (1) determined the level of investments in securities: market value at the time of purchase, par value, market value at the time of measurement, or book value of assets represented by the securities; some compilers look at "new issues," while others feel "calls" a more appropriate measure, and some feel neither is appropriate; (2) treated securities in default; (3) established ownership: securities issued in London were purchased by non-Britishers; securities issued in New York could be bought by foreign investors; and (4) monitored changes in ownership after issue, investments made directly by companies, and reinvested earnings. Estimates have been based on contemporary "judgments," calculated on the basis of "issues" presented to foreign publics, derived indirectly from trade balances, or based on assumptions of percentage return on investment from which the level was then derived. Care in evaluating all such estimates is essential.

17. John J. Madden's work, which goes to 1880 only, is useful for the first five years of this period. See his Cambridge University dissertation of 1958, newly published as *British Investment in the United States, 1860–1880* (New York: Garland, 1985.) Its title notwithstanding, it covers British and continental European investments in the United States. Some of the best work on portfolio investment has been done by Matthew Simon; see his *Cyclical Fluctuations and International Capital Movements of the United States* (1955 Ph.D. diss.; New York: Arno Press, 1978) and his "United States Balance of Payments, 1861–1900," *Trends in the American Economy in the Nineteenth Century*, Studies in Income and Wealth, vol. 24 (Princeton, N.J.: Princeton University Press, 1960), 699–707. The work of Jeffrey G. Williamson, *American Growth and the Balance of Payments* (Chapel Hill: University of North Carolina Press, 1964), is invaluable.

18. Individual investors acquired portfolio investments in many British firms that operated in the United States; the firms themselves made direct investments. When the firm was the investor, I have often felt it unnecessary to go behind the firm to the investors in the business entity (at times this is necessary when the ownership relates

to control; it is not necessary in the case of portfolio investors). Another case of comingling involves a foreign insurance company, for example, that made direct investments in selling insurance in the United States. Its U.S. affiliate would then buy American securities to have appropriate assets. These purchases were "portfolio" investments but were made for the direct investment purpose of involvement in the American insurance business. Such investments became part of the assets of the foreign insurance company in the United States and thus part of the stock of foreign investment in America.

19. Economists are now measurement conscious, but remember how hard it was to determine Iranian assets in the United States at the time of the 1979–80 hostage crisis. The London School of Economics lectures of Ellis T. Powell, *The Mechanism of the City* (London: P. S. King, 1910), are particularly good on the workings of the international market for securities. Any attempt to measure the level of foreign investment based solely on new "issues" is instantly suspect, because of the active international trade in already-issued securities.

20. I know of no one who challenges this. I was, however, startled to see Alfred S. Heidelbach's 1895 data, *Commercial and Financial Chronicle*, 60 (March 30, 1895): 543, wherein he estimated that Americans would pay out to foreigners $75 million in "dividends and interest upon American securities held abroad" (presumably this was mainly on portfolio investments) and another $75 million "for profits of foreign corporations doing business here and of non-residents, derived from real estate investments, partnership profits, &c." (that is, direct investments). Were direct investments more profitable than portfolio ones? Probably. If not, these figures suggest that direct investments equaled or exceeded portfolio ones in that year. Was 1895 an atypical year? Possibly. These are estimates, and the *Chronicle* had many criticisms of Heidelbach's methodology. Nonetheless, the figures do make us pause.

21. In 1914 C. K. Hobson (in *Export of Capital* [London: Constable, 1914], 123–124) noted the "desire of investors to secure a return by investing in business abroad, while retaining substantial control over management." Although Hobson's attention was primarily to portfolio investments, he recognized the importance of the retention of control.

22. Today the practice of economists and statisticians is to define "direct" investment as those interests *that carry control* (as noted earlier, I have followed this definition). Again, by the current U.S. Department of Commerce definition, once there is control, investments can be made in equity *and* intracompany loans, or they can be made directly into physical assets. Some past writings often used the phrase "direct investments" to refer to those that bypassed the market. See discussion of the "definition" problems in Mira Wilkins, "Modern European Economic History and the Multinationals," *Journal of European Economic History*, 6 (Winter 1977): 585. At that time, 1977, intracompany loans by foreign direct investors were not included in the U.S. Department of Commerce definition of "foreign direct investment."

23. My choice of these figures was cautious. See notes to Table 5.4. Obviously there are large areas of disagreement. I am not alone in preparing a table of this sort for these years. Matthew Simon, for example, did this in his 1955 dissertation, *Cyclical Fluctuations*, 684–687 (to 1899 only). My table differs from others in being more discriminate; I excluded many estimates that Simon included, but added others. Simon had some estimates for England only, whereas I omitted all estimates that were solely for one nationality. Simon's work was immensely helpful. Madden did not know of Simon's dissertation, so his estimates were independent of those presented by Simon. Simon was unaware of the detailed estimates made by the British statistician Ernest Seyd, "The Fall in the Price of Silver, its Consequences, and their Possible Avoidance,"

Journal of the Society of Arts, 24 (March 10, 1876): 311. Seyd gives no source for what seem to be "ballpark" guesses. They are clearly rough, albeit quite detailed. I did not put them in the body of the table (they are in the notes) because they needed so much in the way of qualification. Thus his $1,020 million for federal and state debts is plausible. His $486 million on railroad bonds is designated for those "placed in Europe in the last twenty years"; this figure does not appear to take into account defaults or repatriations. Nonetheless, Seyd's total on railroad bonds is lower than that in Madden's *British Investments,* 78–79. Seyd's $244 million for railway shares, mining shares, and other claims held in Europe seems acceptable. Likewise, the $97 million European holdings of American "lands and mortgages, &c." is possible. In short, his total $1,847 million is feasible.

There is a paucity of statistics on the growth of American railroad securities held abroad. Margaret Myers, *The New York Money Market* (New York: Columbia University Press, 1931), 290–291, gave the plausible figure "more than $1.5 billion" for foreign holdings of U.S. railroad securities in 1883 (and secondary sources often cite her number); but when I went to her carefully footnoted source, this figure proved to be "the amount of American railway securities quoted in London," which, of course, in no way represented the "foreign holdings" in U.S. railroad securities. Thus I had to delete her figure. I included Georges Martin's 1897 statistics (that the capable statistician Michael G. Mulhall cited in his *Dictionary of Statistics,* 4th ed. [London, 1899], 653). I have not seen this figure in any other place and know nothing about Martin's methodology. His estimate seems possible. By contrast, I put Cleona Lewis' 1897 estimate in a note, since it was Bacon's for 1899!

There is, however, no evidence of a rise in foreign investment in the United States, 1897–1899, that is suggested by the juxaposition of Martin's and Bacon's numbers, unless both figures are at "market" and this reflects the rise in market values that did occur in these years. My research does convince me, however, that the approximately $7 billion figure for July 1, 1914, provided by Lewis is far superior to the smaller ones sometimes presented. See, for example, Raymond W. Goldsmith, *A Study of Savings in the United States* (Princeton, N.J.: Princeton University Press, 1955), I, 1089, 1090. But in his most recent work, *Comparative National Balance Sheets* (Chicago: University of Chicago Press, 1985), 300, Goldsmith relies on data that, in turn, depend on Lewis' contribution. Williamson, *American Growth and the Balance of Payments,* 259, accepted Lewis' 1914 estimate of $6.75 billion; this was her modification of the statistics to value common stock at market rather than at par. See Cleona Lewis, *America's Stake in International Investments* (Washington, D. C.: Brookings Institution, 1938), 546. Market is obviously preferable to par in establishing the level of foreign investment. I used the higher figure only because I identified other stakes that Lewis did not know about, and I believe these more than offset the discrepancy between market and par. Douglass C. North, "International Capital Movements in Historical Perspective," in *U.S. Private and Government Investment Abroad,* ed. Raymond Mikesell (Eugene: University of Oregon Books, 1962), 24, writes, "Foreign investments in the United States [on the eve of World War I] amounted to some $6,800 million." With the trade in securities, plus changing values in the marketplace, within any year there were major fluctuations in the level of foreign investment in the United States.

24. Nathaniel T. Bacon, "American International Indebtedness," *Yale Review,* 9 (Nov. 1900): 265–285. See also Lewis, *America's Stake,* 523–529, for an appraisal of his statistics. Bacon's study was stimulated by an 1895 discussion of data presented by Alfred S. Heidelbach of Heidelbach, Ickelheimer & Co. on "Why Do We Export Gold?" Heidelbach contended that in payment of our international indebtedness, foreigners had taken American securities rather than requiring payment in gold. See *Commercial*

and Financial Chronicle, 60 (March 30, April 6, April 13, 1895), 542–544, 585, 630–633. Neither Lewis nor Bacon (nor Heidelbach) appears to have been aware of Seyd's 1876 figures. As indicated in note 23 above, while Seyd's numbers seem possible, he gives no sources and I thus hesitate to call his work a "contemporary scholarly approximation." Likewise, neither Bacon nor Lewis (nor Heidelbach) appears to have known of the French statistician Georges Martin's figures—and as I also indicated in note 23, I know nothing of his methodology.

25. Bacon secured letters of introduction to "financiers" in London, Paris, Amsterdam, Frankfurt, and so on, and obtained information from them. He also talked with men at the Inland Revenue Office in Britain and then made "assumptions" from what he learned. As an example of his care, on his estimate of British investment in the United States he noted, "I feel considerable confidence that the error in it will not exceed 25 per cent, as of January 1, 1899." (Bacon, "American International Indebtedness," 268). Paish is well known for his studies on *British* foreign investments. For British foreign investments, he "examined the reports, balance sheets, and income statements of several thousand companies" (George Paish, "Great Britain's Capital Investments in Individual Colonial and Foreign Countries," *Journal of the Royal Statistical Society*, 74 [Jan. 1911]: 167). Nonetheless, his data on British overseas investment have been sharply criticized (see this chapter, end of note 44). Paish, in his considerations of the U.S. investments of other nationalities, was very casual. His *overall* figures on foreign investment in the United States in 1908 are presented in U.S. Senate, National Monetary Commission, *Trade Balances of the United States* [by George Paish], 61st Cong., 2nd sess., 1910, S. Doc. 579, 174–175. When Paish discussed the investments of other than British investors, he added continual qualifications: "estimates," "appears," "approximately," "about."

26. Subsequent series on foreign investment in the United States for all or part of the period 1875–1914 were prepared by Charles J. Bullock, John H. Williams, and Rufus S. Tucker, "Balance of Trade of the United States," *Review of Economic Statistics*, 1 (July 1919): 224–231; Paul Dickens, "The Transition Period in American International Financing: 1897 to 1914," Ph.D. diss., George Washington University, 1933; Eugene Staley, *War and the Private Investor* (Garden City, N.Y.: Doubleday, 1935); U.S. Department of Commerce, Bureau of Foreign and Domestic Commerce, *Foreign Investments in the United States* (Washington, D.C. 1937), 22–23, 28; Lewis, *America's Stake* (1938); Goldsmith, *A Study of Savings* (1955), I, 1089–90; Simon, *Cyclical Fluctuations* (1955), 685–687; and Madden, *British Investment in the United States, 1860–1880* (1958). Meanwhile, in July 1954 the *Survey of Current Business*, 14, summarized the U.S. balance of payments in the years 1850–1914, using data from Bullock, Williams, and Tucker. Simon Kuznets, *Capital in the American Economy* (Princeton, N.J.: Princeton University Press, 1961), 120–121, cites this as his source, but he revised the figures. Other series include Simon, "U.S. Balance of Payments, 1861–1900" (1960), 699–707; U.S. Bureau of the Census, *Historical Statistics of the United States* (Washington, D.C., 1960), 565; North, "International Capital Movements in Historical Perspective" (1962); Williamson, *American Growth* (1964), 255–258; and John Dunning, *Studies in International Investment* (London: Allen & Unwin, 1970), 151. The oft-cited U.S. Bureau of the Census, *Historical Statistics of the United States* (1975), pt. 2, 869, adds nothing on foreign investment in the United States that was not in the 1960 edition of this same work. I have consulted all these contributions and incorporated in my materials the data developed by these scholars. In short, there are many compilers of series on foreign investment in the United States. I am indebted to all of them.

27. Cleona Lewis has indicated in *America's Stake*, 546, that of the $7,090 million in long-term foreign investments in the United States on July 1, 1914, $1,210 million was

in "foreign-controlled enterprises." When she included "foreign-controlled railroads" (Canadian and one British), she raised this "direct investment" figure to $1,310 million (ibid., 558). Goldsmith, *A Study of Savings*, 1090, thought that in 1914 "direct" investment equaled $875 million out of a total of $5 billion in foreign investments in the United States. He used the term to mean investments other than those in stocks and bonds.

28. These figures from *Historical Statistics of the United States* (1960) are based on Simon's data, "U.S. Balance of Payments." Simon, *Cyclical Fluctuations and the International Capital Movements of the United States, 1864–1897*, gives a year-by-year explanation for the period he covers. The word *net* is used in the foreign investment literature in two different (often confusing) ways: first, as I have used it here, as merging outgoing U.S. investment abroad with incoming foreign investment in the United States. This *net* approach is not satisfactory in measuring the amount of foreign investment in America, since it does not segregate it from U.S. investment abroad; thus in Table 5.3, for example, my figures are "gross" ones. Net figures in this sense can be used, however, to help us understand—as in my text—some patterns in capital flows and are useful in defining, vis-à-vis levels of investment, America's "net" debtor status. Second, when dealing separately with either U.S. or foreign investment, the scholar must make sure that in each case the results are net of opposing flows (repatriations) and net of repudiations (defaults and so on). This second use of *net* is essential, and all my figures are net in this usage. Unless otherwise explained, I will employ the word *net* only in the first manner.

29. Lewis, *America's Stake*, 156, 560. Actually, this is not a great difference considering the crudity of the numbers—but I would accept the "trend" for 1869–1914. Lewis used national wealth figures given by the U.S. Census Bureau for 1870, 1880, 1890, 1900, 1904, and 1912 and plotted these along with "foreign obligations" (securities, direct investments, and unfunded commercial and bank debt) figures for 1869, 1899, 1908, and 1914. Her percentages were derived from her chart (p. 154). I have not cited earlier her similar 1790–1869 figures because of lack of confidence in them. These 5 percent–4 percent figures, however, should be compared with my 1776 calculations given at the conclusion of Chapter 1. Since her figures did include commercial and bank debt, the appropriate comparison would be with my less than 4 percent rather than with my 1 percent figure. All of these estimates are, of course, very crude.

30. Myers, *The New York Money Market*, 188. In 1863, however, with the Civil War, foreign investment had dropped very sharply.

31. In 1955 Simon Kuznets published figures based on, as he himself noted, "scanty" data on the foreign investors' role in domestic capital formation. He concluded that capital imports did not account for sizable proportions of U.S. domestic capital formation. (Simon Kuznets, "International Differences in Capital Formation and Financing," National Bureau of Economic Research, *Capital Formation and Economic Growth* [Princeton, N.J.: Princeton University Press, 1955], 19–20, 34–38). In 1961 he republished very similar figures (see Table 5.A), which show a steady fall in the contribution of foreign capital. He also provided new figures for overlapping decades (see Table 5.B), which showed a somewhat different pattern (*Capital in the American Economy*, 131).

Whereas earlier writers believed America was a net importer of capital in the years 1896–1914 (see Bullock, Williams, and Tucker, "The Balance of Trade," 231, and *Survey of Current Business*, July 1954, 14), Kuznets accepted revisions in the balance-of-payment data made by Goldsmith, *A Study of Savings* (1955), who found the United States to be a *net* capital exporter, 1897–1914; Goldsmith—as read by Kuznets—thought U.S. capital outflow to be greater than others had estimated, while the foreign capital inflow

Table 5.A. Net changes in claims against foreign countries as a percentage of U.S. domestic capital formation and national product in current prices, 1869–1908

| | Net changes in claims as a percentage of | | | |
Decade	Domestic net capital formation	Domestic gross capital formation	Net national product	Gross national product
1. 1869–1878	−10.7	−6.5	−1.4	−1.3
2. 1879–1888	−3.1	−1.8	−0.4	−0.4
3. 1889–1898	1.1	0.6	0.2	0.1
4. 1899–1908	8.0	4.3	1.1	1.0
Average of decades	−1.2	−0.8	−0.1	−0.2

Source: Simon Kuznets, *Capital in the American Economy* (Princeton, N.J.: Princeton University Press, 1961), p. 133. Minus sign indicates net capital imports. I have added the averages..

Table 5.B. Net changes in claims against foreign countries as a percentage of U.S. domestic capital formation and national product in current prices, 1874–1913

| | Net changes in claims as a percentage of | | | |
Decade	Domestic net capital formation	Domestic gross capital formation	Net national product	Gross national product
1. 1874–1883	−0.2	−0.1	[a]	[a]
2. 1884–1893	−5.2	−2.8	−0.7	−0.6
3. 1894–1903	8.8	4.9	1.3	1.2
4. 1904–1913	2.3	1.2	0.3	0.3
Average of decades	1.4	0.8	0.8	0.5

Source: Simon Kuznets, *Capital in the American Economy* (Princeton, N.J.: Princeton University Press, 1961), p. 133. Minus sign indicates net capital imports. I have added the averages.
[a] Less than .05 percent

was less (Kuznets, *Capital in the American Economy,* 125). As I have indicated earlier (this chapter, note 23), Goldsmith subsequently used different figures on foreign investment, accepting a larger foreign investment in the United States. Kuznets' material is important in its attempt to determine the contribution of foreign capital, but I find his results unconvincing for several reasons: (1) My research indicates that his underlying figures understated the foreign capital *inflow*. I have gone back and wherever possible checked all his figures. (2) His figures are net, but we need to look at the foreign capital inflows and outflows separately in studying the rise in foreign investment. (3) I find the 10.7 percent contribution to domestic net capital formation in the 1870s (1869–1878) confusing: this was a time of massive defaults in railroad, state government, and mining securities. How are such defaults treated? As inflows—contributions to capital formation because the monies flowed in (and because Kuznets' figures are net, presumably they were not matched by capital exports)? Perhaps. More likely, this decade's figures would be inflated by monies that went into U.S. federal government securities—transactions that left a measurable trail. (4) The broad brush treatment fails to disaggregate. It seems clear, for example, that foreign investment contributed virtually nothing to *residential* construction—an important component of domestic capital formation. (5) The figures do not help in understanding the catalytic role of foreign capital in domestic capital formation, which will become apparent in the chapters that follow. (6) My research convinces me that there was a substantial rise in capital inflow, 1909–1913. See Figure 5.1, which is not fully reflected in Kuznets' 1904–1913 figures.

Using the Simon-Goldsmith net foreign capital import series and unpublished Kuznets series on net capital formation, in 1964 Jeffrey G. Williamson presented a different rendition. For his presentation, he selected peak years of capital imports (see Table 5.C). Williamson concluded, "the inflow of foreign capital is not, it seems, an insignificant proportion of net capital formation" (*American Growth,* 142). His figures suggest that the impact lessened over time.

Kuznets' figures in his fourth column, Tables 5.A and 5.B, should be compared with those most recently put forth in Michael Edelstein's excellent work. See Table 5.D. For net foreign investment flows, Edelstein used data of Matthew Simon, based on balance-

Table 5.C. Relative importance of net capital imports in net U.S. capital formation, peak years 1869–1912 (average per year)

Period	Percentage
1869–1876	15.5
1882–1893	10.3
1906–1912	2.5

Source: Jeffrey G. Williamson, *American Growth and the Balance of Payments* (Chapel Hill: University of North Carolina Press, 1964), p. 142.

Table 5.D. Net foreign investment flows to gross national product, the U.S. case, 1869–1908, 1874–1913 (average per year)

Decade		Percentage
1.	1869–1878	−1.1
2.	1879–1888	−0.8
3.	1889–1898	−0.5
4.	1899–1908	0.5
1.	1874–1883	0.1
2.	1884–1893	−1.5
3.	1894–1903	0.8
4.	1904–1913	a

Source: Michael Edelstein, *Overseas Investment in the Age of High Imperialism: The United Kingdom, 1850–1914* (New York: Columbia University Press, 1982), p. 234. These figures are in 1860 prices. Minus sign indicates net capital inflow.
 a Not estimated.

of-payments material. He cites Simon's 1960 work, which carries the series only to 1900, so it is not clear what his source was for 1899–1908 (Simon, "The United States Balance of Payments, 1861–1900," 699–705). As noted earlier, I feel very strongly that if we are to study the impact of foreign investment in the United States, it is not the *net*

U.S. and foreign investment figures that are important, but the *foreign* capital inflow and outflow figures and, *much more important*, the level of investment figures, the long–term claims on U.S. assets at any particular time. While Edelstein's first set of dates suggests the steady decline in the importance of foreign investment, his use of overlapping decades (as was the case with Kuznets' 1961 work) does *not* confirm such a linear pattern.

32. Douglass C. North, Terry L. Anderson, and Peter J. Hill, *Growth and Welfare in the American Past*, 3rd ed. (Englewood Cliffs, N.J.: Prentice-Hall, 1983), 34. In 1962, when Douglass North had been researching foreign investment questions, he was much more accurate, noting then how much more needed to be known on international capital movements during the century preceding World War I, and even more important, in 1962 he would correctly write that in the years 1875–1914, the United States was "absorbing record amounts of foreign capital." See his "International Capital Movements in Historical Perspective," 10–43, esp. 10, 15. D. C. M. Platt, *Foreign Finance in Continental Europe and the United States, 1815–1870* (London: George Allen & Unwin, 1984), 141, joins the group, quoting S. B. Saul for support: "Foreign capital, for the United States, was the gilt on the gingerbread. It was at its most influential, relatively speaking, in the second and third quarters of the nineteenth century. But by the end of the century it was 'negligible compared with the level of internal savings.' " Platt does concede, however, that the influence of foreign finance was in certain circumstances "disproportionate" relative to its volume and that it did release domestic capital for productive employment.

33. This conclusion is based on my own survey of recent American economic history textbooks, but see also Edelstein, *Overseas Investment*, 235, for an excellent summary of how economists in the last half of the 1970s, when dealing with U.S. developments in the late nineteenth century, ignored foreign borrowings (Lance Davis and Robert E. Gallman), relegated them to a "residual" role (Jeffrey G. Williamson—a shift from his earlier views), or in the same vein considered them as alleviating periodic pressures on the U.S. balance of payments (Paul D. David). I thus face a galaxy of economic stars—several of whom have actually studied foreign investment—when I seek to show the importance of this investment. It is essential to note that some economists, who, during the 1950s and 1960s, studied the history of foreign investment in the United States, had by the 1970s and 1980s turned their attention to other topics. Likewise, the textbook writers' neglect was not always the case. In the very influential textbook by Lance E. Davis, Jonathan R. T. Hughes, and Duncan M. McDougall, *American Economic History* (Homewood, Ill.: Richard D. Irwin, 1961), chap. 14 was devoted to "The Role of Foreign Savings in National Development," and although the emphasis was on the pre-1875 years, there was a full recognition of the U.S. net long-term indebtedness in 1914 and an awareness that "during the period 1820 to 1914 we had successfully mobilized vast sums from abroad to supplement our own savings in the financing of our economic development" (p.252).

34. Part of the problem has been that a number of influential works have stopped at 1861, 1875, or 1880 for example, Ralph Hidy, *The House of Baring* (Cambridge, Mass.: Harvard University Press, 1949), and Leland H. Jenks, *The Migration of British Capital to 1875* (New York: Barnes & Noble, 1973). John Madden influenced Jeffrey Williamson and Platt—and his research stopped abruptly in 1880. I think a more crucial impediment to recognizing the importance of foreign investment in the United States for the entire period 1875–1914 has been the writing of the history of this era as a time when the United States became a world power. This theme often blinded its authors to America's debtor nation status in 1914, which somehow seemed anachronistic.

35. Williamson, *American Growth*, 142. As I wrote this, Martin Feldstein (in the *New*

York Times, Nov. 18, 1984) was noting the present-day unprecedented capital inflow from abroad—at an annual rate of $100 billion! He writes, "That is enough capital inflow to finance about two-thirds of the structural budget deficit or about 40 per cent of all current net investment."

36. The figures in Edelstein, *Overseas Investment*, 234, correctly suggest the contrary. Edelstein estimates that net foreign investment flows into the United States as a percentage of GNP was 0.6 in 1834–1843, whereas it was 1.5 in 1864–1873, 1.1 in 1869–1878, and 1.5 in 1884–1893. As noted, Kuznets, *Capital in the American Economy*, 133, 134, believed that in 1869–1878, the contribution of foreign capital was "at its highest," reaching in 10.7 percent of net capital formation in the United States, whereas Williamson, *American Growth*, 142, found the foreign contribution to net capital formation, on average, 1869–1876 (*sic*), to be 15.5 percent. Irving B. Kravis concluded that although foreign capital inflows "financed significant fractions of U.S. net capital formation during certain periods of U.S. economic history," overall their contribution was "relatively modest"; but he saw a greater contribution in the later than in the earlier years—"probably around 4 percent in the forty years preceding the Civil War and a little over 6 percent in the period 1869–1914" ("The Role of Exports in Nineteenth Century United States Growth," *Economic Development and Cultural Change*, 20 [April 1972]: 403). Foreign investment's contribution to net capital formation may well have "dwindled" in the years 1890–1914.

37. My own research confirms the general high quality of Cleona Lewis' estimates on foreign investment. Every student of foreign investment in the United States should use her pioneering work.

38. The "gold standard" had an important impact on American development, as every basic American history text shows.

39. The research of Leland Jenks and Dorothy Adler has already confirmed this point, and I will do so in more detail. See Leland H. Jenks, "Britain and American Railway Development," *Journal of Economic History*, 11 (Fall 1951): 375–388, and Dorothy Adler, *British Investment in American Railways, 1834–1898* (Charlottesville: University Press of Virginia, 1970).

40. *Banker's Magazine*, New York, 45 (Aug. 1890): 88.

41. I am in fact able to document the existence of foreign investment (or a foreign investor registered to do business) in every state and territory of the United States in these years. Anne T. Ostrye, *Foreign Investment in the American and Canadian West, 1870–1914: An Annotated Bibliography* (Metuchen, N.J.: Scarecrow Press, 1986) is useful for "the land west of the eastern borders of the Dakotas, Nebraska, Kansas, Oklahoma, and Texas to the Pacific Coast."

42. Cleona Lewis, *America's Stake* (1938), was an early student of American economic growth who did not shortchange foreign direct investment in the United States. Subsequent recent accounts of aspects of foreign direct investment in the United States, 1875–1914, have relied heavily on her materials. See David Stanley McClain, "Foreign Investment in United States Manufacturing and the Theory of Direct Investment," Ph.D. diss., Massachusetts Institute of Technology, 1974, chap. 1. McClain, "Foreign Direct Investment in the United States: Old Currents, 'New Waves,' and the Theory of Direct Investment," in *The Multinational Corporation in the 1980s*, ed. Charles Kindleberger and David B. Audretsch (Cambridge, Mass.: MIT Press, 1983), 279, writes, "It is by now a cliché to observe that, though foreign direct investment in the United States accelerated dramatically in the 1970s, foreign involvement in the business affairs of this country has been a central ingredient of economic growth since the founding of the Republic." He cites his dissertation's chapter 1. Students of foreign direct investment—of multinational enterprise—have seen foreign investment in America as important.

On European direct investment in the United States, 1875–1914, see Lawrence G. Franko, *The European Multinationals* (Stamford, Conn.: Greylock, 1976), and Francesca Sanna Randaccio, "European Direct Investments in U.S. Manufacturing," B. Litt. thesis, Wolfson College, Oxford University, 1980. Peter J. Buckley and Brian R. Roberts, *European Direct Investment in the USA before World War I* (London: Macmillan, 1982), has so many errors in it as to render it almost unusable. I will refer later to other studies that cover only a single nation's investors. Note that none of these recent authors on European direct investment in the United States was a specialist on *American* economic history. Their expertise was on multinational enterprise. One reason that the multinational enterprise type of investment was (in the past) so often shortchanged by economists was that much of it did not go through securities markets and thus did not leave traces there. It had to be monitored by different investigative methods.

43. John W. Kendrick's National Bureau of Economic Research estimate of the U.S. gross national product in 1914 is in U.S. Department of Commerce, *Long Term Economic Growth, 1860–1965* (Washington, D.C., 1966), 167.

44. There is an abundant literature on Britain as a capital exporter, 1875–1914. Very influential were George Paish's four contemporary studies: "Our New Investments in 1908," *Statist*, 43 (Jan. 2, 1909): 19–21; "Great Britain's Capital Investments in Other Lands" and "Comments," *Journal of the Royal Statistical Society*, 72, pt. 3 (Sept. 1909): 465–495; "Great Britain's Capital Investments in Individual Colonial and Foreign Countries" and "Comments," *Journal of the Royal Statistical Society*, 74, pt. 2 (Jan. 1911): 167–200; and "The Export of Capital and the Cost of Living," *Statist Supplement*, 79 (Feb. 14, 1914): i–viii. These are all conveniently reprinted in Mira Wilkins, ed., *British Overseas Investments, 1907–1948* (New York: Arno Press, 1977). Edgar Crammond's three articles in *Quarterly Review*, 207 (July 1907): 245–272; 215 (April 1911): 43–67; and 224 (June 1915): 193–222, have attracted far less attention than the Paish contributions. C. K. Hobson, *The Export of Capital* (1914; rpt. New York: Garland, 1983), remains useful, as does his "British Oversea Investments, Their Growth and Importance," *Annals of the American Academy of Political and Social Science*, 68 (Nov. 1916): 23–35. Herbert Feis, *Europe: The World's Banker* (New Haven: Yale University Press, 1930), is valuable. Other helpful studies published in the 1930s include Staley, *War and the Private Investor* (1935); Carl Iversen, *Aspects of the Theory of International Capital Movements* (Copenhagen: Levin & Munksgaard, 1936); and Royal Institute of International Affairs, *The Problem of Foreign Investment* (London: Royal Institute of International Affairs, 1937). The United Nations, *International Capital Movements during the Inter War Period* (Lake Success, N.Y.: United Nations, 1949), has some pre–World War I data.

J. H. Lenfant, "British Capital Export, 1900–1913," Ph.D. diss., University of London, 1949, has been influential. In the 1950s the classic Alec K. Cairncross, *Home and Foreign Investment, 1870–1913* (Cambridge: Cambridge University Press, 1953), and Brinley Thomas, *Migration and Economic Growth* (Cambridge: Cambridge University Press, 1954), broke new ground. A. H. Imlah, "British Balance of Payments and Export of Capital, 1816–1913," *Economic History Review*, 2nd ser., 5 (1952): 208–239, and his *Economic Elements in the Pax Britannica* (Cambridge, Mass.: Harvard University Press, 1958), likewise offered valuable statistics on British capital exports, based on balance-of-payments reconstructions.

Charles H. Feinstein, "Home and Foreign Investment: Some Aspects of Capital Formation, Finance and Income in the United Kingdom, 1870–1915," Ph.D. diss., Cambridge University, 1959, used Imlah's 1952 estimates on capital exports and sought to provide more information on the destinations of the British capital exports. Feinstein—using Imlah's 1958 figures—published data on British overseas assets (net of liabilities) in his *National Income, Expenditure and Output of the United Kingdom* (Cambridge: Cambridge University Press, 1972), 205, T110. R. C. O. Matthews, C. H. Feinstein, and J. C. Odling-Smee, *British Economic Growth, 1856–1973* (Stanford, Calif.: Stanford University Press, 1982), has valuable data on British foreign investment.

Meanwhile, S. B. Saul, *Studies in British Overseas Trade, 1870–1914* (Liverpool: Liverpool University Press, 1960), covered foreign investment as well as trade. John H. Adler, ed., *Capital Movements and Economic Development* (London: Macmillan, 1967), has useful articles by Brinley Thomas and Matthew Simon. In 1968 A. R. Hall, ed., *The Export of Capital from Britain, 1870–1914* (London: Methuen, 1968), presented a collection of papers, including Matthew Simon's "The Pattern of New British Portfolio Foreign Investment, 1865–1914," that had first appeared in *Capital Movements and Economic Development*, ed. Adler. Simon collated the results of 41,000 separate transactions and came up with annual series for British new *portfolio* investments (creations and calls). His figures omitted foreign direct investments, international transactions in outstanding securities, British purchases of securities on markets outside England, and private placements of foreign issues in Great Britain. His methodology may well have resulted in his exclusion of much of the Scottish overseas investment. Also based on the same data (but "calls" only) is Matthew Simon, "The Enterprise and Industrial Composition of New Portfolio Foreign Investment, 1865–1914," *Journal of Development Studies*, 3 (April 1967): 230–292. Arthur I. Bloomfield, *Patterns of Fluctuation in International Investment before 1914* (Princeton, N.J.: Princeton University Press, 1968), attempted to put the British overseas investment in a broad context. P. L. Cottrell, *British Overseas Investment in the Nineteenth Century* (London: Macmillan, 1975), is helpful.

A recent and extremely valuable contribution to the literature is Edelstein, *Overseas Investment in the Age of High Imperialism: The United Kingdom, 1850–1914* (1982). In addition, Irving Stone, of Baruch College, City University of New York, is in the process of "reconstructing, correcting and reformulating the presentation of the [British] capital export data" for 1875–1914, based on data that he, Matthew Simon, and Leland Jenks assembled (Stone to Mira Wilkins, June 20, 1983). I have not seen his series. See also Lance E. Davis and Robert A. Huttenback, "The Export of British Finance, 1865–1914," in *Money, Finance and Empire, 1790–1960*, ed. A. N. Porter and R. F. Holland (London: Frank Cass, 1985), 28–76, and Davis and Huttenback, *Mammon and the Pursuit of Empire: The Political Economy of British Imperialism, 1860–1912* (Cambridge: Cambridge University Press, 1986). Because their interest is in the British Empire, their data on the United States are minimal. D. C. M. Platt, in *Britain's Investment Overseas on the Eve of the First World War* (New York: St. Martin's Press, 1986), argued that the commonly accepted 1913–1914 figure on British capital abroad—that of Paish—is too high, the portfolio component by some 30 percent (p. 5).

45. Edelstein, *Overseas Investment*, 25.

46. As noted, I used both Hobson's and Imlah's (1958) figures. See Edelstein, *Overseas Investment*, 17, for a similarly shaped chart, reflecting Simon's and the Imlah-Feinstein estimates. Simon, "The Pattern," in *The Export*, ed. Hall, 38–39, compared the figures of Imlah, Hobson, and Simon by year.

47. Iverson, *Aspects*, 331. As indications of their importance, Edelstein suggests that a rough calculation of the nominal value of outstanding home and overseas long-term negotiable securities indicates that in 1870 overseas totals were about 33 percent of such U.K. assets; in 1914 their share was 45 percent. Overseas accumulations were about 14 percent of U.K. reproductive capital stock in 1870 and up to about 31 percent in 1914 (Edelstein, *Overseas Investment*, 113). According to Goldsmith, *Comparative National Balance Sheets*, 112, foreign investment on the eve of World War I amounted to more than one-third of Britain's domestic financial assets and "an extraordinary full one-half" of Britain's domestic tangible assets.

48. D. C. M. Platt, "British Portfolio Investment Overseas before 1870: Some Doubts," *Economic History Review*, 2nd ser., 33 (Feb. 1980): 1–16; Platt, *Foreign Finance in Continental Europe and the United States, 1815–1875* (London: George Allen & Unwin, 1984), 181; and Platt, *Britain's Investment Overseas*. Based on an evaluation of Paish's methodology, Dickens, "The Transition Period," 121, thought that Paish's figures for British investment in the United States (and implicitly the rest of the world) were "exorbitant," "excessively high." By contrast, Simon Kuznets' 1955 figures on U.K. foreign investment as a percentage of its domestic net capital formation reveal a huge impact: 1870–1879, 54.2; 1880–1889, 78.8; 1890–1899, 46.2; 1900–1909, 51.1; 1904–1913, 95.8 (Kuznets, "International Differences," 70, using Imlah's 1952 figures; Platt believes that Imlah's figures and those of Paish were not independent of one another.)

49. Robert Gilpin, *U.S. Power and the Multinational Corporation* (New York: Basic Books, 1975), 11. Gilpin's comments reflected the accepted view. Thus Brinley Thomas, "International Capital Movements to 1913," in *Capital Movements*, ed. Adler, 15, wrote of British investment, "It had been largely portfolio rather than direct investment, and mainly in securities yielding a fixed return."

50. Gilpin wrote before the "international debt crisis" of the early 1980s. Clearly the international capital movements of the 1980s involved banks on a major scale.

51. There is now (in the mid-1980s) a general awareness of this. All of Matthew Simon's statistical work, for example, was on "portfolio" investments. John Clapham, in *An Economic History of Modern Britain* (Cambridge: Cambridge University Press, 1968), vol. 3, did not err and did not omit British direct investments overseas. There were earlier studies of British direct investments in the United States (see this chapter, note 61). In 1974 and 1977 I wrote on the need for research on the history of British and continental European multinational enterprise. See Mira Wilkins, "Multinational Enterprises," in *The Rise of Managerial Capitalism*, ed. Herman Daems and Herman van der Wee (Louvain: Leuven University Press, 1974), 213–235, and Wilkins, "Modern European Economic History and the Multinationals," *Journal of European Economic History*, 6 (Winter 1977): 575–595. After Raymond Vernon's project on American multinationals had been virtually completed, he turned to study foreign multinationals. His student John Stopford, in "The Origins of British-based Multinational Manufacturing Enterprises," *Business History Review*, 48 (Autumn 1974): 303–335, looked at the history of British direct investments overseas. See also Alfred D. Chandler, Jr., "The Growth of the Transnational Industrial Firm in the United States and in the United Kingdom: A Comparative Analysis," *Economic History Review*, 2nd ser., 33 (Aug. 1980): 396–410. Geoffrey Jones has written a number of scholarly papers on the history of British business abroad. See, for example, his "The Expansion of British Multinational Manufacturing, 1890–1939," in *Overseas Business Activity*, ed. Akio Okochi and Tadakatsu Inoue (Tokyo: University of Tokyo Press, 1984), 125–153, and his edited *British Multinationals: Origins, Management and Performance* (Aldershot: Gower, 1986). See also Stephen Nicholas, "British Multinational Investment before 1939," *Journal of European Economic History*, 11 (Winter 1982): 605–630. Irving Stone, "British Direct and Portfolio Investment in Latin America," *Journal of Economic History*, 37 (Sept. 1977): 690–722, pointed out that British direct investment in Latin America had been shortchanged. P. Svedberg, "The Portfolio-Direct Composition of Private Foreign Investment in 1914 Revisited," *Economic Journal*, 87 (Dec. 1978): 763–777, likewise, paid new attention to British direct investments abroad. See also John Dunning, "Changes in the Level and Structure of International Production: The Last One Hundred Years," in *The Growth of International Business*, ed. Mark Casson (London: George Allen & Unwin, 1983), 84–139. There have, moreover, been a number of book-length case studies of individual British multinational enterprises.

52. Such British companies were ubiquitous in British business abroad. They are described in Mira Wilkins, "The Free-Standing Company," *Economic History Review,* 2nd ser., 41 (May 1988): 259–282.

53. This was especially true of the most innovative industrial and service enterprises. In "The History of European Multinational Enterprise: A New Look," *Journal of European Economic History,* 15 (Winter 1986): 483–510, I argue that whereas "service sector" multinationals were a late phenomenon in the American case, they were an early one for the British. Often British investors would use "managing agents," which were international businesses in the "service sector."

54. The British Inland Revenue Department divided identifiable income from abroad into three groups: Group I included foreign government securities, dividends, and interest on dominion and foreign stocks, shares (including railway companies), payable in Great Britain, and other "foreign and dominion coupons and dividend warrants payable in Great Britain." Group II included "profits from certain concerns trading abroad and having assets abroad," "businesses controlled in this country": "(a) railways, tramways, etc. operating abroad; cables, telegraphs, and telephones situated abroad; (b) mines, oil wells, and nitrate fields situated abroad; (c) tea, coffee, rubber, sugar, etc, plantations abroad; (d) gas, water, harbor, mortgage, financial, manufacturing, and trading undertakings operating abroad." Many of these appear to be what I have called free-standing companies—and most were direct investments. Group III—for which I do not have income figures—included traditionally defined multinational enterprises: "shipping, banking, and insurance companies having branches abroad and manufacturing and trading concerns with works or branches abroad." The income from group I in 1913–1914 was £86.8 million, and from group II totaled £178.2 million. Were we to add the unknown income from group III, income from foreign direct investment would far exceed that from portfolio stakes. See the figures in Gustav Cassel, *Foreign Investments* (Chicago: University of Chicago Press, 1928), 140, 141, 126.

55. This point is made by Simon, "The Enterprise and Industrial Composition," 282, and by Karl Erich Born, *International Banking in the 19th and 20th Centuries* (New York: St. Martin's Press, 1983), 118.

56. Royal Institute of International Affairs, *The Problem,* 117; Bloomfield, *Patterns,* 3; and M. Edelstein, "Foreign Investment and Empire, 1860–1914," in *The Economic History of Britain since 1700,* ed. Roderick Floud and Donald McCloskey, 2 vols. (Cambridge: Cambridge University Press, 1981), II, 74.

57. The predominant role of the United States seems undisputed. Simon, "The Pattern," in *The Export of Capital,* ed. Hall, 27, writes that "aggregate new British long-term portfolio investment in the United States [1865–1914] . . . constituted almost 21 per cent of the total." See Cairncross, *Home and Foreign Investment,* 185, for clear evidence of the preeminent position of the United States in British investment worldwide, 1871–1914. In an appendix, Jeffrey G. Williamson charted British net capital exports and U.S. net capital imports. It is remarkable how synchronized the swings were in the years 1875–1914 (*American Growth,* 237). See also Dunning, *Studies,* 151 (chap. 4 is on British investment in the United States, 1860–1913).

Both Dunning and A. G. Kenwood and A. L. Lougheed, *The Growth of the International Economy* (London: Allen & Unwin, 1983), 43, calculated British investment in the United States as a percentage of total British overseas investment as 27 percent for 1870. Dunning's percentage was derived by comparing Cairncross' figures with Imlah's. If the reader compares Tables 5.5 and 5.8 in my text, it would seem that British investment in the United States in 1899 was running around 30 percent of British foreign investment; Dunning's figure for 1899 was 20 percent. My own calculations for 1913–1914 show British investment in the United States as slightly more than 20 percent of the total British investment worldwide. For 1913 I compared Paish with Paish (see his Feb. 24, 1914, estimates on British investment in the United States and worldwide, *British Overseas Investment*, ed. Wilkins); I then rechecked these figures against those developed by Cleona Lewis. Dunning compared Paish with Imlah and came up with an 18 percent figure. Feis, *Europe: The World's Banker*, 23, accepts the one-fifth figure for 1913–1914, as does Edelstein, *Overseas Investment*, 77. Qualitative evidence suggests a percentage decline from 1899 to 1913 in American stakes as the British spread their international investments farther afield.

58. The 1876 figure of £234 million as the estimated nominal value of British hold-ings of U.S. securities is given in Madden, *British Investment*, 78 (table 14). For the 1914 figure see my Table 5.8. Although most scholars agree on the preeminent position of the United States in the level of (stock of) British overseas investment in the years 1875–1914, the actual charting of the level of that investment is depressingly imperfect. As noted earlier, the level varied from hour to hour—because it was easy to trade American securities. Matthew Simon's *Cyclical Fluctuations and the International Capital Movements* demonstrates how difficult the tracking is. The breakdown by nationality is more problematic than the aggregate. The more precision, the more vulnerable the figures become. D. C. M. Platt's criticisms of the measurement of the overall amount of British foreign investment makes us ponder whether the multitude of figures on British stakes in the United States are truly meaningful. The totals for July 1, 1914, given in Table 5.8 for British investments in the United States are those of Harvey Fisk, Cleona Lewis, and myself. They are to be compared with George Paish's figure for December 1913 on British "capital publicly invested in the United States": $3.7 billion (in *Statist*, 79 [Feb. 14, 1914]: vi). None of the three estimates in Table 5.8 was totally independent of Paish's; all three authors knew Paish's figure, and then developed their own.

59. On Dundee, W. Turrentine Jackson, *The Enterprising Scot* (Edinburgh: Univer-sity of Edinburgh Press, 1968), 66 and passim, is invaluable. See also "Scottish Capital Abroad," *Blackwood's Edinburgh Magazine*, 136 (Oct. 1884): 468–480; Bruce Lenman and Kathleen Donaldson, "Partners' Incomes, Investment and Diversification in the Scott-ish Linen Area, 1850–1921," *Business History*, 13 (Jan. 1971): 10; and Michie, *Money, Mania, and Markets*, 177, 228, 268. Michie describes the Dundee Stock Exchange as mainly a market in "stocks and shares" of companies formed to invest in the United States. Peter L. Payne, *The Early Scottish Limited Companies, 1856–1895* (Edinburgh: Scottish Academic Press, 1980), 51, notes that each Scottish city—Dundee, Edinburgh, Aberdeen, Glasgow—had its special American connections. W. A. Thomas, *The Pro-vincial Stock Exchanges* (London: Frank Cass, 1973), chap. 14, deals with Scottish stock exchanges and provides substantial material on the American securities traded on these exchanges, much of it based on Jackson, *Enterprising Scot*. Thomas does not emphasize American securities on English provincial exchanges, except to note the substantial market for American rails in Liverpool (*Provincial Stock Exchanges*, 190). See, however, *Stock Exchange Official Intelligence, 1914*, which indicates that a number of companies doing business in America were traded on provincial exchanges. Particu-larly good on the Liverpool–London–United States interconnections in trade and fi-nance is Stanley Chapman, *The Rise of Merchant Banking* (London: Allen & Unwin, 1984), passim. I have found a number of British investments in the United States from Manchester, Hull, Bradford, Sheffield, Birmingham, and so forth.

60. The London financial world followed developments in the United States closely.

61. As noted earlier, Cleona Lewis, *America's Stake* (1938), did not err and omit direct investment. Her important contribution was often forgotten in the plethora of post–World War II literature. In 1953 Roger V. Clements, "British Controlled Enter-

prise in the West between 1870 and 1900 and Some Agrarian Reactions," *Agricultural History*, 27 (Oct. 1953): 132, pointed out that economic historians had paid attention to the ebb and flow of securities across the Atlantic and to "the anonymous British capital put into American railroads," but had neglected the British monies that went into enterprise "that demanded and received conscious supervision on the part of the investors." In the same article Clements noted that throughout the American West, "in a wide variety of enterprises . . . English control was foremost, whether through directors, special emissaries, technical experts, or resident local managers" (p. 134). Clark Spence, *British Investments and the American Mining Frontier, 1860–1901* (Ithaca, N.Y.: Cornell University Press, 1958) studied direct investments in mining. In 1959–60 John Dunning (now of the University of Reading) received a Rockefeller Foundation grant to do research on British manufacturing in the United States; he interviewed managers at some sixty companies, collected large amounts of historical information, and then never published a book utilizing the data he had obtained. His assistant, T. C. Coram, in "The Role of British Capital in the Development of the United States, ca. 1600–1914," master's thesis, University of Southampton, 1967, used some of Dunning's material. Dunning generously permitted me to read his original interviews; I profited immensely from scrutinizing his systematically collected raw materials on the direct investments. Jackson, *The Enterprising Scot* (1968), and Kerr, *Scottish Capital on the American Credit Frontier* (1976), both deal with important aspects of British direct investment in the United States. The new general works on British multinationals always include materials on their U.S. stakes. Thus the gap is being filled.

62. The individual British "investors" made domestic "portfolio" investments, while the *companies* they invested in made the *direct* investments in the United States.

63. What I call free-standing companies have sometimes been called syndicate investments, for example, in Coram, "The Role of British Capital." Free-standing British companies involved in acquiring American brewery firms were labeled in the popular press "Syndicate Breweries." See Table 9.4. The designation *free-standing* is my own, and my text explains my meaning. See also Wilkins, "The Free-Standing Company."

64. This point on liquidity was suggested to me by Robert Aliber (Feb. 1984).

65. These companies create headaches for tabulators of foreign portfolio and direct investment, since (1) they went through capital markets and thus are typically included with portfolio investment estimates, and (2) when the British corporate structure dissolved, generally the individual investor in the British company would then become a *foreign* portfolio investor, since he now owned stock in, say, a New Jersey company rather than in a London one.

66. On the general relationship between service sector firms and free-standing ones, see Wilkins, "The Free-Standing Company."

67. Although it has been argued that the British role is exaggerated, because other nationalities bought securities in London, I know of no one who argues against the preeminence of British capital over that of other nationalities in America in these years.

68. Cleona Lewis' figures are to be preferred over Paish's. Simon's figures measure something different from those of Lewis, Paish, or Madden.

69. These multimillion-dollar investments were noted in Worthy P. Sterns, "The International Indebtedness of the United States in 1789," *Journal of Political Economy*, 5 (Dec. 1897): 28. See also Bacon, "American International Indebtedness," 269 (on Astor). It is not clear whether Bacon considered Astor as "British." Estimates by Simon, Paish, and Lewis appear not to have included these large "British" investments in the United States. Gustavus Myers, *History of the Great American Fortunes* (New York: Modern Library, 1936), who is not always accurate, writes that as of December 31, 1915, William

Waldorf Astor's real estate holdings in New York came to $60 million (p. 169); he also writes that Consuelo Vanderbilt was not alone in marrying a titled Englishman—that more than 500 American women (daughters of the newly rich of this era) married titled foreigners. A 1909 estimate cited by Myers indicated that more than $220 million followed these women to Europe (p. 378n)—much of this, I should note, would be a "unilateral transfer" rather than a continuing claim on U.S. assets (that is, a long-term foreign investment). Indeed, if Myers is correct (p. 378), Sterns is wrong on the Vanderbilt story; by his marriage agreement, the Duke of Marlborough seems to have had a claim only on the income of the railway shares rather than the shares themselves. It matters not; my point here is simply that the migration of Americans abroad could and did create in some instances (and certainly in the case of William Waldorf Astor) "British" investment in the United States that has usually been neglected. Such investments were clearly not typical, yet today's statistics would include them. For years, for example, the huge U.S. investments of J. Paul Getty (an American who was a British resident) were counted by the U.S. Department of Commerce as "British" direct investments in the United States!

70. Throughout the years 1875–1914, the United States ranked in first place as Britain's most important trading partner. For a clear demonstration of this fact, see total values of imports and exports in the trade of Great Britain by trading partners, in P. N. Davies, "British Shipping and World Trade," in *Business History of Shipping*, ed. Tsunehiko Yui and Keiichiro Nakagawa (Tokyo: University of Tokyo Press, 1985), 56–57.

71. Cairncross, *Home and Foreign Investment* (1953); Thomas, *Migration and Economic Growth* (1954); Brinley Thomas, ed., *Economics of International Migration* (London: Macmillan, 1958); Thomas, *International Migration and Economic Development* (1961), 11.

72. Thomas emphasized push for the British to the exclusion of pull of the United States; pull is, however, needed to explain why the British invested heavily in the United States and not in West Africa or China, for example.

73. On French foreign investment, there is a large literature. Everyone relied heavily on Alfred Neymarck, who attempted to provide statistical data on the large French capital exports. Appendix A of Harold Moulton and Cleona Lewis, *The French Debt Problem* (New York: Macmillan, 1925), 321–340, gives a good summary of the literature and makes estimates. See also Harry D. White, *The French International Accounts, 1880–1913* (Cambridge, Mass.: Harvard University Press, 1933); Feis, *Europe: The World's Banker*, chap. 2; Staley, *War and the Private Investor*, 526–527; Rondo Cameron, *France and the Economic Development of Europe, 1800–1914* (Princeton, N.J.: Princeton University Press, 1961); Rondo Cameron, "Economic Relations of France with Central and Eastern Europe, 1800–1914," *Journal of European Economic History*, 10 (Winter 1981): 537–552; Maurice Lévy-Leboyer, *La position internationale de la France* (Paris: Éditions de l'École des Hautes Études en Sciences Sociales, 1977); Émile Becque, *L'internationalisation des capitaux* (Montpellier: Imprimerie Générale due Midi, 1912); and Yves Guyot, "The Amount, Direction and Nature of French Investments," *Annals of the American Academy of Political and Social Sciences*, 68 (Nov. 1916): 36–54.

74. Iverson, *Aspects*, 331–332. George W. Edwards, *The Evolution of Finance Capitalism* (London: Longmans, Green, 1938), 55, indicates that in 1906, 51 percent of the securities listed on the Paris Bourse were foreign ones.

75. A study of French investment in the United States (1875–1914) would make an excellent Ph.D. dissertation. No one really knows the size. See notes to Table 5.8. Lévy-Leboyer's figures on the rise of French investments in the United States are 1880, $77 million; 1896, $96 million; 1902, $116 million; and 1913, $386 million (*La position*, 25). I translated the figures given in francs at 1 fr. = $.193.

76. There is considerable variation in the estimates of French investment in the

United States, July 1, 1914. The *Federal Reserve Bulletin*, 7 (Oct. 1922): 1181, gave a figure of about $500 million, but added to its estimates the caveat: "however credible they may be." As indicated in the notes to Table 5.8, Harvey Fisk's gross approximation of $1 billion for 1914 is far too large. Lewis, *America's Stake*, 546, selects a $410 million figure for French investment in the United States in 1914. I chose a higher figure, since I uncovered some French investments that Lewis did not know of and also added French investment through Swiss intermediaries and some made through purchases in Brussels and other markets. See Table 5.8 for other estimates. There were not that many American bonds listed on the Brussels Bourse. "Foreign Stocks on the Brussels Bourse, 1912," *Bulletin de l'Institut International de Statistique*, 20, pt. 2, 1364–65, gives the U.S. railroad bonds. Far more French investment in the United States went through Switzerland and England than through Belgium.

77. I was very surprised at the number of French direct investments that I identified. None went through money markets. Much of the large literature on French foreign investments has ignored these stakes. All the ones in the United States that I found had to be ferreted out individually by using French company and industry data, U.S. and French town histories, and information and hints from French and American scholars, whose help I acknowledge in the appropriate places. Most of these investments appear to have had little to do with French banks.

78. Robert W. Tolf, *The Russian Rockefellers: The Saga of the Nobel Family* (Stanford, Calif.: Hoover Institution Press, 1976), chap. 12.

79. Charles F. Speare, "Selling American Bonds in Europe," *Annals of the American Academy of Political and Social Sciences*, 30 (1907): 278, 293. New York State amended its banking law in 1911 to require supervision of New York financial institutions that branched abroad. That year Equitable Trust Company of New York received approval from the New York Superintendent of Banks to maintain a branch office in Paris as did the Farmers' Loan and Trust Company of New York to maintain such offices in Paris and London. The offices were subject to the examination of the New York Superintendent of Banks, who reported that these branches, under his supervision, were expected to be valuable in increasing foreign investment in the United States and, specifically, in opening the French market to American securities (New York Superintendent of Banks, *Annual Report for 1911*, 18–19). On the influx of American securities (mainly railroads but others as well) onto the French market in 1910–1912, see, for example, the articles of "Lysis," June 2, 9, 1910; June 22, 29, and July 7, 1911; and March 14, and Dec. 5, 1912, reprinted in Lysis (pseud. for Eugene Letailleur), *Politique et finance d'avant-guerre* (Paris: Payot & Cie., 1920), 117–121, 303–313, 428–431, 572.

80. Some Americans—such as James Stillman—who lived in Paris had large U.S. investments. See *New York Times*, July 4, 1914, p. 1. The occasion for the *New York Times* story was a new French tax imposed on income from foreign investments. Stillman, chairman of the board of National City Bank, lived in Paris after 1909.

81. Feis, *Europe: The World's Banker*, 51; Lévy-Leboyer's figures in *La position*, 25, actually show a rise in French investment in Russia in absolute and percentage terms (1896, 24.3 percent; 1913, 26.3 percent); see Georges Manchez, *Sociétés de dépôts, banques d'affaires* (Paris: Librairie Delgrave, 1918), 58, on the relatively *low* level of French investment in the United States. Guyot, "The Amount," 43, and others note that while French statesmen "groaned over the exportation of capitals to foreign lands, for political reasons they encouraged investment of capital in Russia."

82. Charles P. Kindleberger, *Manias, Panics, and Crashes* (New York: Basic Books, 1978), Feis, *Europe: The World's Banker*, 51, 23; and Lévy-Leboyer, *La position*, 25.

83. Feis, *Europe: The World's Banker*, 55.

84. White, *French International Accounts*, 90.

85. Charles Kindleberger made this point in correspondence with me. See David S. Landes, *Bankers and Pashas* (1958; rpt. New York: Harper Torchbook, 1969), 17–24, for other ties between French and Swiss banking; see also Bacon, "American International Indebtness," 273.

86. Jacob Viner, "Political Aspects of International Finance," *Journal of Business*, 1 (April 1928): 160, writes, "French financial houses have considerable influence over the Brussels Bourse, and French investors have grown accustomed to buying securities listed on the Brussels Bourse because of the practice of some French banking houses of making their flotations in part or in whole in Brussels in order to evade French security taxes." This *may* account for some of the (1897–1913) "Belgian" investment in the United States that Paul Dickens—and no one else—uncovered (Dickens, "The Transition Period," 129). However, as I indicated in this chapter, note 76, I do not believe much French investment in the United States went through Brussels.

87. The "Register of Companies" records in London include stockholder records of British firms. Thus, for example, the Nouveau Monde Gold Mining, Ltd., London, set up in May 1887 to purchase mines in Colorado, had numerous French investors (Memorandum of Association, Nouveau Monde Gold Mining Company, Ltd., Western Range Cattle Industry Study, reel 51, Library of Congress, Acc. 11,092). Other companies had Frenchmen as shareholders with much smaller stakes. Indeed, often French investors owned minority interests in British companies, which conducted business in America. The French went through London for investments in mining not only in America but also in Spain (so this practice was not distinctive to the United States—or to English-language-country investments).

88. Michael Arboux, *Les valeurs mobilières étrangères sur le marché français* (Paris: Recueil Sirey, 1913), 229, notes that French engineers representing French capital in the United States had been pushed aside by the Yankees. The French took the risks but had no voice in how the capital was used.

89. In Table 5.5, for consistency I used the United Nations estimates. As indicated in the notes to that table, in the case of Germany I think the U.N. choice of $5.8 billion is low. I returned to the original estimates, which are (with one exception) given in marks, and used a rate of exchange of $.238 = 1 mark. The $5.8 billion figure, as far as I can tell, seems to have been *net* of foreign investment in Germany; the high $8.6 billion figure probably involved some double counting and also neglected the fact that securities were sold or redeemed as well as purchased.

Germans conducted a number of studies of their nation's foreign investments in the pre–World War I years. See, for example, J. Riesser, *The German Great Banks* (1911; rpt. New York: Arno Press, 1977), 546, 803, and Karl Helfferich, *Germany's Economic Progress and National Wealth, 1888–1913* (New York: Germanistic Society of America, 1914), 112–113. Helfferich, whose figures are frequently quoted, was a professor of political economy and a director of the Deutsche Bank; in 1920 he married the daughter of the Deutsche Bank former chief executive, Georg von Siemens. See Fritz Seidenzahl, *100 Jahre Deutsche Bank, 1870–1970* (Frankfurt: Deutsche Bank, 1970), 8 and passim, and Paul H. Emden, *Money Powers of Europe* (London: Sampson Low, Marston, 1937), 219. Helfferich's estimate for 1913 was 20 billion marks, or $4.8 billion; he seems to have omitted some very significant German foreign investments.

After the war, John Maynard Keynes, *Economic Consequences of the Peace* (New York: Harcourt, Brace & Howe, 1920), 175, summarized the pre–World War I German studies and chose the figure for 1913–14 of $6.25 billion for *net* foreign investments (net of property in Germany owned by foreigners). He thought this figure was high and that $5 billion as a net figure would probably be a better choice. Keynes believed Helfferich's figures were net of property in Germany owned by foreigners (ibid., 175). Actually

Helfferich himself described them as net of "securities redeemed or bought back by foreign countries," which is not the same (*Germany's Economic Progress*, 112–113). See this chapter, note 28, above.

In 1922 a study was made by Friedrich Lenz, "Wesen und Struktur des deutschen Kapitalexports vor 1914," *Weltwirtschaftliches Archiv*, 18 (1922): 42–54, with his figures given on p. 48. He estimated that German investment abroad in 1914 (gross, not net of foreign investment in Germany) was 31 billion marks (or roughly $7.3 billion).

Harold G. Moulton and Constantine E. McGuire, *Germany's Capacity to Pay: A Study of the Reparation Problem* (New York: McGraw-Hill, 1923), 260, provided a more complete summary than Keynes had of the various statistics put forth on German foreign investments (their summary, prepared by Cleona Lewis, did not, however, include the Lenz estimate). It contained one made by August Müller (after the war) for 1913, which was $8.33 billion. This was a summary of the total ownership by Germans of foreign securities and enterprises, with no allowance for the foreign investments in Germany or for duplication (ibid., 280). A census of the foreign securities owned by German nationals had been taken in Germany under a decree of August 23, 1916. It showed foreign ownership to be 16,248 million marks; Germans also reported to their government the export of foreign securities worth 2 billion gold marks from the middle of 1914 to August 1916. In short, the German government was able to obtain information on 18,248 million marks in securities (or at the prewar exchange rate of 4.2 marks, $4.3 billion). Moulton and McGuire concluded that because the returns would have understated the total, after deductions were made for German securities owned by foreigners, an estimate of 20 billion marks (or roughly $4.8 billion) would be a legitimate *net* figure (ibid., 279–280). This is the very low end of Keynes's net estimate (Keynes made the conversion at the rate 1 mark = $.20).

Other summaries were subsequently prepared by Walter Herman Carl Laves, *German Governmental Influence on Foreign Investments, 1871–1914* (1927; rpt. New York: Arno Press, 1977), 208–209; Feis, *Europe: The World's Banker* (1930), 71; and Staley, *War and the Private Investor* (1935), 528–529. Each author incorporated slightly different data, but the basic formats were identical. Staley provided the highest estimate for 1913–14 or $8.56 billion, made in 1915, by P. Arndt. Laves (p.208) included the Lenz estimate but added in short-term trade financing (3 billion marks) without indicating this, thus inflating the $7.3 billion figure to $8.09 billion. For 1914 Feis put the gross figure at between $5.2 billion and $6.6 billion, with $6.6 billion "as the highest total within the range of possibilities." He settled on 23.5 billion marks, or $5.6 billion (*Europe: The World's Banker*, 71, 74).

A sizable amount of German pre–World War I investment was direct investment (carrying ownership and control). Some of the low estimates of German foreign investment clearly neglected the foreign direct investments; Lenz, for example, did not, and that is why I feel more confident about his figures. Recently, new attention has been paid to German direct investment abroad. See, for example, Franko, *European Multinationals*, and Peter Hertner, "Fallstudien zu deutschen multinationalen Unternehmen vor dem Ersten Weltkrieg," in *Law and the Formation of the Big Enterprises in the 19th and Early 20th Centuries*, ed. Norbert Horn and Jürgen Kocka (Göttingen: Vandenhoueck & Ruprecht, 1979), 338–419. See also his "German Multinational Enterprise before 1914," unpublished paper, 1983. In the latter, Hertner accepts a rough figure of 30 billion marks for German investment abroad in 1914 (or $7.14 billion). Born, *International Banking*, 133, however, with his emphasis on banking and portfolio interests, goes back to Feis's $5.6 billion figure. All the authors mentioned above (except Keynes, whose figures—at least in the American edition of *The Economic Consequences*—were given in dollars) provide their values in marks. I have made the conversions. For consistency I have sought a gross figure—not net of foreign investment in Germany.

90. These figures are from Iverson, *Aspects*, 332. The percentages are, of course, dependent on how one calculates the size of both the foreign investment and national wealth. Earlier, Helfferich, *Germany's Economic Progress*, 113, put the figure for 1913 at roughly 6 percent, and Feis, in *Europe: The World's Banker*, 72, put it at 7 percent.

91. This is my own conclusion based on a careful reading of all available evidence. The figures in Feis, *Europe: The World's Banker*, 74, show this conclusively. Thomas R. Kabisch, *Deutsches Kapital in den USA* (Stuttgart: Klett-Cotta, 1982), 26–27, concurs. On the other hand, Fisk, *Inter-Ally Debts*, 316–317, gives a tabulation of Karl Helfferich that puts Russia in first place. I have looked at the substantial materials on German investment in Russia and on German investment in the United States. P.V. Ol', *Foreign Capital in Russia* (1922), translation and introduction by Geoffrey Jones and Grigori Gerenstain (New York: Garland, 1983), has particularly useful data on German investment in Russia. My research convinces me that German investment in the United States far exceeded that in Russia in 1913–14. Indeed, Fisk himself, in one place (p. 312), gives German stakes in the United States at $1.25 billion, that is, a level far greater than the German investments in Russia (p.317). Possibly Germany's 1914 investments in Austria-Hungary could have been larger than in the United States. I doubt it.

92. Lewis, *America's Stake*, 546, gives $950 million, whereas Fisk, *Inter-Ally Debts*, 312, gives $1,250 million. In Table 5.8 I chose a midway point between the two estimates: $1,100 million. In May 1914 Richard Hauser of the Deutsche Bank believed that Germans held $1 billion worth of U.S. securities (this figure presumably excluded many direct investments). See *Commercial and Financial Chronicle*, 98 (May 30, 1914): 1649. By contrast, Feis, *Europe: The World's Banker*, 74, estimated German investments in the United States and Canada in 1914 to be 3.7 billion marks, or $881 million (at the rate of 4.2 marks to the dollar); very little of this amount would have been in Canada. Feis's figure seems to me too low. After 1897 Germans had a special tax on income on foreign securities (Riesser, *The German Great Banks*, 532–533). Many Germans purchased U.S. securities in London, New York, Amsterdam, Basle, or (much less often) Paris. While French ties in Switzerland were overwhelmingly with Geneva, Frankfurt and Basle had very close associations. One sees this clearly in Hans Bauer, *Swiss Bank Corporation, 1872–1972* (Basle: Swiss Bank Corp., 1972), passim. In analyzing Cleona Lewis' methodology on German investments, I find it very vulnerable. Her "other securities" category includes German holdings in U.S. loans to Cuba, Japan, Argentina, and China, which should not be considered as German investments in the United States. It also included securities issued after 1914. Strangely, enemy aliens held $641,800 worth of the First Liberty Loan of 1917. On this, compare Alien Property Custodian, *Report, 1918–1919*, 431–433, and Lewis, *America's Stake*, 536–537, 123–124. Nonetheless, when I compare Lewis' figures with the total of Hauser, cited above, her figures are low, not high. In short, despite the vulnerability of her methodology, a rough $950 million estimate (I prefer $1,100 million) does not seem far out of line.

93. Eleven hundred million dollars divided by $7,300 million equals 15.1 percent; $950 million divided by $6,000 million equals 15.8 percent; $1,250 million divided by $7,300 million equals 17.1 percent.

94. The user of Alien Property Custodian data must remember that the materials are as of 1917, not 1914, and must be adjusted to reflect 1914 investments. There was a substantial change in German investment in the United States in 1914–1917 (in net, probably an increase in direct investments and a decrease in portfolio ones). The changes and the reasons for them will be discussed in Volume 2 of my history of foreign investment in the United States. The unpublished data are in Record Group 131, National Archives, Suitland, Maryland (this record group is cited henceforth as in

Washington, D.C., since the administrative office is there; the actual records are in Suitland). The Alien Property Custodian, *Report, 1918–1919*, carefully used, is invaluable. In addition, I have uncovered substantial material on German investments in the United States in Record Group 59 (State Department Records), National Archives, Washington, D.C. For published material on German investment in the United States, I found particularly useful Dietrich G. Buss, *Henry Villard* (1976 diss.; New York: Arno Press, 1978); Franko, *The European Multinationals;* and Kabisch, *Deutsches Kapital in den USA.* Kabisch relied heavily on the published Alien Property Custodian data, but he also used German business archives. His very capable 1982 work came to my desk after I had almost completed the German investment sections of this book. Kabisch's appendix, pp. 331–352, has a useful alphabetical list of German enterprises in the United States in 1917, as identified by the Alien Property Custodian.

95. Alien Property Custodian, *Report, 1918–1919*, 13–14.

96. Speare, "Selling American Bonds in Europe," 277.

97. Henri Hauser, *Germany's Commercial Grip on the World* (New York: Charles Scribner's Sons, 1918), passim. See also Peter Hertner, "German Multinational Enterprise before 1914: Some Case Studies," in Hertner and Geoffrey Jones, *Multinationals: Theory and History* (Aldershot: Gower, 1986).

98. Based on the U.S. Bureau of the Census, *Historical Statistics of the United States* (1960), 57.

99. Jürgen Kocka, "The Rise of the Modern Industrial Enterprise in Germany," in *Managerial Hierarchies*, ed. Alfred D. Chandler, Jr., and Herman Daems (Cambridge, Mass.: Harvard University Press, 1980), 99, contrasts pre–World War I large German and British enterprises, finding the former clustered in capital-intensive, technologically advanced industries and the latter in textiles and food, "while [British] firms in the so-called new industries—chemicals, electrical and other machinery, and transportation equipment—were not yet so well represented." These comments are suggestive when looking at international investments by nationality. British direct foreign investments were in different sectors from those of the Germans, whether we talk about textiles, food, transportation equipment, or other industries. In 1898 Charles A. Conant, "The Economic Basis of Imperialism," *North American Review*, 167 (Sept. 1898): 336, wrote that German capital was finding its way all over the world from Buenos Aires to Calcutta. "German capital," he continued, "is also largely invested in breweries, paper mills, soap factories, textile mills and machine shops in the United States." As far I can tell, the main German investments in the first two industries mentioned were those of immigrants rather than those of foreign direct investors. I do not know about soap. The textile mills and machine shops were indeed foreign direct investments.

100. Alien Property Custodian, *Report, 1918–1919*, 185.

101. Ibid.

102. Ibid., 188.

103. On Henckels, see Heinrich Kelleter, *Geschichte der Familie J. A. Henckels* (Solingen, 1924), 186, 191, 192; on Jaeger's underwear, see Frank Presbrey, *The History and Development of Advertising* (1929; rpt. New York: Greenwood Press, 1968), 361, and Chapter 10 in my book.

104. Staley, *War and the Private Investor*, 532, put Dutch investment abroad at $2 billion in 1913–14. The *Economist*, 76 (March 15, 1913): 638, made an estimate of investments in foreign securities of about $1.2 billion. For comparisons see Table 5.5. I know of no book in English on Dutch investment abroad, 1875–1914. Standard works such as Feis, *Europe: The World's Banker*, do not even have a chapter on Dutch investments.

105. This figure is from Iverson, *Aspects*, 332.

106. See Table 5.8. There is no book in English on Dutch investments in the United States covering these years, but in Dutch, K. D. Bosch, *Nederlandse Beleggingen in de Verenigde Staten* (Amsterdam: Uitgeversmaatschappij Elsevier, 1948) is invaluable. I have also found helpful Bert C. Forbes, "Investments by Hollanders in America," *Van Norden Magazine,* Oct. 1909, 59–65 (microfiche in New York Public Library); *Economist,* 76 (March 15, 1913): 638; Lewis, *America's Stake;* and, in addition, data on the particular industries in which the Dutch invested.

107. Forbes, "Investments," 60.

108. Bosch, *Nederlandse Beleggingen,* 345–348. In March 1914 Dutch ownership of U.S. Steel (common and preferred stock at par value) alone totaled $38.5 million (Lewis, *America's Stake,* 126). See *Moody's, 1914* for some of the American industrial securities listed in Amsterdam.

109. *Economist,* 76 (March 15, 1913): 638. The *Economist* guessed Dutch holdings in U.S. securities in 1913 were 1 billion florins, or about $400 million.

110. Eugene Staley, *War and the Private Investor,* put total Dutch investment abroad in 1914 at $2 billion. See Table 5.5. My estimate of Dutch investment in the United States of $650 million in 1914 comes to roughly one-third of Staley's worldwide total. The numbers differ from those in the *Economist,* but the ratios coincide.

111. In 1913 the British proportion was about 20 percent; the German, about 16 percent; and the French, about 5 percent.

112. The importance of Amsterdam for American securities was generally acknowledged. See, for instance, Powell, *The Mechanism of the City* (1910), 98.

113. In 1899 Nathanial Bacon thought "Swiss" investments in the United States larger than French interests! Yet he qualified his statement, adding that a number of customers of Geneva's bankers, whose investments he recorded as "Swiss," would actually be French ("American International Indebtedness," 272–273). About 1912 L. Dubois, managing director of the Swiss Bank Corporation (SBC), Basle, told his board that "a substantial portion of the securities issued in Switzerland are bought by our foreign customers." SBC was at this time very much involved in issues of American railroads (Bauer, *Swiss Bank Corporation, 1872–1972,* 190, 188). See ibid., 201, for figures on Swiss investment abroad in 1913. The American house of Hallgarten & Co. specialized in selling American securities in Switzerland, Sweden, Germany, Austria, France, England, and Denmark. See "History of Hallgarten & Co.," draft typescript, 1950, 6 (copy from Moseley, Hallgarten, Estabrook & Weeden Holding Corporation).

114. The first person to attempt to document the history of European direct investment was Franko, *The European Multinationals.* I found this book very useful in my preliminary research. On Swiss business abroad, see Ernst Himmel, *Industrielle Kapitalanlagen der Schweiz im Auslande* (Langensalz: Druck von Herman Beyer & Söhne, 1922). On Swedish foreign direct investment, Ragnhild Lundström, "Swedish Multinational Growth before 1930," in *Multinationals,* ed. Hertner and Jones, is invaluable.

115. Jacob Viner, *Canada's Balance of International Indebtedness, 1900–1913* (Cambridge, Mass.: Harvard University Press, 1924).

116. Herbert Marshall, Frank Southard, and Kenneth Taylor, *Canadian-American Industry* (New Haven: Yale University Press, 1936). Also useful on Canadian business in the United States is R. T. Naylor, *History of Business in Canada, 1867–1914* (Toronto: James Lorimer, 1975).

117. Britishers who made their money in Canada, Australia, or India would often return to the United Kingdom to live out their remaining years. As I review the period 1875–1914, I can think of only one wealthy American who, after migrating and making his fortune, returned to the United Kingdom. Some, such as Carnegie, bought second homes in the old world. The pattern, however, in the case of the

United States in these years, was that once a man decided to immigrate, the immigrant became an American. (William Waldorf Astor, who retired in England, was of course, American-born; George Smith retired to England in 1861, before the 1875–1914 period—see Chapter 6.)

118. Lewis, *America's Stake*, 546. Lewis (p. 552) notes that in 1914 Canadian banks held $46 million of foreign railroad securities, most of which were presumed to be American. Yet this statement is hard to reconcile with her data (p. 546) as given in Table 5.16. If Canadian banks held, say, $40 million in U.S. railway securities, that leaves a mere $8 million for other Canadian investors—a far too small a figure—compared with her estimate of $95 million in "other" U.S. securities. It is not clear, moreover, how she handled the securities held by Canadian insurance companies that did business in the United States.

119. Christopher Armstrong and H. V. Nelles, "A Curious Capital Flow: Canadian Investment in Mexico," *Business History Review*, 68 (Summer 1984): 190.

120. The stakes in public utilities seem to constitute an exception to this generalization.

121. Bacon, "American International Indebtedness," 274.

122. New York State Superintendent of Banking, *Annual Report, 1913*, 15. Vincent P. Carosso, *The Morgans* (Cambridge, Mass.: Harvard University Press, 1987), 851 n. 163, found sizable European investments in the Bank. See also Chapter 13.

123. Lewis, *America's Stake*, 546. The sum Lewis included was $3.2 million for the Mexican government railroad.

124. H. G. Moulton, *Japan, an Economic and Financial Appraisal* (Washington, D.C.: Brookings Institution, 1931), 391, gives the unpublished Bank of Japan estimates. These data were prepared for Moulton by the Bank (information from Professor Hiroaki Yamazaki, Tokyo, July 1984). The figures were broken down as follows: the 461 million yen included 54.7 million yen in loans to China, 6.45 million yen in "foreign securities," and 400 million yen in business enterprise abroad. Of the investment in business enterprises, 310 million yen was assigned to China (including Manchuria), 50 million yen to the United States (including Hawaii), and 40 million yen to the rest of the world. Moulton's own estimate for Japanese foreign investment in 1913 (p. 392) was 600 million yen. He accepted the figure of 50 million yen in the United States and Hawaii. John Dunning, "Changes in the Level and Structure of International Production" in *The Growth of International Business*, ed. Mark Casson (London: George Allen & Unwin, 1983), 87, estimated that Japanese foreign direct investments worldwide in 1914 totaled $20 million. This was a pure guess. If the Bank of Japan figures are to be trusted, then Dunning's number is roughly 10 percent of what it should be!

125. Mira Wilkins, "Japanese Multinational Enterprise before 1914," *Business History Review*, 60 (Summer 1986): 218–223. I established that the bulk of the pre-1914 investments were in the continental United States, not in Hawaii.

126. *Moody's Manual, 1914*.

127. Ibid.

128. Ibid. (Intercontinental Rubber, an American company, owned one-half of its preferred shares.) Could this have been part of the "Belgian" investment in the United States that Dickens identified? See Table 5.8, note e. As indicated in that table (note p), I found Dickens' figure too high.

129. In addition, American international businesses such as Eastman Kodak and United Fruit raised funds abroad. Eastman Kodak paid regular dividends in London; United Fruit paid interest on its 1911 bond issue in London (*Moody's Manual, 1914*). The "foreign" investments in these U.S.-headquartered multinational enterprises were portfolio ones. Stone, "British Direct and Portfolio Investment in Latin America before

1914," 722, makes the point that the British frequently invested in Latin America through American-controlled companies.

130. Thomas, *Migration and Economic Growth* (1973), 158, 174, 233, and his *International Migration and Economic Development*, 10–11.

131. The pattern did not occur, for example, in relation to Italian immigration; Italy was a *capital-importing* country. There probably was an "income-level" or "class" issue involved as well. Many of the Germans and Scots came from "middle-class" families. The income level of Italian immigrants tended to be lower.

132. Douglass C. North, "Transaction Costs in History," *Journal of European Economic History*, 14 (Winter 1985): 560.

133. Charles P. Kindleberger, *American Business Abroad* (New Haven: Yale University Press, 1969), and Mira Wilkins *The Maturing of Multinational Enterprise: American Business Abroad from 1914 to 1970* (Cambridge, Mass.: Harvard University Press, 1974), Raymond Vernon, John Dunning, and Mark Casson, students of multinational enterprise, have in a number of different works emphasized the importance of advantage, particularly technological advantage. See, for example, W. D. Gruber, D. Mehta, and R. Vernon, "The R & D Factor in International Trade and International Investment of U.S. Industries," *Journal of Political Economy*, 75 (Feb. 1967): 20–37; John H. Dunning, *International Production and the Multinational Enterprise* (London: George Allen & Unwin, 1981); and P. J. Buckley and M. Casson, *The Future of the Multinational Enterprise* (London: Macmillan, 1976). Likewise, see Richard E. Caves, *Multinational Enterprise and Economic Analysis* (Cambridge: Cambridge University Press, 1982).

134. Based on Commissioner of Patents, *Annual Report* for the years 1885–1914. The reports use the word *citizens* but *foreign* seems to have been, in fact, determined by residence.

135. There was no separate category for Scotland.

136. Jonathan Liebenau, "The Use of American Patents by German and American Industries, 1890–1935," unpublished paper, 1978.

137. K. Pavitt and L. Soete, "International Differences in Economic Growth and the International Location of Innovation," unpublished paper, University of Sussex Research Unit, 1981.

138. Tedious scrutiny of the patents in the U.S. Patent Office could provide the desired information. See Alien Property Custodian, *Report, 1918–1919*, appendix, 437–465. An article on one industry that gives immensely valuable details is B. Herstein, "Patente und Chemische Industrie in den Vereinigten Staaten," in *Die Chemische Industrie in den Vereinigten Staaten und die Deutschen Handelsbeziehungen*, ed. Hermann Grossman (Leipzig: Verlag von Veit & Comp., 1912), 75–85.

139. In Charles T. Davis, *The Manufacture of Leather* (Philadelphia: H. C. Baird & Co., 1885), "every process or machine used in leather manufacture that has been patented in the United States since 1790 to the close of 1883 is mentioned," by date, inventor, and residence of inventor.

140. Jonathan Liebenau tells me that is possible to go through the patent applications to find out both inventor and assignee (by name and nationality). The names of the assignees are given in the Patent Office's *Gazette*. Marianne Burge, a partner in Price Waterhouse, pointed out to me (in 1981) that foreign investors preferred to keep patent ownership in the hands of the parent firm (if there was expropriation, the "property" was held by the parent abroad and not in the host country). I have found that this was also the case in 1914 (Alien Property Custodian, *Report, 1918–1919*, 105), but that the distinction did not trouble the Alien Property Custodian during World War I. Thus the foreign-owned Atlantic Communication Company had only a license to use Telefunken's wireless patents, but the Alien Property Custodian seized the patents anyway

(ibid., 105–106). In short, there was no concern by Americans over whether a patent was held by a German parent or its U.S. subsidiary; in both cases it was taken over as "enemy property" in the United States during the war years. In most instances, as noted, the German patents continued to be held by the parent enterprise in Germany.

141. For the role of brand names in providing "consistency of quality," see Dunning, "Changes in the Level," 97. A systematic study of the history of these property rights and foreign direct investment is sorely needed.

142. See the splendid summary of the literature in Caves, *Multinational Enterprise,* 204–207.

143. Often the licensor lacked "some assets needed for foreign [direct] investment" (ibid., 205).

144. There has been considerable discussion in books and articles on multinational enterprise of E. M. Graham's views on threat and counterthreat. See his "Oligopolistic Imitation and European Direct Investment in the United States," Ph.D. diss., Harvard Business School, 1975. His approach is not identical to what is presented in my text. While my findings do not fit neatly into his theoretical analysis, they do suggest the usefulness of looking at "threats" and responses—in particular circumstances in the years 1875–1914.

145. Jones, ed., *British Multinationals,* 10, found noteworthy the high number of pre-1914 joint-ventures by British multinationals worldwide. My research confirms the early preference for joint-venture arrangements by all foreign multinationals, not just British ones.

146. Lest these comments seem abstract, examples are in order. (More details will follow in my text.) The partnership of Balfour, Williamson & Co., Liverpool, had a San Francisco house, Balfour, Guthrie, with overlapping partners, but the control was clearly and consistently from Britain (with delegated management); investments were made in a number of corporations, incorporated in the United States and Britain. Merck in the United States came to be incorporated, but the parent was the family partnership in Germany. Alfred Booth & Co., Liverpool, and Booth & Co., New York, at origin, had identical partners; they invested in the United States in trade and manufacturing. Price, Waterhouse (a partnership in Britain) invested in a U.S. house, with overlapping partners (British partners held control).

147. There is a substantial literature on these relationships. See, for example, Robert Liefmann, *Cartels, Concerns and Trusts* (1932; rpt. New York: Arno Press, 1977). Liefmann, in 1897, identified some forty different international groupings in which Germans participated mainly with British, French, Belgians, or Austrians. See his *Die Unternehmerverbände, Konventionen, Kartelle* (1897). Henry W. Macrosty, *The Trust Movement in British Industry* (London: Longmans, Green, 1907), discusses international agreements. See also U.S. Federal Trade Commission, *Report on Cooperation in American Export Trade* (Washington, D.C., 1916); Alfred Plummer, *International Combines in Modern Industry* (1938; rpt. Freeport, N.Y.: Books for Libraries Press, 1971); and Ervin Hexner, *International Cartels* (Chapel Hill: University of North Carolina Press, 1946).

148. In the chapters that follow, I will provide details on these changing accords—by industry. Effects changed over time as well. Work is in process by Mark Casson, who is attempting to develop a theory of cartels. See his "Multinational Monopolies and International Cartels," in Peter J. Buckley and Mark Casson, *The Economic Theory of the Multinational Enterprise* (New York: St. Martin's Press, 1985), chap. 4.

149. The phrase is from H. van der Haas, *The Enterprise in Transition* (London: Tavistock Publications, 1967).

150. Some state as well as local government securities may be included when authors refer to "municipals."

151. U.S. Secretary of the Treasury, *Annual Report, 1874.*

152. U.S. Secretary of the Treasury, *Annual Report, 1875.*

153. Council of the Corporation of Foreign Bondholders, *Annual Report, 1874* (issued Feb. 1875), 25.

154. U.S. Secretary of the Treasury, *Annual Report, 1876,* x, and U.S. Department of Treasury, *Specie Resumption and Refunding of the National Debt,* 46th Cong., 2nd sess., 1880, H. Exec. Doc. 9, 2, contains copy of the contract.

155. See contract of June 9, 1877, in ibid., 61, and also U.S. Secretary of the Treasury, *Annual Report, 1877.*

156. U.S. Secretary of the Treasury, *Annual Report, 1878,* xviii.

157. U.S. Secretary of the Treasury, *Annual Report, 1879,* xv.

158. See U.S. Department of Treasury, *Specie Resumption,* passim; Alexander Dana Noyes, *Thirty Years of American Finance* (1900; rpt. New York: Greenwood Press, 1969), 28–47; and Fritz Redlich, *The Molding of American Banking* (1951; rpt. New York: Johnson Reprint Company, 1968), pt. 2, 367–369.

159. This is fully evident in the correspondence reprinted in U.S. Department of Treasury, *Specie Resumption.*

160. See ibid., 15, 12, for Conant's letter of appointment.

161. The securities moved from London to the Continent. Rondo Cameron estimated that near the peak, the French in 1877 may have owned as much as 2 billion francs' worth of U.S. government securities (that is, approximately $400 million dollars' worth). He notes that although the French purchases of U.S. government securities assumed "large proportions" in the 1870s, the securities were usually purchased in London and were of a quite different character than much of French foreign investment ("French Foreign Investment, 1850–1880," Ph.D. diss., University of Chicago, 1952, 74, 80). The $400 million figure should be viewed in the context of Table 5.8. If it is accurate, it suggests a sharp drop in French investment in the United States in the late nineteenth century. It also should be compared with Madden's numbers: Madden believed the *total* investment in U.S. federal government securities from the European continent was $121.5 million in 1876 (*British Investment,* 79). I would trust Cameron over Madden on these numbers, but the problems of estimation are very much in evidence.

162. For a long time I wondered why. Harry H. Pierce, "Anglo-American Investors and Investment in the New York Central Railroad," in *An Emerging Independent American Economy, 1815–1875,* ed. Joseph R. Frese and Jacob Judd (Tarrytown, N.Y.: Sleepy Hollow Press, 1980), 135–136, 156, helped to suggest the reason. After the death of Thomas Baring III (1799–1873), the senior partner in Baring Brothers, London, was the Harvard-educated Bostonian Russell Sturgis. See Ralph Hidy, *The House of Baring* (Cambridge, Mass.: Harvard University Press, 1949), 395. During the Civil War, his Boston background notwithstanding, Sturgis had been outspoken on behalf of the confederacy—so much so that when Senator John Sherman, the brother of General William T. Sherman, visited London in 1867, Baring's U.S. representative (Samuel Ward) urged that Sturgis be kept "out of sight during the Senator's visit" (Pierce, "Anglo-American," 135–136, 156). In 1877–1881 Russell Sturgis was the senior partner in Baring Brothers, and John Sherman was U.S. Secretary of the Treasury. These two individuals' positions seem to provide one explanation of the absence of Baring's involvement. The lack of a Baring role was all the more conspicuous since the Barings had been brought into the 1871–1873 refunding (before Sherman moved to Treasury and before Sturgis assumed the position of senior partner). See Chapter 4. Platt, who had access to House of Baring papers, pre-1875, concluded that the Barings were "anxious to do all they could for the North" during the Civil War (*Foreign Finance,* 149).

163. Sherman to Conant, Oct. 4, 1877, in U.S. Department of Treasury, *Specie Resumption*, 162.

164. Conant to Sherman, May 12, 1877, in ibid., 38.

165. U.S. Department of Treasury, *Specie Resumption*, 295–297, and John Sherman, *Recollections* (Chicago: Werner, 1895), II, 627, 638–642.

166. U.S. Secretary of the Treasury, *Annual Report, 1879*.

167. U.S. Census Office, *Report on Valuation, Taxation, and Public Indebtedness of the United States—Tenth Census* (Washington, D.C., 1884), 490, 518. In 1880 twenty New York banking firms received the coupons from foreign owners, collected the cash from the New York subtreasury, and remitted the interest abroad. Of the $221 million principal on which these twenty banking houses collected on behalf of the foreign owners, five New York houses handled about $187 million, or almost 85 percent of the total. See ibid., 518. The census report does not name the banking houses. I have, however, little doubt that in the top four were August Belmont & Co., Drexel, Morgan & Co., J. & W. Seligman & Co., and Morton, Bliss & Co. The Census Office did not monitor about $155 million principal on which there were coupons paid (but not paid by the twenty banking houses). Undoubtedly some of this $155 million was held by foreign investors.

168. U.S. Secretary of the Treasury, *Annual Report, 1881*.

169. August Belmont to Thomas F. Bayard, Jan. 28, 1881, cited in David Black, *King of Fifth Avenue* (New York: Dial Press, 1981), 587.

170. *Banker's Magazine*, New York, 38 (Jan. 1884): 577.

171. Paul Studenski and Herman E. Krooss, *Financial History of the United States*, 2nd ed. (New York: McGraw-Hill, 1963), 217, and Noyes, *Thirty Years*, 158. This was part of a general liquidation of American securities by British investors.

172. Studenski and Krooss, *Financial History*, 218, 226–228; Noyes, *Thirty Years*, 236ff; Lewis, *America's Stake*, 66; and Redlich, *The Molding of American Banking*, pt. 2, 370. I found a copy of the Agreement of Feb. 8, 1895, in the Confidential Letterbooks of August Belmont in the Belmont Family Papers, Special Collections, Columbia University Library. August Belmont had died in 1890; his son, also named August, was now the principal in August Belmont & Co. Sometimes the firm's correspondence carried the firm's signature, sometimes Belmont's.

173. August Belmont to Lord Rothschild, Feb. 27, 1895, in Belmont Family Papers.

174. Adler, *British Investment*, 163.

175. Studenski and Krooss, *Financial History*, 229.

176. The Rothschild Archives, London, contains some interesting correspondence on this. See especially Baron Alphonse de Rothschild, Paris, to his cousins, London, Jan. 29, 1895, RAL T16/90.

177. J. P. Morgan's father, J. S. Morgan, had died in April 1890. The firm, J. S. Morgan & Co., however, continued.

178. On December 23, 1895, Belmont cabled N. M. Rothschild & Sons, "Please telegraph confidentially whether you would be willing entertain negotiation." On December 24, 1895, the London firm replied, "We cannot under the circumstances present enter into any negotiation for bond issue which in our judgement would be a complete failure here or even take part in American syndicate." Belmont persisted, cabling London on December 26, 1895: "Conferred with J. P. Morgan . . . Would be a great calamity for all your interests . . . if you did not take leading part in proposed bond transaction. The risk much less than on last occasion and good to be accomplished even greater. Scope of the measure will doubtless be broader and more efficacious. Trust you will not underrate the importance of your intervention in these critical times . . . My personal interests and those of August Belmont & Co. entirely subordi-

nate." N. M. Rothschild & Sons was unmoved, replying on December 27, 1895, "We have not changed our feelings of friendship and goodwill for America and her people still we cannot and we will not take any part either leading or subordinate in an American Bond Syndicate until we are assured both by the American and the English Governments that the pending question [the Venezuelan boundary dispute] is satisfactorily arranged." Belmont did not give up, cabling London on December 30, 1895: "Strictly confidential . . . J. P. Morgan recently not communicative. We learn on satisfactory authority Deutsche Bank Berlin proposes with J. P. Morgan & Co. to take entire Government issue $100,000,000 and syndicate has practically been formed to take the loan when the Government is ready. Have you had any further communication with J. S. Morgan & Co.? Do we understand your position is unchanged? We have just seen the syndicate paper which is in the name of J. P. Morgan & Co. alone and leaves entire management in their hands." The London Rothschilds ended the matter with a final cable on December 31, 1895: "Our position is absolutely unchanged . . . do not think syndicate will place any appreciable amount of bonds in Europe" (RAL II/51/14B).

179. Studenski and Krooss, *Financial History*, 230.

180. Ibid., 231. On January 1, 1896, Geheimerath von Hansemann, Berlin, had written Lord Rothschild, "There is some restricted interest here mainly of the Deutsche Bank, as to a U.S. loan, astonishing indeed with the present tendencies in the U.S." (RAL T16/118). The reference is certainly to the silver agitation in the United States rather than to Cleveland's Venezuelan policy.

181. Studenski and Krooss, *Financial History*, 240 n.1.

182. Bacon, "American International Indebtedness," 269, 271.

183. Speare, "Selling American Bonds in Europe," 270.

184. Paish, "Great Britain's Capital Investment" (Sept. 1909), 479.

185. Paish, "Great Britain's Capital investment" (Jan. 1911), 176. In 1911 only one issue of U.S. government bonds was quoted on the official list of the London Stock Exchange. It was the issue originally handled by N. M. Rothschild & Sons and J. S. Morgan & Co. in 1895. See *Stock Exchange Year Book*, 182.

186. On these, see Studenski and Krooss, *Financial History*, 270, and Alien Property Custodian, *Report, 1918–1919*, 432. Other U.S. government holdings listed in this last tally were U.S. government bonds issued in 1917.

187. *Commercial and Financial Chronicle*, 19 (Nov. 14, 1874): 493.

188. See its *Annual Reports*, for example, *Annual Report, 1874* (Feb. 1875). See also April 1889 correspondence in FO 5/2066, Public Record Office, London.

189. When in the 1880 U.S. census there was a summary of state debts, those repudiated by the states were excluded; in justifying the exclusion, the census declared it should not pass judgment. See U.S. Census Office, *Report on Valuation*.

190. Massachusetts State 5 percents, £309,500, at 98. Based on a list of "Foreign, Colonial and Commercial Loans," in Baring Archives London, AC 29. This sum was small for the Barings in the 1870s.

191. R. H. Inglis Palgrave, "An English View of Investments in the United States," *Forum*, 15 (April 1893): 197.

192. Bacon, "American International Indebtedness," 265–266.

193. Reported in *Banker's Magazine*, New York, 33 (Sept. 1878): 190.

194. Bacon, "American International Indebtedness," 269, and Bosch, *Nederlandse Beleggingen*, 526. The Dutch had invested heavily in state bonds, at greatly discounted prices. They held on, hoping against hope for appreciation. Their losses were particularly large. For example, during Reconstruction, Florida had issued to two railroad companies $4 million in state bonds in exchange for the bonds of the roads. The Florida

state bonds were sold in Holland. The railroad defaulted on *their* bonds; the Florida Supreme Court declared the state's bonds illegal. In 1880 the U.S. Supreme Court held that the Florida bonds had been "steeped in fraud" and that the Dutch holders should have some redress. The latter obtained liens against the railroads. The railroads were then sold for $355,000—a far cry from the $4 million in state bonds issued. See B. U. Ratchford, *American State Debts* (Durham, N.C.: Duke University Press, 1941), 186–187, 173, 179. The Dutch had bought the $4 million in bonds at $2.8 million; even so, they proved no bargain.

195. Bacon, "American International Indebtedness," 271. Compare this to the immense 1850s interest in Germany in American cities' securities. See Chapter 4, note 24.

196. Bacon, "American International Indebtedness," 271–272.

197. *Economist*, 76 (March 15, 1913): 653. As early as 1877, Charles F. Conant was describing the London *Economist* as "unfriendly to all American securities" (Conant to Sherman, July 14, 1877, U.S. Department of Treasury, *Specie Resumption*, 105).

198. Dickens, "The Transition Period," 248–269; Bosch, *Nederlandse Beleggingen*, 521; and Alien Property Custodian, *Report 1918–1919*, 435. Carosso, *The Morgans*, 542–543, 828 n.55, indicates the difficulties of New York City in the Panic of 1907 and the Morgan role in selling its bonds abroad.

199. Paish, "Great Britain's Capital Investment" (Sept. 1909), 479. These figures do not coincide with those of Dickens, who estimated that in November 1908, $2.1 million of New York City notes were sold in London, and in June 1909, when New York City gold bonds were offered, an estimated $5.5 million worth were bought in London. Probably some of the London purchases were made by investors on the European continent.

200. Paish, "Great Britain's Capital Investment," 188.

201. Ibid., 189.

202. Ibid., 176.

203. Ibid. This is not inconsistent with the $32.6 million of New York City bonds that Dickens found were taken up in London in the years 1907–1910. The rest of the $61.6 million of the New York City offering was taken up in 1911–1914.

204. See Chapter 15.

205. *Best's Insurance Reports* in many instances gives the portfolios of U.S. "branches" of foreign insurance companies.

206. Measured by "level" of foreign investment. The only possible exception, if the figures are to be trusted, may have been from roughly 1857–1861 to 1864, when the level of foreign investment in railway securities could have reached first rank. See Table 4.1 and read notes carefully.

6. Railroads and Land

1. All sources agree on this. Jeffrey G. Williamson, *American Growth and the Balance of Payments* (Chapel Hill: University of North Carolina Press, 1964), 136, estimated that roughly 60 percent of the stock (the level) of private U.S. assets held abroad during the entire period 1870–1915 was in railroads. In fact, he found that so important was this sector that in his analysis he could "treat demand for net foreign long term investment as emanating almost entirely from conditions in the railroad sector." Alas, no book has been devoted exclusively to foreign investment in U.S. railroads. Dorothy R. Adler's superb *British Investment in American Railways, 1834–1898* (Charlottesville: University Press of Virginia, 1970) covers only British investments and stops in 1898. Two articles by Leland Jenks—both on British investments only—are useful: "Railroads as an

Economic Force in American Development," *Journal of Economic History*, 4 (May 1944): 1–20, and "Britain and American Railway Development," *Journal of Economic History*, 11 (Fall 1951): 375–388.

Harry H. Pierce's published work has emphasized pre-1875 investment, although he occasionally strays into the years 1875–1914. See his "Foreign Investment in American Enterprise" and "Discussion" in *Economic Change in the Civil War Era*, ed. David T. Gilchrist and W. David Lewis (Greenville, Del.: Eleutherian Mills–Hagley Foundation, 1965), 41–61, and his "Anglo-American Investors and Investment in the New York Central Railroad," in *An Emerging Independent American Economy, 1815–1875*, ed. Joseph R. Frese and Jacob Judd (Tarrytown, N.Y.: Sleepy Hollow Restorations, 1980), 127–160; see also his *Railroads of New York* (Cambridge, Mass.: Harvard University Press, 1953). On Dutch investments in U.S. railroads, K. D. Bosch, *Nederlandse Beleggingen in de Verenigde Staten* (Amsterdam: Uitgeversmaatschappij Elvesier, 1948), 136–178, 521–530, is useful. Likewise, Dietrich G. Buss, *Henry Villard* (New York: Arno Press, 1978), is good on German investments. Michael Edelstein, *Overseas Investment in the Age of High Imperialism: The United Kingdom, 1850–1914* (New York: Columbia University Press, 1982), emphasizes the importance of American railroads in British investments.

I have used railway histories, business biographies, merchant bank histories, and bank archives, plus much miscellaneous other data; my research points to the need for a major study of foreign investments in U.S. railroads, 1875–1914, that includes not merely British investment in American railroads but also German, Dutch, French, Swiss, and other interests as well. Such a study would require intensive use of railroad and bank archives. This chapter should set the stage for such a volume. As Muriel Hidy pointed out to me, although the literature on American railroads is enormous, historians have shortchanged the complications of railway finance. It is little wonder. Each railroad had different financial requirements in different periods. Each turned—at different times—to different financial intermediaries. A railroad might be associated with one banker in one period and with others at a later date. Alliances between and among bankers in financing any single railroad shifted over time.

2. U.S. Bureau of the Census, *Historical Statistics of the United States* (Washington, D.C., 1960), 427, 429. Figures are for Dec. 31, 1874, and June 30, 1914.

3. Yet far more research has been done on foreign investments in U.S. railroads of the pre–Civil War years and of the late 1860s and early 1870s than on those of 1875–1914. Adler, *British Investment*, 203–210, for example, lists railroad issues, 1865–1880. She stops in 1880. This was not because the issues stopped; they continued.

4. See, for example, *Economist, Statist, Financial Times, Financial News,* and London *Times* for British reporting. The newspaper files of the Council of the Corporation of Foreign Bondholders, now located in Guildhall, London, have twenty-six volumes devoted to American railways. Poor's *Manual of the Railroads of the United States* was considered "an indispensable volume in the office of the [British] broker, banker, and capitalist." See *Statist*, 20 (Oct. 15, 1887): 424, and Alfred D. Chandler, *Henry Varnum Poor* (Cambridge, Mass.: Harvard University Press, 1956), 246–270, on the manual. According to Julius Grodinsky, *Jay Gould* (Philadelphia: University of Pennsylvania Press, 1957), 12, Herapath's *Railway Journal*, published in England, gave good but always optimistic coverage of American railroads. Its articles sounded like "stock brokers letters." Dutch and German financial journals regularly reported on U.S. railroads. Bankers and brokers made information available to their clients. See, for example, David Kynaston, "The Late-Victorian and Edwardian London Stockbroker as Investment Adviser," unpublished paper, 1982.

5. Albro Martin, "The American Political Economy," Harvard Business School Reprint Series, 1980, 96. For a time American scholars expressed doubts on the vital

nature of railroads. See Robert Fogel, *Railroads and American Economic Growth* (Baltimore: Johns Hopkins University Press, 1964). Most, however, now accept their highly significant role. See, for example, Paul A. David, *Technical Choice, Innovation and Economic Growth* (Cambridge: Cambridge University Press, 1975), 291–314, and Alfred D. Chandler, *The Visible Hand* (Cambridge, Mass.: Harvard University Press, 1977).

6. Chandler, *Visible Hand*.

7. This point is made by Arthur M. Johnson and Barry E. Supple in *Boston Capitalists and Western Railroads* (Cambridge, Mass.: Harvard University Press, 1967), 345.

8. François Caron, *Economic History of Modern France* (New York: Columbia University Press, 1979), 61.

9. European (especially British and French) investors, experienced with domestic railroads, next went, in a logical progression, to international railroad investments. There is substantial evidence that many railroads in the United States were by 1875–1914 seen as "first-class" securities. American railroad bonds had varying maturities; many were 30-, 40-, or 50-year issues, but there were also railroad bonds with 90- and 100-year maturities! In those cases, the investor was often essentially buying an annuity. A table in the back of an investment guide to American railroads explained the annual interest realized—at various coupon rates—when the bond was bought at prices above and below par. See S. F. van Oss, *American Railroads as Investments* (London: Effingham Wilson, 1893), for bond maturities. The table is on pp. 814–815.

10. Nathaniel T. Bacon, "American International Indebtedness," *Yale Review*, 9 (Nov. 1900): 270. The comment was made about German investors but was true more generally.

11. All sources concur on the predominance of bonds in foreign investors' holdings, but not on the mix. A Dow-Jones estimate, for example, in 1914 of about $4 billion in U.S. railway securities held in Europe indicated that about 10 percent was in shares and 90 percent in bonds (*Bradstreet's*, Oct. 31, 1914, 690). A study by L. F. Loree found that as of Jan. 31, 1915, U.S. railway securities (par value) in "foreign hands" consisted of the following mix: 29 percent in shares, 69 percent in bonds, and 2 percent in short-term notes (*Commercial and Financial Chronicle*, 104 [March 31, 1917]: 1216). Cleona Lewis, *America's Stake in International Investments* (Washington, D.C.: Brookings Institution, 1938), 41, based on the 1919 *American Dollar Securities Report* (Cmd. 212), believed that in 1914 British holdings in bonds were roughly two-and-one-half times their holdings in shares. See also Lewis, *America's Stake*, 558. On the other hand, 1919 data on "enemy"-owned railway securities reveal that Germans, Austrians, and "other enemies" held more railroad shares than bonds, in a ratio of 1.8 to 1 (my own calculations, based on U.S. Alien Property Custodian, *Report, 1918–1919*, 375), but this does not negate the earlier generalizations, since this 1919 summary did not reflect the 1914 ratios; it seems likely that in the "enemies'" disposal of railroad securities between 1914 and 1917, bonds sold more easily than shares. Indeed, Lewis, in *America's Stake*, 123, writes that before April 1917 Germans had sold the greater part "of the pick" of their U.S. securities. Buss indicated that in the 1880s, German bankers invested only in railroad bonds, not in shares (*Henry Villard*, 179).

12. I cannot discern any trend in the variations, although it does seem that in the 1880s there was more involvement in shares than in prior or subsequent decades.

13. As Jacob Schiff of Kuhn, Loeb—who had constant contacts with foreign investors—put it, "stocks go wrong more frequently than bonds." See his testimony (Jan. 16, 1913) in U.S. House, Subcommittee of the Committee on Banking and Currency, *Money Trust Investigation*, 62nd Cong., 2nd sess., 1912–13, 1676. Edelstein, *Overseas Investment*, 123, 125, found that the realized return on "first- and second-class" U.S. rails, 1870–1913, was about 2.4 percent higher for common stock equity than for

preference shares and bonds, a difference that presumably reflected perceived risk. In the late nineteenth and early twentieth centuries, the word *stocks* was sometimes used to refer to what we today call bonds. I have been very careful to check the context in which the word was used to determine whether it referred to shares (equity) or bonds (debt), or both. Schiff was using the word in its modern usage as synonymous with *shares*.

14. The early "mortgage" bonds were, in fact, secured by real property. Then promoters devised the "collateral trust mortgage" bonds that were "secured" by the deposit of stocks and bonds of other companies. See the excellent description in Keith L. Bryant, *Arthur E. Stilwell* (Nashville: Vanderbilt University Press, 1971), 32–33. In short, all "mortgage" bonds were not alike—and all were not backed by real property. For Jay Gould's shenanigans with mortgage bonds, see Grodinsky, *Jay Gould,* passim. The *Stock Exchange Official Intelligence for 1914,* London, 274ff., gives substantial data on U.S. railroad bonds "known in London." One is impressed with the immense variety of types of bonds.

15. See, for example, *Economist,* 45 (Jan. 8, 1887): 39.

16. Ronald B. Weir, *A History of the Scottish American Investment Company Limited, 1873–1973* (Edinburgh: Scottish American Investment Co., 1973), 10.

17. *Economist,* 51 (Feb. 25, 1893): 229.

18. Weir, *A History,* 11.

19. A railroad had to be completed between two points to have any operating revenues.

20. Union Pacific stock, for example, sold in England (in the decade 1882–1892) at prices ranging from $35 to $135. These dollar prices were given in *Economist,* 50 (May 14, 1892): 63.

21. The Dutch seemed far less conservative than the English investor.

22. In the depression of the mid-1870s, the German banking house Jacob S. H. Stern asked Henry Villard "to examine the condition of American roads with depreciated securities to determine where the potential for sustained profits lay" (Buss, *Henry Villard,* 43).

23. While much is made in the literature on the European proclivity to buy bonds, far less emphasis has been placed on the price fluctuations in these "conservative" investments. Everyone notes how profits were made on U.S. government securities purchased below par. The same was true of railroad bonds. Profits and losses to the investor typically related not to nominal interest payments, but to the changes in the value of such securities. Edelstein, *Overseas Investment,* is one of the few authors to take this into account. Since he dealt with only the "best" securities, his data omit some of the more extreme cases. Adler, *British Investment,* 143, notes the "capital gains" of investors in the 1870s as a reason for the subsequent attraction of American railroads. The Scots, as distinct from the English, often bought bonds at deep discounts, selling when the value rose and, accordingly, gaining excellent returns when appreciation is included.

24. See Chapter 4, note 205.

25. D. C. M. Platt, "British Portfolio Investment Overseas," *Economic History Review,* 2nd ser., 33 (Feb. 1980): 1–16, makes this point.

26. Bearer bonds were often held abroad, in small part for secrecy reasons, but mostly to assist in their transfer. Bonds were also held in street names, as a convenience. Shares, likewise, were frequently in broker's or bankers' names rather than in the name of the actual owner. On bearer bonds, see Bacon, "American International Indebtedness," 226, and Adler, *British Investment,* xi. Securities were also transferred without the new owner's bothering to make name changes on the assumption that the

bond itself was the negotiable instrument. On the subsequent complications facing Dutch purchases of American securities from Germans, see S. H. Cross, the Hague, to Director, Bureau of Foreign and Domestic Commerce, Feb. 20, 1924, in Record Group 151, 620 Germany, National Archives, Washington, D.C. Albro Martin, who has had a great deal of expeience with railroad archives, comments on how difficult lists of investors are to use. "So much stock is held by institutions or individuals in their name for beneficial ownership by others that such a list would not necessarily tell one anything" (Martin to Mira Wilkins, April 21, 1982).

27. In addition, Dorothy Adler points out that often *before* offering a railroad issue to the public, merchant bankers would extend credit to the railroad. The issue would then be used to reimburse the British banker; as the financial press realized, this would not affect foreign exchange, because the proceeds had long since been transferred to the United States (Adler, *British Investment*, 150). For our purposes, this is simply another manner by which a short-term trade debt became a long-term "foreign investment" in U.S. railroads.

28. J. Riesser, *The German Great Banks* (1911; rpt. New York: Arno Press, 1977), 532–533.

29. See, for example, Gaspard Farrer to Lord Roberts, Sept. 4, 1901, Baring Archives, London (henceforth cited as BAL), on British purchases in New York.

30. Based on data in banking house archives.

31. On these particular holdings, see *Best's Insurance Reports*.

32. Measuring foreign investment in U.S. railroads by monitoring new "issues abroad" (as has been done) fails to represent the level of investment because it does not reflect the actual investment process. While such a measure exaggerates, on the one hand, it omits many investments and thus, on the other hand, may greatly understate the level of investment at any particular time.

33. In the fall of 1914, as Europe was newly and deeply involved in war, U.S. Treasury officials sought out figures "which would show with some close approximation the amount of American securities held abroad." L. F. Loree, president of the Delaware and Hudson Company, "whose position in the railroad world made it possible to obtain data from the railroads of the country," was deputized to assemble uniform information on U.S. railroad securities held abroad as of Jan. 31, 1915. For stocks, he looked at entries in the transfer books of the issuing company. For bonds, he in the main identified ownership by the "slips" (income tax certificates) filed with the corporations by the payee under the provisions of the new federal income tax law. His 1915 figures were at par value. He verified that $2,576,000,000 stocks and bonds of American railroads were held abroad as of Jan. 31, 1915, and he estimated that in addition $150 million of foreign-owned railroad securities were held in American names, thus making a total of $2.7 billion foreign held. His results were first reported in the *Annalist*, June 28, 1915, 674, which commented that had his canvass been made "one or two or three years ago the total would have been considerably higher." See also *Commercial and Financial Chronicle*, 104 (March 31, 1917): 1216, and discussion of the data in Lewis, *America's Stake*, 531–533. Lewis made her own estimates by adjusting Loree's figures to June 30, 1914. Loree's statistics as published in the *Annalist* and the *Commercial and Financial Chronicle* differed somewhat—with the latter giving for Jan. 31, 1915, slightly higher numbers ($2.7 billion verified to be held abroad—*excluding* foreign-owned railroad securities held in American names). Lewis used data from the *Chronicle* and made her own breakdown by nationality.

34. Based on data in *Best's Insurance Reports*, which give both par and market values for "blue-chip" railway securities held by U.S. branches of foreign insurance companies. Cleona Lewis estimated that if common stock holdings in railroads were calcu-

lated at market value rather than at par, total foreign investment in U.S. railroads in 1914 would be $3.93 billion (*America's Stake*, 546, 558). She did not recalculate bonds at market price.

35. The British statistician George Paish put British holdings of U.S. railroad securities at $2.8 billion in 1910, a sum equal to 85 percent of British investment in America. See George Paish, "Great Britain's Capital Investment in Individual Colonial and Foreign Countries," *Journal of the Royal Statistical Society*, 74 (Jan. 1911); 176, reprinted in *British Overseas Investments, 1907–1948*, ed. Mira Wilkins (New York: Arno Press, 1977). For 1913–14 he raised his estimate to $3 billion, or 82 percent of British stakes in the United States ("The Export of Capital and the Cost of Living," *Statist*, 89 [Feb. 14, 1914]: vi, reprinted in *British Overseas Investments*, ed. Wilkins). Cleona Lewis' figures give British railway stakes in the United States in 1914 as $2.8 billion, or 66 percent of all British holdings in America (smaller than the Paish's estimate but still a large percentage). Lewis, *America's Stake*, 546. I have found Lewis' figures to be the best available. Paish's numbers have been subject to criticism. See, for example, John Maynard Keynes, "Discussion," *Journal of Royal Statistical Society*, 74 (Jan. 1911): 195, reprinted in *British Overseas Investments*, ed. Wilkins. Nonetheless, both Robert M. Kindersley and Lewis—using different methodologies—found Paish's 1913–14 estimate of British investments in U.S. railroads to be within reason. Kindersley, "A New Study of British Foreign Investment," *Economic Journal*, 39 (March 1929): 9–10, reprinted in *British Overseas Investments*, ed. Wilkins, notes that British wartime requisitions of American railway stocks and bonds were estimated at £623 million (or $3.03 billion at $4.86). Presumably Kindersley got this number from the British Treasury or the Bank of England. It does not appear in Gt. Brit., Parl. Papers, XIII-I, *Report of the American Dollar Securities Committee*, Cmd. 212 (1919). If, as is generally believed, British investments in U.S. railroads were lower in 1915 (when requisitioning began) than in 1913, by Kindersley's figures Paish's estimate would be low rather than high—as critics have charged. Lewis did not use Kindersley's estimate. When she read the parliamentary report, she was so troubled by it that she went to the British Treasury, which told her it was filled with misprints. See Lewis, *America's Stake*, 537–546, for an analysis. As noted earlier, she reconstructed British and other nationalities' investments in American railroads (at par) from the January 1915 data of L. F. Loree to arrive at her July 1, 1914, figure of $2.8 billion for British investments in U.S. railways (ibid., 546, 532–533). While hers is lower than Paish's estimate, it is close enough considering the inadequacy of the data. For the French, if we rely on Lewis' figures, railroads in 1914 represented 71 percent of their investments in the United States (ibid., 546). Although the underlying figures are clearly questionable, I feel reasonably sanguine with the relatively high railroad investments in the French and British holdings vis-à-vis those of the Dutch and Germans. The Dutch and Germans appear to have been less "conservative" investors.

36. This would not have been true of, say, 1890, when German and Dutch interests would have been far greater than the French ones. According to Table 6.1, in 1914 French interests were only slightly less than those of the Germans and Dutch. As will be apparent in the text, much of the French investment was made in the decade before World War I.

37. *Banker's Magazine*, New York, 30 (May 1876): 846. The journal thought that the high rate of default on foreign-held bonds was due to the foreign investor's "reckless choice of bad investments."

38. Ibid., 42 (July 1887): 9.

39. Charles Kindleberger, *Manias, Panics, and Crashes* (New York: Basic Books, 1978), 133. More specifically, the Baring Crisis thwarted the plans of the Union Pacific;

the St. Paul, Minneapolis and Manitoba; the Louisville and Nashville; and, in time (1893), the Atchison, Topeka and Santa Fe to raise monies in London.

40. Duke of Marlborough, "Virginia Mines and American Rails," *Fortnightly Review*, n.s., 49 (Jan. 1891): 581–582.

41. Charles Duguid, *The Story of the Stock Exchange* (London: Grant Richards, 1901), 246, 249, 251; see also W. Turrentine Jackson, *Enterprising Scot* (Edinburgh: Edinburgh University Press, 1968), 251, for the dreary mid-1890s.

42. E. G. Campbell, *The Reorganization of the American Railroad System, 1893–1900* (New York: Columbia University Press, 1938), 27–28, 30, and Paish, "Great Britain's Capital Investments" (Jan. 1911), 175, in *British Overseas Investments*, ed. Wilkins, for effects in Britain.

43. Adler, *British Investment*, xiii.

44. Campbell, *Reorganization*, 256–302. The Illinois Central, for example, did well all during the 1890s.

45. William Z. Ripley, *Railroads: Finance and Organization* (New York: Longmans, Green, 1915), 8.

46. Foreign holders of Great Northern shares exchanged their holdings for Northern Securities Company stock in 1901. In 1904 the Supreme Court decreed the dissolution of Northern Securities Company. By 1905, however, the shareholders had not yet gotten back their Great Northern securities, so the figures in Table 6.2, in this one case, seem deceptive. In July 1903 a knowledgeable individual reported that one-fifth of Northern Securities Company stock was held in Europe, and the amount was rising (Gaspard Farrer to E. J. Tuck, July 25, 1903, Gaspard Farrer Letterbook, BAL). Likewise, in the consolidation movement at the turn of the century, shares held by European investors were often exchanged for collateral trust bonds of the parent, thus reducing the equity holdings, but not the investment (Ripley, *Railroads*, 8). There were unquestionably divestments, but this table, in short, may exaggerate them.

47. George Paish, "Our New Investments," *Statist*, 63 (Jan. 2, 1909): 21, in *British Overseas Investments*, ed. Wilkins.

48. Paish "Great Britain's Capital Investments" (Jan. 1911), 174, in *British Overseas Investments*, ed. Wilkins.

49. Ibid., 175.

50. Pierce, "Foreign Investment," 48, and Lewis, *America's Stake*, 51, 120. Actually it was a Pennsylvania Company loan, guaranteed by the Pennsylvania Railroad. See Robert T. Swaine, *The Cravath Firm* (New York: privately printed, 1946), I, 716.

51. Ripley, *Railroads*, 9, and Charles E. Speare, "Selling American Bonds in Europe," *Annals of the American Academy of Politican and Social Science*, 30 (1907): 278.

52. Lewis, *America's Stake*, 51, and another for $5 million in 1910.

53. Ibid., 120.

54. Pierce, "Foreign Investment," 59; Ripley, *Railroads*, 8–9; and Lewis, *America's Stake*, 120. For contemporary French discussions of the influx of American railway securities, see Lysis [Eugene Letailleur], *Contre l'oligarchie financière en France*, 9th ed. (Paris: Aux Bureaux de 'La Revue,' 1908), 99, 143, 149, 152; M. George Aubert, *La finance américaine* (Paris: Ernest Flammarion, 1910), 191; and 1910–1912 articles in Lysis, *Politique et finance d'avant-guerre* (Paris: Payot, 1920), 116–121, 124–125, 129–130, 304–306, 309–310. See also Edmond Baldy, *Les banques d'affaires en france depuis 1900* (Paris: Librairie Générale de Droit, 1922), 160, 191.

55. In June 1915, when the French government arranged a loan from three U.S. banks, the intermediary was Rothschild Frères. The loan was $30 million, and the promissory notes of Rothschild Frères were to be secured by the deposit (as collateral) of bonds of the Chicago, Milwaukee and St. Paul Railroad and the Pennsylvania

Railroad. See Charles C. Tansill, *America Goes to War* (1938; rpt. Gloucester, Mass.: Peter Smith, 1963), 89.

56. See Buss, *Henry Villard*; Fritz Seidenzahl, *100 Jahre Deutsche Bank* (Frankfurt: Deutsche Bank, 1970), chap. 5; and Karl Helfferich, *Georg von Siemens* (Berlin: Verlag von Julius Springer, 1923), II, pt. 4, chap. 4.

57. Walter Herman Carl Laves, *German Governmental Influence on Foreign Investments, 1871–1914* (1927 Ph.D. diss.; New York: Arno Press, 1977), 62.

58. Bryant, *Arthur E. Stilwell*, 78. Robert Edgar Riegel, *The Story of the Western Railroads* (Lincoln: University of Nebraska Press, 1926), 139, adds to the list the California Pacific, the St. Paul and Pacific, the Central Pacific, the Union Pacific, the Denver Pacific, the Oregon and California, the Kansas and Pacific, and the Atchison, Topeka and Santa Fe. The Interstate Commerce Commission (ICC) identified as of January 1, 1909, $70 million invested by thirteen Dutch financial groupings in common and preferred shares of an equal number of American railroads, with the most Dutch interest in the Kansas City Southern ($17.7 million) and in the Missouri, Kansas and Texas ($13.0 million). Data obtained by Bert C. Forbes, "Investments by Hollanders in America," *Van Norden Magazine*, Oct. 1909, 65 (microfiche in New York Public Library). I have been unable to locate the original ICC report. As reported by Forbes, it ignored the far larger stake in bonds. Augustus J. Veenendaal, Jr., is writing a book on the extensive Dutch investments in American railroads.

59. *Economist*, 76 (March 15, 1913), 638.

60. Ripley, *Railroads*, 44, and Paul A. Dickens, "The Transition Period in American International Financing: 1897–1914," Ph.D. diss., George Washington University, 1933, 111.

61. Ripley, *Railroads*, 9.

62. Dickens, "The Transition Period," 104, believed this.

63. Margaret G. Myers, *The New York Money Market* (New York: Columbia University Press, 1931), 292, for example.

64. Of course, the different measures used by Adler and Paish make these figures not fully comparable. See this chapter, note 35, on Paish's figures.

65. This point is made by Ripley, *Railroads*, 8–9, and Dickens, "The Transition Period," 104.

66. This figure includes common stock, preferred stock, and unmatured funded debt, issued and nominally outstanding, as well as those securities actually outstanding. See U.S. Bureau of the Census, *Historical Statistics of the United States* (Washington, D.C., 1975), pt. 2, 735.

67. Pierce, "Anglo-American," 138–154. In 1879 J. P. Morgan formed a syndicate to sell the Vanderbilt shares in London (Chandler, *Visible Hand*, 158). August Belmont & Co. was involved in the underwriting (N. S. B. Gras and Henrietta M. Larson, *Casebook in American Business History* [New York: Appleton-Century-Crofts, 1939], 552). See also Lewis Corey, *House of Morgan* (New York: G. Howard Watt, 1930), 139–142, who argued that Vanderbilt wanted to sell some stock to numerous individual holders to avoid the cry of "monopolist" owner. J. S. Morgan & Co., after the issue, became general agents of the New York Central in London. On October 15, 1881, August Belmont & Co. was writing to W. H. Vanderbilt that N. M. Rothschild & Sons "are large holders of and dealers in the stocks of the different Roads with which you are connected." The letter related to facilitating the "authentication of transfers executed abroad." See letter in Rothschild Archives, London (henceforth cited as RAL) II/51/OB.

68. Adler, *British Investment*, 147: T. W. Powell was the representative.

69. Chandler, *Visible Hand*, 155 (system building), and Ripley, *Railroads*, 5, 9. *The American Iron and Steel Association Bulletin*, 34 (Dec. 10, 1900): 201, using the *Philadelphia*

Evening Telegraph as a source, documented the decline of foreign ownership of shares of the Pennsylvania Railroad in the 1890s (in percentages): 52 (1890), 48 (1893), 47 (1894), 45 (1897), 43 (1898), 36 (1899), and 29 (1900). In 1900, with the advance in price of the shares, many people who had held the stock for years sold out. The *Stock Exchange Official Intelligence for 1914*, London, 300, noted that "Pennsylvania railroad dividend cheques, payable in sterling," could be received by mail in Great Britain "on deposit of the Company's permanent dividend form with the Financial Agents." The "London Fiscal Agents" were listed as London Joint Stock Bank, Ltd.

70. On the $50 million franc-denominated loan of 1906, see the text of this chapter. In 1908 the Barings and the Rothschilds cooperated in an issue (£4 million at 96) of Consolidated Mortgage bonds for the Pennsylvania Railroad. See the list of "Foreign, Colonial, and Commerical Loans" in the BAL. On the various Pennsylvania Railroad bonds "known in London," see *Stock Exchange Official Intelligence for 1914*, 300–301.

71. Edward H. Mott, *Between the Ocean and the Lakes: The Story of the Erie* (New York: John S. Collins, 1901), shows the importance of British investments in this railroad.

72. Anna Robeson Burr, *The Portrait of a Banker: James Stillman* (New York: Duffield, 1927), 244.

73. Paul W. Gates, *The Illinois Central Railroad and Its Colonization Work* (Cambridge, Mass.: Harvard University Press, 1934), 76.

74. Solomon Huebner, "Distribution of Stockholders in American Railroads," *Annals of the American Academy of Political and Social Science*, 22 (1903): 477. Was this the block of stock that moved to Europe in the late 1850s (see Chapter 4)? Did it go first to England and then to Holland? In 1902 Stuyvesant Fish stated that when he was first employed by the Illinois Central (in 1877), less than one-seventh of its stock was owned in the United States, while over one-half was owned in England and almost 30 percent by a company in Holland. See Gates, *The Illinois Central*, 76–77, and Chandler, *Visible Hand*, 184 (on when Fish joined the Illinois Central). George Kennan, *E. H. Harriman* (Boston: Houghton Mifflin, 1922), I, 71, identifies the Dutch holder of the stock as Boissevain Brothers.

75. Bryant, *Arthur E. Stilwell*, 78.

76. Grodinsky, *Jay Gould*, 324–326, 337, 425. As Grodinsky, Gould's sympathetic biographer, put it, Jay Gould "used every stock rigging device then known" (p. 19).

77. Keith L. Bryant, *History of the Atchison, Topeka and Santa Fe Railway* (New York: Macmillan, 1974), 151.

78. Bryant, *Arthur E. Stilwell*, 32ff.

79. Buss, *Henry Villard*, 156–157.

80. Eugene V. Smalley, *History of the Northern Pacific Railroad* (1883); rpt. New York: Arno Press, 1975), 244; Henry Villard, *Memoirs*, 2 vols. (Boston: Houghton Mifflin, 1904), II, 315; and Buss, *Henry Villard*, 159. On the extravagant methods Villard used to attract German capital to the Northern Pacific, see Buss, *Henry Villard*, 139–145, and Villard, *Memoirs*, II, 309–313.

81. Buss, *Henry Villard*, 182; James Blaine Hedges, *Henry Villard and the Railways of the Northwest* (New Haven: Yale University Press, 1930), 176; and Stuart Daggett, *Railroad Reorganization* (Boston: Houghton Mifflin, 1908), 275. After December 1890 Villard no longer represented the Deutsche Bank, but the Bank's important role in relation to the Northern Pacific continued until 1901. On the termination of Villard's advisory relationship, see Buss, *Henry Villard*, 181, and Villard, *Memoirs*, II, 342–358. In 1914 the *Stock Exchange Official Intelligence*, 298, indicated that holders of Northern Pacific bonds could collect interest on their securities in London at the Deutsche Bank; thus even after 1901 the Bank remained involved.

82. Albro Martin, *James J. Hill and the Opening of the Northwest* (New York: Oxford

University Press, 1976), 385. Dr. John Orbell of Baring Brothers & Co., Ltd., wrote me (August 19, 1987) that "according to our records only £2,000,000 bonds were sold" out of the authorized £6,000,000.

83. *Commercial and Financial Chronicle,* 48 (Feb. 25, 1899): 378. In August 1889 Henry Villard had purchased on behalf of the Deutsche Bank and Lazard Speyer-Ellissen $9.75 million worth of Central Pacific securities (Buss, *Henry Villard,* 185). As of August 1899, Bacon estimated that Germans held $12 million to $15 million in Central Pacific securities ("American International Indebtedness," 270). See Swaine, *Cravath Firm,* I, 613–616, on the British, German, and Dutch roles in the 1899 readjustment of the Central Pacific debt.

84. Bacon, "American International Indebtedness," 270. In 1880 the Southern Pacific had a $10 million bond issue in London (Adler, *British Investment,* 210).

85. Bacon, "American International Indebtedness," 270.

86. *Economist,* 50 (May 14, 1892), 63. In 1896, when the Union Pacific reorganization was in process, there was concern about reactions in "financial circles" in Europe (Kennan, *E. H. Harriman,* I, 122).

87. "American Railway Dividend Account Book," 1913, RAL II/16/19. Williamson, *American Growth and the Balance of Payments, 1820–1913,* 153, is wrong when he states, "After 1870 English capital was predominantly in the rails of the developed and urbanized regions of the East, which left the task of Western expansion to the American, Dutch, and German investor." Certain British investors may have been slower to become involved in western rails, but ultimately they shared the task with the other nationalities. Williamson's error was caused by his reliance on a study of British investment that only went to 1880. He incorrectly assumed that what was true of 1870–1880 was also true of 1880–1914.

88. Heather Gilbert, *The End of the Road: The Life of Lord Mount Stephen, 1891–1921* (Aberdeen: Aberdeen University Press, 1977), 287. See Cyrus Adler, *Jacob H. Schiff* (Garden City, N.Y.: Doubleday, 1928), I, 116, on the 1908 Union Pacific bond issue. Sterling bonds of the Union Pacific had their principal and interest payable at Baring Brothers, London. See *Stock Exchange Official Intelligence for 1914,* 308. In 1908 Baring Brothers had a London "tranche" with Glyn, Mills, in a £4,000,000 4 percent Union Pacific issue at 95½, while in 1910 it took part (also with Glyn, Mills) in a £1,500,000 (at 97) first lien and refunding mortgage bond issue for the Union Pacific. Data from the list of "Foreign, Colonial, and Commercial Loans" in the BAL.

89. John F. Stover, *The Railroads of the South* (Chapel Hill: University of North Carolina Press, 1955), and Adler, *British Investment,* esp. 192–193. There is some question as to whether the Baltimore and Ohio should be classed as a southern railway. It served midwestern as well as southern cities. The Baltimore and Ohio had long looked for British aid. Baring Brothers had been its bankers. So had Morgan. In 1914 its London agents were Speyer Brothers. See Edward Hungerford, *The Story of the Baltimore and Ohio Railroad, 1827–1927,* 2 vols. (New York: G. P. Putnam, 1928), II, 177; Adler, *British Investment,* 208, 210; Swaine, *Cravath Firm,* I, 594–597; and *Stock Exchange Official Intelligence for 1914,* 276. In 1877 the Alabama Great Southern was acquired by the banking firm Emile Erlanger & Co., London (Greenberg, *Financiers and Railroads,* 131, and Adler, *British Investment,* 128–131). See Adler, *British Investment,* 134–136, on the Norfolk and Western and the Louisville and Nashville. Norfolk and Western 4 percent Gold Bonds were among the few U.S. railroads listed on the Brussels Bourse ("Foreign Stocks on the Brussels Bourse—1912," *Bulletin de l'Institut International de Statistique,* XX, pt. 2, 1365). Presumably this meant it was attracting investment from the continent as well. It did attract Dutch investment (Swaine, *Cravath Firm,* I, 511).

90. According to the *Courier Journal,* cited in Maury Klein, *History of the Louisville and Nashhville Railroad* (New York: Macmillan, 1972), 176. Louisville interests still were majority owners.

91. August Belmont & Co. to N. M. Rothschild & Sons, Dec. 3, 1895, RAL II/51/14B. The Louisville and Nashville Railroad had at one point attracted the interest of Baring Brothers, then of Sir Ernest Cassel, and finally of the London Rothschilds.

92. When I went to the Minnesota Historical Society, St. Paul, to study British investments in the Pillsbury-Washburn Company and told the librarian that I was doing research on foreign investment in the United States, her first—and correct response—was, Do you want to look at our railway collections? The Minnesota Historical Society has the James J. Hill Papers, the Northern Pacific Papers, the Great Northern Papers, and other railroad collections. A large number of railroads with connections into Chicago and St. Paul/Minneapolis attracted foreign investments. Aside from the ones mentioned in the text, we can also note the Chicago, Milwaukee and St. Paul; the Chicago, Burlington and Quincy; and the Chicago Great Western. The last road, formed in 1892 as a merger of the Minnesota and Northwestern and the Chicago, St. Paul and Kansas City, was at once floated in London and has been described as being "foreign owned" in 1914. See Adler, *British Investment,* 149; Ripley, *Railroads,* 8; and this chapter, note 164 and Chapter 13, note 186.

93. *Commercial and Financial Chronicle,* 104 (March 31, 1917): 1216.

94. Jenks, "Britain and American Railway Development," 376. Matthew Simon found that this section became "the largest department of the London Stock Exchange" ("The Pattern of New British Portfolio Foreign Investment, 1865–1914," in *The Export of Capital from Britain, 1870–1914,* ed. A. R. Hall [London: Methuen, 1968], 27).

95. Jenks, "Britain and American Railway Development," 377.

96. W. Turrentine Jackson, *The Enterprising Scot* (Edinburgh: Edinburgh University Press, 1968), 54.

97. E. Victor Morgan and W. A. Thomas, *The Stock Exchange: Its History and Functions* (London: Elek Books, 1962), 281.

98. For the nominal capitalization, I used U.S. Bureau of the Census, *Historical Statistics of the United States* (1975), 735.

99. Adler, *British Investment,* 143.

100. Edelstein, *Overseas Investment,* 94, 95, 97.

101. Ibid., 136.

102. Based on Bosch, *Nederlandse Beleggingen in de Verenigde Staten,* 139. The real growth was in "Dutch and colonial listings," which in 1910 for the first time exceeded "foreign" listings.

103. Ibid.

104. A. Sartorius Freiherrn von Waltershausen, *Das Volkswirtschaftliche System der Kapitalanlage im Auslande* (Berlin: Georg Reimer, 1907), 42–43.

105. The form in which the security was issued was a matter of discussion between the railroad management and the merchant bankers. See, for example, letters from August Belmont to N. M. Rothschilds & Sons, July 12, 1881; July 16, 1881; and July 29, 1881, RAL II/51/OB, on a possible Baltimore and Ohio loan in dollars or sterling; this particular loan did not come to pass, either in dollars or in sterling by the Rothschilds at this time.

106. Pierce, "Foreign Investment," 52.

107. The Deutsche Bank insisted on a guaranteed rate of exchange of 4.2 marks to the dollar (Buss, *Henry Villard,* 178).

108. Adler, *British Investment,* 146–147, indicates that the distinction between the smaller merchant banking houses and the largest stockbrokers was minimal. See W. J.

Reader, *A House in the City* (London: B. T. Batsford, 1979), passim, for the ease with which Foster & Braithwaite, a large stockbroker, sold American railroad securities.

109. Adler, *British Investment*, 143–145 (on the seven). There are several histories of "The House of Brown," including Edwin J. Perkins, *Financing Anglo-American Trade* (Cambridge, Mass.: Harvard University Press, 1975), which stops at 1880; John Crosby Brown, *A Hundred Years of Merchant Banking* (New York: privately printed, 1909); and John A. Kouwenhoven, *Partners in Banking* (Garden City, N.Y.: Doubleday, 1968). Regrettably, they do not deal with the financing of American railroads, nor does Aytoun Ellis, *Heir of Adventure: The Story of Brown, Shipley & Co.* (London: Brown, Shipley, 1960). On the role of Brown, Shipley (the Brown's London house) in U.S. railroad finance, see Adler, *British Investment*, 81, 145n, 152, 164. Henry Clay, *Lord Norman* (London: Macmillan, 1957), 10, 16–59, shows Brown, Shipley was primarily an acceptance house. Dolores Greenberg, *Financiers and Railroads, 1869–1889* (Newark: University of Delaware Press, 1981), does well on Morton, Bliss. In 1896 George Bliss died; the firm was dissolved in 1897 (ibid., 214). Morton, Rose was its London house. See Linton Wells, "House of Seligman," 1931, unpublished history (microfilm of typescript in New York Historical Society Library), 641–700, on the Seligman firm's intermediation of U.S. railroad securities abroad—road by road, 1875–1914. The Seligmans were involved with the sale abroad of securities of the New York Central; the St. Louis and San Francisco; the Atlantic and Pacific; the Illinois Central; the Pennsylvania Railroad; the Chicago, Milwaukee and St. Paul; the Oregon Railway and Navigation Company; the Chicago, Burlington and Quincy; the Chicago and North Western; the Denver and Rio Grande; and the Northern Pacific.

110. On these houses, see the text of this chapter and, particularly, Chapter 13. Initially I had included Drexel, Morgan as an "American house" with a London outlet. Vincent Carosso, *The Morgans* (Cambridge, Mass.: Harvard University Press, 1987), however, shows that J. S. Morgan & Co., London, was—at least until the mid-1880s—the lead firm of the Morgan group; Carosso's volume documents the London firm's important role in U.S. railroad finance. Speyer is difficult to classify by nationality. It seems legitimate to refer to it as a German-headquartered house in the late 1870s. (By 1914 Speyer & Co. was so well established in New York that it seems wise to call it a New York firm.)

111. The predecessor of Hallgarten & Co. was founded by an immigrant from Frankfurt in 1850. Hallgarten & Co. had wide contacts on the European continent; a "draft" history of the firm described it as "a channel through which moved much" of the foreign capital that went into U.S. railroad expansion (ESW, "History of Hallgarten & Co." typescript, April 28, 1950, 4). According to this text, Hallgarten & Co. by the early twentieth century "probably sold more American [railroad and industrial] securities" in Switzerland, Sweden, Germany, Austria, France, England, and Denmark "than any other establishment of the same character" (ibid., 6). I believe this exaggerates Hallgarten's role, but how much is uncertain.

112. Greenberg, *Financiers and Railroads*, 169.

113. I am using the term *investment banker* to encompass the British merchant banks. See Stanley Chapman, *The Rise of Merchant Banking* (London: Allen & Unwin, 1984), 96–97.

114. R. H. Inglis Palgrave, "An English View of Investments in the United States," *Forum*, 15 (April 1893): 198. Maitland, Phelps & Co. was involved in the financing of the Denver and Rio Grande. See Linton Wells, "House of Seligman," 671. Maitland, Phelps was closely associated with J. K. Gilliat & Co., London.

115. Vincent P. Carosso, "The Morgan Houses: The Seniors, Their Partners, and Their Aides," in *American Industrialization, Economic Expansion, and the Law,* ed. Joseph

R. Frese and Jacob Judd (Tarrytown, N.Y.: Sleepy Hollow Restorations, 1981), 1–36, on who's who among the Morgan houses.

116. Campbell, *Reorganization*, 145–216. In the midst of the dismal 1890s, J. P. Morgan in one day in May 1895 sold 45,717 shares of New York Central stock in London at 105 (ibid., 264). On Morgan's "immense" influence on railroad finance at the end of the nineteenth century, see ibid., 328–333. When J. S. Morgan died in 1890, within the Morgan houses the New York one became the clear leader (Carosso, *The Morgans*).

117. See P. L. Cottrell, "Investment Banking in England, 1856–1882: A Case Study of the International Financial Society," Ph.D. diss., University of Hull, 1974, 740–743, 783–787, for the International Financial Society's role with J. S. Morgan & Co. in selling U.S. railway bonds in England, 1875–1882. Stanley Chapmen has prepared an unpublished study on Kleinwort, Benson. See also Pierce, "Anglo-American," 142–145; Adler, *British Investment*, 149–150; and the prospectuses of railway issues. Robert Benson was closely associated with the Chicago Great Western. Chapter 13 has more on these firms.

118. Carosso, "The Morgan Houses," and Pierce, "Foreign Investment," 53.

119. Edward Tuck was born in Exeter, New Hampshire, in 1842 and attended Dartmouth College. He became U.S. Vice Consul in Paris in 1862 and in 1865 Acting Consul. The next year he joined the Paris house of John Munroe & Co., New York, becoming a partner in both the New York and Paris banks in 1871. Ten years later he retired from active business but kept in close contact with U.S. railway affairs. In 1887 he became a director of Chase National Bank, New York. The next year James J. Hill became a director of that bank. Tuck corresponded with Hill and his friends. On Tuck and Chase National, see William Ten Eck Hardenbrook, *Financial New York* (New York: privately printed, 1897), 275, 271. On Tuck and Hill, see Martin, *James J. Hill*. Martin describes Tuck as a "rich Eastern Democrat" (p. 308), with a villa at Monte Carlo and an apartment on the Champs Élysées (pp. 429, 437). Tuck came to make the Great Northern "his chief hobby" (p. 437) and was a promoter of the railroad in Europe (p. 498). Professor Franklin Brooks of Vanderbilt University, who is preparing a biography of Edward Tuck, has found evidence that Tuck directed French investment to Hill's properties (Brooks to Wilkins, July 1, 1982).

120. Leland H. Jenks, *The Migration of British Capital to 1875* (New York: Barnes & Noble, 1971), 268; Adler, *British Investment*, 131; and Chapter 4, note 94. The Erlangers were involved with the Alabama Southern.

121. Martin, *James J. Hill*, passim, and Weir, *A History*, 8, 15.

122. Vincent Carosso, *Investment Banking in America* (Cambridge, Mass.: Harvard University Press, 1970), 91.

123. Pierce, "Foreign Investment," 56, contains a good description of the functioning of these administrative bureaus. See also Bosch, *Nederlandse Beleggingen*, passim.

124. Buss, *Henry Villard*, 183–185.

125. The phrase is from Charles F. Speare, "Selling American Bonds in Europe," *Annals of the American Academy of Political and Social Sciences*, 30 (1907): 274.

126. The best book on Kuhn, Loeb is Cyrus Adler's biography of its senior partner: Cyrus Adler, *Jacob H. Schiff* (Garden City, N.Y.: Doubleday, 1928), vol. 1.

127. E. Rosenbaum and A. J. Sherman, *M. M. Warburg & Co., 1798–1938: Merchant Bankers of Hamburg* (New York: Holmes & Meier, 1979), 86, 88, 94.

128. Adler, *Jacob H. Schiff*, and Fritz Redlich, *The Molding of American Banking* (New York: Johnson Reprint Corp., 1968), pt. 2, 386.

129. See, for example, the prospectus on the Louisville and Nashville Railroad, 1891. Kuhn, Loeb was ubiquitous in American railroad finance—often in association with foreign banking houses. Otto Kahn, who became a partner in Kuhn, Loeb in 1897, had

studied banking in Germany and had worked in the London branch of the Deutsche Bank (Kennan, *E. H. Harriman*, I, 130).

130. Speare, "Selling American Bonds," 278.

131. Bacon, "American Indebtedness," 272.

132. Carosso, *Investment Banking*, 91.

133. William K. Vanderbilt was the son of William H. Vanderbilt.

134. George J. Gould was Jay Gould's son.

135. Frederick A. Cleveland and F. W. Powell, *Railroad Finance*, (New York: D. Appleton, 1912), 279–280. Kuhn, Loeb had placed the $50 million Pennsylvania Railroad bond issue in Paris (Carosso, *Investment Banking*, 84, and Swaine, *Cravath Firm*, I, 716).

136. Carosso, *Investment Banking*, 92, 93. Carosso excluded J. & W. Seligman from the 1914 list. It still existed but was no longer in the top five. Joseph Seligman had died in April 1880. In 1897 his son reorganized the firm. Seligman & Stettheimer, its Frankfurt house, closed in 1900. The brother of Joseph who ran the Paris house died in France in 1910. Seligman Brothers, London, however, continued. See Wells, "House of Seligman." Likewise, by 1914 the house of Brown still existed but was not in the top rank in negotiating U.S. railroad issues.

137. Lord Mount Stephen, about whom the reader will learn more in the pages to follow. The names are given in Gilbert, *End of the Road*, 274. I have added the comments.

138. R. S. Sayers, *The Bank of England, 1891–1944*, 3 vols. (Cambridge: Cambridge University Press, 1976), III, 362, and data from the Museum and Historical Research Section, Bank of England. On his son, Vivian Hugh Smith (1867–1956), later Lord Bicester, see J. A. S. L. Leighton-Boyce, *Smiths the Bankers, 1658–1958* (London: National Provincial Bank, 1958), 307–308. On Smith's social and business friendships, see comments of Lord Rothschild (on the occasion of Smith's death) at the annual meeting of the Alliance Assurance Company, Ltd., in *Economist*, 70 (April 23, 1910), 907–908; Bo Bramsen and Kathleen Wain, *The Hambros, 1779–1979* (London: Michael Joseph, 1979), 298, 300, 334–335; and Leighton-Boyce, *Smiths*, 273, 308, 310.

139. Data in the RAL. See also *Bankers' Magazine*, London, 99 (June 1915): 784, and Chapter 13 for more details.

140. G. S. Morison followed W. H. Swift, who had been the Baring's U.S. adviser on railroads from the mid-1850s to the mid-1870s. W. H. Swift died in 1879. The BAL contains numerous reports on American railroads prepared by Morison—from 1875 onward.

141. My data on Lord Revelstoke come from information in the BAL and *Bankers' Magazine*, London, 127 (June 1929): 877–880. See Chapter 13 for more on the Barings.

142. On Ernest Cassel, I am indebted to Patricia Thane, whose biographical sketch of Sir Ernest is in the *Dictionary of Business Biography*. On Bischoffsheim & Goldschmidt and American railroads, see Adler, *British Investment*, 205–207. On Cassel, see also Paul H. Emden, *Money Powers of Europe* (1937; rpt, New York: Garland, 1983), 331–342. *Banker's Magazine*, New York, 80 (May 1910): 767, suggests the Harriman connections (E. H. Harriman, of course, died in 1909). When Cassel died in 1921, he left an estate in excess of £7.3 million. He was one of Britain's wealthiest men (W. D. Rubinstein, "British Millionaires, 1809–1949," *Bulletin of the Institute of Historical Research*, 47 [1974]: 215). Cassel was a friend of King Edward VII, as was Lord Rothschild (Christopher Hibbert, *Edward VII* [London: Allen Lane, 1976], 173–174).

143. On Robert Fleming, who was incidentally the grandfather of Ian Fleming (of James Bond fame), I have found useful W. G. Kerr, *Scottish Capital on the American Credit Frontier* (Austin: Texas State Historical Association, 1976); Gilbert, *End of the Road*;

Jackson, *Enterprising Scot;* Adler, *British Investment;* Adler, *Jacob H. Schiff,* I, 13; Swaine, *Cravath Firm,* vol. 1; and John Scott and Michael Hughes, *The Anatomy of Scottish Capital* (London: Croom Helm, 1980). See also Chapter 14.

144. Here I am talking about the first tier of foreign investors (obviously there were investors, in turn, in the foreign-headquartered companies). In addition, there were charities, such as the King's Hospital Fund, which held donated U.S. railroad securities.

145. Among the few exceptions I have found were (1) the British-incorporated holding company, the Alabama, New Orleans, Texas and Pacific Junction Railways Co., Ltd. (June 1881), and (2) the New York, Pennsylvania and Ohio First Mortgage Trust, Ltd. (July 1896). See Adler, *British Investment,* 129, and George Glasgow, *The English Investment Trust Companies* (New York: John Wiley, 1931), 142, 134. There were others, but they were atypical. By contrast, railroads located in many parts of the world were frequently owned by companies incorporated in London. The Sao Paulo Railway, for example, had a London board. See Ellis T. Powell, *The Mechanism of the City* (London: P. S. King, 1910), 144.

146. Canadian brokers, in particular, bought securities for individual Canadian investors on the New York Stock Exchange. As noted earlier, some U.S. railroads were also traded in Geneva, Zurich, Basle, Brussels, and Antwerp.

147. Rubinstein, "British Millionaires, 1809–1949," 204, notes that he often found American railway shares on the inventories drawn up by executors at the time of a testator's death. The death of a wealthy investor transferred securities to his heirs and created a new generation of investors.

148. The investor, for example, may have handled a construction contract and been paid in securities.

149. On reading Grodinsky, *Jay Gould,* I asked whether there were foreign investors who behaved like Gould. The answer is no. Although the *Economist* ran censorious comments about "speculation," there was little of the sort of extreme behavior that characterized men on Wall Street.

150. Pierce, "Anglo American," 152.

151. Huebner, "Distribution of Stockholders," 477. The par value of Illinois Central shares was $100.00 (*Stock Exchange Official Intelligence for 1914,* 289).

152. Martin, *James J. Hill,* 128. The Dutch bought the securities far below par.

153. Alien Property Custodian, *Report, 1918–1919,* 13.

154. See, for example, S. G. & G. C. Ward to Baring Brothers, Oct. 15, 1875, BAL, HC 5.2.30, pt. 16; S. G. Ward to Baring Brothers, Jan. 4, 1876, in ibid., pt. 18; S. G. & G. C. Ward to Baring Brothers, Sept. 5, 1876, in ibid., pt. 21; and S. G. Ward to J. Hickson, Dec. 24, 1876, and Hickson to Ward, Dec. 28, 1876, in ibid., pt. 22. On Baring Brothers' paying full interest on the sterling bonds (£600,000) issued by them, see *Economist,* 24 (Feb. 5, 1876): 169.

155. Rather, Ward wrote that he would be in touch when Hickson returned to Montreal. See Ward to Hickson, Jan. 8, 1877, BAL, HC 5.2.30, pt. 22. Of course, Ward forwarded the entire correspondence to London.

156. Daggett, *Railroad Reorganization,* 45.

157. Lewis, *American's Stake,* 105.

158. Adler, *British Investment,* 173ff. One book Adler did not use but that is very useful on the foreign involvement in the reorganizations of many U.S. railroads, including the Denver and Rio Grande (1885), the St. Louis, Arkansas and Texas (1889), the Ohio and Mississippi (1891), the Union Pacific (1893), the Atchison, Topeka and Santa Fe (1893–1896), the Norfolk and Western (1895), the Baltimore and Ohio (1898), and the Central Pacific (1898) is Swaine, *Cravath Firm,* I, passim.

159. Daggett, *Railroad Reorganization*, 343–346, and passim. Daggett makes the point that shareholders and bondholders often had different interests; thus different committees represented them. He discusses foreign involvement in the reorganization of the Philadelphia and Reading (1874, 1881, 1889, 1893), the Eastern Tennessee, Virginia and Georgia Railroad (1886), the Baltimore and Ohio (1887), the Atchison, Topeka and Santa Fe (1889, 1894–95), the Union Pacific (1893–94), and the Northern Pacific (1893). On other committees—the Dutch committee for the Missouri, Kansas and Texas (1884), the London committee for the Wabash (1885–86), the British committee for the Missouri Pacific (1886), a new Dutch committee for the Missouri, Kansas and Texas (1887–88)—see Grodinsky, *Jay Gould*, 424, 429–433, 443–444, 539–540.

160. Adler, *British Investment*, 189. See also Swaine, *Cravath Firm*, I, 372, 378, for example.

161. Thus, for example, R. D. Peebles of the British-controlled London and San Francisco Bank, Ltd., was in 1880 on the reorganization committee for the Oregon and California Railroad. See Buss, *Henry Villard*, 107, and Swaine, *Cravath Firm,*, I, 378.

162. Adler, *British Investment*, 173, and A. Emil Davies, *Investments Abroad* (Chicago: A. W. Shaw, 1927), 146–157.

163. *Economist*, 45 (Feb. 5, 1887): 184. Dorothy Adler notes that "the fact that the Pennsylvania [Railroad] did not agree to British participation on its board of directors was a cause of complaint by the London press for many years." Nonetheless, the Pennsylvania management "kept constantly in touch with British share and bondholders" (Adler, *British Investment*, 175, 176n).

164. Palgrave, "An English View," 195–196; see Sayers, *Bank of England*, III, 360, for data on Gilliat. While he was the governor (1883–1885), his firm (J. K. Gilliat & Co.) had taken the initiative in the reorganization of the Denver and Rio Grande, 1884–85 (Adler, *British Investment*, 147–148, 173–174). On the Chicago, St. Paul and Kansas City Railroad, see *Investors' Review*, London, 2 (Nov. 1893): 637–645. The prospectus for the railroad had been issued in London in April 1887 by Robert Benson & Co. Its successor in the 1890s was the Chicago Great Western. See also H. Roger Grant, *The Corn Belt: A History of the Chicago Great Western Railroad Company* (DeKalb: Northern Illinois University Press, 1984), 32–33.

165. An 1894 extract from typescript, Edwin Waterhouse, "His Story," n.d., in the Price Waterhouse Archives, London, pp. 94–95. Lidderdale was the governor of the Bank of England during the Baring Crisis.

166. See *Economist*, 76 (March 15, 1913), 638.

167. Martin, *James J. Hill*, 120–122. The U.S. representative of the Dutch bondholders, John S. Kennedy, in exchange for his "intermediation" role, received from the grateful U.S. and Canadian principals a one-fifth interest in the reorganized railroad! This was discovered by Heather Gilbert, "The Unaccountable Fifth," *Minnesota History*, 42 (Spring 1971): 175–177; see also Martin, *James J. Hill*, 154, 193. The Dutch bankers involved were Chemet & Weetjen; Kerkhoven & Co.; Lippmann, Rosenthal & Co.; Wurfbain & Son; and Tutein Nolthenius & De Haan—all of Amsterdam; H. C. Voorhoeve & Co. of Rotterdam; and Johann Carp of Utrecht. The latter seems to have headed the Committee of Dutch Bondholders. See Joseph G. Pyle, *James J. Hill* (Garden City, N.Y.: Doubleday, Page, 1917), II, 432, and I, 185.

168. Greenberg, *Financiers and Railroads*, 122–128, 202; on Oyens' other activities, see Bosch, *Nederlandse Beleggingen*, 170.

169. Klein, *History of the Louisville and Nashville*, 202.

170. Ibid., 214. See Bosch, *Nederlandse Beleggingen*, 171–172, for the role of the administrative office of Wertheim & Gompertz regarding the Louisville and Nashville

Railroad in 1884. Sir Ernest Cassel was active in this reorganization (Emden, *Money Powers*, 333).

171. Adler, *British Investment*, 182.

172. Bosch, *Nederlandse Beleggingen*, 172. For background on the Dutch investment in the Florida Central, see Max Winkler, *Foreign Bonds* (1933; rpt. New York: Arno Press, 1976), 274–275.

173. Schiff to Cassel, May 27, 1889, in Adler, *Jacob H. Schiff*, I, 53.

174. Grodinsky, *Jay Gould*, 540.

175. "Reorganisation Reminiscences," *Investors' Review*, 4 (July 1894): 21–24. Herbert O. Brayer, *William Blackmore* (Denver: Bradford Robinson, 1949), II, 274, confirms that the unidentified railroad was the Denver and Rio Grande. The London *Investors' Review* was very cynical in its approach, and the tone of these reminiscences reflected the general views of the journal. For a far more favorable appraisal of the same reorganization, see Swaine, *Cravath Firm*, I, 371–373.

176. Grodinsky, *Jay Gould*, 590. Jay Gould died in December 1892 (p. 591). George Gould, his son, played the leading role in this "Gould" victory.

177. Swaine, *Cravath Firm*, I, 499–501.

178. See ibid., 373, for the role of the Dutch committee in the reorganization of the Denver and Rio Grande in 1885.

179. Francis Edwin Hyde, "British Capital and American Enterprise in the Northwest," *Economic History Review*, 6 (April 1936): 201–208. On the role of German capital in this railroad in 1885, see Swaine, *Cravath Firm*, I, 378.

180. Swaine, *Cravath Firm*, I, 376–377. The Germans held about $12 million of the $16 million first mortgage bonds. See Grodinsky, *Jay Gould*, 550.

181. In 1898 the Association Nationale de Porteurs Français de Valeurs Mobilières (National association of French holders of securities) was formed; it acted to protect the rights of French owners of foreign securities (Winkler, *Foreign Bonds*, 156–157). I did not find it to be active in American railway matters. There were "Paris" protective committees in relation to U.S. railroad investment, but they bore no comparison with the British, Dutch, and German involvements.

182. My data on George Smith are mainly from Alice E. Smith, *George Smith's Money* (Madison: State Historical Society of Wisconsin, 1966), esp. 139–163. The letter introducing Mitchell was Smith to Edward Baring, Jan. 15, 1877, and is the Baring Papers, Public Archives, Ottawa, vol. 23, p. 012055. After Mitchell died in 1887, George Magoun (of Kidder, Peabody—a firm with which Baring had a special relationship) joined the board of this railroad. The quotation is from Smith, *George Smith's Money*, 161. The exact amount of Smith's holdings in U.S. railroads is uncertain; Alice Smith is very imprecise. She writes "until about the time of World War I the George Smith interests in London held approximately $20,000,000 in bonds and stocks" of the Chicago, Milwaukee and St. Paul (p. 155). In the late nineteenth century, that railroad came under the aegis of the so-called Big Four (Smith, the meatpacker Philip D. Armour, William Rockefeller interests, and Charles W. Harkness interests—the last two associated with Standard Oil). If at the time of his death Smith held 19,000 shares (ibid., 176), his "equity" in the railroad was far less than that of the other three interests. I do not know the size of his bond holdings. I am uneasy about the $20 million figure, since it does not mesh well with other information. I include it only to indicate his biographer's perception of the size of the holding. In November 1899, at the time of Smith's death, 19,000 shares of the common stock of the Chicago, Milwaukee and St. Paul would have had a market value of about $2.4 million (based on November quotations given in the *Commercial and Financial Chronicle*, 70 [Jan. 6, 1900]: 22.) Was the difference made up in bond holdings?

183. Smith, *George Smith's Money*, 170. Alice Smith says she consulted George Smith's will at Somerset House, but that it was "years" before the value of the estate was determined; for the $52 million figure, she cites the *New York Times*, May 8, 1907. If Alice Smith's figures are correct, the £10.7 million estate would be more than 3.5 times that of the wealthiest man to die in 1899, in Britain, by Rubinstein's calculations. See his "British Millionaires," 211. Ibid., 223, lists "George 'Chicago' Smith," as a "foreigner," with the wrong date of death (1900 instead of 1899) and notes that "secondary sources" attributed to him a fortune of £5 million; but Rubinstein found him "unlisted" on the printed probate calendar, which is odd because Alice Smith writes that she found the will in Somerset House. The problem may lie in the long period taken in calculating the value of the estate. It may also mean that Smith had smaller holdings in U.S. railroads than his biographer implies (for marketable holdings could have easily been invento-ried).

184. Smith, *George Smith's Money*, 158–159.

185. There is no indication that George Smith and Donald Smith were relatives or even knew each other.

186. The calculations are my own based on data provided in Martin, *James J. Hill*, 210.

187. See Pyle, *James J. Hill*; Martin, *James J. Hill*; the two-volume life of Lord Mount Stephen, Heather Gilbert's *Awakening Continent* (Aberdeen: Aberdeen University Press, 1965), and her *End of the Road*; Merrill Denison, *Canada's First Bank: A History of the Bank of Montreal* (New York: Dodd, Mead, 1967), vol. 2; and W. Kaye Lamb, *History of the Canadian Pacific Railroad* (New York: Macmillan, 1977). Neither Dorothy Adler, nor Jenks, nor Pierce has published anything on Lord Mount Stephen; none of these experts on British investment in U.S. railroads even mentions him. Yet the moment one begins to read about Hill's railroads, his name is ubiquitous.

188. Martin, *James J. Hill*, 659.

189. Buss, *Henry Villard*, 248; Lewis, *America's Stake*, 34; and Helfferich, *Georg von Siemens*, II, 255–272, on von Siemen's role in the reorganization.

190. Martin, *James J. Hill*, 441.

191. As early as May 1889, Hill realized the necessity of gaining control of the Northern Pacific and was writing to Stephen in that vein (Pyle, *James J. Hill*, I, 450).

192. Martin, *James J. Hill*, 455.

193. Gilbert, *End of the Road*, 180.

194. Martin, *James J. Hill*, 441–463. See also Seidenzahl, *100 Jahre*, 94–97, and Gilbert, *End of the Road*, 75–96, 167ff, which should be read with Martin.

195. Quoted in Pyle, *James J. Hill*, II, 106. The friend would be either Lord Mount Stephen or Lord Strathcona, probably the latter. See this chapter, note 208, for a slightly different rendition of the same story. Although the numbers do not coincide, the point is the same.

196. Gaspar Farrer to E. J. Tuck, July 25, 1903, Gaspar Farrer Letterbook, BAL.

197. Martin, *James J. Hill*, passim and Gilbert, *End of the Road*, passim.

198. Harriman to Stillman, Oct. 23, 1908, quoted in Burr, *Portrait of a Banker*, 241.

199. Biographical data are from Denison, *Canada's First Bank*, II, 410–413, and Beckles Willson, *The Life of Lord Strathcona and Mount Royal*, 2 vols. (Boston: Houghton Mifflin, 1915); Albro Martin found the Hill papers had "disappointingly few letters from Don-ald Smith" (*James J. Hill*, 659). I am deeply indebted to Alastair Sweeny, who is completing a biography of Lord Strathcona. Sweeny writes me that there is a sizable Smith-Hill correspondence in the papers of the Hudson's Bay Company (Alastair Sweeny to Mira Wilkins, May 17, 1983, and Aug. 17, 1983).

200. Sweeny to Wilkins, May 17, 1983.

201. Willson, *Lord Strathcona*, II, 61. See Pyle, *James J. Hill*, I, 109, for the first meeting of Smith and Hill.

202. Muriel Hidy to Mira Wilkins, April 12, 1983.

203. Sweeny to Wilkins, May 17, 1983.

204. Ibid. (controlling shareholder). This is not in the Denison history of the bank, although all the positions he held are included in the bank history. Willson's book is useless on this.

205. R. W. Ferrier, *The History of the British Petroleum Company* (Cambridge, Cambridge University Press, 1982), vol. 1.

206. Sweeny to Wilkins, May 17, 1983.

207. December, 1915, quoted in Pyle, *James J. Hill*, I, 168.

208. Albert Bigelow Paine, *George Fisher Baker* (New York: G. P. Putnam's Sons, 1938), 204–206, contains a charming version of Lord Strathcona's role in the events of May 1901, when Harriman sought control of the Northern Pacific. Hill, Paine writes, wired his friends (Lord Strathcona, the Barings, and Lord Mount Stephen) and asked them to "stand by." Robert Bacon at Morgan's had visions of the English contingent selling. "Mr. Hill was cool but finally said, a little impatiently—'Damn it, Bacon, don't worry. My friends will stand without hitching.' " Northern Pacific stock shot up in value. Most people sold, but Hill's English friends "did not sell a share. Lord Strathcona, approached with an offer of $700 a share for his holdings, . . . shook his head: . . . 'I have had word from Mr. Hill . . . not to part with my stock or be disturbed by a little flurry.' " According to Paine, at that time Lord Strathcona owned some 30,000 shares, and the "little flurry" would have meant a $20 million profit. Paine concluded, "No better example could be found of financial faith and loyalty. But J. J. Hill's friends were like that; they would, as he said, 'stand without hitching.' " By way of confirmation of Lord Strathcona's loyalty, when his grandson married, the couple honeymooned in the United States, where in 1922 the heirs of James Hill entertained the newly-weds lavishly. Many years later the bride (Lady Lorna Howard, daughter of British Prime Minister Stanley Baldwin) recalled that Hill had left instructions that his heirs should never forget the help that Lord Strathcona gave him in his 1901 fight with Harriman. Lady Lorna Howard (at age eighty-eight) told this story to her nephew, B. J. Howard, in February 1984 (B. J. Howard to Mira Wilkins, March 20, 1984).

209. There was, for example, James Ross of Montreal who had been one of the chief contractors on the Canadian Pacific Railroad; he was elected in 1899 a director of the Bank of Montreal "to represent reorganized Cape Breton iron and coal interests" and remained a director until his death in 1913. At the time of his death, he held $3 million in American securities. On his holdings, see Jacob Viner, *Canada's Balance of International Indebtedness, 1900–1913* (Cambridge, Mass.: Harvard University Press, 1924), 90; on his biography, see Denison, *Canada's First Bank*, II, 281, 422.

210. It is astonishing that neither George Smith, nor Donald Smith, nor George Stephen was mentioned in Cleona Lewis' excellent *America's Stake*. Yet these three men were among the largest individual foreign investors in the United States, and the last two were truly influential. William Waldorf Astor's holdings (in real estate) were probably larger; see also, Chapter 5 on Consuelo Vanderbilt and the Duke of Marlborough.

211. Johnson and Supple, *Boston Capitalists*, 319.

212. Bryant, *History of the Atchison, Topeka and Santa Fe*, 151.

213. Data in the RAL. There is evidence that many other British merchant banks owned U.S. railroad securities.

214. Denison, *Canada's First Bank*, II, 251.

215. Stephen Randall, "The Development of Canadian Business in Puerto Rico,"

Revista/Review InterAmericana, 7 (Spring 1977): 11. In 1910 the Royal Bank of Canada deposited securities of the Union Pacific, the Chicago, Burlington and Quincy, the Rock Island, the Great Northern, and the Southern Pacific (ibid.).

216. R. T. Naylor, *The History of Canadian Business, 1867–1914* (Toronto: James Lorimer, 1973), II, 244.

217. See C. A. E. Goodhart, *The Business of Banking, 1891–1914* (London: Weidenfeld & Nicholson, 1972), 478, on the 1913 U.S. railroad portfolio of the Metropolitan Bank of England and Wales. Goodhart is also splendid on the U.S. railway holdings of the Union Bank of London and its successor, 1894–1914 (p. 508–513). This material is particularly valuable because it shows both purchases and sales of securities. In 1883 the chairman of the Consolidated Bank, London, was asked about the position of that bank with regard to Atlantic and Great Western Railroad securities (see Chapter 4). He replied that although the account was not yet closed, "they expected to get very little value for what they held." T. E. Gregory does not reveal the size of the holdings (*The Westminster Bank through a Century* [London: Westminster Bank, 1936], II, 64). Geoffrey Jones discovered that in 1909–10 the Imperial Bank of Persia acquired securities of the Pennsylvania Company (£5,670), the Rock Island, Arkansas and Louisiana Railway (£5,790), the Illinois Central (£5,220), the Minneapolis, Sault St. Marie and Atlantic Railway (£6,225), and the Northern Pacific (£6,375). These securities were part of the bank's investment portfolio in 1913–14. These data are drawn from the archives of the Hongkong Bank Group, provided to me by Jones (April 3, 1985). I also have data on the U.S. railroad securities in the 1913–14 portfolios of the London City and Midland Bank and Lloyds Bank, courtesy of these banks' archivists (Edwin Green to Mira Wilkins, April 19, 1985, and J. M. L. Booker to Mira Wilkins, June 3, 1985).

218. R. E. Tyson, "Scottish Investment in American Railways: The Case of the City of Glasgow Bank, 1856–1881," in *Studies in Scottish Business History*, ed. Peter L. Payne (London: Frank Cass, 1967), 390.

219. See W. J. Reader, *A House in the City* (London: B. T. Batsford, 1979) on Foster & Braithwaite.

220. Swaine, *Cravath Firm*, I, 623.

221. See Chapter 14. Jackson, *Enterprising Scot*, 13–16, 21; H. Burton and D. C. Corner, *Investment and Unit Trusts in Britain and America* (London: Elek Books, 1968), 18–19; and Weir, *A History*, 10, 18.

222. Barry Supple, *The Royal Exchange Assurance: A History of British Insurance, 1720–1950* (Cambridge: Cambridge University Press, 1970), 345. See Chapter 15 of my book on Prudential's holdings.

223. *Best's Insurance Reports of 1914.*

224. This is my estimate based on data in these reports.

225. B. W. E. Alford, *W. D. & H. O. Wells* (London: Methuen, 1973), 136.

226. T. C. Barker, *The Glassmakers: Pilkington* (London: Weidenfeld & Nicholson, 1977), 238–239. Its December 31, 1914, portfolio also contained the Atchison, Topeka and Santa Fe (£5,000), the Atlantic and St. Lawrence Railway (£8,000), the Baltimore and Ohio Railroad (£10,000), the Northern Pacific (£6,000), the Oregon and Washington Railroad and Navigation Company (£5,000), the St. Louis Iron Mountain and Southern (£9,000); the St. Paul, Minneapolis and Manitoba (£7,000), and the Southern Pacific (£12,000).

227. Data from Shell Archives, London. Two items in the Shell portfolio appear of special interest: (1) the heavy predominance of "short notes" and (2) a rise in its U. S. railroad investment in 1914. I found year-end (Dec. 31) data. My mistaken assumption was that year-end 1914 figures would be lower than year-end 1913 (the literature mentions massive selling by Britishers of U.S. securities in July 1914). Note also that in

1913 Shell's holdings in U.S. "rails" were denominated in both dollars and pound sterling, depending on the security.

228. Burmah Oil Company, Ltd., "Assets 1913." From company archives. These data were furnished me by T. A. B. Corley.

229. Peter Mathias, *The Retailing Revolution* (London: Longmans, Green, 1967), 130.

230. It is not clear whether these were long-term investments or just temporary holdings in liquid assets until monies from profits could be reinvested in the business. Railroad securities were indeed liquid; yet in many cases, where I have evidence, the securities were held over a year (that is, they were technically long-term investments).

231. C. K. Hobson, *The Export of Capital* (London: Constable, 1914), 15–16, makes this point. Riegel, *Western Railroads*, 43–44, says that the western railways with federal land grants were required to use American iron and steel.

232. Adler, *British Investment*, 131, 128–129. See Stover, *Railroads of the South*, 246, and 92, 136–137, 215, for details on the Erlanger system. Stover says the majority of the common stock in this road passed from British to American hands in the spring of 1890. Adler, *British Investment*, 131, indicates that British interests in the system were retained until 1924. The *Stock Exchange Official Intelligence for 1914*, London, 274, lists only one American railroad incorporated in London—the Alabama, New Orleans, Texas and Pacific Junction Railways Company, Ltd. (registered in 1881). The chairman of the board of directors in 1914 was Baron Emile B. d'Erlanger. The *Stock Exchange Official Intelligence for 1914* says that this railroad controlled the Vicksburg, Shreveport and Pacific Railroad. The Alabama Great Southern is listed as controlled by the Southern Railway. Morgan, Grenfell & Co. was its London "fiscal agents" in 1914.

233. Adler, *British Investment*, 75, 81–82, 89, 94–95, 170, and Daggett, *Railroad Reorganization*, 96. When Hugh McCalmont (1809–1887) died, he was one of Britain's wealthiest men—leaving an estate of £3.1 million. His fortune had been made through his involvement with the Philadelphia and Reading. On his estate, see Rubinstein, "British Millionaires," 209. In 1889 there were still large British holdings in the Philadelphia and Reading; see Ripley, *Railroads*, 5, and Daggett, *Railroad Reorganization*, 119, 126.

234. Adler, *British Investment*, 131, 188. The three railways listed in connection with A. B. Stickney were successors to one another. The "British banking houses" involved included McCalmont, Robert Fleming (as an individual rather than as a "house"), Erlanger, Baring, J. S. Morgan, and Robert Benson.

235. Thomas Cochran, *Railroad Leaders* (Cambridge, Mass.: Harvard University Press, 1953), 66. See Buss, *Henry Villard*, 67–110, and Hyde, "British Capital," 201–208, for background. Hyde's article shows how Villard used British capital to cast off German control, "the irksome burden of German finance" (p. 208). Not long thereafter Villard would be once again seeking German monies for U.S. railroads.

236. Thomas Baring to Baring Brothers, Feb. 13, 1877, BAL, HC 5.2.30, pt. 22; see also S. G. Ward to Baring Brothers, Jan 9, 1877, and Thomas Baring to Baring Brothers, Feb. 20 and 26, 1877, in ibid. For who's who among the Barings, see notes to Chapter 13.

237. G. S. Morison to S. G. Ward, Oct. 12, 1885, BAL, HC 5.2.30, pt. 54.

238. Thomas Baring to "Ned" (Lord Revelstoke), April 18, 1886, BAL, HC 5.1.27, pt 2.

239. Ibid., April 22, 1886, BAL, HC 5.1.27, pt. 2. When in September 1887 it looked as if Baring Brothers might be involved in financing the Baltimore and Ohio, a condition of their involvement was that management should be placed "in competent hands, satisfactory to the syndicate" (Daggett, *Railroad Reorganization*, 11–12).

240. Thomas Baring to "Ned", April 22, 1886, BAL, HC 5.1.27, pt. 2.

241. Ibid., Aug. 6, 1886, BAL, HC 5.1.27, pt. 2.

242. Johnson and Supple, *Boston Capitalists*, 325, 327.

243. Bryant, *History of the Atchison, Topeka*, 156–157. The expansion meant the earlier reforms "were an exercise in futility" (ibid., 158).

244. Ibid., 163–164 and Campbell, *Reorganization*, 74–75, 77–83.

245. Bryant, *History of the Atchison, Topeka*, 164–165; Swaine, *Cravath Firm*, I, 506; and Campbell, *Reorganization*, 217–232.

246. Bryant, *History of the Atchison, Topeka*, 167.

247. Ibid., 168.

248. Swaine, *Cravath Firm*, I, 507; Campbell, *Reorganization*, 218, notes that in 1894 three-fourths of the railroad's bonds were held in England and on the Continent.

249. On April 23, 1896, Victor Morawetz, a lawyer, wrote the representative of the Dutch committee, John Luden, "The Boston people are extremely bitter on account of our failure to keep the Frisco property . . . and all this they charge to the foreigners" (Swaine, *Cravath Firm*, I, 508).

250. On the Baltimore and Ohio, see ibid., I, 595, 597, and *Stock Exchange Official Intelligence for 1914*, 276. In 1898 and 1908, Speyer Brothers, London, Speyer & Co., New York, and Kuhn, Loeb, New York, had been "reorganization managers" for the Baltimore and Ohio. See *Money Trust Investigation*, 1732, 1712.

251. In 1886 August Belmont, Jr., joined the board of the Louisville and Nashville Railroad; he served as a "strong" chairman of the board of that railroad in the years 1891–1903. The railroad hoped that Belmont might be able to secure financial support from the Rothschild houses. This proved to be the case, and the Rothschild account books show that by year-end 1895, N. M. Rothschild & Sons held 21,297 shares of Louisville and Nashville (L & N) (which the firm valued at £293,851) and £64,830 of that railroad's mortgage bonds. The Rothschild holdings in the L & N were larger than in any of the seventeen other American railroads in which it had interests. Belmont sent London substantial information on the L & N. In 1902, when John W. Gates sought to corner the market for L & N stock, foreign owners sold. In 1903 August Belmont resigned as chairman (Klein, *History of the Louisville and Nashville*, 242–243, 251, 311–312, and Adler, *Jacob H. Schiff*, I, 58). Before Belmont assumed the chairmanship, the L & N had failed to dispose of a bond issue in Europe because of the Baring Crisis (Adler, *Jacob H. Schiff*, I, 56). On the Rothschild holdings, see American Account Book for 1895 in RAL II/3/27; on the general information flows, see, for example, cables sent to N. M. Rothschild & Sons, Dec. 23, 26, 1895 (RAL II/51/48). Both the Rothschild Archives in London and the Belmont Family Papers, Special Collections, Columbia University, contain substantial materials on the L & N. The latter collection has Belmont-Rothschild correspondence and also correspondence between Belmont and Sir Ernest Cassel.

252. Kennan, *E. H. Harriman*, I, 71: Swaine, *Cravath Firm*, I, 500, 511; Nelson Trottman, *History of the Union Pacific* (New York: Ronald Press, 1923), 252; and Campbell, *Reorganization*, 233.

253. Swaine, *Cravath Firm*, I, 614–615.

254. Forbes, "Investments by Hollanders," 64.

255. Buss, *Henry Villard*, 181, 248.

256. Campbell, *Reorganization*, 43–44.

257. Buss, *Henry Villard*, 248; Seidenzahl, *100 Jahre*, chap. 5; Helfferich, *Georg von Siemens*, II, 255–272; and Martin, *James J. Hill*, 441–456. On Edward D. Adams, see *National Cyclopaedia of American Biography*, X, 419.

258. Daggett, *Railroad Reorganization*, 296.

259. Gilbert, *End of the Road*, 30.

260. Indeed, in April 1911 Jacob Schiff wrote E. D. Adams that since the Deutsche

Bank was one of the large interests involved in the Missouri Pacific, he (Adams) should be participating in the attempt to find a new president for that railroad (Adler, *Jacob H. Schiff*, I, 127).

261. Adler, *British Investment*, xiii.

262. Ibid., 179–184.

263. Adler, *Jacob H. Schiff*, I, 151.

264. Adler, *British Investment*, 150. For details, see Maury Klein, *The Life and Legend of Jay Gould* (Baltimore: John Hopkins University Press, 1986), 454–455.

265. On Robert Garrett's ouster in 1887, see Campbell, *Reorganization*, 130–131. When Garrett interests regained control, a syndicate set up in England to do the badly needed financing refused to go ahead with the plan (ibid., 131). See also this chapter note 239.

266. J. Laurence Laughlin, *The Credit of Nations* (New York: Charles Scribner's Sons, 1918), 279. Was the unspecified "guilty" railroad the Atchison, Topeka and Santa Fe? Probably.

267. Swaine, *Cravath Firm*, I, 613–616.

268. Cochran, *Railroad Leaders*, 403. The letter was to Charles F. Cox, vice president of the Canada Southern.

269. Klein, *History of the Louisville and Nashville*, 244, 249, 255. By 1888 August Belmont, Jr., was on board of the Louisville and Nashville Railroad, but not yet chairman. Adler, *British Investment*, 171, discusses this railroad in the context of British "banker-railroad relations." This was *not* the first stock dividend. During the Civil War, the Philadelphia and Reading—a British-dominated railroad—issued a stock dividend. See Chapter 4, note 106.

270. Gilbert, *End of the Road*, 287.

271. The Scottish American Investment Co., Ltd., had, for example, a policy of not investing more than one-tenth of its capital in any one security, but before it invested, it wanted to be sure the management of the railroad was in the hands of "competent and honest men" (Weir, *A History*, 9–10).

272. See Adler, *British Investment*, 116n, and Daggett, *Railroad Reorganization*, 45, for his service on the Erie Committee, 1875–76. See also Adler, *British Investment*, 174n, on the Denver and Rio Grande Committee, 1885. Swaine, *Cravath Firm*, I, 372, excerpts part of Fleming's report on the Denver and Rio Grande. In 1886 Fleming headed a reorganization committee for the Missouri Pacific (Grodinsky, *Jay Gould*, 443–444). He represented foreign bondholders in the reorganization of the East Tennessee, Virginia and Georgia Railroad in 1886 (Daggett, *Railroad Reorganization*, 155).

273. Adler, *British Investment*, 148, and Swaine, *Cravath Firm*, I, 380.

274. Adler, *Jacob Schiff*, I, 123–124.

275. Swaine, *Cravath Firm*, I, 502–509. In 1894, when he was defending British investors' interests in the Atchison, Topeka, he also participated (with A. A. Boissevain & Co., of Amsterdam) in the reorganization of the Norfolk and Western Railroad (Adler, *Jacob Schiff*, I, 68).

276. *Stock Exchange Official Intelligence for 1914*, 280.

277. Daggett, *Railroad Reorganization*, 346, makes this point; I have also made it earlier in another context.

278. Ibid., 345, wrote these comments about bankers and financiers, in general—not particularly foreign ones.

279. Robert Fleming came to set up his own banking house; yet even before that, he was a direct participant in railroad reorganizations.

280. This is not preposterous. E. H. Harriman had such plans for China (which, to be sure, never materialized). See H. J. Eckenrode and Pocohontas Wight Edmunds, *E.*

H. Harriman (New York: Greenberg, 1933), 98–99. Foreign steamship companies apparently thought about developing close ties with U.S. railroads, although I have not been able to establish direct investment connections; some British railroads did have steamship investments. The North German Lloyd Line made "an alliance" with the Baltimore and Ohio (Chandler, *Visible Hand*, 157).

281. See Lewis, *America's Stake*, 546, 567, for a detailed breakdown.

282. Ibid., 569.

283. To complicate matters, there were in the early years, especially, substantial U.S. portfolio holdings in the Canadian Pacific (CP), but the British investments came to be preeminent. See Greenberg, *Financiers*, 200, on the early financing of the CP. Denison, *Canada's First Bank*, II, 214, says that in 1883 about half the total shares of the CP were owned in the United States. Herbert Marshall, Frank A. Southard, and Kenneth W. Taylor, *Canadian-American Industry* (New Haven: Yale University Press, 1936), 194, found that in 1906 the ownership of the CP was 11 percent Canadian, 61 percent British, 15 percent U.S., and 13 percent "other." By June 1, 1914, a Dow-Jones study indicated that two-thirds of the stock (common and preferred) of the Canadian Pacific was held in England (*Bradstreet's*, Oct. 24, 1914, 690).

As for the Grand Trunk, Marshall, Southard, and Taylor, *Canadian-American Industry*, 190, write that it was from its origin "controlled in England, largely financed in England, and governed by a London board." Denison, *Canada's First Bank*, II, 187, notes that in about 1876 the Grand Trunk's management control was transferred from London to Montreal after a long and bitter conflict between the interests representing the English shareholders and those charged with railroad operations in Canada. But four years later, in 1880, when Sir John Macdonald was involved in the plans for the Canadian Pacific, he had discussions in London with Sir Henry Tyler, president of the Grand Trunk Railroad Co. (Gilbert, *Awakening Continent*, 67, 69). Most of the Canadian Northern's securities had been sold in Britain (Lamb, *History of the Canadian Pacific*, 290).

284. Marshall, Southard, and Taylor, *Canadian-American Industry*, 188ff. The track mileage is given as of 1937 in ibid., 191, but the construction was nearly complete by 1914, and the mileage built approximately the same. See also William J. Wilgus, *The Railway Interrelations of the United States and Canada* (New Haven: Yale University Press, 1937).

285. Marshall, Southard, and Taylor, *Canadian-American Industry*, 191-193 (excess of 5,000 miles), and Lamb, *History of the Canadian Pacific*, 167, 237, 238. Lamb gives no figures for U.S. mileage in 1914. Canadian mileage was less than 12,000 in 1914, compared with 17,000 in the mid-1930s. Viner, *Canada's Balance of International Indebtedness*, 90, says Canadian railways owned or controlled 7,197 miles of road in the United States in 1912. See Lewis, *America's Stake*, 567, for the names of the Canadian-controlled railways in the United States in 1914.

286. See "Armour 1867–1953," Harvard Business School Case, 1954, 3; R. A. Clemen, *American Livestock and Meat Industry* (1923; rpt. New York: Johnson Reprint Co., 1966), 234; and Adler, *British Investment*, 194.

287. Lamb, *Canadian Pacific*, 3, and Denison, *Canada's First Bank*, II, 188.

288. Cochran, *Railroad Leaders*, 398.

289. Ibid., 404 (Oct. 2, 1888).

290. See Lamb, *History of the Canadian Pacific*, passim.

291. See Martin, *James J. Hill*, passim, but see ibid., 570–571, for Hill's competitive behavior. See also Lamb, *History of the Canadian Pacific*, 195–204 and 459 n.10. The ties between Hill's railroad and the Canadian Pacific (CP) were long-standing. Hill was involved in the original syndicate for the CP. On May 3, 1883, Hill resigned his

membership on the board of the CP, and on July 12, 1883 Stephen resigned as a director of Hill's St. Paul, Minneapolis and Manitoba. On doing so, Stephen wrote that he had no intention of reducing his stock interest in Hill's road, "so long at least as the policy of the company is not hostile to the Canadian Pacific Railway." He looked forward to "an intimate and friendly alliance" between the two railroads. See Pyle, *James J. Hill*, I, 298ff., esp. 322–324. Stephen's influence on the CP extended far beyond the time he was a director. Stephen's time as president of the CP (1881–1888) had been rewarding in his successes, but also frustrating (he had been under severe personal attack). On the other hand, it was Hill's railroads that had made Stephen a millionaire, and he referred to Hill's original railroad venture as their "blessed old road" (Martin, *James J. Hill*, 443). There is some indication that Lord Mount Stephen was more sympathetic to Hill than to the CP when their interests conflicted. This is not to say that Stephen in any way worked contrary to the interests of the CP. See Gilbert, *End of the Road*, 16, and her *Awakening Continent*, passim. From 1888 both Stephen and Smith had more invested in Hill's railroads than in the Canadian Pacific (Martin, *James J. Hill*, 375).

292. I consider Stephen and Smith "Canadian investors" when they lived in Canada, and English investors after they changed their residence. On Smith's role in relation to the Canadian Pacific, see Lamb, *History of the Canadian Pacific*, 81, 106, 196, 204, 238. After Stephen formally left the four-man executive committee of the Canadian Pacific (CP) in 1892, Smith remained a member; when Smith became High Commissioner for Canada in 1896, he still retained his directorship of the CP—until his death in 1914. Also, on the executive committee of the CP in 1892 was R. B. Angus, who had earlier been associated with Hill's railroad ventures and who would become president of the Bank of Montreal, 1910–1913. See Denison, *Canada's First Bank*, II. Lamb's *History of the Canadian Pacific* and Albro Martin's *James J. Hill* were published within a year of each other and should be read together on Hill, Stephen, Smith, and the CP. Many of same individuals and institutions in London were involved with Hill and with the CP. One man associated with both Hill and the CP was Thomas Skinner. Skinner, who was born in Bristol, England, in 1841, began in 1874 to publish the *Stock Exchange Manual*. He served for a time as London agent for the CP and was considered an expert on Anglo-Canadian matters (W. G. Kerr, *Scottish Capital on the American Credit Frontier* [Austin: Texas Historical Association, 1976], 92–94, and Gilbert, *End of the Road*, 33, 71 322). Martin, *James J. Hill*, 413, reports that Skinner, "one of the most efficient London brokers" (p. 376), was one of a group of four (including Hill and Stephen), who signed the so-called London agreement of May 10, 1895, "to acquire the Northern Pacific on behalf of the Great Northern." Martin (p. 413) says Skinner acted for the Deutsche Bank in the 1895 agreement, which I doubt. Lamb (p. 204) tells us that in 1896 Thomas Skinner was a director of the CP. We find serving as chairman of the board of the Pillsbury-Washburn Flour Mills Co., Ltd., in 1910—a company with a St. Paul–Minneapolis connection. See Report of the General Meeting of that company, Sept 23, 1910, in John S. Pillsbury and Family Papers, Minnesota Historical Society, St. Paul. By 1915, if not earlier, Skinner headed the Bank of Montreal's London Advisory Committee (Denison, *Canada's First Bank*,. II, 330). Skinner was never a director of the Bank of Montreal; Kerr is wrong on that. Skinner was, however, in 1914, the deputy governor of the Hudson's Bay Company (Willson, *Lord Strathcona*, II, 463); Strathcona, of course, was the governor.

293. On Stephen's and Smith's roles when the Grand Trunk tried to acquire the "Soo" railroad, see Martin, *James J. Hill*, 288. Hill, of course, was Canadian born, but I don't think that made the difference.

294. Lewis, *America's Stake*, 546.

295. Adler, *British Investment*, 195.

296. Lewis, *America's Stake*, 316.

297. As noted, the Atlantic Ocean notwithstanding, it could conceivably have existed had British railroad owners acquired steamship and railroad holdings in the United States.

298. Jenks, "Britain and American Railway Development," 378. This is picked up by many writers. See, for instance, Roger V. Clements, "British-Controlled Enterprise in the West between 1870 and 1900 and Some Agrarian Reactions," *Agricultural History*, 27 (Oct. 1953): 133: "The enormous British investment in American railways remained strikingly passive and uninfluential"; and ibid., 135, where Clements contrasts the British exercise of control over other investments in the United States with those in railroads.

299. Adler, *British Investment*, xiii. Jenks had far more expertise on the pre-1875 investments than on the later stakes.

300. Ibid., 199–200.

301. Among the British "millionaires" who made their fortunes in U.S. railroads were Hugh McCalmont, Lord Mount Stephen, and Lord Strathcona.

302. Edelstein, *Overseas Investment*, 123, 125, looking only at the "best" American railroad securities for 1870–1913, found that the realized return on shares was 8.41 percent and on bonds 6.03 percent. He omitted securities of railroads that went into default.

303. The default record reveals large losses that Edelstein's coverage omits.

304. Martin, *James J. Hill*, 440. The Harvard economist Ripley, *Railroads*, 10, was equally hostile to foreign investment in general: "Absentee ownership, an evil in any economic connection, has been particularly productive of harm in the case of American Railroads." He is not altogether convincing in explaining his views, but the suggestion was that absentee ownership, "speculation," and lack of interest in operations went together. Perhaps also, Ripley, writing in 1915, was concerned that foreign investment lacked permanence and could be withdrawn with damaging consequences, although he favored its withdrawal. Henry Ledyard's complaint about foreign insistence on dividends to the exclusion of reinvested earnings, quoted earlier, represents the same type of concern.

305. This is a tentative favorable conclusion, and the subject needs far more investigation. Clearly the foreign investors were generally on the side of prudent behavior. They called on outside accountants, especially in the 1890s. See data in Price Waterhouse Archives, London, Box 1. Daggett, *Railroad Reorganization*, 341, concluded in 1908, however, that the foreign investor who intervened to "apportion charges between operating and capital accounts in a way unsuited to American conditions has been upon occasion a cause of disaster." There were a number of reorganizations in which the foreign banker's role was also questionable, owing to lack of knowledge. The *Investors' Review*, London, in the early 1890s was critical of the role of the British in reorganizations, arguing that the benefits went to the participants in the reorganization and not to the railroads or to the investors. See, for example, *Investors' Review*, 2 (Nov. 1893): 637–645; 4 (July 1894): 21–24; and 4 (Sept. 1894): 171–173.

306. Marlborough, "Virginia Mines and American Rails," *Fortnightly Review*, n.s., 69 (March 1891): 792.

307. One is struck by how many studies of U.S. railroad operations fail even to mention any foreign role! Muriel Hidy, in a personal comment, attributed this not to the passivity of the investors but to the inadequacy of railroad historians in dealing with railroad finance. Some books deal with railroad finance—that is, the types of bonds issued—but not with the sources of capital.

308. They wanted information to be sure everything was proper. One man who

handled British investments in American railroads wrote, for example, in distress over the Great Northern's *Annual Report, 1894–95,* adding, "The investor is a patient beast and will stand anything so long as he understands" (Gaspard Farrer to Lord Mount Stephen, Nov. 26, 1895, quoted in Gilbert, *End of the Road,* 66).

309. On the railroad's land sales, see John D. Hicks, *The Populist Revolt* (Minneapolis: University of Minnesota Press, 1931), 11–15. A total of 180 million acres were given to the railroads in federal land grants; more than 100 million were finally "patented by the railroad companies" (Riegel, *Western Railroads,* 41–43). Typically railroads sold land abroad to potential settlers, to people in Europe who would immigrate to the United States. Such sales (also made by land companies) are not included in this study because the owner of the land became an American resident. Railroads also sold to speculators—in the United States and in Europe—who bought land and planned future subdivisions. Railroads sold to cattle ranchers, domestic and foreign. See ibid., 282–283. Basically, railroads wanted buyers who would use the land; they wanted the output of farms to be carried on the railroads, providing traffic and, of course, revenues. On railroad land sales to Scottish investors, see Jackson, *Enterprising Scot,* 31, 101, 104.

310. See Henry Villard letters, Dec. 17, 1881, and May 4, 1882, in Northern Pacific, President Letters Sent, vol. 24, Minnesota Historical Society, St. Paul, Minn. These were letters to nonresident foreigners. U.S. Sen., 48th Cong., 1st sess., 1884, Exec. Doc. 181, 2, noted the investment of Sykes & Hughes, an English firm doing business in Northern Dakota; Sykes & Hughes was also said to own 85,000 acres in Iowa and Minnesota in 1884. See Jacob Van der Zee, *The British in Iowa* (Iowa City: State Historical Society of Iowa, 1922), 116. See ibid., 260n, about the May 1881 visit of a "Mr. Sykes of Manchester" (Stockport is near Manchester) to Iowa to look at his lands. He probably acquired the North Dakota land from the Northern Pacific on that trip. According to Larry A. McFarlane, "British Agricultural Investment in the Dakotas, 1877–1953," *Business and Economic History,* ed. Paul Uselding, 2nd ser., V (1976), 115, 119, 125, the Richard Sykes Estate, Manchester, attempted to attract settlers to lands near the James River Valley of North Dakota. Richard Sykes in 1881 published *Land and Farming in North Dakota on the Northern Pacific Railroad.*

311. There were four Close brothers, all born in England: John Brooks (b. 1850), James Brooks (b. 1851), William Brooks (b. 1853), and Frederick Brooks (b. 1854). The last three migrated to America, while John Brooks Close remained in Manchester, providing his younger brothers "with a good deal of money to invest, not only for himself but also for his English friends." See Van der Zee, *The British in Iowa,* 57, 258, 69. The brothers' first ventures were in buying land in Iowa, starting in 1878 (ibid., 57, 61, 99, 121). Their firm Close Brothers by 1879 had offices in London and Manchester to encourage immigration to Iowa (p. 77). By 1884 they had more land in Minnesota than in Iowa (p. 116). The three older Close brothers had gone to Cambridge University, where they were oarsmen. Another Cambridge oarsman was Constantine W. Benson, son of the Robert Benson who had acted on behalf of the Illinois Central in London; Constantine was the brother of Robert Benson, who would become active in Robert Benson & Co. and Merchants' Trust, Ltd. C. W. Benson became a partner of the Close brothers, 1880–1884, in Close, Benson, and Co., and seems to have opened doors for them in London. See ibid., 81, 100, 102–103, 114, 170, 277n. Van der Zee did not realize the Illinois Central connection. See Gates, *The Illinois Central,* 224, 317, 348. In an article discussing the Chicago, St. Paul and Kansas City Railroad, whose securities were "sponsored" by Robert Benson & Co. in London in 1886, the *Investors' Review,* 2 (Nov. 1893): 640, commented on Robert Benson's interest in Iowa and his role in relation to that railroad's successor, the Chicago Great Western.

312. Van der Zee, *The British in Iowa,* 103ff. The Close brothers managed this company, 1881–1884, when C. W. Benson took over the management. The Duke of Sutherland was said to have a large interest in this venture (ibid., 105, 114, 104, 107). The Iowa Land Company Ltd., was reported to have raised between $1.125 million and $2.5 million in England (p. 104). The company invested in Minnesota as well as in Iowa (pp. 1–6). It also had some foreclosed land in South Dakota (see McFarlane, "British Investment—Dakotas," 115).

313. Larry A. McFarlane, "British Investment in Midwestern Farm Mortgages and Land, 1875–1900: A Comparison of Iowa and Kansas," *Agricultural History,* 47 (Jan. 1974): 189. In November 1921 William B. Close, then in London, wrote Van der Zee that the Kansas Land Company's 100,000 acres had been sold "within a year" at double the price. He indicated that the acreage in Kansas purchased from the Atchison was 100,000 and, at the same time, the Close brothers had bought a third 100,000 acres in the Texas Panhandle, acreage that was sold in the 1890s at a loss (Van der Zee, *The British in Iowa,* 118). In 1885 Close Brothers incorporated their firm and headquartered themselves in Chicago, carrying on a farm mortgage business, borrowing money at 4 to 5 percent in England, and, according to Van der Zee, "realizing from six and one half to seven percent net on their loans in this country" (ibid., 118). Close Brothers apparently intermediated British monies into Wisconsin; see Table 6.8. They were involved in a Colorado irrigation project and participated in the White Pass and Yukon Railway in Alaska, which they financed from London. Frederick died in 1890 and James in 1910. John Brooks Close, who had remained in England and supplied his younger brothers with capital, died on March 20, 1914. At a date unknown, William Brooks Close returned to live in England (ibid., 106, 118–119, 248). In 1914 he was chairman of Mortgage and Debenture Company, Ltd., London (registered June 17, 1897). This company, with a capital of £500,000, advanced money in the United States and Canada "on first charges on real estate or other securities" (*Stock Exchange Official Intelligence for 1914,* 1047).

314. Winkler, *Foreign Bonds,* 266 (Alabama and Chattanooga). On the Texas and Pacific, see Lewis, *America's Stake,* 82. A few years later Robert Fleming would be involved in reorganizing the Texas and Pacific on behalf of foreign investors. See text of this chapter.

315. Virginia H. Taylor, *The Franco-Texan Land Company* (Austin: University of Texas Press, 1969), 113ff. The $4.1 million was the face value of the railroad bonds surrendered for stock in the land company.

316. J. Fred Rippy, "British Investments in Texas Land and Livestock," *Southwestern Historical Quarterly,* 58 (Jan. 1955): 332.

317. On the Société Foncière et Agricole des États Unis, see Taylor, *Franco-Texan Land Company,* 166ff. On the principal Dutch company, see my text.

318. On the United States Mortgage Company, see H. Peers Brewer, "Eastern Money and Western Mortgages," *Business History Review,* 50 (Autumn 1976): 362–372, and Ivan Wright, *Farm Mortgage Financing* (New York: McGraw-Hill, 1923), 318. According to Brewer, by the mid-1870s the Europeans were generating more funds from the sale of bonds than the firm's New York board could lend, and profits were penalized as interest-bearing liabilities increased relative to interest-bearing assets (Brewer, "Eastern Money," 371). Yet the firm survived and, according to Perine, in January 1893 began a trust and deposit business; it was in 1895 renamed United States Mortgage and Trust Company. See Edward Ten Broeck Perine, *The Story of the Trust Companies* (New York: G. P. Putnam's Sons, 1916), 202–204. Wright (p. 318) says it gave up mortgage lending in the 1890s.

319. On these land mortgage companies, see Allan G. Bogue, *Money at Interest*

(Ithaca, N. Y.: Cornell University Press, 1955), 77, and passim. Land mortgages carried high interest rates and thus seemed particularly attractive (ibid., 88). See also Wright, *Farm Mortgage Financing*, 315–322, and Brewer, "Eastern Money," 356–380. On British interests, see Larry A. McFarlane, "British Investment and the Land: Nebraska, 1877–1946," *Business History Review*, 57 (Summer 1983): 237–272; his "British Investment—Iowa and Kansas," 179–198; and his "British Investment— Dakotas," 116. See also Jackson, *Enterprising Scot*, 254–255; Bogue, *Money at Interest*, 88, 90, 117, 128–129, 132–136, 191–192; and Kerr, *Scottish Capital*, 190. In 1887 Jarvis-Conklin Mortgage Trust established a London office to intermediate monies to the United States (Clyde William Phelps, *The Foreign Expansion of American Banks* [1927; rpt. New York: Arno Press, 1976], 133). By 1887 J. B. Watkins Land Mortgage Company also had a London branch (Bogue, *Money at Interest*, 132). Its predecessor company, J. B. Watkins and Co., had opened the office in London in 1878 (see Inventory of the Jabez Bunting Watkins Collection at the University of Kansas, in *Business History Newsletter* [Oct. 1983], 6). The Lombard Investment Company brought in Dutch and German as well as British money (Swaine, *Cravath Firm*, I, 548). McFarlane, "British Investment—Dakotas," 121, identified ten American mortgage companies that transferred British money into the United States. He wrote, "In London, Edinburgh, and other British cities all 10 firms opened branch offices and retained agents to sell debentures with four-to-seven-year terms and 4 to 6 percent interest, or guaranteed farm mortgages bearing 6 percent or more." Seven of these firms entered the Dakotas in the 1880s, and three in the 1890s (data from McFarlane, Jan. 27, 1986).

320. In Kansas between 1889 and 1893, there were 11,122 foreclosures on farm mortgages (Riegel, *Western Railroads*, 286). It is important, however, to note that mortgage companies, domestic or foreign, did not want to foreclose; they made profits through making loans, not through owning land. See McFarlane, "British Investment— Iowa and Kansas," 196.

321. U.S. House, "Land Titles to Aliens in the United States," 48th Cong., 2nd sess., H. Rept. 2308, Jan. 20, 1885, 2.

322. Ibid. The 21-million-acre figure was frequently cited, but the *National Economist Almanac of 1890* stated that 61.9 million acres were "owned by aliens." Quoted in N. B. Ashby, *The Riddle of the Sphinx* (Chicago: Mercantile Publishing, 1892), 93. No source was given.

323. U.S. House, "Land Titles," 2.

324. This was also true of the French and Dutch firms. Société Foncière et Agricole des États Unis (formed in 1879) had as its president the Comte de Constantin. The Dutch Maxwell Land Grant Company had barons as directors. One western historian (Herbert O. Brayer) entitled an article on cattle ranches "When the Dukes Went West," *The Westerners Brand Book*, IV (1948), 55–76. See also Lewis Nordyke, *Cattle Empire* (New York: William Morrow, 1949), chap. 5, on "Prairie Lords," esp. p. 77.

325. See Jim Berry Pearson, *The Maxwell Land Grant* (Norman: University of Oklahoma Press, 1961), 72–280. The Dutch were still involved in 1961. For Sherwin's lifestyle and ouster, I relied on the letters of a young Dutchman (Albert Verwey) reprinted in Brenda M. Wolvekamp-Baxter, "New Mexico, 1883: The Maxwell Grant and the Cimarron Country in the letters of Albert Verwey," *New Mexico Historical Review*, 59 (April 1979): 125–147. Verwey refers to Sherwin's reigning over 1,200,000 acres. People were notably vague when it came to that much land. On the Maxwell Land Grant Company, see also Bosch, *Nederlandse Beleggingen*, 180–181, 663–666. Bosch gives the capital of the Maxwell Land Grant Company as £1 million. In Washington, D.C., it was not uncommon to talk about the "Holland Land Company" in New

Mexico. See, for example, *Congressional Record*, 51st Cong., 1st sess., Aug. 20, 1890, 8878.

326. On Scully, see Homer E. Socolofsky, *Landlord William Scully* (Lawrence: Regents Press of Kansas, 1979), and his earlier "William Scully: Ireland and America, 1840–1900," *Agricultural History*, 48 (Jan. 1974): 155–175. Still useful is Paul Wallace Gates, *Frontier Landlords and Pioneer Tenants* (Ithaca, N.Y.: Cornell University Press, 1945), 34–61, and John Davis, "Alien Landlordism in America," in *The Land Question from Various Points of View*, ed. C. F. Taylor, (Philadelphia: C. F. Taylor [1898]), 55–59. Scully's land holdings were not included on the 1884 lists. See Table 6.8. A *Philadelphia Bulletin* article of 1909, cited in Lewis, *America's Stake*, 568, gave the "Scully estate" as 2 million acres. This is clearly an error. Scully died in 1906. His wife was his heir. She was an American citizen and retained a house in Washington, D.C., but from 1912 to her death in 1932, she "usually" resided in London (Socolofsky, *Landlord*, 137, 146). Scully himself had become a U.S. citizen in 1900, but he seems to have lived in London much of the time between 1900 and 1906. I would—using residence as a criteria—call the Scully properties those of a "foreign" investor.

327. McFarlane, "British Investment—Nebraska," 271, and his "British Investment—Dakotas," 122. McFarlane to Wilkins, Jan. 23, 1984, indicates that he plans to modify the Missouri percentage, but "it should not change by more than one percent" (that is, it will remain small).

328. McFarlane, "British Investment—Iowa and Kansas," 197. McFarlane's figures are for 1890. According to Van der Zee, the "zenith" for British land ownership in Iowa and Minnesota was in 1884. See his *The British in Iowa*, 114. The year 1890 is six years after the intense agitation against British ownership had begun.

329. The British Land and Mortgage Company of America, Ltd., opened its American "field office" in Manhattan, Kansas, in 1883. It had two livestock farms, a wheat farm, a grain elevator, and a flour mill and became active in farming. After losses, the firm sold its properties. See McFarland, "British Investment—Iowa and Kansas," 191. (the exact date of the sale of the land is not clear, but it was probably in the late 1880s.) On the Duke of Sutherland, see Van der Zee, *British in Iowa*, 103–104, 107.

330. James Macdonald, *Food from Far West* (London and Edinburgh: William P. Nimmo, 1878), 82. I am excluding resident investors; perhaps his partner, Alexander Grant remained in Britain.

331. C. Vann Woodward, *Origins of the New South* (Baton Rouge: Louisiana State University Press, 1951), 119; Mira Wilkins, *Foreign Enterprise in Florida* (Gainesville: University Presses of Florida, 1979), 11; Edward Crapol, *America for Americans* (Westport, Conn.: Greenwood, 1973), 114; and *Stock Exchange Year Book, 1890*, 556. The idea seems to have been that the company would provide mortgages on the land it sold. The Florida Land and Mortgage Company last appears in the *Stock Exchange Official Intelligence* in 1899; it was replaced by the Land and Trust Company of Florida, which seems to have disappeared after 1906. See ibid.

332. Woodward, *Origins*, 119; and Crapol, *America for Americans*, 114. On this investment, see Robert L. Brandfon, *Cotton Kingdom of the New South* (Cambridge, Mass.: Harvard University Press, 1967), 52–59.

333. Joseph C. Bailey, *Seaman A. Knapp* (New York: Columbia University Press, 1945), 109–123, and Bogue, *Money at Interest*, 191–197, 126. This large holding does not appear to be included in the 21 million acres identified by the House Committee (Table 6.8). According to *Stock Exchange Official Intelligence for 1914*, 1057, NALTC's original land acquisition was 850,000 acres. That is not inconsistent with my text, since the 1.5 million acres joins Watkins' holdings with those of NALTC.

334. *Stock Exchange Official Intelligence for 1914*, 1057.

335. See 1889 and 1903–1906 extracts from Edwin Waterhouse, "His Story," n.d., in the Price Waterhouse Archives, London, 43, 113–118, 126, 128–132, and *Stock Exchange Official Intelligence for 1914*, 842.

336. Jackson, *Enterprising Scot*, 222–231.

337. Ibid., 232.

338. Ibid., 222ff.

339. Ibid., 220–222.

340. Muscogee Lumber Company, Seminole Lumber Company and Geo. W. Robinson & Co. See *Burdett's Official Intelligence, 1895*, 1156–57. On Southern States Land and Timber Company, Ltd., see also James Stillman to Archibald Balfour, March 19, 1891, Stillman Papers, Special Collections, Columbia University Library. Stillman, on learning that the United States Trust and Guarantee Corporation, Ltd., owned stock in this firm, urged it to sell such securities. He wrote, "The expenses of administration seem to me enormous. My impresion is that the company [Southern States Land and Timber Company, Ltd.] has paid an exorbitant price for its property, that the timber is being cut off rapidly, which is about all the value there is to the property and that the land cannot be disposed of for agricultural purposes for very many years." Also on this firm, see the *Investors' Review*, London, 4 (July 1894): 64. Lord Rosebery had a sizable investment. This firm last appeared in *Burdett's Official Intelligence* in 1898.

341. Bacon, "American International Indebtedness," 269, and Palgrave, "An English View," 197–198. The four major U.S. mortgage companies went bankrupt in 1893. On the losses, see Jackson, *Enterprising Scot*, 254–255, and Chapter 14.

342. Wallis Hunt, *Heirs of Great Adventure* (London: Balfour, Williamson, 1960), II, 25, for the large 1910 venture ("Brentwood") in California.

343. The initial purchase involved 65,000 acres; the amount was later raised to 180,000 acres. See Maurice Corina, *Trust in Tobacco* (London: Michael Joseph, 1975); Dickens, "The Transition Period," 243; and *Moody's, 1914* (on the extended acreage).

344. Dickens, "The Transition Period," 244–245.

345. *Moody's, 1914*. This brief (1903–1908) foray into what seems to have been backward integration by Bryant & May came soon after that company had clarified its relationship with its joint-venture partner, the leading American match producer— Diamond Match Company. The latter had built a factory in England in 1896 and in 1897 formed a British affiliate (Diamond Match Company, *Annual Report, 1897*). In 1901 Bryant & May acquired Diamond Match's British affiliate, along with its factory; in exchange, Diamond Match obtained controlling interest in Bryant & May. According to a 1949 investigation, between 1912 and 1920 a large part of the American-owned shares in Bryant & May were acquired by British shareholders; Diamond Match continued to hold a minority interest (Report of Commissioner, Combines Investigation Act, Department of Justice, *Matches*, Ottawa, Dec. 27, 1949, 7).

In 1901 a division-of-market agreement was made between Diamond Match and Bryant & May. *Perhaps* in 1903 Bryant & May's "parent," Diamond Match, wanted aid in financing the timberland purchase. *Perhaps* as Diamond Match became less interested in Bryant & May, it was pleased to have the latter out of the United States. I do not know why in 1908 Bryant & May sold its interest in the California venture. As will be evident in other cases (tobacco, for example), international division-of-market arrangements did not preclude supply-oriented—that is export-related—investments by European companies in America (Imperial Tobacco, for example, had such stakes after it agreed not to manufacture in the United States for the American market—see Chapter 9). On Bryant & May's international business connections with Diamond Match, see Håken Lindgren, *Corporate Growth: The Swedish Match Industry in a Global*

Setting (Stockholm: Liber Förlag, 1979), 57–58, 382, 294, 287. Lindgren does not indicate when Diamond Match became a minority holder of Bryant & May securities, although he says (p. 382), citing a 1950s source, that the transition took place "very rapidly." (Between 1912 and 1920, as cited in the 1949 investigation above, is hardly "very rapid.") If Bryant & May was still under American control in the period 1903–1908, when the timberland investment was made (which seems likely), probably its investment should be viewed as that of an American company using its British affiliate and should not be included at all as a "foreign" direct investment. (I have, for example, excluded the U.S. investments of the known-to-be-American-controlled British-American Tobacco Company in the pre–World War I years on that basis—see Chapter 9.) On the other hand, Bryant & May did raise monies in the United Kingdom for this investment, so some "foreign" investment is in evidence. Karl-Gustaf Hildebrand, *Expansion Crisis Reconstruction, 1917–1939* (Stockholm: Liber Förlag, 1985), 25, suggests another reason behind this Bryant & May investment in American timberland: Diamond Match possessed match-making machines that it sold abroad; the machines were not suitable for the woods used by Bryant & May. What could be more obvious: Bryant & May—under the control of Diamond Match—would invest in and import American matchwood species and thus be able to use its parent's machines!

346. Bosch, *Nederlandse Beleggingen*, 182–183.

7. Precious Metals and Coal, Iron, Steel

1. Clark C. Spence, "British Investment and the American Mining Frontier, 1860–1914," *New Mexico Historical Review*, 36 (April 1961): 121—henceforth cited as "British Investment." Spence's article excluded the Southeast, the Pacific Coast states, and Alaska. The companies incorporated between 1860 and 1901 (518 of them) were listed in his earlier book, *British Investments and the American Mining Frontier, 1860–1901* (Ithaca, N.Y.: Cornell University Press, 1958), 241–260. Even earlier, Spence wrote "British Investment and Oregon Mining, 1860–1900," *Oregon Historical Quarterly*, 57 (June 1957); 101–112—henceforth cited as "British Investment—Oregon." On British investment in California mining, see Albin Joachim Dahl, "British Investment in California Mining, 1870–1890," Ph.D. diss., University of California, Berkeley, 1961.

2. Spence, *British Investments*, 233. He never defines *significant*. The sums in mining (both U.S. and foreign) were small, for example, compared with investments (domestic and foreign) in the railroads. It is the contribution of foreign investors in mining relative to that of U.S. investors in this sector that appears significant.

3. Edward Ashmead, *Twenty-five Years of Mining, 1880–1904* (London: Mining Journal, 1909), 81–90. Ashmead included geographical regions excluded by Spence. See also Alfred P. Tischendorf, "North Carolina and the British Investor, 1880–1910," *North Carolina Historical Review*, 32 (Oct. 1955): 512–518; Tischendorf studied mining investments in that single state in that thirty-year period.

4. See Chapter 4 on the Emma mine; Spence, *British Investments*, chap. 8; and Rodman W. Paul, *Mining Frontiers of the Far West, 1848–1880* (New York: Holt, Rinehart & Winston, 1963), 152–153.

5. T. A. Rickard, *Retrospect* (New York: McGraw-Hill, 1937), 36.

6. *Mineral Industry, 1893*, 806–807.

7. W. Turrentine Jackson, *The Enterprising Scot: Investors in the American West after 1873* (Edinburgh: Edinburgh University Press, 1968), 188–189, lists thirty-seven western American mining enterprises registered in Scotland in the years 1872–1913. Of these, all except eight were wound up within ten years of their formation; only three survived past 1913, and one of those had virtually shut down in 1913! The companies

had properties in California, Colorado, Utah, Arizona, Idaho, South Dakota, Missouri, and Nevada.

8. Spence, "British Investment," 127. And even this is deceptive, for, as noted, it was common practice for a mining company to pay an initial dividend out of borrowings, issue a glowing report, and hopefully attract a wave of new capital.

9. Spence, British Investments, 68–69. According to Mineral Industry, 1893, 236, between 1882 and 1893 Arizona Copper Company paid no dividends. Spence, "British Investment," 127, however, notes that the Arizona Copper Company was "the only British [mining] concern in the Southwest which returned at least one hundred per cent on the original investment."

10. Cleona Lewis, America's Stake in International Investments (Washington, D.C.: Brookings Institution, 1938), 113, feels that in the years 1904–1914, especially, many foreign investors transferred their mining investments from the United States to other areas—to take advantage of new discoveries elsewhere.

11. Based on my own scrutiny of shareholder records. For the most part, owners were British; albeit because London was the center for "mining finance," frequently investors from the European continent made their "foreign" (including U.S.) investments through companies set up in the city.

12. H. Osborne O'Hagan, Leaves from My Life (London: John Lane, 1929), I, 79–83.

13. Mineral Industry, 1892, 483, 490.

14. An individual, a group of friends, or a family group that registered a mining company might never go outside the group for funding. The firm would never be traded.

15. Some companies went through three or four reorganizations, reemerging with new names and new sponsors. See Stock Exchange Year Book and Register of Companies, London. Records on a number of these short-lived mining ventures—mainly those in Colorado—were microfilmed in connection with the "Western Range Cattle Industry Study," Manuscript Room, Library of Congress, Acc. 11,092 (henceforth cited as WRCIS). Sometimes companies were registered, but promoters failed in their attempt to float them (Dahl, "British Investment," 130–132). It was not only British mining companies in America that had short lives. Peter Payne estimated "the average length of life of dissolved Scottish companies" (my italics) was 16.4 years, while that of the overseas mining and quarrying companies was a mere 6.4 years—the shortest duration of any industrial category he studied (The Early Scottish Limited Companies, 1856–1895 [Edinburgh: Scottish Academic Press, 1980], 101).

16. Spence, British Investments, 92–93; see also Rickard, Retrospect, 30.

17. Spence, British Investments, 170, quoting an 1875 report, and 174, an 1876 report. See also Jackson, Enterprising Scot, 14, and Spence, British Investments, chap. 6, on British attempts to introduce management.

18. Quoted in Spence, British Investments, 198.

19. Mineral Industry, 1893, 808. On Vincent, see W. Turrentine Jackson, "British Impact on the Utah Mining Industry," Utah Historical Quarterly, 31 (1963): 352, 367–369. When in 1886 a French firm, Société Anonyme des Mines de Lexington, appointed Giovanni Lavagnino as its engineer manager, an American editor commented that "if the company were to appoint the entire French corps of mining engineers, it could not make its mines pay, nor bring back its badly invested money." Management from abroad, in short, sometimes was futile if the whole affair was a scam. See Clark C. Spence, Mining Engineers and the American West (New Haven: Yale University Press, 1970), 9–10.

20. Jackson, "British Impact," 370. These comments were made in relation to British investments in Utah, which did involve special difficulties, but the problems

were not unique to Utah. Spence, "British Investment," 130–132, is particularly useful on the difficulties the British had in managing over distance. He claims that a sizable minority of those sent to intervene were selected "for their appeal to the 'lord-loving [British] public,' rather than for administrative or mining experience" (p. 130).

21. Spence, *Mining Engineers*, 22–23, 137, 265. Hamilton Smith was born in Kentucky. I do not know the birthplace of DeCrano. Spence calls him an American. For the quotation, see Memorandum of Association, p. 33, Tomboy Gold Mines Company, Ltd., June 7, 1899, WRCIS, reel 72. On the Exploration Company, see Rob Turrell and Jean-Jacques van Helten, "The Rothschilds, the Exploration Company and Mining Finance," *Business History*, 28 (April 1986): 181–205.

22. Rickard, *Retrospect*, 29, 37, 48, 53–54, 75–76.

23. Lewis, *America's Stake*, 90. For more on the U.S. subsidiary (established in 1911), see data in Companies Registration Office, London—microfilm in Bancroft Library, University of California, reel 33.

24. See Williams Haynes, *American Chemical Industry*, 6 vols. (New York: Van Nostrand, 1945–1954), II, 149, on Wilkinson. Gold Fields' interests had California business before Gold Fields American Development Company, Ltd., was formed in 1911. The Consolidated Gold Fields of South Africa, Ltd., whose predecessor was established in 1887, was Cecil Rhodes's company. See Lewis Michell, *The Life and Times of Cecil John Rhodes*, 2 vols. (1910; rpt. New York: Arno Press, 1977), I, 197; A. P. Cartwright, *The Gold Miners* (Cape Town: Purnell, 1962), 85; and Paul Johnson, *Consolidated Gold Fields* (New York: St. Martin's Press, 1987), 21–22, 28–29, 38.

25. Act of March 3, 1887, 24 U.S. Stats. 476.

26. Spence, *British Investments*, 205–213. See also Chapter 16. One way of bypassing the statute was to lease a mine; another was to place the title in the hands of an American who signed a private agreement that the title was actually the property of the foreign-owned corporation. Some investors simply ignored the legislation.

27. Spence's figure of 584 (in "British Investment," 121) excluded companies incorporated in the United States that were owned directly by British residents (that is, not through a British-incorporated company), U.S. enterprises that raised money by selling bonds in the United Kingdom, and British enterprises in the Far West (California, Oregon, and Washington) and in the Southeast. He also omitted Alaska. His figure was confined to mining and milling companies, whereas I am covering "mineral industries." In addition, he excluded all non-British foreign investments in the United States. Many mining companies were small ventures and not chartered in the United Kingdom. A biographer of Weetman Pearson (later Lord Cowdray) casually wrote that before 1914 Pearson, with Robert Price, M.P., "controlled" mines in "Colorado, Montana, Maine [sic]," as well as in Mexico, Australia, and Russia; the "mine" in Maine obviously referred to the place of incorporation, not the location of the mine (Robert Middlemas, *Master Builders* [London: Hutchinson, 1963], 220). Spence's figures did cover 1860–1874; some of the companies were out of business by 1874 and thus should be excluded from my total. I have identified many firms not covered by Ashmead.

28. See figures on gold and silver production in *Journal of the Society of the Arts*, 24 (March 17, 1876): 365.

29. See figures that I compiled for *Harper Encyclopedia of the Modern World* (New York; Harper & Row, 1970), 704, 707. One reader questioned whether "steel" should be considered under the rubric "mineral industries." I am following the path of the pre-1914 *Mineral Industry* yearbooks in including steel.

30. J. E. Spurr, ed., *Political and Commercial Geology and the World's Mineral Resources* (New York: McGraw-Hill, 1920), 464, 466.

31. Ibid., 467–468. California investments, however, continued. Thus, for example,

in April 1910 subscription lists opened in London for bonds of the California-incorporated Natomas Consolidated of California (founded in 1908). Applications to purchase the offering of $5 million 6 per cent first-mortgage twenty-year gold bonds (at par) were to be made to the Hirsch Syndicate, Ltd., London. The California gold-mining company had three London directors "appointed by the purchasing syndicate" (Lord Ribblesdale, Sir Charles Day Rose, and Albert Reitlinger). See *Economist*, 70 (April 2, 1910): 760–761, and *Stock Exchange Official Intelligence for 1914*, 1050–51.

32. On the new 1874–1888 gold-mining investments in California, see Dahl, "British Investment," passim.

33. Spence, *British Investments*, 60, 124. On this property, see *Mineral Industry, 1892*, 178, 477 (on its dividends of $2.6 million, 1883–1892), 223, and 483.

34. Spurr, *Political and Commercial*, 467; Jackson, *Enterprising Scot*, 201ff; and Spence, *British Investments*, 63. For the seventeen companies, see WRCIS, reels 43–45, 63–65.

35. Spence, *British Investments*, 28–29, 107–108, and Jackson, *Enterprising Scot*, 202. Stratton's Independence, Ltd., was established in 1899 with a capital of £1,100,000. WRCIS has eight microfilm reels (reels 65–72) on its shareholders in the period 1899–1915. The sales price of $10 million is repeated in all the literature. The price in the sales agreement, however, was £1 million, less than half the $10 million. Very prominent individuals and firms were investors in this mining activity at the start. See the letter from Geo. Butcher to Registrar of Joint-Stock Companies, May 7, 1908, on the 4,500 stockholders (WRCIS, reel 69). By 1902 key British bankers were convinced that the company was greatly overcapitalized. See Gaspar Farrer to J. W. Sterling, June 11, 1902, Baring Archives, London (henceforth cited as BAL). T. A. Rickard, *A History of American Mining* (New York: McGraw-Hill, 1932), 146, writes of how the stock in this London company "became the sport of reckless promotion." This is clear in WRCIS, reels 65–72, which document the entire process. See also Marshall Sprague, *Money Mountain: The Story of Cripple Creek Gold* (Boston: Little, Brown, 1953), 68–75, 111–132, 162–165 (on Winfield Stratton), 128–129, 211–215 (on Verner Z. Reed, the promoter), and 314 (for the returns to the investors). According to Sprague, Stratton was paid $10 million and Reed $1 million, making the British investment $11 million!

36. Spence, *British Investments*, 243, 68; Cleona Lewis, *America's Stake*, 91. In 1902 Gaspard Farrer wrote J. W. Sterling (June 11, 1902), BAL, that the buyers of the Camp Bird mine included Leopold Hirsch & Co. (participants in South African mining and connected with Wernher, Beit & Co.), about 200,000 shares; Chaplin, Milne, Grenfell & Co., about 200,000 shares; and Venture Corporation and friends, 300,000 shares; in addition, 100,000 shares were taken up in the United States. The Venture Corporation's involvement with the Stratton mine, Farrer thought, would prejudice the British public against Camp Bird, although Hirsch's participation was a favorable sign.

37. Lysis [Eugene Letailleur], *Politique et finance d'avant-guerre* (Paris: Payot, 1920), 304. The Paris Bourse had a kind of "curb" or subsidiary exchange called the Coulisse, on which securities not listed on the "cote officielle," or official list, of the Paris Bourse were traded. See Jacob Viner, "Political Aspects of International Finance," *Journal of Business*, 1 (April 1928): 159. In 1914 Camp Bird, Ltd., faced a crisis when its British chairman of the board, Arthur M. Grenfell, went into bankruptcy, having misused Camp Bird's money in the process. See George H. Nash, *Life of Herbert Hoover* (New York: W. W. Norton, 1983), 563–566. Chaplin, Milne, Grenfell suspended payments in June 1914 (ibid., 564).

38. Paul Dickens, "The Transition Period in American International Financing, 1897 to 1914," Ph.D. diss., George Washington University, 1933, 98. The British Rothschilds were involved in the "Alaska Mexican Gold Mining Co." See N. M. Rothschild & Sons to that firm, June 12, 1895, Rothschild Archives, London (henceforth cited as RAL),

II/10/74. Earlier, in 1890, their Exploration Company, London, had obtained a major stake in the Alaska Treadwell Gold Mining Company (Rickard, *A History*, 59). Rickard reports that the Juneau mines in Alaska were owned by "a private company that included among its principal shareholders Wernher, Beit & Co., the South African promoters and financiers, [and] also the old Exploration Company of London" (ibid., 73). For other British investments in Alaska, see ibid., 68.

39. Clifford H. Ince, *The Royal Bank of Canada: A Chronology, 1864–1949* (n.p., n.d.), 12–13.

40. See Donald Hugh Welsh, "Pierre Wibaux, Bad Lands Rancher," Ph.D. diss., University of Missouri, 1955, 260–264, on French investment in the Clover Leaf Gold Mining Company with its mines in South Dakota. On New Mexico, see Jim Berry Pearson, *The Maxwell Land Grant* (Norman: University of Oklahoma, 1961), 179–182 (Aztec mine—1894), and Nash, *Herbert Hoover*, 47, 604 n. 89, 55 (Rothschilds and Steeple Rock Development Co.—1896). See also U.S. Senate, *Mining Interests of Aliens*, 50th Cong., 2nd sess., 1889, S. Rept. 2690, 18.

41. Spurr, *Political and Commercial*, 467–468.

42. Spence, *British Investments*, 48, 68, and Lewis, *America's Stake*, 91. For the earlier unsuccessful British experiences in Idaho gold mining and then the De Lamar Mining Company, see W. Turrentine Jackson, "British Capital in Northwest Mines," *Pacific Northwest Quarterly*, 47 (July 1956): 77–82, 84–85.

43. Tischendorf, "North Carolina," 512–518.

44. Spurr, *Political and Commercial*, 496.

45. Turrell and van Helten, "The Rothschilds," 183, suggest that the Rothschilds' key role in buying and selling gold in London had led to their investments in gold mining. See also Chapter 3, note 249.

46. Spurr, *Political and Commercial*, 480. Regrettably, I do not have 1914 figures.

47. Once South African gold mining began, many of the British interests were diverted in that direction, although—as noted in the text—companies that were involved in South Africa were also in American mining. Consolidated Gold Fields of South Africa's principal U.S. subsidiary was Gold Fields American Development Company, Ltd., which in turn had interests in the Yuba Consolidated Gold Fields and other American gold-mining companies (Lewis, *America's Stake*, 90). U.S. gold production figures are in U.S. Bureau of the Census, *Historical Statistics of the United States* (Washington, D.C., 1960), 371. On South African production, see figures I prepared for *Harper Encyclopaedia*, 712.

48. William Letwin, ed., *A Documentary History of American Economic Policy since 1789* (New York: W. W. Norton, 1972), 256.

49. Milton Friedman and Ana Jacobson Schwartz, *A Monetary History of the United States, 1867–1960* (Princeton, N.J.: Princeton University Press, 1963), 91.

50. S. G. Checkland, *The Mines of Tharsis* (London: George Allen & Unwin, 1967), 126–133, is excellent on the development of the MacArthur-Forrest process. The Cassel Gold Extracting Company, Ltd. (renamed Cassel Cyanide Company in 1906), Glasgow, acquired ownership of the MacArthur-Forrest process patents in 1887. Between 1888 and 1893 the process was tested in the major gold fields of the world, including the United States, and the Cassel Company began to license the process. According to Checkland, it formed a subsidiary in the United States to license the use of the MacArthur-Forrest process. By 1896, however, in the Transvaal, England, and Germany, the patents were ruled void, and the process was free for all to use. The Cassel Company became a major cyanide producer in the United Kingdom—but not in the United States. For the relationship between DEGUSSA and the Cassel Gold Extracting Company, see L. F. Haber, *The Chemical Industry, 1900–1930* (Oxford: Clarendon Press,

1971), 77. Keep this story in mind and then read Jackson, *Enterprising Scot*, 159–161, 188, for what happened on the American side between and among (1) the Glasgow company, Cassell [sic] Gold Extracting Company, Ltd., (2) a Denver company "with rights to the MacArthur-Forrest process," (3) the Tabor Investment Company (with interests in Colorado gold mines), and (4) the Gold and Silver Extraction Company of America, Ltd. (which had a director from the Cassel Gold Extracting Company, Ltd). The Gold and Silver Extraction Company of America, Ltd., was formed in Glasgow in 1893 with a capital of £110,000. It acquired the Simpson process patent (which was apparently similar to the MacArthur-Forrest one). Even after 1896, when the Mac-Arthur-Forrest process became free for all to use, this company was still attempting to raise monies from Scottish investors. It went out of business in 1904. This firm was at formation a subsidiary of the Cassel Gold Extracting Company, but by 1899 its parent was selling shares. See data in Companies Registration Office, Edinburgh—microfilm in the Bancroft Library, University of California, reel 16/B.

51. L. F. Haber, *The Chemical Industry during the Nineteenth Century* (Oxford: Clarendon Press, 1969), 125. The metal-brokering business of Cohen (1790–1856) became, in 1881, Metallgesellschaft.

52. Data from James Gifford to W. W. Wilson, Jan. 22, 1926. Du Pont Papers, Eleutherian-Mills Historical Library, Wilmington, Del. This document describes Franz Roessler as the son of the founder of DEGUSSA. It is not clear whether he was the son or grandson of Ernest Friedrich Roessler.

53. Alien Property Custodian, *Report, 1918–1919*, 56, henceforth cited as *APC Report*.

54. Haynes, *American Chemical Industry*, I, 282.

55. Ibid.; *APC Report*, 56; and Haber, *Chemical Industry, 1900–1930*, 77. The Aluminium Company, Ltd. (formed in England in 1887–88) was involved, because for many years DEGUSSA had purchased its metallic sodium requirements from this firm. The Aluminium Company had produced metallic sodium in order to make aluminum by the Deville process, which was superseded by the more efficient Hall-Héroult method (see Chapter 8 of my book). Aluminium Company, Ltd., had stopped making aluminum but continued manufacturing metallic sodium, using a technology developed by the American Hamilton Y. Castner and selling its output to DEGUSSA. When in 1890 Castner devised a superior method of obtaining metallic sodium by electrolysis of fused salt, the Aluminium Company, Ltd., acquired rights to this new process. In 1900 the British firm Castner-Kellner Alkali Company would acquire Aluminium Company, Ltd. On Aluminium Company, Ltd., see *Mineral Industry, 1892*, 13–14; *Mineral Industry, 1901*, 594–595; and Haber, *Chemical Industry, 1900–1930*, 77.

56. *APC Report*, 56.

57. Ibid., 37. Martha Moore Trescott, *The Rise of the American Electrochemicals Industry, 1880–1910* (Westport, Conn.: Greenwood Press, 1981), 68, quotes two historians of the Niagara Falls electrochemical industry to the effect that "R & H operated the plant and acted as sales agent for the products of the plant, among which were metallic sodium, sodium cyanide and sodium peroxide." Data from 1914 in Record Group (RG) 59, 165.102/196, and later information in RG 131, Box 200, National Archives, Washington, D.C., verify the manufacture of metallic sodium at Niagara Falls but suggest that the cyanide *may* have been produced at the German-owned plant in Perth Amboy, New Jersey.

58. Data in RG 131, Box 200. See also Trescott, *Electrochemicals Industry*, 68.

59. Erich W. Zimmermann, *World Resources and Industries* (New York: Harper & Bros., 1933), 731.

60. See Chapter 4. After its fiasco and other bad experiences with Utah silver

mines, the British tended to shy away from all investments in Utah (Jackson, "British Impact," 372). Between 1875 and 1900 only one new British silver-mining company was successfully launched in that state, compared with about fifteen in the years 1871–1873 (ibid., 374). The British were less cautious in other states.

61. *Mineral Industry, 1892,* 476.

62. Spence, *British Investments,* 68, 245, 264.

63. Ibid., 241–260.

64. Paul, *Mining Frontiers,* 111.

65. *Mineral Industry, 1892,* 477, 478, 490. Actually it mined both silver and gold. See U.S. Senate, *Mining Interests of Aliens,* 17.

66. *Mineral Industry, 1893,* 311.

67. Rickard, *Retrospect,* 53.

68. The Anaconda mine, for example, began as a silver mine. It became the pre-eminent copper mine, but for many years, because it produced silver as a by-product, it also had the country's largest silver output. See Thomas R. Navin, *Copper and Copper Mining* (Tucson: University of Arizona Press, 1978), 202–203.

69. Spurr, *Political and Commercial,* 498, 500, and Zimmermann, *World Resources,* 737.

70. The Rothschilds (British and French) were heavily involved in silver, in part because of their role in copper and lead, but also independently. See John McKay, "The House of Rothschild (Paris) as a Multinational Industrial Enterprise, 1875–1914," in *Multinational Enterprise in Historical Perspective,* ed. Alice Teichova et al. (Cambridge: Cambridge University Press, 1986), 76–78. I found in the RAL the following data on the Rothschild's silver trade: In 1897 the Rothschilds in London agreed to act "as agents for the sale of silver in Europe, and intended for shipment to Europe, of the silver produced by the works of Messrs. Guggenheim [,] The Omaha Smelting Co [,] and the Cons-Kansas City Smelting and Refg. Co. . . . In disposing of this silver the Messrs. Rothschild will bring to bear in behalf of and the interest of the smelters the full advantage of their superior knowledge and information concerning demand for and sources of demand for silver and the market conditions surrounding same, and except as to Commission from Government Clients, the Messrs. Rothschild shall give to the smelters the full results of sales. . . The smelters shall pay to the Messrs. Rothschild for the selling of silver a Commission of 1/8% on sales by them made" (undated [1897] memorandum, RAL VII/36/0).

A large quantity of silver was sold by the Rothschilds under this arrangement (see RAL VI/11/64, and RAL I/0/110–111), whereby the Rothschilds acted as broker. The Guggenheims were pleased that the Rothschilds were able—through their timing of the sales—to obtain "above the London official [price]," but urged on them "the advisability" of the policy "of selling our silver . . . by distributing sales over the week in which silver is shipped in preference to anticipating the market" (M. Guggenheim's Sons to N. M. Rothschild & Sons, Feb. 16, 1900, RAL VII/36/5). In April 1901 the Guggenheims acquired control over American Smelting and Refining Company, and on April 19 they cabled the Rothschilds: "Merger has been effected. In order promote best interests all stockholders, promote harmony, avoid conflict of interests it has been deemed advisable to sell all silver through United Metals Selling Co. We . . . regret necessity for discontinuing present channel." The Guggenheims followed up this cable with a letter explaining that "certain very prominent interests" were "absolutely im-movable on the matter of the silver sales" and had the Guggenheims not waived their "desire to continue transactions through your house . . . the consolidation would have been defeated . . . We shall hope that nevertheless a most friendly feeling will continue to exist between your house and our own" (M. Guggenheim's Sons to N. M. Rothschild & Sons, April 19, 1901, RAL VII/36/11). The United Metals Selling Company was a Lewisohn Brothers' company; see John Moody, *Truth about Trusts* (Chicago: Moody's, 1904), 49–51, and Mira Wilkins, *The Emergence of Multinational Enterprise* (Cambridge, Mass.: Harvard University Press, 1970), 268n. On the silver sales, I am indebted to suggestions from Dr. Stanley Chapman and help from the Rothschild archivists (Yvonne Clarke and Simone Mace).

71. For useful discussion, see English Committee of the Alabama 8 per cent Gold State Bonds of 1870, *Hill Country of Alabama, USA* (London: E. & F. N. Spon, 1878), 6–9 (henceforth cited as *Hill Country*).

72. Quoted in ibid., 22. The description of Sir Lowthian Bell is from T. H. Burnham and G. O. Hoskins, *Iron and Steel in Britain, 1870–1930* (London: George Allen & Unwin, 1943), 33. It is not clear exactly when Sir Lowthian Bell made this statement. He visited the United States in 1874 and published a report on his trip in 1875. He returned again in 1876. See Dorothy Adler, *British Investment in American Railways, 1834–1898* (Charlottesville: University Press of Virginia, 1970), 125, and *American Iron and Steel Association Bulletin*, 27 (Feb. 22, 1893): 60. The statement quoted could have been made at any time between 1874 and 1878.

73. The American town was first called Middlesborough and then renamed Middlesboro; the British name was Middlesbrough.

74. Ethel Armes, *The Story of Coal and Iron in Alabama* (1910; rpt. New York: Arno Press, 1973), 377. For the Quaker connections, see Paul Emden, *Quakers in Commerce* (London: Sampson Low, Marston, 1939), 43–58.

75. Armes, *Coal and Iron*, 378. According to *American Iron and Steel Bulletin*, 27 (Feb. 22, 1893): 60, Thomas Whitwell was in the United States in 1874 with Sir Lowthian Bell (then simply Mr. Bell).

76. Armes, *Coal and Iron*, 384, and *Hill Country*, 66.

77. Armes, *Coal and Iron*, 384–385. The Philadelphia representative of Thomas Whitwell had gone to South Pittsburg to build the furnaces. See ibid., 288–289, on this Swiss-born, British-educated engineer.

78. Ibid., 389, 387.

79. Ibid., 387.

80. Ibid., 389–390. By the end of 1876, the company had spent £88,738; it had a second stock issue in Britain in 1877 (*Hill Country*, 66).

81. On Whitwell's modern blast furnace stove and on the man, see W. T. Hogan, *Economic History of the Iron and Steel Industry*, 5 vols. (Lexington, Mass.: Lexington Books, 1971), I, 28–29; J. C. Carr and W. Taplin, *History of the British Steel Industry* (Cambridge, Mass.: Harvard University Press, 1962), 51n; and Adler, *British Investment*, 122.

82. The quote is from a 1910 book (Armes, *Coal and Iron*, 390).

83. Ibid., 390; Victor S. Clark, *History of Manufactures*, 3 vols. (Washington, D.C.: Carnegie Institution, 1929), II, 213; and C. Vann Woodward, *Origins of the New South* (Baton Rouge: Louisiana State University Press, 1951), 126.

84. Statement of Robert Percival Porter, quoted in Armes, *Coal and Iron*, 305.

85. Ibid., 390. I do not know how the $1.4 million compared with what the British had invested. Note that they got no cash—only stocks and bonds of the Tennessee company.

86. Dillwyn Parrish had been a delegate for the "London Protective Committee" set up by the merchant banking firm of J. K. Gilliat & Co. after the 1884 default of the Denver and Rio Grande Railway and had traveled to the United States in 1885. Dorothy Adler has identified him as closely associated with Scottish investment trusts. In the 1880s Alfred Parrish, described by Armes, *Coal and Iron*, 335, as British, but by Dorothy

Adler as from Philadelphia, was president of the Birmingham, Sheffield and Tennessee River Railroad (later the Northern Alabama); Dillwyn Parrish represented British bond-holders on that road. See Adler, *British Investment*, 148, 149, 177. A "D. Parrish" (surely the same man) in the summer of 1888 unsuccessfully approached Frederick Pabst on the possibility of a brewery consolidation. He was said to represent "London finan-ciers" (Thomas C. Cochran, *The Pabst Brewing Co.* [New York: New York University Press, 1948], 153). The 1892 *Directory of Directors* lists Dillwyn Parrish as a director of the English and Scottish American Mortgage and Investment Company, the London and New York Investment Company, the Northern Alabama Development Company, the American Association, Ltd., and the Exploration Company Ltd. This last was the British Rothschild unit. I found nothing on Dillwyn Parrish in the Rothschild Archives. Was "E. H. Watt" associated with Watts, Ward & Co., Cardiff? See text on the American Association, Ltd.

87. Armes, *Coal and Iron*, 331–333. The city of Bessemer was a suburb of Birming-ham, Alabama. Thomas D. Clark and Albert D. Kirwan, in *The South since Appomattox* (New York: Oxford University Press, 1967), 158, note that DeBardeleben was born in South Carolina, which would explain the connections with Roberts.

88. Armes, *Coal and Iron*, 339.

89. Ibid., 423. When in 1890 the Duke of Marlborough visited the United States, he noted that an "English" company was making steel in Birmingham, Alabama (Duke of Marlborough, "Virginia Mines and American Rails," *Fortnightly Review*, n.s., 49 [June 1891]: 783). This was probably a reference to the DeBardeleben firm. In April 1891 the American banker James Stillman was recommending DeBardeleben Coal and Iron Company securities *and* Tennessee Coal and Iron Company bonds to British investors (James Stillman to Archibald Balfour, London, April 24, 1891, Stillman Letterbook, Stillman Papers, Columbia University).

90. Armes, *Coal and Iron*, 537.

91. Ibid., 390, 425; Adler, *British Investment*, 139; and U.S. Steel, *Annual Report, 1907*.

92. Lewis, *America's Stake*, 83; Adler, *British Investment*, 129–130; and *Stock Exchange Official Intelligence for 1914*, 121, which lists it under the rubric "iron, coal, and steel."

93. Adler, *British Investment*, 139. This chapter, note 86, indicates that Dillwyn Parrish was a director of Northern Alabama Development Company in 1892, which is not surprising, considering his ties with the DeBardeleben group and the Birmingham, Sheffield and Tennessee River Railway—as well as Northern Alabama Development Company's contract with the Tennessee Coal, Iron and Railroad Company.

94. Adler, *British Investment*, 139, 123.

95. Ibid., 135; and Vann Woodward, *Origins*, 126. See Chapter 4.

96. Adler, *British Investment*, 136n, 148–149.

97. *Economist*, 47 (Nov. 2, 1889): 1400. For Vivian Gray & Co.'s association with the Norfolk and Western, see Adler, *British Investment*, 135.

98. Clark, *History of Manufactures*, II, 212. Clark himself thought it was not compa-rable to the "big Pittsburgh stacks."

99. See *Stock Exchange Year Book, 1890*, 526, for foundation date and directors of American Association, Ltd. The latter owned shares in the Middlesborough Town Company, which developed the town. See Maury Klein, *History of the Louisville and Nashville Railroad* (New York: Macmillan, 1972), 280, on the location of the 60,000 acres. *American Iron and Steel Association Bulletin*, 24 (April 16, 1890): 105, quoting from Ry-land's *Iron Trade Circular*, Birmingham, England, gives details on Watts, Ward & Co. The Watts Steel and Iron Syndicate, Ltd., seems to have had an American counterpart company, the Watts Iron and Steel Company. On the latter see Klein, *Louisville and*

Nashville Railroad, 281, and Duke of Marlborough, "Virginia Mines and American Rails," 792, both of which mention the building of the first two furnaces. A contract was made for a steel plant as well. The Duke of Marlborough suggested (in 1891) that steel production actually had gotten under way (p. 783). See *American Iron and Steel Association Bulletin*, 27 (Jan. 11, 1893): 13, and (Feb. 15, 1893): 53, for activities of the Watts Steel and Iron Syndicate, Ltd., in January 1893. According to Clark, *History of Manufactures*, II, 205, "financial stringency" slowed the furnace construction, and the first furnace was not blown in until 1895. Eventually there were the four furnaces plus the steel plant. See Victor S. Clark, *The South in the Building of the Nation* (Richmond, Va.: Southern Historical Society, 1909), VI, 273. Klein, *Louisville and Nashville Railroad*, 280, says that Baring Brothers was involved in the American Association. I have found no other evidence of this. On Middlesbrough, England, see Emden, *Quakers in Commerce*, 50–52. The *Investors' Review*, London, identifies the American Association venture with participants in the Trustees', Executors' and Securities' Insurance Corporation, the Industrial and General Trust, the London and New York Investment Corporation, and the Leopold Salomons' group of companies. See *Investors' Review*, 2 (Nov. 1893): 606; 3 (March 1894): 176; and 3 (Jan. 1894): 13, 36. This was not a Baring Brothers group. Jacob Higson, Manchester, was connected with a short-lived (1888–1894) Colorado gold-mining venture, the Ni-Wot Gold Mines, Ltd. See WICRS, reel 52.

100. *Banker's Magazine*, New York, 44 (August 1889): 82–83.

101. Klein, *Louisville and Nashville Railroad*, 281. See also *American Iron and Steel Association Bulletin*, 24 (April 16, 1890): 105, on the rise of the town.

102. Duke of Marlborough, "Virginia Mines and American Rails," 782–783, 791–792.

103. Klein, *Louisville and Nashville Railroad*, 281–282. By 1893 the American Association was bankrupt—and "its share capital practically worthless." See *Investors' Review*, 2 (Nov. 1893): 606–608, on it and the whole collection of Middlesborough companies: the Middlesborough Town Lands Company, the Coal and Iron Bank of Middlesborough, the Middlesborough Hotel Company, the Cumberland Gas Company, the Middlesborough Electric Company, the Middlesborough Water Company, and the Middlesborough Street Railway Company. See also *American Iron and Steel Association Bulletin*, 27 (Oct. 25, 1893): 317, and (Nov. 22 and 29, 1893): 34.

104. Clark, *History of Manufactures*, III, 27.

105. Klein, *Louisville and Nashville Railroad*, 283.

106. Spurr, *Political and Commercial*, 230; Lewis, *America's Stake*, 93, 564; and *APC Report*, 82.

107. *American Iron and Steel Association Bulletin*, 27 (March 15, 1893): 85.

108. U.S. Senate, *Mining Interests of Aliens*, 18–19, 21–23; see also Spence, *British Investments*, 260, on the Wyoming Coal and Coke Company, Ltd., incorporated in England in 1885.

109. "News from London," *Commercial and Financial Chronicle*, 29 (Aug. 9, 1879): 13.

110. Joseph Daniels, "History of Pig Iron Manufacture on the Pacific Coast," *Washington Quarterly*, 17 (1926): 184–185, and William R. Sherrard, "The Kirkland Steel Mill," *Pacific Northwest Quarterly*, 53 (Oct. 1962): 129–137; data on capitalization from the state archives, Olympia, Washington. See Wallis Hunt, *Heirs of Great Adventure: The History of Balfour, Williamson and Co., Ltd.*, 2 vols. (London: Balfour, Williamson, 1951, 1960), I, 149–150, 166; II, 27 (essential on that firm's involvements). See also R. V. Clements, "British Investments and American Legislative Restrictions," *Mississippi Valley Historical Review*, 42 (Sept. 1955): 220, and *Banker's Magazine*, New York, 44 (Aug. 1889): 83. In Britain the Moss Bay Hematite Iron and Steel Company, Ltd. (Cumberland, England), became a limited liability company in 1881 (*Burdett's Official Intelligence, 1891*, 1868–69).

On Peter Kirk and Charles Valentine, see Charlotte Erickson, *British Industrialists* (Cambridge: Cambridge University Press, 1959), 211, 47. There is no evidence that Balfour, Williamson participated in the manufacturing, only in the mining companies. In 1909 the Workington Iron and Steel Company, Ltd., was formed in Britain; it acquired Moss Bay Hematite Iron and Steel Company, Ltd. I have found no indication that the Workington Iron and Steel Company had American investments. See *Statist*, 81 (Aug. 22, 1914): 475, on the Workington company. Hunt, *Heirs*, II, 27, refers to the Balfour, Williamson investments in the Durham Coal Mine and the Cle Elum Iron Ore Properties as "white elephants."

111. Date of formation in Hogan, *Economic History*, III, 1263.

112. *Banker's Magazine*, New York, 44 (Aug. 1889): 83.

113. Hogan, *Economic History*, I, 223.

114. *Banker's Magazine*, New York 44 (Aug. 1889): 83.

115. *Burdett's Official Intelligence, 1891*, 1374–75.

116. On Smith and Barrow, see Erickson, *British Industrialists*, 29, 152–153, 159.

117. *Burdett's Official Intelligence, 1891*, 1374.

118. Hogan, *Economic History*, III, 1263.

119. *Stock Exchange Official Intelligence for 1914*, 1274. For tax and other reasons, as indicated in Chapter 5, the free-standing London incorporation was often replaced. Instead of a company (Otis Steel Company, Ltd.) making direct investments in America, its British stockholders were now portfolio investors in an American company.

120. I think this was entirely different from the Otis Steel situation, in which J. T. Smith was on the board to attract British investors to a British-incorporated enterprise, not to run the business. The Sanderson firm in the United Kingdom seems to have intended control and direct supervision.

121. I am indebted to Geoffrey Tweedale, "Sheffield Steel and America," *Business History*, 25 (Nov. 1983): 230, and his "Sheffield Steel Industry and Its Allied Trades and the American Market, 1850–1930," Ph.D. diss., London School of Economics, 1983, 178–183, for most of my information on the Sheffield steel men. On Crucible Steel Company, see Clark, *History of Manufactures*, III, 71. In 1905 Halcomb started Halcomb Steel Company in Syracuse. Here again there does not seem to have been Sheffield financing; the Halcomb Steel Company became part of Crucible Steel Company in 1911 (Tweedale, "The Sheffield Steel Industry," 183). Tweedale found a directors' report for Sanderson Brothers, Sheffield, in *Ironmonger*, 92 (Oct. 6, 1900): 34, that stated the "whole" of the U.S. assets had been realized on "very advantageous terms," which seems to suggest that Sanderson Brothers retained no interest in the Crucible Steel Company (Tweedale to Wilkins, Aug. 13, 1984).

122. See Thos. Firth and John Brown, Ltd., "Souvenir of a Visit to the Atlas and Norfolk Works," Sheffield, 1954, booklet in Nuffield College Library, Oxford University; A. C. Marshall and Herbert Newbould, *The History of Firth's (1842–1918)* (Sheffield: Thos. Firth, 1925), 71–72; and on the 1908 furnace, Hogan, *Economic History*, II, 414. See also Tweedale, "Sheffield Steel and America," 231, 234, and his "The Sheffield Steel Industry," 184–186.

123. Tweedale, "Sheffield Steel and America," 231, and his "Sheffield Steel Industry," 190–194. Tweedale writes that one director (in 1905) thought the plant so superior that he would like "to scrap" the firm's British works ("Sheffield Steel" Industry, 192).

124. Tweedale, "Sheffield Steel and America," 233–234, and his "Sheffield Steel Industry," 235–237. Tweedale found in *Implement and Machinery Review*, 36 (May 1, 1910): 103, that the Illinois company of Edgar Allen had a capital of $300,000 (Tweedale to Wilkins, Aug. 13, 1984).

125. Tweedale believes that writers on the American steel industry have not paid adequate attention to this important activity.

126. The bicycle "craze" peaked in 1896 and lasted until 1900 (Hogan, *Economic History*, II, 664).

127. J. Perc Boore, *The Seamless Story* (Los Angeles: Commonwealth Press, 1951), 1, 27, 34–37.

128. Ibid., 43, 52.

129. Ibid., 122–123. According to *Investors' Review*, 7 (June 1896): 342, in the United Kingdom in 1894 Components Manufacturing Company was formed to acquire the business and patent rights of several firms, including "Thomas Warwick & Sons Limited (E. Warwick was its secretary), [and] Hudson & Company Limited." Harvey Du Cros (of Dunlop) was chairman of Components Manufacturing Company.

130. *New York Times*, June 20, 1897, p. 1.

131. Boore, *The Seamless Story*, 45. Stiefel had worked in the Mannesmann Tube works in Wales.

132. Ibid., 52–59. The Tubes (America), Ltd., prospectus was issued in Birmingham, England, on June 28, 1897. Application for quotation was to be made to the Birmingham, Manchester, and Liverpool exchanges (ibid., 56).

133. Ibid., 59–61. The very same companies that Tubes (America), Ltd., would have consolidated were taken over by the new combination led by Shelby Steel. Tubes (America), Ltd., was dissolved in 1899 (*Stock Exchange Official Intelligence for 1914*).

134. Clark, *History of Manufacturing*, III, 128, and Hogan, *Economic History*, I, 283; but Boore, which is the best source on all of this, says nothing about foreign ownership; the board of directors of the new company showed no evidence of English participation. I suspect Clark and Hogan confused this venture with the aborted Tubes (America), Ltd., combination that would have been majority owned by Englishmen. On the other hand, it is possible that subscribers to the stock of Tubes (America), Ltd., were reimbursed in Shelby Steel shares. The English ownership of American Weldless does not appear to have been large enough to make a difference in controlling ownership of Shelby Steel.

135. Hogan, *Economic History*, I, 282–284; Clark, *History of Manufactures*, III, 128–129; and Moody, *Truth about Trusts*, 142–143. Any British stockholders would then have become stockholders in U.S. Steel.

136. W. E. Minchinton, *The British Tinplate Industry* (Oxford: Clarendon Press, 1957) 43–44, 72, 66; Clark, *History of Manufactures*, II, 372–376; and Hogan, *Economic History*, I, 348–355 (on the tariff).

137. On Morewood's U.S. expansion, see *American Iron and Steel Association Bulletin*, 27 (March 9, 1893): 75, and 27 (Oct. 4, 1893): 293.

138. Ibid., 27 (Oct. 18, 1893): 308, and 27 (Dec. 6, 1893): 349.

139. Minchinton, *The British Tinplate Industry*, 67, 72, and D. E. Dunbar, *The Tin-Plate Industry* (Boston: Houghton Mifflin, 1915), 21.

140. Minchinton, *The British Tinplate Industry*, 70, 75, 89. Moody, *Truth about Trusts*, 157–158, says that 95 percent of tinplate production in the United States was controlled by the new American firm. See also Levy, *Monopoly and Competition*, 204, 207, and Dunbar, *The Tin-Plate Industry*, 83, 84.

141. As noted, the Southern States venture had lasted several years after the 1877–78 deaths, but these clearly undermined the viability of the project.

142. In U.S. Steel and Otis Steel, for example.

143. Seymour S. Bernfeld (in collaboration with Harold K. Hochschild), "A Short History of American Metal Climax, Inc.," in American Metal Climax, Inc., *World Atlas* (New York: n.d.[1962]), 7.

144. *APC Report*, 74.-

145. Ibid., 309, and RG 131, Box 102, National Archives, Washington, D.C. Ownership by 1914 was 75 percent by George Hirsch of Gera, Reuss, Germany, and 25 percent by Ignatz Petschek, resident of Austria.

146. *APC Report*, 42.

147. *American Iron and Steel Association Bulletin*, 27 (July 5 and 12, 1893): 205 (on the "expected" visit that month; I presumed it occurred) and ibid., 27 (Aug. 2, 1893): 226, on the Krupp exhibit. F. A. Krupp was the head of the German firm at this time.

148. See ibid., 34 (April 1, 1900): 66, on Piorkowski, "of the German army"—the Krupp representative. According to John F. Thompson and Norman Beasley's history of International Nickel, *For the Years to Come* (New York: G. P. Putnam's Sons, 1960), 42, Krupp had "New York agents" in 1886.

149. *American Iron and Steel Association Bulletin*, 34 (April 1, 1900): 69.

150. With World War I, no Krupp properties in the United States were taken over by the Alien Property Custodian (*APC Report*). According to the *American Iron and Steel Association Bulletin*, 34 (April 1, 1900): 66, the Krupp concern in 1900 employed about 75,000 people, including Essen factory workers and mining and smelting concerns outside Essen. Obviously Krupp was huge.

151. Heinrich Kelleter, *Geschichte der Familie J. A. Henckels* (Solingen, 1924), 185, 186, 191, 192, and *APC Report*, 322. In 1906 in Ohio the Henkel Company was formed; this seems to have had nothing to do with J. A. Henckels. It made the same products and seems to have tried to capture the advantage of the Henckels' name. Its goods, of course, could not use Henckels' famous "twin" trademark. On Henkel Company of Fremont, Ohio, see *American Cutler*, June 1919, 8–10. J. A. Henckels did not manufacture in the United States.

152. Boore, *Seamless Story*, 1–2, 10.

153. Ibid., 10–11, 17.

154. Ibid., 11. The reason why is not clear.

155. Ibid., 14. Eventually the machinery, equipment, and licenses were sold to Benedict and Burnham Manufacturing Company of Waterbury, Connecticut, a firm that the Mannesmanns had earlier—in 1894—licensed to make seamless copper and brass tubes (ibid., 11, 13, 15). The Mannesmann Cycle Tube Works was planned as a major undertaking, with a capital of $10 million (Thomas R. Kabisch, *Deutsches Kapital in den USA* [Stuttgart: Klett-Cotta, 1982], 242).

156. Hogan, *Economic History*, II, 414.

157. Ibid.

158. Pearson, *The Maxwell Land Grant*, 210–218 and passim.

159. Lewis, *America's Stake*, 572. Herbert Marshall, Frank Southard, and Kenneth Taylor, *Canadian-American Industry* (New Haven: Yale University Press, 1936), 182, indicate that Canada Foundries and Forgings, Ltd., had a Buffalo, New York, plant (no date of establishment) that was destroyed by fire in 1922 and not rebuilt. Buffalo City directories for 1910–1922, however, have no listings for Canada Foundries and Forgings, but from 1916 to 1921, Canadian Furnace Co., Ltd., a manufacturer of pig iron, was listed (Buffalo City directories and data from Barbara M. Soper, librarian, Buffalo and Erie County Public Library, April 26, 1982).

160. Albro Martin, *James J. Hill* (New York: Oxford University Press, 1976), 468–469, and W. Kaye Lamb, *History of the Canadian Pacific Railroad* (New York: Macmillan, 1977), 202–204. See also Heather Gilbert, *End of the Road* (Aberdeen: Aberdeen University Press, 1977), 323–329, 334–335 (on British investments in iron ore certificates).

161. Lewis, *America's Stake*, 564. Lewis does not indicate a U.S. location. Could this be an error and the firm associated with the British Firth Sterling Steel Company?

162. Hogan, *Economic History*, II, 776.

163. Ibid.

164. U.S. Federal Trade Commission, *Report on Cooperation in the Export Trade* (Washington, D.C., 1916), II, 81; see also ibid., I, 348–349, which discusses whether U.S. firms were really participants. Hogan, *Economic History*, II, 788, does not include U.S. Steel or other U.S. companies as members in November 1904; Hermann Levy, *Monopoly and Competition* (London: Macmillan, 1911), 261–262, believed that U.S. firms were members from 1905 and notes how effective the cartel was in restricting U.S. exports. On the other hand, there is reason to believe that the U.S. market was not fully protected. Thus in 1908 Charles Schwab of Bethlehem Steel advocated continued high protective tariffs on foreign rail imports. See Robert Hessen, *Steel Titan: The Life of Charles M. Schwab* (New York: Oxford University Press, 1975), 190; but when the tariffs were lowered in 1909, Bethlehem was not badly hurt (ibid., 194). Alfred Plummer, *International Combines in Modern Industry* (2nd ed., 1938; rpt. Freeport, N.Y.: Books for Libraries, 1971), 161–162, writes that American steel-rail makers entered the International Rail Makers Association in 1904; and the association agreement was renewed in 1907 for five years and then in 1912 for three years. Fixed quotes were assigned to national (including U.S.) participants.

165. *FTC Report on Cooperation*, II, 81.

166. *Bradstreet's*, Oct. 24, 1914, 690. This constituted about 25 percent of the common stock and about 8 percent of the preferred. See also *Commercial and Financial Chronicle*, Oct. 20, 1923, 1740, for March 31, 1914, and Dec. 31, 1914 figures.

167. It is likely that some British investments in American Tin Plate Company became portfolio interests in U.S. Steel; likewise, probably some British interests in Shelby Steel Tube Company were exchanged for U.S. Steel stock. As noted in Chapter 4, Carnegie had raised some monies in Britain; I doubt, however, that that portfolio investment remained in 1901. I know of portfolio interests in Federal Steel Company and American Steel and Wire Company that undoubtedly contributed to the portfolio interests in U.S. Steel. Yet these and other predecessor-company investments notwithstanding, clearly after U.S. Steel was formed, its securities were bought (and sold) abroad.

168. Dickens, "Transition," 263.

169. George Paish's estimate for 1910 of $1.7 million British investment in "coal, iron, and steel" (given in Table 5.11) is obviously preposterous; it is far, far too low.

8. Other Minerals

1. On the U.S. copper industry in the early 1880s, see D. W. Fryer, *World Economic Development* (New York: McGraw-Hill, 1965), 404; on Montana Copper, Thomas R. Navin, *Copper Mining and Management* (Tucson: University of Arizona Press, 1978), 304; and on Arizona Copper, W. Turrentine Jackson, *The Enterprising Scot* (Edinburgh: Edinburgh University Press, 1968), chap. 7.

2. T. A. Rickard, *A History of American Mining* (New York: McGraw-Hill, 1932), 351.

3. Wallis Hunt, *Heirs of Great Adventure*, 2 vols. (London: Balfour, Williamson, 1951, 1961), I, 129.

4. Report of E. Cumenge, Paris, Dec. 15, 1894, pp. 1–2, Box 104, Rothschild Papers, French National Archives, Paris (henceforth cited as RAP). All box numbers are provisional.

5. Ed Raquet, Rothschild's, to Administrative Director of Société Metallurgique du Cuivre, Feb. 16, 1889, Box 100, RAP.

6. On the Secretan Syndicate, see M. A. Abrams, "The French Copper Syndicate, 1887–1889," *Journal of Economic and Business History*, 4 (May 1932): 409–428; W. Y. Elliott

et al., *International Control in the Non-Ferrous Metals* (1937; rpt. New York: Arno Press, 1976), 395–397; and Charles E. Harvey, *The Rio Tinto Company* (Penzance: Alison Hodge, 1981), 68–73. The Rothschild Archives, London (henceforth cited as RAL), has many letters from Baron Alphonse de Rothschild in Paris to his cousins in London, 1888–89, on Secretan matters. See RAL T15/17.

7. Elliott, ed., *International Control*, 397.

8. Navin, *Copper Mining*, 204.

9. Mira Wilkins, *The Emergence of Multinational Enterprise* (Cambridge, Mass.: Harvard University Press, 1970), 80.

10. August Belmont to Lord Rothschild, Aug. 21, 1891, Belmont "Confidential Letter Book," Belmont Family Papers, Columbia University Library (on "an option"). See also Belmont to Lord Rothschild, Sept. 25, 1891, in ibid., and Ernest Cassel to Belmont, Oct. 3, 1891, Belmont Family Papers. Jacob Schiff of Kuhn, Loeb apparently kept Cassel informed. See Cyrus Adler, *Jacob H. Schiff* (Garden City, N.Y.: Doubleday, 1928), I, 155–156, for an indication that this was the case. Belmont reported in August 1891 that he had talked with J. B. Haggin on the matter (Belmont to Lord Rothschild, Aug. 21, 1891, Belmont "Confidential Letter Book," Belmont Family Papers). See also ibid., July 15, 1891.

11. According to a report of E. Cumenge, Dec. 15, 1894, p. 2, RAP.

12. Nathaniel Rothschild, London, to August Belmont, July 31, 1894, RAL II/11/0 (see Chapter 13 on the first name of Lord Rothschild). The letter added, "In order, however, that there should be no misunderstanding of any sort or kind, my dear Belmont, it must be clearly understood that we should never for a single moment entertain anything like the financing of American copper and that we should simply and merely undertake to superintend the selling of the same."

13. See correspondence in RAL II/11/0, 1894–95, and RAL II/15/14A, Jan.–June 1895.

14. See data in RAL II/11/0.

15. *Statist*, 36 (Sept. 14, 1895): 323, reported that "the Explorations, with some of its friends, have bought a quantity of shares of the Anaconda Mining Company," subject to investigation by Hamilton Smith, who was in America to look at the mining property. He had a month (that is, until Oct. 15). On Oct. 3, 1895, Alphonse de Rothschild wrote from Paris to his cousins in London, "There is much concern as to the Anaconda affair, should it not realize, it would be a great disappointment and the price of the Rio [Tinto Company] shares will be effected [*sic*] at least temporarily" (RAL T16/107).

16. Elliott, *International Control*, 397. This would be the price at par value. See *Statist*, 36 (Oct. 19, 1895): 477, which reported that the capital of Anaconda had been recast and reached $30,000,000. A quarter of the shares had been taken by the Rothschild and Exploration group. E. Cumenge to Messieurs Mirabaud-Pascard & Co., Paris, Aug. 28, 1896, Box 101, RAP, used the figure $8 million. On Oct. 29, 1895, Jacob Schiff of Kuhn, Loeb wrote Marcus Daly of Anaconda, " I am glad our London friends have adopted the views I endeavored to impress them with"—that is, they purchased the interest in Anaconda (Adler, *Jacob H. Schiff*, I, 156). Navin, *Copper Mining*, 204, states that it was the Hearst stock that was purchased.

17. Isaac F. Marcossen, *Anaconda* (New York: Dodd, Mead, 1957), 92. In 1894 Anaconda had been incorporated as the Anaconda Mining Company. After the Rothschild acquisition, it was reincorporated as the Anaconda Copper Mining Company. See William S. Greever, *The Bonanza West: The Story of Western Mining Rushes, 1848–1900* (Norman: University of Oklahoma Press, 1963), 240. Greever also indicates that it was the Hearst shares that the Rothschilds bought.

18. Wilkins, *Emergence*, 80. By "control," I mean control over the marketing of Anaconda copper in Europe, which was the Rothschilds' main aim. The house did not

own a majority of the stock, but since it owned more than 10 percent, by contemporary U.S. Department of Commerce standards this would be a direct investment.

19. Clark C. Spence, *British Investments and the American Mining Frontier* (Ithaca, N.Y.: Cornell University Press, 1958), 78.

20. Both the Rio Tinto mine and the Boleo mine in 1900 ranked in the top ten leading copper producers worldwide (numbers 2 and 8, respectively). See Navin, *Copper Mining*, 396.

21. Wilkins, *Emergence*, 180, 116, 100; Harvey, *Rio Tinto Company*, 71, 188, 202, 110; and Alfred Plummer, *International Combines in Modern Industry* (2nd ed., 1938; rpt. Freeport, N.Y.: Books for Libraries Press, 1971), 239–240. See Bertrand Gille, *Histoire de la maison Rothschilds, 1848–1870* (Geneva: Libraire Droz, 1967), II, 550–552, on the Rothschilds' involvements in nonferrous metals, 1848–1870. Data in the RAP and RAL show clear interest by the houses in the business activities. The Rothschilds were also very much involved in gold and silver—as indicated in Chapter 7—and in South African diamonds. See the text and this chapter, note 53 on the Rothschilds' nickel business.

22. My 25 percent figure is the total of Anaconda (17 percent), Mountain Copper (4 percent), Arizona Copper (3 percent), and others (1 percent), based on Navin, *Copper Mining*, 396, 399—1900 percentages. On British ownership of the Mountain Copper Company, see J. E. Spurr, *Political and Commercial Geology and the World's Mineral Resources* (New York: McGraw-Hill, 1920), 230, and Cleona Lewis, *America's Stake in International Investments* (Washington, D.C.: Brookings Institution, 1938), 91. S. D. Chapman, "British-Based Investment Groups before 1914," *Economic History Review*, 2nd ser., 38 (May 1985): 234–235, identifies Mountain Copper as part of the "Matheson group" of enterprises. This Scottish group in earlier years had controlled the important Rio Tinto Company in Spain (Harvey, *Rio Tinto*, 188). The best material on Mountain Copper is in the appendix to Albin Joachim Dahl, "British Investment in California Mining, 1870–1890," Ph.D. diss., University of California, Berkeley, 1961, 249–267. The firm was registered in London on Dec. 1, 1896. Around the turn of the century it employed some 1,500 men in mining and at its smelter in Keswick, California. William Keswick (of the Matheson group) had been a principal in the development. See Jackson, *Enterprising Scot*, chap. 7, and W. G. Kerr, *Scottish Capital on the American Credit Frontier* (Austin: Texas State Historical Association, 1976), on the Arizona Copper Company and its Scottish investors. It was organized by the Scottish American Mortgage Company and subsequently dominated by the Scottish American Investment Company.

23. The Ray Copper Mines, Ltd., was floated in London in June 1899, and raised some $700,000 there (Paul Dickens, "Transition Period in American International Financing, 1897–1914," Ph.D. diss., George Washington University, 1933, 239–240, and Navin, *Copper Mining*, 29, 112). Apparently the Ray mine was badly managed (Navin, *Copper Mining*, 112). Harvey O'Connor tells of how "shareholders' sons, sent out to the American wilderness for experience and tempering, scandalized Arizona's mining community by knocking off promptly at four every day for afternoon tea. And indeed at almost any time of day young Englishmen could be seen, outfitted in the best Bond Street riding-habits prancing along mountain trails, riding pad saddles on dock-tailed ponies" (*The Guggenheims* [New York: Covici Friede, 1937], 300–301).

As early as 1901, Ray Copper Mines, Ltd., was deemed a failure. S. G. Checkland, *The Mines of Tharsis* (London: George Allen & Unwin, 1967), 189, attributed the failure to attempting management "from a European head office." Eventually the operations passed into the hands of the Anglo-American Company. In 1905 a railroad finally reached Kelvin, Arizona. Meanwhile, new technology made this mine a workable proposition. The American mining expert D. C. Jackling recognized the mine's potential. Philip Wiseman—an American mining engineer—checked out the property. Navin writes: "Wiseman was not daunted by the knowledge that a British group of mining engineers, backed financially by Lord Kelvin of thermodynamics fame, had failed to make the mine a paying success. When he tried to find the British owners, Wiseman had considerable difficulty locating them!" (*Copper Mining*, 260, 314–315). See also Rickard, *A History*, 298–299. Kelvin, Arizona, was named after Lord Kelvin. The successor company—formed in 1910—was Ray Consolidated Copper. For useful details, see also David Lavender, *The Story of Cyprus Mines Corporation* (San Marino: Huntington Library, 1962), 30–34, 347. At origin, Ray Copper Mines, Ltd., was a typical free-standing company.

24. Based on Navin, *Copper Mining*, 304, 207, 396, 399. These were portfolio investments. As noted earlier, Lewisohn Brothers in 1880 had attracted European shareholders to Montana Copper. This company in 1887 had been merged into the Boston & Montana Consolidated Copper & Silver Mining Company, which would in 1899 be taken over by Amalgamated Copper. Navin (p. 304) suggests that in 1880 the major shareholders in Montana Copper had been "Europeans." In 1888 Jacob Schiff of Kuhn, Loeb & Co. wrote Ernest Cassel about the "Boston & Montana shares" that were "attracting great attention in Europe" (Adler, *Jacob Schiff*, I, 155).

25. W. Turrentine Jackson, "British Impact on the Utah Mining Industry," *Utah Historical Quarterly*, 31 (Fall, 1963): 374, and O'Connor, *The Guggenheims*, 288, 352, 360, 375, 416.

26. There were additional British-financed companies; for example, Copper King, Ltd., was floated in London in January 1899, raised some $315,000, and acquired a mining property in California. See Dickens, "Transition Period," 239–240. Other sources indicate that more monies were raised and spent. Copper King, Ltd., developed the mine, which was near San Francisco, and in April 1901 opened a smelter (R. P. T. Davenport-Hines, "Davison Alexander Dalziel," *Dictionary of Business Biography*, II, 6). By early 1903 the company was insolvent, and bankruptcy proceedings began. The local manager was charged with gross mismangement. The mine and smelter were sold by the receiver in 1905 to an American. See appendix to Dahl, "British Investment," 267, 269–271. This was another short-lived free-standing company.

27. See data in Box 101, RAP.

28. Wilkins, *Emergence*, 80.

29. *Mining Manual* (London), 1912, 587, and Wilkins, *Emergence*, 80–81.

30. Navin, *Copper Mining*, 206–207, 304.

31. Dickens, "The Transition Period," 239.

32. *Mining Manual, 1912*, 585. Navin, *Copper Mining*, 204, notes that at some point (unspecified), a large block of the "Hearst" securities went to a Dutch investment trust. "which for many years was one of the largest holders of Anaconda stock with the privilege of representation on the Board (through Hallgarten & Company of New York)." I have not been able to obtain further information on this.

33. Wilkins, *Emergence*, 80–82. In May 1915 Amalgamated Copper was dissolved and its subsidiary, Anaconda, took over the properties.

34. John Moody, *The Truth about Trusts* (New York: Moody, 1904), 28.

35. Ibid., 16. Amalgamated Copper had been organized by individuals—H. H. Rogers and William G. Rockefeller—associated with Standard Oil (ibid., 4–5, 9). Amalgamated Copper is not in the index of the basic Standard Oil history—Ralph Hidy and Muriel Hidy, *Pioneering in Big Business* (New York: Harper, 1955)—although both men were officers of Standard Oil (New Jersey), 1899–1911 (ibid., 314). One historian suggests, however, that the Paris Rothschilds had once felt kindly toward Standard Oil but

were nervous when the giant oil company seemed to be moving into copper. See F. C. Gerretson, *History of the Royal Dutch* (Lieden: E. J. Brill, 1957), IV, 204. Earlier, the Paris Rothschilds had tried, in vain, to negotiate with Standard Oil to divide world oil markets. On this read Wilkins, *Emergence*, 82, together with Baron Alphonse to cousins, June 11, 1894, RAL T16/64 (which reports that negotiations with Standard Oil were not progressing), and Robert W. Tolf, *The Russian Rockefellers: The Saga of the Nobel Family* (Stanford, Calif.: Hoover Institution Press, 1976), 116–117 (the unidentified Jules Aron was with the Paris Rothschilds; this deals with the breakdown of negotiations in the spring of 1895). The Paris Rothschilds were involved in oil as well as in metals. For the continuing concerns of the London Rothschilds in copper, see, for example, Nathaniel Mayer Rothschild, London, to cousins, Paris, May 31, 1907; July 22, 1907; Oct. 3, 1907; and Oct. 17, 1907, RAL XI/130A/1. The July 22 letter mentions a visit from John D. Ryan, of Amalgamated Copper.

36. In the years 1901–1914, the Scottish-owned Arizona Copper Company was very prosperous. See Jackson, *Enterprising Scot*, 181–182. It would be acquired by Phelps, Dodge in 1921 for stock with a book value of $18.2 million—which turned out to be a "bargain" price (Navin, *Copper Mining*, 55, 232).

37. Mountain Copper in California, which had been one of the world's ten largest copper companies in 1900, was less important in 1914 (Navin, *Copper Mining*, 55, 396). Its decline in copper production was largely offset in 1910–1914 by the rising output of pyrite ore from its Hornet mine, most of which it sent to its smelting facilities on San Francisco Bay, near Martinez, for processing. These facilities were completed in 1905 and, according to Dahl, included plants for manufacturing sulfuric acid and superphosphate fertilizer. The company had a wholly owned subsidiary, San Francisco Chemical Company which produced the sulfuric acid from the processed sulfurous ores (Dahl, "British Investment," 256, 258). The Ducktown Sulphur, Copper and Iron Company, Ltd., in Tennessee had also become engaged in sulfuric acid production as a by-product of its smelting. In 1908 the largest sulfuric acid unit in the world came on stream in Tennessee, which soon was owned by the Tennessee Chemical & Fertilizer Company, apparently a joint-venture between the Ducktown company and the American-owned Tennessee Copper Company. See Williams Haynes, *American Chemical Industry*, 6 vols. (New York: Van Nostrand, 1945–1954), I, 263; III, 173; IV, 81.

38. Figures for 1917 in Spurr, *Political and Commercial*, 229–230.

39. O'Connor, *The Guggenheims*, 288, 352, 360, 375, 416.

40. Lewis, *America's Stake*, 91, 933, 550. Between 1916 and 1923, Kennecott Copper would acquire 100 percent control of the venture (Navin, *Copper Mining*, 262).

41. On the Paris issue in 1912, see Lysis [Eugene Letailleur], *Politique et finance d'avant-guerre* (Paris: Payot, 1920), 572. On the predecessors of Ray Consolidated Copper, see this chapter, note 23. Ray Consolidated Copper was a Guggenheim venture; in 1926 its properties were acquired by a subsidiary of Kennecott Copper. See U.S. Federal Trade Commission, *Report on the Copper Industry* (Washington, D.C., 1947), 311. By 1912 it was making excellent profits (ibid., 134).

42. As noted, Amalgamated had acquired control not only of Anaconda but also of Boston & Montana Consolidated Copper & Silver Mining Company.

43. Navin, *Copper Mining*, 62. Navin described it as British backed in the 1880s. Yet it may not have been free standing. Dahl, "British Investment," 258, indicated that in the early twentieth century, the "New Jersey Refining Co.," *a subsidiary of Mountain Copper*, refined some of the copper that that British-controlled firm mined and smelted in California. Were the New Jersey Extraction Company and the New Jersey Refining Company the same firm? It seems possible.

44. O'Connor, *The Guggenheims*, 134–136, details how the Guggenheims estab-

lished in 1904–05, with the help of Kuhn, Loeb and Sir Ernest Cassel, the American Smelters Securities, and arranged the sale of its preferred stock in France through the Banque de Paris, in Holland through the Bank of Amsterdam, and in Cologne and Frankfurt through Cassel's connections. According to O'Connor, the Guggenheims raised $22 million. In Dec. 1905 Kuhn, Loeb placed 13,000 shares of ASARCO stock in Holland through Hope & Co. and the Bank of Amsterdam (Adler, *Jacob H. Schiff*, I, 157). In 1912, $15.35 million of American Smelters Securities preferred shares were sold in London. See Dickens, "Transition Period," 263.

45. See data in Box 101, RAP, and Plummer, *International Combines in Modern Industry*, 239–240.

46. Herbert Feis, *Europe: The World's Banker* (1930; rpt. New York: W. W. Norton, 1965), 79, notes that because the Germans had little experience in the mining sphere, they did not make giant investments abroad in mining. Feis, however, neglected to note how important the Germans were in the metal trades.

47. It was all a family affair. Metallgesellschaft was incorporated in Germany in 1881, an outgrowth of a metal trading firm founded in the early nineteenth century by *Philipp Abraham Cohen* (1790–1856). Cohen's assaying business became part of DEGUSSA. See Chapter 7 and note 51 in that chapter. One of Cohen's daughters married Rafael Moses (1817–1883) of London; Moses changed his name to *Ralph Merton*, and on Cohen's death he took over and expanded the business of his father-in-law's Frankfurt firm. In 1860 Ralph's son *Henry Ralph Merton* (1838–1872) opened an allied firm in London styled Henry R. Merton & Co. In the 1870s another of Ralph's sons, *Wilhelm Merton* (1848–1916), became the principal manager of the Frankfurt firm and "to an extent, of the London affiliate." Wilhelm Merton was in charge of Metallgesellschaft when it was incorporated in 1881. Two other sons of Ralph (Emile and Zachary) participated in the management of Henry R. Merton & Co., London. Wilhelm Merton married into the Ladenburg family of Frankfurt. In 1881 Zachary Hochschild (1854–1912), who was a cousin-in-law of Wilhelm Merton, was important in Metallgesellschaft. Zachary's brother, Berthold Hochschild (1860–1928), was the first manager of American Metal Company in New York. See Seymour S. Bernfeld, "A Short History of American Metal Climax," in American Metal Climax, Inc., *World Atlas* (n.p.,n.d. [1962]), 2–3, and Walther Dabritz, *Fünfzig Jahre Metallgesellschaft, 1881–1931* (Frankfurt: privately printed, 1931). Bernfeld refers to "Zacharias" Hochschild in one place and to "Zachary" in another; I used Dabritz's spelling of the first name.

48. Bernfeld, "A Short History," 6.

49. Navin, *Copper Mining*, 114–115, and Dabritz, *Fünfzig Jahre*, 93–94.

50. Bernfeld, "Short History," 4.

51. The new approach took place gradually. Its 1892 advertisements (*Mineral Industry*, p. 10) indicated that American Metal was the agent for Williams, Foster & Co., Ltd., and Pascoe Grenfell & Sons, Ltd., both in Swansea. For an extremely useful overview of the Swansea copper-smelting industry, see Harvey, *Rio Tinto*, 150–152.

52. Spurr, *Political and Commercial*, 279; Alien Property Custodian, *Report, 1918–1919*, 76 (henceforth cited as *APC Report*); and Martha Moore Trescott, *The Rise of the American Electrochemicals Industry, 1880–1910* (Westport, Conn.: Greenwood Press, 1981), 96.

53. Metallgesellschaft (a parent of American Metal) had a representative on the board of Société le Nickel. There is correspondence in the RAP, Box 101, between Z. Hochschild of Metallgesellschaft, Frankfurt, and J. Aron of the French Rothschild house. On Société le Nickel's importance, see John F. Thompson and Norman Beasley, *For the Years to Come* (New York: G. P. Putnam's Sons, 1960), 117–118. Copper and nickel were often found together—so there was a direct connection. On November 8,

1895, August Belmont wrote Baron Alphonse de Rothschild that he and "Mr. Ruef" (the Paris Rothschild representative?) had been in daily negotiations with Robert Thompson of the Canadian Copper Company (the predecessor of International Nickel). Belmont hoped the result would be "some working arrangements between your house, himself [Thompson], and the Société le Nickel." Belmont continued: "We had not gone far in our inquiries before I realized the danger threatening the nickel industry unless a working arrangement could be reached. The capacity of both your Company [Société le Nickel] and that of the Canadian Copper is so much greater than the demand that a reckless course in the search of the market at any price on the part of the one or the other, is bound to bring disaster." Belmont followed up this letter with one on November 30, referring to a contract signed with Thompson, which would provide a basis for one with Metallgesellschaft. Belmont was pleased with the results, "for I know how annoying this competition has and might have been" (Belmont to Baron Alphonse de Rothschild, Nov. 8, 30, 1895, Belmont Family Papers). This agreement was obviously the preface to the one with American Metal Company mentioned in the text.

54. Bernfeld, "Short History," 6. I am not certain this is true. Bernfeld places the plant in South Carolina, when it actually was in North Carolina. American Metal was clearly involved in the plans—but the 25 percent figure seems large.

55. Spurr, *Political and Commercial*, 279, 281, and *APC Report*, 73. The capital of this company was $3 million.

56. Ibid., 83.

57. Between 1913 and 1919, American Zinc & Chemical built its own zinc-smelting plant and sulfuric acid works, acquired coal mines, and developed a company town at Langeloth, Pennsylvania. Its investment was in excess of $4 million (*APC Report*, 73–74). The town was named after Jacob Langeloth, a deputy member of the executive board of Metallgesellschaft, who had been directly responsible for the formation of American Metal Company in 1887 (Bernfeld, "Short History," 3). From 1888 to 1911 Langeloth was president and from 1911–1914, chairman of the board of American Metal (ibid., 4, 6, 7).

58. Dabritz, *Fünfzig Jahre*, 78, 85–86.

59. According to Navin, *Copper Mining*, 274, Metallgesellschaft "specifically insisted that the American Metal Company not enter the mining business [in the United States]." The coal mines were a clear exception.

60. *APC Report*, 72.

61. Ibid.

62. Bernfeld, "Short History," 7.

63. Even before this, Aron Hirsch & Sohn had been interested in the U.S. copper trade—and when, in the fall of 1894, rumors circulated about N. M. Rothschild & Sons' interest in making arrangements with U.S. copper producers, Hirsch wrote "to offer" the Rothschilds "our services for selling those quantities of copper which you should judge good to place in Germany" (Aron Hirsch & Sohn to N. M. Rothschild & Sons, Nov. 2, 1894, RAL II/11/0).

64. Bernfeld, "Short History," 6, and *APC Report*, 85.

65. Ibid., 100.

66. Ibid., 85.

67. *APC Report*, 85, and *Moody's, 1914.*

68. Elliott, *International Control*, 670; J. J. Storrow, 44 State St., Boston, to Baron Robert de Rothschild, Oct. 25, 1906, Box 101, RAP, reported on how United States Smelting, Refining, and Mining Company "is getting on." Dickens, "Transition," 246, notes that this company had a common and preferred stock issue in October 1906, of which $500,000 of each was purchased in Britain. Storrow says nothing in his letter on

the stock issue. James Jackson Storrow had become a partner in the Boston banking house of Lee, Higginson in 1900. See Vincent P. Carosso, *Investment Banking in America* (Cambridge, Mass.: Harvard University Press, 1970), 94. For the Lee, Higginson–Rothschild connections, see Chapter 13.

69. Date of incorporation from Department of State, New Jersey; other information from *APC Report*, 65, and Bernfeld, "Short History," 7. An advertisement in *Mineral Industry, 1912* shows USMRC as the owner of the indicated properties; see also *Moody's, 1914*. By 1912 one-third of USMRC was owned by the German controlled L. Vogelstein & Co., and two-thirds by the, American-controlled (with some foreign investments) U.S. Smelting, Refining and Mining Company.

70. *APC Report*, 86.

71. Ibid., 65, 86.

72. Ibid., 86. On this firm, see also Spurr, *Political and Commercial*, 280–281, 300, 310.

73. *APC Report*, 88.

74. Ibid., 88–89.

75. Ibid., 91–92, 99.

76. *Mineral Industry, 1914*, 855, 859, 866.

77. *APC Report*, 65, and U.S. Federal Trade Commission, *Report on Cooperation in American Export Trade* (Washington, D.C., 1916), I, 356–369 (henceforth cited as *FTC Report on Cooperation*).

78. *APC Report*, 68–71; W. R. Ingalls, "How Metals are Sold—Copper," *Engineering and Mining Journal*, 93 (May 4, 1912): 888. The other four major U.S. copper exporters were American.

79. *APC Report*, 68, and *FTC Report on Cooperation*, I, 363.

80. Plummer, *International Combines*, 240.

81. *APC Report*, 67. The agreement controlled the world output of zinc spelter (except in the United States). *FTC Report on Cooperation*, I, 362–363, has details on the International Zinc Syndicate and its predecessors.

82. *APC Report*, 68, and Spurr, *Political and Commercial*, 310–311.

83. Wilkins, *The Emergence*, 81. American Smelting and Refining—a Guggenheim company—did sell its stock in Europe, but it attracted purely portfolio investments. Similarly, Utah Copper and Ray Consolidated—both of which were Guggenheim ventures—raised monies abroad, principally in France. Again, such monies were purely portfolio interests. (See text in this chapter.) Likewise, as noted, the Lewisohns had sold U.S. mining securities in Europe (Navin, *Copper Mining*, 304). German immigrants to the United States maintained international business friendships. See Chapter 7, note 70, for the Guggenheims' use of the British Rothschilds, 1897–1901, in silver sales.

84. *APC Report*, 63.

85. Ibid., 63–64.

86. Testimony of John D. Ryan, U.S. House, Judiciary Committee, *Hearing on the Clayton Act*, 63rd Cong., 2nd sess., 1914, I, ser. 7, pt. 11, 435, 438. See also *FTC Report on Cooperation*, I, 361.

87. In addition, as noted in the text (and see this chapter, note 53), in 1896 American Metal had become involved in the nickel business. In 1902 International Nickel Company was formed—the world's largest nickel producer. Its founder, Robert Thompson, regularly traveled to Europe to hobnob with the Rothschilds in Paris (Thompson and Beasley, *For the Years to Come*, 139). There were price and market-sharing agreements between the Rothschilds and International Nickel (Wilkins, *Emergence*, 137, 100). Bernfeld, "A Short History," 4–5, suggests a close business friendship between Robert Thompson and American Metal that "enabled the [American] Metal

Company to profit generously from the increased foreign demand for nickel." In tracing the ties of American Metal, however, the Alien Property Custodian said nothing about nickel. It could be that since copper and nickel were mined together, the rise in nickel demand gave American Metal increased copper for sale. Yet the connections seem more intimate. In fact, Henry Gardner, a partner in Henry R. Merton & Co., London (one of the parent companies of American Metal), was in 1902 offered the presidency of International Nickel. He turned down the position but, according to historians of the nickel company, remained (until his death in 1944) an adviser to International Nickel and was instrumental in shaping policy. See Thompson and Beasley, *For Years to Come*, 144–145. I am uncertain whether Metallgesellschaft (also a parent of American Metal Company) handled nickel sales, but it seems very likely, especially since it had a representative on the board of Société le Nickel; see also August Belmont to Baron Alphonse de Rothschild, Nov. 30, 1895, Belmont Family Papers, which seems to suggest this.

88. League of Nations, *Report on the Problem of Raw Materials and Foodstuffs*, by Corraco Gini (Geneva, 1921), 224.

89. Philip E. Chazal, *The Century in Phosphates and Fertilizers: A Sketch of the South Carolina Phosphate Industry* (Charleston, S.C.: Lucas-Richardson, 1904), 53–54, states that the South Carolina Phosphate Company, Ltd., generally known as the Oak Point Mines Company, was "an English corporation organized in 1870." Tom W. Shick and Don H. Doyle, "The South Carlina Phosphate Boom and the Stillbirth of the New South, 1867–1920," *South Carolina Historical Magazine*, 86 (Jan. 1985): 9, likewise describe Oak Point Mines as "English owned," in the 1870s. C. C. Hoyer Millar, *Florida, South Carolina and Canadian Phosphates* (London: Eden Fisher, 1892), 160, wrote that in 1878 the Oak Point Mines enterprise was one of eight companies involved in South Carolina river pebble mining. Ibid., 160, 163, indicates that the "Carolina Mining Company" was registered in England (probably in the 1880s) as the Phosphate Mining Company Ltd., and that its "huge" dredge was by 1892 producing over 30,000 tons of phosphates per year. David Roberts, a participant in South Carolina phosphate mining in the 1880s, had British connections (see iron ore discussion in chapter 7); Shick and Doyle, "South Carolina," 18, note Roberts' importance but neither reveal his British associations nor seem to know of them. According to ibid., 22, in 1890 Oak Point Mines was merged with Coosaw Mining, the leading phosphate producer and locally owned; the resulting company was Coosaw Mining (Chazal, *The Century*, 56).

90. Robert T. Swaine, *The Cravath Firm*, 2 vols. (New York: privately printed, 1946, 1948), I, 434. Neither Millar, nor Chazal, nor Shick and Doyle indicate what company or land was purchased or anything at all about this investment.

91. *Burdett's Official Intelligence, 1891*, 848–849.

92. Millar, *Florida, South Carolina*, 61–62, 69. Arch Fredric Blakey, *The Florida Phosphate Industry* (Cambridge, Mass.: Harvard University Press, 1973), 48, indicates that the "Florida Phosphate Company" was an early entry into Florida land pebble mining. He does not explain what happened to the firm. A firm he refers to as the "Florida Pebble Phosphate Co., Ltd. of London," was taken over by Joseph Hull (an American) in 1902 (p. 56).

93. League of Nations, *Raw Materials and Foodstuffs*, 224.

94. *Mineral Industry, 1914*, 596.

95. See League of Nations, *Raw Materials and Foodstuffs*, 231, and Haynes, *American Chemical Industry*, II, 187, on two French and two German enterprises in Florida. See also Blakey, *Florida Phosphate Industry*, 59. Millar, *Florida, South Carolina* (1892), 93–95, noted that a French syndicate had bought (probably in 1891–92) Peninsular Phos-

phate's gravel-rock-mining properties in Marion County, near Ocala, Florida. See statistics in League of Nations, *Raw Materials and Foodstuffs*, 225, 231, 233.

96. *FTC Report on Cooperation*, I, 299.

97. League of Nations, *Raw Materials and Foodstuffs*, 224.

98. Haynes, *American Chemical Industry*, II, 187.

99. Some French investments continued through World War I. See Blakey, *Florida Phosphate Industry*, 59.

100. *Mineral Industry, 1914*, 596. According to Haynes, *American Chemical Industry*, II, 187, the key German firms were in the hard-rock field: J. Buttgenbach & Co. in Holder, Florida, and Schilman & Bene in Ocala, Florida.

101. Haynes, *American Chemical Industry*, II, 185. I.A.C. became International Minerals and Chemical Corporation in 1942.

102. In the colonial era (see Chapter 1) Americans had developed a potash industry, actually an export industry, but after the War of 1812, U.S. exports had declined. American potash was replaced by kelp from Scotland and then by soda ash from the new British chemical industry. The "death blow" to U.S. potash (a forest products industry) came with the opening in 1861 of the Prussian potash mines. Those mineral potassium salts provided the best source of potash, and the American industry disappeared. See Haynes, *American Chemical Industry*, I, 160–164.

103. In the National Archives in Washington, D.C., there are literally hundreds of documents on potash matters in the State Department records, RG 59, 611.627; see esp. 611.627/331: "The Potash Controversy, Statement on behalf of the German Potash Syndicate, Jan. 20, 1911," with annotated comments by M. H. Davis (henceforth cited as "The Potash Controversy"). A small part of the correspondence and other material covering 1909–1911 has been published in *Foreign Relations of the United States, 1910*, 198-243. I used the originals.

104. *Moody's, 1914*.

105. An unofficial, unrevised draft, "History of the International Minerals and Chemical Corporation," typescript, n.d. [1960s?], p. 2, indicates that Waldemar was born in London in 1880, orphaned at age three, and then adopted by Hermann Schmidtmann. This document is hence forth cited as "Draft History."

106. Data in National Archives, esp. "The Potash Controversy."

107. "Draft History," 1–2; date of incorporation from *Moody's, 1914*.

108. See "The Potash Controversy," 18, for Waldemar Schmidtmann's presidency.

109. It came to have a star-studded board of directors that in 1914 included Thomas W. Lamont, Albert H. Wiggin, Benjamin Strong, and E. R. Stettinius. See *Moody's, 1914*. In 1909 all except Stettinius were already on the board ("Draft History," 2). Thomas W. Lamont in 1909 became vice president of First National Bank, New York (and in 1911 he became a partner in J. P. Morgan & Co.). Albert H. Wiggin in 1909 was vice president of Chase National Bank, New York, and president in 1911. Benjamin Strong was vice president of Bankers' Trust and became president in January 1914 (he would become the first governor of the Federal Reserve Bank of New York in October 1914). E. R. Stettinius would become a Morgan partner on January 1, 1916.

110. *Moody's, 1911*, and Investor's Agency, "International Agricultural Corporation," Feb. 18, 1913, Scudder Collection, Columbia University Library. In 1909 its German investment was carried on its books at $4 million (Wilkins, *The Emergence*, 98).

111. Ownership of Sollstedt data in RG 131, Box 161, National Archives. RG 131 includes the records of the Alien Property Custodian. See also data in RG 59, 611.627.

112. Data in RG 131, Box 161.

113. Haynes, *American Chemical Industry*, VI, 306. In April 1913, A. V. Davis wrote A. Badin (of l'Aluminium Français, Paris) that International Agricultural Corporation,

"Which has a strong lot of men as directors," was backing the production of aluminum-carbo-nitride at Niagara Falls (letter of April 22, 1913, included in *U.S. v. Aluminum Company of America*, Exhibits, Eq. 85–73 [SDNY 1937–1942], Exhibit 564, p. 3088). This was a different venture from Niagara Alkali—but it shows some of the interrelationships.

114. "The Potash Controversy," 20, 23.

115. Wilkins, *The Emergence*, 98. See RG 59, 611.627 for details, esp. 611.627/314.

116. M. H. Davis, "Memorandum on Potash Controversy with Germany," Jan. 20, 1911, RG 59, 611.627/338. On the German Kali Works, the representative of the Syndicate in the United States, see RG 59.611.627/141, 230, 324, 329, 331, and Haynes, *American Chemical Industry*, II, 142–143, which suggests that even before the German Kali Works was incorporated in New York (according to Haynes, in 1909), it had had representation in the United States (at least as early as 1903).

117. M. H. Davis, "Memo," Nov. 3, 1911, RG 59, 611.627/457. The State Department was active in defending "American" interests. Not until the spring of 1911 did M. H. Davis, the State Department's chief negotiator, conclude that the Schmidtmanns were anxious "to use" the State Department, not to settle the American contracts (and eliminate the penalties), but rather to force the German Syndicate to give them "favorable terms for the operation of their mines in Germany," and that I.A.C. and Schmidtmann interests "are practically identical." See, M. H. Davis, "Present Phase of the Potash Question," April 8, 1911, Confidential, RG 59, 611.627/457. Assistant Secretary of State Huntington Wilson penciled a note on the memorandum: "'My pretty bird, ye spake too late?' HW."

118. Investor's Agency, I.A.C., Feb. 18, 1913, Scudder Collection, Columbia University Library.

119. "Draft History," 9.

120. My summary oversimplifies what is a very complicated story.

121. Haynes, *American Chemical Industry*, IV, 331, and *Moody's, 1914*. On its large Florida activities, see Blakey, *Florida Phosphate Industry*, 56.

122. *APC Report*, 324; data in RG 131, Box 161; and *Moody's, 1914*, on I.A.C. stock outstanding in 1914.

123. Haynes, *American Chemical Industry*, II, 149–150. On other American interests of Consolidated Gold Fields of South Africa, Ltd., see Chapter 7 and note 228 in this chapter. The Consolidated Gold Fields of South Africa was diversifying in 1909. It made a number of different U.S. investments. See Paul Johnson, *Consolidated Gold Fields* (New York: St. Martin's Press, 1987), 38, 40.

124. Harvey, *Rio Tinto*, 11.

125. Ibid., 188, 110, 202. Both the French and the British Rothschilds appear to have been involved in Rio Tinto. Harvey dates the Rothschild dominance to the late 1880s, but a report of E. Cumenge, Paris, Dec. 15, 1894, pp. 1–2, Box 104, RAP, suggests an association with Rothschild interests in 1884.

126. Harvey, *Rio Tinto*, 78–79.

127. Ibid., 81–82, 87, 161.

128. Ibid., 82, 161, 165.

129. Ibid., 161.

130. Ibid., 162, and Haynes, *American Chemical Industry*, II, 198.

131. Hermann Levy, *Monopoly and Competition* (London: Macmillan, 1911), 242–243, and W. J. Reader, *Imperial Chemical Industries* (London: Oxford University Press, 1970), I, 103.

132. *Economist*, 47 (July 20, 1889): 948–949. The prospectus as printed in the *Economist* says "Lord Thurloe," a typographical error. On the failure of the *New York* flotation of

this company, see *ibid.* (Aug. 10, 1889), 1096. On Oct. 31, 1890, Price, Waterhouse & Co., New York, agreed to do an examination of a collection of salt works in Warsaw, New York, on behalf of North American Salt Company, Ltd. The accounting firm charged $1,907 and met with protests. The bill does not seem to have been paid. See 1890–91 correspondence in Box 1, Price Waterhouse Archives, London. In February 1891, Lord Thurlow was still confident that the "reorganized" North American Salt Company would be a success. See Albert F. Calvert, *A History of the Salt Union* (London: Effingham Wilson 1913), 40. Nothing more was heard about the North American company thereafter.

133. Arthur S. Dewing, *Corporate Promotions and Reorganizations* (Cambridge, Mass.: Harvard University Press, 1914), chap. 8.

134. On the U.S. industry, see N. J. Travis and E. J. Cocks, *The Tincal Trail: A History of Borax* (London: Harrap, 1984), 39–68, and George H. Hildebrand, *Borax Pioneer, Francis Marion Smith* (San Diego: Howell-North Books, 1982), 1–41.

135. Travis and Cocks, *The Tincal Trail*, 69–75 (on Redwood and Sons), 76–138 (on the PBRC and BCL), 139–145 (on "the fall" of Smith); Hildebrand, *Borax Pioneer*, 42–92, esp. 46, 53, 57, on Smith's holdings in PBRC and BCL and the role of Baker; and ibid., 90 (Hildebrand writes that Baker had a $4 million "option" to buy Smith's shares; I am presuming that that was the price actually paid, which seems likely from the context). In addition, on the history of Borax Consolidated, Ltd., I used United States Borax & Chemical Corporation, *The Story of Borax* (Los Angeles: United States Borax & Chemical Corp., 1979), 6–16; *The London Times*, June 12, 1959; Haynes, *American Chemical Industry*, I, 322–323; II, 245–246; and VI, 318–319; John Donaldson, *International Economic Relations* (New York: Longmans, Green, 1928), 324; Harry Foster Bain and Thomas Thornton Read, *Ores and Industry in South America* (New York: Harper & Bros., 1934), 264; Benjamin L. Miller and Joseph T. Singewald, *The Mineral Deposits of South America* (1919; rpt. New York: Arno Press, 1977), 306; *Burdett's Official Intelligence, 1901* and ibid., *1898*; *Mineral Industry, 1901*, 58; and *Mining Manual 1912 (London)*, 623. On Smith's failure, I found George H. Nash, *The Life of Herbert Hoover* (New York: W. W. Norton, 1983), 471, of interest.

136. U.S. House, 63rd Cong., 2nd sess., Feb. 3, 1914, H. Rept. 214, 3, 5, 7, 8, 10, 14.

137. *Mineral Industry, 1892*, 12, 17. The price would drop to 33 cents a pound in 1899. Donald H. Wallace, *Market Control in the Aluminum Industry* (Cambridge, Mass.: Harvard University Press, 1937), 13, 17.

138. *Mineral Industry, 1892*, 13; Wallace, *Market Control*, 6, 33; and Albrecht Strobel, "Aluminium-Industrie-Actien-Gesellschaft Neuhausen (A.I.A.G.) Today: Schweizerische Aluminiumindustrie A.G.-Alusuisse and Its Multinational Activity, 1888–1914," unpublished paper, presented at Florence Conference, 1983. Peter Huber of the Swiss firm Maschinenfabrik Oerlikon and Emil Rathenau of Allgemeine Elektrizitäts Gesellschaft (A.E.G.) were the principal shapers of A.I.A.G. From 1893 on, Carl Fürstenberg of the Berliner Handels-Gesellschaft was also very much involved.

139. Ibid.

140. In 1901 the Swiss company was A.I.A.G.; the French companies were (1) Société Electrométallurgique Française, at Froges, which was formed in 1888 and used Héroult patents, and (2) M. Péchiney's firm, Compagnie de Produits Chimiques d'Alais et de la Camargue, which erected an electrolytic plant under a Hall license in 1898 (earlier it had used the Deville process); the British firm was the British Aluminium Company, formed in 1894 (and not to be confused with Aluminium Company, Ltd.); it had begun operations in 1896 using Héroult patents purchased from A.I.A.G. (Wallace, *Market Control*, 34–37, and Strobel, "A.I.A.G."). Apparently, before A.I.A.G. joined in the agreement, it had projects under way to start its own electrolytic plant in

the United States, but it retreated from this when it felt it could not compete success-fully (Strobel, "A.I.A.G.").

141. Wilkins, *The Emergence*, 87–88.

142. In Europe A.I.A.G. was dominant, but it was "menaced" by Compagnie de Produits Chimiques d'Alais et de la Camargue (Pechiney), directed by Adrien Badin. Badin in 1909 had purchased an exclusive license for the "Serpek technique," which everyone thought would revolutionize the production of aluminum oxide, cutting the costs of bauxite by nearly half. Badin transferred the exclusive license to the Société Générale Nitrures; it was the Serpek technique that gave the French the apparent advantage and became the basis for a combination of the big French aluminum pro-ducers in a holding company, Société l'Aluminium Français, founded in 1912 (Strobel, "A.I.A.G.").

143. A. V. Davis to J. A. Fowler, Feb. 17, 1912, in *U.S. v. Aluminum Company of America*, Exhibits, Eq. 85–73 (SDNY 1937–1942), Exhibit 1011, pp. 5018–19. The "German" company referred to herein was undoubtedly the Neuhausen enterprise (A.I.A.G.), which was mainly German owned.

144. In fact, there does not seem to have been a written reply. Neither the U.S. Department of Justice files in the National Archives nor those in the Justice Department itself contain one, nor do the exhibits in the Alcoa case. See Clarence F. Lyons, National Archives, to Mira Wilkins, May 18, 1981, and Catherine C. McMillan, Justice Depart-ment, to Mira Wilkins, June 2, 1981. It is clear from data provided in *U.S. v. Alcoa* (see this chapter, note 143) that Alcoa's attorneys had discussions with the Justice Depart-ment in March 1912 concerning the consent decree. See, for example, Exhibit 1015. Obviously the "reply" was given orally in the discussions.

145. See article reprinted in *Mineral Industry, 1912*, 18. The actual incorporation in New York, dated Aug. 27, 1912, was filed and recorded on September 11, 1912. See *U.S. v. Alcoa*, Exhibit 562, pp. 3078–83. For background on the French plans, see C. J. Gignoux, *Histoire d'une entreprise française* (Paris: Hachette, 1955), 108.

146. George W. Stocking and Myron W. Watkins, *Cartels in Action* (New York: Twentieth Century Fund, 1946), 242. On l'Aluminium Français, which comprised the leading French producers, see Gignoux, *Histoire*, 108–109, 113–116, and this chapter, note 142.

147. Wallace, *Market Control*, 117.

148. *Mineral Industry, 1912*, 18. He was listed in the incorporation documents as a director and shareholder (*U.S. v. Alcoa*, Exhibit 562, pp. 3082–83). See also Gignoux, *Histoire*, 115.

149. See for example, Lewis, *America's Stake*, 93. Wallace, *Market Control*, 115, notes that all the stock was owned "by Europeans" and the financing came from French and Swiss banks. According to Gignoux, *Histoire*, 116, the initial financing came from Banque Franco-Américaine and then from Crédit Lyonnaise and Banque Louis Dreyfus.

150. According to Bernfeld, "Short History," 6, American Metal acquired one-quarter of the capital. The Certificate of Incorporation shows the involvement of Carl M. Loeb and Theodore Sternfeld of 52 Broadway (the address of American Metal). In 1917 Loeb became president of American Metal. Zachary Hochschild of Metallgesells-chaft was a director of Southern Aluminium Company. See *U.S. v. Alcoa*, Exhibit 562, pp. 3082–84, and Bernfeld, "Short History," 6, 16. As early as 1908, *Mining World* was speculating that American Metal's German connections were considering entering the U.S. aluminum business (Jan. 25, 1908, 157). *Mineral Industry, 1912*, 18, did note American Metal's participation.

151. See Wallace, *Market Control*, 39, on the connection between Metallgesellschaft

and l'Aluminium Français; Wallace apparently did not know of Southern Aluminium's relationship with American Metal or of Hochschild's role on the Southern Aluminium board. The plans for l'Aluminium Français were made in 1911, but the statutes are dated Jan. 16, 1912 (Gignoux, *Histoire*, 108). Strobel, "A.I.A.G.," also gives a 1912 date of formation for l'Aluminium Français.

152. *U.S. v. Alcoa*, Exhibit 146, pp. 788–789.

153. Ibid., Exhibit 562, p. 3079.

154. *Mineral Industry, 1914*, 16. See also, *Mineral Industry, 1913*, 15; specific details appear in this article.

155. See agreement of Oct. 23, 1912, to establish the American Nitrogen Corporation (*U.S. v. Alcoa*, Exhibit 179, pp. 1016–21). This would use the Serpek technique. By April 16, 1913, Badin wished to void the plans for American Nitrogen Corporation. See ibid., Exhibit 564, p. 3099. The joint-venture alumina plant was never built. According to Strobel, "A.I.A.G.," the Serpek technique was dropped in 1913, because technical and economic problems could not be solved. Badin, however, in his April 1913 letter, assured A. V. Davis that "les résultats sont complétement satisfaisants" (ibid., 3093). He had given other reasons for opposing the joint-venture.

156. On June 10, 1912, three days after Alcoa had signed the consent decree, and with full knowledge of the U.S. Justice Department, Alcoa's Canadian subsidiary (Northern Aluminum) made a pact with l'Aluminium Français and others regulating trade *outside* the United States. See *U.S. v. Alcoa*, Exhibit 1009 (consent decree) and Exhibit 143 (June 10 agreement). In showing this agreement to the Justice Department, George Gordon (a lawyer for Northern Aluminum and Alcoa) pointed out that Southern Aluminium's entry showed that Europeans were "free to compete" in the United States. See his letter of Nov. 25, 1912, in ibid., Exhibit 1021, pp. 5050–51.

157. In a confidential letter of April 16, 1913, Badin wrote, "I do not believe that the political conditions in the United States make it advisable to associate our aluminum companies, even only for the fabrication of alumina." He suggested that Alcoa, Southern, and Northern have separate plants. See ibid., Exhibit 564, p. 3098. Exhibits 563 and 564 show a most cordial relationship between Davis and Badin. As noted earlier, according to Strobel, "A.I.A.G.," in 1913 the French were not having success with the new Serpek technique, but there is no evidence that Davis knew this.

158. In 1915, with the war in Europe, Alcoa would acquire Southern Aluminium's facilities. At that time, Southern Aluminium held 19,000 acres of land in North Carolina, had made progress on the dam, and had constructed roads, railroads, and buildings. It had barely begun building the aluminum plant (Ibid., Exhibit 146, pp. 787–792). See also *Mineral Industry, 1914*, 16.

159. There were a few years at the turn of the century when Russian output and exports exceeded those of the United States, but they were exceptional.

160. In addition to those mentioned in Chapter 4, there were some French, Belgian, Dutch, and British investments in Wyoming in 1889. See Lewis, *America's Stake*, 96, and John Ise, *United States Oil Policy* (New Haven: Yale University Press, 1926), 94. There were undoubtedly other miscellaneous stakes.

161. See Tolf, *The Russian Rockefellers*, chap. 3, and Mira Wilkins, "The Internationalization of the Corporation—The Case of Oil," in *The Corporation and Australian Society*, ed. K. E. Lindgren et al. (Sydney: Law Book, 1974), 280.

162. T. A. B. Corley, "Strategic Factors in the Growth of a Multinational Enterprise: The Burmah Oil Company, 1886–1928," in *The Growth of International Business*, ed. Mark Casson (London: George Allen & Unwin, 1983), 216, 219–221, and T.A.B. Corley, *A History of the Burmah Oil Company, 1886–1924* (London: Heinemann, 1983).

163. Gerretson, *Royal Dutch*.

164. Gille, *Histoire*, II, 552; Tolf, *Russian Rockefellers*, 85; and Wilkins, "Internationalization," 280–281.

165. Robert Henriques, *Lord Bearsted (Marcus Samuels)* (London: Barrie & Rockliff, 1960).

166. Wilkins, "Internationalization," 280–281.

167. Hidy and Hidy, *Pioneering in Big Business*, passim.

168. Hunt, *Heirs*, II, 28–31. On other investments by this firm in California oil, see ibid., 83. It was also interested in Peruvian oil and U.S. coal mining (for the latter, see Chapter 7). On the 1904 production figures, see report of the California Oilfields, Ltd., annual meeting, in *Statist*, 56 (Nov. 11, 1905): 873. For its major customer, see Gerald T. White, *Formative Years in the Far West* (New York: Appleton-Century-Crofts, 1962), 253–255, 266, 286, 294, 337, 343–344, 462. The predecessor of Standard Oil of California was the Pacific Coast Oil Company.

169. Robert C. Cotner, ed., *Addresses and State Papers of James Stephen Hogg* (Austin: University of Texas Press, 1951), 501. Apparently they did more than simply gather information. An Englishman named James Roche took a "tentative lease for a forty-acre refinery site at Port Arthur," which he would sell to the Hogg-Swayne Syndicate for a "nice profit" (Cotner, *James Stephen Hogg* [Austin: University of Texas Press, 1959], 544).

170. Dickens, "Transition," 99, 241. According to Lewis, *America's Stake*, 95, 565, in 1913 this company sold out to the British Fremont Oil Company, Ltd. (capital, £43,000), a firm that soon "disappeared" after benefiting only its underwriters! See also *Stock Exchange Official Intelligence for 1914*, 1463, which reports a resolution to wind up Texas Oilfields, Ltd., passed in July 1913.

171. Harold F. Williamson et al., *The American Petroleum Industry, 1899–1959* (Evanston, Ill.: Northwestern University Press, 1963), 83, and Cotner, *Hogg*, 525ff.

172. Cotner, *Addresses*, 501.

173. Cotner, *Hogg*, 541.

174. Ibid., 542–44, and Williamson, *American Petroleum*, 84.

175. Cotner, *Hogg*, 546.

176. Ise, *United States Oil Policy*, 95 (on the English syndicate). On the complex story of foreign investment in Wyoming oil, see U.S. Federal Trade Commission, *Report on the Petroleum Industry of Wyoming* (Washington, D.C. 1921), 19–20, 31; Harold D. Roberts, *Salt Creek Wyoming* (Denver: Midwest Oil Corporation, 1956), 30–108; and Gene M. Gressley, "The French, Belgians and Dutch Come to Salt Creek," *Business History Review*, 44 (Winter 1970): 498–519. In 1902 Société Belgo-Américaine des Pétroles de Wyoming (Belgian and French interests) and in 1906 Petroleum Maatschappij Salt Creek (Dutch interests) were formed for Wyoming investment. These interests joined as partners in Wyoming Oil Fields and Natrona Pipe Line and Refinery Company. Meanwhile, in 1911 another French group invested $600,000 in the Midwest Oil Company. In February 1914, the Midwest Refinery Company (capital, $20 million) was formed to acquire 51 percent (later 100 percent) of the Belgian-French-Dutch owned Franco-Petroleum Company (which operated the Wyoming Oil Fields and Natrona Pipe Line and Refinery Company) and also to acquire the Midwest Oil Company and its contracts. This 1914 transaction merged the interests of all the Belgian, French, and Dutch investors. The Midwest Refinery Company also attracted investment from Colorado promoters and Jersey Standard executives. See Bennett H. Wall and George S. Gibb, *Teagle of Jersey Standard* (New Orleans: Tulane University, 1974), 96–97. Based on their earlier interests, there appear to have been English, Belgian, French, and Dutch investments in Midwest Refinery Company, which in 1914 dominated the oil refining

industry in Wyoming and had twenty-year contracts with producers. I do not know the size of the foreign investment in 1914.

177. Gerretson, *Royal Dutch*, IV, 233.

178. Kendall Beaton, *Enterprise in Oil: A History of Shell in the United States* (New York: Appleton-Centry-Crofts, 1957), 114; Gerretson, *Royal Dutch*, IV, 233; and Augustus J. Veenendaal, Jr., "Railroads, Oil and Dutchmen," *The Chronicles of Oklahoma*, 63 (Spring 1985): 15–21.

179. Gerretson, *Royal Dutch*, IV, 236; U.S. Federal Trade Commission, *Foreign Owner-ship in the Petroleum Industry* (Washington, D.C., 1923), 35; and Lewis, *America's Stake*, 97. Union des Pétroles d'Oklahoma also acquired the properties of Premier Petroleum Company (a Maine-incorporated firm with British investors). See *Stock Exchange Official Intelligence for 1914*, 1457.

180. According to J. Houssiaux, *Le pouvoir de monopole* (Paris: Sirey, 1958), 307. Even so, its assets were a mere $81,130 (427,000 francs). Houssiaux's data exclude a number of companies and the asset figures are highly doubtful. The French economic historian Albert Broder tells me that French firms typically understated assets.

181. Beaton, *Enterprise in Oil*, 135–136. Their investments were in Dundee Petro-leum, Samoset Petroleum, and Alma Oil. In addition, the *Stock Exchange Official Intel-ligence for 1914*, 1449, 1455, 1464, listed the following companies (date registered in London in parentheses) with oil properties in Oklahoma: Kansas-Oklahoma Oil and Refinery Company, Ltd. (1912), Oklahoma Oil Company, Ltd. (1910), and Tulsa Oil Company, Ltd. (1912). I have no reason to believe that there was a connection between the Dutch Oklahoma Petroleum Company and Tulsa Petroleum Company and the British firms with the word *Oil* substituted for *Petroleum*.

182. In 1912 General Petroleum in California had acquired Continental Petroleum; the merger was facilitated with British financing (including Francis Algernon Govett, Leslie Urquhart, and others). That year General Petroleum acquired an option to purchase control of Union Oil, also in California. Herbet Hoover arranged in 1913 for General Petroleum securities to be sold in London. The best source on these trans-actions is Nash, *Herbert Hoover*, 476–469. Weir's associates included two British finan-ciers, Arthur M. Grenfell and R. Tilden Smith (ibid., 469). Union Oil in California and Union Petroleum in Oklahoma had no relationship to each other.

183. *Mineral Industry, 1914*, 555.

184. Nash, *Herbert Hoover*, 469–473. In November 1914 a plan for the reorganization of General Petroleum was made by Americans, with Weir, his syndicate, and the British companies excluded, and by 1916 "the deal" of 1913–14 had, in effect, been rescinded. Nash is far superior to *Mineral Industry, 1913*, 537, and *Mineral Industry, 1914*, 555–556; Dickens, "Transition," 100, 269; F.T.C., *Foreign Ownership*, 21; and R. J. Forbes, *A Chronology of Oil*, 2nd ed. (n.p., 1965), 45, which I had initially used in attempting to decipher this significant (albeit aborted) entry. There was substantial additional British interest in California oil fields. See *Stock Exchange Official Intelligence for 1914*.

185. One of the few it investigated was the 1907 Texas proposition. See list of "Sundry USA Propositions" in Box C30, Pearson Archives, Science Museum, London.

186. See April 4, 1912, Contract, Box C41/2, Pearson Archives.

187. On this company, see Box C49/1, Pearson Archives. Material in Box C50/1 shows that the New York office existed in 1913. Plans for this office are in B. Clive Pearson, "The Anglo Mexican Petroleum Products Co., Ltd. Memorandum re: Orga-nization," Sept. 17, 1912, in Box C50/5.

188. Most other foreign investments, as we have seen, were in one function only. The Wyoming investors, involved in the production of crude and refined oil, and the

Kansas-Oklahoma Oil and Refinery Company, Ltd., which intended to do the same, were exceptional (see this chapter, note 181).

189. Beaton, *Enterprise in Oil*, 49. Gerretson, *Royal Dutch*, IV, 204, has an interesting explanation of the Paris Rothschild connection. He writes that the latter saw Standard Oil as involved in Amalgamated Copper (1899)—see this chapter, note 35—and threatening. Thus in 1903 Alphonse de Rothschild decided to "throw in his lot" with Henri Deterding, Royal Dutch's leader.

190. Hidy and Hidy, *Pioneering in Big Business*, 549, 553; Beaton, *Enterprise in Oil*, 56–57; Hunt, *Heirs*, II, 80–81, 85–86; and White, *Formative Years*, 462, 296–297. The crude oil from Lobitos, first delivered in April 1910, was high in gasoline content.

191. Hidy and Hidy, *Pioneering in Big Business*, 568.

192. Beaton, *Enterprise in Oil*, 57.

193. The date of registration is given in Shell Union Oil Corporation, Organization Papers (1922), Agreement No. 1, Shell Library, London.

194. Even before its association with Royal Dutch, Shell had purchased Texas crude (1901). See Forbes, "Chronology," 34, and Henriques, *Lord Bearsted*, 349.

195. Gerretson, *Royal Dutch*, IV, 233–235.

196. Ibid., 237.

197. Ibid., 238. According to Gignoux, *Histoire*, 116, Banque Franco-Américaine was founded in 1912 and showed signs of weakness in 1913! Gignoux must be wrong about its date of formation. M. Georges Aubert, *La finance américaine* (Paris: Ernest Flammarion, 1910), 163, wrote that the Banque Franco-Américaine had opened "a branch" in New York three or four years ago and had prospered. See also this chapter, note 149, for its interests in Southern Aluminium.

198. Gerretson, *Royal Dutch*, IV, 238. According to Hidy and Hidy, *Pioneering in Big Business*, 509, Teagle sailed for Europe in the spring of 1910 and entered into negotiations with Deterding.

199. Beaton, *Enterprise in Oil*, 60–62.

200. The date of registration is given in Shell Union Oil Corporation, Organization Papers, Agreement No. 1.

201. See Shell, *Reports of Annual Meetings*, June 14, 1911, and June 7, 1912, and Royal Dutch Company, *Report for 1911* (dated June 1912).

202. Beaton, *Enterprise in Oil*, 118, and Gerretson, *Royal Dutch*, IV, 241. See also George Sweet Gibb and Evelyn H. Knowlton, *The Resurgent Years, 1911–1927* (New York: Harper & Bros., 1956), 91–92.

203. Gerretson, *Royal Dutch*, IV, 241. I have been unable to verify a decision made at an April 12 meeting (Shell, in London, tried in vain to do so for me).

204. Beaton, *Enterprise in Oil*, 62.

205. Ibid., 56.

206. See Henriques, *Lord Bearsted*, 521, 525–526; Beaton, *Enterprise in Oil*, chap. 4; Gerretson, *Royal Dutch*, IV, 242; and Swaine, *Cravath Firm*, II, 74–76, for some of the technicalities of the Oklahoma acquisitions.

207. Gerretson, *Royal Dutch*, IV, 243: The date is given in Beaton, *Enterprise in Oil*, 126.

208. Sir Henri Deterding, *An International Oilman* (1934; rpt. New York: Arno Press, 1977), 87–88.

209. Swaine, *Cravath Firm*, II, 76.

210. Gerretson, *Royal Dutch*, IV, 228. California Oilfields, Ltd., paid a 30 percent dividend in 1908, 35 percent in 1909, 35 percent in 1910, 30 percent in 1911, and 30 percent in 1912. See *Stock Exchange Official Intelligence for 1914*, 1442.

211. An excerpt from the August 8, 1913, board minutes was furnished to me by the

Shell Company in London. On Robert Waley Cohen, see Robert Henriques, *Sir Robert Waley Cohen, 1877–1952* (London: Secker & Warburg, 1966). Did Deterding know that in April 1913 Admiral John Fisher had proposed to Winston Churchill that the British Navy make a large supply contract with California Oilfields? See Geoffrey Jones, *The State and the Emergence of the British Oil Industry* (London: Macmillan, 1981), 168. This was not recorded as discussed at the August 8, 1913, board meeting of Shell. Perhaps it was the Fisher discussions that brought this company to Deterding's attention and stimulated him to consider buying this particular property.

212. Gerretson, *Royal Dutch*, IV, 228,

213. Ibid., 242.

214. *London Times*, Oct. 11, 1913.

215. Data from Royal Dutch Company *Annual Reports*.

216. Apparently it had, however, considered selling in August 1908 to Standard Oil, but the latter had preferred to buy the crude oil rather than the property. See White, *Formative Years*, 343–344.

217. Hunt, *Heirs*, II, 81–82, and White, *Formative Years*, 462 (August 1910 three-year contract). It is not clear how this oil was handled within the Standard Oil organization before the dissolution. It seems to have been sold to Standard Oil of California, which refined it; the kerosene output then appears to have been marketed by Standard Oil of New York in the Far East, while the gasoline was sold by Standard Oil of California in that state.

218. Since California Oilfields was already British owned, this involved a transfer from one foreign investor to another.

219. Gerretson, *Royal Dutch*, IV, 244–246.

220. According to ibid., 230, Deterding (in 1913 or 1914) made an offer of £10 million for General Petroleum, which "had acquired" Union Oil—but the negotiations fell through. According to Nash, *Herbert Hoover*, 471, around January 1914 General Petroleum was trying to merge with "California Petroleum." See discussion earlier in this chapter of Andrew Weir's interest in General Petroleum and Union Oil.

221. Gerretson, *Royal Dutch*, IV, 230, and Beaton, *Enterprise in Oil*, 80.

222. White, *Formative Years*, 476. The new refinery went on stream December 1915.

223. Beaton, *Enterprise in Oil*, 79.

224. Ibid., 78.

225. Lewis, *America's Stake*, 95. This figure would seem much too low. Paish estimated that British investment in oil in the United States in 1910—before the Royal Dutch entry—had already reached $17.4 million. See George Paish, "Great Britain's Capital Investments in Individual Colonial and Foreign Countries," *Journal of the Royal Statistical Society*, 74, pt. 11 (Jan. 1911): 176. The California Oilfield purchase in 1913 was $13 million; the 's-Gravenhage Association had a capital of $4.4 million (Beaton, *Shell Oil*, 71, 118). Thus Royal Dutch-Shell investments by year-end 1913, not counting the land for terminals of American Gasoline Company, would already be $17.4 million. And Royal Dutch-Shell made new investments in 1914. I asked Shell-London sources for a figure, but they did not find one readily available. I stress "direct investments," for Shell owned, at year-end 1914, about $1 million in railway securities—mainly "short notes." (Data from Shell-London.) Lewis, *America's Stake*, 565, gives the 1914 "capital stock" of Shell of California as $17.7 million. If that is the figure she used for Shell group investments, it totally excludes the Oklahoma holdings.

226. According to Gerretson, *Royal Dutch*, IV, 225, in 1912 the group formed the Washington Refining Company which built a small refinery in San Francisco to purify imported crude gasoline. Beaton, *Enterprise in Oil*, 75, states that along with the California Oilfields, Ltd., purchase, Shell obtained the Capitol Refining Company, which

operated a small, antiquated refinery across the bay from San Francisco. A third small refinery was built at Coalinga early in 1914 for local consumption (Gerretson, *Royal Dutch*, IV, 230). The fourth operation was the construction of the Martinez refinery.

227. Royal Dutch, *Annual Report, 1914*, gives its production in the U.S. as 4.4 million barrels in California and 0.6 million in Oklahoma, or a total of 5 million barrels. The American Petroleum Institute, *Petroleum Facts and Figures, 1971*, 70, gives U.S. oil output in 1914 as 265.8 million barrels.

228. Data as indicated in my text above and F.T.C., *Foreign Ownership*, 34–35. Balfour, Williamson, before and after it sold California Oilfields to Shell in 1913, sought other California oil properties but found little oil (Hunt, *Heirs*, II, 83). Johnson, *Consolidated Goldfields*, 38, writes that the British Gold Fields group in 1909 acquired shares in oil companies in the United States and Mexico; he gives no additional information.

229. The Bank of Montreal's Chicago branch in 1914 had a capital and surplus of $33 million, which meant that its U.S. investment was far larger than that of Shell's. I have not counted direct investments in railroads as "industrial" ones. These were larger: in 1914, for example, the Canadian Pacific's interests in American railroads totaled $53.2 million (capital stock and funded debt) and those of the Canadian Grand Trunk equaled $22.9 million (capital stock and funded debt). See Lewis, *America's Stake*, 567.

230. John McKay, "The House of Rothschild (Paris) as a Multinational Industrial Enterprise, 1875–1914," in *Multinational Enterprise in Historical Perspective*, ed. Alice Teichova et al. (Cambridge: Cambridge University Press, 1986), 74–86, shows a comparable role for the Rothschilds outside the United States. When the Rothschilds invested in Oklahoma with Royal Dutch-Shell in 1912, that was surely to assist an associated firm.

231. When, during the Secretan affair, the Société Industrielle et Commerciale de Métaux (SICM) bought certain copper company securities as well as inventories, this could possibly be viewed in terms of backward integration. SICM did manufacture. This, however, was more an attempt to corner copper markets than backward integration by a manufacturer in the course of normal business. In any case, it was short-lived.

232. Interestingly, the Pacific Borax and Redwood's Chemical Works, Ltd. (PBRC), and its successor, Borax Consolidated, Ltd. (BCL), were set up in the manner of free-standing companies to tap British capital markets, and like many free-standing firms, the two London borax companies were associated with an investment trust, the Indian and General Investment Trust, Ltd.; both PBRC and BCL had Sir Alexander Wilson from that trust as their chairman of the board (Travis and Cocks, *The Tincal Trail*, 77).

233. This became evident when I compared data in this chapter with Wilkins, *The Emergence*, passim.

9. Food, Drink, Tobacco, and Grocery Products

1. The best material on John Adair and his U.S. investments is in Harley T. Burton, *A History of the JA Ranch* (1927; rpt. Ann Arbor: University Microfilms, 1966), 17–59. Burton prints in full the partnership agreements. See also J. Evett Haley, *Charles Goodnight* (Norman: University of Oklahoma Press, 1936), 293–326. Adair died on May 14, 1885, and his wife continued the partnership. Before Goodnight joined with Adair, he seems to have sought out British monies from the London promoter William Blackmore. Nothing, however, appears to have materialized. See Herbert O. Brayer, *William Blackmore* (Denver: Bradford Robinson, 1949), I, 148, 217, 222, 224, esp. 244n.

2. In the spring of 1877 James MacDonald was dispatched by the *Scotsman* (a newspaper in Edinburgh) to investigate. He traveled throughout the United States. On his return he wrote *Food from the Far West* (London and Edinburgh: William P. Nimmo, 1878). There was a British government inquiry in 1879: "Joint Report of Mr. Clare Read and Mr. Albert Pell, M.P.," Great Britain, House of Parliament, Reports of the Assistant Commissioners, *Agricultural Interests Commission*, Aug. 1880. The report dealt with wheat and other crops as well as with "cattle and meat"; it pointed out that the "average profit of the stockowner has been for years fully 33 per cent" (p. 8). In 1880 W. Baillie Grohlman wrote in *Fortnightly Review* on "Cattle Ranches in the Far West," n.s., 28 (Sept. 1880): 438–457. For the great interest, see W. Turrentine Jackson, *The Enterprising Scot* (Edinburgh: Edinburgh University Press, 1968), 75; his "British Interests in the Range Cattle Industry," in Maurice Frink, W. Turrentine Jackson, and Agnes Wright Spring, *When Grass Was King* (Boulder: University of Colorado Press, 1956), 141–142; and W. G. Kerr, *Scottish Capital on the American Credit Frontier* (Austin: Texas State Historical Association, 1976), 10–18.

3. Aside from those works mentioned in the preceding note, see also James W. Barclay, *The Denver and Rio Grande Railway of Colorado* (London, 1877), 119, in which he praised Colorado as "peculiarly favorable to agriculture and stock raising." This is cited in Robert E. Athearn, *Westward the Briton* (New York: Charles Scribner's Sons, 1953), 124, 186; on Barclay, refer to Kerr, *Scottish Capital*, 64. S. N. Townsend, in *Colorado: Its Agriculture, Stockfeeding, Scenery and Shooting* (London, 1879), 116 (cited in Athearn, *Westward*, 120, 201), wrote that money made money rapidly in the American West. In a similar vein, William Saunders, *Through the Light Continent, or the United States in 1877–8* (London, 1879), also cited in Athearn, *Westward*, 199–200, explained cheap beef from America in terms of "free land"; the "free range" was discussed in Read and Pell's report, p. 8 (see the preceding note).

4. In a list of shareholders of Swan Land and Cattle Company, Ltd., in 1883, for example, two dozen investors identified themselves as "farmers." See List of Shareholders, April 18, 1883, in Acc. 79, Western Range Cattle Industry Study, Western History Research Center, University of Wyoming, Laramie.

5. On August 19, 1876, Lord Dunraven (of Limerick) had set up the Estes Park Company, Ltd. (capital, £33,000), to develop land in Colorado, "to breed, grow and deal in all kinds of stock, cattle, sheep and produce and to carry on the business of a dairy farm." The new company could also develop mineral lands, establish hotels and stores and aid immigration. It was controlled by Lord Dunraven and his friends. See data in Western Range Cattle Study Collection, Library of Congress, Acc. 11,092, reel 46. It was formed at about the same time as Adair's venture and anticipated the avalanche of British companies by about three years. In general, British companies' investments in American cattle ranches have been very well documented in Herbert O. Brayer, "When Dukes Went West," *Westerners Brand Book*, IV (1948), 55–76, and his "The Influence of British Capital on the Western Range Cattle Industry," *Journal of Economic History*, Supplement, 9 (1949): 85–98 (these two articles by Brayer are virtually identical); J. Fred Rippy, "British Investments in Texas Lands and Livestock," *Southwestern Historical Quarterly*, 58 (Jan. 1955): 331–341; Jackson, "British Interests" (1956) and *Enterprising Scot*, chaps. 3, 5 (1968); Richard Graham, "The Investment Boom in British-Texas Cattle Companies, 1880–1885," *Business History Review*, 34 (Winter 1960): 421–445; and Kerr, *Scottish Capital*, chap. 2 (1976). Rippy, Graham, and Kerr put special emphasis on Texas ranches. Lewis Atherton, *The Cattle Kings* (Bloomington: Indiana University Press, 1967), is useful on the British investors.

In addition, there are histories of individual ranches owned by British companies: Larry A. McFarlane, "The Missouri Land and Livestock Company, Limited, of Scotland: Foreign Investment on the Missouri Farming Frontier 1882–1908," Ph.D. diss., University of Missouri, 1963 (copy in New York Public Library); on the Espuela Land and Cattle Company, Ltd., William Curry Holden *The Spur Ranch* (Boston: Christopher, 1934); on Matador, W. M. Pearce, *The Matador Land and Cattle Co.* (Norman: University of Oklahoma Press 1964); on XIT, J. Evetts Haley, *The XIT Ranch of Texas* (Norman: University of Oklahoma Press, 1953), and Lewis Nordyke, *Cattle Empire: The Fabulous Story of the 3,000,000 Acre XIT* (New York: William Morrow, 1949); on Powder River, L. Milton Wood, *Moreton Frewen's Western Adventures* (Boulder: Robert Rinehart, 1986); on Swan, Harmon Ross Mothershead, *The Swan Land and Cattle Company Ltd.* (Norman: Universtiy of Oklahoma Press, 1971); and on Maxwell Cattle Company, Jim Berry Pearson, *The Maxwell Land Grant* (Norman: University of Oklahoma Press, 1961), 97–107.

Also useful are *Burdett's Official Intelligence*, London, and the *Stock Exchange Year Book*, London. The Manuscript Division, Library of Congress, has a collection (on microfilm) called the Western Range Cattle Industry Study Collection (WRCIS), Acc. 11,092, which contains data collected by Herbert O. Brayer, including substantial materials on the Matador Land and Cattle Company, the Prairie Cattle Company, the Swan Land and Cattle Company, and other enterprises. For additional works on British investments in American cattle companies, see Anne T. Ostrye, *Foreign Investment in the American and Canadian West, 1870–1914: An Annotated Bibliography* (Metuchen, N.J.: Scarecrow Press, 1986).

6. The Earl of Airlie headed the Oregon and Washington Trust Company, formed in 1873 (see Chapter 4). He was chairman of the Dundee Mortgage Company, formed in 1876, a predecessor to the Alliance Trust Company (Kerr, *Scottish Capital*, 171). Lord Airlie died in 1881, but his daughter married the manager of Lord Dunraven's cattle ranch in Estes Park, Colorado. His son also went into Colorado cattle ranching, eventually emigrating to Colorado (ibid., 172–173).

7. A wide range of British individuals invested in the cattle companies—merchants, manufacturers, sharebrokers, chartered accountants, bankers. See, for example, the list of 417 shareholders of Swan Land and Cattle Company, Ltd., cited in this chapter, note 4. Kerr, *Scottish Capital*, chap. 2, discusses in detail Scottish shareholders in various U.S. cattle companies. He does not emphasize the stock raisers' involvements, but rather describes a collection of businessmen closely linked with mortgage companies and investment trusts.

8. See Jackson, *Enterprising Scot*, 76, and Kerr, *Scottish Capital*, 10–12, on the promotional literature.

9. For example, among the cattle ranches established in 1883 in the Dakota Territory was the Lang ranch, owned by Sir John Pender and managed by Gregor Lang, a Scot who had been dispatched by Pender to set up and run the business. See Hermann Hagedorn, *Roosevelt in the Badlands* (Boston: Houghton Mifflin, 1921), 8–9, 11, 20, 22, and Lincoln A. Lang, *Ranching with Roosevelt* (Philadelphia: L. B. Lippincott, 1920). Pierre Wibaux obtained French monies for his successful ranching activities in the Dakota and Montana territories. See Donald Hugh Welsh, "Pierre Wibaux, Bad Lands Rancher," Ph.D. diss., University of Missouri, 1955. Wibaux became the largest cattle rancher in the "Bad Lands." He was in England in 1881–82, where he heard all the excited talk about money to be made in cattle ranching in America (ibid., 2).

10. S. G. & C. G. Ward, Baring Brothers' New York agent, forwarded to Baring Brothers a letter from Chase & Higginson, New York, which contained a printed prospectus (1883) for the Union Cattle Company, Cheyenne, Wyoming Territory. Chase & Higginson asked Ward to write Baring Brothers, London, "that in case any inquiries should be made of them relative to the Union Cattle Company of Wyoming

Territory they can safely say that the gentlemen connected with the company are of the highest respectability"(in HC 5.2.30, pt. 48 [Aug.-Dec. 1883], Baring Archives, London [henceforth cited as BAL]).

11. Compare Tables 6.8 and 9.1. There were often ambiguities on how much acreage was owned or controlled. Thus the data on the two tables do not coincide.

12. Jackson, *Enterprising Scot*, 114.

13. Kerr, *Scottish Capital*, 23–2, 21, 173. Alexander McNab (of Clackmannanshire, Scotland) invested in the Matador, Swan, and Espuela companies. Thomas Lawson, another Scot, was the prime mover in the Missouri Land and Livestock Company, and his report endorsed the Swan Land and Cattle Company. See Holden, *The Spur Ranch*, 24; Mothershead, *The Swan Land and Cattle Co.*, 19–29, 100; and McFarlane, "The Missouri Land and Livestock Company," 13.

14. See this chapter, note 9. Pender was a Scot who became a merchant in Glasgow and then in Manchester; he participated in financing Cyrus Field's transatlantic cables and became a "cable magnate." See Chapter 14. He was a member of Parliament, 1862–1866, 1872–1885, and 1892–1896. See *Men and Women of the Time, 1895*, 661–663, and Hugh Barty-King, "Sir John Pender," *Dictionary of Business Biography*.

15. Jackson, *Enterprising Scot*, 100, and Jackson, "British Interests," 223.

16. Richard Perren, *The Meat Trade in Britain, 1840–1914* (London: Routledge & Kegan Paul, 1978), 118, 157.

17. Haley, *Charles Goodnight*, 316.

18. Haley, *The XIT Ranch*, 73. The parent company was the Capitol Freehold Land and Investment Company, Ltd., London. Nordyke, *Cattle Empire*, 76, notes, however, that the London office of the Capitol Freehold company had an annual budget "for office expenses" of $50,000 (£10,000). When the Matador Land and Cattle Company acquired some XIT land in 1902, they learned that the American manager of the XIT ranch had authority to make the sale. See Pearce, *The Matador Land*, 82–85.

19. Pearce, *The Matador Land*, 10–11, 18–20 (Dec. 8, 1884, letter), 32, 41.

20. Mackay himself did not become a director until 1912.

21. Pearce, *The Matador Land*, 41 (June 10, 1891, letter). The home directors' scrutiny of Matador operations became "legendary" (Kerr, *Scottish Capital*, 8n).

22. Holden, *The Spur Ranch*, 20–24. In the case of the Espuela company, it had a full-time "secretary" in London, who transmitted "policies" formulated by the board of directors to the resident manager. All income received by the company was immediately remitted to London. Monies for operating expenses were disbursed from London. Thus control was fully exercised. See ibid., 25–26.

23. Jackson, *Enterprising Scot*, 114 and chap. 5.

24. Kerr, *Scottish Capital*, 39–41.

25. Gene Gressley, *Bankers and Cattlemen* (New York: Alfred Knopf, 1966), 243–248, and Jackson, "British Interests," 256–260. By contrast, Frenchman Pierre Wibaux, who had begun cattle ranching in eastern Montana and in the Dakota Territory in 1883, saw new opportunities after the disastrous 1886–87 winter. His brother, Joseph, a textile manufacturer in France, talked some forty investors from Roubaix, along with a Lille bank, Henry Devilder & Co., into financing Pierre Wibaux's cattle purchases, which included the livestock from the Powder River Cattle Company, a bankrupt English venture (Welsh, "Pierre Wibaux," esp. 118, 147–148, 206). Nonetheless, the 1890s did not bring the prosperity Pierre Wibaux expected, and while he repaid his borrowings from the French investors, by the late 1890s he began to take an interest in nonranching business; by January 1907 he had sold practically all his cattle (ibid., 224, 259).

26. Erastus Wiman, "British Capital and American Industries," *North American Review*, 150 (Jan. 1890): 227. Sir John Pender, for example, pulled out of his investment

in the Dakota Territory after about 80 percent of his cattle herd was lost in the winter of 1886–87 (Lang, *Ranching with Roosevelt*, 251, 253). Possibly the March 1887 Alien Property Act also deterred Sir John Pender from *new* investment. See comments in Table 9.1 for corporate cattle companies' problems.

27. Jackson, *Enterprising Scot*, 137; see also Rippy, "British Investments," 336–341. Pierre Wibaux wrote his brother in France that the problems faced by the English-owned Powder River Cattle Company, for example, were "caused by poor management and considerable unnecessary expenses in England and America as well. They have been buying cattle without counting them" (Welsh, "Pierre Wibaux," 148).

28. Matador, for example, did not start to sell land until the 1920s.

29. Atherton, *The Cattle Kings*, 62–63, 99–100. After eight years in Brazil managing the Brazil Land Cattle and Packing Company, Murdo Mackenzie returned to the Matador company (ibid., 234, 239–240).

30. When Jackson ("British Interests," 318), for example, writes of a "home office," it is about a board of management or a secretary. These home offices did not participate in "downstream" operations—importing, slaughtering, cold storage, or marketing. The memorandum of association of the Swan Land and Cattle Company, 1883, authorized it to acquire land and "to buy, breed, graze, and sell cattle . . . and other live stock, to deal in dead meat, or in manufacturing, converting, or rendering marketable these or other agricultural products of the country, in the United States and elsewhere and to become carriers by land or water for the purposes aforesaid" (Western Range Cattle Industry Study, Acc. 79, Western History Research Center, Laramie, Wyoming). The Marquis de Morès, a Frenchman whose short-lived ventures (1883–1886) may have been completely financed by his father-in-law, the New York banker Louis von Hoffman (and may have attracted no foreign capital, despite the Marquis' boasts of access to French monies), had exceptional integrated activities. He acquired cattle and cattle lands and established a slaughterhouse in Medora (Dakota Territory)—said to be the largest west of Chicago. He organized the Northern Pacific Refrigerator Car Company. His projects failed. See Mary Yeager, *Competition and Regulation: The Development of Oligopoly in the Meat Packing Industry* (Greenwich, Conn.: JAI Press, 1981), 66; Welsh, "Pierre Wibaux," 85; Arnold O. Goplen, "The Career of Marquis de Morès in the Badlands of North Dakota, *North Dakota History*, 13 (Jan.–April 1946): 5–70; and Charles Droulers, *Le Marquis de Morès, 1858–1896* (Paris: Librairie Plan, 1932), 42–51.

31. This was the common practice for all livestock producers. See Robert M. Aduddell and Louis P. Cain, "Public Policy toward 'The Greatest Trust in the World,' " *Business History Review*, 55 (Summer 1981): 221. My text's conclusions refer to "British" investors; although there were French ones, the latter were of substantially less importance, but they too made sales in the domestic market.

32. MacDonald, *Food from the Far West*, 4–5; U.S. House of Representatives, 48th Cong., 2nd sess., 1885, Exec. Doc. 247, 172 (henceforth cited as the "Nimmo Report"). W. D. Zimmerman, "Live Cattle Export Trade between the United States and Great Britain, 1868–1885," *Agricultural History*, 26 (Jan. 1962): 47, describes Eastman as America's largest cattle exporter, 1870–1885. Eastman had in 1859 been made the manager of the cattle business for the New York Central Railroad. Then he went into business on his own, into cattle exports, meat packing, and the shipment of chilled meat in the 1870s (*Who Was Who in America, 1607–1896*). Perren, *Meat Trade*, 126, notes that typically in the late 1870s firms exported both cattle and chilled beef.

33. Letter from Eastman, April 13, 1885, in "Nimmo Report," 172.

34. James T. Critchell and Joseph Raymond, *A History of the Frozen Meat Trade* (London: Constable, 1912), 26.

35. MacDonald, *Food from the Far West*, 5.

36. Critchell and Raymond, *Frozen Meat*, 24.

37. U.S. Treasury, Bureau of Statistics, *Commerce and Navigation of the United States* (Washington, D.C., 1879), for 1878, 234 (fresh "dead" beef) and 200 (cattle). This atypical situation colored the impressions of visitors such as James MacDonald.

38. Critchell and Raymond, *Frozen Meat*, 25.

39. Based on annual reports of U.S. Treasury, Bureau of Statistics, *Commerce and Navigation of the United States*.

40. Jackson, "British Interests," 290.

41. Critchell and Raymond, *Frozen Meat*, 210, 26.

42. Ibid., 210. *Who Was Who in America* indicates that Timothy C. Eastman had a son, but does not give his name. The elder Eastman died in 1893 at the age of seventy-two. The New York business was held by the London company through an American subsidiary (*Stock Exchange Year Book, 1890*).

43. Wiman, "British Capital," 226. This is a bit hard to reconcile with the £900,000 capital of Eastmans, Ltd.; Wiman had a propensity for exaggeration.

44. *Stock Exchange Year Book, 1890* has a list of directors.

45. Robert T. Swaine, *The Cravath Firm* (New York: privately printed, 1946), I, 429. It was typical for a seller of a U.S. property to obtain shares in the new British holding company.

46. Wiman, "British Capital," 172.

47. Swaine, *Cravath Firm*, I, 432–433, citing a letter from the U.S. law firm Seward, Da Costa & Guthrie to British promoter H. Osborne O'Hagan, Dec. 2, 1890. The letter is of interest because it states that Eastman knew the "Nelson" business was in O'Hagan's hands and felt the latter was acting in the interest of the "Nelson crowd." James Nelson & Son, a British concern, had built a factory in Argentina in 1885–86 and was shipping from there to Britain. See J. Colin Crossley and Robert Greenhill, "The River Plate Beef Trade," in *British Imperialism, 1840–1930*, ed. D. C. M. Platt (Oxford: Clarendon Press, 1977), 300, and Perren, *Meat Trade*, 183–184, 193.

48. J. H. Clapham, *An Economic History of Modern Britain* (Cambridge: Cambridge University Press, 1968), III, 240.

49. Critchell and Raymond, *Frozen Meat*, 77.

50. According to ibid., 210. The following statement was made at the Eastmans, Ltd., April 1900 annual metting: "We have decided at an early date to give up importing chilled beef from America . . . and have arranged to lease our New York abattoir on favorable terms to Swift & Co. of Chicago. We still retain the Ottman & Co. and Beinicke & Co. businesses in New York; these businesses are doing very well" (*Commercial and Financial Chronicle*, 70 [April 28, 1900]: 844). Clearly, however, giving up the abattoir and chilled-meat imports meant the end for the heart of the U.S. business.

51. Critchell and Raymond, *Frozen Meat*, 210. In my discussion I have focused on the important Eastmans, Ltd. Kerr, *Scottish Capital*, 13n, 16–17, notes that in the decade after the early 1870s, many British companies were formed to import into the United Kingdom cattle and fresh beef from the United States. For example, there was the British & North Atlantic Steam Navigation Company, Ltd., whose prospectus offered an "improved mode of transporting cattle" from North America, while the American, Foreign and Colonial Meat and Provision Company, Ltd. (1877), would sell "American fresh meat" in Britain. Kerr has nothing on the success or failure of these firms. For other such companies, which were typically short-lived, see WRCIS, reels 23 and 24.

52. Mira Wilkins, *The Emergence of Multinational Enterprise: American Business Abroad from the Colonial Era to 1914* (Cambridge, Mass.: Harvard University Press, 1970), 189–190.

53. Lawrence Oakley Cheever, *The House of Morrell* (Cedar Rapids, Iowa: Torch Press, 1948), 72, 75.

54. This statement is made on the basis of a tedious comparison of the annual dollar values of the exports, listed by product, in U.S. Department of Treasury, Bureau of Statistics, *Commerce and Navigation of the United States, 1878–1890*. Bacon exports were much greater than ham exports. Perren, *Meat Trade*, 170, compares U.S. chilled-beef exports with U.S. bacon and ham exports to the U.K. by weight, 1890–1913. His figures also show the significance of U.S. bacon exports.

55. Cheever, *House of Morrell*, 88–89, 111, 121, 126–127, 143, 146–153 (the quote is from p. 153), 156, 164. In 1904 an investigator from the U.S. Bureau of Corporations talked with John Morrell of "John Morrell Packing Co., Ltd." in Iowa and was told that two-thirds of its products were exported to England (T. A. Carroll, Special Agent to Commissioner of Corporations, July 11, 1904, RG 122, File 666, pt. 5, National Archives, Washington, D.C.). Nothing was said about any foreign ownership. The 1904 employment figures are from ibid.

56. Peter Mathias, *Retailing Revolution* (London: Longmans, Green, 1967), 41–46; Alex Waugh, *The Lipton Story* (Garden City, N.Y.: Doubleday, 1950), 12–39; and Thomas J. Lipton, *Leaves from the Lipton Log* (London: Hutchinson, n.d. [1931?]), 24–112.

57. Mathias, *Retailing*, 98, 109. The Chicago plant operated under the name of Cork Packing House.

58. Ibid., 98, 110. On the Nebraska plant, see "Cudahy Packing Co.," booklet published by that company, 1938.

59. Mathias, *Retailing*, 99, 110, and Lipton, *Leaves*, 185.

60. Mathias, *Retailing*, and Lipton, *Leaves*, 186–187. See also "Cudahy Packing Co.," 1938, which says that in 1887 the Armour Cudahy Packing Company was organized and bought the South Omaha plant. In 1890 Michael and Edward Cudahy purchased the Armour interests in the venture and established the Cudahy Packing Company. The sum of $70,000 (given by Mathias) seems low, but Lipton wrote that he paid nothing for the plant, so eager were local merchants to have the business in South Omaha (Lipton, *Leaves*, 183). At origin, in 1887, the Armour Cudahy Packing Company had a capital of $750,000 (U.S. Federal Trade Commission, *Report on Meat Packing* [Washington, D.C., 1919], 239).

61. Mathias, *Retailing*, 110–111.

62. Lipton, *Leaves*, 188.

63. J. Aubrey Rees, *The Grocery Trade* (London: Duckworth, 1910), II, 247–248, and Mathias, *Retailing*, 112.

64. According to Mathias (*Retailing*, 342), Lipton had incorporated a new company in the United States in 1890, T. J. Lipton, Inc. (U.S.A.).

65. Ibid., 111, and Lipton, *Leaves*, 191 (on Armour: "my good friend").

66. Brayer, *William Blackmore*, 24, 215, and elsewhere, makes passing reference to British interests in raising sheep in the United States. Close Brothers in Iowa engaged in sheep raising. In 1905 the Swan Land and Cattle Company, Ltd., Wyoming, introduced sheep, but for wool rather than for meat (Mothershead, *The Swan Land and Cattle Co.*, 123–124). In the Dakotas, the Marquis de Morès invested in sheep ranching (Atherton, *Cattle Kings*, 136–137). As noted earlier, I am not sure how much money from abroad—if any—was involved in this Frenchman's ranch.

67. Perren, *Meat Trade*, 169.

68. *Stock Exchange Year Book, 1893*, 1012, 986, 1009–10, 1014.

69. International Packing and Provision Company, Ltd., and Fowler Brothers, Ltd., each had a larger capital than the G. H. Hammond Company, Ltd., although Hammond was the most important.

70. See Mary Yeager Kujovich, "The Dynamics of Oligopoly in the Meat Packing Industry: An Historical Analysis, 1875–1912," Ph.D. diss., Johns Hopkins University, 1973, 107–110, 165, 208n.

71. Bessie Louise Pierce, *A History of Chicago* (Chicago: University of Chicago Press, 1857), III, 115–116.

72. H. Osborne O'Hagan, *Leaves from My Life*, 2 vols. (London: John Lane, 1929), I, 230.

73. *Stock Exchange Year Book, 1893*, 1012.

74. Swaine, *Cravath*, I, 429. Such a strategy was not uncommon. Just after the Prairie Cattle Company dividend in 1881, there were a batch of cattle company promotions. There were some interlocking directorates with the cattle companies. Thus, for example, Colin James Mackenzie, who was a director of G. H. Hammond Company, Ltd., was also a director of Swan Land and Cattle Company (*Directory of Directors, 1892*). Mothershead, *The Swan Land and Cattle Co.*, does not, however, indicate any special relationship between the two companies (Hammond is not even in the Mothershead book index).

75. O'Hagan, *Leaves*, I, 330–331.

76. Swaine, *Cravath Firm*, I, 433.

77. British ownership may even have been conducive to such cooperation.

78. Kujovich, "Dynamics," 209, 214, 231, 233–234, 166.

79. *Stock Exchange Year Book, 1893*, 986, and Pierce, *A History of Chicago*, III, 117. The stock was denominated in pounds and the mortgage bonds in dollars. The *Stock Exchange Year Book, 1893* indicates that both companies had the same British "secretary," A. W. Barr, and the same London office. There was, however, only one interlocking director, the British major J. E. Jameson, who was also a director of several American breweries. See *Directory of Directors*.

80. W. T. Caesar, Chicago, to T. Gurney Fowler, London, Feb. 14, 1894, Price Waterhouse Archives, London, Box 1.

81. *Burdett's Official Intelligence, 1896*, 1121, and ibid., 1901, 1132. What seems to have happened was that the British parent company was liquidated. The businesses were then reorganized as American enterprises. The British shareholders lost practically everything, and American owners resumed control.

82. *Stock Exchange Year Book, 1893*, 1009–10; the prospectus was published in *Economist*, 48 (Sept. 27, 1890): 1236; it refers to the properties "to be taken over as at 31st October, 1889." James MacDonald in 1877 had visited the Fowler Brothers' packing house in Chicago, where 400 men and boys were employed in slaughtering, curing, and packing 2,000–3,000 hogs daily (MacDonald, *Food from the Far West*, 188). There is no indication that in 1877 this was a "British company."

83. *Stock Exchange Year Book, 1893*, 1014.

84. Quoted in Jackson, *Enterprising Scot*, 113. Where he got the $19 million figure from is unclear. The *American Iron and Steel Association Bulletin*, 24 (March 5, 1890): 61, reported that the Union Stock Yards of Chicago would probably soon be sold to an English syndicate. The price was $30 million, "and a number of rich Englishmen are ready to exchange that sum of money for controlling interest in it."

85. Harold F. Williamson, ed., *The Growth of the American Economy*, 2nd ed. (Englewood Cliffs, N.J.: Prentice-Hall, 1951), 453.

86. A predecessor of the Cravath firm (Seward, Guthrie & Morawetz) was the prinicipal U.S. law firm involved.

87. Swaine, *Cravath Firm*, I, 424.

88. This company, in turn, owned the Union Stock Yard Company of Chicago. See *Stock Exchange Year Book, 1893*, 985. This transaction was what shocked the press and the chairman of Scottish American Mortgage.

89. *Stock Exchange Year Book, 1891,* 870 (date of establishment). According to the Federal Trade Commission, *Report on Meat Packing* (1919), pt. 1, 240, the New Jersey company "took over" the stockyards in 1891.

90. Swaine, *Cravath Firm,* I, 463.

91. O'Hagan, *Leaves,* I, 311.

92. A. von André, F. B. Blake, B. T. Bosanquet, and the Rt. Hon. H. C. E. Childers. See *Stock Exchange Year Book, 1891,* 870. The presence of Adolf von André, of André, Mendel & Co., "Merchants, London," on this board is of interest. The André family were merchant bankers of note. See T. S. G. Wilson, *French Banking Structure* (Cambridge, Mass.: Harvard University Press, 1957), 137–138; Dan Morgan, *Merchants of Grain* (New York: Viking Press, 1979), passim; *Directory of Directors, 1892;* and Philippe Chalmin, *Negociants et Chargeurs* (Paris: Economica, 1985), 35, 207.

93. See Pierce, *History of Chicago,* III, 141 (for concern).

94. Ibid., 142; Swaine, *Cravath Firm,* I, 464; and O'Hagan, *Leaves,* I, 314.

95. O'Hagan, *Leaves,* I, 314.

96. Ibid. 317–322, and Pierce, *History of Chicago,* III, 142.

97. Pierce; *History of Chicago,* III, 143, and Swaine, *Cravath Firm,* I, 466–469.

98. Based on Swaine, *Cravath Firm,* I, 469; Pierce, *History of Chicago,* III, 143; O'Hagan, *Leaves,* I, 324; and Federal Trade Commission, *Report on Meat Packing* (1919), 240, 283–284, 332, which has nothing on the British role.

99. And Morrell & Co. was not a "British promotion," but a multinational-type enterprise, developing from an existing business.

100. The presence of British sales outlets is indicated in Kujovich, "Dynamics," 308, and in company prospectuses.

101. Kujovich, "Dynamics," 261.

102. Data in RG 122, File 3558–1, National Archives, Washington, D.C., and Cleona Lewis, *America's Stake in International Investments* (Washington, D.C.: Brookings Institution, 1938), 88. The $6.2 million was for Anglo-American Provision ($1.2 million) and the Kansas City plant ($5 million). Compare these prices with the 1902 Lipton sales price of $250,000 noted in my text. Lipton's stake seems quite small in this context. The division of "Fowler" properties between Armour and Swift did not coincide with the earlier parent corporate structures.

103. Data in RG 122, File 3558–1, and Kujovich, "Dynamics," 268, 263–264. They bought the American-incorporated Hammond firms from the British parent. It is rather interesting that the Fowler group of companies commanded a higher price than those of Hammond.

104. Kujovich, "Dynamics," 278, and John Moody, *Truth about Trusts* (New York: Moody, 1904), 257.

105. This is my own rough calculation.

106. The Bureau of Corporation believed that the plants were bought out in the interest of a "more stable combination." See data in RG 122, File 3558–1.

107. Critchell and Raymond, *Frozen Meat,* appendix II.

108. Perrens, *Meat Trade,* 170. Could these source changes be in part a *consequence* rather than a cause of the divestments? Perhaps it was both.

109. Clapham, *Economic History,* III, 277–278.

110. My own calculation, based on $45 million in cattle, $19 million in meat packing, and $19 million in the stockyards.

111. On Dutch stakes, see K. D. Bosch, *Nederlandse Beleggingen in De Verenigde Staten* (Amsterdam: Uitgeversmaatschappij Elsevier, 1948), 180–181, 665–666. On French investments, see Atherton, *Cattle Kings,* 14 and this chapter, notes 9, 25, and 30.

112. When in 1910 Sulzberger & Sons was formed in the United States, some of the

preferred shares of this meat-packing firm were sold in Holland through Adolph Boissevain of Amsterdam (Swaine, *Cravath Firm*, II, 74). Some of these shares may have been sold in London (Paul Dickens, "The Transition Period in American International Financing, 1897 to 1914," Ph.D. diss., George Washington University, 1933). I presume Dickens' reference to Julzberger [*sic*] is to Sulzberger. See also Bosch, *Nederlandse Beleggingen*, 348, which spells Sulzberger, Salzberger. Bosch also indicates that in 1912 Swift common stock was sold in Amsterdam.

113. Wallis Hunt, *Heirs of Great Adventure*, 2 vols. (London: Balfour, Williamson, 1951, 1960), II, 27, 25, 52.

114. Jackson, *Enterprising Scot*, 244. Toward the end of the nineteenth century, sugar refiners of Greenock, Scotland, based originally on West Indian slave-produced sugar cane, met new competition from subsidized continental beet sugar. See W. H. Marwick, *Economic Developments in Victorian Scotland* (London: George Allen & Unwin, 1936), 127. Apparently, one response was to invest in the state of Washington.

115. See Chapter 6.

116. Morton Rothstein, "Multinationals in the Grain Trade, 1850–1914," *Business and Economic History*, 2nd ser., 12 (1983): 85–93. Rothstein writes that Fowler Brothers, Ltd. (the meat packers), also moved into the grain trade on a large scale (ibid., 90). On Fowler Brothers, Ltd., see earlier section of this chapter. See also Morton Rothstein, "American Wheat and the British Market, 1860–1905," Ph.D. diss., Cornell University, 1960.

117. Larry A. McFarlane, "British Investment in Midwestern Farm Mortgages and Land, 1875–1900: A Comparison of Iowa and Kansas," *Agricultural History*, 47 (Jan. 1974): 191.

118. Jackson, *The Enterprising Scot*, 243–244.

119. Hunt, *Heirs of Great Adventure*, I, 182. Larry A. McFarlane, "British Agricultural Investment in the Dakotas, 1877–1953," *Business and Economic History*, 2nd ser., 5 (1976): 114, notes British interests in "local flour mills" in the Dakota Territory. See also Rothstein, "Multinationals," 85–93.

120. Edgar Lee Masters, *Levy Mayer and the New Industrial Era* (New Haven: n.p., 1927), 46; Dorothy Adler, *British Investment in American Railways, 1834–1898* (Charlottesville: University Press of Virginia, 1970), 159n; Wiman, "British Capital," 226; and *Burdett's Official Intelligence, 1895*.

121. *Northwestern Miller*, 28 (Nov. 8, 1889): 521. The chairman, Henry Seton-Karr, M.P., was also a director of the Capitol Freehold Land and Investment Company, Ltd., which had the investment in the XIT ranch in Texas (see above) (*Directory of Directors, 1892*). The connection here is that both activities involved Chicago investors.

122. Wiman, "British Capital," 226. The City of Chicago Grain Elevators, Ltd., registered Oct. 30, 1889 (*Stock Exchange Year Book, 1890*), acquired properties in Chicago once owned by Munger, Wheeler & Co. (*Burdett's Official Intelligence, 1891*). On the importance of Munger, Wheeler & Co., see Rothstein, "Multinationals," 89.

123. Pierce, *History of Chicago*, III, 74.

124. Victor S. Clark, *History of Manufactures*, 3 vols. (Washington, D.C.: Carnegie Institution, 1929), II, 167. I have found no other reference to this acquisition.

125. For Pillsbury's first rank, see Charles Byron Kuhlmann, *The Development of the Flour-Milling Industry in the United States* (Boston: Houghton Mifflin, 1929), 133.

126. For background, see ibid., 131–132; Herman Steen, *Flour Milling in America* (Minneapolis: T. S. Denison, 1963), 284; and John Storck and Walter Dorwin Teague, *Flour for Man's Bread* (Minneapolis: Minnesota Press, 1952), 211. There is some controversy on when the "style" C. A. Pillsbury and Co. was first used. *The City Directory of Minneapolis, 1871* (which may have been published in 1872) lists C. A. Pillsbury and

Co., and the *Northwestern Miller*, 75 (Aug. 12, 1908): 391, uses the 1871 date. Pillsbury's historian, Professor Doniver Lund, and the family genealogies have settled on the 1872 date.

127. The prospectus is given in *Economist*, 47 (Nov. 2, 1889): 1400. W. D. Washburn's Mills were included; they should not be confused with the Washburn-Crosby properties, which were not included (Steen, *Flour Milling*, 64).

128. Kuhlmann, *The Development*, 134–135.

129. *Northwestern Miller*, 28 (Nov. 8, 1889): 521. This trade journal is a particularly good source. It had its own London office and a London correspondent that covered the annual meetings of Pillsbury-Washburn Flour Mills Company, Ltd., which were held in London.

130. Adler, *British Investment*, 160n. The Minneapolis, Sault Ste. Marie and Atlantic was constructed by Canadian interests with British backing (ibid., 195). It became in 1888 part of the Canadian Pacific System (Herbert Marshall, Frank Southard, and Kenneth Taylor, *Canadian-American Industry* [New Haven: Yale University Press, 1936], 192). There were sizable Canadian-British interests in the railroads in the St. Paul–Minneapolis area. See Chapter 6. Most important, it seems to me, the investments in flour in Minnesota must be seen in the overall context of British investment in railroads and land in Minnesota. The Chicago–St. Paul axis attracted extraordinary interest abroad. See, for example, *Investors' Review*, 2 (Nov. 1893): 637–645. Morton, Rose & Co. had been the issuer in London of Minneapolis, St. Paul and Sault Ste. Marie first-mortgage bonds in April 1887. It offered the ordinary shares, the cumulative preference shares, and the mortgage debentures of Pillsbury-Washburn Flour Mills Company, Ltd., in October 1889. See ibid., 604–605, and *Economist*, 47 (Nov. 2, 1889): 1400. As will be evident in the text, James Hill's British friends became heavy investors in Pillsbury-Washburn Flour Mills Company, Ltd.

131. Quoted in *Economist*, 47 (Nov. 16, 1889): 1461.

132. R. H. Glyn was chairman. By 1893 Sir William B. Forwood—a prominent Liverpool merchant and shipper—had joined the board. Forwood's autobiography does not mention Pillsbury-Washburn but describes a man very much involved in American trade. In 1888 he had been elected a director of Cunard Company and the Bank of Liverpool (he was for two years deputy-chairman of the former and became chairman of the latter in 1898). See his *Recollections of a Busy Life* (Liverpool: Henry Young, 1910), passim, and esp. 71–77, 81, 176–177. The *Stock Exchange Year Book* provides the names of directors, and the *Directory of Directors* gives data on their interlocking affiliations.

133. *Northwestern Miller*, 28 (Nov. 15, 1889): 553.

134. Rothstein, "Multinationals," 89. He gives no dates on this connection. *Directory of Directors, 1892* describes Sydney T. Klein as of William Klein & Sons.

135. These were the expenses for 1893–94, a not atypical year. Just under half went for fees to remunerate the directors—by far the largest item of the London office expenses (*Northwestern Miller*, 38 [Dec. 7, 1894]: 904a; see also ibid., 46 [Dec. 16, 1898]: 1052, when expenses had risen to £3,500).

136. Ibid., 37 (Jan. 19, 1894): 90, describes the conduct of the company's foreign trade. It says nothing about Klein.

137. Ibid., 28 (Nov. 29, 1889): 613. A list of prominent shareholders, which includes a number of trust companies, is given in ibid., 46 (Dec. 16, 1898): 1052. The owners of the merged companies were paid, despite the lack of interest on the part of the British public.

138. Kuhlmann, *The Development*, 136ff, and Storck and Teague, *Flour Milling*, 308.

139. By November 1893, ordinary shares—issued at £10—were quoted at £2, while £100 debentures were quoted at £60. See *Investors' Review*, 2 (Nov. 1893): 605.

140. Roger V. Clements, "The Farmers' Attitude toward British Investment in American Industry," *Journal of Economic History*, 15 (June 1955): 158. Charles Pillsbury in 1894 told the British company shareholders, "I used to think that it was necessary for me—in the old days when it was a private partnership . . .—to visit each mill daily." In the same speech, he described a policy once followed and added, "But I do not care to take the responsibility of taking risks with others' money" (*Northwestern Miller*, 38 [Dec. 7, 1894]: 904b, 931). His speech did suggest a somewhat different role as "manager."

141. Conversation with Doniver Lund, Feb. 1982. Lund is completing a history of the Pillsbury Company.

142. *Northwestern Miller*, 38 (Dec. 7, 1894), 897. Apparently the reference was to differences in policy on carrying large inventories of wheat (ibid., 904a and 931).

143. Storck and Teague, *Flour Milling*, 309.

144. Kuhlmann, *The Development*, 169–170, and letter from John S. Pillsbury et al. to shareholders, Pillsbury-Washburn Flour Mills Company, Ltd., Feb. 16, 1899, which states that "a large majority of both classes of shares, ordinary and preferred, are now owned by the original shareholders of this company, and by their friends." A majority of the shares in the British company were held by U.S. citizens who were "unalterably opposed" to the McIntyre combination (*Northwestern Miller*, 47 [Feb. 22, 1899]: 340. Can we conclude that at this point control passed back across the Atlantic?

145. Kuhlmann, *The Development*, 171–172.

146. J. S. Pillsbury to R. H. Glyn, Sept. 20, 1901, John S. Pillsbury and Family Papers, Box 2, Minnesota Historical Society (MHS), St. Paul. This letter was written less than a month before J. S. Pillsbury's death. Seven years later, *The Northwestern Miller* would comment, "While attempts have been made to secure the English stock [in Pillsbury-Washburn Flour Mills Company, Ltd.] and make the company purely American, they have never been completed and the old order of things has been perpetuated from year to year" (75 [Aug. 12, 1908]: 391).

147. Spencer to William de la Barre, May 7, 1907, de la Barre Papers, MHS. Spencer's amazingly frank letters to de la Barre were all "private and confidential." They were to the only man in America Spencer trusted.

148. Ibid.

149. Ibid., June 12, 1907.

150. Ibid., July 22, 1908.

151. Ibid., July 27, 1908.

152. Ibid., Aug. 13, 1908.

153. Ibid.

154. Gaspard Farrer to Thomas Skinner, Sept. 8 and 10, 1908; to Glyn, Sept. 28, 1908; to Robert Meighen, Sept. 29, and Nov. 3, 1908 (quotation is from Nov. 3 letter); and to Lord Mount Stephen, Oct. 8, 1908, in Gaspard Farrer Letterbook, BAL.

155. Spencer to de la Barre, July 6, 1910, de la Barre Papers, MHS. The "agreement" appears to have been a contract retaining his services.

156. Or so Klein described himself. See *Northwestern Miller*, 83 (Oct. 10, 1910): 361.

157. Spencer to de la Barre, July 6, 1910, MHS. Klein did not have a large enough interest in the new operating company to constitute a major voice, much less control. His "boy" was not in a significant position.

158. Pillsbury-Washburn Flour Mills Company, Ltd., came out of the receivership in 1910. It had a capital of £946,100 in 1914 (Lewis, *America's Stake*, 566). In 1923 the company sold out to the American operating entity, and the properties and operations were united in the hands of the U.S.-incorporated company (Kuhlmann, *The Development*, 172).

159. See *Burdett's Official Intelligence, 1901* for the corporate change and W. J. Caesar, Chicago, to J. Gurney Fowler, Feb. 14, 1894, Price Waterhouse Archives, Box 1, London, for the explanation. Why pay British directors if they added nothing?

160. *Stock Exchange Year Book, 1911.*

161. Hunt, *Heirs of Great Adventure,* II, 25 (quoting James Guthrie), 79–80 (on Crown Mills). See also Steen, *Flour Milling,* 380.

162. Rothstein, "Multinationals," 88.

163. P. L. Payne, "The Emergence of the Large Scale Company in Great Britain, 1870–1914," *Economic History Review,* 2nd ser., 20 (Dec. 1967): 539, lists twelve brewery companies in the top thirty British industrials ranked by size of capital in 1905.

164. For example, in 1892 Major J. Eustace Jameson was a director of the Chicago Packing and Provision Company, Ltd., St. Louis Breweries, Ltd., and San Francisco Breweries, Ltd. Russell H. Monro was a director of Eastmans, Ltd., and the Bartholomay Brewing Company, Ltd., City of Chicago Brewing and Malting Company, Ltd., and the St. Louis Breweries, Ltd. (*Directory of Directors, 1892*). Henry Seton-Karr, M.P., was in 1895 a director of the Capitol Freehold Land and Investment Company, the Chicago and North-West Granaries, and the Goebel Brewery Company (a reconstruction of the Detroit Breweries). See *Investors' Review,* 7 (March 1896): 145.

165. J. E. Vaizey, "The Brewing Industry," in *Effects of Mergers,* ed. P. Lesley Cook and Ruth Cohen (London: George Allen & Unwin, 1958), 403; Clapham, *Economic History,* III, 210, 257; and O'Hagan, *Leaves,* 240–255.

166. South African breweries were also promoted in London (*Economist,* 47 [Nov. 2, 1889]: 1400). Interestingly, the Barings were *not* participants in any of the American brewery issues. See Lance E. Davis and Robert A. Huttenback, *Mammon and the Pursuit of Empire* (Cambridge: Cambridge University Press, 1986), 90–91, on the general activities in brewery promotions.

167. See, for example, Thomas C. Cochran, *The Pabst Brewing Company* (New York: New York University Press, 1948), and report from New York correspondent in *Economist,* 47 (June 29, 1889): 828, and ibid. (July 27, 1889): 965. On the formation of these "American trusts," see Alfred D. Chandler, Jr., *The Visible Hand* (Cambridge, Mass.: Harvard University Press, 1977), 320–331.

168. Stanley Baron, *Brewed in America: A History of Beer and Ale in the United States* (Boston: Little, Brown, 1962), 268.

169. Ibid., and Cochran, *Pabst Brewing Company,* 405.

170. Cochran, *Pabst Brewing Company,* 153–154.

171. Ibid., 154, citing a November 1888 letter from H. M. Bigelow.

172. O'Hagan, *Leaves,* I, 295.

173. Masters, *Levy Mayer,* 46.

174. Cochran, *Pabst Brewing Company,* 406, 158.

175. Prospectus of Milwaukee & Chicago Breweries, Ltd., March 4, 1891, in *Prospectuses of Public Companies—1891 as Advertised in the Times,* 33.

176. Cochran, *Pabst Brewing Company,* 158–159.

177. Baron, *Brewed in America,* 269.

178. Ibid., 273.

179. Ibid. points out that U.S. breweries also owned retail outlets and that only the phrase "tied houses" was unfamiliar. Vaizey, "The Brewing Industry," 407, was apparently mistaken when he writes that the tied-house system was *absent* in America. It seems, however, clear that although American breweries may have controlled certain saloons, they had nothing on a national scale equivalent to the networks of British pubs.

180. Wiman, "British Capital," 227–228.

181. Ibid., 228.

182. For the prestigious group associated with the Frank Jones Brewing Company, for example, see *Investors' Review* (London) 3 (Jan. 1894): 13. Brewers were often included to reassure investors that there were knowledgeable men on the board (O'Hagan, *Leaves*, I, 295–296).

183. *Economist*, 47 (June 29, 1889): 829. The *Economist's* warnings on the breweries echoed its earlier disparaging views on American railroads.

184. Reported in ibid., 47 (Aug. 17, 1889): 1059.

185. Robert Berger (with the aid of George O. May), "History of Price, Waterhouse & Co. and Jones, Caesar & Co. 1890 to June 30, 1901," typescript, 1947, pt. 2 (compiled in New York), in Price Waterhouse Archives, London. On the dismissals at the St. Louis Breweries, see *Banker's Magazine*, New York, 45 (Sept. 1890): 185.

186. Baron, *Brewed in America*, 270, and Clements, "The Farmers' Attitude," 159.

187. Cochran, *Pabst Brewing Company*, 159.

188. Swaine, *Cravath Firm*, I, 424, identifies Monro as O'Hagan's representative.

189. Monro to Fowler, Aug. 19, 1894, Price Waterhouse Archives, London, Box 1. On the brewing involvements of Monro, see *Directory of Directors*.

190. Nathaniel T. Bacon, "American International Indebtedness," *Yale Review*, 9 (Nov. 1900): 266.

191. Lewis, *America's Stake*, 99.

192. John Vaizey, *The Brewing Industry, 1886–1951* (London: Isaac Pitman, 1960), 15; see also *Economist*, 67 (Dec. 19, 1908): 1170–71.

193. Ibid., 1171.

194. See Table 5.11.

195. Lewis, *America's Stake*, 99, 565.

196. *Stock Exchange Official Intelligence for 1914*, 430–509, provides data on sixteen British companies with American breweries. The text reflects the sad performance. Bartholomay Brewing Company (of Rochester), Ltd.—last dividend on ordinary shares, 1½ percent in December 1897 (p. 430); John F. Betz and Son's Brewery, Ltd.—no dividend had been paid on ordinary stock (p. 445)—and so forth. Davis and Huttenback, *Mammon and the Pursuit of Empire*, 91, note that Goebel Brewing Company (which was the reorganized Detroit Breweries, Ltd.) earned an annual average of 15.5 percent in the years 1905–1912. Between 1908 and 1913, it paid dividends of between 17.5 and 20 percent on ordinary shares (*Stock Exchange Official Intelligence for 1914*, 458). It was exceptional.

197. Alien Property Custodian, *Report, 1918–1919*, 150 (henceforth cited as *APC Report*).

198. Ibid., 356.

199. Ibid., 150, 323, 329, 355–356. Residence of owner, not citizenship, determines direct foreign investments by U.S. Department of Commerce standards. Krueger's brewery had been included in the U.S. Brewing Company merger. See Table 9.2.

200. *APC Report*, 347.

201. Clark, *History of Manufactures*, II, 167. Lewis also writes of an unnamed liquor company that was British owned. "T. B. Ripey," a distiller in Anderson, Kentucky, sold (in 1889) to an English syndicate represented by a New York promoter, M. Hoffheimer, a two-thirds interest in his distilleries, which were valued at $500,000. Ripey was retained as manager for five years at $8,000 a year. All his brands of whiskey, together with all rights, titles, and interests in the distilleries, passed to the English syndicate with the sale. See *American Iron and Steel Association Bulletin*, 24 (Jan. 1 and 8, 1890): 2. In February 1890 a Chicago paper reported on a conference in that city between E. C. Depeyer, representing an English syndicate, and Jacob and Samuel

Wolner (surely Woolner) of the Whiskey Trust, wherein the two parties agreed to the sale of controlling interest in the trust to the English syndicate; the papers were to be signed Feb. 27, 1890 (ibid., 24 [March 5, 1890]: 61). I cannot find any evidence that an "English syndicate" took over control of the giant Distillers' and Cattle Feeders' Trust.

202. Ross Wilson, *Scotch: The Formative Years* (London: Constable, 1970), 150–151.

203. See, for example, *Hiram Walker & Sons, Ltd.* v. *Mikolas et al.,* 79 Fed. Rep. 955 (April 8, 1897).

204. *APC Report,* 149–151.

205. Jean Heer, *World Events, 1866–1966: The First Hundred Years of Nestlé* (Rivaz, Switzerland, 1966), 28–29, 39, 43, 56–57, 65–66, 72–77; Thomas Horst, *At Home Abroad* (Cambridge, Mass.: Ballinger, 1974), 36; and Mira Wilkins, "Cross Currents: American Investments in Europe, European Investments in the United States," *Business and Economic History,* 2nd ser., 6 (1977): 27–29. The Feb. 15, 1902, agreement is printed in full in U.S. Federal Trade Commission, *Report on Milk and Milk Products* (Washington, D.C. 1921), 156–163.

206. Heer, *Nestlé,* 34, 60, 64, 79, and *Fortune,* Feb. 1946, 122.

207. *Fulton, New York, 1901* (Fulton, N.Y.: Morrill Press, 1901), 65.

208. Heer, *Nestlé,* 88.

209. Horst, *At Home Abroad,* 36. See the full agreement in F.T.C., *Report on Milk,* 164–167.

210. Heer, *Nestlé,* 117.

211. I. J. Isaacs, compiler, *The City of Fulton, Its Interests and Industries, 1913* (Fulton, N.Y., 1913), 33.

212. Ibid., 35. See also, *Forward with Fulton* (Fulton, N.Y.), May 30–June 2, 1962, 5.

213. Heer, *Nestlé,* 85.

214. Ibid., 86.

215. Geoffrey Jones, "Multinational Chocolate, Cadbury Overseas, 1918–1939," *Business History,* 26 (March 1984): 61.

216. Heer, *Nestlé,* 144.

217. See data in Box 235, folder (fl.) 6, Thomas W. Lamont Papers, Harvard Business School, Boston (henceforth cited as TWL Papers), and Thomas W. Lamont, *Across World Frontiers* (New York: Harcourt Brace, 1951), 25.

218. T. W. Lamont to F. L. Slade, Feb. 25, 1903, Box 235, fl. 9, TWL Papers.

219. *Merchants' Review,* Aug. 10, 1900, in Box 235, fl. 9, TWL Papers.

220. See data in Box 235, fl. 9, TWL Papers, and Lamont, *Across Frontiers,* 32.

221. Letter in Box 235, fl. 11, TWL Papers. The copy does not contain the letterhead, and the list of branches is from another letterhead in Box 235, fl. 12, TWL Papers. See also T. W. Lamont to A. Roussy, April 5, 1905, in Box 235, fl. 11, TWL Papers. August Roussy was a director of Nestlé and son of the chairman (Heer, *Nestlé,* 86, 89).

222. April 4, 1905, letter in Box 235, fl. 11, TWL Papers.

223. Heer, *Nestlé,* 144. This correspondence was with Nestlé rather than with Peter & Kohler, since, as noted, after 1904 Nestlé marketed that firm's chocolates.

224. *1913 Fulton Guide,* 35. That year Lamont, Corliss was negotiating with Hershey to change its labels so as not to enfringe on the original Peter label. See T. W. Lamont to Hershey, Jan. 19, 1907, Box 235, fl. 12, TWL Papers.

225. Heer, *Nestlé,* 105, 144. On June 21, 1909, T. W. Lamont wrote to Henri Montet, c/o Nestlé Chocolate Factory, Fulton, New York, "echoing all your friendly sentiments as to the future relations in the new and united company." Letter in Box 235, fl. 13, TWL Papers.

226. *1913 Fulton Guide,* 35. In March 1913 Henri Montet was listed as Secretary, Lamont, Corliss & Co. See data in Box 235, fl. 17, TWL Papers.

227. Heer, *Nestlé*, 105.
228. C. A. Corliss to T. W. Lamont, Aug. 23, 1912, Box 235, fl. 16, TWL Papers.
229. C. A. Corliss to T. W. Lamont, Nov. 2, 1914, Box 235, fl. 18, TWL Papers. In 1913 the U.S. chocolate company was Peter, Cailler, Kohler Swiss Chocolate Company, factory in Fulton, New York; New York offices: 131 Hudson Street. See *1913 Fulton Guide*, 35.
230. *1913 Fulton Guide*, 35.
231. Heer, *Nestlé*, 106.
232. *1913 Fulton Guide*, 35 (products), and Heer, *Nestlé*, 142–143 (marketing). See T. W. Lamont to J. J. Kohler, Nov. 4, 1914, Box 235, fl. 18, TWL Papers, in which he reports results and states that Lamont, Corliss & Co. "will this year be able to pay, without question, the full 7% dividend upon second preferred stock"; he added that as for common stock, it had clearly a value of about ten times its "nominal " value of $1 a share. Nestlé marketed the baby food itself. See Heer, *Nestlé*, 117.
233. Data in RG 131, Box 257, National Archives, Washington, D.C.
234. Bruno Kuske, *100 Jahre Stollwerck-Geschichte, 1839–1939* (Köln: Stollwerck, 1939), 106. Baker, of course, made "cooking" chocolates. Stollwerck appears to have made a variety of different chocolate products.
235. Iolo A. Williams, *The Firm of Cadbury, 1831–1931* (London: Constable, 1931), 6, 62, 73, 130. It is somewhat of a mystery why Cadbury did so badly in America. William Tallis, works foreman at the Cadbury Bourneville plant, traveled to the United States with young Barrow Cadbury in 1882. The Cadbury family was influenced by Stollwerck factories in Germany; the sons apprenticed there (ibid., 73). Could Stollwerck's expansion in America possibly have reduced Cadbury's incentive to expand in the United States?
236. Geoffrey Jones, "Multinational Chocolate," 61, argues that "national tastes in chocolate and confectionery vary widely, and Cadbury products offered a peculiarly British taste . . . On the Continent, or even in the United States, Cadbury found it almost impossible to develop a market for its products."
237. The material on Mackintosh comes from Geo. W. Crutchley, *John Mackintosh: A Biography* (London: Hodder & Stoughton, 1921), 31–34, 44ff., 86–87, 92–96, 99, and H. A. Thomson, ed., *By Faith and Work: The Autobiography of the First Viscount Mackintosh of Halifax* (London: Hutchinson, 1966), 32–34. His son says that the J. Walter Thompson contract was in 1903; Crutchley says 1904. In view of the advertising heralding Mackintosh's second visit, the 1903 date on the arrangements seems more plausible. Irving Cox, Secretary, Lamont, Corliss & Co. to August Roussy, April 4, 1905, Box 235, fl. 11, TWL Papers, lists Mackintosh as a client. Lamont, Corliss had close relations with J. Walter Thompson. See data in Box 235, fl. 12, TWL Papers. Mackintosh also established factories in Germany, Canada, and Australia (Crutchley, *Mackintosh*, 82–83). It is possible that arrangements could have been with J. Walter Thompson in London. In 1899 the American advertising agency had opened a London office "to induce European businessmen to sell and advertise in America, and to let Thompson handle their advertising in the U.S." (*Advertising Age*, Dec. 7, 1964, 32).
238. *Sears, Roebuck Catalogue, 1897*, 9–10, 12–14. Frank Presbrey, *The History and Development of Advertising* (1929; rpt. New York: Greenwood Press, 1968), 361, includes Liebig's Extract of Beef as among the products advertised in national periodicals in the United States in the 1880s and 1890s.
239. *Investors' Review*, 3 (May 1894): 301, reported that the American subsidiary (and a Russian one set up at the same time) "proved veritable starvelings, incapable of paying even the full interest on their debentures." Yet according to C. A. Read to John Dunning, June 22, 1960, and Dunning interview, July 8, 1960, the American subsidiary

continued in business, as a manufacturer (Dunning data, University of Reading, Reading, England). In 1897 a report to the annual meeting of Spratt's Patent (America), Ltd., the U.S. affiliate, indicated good progress. The "prejudice" in the United States against the company's product had disappeared, and the expectation was that "before long" there would be return on investments (London *Times*, Aug. 28, 1897). The British firm did not withdraw from the American market until 1958. "Spratt's Patent" also sold mange and worm cures for dogs, as well as a dog soap (*Sears, Roebuck Catalogue, 1897*, 593).

240. Lea & Perrins Worcestershire Sauce, for example, had long been exported to the United States. John Duncan & Sons (an American firm) had sold the sauce in America since the 1830s; in 1900 the agent began to manufacture, *under license* (Dunning data). Lamont, Corliss & Co. had an inquiry in April 1909 as to whether it would care to have the Lea & Perrins Worcestershire Sauce account "for this country," but C. A. Corliss thought it would be difficult to get the account away from John Duncan's Sons (R. H. Cory, New York, to T. W. Lamont, April 20, 1909, Box 235, fl. 13, TWL Papers). Crosse & Blackwell had exported to the United States from the 1840s and had an agent in Boston (Dunning data). The British biscuit maker Huntley & Palmers appointed a U.S. representative in 1888 to act for it and for the British candymaker Rowntree's of York. See T. A. B. Corley, *Quaker Enterprise in Biscuits: Huntley & Palmers* (London: Hutchinson, 1972), 90–92, 126, 161.

241. By 1891 Fabrique de Produits Maggi, S.A., a Zurich firm, marketed pea and bean soup powders, seasonings, and then later would introduce the first meat bouillon cubes in the United States. Maggi sold through an agent (Heer, *Nestlé*, 70–71). Among the "German" products was Loriot peppermints made by a Strasbourg firm, Ungemach, A.G., and sold through Lamont, Corliss & Co. (C. A. Corliss to Lamont, Corliss & Co., Aug. 23, 1912, Box 235, fl. 16, and Lamont to Frederick Coudert, June 26, 1915, Box 235, fl. 19, TWL Papers).

242. Yosuke Kinugasa, "Japanese Firms' Foreign Direct Investment in the U.S.," in *Overseas Business Activities*, ed. Akio Okochi and Tadakatsu Inoue (Tokyo: University of Tokyo Press, 1984), 54–55, 57.

243. This was pointed out to me by Alfred D. Chandler, Jr.

244. *APC Report*, 155; RG 131, Box 171, National Archives, and *New York Times*, March 2, 1981.

245. L. Roselius to T. W. Lamont, April 17, 1909, Box 235, fl. 13, TWL Papers.

246. Data in RG 131, Box 171, National Archives.

247. *APC Report*, 153–154. Thomas R. Kabisch, *Deutsches Kapital in den U.S.A.* (Stuttgart: Klett-Cotta, 1982), 281, 367 (on Heinrich Franck Söhne & Co.). A number of German firms imported coffee, including the large Crossman & Sielcken, with a capital of $5.3 million, practically all German owned. A. Held & Co. (75 percent German owned) brought coffee from South America (and surely from Central America) into the United States, as did Schutte Bunemann Company (also 75 percent German owned). See *APC Report*, 143–144. Germans were large investors in growing and/or buying coffee in Guatemala, Colombia, and Venezuela, as well as elsewhere in Latin America.

248. Data in Unilever Archives, London (Unilever would later acquire Lipton's American business), indicate that the *tea* firm was "founded" in the United States in 1893 in Chicago. The *company* that Unilever would later acquire was incorporated July 8, 1915. I am uncertain exactly where T. J. Lipton, Inc. (U.S.A.)—which according to Mathias, *Retailing*, 342, was incorporated in 1890—fits into this picture. (See this chapter, note 64.)

249. Rees, *The Grocery Trade*, II, 247–248. Lipton-London and Lipton-U.S. divided world markets, confining Lipton-U.S. to business in America (Mathias, *Retailing*, 343).

250. "History Outline" in Unilever Archives, London.

251. John Dunning interview with the Tetley company, March 31, 1960 (Dunning data).

252. Douglas A. Simmons, *Schweppes* (London: Springwood Books, 1983), 44, 48.

253. John J. Riley, *A History of the American Soft Drink Industry* (1958; rpt. New York: Arno Press, 1972), 116–118. For context, Coca-Cola was founded in 1886.

254. *Sears, Roebuck Catalogue* and Presbrey, *The History,* 338.

255. The Germans were key in the coffee trade (see this chapter, note 247). Lipton had a very extensive network for obtaining tea. Coffee and tea were basic products. Cocoa was a specialty item.

256. Wilkins, *The Emergence,* 92, and B. W. E. Alford, *W. D. & H. O. Wills* (London: Methuen, 1973), chap. 11, esp. 268.

257. *Moody's, 1914.* BAT had a factory, started in 1904 in Petersburg, Virginia, for export (Dunning data). This appears to have been a cigarette factory (information from Philip Shepherd). The British-American Tobacco Company in 1911 manufactured cigarettes in the United States for export, especially to China. See Reavis Cox, *Competition in the American Tobacco Industry* (New York: Columbia University Press, 1933), 37, 71, 73. BAT was also a large purchaser of U.S. tobacco, buying (in 1911) almost 17 percent of the total Virginia and North Carolina tobacco leaf crop (ibid., 32).

258. Maurice Corina, *Trust in Tobacco* (London: Michael Joseph, 1975), 95.

259. Ibid., 107–108, 110, 122. See also Hermann Levy, *Monopoly and Competition* (London: Macmillan, 1911), 269–270.

260. Cox, *Competition,* 38.

261. Corina, *Trust in Tobacco,* 110, 112.

262. *Burdett's Official Intelligence, 1891,* 956–957, indicates that Philip Morris & Co. was registered on Dec. 4, 1888, when the "former company" (no date of origin given) was dissolved.

263. Philip Morris, *Annual Report, 1980* (on 1847 date and word coinage), and Nannie Mae Tilley, *The Bright-Tobacco Industry* (Chapel Hill: University of North Carolina Press, 1948), 506 (on the Crimean War officer). I am grateful to Philip Shepherd for directing me to these references.

264. Corina, *Trust in Tobacco,* 23, 51, 69, 75, tells us that the first Philip Morris Corporation in New York listed among its principal assets a brand sold in London called Marlboro, and that it sought to promote English brands in the U.S. market, "behind Duke's back." In the years 1900–1914 Philip Morris was not an important British company. When, for example, the British *Cigarette World and Tobacco News,* 9 (Sept. 15, 1904): 274, described the British cigarette industry, it did not even mention Philip Morris. In February, 1904, however, Philip Morris & Co., Ltd., did join other British cigarette manufacturers in a "Memorial to the Chancellor of the Exchequer," asking for higher duties on imported cigarettes (ibid. [Feb. 15, 1904]: 51); apparently it was concerned over "continental competition." Thus there is no question of its British existence at the same time that it was developing an American presence. Yet that existence did not amount to much. The year 1894 was the last in which Philip Morris & Co., Ltd., appeared in *Burdett's Official Intelligence.* Cox, *Competition in American Tobacco,* 330, reports that early in 1919 Tobacco Products Corporation bought the American interests of the British Philip Morris & Co., Ltd. *Moody's, 1981* says that "Philip Morris & Co., Ltd., Inc." was incorporated in Virginia on Feb. 21, 1919, and acquired the assets of Philip Morris & Co., Ltd., "a New York corporation." According to a Philip Morris executive, Alfred E. Lyon, who was employed by Tobacco Products Corporation in 1919 and who in 1929 started working for Philip Morris, it was not until 1933 that the brand "Philip Morris cigarettes" first appeared, and that year "Call for

Philip Morris" became the firm's slogan. By that time (and probably from 1919 onward, if not earlier), the firm was clearly American. Alfred Lyon (born 1886) would recall in 1952 that before 1933, "Marlboro Cigarettes were the main source of our income." See *America's Twelve Master Salesmen* (New York: B. C. Forbes, 1952), 91–102. But see also Hal Morgan, *Symbols of America* (New York: Penguin Books, 1987), 95, who dates the original *drawing* of a Philip Morris bellhop with the phrase " 'Call for Philip Morris,' Bond Street Cigarettes" to 1919.

265. When I puzzled where to include Lever's soap in my book, Dr. William J. Reader wisely steered me in this direction.

266. Charles Wilson, *Unilever* (New York: Frederick A. Praeger, 1968), I, 90. As early as 1887 his company had registered the trademark Sunlight in the United States. See June 3, 1903, agreement between Lever Brothers, Ltd., and Lever Brothers Company, assigning the trademarks and goodwill to the latter company, in Unilever PLC Archives, London.

267. Wilson, *Unilever*, I, 90.

268. On the New York office, see A. J. Wolfendale to W. H. Lever, Nov. 20, 1895, Lever Correspondence (henceforth cited as L. Corr.), 367, Unilever Archives, London (henceforth cited as UAL).

269. History Section of Legal Department, Lever Brothers and Unilever, Ltd., London, Dec. 1947, "Answers to Questionnaire pertaining to Early History of Lever Brothers Company, Cambridge, Mass." in "Historical File," UAL.

270. Ibid., and Wilson, *Unilever*, I, 99, 104.

271. Manuscript notes by P. J. Winser, Oct. 28, 1897, L. Corr., 1699, UAL.

272. Wilson, *Unilever*, I, 104, 56. Already by the early 1890s Brooke's Soap, Monkey Brand, was "greatly advertised" in the United Kingdom and was "well known" there. T. R. Nevett, *Advertising in Britain* (London: Heinemann, 1982), 73, contains an elegant full-page advertisement from the *Illustrated London News*, Jan. 23, 1892, 21, for Brooke's Soap. The words *Monkey Brand* were not there, but the advertisement contained pictures of monkeys. This British advertisement appeared seven years before the Lever acquisition. The ad read: "MAKES COPPER LIKE GOLD . . . MAKES BRASS LIKE MIRRORS . . . FOR POTS AND PANS . . . IT WON'T WASH CLOTHES." The monkeys see their reflections in the shining metal. Brooke's Soap was well known in England before Lever purchased the Philadelphia manufacturer. See also *Investors' Review*, 7 (April 1896): 249, and Blanche B. Elliott, *A History of English Advertising* (London: B. T. Batsford, 1962), 176. It seems likely that Lever's U.S. investment in this case was a response to an American business abroad.

273. W. H. Lever to S. Gross, Nov. 18, 1902, L. Corr. 182d, UAL.

274. Financial data from "Historical File," UAL.

275. According to data from Unilever PLC, Lever Brothers, Ltd., Boston Works, had been incorporated in October 1899.

276. W. H. Lever to S. Gross, April 22, 1903, L. Corr., 182d, UAL.

277. I know he was there from A. J. Wolfendale to W. H. Lever, Feb. 15, 1904, L. Corr., 367, UAL.

278. W. H. Lever to Dr. H. D. Thomas, March 11, 1907, L. Corr., 6022, UAL.

279. Financial data from "Historical File," UAL.

280. "The Lever Story, 1895–1959," pamphlet in "Historical File," UAL.

281. W. H. Lever to Lever Brothers Company, Aug. 14, 1904, and ibid., Aug. 23, 1904, both in L. Corr., 1482, UAL.

282. Ibid., Sept. 3, 1904, L. Corr., 1482, UAL.

283. Wilson, *Unilever*, I, 50.

284. W. H. Lever to Sidney Gross, Dec. 16, 1902, L. Corr., 182d, UAL.

285. Ibid.

286. W. H. Lever to Directors, Lever Brothers, Ltd., Boston Works, March 21, 1903, L. Corr., 1482, UAL.

287. TWL Papers.

288. Wilson, *Unilever*, I, 205.

289. C. A. Corliss to T. W. Lamont, July 12, 1912, Box 235, fl. 16, TWL Papers.

290. Wilson, *Unilever*, I, 205. In 1912 Lever in America once again showed net losses. Financial data from "Historical File," UAL. Small profits reappeared in 1913.

291. Lever to H. G. Hart, July 1, 1919, L. Corr., 8408, UAL.

292. See letter from Milton C. Mumford, President, Lever Brothers Company, New York, to Norman H. Stouse of J. Walter Thompson, Nov. 13, 1964, which notes, "JWT. . . has been working with Lever Brothers continually for 59 years" (*Advertising Age*, Dec. 7, 1964, 111). As indicated in this chapter, note 237, Lamont, Corliss & Co. often worked with J. Walter Thompson.

293. Wilson, *Unilever*, I, chap. 9.

294. Ibid., 126, 133.

295. Ibid., 137, 204.

296. Ibid., 204.

297. See Lewis, *America's Stake*, 566, on capital stock; "Historical File," UAL, on employment; and data from Unilever PLC, on sales. By way of comparison, in 1904 Lamont, Corliss & Co., before it obtained the Swiss chocolate and Lever accounts, was already doing about $2.25 million in business (T. W. Lamont to Arthur H. Lockett, March 4, 1904, Box 235, fl. 9, TWL Papers).

298. Basil Reckitt, *The History of Reckitt and Sons Ltd.* (London: A. Brown, 1951), 52, 101.

299. "Lever Golden Jubilee—USA—1895–1945," 1945 booklet in UAL.

300. Ibid.

301. The 1892 advertisement for "Brooke's Soap" (see this chapter, note 272) indicated that it was sold by "iron mongers, grocers, and chemists." ("Chemists" were for Britain what "drug stores" were for America.) Stollwerck also did some of its marketing through drug stores (Kuske, *100 Jahre*, 14, 104).

302. Ann Francis, *A Guinea a Box* (London: Hale, 1968), 118.

303. Augustus Muir, *Nairns of Kirkcaldy* (Cambridge: W. Heffer, 1956), 88.

304. Quoted in Presbrey, *History of Advertising*, 396.

305. See T. A. B. Corley, "From National to Multinational Enterprise: The Beecham Business, 1848–1945," unpublished paper, 1983, and London *Times*, Oct. 27, 1911; Oct. 25, 1912; Oct. 23, 1913. Thomas J. Barratt became a partner in A. & F. Pears in 1865 at the age of twenty-four; Barratt was personally responsible for the brilliant advertising. He died in 1914. See obituaries in ibid., April 27, 1914, and *New York Times*, April 27, 1914. In 1917, after Lever in the United Kingdom acquired A. & F. Pears, Ltd., Lever Brothers Company began to manufacture Pears' soaps in the United States at Lever's Cambridge plant ("Lever Golden Jubilee" booklet).

306. See Håkan Lindgren, *Corporate Growth: The Swedish Match Industry in Its Global Setting* (Stockholm: Liber Förlag, 1979), 56–58, 294, 382. According to Lindgren, *Corporate Growth*, 78, Forenade "acquired" Stromborg Export and Import Company; see ibid., 102, on Diamond Match's demand. See also Karl-Gustaf Hildebrand, *Expansion, Crisis, Reconstruction, 1917–1939* (Stockholm: Liber Förlag, 1985), 34, 429 n.9.

307. See this chapter, note 241.

308. See this chapter, note 240.

309. See text of this chapter.

310. See this chapter, note 240.

311. Alfred Chandler, "The Emergence of Managerial Capitalism," paper delivered at American Historical Association meeting, Dec. 1983, argued that Britain had become the first "consumer society" and these products reflected the needs of that market.

312. Steen, *Flour Milling*, 293, says that Washburn Crosby (the predecessor of General Mills) reached first place in 1909. Of course, by 1909 Pillsbury-Washburn Flour Mills Company, Ltd., was in receivership, and as we have seen, after 1899 the controlling stockholders in this "British" company were American—so should we blame the British investors?

313. C. K. Hobson, *The Export of Capital* (London: Constable, 1914), 73.

314. And those in beer were holdovers from an earlier era—not new investments.

10. Textiles, Apparel, Leather Goods, and Related Products

1. My initial surprise was an outcome of my having been brought up on the extensive 1960s and 1970s literature on multinational enterprise, which, based mainly on U.S. business abroad, found little involvement by firms in the textile industry in operations outside their home country.

2. I have found some cases in which British merchant bankers in the years 1875–1914 became owners of cotton plantations through debt defaults, but their investments (known by the price obtained when the properties were sold) were in the tens of thousands of dollars—that is, quite small—and thus to introduce details on such short-lived holdings seems unnecessary.

3. W. Turrentine Jackson, *The Enterprising Scot* (Edinburgh: Edinburgh University Press, 1968), 253–254, 274–275.

4. The best source on this investment is Robert L. Brandfon, *Cotton Kingdom of the New South* (Cambridge, Mass.: Harvard University Press, 1967), 117–131. See also Cleona Lewis, *America's Stake in International Investments* (Washington, D.C.: Brookings Institution, 1938), 84n, 571; U.S. Federal Trade Commission, *Report on Cooperation in American Export Trade* (Washington, D.C., 1916), I, 250; and interview with Delta and Pine Land Company, Oct. 2, 1975, files of Duane Kujawa. *The Stock Exchange Official Intelligence for 1914*, 668, notes that in 1911 the Fine Cotton Spinners' and Doublers' Association, Ltd., acquired a controlling interest in two companies "owning cotton lands in Memphis, Tenn. USA." This relates to the Mississippi cotton plantations. Memphis, on the Mississippi River, was at the northern boundary of the Yazoo Delta (Brandfon, *Cotton Kingdom*, 25).

5. M. T. Copeland, *The Cotton Manufacturing Industry in the United States* (Cambridge, Mass.: Harvard University Press, 1912), 342n, 359.

6. Brandfon, *Cotton Kingdom*, 127–129. Also in 1911 a Dutch company, Delta Landbouw Mij. (Delta Planting Company; Delta Farms Company), acquired 8,000 acres of cotton land in Mississippi. See K. D. Bosch, *Nederlandse Beleggingen in de Verenigde Staten* (Amsterdam: Uitgeversmaatschappij Elsevier, 1948), 450. Brandon says nothing about these Dutch investments. They were certainly less important than those of the Fine Cotton Spinners' and Doublers' Association.

7. Brandfon, *Cotton Kingdom*, 129–131. Compare this with Lever's decision on his Mississippi cottonseed oil plant (see Chapter 9).

8. In 1905 the Swan Land and Cattle Company, Ltd., sold its cattle and started to raise sheep for wool. It did not fare well. By 1914, however, it described itself as in the "sheep raising business in Wyoming." See Harmon Ross Mothershead, *The Swan Land and Cattle Company Ltd.* (Norman: University of Oklahoma Press, 1971), 123–124, and *Stock Exchange Official Intelligence for 1914*, 1083. See also Chapter 9, note 66.

9. I mention them only to complete this chapter's coverage. They did after all exist as "textile–related" foreign investments.

10. Asher Isaacs, *International Trade, Tariffs, and Commercial Policies* (Chicago: Richard D. Irwin, 1948), 196–197.

11. S. B. Saul, *Studies in British Overseas Trade, 1870–1914* (Liverpool: Liverpool University Press, 1960), 146, and Victor S. Clark, *History of Manufactures*, 3 vols. (Washington, D. C.: Carnegie Institution, 1929), II, 167. Neither gives names. British immigrants came to American mills (R. T. Berthoff, *British Immigration to Industrial America* [Cambridge, Mass.: Harvard University Press, 1953], 32–36). These could have been "immigrant" firms.

12. Standard sources do not single them out for mention. In fact, when Samuel Andrew, secretary of the Oldham Master Cotton Spinners' Association, was asked in 1886, "Is it not the fact that English manufacturers have been and are now establishing manufactories abroad?" he replied, "I do not think, it is to any great extent true. I know, however, English manufacturers who have mills at Rouen" (Great Britain, Parliamentary Papers, Second Report of the Royal Commission on Depression of Trade and Industry, XXII [c. 4715], 1886, 154, par. 4525). Andrew said *nothing* on British investments in mills in America. The large British Rylands & Sons that combined spinning, weaving, bleaching, and dyeing with the manufacture of clothing did have salesmen in the United States, but there is no indication that it manufactured in this country. See Copeland, *Cotton Manufacturing*, 345, 368, on Rylands.

13. Testimony in the Tariff Commission, *Report on the Textile Trades* (London: P. S. King, 1905), II, pt. 1, "The Cotton Industry," par. 526. The "tariff commission" was a private British group, not a governmental body. Henceforth cited as *Tariff Commission Report*.

14. *Burdett's Official Intelligence, 1895*, 1184–85; it also had a German subsidiary. See, in addition, John Dunning data, University of Reading, Reading, England.

15. 1960 interview in Dunning data.

16. *Bulletin of the National Association of Wool Manufacturers*, 27 (Dec. 1898): 420, noted that in October 1898 the Pomeroy Mills, Pittsfield, Massachusetts, were leased to Hellewell & Co., Leeds, England, "for the manufacture of cotton warp, carriage cloths, etc.," another specialized group of products.

17. William Ashley, *The Tariff Problem*, 2nd ed. (London: P. S. King, 1903), 77, noted that Sir Titus Salt, Bart., Sons & Co., Ltd., Saltaire (dress goods and the like) had invested in the United States in "recent years." My best information on this investment comes from Denys Salt to Mira Wilkins, Aug. 2, and Dec. 14, 1982, who wrote that the Salt's Textile Company was set up in Bridgeport, Connecticut, after the passage of the 1890 McKinley tariff. Salt believed it was wholly owned by Sir Titus Salt, Bart., & Sons, Ltd., and employed about 1,500 people. Its products were sold to jobbers and manufacturers throughout the United States. On Sir Titus Salt, Bart., Sons & Co., Ltd., at Saltaire in England, see *Bulletin of the National Association of Wool Manufacturers*, 22 (Sept. 1892): 299–302, and 25 (Dec. 1895): 356.

18. *Tariff Commission Report*, II, pt. 2, "The Wool Industry," par. 1683.

19. Ibid., par. 1624.

20. Ibid., par. 1765. Other firms in the "woolen industry" mentioned in these 1905 tariff hearings, which had "set up mills" in the United States, were "Priestley of Bradford . . .; Marshalls, of Leeds . . . this firm is reported to have had at one time employed 4,000 hands in Leeds . . . Lister, of Huddersfield," with imitation seal skin, cloth (ibid., par. 1486). Some of these firms closed down entirely in Great Britain. The impact of British immigrants on the American woolens industry is indicated by Berthoff, *British Immigrants*, 38–39, which is often vague on whether "British manufactur-

ers" migrated or continued to retain plants and residence in their home country, thus making "foreign" investments.

21. Ashley, *The Tariff Problem*, 77.

22. J. Neville Bartlett, *Carpeting the Millions: The Growth of Britain's Carpet Industry* (Edinburgh: John Donald, n.d. [1977?]), 60–61, 106.

23. *Tariff Commission Report*, II, pt. 5, "The Carpet Industry," Witness No. 71, pars. 2932–33. The date coincides with that in Bartlett, *Carpeting*, 60 (for Firth).

24. Ibid., Firm No. 4292, par. 2997. I presume Witness No. 71 did not come from Firm No. 4292, and this witness was not from Firth. I do not believe T. F. Firth & Sons was the only British carpet maker to invest in the United States. This firm could, however, conceivably have been Firth. The report wanted to make the point that many companies were investing in America and might well have used this deceptive strategy.

25. Ibid., par. 2931.

26. Bartlett, *Carpeting*, 61, based on 1909–1912 data in the Crossley firm's archives. Crossley's Austrian and Russian plants were built in the 1880s (ibid., 60). Bartlett (p. 61) reports that John Crossley & Sons, Ltd., had in 1870 turned down an offer by a leading customer to provide capital for an American factory and in the late 1890s had again rejected a similar proposal.

27. Bruce Lenman and Kathleen Donaldson, "Partners' Incomes, Investment and Diversification in the Scottish Linen Area, 1850–1921," *Business History*, 13 (Jan. 1971): 15.

28. W. & J. Sloane today is mainly known as a retailer of fine furniture. It continues to sell carpets, but one would probably not go to this firm's stores for linoleum. Bartlett, *Carpeting*, 37, describes W. & J. Sloane as well-known importers and distributors of carpets in the 1870s.

29. If W. & J. Sloane had an interest, the relationship would be not unlike that of Lamont, Corliss & Co. and the chocolate works in Fulton, New York—described in Chapter 9—albeit W. & J. Sloane sold at retail, whereas Lamont, Corliss did not. Likewise, there is no indication that Nairn had an interest in W. & J. Sloane.

30. Augustus Muir, *Nairns of Kirkcaldy* (Cambridge: W. Heffer, 1956), 68, 85–89, 92, 101–102.

31. *Stock Exchange Official Intelligence for 1914*, 690.

32. Berthoff, *British Immigration*, 45, 43, writes of British silk and lace manufacturers "who set up branch mills in America"—in Pennsylvania, Connecticut, and New York. Berthoff is, however, not explicit on ownership, and his use of the word *branch* notwithstanding, some of these could be plants of British manufacturers who migrated to the United States.

33. Denys Salt to Wilkins, Dec. 14, 1982. "Salt's Textile Manufacturing Co." with a New York address is listed on the March 1914 membership list roster of the Silk Association of America, *Annual Report, 1914*, 122. Several Manchester silk producers (H. T. Gaddum and Watts & Son) had New York sales agents in the late 1880s. See William C. Wyckoff, *American Silk Manufacture* (New York: Silk Association of America, 1887), 138. These agents appear to have sold spun silk. I have no evidence that these firms ever manufactured in the United States. William Watson of Lister & Co., Manningham Mills, Bradford, which was in the early twentieth century the most important British producer of silk plushes, noted in 1905 that his firm had considered manufacturing in the United States and that he had traveled across the Atlantic several times, but had decided not to invest— since there were "sufficient" firms there to meet demand. See *Tariff Commission Report*, II, pt. 6, "Silk Industry," pars. 3311, 3318. On the Manningham Mills and S. Cunliffe Lister (Lord Masham), see *Bulletin of the Association of Wool Manufacturers*, 25 (Dec. 1895): 356–357.

34. Berthoff, *British Immigration*, 43, 45. See note 32 above. The *Tariff Commission Report*, II, pt. 4, "Lace Industry," par. 2730, says that because of the high U.S. tariffs, British manufacturers established lace-manufacturing plants in "Chicago, Philadelphia, Maine [*sic*], and Baltimore." Note the different locales from those cited in Berthoff.

35. *Tariff Commission Report*, II, pt. 7, "Flax, Hemp & Jute Industies," pars. 3829, 3843. R. H. Reade, chairman and managing director of the York Street Flax Spinning Company, Ltd., Belfast, testified that his company (flax spinners, weavers, bleachers, dyers, and distributors) had its own places of business in New York, London, Paris, and Berlin. "We and many other Irish firms have started factories for stitching and hemming in New York," because of the duties. The first U.S. "branch" of the York Street Flax Spinning Company had opened in New York in 1871 (Emily Boyle, "John Mulholland," *Dictionary of Business Biography*, IV, 375).

36. Henry W. Macrosty, *The Trust Movement in British Industry* (London: Longmans, Green, 1907), 166.

37. Calico Printers' Association, Board of Directors Minutes, January 28, 1904 (I am indebted to Dr. Anthony Howe for this reference). Calico Printers' Association was a huge merged enterprise. Its December 1899 prospectus announced the amalgamation of fifty-nine British companies (Macrosty, *The Trust Movement*, 149). In 1899 three groups of promoters—at least one of which claimed to have British capital behind it—sought to purchase and combine thirty print cloth factories in Fall River and New Bedford, Massachusetts (these works had 2.25 million spindles). The merger never materialized; although there was a "print cloth pool" and a selling combination, I have found no evidence of British business influence on either. See Clark, *History of Manufactures*, III, 181–182. My *guess* is that the promoters in 1899 were seeking, in vain, to try to expand the *British* merger—Calico Printers' Association—into America; as I will show, this had been done in 1897–98 with the English Sewing Cotton Company–American Thread arrangements.

38. Report of Shareholders Meeting, Year ending Dec. 31, 1912, in *Economist*, 76 (March 1, 1913), 534. See also 1911 report in ibid., 74 (March 2, 1912): 482–483.

39. Report of Shareholders Meeting, Year ending Dec. 31, 1913, *Economist*, 78 (Feb. 28, 1914): 548. The chairman referred to a company plant in Germany, where numerous difficulties had been overcome (ibid.).

40. Report of Shareholders Meeting, Year ending Dec. 31, 1914, *Economist*, 80 (Feb. 27, 1915): 448.

41. "German Textile Factories in America," *Bulletin of the National Association of Wool Manufacturers*, 29 (Dec. 1899): 380; ibid., 29 (March 1908): 58, 127–128 (on advocacy of high tariff); Alien Property Custodian, *Report, 1918–1919* (henceforth cited as *APC Report*), 128–129; Clark, *History of Manufactures*, III, 198; and Arthur H. Cole, *American Wool Manufacture* (Cambridge, Mass: Harvard University Press, 1926), II, 163 (quote). The German firms were based in Gera, Greiz, and Leipzig.

42. Clark, *History of Manufactures*, III, 195.

43. On this *German* industry, see W. O. Henderson, *The Rise of German Industrial Power* (Berkeley: University of California Press, 1975), 145–146, 238. The German firms in Passaic, New Jersey, were truly important ones. Botany Worsted Company had started modestly, importing "cashmeres in the gray, to be finished at their mills in this country." The goods in gray came from the parent firm—Stoehr & Co., Leipzig (*Bulletin of the National Association of Wool Manufacturers*, 22 [Sept. 1892]: 312). By 1912 Botany Worsted Mills made "Fine Ladies Dress Goods, Cloths and Men's Wear Goods and Fine Worsted Yarns—Dry Spun." It had "Dress Goods Sales Rooms" in ten U.S. cities. See ibid., 42 (March 1912), advertisement. On the Forstmann family enterprise (which

for several generations had been engaged in wool manufacture in Germany) and its American mills, see, for example, ibid., 37 (Dec. 1907): 439; 41 (Sept. 1911): 457; and 42 (March 1912): advertisement.

44. Data in Record Group 131, Box 254, National Archives, Washington, D.C. See also Silk Association of America, *Annual Report, 1910*, 47. The employment figures are from *Moody's 1920*, 1135, but data suggest that the number applies to 1914.

45. In September 1899 the U.S. Vice-Consul General (Simon W. Hanauer) at Frankfurt reported that manufacturers of silk textiles from Crefeld planned to start branch factories in America. Crefeld was the most important German silk textile center. See *Bulletin of the National Association of Wool Manufacturers*, 29 (Dec. 1899): 380. It is not clear whether they actually did so. William Schroeder & Co., Crefeld, had mills in Germany and Switzerland and was one of the largest silk manufacturers in Europe. It had a branch house in New York, founded in 1870. It does not seem to have had American mills (Silk Association of America, *Annual Report, 1907*, 49). Herman Simon and his brother Robert (who died in 1901), both from Frankfurt, had migrated to the United States. Their mill at Easton, Pennsylvania, began in 1883. By 1913 R. & H. Simon was "a great industrial enterprise," with silk mills at Union Hill, New Jersey, and Easton. On his death, Sept. 27, 1913, Herman Simon was the active head of R. & H. Simon and known as the largest "individual silk owner in the world." His company, R. & H. Simon, had (as of 1917) minority foreign ownership: 18 percent. On R. & H. Simon, see Silk Association of America, *Annual Report*, 1886, 111; obituary for Herman Simon, ibid., 1914, 36; and *APC Report*, 346. On Audiger & Meyer Silk Company, Paterson, New Jersey, see Silk Association of America annual reports. It last appears on the Silk Association membership rolls in 1907. Nonethless, the *APC Report* (p. 297) suggests that it still existed in 1914 and was 68 percent German owned.

46. *APC Report*, 132.

47. Ibid., 131–132.

48. Ibid., 133.

49. The French were large exporters of textiles—silk, wool, and cotton. For their importance in French foreign trade, see François Caron, *An Economic History of Modern France* (New York: Columbia University Press, 1979), 106.

50. A. P. Thomas, *Woonsocket: Highlights of History, 1800–1976* (East Providence, R.I.: Globe Printing, 1976), 108–118, discusses the French mills. I am deeply indebted to Professor Donald Marchand for directing me to this reference. See also Cole, *American Wool Manufacture*, II, 163.

51. Thomas, *Woonsocket*, 108, 111. Before his death in 1985, Robert Lepoutre wrote that his father (Auguste Lepoutre) had gone to America in 1899 to explore the possibilities of manufacturing there; the son recalled the story about the priest (1985 notes of Robert Lepoutre, Roubaix, courtesy of Jean-François Hennart, Feb. 3, 1986).

52. Thomas, *Woonsocket*, 109. In 1911 a representative of one of the German-owned firms in Passaic, New Jersey, testified that when its American works was built, its German owners were obliged "in order to be able to compete . . . to import most of its machinery . . . This is especially true of machinery used in what is known as the French system of worsted spinning, which is being adopted more and more each year" (Clark, *History of Manufactures*, III, 198). The German Forstmann & Huffmann, Passaic, New Jersey, advertised in 1912 "Fine Dry-Spun Worsted Yarns (French System)." See *Bulletin of the National Association of Wool Manufacturers*, 42 (March 1912).

53. Thomas *Woonsocket*, 108–118.

54. Émile Becque, *L'internationalisation des capitaux* (Montpellier: Imprimerie Générale du Midi, 1912), 212–213, wrote of the French silkmakers in the United States, but gave no names. Clark, *History of Manufactures*, III, 216, recorded that "some silk mills

[in the United States] . . . were virtually links in an international chain of establish-ments." He could have been talking about the Swiss, German, or British mills, but I believe he was referring to some French-owned ones.

55. Michel Laferrère, *Lyon: ville industrielle* (Paris: Presses Universitaires de France, 1960), 12, 142n, and A. Beauquis, *Histoire économique de la soie* (Paris: H. Dunod et E. Pinat, 1910), 494–495. Wyckoff, *American Silk Manufacture*, 137, indicates that in 1887 Guerin, Vve & Fils, Lyon, had a sales branch in New York, and E. Paladine served as agent in New York for P. H. Barbezat, Lyon. J.-L. Duplan, *Lettres d'un vieil américain* (Paris: Payot, 1917), 83, wrote that in 1875, 90 percent of the silk consumed in the United States came from France.

56. Laferrère, *Lyon*, 187–188. On the plant's location, see Silk Association of Amer-ica, *Annual Report, 1909*, 35. Duplan Silk Company also had a presence in New York City first on Broome Street and then on Union Square. See ibid., 1911, 78, and 1913, 91. For a presentation of Jean L. Duplan, see ibid., 1914, 47.

57. I am indebted to Professor Pierre Cayez for his aid in my research on the French silk companies (Cayez to Wilkins, Jan. 5, 1983). The Department of State, Augusta, Maine, confirms the incorporation of the J. B. Martin Company, on Oct. 2, 1909 (letter to Wilkins, March 18, 1983). J. B. Martin Company continued to use the Norwich, Connecticut, address. See Silk Association of America, *Annual Report, 1914*, 121. By the early 1900s, United Piece Dye Works had a plant in Lodi, New Jersey. United Piece Dye Works first appears on the membership roster of the Silk Association of America in March 1904; see ibid., 1904, 70, and also ibid., 1910, 51, for presentation by Albert Blum of the United Piece Dye Works, of "Lodi, N.J. and New York City," on piece dyeing, printing, and finishing. Blum—who had been associated with the Alexander Dye Works, Lodi, New Jersey (the predecessor of the United Piece Dye Works)—ran this firm. It is not clear exactly when Edmond Gillet became involved. My source for his role is Cayez to Wilkins, Jan. 5, 1983.

58. Duplan, *Lettres*, 84–87. "J.-L. Duplan" and "Jean L. Duplan" of Duplan Silk Company are undoubtedly the same person.

59. Silk Association of America, *Annual Report, 1901*, 21, 48, 120. The Schwarzen-bach firm in Switzerland had in 1860 inaugurated the first silk power-loom weaving in Europe. In 1885 Robert Schwarzenbach had visited the United States and acquired a factory site in West Hoboken. His cousin, Ernest A. Otz—who arrived in America in January 1879 as a representative of J. Schwarzenbach-Landis (silk manufacturers, Zu-rich)—together with Jacques Huber and Robert Schwarzenbach (1839–1904; he re-mained in Switzerland) established Schwarzenbach, Huber & Co. on Jan. 1, 1888. The new firm was formed "on the determination of the Schwarzenbachs to establish silk manufacturing plants in America." See ibid., 1902, 39–40; ibid., 1904, 40 (obituary for Otz); and ibid., 1905, 60–61 (obituary for Robert Schwarzenbach). On Schwarzenbach and other Swiss silkmakers in America, see also Ernst Himmel, *Industrielle Kapitalan-lagen der Schweiz im Ausland* (Langensalza: Hermann Beyer, 1922), 13, 36, 42, and esp. 124–125. Himmel was unaware that Schwarzenbach had an American business as early as the 1880s.

60. Data on this business were mentioned in Hans Bauer, *Swiss Bank Corporation, 1872–1972* (Basle: Swiss Bank Corporation, 1972), 168–169, only because A. Simonius, chairman of the SBC, traveled on the Titanic in 1912 when he went to inspect this branch! SBC had interests in the Swiss manufacturing venture.

61. Julius Landmann, *Die Schweizerische Volkswirtschaft* (Einsidein, Switzerland: Ver-lagsanstalt Benziger, 1925), 189. See ibid., 177ff., on the importance of the Swiss embroidery industry. In the early 1870s an uncle of Meyer Guggenheim's wife had started a Swiss factory for embroidering by machine. Meyer, who would be its sales

representative in the United States, sent his sons to St. Gall, the Swiss embroidery center, and opened a New York office for Swiss manufacturers. It was the start of Meyer Guggenheim's fortune. See Harvey O'Connor, *The Guggenheims* (New York: Covici, Friede, 1937), 37–40. Guggenheim was strictly an importer; he never did any manufacturing. On the Swiss importance in the U. S. embroidery industry, see Himmel, *Industrielle Kapitalanlagen*, 126–127, and the unpaged "Recapitulation." As of 1914, Swiss investments in the U.S. embroidery industry were larger than in any other American manufacturing sector. The investment was 47.5 million francs (about $9.2 million) in the multiplant Schweizerisch-Amerikanischen Stickerei-Industrie-Gesellschaft.

62. *Tariff Commission Report*, passim. For complete transfers, see, for example, pt. 7, par. 4241. Nairn, which asked for a tariff after entry, was exceptional.

63. *American Iron and Steel Association Bulletin*, 23 (Dec. 11, 1889): 341, noted that "it is stated that a syndicate of English and New York capitalists is buying up and consolidating all the cotton-duck mills in the country, the industry being centered in Baltimore. For this purpose $15,000,000 to $18,000,000 would be required." I have no evidence that the "English" made such an investment.

64. In April 1899 the *Fall River News* had marveled that one of the biggest combinations yet conceived was in the process of formation: "It is nothing less than the purchase by an English syndicate of the entire cotton yarn industry of the United States, a purchase which will require considerably over $100,000,000 capital . . . It seems that the New Bedford banks grew weary of carrying the load and sought relief. They finally interested some wealthy English capitalists." The news account greatly exaggerated both the size of the combination and the role of the British. The New England Cotton Yarn Company (incorporated in July 1899) had an authorized capital of $5 million in common stock and $6.5 million in preferred stock, and $6.5 million in 5 percent mortgage bonds. The preferred stock and the bonds were offered for public subscription at par by Kidder, Peabody in New York and Baring Brothers in London. See Arthur S. Dewing, *Corporate Promotions and Reorganization* (Cambridge, Mass.: Harvard University Press, 1914), 305, 309n, 313–314. Paul D. Dickens estimated that the amount raised in London was $5 million. See his "Transition Period in American International Financing," Ph. D. diss., George Washington University, 1933, 244.

65. I have excluded from my study, here as earlier, the impact of immigrants, some of whom carried capital to America, but whose activities did not result in continuing long-term foreign investments.

66. Philip Scranton, *Proprietary Capitalism: The Textile Manufacture at Philadelphia, 1800–1885* (Cambridge: Cambridge University Press, 1983), 339.

67. This conclusion is based on available secondary sources. It is beyond the scope of my present study to delve into the records of the multitude of immigrant manufacturers. Take the Schofields, for example. Sevill Schofield was born in 1832 at Lees near Oldham "to a Lancashire textile district family." With his parents and all five siblings, he arrived in the United States in 1845. The family went to Philadelphia, where his father, Joseph, undertook to contract labor to operate mills "for other parties." Sevill went to work in a mill. Over time, Joseph and then Sevill owned their own mill. By 1857 Sevill was running the family firm, making spun cotton and carpet yarns. The business grew. In the 1880s his son entered the partnership (ibid., 57–62). *Burdett's Official Intelligence, 1891*, London, lists a firm called J. K. Schofield & Co., Ltd., cotton spinners and manufacturers, Springfield Mill, Bury, Lancashire. Was there a transatlantic relationship? It is doubtful, although possibly J. K. Schofield and Sevill Schofield were relatives. The Merrimack Valley Textile Museum manuscript collection has data on immigrant manufacturers. Thus Charles Fletcher (1839–1907) became a major figure in the U.S. woolen industry. He was born in Thornton, England, and trained in the

mills at Bradford. He came to the United States in 1864, established his own mills, founded the Pocasset Worsted Company (in Thornton, Rhode Island), and was one of the first directors of the American Woolen Company. See Helena Wright, *The Merrimack Valley Textile Museum: A Guide to the Manuscript Collections* (New York: Garland, 1983), 100. Foreign investment does not appear to have been involved.

68. Edward Stanwood, "Cotton Manufacture," in U.S. Department of Interior, Census Office, *Report on Manufacturing Industries in the United States*, 11th Census, 1890 (Washington, D.C., 1895), pt. 3, 180.

69. James Coats built a small thread mill in Scotland in 1826. His two sons, James and Peter, under the name J. & P. Coats, took over his thread business on July 1, 1830. See "Text of the 150 Year Exhibition," Renfrew District Libraries, Scotland, panel 9. I am indebted to Dr. Stephen Young for these data.

70. Leslie Hannah and J. A. Kay, *Concentration in Modern Industry* (London: Macmillan, 1977), 1, says that it was the largest British firm in 1900.

71. See D. A. Farnie, *The English Cotton Industry and the World Market, 1815–1896* (Oxford: Clarendon Press, 1979), 155, on the technology.

72. Ibid., 28.

73. Ibid., 28, 195, and Mathew Blair, *The Paisley Thread Industry* (Paisley: Alexander Gardner, 1907), 52, 73. Farnie, *English Cotton*, 155, using data from W. D. Rubinstein, "British Millionaires, 1809–1949," *Bulletin of the Institute of Historical Research*, 74 (November 1974): 202–223, concluded that of the twenty-four millionaires from the British cotton industry who died between 1830 and 1942, sixteen (including eleven from the Coats family) were thread manufacturers. See also W. D. Rubinstein, *Men of Property* (New Brunswick, N.J.: Rutgers University Press, 1981), 84.

74. "Photographs and Brief Description of the Establishment of the Conant Thread Company, Pawtucket, R. I.," 1878. Copy in Pawtucket Library. This brochure was prepared as "A souvenir of the visit of Sir Peter Coats during the Winter of 1877–1878." Since the brochure was probably written by Americans, I presume this reference is to several million "dollars," not pounds. This is confirmed by data in Sir Alec Cairncross, "The Early Growth of Messrs. J. & P. Coats," unfinished paper (ca. 1956).

75. Information from J. B. K. Hunter, April 27, 1986. Profits from the American operations *as a percentage of total Coats profits* varied substantially. According to Hunter, the historian of J. & P. Coats, they were at their peak in the 1870s (Hunter to Wilkins, April 27, 1986).

76. Robert Grieve, *An Illustrated History of Pawtucket* (Pawtucket, R. I.: Pawtucket Gazette & Chronicle, 1897), 275, and R. I. Historical Preservation Commission, Pawtucket, *Statewide Historical Preservation Report*, P-PA-1, Oct. 1978, 17. I am indebted to Mr. Paul Arsenault, Reference Librarian, Pawtucket Public Library, for the data on Coats's Pawtucket Mills. See Cairncross, "The Early Growth" (on the size of investment), and J. B. K. Hunter to Wilkins, April 27, 1986 ("almost 100 percent").

77. Grieve, *An Illustrated History*, 17, and Hunter to Wilkins, April 27 and Aug. 22, 1986 (on reasons for name change in 1893 and the role of Alfred M. Coats). I used the *National Cyclopaedia of American Biography* (1932), XXII, 57–58, for the date of Conant's death. He was born in 1827.

78. "150 Year Exhibition," panel 18.

79. Hunter to Wilkins, April 27, 1986.

80. Frank Presbrey, *The History and Development of Advertising* (1929; rpt. New York: Greenwood Press, 1968), 338.

81. Stanwood, "Cotton Manufacture," 181. "Kearny" and "Newark" as place names seem at times to have been used interchangeably; they were neighboring cities. Hunter uses the place name "East Newark" for these mills.

82. "Text of 150 Year Exhibition," panel 7. This merger put the two U.S. plants of the Clark enterprise—in Newark-Kearny—under common Scottish ownership.

83. The 1881 date is from the *Industrial Commission Report,* 19 vols. (Washington, D.C., 1899–1903), XIII (1901), 343.

84. Hunter to Wilkins, April 27, 1986.

85. *Banker's Magazine,* New York, 41 (Aug. 1889): 83, noted, however, that the thread mills in New Jersey and Rhode Island were perhaps the best-known examples of "great enterprises" of "Englishmen" [*sic*] in America.

86. See Robert Bruce Davies, *Peacefully Working to Conquer the World: Singer Sewing Machines in Foreign Markets, 1854–1920* (New York: Arno Press, 1976) and Mira Wilkins, *The Emergence of Multinational Enterprise: American Business Abroad from the Colonial Era to 1914* (Cambridge, Mass.: Harvard University Press, 1970), 37–45.

87. Macrosty, *The Trust Movement,* 126. See Testimony of Lyman Hopkins, April 9, 1901, *Industrial Commission Report,* XIII, 350, on the English companies' pre-1896 exports, and data from J. B. K. Hunter, April 27, 1986.

88. Macrosty, *The Trust Movement,* 127; Blair, *Paisley Thread,* 52; and data from J. B. K. Hunter, April 27, 1986.

89. Hunter to Wilkins, Aug. 22, 1896 (on the figure of 6,000), and Grieve, *An Illustrated History of Pawtucket* (1897), 275 (on the Pawtucket venture).

90. H. E. Blyth, *Through the Eye of a Needle: The Story of English Sewing Cotton* (n.p., n.d. [1947?]), 10–19, gives details on the fourteen firms, which included some that traced their roots back to the eighteenth century, one that had German and French factories, and another with a Montreal mill. English Sewing Cotton included some of the most famous names in the cotton trade (for example, the Strutt mills and the Arkwright company mills).

91. Macrosty, *The Trust Movement,* 129–130. See also Archibald Coats, comments at the Fifteenth Annual Meeting of J. & P. Coats, reported in *Statist,* 56 (Nov. 11, 1905): 869.

92. J. H. Clapham, *An Economic History of Modern Britain* (Cambridge: Cambridge University Press, 1968), III, 225, 231, 288, 305, 311; Blair, *Paisley Thread,* 63; and Macrosty, *The Trust Movement,* 135.

93. John Moody, *Truth about Trusts* (New York: Moody, 1904), 234. The *Industrial Commission Report,* XIII, 361, lists thirteen firms (with one different from Moody), but on p. 343, the report lists fourteen firms in the American Thread merger.

94. *Industrial Commission Report,* XIII, 363, and Stanwood, "Cotton Manufacture," 180. A predecessor of Willimantic Linen Company started in the 1840s. Willimantic Linen had had earlier run-ins with Clark Thread. Before Coats acquired Clark & Co., Willimantic Linen had sued Clark Thread (in the United States) for infringement of its patent on thread-winding machinery. Clark Thread argued that its machine was based on a prior British patent. Although Willimantic won in the lower court, the U.S. Supreme Court found in favor of Clark Thread. See *Clark Thread Company, Appl.* v. *Willimantic Linen Company,* 140 U.S. 481 (1891). Hezekiah Conant had worked for nine years (1857–1868) for Willimantic. See Richard Bayles, ed., *History of Providence County Rhode Island* (New York: W. W. Preston, 1891), 450–451.

95. *Industrial Commission Report,* XIII, 358.

96. Hopkins testimony, ibid., 346, 348, 350.

97. See ibid., I, 1139ff, esp. 1155, for his testimony of Dec. 12, 1899, in favor of giant corporations. On the lawyer John Dos Passos, see biography of his son: John H. Wrenn, *John Dos Passos* (New York: Twayne, 1961), 21. The novelist was born in 1896.

98. Hopkins testimony, *Industrial Commission Report,* XIII, 353.

99. Moody, *Truth about Trusts,* 234.

100. Hopkins testimony, *Industrial Commission Report*, XIII, 353.

101. Ibid.

102. U.S. Federal Trade Commission, *Report on Cooperation in the Export Trade* (Washington, D.C., 1916), I, 253.

103. *Industrial Commission Report*, XIII, 354, 361 (list of directors).

104. Ibid., 354, 356.

105. Estimates of American Thread Company's market share in 1901 ranged from a little less than one-third (Hopkins testimony, *Industrial Commission Report*, XIII, 348) to about 50 percent (Moody, *Truth about Trusts*, 235). Coats was said to have one-third (Hopkins testimony, *Industrial Commission Report*, XIII, 356); it is not clear, however, whether the Coats figure was just for the Pawtucket, Rhode Island, mills or for the entire Coats group of mills. Coats's sales in the United States in 1899 were said to be double those of Clark's ("Text of 150 Year Exhibition," panel 18).

106. Hopkins testimony, *Industrial Commission Report*, XIII, 351–352.

107. *Statist*, 56 (Nov. 11, 1905): 869.

108. Hopkins testimony, *Industrial Commission Report*, XIII, 348–349. That wages in the U.S. thread factories of Scottish manufacturers were about double those in Scotland is also noted in Gordon Donaldson, *The Scots Overseas* (London: Robert Hale, 1966), 115; Donaldson's context leads us to believe that he is talking about an earlier period than Hopkins was—probably the late 1860s and 1870s.

109. *Statist*, 72 (July 27, 1912): 318.

110. Hopkins testimony, *Industrial Commission Report*, XIII, 346; Dunning data; and Clark, *History of Manufactures*, III, 181.

111. "Text of 150 Year Exhibition," panels 18 and 4. There is no mention of the Kearny mills, which at some point in the 1880s or 1890s seem to have been merged with the Newark mills. Coats in these years continued to have problems with imitators and infringers on its name. In the early twentieth century, its American attorney urged the New York legislature to require standard lengths of thread on spools to defeat the "unfair competition" of thread manufacturers, who copied the Coats spools with heavier cores and less thread. Throughout the country, its law firm pursued suits on Coats's behalf to protect the trade rights to the name Coats that were being infringed upon by one John Coates. See Robert T. Swaine, *The Cravath Firm* (New York: privately printed, 1946), I, 770, 772. The name-infringement matter was far from new. See *Journal of the Society of the Arts*, 24 (Nov. 26, 1875): 20, and Chapter 4, note 266. Apparently the copied name bothered Coats more in the twentieth century than in 1862.

112. Blair, *The Paisley Thread Industry*, 52. In 1910 J. & P. Coats had five mills in Pawtucket, Rhode Island. J. B. K. Hunter wrote me (April 27, 1986) that in the early 1880s the Pawtucket mills were equal in size to those of Coats at Paisley. The *Economist* reported that Coats's Pawtucket employees had complained that two years earlier their wages had been reduced by 10 percent and now the cost of living was rising. The workers struck. Management responded by shutting down the five mills, and 2,500 textile workers were out of work. See *Economist*, 70 (Feb. 5, 1910): 279.

113. Final Decree in the *United States v. American Thread et al.*, Equity No. 312, District Court of New Jersey, June 2, 1914.

114. "Fighting" in antitrust parlance of this era meant unfair price cutting. "Fighting ships," for example, were not military ones, but those engaged in predatory pricing tactics designed to put competitors out of business.

115. *FTC Report on Cooperation*, I, 253, and *Statist*, 88 (July 15, 1916): 130.

116. *Statist*, 88 (July 15, 1916): 130.

117. Graham Turner, *Business in Britain* (Boston: Little, Brown, 1969), 402.

118. J. & P. Coats's business would fare better than that of American Thread. The

latter would concentrate on industrial threads, whereas the Coats and Clark mills produced for the general thread market. See J. Herbert Burgy, *The New England Cotton Textile Industry* (Baltimore: Waverly Press, 1932), 201. For many years, however, American Thread Company was far larger than its parent, English Sewing Cotton Company, Ltd. (Turner, *Business in Britain*, 403).

119. The best source on this is Linen Thread Company, Ltd., *The Faithful Fibre* (Glasgow: Linen Thread, 1956), 25, 27, 29.

120. Berthoff, *British Immigration*, 44 (on the Paterson mill).

121. Linen Thread Company, *Faithful Fibre*, 25.

122. See Chapter 4.

123. Linen Thread Company, *Faithful Fibre*, 27, 29, and Clark, *History of Manufactures*, II, 459.

124. According to Clark, *History of Manufactures*, II, 460. This may well have been a firm that closed in Britain and set up anew in America, or one run by immigrant Scots.

125. Linen Thread Company, *Faithful Fibre*, 33. The Hilden mills were in Lisburn, northern Ireland.

126. See *Stock Exchange Official Intelligence for 1914*, 748, for 1898 capitalization.

127. Linen Thread Company, *Faithful Fibre*, 53. The Barbour mill at Paterson, New Jersey, alone was in 1905 said to be equal in size to the giant Barbour enterprise in northern Ireland (R. H. Reade, Belfast, testimony, *Tariff Commission Report*, pt. 7, par. 3845).

128. Macrosty, *The Trust Movement*, 136–137.

129. American Thread Company made linen as well as cotton thread.

130. Coats appears to have sold part of its holdings in English Sewing Cotton Company in order to invest in Fine Cotton Spinners'. See Macrosty, *The Trust Movement*, 132, and FTC, *Report on Cooperation*, I, 252. Coats developed close relations with Fine Cotton Spinners'. In 1889 Coats had begun buying Sea Island cotton regularly from the Florida Manufacturing Company (I have been unable to determine anything about this firm, its size, its functions, or even its location within Florida); in 1900 Coats and Fine Cotton Spinners' jointly invested in an Egyptian cotton shipping firm (Carver Brothers), and at the same time Coats offered Fine Cotton Spinners' "certain reciprocal arrangements re: American cotton" (Fine Cotton Spinners', Executive Directors Minutes, April 25, 1900) that involved the two British companies and Clark Thread Company, Newark, New Jersey, in the takeover of the Florida Manufacturing Company. My sparse information on this investment comes from Anthony Howe to Mira Wilkins, May 1 and Sept. 11, 1986, and J. B. K. Hunter to Mira Wilkins, Aug. 22, 1986. Howe writes (letter of Sept. 11, 1986) that the first year Fine Cotton Spinners' received a 13.5 percent return (dividend) on its £18,271 investment. This joint-venture investment in the Florida Manufacturing Company appears to have been small compared with Fine Cotton Spinners' 1911 investment in growing cotton in Mississippi.

131. Jackson, *Enterprising Scot*, 221, 229 (on Coats's interests in 1882–1884 in timberland in Michigan and Archibald Coats's £7,000 investment in the Humbolt Redwood Company in California). I have no evidence that the family intended to use Michigan or California timber for spools, but Blair, *Paisley Thread*, 77, indicates that the bulk of wood used in Paisley in 1907 was imported from the north of Europe and North America. See Jackson, *Enterprising Scot*, 192–193, 202, on the Coats family mining and smelting investments in Utah, Nevada, and Colorado, including the Glasgow and Western Exploration Company group (after 1896). In the case of the latter, the Coats family actually took the initiative in organizing the enterprise and throughout held controlling interest. The Glasgow and Western Exploration Company, Ltd., and its subsidiaries mined and built a smelter, tunnels, and railways. It spent about $5 million

on its mining and smelting projects (Lewis, *America's Stake*, 571). The group operated in Utah, Nevada, and Colorado. In 1913 "liabilities forced the termination of the Glasgow and Western. Business continued until 1921 when all the properties had at last been sold or liquidated" (Jackson, *Enterprising Scot*, 193)

132. Many years later, in the 1920s, this process would be employed in the United States by the Tubize Artificial Silk Company. See Jesse W. Markham, *Competition in the Rayon Industry* (Cambridge, Mass.: Harvard University Press, 1952), 8, and D. C. Coleman, *Courtaulds* (Oxford: Clarendon Press, 1969), II, 147.

133. Coleman, *Courtaulds*, II, 30, and chaps. 2 and 3.

134. Ibid., 79

135. Ibid., 18–19.

136. Ibid., 104, and Markham, *Competition*, 15.

137. Coleman, *Courtaulds*, II, 83.

138. Ibid., and chaps. 4 and 5.

139. Ibid., II, chap. 5

140. Ibid., II, 108.

141. Formed as American Viscose Company (1910); a new company, the Viscose Company (1915), reorganized into American Viscose Corporation (AVC) in 1922; the Viscose Company existed as a subsidiary of AVC until 1937, when AVC became the operating enterprise.

142. Coleman, *Courtaulds*, II, 119.

143. Markham, *Competition*, 22.

144. Coleman, *Courtaulds*, II, 113, 142, 151.

145. *APC Report*, 458–459, 325, 561–562; *Guide to the Exhibits of American Wool Manufacturers, World's Columbian Exposition* (Chicago, 1893), 27; and Presbrey, *History of Advertising*, 361.

146. A. H. John, *A Liverpool Merchant House* (London: George Allen & Unwin, 1959), 27–28, 49–51. Clark, *History of Manufactures*, III, 234, notes that half the leather gloves made in the United States at this time were manufactured in Fulton County, New York, and more than one-fourth in Gloversville.

147. John, *Liverpool Merchant House*, 74.

148. Ibid., passim.

149. Ibid., 78; Clark, *History of Manufactures*, III, 278; and Williams Haynes, *American Chemical Industry*, 6 vols. (New York: D. Van Nostrand, 1945–1954), I, 246.

150. John, *Liverpool Merchant House*, 78.

151. Ibid., 77.

152. Clark, *History of Manufactures*, III, 227.

153. John, *Liverpool Merchant House*, 79.

154. Ibid., 79–80.

155. Clark, *History of Manufactures*, III, 228. As in the case of U.S. Leather, no foreign investment appears to have been involved.

156. John, *Liverpool Merchant House*, 81.

157. Based on ibid., 79.

158. Ibid., 82.

159. Clark, *History of Manufactures*, III, 229.

160. John, *Liverpool Merchant House*, 83.

161. Ibid., 84.

162. Ibid., 86–87.

163. Ibid., 85–86.

164. Ibid., 87.

165. I find it hard to emphasize this, because after Schultz's initial experimental

work at Booth's Gloversville factory in the 1880s, the latter facility did not actually adopt the process until 1894!

166. L. F. Haber, *The Chemical Industry during the Nineteenth Century* (Oxford: Clarendon Press, 1969), 145, and Clark, *History of Manufactures*, III, 221.

167. *APC Report*, 36.

168. Charlotte Erickson, *American Industry and the European Immigrant* (Cambridge, Mass.: Harvard University Press, 1957), 133, 242 n.54, citing a report on technical education in Pennsylvania.

169. Haynes, *American Chemical Industry*, I, 312.

170. Ibid., I, 308; VI, 174–175. Why else would Farbenfabriken of Elberfeld Company (Bayer's New York sales company) have advertised in the *Bulletin of the National Association of Wool Manufacturers*, 35 (March 1905), that it was "Sole Agents for The Hudson River Aniline Color Works"?

171. Erich W. Zimmermann, *World Resources and Industries* (New York: Harper & Bros., 1933), 748.

172. Haber, *The Chemical Industry during the Nineteenth Century*, 143.

173. Haynes, *American Chemical Industry*, VI, 10, 392. See Chapter 11 for more details.

174. See Chapter 11. The Castner-Kellner Alkali Company, Ltd. was formed in the United Kingdom in 1895.

175. Martha Moore Trescott, *The Rise of the American Electrochemical Industry, 1880–1910* (Westport, Conn.: Greenwood Press, 1981), 67. It seems unlikely that this was liquid chlorine, for the credit goes to Goldschmidt Detinning Company for producing in October 1909 the first liquid chlorine in the United States (which was not sold to the textile industry). See Roy A. Duffus, Jr., *The Story of M & T Chemicals Inc.* (New York: Codella Duffus Baker, 1965), 9, 12. In fact, Haynes, *American Chemical Industry*, III, 4, describes Castner Electrolytic Alkali Company as a producer of bleaching "powder." Haynes writes that in the first decade of the twentieth century, "bleaching powder was the chief cog in the expanding wheels of the alkali business" (ibid.). United Alkali Company invested in the United States in chlorate manufacturing (see Chapter 11). I can find no evidence that this was motivated by textile industry demand.

176. See letterhead, Jan. 3, 1911, letter in RG 59, 611.627/293, National Archives, Washington, D.C.

177. Duffus, *M & T Chemicals*, 6–9, 13.

178. Haynes, *American Chemical Industry*, VI, 356; *APC Report*, 344; and Sheldon Hochheiser, *Rohm and Haas* (Philadelphia: University of Pennsylvania Press, 1986), 3–14.

179. See Mira Wilkins, *The Emergence of Multinational Enterprise* (Cambridge, Mass.: Harvard University Press, 1970), 188; FTC, *Report on Cooperation*, I, 191–192. A new American subsidiary was formed, the New York Quebracho Extract Company. See also Agnes H. Hicks, *The Story of the Forestal* (London: Forestal Land, Timber and Railways, 1956), 4, 15, 21, which suggests the American acquisition occurred in 1912.

180. In England in the 1890s, Howard & Bullough had 6,000 employees. See S. B. Saul, "The Engineering Industry," in *The Development of British Industry and Foreign Competition, 1875–1914*, ed. Derek H. Aldcroft (London: George Allen & Unwin, 1968), 192, 193–194. On its American company, see Thomas R. Navin, *The Whitin Machine Works since 1831* (Cambridge, Mass.: Harvard University Press, 1950), 241–242.

181. Navin, *Whitin Machine Works*, 245–249.

182. Ibid., 281–282.

183. Ibid., 353.

184. Dickens, "The Transition Period," 261.

185. Navin, *Whitin Machine Works*, 5. Clark, *History of Manufactures*, III, 198, found

that in 1912, 23 percent of the looms, but 78 percent of the other machinery employed in all branches of the U.S. woolen industry, were of foreign manufacture. See also Saul, "The Engineering Industry," 194. There were also machinery imports from France. On one importer, Atkinson, Haserick & Co., see Wright, *The Merrimack Valley Textile Museum*, 239.

186. Clark, *History of Manufactures*, III, 198.

187. *APC Report*, 146.

188. Clark, *History of Manufactures*, III, 220.

189. See Wilkins, *The Emergence*, passim. I write "as such," because machinery makers, particularly Singer sewing machines, were in a textile-related industry.

190. For others, see *Tariff Commission Report*, pt. 2, par. 1486, and Ashley, *The Tariff Problem*, 77.

191. Is sewing thread a "convenience good" like chocolates, soap, and matches—low-priced goods that the consumer picks up on the basis of a known, advertised name? See F. M. Scherer, *Industrial Market Structure and Economic Performance* (Boston: Houghton Mifflin, 1980), 5, on "convenience goods." The examples he gives are toothpaste, razor blades, and cigarettes.

192. For similarity to U.S. business in other countries in these broad terms, see Wilkins, *Emergence of Multinational Enterprise*.

193. See, for example, Louis Galambos, *Competition and Cooperation* (Baltimore: Johns Hopkins University Press, 1966), 15. Some theories of multinational enterprise would explain (at least in part) the absence of American business abroad in textiles as attributable to the absence of concentration.

194. Tariffs played an important role in determining when and which particular dyes were made in the United States.

195. Textile product imports were 20.8 percent of consumption in 1869 and only 8.6 percent in 1909. See Lance E. Davis et al., *American Economic Growth* (New York: Harper & Row, 1972), 572.

11. The Chemical Industry

1. See Chapter 7.

2. See Chapter 8.

3. Electrochemical output of mineral products can be classified as a part of the mining, chemical, or electrical industry. See Martha Moore Trescott, *The Rise of the American Electrochemicals Industry, 1880–1910* (Westport, Conn.: Greenwood Press, 1981). Thus the investments of American Metal Company in electrolytic refining could be considered under the rubric "chemical industries," as could the British investments in electrolytic refining (New Jersey Extraction Company), the German stakes in Niagara Alkali Company, and the French ones in Southern Aluminium, all of which were noted in Chapter 8.

4. Many put it in this category.

5. U.S. Senate, Judiciary Committee, *Alleged Dye Monopoly, Hearings*, 67th Cong., 1922, 749 (henceforth cited as *1922 Dye Hearings*).

6. Williams Haynes, *American Chemical Industry*, 6 vols. (New York: D. Van Nostrand, 1945–1954), I, 330. For example, Herman Seydel, born in Brussels, came to the United States as a color chemist for the German firm Kalle & Co. in 1896; from 1899 to 1904 he was a sales representative in this country for another German enterprise, the Berlin Aniline Works. In 1904 he founded his own business, which eventually (in 1920) came to be called Seydel Chemical Company (ibid., VI, 370). As my notes will indicate,

I am deeply indebted to Haynes's monumental six-volume study in preparing this chapter. Garland Publishing reprinted it in 1983.

7. Ibid., I, 330. These firms by 1914 were doing full manufacture in America.

8. See text below.

9. Alien Property Custodian, *Report, 1918–1919*, 61 (henceforth cited as *APC Report*). Forty-five hundred were sold to the Chemical Foundation, plus 1,200 additional patents of Bayer (*1922 Dye Hearings*, 287). Some patents sold to the Chemical Foundation were not related to the chemical industry (ibid., 105), but the vast bulk were. The best data on patents in the U.S. chemical industry—by nationality and product, 1900–1910—are in Hermann Grossmann, *Die Chemische Industrie in den Vereinigten Staaten* (Leipzig: Verlag von Veit & Comp., 1912). My thanks go to Jonathan Liebenau for directing me to this material. See also Haynes, *American Chemical Industry*, III, 483–491.

10. James M. Gifford to W. W. Wilson, Jan. 22, 1926, in Du Pont Archives, Eleutherian Mills Historical Library, indicates that 30 percent of the shares in Niagara Electro Chemical Company were issued to Aluminium Company, Ltd., in exchange "for processes." Aluminium Company held the key patents. On Th. Goldschmidt, see Roy A. Duffus, Jr., *The Story of M & T Chemicals Inc.* (New York: Cordella Duffus Baker, 1965), 10, 16.

11. *APC Report*, 454ff. Much more has been written on chemical patents than on trademarks. The latter, however, were very important.

12. Ibid., 25, and Haynes, *American Chemical Industry*, I, 392–393. Grossmann, *Chemische Industrie*, 76, shows that between 1900 and 1910 in chemicals more German-held patents were granted in the United States than U.S.-held ones!

13. See Ross J. S. Hoffman, *Great Britain and German Trade Rivalry, 1875–1914* (Philadelphia: University of Pennsylvania Press, 1933), and Henri Hauser, *Germany's Commercial Grip on the World* (New York: Charles Scribner's Sons, 1918) for the German export challenge.

14. *APC Report*, 30–31.

15. Aluminum—an electrochemical industry—was also characterized by intercontinental accords. See Chapter 8.

16. W. J. Reader, *Imperial Chemical Industries* (London: Oxford University Press, 1970), I, 16–26 (henceforth cited as *I.C.I.*).

17. Ibid., 21.

18. Ibid., 26.

19. Ibid., 487.

20. Ibid., 20, 60, 68.

21. Ibid., 70.

22. Ibid., 490, 61, 81–85.

23. Ibid., 85–86. No U.S. companies took part in either the first or the second "International Conventions."

24. Ibid., 86–87.

25. Ibid., 156–157.

26. Ibid., 158.

27. Ibid., 157–158, 482.

28. Ibid., 159, and Alfred D. Chandler and Stephen Salsbury, *Pierre S. du Pont and the Making of the Modern Corporation* (New York: Harper & Row, 1971), 170–171. It probably was not renewed, since everyone was conforming to its terms and thus renewal was unnecessary.

29. Reader, *I.C.I.*, I, 159, 161. A copy of the Oct. 26, 1897, agreement is in William L. Stevens, ed., *Industrial Combinations and Trusts* (New York: Macmillan, 1913),

176–183. See also Mira Wilkins, *Emergence of Multinational Enterprise* (Cambridge, Mass.: Harvard University Press, 1970), 89–90, and Chandler and Salsbury, *Pierre S. du Pont*, 171–172.

30. Reader, *I.C.I.*, I, 198, 200–204, 212–231; Chandler and Salsbury, *Pierre S. du Pont*, 192–193, 197–199, 299, 650 n.83; Stevens, ed., *Industrial Combinations and Trusts*, 463–471; and Du Pont, *Annual Report, 1912*.

31. Reader, *I.C.I.*, I, 196, 172.

32. Quoted in ibid., 196.

33. Ibid., 194–215.

34. Ibid., 173.

35. See Chapter 4. Bayer's original German plant was at Elberfeld. By 1914 Bayer's German headquarters was Leverkusen. Carl Rumpf was in the early 1870s Bayer's New York representative. Rumpf returned to Germany in about 1880 (Haynes, *American Chemical Industry*, VI, 174). He appears to have been followed by E. Sehlbach & Co., which was succeeded by the Farbenfabriken of Elberfeld Company, and then by Bayer Company, Inc. See ibid. and Herman Metz testimony in *1922 Dye Hearings*, 749. "Farbenfabriken of Elberfeld Co." was in existence in 1897. See advertisement in *Bulletin of the National Association of Wool Manufacturers*, 27 (1897). In 1905 its advertising identified I. J. R. Muurling as president and Wm. Diestel as treasurer.

36. Bayer Company, Inc., New York, letterhead (Oct. 3, 1914) gives branch offices. See letterhead in Record Group (RG) 59, 165.102/11, National Archives, Washington, D.C.

37. Haynes, *American Chemical Industry*, VI, 174.

38. Ibid., I, 308; VI, 174–175. Data in RG 131, Box 147, NA, reveals that the Hudson River Aniline Color Works was originally incorporated in August 1882. It was reincorporated in the state of New York in 1903. The capital of the 1903 company was initially $41,000. The plant was in Rensselaer, near Albany, but the firm seems to have had an office in Albany, and its advertisements referred to the Hudson River Aniline Color Works, Albany, New York. See *Bulletin of the National Association of Wool Manufacturers*, 35 (March 1905) and 36 (March 1906). The New York Department of State, Division of Corporations, confirms the 1882 incorporation (letter of Aug. 15, 1985).

39. Haynes, *American Chemical Industry*, VI, 175. Waldman's competing company did not prove successful.

40. John Joseph Beer, *The Emergence of the German Dye Industry* (Urbana: University of Illinois Press, 1959), 124–125; L. F. Haber, *The Chemical Industry during the Nineteenth Century* (Oxford: Clarendon Press, 1958), 134; and Haynes, *American Chemical Industry*, I, 312. Bayer had first introduced aspirin in Germany in 1898. See L. F. Haber, *The Chemical Industry, 1900–1930* (Oxford: Oxford University Press, 1971), 128.

41. Ford, Bacon, Davis, "Report on Bayer Co.," Nov. 7, 1918, in RG 131, Box 34, NA.

42. On the need for imports, Herman Metz, "Memo," Aug. 12, 1914, RG 59, 165. 102/2, NA.

43. Based on data in RG 131, Boxes 147 and 34, NA. On June 12, 1913, Hudson River Aniline Color Works, owned by the German Bayer Company, sold all its real estate in the vicinity of Rensselaer, New York, to Synthetic Patent Company, for $50,000. The property had been carried on the books at $178,479! Synthetic Patent had been formed on June 4, 1913, with a capital of $50,000. It not only acquired the real estate in Rensselaer, but it also paid $225,000 for all the U.S. letter patents standing on record in the name Farbenfabriken of Elberfeld Company, a company that had served as the sales arm in New York for the Bayer group. On June 12, 1913, the Hudson River company also sold its stock of merchandise, raw materials, and factory equipment to

Bayer Company, Inc. for $316,598. The latter was incorporated in New York on June 3, 1913; it acquired the Hudson River company's assets and also the trademarks, goodwill, and the like, of Farbenfabriken of Elberfeld. The Bayer Company, Inc., had a capital of $750,000 at origin. Since these were all intracompany transactions, it is not clear how meaningful these figures are in determining the actual size of the investment.

44. Haynes, *American Chemical Industry*, I, 313.

45. *APC Report*, 34.

46. Haynes, *American Chemical Industry*, III, 312–314 (on Gref).

47. In 1918 the stock in Bayer and Synthetic Patents (see note 43 above) were sold at public auction for $5.3 million (*APC Report*, 220). This price reflected the sizable 1914–1918 expansion, so it cannot be perceived as that of 1914. On the other hand, it was probably a low price for 1918. The figures given in note 43 are lower—but, as mentioned, they are probably not a reliable guide to the size of the investment. For the early years, Bayer's pharmaceuticals appear to have been sold through Schieffelin & Co., a drug wholesaler, but after production began, the Bayer organization took over the distribution. See Tom Mahoney, *The Merchants of Life* (1959; rpt. Freeport, N.Y.: Books for Libraries, 1972), 212, and 7–8, 163 (on Schieffelin & Co.).

48. A German chemist in 1898 had discovered heroine, an artificial alkaloid obtained from morphine. U.S. House, Committee on Ways and Means, *Prohibiting the Importation of Opium for the Manufacture of Heroine, Hearings*, 68th Cong., 1st sess., 1924, 1–2, 30–35, 46. See also Haynes, *American Chemical Industry*, III, 300 (on Bayer's role), and Hal Morgan, *Symbols of America* (New York: Penguin Books, 1987), 83, which shows the trade name in 1898 as "Heroin." By 1912 it was "Heroine" (Haynes, *American Chemical Industry*, III, 313).

49. Haber, *Chemical Industry during the Nineteenth Century*, 135.

50. Haynes, *American Chemical Industry*, III, 314, indicates that Bayer in the United States first started to advertise to the general public in 1916, and that up to this time the medical profession had considered aspirin "an ethical prescription product." It was first sold in powder rather than in pill form (Mahoney, *Merchants of Life*, 212). Fascinating material on Bayer's pre–World War I U.S. marketing is in *Bayer Company, Inc.*, v. *United Drug Company*, 272 Fed. Rep. 505 (SDNY 1921). Apparently, the drug was sold over-the-counter by retail druggists, who often used their own rather than the Bayer name.

51. Haynes, *American Chemical Industry*, I, 313, and VI, 292–293; Haber, *Chemical Industry, 1900–1930*, 181; and *APC Report*, 36. The other four, constituting about 12 percent of U.S. production, were W. Beckers Aniline & Chemical Works (5 percent), Central Dyestuff & Chemical Company (3–4 percent), Consolidated Color & Chemical Company (2–3 percent), and Hub Dyestuff & Chemical Company (less than 1 percent). All except Consolidated Colors (a Hoechst enterprise) were U.S. owned. Dr. William G. Beckers was of German "origin" (*APC Report*, 51), as, of course, were Jacob Schoellkopf, Frederick Heller, and Henry Merz. Beckers had come to the United States as a color technician for Bayer (Haynes, *American Chemical Industry*, III, 234–235). The Brooklyn firm, founded by Thomas and Charles Holliday (sons of Read Holliday)—see Chapter 4—is not included in the list. In 1881, when there were seven dyemakers in the United States, the Holliday firm was the only one that worked from its own intermediates, producing benzol, nitrobenzol, dinitrobenzol, aniline, and its salts. It survived the tariff reductions of 1883. In 1889 Edgar Holliday took over its active management. A company was incorporated in 1890 with $250,000 capital. I do not know the investment relationship (if any) between the U.S. Holliday interests and Read Holliday & Sons, Ltd., in England.

On the American Holliday firm, see Haynes, *American Chemical Industry*, I, 303, 307, 312. Herman Metz, *1922 Dye Hearings*, 750, referred to "Read Holliday & Son" as an *importer* of dyes into the United States in the 1890s, representing the English company. When, after 1883, duties were removed on dyestuff intermediates (see ibid., 102) and lowered on end-products, the Hollidays (in America) had campaigned for higher tariffs; but in 1890 the dyestuff tariffs were further reduced (Haynes, *American Chemical Industry*, I, 312). Probably the American Hollidays then shifted from being manufacturers to becoming simply importers. A 1914 commemorative brochure for Read Holliday & Sons, Ltd. (quoted in Haber, *Chemical Industry during the Nineteenth Century*, 145), notes that a son (Edgar?) of Thomas Holliday opened branches of the U.S. business in Boston and Philadelphia. In 1916, when Americans were paying new attention to the coal-tar industry, R. W. Kemp, grandson of the founder of Read Holliday & Sons, Ltd., organized and headed Holliday-Kemp in the United States (Haynes, *American Chemical Industry*, III, 237). Reader, *I.C.I.*, I, 438, writes of Read Holliday's American company in 1922.

52. Haynes, *American Chemical Industry*, VI, 175. By way of comparison, Bayer in Germany in 1913 employed 10,600 people (Harber, *Chemical Industry, 1900–1930*, 128).

53. Haber, *Chemical Industry, 1900–1930*, 29.

54. *APC Report*, 38.

55. This statement, dated Aug. 20, 1914, was forwarded to the State Department by Joseph P. Tumulty, secretary to President Woodrow Wilson. Tumulty (on White House stationery) noted the statement's importance. See RG 59, 165.102/13, NA.

56. Reader, *I.C.I.*, I, 258.

57. *APC Report*, 32, and Haber, *Chemical Industry, 1900–1930*, 121. In 1904–1908, two loose combinations united Germany's largest dyestuff firms. One, organized by Carl Duisberg, joined Bayer, Badische, and AGFA. The second combined Hoechst, Cassella, and Kalle (*APC Report*, 33, and Haber, *Chemical Industry, 1900–1930*, 124–128). In the United States, each German firm continued to have separate representation.

58. Haynes, *American Chemical Industry*, VI, 183; I, 312.

59. *APC Report*, 34.

60. Haynes, *American Chemical Industry*, VI, 183, and *1922 Dye Hearings*, 180–181. On A. Poirrier of Paris and Lyon, see Michel Laferrère, *Lyon: ville industrielle* (Paris: Presses Universitaires de France, 1960), 493. In the 1890s, in the United States, Sykes & Street, later Walter F. Sykes, represented A. Poirrier, as importers (*1922 Dye Hearings*, 750).

61. *APC Report*, 53. The firms were (with date of origin in parentheses): Wm. Pickhardt and Kuttroff (1871), Kuttroff, Pickhardt & Co. (1899), Continental Color and Chemical Company (1906), and the Badische Company (1907). See *1922 Dye Hearings*, 181.

62. *1922 Dye Hearings*, 181.

63. *APC Report*, 39, 53–55. Kuttroff had become an experienced importer who worked in close harmony with his German supplier.

64. Haber, *Chemical Industry, 1900–1930*, 132.

65. *1922 Dye Hearings*, 749; advertisement for New York and Boston Dyewood Company in *Bulletin of the National Association of Wool Manufacturers*, 27 (1897); and data from Department of State, Albany, New York, March 19, 1981. On the offices, see Lutz Alt, "The Photo-Chemical Industry: Historical Essays in Business Strategy and Internationalization," Ph. D. diss. MIT, 1986, 35.

66. *1922 Dye Hearings*, 276, 749.

67. Ibid., 750 (1894 or 1895), 276 (1902).

68. Ibid., 750. See advertisement for H. A. Metz & Co., New York, with branches

in Boston, Providence, Charlotte, San Francisco, Philadelphia, Chicago, Atlanta, and Montreal, plus "laboratories" in Newark, New Jersey, in *Bulletin of the National Association of Wool Manufacturers*, 40 (March 1912). According to other data, in 1912 H. A. Metz & Co. took over all the assets of Victor Koechl & Co., which was thereafter known as the "Pharmaceutical Department" (*1922 Dye Hearings*, 278).

69. Metz at the *1922 Dye Hearings*, 750, testified that it was established in 1899; but on p. 744 he gave the date as 1893 or 1894. Other data indicate the date was 1902.

70. Haynes, *American Chemical Industry*, I, 313. Metz's younger brother, Dr. Gustave P. Metz, became production manager for Consolidated Color & Chemical Company, 1902–1912, and was "consultant" to Farbwerke Hoechst, 1913–1917 (ibid., III, 319n).

71. *1922 Dye Hearings*, 276, 754. According to *APC Report*, 51, for many years prior to 1912, Hoechst had held a majority of the H. A. Metz firm.

72. *APC Report*, 52, and Haber, *Chemical Industry, 1900–1930*, 121–122, 131–132.

73. Discussions with Jonathan Liebenau, London, October 1981, made me realize the importance of Salvarsan. See also U.S. Senate, Committee on Patents, *Salvarsan Hearings*, 65th Cong., 1st sess., 1917. Paul Ehrlich's research had been financed by Leopold Cassella & Co. There was a close relationship between this company and Hoechst; Ehrlich had assigned his Salvarsan patent to Hoechst (Mahoney, *Merchants of Life*, 10).

74. This seems to have been a way of coping with what has recently been called "transfer price" problems.

75. *APC Report*, 51. It was practically 100 percent owned by Hoechst (all except ten shares were German owned).

76. *1922 Dye Hearings*, 278.

77. *APC Report*, 51–52. In 1912 a group of Philadelphia lawyers had sued an officer of Bayer's U.S. subsidiary in a case involving the bribing of purchasing agents. In the course of the litigation, the lawyers realized that it might be possible to use the Sherman Antitrust Act, arguing that the associations with the parent in Germany constituted a restraint of trade. German businesses in the United States got very nervous (*APC Report*, 41). See also Howard Watson Ambruster, *Treason's Peace* (New York: Beechhurst Press, 1947), 5–10, and *1922 Dye Hearings*, 278–279.

78. *APC Report*, 41–42, 51–52, and *1922 Dye Hearings*, 278–279.

79. RG 59, 165.102, NA, has substantial material on Metz. See 165.102/90 for his letterhead (Oct. 3, 1914 letter).

80. *1922 Dye Hearings*, 745, 748.

81. Data from Department of State, Albany, N.Y., March 19, 1981.

82. *APC Report*, 39, 363, 41–42, 49.

83. Haynes, *American Chemical Industry*, I, 312. When in 1899 General Chemical was formed—the first important *American* merger in the chemical industry—Matheson was a director (ibid., I, 265).

84. Haber, *Chemical Industry, 1900–1930*, 132–133.

85. See its letterhead in RG 59, 165.102/40, NA (Aug. 24, 1914, letter). By 1908 Matheson was sufficiently prosperous to buy most of Key Biscayne, an island off the South Florida coast (near downtown Miami).

86. Haynes, *American Chemical Industry*, VI, 370 and *APC Report*, 326. According to data in RG 131, Box 172, Kalle Color & Chemical Company, incorporated in New York in 1913, had as of February 1914 as stockholders or record: Herman Raith, Stuttgart, Germany (500 shares); Mathieu Rais, Manchester, England (500 shares); and Edgar Fischer, New York (500 shares). The German-born Fischer became a naturalized American on July 9, 1914.

87. *APC Report*, 55. On Griesheim, see Haber, *Chemical Industry, 1900–1930*, 114–115.

According to Metz, at one time (in the 1890s) A. Klipstein was the Swiss CIBA (Gesellschaft für Chemische Industrie) representative (importer) in the United States. See *1922 Dye Hearings*, 750.

88. *APC Report*, 56, and Lawrence G. Franko, *The European Multinationals* (Stamford, Conn: Greylock, 1976), 164.

89. *1922 Dye Hearings*, 749.

90. There were some Swiss and French involvements, but they were minor vis-à-vis the German role. According to W. J. Reader, *I.C.I.*, I, 261–262, 277, 437, the British dyestuff firm I. Levinstein & Co., Ltd., which was in 1890–1895 one-third owned by the Levinstein family, one-third by Bayer, and one-third by AGFA, had stationed Edgar Levinstein (the son of founder Ivan Levinstein) in Boston, Massachusetts, "for years . . . in charge of the family business." Edgar Levinstein ran and apparently largely owned I. Levinstein & Co., Inc., Levinstein, Ltd.'s, selling company in the United States. See also *1922 Dye Hearings*, 750. In 1881 William Lesser, who had been with the English firm Levinstein, Campbell & Co. (a predecessor of I. Levinstein & Co., Ltd.), joined Albany Aniline & Chemical Works as sales manager. When the "Bayer group" defected to form the Hudson River Aniline Color Works, Lesser went along. Later he would visit Bayer laboratories in Germany for the latest technology (Haynes, *American Chemical Industry*, I, 308).

91. Haber, *Chemical Industry, 1900–1930*, 134.

92. See Greeley & Giles, "Report on Merck & Co.," Oct. 2, 1918, RG 131, Box 187, NA. Peter Hertner found an 1890 contract in the Merck Archives, Darmstadt, between the German firm and George Merck relating to the establishment of the American "partnership" between George Merck and Weicker. See Peter Hertner, "German Multinational Enterprise before 1914," in *Multinationals: Theory and History*, ed. Hertner and Geoffrey Jones (Aldershot: Gower, 1986), 116.

93. Haynes, *American Chemical Industry*, I, 330; VI, 271. See also George Merck to Alien Property Custodian, April 4, 1918, RG 131, Box 186, NA. In 1904, after clashing with George Merck, Weicker, who had married a wealthy American—with financial assistance from his father-in-law—left the American Merck company and bought control of E. R. Squibb & Sons (Mahoney, *Merchants of Life*, 193). By this time the thirty-six-old Merck was fully in charge.

94. U.S. House, Committee on Ways and Means, *Importation and Use of Opium, Hearings*, 61st Cong., 3rd sess., 1910–11, 145–146.

95. *APC Report*, 59, and Haynes, *American Chemical Industry*, III, 292.

96. George Merck to Alien Property Custodian, April 4, 1918.

97. Ibid. and other data in RG 131, boxes 156 and 187, NA.

98. *APC Report*, 343.

99. Ibid., 461.

100. U.S. Department of Commerce, *Foreign Direct Investment in the United States*, 9 vols. (Washington, D.C., 1976), V, G–93. I have not found any other evidence of a direct investment; the Commerce Department study does not cite a source. Data in RG 59, 165.102/16, NA, for September 1914 do, however, indicate that Knoll & Co. had been exporting to the United States before war broke out in Europe.

101. Haynes, *American Chemical Industry*, III, 484–485.

102. See Hans Hollander, *Geschichte de Schering Aktiengesellschaft* (Berlin: Schering, 1955), 14–15, on the start of Schering & Glatz. See also Haynes, *American Chemical Industry*, III, 483–484. The *APC Report* has nothing on Schering & Glatz, which, however, appears to have survived the war (with that name). See Haynes, *American Chemical Industry*, III, 322; VI, 470. On Schering & Glatz, see also Mahoney, *Merchants of Life*, 253.

103. Haynes, *American Chemical Industry*, VI, 209.

104. The quotation is from U.S. Federal Trade Commission, *Report on Cooperation in American Export Trade* (Washington, D.C., 1916), II, 432. It was a reply to an inquiry sent out in 1914 or 1915.

105. This could be a reference to the connections between Fries Brothers and Société Chimiques des Usines du Rhône. See "Fine Chemicals" section of this chapter and Haynes, *American Chemical Industry*, VI, 171. The French firm did make pharmaceuticals in France (Haber, *Chemical Industry, 1900–1930*, 159). Fries Brothers made saccharin, which could have been designated as a "pharmaceutical." It might also refer to the factory of Antoine Chiris (see the "Fine Chemicals" section of this chapter). I know this firm manufactured pharmaceuticals at a later date. See Haynes, *American Chemical Industry*, III, 320 (referring to 1922).

106. This might be called a U.S. business in England. It was not. It had no American parent. On its early history, see Mahoney, *Merchants of Life*, 95–106, 113.

107. Haynes, *American Chemical Industry*, VI, 61.

108. Fred A. Coe, Jr., *Burroughs Wellcome Co., 1880–1980* (New York: Newcomen Society, 1980), 11. The firm first registered Tabloid as a trademark in 1884 (Mahoney, *Merchants of Life*, 99).

109. *Economist*, 47 (Nov. 23, 1889): 1510; H. Osborne O'Hagan, *Leaves from my Life*, 2 vols. (London: John Lane, 1929), II, 32–38; and *New York Times*, Jan. 28, 1923 (on Warner's 1893 losses). T. A. B. Corley to Wilkins, July 19 and Sept. 10, 1986, writes that in 1899 Warner "forfeited" his shares in the British company in settlement of his debts to the firm; the latter was by then British controlled.

110. Ann Francis, *A Guinea a Box* (London: Hale, 1968), 64, 70, 118, 146–147, 154. According to T. A. B. Corley, "From National to Multinational Enterprise: The Beecham Business, 1848–1945," unpublished paper, 1983, Joseph Beecham arranged with the company's agent, B. F. Allen, to have the pills made in Brooklyn. There was no formal agency contract, only a verbal agreement whereby Allen paid the factory employees and then was reimbursed by the British company.

111. This was a constant problem for British (and German) sellers of consumer goods. J. & P. Coats had the same complaints; so did the German stainless steel cutlery maker, Henckels, and the German Heinrich Franck Söhne & Co.—for example.

112. T. A. B. Corley to Mira Wilkins, June 27, 1982. My guess is that this probably was sixty crossings, or thirty trips—still a formidable number, considering that Joseph Beecham died in 1916. Since his interest in American business seems to have begun in the late 1880s, he appears to have made annual trips to America thereafter.

113. Corley, "From National to Multinational," suggests that Beecham's reasons for beginning manufacturing in 1890–91 were: (1) Beecham was importing pill boxes from New England; why ship them to the United Kingdom and then back to the United States? (2) Beecham wanted to manufacture near his customers; (3) Americans preferred sugar-coated pills; and (4) tariff barriers were high. He also suggests that local manufacture was a way of avoiding imitators. I do not see the last item as a plausible reason. Another consideration in the original decision to manufacture may have been that the McKinley tariff eliminated duties on raw sugar, which would bring down the cost of U.S. production. See F. W. Taussig, *Tariff History of the United States*, 8th rev. ed. (New York: Capricorn Books, 1964), 275–282.

114. Indeed, Pears' Soap (discussed with the other soaps in Chapter 9) was marketed through drug outlets. On Pears' Soap marketing, see "Lever Golden Jubilee—USA, 1895–1945" (booklet, 1945), 5, in Unilever Archives, London. In 1909 Joseph Beecham joined the board of A. & F. Pears, Ltd., London. On the connections, see Corley, "From National to Multinational." In 1910 Thomas J. Barratt, chairman and

managing director of A. & F. Pears, Ltd., told the stockholders that Beecham "has relieved me of journeys to the United States whence he is now returning after a visit in the interests of his own and our business" (London *Times*, Oct. 27, 1910). In 1911, when Barratt considered establishing a Pears' Soap factory in the United States, he traveled with Joseph Beecham (ibid., Oct. 27, 1911).

115. Alfred D. Chandler, "Global Enterprise," unpublished paper, 1982, makes the point that the Germans pioneered in selling drugs to doctors and hospitals. Franko suggests the reason lay in the early adoption in Germany of government health insurance, which created a sizable demand (*European Multinationals*, 36). Other reasons include the German science-based industry. Since in many cases they sold prescription drugs, selling through doctors was the only possible route. As noted earlier, even aspirin was initially promoted through doctors.

116. Haynes, *American Chemical Industry*, III, 313. In 1912 Aspirin sold at $4.40 a pound; but under its chemical name, $0.65 a pound. For other products the case was similar: Veronal, $21.00/lb. v. $5.75/lb.; Heroine, $8.80/oz. v. $6.45/oz. (imported by Bayer); Aristol, $1.80/oz. v. $0.36/oz. (ibid., 313, 300). Veronal was a barbituate discovered by Merck & Co. in 1904 (Haber, *Chemical Industry, 1900–1930*, 128). Apparently Bayer independently had developed the same product, and the two firms agreed to share the process (Haber, *Chemical Industry during the Nineteenth Century*, 135). The Pure Food and Drug Act of 1906 had required labels to indicate the opium, cocaine, heroine, and morphine content of products. The Harrison Act, passed in December 1914, put the first rigid controls on the sale of narcotics. Not until 1924 was the importation of crude opium for the purpose of making and selling heroine prohibited (Haynes, *American Chemical Industry*, III, 414, 300–303).

117. As indicated earlier, Salvarsan was a brand name.

118. A witness before a U.S. Congressional Committee in 1906 estimated that 50,000 patent medicines (nostrums) were made and sold in America! See James Harvey Young, *The Medical Messiahs* (Princeton, N.J.: Princeton University Press, 1967), 23.

119. Haynes, *American Chemical Industry*, VI, 172; III, 331.

120. Ibid., VI, 171. By 1913 Société Chimiques des Usines du Rhône was the leader in French "organic chemicals." It specialized in pharmaceuticals, photochemicals, essences (vanillin and courmarin), and cellulose acetate film (Haber, *Chemical Industry, 1900–1930*, 159). In 1928 it became part of Rhône-Polenc, S.A. (ibid., 305). I do not know the extent of its ownership of Fries Brothers.

121. Haynes, *American Chemical Industry*, VI, 171–172; I, 329.

122. Ibid., I, 327–328; VI, 207; and *APC Report*, 457.

123. Haber, *Chemical Industry, 1900–1930*, 222.

124. Haynes, *American Chemical Industry*, VI, 283; I, 328. In 1914 Monsanto was heavily dependent on German imports (Monsanto to U.S. Department of State, Aug. 31, 1914, RG 59, 165.102/12, NA).

125. Haber, *Chemical Industry, 1900–1930*, 22.

126. *APC Report*, 310. Curiously, Haynes has nothing on this U.S. plant, although he does have data on Constantine Fahlberg (Haynes, *American Chemical Industry*, I, 328).

127. Haynes, *American Chemical Industry*, III, 331, and *APC Report*, 467.

128. Haynes, *American Chemical Industry*, III, 515.

129. Haber, *Chemical Industry during the Nineteenth Century*, 146. On General Chemical Company, Haynes, *American Chemical Industry*, I, 264–265; III, 5–6. J. M. Goetchius of General Chemical would later comment that in 1911 men from Badische inspected the firm's facilities. The response was that the Germans wanted to order apparatus from the Americans (ibid., I, 265–266). Note that W. J. Matheson—who represented Cassella, one of the six major German dyestuff companies, in the United States—was

in 1899 a founding director of General Chemical (ibid., 265). General Chemical would be merged into Allied Chemical & Dye Corporation in 1920 (ibid., VI, 9).

130. On the Ducktown company, see Haynes, *American Chemical Industry*, I, 263, and IV, 81; and Duane A. Smith, *Mining America: The Industry and the Environment, 1800–1980* (Lawrence: University Press of Kansas, 1987), 96–98. I have not mentioned the British-owned San Francisco Chemical Company that produced sulfuric acid, as an adjunct to its parent's pyrite mining (see Chapter 8, note 37), since San Francisco Chemical was a very small factor in U.S. sulfuric acid output.

131. *Mineral Industry, 1892*, 57.

132. Reader, *I.C.I.*, I, 106, and *Mineral Industry, 1892*, 63.

133. Reader, *I.C.I.*, I, 5–8; Haber, *Chemical Industry during the Nineteenth Century*, 89; and Haber, *Chemical Industry, 1900–1930*, 3.

134. Haynes, *American Chemical Industry*, I, 270–272; VI, 391. The best sources I have found on Rowland Hazard are two articles in the *Bulletin of the National Association of Wool Manufacturers*, 28 (Sept. 1898 and Dec. 1898): 264–266 and 313–341. His textile enterprise was the Peace Dale Manufacturing Company, Peace Dale, Rhode Island.

135. According to Haynes, *American Chemical Industry*, I, 272; VI, 392. Edward N. Trump, "Looking Back at 50 Years in Ammonia-Soda Alkali Industry," *Chemical and Metallurgical Engineering*, 40 (March 1933): 127, reported that one-third of the initial capital was supplied by the Solvays and two-thirds by Hazard, William Cogswell, and a small group of their friends in Syracuse. Trump says nothing, however, about ownership per se. Moreover, he may not have been privy to the original ownership relationships.

136. Haynes, *American Chemical Industry*, I, 272, and VI, 392; Trump, "Looking Back," 128–129. The historian W. J. Reader writes, "The 'detailed tabulation' you refer to was in fact a comparison of costs between the various factories in the Solvay Group . . . they were drawn up in a very sophisticated way being based not on money values, but on hours worked and quantities of materials used" (Reader to Wilkins, Jan. 24, 1981).

137. Haynes, *American Chemical Industry*, I, 272.

138. Ibid., 271–272; Trump, "Looking Back," 126; and Jacques Bolle, *Solvay, l'invention, l'homme, l'entreprise industrielle, 1863–1963* (Brussels: Solvay, 1963), 130.

139. Haynes, *American Chemical Industry*, I, 272, and Haber, *Chemical Industry during the Nineteenth Century*, 148.

140. Trump, "Looking Back," 128.

141. Haynes, *American Chemical Industry*, VI, 392.

142. Ibid., I, 272.

143. Ibid., VI, 392–393.

144. Trump, "Looking Back," 128. Trump joined S.P.C. in 1882.

145. Haynes, *American Chemical Industry*, VI, 392–393.

146. Ibid., 392 (1897), and I, 272 (1898).

147. Haber, *Chemical Industry during the Nineteenth Century*, 149.

148. Reader, *I.C.I.*, I, 222.

149. Ibid., I, 100.

150. Haynes, *American Chemical Industry*, I, 272.

151. Reader, *I.C.I.*, I, 95, and Haynes, *American Chemical Industry*, VI, 10 (quotation).

152. Haynes, *American Chemical Industry*, VI, 392. The Belgians—Solvay & Cie.—did have an interest in Semet-Solvay in 1920. See Cleona Lewis, *America's Stake in International Investments* (Washington, D.C.: Brookings Institution, 1938), 566. Reader, *I.C.I.*, throws no light on the financing.

153. Trump, "Looking Back," 128.

154. Haynes, *American Chemical Industry*, VI, 367–368.

155. Reader, *I.C.I.*, I, 222–223, 291.

156. Ibid., 97.

157. Ibid., 64, 97, 96.

158. Ibid., 98.

159. The $200,000 figure appears in BPB.B169ff, Jan. 7, 1889, in I.C.I. Archives, furnished me by W. J. Reader. It seems likely that the shares were acquired from the American group.

160. Reader, *I.C.I.*, I, 100, 293, 139. With this proxy, if the American owners voted as a block, they had sufficient stock to exercise control.

161. It appears to have had "just under" 50 percent of the shares in 1881 and 45.9 percent in 1914. My guess is that the 1887 holdings were "just under" 50 percent.

162. Reader, *I.C.I.*, I, 140, 64, 98.

163. Ibid., 100.

164. BPB.B.169ff, Jan. 7, 1889, letter in I. C. I. Archives, furnished me by W. J. Reader.

165. Reader, *I.C.I.*, I, 64.

166. Ibid., 223.

167. Ibid., 222.

168. Haber, *Chemical Industry, 1900–1930*, 177.

169. Both companies would become part of Allied Chemical in 1920.

170. My calculations based on Reader, *I.C.I.*, I, 292, and E. N. Trump to Roscoe Brunner, May 13, 1917, in MDW 94/3/7, I.C.I. Archives, furnished me by W. J. Reader.

171. Trump, "Looking Back," 128–129.

172. It became in 1943 Wyandotte Chemicals Corporation.

173. Reader, *I.C.I.*, I, 222–223. In 1914 Michigan Alkali produced 270,000 tons of soda ash, compared with Solvay Process' 450,000 tons. Haynes, *American Chemical Industry*, I, 273, points out that by the end of the 1800s "the original Solvay patents" had long expired; the courts ruled that the supplementary patents on improvements were "insufficiently essential to successful operation to prevent others from employing similar methods." Thus the door had opened to the many new entries.

174. Haynes, *American Chemical Industry*, I, 273.

175. Haber, *Chemical Industry, 1900–1930*, 177.

176. Haynes, *American Chemical Industry*, I, 273. This company was renamed Mathieson Chemical Company in 1948, and six years later it merged with Olin Industries to become Olin-Mathieson Chemical Company (Haber, *Chemical Industry during the Nineteeth Century*, 150).

177. Haynes, *American Chemical Industry*, VI, 264, and Reader, *I.C.I.*, I, 108.

178. Haynes, *American Chemical Industry*, VI, 264.

179. Reader, *I.C.I.*, I, 229.

180. In 1895, when Castner-Kellner Alkali Company, Ltd., was formed in the United Kingdom, it acquired from the Aluminium Company (U.K.) English rights to Castner's alkali and chlorine patents (*Mineral Industry, 1901*, 604). The American rights appear to have gone to Mathieson Alkali.

181. Haynes, *American Chemical Industry*, VI, 264, 114, and *Mineral Industry, 1901*, 559.

182. Haber, *Chemical Industry during the Nineteenth Century*, 150, and Joseph W. Richards, quoted in Trescott, *Electrochemicals Industry*, 67 ("American representative"). *Mineral Industry, 1901*, 599, says that Castner Electrolytic Alkali Company (CEAC) was formed in 1900 with a capital of $3 million to purchase and to use the Castner patents in the United States and to acquire the Mathieson Alkali electrochemical works at

Niagara Falls; Mathieson Alkali owned $2 million of the shares of CEAC. Haynes, *American Chemical Industry*, VI, 264–265, reports that in 1917 Castner Electrolytic Alkali was merged back into Mathieson Alkali—and took the name Mathieson Alkali Works, Inc. The *Stock Exchange Official Intelligence for 1914*, London, 609–610, confirms the incorporation of Castner Electrolytic Alkali Company on June 29, 1900 (in Virginia), to manufacture caustic soda and bleaching powder. It had properties at Niagara Falls. The London agent for the debenture trustees was Castner-Kellner Alkali Company, Ltd. Paul D. Dickens, "The Transition Period in American International Financing: 1897–1914," Ph.D. diss., George Washington University, 1933, indicates that in July 1900 "Castner Electrolytic Alkali Co. of U.S.A." offered fifteen-year-first-mortgage sterling debentures in London (he estimates some $729,900 was taken up there).

183. Trescott, *Electrochemicals Industry*, 64, lists electrochemical companies in order of arrival at Niagara Falls. Pittsburgh Reduction Company (later Alcoa) and Carborundum Company had started there in 1895; these two U.S.-owned companies and the three firms involving foreign investment made up the pioneering five entries.

184. Haber, *Chemical Industry, 1900–1930*, 179. Although after 1900 the British Castner-Kellner Alkali Company, Ltd., apparently had minority interests in the Castner Electrolytic Alkali Company at Niagara Falls and in the Niagara Electro Chemical Company, also at Niagara Falls, these American firms do not appear to have had any relation to each other, at least none that I have been able to discern. Each specialized in different products in the heavy-chemical industry.

185. *APC Report*, 56.

186. James Gifford to W. W. Wilson, Jan. 22, 1926, Du Pont Papers (on the date of Perth Amboy Works' incorporation); Haber, *Chemical Industry, 1900–1930*, 123; and *APC Report*, 56.

187. *APC Report*, 344. Ibid., 65, shows Roessler & Hasslacher with interests in the United States in General Bakelite Company, Enamel Company of America, and Chlorine Product Company. On General Bakelite, see Haynes, *American Chemical Industry*, III, 378–380.

188. See data in RG 131, Box 200, NA, and Thomas R. Kabisch, *Deutsches Kapital in den USA* (Stuttgart: Klett-Cotta, 1982), 262–270, on the DEGUSSA group of companies in the United States.

189. Haynes, *American Chemical Industry*, VI, 313, and Haber, *Chemical Industry during the Nineteeth Century*, 151. For more details on the Oldbury Electro-Chemical Company, see the business history of its parent: Richard E. Threlfall, *The Story of 100 Years of Phosphorous Making* (Oldbury: Albright & Wilson, 1951), 94, 153–163, 260–263.

190. Aside from those firms mentioned in the text, in the mid-to-late 1890s National Electrolytic began operations at Niagara Falls. It was basically American owned but used the patents of William Taylor Gibbs, a British-born Canadian resident. Gibbs obtained an interest (not a controlling one) in National Electrolytic (Threlfall, *Phosphorus Making*, 281–283, 290). This firm started to produce chlorates after the imposition of the duty on them in 1898 (Haynes, *American Chemical Industry*, I, 282). Trescott, *American Electrochemicals Industry*, 64, did not rank it as an innovator at Niagara Falls, since she dated its entry as "about 1902," which appears to be an error. Haynes (I, 282), Threlfall (p. 281), and Trescott herself (p. 80) all suggest the earlier date. It probably should be included among the first entries.

191. *Mineral Industry, 1892*, 64. For its sales agents in the United States, see Haynes, *American Chemical Industry*, I, 276.

192. Edward Salisbury Clark, "An Outline History of the North American Chemical Company of Bay City, Michigan: 1898–1928," typescript, 1928. I am indebted to Mary B. McManman of the Bay City Library for making this source available to me. The

president of North American Chemical (1898–1914) was John Brock, who resided in England (ibid., 39). Brock was the "working head" of United Alkali (Reader, *I.C.I.*, I, 106). Other material on the North American Chemical Company is in Leslie Arndt, *The Bay County Story* (Linwood, Mich.: privately printed, 1982), 149; Haber, *Chemical Industry during the Nineteeth Century*, 151; Haynes, *American Chemical Industry*, I, 282; Haber, *Chemical Industry, 1900–1930*, 28; Threlfall, *Phosphorus Making*, 262; and Reader, *I.C.I.*, I, 228. North American Chemical seems to have been more successful in its earlier than in its later years. United Alkali in the United Kingdom had far more products than North American Chemical, whose product line was very limited. It made no attempt to introduce the old-fashioned Leblanc process of alkali making into the United States. I puzzled for a while on why the company started to look at Detroit, until I realized that in 1895–1897 Solvay Process Company had built a plant there. United Alkali would have been aware of this.

193. Threlfall, *Phosphorus Making*, 287. In 1902 the British firm Albright & Wilson, Ltd., acquired controlling interest in E.R.C.; it made arrangements for the transfer of the hypophosphite plant to its U.S. subsidiary, Oldbury Electro-Chemical Company, at Niagara Falls (ibid., 288–289, 154).

194. Haynes, *American Chemical Industry*, VI, 305, and *APC Report*, 37.

195. See letterhead, Jan. 3, 1911, letter in RG 59, 611.627/293, NA.

196. Good details on this venture are in Duffus, Jr., *The Story of M & T Chemicals*, 1–16. The $3 million in capital was made up of $2 million in common shares and $1 million in cumulative preferred shares. American Can Company owned $500,000 of the common shares of Goldschmidt Detinning Company. Most of the $1 million in cumulative preferred and the remaining $500,000 of common shares (remember $1 million was owned by Th. Goldschmidt, Essen) were sold to the public, although some went to German suppliers.

197. Ibid, 9–12. In 1911 the capital of Goldschmidt Detinning was raised from $3 million to $3.75 million; the newly issued stock went to Th. Goldschmidt in exchange for the alkaline detinning technology (ibid., 15–16). This increased the German firm's holdings to 47 percent. Th. Goldschmidt was the largest single shareholder in the U.S. company. In 1916, with war conditions, the German firm sold its $1.75 million par value interest in Goldschmidt Detinning for $1 million (ibid., 24). In 1915 the detinning company had purchased Goldschmidt Thermit Company for $500,000 cash (ibid., 20). The latter may have been owned by Th. Goldschmidt.

198. Robert T. Swaine, *The Cravath Firm* (New York: privately printed, 1946), II, 110.

199. Haber, *Chemical Industry, 1900–1930*, 114.

200. List prepared by Alfred D. Chandler.

201. The Alien Property Custodian Report has nothing on this firm, nor does Haynes, nor does Kabisch, *Deutsches Kapital in den USA*.

202. Haynes, *American Chemical Industry*, I, 283.

203. Trescott, *Electrochemicals Industry*, 15–16, discusses the international dimensions of the electrochemical activities—the scientific and engineering work, the patent activity, the industrial developments, and the education. She does not, however, consider international investments. She would undoubtedly add French influences to my list (but more on the *electro*chemical than on the purely chemical side).

204. Reader, *I.C.I.*, I, 230, 290.

205. Haber, *Chemical Industry, 1900–1930*, 177. The English Caustic Soda Makers Association included United Alkali; Brunner, Mond; Castner-Kellner; and other British chemical companies (ibid., 138–139).

206. See Haynes, *American Chemical Industry*, VI, 433–434 (on Linde and Linde Air Product Company); Haber, *Chemical Industry, 1900–1930*, 30–31 (on Linde), 144 (on

Gesellschaft für Lindes Eismachinen); *Stock Exchange Official Intelligence for 1914*, 588 (on British Oxygen Company); and Haynes, *American Chemical Industry*, III, 159 (on Cecil Lightfoot). In October 1917 Union Carbide and Carbon Corporation was formed and acquired Linde Air Products. *APC Report*, 395, lists among the alien-owned shares of "inactive" U.S. industrials 4,237 shares (at par and market value of $423,700) of Linde Air Products. By that time Linde Air Products was already part of Union Carbide. The amount, I am guessing, might be the holding of Linde or his German company. Since Linde was an organizer of the U.S. firm and since his company obtained a minority interest in British Oxygen, it seems likely that he or his German company would have held a minority interest in Linde Air Products. See also Monopolies and Restrictive Practices Commission, *Report on the Supply of Certain Industrial and Medical Gases* (London: H.M.S.O., 1956), 9–10, 19, for some verification of this assumption. Alfred Chandler, using German sources, found confirmation that Linde's license was accompanied by his taking shares in exchange. Earlier Linde had licensed an American company to produce and to distribute his refrigerating machinery.

207. According to Dunning data, University of Reading, Reading, England (International Paints), and Haynes, *American Chemical Industry*, II, 248 (Rollin Chemical).

208. Taussig, *Tariff History*, 472. Similar descriptions are in Haynes, *American Chemical Industry*, for example, I, 312.

209. Haynes, *American Chemical Industry*, III, 225. On Little, see ibid., I, 396–397.

210. *1922 Dyestuffs Hearings*, 102–103, traces the history of U.S. tariffs on coal-tar dyes and dyestuffs from 1864 to 1916. Between 1864 and 1883, there was modest protection of both colors and intermediates. After 1883, duties were removed on dyestuffs (intermediates). In the Dingley tariff of 1897, the Payne-Aldrich tariff of 1909, and the 1913 tariff, coal-tar dyes (colors) had a duty of 30 percent, whereas intermediates continued to be admitted duty free. Existing U.S. "dyestuff" plants typically made dyes and depended on imported intermediates.

211. A number of the accounts of the origins of Solvay Process Company note the important role of William B. Cogswell, who made the initial contacts with Ernest Solvay. See, for instance, Haber, *Chemical Industry during the Nineteeth Century*, 148, and Trump, "Looking Back," 126. Cogswell became general manager of Solvay Process; he was an employee of Rowland Hazard. Hazard died in 1898; his son Frederick R. Hazard (1858–1917), who had also worked at the family's Rhode Island woolen mills, became of key importance in Solvay Process. See Haynes, *American Chemical Industry*, I, 272–273. For the important role of Rowland Hazard, see also T. Bolle, *Solvay*, 85.

212. Haynes, *American Chemical Industry*, III, 3.

213. *APC Report*, 34–35, particularly emphasizes the corruption of purchasing agents, of buyers of dyestuffs. See also U.S. Department of Commerce, *The German Dyestuffs Industry* (Washington, D.C., 1924), 57; Haynes, *American Chemical Industry*, I, 312; and Ambruster, *Treason's Peace*, 1–14. Ambruster (pp. 2–3) saw the large German firms in the pre–World War I period acting in coordination with the German government to strangle America's organic chemical industry: "The completeness with which we [the United States] failed to develop this militarily strategic industry attests to the determination of purpose and the typical German thoroughness with which the representatives of *Kultur* carried out, within our borders, their coordination of industry with the forces of war."

214. Morris R. Poucher, who worked for Badische in the United States before World War I, told Williams Haynes that for many years Badische had a half-dozen suits current in the patent or customs court (Haynes, *American Chemical Industry*, I, 312n). Bayer's chief executive in the United States, Anthony Gref, was a skilled patent attor-

ney (ibid., III, 312). Badische, in particular, entered into numerous licensing arrangements, perhaps the most important being with General Chemical Company.

215. There is no indication that had there been very high tariffs or other reasons for U.S. manufacture, the Germans would not have licensed U.S. firms and/or manufactured through subsidiaries or affiliates in the United States.

216. Taussig, *Tariff History*, 473.

217. See Haynes, *American Chemical Industry*, VI, 114–115, and Haber, *Chemical Industry during the Nineteenth Century*, 150.

218. Only two free-standing companies are mentioned in the entire chapter. One was H. H. Warner and Co., Ltd.; it was clearly exceptional—and of little consequence (except as a means of enriching Warner himself). The other was the Ducktown Sulphur, Copper and Iron Company, Ltd., which became an innovator after being taken to court for polluting—again, an atypical pattern for the pre–World War I chemical industry.

12. Other Manufacturing

1. There are two useful histories of Massey-Harris: Merrill Denison, *Harvest Triumphant* (Toronto: Collins, 1949), and E. P. Neufeld, *A Global Corporation: A History of the International Development of Massey-Ferguson Ltd.* (Toronto: University of Toronto Press, 1969).

2. Denison, *Harvest Triumphant*, 159.

3. Ibid., 171.

4. The best source on International Harvester's foreign manufacturing plants (sequence and products) is that company's *Annual Report, 1909;* see also the 1907 annual report for more details on the Canadian plant.

5. Ibid., 1909, and Fred V. Carstensen, *American Enterprise in Foreign Markets* (Chapel Hill: University of North Carolina Press, 1984), 142ff.

6. Denison, *Harvest Triumphant*, 164, 179.

7. It is not clear why U.S. costs would be lower. Economies of scale? Cheaper power? Lower-cost transport for inputs and outputs? These are possibilities.

8. Denison, *Harvest Triumphant*, 182–184, and Neufeld, *A Global Corporation*, 20–21.

9. According to Neufeld, *A Global Corporation*, 20. Denison, *Harvest Triumphant*, 185, says that "in 1912" the Deyo-Macey Company "was purchased outright."

10. Denison, *Harvest Triumphant*, 171, writes that in 1906 Massey-Harris began to market an unspecified line of American stationary gasoline farm engines in Canada. I presume this was the Deyo-Macey line.

11. Based on Denison, *Harvest Triumphant*, 185. According to Neufeld, *A Global Corporation*, 20, Massey-Harris actually moved the machinery to Weston (a suburb of Toronto) in 1916 and began producing such engines there in that year.

12. Denison, *Harvest Triumphant*, 184, and Neufeld, *A Global Corporation*, 20–22.

13. Denison, *Harvest Triumphant*, 184, and Neufeld, *A Global Corporation*, 22. In 1914 the authorized capital was $1,750,000. See Cleona Lewis, *America's Stake in International Investments* (Washington, D.C.: Brookings Institution, 1938), 566.

14. The only possible larger Canadian manufacturing investments might be those of S. J. Moore (see text of this Chapter).

15. Robert T. Swaine, *The Cravath Firm*, 2 vols. (New York: privately printed, 1946), I, 546.

16. See Chapter 7.

17. James M. Laux, *In First Gear: The French Automobile Industry to 1914* (Montreal:

McGill-Queen's University Press, 1976), 99. Whether these were "independent" agencies is not clear.

18. Patrick Fridenson, *Histoire des usines Renault* (Paris: Seuil, 1972), 54.

19. Mira Wilkins, "Multinational Automobile Enterprises and Regulation: An Historical Overview," in *Government, Technology, and the Future of the Automobile*, ed. Douglas H. Ginsburg and William J. Abernathy (New York: McGraw-Hill, 1978), 224.

20. Charles W. Bishop, *La France et l'automobile* (Paris: Editions M.-Th. Genin, 1971), 300.

21. Michel Laferrère, *Lyon: ville industrielle* (Paris: Presses Universitaires de France, 1960), 371, 374; Jean-Pierre Bardou, Jean-Jacques Chanaron, Patrick Fridenson, and James M. Laux, *La révolution automobile* (Paris: Albin Michel, 1977), 49; and G. N. Georgano, ed., *Encyclopedia of American Automobiles* (New York: Rainbird Reference Books, 1971), 15.

22. Brochure of Mercedes-Benz Sales, Inc., n.d. [1962?], and F. Schildberger, "75 Years of Mercedes Ties with the United States," in *Mercedes in aller Welt* (Stuttgart: Daimler-Benz, 1963), 211.

23. "Power of Attorney," Oct. 6, 1888, Steinway Archives, Long Island City, N.Y.

24. Ibid.

25. I obtained capitalization data from the Corporations Bureau, Albany, N.Y., Jan. 28, 1977. Earlier I had written to John Steinway, asking what percentage of the capital was represented by Daimler's sixty-six shares. He replied, "I have no idea what the original capitalization of the Daimler Motor Company was. I have never been able to find the business records. However, my grandfather died in 1896 and his estate lists 1180 shares of Daimler Motor. I suspect the 66 to Gottlieb Daimler was a small token" (Steinway to Mira Wilkins, Jan. 20, 1977). I do not know whether the capital of Daimler Motor Company was the same in 1888 and 1896. If in 1888 shares were $100, which is possible, Daimler's interest would have been $6,600 of $200,000, or 3.3 percent (and if in 1888 Steinway held 1,180 shares, his holdings would equal 59 percent). If in 1888 the shares were $1,000, Daimler's holdings would be 33 percent (and in order for Steinway to have 1,180 shares in 1896, the capital would have had to be increased). In any case, it is clear that Daimler held a minority interest. (I do not, moreover, know if all the "authorized capital" was actually issued.)

26. Friedrich Schildberger, "Die Entstehung des industriellen Automobilbaues in den Vereinigten Staaten bis zur Jahrhundertwende und der deutsche Einfluss," *Automobil-Industrie*, Jan. 1969, 56.

27. Ibid.; William Greenleaf, *Monopoly on Wheels* (Detroit: Wayne State University Press, 1961), 32; and data from John Steinway, Jan. 20, 1977.

28. This advertisement was found by Professor Cyril Ehrlich, a historian of the piano industry.

29. Schildberger, "Die Entstehung," 57–58.

30. It was organized on Aug. 2, 1898. Data from the Corporations Bureau, Albany, N.Y., Feb. 10, 1977.

31. A 1906 brochure advertising the American Mercedes describes the Daimler Manufacturing Company as "closely affiliated with the parent company" and "operating under American patent and shop rights." Daimler Motoren Gesellschaft had been founded in 1890 (Bardou et al., *La révolution*, 24).

32. John Steinway recalled that his uncle, Louis von Bernuth, ran the company at one time. Data from John Steinway.

33. The "Mercedes" first appeared in Germany in 1901, produced by Daimler Motoren Gesellschaft.

34. 1906 brochure.

35. Bardou et al., *La révolution*, 60. The Fiat Company had been formed in Italy in 1899 (ibid., 61).

36. Louis T. Wells, "Automobiles," in *Big Business and the State*, ed. Raymond Vernon (Cambridge, Mass.: Harvard University Press, 1974), 231, 295. Georgano, ed., *Encyclopaedia*, 78, states that the Fiat Motor Company in the United States "was an independent concern, formed with American capital to manufacture Fiat cars under license." There could, of course, have been an Italian minority interest. Others refer to it as the manufacturing "branch" of Fiat in the United States. See Patrick Fridenson, "The Growth of Multinational Activities in the French Motor Industry," in *Multinationals: Theory and History*, ed. Peter Hertner and Geoffrey Jones (Aldershot: Gower, 1986), 157. Valerie Castronovo, *Giovanni Agnelli* (Torino: Einaudi, 1977), 47–48, writes that the U.S. venture was comanaged by the Italians and Americans.

37. Chambre Syndicate des Constructeurs d'Automobiles, *Annuaire* (Paris, 1914). I am indebted to Patrick Fridenson for this reference. Georgano has nothing on this.

38. Wilkins, "Multinational Automobile Enterprises," 224–226, and Alfred D. Chandler, Jr., *Giant Enterprises* (New York: Harcourt, Brace, 1964), 3.

39. Mira Wilkins and Frank Ernest Hill, *American Business Abroad: Ford on Six Continents* (Detroit: Wayne State University Press, 1964), 53.

40. Kathleen Edith Dunlop, "The History of the Dunlop Rubber Company, Ltd., 1888–1939," Ph.D. diss. University of Illinois, Urbana, 1949, 28, 114–16. Initially bicycles as well as tires were shipped.

41. Dr. Geoffrey Jones, who used the Dunlop Archives, has been extremely helpful to me in reconstructing the story of Dunlop in America. See his "Growth and Performance of British Multinational Firms before 1939: The Case of Dunlop," *Economic History Review*, 2nd ser., 38 (Feb. 1984): 35–53, and his "Expansion of British Multinational Manufacturing," in *Overseas Business Activities*, ed. A. Okochi and T. Inoue (Tokyo: University of Tokyo Press, 1984), 129–130. Sir Arthur du Cros says that his father (Harvey, Sr.) first arrived in America on Christmas Day, 1890. See Arthur du Cros, *Wheels of Fortune* (London: Chapman & Hall, 1938), 47. The Corporations Bureau, Albany, N.Y., Dec. 8, 1981, writes me that the American Dunlop Tire Company, a New Jersey corporation, received authority to do business in New York on July 21, 1893. Jones, "The Growth," 38, says that the new American Dunlop company was a "wholly-owned foreign manufacturing subsidiary."

42. Dunlop, "The History," 117 (1899). Jones in both papers gives the date as 1898. L. M. Bergin, Testimony of July 20, 1922, Dunlop Archives (data from Jones), gave the date as 1898–99. As I have shown, in 1898–1900 a number of British companies were pulling back from U.S. business. Moreover, it looked at that time as though the bicycle market had peaked.

43. Glenn D. Babcock, *History of United States Rubber Company* (Bloomington: Bureau of Business Research, Graduate School of Business, Indiana University, 1966), 73–74. The United States Rubber Company had been formed in 1892.

44. Victor S. Clark, *History of Manufactures*, 3 vols. (Washington, D.C.: Carnegie Institution, 1929), III, 236. The Rubber Goods Manufacturing Company, formed in 1899, brought together a large number of plants, securing control of the most important ones making bicycle tires. Ibid., and John Moody, *Truth about Trusts* (New York: John Moody, 1904), 269.

45. Babcock, *History of U.S. Rubber*, 114.

46. *Saturday Evening Post*, March 1, 1913, 63.

47. L. M. Bergin testimony (obtained from Dr. Jones).

48. *Saturday Evening Post*, March 1, 1913, 63.

49. L. M. Bergin testimony.

50. Babcock, *History of U.S. Rubber*, 117.

51. The reentry of Dunlop into American business will be covered in Volume 2 of my history of foreign investment in the United States.

52. Barbou, *La révolution*, 28.

53. On its foreign plants, see letterhead of the Michelin Tire Company, Frederick W. Taylor Papers, Stevens Institute of Technology, Hoboken, N.J. James Laux has pointed out to me that according to *The Automobile*, March 28, 1907, Michelin had sold 16,000 tires in the United States in 1906 (all imports); there was a 35 percent tariff, and thus the company had decided that the potential market warranted its manufacturing in the country.

54. Ibid., Oct. 3, 1907.

55. Taylor to Edouard Michelin, Aug. 29, 1912, Taylor Papers.

56. Marcel Michelin to Taylor, Sept. 11, 1912, Taylor Papers.

57. Hathaway Report of Oct. 4, 1912, Taylor Papers.

58. Ibid.

59. Branch list on letterhead, Michelin Tire Company, Taylor Papers. Hal Morgan, *Symbols of America* (New York: Penguin Books, 1987), 222, has a Michelin advertising poster, circa 1910. Was this used in the United States? Probably.

60. Typescript of Works Progress Administration, "History of Milltown," 1936, 30–34.

61. Ibid., and *Milltown Review*, April 25, 1930, and Sept. 11, 1930.

62. On the limited U.S. tire companies' pre-1914 role abroad, see Mira Wilkins, *The Emergence of Multinational Enterprise: American Business Abroad from the Colonial Era to 1914* (Cambridge, Mass.: Harvard University Press, 1970).

63. In meat, flour, and brewing, for example (see Chapter 9). The *American Iron and Steel Association Bulletin*, 24 (March 5, 1890): 61, quoted a dispatch from Trenton, New Jersey, dated Feb. 13, 1890, on negotiations between "the English syndicate and the Central Rubber Trust of this city" having been concluded that day by a sale of five factories in Trenton to the English capitalists. The amount involved was "over $3 million." I have been unable to learn more about this, which does *not* seem to relate to the New York, Belting and Packing Company acquisitions. Trenton is near Philadelphia; New York Belting and Packing Company's ventures were in Passaic, New Jersey, near New York City (just north of Newark).

64. Durant in 1871 had become the founder of Wellesley College.

65. On New York Belting and Packing Company, Ltd. see its prospectus, published in the London *Times*, Jan. 26, 1891, and Babcock, *History of U.S. Rubber*, 44–47. The Belmont involved was August Belmont, Jr., whose father died in 1890. The English Association of American Bond and Shareholders often acted on behalf of British investors. On its role vis-à-vis another one of Belmont's ventures (the Louisville and Nashville Railroad), see Ernest Cassel to Belmont, June 27, 1891, and Sept. 5, 1891, Belmont Family Papers, Special Collections, Columbia University Library.

66. Thomas Chalmers, *100 Years of Guttapercha: R. & J. Dick, Ltd.* (Glasgow: privately printed, n.d. [1947?]), 17, 40–44, and Lewis, *America's Stake*, 566.

67. Based on John Dunning, interview, July 20, 1960, at British Belting and Asbestos, Ltd., in England. Dunning's notes indicate that the U.S. subsidiary was established sixty-three years earlier and that the "pre-1925 plant was at Paterson and Boston; . . . date of establishment, 1904" (Dunning data, University of Reading, Reading, England).

68. See Williams Haynes, *American Chemical Industry*, 6 vols. (New York: D. Van Nostrand, 1945–1954), VI, 177–178.

69. On all these companies, see Alien Property Custodian, *Report, 1918–1919*, 119–120 (henceforth cited as *APC Report*).

70. Ibid., 117; ranking from unpublished list prepared by Alfred D. Chandler, Jr.

71. Jürgen Kocka, "The Rise of the Modern Industrial Enterprise in Germany," in *Managerial Hierarchies*, ed. Alfred D. Chandler, Jr., and Herman Daems (Cambridge, Mass.: Harvard University Press, 1980), 104.

72. *APC Report*, 117–118, and, more important, data in Record Group 131, Box 212, National Archives, Washington, D.C.

73. In 1914 (subsequent to the outbreak of war in Europe), the majority interest in H. Koppers Company was bought by Americans; by 1917 the Germans retained 20 percent. See Fred C. Foy, *Ovens, Chemicals, and Men! Koppers Company, Inc.* (New York: Newcomen Society, 1958), 11–13; Haynes, *American Chemical Industry*, VI, 242; and *APC Report*, 327. Data from Alfred D. Chandler, Sept. 18, 1987, on Semet-Solvay and Koppers.

74. W. Robert Nitske and Charles Morrow Wilson, *Rudolf Diesel* (Norman: University of Oklahoma Press, 1965), 184–185 (on the Deutz firm), and Gustav Goldbeck, *Kraft für Die Welt* (Düsseldorf: Econ-Verlag, 1964), 46, 73, 91, 229 (on its American factory). Nitske and Wilson, *Rudolf Diesel*, 254, write that "the Otto Engine Company under license from the German Deutz firm, began building diesel engines at its plant in Philadelphia" in 1910. Was this the same facility?

75. *APC Report*, 122.

76. Ibid., 119, 347, 564. Standard German economic histories do not even mention Koerting!

77. See data in RG 131, Box 200, National Archives, for details. See also this chapter, note 108.

78. *APC Report*, 299, 220, 148.

79. Bruno Kuske, *100 Jahre Stollwerck-Geschichte, 1839–1939* (Köln: Stollwerck, 1939), 87–93, 104–107; *Moody's Public Utilities and Industrials, 1916*, 1863; and Gyula Meleghy, "Die Vermittlerrolle der Banken bei deutschen Investitionen in Nord- und Mittelamerika bis zum Ersten Weltkrieg," Ph.D. diss., University of Cologne, 1983, 216–242, 302–304. In 1911 Ludwig Stollwerck was chairman of the board.

80. *APC Report*, 120–121, 327. The New York Public Library has early-twentieth-century (pre–World War I) descriptive catalogues prepared by Kny-Scheerer Company, New York. One, for example, offers "dissecting and microscopic instruments." The spelling *Kny-Scheerer*, while odd, is correct and is used on the catalogues.

81. W. J. Reader, *Weir Group* (London: Weidenfeld & Nicolson, 1971), 37–38.

82. On this firm, see *Stock Exchange Year Book, 1893* and *Burdett's Official Intelligence, 1891*. All the ordinary shares were taken by the American vendors. The British were offered debentures and preference shares.

83. *Moody's, 1914*. International Steam Pump Company, *Annual Report, 1901* (Scudder Collection, Columbia University), indicates that among the assets of ISPC were £200,000 ordinary shares of Blake and Knowles Steam Pump Works, Ltd., and among the liabilities of ISPC's subsidiary, George F. Blake Manufacturing Company, were $1 million in mortgage bonds and $500,000 in preferred stock of Blake and Knowles Steam Pump Company, Ltd. ISPC, *Annual Report, 1904*, indicates that the Blake and Knowles Steam Pump Works, Ltd, was dissolved in 1903—and replaced by a New Jersey company of the same name.

84. S. B. Saul, "The Engineering Industry," in *The Development of British Industry and Foreign Competition*, ed. Derek H. Aldcroft (London: George Allen & Unwin, 1968), 205. I do not know where these were. In addition, the *Stock Exchange Official Intelligence for 1914*, 713, indicates that a firm, Humphrey Pump Company, Ltd., registered on June

6, 1913, and formed to acquire Pump and Power Company, Ltd., held the patents for Humphrey's internal combustion pump and $172,600 in common stock (out of a total of $1 million) and $12,600 in preference stock of the Humphrey Gas Pump Company (Syracuse, New York). I know nothing of this minority stake.

85. The United States Rolling Stock Company appears to have been formed in 1871 by British investors to provide equipment for the Atlantic and Great Western Railroad. Bischoffsheim & Goldschmidt offered the rolling stock company's shares in London that year—a £100,000 issue. Its president in 1878 was General George B. McClellan. By 1893 the company was in financial difficulty, and in 1894 it reappeared as the United States Car Company. In 1897 it was once again in arrears, reemerging from this reorganization as the Illinois Car and Equipment Company. It had by this time three U.S. plants. The new company, however, under "the absentee management of its English owners continued to be unprofitable." By 1903 it was leasing its plants. See Swaine, *Cravath Firm* I, 315, 480–481, 645–646, and Dorothy Adler, *British Investment in American Railways* (Charlottesville: University Press of Virginia, 1970), 113, 205, 206. The Illinois Car and Equipment Company, with its headquarters in Chicago, had a London board of directors and a London "secretary" in 1914 (*Stock Exchange Official Intelligence for 1914*, 717). The company was incorporated in New Jersey. It owned all the stock of the Illinois Car Company.

86. *American Iron and Steel Association Bulletin*, 23 (Dec. 11, 1889): 341, and Clark, *History of Manufactures*, II, 341. See Chapter 7 on other large British investments in iron in Alabama.

87. *Stock Exchange Year Book, 1911.* and "History of Fraser & Chalmers," unsigned typescript, March 31, 1953, copy in Milwaukee County Historical Society Research Collection (MCHSRC).

88. "History of Fraser & Chalmers," and H. Schiffin "Brief Historical Sketch of the Origin and Growth of Gates Iron Works and Fraser & Chalmers," Oct. 1, 1942, copy in MCHSRC.

89. Perhaps they thought costs would be lower in Britain. Certainly shipping from the United Kingdom to South Africa was superior in terms of cost and regularity to that from the United States to South Africa. No imperial preference issue seems relevant for 1890. I find not entirely satisfactory the only explanation that I have seen—that is, that "as these mines were all being developed by British capital, this British capital demanded their machinery be manufactured in England" (Schifflin, "Brief Historical Sketch").

90. "History of Fraser & Chalmers."

91. Ibid.

92. Walter Peterson, *An Industrial Heritage* (Milwaukee: Milwaukee Historical Society, 1978), 107.

93. *Economist*, 57 (Dec. 15, 1900): 1782.

94. "History of Fraser & Chalmers."

95. *Statist*, 56 (Dec. 16, 1905): 1024. He added, "But even if we had a large control or even the sole control, I am afraid that we could not have changed the conditions which have arisen there."

96. Peterson, *An Industrial Heritage*, 137.

97. Ibid., 109, and *Commercial and Financial Chronicle*, 83 (July 14, 1906): 90.

98. Peterson, *An Industrial Heritage*, 141.

99. Ibid., 142.

100. *Statist*, 74 (Nov. 23, 1912): 584.

101. That is, when it accepted the merger. The quotation is from the *Stock Exchange Year Book, 1911.*

102. "History of Fraser & Chalmers."

103. See Lewis, *America's Stake*, 571, and *Stock Exchange Official Intelligence for 1914*, for industry identification.

104. For all the material on Swedish direct investment in the United States, I am deeply indebted to Ragnhild Lundström, "Early Swedish Multinationals," paper prepared for the European Science Foundation Conference on Multinationals, Sept. 1983, her sources therein, plus Lundström to Wilkins, Oct. 30, 1983. A revised version of this paper has been published in *Multinationals: Theory and History*, ed. Peter Hertner and Geoffrey Jones (Aldershot: Gower, 1986), 135–156. I have been able to verify that the Empire Cream Separator Company was incorporated in New Jersey, but the Department of State, Trenton, N.J., wrote me (May 18, 1984) that they do not know the date of the incorporation!

105. Lundström to Wilkins, Oct. 30, 1983; the subsidiary, American Lux Light Company, was incorporated in New York on June 8, 1906. Its principal location of business was in Chautauqua County, New York, in the far western portion of the state. Data from New York Department of State, Nov. 17, 1983.

106. Lundström to Wilkins, Oct. 30, 1983. McIntosh & Seymour Corporation was incorporated in New York on Nov. 24, 1913. Its principal location of business was in Cayuga County, in upstate New York (Cayuga County is north of Ithaca and west of Syracuse). McIntosh & Seymour Corporation was merged into American Locomotive Company on Aug. 31, 1936. Data from the New York Department of State, Nov. 17, 1983. Rudolf Diesel's approach to international business was to license German and foreign firms. On AB Diesels Motorer and its own innovations and on McIntosh & Seymour Corporation, see Nitske and Wilson, *Rudolf Diesel*, 168, 256. It became an important company.

107. Ibid., 126, 150, 178–179, 191, 201–202, 253–254. Apparently Rudolf Diesel received shares amounting to $150,000 in this company (ibid., 201–202, 205). This was a small minority interest (the firm's capital was $2.1 million). The best material on Rudolf Diesel's attempts to introduce his engine into America is in Richard H. Lytle, "The Introduction of Diesel Power in the United States, 1897–1912," *Business History Review*, 42 (Summer 1968): 115–148. Diesel on October 9, 1897, sold his American rights to the Diesel patents to Busch for $238,000 and a 6 percent royalty on all engines sold. See also Saul, "Engineering Industry," 218, for insights on Rudolf Diesel's "mis-sale" of his rights.

108. The Swedish-German connections were substantial. The German Norma Compagnie, GmbH, Cannstadt—owner of Norma Company of America and makers of ball bearings—was reported to be 50 percent owned by the Swedish SKF as of 1912. See Charles Higham, *Trading with the Enemy* (New York: Delacorte Press, 1983), 252. On the Norma Company's U.S. investments, see text above.

109. M.A.N. did, however, license the New London Ship and Engine Company (a supplier of Electric Boat Company) to produce marine diesel engines (Lytle, "The Introduction of Diesel Power," 135).

110. See Georg Siemens, *History of the House of Siemens*, 2 vols. (1957; rpt. New York: Arno Press, 1977), passim. On Rathenau, see Felix Pinner, *Emil Rathenau und das elektrische Zeitalter* (1918; rpt. New York: Arno Press, 1977). See also Wilkins, *The Emergence*, 154. At times the relationship between Siemens and A.E.G. would be uneasy and even fraught with conflict. See Hugh Neuburger, "The Industrial Policy of the Kreditbanken, 1880–1914," *Business History Review*, 51 (Summer 1977): 205.

111. Wilkins, *The Emergence*, 54.

112. Rathenau to Edison, Feb. 19, 1889, Edison Archives, West Orange, N.J.; Siemens, *House of Siemens*, I, 100; and Neuburger, "The Industrial Policy," 193–195.

113. Dietrich G. Buss, *Henry Villard* (New York: Arno Press, 1978), 188. Edison's biographer confirms that Villard was an enthusiastic supporter of Edison and an investor in Edison Electric Light early in 1880. See Matthew Josephson, *Edison* (New York: McGraw-Hill, 1959), 236.

114. Buss, *Henry Villard*, 196.

115. Ibid., 197, and Siemens, *House of Siemens*, I, 100. See Buss, *Henry Villard*, 157, for Villard's earlier associations with Georg von Siemens. Siemens had gone on the famous 1883 "celebration trip" for the Northern Pacific, which had been arranged by Villard (ibid., 140ff).

116. Siemens, *House of Siemens*, I, 100.

117. Buss, *Henry Villard*, 197.

118. Ibid., 198.

119. Ibid., 199.

120. Ibid., 200

121. Ibid.

122. Ibid., 200–201.

123. Plan for Edison General Electric Company, Edison Archives, n.d. [1888].

124. For these figures, Buss, *Henry Villard*, 208–209, cites "To the stockholders of the Edison Electric Light Co.," April 26, 1889, Henry Villard Papers, vol. 63, Harvard Business School. Buss, *Henry Villard*, 209, states that the total was $8.2 million, which I suspect is either an arithmetic mistake or a typographical one.

125. Buss, *Henry Villard*, 184.

126. See Wilkins, *The Emergence*, 52–58, on how Edison lost control over the foreign business. See Karl Helfferich, *Georg von Siemens*, 3 vols. (Berlin: Verlag von Julius Springer, 1923), II, 97, for more on the German role.

127. Buss, *Henry Villard*, 208, 214.

128. Ibid., 202.

129. Ibid. There may have been other reasons for the acquisition as well. On Sprague, see Melvin Kranzberg and Carroll W. Pursell, ed., *Technology and Western Civilization*, 2 vols. (New York: Oxford University Press, 1967), I, 572–574, which explained the acquisition as a consequence of "the strength of Sprague's position in the field" (p. 574). The author failed to realize the concerns of Siemens & Halske, although he noted that the first streetcar line had been built by the German firm in 1879 (p. 572). See also Harold C. Passer, *The Electrical Manufacturers, 1875–1900* (Cambridge, Mass.: Harvard University Press, 1953), 239–249, on Sprague, and his "Frank Julian Sprague, Father of Electric Traction, 1857–1934," in *Men in Business*, ed. William Miller (New York: Harper Torchbooks, 1962), 212–237. Passer (ibid., 229) wrote that Edison General Electric Company, by absorbing Sprague, "made certain that its largest customer would not take his business elsewhere. Over 65 per cent of the motors manufactured at the Schenectady plant [of Edison G.E.] were sold to Sprague in 1889." Passer says nothing about Siemens & Halske's role in the acquisition and apparently knew nothing about it.

130. Ibid., 228–229, and Josephson, *Edison*, 327–353.

131. Alfred D. Chandler, *The Visible Hand* (Cambridge, Mass.: Harvard University Press, 1977), 427.

132. Buss, *Henry Villard*, 212. Edison had inquired of Siemens Brothers in London on their prices in the fall of 1889 and decided that the cables could be made in the United States. See Edward Dean Adams, *Niagara Power* (Niagara Falls, N.Y.: Niagara Falls Power Co., 1927), I, 146.

133. Buss, *Henry Villard*, 211–212.

134. Ibid., 218–219. I have followed Buss on this, because he had access to the

records. Henry Villard, *Memoirs* (Boston: Houghton Mifflin, 1904), II, 325, suggests that Villard had opposed the merger.

135. Josephson, *Edison*, 365.

136. Ibid., 364. Josephson knew of the German involvement, but not the extent of it. Just how the withdrawal occurred (to whom the stock was sold) is not clear. In all probability Morgan acquired the German interest.

137. Siemens, *House of Siemens*, I, 128–129. This volume does not link the trip with the retreat from Edison G.E., but it seems almost obvious.

138. See memorandum, April 9, 1892, in Siemens Archives, Munich, SAA (Siemens Archiv-Akte) 68/L:262. I am indebted to Dr. Harm Schröter for photocopies of documents from the Siemens Archives.

139. Siemens, *House of Siemens*, I, 128–129, 306, 320–322.

140. Passer, *Electrical Manufacturers*, x. See John Winthrop Hammond, *Men and Volts: The Story of General Electric* (Philadelphia: J. B. Lippincott, 1941), 214, 218–219, on the importance of the Siemens & Halske Company of America. In May 1894 the sales manager of the eastern district for General Electric found that in dc generators, its principal competitor was Siemens & Halske. The latter's apparatus was 15 percent lower in price than General Electric's and "well-built, highly finished, and in every way satisfactory" (Passer, *Electrical Manufacturers*, 127).

141. Siemens, *House of Siemens*, I, 309. In August 1895 a G.E. sales manager reported that in his district G.E. got 60 percent of the lighting equipment business, Siemens & Halske got 15 percent, Westinghouse obtained 15 percent, with the rest to smaller companies (Passer, *Electrical Manufacturers*, 126). See ibid., 334, on Siemens & Halske's enlargement of facilities in Chicago in 1895.

142. Siemens, *House of Siemens*, I, 104. See also Passer, "Frank Julian Sprague," 231, on Siemens & Halske of America in 1897.

143. *Commercial and Financial Chronicle*, May 13, 1899, 927. The Electric Vehicle Company was founded by Isaac Rice. About this time it was being taken over by William C. Whitney. See Allan Nevins, *Ford* (New York: Charles Scribners' Sons, 1954), 618, 287–288.

144. John Moody, *Truth about Trusts* (New York: Moody, 1904), 249. Hammond, *Men and Volts*, 284, and Passer, *Electrical Manufacturers*, x, 334, confirm the G.E. acquisition in 1900.

145. Ibid., 334, notes the worsening competitive position after 1896. Passer did not realize that the parent company was letting its U.S. business slip from its control—or the move of the American company to other activities.

146. Testimony of "Mr. Walser" of Goss Printing Company, New York, U.S. Industrial Commission, *Report* (Washington, D.C., 1900), VIII, cxviii, 376. Passer, *Electrical Manufacturers*, 334, noted the prolonged strike.

147. Data uncovered by Dr. Schröter in the Siemens Archives seem to indicate that Georg von Siemens' rendition of this story in his history of the House of Siemens is not completely accurate. I have used the archival data for my presentation. See Wilhelm von Siemens, Paris, to Siemens & Halske, Secretariat, April 16, 1903, and Edward D. Adams (the Deutsche Bank representative in the United States) to Deutsche Bank, Secretariat, April 17, 1903, both in SAA 4/LK77 (Wilhelm von Siemens). Siemens & Halske, Berlin, sought help from Adams in voiding its contract with Siemens & Halske Electric Company of America and in eliminating its name from this American corporation. Adams explained that he was a good friend of Charles A. Coffin of General Electric, with whom he had discussed the matter. Coffin was off to Europe and, when visiting Berlin, would try to call on Arthur Gwinner (of the Deutsche Bank) to talk over the Siemens & Halske business. General Electric had paid a "large sum of money" for

Siemens & Halske of America and wanted to be sure Siemens & Halske, Berlin, would not give anyone else the right to use its name or its patents in America. On June 13, 1903, a draft agreement between General Electric and Siemens & Halske, Berlin, was prepared. See copy in SAA 4/LK77 (Wilhelm von Siemens). It apparently was *not* signed. The actual resolution is in Circular 174, Berlin, July 20, 1904, SAA 68/L:262. On April 13, 1908, the certificate of dissolution of Siemens & Halske Electric Company of America was filed in Springfield, Illinois (Edward D. Adams to Deutsche Bank, Secretariat, Berlin, Oct. 26, 1908, SAA 4/LK77 [Wilhelm von Siemens]). Passer, *Electrical Manufacturers*, 334, suggests that G.E. bought Siemens & Halske of America because G.E. was "weak in power patents."

148. Siemens, *House of Siemens*, I, 309–310. See also Georg Siemens, *Carl Friedrich von Siemens* (Freiburg: Verlag Karl Alber, 1960), 57, which notes General Electric's acquisition of Siemens & Halske Electric Company of America and the plans for the final liquidation of the latter.

149. See Wilkins, *Emergence*, 94–95, for details.

150. I have noted the timing on the formation of Siemens & Halske Electric Company of America. It started just as both Siemens and A.E.G. were getting out of Edison G.E. Although I have no evidence, I doubt it was accidental that in 1903, when Siemens & Halske wished to cancel its patent agreement with its ex-subsidiary in the United States, A.E.G. entered into the division-of-territory agreement with General Electric. On the formation of Telefunken, see Harm Schröter, "A Typical Factor of German International Market Strategy: Agreements between the U.S. and German Electrotechnical Industries up to 1939," in *Multinational Enterprise in Historical Perspective*, ed. Alice Teichova et al. (Cambridge: Cambridge University Press, 1986), 161.

151. *APC Report*, 104. In the *New York Times*, Dec. 15, 1940, is an obituary for Karl G. Frank, which indicates that he came to America in 1903 "as representative here of the Siemens Halske Siemens Schuckte-werke." In the *Jahrbuch der drahtlosen Telegraphie—1912–1913*, 202, was a statement that "Telefunken Wireless Telegraph Co. of the United States," New York, had its own factory. A subsequent listing of this company in the same yearbook, however, did not indicate any capital associated with the venture. On the *Jahrbuch* data I used a briefing paper in Box 71, Owen Young Papers, Van Hornesville Community Corporation, Van Hornesville, N.Y. The *APC Report* has nothing on a Telefunken factory.

152. Schröter, "A Typical Factor," 161. See ibid., 163, on a "secret understanding" between General Electric and Carl Friedrich von Siemens (of Siemens & Halske), made "shortly before the war," that would bring G.E. and Siemens into closer association. Carl Friedrich von Siemens (b. 1872) was Werner von Siemens' son by his second marriage—and very much younger than his stepbrothers, Arnold and Wilhelm. In the early twentieth century Carl Friedrich von Siemens was active in Siemens Brothers & Co., Ltd., in Britain, which had been founded by his uncle, Sir William Siemens. See J. D. Scott, *Siemens Brothers, 1858–1958* (London: Weidenfeld & Nicolson, 1958), 75, 22, 263. See also Siemens, *Carl Friedrich von Siemens*.

153. On Westinghouse's pre–World War I business abroad, see Wilkins, *Emergence*, 95–96. See also Swaine, *Cravath Firm*, II, 33ff, for Westinghouse's difficulties. Lord Rothschild to Paris cousins, Oct. 27, 1907, Rothschild Archives London XI/130A/1, wrote on "the difficult position in which the Société Générale [Paris] has been placed by (we trust) the temporary embarrassment of Westinghouse."

154. Theodor Heuss, *Robert Bosch: Leben und Leistung* (Stuttgart: Rainer Wunderlich Verlag, 1946), 121, passim.

155. Lawrence G. Franko, *European Multinationals* (Stamford, Conn.: Greylock, 1976), 164.

156. American Bosch Corporation Prospectus, Oct. 25, 1938, 3, Scudder Collection, Columbia University, and Heuss, *Robert Bosch*, 177.

157. Heuss, *Robert Bosch*, 213, 218–219, and American Bosch Corporation Prospectus, Oct. 25, 1938, 7.

158. *APC Report*, 108–111, 187.

159. Gleason L. Archer, *History of Radio to 1926* (New York: American Historical Society, 1938), 89, and U.S. Federal Trade Commission, *Report on the Radio Industry* (Washington, D.C., 1924), 11, 185.

160. See this chapter, note 151.

161. *APC Report*, 120.

162. Geoffrey Jones, "The International Expansion of the Gramophone Company: An Anglo-American Multinational, 1898–1931," *Business History Review*, 59 (Spring 1985): 81. I probably should not even call it an investment. It was essentially a payment for anticipated research results.

163. See *Moody's, 1920*, 836.

164. Wilkins, *Emergence*, 51, 200, 213.

165. Lundström, "Early Swedish Multinationals," sources therein, and Lundström to Wilkins, Oct. 30, 1983.

166. R. M. Morgan, *Callender's 1882–1945* (Prescott, Merseyside: BICC, 1982), 1, 5, 19, 20, 26, 28, 37, 167–170. When the American factory closed, production was concentrated at Erith, in Britain.

167. On June 24, 1890, the Okonite Company of New York was merged with Shaw & Connolly of Manchester, England, and both were taken over by the new International Okonite Company, Ltd. (*Stock Exchange Year Book, 1893*). On October 27, 1893, the International Okonite Company Ltd., was renamed Okonite Company, Ltd. See *Burdette Official Intelligence, 1895*, 1118–19. Until 1913 the Okonite Company was included in the *Stock Exchange Official Intelligence*, London. It was not included in the 1914 edition of this important securities manual. In 1924 this firm—now described as an American company—became the Okonite-Callender Company of New Jersey, associated with the British firm Callender's Cable and Construction Company (Morgan, *Callender's*, 78).

168. The telephone it produced had features different from the one made by Western Electric. Data from Ragnhild Lundström.

169. See Gerard Jacob-Wendler, *Deutsche Elektroindustrie in Lateinamerika: Siemens and AEG, 1890–1914* (Stuttgart: Klett-Cotta, 1982), on the role of German electrical industry giants in Latin America.

170. The specifics are included earlier in the chapter.

171. See Chapter 7 for details on the tubing investments.

172. J. D. Scott, *Vickers* (London: Weidenfeld & Nicolson, 1962), 43.

173. Clive Trebilcock, *The Vickers Brothers* (London: Europa Publications, 1977), 133.

174. Ibid., 137.

175. Ibid., 136. In 1886 a U.S. Navy Act had required shipbuilders to use only domestic material in warship construction. See John G. B. Hutchins, *The American Maritime Industries and Public Policy, 1789–1914* (Cambridge, Mass.: Harvard University Press, 1941), 458. Naval contracts had encouraged Bethlehem Iron Company to arrange for the Whitworth Company in England in 1886 to supply equipment, technicians, and information to remodel the Bethlehem steel works. Bethlehem had also obtained plans and equipment from Schneider-Creusot for steel armor plate. European armaments technology was clearly in advance of America's. See ibid., and Clark, *History of Manufactures*, II, 271, 313–316.

176. Trebilcock, *Vickers Brothers*, 137. In May 1899 Charles Harrah, president of

Midvale Steel, told Charles Schwab, then president of Carnegie Steel, that Vickers, Sons & Maxim was "about to buy Midvale." Two weeks later Schwab got a telegram from Vickers denying any intention of entering armor production in the United States. See Robert Hessen, *Steel Titan, The Life of Charles M. Schwab* (New York: Oxford University Press, 1975), 99, 320. Vickers' plans were more ambitious.

177. Trebilcock, *Vickers Brothers*, 138. See also Clark, *History of Manufactures*, III, 143, and *American Iron and Steel Association Bulletin*, 24 (Dec. 10, 1900): 205.

178. One suspects that the plans for this was what Harrah had been referring to. See note 176 above.

179. Trebilcock, *Vickers Brothers*, 138.

180. Ibid., 138–139.

181. In 1912, when Frederick Taylor was planning visits for Marcel Michelin to various works operated under the principles of scientific management, he noted that the Watertown arsenal could not be included, "as there is a law in our country preventing anyone who is not a citizen of the United States from visiting either the arsenals or the navy yards" (F. W. Taylor to Edouard Michelin, Aug. 29, 1912, Taylor Papers). No American shipyard was fully integrated; all depended on outside steel companies (Hutchins, *American Maritime Industries*, 465–466). No ship building—either for civilian or for military purposes—was done in the United States by foreign-owned companies, submarines excepted.

182. For data on Vickers and Electric Boat, see Scott, *Vickers*, 62–67, and Trebilcock, *Vickers Brothers*, 99–102, 155. For background on Isaac L. Rice, see *National Cyclopaedia of American Biography*, XI (1901), 447–448. On Siemens & Halske of America, see text above.

183. Trebilcock, *Vickers Brothers*, 100.

184. I have deciphered this complicated story, using data from Eberhard Faber, Inc., Crestwood, Pennsylvania, April 29, 1983; from Faber-Castell Corporation, Parsippany, New Jersey, Jan. 13, 1986; from A. W. Faber-Castell, Stein bei Nürnberg, Germany, Feb. 14, 1986 (via Oskar Schwarzer, Universität Erlangen-Nürenberg); from *von Faber et al. v. Faber*, 124 Fed. Rep. 603 (SDNY 1903); and from *von Faber-Castell v. Faber*, 139 Fed. Rep. 257 (CCA2 1905). See also *APC Report*, 556.

185. It distributed in the United States Bibles and secular books published by Oxford University Press in Britain. See *Oxford Publishing since 1478* (London: Oxford University Press, 1966), 9–10.

186. Charles Morgan, *The House of Macmillan* (London: Macmillan, 1944), 4, 82–83, 163–164.

187. Lewis, *America's Stake*, 571.

188. *Stock Exchange Official Intelligence for 1914*, 897, identifies Raphael Tuck & Sons, Ltd., as a book publisher.

189. My source on Nelson is W. Turrentine Jackson, *The Enterprising Scot* (Edinburgh: Edinburgh University Press, 1968), 14, who writes that Nelson visited the United States several times in connection with the New York branch. His source was *The Scotsman*, Oct. 21, 1892. No functions of the branch are indicated.

190. *APC Report*, 290, 152.

191. Ibid., 317, 185, 462–463.

192. Ibid., 186.

193. Haynes, *American Chemical Industry*, III, 361, and Ervin Hexner, *International Cartels* (Chapel Hill: University of North Carolina Press, 1945), 375.

194. Clark, *History of Manufactures*, III, 253–256, and U.S. Federal Trade Commission, *Report of Cooperation in American Export Trade*, 2 vols. (Washington, D.C., 1916), II, 44.

195. *APC Report*, 147, 290, 315, 566, 569. The German-American Portland Cement Company was later renamed the LaSalle Portland Cement Company.

196. *FTC Report on Cooperation*, II, 44.

197. Wallis Hunt, *Heirs of Great Adventure* (London: Balfour, Williamson, 1960), II, 78; Lewis, *America's Stake*, 101–102, 566; and *Stock Exchange Official Intelligence for 1914*, 807.

198. Virginia H. Taylor, *Franco-Texan Land Company* (Austin: University of Texas Press, 1969), 195–196, 199.

199. Jim Berry Pearson, *The Maxwell Land Grant* (Norman: University of Oklahoma Press, 1961), 168–171, 219–221.

200. Roger V. Clements, "British Controlled Enterprise in the West between 1870 and 1900," *Agricultural History*, 27 (Oct. 1953): 132–141.

201. *APC Report*, 293.

202. Haynes, *American Chemical Industry*, VI, 177–178. The American company was renamed General Ceramics during World War I. See also *APC Report*, 314.

203. *APC Report*, 145. See Cyril Ehrlich, *The Piano* (London: J. M. Dent, 1976), passim on the American piano industry, and p. 139, on Sterling.

204. See *APC Report*, 292, 293.

205. See Herbert Marshall, Frank A. Southard, Jr., and Kenneth W. Taylor, *Canadian-American Industry* (1936; rpt. New York: Russell & Russell, 1970), 178–180. S. J. Moore had in 1879 opened a small printing shop in Toronto and organized the Carter-Crume Company to produce and sell the books. In the 1880s he established a factory in Buffalo, and his American business came to exceed his Canadian operations. In 1893 he organized the Niagara Silver Spoon Company to manufacture and sell souvenir silver spoons. In 1901 Moore merged this firm with other silverware companies in Massachusetts and Connecticut and organized William A. Rogers, Ltd. Some time before 1909, through his Buffalo friends, Moore invested in the F. N. Burt Company, a maker of small paper boxes. In 1909 the F. N. Burt Company, Ltd., was formed to acquire F. N. Burt Company, Inc., along with three Canadian companies owned by Moore. In 1911 the largest of the Moore companies was formed, the American Sales Book Company, Ltd., incorporated in Ontario in 1911, to acquire and consolidate Moore properties in Niagara Falls, New York; Elmira, New York; and Long Island. On the American Sales Book Company, see *Moody's, 1928*, 2245. Moore's U.S. investments were substantial. Cleona Lewis, *America's Stake*, 566, indicates that the "capital stock" of the American Sales Book Company, Ltd., in 1914 was $3.94 million. See R. T. Naylor, *The History of Canadian Business, 1867–1914* (Toronto: James Lorimer, 1973), II, 247–248, for other far smaller miscellaneous Canadian investments in industrial properties in the United States.

206. Letter from Charles Jones to Mira Wilkins, June 24, 1987 (on Crittall & Co.) and Dunning data, University of Reading, Reading, England (on Morgan Crucible).

207. See Fred Carstensen, "International Harvester," 1985 Bellagio paper, forthcoming; London City and Midland Bank Balance Sheet, Dec. 1913, Midland Bank Group Archives (data from Edwin Green, archivist); and Paul Dickens, "The Transition Period in American International Financing, 1897 to 1914," Ph.D. diss., George Washington University, 1933, 261.

208. Minutes of Board of Directors meeting, Studebaker Brothers Manufacturing Company, Jan. 27, 1911. Data given me by Donald F. Davis, May 29, 1981.

209. See Dickens, "The Transition Period," 258. He estimated that $3 million of the $13.5 million preferred shares were acquired by foreign investors.

210. K. D. Bosch, *Nederlandse Beleggingen in de Verenigde Staten* (Amsterdam: Uitgeversmaatschappij Elsevier, 1948), 348, common and preferred shares.

211. Data from Donald F. Davis, May 29, 1981. As of Dec. 18, 1919, the Dutch

administrative trust held 7,700 common and 3,070 preferred shares of the 300,000 common and 150,000 preferred shares outstanding. These securities all appear to have been acquired before World War I.

212. Dickens, "The Transition Period," 263.

213. Ibid., 253.

214. Ibid., 264.

215. Carl W. Ackerman, *George Eastman* (Boston: Houghton Mifflin, 1930), 129ff, esp. 129, 132, 142–143, 173–175. Part of the rationale for an English "promotion" was to obtain publicity. Just as earlier promoters of breweries had tried to convince American brewers to have a London company for advertising purposes (see Chapter 9), this had been the plan for Eastman Kodak, Ltd. Sir James Pender (1841–1921) was the son of the famous cable "magnate" (see Chapter 14). Lord Kelvin had other American associations (see Chapter 8, note 23, for his involvements in the U.S. copper industry). At about the same time that Eastman Kodak changed from a British to a New Jersey incorporation, the Americans involved in Pillsbury and Borax Consolidated also desired to move the legal "headquarters" of their enterprises across the Atlantic. Neither did so. The suggestion in the Pillsbury case was that the parent company was superfluous; I did not find anything in Pillsbury documents to indicate that there was a tax issue involved. Francis Marion Smith, when he wanted to transfer the Borax Consolidated headquarters to New York (and dissolve the British registered company), suggested that the Borax company follow the Kodak lead (N. J. Travis and E. J. Cocks, *The Tincal Trail* [London: Harrap, 1984], 142). The *Stock Exchange Official Intelligence for 1914*, London, 654, lists Eastman Kodak Company as incorporated under the laws of New Jersey, Oct. 24, 1901. Its directors still included Sir James Pender.

216. See Chapter 8.

217. Thus, Siemens & Halske wanted Villard to buy Sprague to cut back competition in Europe—a good case of cross-investment—but Siemens & Halske's involvement in Edison General Electric lasted only a brief period.

218. However in 1889, associated with the general move of British promoters into the United States, there were British *attempts* both to bring harvester manufacturers into a "single trust" and to create a combination of American plowmakers. These plans for free-standing companies came to naught. Cyrus McCormick, Jr., for example, was not interested. Fred Carstensen found data on these British activities in the McCormick Collection at the State Historical Society of Wisconsin, Series W, Box 1, files: American Harvester Company, Correspondence, May-October 1889 and October–December 1889. See Carstensen to Wilkins, April 1, 1986. In 1889–90 three separate "promoters"— each backed by British capital—tried to create the combination of plow manufacturers. Wayne Broehl is splendid on their futile efforts in this respect. See his *John Deere's Company* (New York: Doubleday, 1984), 258–270.

219. This particularly struck Alfred Chandler as he read the first draft of this manuscript.

220. See Mira Wilkins, "The History of Multinational Enterprise: A New Look," *Journal of European Economic History*, 15 (Winter 1986): 483–510.

13. Banking Services

1. The listed English solicitors referred business to American law firms and thus served as "indirect" conduits of foreign investments. See Robert T. Swaine, *The Cravath Firm*, 2 vols. (New York: privately printed, 1946), I, 149, 367, 458; II, 110, 238. Freshfield's of London may have been directly involved in the Baltimore and Ohio reorga-

nization of 1878 (see ibid., I, 597), but this was exceptional. American lawyers such as Levy Mayer in Chicago, the predecessors of the Cravath firm and the Cravath firm, and Shearman & Sterling in New York, for example, were active facilitators of the entry of foreign investment. See Edgar Lee Masters, *Levy Mayer and the New Industrial Era* (New Haven: n.p., 1927), and Swaine, *Cravath Firm*, vols. 1 and 2. The lawyer John Sterling was U.S. trustee for Lord Strathcona (Alastair Sweeney to Mira Wilkins, May 17, 1983). See also John A. Garver, *John William Sterling* (New Haven: Yale University Press, 1929).

2. John Dos Passos was the great merger lawyer; J. P. Morgan, the private banker; Henry Villard and Arthur E. Stilwell, promoters; and James L. Lombard, the dean of mortgage company organizers.

3. Mira Wilkins, *The Maturing of Multinational Enterprise: American Business Abroad from 1914 to 1970* (Cambridge, Mass.: Harvard University Press, 1974), 19. This seems to have attracted more short-term than long-term foreign investment.

4. In banking terminology, the word *agency* often describes a direct investment rather than an independent firm. For most students of industrial multinational enterprise, the word *agent* usually means "independent" agent. In banking terminology an agent, as distinct from an agency, *could* also be independent.

5. At least none that I have traced. For a long time the first place in Table 13.1 of the Imperial Bank of Russia puzzled me. The Imperial Bank of Russia, or the Bank of Russia, or the "State Bank," as it was often called, kept the large Russian Treasury deposits. From 1895 through 1914, Russian Treasury deposits in this bank far exceeded private ones. See Manuel Larkin, "The Russian Imperial Bank," master of philosophy thesis, University of Chicago, 1910, 9, copy in New York Public Library, and Olga Crisp, "Russia, 1860–1914," in *Banking in the Early Stages of Industrialization*, ed. Rondo Cameron (New York: Oxford University Press, 1967), 200.

6. I will note the actual investments later in this chapter.

7. The Hongkong and Shanghai Banking Corporation, as I will show, had a license to carry on the business of banking in California—but its bank there was basically engaged in international, not domestic, business. Data of J. R. Jones, ca. 1964, in File J4, Archives, Hongkong and Shanghai Banking Corporation, Hong Kong.

8. Harold van B. Cleveland and Thomas F. Huertas, *Citibank, 1812–1970* (Cambridge, Mass.: Harvard University Press, 1985), 38–39.

9. See section 9 of the act, which is printed in full in Ross Robertson, *The Comptroller and Bank Supervision* (Washington, D.C., 1968), 195–212. Section 9 is on p. 197. This book is very useful on the evolution of America's dual banking system. See also Clyde William Phelps, *The Foreign Expansion of American Banks* (New York: Ronald Press, 1927), chap. 12.

10. I am not arguing that this curbed foreign "takeovers," but rather that it deterred foreign investors from founding new national banks, since such banks would be very constrained in operations. There was nothing in the law that said foreign investors could not found national banks.

11. Statistics for 1887–1897 on national bank ownership, provided by John A. James, *Money and Capital Markets* (Princeton, N.J.: Princeton University Press, 1978), 173, and divided between "country banks" and "reserve city banks," reveal that in no region of the United States were "national banks–country banks" more than 40 percent owned out-of-state. As for "national banks–reserve city banks," in no city were more than 44 percent of the shares in individual banks held out-of-state. James (p. 172) suggests that the out-of-state holdings were in "a large amount" owned by people living in nearby states and the rest by northern and eastern capital. He never even hints that any portion (much less a significant portion) was held out-of-country—that is, in

Europe or Canada. Some small portion of the out-of-state holdings in national banks was undoubtedly held out-of-country, but the amount was not important. Nathaniel T. Bacon, "American International Indebtedness," *Yale Review*, 9 (Nov. 1900): 266, called the amount, in 1899, "infinitesimal."

12. Robertson, *The Comptroller*, 64–67. For additional reasons for the rise of state banking, see James, *Money and Capital*, 36–38, 226. By 1892 the number of state-incorporated banks exceeded the number of national banks, and by 1914 the United States had 17,498 state banks and 7,518 national banks (Robertson, *The Comptroller*, 67).

13. Ibid., 61–71.

14. Letter in FO 5/2043, Public Record Office, London. It is not clear when the state of New York put the restrictions on the taking of deposits by foreign bank's agencies, or even whether there were actual statutory restrictions. There is no evidence, however, that the Bank of Montreal (which established its own agency in 1859) ever took deposits in New York, although it did in Chicago. This would lead one to believe the restrictions were long-standing, but an 1880 New York banking law has an explicit reference to foreign corporations that "receive deposits" through agencies in the state, or make loans, "or are in any manner engaged in business as bankers." See *Banker's Magazine*, New York, 25 (July 1880): 3, and 25 (Aug. 1880): 140. This notwithstanding, in December 1881 a French banker was complaining that Crédit Lyonnais' New York agency could not take deposits by virtue of New York state law. See Jean Bouvier, *Le Crédit Lyonnais de 1863 à 1882* (Paris: S.E.V.P.E.N., 1961), II, 569. I have gone through *Banker's Magazine* (New York) and the New York State Banking Department, *Annual Reports*, and cannot find any change in the years 1880–1886 that explicitly prohibited New York agencies of foreign banks from taking deposits. Nonetheless, as my text and the Crédit Lyonnais data make evident, this was the way the law was interpreted at least by the 1880s and probably earlier, given the behavior of the Bank of Montreal. Can it be that the phrases in the 1880 law were simply pro forma? As I trace banking history, I find that often what was not specifically authorized was forbidden. Could this have been the case in this instance?

15. In response to its inquiry, the Banking Department, Albany, New York, wrote the U.S. Bureau of Foreign and Domestic Commerce, June 10, 1919, on the 1914 legislation, which was still in force in 1919: "A foreign banking corporation . . . may be licensed by the Superintendent of Banks to maintain an agency in this state for the transaction of the following business only: The business of buying, selling, paying or collecting bills of exchange, or issuing letters of credit or of receiving money for transmission or transmitting the same by draft, check, cable, or otherwise, or of making sterling or other loans, or transacting any part of such business." See also Banking Department, Albany, New York, to A. S. Chadwick, Dec. 5, 1919. Both letters are in RG 151, 600 US 1919–1935, National Archives, Washington, D.C. *The Commercial and Financial Chronicle*, 97 (May 30, 1914): 1650, is useful on the 1914 legislation, and also A. S. J. Baster, *International Banks* (1935; rpt. New York: Arno Press, 1977), 31.

16. *Banker's Magazine*, New York, 88 (March 1914): 397, and *Bankers' Magazine*, London, 97 (March 1914): 475.

17. On London City and Midland, see Thomas Balogh, *Studies in Financial Organization* (Cambridge: Cambridge University Press, 1950), 1, 13, 16, 112–113.

18. London City and Midland's first correspondent relationship in the United States was with the Bank of British North America, which had a New York agency and a branch in California. This association lasted from 1893 to 1907. By June 1914 London City and Midland had as correspondents in *New York* (the date of establishing the relationship is in parentheses) New York Produce Exchange Bank (Dec. 1898), National City Bank (June 1904), Kountze Brothers (Dec. 1904), Corn Exchange Bank (Dec. 1908),

Hanover National Bank (Dec. 1908), Merchant's National Bank (Dec. 1908), National Park Bank (Dec. 1908), Bank of the Manhattan Company (June 1909), Bankers' Trust Company (June 1909), National Bank of Commerce (Dec. 1909), Mechanics' and Metals National Bank (Dec. 1910), Fourth National Bank (Dec. 1912), and the Citizens' Central National Bank (Dec. 1913)—thirteen New York banks in all. In addition, it had in June 1914 five correspondent banks in *Philadelphia*—Centennial National Bank (Dec. 1898), Tradesmen's National Bank (Dec. 1904), Fourth Street National Bank (Dec. 1909), Girard National Bank (Dec. 1909), and Philadelphia National Bank (Dec. 1910); two in *Chicago*—First National Bank of Chicago (Dec. 1898) and National Bank of the Republic (Dec. 1898); one in *Milwaukee*—First National Bank of Milwaukee (Dec. 1898); one in *Indianapolis*—Merchants' National Bank of Indianapolis (Dec. 1989); three in *New Orleans*—Whitney National Bank (June 1901), Canal-Lousiana Bank and Trust Company (Dec. 1905), and Hibernia Bank and Trust Company (Dec. 1908); three in *Boston*, People's National Bank of Roxbury (Dec. 1902), First National Bank (Dec. 1910), and National Shawmut Bank (Dec. 1912); one in *Hutchinson, Kansas*—First National Bank (June 1904); two in *St. Louis, Missouri*—Mercantile Trust Company (June 1904) and Third National Bank (Dec. 1905); one in *Pittsburgh*—Columbia National Bank of Commerce (Dec. 1905); one in *Oakland, California*—Oakland Bank of Savings (Dec. 1907); three in *San Francisco*—Anglo and London Paris National Bank (Dec. 1909), Crocker National Bank (Dec. 1910), and Bank of Italy (Dec. 1911); one in *Dallas*—City National Bank (Dec. 1909); two in *Minneapolis*—North Western National Bank (Dec. 1909) and Scandinavian National Bank (Dec. 1909); and one each in *Santa Barbara, California*—Santa Barbara National Bank (June 1910); *Manchester, New Hampshire*—Merchants National Bank (June 1910); *Kalamazoo, Michigan*—Kalamazoo City Savings Bank (Dec. 1910); and *Cincinnati*—German National Bank (Dec. 1912). In addition, other correspondent banks were appointed, but the relationships did not survive to 1914. Data from annual reports of London and Midland Bank, Ltd., 1893–1897, and London City and Midland Bank, 1898–1914, sent to me by the Midland Bank archivist, Edwin Green (letter of April 15, 1985).

19. Sir Edward H. Holden took his first trip to the United States in 1904 and was convinced that Midland should play a more active international role (Edwin Green, "Sir Edward Hopkinson Holden [1848–1919]," *Dictionary of Business Biography*, III, 294). Edgar Jones, *Accountancy and the British Economy* (London: B. T. Batsford, 1981), 106, notes London City and Midland's 1912 plans to extend its operations in the United States. M. Georges Aubert, *La finance américaine* (Paris: Ernest Flammarion, 1910), 165, wrote that Sir Edward Holden, of London City and Midland Bank, and Felix Schuster, of the Union Bank of London and Smiths, were both making trips to the United States with the goal, which they did not hide from their colleagues or stockholders, of embarking on new business of interest to their banks. Edwin Green writes me that the reference in Edgar Jones's book is to the extension of correspondent links rather than branch banks or representative offices (Green to Wilkins, April 15, 1985). Nonetheless, Sir Edward's complaints in early 1914 suggest that he was thinking in broader terms, and Green, in the *Dictionary of Business Biography*, 294, notes that Sir Edward dropped the idea of a New York branch because of the restrictive legislation.

20. *Commercial and Financial Chronicle*, 97 (May 30, 1914): 1640.

21. F. Cyril James, *The Growth of Chicago Banks*, 2 vols. (New York: Harper & Bros., 1938), I, 495. See also State of Illinois, Banking Department, to U.S. Bureau of Foreign and Domestic Commerce, June 9, 1919, RG 151, 600 US 1919–1935, National Archives.

22. James, *Growth of Chicago Banks*, I, 495–496; II, 1191, 1172, 1318.

23. Ibid., I, 496–497.

24. Ibid., I, 521; II, 1191, 1172, 1318.

25. Ibid., II, 1362.

26. D. L. C. Galles, "Bank of Nova Scotia," *Minnesota History*, 42 (Fall 1971): 273. The Bank of Nova Scotia had opened a "branch" in Minneapolis in 1885 to make loans, buy and sell exchange, and make collections in all parts of Canada. Its Minneapolis branch did not take deposits. The bank decided in 1892 to close its Minneapolis business rather than have the unnecessary expense of operating in both Chicago and Minneapolis (ibid., 268–276). It opened in Chicago in 1892. See James, *Growth of Chicago Banks*, I, 590, on the new foreign bank branches.

27. Ibid., II, 1218, 1211.

28. Ibid., 826, 824. It is curious, however, that when the Pujo Committee in 1913 investigated the concentration of control over credit and looked at the five "largest banks" in Chicago—its references were solely to domestic ones: the Continental and Commercial Bank, the First National Bank, the Corn Exchange Bank, the Merchant's Loan and Trust Company, and the Illinois Trust and Savings Bank. See U.S. House, Subcommittee of the Committee on Banking and Currency, *Money Trust Investigation* (Washington, D.C., 1913), pt. 23, 1640–41.

29. The only way I can explain the Pujo Committee's exclusion of it is the committee counsel's general lack of interest in international institutions, which is manifest throughout his questioning. My source on the size and role of the Canadian banks is the excellent historian of Chicago banking F. Cyril James; Vincent P. Carosso, "The Wall Street Money Trust from Pujo through Medina," *Business History Review*, 47 (Winter 1973): 425–428, shows the "political" focus of the Pujo Committee inquiry.

30. James, *Growth of Chicago Banks*, II, 912. Merrill Denison, *Canada's First Bank: A History of the Bank of Montreal*, 2 vols. (New York: Dodd, Mead, 1967), II, 180, 197. Regrettably, Denison says little about the Chicago branch, 1875–1914. He does note (II, 260) that in Chicago during the Panic of 1893, as currency became scarce, "in some cases Canadian currency was actually resorted to for the purposes of commerce and the payment of wages." Likewise, in 1907 the Chicago branch of the Bank of Montreal came to the aid of midwestern banks, bringing in currency from Canada (ibid., 295).

31. Charles P. Kindleberger, *The Formation of Financial Centers* (Princeton University, International Finance Section, Department of Economics, 1974), 8, makes the point that "the geographical pattern of banking was linked to commerce." Green, "Sir Edward Hopkinson Holden," 294, suggests that Holden considered a Chicago branch for London City and Midland in 1904. Nothing came of it. It was not illegal, just illogical. The bank maintained correspondents in Chicago.

32. Stephen A. Caldwell, *A Banking History of Louisiana* (Baton Rouge: Louisiana State University Press, 1935), 109.

33. In 1885 H. D. Forsyth, New Orleans, was writing to S. G. Ward, Baring's representative, Oct. 3, 1885, Baring Archives, London (BAL), HC 5.2.30, pt. 54, on the reorganization plan for the Citizens' Bank. Forsyth indicated that a "Mr. B. Neugass [sic] of London" and his associates were expected to buy the greater portion of the new stock. Forsyth wondered if Baring Brothers might become subscribers. Forsyth doubted it, "although it would be much appreciated here." There is no indication of Baring's response, or if the purchase was made. See this chapter, note 189, on Newgass and his American interests. Newgass—in his Liverpool days—had been associated with Lehman Brothers at a time when the latter was heavily involved in the cotton trade and had an office in New Orleans. Data from Stanley Chapman. Caldwell, *Banking History*, has nothing on Newgass.

34. Victor Ross, *The History of the Canadian Bank of Commerce* (Toronto: Oxford University Press, 1922), II, 296.

35. Ibid., 297. Probably a "correspondent" arrangement.

36. D. E. Kaufmann, *La banque en France* (Paris: M. Giard & E. Briére, 1914), 249–250.

37. Caldwell, *Banking History*, 110.

38. Chamber of Commerce of the United States, Finance Department, *Laws and Practices Affecting the Establishment of Foreign Branches of Banks* (Washington, D.C.: Chamber of Commerce of the U.S., 1923), 15. The law was amended in 1906, but no changes were made in these provisions.

39. Ibid., 15.

40. Phelps, *Foreign Expansion*, 18.

41. On the San Francisco Clearing House, see Ira B. Cross, *Financing an Empire*, 4 vols. (Chicago, S. J. Clarke, 1927), II, 884. The Anglo-Californian Bank, Ltd., was the Seligman bank, and while chartered in London, it also involved significant U.S. interests. According to Linton Wells, "House of Seligman," 1931, microfilm of typescript, New York State Historical Society Library, p. 195, in 1888 the Seligmans relinquished control and sold practically all their shares to Lazard Frères. On the Anglo-Californian Bank, Ltd., see ibid., 178ff.

42. Davidson & Co. closed its doors in 1878, and its business was taken over by "A. Gansel & J. Cullen" until 1880, when it apparently shut for good. "Albert Gansel" had come from the Rothschild agency in Naples. See Cross, *Financing an Empire*, I. 51. (Rothschild records spell the name "Gansl" and give the firm name as Gansl & Cullen.) In September 1880 the Bank of California agreed to act as correspondent for N. M. Rothschild & Sons, London (Bank of California to N. M. Rothschild & Sons, Sept. 7, 1880, Rothschild Archives London [RAL] II/50/0).

43. Lazard Frères was founded in 1847 in New Orleans by three brothers from Lorraine, France. It was involved in the cotton trade. See J. S. G. Wilson, *French Banking Structure and Credit Policy* (Cambridge, Mass.: Harvard University Press, 1957), 147. In 1849 the brothers moved to San Francisco, where the firm was reestablished; soon it was dealing in gold and silver and the related exchange business (Cary Reich, *Financier* [New York: William Morrow, 1983], 27). It opened an office in New York, and "several members of the firm" returned to Europe, where a Paris house was started (in 1849 according to Phelps; in 1852, to Wilson; by 1852, to Reich; in 1856, to Truptil). In 1876 its offices in New York, San Francisco, and Paris became private banking houses. Meanwhile, in 1870, according to Truptil, a branch was opened in London as Lazard Brothers & Co., and in 1877 Lazard Brothers & Co., Ltd., was formed in London and was involved in general banking business.

The controlling interest in Lazard Frères in New York was American. This seems to be the case with the San Francisco house. The family group acted in concert. See C. W. Phelps, *Foreign Expansion of American Banks* (1927; rpt. New York: Arno Press, 1976), 8, 10, and R. J. Truptil, *British Banks and the London Money Market* (London: Jonathan Cape, 1936), 142. Cross, *Financing an Empire*, I, 425–426, reported that in September 1876 the San Francisco newspapers announced that the "old importing house," Lazard Frères, would in the future devote itself to the banking business. The firm was described as having excellent French connections and as having represented the French government on the Pacific Coast. Lazard Frères in San Francisco became a leader in foreign exchange transactions (ibid., III, 64).

In 1884 Lazard Frères in California became the London, Paris and American Bank, Ltd., with a British charter and a capital stock of £400,000. In 1891 the latter was advertising in the London *Times* as having its head office in London and the "branch" in San Francisco; Lazard Frères was listed as its New York "agents," while Lazard Frères et Cie. was its Paris "agents." (See London *Times*, March, 9, 1891, 14.) In 1908 a California group headed by Herbert Fleischhacker assumed control and reorganized that bank as the London, Paris National Bank (capital, $2 million); Fleischhacker, an

American citizen (born in San Francisco), was the son-in-law of Sigmund Greenebaum, president of the London, Paris and American Bank, Ltd. At this point, according to Wilson, *French Banking Structure*, 146, Lazard Frères sold out. (Truptil, *British Banks*, 142, writes that the Lazard Frères group sold in 1884.) In 1908 or 1909 the London, Paris National Bank was merged into the Anglo and London Paris National Bank (capital, $26 million), a merger that joined it with the bank that the Seligmans had founded, the Anglo-Californian Bank, Ltd. As noted earlier (in note 41), according to Linton Wells, in 1888 the Seligmans had relinquished their control of the Anglo-Californian Bank and sold practically all their shares to Lazard Frères. On the merger, see Cross, *Financing an Empire*, I, 268, 426; III, 69. The 1908 date is given in ibid., II, 716; in other places Cross gives the 1909 date.

44. Cross, *Financing an Empire*, II, 884.

45. There were nine, if we include the seven in Table 13.2, plus Davidson & Co. and Belloc Frères, but the "foreign" designation of Lazard Frères is, as noted in Table 13.2, very doubtful, so eight might be a more accurate number.

46. Cross, *Financing an Empire*, III, 145. Cross says the Hongkong Bank always "confined" itself to the foreign exchange business and the purchase-of-silver-bullion business. Data in the Kidder, Peabody & Co. Papers indicate other functions. In 1892 Kidder, Peabody gave instructions that monies from the sale of San Francisco real estate be deposited to the firm's credit in the Hongkong and Shanghai Bank in San Francisco. See Kidder, Peabody, Boston, to Lloyd & Wood, San Francisco, May 11, 1892, Kidder, Peabody Confidential Letters, Kidder, Peabody Collection, vol. 5, Harvard Business School Library. The Hongkong Bank historian, Frank H. H. King, has looked at the balance sheets of the California branch and writes me that it was not a deposit-taking institution (King, Hong Kong, to Mira Wilkins, June 24, 1984). J. R. Jones, "History of the Bank in California," ca. 1964, File J4, Archives, Hongkong and Shanghai Banking Corporation, notes that when the "office" opened in 1875, it was to supervise "the purchase and export of Mexican dollars and bar silver to China and [the] selling [of] Hong Kong exchange to the thousands of Chinese who had settled in the Western States of America." In 1912 the bank obtained a license to carry on the business of banking in California, under its own name. "To comply with the law," its balance sheet showed a capital of $50,000 (ibid.; quotation from King in King to Wilkins, June 24, 1984). The Bancroft Library, University of California, contains a signature book of the Hongkong and Shanghai Banking Corporation, San Francisco, recording amounts of deposit in the period 1906–1936. This volume appears to have represented sums collected from local Chinese for remittance home. The sums were sizable.

47. See Cross, *Financing an Empire*, I, 257, and Ross, *Canadian Bank of Commerce*, I, 300–346, for the Bank of British Columbia's history in California. Ross writes that the Bank of California and, after 1875, the Nevada Bank were the only institutions in California to outdistance the Bank of British Columbia. See ibid., 322.

48. Cross, *Financing an Empire*, I, 258.

49. Ross, *History*, II, 558 (on branches of Canadian Bank of Commerce). Nonetheless, A. C. Kains, the first San Francisco manager of the Canadian Bank of Commerce, became in 1914 the first governor of the Federal Reserve Bank of San Francisco (Cross, *Financing an Empire*, II, 645).

50. Cross, *Financing an Empire*, I, 258. For the founders of the bank see Chapter 4, note 290. In 1875 the London and San Francisco Bank, Ltd., had its London office at 22 Broad St. Its directors included Henry L. Bischoffsheim, J. F. Flemmich, E. H. Green, Junius S. Morgan, J. May, J. Parrott, Frederick Rodewald, Robert Ryrie, Baron Herman Stern, and Rudolph Sulzbach (*Stock Exchange Year Book, 1875*). In 1880 the London and

San Francisco Bank, Ltd., was reorganized. It moved its London office to 73 Lombard St. In the early 1890s its directors included George W. Campbell (of Finlay, Campbell & Co., East India merchants), Henry Goschen (of Frühling & Goschen, merchants and foreign bankers), Charles Hemery (of George Hemery & Sons, merchants), William Neubold (who was involved in Latin American railroads), Robert Davie Peebles (managing director), Robert Ryrie (East India merchant), and Norman Dunning Rideout (from California). See *Stock Exchange Year Book, 1890,* and *Directory of Directors, 1892* (advertisement for bank and director identification). Drexel, Morgan & Co. was the agent for the bank in New York.

51. Cross, *Financing an Empire,* I, 258. The Bank of California was in 1905 a state bank. It later became a national bank and, because of this history, was in 1927 the only national bank in the entire United States with branches outside the state in which its home office was located (ibid., II, 905).

52. Ibid., II, 641. Actually as early as 1880 (the year the bank was founded), the Japanese Finance Ministry had given it permission to start a branch, agency, or representative office in San Francisco. See Shinji Arai, *History of the Yokohama Specie Bank* (Tokyo, 1981), II, 38 (in Japanese). In 1886 it set up a representative office or agency in San Francisco (Yokohama Specie Bank, *History of the Yokohama Specie Bank* [Tokyo 1920]; in Japanese). I am indebted to Professor Hiroaki Yamazaki for this information. The San Francisco office became a "branch bank" in 1899 (Arai, *History,* II, 91).

53. Cross, *Financing an Empire,* II, 641.

54. Phelps, *Foreign Expansion,* 202, and data obtained in Japan from Yokohama Specie Bank balance sheets.

55. Cross, *Financing an Empire,* III, 517.

56. On the seven, see ibid., II, 655, 665, 683, 689, 693, 696. Some were private. Some were state chartered.

57. Frank Freidel, *America in the Twentieth Century* (New York: Alfred A. Knopf, 1960), 47.

58. Cross, *Financing an Empire,* II, 727–728. Of the seven banks formed in 1903–1907, five were shut by California authorities and two had by 1909 already gone into voluntary liquidation!

59. A. S. J. Baster, *International Banks* (1935; rpt. New York: Arno Press, 1977), 159, and Cross, *Financing an Empire,* III, 50. The 1913 branch of the Yokohama Specie Bank in Los Angeles was a branch of the San Francisco unit, not of a foreign bank.

60. Cross, *Financing an Empire,* II, 696.

61. In 1924 the assets of the Nippon Bank were sold to the Sumitomo Bank of California, Sacramento (ibid., 699). I did not include the Nippon Bank in Table 13.2 because of my uncertainty as to whether it was owned by nonresident foreign investors.

62. See this chapter, note 46. Its 1912 legal change was either a response to the 1909 law or in anticipation of the 1913 one, or both.

63. California's 1913 law is detailed in Chamber of Commerce of the United States, *Laws and Practices,* 15–16.

64. U.S. Senate, National Monetary Commission, *Digest of State Bank Statutes,* 61st Cong., 2nd sess., 1910, S. Doc. 353, 693.

65. Phelps, *Foreign Expansion,* 202.

66. Clifford H. Ince, *The Royal Bank of Canada: A Chronology, 1864–1969* (n.p., n.d.), 13, 15, 16, 112.

67. Denison, *Canada's First Bank,* II, 276, 353, gives few details about the Spokane branch.

68. The only other branch of a foreign commercial bank in the United States in this

period not mentioned in the text that I know about was that of the Bank of Nova Scotia in Boston.

69. As noted, while the Hongkong Bank had a license to carry on the business of banking in California, it was basically involved in international transactions.

70. Richard E. Sylla, *The American Capital Market, 1846–1914* (1968 diss.; New York: Arno Press, 1975), 26.

71. According to Clyde William Phelps, by the Federal Reserve Act of 1913, national banks were "for the first time in our history allowed to accept drafts drawn upon them" (*Foreign Expansion*, 109). Likewise, as noted, until 1914 (when the Federal Reserve System was established), America's national banks could not branch abroad (ibid., 92). Thus the country's largest banks—its national banks—were fettered.

72. Ellis T. Powell, *The Evolution of the Money Market (1385–1915)* (London: Financial News, 1915), 375–376, wrote that "the unique solidity and responsibility of the great English accepting firms and banks" were key to making London the great financial center of the world. He continued, "There is no reason, on the face of things, why American private financial firms should not do a large acceptance business. (The American national banks are forbidden by law to give acceptances.) But the fact is that they do not attempt it because the endeavor would bring their credit, excellent as it is, into disadvantageous contrast with that of the London houses." The International Banking Corporation had begun playing a role in financing American trade. See Mira Wilkins, *The Emergence of Multinational Enterprise* (Cambridge, Mass.: Harvard University Press, 1970), 107. On Brown Brothers and Brown, Shipley & Co.'s role in financing U.S. trade, see Henry Clay, *Lord Norman* (London: Macmillan, 1957), 9–10, 16, 53–54, 57. It was not until the passage of the April 1914 legislation that banks incorporated in the state of New York were permitted—by statute—to accept drafts and bills of exchange drawn against shipments of goods to and from foreign countries (W. P. G. Harding, "The Results of the European War on America's Financial Position," *Annals of the American Academy of Political and Social Science*, 60 [July 1915]: 113). See Cleveland and Huertas, *Citibank*, 42–44, for National City Bank's rising interest in this business.

73. U.S. Federal Trade Commission, *Report on Cooperation in American Export Trade* (Washington, D.C., 1916), I, 22, 40, 63–64. In 1901–1903 America was the world's greatest exporting nation, with average annual exports of $1.41 billion, compared with $1.38 billion for England and $1.12 billion for Germany. In 1911–1913 the United States ranked after England, with average annual exports for England of $2.38 billion; for the United States, $2.29 billion; and for Germany, $2.16 billion (ibid., I, 17).

74. Actually, twenty-one "foreign" banks were licensed; one was from Connecticut, the International Banking Corporation. I exclude it because it was not an "out-of-country" bank.

75. The word *agency* in this context was an owned establishment of the foreign bank, a foreign direct investment. It was not independent. The word *branch* was not used, because a branch would have had greater privileges than an agency. As noted earlier, foreign bank branches were forbidden under New York state law.

76. On British banks involved with Latin American business, David Joslin, *A Century of Banking in Latin America* (London: Oxford University Press, 1963), is invaluable.

77. J. R. Jones, "New York," ca. 1964, in File J4, Archives, Hongkong and Shanghai Banking Corporation, Hong Kong, has substantial data on the history of the bank in New York.

78. Banco Nacional de Cuba (the National Bank of Cuba) was that nation's largest. It was founded in 1901, with a capital of one million dollars and took over the earlier Cuban business of the North American Trust Company. At origin it was the fiscal agent for the occupation government (as its predecessor had been), and then it served the

same purpose for the Cuban government. It probably had representation in New York from its origin, that is, from 1901 onward. By 1914 it had a capital and surplus of 6.9 million pesos, deposits of 23.7 million, and "total resources" of 32.7 million (the peso in 1914 was on par with the dollar). As far as I know, the North American Trust Company was U.S. owned; in 1914 it seems likely that this was still the case with the National Bank of Cuba, although Vincent Carosso found that in the early twentieth century (ca. 1905–1910), about one-fifth of the National Bank of Cuba's capital (10,000 shares) was held by Morgan, Harjes, Morgan's Paris house. Its president was an American, and its internal correspondence was in English. (By 1928, however, 25,001 out of 50,000 shares had passed into the hands of José Lopez-Rodriguez, a resident of Cuba of Spanish nationality. Lopez-Rodriguez appears to have gained this control in 1919–20.) See Henry C. Wallich, *Monetary Problems of an Export Economy: The Cuban Experience, 1914–1947* (Cambridge, Mass.: Harvard University Press, 1950), 51–53, 56, and Vincent Carosso, *The Morgans* (Cambridge, Mass.: Harvard University Press, 1987), 851 n.163.

79. On the Yokohama Specie Bank, see Mira Wilkins, "American-Japanese Direct Foreign Investment Relationships, 1930–1952," *Business History Review*, 56 (Winter 1982): 507. There are several histories in Japanese of the Yokohama Specie Bank (see this chapter, note 52). As indicated in that note, a representative office existed in San Francisco in 1886. Another one opened in Hawaii in 1892 (before annexation); both the San Francisco and the Honolulu offices became "branches" in 1899 (Yokohama Specie Bank, *The History*, and Arai, *History*, II, 91). In 1914 the New York agency of the Yokohama Specie Bank ranked fifth after the home office and the London, Bombay, and Shanghai branches in its transactions (Japan, Ministry of Finance, *Business Report of Banking and Trust Business* [Tokyo, 1916], 69—in Japanese). I am indebted to Professor Hiroaki Yamazaki for translations.

80. Silk Association of America, Annual Reports, for example, *Annual Report, 1910*, 81.

81. Japan, Ministry of Finance, *Business Report*, 75, and Arai, *History*, II, 100–101.

82. New York Superintendent of Banking, *Annual Report for 1911*, 14.

83. See this chapter, note 18.

84. Lloyds Bank, *Annual Report, 1914*.

85. The best histories of the Bank of England are J. H. Clapham, *Bank of England*, 2 vols. (Cambridge: Cambridge University Press, 1966), and R. S. Sayers, *The Bank of England, 1891–1944*, 3 vols. (Cambridge: Cambridge University Press, 1976).

86. Swaine, *Cravath Firm*, I, 14, 149, 367. Swaine says that R. M. Blatchford held the position for more than forty years after 1826, but in 1884 Blatchford's grandson wrote of the Cravath firm's English clients as an outgrowth of the connections established by Blatchford with the Bank of England, The suggestion was that the Bank of England still used the law firm.

87. John Saunders Gilliat, William Lidderdale, the first and second Lord Revelstoke, Alfred Charles Rothschild, Everard Hambro, and Edward Charles Grenfell are examples of Bank of England directors with interests in America. Mark Wilks Collet (governor, 1885–1887) had been involved in Anglo-American commercial relations from 1832 and in 1851 had joined Brown, Shipley & Co. in Liverpool. On Collet, see Aytoun Ellis, *Heir of Adventure: The Story of Brown, Shipley & Co.* (London: Brown, Shipley, 1960), 56–58, 93, 100, and Clay, *Lord Norman*, 7–11. Collet's grandson, Montagu Collet Norman (1871–1934), spent several years in the United States; he was first elected a Bank of England director in 1907 (ibid., 18–29, 55). For a highly colored view of the Bank of England's American involvements, see *Investors' Review*, London, 3 (March 1894): 131–134, which discusses the relations of the Merchants' Trust, the Bank,

and American business. The *Investors' Review* had a vendetta with the Bank of England, which it labeled a "paralytic bank" (see 3 [Jan. 1894]: 1–17). The journal was not always accurate; one can take major exception to its conclusions; yet it provides some otherwise not available data of interest on the Bank of England's role in connection with American securities. See ibid., 2 (Nov. 1893): 644, and the comments on the "Maple Leaf"—the Chicago, St. Paul and Kansas City Railroad Company: "It is saddening to find the Bank of England mixed up to any extent with business of this kind, and the directors who permitted, or ordered, it to become the tout-in-ordinary for this waif American railroad of foreign origin [earlier, p. 637, the *Review* had pointed out that "foreign gentlemen" had planned the road] ought never to have done anything of the sort." The bank's directors could be involved, said the *Review*, but "they ought to keep the Bank rigorously free from participation" (ibid., 645). According to ibid., 3 (Jan. 1894): 13, more than a half-dozen "members of the Bank [of England] board or of their relations and firms" were involved in the Frank Jones Brewing Company—an American investment. An 1894 extract from Edwin Waterhouse, "His Story," typescript in Price Waterhouse Archives, London, p. 94, discussed the London Finance Committee of the Chicago Great Western Railroad. Waterhouse was a member, and the committee involved "our friend Mr. Lidderdale," who was chairman; A. F. Wallis (one of his colleagues at the Bank of England); and Howard Gilliat. The committee acted to reorganize the railroad's finances. The Chicago Great Western was the successor to the Chicago, St. Paul and Kansas City Railroad. As I went through stockholder lists of British-registered companies that did business in America, names associated with the Bank of England were present. Indeed, the more one looks, the more surprising are the places where bank directors are mentioned. Thus, not long after the gold strike at Cripple Creek, Colorado, who should appear as a visitor there but William Lidderdale (his visit seems to have been in 1892). See Marshall Sprague, *Money Mountain : The Story of Cripple Creek Gold* (Boston: Little, Brown, 1953), 99.

88. I have no doubt about this generalization.

89. During the Boer War, when the British briefly turned to the United States for financing, J. P. Morgan & Co. in 1900 acted "as agent of the Bank of England" and took subscriptions in the United States for the British National War Loan. See Vincent Carosso, *Investment Banking in America* (Cambridge, Mass.: Harvard University Press, 1970), 80. Subsequently the Bank of England authorized Morgan; Kidder, Peabody; and Baring, Magoun to accept subscriptions in the United States for a British loan (ibid.).

90. In fact, it was these very "bankers," who kept the Bank of England informed. I discuss them in detail later in this chapter.

91. None appeared on the 1912–1914 lists.

92. The Bank of British North America, headquartered in England, had its principal operations in Canada and was often called a Canadian bank.

93. *Banker's Magazine*, New York, 34 (June 1880): 918. The Bank of Nova Scotia is not on this list. I suspect that years earlier it had closed its 1832 New York agency and had not yet reopened it. Galles, "Bank of Nova Scotia," dealing with that bank in the 1880s, says nothing about a New York agency and (using a 1900 history of the bank as a source) says that the Minneapolis branch (1885–1892) was the bank's "first venture outside maritime Canada" (p. 268). It was a later (1932) bank history that identified the 1832 agency!

According to Bouvier, *Le Crédit Lyonnais*, II, 569–572, Crédit Lyonnais had a New York agency in the years 1879–1882. On the Netherland Trading Society, see R. S. Sayers, ed., *Banking in Western Europe* (Oxford: Oxford University Press, 1962), 199. The Netherland Trading Society started its New York agency in late 1878 or early 1879. Oliver S. Carter, Stanton Blake, and Henry Hawley were appointed to manage it.

Banker's Magazine, New York, 33 (Feb. 1879): 648, reported, "Their business will include the purchase and sale of bonds, stocks, and other securities, the buying and selling of exchange, and other transactions of a mercantile nature." Carter and Hawley were New York merchants, while Blake was with the banking house Blake Brothers & Co. of New York and Boston. I do not know when the Netherland Trading Society closed its New York agency, but Blake Brothers retained long-standing and important Dutch connections. See the advertisement for Nederlandsche Handel-Maatschappij (the Netherland Trading Society)—office: 142 Pearl St.—in *Commercial and Financial Chronicle,* 32 (Jan. 1, 1881): 24. On the same page are advertisements for Nederlandsche Indische Handelsbank, Amsterdam, and Adolph Boissevain & Co., Amsterdam; the former listed Blake Brothers & Co., New York, as agent, and the latter listed the same firm as its New York correspondent.

94. August Belmont to N. M. Rothschild & Sons, April 30, 1880, RAL T59/34. See also Denison, *Canada's First Bank,* II, 196–197. Charles Smithers, the bank's general manager, told Canadians at the Bank of Montreal annual meeting in 1880 that in response to the legislation he had "called in about four and a half million dollars in the course of a few days."

95. *Banker's Magazine,* New York, 34 (June 1880): 920; 35 (July 1880): 3; and 35 (Aug. 1880): 141–142.

96. Bouvier, *Crédit Lyonnais,* II, 572.

97. I can trace the BBNA's presence back to the mid-1850s (the Bank of Montreal and the Bank of Nova Scotia had earlier New York "agents," but the continuity was interrupted). Data from Annual Reports of London City and Midland Bank and Lloyds Bank sent me by Edwin Green (April 15, 1985) and J. M. L. Booker (June 3, 1985) show the BBNA acting for those banks.

98. See Chapter 6. Compare Denison, *Canada's First Bank,* II, 419–420, and Albro Martin, *James J. Hill and the Opening of the Northwest* (New York: Oxford University Press, 1976), passim.

99. Denison, *Canada's First Bank,* II, 183, 186–187 (a $3 million issue). Denison is wrong in calling it the first. Dabney, Morgan & Co., New York, "some years" before 1871 negotiated a 7 percent Peruvian loan of $2 million, albeit this loan was originated by J. S. Morgan & Co., London. As of July 1, 1871, the *New York Times,* April 9, 1871, p. 6, announced that loan would be reduced by bonds drawn for redemption to the amount of $531,500. The remainder of the loan outstanding was $1,594,500. (Vincent Carosso is my source for the origination of the loan.)

100. Denison, *Canada's First Bank,* II, 194, 196.

101. Ibid., 196.

102. R. T. Naylor, *History of Business in Canada,* 2 vols. (Toronto: James Lorimer, 1975), II, 240. This includes, of course, short-term and call loans; these figures are probably not exactly comparable to the ones in Table 13.4.

103. Denison, *Canada's First Bank,* II, 205.

104. Ibid., 251.

105. "Trust companies" engaged in banking and were virtually unregulated. The date of establishment of the Transatlantic Trust Company was obtained from Elizabeth Jaggers, Banking Department, State of New York, to Mira Wilkins, Aug. 19, 1985. Details on its ownership and functions are in Alien Property Custodian, *Report, 1918–1919,* 134–137. In New York, as indicated, the agencies of the Banco di Napoli and the Bohemia Joint Stock Bank seem to have helped immigrants with remittances, as did the Yokohama Specie Bank and the Hongkong Bank in California. See chapter 14, note 30, on American trust companies that served as intermediaries to bring foreign monies into the United States.

106. It is very difficult to portray the truly international character of finance in the years 1875–1914. Most authors tend to be national in focus. The popular Paul H. Emden, *Money Powers of Europe* (London: Sampson Low, Marston, 1937) is exceptional in capturing the complex international interrelationships of the major financial institutions.

107. The literature has tended to emphasize the roles of these two houses before 1875 and not in the great era of international lending, 1875–1914. This is an error—based, I would argue, on the paucity of research on the activities of these merchant bankers in the four decades before World War I. "Merchant banks" in Britain were in a very special position. In 1871 F. A. Hamilton of Brown, Shipley & Co. (an American house in London and Liverpool) wrote Lord Salisbury on the occasion of a "Bank Holiday" bill that "there are many Houses, such as Messrs. Rothschild, Baring Brothers & Co. and my own firm Brown, Shipley & Co., who are not legally bankers, but merchants, tho' their transactions in Bills of Exchange, Home and Foreign Monetary operations are on a much larger scale than many Bankers." (The bill was modified to include them.) See Ellis, *Heir of Adventure*, 102–104. The best work on British merchant banks is Stanley Chapman, *The Rise of Merchant Banking* (London: Allen & Unwin, 1984).

108. On the basis of existing records, it seems impossible to determine what percentage of all American securities transactions went through the Morgan London house. Many other firms participated. On the role of the Morgans, I am deeply indebted to the excellent study of Carosso, *The Morgans*, which provides numerous details unavailable elsewhere. It is the authoritative work on the Morgans. The Morgan house in Paris was Morgan, Harjes & Co. It was far less important than the London and New York firms, but it did offer American securities in France—the same ones handled by the London and New York houses. My material on the Morgan houses in this chapter is less detailed than that on the Barings and the Rothschilds despite the Morgans' importance, because after 1890 the headquarters of this house became American—and this chapter deals with "foreign" banks and banking houses.

109. See Chapter 5.

110. Until the end of 1885, the Barings were represented in New York by the firm S. G. & G. C. Ward. Samuel Gray Ward and George Cabot Ward were sons of Thomas Wren Ward (1786–1858) of Boston, who had become Baring's U.S. representative in 1829. See House Correspondence—North American, New York, BAL, HC 5.2.30 (1872–1886), and Ralph Hidy, *House of Baring* (Cambridge, Mass.: Harvard University Press, 1949), 98. In 1878 Kidder, Peabody became Baring's "correspondents" in both New York and Boston (BAL, HC 5.1.27). See also Vincent Carosso, *More Than a Century of Investment Banking: The Kidder, Peabody & Co. Story* (New York: McGraw-Hill, 1979), and Arthur M. Johnson and Barry E. Supple, *Boston Capitalists and Western Railroads* (Cambridge, Mass.: Harvard University Press, 1967), 319. The Baring Archives in London contain extensive correspondence to Baring Brothers from S. G. & G. C. Ward (1872–1886); correspondence with Kidder, Peabody; other correspondence with Baring, Magoun & Co.; and the Gaspard Farrer Letterbooks. All attest to Baring's continuing interest in U.S. business.

111. This marked the end of Baring's long association with the Ward family.

112. Carosso, *More Than a Century*, 17, 33, and Johnson and Supple, *Boston Capitalists*, 319. Between 1873 and 1882 the senior partner in Baring Brothers, London, was the Bostonian Russell Sturgis (1805–1887). His main interests were in the Far East. When he retired in 1882, the leadership role passed to Edward Charles Baring (1828–1897), as of 1885 the first Lord Revelstoke, who had as a young man traveled extensively in America and had an abiding interest in the country (Hidy, *House of Baring*, 395, 44).

Thomas Baring (1839–1923), who became the Kidder, Peabody partner in 1886, was Lord Revelstoke's brother (*Burke's Peerage; Bankers' Magazine*, London, 116 [July 1923]; 28). From the mid-1880s, a new generation of Barings took interest in American business, including John Baring (1863–1929), son of Edward C. and the second Lord Revelstoke (as of 1897), and his brothers Cecil Baring (1864–1934) and Hugo Baring (1876–1949). John Baring became a full partner in Baring's in 1890, and when shortly thereafter his father retired, the London business was led by him and his cousin Francis Henry Baring (1850–1915), son of Baron Northbrook. When Francis Baring retired in 1902, Gaspard Farrer—who had major interests in American finance—became a partner (*Bankers' Magazine*, London, 127 [June 1929]; 877–880). George C. Magoun (1841–1893) had opened the Kidder, Peabody New York office in 1862; he became a partner in Kidder, Peabody in 1872 (Carosso, *More Than a Century*, 33).

113. On these, see data in BAL, HC 5.2.30. See specifically S. G. Ward to Baring Brothers, Feb. 19, 1891, BAL, HC 5.2.30, pt. 59, for a summary of what the American agent saw as his accomplishments. On the Atchison, Topeka, see Chapter 6. Baring's interests in the Eastern Railway stemmed back to 1852. See Ralph W. Hidy and Muriel E. Hidy, "Anglo-American Merchant Bankers and Railroads of the Old Northwest, 1848–1860," *Business History Review*, 34 (Summer 1960): 154.

114. See Prospectus and discussion in BAL, HC 5.1.27, pt 2.

115. Keith Bryant, *History of the Atchison, Topeka and Santa Fe Railroad* (New York: MacMillan, 1974), 151.

116. See Chapter 8.

117. Martin, *James J. Hill*, 385. This was for the Great Northern Railroad. Compare its size with issues (1865–1880) listed in Dorothy Adler, *British Investment in American Railways, 1834–1898* (Charlottesville: University Press of Virginia, 1970), appendix 1. Regrettably, Adler's list stops in 1880.

118. U.S. Federal Trade Commission, *Report on the Copper Industry* (Washington, D.C., 1947), 184, suggests this, as did *Banker's Magazine*, New York, 45 (Dec. 1890): 406. In June 1890 Baring Brothers gave N. M. Rothschild & Sons a check for £20,000, "being the approximate amount overpaid by you against our delivery of warrants representing about Tons 833 of Anaconda Matte. We are [the June 17 letter continued] writing today to the Bank of France to ask them to furnish us with the balance of about 270 Tons Matte, which we have still to deliver on their behalf to fulfill the contract made with the Exploration Company for 8600 Tons" (Baring Brothers to N. M. Rothschild & Sons, June 17, 1890, RAL XI/4/54). The letter indicates the scale of Baring Brothers' involvements. Every study of British banking and British finance deals with the 1890 Baring Crisis and associates it with Baring's Argentine commitments. One of the best treatments of the Baring Crisis is in Clapham, *Bank of England*, II, 326–339. The copper involvements were not crucial; they only made Baring's more vulnerable.

119. Balogh, *Studies in Financial Organization*, 1, makes the point that while the *Economist* (in the spring of 1914) classified Baring Brothers & Co. as a "joint-stock bank" and while this classification might be "juridically correct," it was not accurate "from a functionally analytical point of view."

120. J. C. Gilbert, *A History of Investment Trusts in Dundee, 1873–1938* (London: P. S. King, 1939), 29. As late as 1894, however, Thomas Baring remained on the board of the Atchison, Topeka and Santa Fe. See Bryant, *Atchison, Topeka*, 165. Baring apparently sold its U.S. securities because they were negotiable and were a way to raise money in time of need.

121. See Chapter 6; Adler, *British Investment*, 160–161; and E. G. Campbell, *Reorganization of the American Railroad System* (New York: Columbia University Press, 1938),

13, 43–44. On the impact on U.S. money markets, see, for example, Alexander Dana Noyes, *Thirty Years of American Finance, 1865–1897* (1900; rpt. New York: Greenwood Press, 1969), 158. In the United States there was a double wallop: In July 1890 Congress had passed the Sherman Silver Purchase Bill, which upset the international financial community. Then came the Baring Crisis. See Matthew Simon, *Cyclical Fluctuations and the International Capital Movements of the United States, 1865–1897* (1955 diss.; New York: Arno Press, 1978), 466–475. The British retreat from American securities began before "the City" knew of Baring's problems.

122. See Carosso, *More Than a Century,* 33–34, 188, and Heather Gilbert, *End of the Road* (Aberdeen: Aberdeen University Press, 1977), II, 256n. When Baring, Magoun & Co. was formed, Thomas Baring withdrew as a partner of Kidder, Peabody, joining instead the new Baring partnership in New York.

123. Campbell, *Reorganization,* 211.

124. Martin, *James J. Hill,* 502, and Gilbert, *End of the Road,* 196ff. See also Chapter 6.

125. Farrer to Bacon, Oct. 11, 1901, Farrer Letterbook, BAL. This may have been Farrer's *own* activity rather than Baring Brothers business. It is included as indicative of the kinds of business bankers engaged in. One wonders why Farrer did not assume that J. S. Morgan & Co. would take care of this.

126. As Heather Gilbert has shown, Farrer was most intimate with Lord Mount Stephen.

127. Garver, *John William Sterling,* 87. For years Farrer crossed the ocean every June to visit with Sterling and to go with him "to the well furnished fishing lodge at Grand Metis, in Canada, which Lord Mount Stephen insisted that Mr. Sterling should occupy every year for a month during the salmon season, with any friends whom he chose to invite."

128. Ibid., 86. Data also from Alastair Sweeny, biographer of Lord Strathcona, on the latter's connection with Sterling.

129. Garver, *John William Sterling,* 87–88, 90.

130. This cannot be overemphasized. The world of international finance, 1875–1914, was one where friendship counted, where the knowledge and information from such friendship networks were crucial.

131. Gilbert, *End of the Road,* 198.

132. For the Barings' and Farrer's role in relation to the formation of Northern Securities, see ibid., 198–209.

133. Ibid., 287, and Cyrus Adler, *Jacob H. Schiff* (Garden City, N.Y.: Doubleday, 1928), I, 116 (on the 1908 Union Pacific bond issue).

134. Carosso, *More Than a Century,* 31; Adler, *Jacob H. Schiff,* I, 172; and Swaine, *Cravath Firm,* I, 734–735.

135. Swaine, *Cravath Firm,* I, 734–735.

136. John A. Garver, in his biography of John W. Sterling, makes the error of describing Farrer as "the head" of Baring Brothers (*John William Sterling,* 87). The error gives a hint of Farrer's importance. Likewise, *Banker's Magazine,* London, 127 (June 1929): 879, in its obituary article on John Baring (Lord Revelstoke) noted that the latter was "brilliant" and was assisted by the "sound and far-reaching judgment" of his partner, Gaspard Farrer.

137. U.S. Treasury, *Specie Resumption and Refunding of National Debt,* 46th Cong., 2nd sess., 1880, H. Exec. Doc. 9.

138. Ibid., 61.

139. So I was told by Richard Davis, historian of the English Rothschilds. I have not seen the Rothschild profit and loss accounts.

140. *Commercial and Financial Chronicle,* 32 (Feb. 1881): xii.

141. Richard Davis, *The English Rothschilds* (Chapel Hill: University of North Carolina, 1983), passim, calls him Nathan, as does *Burke's Peerage*. However, data in the
Rothschild Archives refer to him as Nathaniel. Apparently his mother called him
Nathaniel, since her father-in-law was Nathan (Davis, *The English Rothschilds,* 63, and
information from the archivist, Rothschild Archives London). August Belmont, Sr.,
also called him Nathaniel. See note 146 below. August Belmont, Jr., addressed him as
Lord Rothschild (see, for example, Belmont to Lord Rothschild, May 22, 1909, RAL
II/96/1). Lord Rothschild himself seems to have used "Nathaniel" in his own corre-
spondence for a number of years.

142. Bo Bramsen and Kathleen Wain, *The Hambros* (London: Michael Joseph, 1979),
298–299. Lord Rothschild became an intimate friend of the Prince of Wales (King
Edward VII). See Christopher Hibbert, *Edward VII* (London: Allen Lane, 1976), 173.

143. Jean Bouvier, *Les Rothschild* (Paris: Fayard, 1967), 296.

144. Shepard B. Clough and Charles W. Cole, *Economic History of Europe* (Boston:
D. C. Heath, 1941), 637.

145. See correspondence in RAL XI/101, for example.

146. Adler, *British Investment,* 91n and appendix 1. Perhaps William Moorhead's
letter of October 1869 to Jay Cooke, cited in Henrietta Larson, *Jay Cooke* (Cambridge,
Mass.: Harvard University Press, 1936), 266, still represented the Rothschild viewpoint. They had refused to invest in or market the Northern Pacific bonds because they
thought those involved both risk and trouble in management; the amount Cooke
wanted them to take was too large; and most important, no road had yet been built nor
any considerable amount of cash capital paid in. In short, the Rothschilds were careful
investors. On May 9, 1879, less than a month before Baron Lionel's death, August
Belmont wrote his own son, Perry Belmont, "When Nathaniel tells you that he wishes
me to send orders for bonds and railroad shares to them which they will execute at a
low commission for my account and risk . . . he puts the cart before the horse. It is for
the wealthy House of Rothschild with all their power and influence to give us orders
for their account." August Belmont concluded his letter, complaining of "the utter
want of appreciation of the importance of American business on the part of the
Rothschilds, and a disregard of the changes produced by cables and by the great
competition of Bankers, Banks, and syndicates." (August Belmont to Perry Belmont,
May 9, 1879, in Perry Belmont, *An American Democrat* [1941; rpt. New York: AMS
Press, 1967], 207). N. M. Rothschild & Sons' "American Railway Dividend Account
Book" starts in 1876, but not until the 1880s was the full involvement in evidence (RAL
II/16/0).

147. RAL II/16/3. See also Belmont letters, RAL II/51/0B. When the London house
desired August Belmont to buy for its account 1,000 shares of the Chicago, Rock Island
and Pacific Railroad, the New York firm bought gradually so as "to avoid advancing the
market" (August Belmont & Co. to N. M. Rothschild & Sons, Sept. 23, 1881, RAL
II/51/0B).

148. David Black, *The King of Fifth Avenue: The Fortunes of August Belmont* (New York:
Dial Press, 1981), 658.

149. See Chapter 6.

150. See Chapter 8.

151. See Chapter 12.

152. Edward D. Adams, *Niagara Power, History of the Niagara Falls Power Company,
1886–1918* (Niagara Falls, N.Y.: Niagara Falls Power Co., 1927), I, 295. See also Chapter
15.

153. American Account Book, 1895, RAL II/3/27.

154. Fritz Redlich, *The Molding of American Banking* (New York: Johnson Reprint

Corp., 1968), pt. 2, 370. Both the French and the British Rothschilds were involved (RAL T16/91–92). See also Chapter 5.

155. The London Rothschilds also participated. On Nov. 6, 1901, Lee, Higginson & Co., Boston, wrote Lord Rothschild, "Much interest [in the United States] centers in the copper situation. Undoubtedly you, with your large interests in copper, are much better informed in regard to this than we can be" (RAL II/53/0B).

156. See Chapters 7 and 8; George H. Nash, *The Life of Herbert Hoover* (New York: W. W. Norton, 1983), 604 n.89, 47, 55; and Clark C. Spence, *Mining Engineers and the American West* (New Haven: Yale University Press, 1970), 137–138, 265, 272, who describes the Exploration Company, Ltd., as active in the Alaska Treadwell mines and the Tomboy Gold Mines Company, Ltd., as well as in Anaconda. The Exploration Company was also said to control the Steeple Rock Development Company, which operated the Carlisle (gold) mine in New Mexico (1896–97). In addition, it was apparently involved in other promotions in Idaho, Montana, and Colorado. All its mining engineers, including Thomas Mein, appear to have been Americans (at least according to Spence). When in 1890 Fraser & Chalmers, Ltd., had been registered in London, the Exploration Company, Ltd., acted as the "promoters and trustees for the debenture holders." Edmund G. DeCrano, a managing director of the Exploration Company, Ltd., was a director of Fraser & Chalmers, Ltd. ("The History of Fraser & Chalmers," unpublished typescript, March 31, 1953, pp. 2–3, Milwaukee County Historical Society, Milwaukee, Wisconsin). The best work on the Exploration Company is Rob Turrell and Jean-Jacques van Helten, "The Rothschilds, the Exploration Company and Mining Finance," *Business History*, 28 (April 1986), 181–205. Ibid., 188–189, notes that in 1895 the Exploration Company promoted a Parisian firm, Compagnie Français des Mines d'Or et d'Exploration, whose major shareholders included Rothschild Frères, Baron James de Hirsch, and the Société Générale (Paris). I found the Compagnie to be a major participant (in 1899) in the promotion of the Tomboy Gold Mines Company, Ltd. (Western Range Cattle Industry Study [WRCIS], Manuscript Room, Library of Congress, Acc. 11,092, reel 72.)

157. For details see Chapter 7, note 70. In its initial 1897 memorandum on this matter, the British Rothschilds wrote "of the importance of this arrangement." See memorandum in RAL VII/36/0.

158. See Chapter 8.

159. See Chapter 15.

160. Black, *August Belmont*, 591, 639, 640, 658, 704, writes of the uneasy relations between August Belmont & Co. and both the London and the Paris houses in the years 1881–1887. Correspondence in the RAL confirms this. (See, for example, August Belmont & Co. to N. M. Rothschild & Sons, March 1, 1881, RAL II/51/0A.) Nonetheless, the stresses in the association should not be exaggerated. The Rothschilds were dependent on August Belmont & Co.; but they made their own decisions in a context far broader than the United States. In the 1880s in London, Paris, and New York, there emerged a new leadership generation of both Rothschilds and Belmonts. It is very important that August Belmont & Co. was never the Rothschilds' sole source of American information. The international banking community had many informal relationships, especially in transatlantic business. Thus, for example, Edward D. Adams, when he was a partner in Winslow, Lanier & Co. in the 1880s, always visited with Lord Rothschild when he was in London. See Adams, *Niagara Power*, I, 297.

161. Black, *August Belmont*, 723–724, 658. Accordingly, all references to August Belmont after 1890 are to the son. Early in 1891 August Belmont became chairman of the board of the Louisville and Nashville Railroad. See Maury Klein, *History of the Louisville and Nashville Railroad* (New York: Macmillan, 1972), 252.

162. See text and this chapter, note 42.

163. Adler, *Jacob H. Schiff*, I, 194.

164. Lee, Higginson & Co., Boston, to Lord Rothschild, Nov. 6, 1901, RAL II/53/0B.

165. Lee, Higginson & Co., Boston to N. S. [*sic*] Rothschild & Sons, Nov. 13, 1901, RAL II/53/0B.

166. See correspondence, RAL II/53/0B.

167. See 1913 American Accounts, RAL II/3/27. I have cited only the securities' account with Lee, Higginson. This by no means is indicative of the Rothschilds' total American interests. On United States Smelting, Refining and Mining Company, see Chapter 8.

168. All these January 1907 letters are from Lord Rothschild, London, to his cousins in Paris. They are in RAL XI/130A/1. On Harriman and the Union Pacific at this time, see James Blaine Walker, *The Epic of American Industry* (New York: Harper & Bros., 1949), 284.

169. 1907 letters from Lord Rothschild, London, to cousins, Paris, RAL XI/130A/1.

170. Ibid.

171. By 1910–1914 August Belmont & Co. was probably not in the pivotal position of prior years. Thus, when the Pujo Committee looked into the concentration of U.S. credit (1912–13), there was no mention of August Belmont & Co. in the hearings. See U.S. House of Representatives, Subcommittee of the Committee on Banking and Currency, *Money Trust Investigation* (Washington, D.C., 1912–13). Carosso, *Investment Banking in America*, 44, writes that by 1900 the two principal firms selling industrials in New York were Baring, Magoun and August Belmont. His last mention of August Belmont & Co. was for 1900. See ibid., 91. It seems that after his difficulties with the Interborough Rapid Transit Company in 1907, August Belmont adopted a much lower profile. Nonetheless, when in November 1909 the Wright Company was incorporated with a paid-in capital of $200,000 to acquire the Wright Brothers airplane patents, August Belmont numbered among the original stockholders. See Walker, *The Epic of American Industry*, 364. I have not found evidence of Rothschild involvement.

172. S. D. Chapman, "The Evolution of Merchant Banking in Britain in the Nineteenth Century," in *Transformation of Bank Structures in the Industrial Period*, ed. V. I. Bovykin (Budapest: Adadémiai Kiado, 1982), 26–27.

173. Sir Ernest Cassel had started his banking career as a clerk in Bischoffsheim & Goldschmidt, a firm he left in 1884, although he continued to have an office at their Throgmorton St. address. In 1910 he became a partner in S. Japhet & Co. In between, he acted independently or in association with various financial houses on numerous international projects—both American and non-American. See Patricia Thane, "Sir Ernest Joseph Cassel (1852–1921)," *Dictionary of Business Biography*. See also Chapter 6.

174. This is not strange, considering the long-term attraction of America to British investors. See Chapman, *The Rise of Merchant Banking*, passim. On pp. 202–204 Chapman gives a list of merchant bankers and their geographical spheres of influence.

175. A member of the family, H. A. Schroeder, lived in Alabama, and the London firm had handled Alabama's state debts. The Alabama Schroeder was president of the Southern Bank of Alabama in Mobile until his retirement in 1875. The London Schroeder house continued to be associated with Alabama business, including railroad business. See Adler, *British Investment*, 126, and Leland Jenks, *Migration of British Capital* (New York: Harper & Row, 1973), 421.

176. See Chapter 8.

177. *Stock Exchange Official Intelligence for 1914*, 306.

178. Bramsen and Wain, *The Hambros, 1779–1979*, 301. The same was true of the next generation of Hambros and Morgans. See ibid., 328–329. Of the £1 million that C. J.

Hambro & Son had invested in securities in 1898, 30 percent of the total was in American railroads (ibid., 330).

179. Adler, *British Investment*, 150. It issued, for example, Marietta and North Georgia Railroad bonds. See *Investors' Review*, London, 3 (March 1894): 132, and Bramsen and Wain, *The Hambros*, 309; 306–307 (for the importance of its American investments). Everard Hambro (1842–1925) knew everybody of significance in the London banking world. He also took part in the Exploration Company, Ltd. (see Turrell and van Helten, "The Rothschilds," 185), and was directly involved in American mining ventures; he acquired 5,000 shares of Stratton's Independence, Ltd., in 1899, for example (WRCIS, reel 65).

180. Its main involvement had been in the early 1870s (see Chapter 4), but it took years to unscramble the problems (Adler, *British Investment*, 113–115, and Emden, *Money Powers*, 330, 332).

181. From the 1850s until 1882; see Chapter 6. After 1885 the Morgans became involved with this railroad.

182. According to Adler, *British Investment*, 147.

183. See Dietrich G. Buss, *Henry Villard* (New York: Arno Press, 1978), 183–185.

184. When Jay Cooke was marketing the U.S. refunding loan in 1871, his European bankers' list was headed by "R. Raphael and Sons (including $1,000,000 joint account with Von Hoffman . . .)." See Chapter 4, note 152, and Wells, "House of Seligman," 148. August Belmont wrote to N. M. Rothschild & Sons, London, Feb. 19, 1880, RAL T59/33, noting the "intimate relations and immense transactions" in U.S. government bonds between the First National Bank, New York, and "the Raphaels in London and their agents v. Hoffman here [in New York]." I wrote to R. Raphael & Sons, London, asking whether their records indicated the period that Louis von Hoffman acted as their agent. M. H. Tollemache of Raphael, Zorn replied (Feb. 20, 1985) that since most of their records were destroyed during the war, it was impossible to establish the exact period; however, von Hoffman was in that role at least as late as 1890. Tollemache added, "It has always been my understanding that we had a joint account with von Hoffman & Co. for the purpose of American arbitrage."

Louis von Hoffman was active in railroad finance. See Dolores Greenberg, *Financiers and Railroads, 1869–1889, A Study of Morton, Bliss & Co.* (Newark: University of Delaware Press, 1980), 13. In the late 1860s the firm became involved with the London shareholders of the Erie (Adler, *British Investment*, 97n). At the start of 1870 L. von Hoffman & Co. was the depository for the London committee, and shares had been sent to New York for registration "in the name of Heath and Raphael" (ibid., 100). Edward Harold Mott, *Between the Ocean and the Lakes: The Story of Erie* (New York: John S. Collins, 1901), 178, suggests that this may be a reference to Robert A. Heath and Henry A. Raphael. In 1873 the Raphael firm and the Union Bank of London had floated in London a large issue of the New York Central (Adler, *British Investment*, 207). Louis von Hoffman (1815–1909) had founded the firm of Louis von Hoffman & Co. with his father (*New York Times*, Feb. 5, 1909). Von Hoffman's daughter married a French nobleman, the Marquis de Morès, who made major investments in cattle and sheep and meat packing in the Dakotas in the 1880s, using von Hoffman's monies. See Lewis Atherton, *Cattle Kings* (Bloomington: Indiana University Press, 1961), 37, 59, 136. It is not clear how much (if any) "foreign" money went into de Morès' ventures.

185. On Robert Fleming & Co., see Chapter 14.

186. Robert Benson & Co., which had been a representative of the Illinois Central from the mid-1850s, failed in 1875, after the death of the senior partner. A few months later, Robert Benson's son (also Robert) resolved to continue his father's business in American securities. Another son, Constantine W. Benson, became a partner (1880–

1884) of the Close brothers, who were developing land in Iowa; Robert Benson became a publicist for such land. C. W. Benson in 1884 took over the management of the Iowa Land Company, Ltd. In the mid-1880s the London firm resumed the name of Robert Benson & Co. Robert Benson & Co. was the issuing house in London for Chicago, St. Paul and Kansas City first-mortgage bonds and for Minnesota and North-Western Railway bonds. These companies were the predecessors of the Chicago Great Western. In 1892, when the Chicago Great Western was formed, Robert Benson arranged the financing. See H. Roger Grant, *The Corn Belt: A History of the Chicago Great Western Railroad Company* (DeKalb: Northern Illinois University Press, 1984), 32–33; Adler, *British Investment*, 147, 149, 192n; and Jacob Van der Zee, *The British in Iowa* (Iowa City: Iowa State Historical Society, 1922), 102–103, 114, 170, 277n. The firm was very much involved in the Merchants' Trust (*Investors' Review*, London, 3 [March 1894]: 131–135). In 1914 it was the London agent for the Long Island Railroad (*Stock Exchange Official Intelligence for 1914*, 294). Robert Benson & Co.'s American business was formidable. For general data on Robert Benson and the firm, see Chapman, *The Rise of Merchant Banking*, 129.

187. Among its U.S. involvements, Kleinwort, Sons & Co. served as London agents for American Smelting and Refining. See *Stock Exchange Official Intelligence for 1914*, 538. See Chapter 12 for its relationship to Studebaker Corporation. Kleinwort, Sons & Co., at the initiative of Goldman, Sachs, had developed a connection with that firm. See Stephen Birmingham, *Our Crowd* (New York: Dell, 1967), 163–164; Hermann Wallich and Paul Wallich, *Zwei Generationen im deutschen Bankwesen, 1833–1914* (Frankfurt: Fritz Knapp Verlag, 1978), 278, 284; and Walter E. Sachs Reminiscences, Oral History Collection, Columbia University, New York, 2 pts., 1956, 1964, pt. 1, 21, pt. 2, 220, for Kleinworts' association with Goldman, Sachs.

188. See Chapter 6 on Erlanger's railroad involvements.

189. Benjamin Newgass (whose name was often misspelled in contemporary references) began his career as a commission merchant in Liverpool. Chapman, *The Rise of Merchant Banking*, 77, writes that he was in partnership with Lehman Brothers (New York) in 1873. The Newgass firm was in 1873 the largest importer of cotton in Liverpool (data from Baring Brothers Mss., provided me by Stanley Chapman). The partnership with Lehman Brothers ended in 1875 (Brandt Circulars, 1875, 180–181, Nottingham University Library—information from Chapman). Newgass invested in American land. See U.S. House of Representatives, 48th Cong., 2nd sess., 1885, Exec. Doc. 247, 46, and Table 6.8 in this book. He moved to London (exact date unknown); in 1885 he was planning to invest in the Citizens' Bank in New Orleans (see this chapter, note 33). He acquired and traded U.S. railroad shares and bonds. In 1886, with Robert Fleming, he was a member of the London Committee of Bondholders in the Rio Grande Division of the Texas and Pacific Railroad (Adler, *British Investment*, 158 n.89). He had the reputation of being a "keen operator" in American business, "coining money" in the 1886 Stock Exchange boom (Chapman, *The Rise of Merchant Banking*, 77). Turrell and van Helten, "The Rothschilds," 185, found John Dudley-Ryder of Benjamin Newgass & Co. to be a director and shareholder of the Exploration Company, Ltd. (1889–1925). Dorothy Adler believed that Benjamin Newgass & Co. was a large seller of Union Pacific shares in late October 1890 (*British Investment*, 160–161). Chapman, in preparing his history of British merchant banking, encountered numerous references to Newgass' American business (*The Rise of Merchant Banking*, 77, 190 n.22), as have I. On his land holdings, for example, see John Davis, "Alien Landlordism," in *The Land Question from Various Points of View*, ed. C. F. Taylor (Philadelphia: C. F. Taylor [1889]), 43, and Lewis, *America's Stake*, 569. The *Stock Exchange Official Intelligence for 1914*, 275, indicated that the Atlantic and Danville Railway Company (organized in Virginia in 1894) had as

its president, B. Newgass, London, England, and as its London agents B. Newgass & Co., Lombard Street. In 1914 a Brown, Shipley in-house letter called Newgass a "shrewd old man" (quoted in Chapman, *The Rise of Merchant Banking*, 72).

190. See Greenberg, *Financiers and Railroads*, on Morton, Rose & Co. In London, Morton, Rose & Co. issued Chicago, Burlington and Quincy securities. It was the agent in London for the Burlington and for the Chicago, Milwaukee and St. Paul (*Investors' Review*, London, 3 [March 1894]: 132).

191. Its principal partner, Arthur M. Grenfell, was chairman of the prosperous Camp Bird mining company in Colorado. Nash, *The Life of Herbert Hoover*, 563–566, is useful on Chaplin, Milne, Grenfell. See also *New York Times*, June 7, 1914, 1. The firm suspended business on June 6, 1914.

192. Adler, *British Investment*, 146. The American firm was Blake Brothers, New York and Boston.

193. Hans Bauer, *Swiss Bank Corporation, 1872–1972* (Basle: Swiss Bank Corp., 1972), 137.

194. Phelps, *Foreign Expansion of American Banks*, 10, indicates that the New York firm was American controlled. See also this chapter, note 43.

195. On the 1914 partners in the London house, see *Stock Exchange Official Intelligence for 1914*, 423. On the Speyer houses, see this chapter, note 216.

196. Other British participants included Frühling & Goshen; Frederick Huth & Co.; Smith, Payne & Smiths; H. S. Lefevre & Co.; Thomson, Bonar & Co.; and S. Japhet & Co., for example. The Rand house Wernher, Beit & Co. and the Hirsch group (Leopold Hirsch & Co.) that specialized in other areas of the world had American mining involvements, as did the Matheson Investment Group. The International Financial Society took part in American issues in these years. See P. L. Cottrell, "Investment Banking in England, 1856–1882: A Case Study of the International Financial Society," Ph.D. diss., University of Hull, 1974, 740–743, 783–787. On the Matheson Investment Group, see S. D. Chapman, "British-Based Groups before 1914," *Economic History Review*, 2nd ser., 38 (May 1985): 233–235.

197. Powell, *The Evolution*, 389.

198. The leading investment bankers in Britain operated on the basis of trust. J. P. Morgan, schooled by his father, expressed a similar view in 1912, when he was interrogated at the Pujo Committee hearings:

Untermyer: "You are responsible for the securities issued?"
Morgan: "Morally, yes . . ."
Untermyer: "You do not consider you are under any obligation to protect the securities you issue."
Morgan: "Unless there is trouble."

See Morgan testimony, Dec. 19, 1912, U.S. House, Subcommittee of the Committee on Banking and Currency, *Money Trust Investigation* (Washington, D.C., 1913), 1064.

199. Carosso, *Investment Banking in America*, 78.

200. For example, Barclay, which I believe did not typically deal in U.S. securities, on occasion acted to intermediate British funds into the United States. Thus in 1887 H. G. Chalkley of the London branch of the American mortgage company J. B. Watkins Land Mortgage Company arranged for Barclay's "to accept" the firm's debenture bonds and "to advance £1 for each $6.00 of bonds." See Allan G. Bogue, *Money at Interest* (Ithaca, N.Y.: Cornell University Press, 1955), 132. In April 1894, when a receiver was appointed for J. B. Watkins Land Mortgage Company, the latter's liabilities included "Loans from Barclay & Co., Bankers, London, secured by Debenture Bonds," $97,500 (ibid., 202). Bogue described Chalkley as "a Quaker financial agent" and explains this as the basis for the Barclay & Co. connections. See Allan G. Bogue,

"The Administrative and Policy Problems of the J. B. Watkins Land Mortgage Company, 1873–1914," *Bulletin of the Business History Society*, 27 (March 1953): 31.

W. G. Kerr writes that the Scottish American Mortgage Company, which intermediated funds to the United States, had three Scottish bankers: the Royal Bank of Scotland, the Union Bank (Scotland), and the British Linen Company Bank. (It also used Glyn, Mills & Currie in London.) Its "reserve-fund" was invested in Royal Bank or British Linen Company Bank shares (W. G. Kerr, *Scottish Capital on the American Frontier* [Austin: Texas State Historical Association, 1976], 108, 114–115). It is not clear from Kerr's work, however, that the Scottish banks themselves were directly involved in U.S. investments, although other evidence would indicate this.

Personal ties of British bank directors with U.S. investment intermediaries were numerous. Sir George Warrender of Edinburgh, in the late nineteenth century a director of the Royal Bank of Scotland, was also the first chairman of the board of the Scottish American Investment Company, Ltd., and served on the boards of Arizona Copper Company, the Scottish American Investment Trust, and the Anglo-American Debenture Corp. See Ronald B. Weir, *A History of the Scottish American Investment Co., Ltd.* (Edinburgh: Scottish American Investment Company, Ltd., 1973), 7, 15.

Sir William B. Forwood, a director of the Bank of Liverpool and chairman from 1898, had numerous American interests. See *Directory of Directors, 1892: The Investors' Review*, 3 (April 1894): 200–203; and William B. Forwood, *Recollections of a Busy Life, Being the Reminiscences of a Liverpool Merchant, 1840–1910* (Liverpool: Henry Young, 1910).

201. Glyn, Mills, frequently classed as a commercial bank (it took deposits), certainly acted as a "merchant bank" and participated in U.S. railroad finance. In U.S. business it was associated with Winslow, Lanier & Co. On Glyn, Mills, see Balogh, *Studies*, 11–12, 309. It was involved—with Baring Brothers—in 1908 and 1910 in the Union Pacific Railroad issues ("Foreign, Colonial, and Commercial Loans" list in BAL). The Convertible Gold Bond issue of 1910 of the Chesapeake and Ohio Railway had its principal and interest payable in New York, but at its holder's option the payment could be made at Glyn, Mills, Currie & Co., London, at $4.87 per pound. See *Stock Exchange Official Intelligence for 1914*, 279. See Chapman, "The Evolution," 26 and 30, for the exceptional role of Glyn, Mills. I am indebted to Vincent Carosso for information on Glyn, Mills's relation to J. S. Morgan & Co.

202. See Chapter 15. Carosso tells me such compensation arrangements were not unusual.

203. See, for example, the June 22, 1908, reorganization plan for the Baltimore and Ohio Railroad; the London and Westminster Bank, Ltd., was the depository (U.S. House, Subcommittee of the Committee on Banking and Currency, *Money Trust Investigation*, pt. 23, 1712). After the Kansas City, Mexico and Orient Railway Company went into receivership in 1912, British holders of bonds were "invited" to deposit them with Glyn, Mills, Currie & Co., London (*Stock Exchange Official Intelligence for 1914*, 289).

204. British banks took part in U.S. trade financing. If loans related to this activity defaulted, "settlement" arrangements might thrust the bank into "long-term" finance. The City of Glasgow Bank had loaned monies domestically; with domestic defaults, it had become the owner of U.S. railroad securities, taken as collateral. For the bank's U.S. involvements, see R. E. Tyson, "Scottish Investment in American Railways: The Case of the City of Glasgow Bank, 1856–1881," in *Studies in Scottish Business History*, ed. Peter L. Payne (London: Frank Cass, 1967). The City of Glasgow Bank itself failed in 1878.

205. See R. C. Michie, *Money, Mania and Markets* (Edinburgh: John Donald, 1981), 156, on a loan to the Oregon Railway Company.

206. *Issues Advertised in the Times, 1891*, 33, 37.

207. When Chaplin, Milne, Grenfell, which acted as London "banker" for Camp Bird, Ltd., in Colorado, went into receivership, Camp Bird had £16,000 on deposit with Chaplin, Milne, Grenfell (Nash, *Herbert Hoover*, 564). When Natomas Consolidated of California sought to raise money in London, the Hirsch Syndicate, Ltd., handled the subscription. The London "bankers" were London County and Westminster Bank, Ltd. (*Economist*, 70 [April 2, 1910]: 760–761).

208. See C. A. E. Goodhart, *The Business of Banking* (London: Weidenfeld & Nicolson, 1972), 478, 508–513. I am indebted to Edwin Green of the Midland Bank for providing me with a list of London City and Midland Bank's American securities—as of December 1913. With the exception of New York City securities and some £102,600 in International Harvester 5 percent notes, the American portfolio was entirely in railroads. It totaled £530,000, which was 6.8 percent of its investment portfolio. Likewise, J. M. L. Booker, archivist, Lloyds Bank, found that that bank held in 1913–14 a number of different U.S. railroad securities plus Chicago Elevated Railway and New York City revenue bills (based on Lloyds Bank Investment Committee Minute Book).

209. Aubert, *La finance américaine*, 166. The Union Bank of London and Smiths participated in U.S. railroad underwritings (Goodhart, *The Business of Banking*, 138). Smith, Payne & Smiths—which in 1902 had merged with the Union Bank of London to form the Union Bank of London and Smiths—had had U.S. business involvements long before the merger. On the merger, see ibid., 397. So had the Union Bank; see Chapman, *The Rise of Merchant Banking*, 136. In 1888, when Hanover National Bank, New York, established a foreign department, its first account was with Smith, Payne & Smiths, London. "The initial transaction consisted of sales of checks for customers and collection of items on London and various cities of the Empire" (Roger Holden, "The Story of Central Hanover," typescript, 1930, Manufacturers Hanover Trust Company History Center, New York). See this chapter, note 18, on London City and Midland's New York correspondents. New York's two largest banks were National City and First National. London City and Midland's had National City Bank as a correspondent. Cleveland and Huertas, *Citibank*, 33, describes George F. Baker's First National Bank as less an originator of issues than an ally of others, such as J. P. Morgan.

210. In addition, British-owned "foreign and colonial" banks acquired existing American railroad securities for their investment portfolios. Such securities appear to have been purchased in London through ordinary brokerage channels. Thus the Imperial Bank of Persia—strictly as an investment—owned American railroad securities in 1909–1914 (data from the Archives of the Hongkong Bank Group, provided me by Geoffrey Jones [April 3, 1985]). See Chapter 6 for details on the bank's holdings.

211. Henri Hauser, *Germany's Commercial Grip on the World* (New York: Charles Scribner, 1918), 43, and J. Riesser, *The German Great Banks and Their Concentration* (1911; rpt. New York: Arno Press, 1977), passim.

212. Clough and Cole, *Economic History of Europe*, 637. Bleichroeder had very early participated in American finance. For a time, according to Emden, *Money Powers*, 397, S. Bleichroeder "controlled" the New York banking house Ladenburg, Thalmann & Co. It was Ladenburg, Thalmann & Co. that founded what became American Metal Company (see Chapter 8). There were also W. H. Ladenburg & Soehne, Mannheim; E. Ladenburg, Frankfurt; and W. Ladenburg & Co., London. On all of them, see Emden, *Money Powers*. On the Mendelssohns' involvement (in 1886) in an issue of 4½ percent gold bonds of the St. Paul, Minneapolis and Manitoba, see Hans Fürstenberg, *Carl Fürstenberg* (Berlin: Verlag Ullstein, 1931), 166; Robert Warschauer & Co., Berlin, also participated in this issue (ibid.).

In 1901 Disconto-Gesellschaft took over M. A. Rothschild & Soehne, Frankfurt, and in 1904 the Dresdner Bank absorbed Erlanger & Soehne, Frankfurt (Emden, *Money*

Powers, 268n, 397–398). The Rothschilds and the Erlangers, of course, continued in London. Gebrüder Sulzbach, Frankfurt, also active in U.S. business (for example, in the London and San Francisco Bank), survived, but not as an important participant in U.S. business (ibid., 258, 398). Data in Kindleberger, *The Formation of Financial Centers*, 26–27, suggest that the end to the Erlanger and Rothschild houses in Germany was symbolic of the shift in importance from Frankfurt to Berlin as the German financial center. German banking from the 1860s onward had become increasingly concentrated in Berlin. In the early twentieth century Mendelssohn and Bleichroeder in Berlin and M. M. Warburg in Hamburg were marketing U.S. securities. On Warburg, see E. Rosenbaum and A. J. Sherman, *M. M. Warburg & Co., 1798–1938* (New York: Holmes & Meier, 1979), 103. Frankfurt, however, maintained its long-standing important American associations, and the post–Civil War profits made in that city from U.S. business were often reinvested in the United States, especially in railroads; Lazard Speyer-Ellissen and Jacob S. H. Stern, in particular, continued to be heavily involved in U.S. business.

213. The Deutsche Bank was identified with electrical undertakings and transatlantic enterprises; it was the only German bank in 1914 to rank in the world's top ten; see Table 13.1. The Disconto-Gesellschaft was especially active in transport. The Dresdner Bank specialized in textiles, chemicals, and mining. The Darmstädter Bank had no particular industrial or geographical niche. On these banks, see Riesser, *The German Great Banks*, passim. See also Edgard Depitre, *La mouvement de concentration dans les banques allemandes* (Paris, 1905), and the review of Depitre's volume by R. H. Inglis Palgrave in *Economic Journal*, 16 (June 1906); 248–250.

214. Emden, *Money Powers*, 240–245, described the Berliner Handels-Gesellschaft as an institution "entirely sui generis." It was "first and foremost an issuing and Stock Exchange bank, and accordingly included among its assets more investments than any other bank . . . No other bank approached it in the art of making issues." The most useful source on this bank is Fürstenberg, *Carl Fürstenberg*.

215. Walter Herman Carl Laves, *German Governmental Influence on Foreign Investments, 1871–1914* (1927; rpt. New York: Arno Press, 1977), 8–9.

216. Speyer & Co., New York, which was—as noted in Chapter 6—one of the major investment banks in that city in 1914, maintained its partnership interconnections with the old Frankfurt banking house of Lazard Speyer-Ellissen, as well as with Speyer Brothers, London. In 1914 Speyer & Co.'s senior partner was James Speyer, who had been born in New York in 1861, where James's father, Gustavus, and his uncle, Philip Speyer, ran the predecessor firm to Speyer & Co. In 1864 Gustavus returned to Germany; James grew up in Frankfurt and apprenticed with the parent firm in that city. In 1885 he joined Speyer & Co. in New York and became its senior partner in 1899. In 1892 Eduard Beit (of Hamburg) had married Gustavus' daughter. In 1910 there were no more Speyers in Frankfurt, and Eduard Beit received a Prussian title—Beit von Speyer. Beit—the brother-in-law of James Speyer—became the senior partner of Lazard Speyer-Ellissen. He had interests in Speyer & Co., New York. The London house was headed by another member of the family, Sir Edgar Speyer. The Deutsche Bank worked in close conjunction with Lazard Speyer-Ellissen and Speyer & Co. in its many U.S. investments. See *New York Times*, Nov. 1, 1941 (James Speyer obituary); Emden, *Money Powers*, 274–277; and Stephen Birmingham, *Our Crowd* (New York: Dell, 1967), 406. Of Speyer, Emden, *Money Powers*, 274, writes that "by far the strongest connection between Frankfurt and Germany on the one hand and New York (and to a great extent London also) on the other was brought about and maintained by the Speyers; the outstanding position which they occupied in German-American affairs rested in the first place on their great capital strength, and secondly, on the fact that the firms which

the members of the family established remained most closely connected amongst each other, as the leading partners of one house were at the same time partners in all the others." See also testimony of James Speyer, U.S. Senate, Committee on Finance, *Sale of Foreign Bonds, Hearings,* 72nd Cong., 1st sess., 1932, 605–606, 609, on copartnership relationships.

Kuhn, Loeb & Co., likewise, was in 1914 a key American investment banking house. See Chapter 6. On Goldman, Sachs & Co., see Walter E. Sachs Reminiscences, pt. 1, 18 (on the firm's relationship with Disconto-Gesellschaft), pt. 2, 54, 55, 127 (on Frankfurt connections). Hallgarten & Co. was founded by the Frankfurt immigrant Lazarus Hallgarten. See "History of Hallgarten & Co.," draft typescript, April 28, 1950, 1 (I am indebted to Jon Buckley of Moseley, Hallgarten, Estabrook & Weeden Holding Company for a copy). The J. & W. Seligman connections with Frankfurt ended when in 1900 Seligman & Stettheimer closed its doors. J. & W. Seligman continued in New York; so did Seligman Brothers in London; but in 1914 J. & W. Seligman was no longer in the front rank of U.S. investment banks, as it once had been. See Wells, "House of Seligman." On Ladenburg, Thalmann & Co., see this chapter, note 212.

217. Riesser, *The German Great Banks,* 435, 478.

218. Ibid., 61, 447, 502. I am assuming that Riesser's use of E. vom Baur rather than G. vom Baur (on p. 447) was a typographical error and not a name change in the American house.

219. Emden, *Money Powers,* 244, writes that in 1903 Carl Fürstenberg of the German bank became a "sleeping partner" in Hallgarten & Co., New York. According to the draft history of Hallgarten & Co., "History of Hallgarten & Co.," Charles (*sic*) Fürstenberg was a partner in 1904–1912; Hans Winterfeldt, in 1904–1908, and Dr. Ludwig Treitel, in 1908–1912. The draft history states that Fürstenberg and Winterfeldt "had been officers of a Berlin Bank before becoming partners." In 1904 Hallgarten & Co. had eight partners. On Carl Fürstenberg, who took over the management of the Berliner Handels-Gesellschaft in 1883 and remained in charge until his death in 1933, see Emden, *Money Powers,* 241–245, and Fürstenberg, *Carl Fürstenberg.* The latter indicates that Hans Winterfeldt went to America on behalf of Berliner Handels-Gesellschaft and took an active interest in Hallgarten & Co. He left the latter in 1908 to join Speyer & Co. He was replaced by Treitel, the step-son of Carl Fürstenberg (see ibid., 197, 330, 449, 525–531). Fürstenberg was a "silent partner" in Hallgarten & Co., while Winterfeldt and then Treitel took an active interest in the firm. In 1908 Max Horowitz also became a partner, and in 1912 he represented Berliner Handels-Gesellschaft. Replacing Treitel in 1912 was Treitel's "good friend" Albert Rothbart. See "History of Hallgarten & Co.," and Wallich and Wallich, *Zwei Generationen im deutschen Bankwesen,* 301.

220. Walter E. Sachs of Goldman, Sachs, & Co. many years later (in 1956) described the relationship between Goldman, Sachs & Co. and Disconto-Gesellschaft before World War I: "We were very close to them, and as a result, I [Walter E. Sachs in 1907 as a young man] had the unique experience of being allowed to sit at the so-called 'directors'—that means the managers'—table and see the books." Sachs recalled that the German banks "gave us credit which we lent out to American merchants" (Walter E. Sachs, Reminiscences, pt. 1, 18, 21). Although Sachs does not say so, it seems likely that Disconto-Gesellschaft also distributed securities for Goldman, Sachs in the German market. According to Riesser, *The German Great Banks,* 446, the Dresdner Bank "entered into a close alliance with the banking house J. P. Morgan & Co. of New York, London, and Paris, for the purpose of common action in the field of international finance and issue operations and of extending the German market for American securities."

221. Ibid., 435, on its general involvements.

222. See Karl Helfferich, *Georg von Siemens* (Berlin: Julius Springer, 1923), II, 231–233, and also Dietrich G. Buss, *Henry Villard* (New York: Arno Press, 1978), 139–145, on Siemens' first exhilarating trip in 1883 sponsored by the Northern Pacific.

223. Helfferich, *Georg von Siemens*, II, 14–21, 33.

224. Ibid., 225.

225. On Villard and the Deutsche Bank, see Buss, *Henry Villard*, 157, 171–185, 200, and Henry Villard, *Memoirs* (Boston: Houghton Mifflin, 1904), II, 315ff. *Who Was Who in America*, I, 5–6, gives the dates of Adams' tenure as Bank representative. Edward D. Adams (1846–1931) was an experienced banker. He had been a member of the firm Winslow, Lanier & Co. (1879–1893) before becoming the Deutsche Bank representative, and he knew American railroads well, having taken part in numerous railroad reorganizations. Adams had common interests with the Deutsche Bank not only in American railroads but also in the electrical industry. See Matthew Josephson, *Edison* (New York: McGraw-Hill, 1959), 349 (on Adams trying to convince Edison in 1889 to take a look at what was being done at the Westinghouse plant on engineering ac alternators and transformers).

Adams had been a director of Edison Electric Illuminating Company of New York (1884–1889), a position he resigned when in 1890 he became president of the Cataract Construction Company (Adams, *Niagara Power*, I, 164). The Cataract enterprise was developing electric power at Niagara Falls, and in all the years that Adams was the Deutsche Bank's representative, he was associated with this huge hydroelectric project. Adams in 1927 wrote a two-volume history of the development of hydroelectric power at Niagara Falls (*Niagara Power*). In it he never mentioned the Deutsche Bank. It, however, shows his deep knowledge of and commitment to electrical innovations. See Chapter 14 for his involvements at Niagara Falls. From 1893 onward, Adams represented the Deutsche Bank in the reorganization of the Northern Pacific. See Chapter 6. In 1926 Edward Everett Bartlett published in New York a privately printed short tribute to Adams: *Edward Dean Adams*. It is to be used with caution, but it does note that on April 9, 1925, on Adams' seventy-ninth birthday, the Deutsche Bank's top management cabled him: "The Northern Pacific reorganization brought us into close touch . . . Daily intercourse between us of many years' duration followed" (ibid., 25).

226. The history of the Deutsche Bank, Fritz Seidenzahl, *100 Jahre Deutsche Bank, 1870–1970* (Frankfurt: Deutsche Bank, 1970), devotes a full chapter to the Northern Pacific.

227. He became chairman of the board in 1889. He resigned from the board in 1893. Deutsche Bank interests remained. See Villard, *Memoirs*, II, 327, 332, 365, and Seidenzahl, *100 Jahre*, chap. 5.

228. See Chapter 6. See also Seidenzahl, *100 Jahre*, chap. 5; Helfferich, *Georg von Siemens*, II, 233ff; Stuart Daggett, *Railroad Reorganization* (Boston: Houghton Mifflin, 1908), 273–296; and Gilbert, *End of the Road*, 75, 82, 95, 130, 168, 173, 180.

229. On the date von Gwinner joined the management board, see Seidenzahl, *100 Jahre*, 443. See Chapter 6 on his role with respect to the Northern Pacific. See also Arthur von Gwinner, *Lebenserinnerungen* (Frankfurt: Fritz Knapp Verlag, 1975), 62–78, 121–152.

230. Emden, *Money Powers*, 236.

231. Buss, *Henry Villard*, 172–173.

232. See Chapter 6 on the Deutsche Bank and U.S. railroads.

233. See Chapter 12 and Josephson, *Edison*, 353–354, 363–364.

234. Hugh Neuburger, *German Banks and German Economic Growth from Unification to World War I* (New York: Arno Press, 1977), 92.

235. Helfferich, *Georg von Siemens*, II, 97. Adams, *Niagara Power*, says nothing on

this. Adams—in his role as Deutsche Bank representative—may well have kept the bank attuned to what was happening in American electric power developments. Data in the Siemens Archives, Munich, show that when Siemens & Halske, Berlin, had a business problem in the United States, the firm turned to the Deutsche Bank, Berlin, which at once called on Edward D. Adams. See, for example, Adams to Deutsche Bank (Secretariat), April 17, 1903, and Arthur Gwinner to Wilhelm von Siemens, April 27, 1903, both in Siemens-Archiv-Akte (SAA) 4/LK77 (Wilhelm von Siemens). I am indebted to Dr. Harm Schröter for this material. See also Chapter 12.

236. Alien Property Custodian, *Report, 1918–1919*, 42–43, 559–560, 569. Edward Adams was chairman of the board of Lehigh Coke Company, 1910–1917 (Bartlett, *Adams*, 38).

237. Redlich, *The Molding of American Banking*, pt. 2, 370–371.

238. Seidenzahl, *100 Jahre*, chap. 11. I have no evidence, however, that the Deutsche Bank made any investments in the U.S. oil industry, which seems unlikely.

239. See Chapter 12.

240. *Commercial and Financial Chronicle*, 83 (July 14, 1906): 90. While the Chalmers' side of Allis-Chalmers Company comprised immigrant Scots, Alfred Chandler reminds me that the Allis side comprised immigrant Germans. Does this account for the Deutsche Bank connection? According to Bartlett, Adams had become a director of Allis-Chalmers in 1901 (*Adams*, 37).

241. Emden, *Money Powers*, 236, writes of the close relations between the influential Speyer family and the Deutsche Bank.

242. Ibid., 232, 233, 260. In fact, reading between the lines, it may well have been the Deutsche Bank's relationships with the Frankfurt firm Jacob S. H. Stern that was responsible for its initial heavy U.S. involvements. As early as April 1872, Henry Villard had involved the Stern firm with Wisconsin Central bonds. In 1881 Henry Villard had gotten Jacob S. H. Stern into financing the Oregon Railway and Navigation Company. The Stern firm had made money on Villard's handling of the Kansas and Pacific receivership (Villard had become a receiver in 1876). Otto Braunfels had been with Georg von Siemens on the Northern Pacific celebration trip in 1883. See Buss, *Henry Villard*, 29, 43, 122–123; and Villard, *Memoirs*, II, 310.

243. Cyrus Adler, *Jacob H. Schiff* (Garden City, N.Y.: Doubleday, 1928), I, 195.

244. On both, see Buss, *Henry Villard*, 183–185, and Wallich and Wallich, *Zwei Generationen im deutschen Bankwesen*, 278, 291. Müller, Schall & Co. was apparently German owned (Alien Property Custodian, *Report, 1918–1919*, 216).

245. Paul Dickens, "The Transition Period in American International Financing: 1897 to 1914," Ph.D. diss., George Washington University, 1933, 117–118, 244, 246.

246. Some of these banks were involved at home with businesses that had invested in America: the Disconto-Gesellschaft (and Hermann Schmidtmann), the Dresdner Bank (and Orenstein & Koppel), and all the banks with the German insurance companies (Riesser, *The German Great Banks*, 484, 495, passim). How, if at all, these German associations were extended across the Atlantic is not clear.

When Albert Ballin of the Hamburg-American Lines was negotiating transatlantic shipping agreements, a director of Disconto-Gesellschaft participated (Bernhard Huldermann, *Albert Ballin* [London: Cassell, 1922], 55). The Disconto-Gesellschaft held Pennsylvania Railroad shares on behalf of German investors (Harry H. Pierce, "Foreign Investment in American Enterprise," in *Economic Change in Civil War Era*, ed. David T. Gilchrist and W. David Lewis [Greenville, Del.: Eleutherian Mills–Hagley Foundation, 1965], 57). See this chapter, note 220, on the Disconto-Gesellschaft connection with Goldman, Sachs & Co. and Morgan's association with the Dresdner Bank.

Thomas R. Kabisch, *Deutsches Kapital in den USA* (Stuttgart: Klett-Cotta, 1982), 196,

has data on these German banks' U.S. business in the years 1870–1905. His material
shows the paramount position of railroads in their U.S. involvements and the relative
importance of the Darmstädter Bank in such issues. The reason for the latter would lie
in the associations between the Darmstädter Bank and Hallgarten & Co., New York.
See Table 13.5. In 1906, with plans for greater U.S. business, the Darmstädter Bank (in
cooperation with other German and American banking houses) founded the Amerika-
Bank, Berlin, which never seems to have done very much (the Panic of 1907 frightened
investors), and it went into liquidation in 1909 (Riesser, *The German Great Banks*, 448,
507)

Karl Erich Born, *International Banking in the 19th and 20th Centuries* (New York: St.
Martin's Press, 1983), 129, dates the participation of the Berliner Handels-Gesellschaft
in U.S. railway financing from 1884. A typical combination of participants was, for
example, the one in July 1886 when J. & W. Seligman & Co. underwrote $5 million of
St. Louis and San Francisco 5 percent fifty-year general mortgage bonds at 90 and then
formed a syndicate that included Berliner Handels-Gesellschaft; Kidder, Peabody &
Co.; E. W. Clark & Co.; Seligman & Stettheimer; Kuhn, Loeb & Co.; Hallgarten & Co.;
Brown Brothers; and Morton, Bliss & Co. (Wells, "House of Seligman," 643–644, 648).
The Kidder, Peabody Papers reveal some of the international relations: on the Atchi-
son, Topeka financing, Francis H. Peabody wrote George Magoun on Nov. 30, 1887,
"Could not Mr. Baring get some other house—possibly Hope & Co. or the Berliner
Handelsgesselchaf [*sic*] to join and take one-half of the Terminal 5s and one-half of
these 6s?" (Peabody to Magoun, Nov. 30, 1887, Kidder, Peabody Collection, vol. 5,
1888–1895). Fürstenberg, *Carl Fürstenberg*, 165–166, 196, 309, 446, 527–532, is very good
on Berliner Handels-Gesellschaft's handling of American issues in Germany. In the
early spring of 1911, the German government refused the listing of the bonds of the
Chicago, Milwaukee, and St. Paul Railroad on the Berlin Exchange (see Chapter 16);
these bonds were handled by the Berliner Handels-Gesellschaft. For more on some of
the specific German banks involved in particular U.S. issues, 1875–1914, see Gyula
Meleghy, "Die Vermittlerrolle der Banken bei deutschen Investitionen in Nord- und
Mittelamerika bis zum Ersten Weltkrieg," Ph.D. diss., University of Cologne, 1983,
270–283.

247. Bouvier, *Le Crédit Lyonnais de 1863 à 1882*, I, 252. This book is marvelous on that
bank's U.S. activities. Regrettably, Bouvier's history goes only to 1882.

248. Ibid., II, 569–572.

249. See data earlier in this chapter.

250. See Chapter 8. See Aubert, *La finance américaine* 163, for Crédit Lyonnais'
minor—unimportant—role in New York in 1909–10. Aubert suggests that the reason
Crédit Lyonnais did not have a New York agency was the great difficulty in finding a
man suitable to direct such an important business (ibid., 164).

251. Edmond Baldy, *Les banques d'affaires en France depuis 1900* (Paris: Librairie Générale de Droit & de Jurisprudence, 1922), 190–191. In 1895 Société Générale participated
in Compagnie Français des Mines d'Or et d'Exploration, which in turn took part in
American mining finance. See this chapter, note 156.

252. See Nathaniel Mayer Rothschild, London, to cousins, Paris, Oct. 27, 1907, RAL
XI/130A/1, wherein the writer thanks his Paris cousin "Jimmy" (1878–1957) for the
latter's letter on the difficult position in which Société Général had been placed by the
"embarrassment of Westinghouse."

253. See Chapter 8.

254. James, *Growth of Chicago Banks*, II, 1211, and Kaufmann, *La banque en France*, 237
(Kaufmann says that the Chicago "agency" was liquidated in 1899); see ibid., 249–250,
on the New Orleans agency. James calls the Chicago outlet a "branch." See Aubert, *La*

finance américaine (1910), 163, on the Comptoir d'Escompte's insignificant role in New York at that time.

255. Its founders included Henri Bamberger (a nephew of Louis Bischoffsheim) and Edouard Hentsch. See Rondo Cameron, *France and the Economic Development of Europe* (Princeton, N.J.: Princeton University Press, 1961), 197. Both the Bischoffsheim and the Hentsch names were familiar in American investment activities. See Emden, *Money Powers*, 163, for the role of Bischoffsheim & Goldschmidt in the founding of the Banque des Pays-Bas. As noted earlier, Bischoffsheim & Goldschmidt were very active in U.S. railroads. Chapman, "The Evolution," 25, calls Bischoffsheim & Goldschmidt "Paris based."

256. Henry Collas, *La Banque de Paris et des Pays-Bas* (Dijon: Imprimerie Barbier, 1908), 17. Details are lacking.

257. Ibid., passim.

258. Kaufmann, *La banque en France* (1914), 222, writes that the Banque de Paris et des Pays-Bas participated along with Société Générale in a number of American transactions involving the Barings and Kuhn, Loeb.

259. Adler, *Jacob Schiff*, I, 195.

260. Baldy, *Les banques d'affaires*, 160.

261. Ibid.

262. Collas, *La Banque de Paris*, 154.

263. Baldy, *Les banques d'affaires*, 160.

264. Collas, *La Banque de Paris*, 66.

265. Baldy, *Les banques d'affaires*, 166. See also Swaine, *Cravath Firm*, II, 118.

266. Baldy, *Les banques d'affaires*, 114, 166.

267. Aubert, *La finance américaine* (1910), 163. Aubert indicates that it was "a branch," but that cannot be, since New York law forbade branches of foreign banks. For its activities in oil and aluminum, see Chapter 8. According to Aubert, the New York manager was M. H. Brunner, a man with thirty years of experience in American business. C. J. Gignoux, *Histoire d'une entreprise française* (Paris: Hachette, 1955), 116, writes that the Banque Franco-Américaine was faltering by 1913—so the prosperity does not appear to have lasted.

268. The point is made by Herbert Feis, *Europe: The World's Banker* (1930; rpt. New York: Kelley, 1964), 38, and others as well. Hottinguer & Cie. remained of importance in American business (Kaufmann, *La banque en France*, 172). Harry White, *The French International Accounts, 1880–1913* (Cambridge, Mass.: Harvard University Press, 1933), 279, writes that "the large private banking firms like Rothschild, Vernes, Mallet, had been largely superseded as leaders in the underwriting field, and were forced to cooperate with the large banks, since the latter controlled most of the agencies thru [*sic*] which securities were sold."

269. See this chapter, note 108, on Morgan, Harjes and note 43 on Lazard Frères. Munroe & Co., which began as an American bank in Paris in 1851, was the successor to a merchandising firm of that name. From the 1850s onward the firm was an active seller of American securities. Edward Tuck was for many post–Civil War years a partner in both the New York and the Paris firms (he was involved with putting French investors into James L. Hill's railroads). In 1900 John Munroe's daughter married Henri Hottinguer—uniting two firms that were both active in American securities. John Munroe died later that year, but his Paris firm continued. On Munroe & Co., I have used Cleona Lewis, *America's Stake in International Investments* (Washington, D.C.: Brookings Institution, 1938), 192; data from Franklin Brooks, July 1, 1982 (Brooks is writing a biography of Tuck); Max Gérard, *Messieurs Hottinguer, banquiers à Paris* (Paris: Hottinguer, 1972), II, 670–671; and Charles P. Kindleberger, *Multinational Excursions*

(Cambridge, Mass.: MIT Press, 1984), 120 (Kindleberger writes that the firm continued in existence until 1930).

270. White, *French International Accounts*, 279–280. Aubert, *La finance américaine* (1910), 160–169, thought that French banks should do more American business.

271. Riesser, *The German Great Banks*, 503.

272. The Boissevain name was ubiquitous in American business. The Dutch firm had a London house (a copartnership with Americans)—Blake, Boissevain & Co.—which often acted for Boissevain family interests. Thus in 1896 we find Howland Davis of Blake, Boissevain & Co. joining the board of the Baltimore and Ohio Railroad. See E. G. Campbell, *The Reorganization of the American Railroad System, 1893–1900* (New York: Columbia University Press, 1938), 137. A. A. H. Boissevain himself participated in 1894 in the reorganization of the Union Pacific (ibid., 233). See also Chapter 6 and Adler, *British Investment*, 146. Blake, Boissevain worked closely with Blake Brothers, New York and Boston, and Speyer & Co., New York.

273. I do not have the space to deal separately with each of these Dutch firms and their American connections. On Tutein Nolthenius & De Haan, see Augustus J. Veenendaal, Jr., "The Kansas City Southern Railway and the Dutch Connection," *Business History Review*, 61 (Summer 1987): 291–316.

274. Bacon, "American International Indebtedness," 271–272. See also Bouvier, *Crédit Lyonnais*, II, 564.

275. Alex Lombard, *Notice sur la position financière actuelle des états de l'amerique du Nord* (Geneva: Imprimerie de Ch. Gruaz, 1841) and his *Notes financières et statistiques sur L'état d'Ohio* (Geneva, 1847); Bacon, "American International Indebtedness," 271–272; Bouvier, *Crédit Lyonnaise*, II, 568; and Bauer, *Swiss Bank Corporation*, 368.

276. Switzerland has been described in these years as the "Eldorado of French capitalists" (Nicholas Faith, *Safety in Numbers* [New York: Viking Press, 1982], 68). See also Bacon, "American International Indebtedness," 273.

277. Bauer, *Swiss Bank Corporation*, 195 (for relative size of Swiss banks), passim (for Frankfurt connections), 135, 137 (London office), 188 (quote). As noted earlier, when Blake, Boissevain & Co., London, went into liquidation on January 1, 1901, the Swiss Bankverein took over many of its customers. George F. Blake joined the Bankverein in London as manager. The Boissevain firms in Amsterdam and New York were retained as connections (ibid., 137).

278. *Stock Exchange Official Intelligence for 1914*, London, 280. This was undoubtedly because the Swiss Bankverein took over the customers of Blake, Boissevain & Co., London.

279. Bauer, *Swiss Bank Corporation*, 165.

280. See Chapter 8.

281. Bauer, *Swiss Bank Corporation*, 168–169, for example, Stickereiwerke Arbon, A. G.

282. Ibid., 192. The bankrupt New York company is not identified by name.

283. Faith, *Safety in Numbers*, 41.

284. Information from Dr. R. Lundström.

285. Paul Dickens, "The Transition Period," in appendix A, schedule II, 236–270, prepared a list of issuers (companies), class of securities (type of stock or bond), foreign market in which offered, size of issue, foreign share, and price. He added up his column on "foreign share" to obtain the totals in the table. In many cases he indicated that he personally made the *estimate* of "foreign share."

286. These are nominal values of "new issues." These figures do not tell us how much was actually remitted to the United States, nor do they tell us the level of investment, since already-issued securities continued to be actively traded. As Dickens

himself recognized (ibid., 115), "the flow of securities from American to foreign ownership and back was continuous." Also, although Dickens appears to have covered London issues well, I have found a number of omissions of issues on the Continent. Thus his figures for "new issues" may well be low. On the other hand, "issues" in London and on the Continent were often comingled, with an international syndicate offering the same security on several markets.

287. As noted, however, the amount channeled was not the $2.6 billion total. The actual amount is unknown.

288. See Chapter 14, note 91.

289. The government-borrowing shown in Table 13.6 was, in the main, by New York City, and American investment banks took the lead—albeit in cooperation with foreign banks—in introducing that city's securities abroad. See, for example, the *London Times*, April 27, 1914.

14. Financial, Commercial, and Communication Services

1. P. L. Cottrell, "Investment Banking in England, 1856–1882," Ph.D. diss., University of Hull, 1974, 741; Dorothy Adler, *British Investment in American Railways* (Charlottesville: University Press of Virginia, 1970); and W. J. Reader, *A House in the City* (London: B. T. Batsford, 1979), passim, which is on Foster & Braithwaite. Reader (pp. 52–53) points out that Foster & Braithwaite were considered American specialists. His book contains a substantial amount on this firm's interests in numerous American railways.

2. Adler, *British Investment*, 146. E. F. Satterthwaite's firm went bankrupt in 1894 (Reader, *A House in the City*, 53).

3. Sometimes the line between "stockbroker" and "merchant banker" was thin. Adler, *British Investment*, refers to Vivian, Gray as a stockbroker on p. 147 and as a merchant banking house on p. 149n. See ibid., 147, 135–136, and Reader, *A House in the City*, 53 (on Heseltine, Powell). Heseltine, Powell & Co. often acted to guarantee the signature of European holders of American railway securities when the latter wished to make transfers. It served in this capacity for securities of the Atchison, Topeka and Santa Fe; the Baltimore and Ohio; the Chicago Great Western; the Chicago, Milwaukee and St. Paul; the Denver and Rio Grande; Northern Securities; and the Pittsburgh, Fort Wayne and Chicago. See *Stock Exchange Official Intelligence for 1914*, 312–314. Canadian stockbrokers also put Canadian investors into U.S. portfolio investments.

4. David Kynaston, "Harry Panmure Gordon (1837–1902)," *Dictionary of Business Biography*, II, 611–613, and H. Panmure Gordon, *The Land of the Almighty Dollar* (London: Frederick Warne, 1892), 174–175. On British stockbrokers and the ease with which they handled American securities, see David Kynaston, "The Late-Victorian and Edwardian Stockbroker as Investment Adviser," unpublished paper, 1982.

5. John J. Madden, *British Investment in the United States, 1860–1880* (1958 diss.; New York: Garland, 1985), 123, suggests that the stockbrokers—unlike the merchant bankers—did not tie up capital for long periods in American railroads; they were, he believed, more apt to act as commission agents in new issues. On the other hand, as I went through the records of stockholders in free-standing companies (1875–1914), often "stockbrokers" were listed as owners of record.

6. See S. F. Van Oss, *American Railroads as Investments* (London: Effingham Wilson, 1893) and Augustus J. Veenendaal, Jr., "Railroads, Oil and Dutchmen," *Chronicles of Oklahoma*, 63 (Spring 1985): 4–27.

7. The merger behavior was the typical pattern of the bevy of promotions, 1889–90. See Erastus Wiman, "British Capital and American Industries," *North American Review*,

150 (Jan. 1890): 220–234, and *Banker's Magazine*, New York, 44 (August 1889): 81–85. In 1899, as an example, an English promoter, Harry S. Foster, merged a group of American manufacturers of automatic weighing machines and formed the American Automatic Weighing Machine Company, Ltd.; this London promotion, like so many of them, was unsuccessful. See Robert T. Swaine, *Cravath Firm and Its Predecessors* (New York: privately printed, 1946), I, 641. The *Stock Exchange Year Book* and *Burdett's Official Intelligence* are good sources for the numerous promotions. The British press saw London as overrun with American promoters, but the many British promoters were as eager as any American to make money "putting together" these propositions to attract British savings.

8. Paul Dickens, "The Transition Period in American Finance," Ph.D. diss., George Washington University, 1933, 6.

9. Swaine, *Cravath Firm*, I, 311, 544, 420.

10. Herman E. Krooss and Martin R. Blyn, *A History of Financial Intermediaries* (New York: Random House, 1971), 130–131.

11. P. L. Cottrell, *Industrial Finance, 1830–1914* (London: Methuen, 1980), 181; Michael Edelstein had made this identical point earlier. London's first-class merchant banking houses handled large issues. There were efficiencies in doing so: "the first class merchant bankers ignored small and medium sized issues from overseas" (Michael Edelstein, "Rigidity and Bias in the British Capital Market, 1870–1913," in *Essays on a Mature Economy: Britain after 1840*, ed. Donald N. McCloskey [Princeton, N.J.: Princeton University Press, 1971], 86–87).

12. James B. Jefferys, *Business Organisations in Great Britain, 1856–1914* (New York: Arno Press, 1977), 306.

13. There are two excellent books covering O'Hagan's activities: (1) his memoirs: H. Osborne O'Hagan, *Leaves from My Life*, 2 vols. (London: John Lane, 1929), and (2) the history of an American law firm with which O'Hagan dealt: Swaine, *Cravath Firm*, vol. 1, passim.

14. This company was incorporated in London on Oct. 3, 1890. Its auditors were Price, Waterhouse; its bankers, Lloyds Bank. It was formed to conduct in the United States the same business as that of the City of London Contract Corporation, Ltd. (registered June 5, 1882)—that is, to handle matters connected with promotions. See *Burdett's Official Intelligence, 1895*, 1088–89, 994–995. One-fourth of the London and Chicago company was owned by CLCC, one-fourth by the British public, and one-half by the American public. See Swaine, *Cravath Firm*, I, 469–470, for details.

15. Swaine, *Cravath Firm*, I, 424. In several of the CLCC's promotions, it used a New York law firm to deal with business problems—beyond simply legal questions (ibid., 627). R. H. Monro was on the board of the London and Chicago Contract Corporation, Ltd., but not on the board of the City of London Contract Corporation, Ltd. (*Burdett's Official Intelligence, 1895*).

16. He would purchase properties and then resell them.

17. On its role as promoter, see Swaine, *Cravath Firm*, I, 765. See also *Investors' Review*, 1 (Jan. 1892): 55; 2 (Nov. 1893): 606–607; 3 (Jan. 1894): 13, 15, 36; 3 (March 1894): 176–177; 3 (April 1894): 200–202; 4 (July 1894): 64; 5 (May 1895): 204.

18. "The Winchester House" was a property that, as the *Investors' Review* put it, "never did any good. No dividend was ever earned." In 1887 this piece of British real estate had been transferred to the newly created trustees' corporation (ibid., 2 [Jan. 1894]: 13).

19. Pender had been involved in helping Cyrus Field finance the first transatlantic cable (see Chapter 4). On his continuing role in cables, see text to follow. He also invested in cattle ranching in the Dakotas (see Chapter 9).

20. See *Investors' Review*, as cited in this chapter, note 17. For the Trustees' Corporation's investments in Cataract Construction (which was neither a sham nor a Trustees' Corporation creation), see Edward D. Adams, *Niagara Power* (Niagara Falls, N.Y.: Niagara Power Co., 1927), I, 295. None of the "industrial" companies noted did well.

21. *Investors' Review*, 3 (Jan. 1894): 13, 15.

22. Ibid., 1 (Jan. 1892): 55. The American Association, Ltd., for example, was bankrupt—see Chapter 7.

23. See George Glasgow, *The English Investment Trust Companies* (New York: John Wiley, 1931), 100 (its name was changed to Trustees Corporation in Aug. 1917), 66 (on International Investment Trust), 74 (on London and New York Investment Corporation), 106 (on United States Debenture Corporation). In the *Stock Exchange Official Intelligence for 1914*, 1090, the Trustees, Executors and Securities Insurance Corporation, Ltd. (the apostrophes were dropped) was described as chaired by G. A. Touche, M.P., and as "formed [in 1887] to (1) act as trustee, agent, executor and administrator; (2) undertake the safe custody and insurance of Bonds, Shares, etc., deposited with the Corporation; (3) issue warrants and certificates against securities deposited; and (4) undertake the issue of foreign, colonial and municipal loans and payment of coupons thereon." Its head office was Winchester House, London, a building on which it had a long-term lease.

24. Clark C. Spence, *British Investments and the American Mining Frontier, 1860–1901* (Ithaca, N.Y.: Cornell University Press, 1958), 48. The Mining and Financial Trust Syndicate, Ltd., did not survive. It was last listed in the *Stock Exchange Official Intelligence* in 1905. Albin Joachim Dahl, "British Investment in California Mining, 1870–1890," Ph.D. diss., University of California, Berkeley, 1961, 128, 135–141, 242, is particularly useful on British promoters of American mining ventures.

25. O'Hagan's own book has nothing on his fees. I sought in vain an "American" promotion with business in the United States rather than in Trinidad. I have no reason, however, to believe the costs would have been different. The costs of the Trinidad issue came to 17.5 percent. When Deere & Co. management was talking in 1889–90 with promoters about a British-financed merger of plow companies, "the outside limit of commissions and promoter's fees was considered to be 20%," or so a Deere & Co. executive believed. See Wayne C. Broehl, *John Deere's Company* (New York: Doubleday, 1984), 267. But the Duke of Marlborough, "Virginia Mines and American Rails," *Fortnightly Review*, n.s., 49 (June 1891): 793, wrote: "The promoters on both sides [of the Atlantic], the lawyers, the trust companies, etc., will have had their share of the plunder. In New York no one discusses a financial scheme for England at a lower rate than setting aside from 33 to 35 percent for expenses connected with the bringing out of a company." If the Duke of Marlborough was not exaggerating, A. L. Barber got a "bargain." Deere & Co. never went through with a London promotion.

26. Take the case, for example, of New Orleans–born Paul P. de Bellet, who from France in 1878 wrote General P. G. T. Beauregard (the Confederate general) suggesting that Beauregard get a six-month option on a Calcassieu, Louisiana, sulphur mining company. "With all the stock of the old company, we can then organize a new company under your management and issue some shares and bonds here in Paris, guaranteed by the charter, franchises, and stock of our company . . . Your name will go far, very far, in assuring our success" (Virginia H. Taylor, *The Franco-Texan Land Company* [Austin: University of Texas Press, 1969], 153–154). Such were the schemes of "typical" promoters.

27. Stockholder lists of the British-incorporated companies show this to be the case.

28. Herbert Feis, *Europe: The World's Banker* (1930; rpt. New York: W. W. Norton, 1965), 8–10.

29. J. C. Gilbert, *A History of Investment Trusts in Dundee* (London: P. S. King, 1939), 1; Ronald Weir, *A History of the Scottish American Investment Company Limited, 1873–1973* (Edinburgh: Scottish American Investment Co., 1973); and E. T. Powell, *The Evolution of the Money Market* (London: Financial News, 1915), 469, and his *Mechanism of the City* (London: P. S. King, 1910), 34–35.

30. In the years before 1914, the *investment* trust company, as such was not an American form. There was, however, a heterogeneous group of U.S.-headquartered "trust companies," some of which brought foreign capital into American investments. With the exception of Transatlantic Trust Company (see Chapter 13), I have not found any U.S. trust companies that were foreign-controlled in 1875–1914.

According to Krooss and Blyn, *A History of Financial Intermediaries*, 102, 138, at the end of the Civil War the United States had only seven trust companies, but by 1908 some 1,470 existed. Included was the *Mercantile Trust Company*, which in 1876 set up a London office to raise money for western mortgages. The office was no success, and by 1880 the Mercantile Trust Company was virtually out of the mortgage business and into a "business based on deposits and commercial loans." See H. Peers Brewer, "Eastern Money and Western Mortgages in the 1870s," *Business History Review*, 50 (Autumn 1976): 35.

I do not know whether I should include the prominent *United States Trust Company* (founded in 1853) among the American intermediaries of foreign monies, but fragmentary evidence suggests that it probably played such a role. Its founder, John A. Stewart, took part in the 1871 establishment of United States Mortgage Company. (See Ivan Wright, *Farm Mortgage Financing* [New York: McGraw-Hill, 1923], 318.) In addition, Stewart served on the New York advisory board of the Scottish American Investment Company in the 1870s. (Weir, *The Scottish American Investment Company*, 8.) The USMC and the SAIC brought foreign capital to America. I do not believe there was a direct association between the United States Trust Company and the United States Trust Corporation, Ltd., London, although some of the same circle of individuals appear to have participated in both.

The *Jarvis-Conklin Mortgage Trust Company* opened an office in London in 1887 to attract British monies into American mortgages. When the U.S. parent went bankrupt in the Panic of 1893, the London office was taken over by the *North American Trust Company;* this New York-headquartered firm changed its name in 1905 to *Trust Company of America*. In 1912 the *Equitable Trust Company of New York* (name adopted in 1902 and not to be confused with an 1870s firm of the same name) acquired the Trust Company of America with its London office and the original Jarvis-Conklin-installed management of that office. Meanwhile, in 1910 Equitable Trust Company of New York had opened a Paris branch, which served as an information bureau for "clients of the bank visiting or living in Paris." It seems to have handled American securities for French investors. Equitable Trust Company also carried on a sizable foreign exchange business in New York. (See Clyde William Phelps, *The Foreign Expansion of American Banks* [1927. New York: Arno Press, 1976], 133–135; New York, Superintendent of Banks, *Annual Report for 1911*, 18–19; and Edward Ten Broeck Perine, *The Story of the Trust Companies* [New York: G. P. Putnam's, 1916], 216–219.)

By 1914 the largest U.S.-headquartered trust company was *Guaranty Trust Company of New York*. In 1897, it had established an office in London, which may well have been more to aid U.S. business abroad than to move European funds into the United States. In 1912 Guaranty Trust Company acquired *Standard Trust Company*, New York, which had some minority foreign ownership and was instrumental in bringing foreign capital into U.S. investments (see this chapter, note 96). Guaranty Trust Company had by 1914 a large foreign department in New York. (See Perine, *The Story of Trust Companies*, 199; Phelps, *Expansion*, 137; and Swaine, *Cravath Firm*, I, 591–594.)

Farmers' Loan and Trust Company, as far back as the 1830s, had been intermediating European monies into the United States (see Chapter 3). In 1906 it opened branches in London and Paris. In 1911 the New York Superintendent of Banks expected that those branches would raise foreign investments in U.S. securities and give American institutions a share in the profits of international financial operations. (See Phelps, *Foreign Expansion*, 139, and Superintendent of Banks, *Annual Report* for 1911, 18–19.)

In addition, the *Empire Trust Company*, New York, organized in 1902, started a London office in June 1913 (Phelps, *Foreign Expansion*, 141–142). The *Old Colony Trust Company* of Boston, had "a quarter of a century after its foundation in 1890," customers from all over the world—from Canada, Mexico, the West Indies, Central America, South America, England, France, Switzerland, Italy, Germany, Syria, China, Japan, and Australia (Perine, *The Story of Trust Companies*, 189–190).

The *Knickerbocker Trust Company*, New York (which suspended payments on October 22, 1907, bringing on the 1907 Panic), was involved in transactions related to foreign investments. The records of Stratton's Independence, Ltd. (a British-incorporated owner of an American mine), show Knickerbocker Trust Company in 1899 as owner of 100,000 shares (about 9 percent of the capital); Knickerbocker Trust Company in 1899–1900 appears to have sold most of these shares in England. (See Register of Companies, London, Stratton's Independence, Ltd., Western Range Cattle Industry Study, Manuscript Room, Library of Congress, Acc. 11,260, reels 65 and 66. Henceforth cited as WRCIS).

Because of restrictions on American commercial banks imposed by national and state legislation, many trust companies in the United States by the 1890s served as commercial banks, having the added privilege of pursuing fiduciary business. In 1903 *Bankers Trust Company* was organized by American bankers; unlike some other trust companies, it was not designed to compete with banks. Its clientele included foreign governments, but what exactly it did for them is unclear. (See Perine, *The Story of Trust Companies*, 222–228.)

All these, as well as other U.S. trust companies, appear to have handled foreign investors' savings, placing them in appropriate investments. In that they served as "trustees," their functions were not unlike those of the British investment trust companies.

31. Among the "dropouts" with American business were American and General Mortgage and Investment Corporation, Ltd., and the British and American Trustee and Finance Corporation, Ltd. (based on a comparison of a list of trust companies established [or organized] in the years 1879–1890 given in *Investors' Review*, 1 [Jan. 1892]: 51–55, and the lists in *Stock Exchange Official Intelligence for 1914* and in Glasgow, *The English Investment Trust*). On the behavior of some of the British trusts of the late 1880s, see U.S. Securities and Exchange Commission, *Investment Trusts in Great Britain*, 76th Cong., 1st sess., 1939, H. Doc. 380, 6–7. This report was prepared by Thomas Balogh and Ernest Doblin.

32. A glance through the *Stock Exchange Official Intelligence for 1914*, for example, reveals "financial trusts" with specialities in railroads, breweries, rubber, tea, or telegraphs; those with geographical specialities in America, Malaya, Russia, or India; and then general investment companies.

33. Matthew Simon, *Cyclical Fluctuations and the International Capital Movements of the United States* (1955 diss.; New York: Arno Press, 1979), chap. 4.

34. Gilbert, *A History*, 6. Gilbert does not indicate how he treated railroad defaults. The returns on U.S. rails have been variously calculated. See Michael Edelstein, *Overseas Investment in the Age of High Imperialism* (New York: Columbia University Press,

1982), 94. See also Jeffrey G. Williamson, *Late Nineteenth-Century American Development* (Cambridge: Cambridge University Press, 1974), 97, for real as well as nominal yields on U.S. rails. There is no question that interest rates were higher in the United States than in Great Britain.

35. Gilbert, *A History*, 24.

36. Ibid., 7–8. Glasgow, *The English Investment Trust*, divides his classification of trusts into pre–Baring Crisis and post–Baring Crisis ones. For the proliferation of investment companies, trust companies, and finance companies, 1886–1890, a good source is *Investors' Review*, 1 (Jan. 1892): 51–55. A list is included, comparing the "original value" of the investment trust securities as issues and their "present market value."

37. Gilbert, *A History*, 9. There are several splendid studies of Scottish investment trusts, and particularly on their role in the United States. The Gilbert and Weir books, cited above, are excellent, as are W. Turrentine Jackson, *The Enterprising Scot* (Edinburgh: Edinburgh University Press, 1968), with substantial information on the investment trusts, and W. G. Kerr, *Scottish Capital on the American Credit Frontier* (Austin: Texas State Historical Association, 1976). See also Ranald C. Michie, "Crisis and Opportunity: The Formation and Operation of the British Assets Trust, 1897–1914," *Business History*, 25 (July 1983): 125–147. Published data on the English investment trusts in the United States are far leaner. There is Glasgow's 1931 work cited above. *Investors' Review*, 1892ff, included substantial information on the English trust companies; it was a sharp critic of their doubtful investments. H. Burton and D. C. Corner, *Investment and Unit Trusts in Britain and America* (London: Elek Books, 1968), 15–43, is somewhat useful. Apparently none of the English trusts headquartered outside London survived to be included in Glasgow's 1931 work! All the English trusts he lists were headquartered in London. Some of those started in the provincial markets appear to have gravitated to London. The *Stock Exchange Official Intelligence for 1914* does, however, include some investment trusts with English non-London headquarters. One would like to know more, for example, about the J. R. Ellerman's group of trusts, the London General Investment Trust (1889), the Brewery and Commercial Investment Trust (1890), and the Debenture Securities Investment Company (1895). The founding date is in parentheses. Ellerman had a number of U.S. interests, as did these trusts. On Ellerman and his trusts, see the very minimal materials in James Taylor, *Ellermans: A Wealth of Shipping* (London: Methuen, 1921), 119–121.

38. Glasgow, *The English Investment Trust*. An example of the interlocking relationships is evident in the founders of the London and New York Investment Corporation, Ltd. (1889), which included Dillwyn Parrish, English and Scottish Investment Company, Ltd.: A. D. Clarke, Bankers Investment Trust, Ltd.; Ernest Noel, Mercantile Investment and General Trust Company, Ltd.; and G. A. Touche, Industrial and General Trust, Ltd. (Adler, *British Investment*, 214–216). The directors often interlocked with London-headquartered companies in which the trusts invested (based on *Directory of Directors*). Likewise, in 1939 a study prepared for the U.S. Securities and Exchange Commission, *Investment Trusts in Great Britain*, 17–18, identified (as of 1935) eleven British investment trust "groups" and noted that the interconnections went beyond these groups. Prior to 1914 it was already possible to talk of investment trust groups and interlocking directorates. As ibid., 6, pointed out, in the late 1880s "the same persons reappeared on the boards of a large number of new trusts."

39. John Scott and Michael Hughes, *The Anatomy of Scottish Capital* (London: Croom Helm, 1980), 25ff., and Jackson, *Enterprising Scot*, passim.

40. For example, Robert Benson & Co. was associated with the Merchants' Trust, Ltd., while Robert Fleming & Co. had many investment trust company associations.

Vincent Carosso tells me that J. S. Morgan & Co. had some Scottish investment trusts "among its institutional clients, both as underwriters and buyers."

41. There were the Ellerman group and the Touche group of trusts.

42. This investment trust began basically in handling mortgage lending in the United States.

43. Gilbert, *A History*, 10, 40–64.

44. See Glasgow, *The English Investment Trusts*, 102, on corporate name change, and Adler, *British Investment*, 216–219, for the names of the participants in 1890.

45. Thomson, Bonar & Co. was a British merchant banking house with some involvements in American railroad investments and finance. See Stanley Chapman, *The Rise of Merchant Banking* (London: Allen & Unwin, 1984), 97, 144, 204.

46. Lloyds Bank had long had business in the United States. The Huth family (F. Huth & Co.) had likewise long been identified with American trade and finance.

47. In 1890 this was America's largest "mortgage-granting" company.

48. Thomas, Wade, Guthrie & Co. had American involvements of its own; see Chapter 15.

49. Adler, *British Investment*, 216.

50. Over 100 letters written by James Stillman relating to the business of the United States Trust and Guarantee Corporation, Ltd., 1890–1896, are in his Letterbooks, Stillman Papers, Special Collections, Columbia University. The best and most numerous letters are from Stillman to Archibald Balfour. There are also letters to John Munroe & Co., New York, and to the Lombards (principally William A. Lombard). See esp. James Stillman to Archibald Balfour, Dec. 30, 1890, wherein he outlines his strategy to invest in banks throughout the country; ibid., Jan. 16, 1891, for more on the strategy; and ibid., Jan. 20, 1891, on the actual purchases. On the United States Trust and Guarantee Corporation, Ltd.'s holdings in Lombard Investment Company, see James Stillman to W. P. Manley, March 11, 1893, and Stillman to Archibald Balfour, Sept. 22, 1893. Stillman did not handle all the investments for the firm—and he often wrote inquiring about particular investments that the British firm had made in London in companies that did business in the United States. For other materials on the early history of the United States Trust and Guarantee Company, Ltd., and the British investors, see *Investors' Review*, 4 (Oct. 1894): 244. For the group involved in 1914, see *Stock Exchange Official Intelligence for 1914*, 1133. In 1914 both James Stillman and F. A. Vanderlip served on the seven-man London board of directors. There also continued to be in 1914 a U.S. Advisory Board.

51. Dorothy Adler lists the Scottish American Investment Trust in 1876 as marketing an issue of the Albany and Susquehanna (*British Investment*, 209). On the investment trusts' role in promoting and underwriting in the late 1880s, see U.S. Securities and Exchange Commission, *Investment Trusts in Great Britain*, 7. In August 1899 the Anglo-American Debenture Corporation owned 999,900 of the 1,100,000 shares total of the new Stratton's Independence, Ltd., a Colorado mining venture. By the end of 1900 it had sold all these shares (WRCIS, reel 61).

52. Glasgow, *The English Investment Trust*, 96 (date of name change), and Adler, *British Investment*, 151, 208.

53. For names, see *Northwestern Miller*, 40 (Dec. 16, 1898): 1052. See ibid., 27 (Nov. 29, 1889); 613, for what happened to unsubscribed stock. On the investments of the London and New York Investment Corporation as of Dec. 31, 1893, see *Investors' Review*, London, 3 (March 1894): 176–177. For the general process by which the trust companies picked up "'fag-ends of issues," see ibid., 1 (Jan. 1892): 43–46. Major holders of shares in the San Francisco Breweries, Ltd., for example, included the American Brewing and General Securities Trust, the North of England Trustee Deben-

ture and Assets Corporation, the Trust and Loan of China, Japan and the Straits (!), and "the Imperial and Foreign Investment and Agency [sic]." The last, as noted earlier, involved many of the same principals as the United States Trust and Guarantee Corporation, Ltd. Similarly, Otis Steel Company, Ltd.'s major British owners included the Industrial and General Trust, the International Investment Trust, the United States and South American Trust, the London Trust Company, and the United States Debenture Corporation (Ibid., 43, 45).

54. Powell, *Mechanism of the City*, 5–6.

55. R. H. Inglis Palgrave, "An English View of Investments in the United States," *Forum*, 15 (April 1893): 199; contrast this article with the ones appearing shortly thereafter in *Investors' Review*, London, which suggested that the "well-known" men had been behaving improperly in lending their names to such activities. See, for example, ibid., 3, (Jan. 1894): 13ff, and 5 (May 25, 1895): 302–304. The last of these articles was on the occasion of the liquidation of the English and Scottish Mercantile Investment Trust, Ltd., a company born in 1886, whose "death" came in July 1894. The article noted that the Trust had "filled its bag with . . . Otis Steel shares, Pillsbury-Washburn shares, City of Chicago Grain Elevator shares, Trustees', Executors', etc., Corporation shares, Middlesboro' Town Lands shares . . . and the Trust now lies in its grave with a ghastly legacy of debts to pay and no money to prosecute its destroyers with" (ibid., 304).

56. *Investors' Review*, London, 3 (March 1894): 129–141.

57. *Statist*, 75 (March 8, 1913): 501. The Merchants' Trust was founded in 1889. Its original board consisted of Col. Robert Baring (brother of Lord Revelstoke), Robert Benson (of R. Benson & Co.), C. E. Bright (a director of Antony Gibbs & Sons), W. M. Campbell (a director of the Bank of England), H. Gilliat (of J. K. Gilliat & Co.), C. Hambro (brother of the head of C. J. Hambro & Son), and Lord Kinnaird (partner in Ransom, Bouverie & Co., which merged into Barclay, Bevans & Co.). See *Investors' Review*, London, 3 (March 1894): 129–141. All these men and their firms were highly knowledgeable about American investments, especially U.S. railroads.

58. Based on George Glasgow, *The Scottish Investment Trust Companies* (London: Eyre & Spottiswoode, 1932), passim and his *English Investment Trust*, passim: Burton and Corner, *Investment and Unit Trusts*, 43; and references in this chapter, note 37.

59. Gilbert, *A History*, 30.

60. Jackson, *Enterprising Scot*, 251. Fleming's original company (1873) was the Scottish American Investment Trust. In 1879 three successors were formed, the First, Second, and Third Scottish American Trust Companies. All three were under the same management. See ibid., 21–23, and Gilbert, *A History*, 13–27. See also *Stock Exchange Official Intelligence for 1914*, 1112, 1129, 1132.

61. See Chapter 6.

62. Scott and Hughes, *The Anatomy*, 74, and Glasgow, *The English Investment Trust*, 70–71.

63. According to Burton and Corner, *Investment and Unit Trusts*, 42.

64. According to Gilbert, *A History*, 30, and Jackson, *Enterprising Scot*, 71.

65. Scott and Hughes, *The Anatomy*, 74.

66. Swaine, *Cravath Firm*, I, 372, suggests that Fleming may have had a London address as early as 1885. There is no biography of Fleming. Adler, *British Investment*, passim, has substantial data on Fleming and American railroad securities. On the continuing Fleming role, see Securities and Exchange Commission, *Investment Trusts in Great Britain*, 18, 22. Chapman, *The Rise of Merchant Banking*, 99, has looked at Fleming's "syndicate books," 1900–1912. They show him to be heavily involved in American railroads, public utilities, and industrials. Of the 445 accounts, only 8 appeared to be for British companies, with most of the remainder for U.S. enterprises.

67. Not to be confused with Fleming's Scottish American Investment Trust.

68. Weir, *Scottish American Investment Company*, 10, 18.

69. The Alliance Trust Company, Ltd., Dundee, was organized in 1888. See Kerr, *Scottish Capital*, 166ff.

70. Jackson, *Enterprising Scot*, 62 (in 1881). Most of the office buildings in Kansas City and Portland were sold at a profit in 1886. See ibid., 66.

71. For added details on these men, see Gilbert, *A History*, 34, passim; Jackson, *Enterprising Scot*, 13ff.; and Weir, *The Scottish American Investment Company*, 3 (esp. good biographical data on William J. Menzies). See Kerr, *Scottish Capital*, 168–171, on Mackenzie.

72. Jackson, *Enterprising Scot*, 69, 71.

73. Weir, *The Scottish American Investment Company*, 7, 15, and Kerr, *Scottish Capital*, 62. See also Chapter 13, note 200, on Sir George Warrender.

74. Weir, *The Scottish American Investment Company*, 8, 15.

75. William J. Menzies, *America as a Field for Investment* (Edinburgh: William Blackwood, 1892), 19.

76. Gene M. Gressley, *Bankers and Cattlemen* (New York: Alfred A. Knopf, 1966), 192–205, and Gene M. Gressley, "Brokers to the British: Francis Smith & Co.," *Southwestern Historical Quarterly*, 71 (July 1967): 7–25. The Northern Counties Investment Trust Company, Ltd., established in 1889, was headquartered in Bradford, England. See *Stock Exchange Official Intelligence for 1914*, 1059. The Dundee company was a predecessor of the Alliance Trust Company.

77. Gilbert, *A History*, 18, and Kerr, *Scottish Capital*, 29.

78. On cattle ranches, see Chapter 9.

79. These investments are particularly well documented in *Investors' Review*, 1892ff. When the American Trust Company, Ltd., Edinburgh (started in 1899), began to invest in American Beet Sugar, American Steel Wire, American Cotton Oil, and Federal Steel, there was bitter disagreement among the directors over the investments in these industrials (Jackson, *Enterprising Scot*, 261). In the early twentieth century, however, the trusts did invest in major U.S. industrials. The British Investment Trust, Ltd., started in 1889 in Edinburgh by Robert Fleming and John Guild, had, for example, in 1913 £2.5 million invested in U.S. securities, of which £1 million was in industrials (ibid., 56, 269). In the late 1880s and 1890s the English trusts often owned shares of British-incorporated U.S. industrials. The early 1900s investments in U.S. industrials were mainly in U.S.-incorporated ones. Edelstein, *Overseas Investment*, 60, notes that in the late 1880s British investment trusts first became involved in underwriting industrial securities; some were "industrials" with U.S. plants.

80. Data on the portfolio of United States Investment Trust and Guarantee Corporation, Ltd., in 1890–91, in the Stillman Papers, shows that the bulk of its investments were not in railroad securities. This was, likewise, not the case with many of the trust companies discussed in *Investors' Review*, 1892ff. So too by 1914 the very prudent Alliance Trust Company, Ltd., Dundee, still had over 50 percent of its U.S. portfolio in mortgages (see next section of this chapter); in this regard it appears to have been exceptional.

81. Others, for example, with sizable U.S. investments in 1914 included American Trust Company, Ltd. (Edinburgh); British Investment Trust, Ltd. (Edinburgh); First Scottish American Trust Company, Ltd. (Dundee); Foreign, American and General Investment Trust Company, Ltd. (London); International Financial Society, Ltd. (London); International Investment Trust, Ltd. (London); Investment Trust Corporation, Ltd. (London); London Scottish American Trust, Ltd. (London); Mercantile Investment and General Trust, Ltd. (Bradford); Scottish American Investment Company

(Edinburgh); Scottish Investment Trust Company, Ltd. (Edinburgh); Second Scottish American Trust Company, Ltd. (Dundee); Second Scottish Edinburgh Trust, Ltd. (Edinburgh); Second Scottish Investment Trust Company, Ltd. (Edinburgh); Third Edinburgh Investment Trust, Ltd. (Edinburgh); Trustees, Executors and Securities Insurance Corporation, Ltd. (London); United States and South American Investment Trust Company, Ltd. (London); United States Debenture Corporation, Ltd. (London); United States Investment Corporation, Ltd. (Edinburgh); and United States Trust Corporation, Ltd. (London).

82. Robert M. Kindersley, "A New Study of British Foreign Investments" (1929), 10, reprinted in *British Overseas Investments, 1907–1948*, ed. Mira Wilkins (New York: Arno Press, 1977).

83. Madden, *British Investment*, 75.

84. William J. Kerr, "Scottish Investment" in *Studies in Scottish Business History*, ed. P. L. Payne (London: Frank Cass, 1967), 370; Kerr, *Scottish Capital*, passim; Michie, "Crisis and Opportunity," 137–139; and Jackson, *Enterprising Scot*, passim. Although Kerr and Jackson referred specifically to the Scottish enterprises, this was also true of the English ones. See Adams, *Niagara Power*, I, 297.

85. Technically, when the British financial intermediary (Bfi) invested in a London company (which in turn invested in the United States), this should be viewed as a domestic investment by the Bfi to avoid double counting. If it invested in U.S. securities, irrespective of whether they were acquired in London or in New York, these were investments in America.

86. Given all these comments, one should expect an estimate of the size of investments by investment trust companies in America. Alas, I do not have adequate data to prepare such an estimate.

87. The United States Trust and Guarantee Corporation, Ltd., had investments in the Scottish American Mortgage Company, Ltd., for example. See James Stillman to Archibald Balfour, Feb. 24, 1891, Stillman Papers. As noted, it also invested in the Lombard Investment Company.

88. Lavington, *The English Capital Market*, 119.

89. John A. James, *Money and Capital Markets in Postbellum America* (Princeton, N.J.: Princeton University Press, 1978), 237. To be sure, many national banks made such loans anyway. See Richard H. Keehn and Gene Smiley, "Mortgage Lending by National Banks," *Business History Review*, 51 (Winter 1977): 474–491.

90. On the American trust companies, see this chapter, note 30, and Wright, *Farm Mortgage Financing*, passim, on the U.S. mortgage companies.

91. In this chapter I am going to discuss "the typical" path of the British investor in providing mortgage monies. Quite atypical was the Oregon and Washington Mortgage Savings Bank (capital, £60,000), located in Portland, Oregon, and established in 1876 by William Reid, who migrated to Oregon, and by "several Scottish capitalists." It was the first savings bank of deposit in Oregon and used both Oregon and Scottish monies to invest in real estate mortgages. By 1881 this bank had $3,700,000 in loans outstanding. See H. K. Hines, *An Illustrated History of the State of Oregon* (Chicago: Lewis, 1893), 310, and Jackson, *Enterprising Scot*, 28. In 1882 it was put by the Scots involved (the William Mackenzie group) under the same management as Dundee Mortgage—in Oregon and Dundee (Gilbert, *A History*, 47). Another "bank" was the Land Mortgage Bank of Texas, Ltd., registered in Britain in 1886. Large and successful, it engaged in mortgage lending on land (it was finally liquidated in 1922). See Lewis, *America's Stake*, 86, 563, 574, and Kerr, *Scottish Capital*, 194. It was headquartered in Bradford, England—and its shares were quoted on the Bradford and Leeds exchanges. It had a capital of £1 million. See *Stock Exchange Official Intelligence for 1914*, 405. Despite its designation as a "bank,"

it appears to have functioned as an investment company. I have no evidence that it took deposits in Texas.

92. Three of the major U.S. mortgage companies—the Lombard Investment Company, the Jarvis-Conklin Mortgage Trust Company, and the Equitable Mortgage Company—were located in Kansas City (Wright, *Farm Mortgage Financing*, 321). They attracted East Coast as well as foreign investment. The best recent work on British interests in farm mortgages is in a series of articles by Larry A. McFarlane. See his "British Investment in Midwestern Farm Mortgages and Land, 1875–1900: A Comparison of Iowa and Kansas," *Agricultural History*, 47 (Jan. 1974): 179–198; his "British Agricultural Investment in the Dakotas, 1877–1953," *Business and Economic History*, 2nd ser., 5 (1976): 112–126; and his "British Investment and the Land: Nebraska, 1877–1946," *Business History Review*, 57 (Summer 1983): 258–272. McFarlane divides British mortgage lending into three categories: (1) through Scottish firms, (2) through English ones, and (3) through American enterprises.

93. Compare Glasgow, *The Scottish Investment Trust*, with his *English Investment Trust* to see the "mortgage thrust" of the Scottish enterprises. Kerr, *Scottish Capital*, 198, says that "much of" the investment trust funds of Scottish firms in the United States went into farm mortgages. Many Scottish trusts were at origin mortgage companies. For the close associations between the Scottish investment trusts and mortgage companies, Kerr, *Scottish Capital*, passim, and Jackson, *Enterprising Scot,*, passim, are excellent. This was especially true of the Mackenzie group of companies.

94. On the Lombard Investment Company, see Wright, *Farm Mortgage Financing*, 315, 318–322. It began in Iowa. In 1882 it was organized in Boston and in Kansas City, Missouri. It moved its headquarters to Kansas City in 1885. In the "heyday of his glory," James L. Lombard was selling securities in several European countries. As noted earlier the United States Trust and Guarantee Corporation, Ltd., London, was in 1893 the largest shareholder in the Lombard Investment Company. On the J. B. Watkins Land Mortgage Company, see Allan G. Bogue, *Money at Interest: The Farm Mortgage on the Middle Border* (Ithaca, N.Y.: Cornell University Press, 1955). An analysis of 1,800 investors on a register of the late 1880s of J. B. Watkins Land Mortgage Company revealed that some 28 percent of the investors resided in Great Britain and Ireland, with Englishmen the overwhelming majority in this group (ibid., 134, 136). On Jarvis-Conklin Mortgage Trust Company, see Phelps *Foreign Expansion of American Banks*, 133. On Equitable Mortgage Company, see McFarlane, "British Investment—Iowa and Kansas," 196, 198, who writes that in 1888 this firm opened a chain of seventy-seven investment offices in Britain and by 1892 had sold $3,637,500 in mortgage bonds to foreign capitalists.

95. For example, see *Burdett's Official Intelligence.*

96. On loans on urban real estate, for example, see Jackson, *Enterprising Scot*, 16 (San Francisco), 17–18 (Chicago), 31 (Kansas City). McFarlane to Wilkins, Jan. 23, 1984, indicates that he is planning to write an article on British investments in urban real estate and urban lending. The largest "British" investment in urban real estate took place when William Waldorf Astor changed his residence to Great Britain in the 1890s and his New York real estate became "British" investments; although much of this was owned property, I assume some of it involved mortgage lending. See Chapter 5.

In 1897 the American lawyer W. D. Guthrie, whose New York firm (Seward, Guthrie & Steele) had been handling the business of a number of European investors in the United States, asked himself: "Why . . . should the Seward firm be turning all the mortgage trustee, stock transfer agent and register business—not to mention business in connection with funds sent by foreign clients for investment in the United States—over to unrelated trust companies? Why should not the Seward partners have a trust company of their own?" Thus in January 1897 Guthrie organized the Standard Finance & Trust Company (capital, $100,000), with control held by the partners. He believed that "there is a very large field here for investment of foreign capital secured by mortgages upon city property," in New York and Chicago primarily. The new firm proved successful, and in 1898 Guthrie organized the Standard Trust Company of New York, with a capital of $500,000. Guthrie's law firm did substantial business with the British promoter H. Osborne O'Hagan, and because O'Hagan would be directing business to the new company, he was offered $50,000 of the shares (or a 10 percent interest) and was made a director of Standard Trust Company. The venture was a great success; in 1912 Standard Trust Company was merged into Guaranty Trust Company of New York (Swaine, *Cravath Firm*, I, 591–594). The published literature has far more discussion on foreign farmland ownership and agricultural credit (because of the populist opposition) than on urban real estate and real estate mortgages. I believe foreign investments in farmland mortgages were far in excess of those in urban real estate. Lending on urban real estate, however, did exist and seems to have been on office buildings, hotels, and town lots but not on housing per se. I have found nothing to indicate that foreign investors were involved (except in rare instances) in mortgages for urban one-family residences. In large urban areas, foreign investors may have participated in some financing of multifamily residential properties (apartment houses).

97. McFarlane makes this point in his "British Investment—Iowa and Kansas," 184–185, as do Jackson and Kerr. Jackson, *Enterprising Scot*, 19, reports that Illinois by 1879 was no longer a satisfactory field for foreign farm mortgage investments, because interest rates had dropped to 6 percent. He writes that Scottish investors looked to Iowa and southern Minnesota, where 8 percent rates were possible. Kerr, *Scottish Capital*, 192, noted that in 1891 when Kansas passed legislation that provided for "surveillance" of foreign mortgage companies' activities, it was "pretty much of an academic exercise. By the late 1880s and early 1890s, British and Scottish companies had long since turned their investment sights toward Texas and the South." British investors moved from midwestern to southeastern, southwestern, and Pacific Coast locations. Within regions, however, there also were differences. In the north central states, for example, the Dakotas had for many years the highest rates.

98. John Davis, "Alien Landlordism in America," in *The Land Question from Various Points of View*, ed. C. F. Taylor (Philadelphia: C. F. Taylor, [1898]), 56.

99. This *direct* lending was in contrast to the behavior of companies that invested in other ones, which in turn made the loans. Aside from the Scottish investment trust companies already mentioned (which held mortgages), these men were associated with the Dundee Mortgage and Trust Investment Company, Ltd. (Mackenzie and Fleming)—a predecessor of the Alliance Trust Company, Ltd.—and the Arizona Trust and Mortgage Company, Ltd. (William J. Menzies). Dundee Mortgage and Trust Investment Company was active in Muscatine, Iowa, because William Mackenzie's brother George settled there, forming the Muscatine Mortgage Company and the Muscatine Mortgage and Trust Company in 1882 and 1883 (Kerr, *Scottish Capital*, 182). Mackenzie's Oregon and Washington Trust Investment Company was formed in 1873 to invest in land mortgages (Gilbert, *A History*, 33). It merged with Dundee Mortgage and Trust Investment Company, Ltd., in 1879 (ibid., 43). The latter and the Dundee Investment Company, Ltd. (another of Mackenzie's companies and the successor to the Dundee Land Investment Company, Ltd.), merged in 1889 into the new Alliance Trust, formed in April 1888 (ibid., 56–57, 64). The Alliance Trust, as noted, was at origin a mortgage-granting company.

100. The very successful Scottish American Mortgage Company, Ltd., was formed in 1874. See Jackson, *Enterprising Scot*, 17–19, 36–37; Kerr, *Scottish Capital*, 98ff.; and

Chapter 4. See also Stillman to Archibald Balfour, March 19, 1891, Stillman Papers (describing it as "well managed").

101. Jackson, *Enterprising Scot*, 41–42, and Scott and Hughes, *The Anatomy*, 26–27. This had nothing to do with the United States Mortgage Company, established in New York in 1871; at least I have been unable to establish a connection.

102. Scott and Hughes, *The Anatomy*, 25, and Jackson, *Enterprising Scot,*, 42. American Mortgage made loans in Missouri, Iowa, the Dakotas, Oregon, Washington, Georgia, Alabama, and Mississippi (ibid., 19). On the Edinburgh American Land Mortgage Company, Ltd., see ibid., 19–21. On the Oregon Mortgage Company, see Hines, *An Illustrated History of the State of Oregon*, 310.

103. Glasgow, *The Scottish Investment Trust*, 96, and Kerr, *Scottish Capital*, 63. Guild, born in 1820, had begun his career as a merchant; he was involved in shipping. He became "intimately associated" with Fleming and Mackenzie, although their senior by more than twenty-five years. Guild served as chairman of the Scottish American Investment Trusts (the so-called Fleming companies) and also as chairman of the Dundee Mortgage and Trust Investment Company and later chairman of the Alliance Trust (the Mackenzie companies). See ibid. and Jackson, *Enterprising Scot*, 56–57, 67, 69. Published sources have far less on him than on his younger associates. Kerr, however, called Guild an "Olympian figure in the investment-trust world, as much a founding father as Robert Fleming and probably as knowledgeable on American securities" (*Scottish Capital*, 63).

104. Powell, *Evolution of the Money Market*, 473. This firm appears to have been founded in the 1880s. McFarlane, "British Investment—Iowa and Kansas," 43n, found its surviving records too vague to obtain estimates of its actual lending. It last appeared in the *Stock Exchange Official Intelligence* in 1903.

105. McFarlane, "British Investment—Iowa and Kansas," 191, and his "British Investment—Nebraska," 266. It was associated with the Lombard Investment Company.

106. McFarlane, "British Investment—Nebraska," 261; "British Investment—Iowa and Kansas," 198; and "British Investment—Dakotas," 115, list English firms participating in U.S. mortgage lending. A number of these companies had headquarters outside London: in Hull, Liverpool, Manchester, and Norwich, for instance. In Nebraska, Iowa, Kansas, and the Dakotas, McFarlane's data suggests that in 1890 English lending was in excess of Scottish lending.

107. Kerr, *Scottish Capital*, 55. What follows is based to a large extent on his description of Scottish company behavior, particularly in Texas.

108. In the Dakota territories in the early 1880s, interest rates were particularly high; the farmer paid 12 to 18 percent for mortgage monies. Mortgage companies appeared everywhere—"with active agents in all towns. These largely handled English monies," paying 10 percent to the foreign investor, with the difference going to the American agents. See John Jay Knox, *History of Banking in the United States* (1903; rpt. New York: Augustus Kelley, 1969), 801.

109. Kerr, *Scottish Capital*, 9, 56, 70, 111.

110. Ibid., 111.

111. Ibid., 70.

112. The investors could buy either the debentures that had fixed income or the shares in the trusts or mortgage companies that issued dividends based on profits. The choice depended on the individual investor's attitude toward risk.

113. Barry Eichengreen, "Mortgage Interest Rates in the Populist Era," *American Economic Review*, 74 (Dec. 1984): 997, attributed the first debentures based on mortgages to the Iowa Loan and Trust Company, 1881. The Scots in the 1870s were already

following this practice for American mortgages and were the true innovators. Likewise, the U.S. Mortgage Company in the 1870s also issued debentures against mortgages. The Iowa Loan and Trust Company never claimed to be the innovator. See Howard H. Preston, *History of Banking in Iowa* (1922; rpt. New York: Arno Press, 1980), 278–279 (on "debenture companies" and farm mortgages).

114. Glasgow, *The Scottish Investment Trust*, 11. The Scottish firms also issued "debenture stocks" (ibid., 11–12).

115. To repeat, some Scottish "investment trusts"—the Oregon and Washington Trust Investment Company (formed in 1873) is a case in point—were actually land mortgage companies. See this chapter, notes 93 and 99.

116. Kerr, *Scottish Capital*, 201. The Scottish firms controlled the lending activities.

117. Ibid., 197.

118. Kerr in ibid. notes the general neglect of "provincial markets" when scholars have dealt with British foreign investment.

119. McFarlane, "British Investment—Iowa and Kansas," 192. With the exception of Close Brothers, the English mortgage companies that he includes on his roster had their origins in the 1880s or later; and Close Brothers probably did not get into mortgage lending until the 1880s. See Jacob van der Zee, *The British in Iowa* (Iowa City: State Historical Society of Iowa, 1922). Scots in Dundee had become familiar with American land mortgages in the 1860s, and as early as 1873, with the Oregon and Washington Trust Investment Company, the Scots were already making direct investments in providing land mortgages on the Pacific Coast. See Chapter 4. See also McFarlane, "British Investment—Dakotas," 118–119, on diversified investments. The generalization on the extent of the Scottish head start needs qualification: Balfour, Williamson, Liverpool, through its California house, was making farm mortgages in the West at least by 1878 and probably earlier—see text of this chapter; it was not engaged in midwestern lending and, as will be evident, followed the Scottish "model."

120. In *some* instances, however, certain individuals appear to have been involved in both English investment trust companies and mortgage companies, so here too there were interlocking relationships.

121. See Kerr, *Scottish Capital*, and Jackson, *Enterprising Scot*.

122. Kerr, *Scottish Capital*, 57–58.

123. McFarlane, "British Investment—Dakotas," 120.

124. Francis Smith, for example, acted on behalf of both English and Scottish firms in Texas. The Georgia Loan and Trust Company in Americus, Georgia, was an agent for English and Scottish companies in Georgia, Alabama, Tennessee, and Florida. So too in Arkansas the same local agent represented Scottish and English mortgage lenders (Kerr, *Scottish Capital*, 163).

125. On the cattle companies, see Chapter 9.

126. Remember, however, that all the capital was not necessarily issued, subscribed, or called from the investors.

127. J. Evetts Haley, *Charles Goodnight* (Norman: University of Oklahoma Press, 1936), 344–345, and Kerr, *Scottish Capital*, 50–87.

128. McFarlane, "British Investment—Iowa and Kansas," 188–189, and "British Investment—Nebraska," 265, 266.

129. Kerr, *Scottish Capital*, 173, and Herbert O. Brayer, *William Blackmore* (Denver: Bradford Robinson, 1949), II, 211, 256, 261.

130. Jackson, *Enterprising Scot*, 62–63, 67. Brayer, *William Blackmore*, II, 211, described the firm (in 1877) as engaged in land speculation in Colorado. The Colorado Mortgage and Investment Company of London, Ltd., was organized in 1877. In the early 1880s it built the High Line irrigation canal in Colorado—an eighty-three-mile-long irrigation

ditch—at the cost of $640,000. It lent money on mortgages and had subsidiary companies involved in Denver real estate (it built the Windsor Hotel) and in brick manufacturing. See Clements, "British-Controlled Enterprise in the West between 1870 and 1900," *Agricultural History*, 27 (Oct. 1953): 137–141. Clearly the irrigation project was part of "land development." Irrigated land commanded higher prices and would attract settlers (and provide returns for the mortgage business). It was unsuccessful and was last listed in *Burdett's Official Intelligence* in 1898. In 1893 another company, the Colorado Mortgage and Investment Company, Ltd., was formed in London. It paid a 5 percent dividend its first year and then never again! See *Stock Exchange Official Intelligence for 1914*, 1008. In 1897, of the 3,000 shares outstanding in the Windsor Hotel Company, Ltd., the Colorado Mortgage and Investment Company, Ltd., owned 1,200 and James W. Barclay owned 657. See WRCIS, reel 64.

131. See Chapter 9.

132. Joseph Canon Bailey, *Seaman A. Knapp* (New York: Columbia University Press, 1945), 123–124. The venture, however, became a losing proposition when the bounties granted to domestic sugar growers (under the 1890 McKinley Act) were removed in 1894.

133. Jackson, *Enterprising Scot*, 133, and *Stock Exchange Official Intelligence for 1914*, 1098.

134. This is a reference to Mackenzie's Dundee Mortgage and Trust Investment Company, Ltd. See Gilbert, *A History*, 40.

135. Wallis Hunt, *Heirs of Great Adventure*, 2 vols (London: Balfour Williamson, 1951, 1960), I, 95, 147–148; II, 25; and Morton Rothstein, "A British Firm on the American West Coast," *Business History Review*, 37 (Winter 1963): 403–404.

136. Hunt, *Heirs of Great Adventure*, I, 148.

137. Hines, *History of Oregon*, 310. The Hines book was published in 1893, and its biographical data on Reid go beyond 1885; there is, however, a suggestion that Reid broke with his Scottish backers in 1885—over a complicated matter related to railroads (ibid., 311).

138. Kerr, *Scottish Capital*, 189.

139. For 1890, McFarlane estimated the farm mortgage loans of two Scottish and seven English firms in Kansas to be $2.7 million (with another $2 million invested through U.S. firms), and those of four Scottish and three English firms in Iowa, $1.2 million (with another $0.7 million invested through U.S. firms). For Nebraska, he found that three Scottish firms had outstanding $0.4 million in loans, while nine English firms had $2 million outstanding (another $1 million went through American intermediaries). See McFarlane, "British Investment—Iowa and Kansas," 197–198, and his "British Investment—Nebraska," 266. For the same year, three Scottish and eleven English firms had $2.7 million outstanding in mortgages in South Dakota (with another $1.6 million through U.S. firms), and two Scottish and six English companies had $1.3 million in North Dakota (with another $0.9 million through U.S. firms). See McFarlane, "British Investment—Dakotas," 115–116. McFarlane's figures are all "minimums." In sum, as of 1890 he was able to estimate approximately $16.5 million in British mortgage loans outstanding in Kansas, Iowa, Nebraska, and the Dakotas.

140. Putting together the Oregon data and Kerr's and McFarlane's figures; recognizing that the Oregon material is for 1885 (not 1889 or 1890) and involves "flow" not stock (that is, loans made, not loans outstanding); and accepting that Kerr's and McFarlane's figures are low and omit some foreign mortgage loans in the covered areas and do not include many other sections of the United States where lending took place, we are still far from Congressman Davis' $3 billion figure. We can also compare Davis' 50 percent of U.S. mortgages figure with percentage estimates by McFarlane, "British

Investment—Nebraska," 271, who calculated that foreign capital in 1890 financed about 4 percent of the farm loans in *Nebraska* and *Minnesota*, almost 10 percent in *North Dakota*, and 14.5 percent in *South Dakota*. McFarlane thought that by 1890—with lower interest rates in *Iowa* and *Kansas* and very adverse antiforeign sentiment in Kansas—the figures for those two states were a mere 1 and 2 percent. I find the 2 percent figure for Kansas extraordinarily low, considering the opposition that arose there. In his "British Investment—Iowa and Kansas," 196–197, McFarlane stated that 1 and 2 percent for Iowa and Kansas, respectively, were "preliminary 'lower limit' " estimates. McFarlane provides no figures for southern or far-western states, but if his estimates are anywhere near the mark (and I suspect they are in most instances quite accurate), Davis' numbers are far too high.

141. George K. Holmes, "A Decade of Mortgages," *Annals of the American Academy of Political and Social Science*, 4 (1894): 904–918. Holmes deals with domestic mortgage lending. He does not deal with the foreign investor.

142. Kerr, *Scottish Capital*, 193, argues that "the British mortgage companies increased competition on the frontiers of American credit and so drove rates down." When in the late 1870s interest rates in Kansas had fallen, the American J. B. Watkins, who was providing mortgages there, "followed a policy of dropping the rate first on [mortgage-backed] securities intended for England, where the long-term interest rate was lower than the long-term rate in eastern America" (Bogue, *Money at Interest*, 117). This seems to mean that Watkins could continue offering mortgages at the lower rates—as a consequence of his having access to the cheaper money.

143. The quotation is from Jackson, *Enterprising Scot*, 245 (my italics). See also Bogue, *Money at Interest*, 189ff., and Wright, *Farm Mortgage Financing*, 321–323.

144. The Colonial and United States Mortgage Company, Hull, was forced to make capital calls on its shares (Jackson, *Enterprising Scot*, 254). It did not, however, go under. See McFarlane, "British Investment—Iowa and Kansas," 190; McFarlane, "British Investment—Dakotas," 115; and *Stock Exchange Official Intelligence for 1914*, 1007. The Anglo-American Land Mortgage and Agency Company, associated with the Lombard Investment Company, was unable to pay the principal on its maturing debentures. It went into receivership in November 1894 (Jackson, *Enterprising Scot*, 254, and *Investors' Review*, 4 [Dec. 1894]: 370). It apparently revived, and in 1905 its name was changed to Anglo-American Assets Company. A spectacular case of success and failure was the Yorkshire Investment and American Mortgage Company, Ltd., formed in 1886, with head offices in Bradford, England. Its U.S. agent was the Jarvis-Conklin Mortgage Trust Company, Kansas City. By the fall of 1891, it had £558,284 invested in the United States ($2.7 million), and that year it paid two dividends, each of 10 percent. By 1897, however, this company could no longer remain in business "by reason of its liabilities," and it began winding up its affairs. See data in WRCIS, reel 55.

145. Jackson, *Enterprising Scot*, 254–255. Jackson mentions Equitable Mortgage Company, the Jarvis-Conklin Mortgage Trust, and the Lombard Investment Company. The fourth was the J. B. Watkins Land Mortgage Company.

146. Palgrave, "An English View of Investments," 197–198. This is the same article that I quoted earlier in praise of "the investment trusts." It clearly demonstrates that in the Englishman's mind, the English "investment trust" with its interests in railroad bonds and other securities was not identified with mortgages on land.

147. Kerr, *Scottish Capital*, 9.

148. Williamson, *Late Nineteenth-Century*, 98. He refers only to the Midwest, but it was true of the West and South as well. McFarlane, "British Investment—Nebraska," 260, notes the drop in the costs of mortgage credit in Nebraska, where "average interest rates" were as much as 12 percent in the 1870s, 8.7 percent in 1880, and 8.4

percent in 1890, and had dropped to 5.7 percent in 1900. While rates fell, there continued to be sharp regional differences. Whereas in Boston in 1893–1897, for example, the "average weekly discount rate" was 3.8 percent, in Birmingham, Alabama, and Houston, Texas, it was 8 percent, and in Denver, 10 percent (James, *Money and Capital Markets*, 10). The differences had been even greater in the 1880s (ibid., 14). "Discount rates" and "mortgage rates" were obviously different, but the differentials were comparable. It was in the South and the West that the Scottish mortgage companies found their best opportunity. Nonetheless, lower rates did mean fewer good mortgage possibilities.

149. Nathaniel T. Bacon, "American International Indebtedness," *Yale Review*, 9 (Nov. 1900): 268–269. On the fate of the Lombard Investment Company, see New York State, Superintendent of Banking, *Annual Report Relative to Foreign Mortgage, Loan, Investment, and Trust Companies, 1891–1893* ("Foreign" in this source's title meant out of state; no out-of-country companies were included in these reports), and Wright, *Farm Mortgage Financing*, 315, 318–32, for more details on the Lombard Investment Company.

150. Kerr, *Scottish Capital*, 162, noted that the Scottish American Mortgage Company in the 1890s continued strong in its Texas and southern lending. It was making loans in Texas, Georgia, Alabama, Florida, Mississippi, Arkansas, and Tennessee, as well as in Washington, Minnesota, South Dakota, and Illinois. By 1890 the South (including Texas) accounted for 65 percent of its loans. Its new agency in Washington was just starting, but aside from Minnesota, "the north-central states [had] lost importance for the company" (ibid., 162–165).

151. Writing in 1923, Ivan Wright stated, "Strange as it may seem to the people of the United States, the European investors consider the American farm mortgage a good security upon which to loan money" (*Farm Mortgage Financing*, 172). Likewise, as noted earlier, Lavington, *English Capital Market* (1921) wrote of trusts and finance companies and of their investments in "real estate in the United States." The *Stock Exchange Official Intelligence for 1914* lists a large number of British mortgage companies engaged in business in the United States.

152. Hunt, *Heirs of Great Adventure*, I, 187; II, 25, 27.

153. Kerr, *Scottish Capital*, 108.

154. Glasgow, *The Scottish Investment Trust*, 54; at $4.86, that is roughly $9.6 million.

155. Jackson, *Enterprising Scot*, 258, provides an 1895 list of sixteen Dundee and Edinburgh mortgage companies with U.S. investments. He gives their capital and debentures. The three largest (and their capital and debentures in 1895) were the Alliance Trust Company, Ltd., Dundee (£1,500,000; £2,070,000); the new Investors' Mortgage Security Company, Ltd., Edinburgh (£1,000,000; £786,726); and the Scottish American Mortgage Company, Edinburgh (£1,274,672; £552,947). Davis, "Alien Landlordism," 54–68, indicates that in 1898 the issue of foreign mortgages in the Midwest was still very much alive. See also McFarlane's work on the north central states.

156. Gilbert, *A History*, 7 (on difficulties in 1893), 10 (on size of the Alliance Trust), 95 (on mortgage percentages), and Jackson, *Enterprising Scot*, 282 (on size of investments in mortgages).

157. The figures are from Glasgow, *The Scottish Investment Trust*, 96. Glasgow says that the company specialized in American mortgages. See also Jackson, *Enterprising Scot*, 249–250, 272, which indicates that the company invested throughout the West and South and into Canada.

158. Cleona Lewis, *America's Stake in International Investments* (Washington, D.C.: Brookings Institution, 1938), 87n.

159. Kerr, *Scottish Capital*, 189.

160. This is my interpretation. Kerr felt the rise was important.

161. In addition to the firms mentioned, in 1913–14 numerous other Scottish mortgage companies remained in the U.S. market. For example, the Edinburgh American Land Mortgage Co., Ltd. (1878); the Western and Hawaiian Investment Co., Ltd., Dundee (1883); the Oregon Mortgage Co., Ltd., Edinburgh (1883); the United States Mortgage Co. of Scotland, Ltd., Edinburgh (1884); the United States Investment Corp., Ltd., Edinburgh (1890); the Edinburgh North-American Investment Co., Ltd. (1892); the American Mortgage Co. of Scotland, Ltd., Edinburgh (1906); and Western Ranches and Investment Co., Ltd., Edinburgh (1910). The date of formation is in parentheses. In 1909 the Oregon Mortgage Co., Ltd., had $2.8 million in loans in Washington, Oregon, Montana, and Idaho. See Jackson, *Enterprising Scot*, 273 (on the Oregon Mortgage). There were also remaining English companies—for example, the British and American Mortgage Co., Ltd., London (1877); the American Freehold-Land Mortgage Co., Ltd., London (1879); the Colonial and United States Mortgage Co., Ltd., Hull (1880); the Canadian and American Mortgage and Trust Co., Ltd., Liverpool (1884); the London and North-West American Mortgage Co., Ltd., London (1886); the Trust and Mortgage Co. of Iowa, Ltd., London (1889); the Alliance Mortgage and Investment Co., Ltd., Manchester (1890); and the Mortgage and Debenture Co., Ltd., London (1897), which was a Close Brothers company. *Stock Exchange Official Intelligence for 1914* is useful on the English companies.

162. Jackson, *Enterprising Scot*, 266–271, esp. 268.

163. Hunt, *Heirs of Great Adventure*, II, 27.

164. Many of the Scottish mortgage companies would in time become transformed into "investment trusts" (Glasgow, *The Scottish Investment Trust*, passim). The word *craze* is from Wright, *Farm Mortgage Financing*, 323.

165. By 1909–1913, however, most of the still-surviving English companies with U.S. mortgages were paying regular dividends. The London and North-West American Mortgage Company, Ltd., which was realizing its assets consisting of mortgages and real estate in the United States, was exceptional. See *Stock Exchange Official Intelligence for 1914*, 980–1100.

166. This is suggested in the work of McFarlane and of Preston, *Banking in Iowa*, 278–279.

167. Jackson, *Enterprising Scot*, 163.

168. See Hines, *History of Oregon*, 310–311, for William Reid's move from mortgage lending to railroad investments. (In each case, he brought in Scottish investment.)

169. K. D. Bosch, *Nederlandse Beleggingen in de Verenigde Staten* (Amsterdam: Uitgeversmaatschappij Elsevier, 1948), 175–178, 351.

170. Edmond Baldy, *Les banques d'affaires en France depuis 1900* (Paris: Librairie Générale de Droit, 1922), 114, 166. See also Linton Wells, "House of Seligman," unpublished manuscript, 1931, New York State Historical Society, 472. Anne T. Ostrye, *Foreign Investment in the American and Canadian West, 1870–1914: An Annotated Bibliography* (Metuchen, N.J.: Scarecrow Press, 1986), 128 (item 573), indicates that data on the Société Financière Franco-Américaine (1905–1918) exist in the French National Archives.

171. Hans Bauer, *Swiss Bank Corporation* (Basle: Swiss Bank Corp., 1972), 161.

172. *Economist*, 48 (May 3, 1890): 557, and J. Riesser, *The German Great Banks* (1911; rpt. New York: Arno Press, 1977), 435. Otto Braunfels was associated with the Frankfurt banking house of Jacob S. H. Stern. See Fritz Seidenzahl, *100 Jahre Deutsche Bank* (Frankfurt: Deutsche Bank, 1970), 56; see also Thomas R. Kabisch, *Deutsches Kapital in den USA* (Stuttgart: Klett-Cotta, 1982), 75, 185–186, on D.A.T.G.

173. Riesser, *German Great Banks*, 478.

174. Ibid., 436. It carried on the second function of the original company, but its principal activity "became the examination of the accounts of stock companies and the undertaking of trustee operations and those of pledge holding."

175. Powell, *Evolution*, 478.

176. Above I noted the participation of Iselin & Co. in the S.F.F.A. Iselin & Co., New York, was of Swiss origins, and in the early 1870s, when the Schweizerischer Bankverein considered establishing a U.S. bank, it planned to involve Iselin & Co. See Bauer, *Swiss Bank Corporation*, 48. In 1914 A. Iselin & Co., New York, was listed as a correspondent of Lloyds Bank, London (information from J. M. L. Booker, archivist, Lloyds Bank).

177. Bauer, *Swiss Bank Corporation*, 161. The Dutch syndicate was not named; it could easily have been Vereenigde Amerikaansche Fondsen, since the Swiss bank had ties with the Boissevains, or perhaps it was the Syndicaat van Amerikaansche Industrieele Aandeelen.

178. I have not found any that were not associated with banks.

179. For example, Robert Fleming acted as "investment banker" and investment trust adviser; so did Robert Benson and J. S. Morgan. The Scottish American Investment Company, Ltd., had ties with John S. Kennedy, J. Tod Kennedy, and J. P. Morgan & Co., American "banking houses."

180. Based on Bosch, *Nederlands Beleggingen*, 441.

181. See the fine article by John Fahey, "When the Dutch Owned Spokane," *Pacific Northwest Quarterly*, 72 (Jan. 1981): 2–10. The State of Washington had alien property laws in force in the mid-1890s.

182. Swaine, *Cravath Firm*, I, 548, and Bacon, "American International Indebtedness," 270.

183. Alien Property Custodian, *Report, 1918–1919* (henceforth cited as *APC Report*).

184. Rondo Cameron, *France and the Economic Development of Europe, 1800–1914* (Princeton, N.J.: Princeton University Press, 1961), 131. Brewer, "Eastern Money and Western Mortgages in the 1870s," 362–372, gives details of United States Mortgage Company's activities in intermediating monies from Europe to the United States. The company had two boards of directors, one of which met in New York and the other in Paris.

185. Wright, *Farm Mortgage Financing*, 318. Brewer only discussed the firm in the 1870s but adds a footnote to the effect that in the mid-1890s it finally became aggressive and truly prosperous. According to Perine, *The Story of Trust Companies*, 202, the United States Mortgage Company first undertook a trust and deposit business in 1893 and changed its name to United States Mortgage and Trust Company in 1895.

186. M. Georges Aubert, *La finance américaine* (Paris: Ernest Flammarion, 1910), 167–168.

187. F. Cyril James, *The Growth of Chicago Banks* (New York: Harper & Bros., 1938), 1362.

188. Lewis, *America's Stake*, 86–87. Cleona Lewis in my view underestimated the number of British providers of mortgages but did not underestimate the total amount loaned. As noted, the loans tended to be relatively short term, three to five years, so that the same monies were turned over, and this served to reduce the amounts outstanding at any specified date. Cleona Lewis assumed that 1916–17 mortgage loans (figures that she discovered) by foreign investors were lower than in 1914. Bosch, *Nederlandse Beleggingen*, 441, shows that Lewis' assumption in relation to the Dutch mortgage bank loans was in error. Her Dutch estimates were, accordingly, inflated. Cleona Lewis' source was the *Commercial and Financial Chronicle*, April 1, 1916, 1207, and Sept. 15, 1917, 1046. In this chapter I have shown that five British firms had about

$35 million outstanding in U.S. mortgages in 1913–14. There were many other lenders, as indicated in this chapter, note 161; in Chapter 15 I show that British insurance companies provided monies for U.S. real estate loans. We must remember to include British investments in urban real estate mortgages, as well as in farmland. Thus, to increase the $35 roughly fivefold, add another $29.3 million for the Dutch mortgage bank investments, and about $3 million for other miscellaneous stakes does not seem unreasonable.

189. Hunt, *Heirs of Great Adventure*, I and II, passim. The quotation is from II, 27.

190. A. H. John, *A Liverpool Merchant House Being the History of Alfred Booth & Co., 1863–1958* (London: George Allen & Unwin, 1959), 24; Adler, *British Investment*, 147, 149, 187n; and Morton Rothstein, "Multinationals in the Grain Trade, 1850–1914," *Business and Economic History*, 2nd ser. 12 (1983): 87.

191. Antony Gibbs & Sons, Ltd., *Merchants and Bankers, 1808–1958* (London: Antony Gibbs, 1958), 33, 102, 36; Thomas C. Cochran, *The Pabst Brewing Co.* (New York: New York University Press, 1948), 155 (Pabst and Anheuser-Busch).

192. See Walther Däbritz, *Fünfzig Jahre Metallgesellschaft* (Frankfurt, 1931), 162, 292–298.

193. Mitsui & Co., *100 Year History*, 13, 31–32, 295, 34, 68–69, 50, 71, 77–78 (general); and Kazuo Yamaguchi et al., "100 Year History of Mitsui & Co.," unpublished 1978 manuscript in Japanese, I, 207 (San Francisco branch) and 357 (Southern Products). I am indebted to Professor Hiroaki Yamazaki, July 1984, for helping me with this Japanese-language volume. I obtained the employment data on Mitsui's U.S. business from the Japanese Business History Institute, Tokyo. Likewise, I have used the Mitsui & Co., *Semi-Annual Report, Nov. 1913–April 1914*, in Mitsui & Co. Archives, Tokyo. The annual report is in Japanese, and again Professor Yamazaki was very helpful. By way of comparison, Mitsui & Co. had forty-eight employees in its Shanghai branch, forty-one in Hong Kong, and eighteen in London.

194. The *1880 American Silk Goods Directory* lists K. Yamao, Agent of Mitsui & Co., Yokohama, with a New York address at 46 Murray St. Also listed in New York City as importers of raw silk were Nanishiro Adachi (same address); Oria Kai, Agent for Yamato Trading Company, Japan (51 Mercer St.); Sato & Arai, Agents of Shiro Tashiro, Yokohama (55 Walker St.); and O. Yamada and M. Fukui (58 Walker St.). The directory is printed in W. C. Wyckoff, *Silk Goods of America*, 2nd ed. (New York: Silk Association of America, 1880), 131. By 1882 Mitsui & Co. was no longer listed as the Mitsui & Co. history would lead us to expect. Oria Kai (a Japanese weaving association) remained as "Agent" for Yamato Trading Company, which now advertised its home office in Tokyo and branches in Yokohama, Japan; London, England; and Vladivostock, Russia. It had a "corresponding house" in Lyon, France. In 1882 R. Arai was listed as "N.Y. General Representative" of the Doshin Silk Company (Doshin Kaisha), Yokohama, which also had a branch office in Lyon. The 1882 directory and advertisements for these firms is in W. C. Wyckoff, *Silk Manufacture in the United States* (New York: n.p., 1883), 139, 145, 146. By 1887 all the Japanese names had disappeared except that of R. Arai, who was identified in the Silk Association Directory as Agent for Doshin Silk Company, Yokohama (W. C. Wyckoff, *American Silk Manufacture* [New York: Silk Association of America, 1887], 137). The "Arai" of Sato & Arai and R. Arai was the grandfather of Mrs. Haru Matsukata Reischauer, who, in her *Samurai and Silk* (Cambridge, Mass.: Harvard University Press, 1986), 190ff., tells of Rioichiro Arai as a silk importer and also of Momotaro Sato (who came to the United States in 1867, opened a small store in New York selling general merchandise, and then returned to Japan to recruit Japanese employees). In 1876 Arai had gone to America and in 1878 formed a partnership with Sato to handle raw silk imports. He then became a significant silk importer.

195. Nobuo Kawabe, "Japanese Business in the United States before World War II: The Case of Mitsubishi Shoji Kaisha, the San Francisco and Seattle Branches," Ph.D. diss., Ohio State University, 1980, 18. This dissertation has been published in Japanese.

196. Mitsui & Co., *100 Years*, 70.

197. Williams Haynes, *American Chemical Industry* (New York: D. Van Nostrand, 1954), II, 274. The context indicates that this was before World War I, although it is not explicitly stated.

198. Mitsui & Co., however, had lines of credit with European banks (Mitsui & Co., Semi-Annual Report, Nov. 1913–April 1914).

199. I have found D. H. Aldcroft, "The Mercantile Marine," in his edited volume *The Development of British Industry and Foreign Competition, 1875–1914* (London: Allen & Unwin, 1968), 326–363, particularly useful on British shipping.

200. On the growth of German shipping, see John G. B. Hutchins, *The American Maritime Industries and Public Policy, 1789–1914* (Cambridge, Mass.: Harvard University Press, 1941), 525. Henri Hauser, *Germany's Commercial Grip on the World* (New York: Scribner's Sons, 1918), 106–107, writes that in 1914 the North German Lloyd and Hamburg-American represented 40 percent of Germany's commercial merchant marine. The Hamburg-American, with its "sixty-eight lines," touched at all American ports. On the extraordinary expansion of the Hamburg-American under Ballin's leadership, see Bernhard Huldermann, *Albert Ballin* (London: Cassell, 1922), esp. 69–130. See also Ross J. S. Hoffman, *Great Britain and the German Trade Rivalry* (Philadelphia: University of Pennsylvania Press, 1933), 200–231.

201. *APC Report*, 126. The two German firms, through American subsidiaries, "owned" (the North German Lloyd had a 999-year lease) the piers. When the U.S. government took possession of these docks in 1918, it determined their value at $7.1 million, a sum that would eventually be paid to the Alien Property Custodian.

202. Hutchins, *American Maritime Industries*, 515. The Osaka Shōsen Kaisha also provided regular transpacific service, Hong Kong to Tacoma. For invaluable details on which lines serviced which routes, see U.S. House of Representatives, Committee on Merchant Marine and Fisheries, *Investigation of Shipping Combinations* (Washington, D.C., 1913), and U.S. House of Representatives, Committee on Merchant Marine and Fisheries, *Steamship Agreements and Affiliations in the American Foreign and Domestic Trade* (Washington, D.C., 1914). On the Japanese transpacific service, William D. Wray, *Mitsubishi and the N.Y.K., 1870–1914* (Cambridge, Mass.: Harvard University Press, 1984), 408–412, is useful, as is Keiichiro Nakagawa, "Japanese Shipping," in Tsunehiko Yui and Keiichiro Nakagawa, *Business History of Shipping* (Tokyo: University of Tokyo Press, 1985), 6–7. There was substantial Norwegian and Swedish shipping that called at American ports. There was the Scandanavian-American Line. There was also an important Italian line (Navigazione Generale Italiana) and a Brazilian one (Lloyd Brazileiro), for example. According to the New York agent of Lloyd Brazileiro, that line was owned by the Brazilian government (*Shipping Combinations*, 49).

203. See Chapters 3 and 16. The law was not well enforced, and it is possible that American subsidiaries of certain foreign shippers may have been involved in the coastwide trade.

204. Thomas R. Navin and Marian V. Sears, "A Study in Merger: Formation of the International Mercantile Marine Company," *Business History Review*, 28 (1954): 291–300. On Ellerman, see Taylor, *Ellermans*, 12, 41.

205. The best work on IMM is Navin and Sears, "A Study," 291–328. I have also used data from *Shipping Combinations*, esp. 573–602; N. S. B. Gras and Henrietta Larson, *Casebook in American Business History* (New York: Appleton-Century-Crofts, 1939), 566–596; Lewis Corey, *The House of Morgan* (New York: G. H. Watt, 1930),

304–307; and *Moody's*. On the White Star Line, see W. H. Bunting, *Portrait of a Port: Boston, 1852–1914* (Cambridge, Mass.: Harvard University Press, 1971), 426, and Gras and Larson, *Casebook*, 578; on Ellerman, Taylor, *Ellermans;* on the Dominion Line, N. R. P. Bonsor, *North Atlantic Seaway* (Prescot, Lancashire: T. Stephenson, 1955), 243–248. Bonsor is excellent on all the passenger lines. Vivian Vale, *The American Peril: Challenge to Britain on the North Atlantic, 1901–04* (Manchester: University Press, 1984), adds details on international shipping and the IMM.

206. See Huldermann, *Albert Ballin*, 55–57, and even better, Lamar Cecil, *Albert Ballin* (Princeton, N.J.: Princeton University Press, 1967), 49–57.

207. Navin and Sears, "A Study," 308, and Cecil, *Albert Ballin*, 53n.

208. For the alarm in Britain, see Mira Wilkins, *The Emergence of Multinational Enterprise* (Cambridge, Mass.: Harvard University Press, 1970), 70–71.

209. Francis W. Hirst, *Monopolies, Trusts, and Cartels* (London: Methuen, 1905), 140.

210. Gras and Larson, *American Business History*, 580–582. Initially the American planners had hoped for U.S. subsidies for an all-American shipping enterprise. When Congress failed to pass the subsidy bill, it was no longer important that this venture be all-American.

211. Hirst, *Monopolies*, 140.

212. Gras and Larson, *Casebook*, 583, and *Shipping Combinations*, 573–575.

213. It reemerged finally as U.S. Lines. In 1913 the American vice president of IMM, Philip A. S. Franklin, had told a U.S. congressional committee that "it is difficult to say where the actual ownership . . . of the I.M.M. Co. is; but the I.M.M. Co. is controlled here [in the United States]." Presumably this was because the voting trust's majority remained American. IMM bonds could be registered, but very few of them were, and Franklin reported that "you could not possibly tell where the bonds were held" (*Shipping Combinations*, 573–575). It is odd to think of IMM as "U.S. controlled" when its president was British and lived in London. IMM was listed on the Amsterdam exchange, so undoubtedly there were some Dutch portfolio investments (Bosch, *Nederlandse Beleggingen*, 347). Remember also that IMM had a 25 percent interest in the Holland-America Line.

214. Aldcroft, "The Mercantile Marine," 327; Hirst, *Monopolies*, 140; and P. N. Davies "British Shipping and World Trade," in *Business History of Shipping*, ed. Yui and Nakagawa, 78.

215. U.S. House of Representatives, Committee on the Merchant Marine and Fisheries, *Free Ship Bill Hearings*, 62nd Cong., 2nd sess., 1912, 371–372. In 1890 it had been 83.3 percent of imports and 90.6 percent of exports. For the British share, see Aldcroft, "Mercantile Marine," 329, 362–363.

216. The literature generally deals with "flags" rather than "ownership," but it seems clear that foreign ownership was preeminent. See this chapter, note 222.

217. The best discussion of the term *conference* is in *Shipping Combinations*, 1361. Conference lines were those that literally held conferences on schedules for sailings, rates, pooling, and rebates. However the word was used, it carried with it the idea of cooperation.

218. Ibid., 1360. This committee went so far as to claim that without the agreements, the weak would fall by the wayside and monopoly would have emerged!

219. *Steamship Agreements*, 415, and Hutchins, *American Maritime Industries*, 525–526. The earliest agreement discussed was the North Atlantic Steamship Lines Agreement, concluded in Hamburg in January 1892 (*Steamship Agreements*, 26). There were earlier ones. The first was said to be the Calcutta Conference of 1875. See Ervin Hexner, *International Cartels* (1946; rpt. New York: Greenwood Press, 1971), 387. The Alexander Committee (the House Committee on Merchant Marine and Fisheries) documented the

agreements in force in 1913; see *Shipping Combinations* and *Steamship Agreements*. The agreements covered regularly scheduled lines. In the main, tramp steamers (which were chartered) were not under these accords (*Shipping Combinations,* 1360). The arrangements were often uneasy ones (Hoffman, *Great Britain and the German Trade,* 220–222). For the German role, see Cecil, *Albert Ballin,* 46–62.

220. *Steamship Agreements,* passim.

221. This emerges in the testimony presented in *Shipping Combinations,* passim.

222. This seems true no matter how we define *foreign, company,* or *control.* In shipping, the definitions are often difficult. For example, the American William Boyd testified before a congressional committee that the American Rio Plata Line belonged "to us." Boyd had organized it and "induced those owners to put their boats in our service." The steamers themselves, however, were British owned, and the Line's ships all operated under a British flag (*Shipping Combinations,* 385–386). I can call such an arrangement American without contradicting the general statement, so extensive was the undisputed and unambiguous foreign role. Much more important, I can even classify all the IMM lines as American controlled—following Franklin's statement (see note 213 above)—without countering this generalization.

As noted, normal use of the term *foreign tonnage* in the shipping literature does not relate to ownership or control but to the flag that the ship flies. Thus a British flag ship that was American owned or controlled (directly or indirectly) would be called British. Although foreign-owned and controlled steamship companies handled less tonnage than the statistics on foreign tonnage would suggest, the evidence seems clear that they still carried the bulk of U.S. exports and imports. I have seen no figures that divide foreign trade carriers by ownership (much less by control) rather than by flag. Aldcroft, "The Mercantile Marine," 327, purports to give "owner" (by nationality), but I think he is actually giving "flag" information. Compare ibid., 327, 328, 362–363.

223. For a list of the companies and amount invested, see S. G. Ward & G. C. Ward to Baring Brothers, July 25, 1883, BAL, HC 5.2.30 pt. 47.

224. Ibid. Anglo-American Telegraph Company was the direct successor to the original transatlantic cable company of Cyrus Field (see Chapter 4). Sir John Pender had been one of the original investors in Field's venture. See *Men and Women of Our Times,* 14th ed. (London, 1895), 661–662. For more on Sir John Pender, who has been called the "cable magnate," see *Dictionary of National Biography,* Supplement, 1130; Georg Siemens, *The House of Siemens,* 2 vols. (1957; rpt. New York: Arno Press, 1977), I, 71–73; J. D. Scott, *Siemens Brothers, 1858–1959* (London: Weidenfeld & Nicholson, 1958), 56–58; and Hugh Barty-King, "Sir John Pender," *Dictionary of Business Biography,* IV, 609–614.

The Direct United States Cable Company had been founded in 1873 by William Siemens (the "British" Siemens), assisted by his cousin Georg von Siemens of the Deutsche Bank. It aimed to challenge the position of those cables under Pender's domination. Soon it joined the group, and Pender in time became important in this company as well. On the Direct United States Cable Company, see Scott, *Siemens Brothers, 1858–1958,* 39–40, 56–57, and Karl Helfferich, *Georg von Siemens,* 2 vols. (Berlin: Verlag von Julius Springer, 1923), II, 14–21.

In 1879 the French cable company attempted to confront the British transatlantic "monopoly." It, too, soon came under the control of the "Pender ring" (Georg Siemens, *House of Siemens,* I, 73). In 1883 there was also the American Telegraph and Cable Company (two cables; capital, £2.8 million). Jay Gould had started American Telegraph and Cable in 1880, trying to combat the "foreign monopoly"; he leased the two cables built by his company to Western Union (which he then controlled) and in 1882 made a pool agreement with the Pender group, so for all practical purposes the "foreign monopoly" remained. The Pender group remained supreme in transatlantic communication. See Julius Grodinsky, *Jay Gould* (Philadelphia: University of Pennsylvania Press, 1957), 279, 285; Siemens, *House of Siemens*, I, 73; and Wilkins, *Emergence*, 48.

On December 12, 1883, the Americans John W. Mackay (who had made his money from the Comstock Lode) and James Gordon Bennett (a newspaperman) founded the Commercial Cable Company, which laid two transatlantic cables in 1884 and engaged in a rate war with the Pender pool; the rate war was settled in 1888 (Siemens, *House of Siemens*, I, 74; Scott, *Siemens Brothers*, 64, 191; and Wilkins, *Emergence*, 48). Pender's international cable empire comprised much more than the transatlantic connections; his holding company—the Globe Telegraph & Trust Company—participated in cables worldwide (Scott, *Siemens Brothers*, 56). The Globe Telegraph & Trust Company was formed in 1873. By the time of his death in 1896, Pender's communications system "operated over 50,000 nautical miles of submarine cable, carried two million messages a year, and employed 1,800" individuals (Barty-King, "Sir John Pender," 612).

225. Corey, *House of Morgan*, 222.

226. See *Foreign Relations of the United States, 1899*, 310–314, and ibid., 1920, I, 134, on the German cables.

227. W. J. Baker, *A History of the Marconi Company* (London: Methuen, 1970), 35. Henry Jameson-Davis, Marconi's cousin, was the first "managing director." Baker's work is a history of the British company. Also useful is Hugh G. J. Aitken, *Syntony and Spark—The Origins of Radio* (New York: John Wiley, 1976), 224, and W. P. Jolly, *Marconi* (New York: Stein & Day, 1972), 44.

228. On its history, see Gleason L. Archer, *History of Radio* (New York: American Historical Society, 1938); L. S. Howeth, *History of Communications—Electronics in the United States Navy* (Washington, D.C., 1963); and U.S. Federal Trade Commission, *Report on the Radio Industry* (Washington, D.C., 1924). Particularly helpful on the finances of the American company are the Marquess of Reading, *Rufus Isaacs, First Marquess of Reading* (London: Hutchinson, 1942), I, 225ff., and Frances Donaldson, *The Marconi Scandal* (London: Rupert-Hart, Davis, 1962).

229. Baker, *History of the Marconi Company*, 52.

230. See Reading, *Rufus Isaacs*, I, 233–234, and *Stock Exchange Official Intelligence for 1914*, 1603. Federal Trade Commission, *Radio Industry*, 1, 11, says, at origin, $10 million, about 25 percent of which was held by the parent. This is an error. To be more precise, in 1910–1912 only $1,511,200 appears to have been issued. The parent company held $875,000, or about 58 percent. See Lord Robert Cecil Report, in Donaldson, *The Marconi Scandal*, 273–274.

231. According to Baker, *A History of the Marconi Company*, 73, the American rights to Marconi's inventions were transferred from the parent company to the U.S. affiliate in 1902 for £50,000.

232. Archer, *History of Radio*, 89, says that the plant was in Roselle Park, New Jersey. Baker, *A History of the Marconi Company*, 180, and U.S. Federal Trade Commission, *Radio Industry*, 11, 185, indicate that the plant was in Aldene, New Jersey. I suspect that Aldene and Roselle Park are the same place.

233. Donaldson, *Marconi Scandal*, 272. United Wireless was at that time run by a shareholders' reorganization committee. Its directors were in prison for financial irregularities. Hugh G. J. Aitken, *The Continuous Wave: Technology and American Radio, 1900–1932* (Princeton, N.J.: Princeton University Press, 1985), 192–194, is the best source on United Wireless.

234. Baker, *A History of the Marconi Company*, 130; Archer, *History of Radio*, 101; Donaldson, *The Marconi Scandal*, 272–278; and Aitken, *The Continuous Wave*, 193.

235. David Sarnoff, *Looking Ahead* (New York: McGraw-Hill, 1968), 3.

236. Archer, *History of Radio*, 75, and Baker, *A History of the Marconi Company*, 80.

237. Donaldson, *The Marconi Scandal*, 14.

238. Ibid., 272–274; Reading, *Rufus Isaacs*, 232–237; and Archer, *History of Radio*, 63, 101. Godfrey Isaacs had become managing director of the British company in January 1910 (Jolly, *Marconi*, 172). Of the new monies, $1.5 million would be used to buy up the assets of the United Wireless and reimburse the parent company for its part in the reorganization. The rest would be devoted to building high-power stations. The process of raising the new capital and the resulting scandal in England are well told in Lord Robert Cecil's Report, June 1913, reprinted in Donaldson, *The Marconi Scandal*, 273–389, and in ibid., passim.

239. Donaldson, *The Marconi Scandal*, 273. The March 29, 1912, agreement between Marconi of America and its parent set down the terms of the capital increase (ibid., 274).

240. Ibid., 273.

241. Ibid., 277–278. Marconi of America was to hold its shareholders meeting on April 18, 1912, to endorse the new issue and approve the terms of the March 29 agreement. The trading in the shares; the involvement of Godfrey Isaac's brother, Sir Rufus (the British Attorney-General); and the role of the Post Office contract were all elements in the so-called Marconi scandal. Since the scandal per se had no impact on developments in America, I will not concern myself with it.

242. *New York Times*, July 11, 1914.

243. Howeth, *History*, 208.

244. The British Marconi also had affiliates in Russia, France, Spain, and Canada (Reading, *Rufus Isaacs*, 232).

245. *Stock Exchange Official Intelligence for 1914*, 1603.

246. Reading, *Rufus Isaacs*, 233, and *Stock Exchange Official Intelligence for 1914*, 1603. The credit balance on its profit and loss account on Jan. 31, 1913, was only $224,483. Its investments and loans at cost were $2,632,847 (ibid.).

247. Aitken, *The Continuous Wave*, 194.

248. *APC Report*, 103.

249. Ibid.

250. Ibid.

251. In the post–World War II years, this became A.E.G-Telefunken. As noted in Chapter 12, Telefunken was founded in 1903.

252. *APC Report*, 104, 296.

253. Ibid., 104. On Telefunken's other international activities, see Reading, *Rufus Isaacs*, 227, and 1919 Briefing Paper, Box 71, Owen Young Papers, Van Hornesville Community Corporation, Van Hornesville, N.Y. (pre–World War I business).

254. Howeth, *History*, 152, and Baker, *A History of the Marconi Company*, 130–135. Baker (p. 158) writes that in 1912–1914 "the private Marconi-Telefunken 'War' had been succeeded by a period of peaceful co-existence in which exchanges of technical information backed up by bi-lateral visits . . . were the order of the day."

255. *APC Report*, 103, and Howeth, *History*, 207.

256. *APC Report*, 103, and Howeth, *History*, 225.

257. Federal Trade Commission, *Radio Industry*, 12, for example.

258. *APC Report*, 103. Aitken, *The Continuous Wave*, 159, 283, notes that the Telefunken Von Arco machine was installed at Sayville in 1914, and the French Goldschmidt alternator was installed at Tuckerton that same year.

259. Federal Trade Commission, *Radio Industry*, 12, 14.

260. Aitken, *Syntony and Spark*, 240–243, discusses the audacity of Marconi in proposing to compete with the cable companies. Barty-King, "Sir John Pender," notes that

Sir John (who died in 1896) saw no threat to his cable companies from wireless telegraph.

261. Federal Trade Commission, *Radio Industry*, 12. To be sure, United Fruit had its own radio connections with its vessels, and Federal Telegraph Company of California (formed in 1911) did some ship-to-shore and ship-to-ship radio communication on the West Coast. These were exceptional. The U.S. Navy, of course, had its own stations. See Archer, *History of Radio*, 124.

262. George Paish, "Great Britain's Capital Investment in Individual Colonial and Foreign Countries," *Journal of the Royal Statistical Society*, 74 (Jan. 1911): 176, reprinted in Mira Wilkins, *British Overseas Investment, 1907–1948* (New York: Arno Press, 1977).

263. Bosch, *Nederlandse Beleggingen*, 346. Interestingly, the common stock of Marconi Wireless of America was also listed in Amsterdam (ibid.). For the more extensive London listings, see Paul Dickens "The Transition Period in American International Financing: 1897 to 1914," Ph.D. diss., George Washington University 1933, 236–264.

264. See Lysis [Eugene Letailleur], *Politique et finance d'avant-guerre* (Paris: Payot, 1920), 311 (reprint of his July 7, 1911 article), for a critical discussion of an A.T.T. issue.

265. H. B. Thayer to F. R. Welles, April 25, 1905, Western Electric Archives. Western Electric was the manufacturing subsidiary of A.T.T.

266. On its 1906 bond issue, see Chapter 13.

15. Other Services

1. Beyond these, there was a range of miscellaneous services provided by foreign direct investors. For example, New York Taxicab Company, Ltd., was owned by Frenchmen (the French manufactured taxis; was there a connection?). The Berlitz School in New York was French owned. Tattersall's (of New York), Ltd., formed in England in 1890, acquired the business of the American Horse Exchange and the Easton's National Horse and Cattle Exchange. On these, see Cleona Lewis, *America's Stake in International Investments* (Washington, D.C.: Brookings Institution, 1938), 102; *Stock Exchange Official Intelligence for 1914*, 1637; and *Burdett's Official Intelligence, 1895*, 1164–65.

2. Frank Presbrey, *The History and Development of Advertising* (1929; rpt. New York: Greenwood Press, 1968), 107. Presbrey is vague on when T. B. Browne opened its office in the United States, but the context suggests the 1880s or the 1890s. On T. B. Browne, see T. R. Nevett, *Advertising in Britain* (London: Heinemann, 1982), 104, and Diana and Geoffrey Hindley, *Advertising in Victorian England, 1837–1901* (London: Wayland, 1972), 38, 203. The Hindleys write that Browne produced the "Bubbles" poster for A. & F. Pears and that Browne was the first advertiser to have a specialized trademark department. They say that at the turn of the century this London firm was the largest advertising agency in the United Kingdom, with branches in Glasgow, Manchester, and Paris; they include nothing on its U.S. branch.

3. Presbrey, *The History*, 394–395, 338, 386, 98. Presbrey writes that Pears' Soap began advertising in the United States in 1883. It was an international advertiser when American manufacturers still hesitated about advertising. In 1888 its advertising budget was said to be $200,000, of which $35,000 went to the United States (ibid., 395).

4. I use the word *typically* because certain of the larger trading companies, as we have seen, began manufacturing in the United States and sold their own manufactured products domestically (Balfour, Guthrie and Booth & Co. are examples).

5. If an independent wholesaler was satisfactory, however, companies found no reason to replace him. Pears' Soap—with the most-advertised foreign product in the United States—used an independent agent (Walter Janviers) for thirty-six years, 1884–

1920! Not until 1920 did this company integrate forward into distribution, and by that time Pears' Soap was a subsidiary of Lever Brothers. As noted, Pears' Soap did not manufacture in the United States before World War I.

6. Exceptional was the British candymaker John Mackintosh, Ltd., and it was unsuccessful. Some of the British-owned breweries in the United States had interests in saloons (see Chapter 9 for some of the problems). I assume that the British publishing houses at least on occasion sold directly to American book readers. These, however, were isolated cases.

7. Mira Wilkins, "American-Japanese Direct Foreign Investment Relationships, 1930–1952," *Business History Review*, 56 (Winter 1982): 510. Similarly, F. A. O. Schwarz sold toys and novelties at retail and was 25 percent German owned (Alien Property Custodian, *Report, 1918–1919*, 145).

8. Bruno Kuske, *100 Jahre Stollwerck-Geschichte, 1839–1939* (Cologne: Stollwerck, 1939), 105. See also Chapter 12.

9. See Chapter 9.

10. The Bells became associated with Eastman. See Chapter 9.

11. Peter Mathias, *Retailing Revolution* (London: Longmans, Green, 1967), 343. On British retailing, see James B. Jefferys, *Retail Trading in Britain, 1850–1950* (Cambridge: Cambridge University Press, 1954), and W. Hamish Fraser, *The Coming of the Mass Market, 1850–1914* (London: Macmillan, 1981).

12. Alfred D. Chandler, *The Visible Hand* (Cambridge, Mass.: Harvard University Press, 1977), 234.

13. S. Japhet, *Recollections from My Business Life* (London: privately printed, 1931), 89, 91. The United Cigar and Sears, Roebuck issues were in 1906. The S. S. Kresge one was in 1912. See "History of Hallgarten & Co.," draft typescript, 1950, 6; Hermann Wallich and Paul Wallich, *Zwei Generationen im deutschen Bankwesen, 1833–1914* (Frankfurt: Fritz Knapp Verlag, 1978), 282–284; Walter E. Sachs Reminiscences Oral History Collection, Columbia University, New York, 2 pts. (1956, 1964), pt. 1, 32, 34, 35, 87–88; pt. 2, 220; and Vincent Carosso, *Investment Banking in America* (Cambridge, Mass.: Harvard University Press, 1970), 82–83.

14. Mira Wilkins, *The Emergence of Multinational Enterprise* (Cambridge, Mass.: Harvard University Press, 1970).

15. An excellent work on British insurance firms is Harold E. Raynes, *A History of British Insurance*, rev. ed. (London: Sir Isaac Pitman, 1959); see pp., 264, 270, 274, on the impact of the fires. See also Robert L. Nash, *A Short Inquiry into the Profitable Nature of Our Investments*, 3rd ed. (London: Effingham Wilson, 1881), 92.

16. Marquis James, *Biography of a Business, 1792–1942* (Indianapolis: Bobbs Merrill, 1942), 172.

17. See *Best's Insurance Reports* (*Casualty and Miscellaneous*), *1918–19* (henceforth cited as *Best's—Casualty*). This statement is a bit suspect because many British firms that provided casualty insurance actually had entered the United States many years earlier as providers of *fire* insurance.

18. *Commercial and Financial Chronicle*, 34 (Feb. 4, 1882): 128.

19. Based on *Best's Insurance Reports* (*Fire and Marine*), *1914* (henceforth cited as *Best's—Fire*). *Best's Insurance Reports* are by far the most useful source on foreign insurance companies in the United States.

20. W. G. Kerr, *Scottish Capital on the American Credit Frontier* (Austin: Texas State Historical Association, 1976), 163.

21. P. G. M. Dickson, *The Sun Insurance Office, 1710–1960* (London: Oxford University Press, 1960), 221, puts the Liverpool & London & Globe in first place in 1876. See *Best's—Fire* for the 1914 rankings. For the importance of Liverpool firms, see Barry

Supple, *The Royal Exchange Assurance* (Cambridge: Cambridge University Press, 1970), 214.

22. *Best's—Fire.*

23. Dickson, *The Sun,* 221.

24. Ibid., 221–231. When Sun Insurance made this purchase, the Watertown firm was operating in about thirty states and had 1,400 agents (ibid., 227).

25. Supple, *Royal Exchange Assurance,* 342–343. Royal Insurance Company and Royal Exchange Assurance were different companies.

26. Ibid., 213.

27. Ibid., 246–249, 363. After the San Francisco fire, the Liverpool & London & Globe paid out $4.7 million, while the Royal Insurance Company paid out $7.5 million. See T. Dyer Simpson, *1936 Our Centenary Year* (London: Liverpool & London & Globe, 1936), 62. The British Commercial Union and its associates, the Palatine and Commercial Union of New York, had policies containing conditions that excluded liabilities for losses by fire resulting from earthquakes. Nonetheless, that group eventually paid out almost $4 million as a consequence of the San Francisco fires. See Edward Liveing, *A Century of Insurance* (London: H. F. & G. Witherby, 1961), 100.

28. Supple, *Royal Exchange Assurance,* 249–250.

29. Liverpool & London & Globe organized Globe Indemnity Company, New York, in 1911. It wrote all classes of liability, accident and health, steam boiler, fly wheel plate glass, and burglary insurance and provided fidelity and surety bonds (*Best's—Casualty*). The Royal Idemnity Company, New York, was formed in 1911 by the Royal Insurance Company (ibid.). The Ocean Accident and Guarantee Corp., Ltd., a British insurance office of importance, had entered the United States in 1895, and had begun to write credit insurance. By 1898 it was writing all lines of casualty insurance. In 1910 it became associated with the Commercial Union, a British firm. See Liveing, *A Century of Insurance,* 102–103, and *Best's—Casualty.* Royal Exchange Assurance's net accident premiums in the United States before World War I were approximately 15 percent of its fire premiums (Supple, *Royal Exchange Assurance,* 470, 242).

30. *Best's—Casualty.*

31. Compiled from data in *Best's—Fire.*

32. Compiled from data in *Best's—Casualty.*

33. Wallis Hunt, *Heirs of Great Adventure* (London: Balfour, Williamson, 1951), I, 78, 129.

34. Ibid., 129.

35. *Best's—Fire;* Alien Property Custodian, *Report, 1918–1919,* 435–436; and *Best's—Casualty.*

36. *Best's—Fire.* The Warsaw Insurance Company is listed as Warsaw, Russia.

37. Ibid. *Best's—Fire* includes both insurance and reinsurance companies, intermixed.

38. Ibid.

39. Ibid. They are the only Bulgarian investments in the United States that I have been able to identify.

40. Lewis, *America's Stake,* 111.

41. *Best's—Fire,* 5. The warning was specifically against out-of-country (not merely out-of-state) firms.

42. Dickson, *The Sun,* 229.

43. See Raynes, *History,* 270–271, for New York legislation: 1851, 1859, 1866.

44. Supple, *Royal Exchange Assurance,* 249.

45. For example, the Alliance Assurance Company, Ltd., London, had on various occasions undertaken business in the United States before 1891; that year it acquired

the Union Fire Insurance Company of San Francisco. After the 1906 fire (when its losses were £690,000), it withdrew from American business. See Sir William Schooling, *Alliance Assurance, 1824–1924* (London: Alliance Assurance, 1924), 41, 72–73.

46. For example, Royal Exchange Assurance exited from California in 1908 but increased its U.S. business in general (Supple, *Royal Exchange Assurance*, 250, 242).

47. *Best's—Fire.*

48. John A. Garver, *John William Sterling* (New Haven: Yale University Press, 1929), 74. American life insurance companies followed the same pattern, buying or building abroad to demonstrate stability and reliability. See Wilkins, *The Emergence*, 65.

49. *Best's—Fire.*

50. *Best's—Casualty.* There is no duplication in premiums, although some of the same parent companies are represented.

51. *Best's—Life—1911/1912*, also includes Great West Life Assurance Company, Manufacturers' Life Insurance Company, and North American Life Insurance Company as doing business in the United States. See also *Best's—Life—1916/1917* for same group in 1914. R. T. Naylor, *The History of Canadian Business, 1867–1914* (Toronto: James Lorimer, 1973), II, 246, writes that "by 1914 every major Canadian life company had U.S. branches"; data in *Best's* do not confirm this. On Sun Life, see Joseph Schull, *The Century of the Sun* (Toronto: Macmillan of Canada, 1971), 7, 37–39, which indicates more extensive U.S. business of Sun Life than do *Best's* reports. The reader should not confuse the Canadian Sun Life with the British fire insurance company Sun Insurance Company. They were unrelated.

52. This reflected the nature of the business. As Rayner, *History of British Insurance*, 271, writes, "The life assurance business of British companies in the United States was never very substantial." See also ibid, 276. I have made the same point earlier.

53. Ibid., 271: "U.S.A. assets constituting the insurance reserves."

54. Supple, *Royal Exchange Assurance*, 342.

55. *Best's—Fire.*

56. Ibid.

57. *Best's—Casualty.* There was no overlap.

58. Ibid.

59. *Best's—Fire.*

60. Ibid. So does *Best's—Casualty* for the casualty companies.

61. Nathaniel Mayer Rothschild, London, to cousins, Paris, Oct. 18, 1907, Rothschild Archives London (RAL) XI/139A/1. See also Supple, *Royal Exchange Assurance*, 345–346, for evidence that other parent English and Scottish insurance companies (as distinct from their branches and affiliates) held U.S. securities.

62. Naylor, *History*, II, 246.

63. Schull, *Century of Sun*, 45.

64. Supple, *Royal Exchange Assurance*, 345.

65. Robert T. Swaine, *The Cravath Firm* (New York: privately printed, 1946), I, 547, 767.

66. See the 1967 recollections of William Sutherland (then aged ninety), who joined Arthur Young & Co. in 1903, in *The Arthur Young Journal*, 75th anniversary ed. (Spring–Summer 1969): 33.

67. When the Chancellor of the Exchequer, Reginald McKenna, needed dollars for war purchases in the summer of 1915, he called in Sir Thomas Dewey, chairman of Prudential, and A. C. Thompson, general manager, and asked them how much Prudential Assurance owned in American securities; they replied $40 million (Lord Beaverbrook, *Politicians and the War* [1925; rpt. New York: Archon Books, 1968], 147–149). I checked the balance sheet of Prudential Assurance Company, Ltd. (in the London

Times, March 6, 1914), to see whether this story could be feasible. Prudential had, under the heading "Investments," £19.7 million in "Railway and other debentures and debenture stocks and gold and sterling bonds—Home and Foreign," so the $40 million in American securities could fit under this rubric and was very likely. Prudential Assurance held no mortgages outside the United Kingdom.

68. The Prudential Assurance Company of Great Britain was founded in 1848. Its namesake in the United States (founded in 1874; name changed in 1877 to Prudential Insurance Company of America) was modeled after the British Prudential; in fact, its founder seems to have desired to take advantage of the latter's reputation and visited London for advice. There is no evidence, however, that Prudential Assurance Company, Ltd., financed or in any way "controlled" the American fledgling. See William H. A. Carr, *From Three Cents a Week: The Story of Prudential Insurance Company of America* (Englewood Cliffs, N.J.: Prentice-Hall, 1975), 13–15, 17–18, 27–29.

69. C. W. DeMond, *Price, Waterhouse and Company in America* (New York: Price Waterhouse, 1951), 126.

70. Edwin Waterhouse, "His Story," n.d., p. 16, Price Waterhouse Archives (henceforth cited as PWA), London.

71. See 1877 Prospectus of Southern States Coal, Iron and Land Company, Ltd., formed in 1875 to develop the iron industry in Tennessee. Copy in English Committee of the Alabama 8 percent Gold State Bonds of 1870, *Hill County Alabama U.S.A.* (London: E & F. N. Spon, 1878), British Museum shelfmark 10410cc5. See also Chapter 7.

72. I have called Barrow, Wade, Guthrie & Co. the first, rather than Veysey and Veysey, since William H. Veysey apparently migrated to America—and there remained no Veysey and Veysey in England. See James Don Edwards, *History of Public Accounting in the United States* (University: University of Alabama Press, 1978), 48. Guthrie remained in Britain.

73. James T. Anyon, *Recollections of the Early Days of American Accountancy, 1883–1893* (New York: privately printed, 1925), 9–19.

74. Ibid., 19.

75. Dorothy Adler, *British Investment in American Railways, 1834–1898* (Charlottesville: University Press of Virginia, 1970), 181–182, which indicates that by 1884 at least $17.5 million of the common shares of this railroad were in British and Dutch hands. See Chapter 6.

76. Anyon, *Recollections*, 19. See Chapter 10 on the York Street Flax Spinning Company.

77. Adler, *British Investment*, 218; on this investment trust company, see Chapter 14.

78. On the Chicago office, see biographical sketch of Arthur Smith in Norman Webster, *The American Association of Public Accountants: Its First Twenty Years, 1886–1906* (New York: American Institute of Accountants, 1954), 377.

79. Waterhouse, "His Story," 58.

80. Deloitte, Plender, Griffiths & Co., *Deloitte & Co., 1845–1956* (Oxford: privately printed, 1958), 47. I wonder whether these investigations were pre-1888 or 1888–1890. These locales attracted sizable British investments in the late 1880s.

81. Based on listings in *Burdett's Official Intelligence* and data in PWA, London.

82. Based on data in *Burdett's Official Intelligence*. Adler, *British Investment*, 199n, notes the "early" work of Turquand, Young & Co. on American railroads.

83. Deloitte, *Deloitte*, 47, and DeMond, *Price, Waterhouse*, 11–12. See Chapter 9 on the brewery promotions.

84. *Burdett's Official Intelligence.*

85. W. J. Caesar to J. Gurney Fowler, Oct. 14, 1898, PWA, Box 1; all correspondence unless otherwise specified was in the large Box 1.

86. Deloitte, *Deloitte*, 48, and Lewis D. Jones, New York, to PW & Co., June 16, 1891, PWA. Edwards, *History of Public Accounting*, 51, says that two well-known firms of public accountants opened branch offices in Chicago in 1891. He identified one as Price, Waterhouse; the other was Deloitte, Dever, Griffiths & Co. As noted, Barrow, Wade & Guthrie had a Chicago office earlier.

87. Arthur S. Dewing, *Corporate Promotions and Reorganizations* (Cambridge, Mass.: Harvard University Press, 1914), 142n and 178n.

88. Background on Jones in DeMond, *Price, Waterhouse*, 13.

89. "Heads of Agreement," August 1890, in PWA, Box 1; I did not find the Sept. 11, 1890 document, but PW & Co. to Jones and Caesar, Dec. 29, 1891, summarizes its basic points.

90. Correspondence in Box 1, PWA. Erastus Wiman, author of "British Capital and American Industries," *North American Review*, 150 (Jan. 1890): 220–234, was a Canadian entrepreneur who migrated to the United States and became a partner of R. G. Dun. For more on Wiman, see Naylor, *The History of Canadian Business*, 11, 250. There is no evidence the bill was ever paid.

91. See Chapter 8 for more details.

92. Jones to PW & Co., May 29, 1891, and PW & Co. to Jones, June 9, 1891, PWA.

93. The notion of a "corrupt" America had long existed. Accountants repeatedly told the story of Jay Gould, who, when called to account for defrauding English investors, asked for the stock certificates to verify the amount of investment. When the certificates were returned to him, he shredded them, destroying any evidence against him! See Gary John Previts and Barbara Dubis Merino, *A History of Accounting in America* (New York: Ronald Press, 1979), 137. Indeed, the very need for British accountants was based on improper American practices.

94. On the arrangements with Caesar, see PW & Co. to Jones, June 9, 1891; Jones to PW & Co., June 16, 1891; PW & Co. to Jones and Caesar, Dec. 29, 1891, PWA.

95. DeMond, *Price, Waterhouse*, 18.

96. PW & Co. to Jones and Caesar, April 5, 1892, PWA.

97. My information on the New York and Denver offices comes from a biographical sketch of Ernest Hart, son of the founder of Hart Brothers, Tibbetts & Co. in London, who was with the firm's New York office briefly in 1892 and with the Denver office in 1892–93 (Webster, *American Association*, 352). *Burdett's Official Intelligence 1895* is my source for the Denver Breweries account. J. R. Ellerman, who did not open an American office, also was involved with American breweries. See Chapter 14.

98. As noted above, however, Deloitte was doing work for bankers' reorganization committees.

99. Jones to J. Gurney Fowler, Jan. 31, 1894, PWA.

100. Caesar and Jones to PW & Co., Jan. 27, 1894, PWA. Note the differentiation between "banks" (U.S. commercial banks) and European "banking houses." See Chapter 13.

101. Jones to Fowler, Feb. 12, 1894, and Fowler to Jones, Feb. 26, 1894, PWA.

102. Caesar to Fowler, Feb. 14, 1894, and Fowler to Caesar, Feb. 26, 1894, PWA. The London Guarantee and Accident Company, Ltd., had entered the United States in 1892; it had its U.S. branch in Chicago. See *Best's—Casualty*.

103. Russell Monro to Fowler, Aug. 19, 1894, PWA. Monro was a director of American Breweries and General Securities Trust, Ltd., Bartholomay Brewing Company, Ltd., City of Chicago Brewing and Malting Company, Ltd., Commercial Union Brewery Investment Company, Ltd., and St. Louis Breweries, Ltd. See *Direc-*

tory of Directors. On Monro's relations with O'Hagan, see Swaine, *Cravath Firm,* I, 424.

104. See Robert Berger (with the aid of George O. May), "History of P.W. & Co. and Jones, Caesar & Co., 1890 to June 30, 1901," New York, typescript 1947, pt. 2, chap. 5., pp. 1–3, in PWA.

105. "Why do you write off so much more than 'Deloitte' and other accountants?" inquired Russell Monro, Monro to Fowler, Aug. 19, 1894, PWA.

106. *Northwestern Miller,* 38 (Dec. 7, 1894): 897. The matter of depreciation was one that continued to irritate Americans involved with British-headquartered companies. Thus Francis Marion Smith was "contemptuous"of this "strange British practice" that he saw reducing his dividends; this was apropos of Borax Consolidated, Ltd., and as late as 1901. See N. J. Travis and E. J. Cocks, *The Tincal Trail* (London: Harrap, 1984), 141.

107. Fowler to Jones, Aug. 30, 1894, PWA.

108. PW & Co. to Caesar & Jones, Oct. 10, 1894, PWA.

109. Ibid.; Caesar to PW & Co., Nov. 5, 1894; Jones, Caesar & Co. to PW & Co., Jan. 14, 1985; and PW & Co. to JC & Co., Oct. 25, 1897, PWA.

110. Caesar to PW & Co., Nov. 5, 1894, and enclosure, PWA.

111. PW & Co. to Jones and Caesar, Nov. 21, 1894, first draft and actual letter, PWA.

112. DeMond, *Price, Waterhouse,* 29.

113. Caesar to PW & Co., Jan 16, 1897, PWA.

114. 1897 and 1898 correspondence, PWA.

115. John L. Carey, *The Rise of the Accounting Profession: From Technician to Professional, 1896–1936* (New York: American Institute of Certified Accountants, 1969), 44, and Previts and Merino, *History,* 98.

116. Webster, *American Association,* 338. Caesar did not tell London.

117. See "Profit Accounts" in Box 1, PWA, and Berger, "History," chap. 12, 3–4. Price, Waterhouse was the auditor for New York Belting and Packing Company, Ltd., formed in 1890, in which August Belmont participated. See *Burdett's Official Intelligence.*

118. I did not find the short-term agreement, although it is referred to in the correspondence. The Feb. 1898 draft exists in Box 1, PWA.

119. Caesar to Fowler, Oct. 14, 1898, PWA.

120. Ibid.

121. Caesar to Fowler, Oct. 14, 1898—second letter—PWA.

122. PW & Co. to Caesar, Feb. 8, 1899, PWA.

123. Caesar to A. W. Wyon, Feb. 27, 1899, PWA.

124. Caesar to Fowler, Aug. 1, 1900, PWA. Caesar was born on May 6, 1859 (Webster, *American Association,* 338).

125. Caeasr to Fowler, Aug. 27, 1900, PWA. Abbreviations in the original.

126. I have no evidence on Hart Brothers, Tibbetts & Co. in the United States at this time. Presumably its two offices had closed during the rough years of the mid-1890s.

127. Mary E. Murphy, "Sir George Touche, Bart. C.A., 1861–1935: A Memoir," *Business History Review,* 34 (Winter 1960): 468–469, 473. See also testimony of J. B. Niven, U.S. House, *The Money Trust Investigation* (Washington, D.C., 1913), pt. 13, 952. In 1889 G. A. Touche was already involved in American business as a founder (one among many) of the London and New York Investment Corporation and as a principal in the Industrial and General Trust, Ltd. (Adler, *British Investment,* 214–215).

128. Agreement in Box C2, PW Private-American Agency, PWA.

129. DeMond, *Price, Waterhouse,* 128.

130. Ibid., 60.

131. Ibid., 129.

132. Berger, "History," chap. 17, 1.

133. DeMond, *Price, Waterhouse,* 52, 64, 74, 93, 102, 104, 122, 129, and data in Box C2, PW Private-American Agency, PWA.

134. Data in ibid. Previts and Merino, *History,* 142, note that in 1903, of the fifty-three members of the Illinois state accounting society, twenty-one were from Price, Waterhouse, "practitioners who could not be certified in New York State because they were British subjects, but could be certified in Illinois under board waiver provisions." The profession was first recognized in Illinois in 1903. See [J. C. Burton, ed.], *Arthur Young and the Business He Founded* (New York: privately printed, 1948), 20.

135. Paul Grady, ed., *Memoirs and Accounting Thought of George O. May* (New York: Ronald Press, 1962), 25, 31.

136. See, for example, R. H. Parker, "The Third International Congress of Accounting Historians," *Journal of European Economic History,* 10 (Winter 1981): 746.

137. Deloitte, *Deloitte,* 48, 150.

138. Frank Spencer to William de la Barre, Aug. 13, 1908, de la Barre Papers, Minnesota Historical Society, St. Paul.

139. Ibid., Sept. 3, 1909; and *Northwestern Miller,* 83 (July 27, 1910): 217–218.

140. *Northwestern Miller,* 83 (July 27, 1910): 218.

141. George Soule and Vincent P. Carosso, *American Economic History* (New York: Dryden Press, 1957), 311, and Deloitte, *Deloitte,* 88.

142. Walter Hanson, *Peat, Marwick, Mitchell & Co.* (New York: Newcomen Society, 1978), 8–9, and T. A. Wise, *Peat, Marwick, Mitchell & Co.* (n.p.: Peat, Marwick, Mitchell, 1982) 13–15, 98. (There was a period, 1919–1925, when the arrangements were terminated; ibid., 14–15.)

143. Edgar Jones, *Accountancy and the British Economy, 1840–1980: The Evolution of Ernst & Whinney* (London: Batsford, 1981), 106, and letter from Edwin Green, Midland Bank, to Mira Wilkins, April 15, 1985.

144. Carey, *The Rise,* 34.

145. DeMond, *Price, Waterhouse,* 40–41. The Minutes of the Partners' Meeting in New York, Oct. 21–22, 1910, show new plans to employ American college graduates, "none but the very best men." Minutes in Box C2, PW Private-American Agency, PWA. In the years before World War I, the recommended practical experience for American CPAs was consistently lengthened by state and national organizations. Historians have suggested that this development was an adaptation of the British apprenticeship system to the American environment (Previts and Merino, *History,* 156). To make this suggestion denigrates the more important professionalism that was transferred.

146. My colleague Kenneth Most found for me two histories of Arthur Young: [Burton, ed.], *Arthur Young,* and the 75th Anniversary issue of *The Arthur Young Journal* (1969). Arthur Young (under the style Stuart & Young) had started in Chicago in 1894 (the year Jones, Caesar found so discouraging). Young's initial business was bailing out "Scottish and English investment companies" that had been hard hit by the Panic of 1893. Young knew the directors of these companies "in the old country." In 1895 Stuart & Young opened a Kansas City branch office "largely to facilitate the realization of [the] farm loans" of these investment companies. See Burton, *Arthur Young,* 20–21. On the importance of Kansas City in mortgage lending by investment trusts, see Allan G. Bogue, *Money at Interest* (Ithaca, N.Y.: Cornell University Press, 1955); Ivan Wright, *Farm Mortgage Financing* (New York: McGraw-Hill, 1923), 319, 321; and George Holmes, "A Decade of Mortgages," *Annals of the American Academy of Political and Social Science,* 4 (1894): 904–907, 916–917. I did include Marwick, Mitchell in my earlier discussion because of its ties with the nonresident British firm W. B. Peat & Co.

147. Wise, *Peat, Marwick,* 3. Andersen received his C.P.A. in Illinois in 1908 at the age of twenty-three; he may have been working with Price, Waterhouse in Chicago before that date.

148. Clark C. Spence, *British Investments and the American Mining Frontier* (Ithaca, N.Y.: Cornell University Press, 1958), 70.

149. T. A. Rickard, *A History of American Mining* (New York: McGraw-Hill, 1932), 19.

150. Spence, *British Investments,* 117.

151. Ibid., 70, and H. Osborne O'Hagan, *Leaves from My Life* (London: John Lane, 1929), I, 79–83. Bewick, Moreing & Co. hired Herbert Hoover in 1897. See Wilkins, *The Emergence,* 71, and T. A. Rickard, *Retrospect* (New York: McGraw-Hill, 1937), 69–70.

152. Spence, *British Investments,* 117.

153. George H. Nash, *The Life of Herbert Hoover* (New York: W. W. Norton, 1983), 224.

154. Ibid. 224–225. For the firm's extraordinary worldwide activities, see ibid., 226 and passim.

155. See Spence, *British Investments,* 71, 95, 102–103, and Rickard, *Retrospect,* for the important impact of the Rickard family on Anglo-American mining.

156. Rickard, *Retrospect,* 34, 36–37. See Spence, *British Investments,* 118, for other British mining engineering firms. See also Clark C. Spence, *Mining Engineers and the American West* (New Haven: Yale University Press, 1970), passim.

157. On Beatty's early history with Guggenheim Exploration Company see Nash, *Life of Herbert Hoover,* 388–389.

158. It is hard to overestimate the cosmopolitan character of the mining engineers' profession. London was the center, and when Americans were talented, they were employed by British firms in international explorations and evaluations as well as in international mining management. As noted in Chapter 7, the Rothschild's Exploration Company, Ltd., from 1886 onward used American engineers.

159. On the Hudson River Tunnel, see J. A. Spender, *Weetman Pearson* (London: Cassell, 1930), 52–58; Robert Keith Middlemas, *The Master Builders* (London: Hutchinson, 1963), 181–182; data in Box 67, Pearson Papers, Science Museum, London; and Carl W. Condit, *Port of New York* (Chicago: University of Chicago Press, 1980) I, 249–251.

160. Adler, *British Investment,* 122n.

161. Swaine, *Cravath Firm,* I. 626, 631, is excellent on this venture.

162. Nash, *Life of Herbert Hoover,* 224.

163. Edward D. Adams, *Niagara Power,* 2 vols. (Niagara Falls, N.Y.: Niagara Falls Power Co, 1927), I, 115–120.

164. Ibid., 125–128, 134. Adams identifies George Bliss as a New York lawyer. Could this have been George Bliss of Morton, Bliss & Co.? That George Bliss was not a lawyer, and Adams should have known him and not made the error in identification.

165. This history—Adams, *Niagara Power*—is the basis of much of what is included herein.

166. Ibid., I, 297.

167. Ibid., 297–298.

168. Richard Davis, *The English Rothschilds* (Chapel Hill: University of North Carolina Press, 1983), 134.

169. Adams, *Niagara Power,* I, 295.

170. Ibid., 297.

171. Ibid., 165–166.

172. Ibid., 443.

173. As noted in an earlier chapter, the Deutsche Bank was very much involved in

electrical developments. Sir William Siemens (1823–1883)—brother of Werner Siemens and founder of the British firm Siemens Brothers—had visited Niagara Falls in 1876 and thereafter had marveled at "the amount of force thus eternally spent" with so little consequence. See J. D. Scott, *Siemens Brothers* (London: Weidenfeld & Nicolson, 1958), 22, 43, 263, and Adams, *Niagara Power,* II, 167.

174. Adams, *Niagara Power,* I. 244.

175. In this section I have considered only what seem to me the most important of the British "consulting engineers" in America. The "industry" was enormous—as witnessed by the number of entries in the *Dictionary of Business Biography.* Others, aside from the ones mentioned, had American business. For example, Woodhouse and Rawson United, Ltd., "engineers and electrical contractors," had in 1889 "branches, offices, depots, and agencies" worldwide, including St. Louis, Missouri (*Economist,* 47 [July 20, 1889]: 950). I have tried to be selective, not comprehensive.

176. See this chapter, note 159.

177. On the East River tunnels, see Boxes 8 and 9, Pearson Papers; Middlemas, *The Master Builders,* 191–192; and Condit, *Port of New York,* 391.

178. Elwood Mead, *Irrigation Institutions* (New York: Macmillan, 1907), 57, 344. On British involvement in Colorado irrigation schemes, see Roger V. Clements, "British-controlled Enterprise in the West between 1870 and 1900 and Some Agrarian Reactions," *Agricultural History,* 27 (Oct. 1953): 136–141.

179. *Stock Exchange Official Intelligence for 1914,* 1073.

180. A "construction company" was associated with the Niagara Falls development, as noted, and in the early stages it had sought out British capital in an important fashion.

181. Thomas P. Hughes, *Networks of Power: Electrification in Western Society, 1880–1930* (Baltimore: John Hopkins University Press, 1983), regrettably provides no help on this matter.

182. See Chapter 12. Essentially this agreement meant that Americans bought American electrical machinery and equipment. There were exceptions—but the American market was typically an American one. In water-power machinery, where the Swiss had a substantial technological lead, turbines of Swiss design (by Faesch & Piccard, Geneva, and Escher, Wyss & Co., Zurich) were built in the United States by I. P. Morris Company, Philadelphia. See Adams, *Niagara Power,* II, 227, 433, 439.

183. Karl Helfferich, *Georg von Siemens* (Berlin: Verlag von Julius Springer, 1923), II, 97–98.

184. Adams tried to attract electric-power customers to the Niagara Falls area, thus providing the power company with operating revenues. In one instance he sought out a potential supplier. On hearing in 1891 that E. E. L. Brown was leaving the Maschinenfabrik of Oerlikon (located near Zurich, Switzerland), Adams invited Brown to establish a new engineering works at Niagara Falls and offered to promote such a business. Brown had just founded Brown, Boveri & Co. and declined Adams' invitation (Adams, *Niagara Power,* II, 180).

185. Lewis, *America's Stake,* 73.

186. Ibid., 72. On German investments in U.S. power and light companies, see Alien Property Custodian, *Report, 1918–1919,* 407–416. Cleona Lewis' list barely touches the surface. See *Stock Exchange Official Intelligence for 1914,* 944–975, for additional electric lighting and power companies that did business in the United States and whose securities were available in London.

187. Paul Dickens, "The Transition Period in American International Financing," Ph.D. diss., George Washington University, 1933, 105, 260, 261, and *Moody's 1914.*

188. Swaine, *Cravath Firm,* I, 646, 729–734.

189. John Moody, *The Truth about Trusts* (New York: Moody, 1904), 394. For part of the story, see Charles W. Cheape, *Moving the Masses* (Cambridge, Mass.: Harvard University Press, 1980), 92–95.

190. Dickens, "The Transition Period," 247.

191. Nathaniel Mayer Rothschild, London to cousins, Paris, May 30, 1907, RAL XI/130A/1.

192. See ibid., letters of Aug. 26, Aug. 28, Sept. 2, 1907.

193. Ibid., Nov. 18, 1907.

194. Ibid., Nov. 19, 1907.

195. Ibid., Nov. 19, Nov. 21, Dec. 2, Dec. 9, Dec. 12, Dec. 24, Dec. 30, 1907, and Lionel Rothschild to cousins, Paris, Dec. 6 and Dec. 10, 1907.

196. Nathaniel Mayer Rothschild, London, to cousins, Paris, Nov. 19, 1907, RAL X1/130A/1.

197. Ibid., Nov. 20, 1907.

198. Nathaniel Mayer Rothschild, London, to cousins, Paris, Jan. 6, 1908, RAL X1/130A/2.

199. Dickens, "The Transition Period," 249, 251. A Frenchman, writing about American finance in 1910 and noting the immense opportunities, warned, however, that in some exceptional cases the association of "great" New York "banks" with ventures did not guarantee success. The two examples he cited were Morgan and the shipping trust (I.M.M.) and Belmont and the New York subway system. See M. Georges Aubert, *La finance américaine* (Paris: Ernest Flammarion, 1910), 168.

200. August Belmont to Lord Rothschild, May 22, 1909, RAL II/96/1.

201. See *Stock Exchange Official Intelligence for 1914*, 288.

202. See Dickens, "The Transition Period," 236–269, for names of public utilities in the United States that sought monies abroad in the years 1897–1914.

203. Jacob Viner, *Canada's Balance of International Indebtedness, 1900–1913* (Cambridge, Mass.: Harvard University Press, 1924), 89.

204. Christopher Armstrong and H. V. Nelles, "A Curious Capital Flow: Canadian Investment in Mexico, 1902–1910," *Business History Review*, 58 (Summer 1984): 201.

205. Lewis, *America's Stake*, 566.

206. Ibid., 102.

207. Herbert Marshall, Frank Southard, and Kenneth Taylor, *Canadian-American Industry* (New Haven: Yale University Press, 1936), 261.

208. Schull, *Century of Sun*, 45. See also Marshall, Southard, and Taylor, *Canadian-American Industry*, 261, which did not know of the Sun Life connection but did recognize that the pre–World War I Illinois Traction Company was "evidently Canadian-owned and directed." In 1914 T. B. Macauley of Montreal was listed as "Director" and "Secretary" of Illinois Traction Company (*Moody's 1914*, 386). At that time Thomas Bassett Macauley was also secretary and managing director of Sun Life (Schull, *Century of Sun*, 49). See ibid., 41, for Macaulay's belief that such investments were for the twentieth century what railroad bonds were for the nineteenth.

209. Armstrong and Nelles, "A Curious Capital Flow," 190.

210. Dickens, "The Transition Period," 109.

211. This was true even though there were the consulting engineers and even though Macauley was on the board of directors of Illinois Traction Company. Charles Algernon Moreing was in 1899 president of the St. Lawrence Power Company, but he was not a full-time member of management; he was involved in numerous other activities at the same time.

212. Although Belmont was the Rothschild representative, he was clearly an American private banker in his own right.

16. The Reactions to Foreign Investment in the United States

1. Address of W. W. Miller of Hornblower, Miller & Potter to the first Annual Meeting of the Investment Banker's Association of America, *Report of Meeting, 1912*, 48.

2. Charles F. Speare, "Selling American Bonds in Europe," *Annals of the American Academy of Political and Social Science*, 30 (1907): 269.

3. E. L. McColgin to A. H. Baldwin, Chief of the Bureau of Foreign and Domestic Commerce, U.S. Department of Commerce, Nov. 23, 1912, RG 59, 811.60/1, National Archives, Washington D.C.

4. Edwin E. Ferguson, "The California Alien Land Law," *California Law Review*, 35 (March 1947): 67.

5. See Chapter 6.

6. J. Evetts Haley, *Charles Goodnight* (Norman: University of Oklahoma Press, 1936), 350.

7. See Clark C. Spence, *British Investments and the American Mining Frontier, 1860–1901* (Ithaca, N.Y.: Cornell University Press, 1958), and Roger V. Clements, "British Investment in the Trans-Mississippi West, 1870–1914, Its Encouragement, and the Metal Mining Interests," *Pacific Historical Review*, 29, (Feb. 1960): 35–50.

8. *New Mexico Interpreter* (White Oaks), June 3, 1887, quoted in Jim Berry Pearson, *The Maxwell Land Grant* (Norman: University of Oklahoma Press, 1961), 110–111.

9. U.S. Senate, *Mining Interests of Aliens*, 50th Cong., 2nd sess., 1889, S. Rept. 2690, 2.

10. Ibid., 3, 5.

11. Rep. Smith from Arizona, *Congressional Record*, 51st Cong., 1st sess., Aug. 20, 1890, 8880. The reference must be to Arizona Copper Company.

12. I do not believe this particular investment came about. For other investments by Sheffield steelmakers, see Chapter 7.

13. *Banker's Magazine*, New York, 40 (Feb. 1886): 578.

14. *Northwestern Miller*, 28 (Nov. 8, 1889): 521.

15. Thomas J. Lipton, *Leaves from the Lipton Logs* (London: Hutchinson, n.d. [1931?]), 183.

16. Edward D. Adams, *Niagara Power*, 2 vols. (Niagara Falls, N.Y.: Niagara Falls Power Co., 1927), II, 180, 423. See Chapter 15.

17. *Commercial and Financial Chronicle*, 34 (Feb. 4, 1882): 129.

18. U.S. Senate, *Mining Interests of Aliens* (1889), 11–12. I did not mention these tin deposits in Chapter 8, because although the British company was formed and floated, the development came to naught. A 1920 book would refer to the desposits as "of more scientific interest than commercial importance." See J. E. Spurr, ed., *Political and Commercial Geology and the World's Mineral Resources* (New York: McGraw–Hill, 1920), 330. It is possible to see, in part, Alcoa's acceptance of l'Aluminium Français' entry into the American aluminum industry as associated with the Serpek technique—see Chapter 8.

19. *Bulletin of the National Association of Wool Manufacturers*, 39 (Dec. 1899): 380.

20. American companies often sought out European technology separate from foreign investment. European foreign direct investors often introduced new technology. What I found rare was the search for the package of foreign capital and technology.

21. See Chapter 5. Most did not.

22. By 1900 AB Separator firm was employing 1,000 workers. See Ragnhild Lundström, "Early Swedish Multinationals," in *Multinationals: Theory and History*, ed. Peter Hertner and Geoffrey Jones (Aldershot: Gower, 1986), 141, and Thomas R. Navin,

The Whitin Machine Works since 1831 (Cambridge, Mass.: Harvard University Press, 1950), 241 (on Howard & Bullough).

23. See William Watson's testimony before the Tariff Commission, *Report on the Textile Trades* (London: P. S. King, 1905), II, pt. 6, para. 3318.

24. The three cases I have given were towns in the Northeast. In the 1890s and early twentieth century, these areas were beginning to feel that their manufacturing superiority was being challenged by other regions in the United States.

25. See Chapter 5.

26. I have shown how important this was in the 1830s.

27. Clements, "British Investment in the Trans-Mississippi West," 45, concluded that "except in the field of legislation on property rights, state action while *sometimes* expressing a fairly wide appreciation of alien capital, could not be considered a very powerful influence on its [in] flow" (my italics). Clearly in the metal-mining states (and in New England, which was not included in Clement's study), there was "a fairly wide appreciation of alien capital." In the plains states, it is doubtful that such an appreciation existed in state policies, and in the South the degree of appreciation was very limited.

28. Ibid.

29. Roger V. Clements, "British Investment and American Legislative Restrictions in the Trans-Mississippi West, 1880–1990, "*Mississippi Valley Historical Review*, 42 (Sept. 1955): 220.

30. P. G. M. Dickson, *The Sun Insurance Office, 1710–1960* (London: Oxford University Press, 1960), 223–230.

31. New York Superintendent of Banks, *Annual Report, 1911*, 18–19.

32. Clements, "British Investment in the Trans-Mississippi West," 44–45, adds some other highly miscellaneous state aids—such as time off from work for a Colorado state official to act as agent for a British mine.

33. See Chapter 5.

34. Ibid.

35. See E. L. McColgin to A. H. Baldwin, Baldwin to Wilbur J. Carr, and Carr to Baldwin, Nov. 23, Nov. 26, Dec. 4, 1912, all in RG 59, 811.60/1, National Archives.

36. Richard Hume Werking, *The Master Architects: Building the United States Foreign Service, 1890–1912* (Lexington: University of Kentucky Press, 1977), 228–229, 305. The firm involved was Caraconda Brothers.

37. A few American tariff advocates saw foreign investment as providing jobs, but in no sense can U.S. tariffs be seen as designed to promote foreign investment.

38. Indeed, there might not have been any history at all. This is controversial, and others might argue that an aggressive Henri Deterding would have entered America anyway. My interpretation is that had Standard Oil of New Jersey executive Walter Teagle not been restrained by U.S. antitrust considerations, he and Deterding would have arranged to divide world markets—and the United States would have been the Americans' preserve.

In another fashion, U.S. antimonopoly policies aided Shell. When the group had set out to acquire oil properties in Oklahoma in 1912, in many cases sellers had defective titles, and their interests in so-called departmental leases were in excess of the 4,800-acre limit imposed by federal law. Much of the best Oklahoma oil land was administered by the Indian Bureau of the U.S. Department of the Interior for the Indian owners, and to prevent monopolization of the leases (with Standard Oil in mind), Congress had prohibited anyone from holding more than 4,800 acres of Indian leases. The Interior Department's policy was to ignore corporate entities and to interpret the statute rigidly. This legislation and, more important, the interpretations created substantial difficulties for Royal Dutch-Shell "and required the disposal of all Indian leases in the acquired properties in excess of the 4,800 acre limit." In this connection, the group's New York law firm in 1912 contacted the U.S. Secretary of the Interior (Walter L. Fisher), who revealed his concern as to whether the law firm's clients "were dummies for the Standard Oil companies; the Secretary was assured they were not." As a result, the lawyer involved later recalled, "some of the absurdities of the Department's interpretation of the Federal statutes affecting departmental leases were relaxed, but the statutes and regulations under them continued to be a serious problem" (R. T. Swaine, *The Cravath Firm* [New York: privately printed, 1946] II, 75–76). Swaine cites his own Oct. 23, 1912, letter to Fisher.

Another piece of U.S. legislation that more or less inadvertently may have encouraged foreign investment was the 1877 Desert Land Act. Unlike most U.S. public land legislation that required residence, this act, designed to irrigate arid land, did not. This may have served to attract foreign investors to this category of land investment. See Elwood Mead, *Irrigation Institutions* (New York: Macmillan, 1907), 16–17, 34–36, 56–59, 344, for hints on this connection.

39. With its tariff policies, the U.S. federal government did support (protect) domestic industry.

40. August Belmont & Co. to N. M. Rothschild & Sons, July 29, 1881, Rothschild Archives, London (RAL) II/51/OB.

41. Maury Klein, *History of the Louisville and Nashville Railroad* (New York: Macmillan, 1972), 219.

42. E. H. Harriman to James Stillman, Oct. 23, 1908, quoted in Anna Robeson Burr, *Portrait of a Banker, James Stillman* (New York: Duffield, 1927), 241.

43. W. Turrentine Jackson, "British Impact on the Utah Mining Industry," *Utah Historical Quarterly*, 31 (Fall 1963): 470.

44. Donald Hugh Welsh, "Pierre Wibaux, Bad Lands Rancher," Ph.D. diss., University of Missouri, 1955, 143.

45. It was, after all, the "American" banking house of August Belmont & Co. that advised its principals, the London Rothschilds, in 1881 against investing in the Denver and Rio Grande, in part because the latter securities were apt to be subject to "speculative manipulation," but also because its success was "a matter for the future" and would come only after settlement of the area (August Belmont & Co. to N. M. Rothschild & Sons, Oct. 18, 1881, RAL II/51/OB).

46. *Banker's Magazine*, New York, 33 (April 1879): 749.

47. Ibid., 34 (Jan. 1880): 520–521 (my italics).

48. Ibid., 35 (Aug. 1880): 125.

49. "Taxing Foreign Banking Capital," *Banker's Magazine*, New York, 34 (June 1880): 919.

50. See, for example, the discussion in W. J. Caesar, Chicago, to J. Gurney Fowler, Feb. 14, 1894, Price Waterhouse Archives, London.

51. There may have been some of the same concerns over American bankers' actions, but the concerns were often made more explicit when foreign investors were involved.

52. *Economist*, 47 (July 27, 1889): 965.

53. 234 U.S. 216. See Reavis Cox, *Competition in the American Tobacco Industry* (New York: Columbia University Press, 1933), 38.

54. See data in FO 5/2043, Public Record Office (PRO), London, for 1886 regulations. For later rules and some historical background, see Chamber of Commerce of the United States, *Laws and Practices Affecting the Establishment of Foreign Branches of Banks* (Washington, D.C.: Chamber of Commerce, 1923), and Clyde William Phelps, *The*

Foreign Expansion of American Banks (1927; rpt. New York: Arno Press, 1976), 194–203. Often, before state prohibitions on foreign banks were imposed, examination and regulation occurred. See Chapter 13 for regulations on and then the prohibition of foreign banks in California, as an example.

55. In New York in 1886, for instance, the minimum capital of a foreign insurance company was specified by law; it had to be invested in approved securities; the foreign insurance firm had to register with the state superintendent. See Consul General, New York, to Foreign Office, Oct. 27, 1886, FO 5/2043, PRO, for New York and other state regulations. See also Chapter 15.

56. As Phelps, *Foreign Expansion*, 195, points out, the rules on banks were to protect depositors. *Best's Insurance Report (Fire and Marine Insurance), 1914*, 5, noted that regular licenses served to secure financial responsibility and to protect the insured.

57. Clyde Phelps—a historian of international banking—feels that state laws that were hostile to "foreign" (out-of-state, as well as out-of-country) banks "were adopted primarily because a state wished to protect its business enterprises against *those of other states of the union*" (Phelps, *Foreign Expansion*, 194; my italics). Investors from outside the nation were then treated equally with those from outside an individual state. State laws on out-of-state banks applied to out-of-country banks.

58. Virginia H. Taylor, *The Franco-Texan Land Company* (Austin: University of Texas Press, 1969), 221–223. The more general point is made in Detlev F. Vagts, "The Corporate Alien: Definitional Questions in Federal Restraints on Foreign Enterprise," *Harvard Law Review*, 74 (June 1961): 1528.

59. William Marion Gibson, *Aliens and the Law* (Chapel Hill: University of North Carolina Press, 1940), 75. The reciprocity provision in the 1881 law was reconfirmed in 1905 legislation (ibid., 77). In 1906, however, a new U.S. federal law dropped the reciprocity clause and gave "any owner of a trade-mark who shall have a manufacturing establishment within the United States" the same protection (ibid., 81). The clause seems to have been dropped because of the complexity in enforcement.

60. David M. Pletcher, "1861–1898: Economic Growth and Diplomatic Adjustment," in *Economics and World Power*, ed. William H. Becker and Samuel F. Wells, Jr. (New York: Columbia University Press, 1984), 141 (Pletcher does not note the name of the French cable company nor that it was allowed entry; he does specify the conditions). On the German cable company, see *Foreign Relations of the United States, 1899*, 311–312.

61. The main specific impact on Imperial Tobacco was to lessen the U.S. influence (American Tobacco had to sell its minority stake in Imperial). Imperial had U.S. investments in acquiring tobacco for export; after 1911 these remained untouched by the decision. The effect of the Court action on BAT was to open the way for that company to pass, in the 1920s, to British control. Then BAT's investments in the United States made for export (stakes in both cigarette manufacturing and leaf purchasing) would change from U.S. to British ones.

62. Cox, *Competition*, 28.

63. See Chapter 10.

64. The aim was apparently to eliminate graft paid by German dye companies to American buyers. See Howard Watson Ambruster, *Treason's Peace* (New York: Beechhurst Press, 1947), 5–10, and Alien Property Custodian, *Report, 1918–1919*, 41. The graft was considered an aspect of "predatory pricing," that is, anticompetitive.

65. See Chapters 10 and 11.

66. Typically, as noted earlier, foreign investors used American law firms to provide interpretations of applicable American law.

67. See *Banker's Magazine*, New York, 38 (Jan. 1884): 577, and 40 (Feb. 1886): 578, for

a similar view. But on the same page in the 1886 *Banker's Magazine*, the journal expressed approval of European investment in U.S. manufacturing behind U.S. tariff walls! See section of this chapter on favorable responses. In 1879 *Banker's Magazine* had commented that the great majority of Americans believed it was "a misfortune to have its [the country's] public, corporate, or private securities held abroad. The doctrine of borrowing in the cheapest markets may be theoretically correct, but to popular apprehension, interest paid to foreigners is very much like the rent paid to absentee landlords, which is the standing grievance of Ireland" (*Banker's Magazine*, 33 [April 1879]: 746). In short, the same journal could have different responses at different times, and different ones related to investments in different sectors at the same time.

68. A. D. Noyes, *Thirty Years of American Finance* (1900; rpt. New York: Greenwood Press, 1969), 122–123. For similar fears, see Henry Adams, *Letters*, ed. Worthington Ford, 2 vols. (Boston: Houghton Mifflin, 1930, 1938), II, 103, for his April 1896 concerns over foreign monies—loaned practically on call: "This makes our market excessively sensitive and dangerous."

69. E. C. Stedman, *New York Stock Exchange* (1905; rpt. New York: Greenwood Press, 1969), 298, 348, 352, 354.

70. As will be evident, this was a view of populist leaders as well as some bankers.

71. See the three articles on negative reactions by Roger V. Clements, "British Investment and American Legislative Restrictions"; his "British-Controlled Enterprise in the West between 1870 and 1900 and Some Agrarian Reactions," *Agricultural History*, 26 (Oct. 1953): 132–141; and his "Farmers' Attitude toward British Investment in American Industry," *Journal of Economic History*, 15 (June 1955): 151–159; and Edward P. Crapol, *America for Americans* (Westport, Conn.: Greenwood Press, 1973).

72. Letter of April 17, 1892, cited in Swaine, *Cravath Firm*, I, 467. This was on a matter related to the Chicago stockyards.

73. Robert E. Riegel, *The Story of Western Railroads* (Lincoln: University of Nebraska Press, 1926), 138–140, 290.

74. N. B. Ashby, *The Riddle of the Sphinx* (Chicago: Mercantile Publishing, 1892), 266–267. The hostility toward "absentee ownership" was long-standing. The farmers' assumption was that eastern and European investors were less responsive to local public opinion and local needs. See Solon Justus Buck, *The Granger Movement, 1870–1880* (Cambridge, Mass.: Harvard University Press, 1913), 12–13.

75. Charles Francis Adams, "The Granger Movement," *North American Review*, 120 (April 1875): 397. Adams often used the word *foreign* to refer to eastern as well as European.

76. Ibid., 398. But, Adams noted, "those who did live upon the prairies were not East Indians, and there was very little probability that they would long submit to any very appreciable ignoring of their rights. They had also very respectable grievances to complain of" (ibid., 399).

77. Robert C. Cotner, *Addresses and State Papers of James Stephen Hogg* (Austin: University of Texas Press, 1951), 277–278. The case was *Mortgage Trustees of the Texas and Pacific, the St. Louis and Southwestern, the Tyler Southwestern, the International and Great Northern and the Gulf, Colorado and Santa Fe v. Texas Railroad Commission and C. A. Culberson, Attorney General* (1892).

78. See John D. Hicks, *The Populist Revolt* (Minneapolis: University of Minnesota Press, 1931), 60–66, on farmers' grievances. He does not discuss the foreign investment issue. Others, however, did associate "watered" capital with foreign investment.

79. See U.S. Senate, 48th Cong., lst sess., 1894, Exec. Doc. 127, esp. 2, 31, 38–39, on the unauthorized fencing of public land. On frauds, see Paul Wallace Gates, "The Homestead Law in an Incongruous Land System," in *The Public Lands*, ed. Vernon

Carstensen (Madison: University of Wisconsin Press, 1963), 338. See also Commissioner of General Land Office, *Annual Report, 1885,* 167, 173.

80. See Roger V. Clements, "British-Controlled Enterprise in the West," 135–141, for reactions to British "irrigation" companies. These were basically "land companies" that became involved in irrigation as a means of raising the value of the land. Protestors claimed that the farmer who had "to pay the initial heavy charges for land and water was compelled to mortgage his farm to the company of whom [from which] he was purchasing land and water rights" (ibid., 136).

81. Cotner, *Papers of James Stephen Hogg,* 226, 272–274.

82. Quoted in Crapol, *America for Americans,* 94.

83. *New York Times,* Jan. 24, 1885.

84. An excellent work on William Scully and the reaction to him is Paul Wallace Gates, *Frontier Landlords and Pioneer Tenants* (Ithaca, N.Y.: Cornell University Press, 1945), 34–64. Scully was referred to by name in Congressional reports. See, for example, U.S. House, 49th Cong., 1st sess., 1886, H. Rept. 1951, 3. One author called Scully "the spark . . . necessary to inflame the popular imagination" (James Karr Taylor, "Escheats under Statutes Disqualifying Aliens from Holding Property," masters' thesis, Faculty of Law, Columbia University, 1935, 62).

85. Quoted in the fine biography of Scully by Homer E. Socolofsky, *Landlord William Scully* (Lawrence: Regents Press of Kansas, 1979), 118.

86. U.S. Senate, 48th Cong., 1st sess., 1884, Exec. Doc. 127, 2.

87. William A. Hall to Hon. Mr. Belford, member of Congress from Colorado, Jan. 16, 1884, ibid., 31.

88. Oates sponsored strong legislation against alien owners. See U.S. House, "Land Titles to Aliens in the United States," 48th Cong., 2nd sess., Jan. 20, 1885, H. Rept. 2308, endorsing his bill, HR 5266.

89. Lewis Nordyke, *Cattle Empire* (New York: William Morrow, 1949), 76–77. For more on Archibald Marjoribanks, see Clements, "British-Controlled Enterprise," 134n.

90. Speeches of James Stephen Hogg, in *Papers of James Stephen Hogg,* ed. Cotner, 97 (April 19, 1890), 116–118 (inaugural address, Jan. 21, 1891), 180–181 (March 14, 1892).

91. 1888 flyer, Pearson, *Maxwell Grant,* facing p. 131.

92. Demands of the Farmers' Alliance of Texas, 1886; St. Louis Demands, Dec. 1889; Ocala Demands, Dec. 1890; Cincinnati Platform, May 1891; St. Louis Platform, Feb. 1892; and Omaha Platform, July 1891. Each had an anti–alien property plank. See Vernon Carstensen, ed., *Farmer Discontent, 1865–1900* (New York: Wiley, 1974), 74, 78, 79 (for first three), and Hicks, *The Populist Revolt,* 428, 431, 433, 438, 443 (for all except the first).

93. Quoted in Ashby, *The Riddle of the Sphinx* (1892), 322–326.

94. For biographical data on Leland Stanford (1824–1893), see Richard B. Morris, ed., *Encyclopedia of American History* (New York: Harper & Row, 1976), 1155–56. In fact, in August 1889 German investors had acquired sizable interests in the Central Pacific. Was there a connection between Stanford's May 1890 comments and this purchase? On the German acquisitions, see Dietrich G. Buss, *Henry Villard* (New York: Arno Press 1977), 185. The Central Pacific and the Southern Pacific had raised money in London (Dorothy Adler, *British Investment in American Railways* [Charlottesville: University Press of Virginia, 1970], 207, 210).

95. Ashby, *The Riddle of the Sphinx,* 327: "Debt has ever been the symbol of bondage." See Allan G. Bogue, *Money at Interest* (Ithaca, N.Y.: Cornell University Press, 1955), 150, on the Farmers' Alliance opposition to both mortgages and mortgage lenders. Bogue cites a Nov. 24, 1891, letter of mortgage grantor, J. B. Watkins, to his English representative.

96. Open letter, quoted in speech of James Stephen Hogg (of Texas), Oct. 1, 1892, in *Papers of James Stephen Hogg*, ed. Cotner, 273. These Kansas farmers thought foreclosures were based on a "preconceived purpose to gain possession of these farms" (ibid.). On the Kansas foreclosures, see Hicks, *Populist Revolt*, 84.

97. Ivan Wright, *Farm Mortgage Financing* (New York: McGraw–Hill, 1923), 1, 43.

98. Today, when we take mortgages for granted, it is hard to realize the controversy they once provoked. Thus a writer in the *Annals* of 1894 would discuss the question, "Are mortgages evidences of prosperity, or not?" He pointed to the "voluntary character" of this type of indebtedness that he believed demonstrated "a general consensus of opinion that it is a means of promoting prosperity." Nonetheless, the author recognized, "Let there be a failure of crops, so that the interest burden cannot be shifted upon the consumers, and farmers begin to think of political revolution and of schemes of legislation to lighten their load of debt" (George K. Holmes, "A Decade of Mortgages," *Annals of the American Academy of Arts and Sciences*, 6 [1894]: 913–914).

99. John Davis, "Alien Landlordism in America," in *The Land Question from Various Points of View*, ed. C. F. Taylor (Philadelphia: C. F. Taylor, [1898]), 56–57, 61–63. Davis was one of the intellectual leaders of Kansas populism; edited a Junction City, Kansas, newspaper; and served in Congress, 1891–1895. See Socolofsky, *Landlord*, 113, 169n.

100. Davis, "Alien Landlordism," 61. The passionate feelings were reflected in Davis' quotation from an unidentified American writer on British landlordism in Ireland: "The Saxon Thane was a swinish, licentious brute . . . in the course of time the Dane, a born sea pirate . . . mixed his blood with the Saxon. Then came the Norman, a born land pirate . . . The world . . . saw a new creation . . . the . . . steel-hearted, relentless absentee British landlord; one-third sea pirate, one-third land pirate and one-third hog." To which Davis added, "It is to this brute of greed and cruelty, this merciless hog, this devilfish from over the sea, that we are surrendering our families . . . Forbid it, Heaven! Is there no voice, human or divine, that can awaken the American people to a sense of their danger?" (ibid., 67–68).

101. In the early twentieth century, a new swell of anti–alien land ownership sentiments arose, associated with resident Japanese farming in California. See Dudley O. McGovney, "The Anti-Japanese Land Laws of California," *California Law Review*, 35 (1947): 7. Because these concerns related to settlers, not to nonresidents, they are outside the scope of my study. In the years 1900–1914, hostility to British ownership of land persisted but lost the intensity of the previous two decades.

102. Early in 1902 James S. Hogg spent three months in Europe attempting to interest foreign capital in the Hogg-Swayne Syndicate to develop Texas oil (Cotner, ed., *Papers of James Stephen Hogg*, 501). This was the very same Hogg who as Texas Governor (1891–1895) had denounced British investments in Texas land!

103. *Congressional Record*, 51st Cong., 1st sess., Aug. 20, 1890, 8879. Payson represented prairie counties and was a strong supporter of anti–alien land legislation. See Gates, *Frontier Landlords*, 59.

104. *Congressional Record*, 51st Cong., 1st sess., Aug. 20, 1890, 8878.

105. See Chapter 8 on copper and John D. Ryan's concerns. C. C. Hoyer Millar, *Florida, South Carolina and Canadian Phosphates* (London: Eden Fisher, 1892), 104, quotes (disapprovingly) from an American complaint over "sharp-dealing brothers from England," who depressed the prices of Florida phosphate exports.

106. See U.S. House, 63rd Cong., 2nd sess., Feb. 3, 1914, H. Rept. 214.

107. See Chapter 8.

108. Quoted in *Mineral Industry, 1914*, 555.

109. Ibid., 555–556.

110. George H. Nash, *The Life of Herbert Hoover* (New York: W. W. Norton, 1983), 472.

111. See section on national defense later in this chapter.

112. Quoted in Ashby, *The Riddle of the Sphinx,* 250–251.

113. It is hard to exaggerate the substantial coverage that the surge of British interests in American industry, 1889–90, received. See, for example, the discussion in *Banker's Magazine,* New York, 44 (Aug. 1889): 81–85, on British stakes in breweries and iron and steel works. *The American Iron and Steel Association Bulletin,* 23 (Dec. 11, 1889): 341, reported that (1) an English syndicate was purchasing John Bass's large car-wheel works and boiler and locomotive plants in Fort Wayne, St. Louis, and Chicago, along with Bass's iron and coal mines in Alabama. Price: $3.5 million. (2) An English syndicate represented by the Chicago attorney Edwin Corwin had offered $8.5 million for Elgin National Watch Company. (3) Corwin was planning (with the help of the English syndicate) a consolidation of three Detroit stove companies under Michigan Stove Company. (4) An English syndicate had bought Van Dusen's grain elevator chain. (5) An English and American syndicate was planning to raise $15 million to $18 million to buy all the cotton-duck mills in the country. Some of these investments were not consummated. The largest venture—that involving the cotton-duck mills—never came to pass.

In its Jan. 1 and 8, 1890, issue the same *Bulletin* (vol. 24, p. 2) reported on (1) plans to sell about two dozen tanneries in New England (the Shaw tanneries being the most important) to British investors. Three English accountants were on the scene to investigate. (2) T. B. Ripey, a Kentucky distiller, had sold out to a British syndicate. (3) The Angus Smith system of grain elevators had been sold for $1 million to an English syndicate. Its next issue (Jan. 15, 1890) told of Thomas Stewart of London, at the Grand Pacific Hotel in Chicago, planning to invest $15 million of English capital (p. 10). It also reported that four of the principal paper mills in Glens Falls and Remington, New York, were being sold to an English syndicate. Price: $4 million to $5 million. And so it went, with each subsequent issue of the paper offering new reports. See also for another rendition Erastus Wiman, "British Capital and American Industries," *North American Review,* 150 (Jan. 1890): 220–234.

114. Other reasons for the rejection were: "2. The large capital of the English company would, we fear, subject it to heavy taxation in many of the States in which it would do business. 3. There would be difficulty on account of the tenure of the real estate which the Company requires on its own business. In many States a foreign corporation could not own real estate" (Swaine, *Cravath Firm,* I, 430 [Feb. 20, 1890, letter]).

115. Phelps, *Foreign Expansion,* 195.

116. Silver advocates, agrarians, and debtors in the United States resented creditors (domestic or foreign). The country must have more money. "The Rothschild's, and the interests which profit by a shrunken volume of money, are hostile to any movement on the part of our government to dethrone them" (Ashby, *The Riddle of the Sphinx,* 330).

117. The figure is far in excess of other estimates. See Table 5.4.

118. W. H. Harvey, *Coin's Financial School* (Chicago: Coin, 1894), 89, 132, 135, 138–140, 146, 151. In this context a story related in the latest Rothschild House history is of interest: when in 1892 Chancellor of the Exchequer Sir William Harcourt had wanted a delegate to a Bimetallism Conference, he turned to Lord Rothschild (Nathaniel M. Rothschild), who declined the invitation but recommended his brother Alfred. Sir William asked whether the latter was "a good staunch monometallist (what Mr. Gladstone calls a 'sane man') who will uphold to his death the gold standard." Lord Rothschild reassured Harcourt that he had no need to worry. See Richard Davis, *The English Rothschilds* (Chapel Hill: University of North Carolina Press, 1983), 222, who based this on correspondence in the Harcourt papers.

119. F. Cyril James, *The Growth of Chicago Banks*, 2 vols. (New York: Harper & Bros., 1938), I. 634.

120. Quoted in ibid., 640. The prosilver advocates and the attackers of alien land ownership were often one and the same. See, for example, Davis, "Alien Landlordism," 61, 63n.

121. Adams, *Letters*, II, 103, 110 (July 1896 letter). See his Sept. 1893 letter, wherein he wrote, "In a society of Jews and brokers, a world made up of maniacs wild for gold, I have no place" (ibid., 33).

122. Powderly is quoted in Crapol, *America for Americans*, 97.

123. American businessmen had these worries over a British textile machine producer and over German dyestuff makers, for example.

124. See W. J. Caesar to J. G. Fowler, Oct. 14, 1898, Box 1, Price Waterhouse Archives, London, on the "prejudice" against "foreign" accountants; Caesar to Price, Waterhouse, London, Oct. 14, 1898, in ibid., on the agitation in New York against employment of foreign accountants; and John L. Carey, *The Rise of the Accounting Profession* (New York: American Institute of Certified Public Accountants, 1969), 34, on the jealousy of American accountants.

125. Cotner, ed., *Papers of James Stephen Hogg*, 374–375.

126. Carstensen, ed., *Farmer Discontent, 1865–1900*, 121.

127. See, for example, the testimony of Sidney Story, vice president of Pan American Mail Steamship Company, New Orleans, Jan. 7, 1913, U.S. House of Representatives, Committee on Merchant Marine and Fisheries, *Investigation of Shipping Combinations* (Washington, D.C., 1913), 5–21. Story's firm was put out of business because of the "shipping combinations" (ibid., 5).

128. The specific complaints are summarized in U.S. Federal Trade Commission, *Report on Cooperation in American Export Trade* (Washington, D.C., 1916), I, 36–40. See also *Shipping Combinations*, passim, and U.S. House of Representatives, Committee on Merchant Marine and Fisheries, *Steamship Agreements and Affiliations in the American Foreign and Domestic Trade* (Washington, D.C., 1914), passim.

129. Julius Grodinsky, *Jay Gould* (Philadelphia: University of Pennsylvania Press, 1957), 279.

130. It was apparently a subsidiary of the English Mannesmann Tube Company, which in turn was German controlled.

131. J. Perc Boore, *The Seamless Story* (Los Angeles: Commonwealth Press, 1951), 13, gives details.

132. See Chapter 12. Yet nothing barred Vickers' participation in submarines. As noted in Chapter 12, submarines were not a top priority of the U.S. Navy. By 1912 American regulations forbad foreigners from even visiting U.S. navy yards (F. W. Taylor to E. Michelin, Aug. 29, 1912, Taylor Papers, Hoboken, New Jersey).

133. Gleason L. Archer, *History of Radio* (New York: American Historical Society, 1938), 63, 78.

134. L. S. Howeth, *History of Communications-Electronics in the United States Navy* (Washington, D.C., 1963).

135. U.S. Navy, *Annual Report, 1913*, 17.

136. Howeth, *History*, and Chapter 14.

137. John A. DeNovo, "Petroleum and the U.S. Navy before World War I," *Mississippi Valley Historical Review*, 41 (March 1955): 641–656; Gerald Nash, *United States Oil Policy, 1890–1964* (Pittsburgh: University of Pittsburgh Press, 1968), 5, 8–11, 16–19; and John Ise, *United States Oil Policy* (New Haven: Yale University Press, 1926), 157–158, 309–320.

138. U. S. Secretary of the Navy, *Annual Report, 1913*, 14.

139. *Mineral Industry, 1913,* 537, quoting *Engineering and Mining Journal,* Jan. 31, 1914. Nash, *Herbert Hoover,* 472, puts the Andrew Weir California oil ventures in the context of the British Navy's needs.

140. U.S. Secretary of the Navy, *Annual Report, 1914* (Dec. 1, 1914), 17.

141. Ise, *United States Oil Policy,* 460, notes that Americans also watched the British government in 1914 buy control of the Anglo-Persian Oil Company to secure a future supply of fuel oil for its Navy. On British government activities, see Geoffrey Jones, *The State and the Emergency of the British Oil Industry* (London: Macmillan, 1981), and R. W. Ferrier, *The History of the British Petroleum Company* (Cambridge: Cambridge University Press, 1982), vol. 1.

142. Ise, *United States Oil Policy,* 460.

143. All this was a preview: the issue of foreign corporations and American oil reserves would become of much greater concern in the years 1919–1923.

144. The quotation is from Adams, "The Granger Movement" (April 1875), 395. As noted earlier, Adams often used the word *foreign* to refer to eastern as well as European capital. For details on the Potter Law, see Buck, *The Granger Movement,* 182–205. Regulation of the railroads—state and federal—was often seen as reducing returns to investment. There was, however, no special prejudice against investors from abroad. Thus I am not going to discuss the railroad legislation, since it did not single out the out-of-country investor.

145. William Mackenzie to Earl Granville, Jan. 7, 1881, FO 5/1763, PRO.

146. Gene M. Gressley, *Bankers and Cattlemen* (New York: Alfred A. Knopf, 1966), 193, and his "Brokers to the British: Francis Smith and Company," *Southwestern Historical Quarterly,* 71 (July 1967): 9. They believed the law deprived nonresident corporations of the right to foreclose.

147. Ibid.

148. The sequence of the initial measures (some states passed more than one law) affecting alien nonresident owners was Indiana (1885), Wisconsin, Minnesota, Colorado, Nebraska, Illinois (1887), Iowa (1888), Washington (constitutional provision—1889), Kansas, Idaho, Texas (1891), and Missouri (1895). See state statutes and Clements, "British Investment and American Legislative Restrictions," 219–222; Crapol, *America for Americans,* 103–107; Charles H. Sullivan, "Alien Land Laws: A Re-Evaluation," *Temple Law Quarterly,* 36 (1962): 31n; Gates, *Frontier Landlords,* 58–59; and Douglas W. Nelson, "The Alien Land Law Movement of the Late Nineteenth Century," *Journal of the West,* 9 (Jan. 1970): 52–54.

149. At the eleventh annual meeting (1893), held in Britain, of the shareholders of the Matador Land and Cattle Company, Ltd. (a huge holder of Texas land), the chairman discussed a recent rather alarmist newspaper article on the subject of Texas lands: "From time to time mutters have been heard about the confiscation of land held by aliens in America. These rumours have never resulted in any act of confiscation, and we do not believe that they ever will. Foreigners have rights which the laws of every civilised country recognize, and while it is within the right of any State of the Union to change its laws so as to refuse aliens the privilege of acquiring land within its boundaries, it cannot take away by force the property of any alien who has acquired land by legal title before a law of prohibition was introduced. We are well advised that our titles are beyond challenge, and that the Federal Court is a safe defence against any attempt to deprive an alien of his rights" (W. M. Pearce, *The Matador Land and Cattle Company* [Norman: University of Oklahoma Press, 1964], 51). When it became clear to one large foreign investor, William Scully, that his "alien" status was undesirable—and after Missouri passed its alien land law (1895)—Scully simply declared his intention to become an American citizen (Sept. 20, 1895). He became one on Oct. 17, 1900 (Soco-

lofsky, *Landlord,* 127, 129). This did not stop him from continuing to keep a home in London. That the laws were not applied retroactively protected Scully's earlier holdings.

150. See Chapter 13. Out-of-state branches were also barred, but New York paid special attention to out-of-country banks.

151. See Consul General, New York, to Foreign Office, Oct. 27, 1886, FO 5/2043, PRO. As state measures multiplied, some foreign insurance companies sought to circumvent them. A Sun Insurance Office representative from Great Britain found in 1887 that the firm's American manager had procured "entry into many of the States in which it was then operating by the old fashion method of bribing 'the right man . . . in the right way' " (Dickson, *The Sun Insurance Office,* 231). The home office was appalled, not at the practice, but at the inefficiency involved: at least one insurance superintendent had been paid off twice!

152. Edward Liveing, *A Century of Insurance* (London: H. F. & G. Witherby, 1961), 55.

153. Samuel Kerr to M. J. Dart, Dec. 27, 1890, quoted in Bogue, *Money at Interest,* 165.

154. W. G. Kerr, *Scottish Capital on the American Credit Frontier* (Austin: Texas State Historical Association, 1976), 191.

155. Bogue, *Money at Interest,* 166; a copy of the 1892 law is in *Papers of James Stephen Hogg,* ed. Cotner, 549–551, and background, 158, 179–181. All of the alien property acts threatened foreign mortgage lenders. In most cases the mortgage companies were protected by clauses that gave them the right to foreclose and to hold the land for a short period. See Clement, "British Investment and American Legislative Restrictions," 219. Land was the collateral on the loan, and if a mortgage company did not have the right to foreclose, it had no collateral.

156. Gary John Previts and Barbara Dubis Merino, *A History of Accounting in America* (New York: Ronald Press, 1979), 98. A number of foreign accountants became CPAs in Illinois, which had no such restriction. Some declared they intended to become citizens, and never did.

157. Foreign investors were concerned about taxes. The Cravath law firm and its predecessors offered advice. See Swaine, *Cravath Firm,* I, 430, for example. Gibson, *Aliens and the Law,* 108, records the existence in the pre–World War I years of discrimination against nonresident aliens in state inheritance taxes and property taxes. Illinois sought more taxes from the large foreign landlord William Scully, suing him in 1882 "to recover back personal property taxes" for the years 1875–1881. When it was claimed that he owed taxes based on his rent rolls in Illinois, his defense was that these rolls were "owned in Great Britain, not in Illinois" and therefore not taxable in the state. A local jury found for the plaintiff, but the Illinois Supreme Court reversed the judgment against Scully (Gates, *Frontier Landlords,* 54, and Socolofsky, *Landlord,* 90). In 1887 the Illinois legislature passed a bill preventing "alien landlords from requiring tenants to pay taxes assessed upon the land they rented." Scully responded by raising his rent the equivalent of the taxes due (ibid., 108). In banking, some states imposed special taxes on foreign banks or bank agencies (see Chapter 13). Liveing, *A Century of Insurance,* 55, notes differential state taxation for foreign insurance companies in the 1890s. In 1899 Sir Julian Pauncefote (the British Ambassador) called the attention of U.S. Secretary of State John Hay to legislation in Iowa and laws proposed in Missouri and Nebraska imposing a discriminatory tax on foreign fire insurance companies (*Foreign Relations of the United States, 1899,* 345). This is only a sampling. Clearly the states' power to tax could be, and was, differentially applied to investors from abroad.

158. As noted, on occasion such laws also altered foreign investors' location decisions within the United States.

159. See Matthew Simon, *Cyclical Fluctuations and the International Capital Movements of the United States, 1865–1877* (New York: Arno Press, 1979), 231–234, 467–469.

160. James, *The Chicago Banks*, I, 634.

161. See Chapter 4. See also Act of May 10, 1872, 17 U.S. Stats. 91, and Clark C. Spence, "British Investment and the American Mining Frontier, 1860–1914, "*New Mexico Historical Review*, 36 (April 1961): 134. The British Foreign Office did protest, in vain.

162. 20 U.S. Stats. 88. See Spence, *British Investments*, 196. Jenks Cameron, *The Development of Governmental Forest Control in the United States* (1928; rpt. New York: DaCapo Press, 1972), 216, describes the 1878 legislation as the culmination of efforts "looking to the devisement of some method by which Western agricultural and mining interests might obtain timber without being put to the necessity of stealing it." Cameron says nothing about the antialien clause. See also Victor Westphall, *The Public Domain in New Mexico, 1854–1891* (Albuquerque: University of New Mexico Press, 1965), 113.

163. W. Turrentine Jackson, *The Enterprising Scot* (Edinburgh: Edinburgh University Press, 1968), 224. As noted earlier, the antialien clause was a typical part of federal public domain legislation, at least from the 1841 Preemption Act.

164. Spence, *British Investments*, 196–197. On the impact on the Scottish-financed California Redwood Company, see Jackson, *Enterprising Scot*, 224–231.

165. One in 1883, five in 1884, three in 1885, and nine in 1886. See Spence, *British Investments*, 204.

166. U.S. House, "Land Titles to Aliens in the United States," 48th Cong., 2nd sess., Jan. 20, 1885, H. Rept. 2308, 2. For many years I puzzled over the phrase "the shieks of Asia." My present belief is that it is most likely a reference to Britishers who had gained great wealth in India or East Asia and were investing in America. Frequently the anti-British verbiage included comments that Americans were *not* East Indians and should not be treated like them. This said, I should also be quick to note that there is no evidence of a sizable transfer of wealth from India or East Asia to America by British investors, albeit some of the British trust companies with India or China in their names did become involved in U.S. investments, and some British investment groups that were heavily engaged in Asian business also had U.S. stakes.

167. U.S. House, "Land Titles," and Jackson, *Enterprising Scot*, 107–109. See also L. S. Sackville West, Washington, D.C., to Earl of Granville, Jan. 22, 1885, FO 5/1902, PRO. Why did this legislation originate with the Representative from Alabama? Part of the reason may lie in the earlier heavy foreign investment in Alabama state bonds and railroads, which had been transformed into large land holdings.

168. Act of March 3, 1887, 24 U.S. Stats. 476. The formal title of the act was "An Act to restrict the ownership of real estate in the Territories to American citizens, and so forth." It was often referred to as the alien land law or the Alien Property Act of 1887. See also data in FO 5/1979, PRO. The *federal* legislation became the model for many of the state laws passed after 1887. Throughout, the act contained the word *hereafter* so as not to affect existing investors. Likewise, a provision exempted land acquired in "the collection of debts heretofore created," that is, foreclosures by foreign mortgage companies on properties already mortgaged. Vagts, "The Corporate Alien," 1532, suggests that the classification of corporations as alien by virtue of their shareholdings began with this legislation.

169. Spence, *British Investments*, 205; *Financial News*, July 20, 1887; and also extensive data in FO 5/2043, PRO.

170. See, for example, Calderon Carlisle to Sir L. Sackville West, April 6, 1887, FO 5/1979, PRO, and statement by Rep. Holman, *Congressional Record*, 51st Cong., 1st

sess., Aug. 20, 1890, 8878, suggesting that foreign investors had lobbied against the bill.

171. U.S. Senate, *Mining Interests of Aliens*, 50th Cong., 2nd sess., 1890, S. Rept. 2690. On the other hand, in April 1887 Pierre Wibaux had just arranged French financing of his cattle ranch in the Dakota Territory. The March 1887 legislation affected the *legal* organization of his business but in no way restricted the foreign investment. See Welsh, "Pierre Wibaux," 118–119.

172. According to Land Office rules, a corporation obtaining a patent had to present evidence that it was less than 20 percent owned abroad. No one, however, monitored any subsequent transfer of ownership abroad (Spence, *British Investments*, 210). See also British Consul General, New York, to Lord Salisbury, July 23, 1887, FO 5/1987, PRO.

173. Jackson, *Enterprising Scot*, 113.

174. Quoted in Spence, *British Investments*, 210. Davis, in 1898, agreed: "We have no effective legislation by Congress restricting or suppressing foreign investment in American soil" ("Alien Landlordism," 60).

175. Law of March 2, 1897, 29 U.S. Stats. 618.

176. In 1889 North and South Dakota, Montana, and Washington became states; in 1890, Wyoming; in 1896, Utah. Oklahoma would become a state in 1907 and Arizona and New Mexico in 1912. As states they were no longer covered by the act.

177. Rowland Tappan Berthoff, *British Immigrants in Industrial America, 1790–1950* (Cambridge, Mass.: Harvard University Press, 1953), 39.

178. Robert C. Cotner, *James Stephen Hogg* (Austin: University of Texas Press, 1959), 136. On the Capitol Syndicate and the Capitol Freehold Land and Investment Company, Ltd., see ibid., 134–135; Nordyke, *Cattle Empire*, 62–77, passim; and J. Evetts Haley, *The XIT Ranch of Texas* (Norman: University of Oklahoma Press, 1953), 49, 71–73, passim. I do not know the resolution of the suit.

179. Lawrence Oakley Cheever, *The House of Morrell* (Cedar Rapids, Iowa: Torch Press, 1948), 102.

180. See Jones, Caesar to Price, Waterhouse, Dec. 21, 1897, Price Waterhouse Archives, London. The 1885 Contract Labor Act had exempted professionals. The law, however, had been modified in 1891 to include professionals.

181. The law was not well enforced, and there were numerous ways to circumvent it. See Charlotte Erickson, *American Industry and the European Immigrant, 1860–1885* (Cambridge, Mass.: Harvard University Press, 1957), chaps. 9 and 10. Erickson, commenting on the failure of the contract labor laws after twenty years of operation (1885–1905) to deter recruitment of skilled European workers by "American industry," noted that the relatively new U.S. tin-making, silk, hosiery, and lace industries all received in those years importations of skilled workers from abroad (p. 175). With the exception of hosiery (where I have identified no foreign investment), the other "new industries" did attract foreign direct investments. The law did not prohibit the bringing in of skilled workers; it merely specified that they could not come in under an indenture.

182. This was specified in sec. 9 of the National Bank Act of 1864. See Ross M. Robertson, *The Comptroller and Bank Supervision* (Washington, D.C., 1968), 197. It was repeated in the Federal Reserve Act of 1913.

183. John G. B. Hutchins, *The American Maritime Industries and Public Policy, 1789–1914* (Cambridge, Mass.: Harvard University Press, 1941), 542–543.

184. Letter to Lord Salisbury, July 23, 1887, FO 5/1987, PRO, which referred to events of a few years back. Hutchins never discusses the percentage of shares "allowed" to be held abroad, although he does explicitly state that after 1817 "only

vessels built and owned in the United States could engage" in the coastwise carrying trade (*American Maritime Industries,* 252). There was no set percentage on companies. See Vagts, "The Corporate Alien," 1503–4, for background.

185. See Hutchins, *American Maritime Industries,* 569–571, on railway participation.

186. One of my colleagues in political science (David Zweig) suggested that the Alien Property Act of 1887 also might be viewed in national defense terms, for the defense of sovereignty is "national defense." Clearly the Alien Property Act was an assertion of sovereignty. I have, however, used the phrase "national defense" in the military sense—and the alien property legislation was in no way designed to make us less vulnerable were war to occur.

187. Hutchins, *American Maritime Industries,* 540.

188. Under the Radio Act of August 13, 1912 (37 U.S. Stat. 302), no person or company could operate any apparatus for radio communication between the several states, or with foreign nations, or upon any vessel of the United States without a license from the U.S. Secretary of Commerce and Labor. The Act mandated that licenses would be issued only to U.S. citizens or companies incorporated under the laws of some state or territory of the United States. Nothing was included on ownership of an American corporation, and immediately the U.S. Attorney General interpreted this law as permitting alien control over *corporate* licensees—29 Op. Att'y Gen. 579 (1912)—which effectively nullified any possible antiforeign intent. See U.S. Department of Commerce, *Foreign Direct Investments in the United States* (Washington, D.C., 1976), VII, 300–301, on the Attorney General's opinion.

189. DeNovo, "Pretroleum and the U.S. Navy," 647, and Ise, *United States Oil Policy,* 324. Not until after World War I (in 1920) was a Mineral Land Leasing Act passed (it did affect foreign investors, but it is outside this volume's time period).

190. John Hay to Reginald Tower, April 27, 1899, *Foreign Relations of the United States, 1899,* 346. For a similar earlier response, see Edw. Thornton to Earl Granville, June 13, 1881, FO 5/1761, PRO.

191. Werking, *The Master Architects,* 226, based on Poole's notes for a lecture, March 1935.

192. Export promotion as a way of dealing with debtor status assumes, of course, that foreign investment is a "balancing" item on international accounts and that an annual excess of exports over imports reduces foreign obligations. When one looks at long-term foreign investments as "autonomous" transactions, then export promotion becomes irrelevant. All the other measures discussed looked at foreign investment per se. Export promotion does provide a nation with foreign exchange to pay interest and dividends on foreign obligations.

193. Gates, *Frontier Landlords,* 58, believes that historians of agrarian movements have neglected the issue of alien landlordism, devoting their attention to silver and the malpractices of the railroads, whereas this was a fundamental cause of western discontent. He has only a few allies in this view, yet he ranks among the best of historians in this field.

194. The typical phrase used was "eastern and foreign capital." Bogue's excellent *Money at Interest* discusses at length the intermediation of British monies into American land mortgages, but in his summary when he dealt with populist views toward the moneylender (pp. 262–276), he never once specifically mentions British investors; the "moneylender"—irrespective of nationality—was a "hyena-faced shylock" to the farmer.

195. Nathaniel Mayer Rothschild, London, to cousins, Paris, March 14, 1907, RAL XI/130A/1.

196. Gates would not agree; see note 193 above.

197. In fact, the hearings were entitled "The Money Trust Investigation" (U.S. House, Subcommittee on Banking and Currency, *Money Trust Investigation* [Washington, D.C., 1912–13]). Vincent P. Carosso, "The Wall Street Money Trust from Pujo through Medina," *Business History Review*, 67 (Winter 1973): 425–428, shows the bias in the Pujo probe.

198. See, for example, the testimony of J. P. Morgan, Jacob H. Schiff (of Kuhn, Loeb), Henry P. Davison (of J. P. Morgan & Co.), and Robert Winsor (of Kidder, Peabody), *Money Trust Investigation*, pt. 14, 1003ff; pt. 23, 1660ff; pt. 25, 1850ff; pt. 26, 1995ff.

199. It is all the more remarkable when one realizes how much Samuel Untermyer knew about foreign enterprise in the United States. In 1902 he was the U.S. counsel for the British firm Imperial Tobacco when it made an agreement with American Tobacco to divide world markets. See copy of the 1902 agreement in William S. Stevens, ed., *Industrial Combinations and Trusts* (New York: Macmillan, 1913), 175. It is also remarkable when we find the Superintendent of Banks in New York (in 1911) well aware of the profits of foreign banks in America's international finance. See his *Annual Report, 1911*, 19.

200. See, for example, *Shipping Combinations*, 10.

201. FTC, *Report on Cooperation in the Export Trade*.

202. *Shipping Combinations* and *Steamship Agreements*, passim. The principal focus was on "combinations," and the conclusions related to agreements rather than specifically to foreign combinations or foreign agreements—although this was implicit throughout.

203. Lewis Atherton, *The Cattle Kings* (Bloomington: Indiana University Press, 1967), 118.

204. Primary sources dealing with 1875–1914 have far more discussion of foreign investment than secondary ones; textbooks have the least material.

205. There have been several excellent studies on German and French reactions to their nationals' pre-1914 investments abroad. Chronologically, they are Yves Guyot, "The Amount, Direction and Nature of French Investment," *Annals of the American Academy of Political and Social Science*, 68 (Nov. 1916): esp. 36–38; Walter Herman Carl Laves, *German Governmental Influence on Foreign Investment, 1871–1914* (1927 diss.; New York: Arno Press, 1977); Jacob Viner, "Political Aspects of International Finance," *Journal of Business*, 1 (April 1928): 141–173, and his "Political Aspects of International Finance—II," *Journal of Business*, 1 (July 1928): 324–363; and Herbert Feis, *Europe: World Banker, 1870–1914* (1930; rpt. New York: W. W. Norton, 1965). I have used these, plus many other primary and secondary works.

206. George Paish, "Great Britain's Capital Investments in Other Lands, " *Journal of the Royal Statistical Society*, 72 (Sept. 1909): 480.

207. Ibid.

208. Ibid.

209. Ibid.

210. *Statist*, 79 (Feb. 14, 1913): viii.

211. J. S. Mill, in *Principles of Political Economy*, first published in 1848 (7th ed., 1871), "The perpetual overflow of capital into colonies or foreign countries, to seek higher profits than can be obtained at home . . . [has arrested] the decline of profits in England . . . it does what a fire, or an inundation, or a commercial crisis would have done: it carries off a part of the increase of capital from which the reduction of profits proceeds. Secondly, the capital so carried off is not lost, but is chiefly employed either in founding colonies, which become large exporters of cheap agricultural produce, or in extending and perhaps improving the agriculture of older communities. It is to the emigration of

English capital, that we have chiefly to look for keeping up a supply of cheap food and cheap materials of clothing, proportional to the increase of our population; thus enabling an increasing capital to find employment in the country, without reduction of profit, in producing manufactured articles with which to pay for this supply of raw produce. Thus, the exportation of capital is an agent of great efficacy in extending the field of employment for that which remains: and it may be said truly that, up to a certain point, the more capital we send away, the more we shall possess and be able to retain at home.

"As long as there are old countries where capital increases very rapidly, and new countries where profit is still high, profits in the old countries will not sink to the rate which would put a stop to accumulation; the fall is stopped at the point which sends capital abroad." Quoted from Mill's seventh edition, in the marvelous anthology put together by D. K. Fieldhouse, *The Theory of Capitalist Imperialism* (London: Longman, 1967), 34–35. It was generally accepted in Paish and others that investments were made abroad because the rate of return was higher than at home. Paish did not discuss the effect on interest rates at home. As I will show, others aside from Mill did.

212. *Journal of the Royal Statistical Society*, 72 (Sept. 1909): 482–483. Henry Beaumont thought that "it was a grand thing for the country, for capitalists, and for everybody concerned, to have largely increasing investments in foreign countries" (ibid., 484). C. Rozenraad, president of the Federation of Foreign Chambers of Commerce agreed (ibid.).

213. Edgar Crammond, "British Investments Abroad," *Quarterly Review*, 215 (July 1911): 67.

214. This article is printed in full in John Maynard Keynes, *Collected Writings*, ed. Elizabeth Johnson (London: Macmillan, 1971), XV, 44–59, esp. 56–59. Later Keynes would become far less sympathetic to foreign investment.

215. C. K. Hobson, *Export of Capital* (London: Constable, 1914), 54, 27. With what seems today to be extraordinary naiveté, Hobson wrote, "The capitalist . . . need now have little fear that property which is not under his immediate control will be lost to him. Geographical considerations play a much smaller part than in the past . . . the increased respect for private property, even when belonging to aliens, has been promoted above all by the growing desire all over the world for commercial and industrial development upon capitalist lines" (p. 78). Three years later the Russian Revolution would shatter such illusions; and of course World War I itself created new attitudes toward the property of "enemy aliens."

216. Ibid., 54–55. This is along the lines of J. S. Mill's approach (see note 211 above).

217. Ibid., 61.

218. Ibid., 67, 236.

219. Ibid., 221, 228. He was echoing the 1910 article of Keynes, quoted above, although he does not cite it.

220. Quoted in English Committee of the Alabama 8 percent Gold State Bonds of 1870, *Hill Country of Alabama, USA* (London: E. & F. N. Spon, 1878), 22.

221. Hyde Clarke, *Sovereign and Quasi-Sovereign States: Their Debts to Foreign Countries* (London: Effingham Wilson, 1878), 21.

222. Ibid.

223. R. H. Inglis Palgrave, "An English View of Investments in the United States," *Forum*, 15 (April 1893): 191.

224. Jacob Riesser, *The German Great Banks* (1911; rpt. New York: Arno Press, 1977), 387. Riesser was a professor at the University of Berlin. See also ibid., 391 and 537ff. for favorable comments on foreign investment.

225. Laves, *German Governmental Influences*, 8, 9.

226. M. Georges Aubert, *La finance américaine* (Paris: Ernest Flammarion, 1910).

227. The principal collector of data on foreign security issues in France was Alfred Neymarck. For his comments on world peace (Sept. 1911), see *Bulletin de l'Institut International de Statistique*, 19 (1912): pt. 2, 225.

228. See extract from Jules Ferry in Fieldhouse, *The Theory of Capitalist Imperialism*, 51.

229. George W. Edwards, "Government Control of Foreign Investment," *American Economic Review*, 18 (Dec. 1928): 687–690.

230. Herbert Feis, *Europe*, is particularly useful on these matters. See also Michel Arboux, *Les valeurs mobilières étrangères sur le marché français* (Paris: Recueil Sirey, 1913) on the pros (and cons) of capital export. When Aubert, *La finance américaine* (1910), berated his countrymen for not recognizing the opportunities in America, he frequently noted that he did so as a patriotic Frenchman. Rondo E. Cameron, *France and the Economic Development of Europe, 1800–1914* (Princeton, N.J.: Princeton University Press, 1961), 494–495, writes that "French ministers sought by every means at their disposal to encourage French investments in both government and private securities in Russia. The investors for their part responded with alacrity, but appeals to patriotism and national interest carried little if any weight in their investment decisions . . . French investors found the combination of high yields and apparent solidity of Russian loans and government-guaranteed railway bonds a powerful inducement."

231. Feis writes that the German government "often fought to induce banks and investors to finance projects deemed essential to the advancement of imperial aims" (*Europe*, 169). Yet this is not in a U.S. context. The "imperialist" arguments of French and German government officials—that foreign investment would aid the growth of colonies and spheres of influence—are not relevant to foreign investment in the United States. It was often said that German and French embassies bargained over railroad loans and orders for Krupp and Schneider. See, for example, *Nation*, London, 14 (Nov. 29, 1913): 382. I have not identified such "bargaining" in the U.S. context (1875–1914), unless one includes the French refusal to list U.S. Steel on the Paris Bourse (a negative rather than positive measure; see text of this chapter). Jacob Viner, "International Finance and Balance of Power Diplomacy, 1880–1914," *Southwestern Political and Social Science Quarterly*, 9 (March 1929): 407–451, discusses the pre–World War I "web of diplomacy" and financial negotiations, showing clear instances of French and German governmental promoting (and discouraging) of foreign government loans for diplomatic ends. Viner considers the major debtor nations and then notes explicitly that the United States (as a debtor) was a "nonparticipant" in the financial "diplomacy" (ibid., 449). It was a debtor, but not treated like other debtor countries. Laves found the German Navy to be a strong advocate of foreign investment; the Navy wanted German investors to go abroad so that it could argue for a larger appropriation, since increased foreign investment would need protection (*German Governmental Influence*, 9). Yet the relevance to U.S. investment is not apparent. For the role of the British Admiralty in relation to British overseas investments in oil, see the balanced study by Jones, *The State and the Emergence of the British Oil Industry*. Here, too, the specifics concerning U.S. investment are not explicit. There is some evidence, however, that the *Canadian* government gave aid to the Canadian Pacific—or so U.S. railroadmen thought.

232. Indeed, one is struck by how in the British case the protests seemed almost pro forma; when the British met rebuffs, the Foreign Office dropped its "support" of the British investor. Thus in 1875–76 the Foreign Office protested the U.S. Mining Act of 1872—in vain (Spence, "British Investments," 134). There are many other British, essentially half-hearted, interventions of a similar nature. Bruce M. Russett, *Community and Contention* (Cambridge, Mass.: MIT Press, 1963), 229, 63–67, wrote on British

investment in the United States and U.S. investment in Britain and looked for diplomatic relationships associated with the cross-investment pattern. Although he found British government aid to foreign investment in countries outside the United States, he does not document any specific aids to British investors in the United States. The same conclusion emerges from Jones, *The State and the Emergence of the British Oil Industry*. D. C. M. Platt, *Finance, Trade, and Politics in British Foreign Policy, 1815–1914* (Oxford: Clarendon Press, 1968), 73, argued that from an earlier laissez-faire view, just before World War I, the British government was ready to give support ("propaganda and persuasion rather than physical pressure") to bona fide British capital abroad—a general statement rather than specifically applicable to British investment in the United States.

The German government assisted the German cable company to land its cable in the United States. See *Foreign Relations of the United States, 1899*, 310–314. It aided the Potash Cartel in the U.S. market, when the Cartel was threatened by an Austrian investor in Germany and the United States (see Chapter 8). There were other interventions; yet what seems most evident is the independence of German businesses from German government help; German companies with investments in the United States did not typically need their government's aid. Jeannette Keim, *Forty Years of German-American Political Relations* (Philadelphia: William J. Dornan, 1919), sought to clarify the diplomatic relations between the U.S. and Germany, 1870–1910. She identified *no* issues associated with German investment in the United States, although (like Russett for the British) she discussed German government aid to foreign investors outside the United States—as part of U.S.-German diplomatic relations.

Welsh's "Pierre Wibaux," which deals with a French investment in the United States, based on extensive family correspndence, shows how that international business relationship had no connections at all with diplomatic relations. Wibaux never asked for French government assistance. I believe this was typical of other French investments in the United States. Except on matters of cables and shipping, the French government seemed uninterested in promoting or protecting French interests in the United States.

233. Consular services were undoubtedly more important in other host countries. The private sector "information network" infrastructure between the United States and Europe, 1875–1914, was, as I have shown, well developed.

234. Hobson, *The Export of Capital*.

235. Robert Lucas Nash, *A Short Inquiry into the Profitable Nature of Our Investments*, 3rd ed. (London: Effingham Wilson, Royal Exchange, 1881), 30.

236. E. T. Powell, *The Mechanism of the City* (London: P. S. King, 1910), 145.

237. See Spence, *British Investments*, 198, for a comment (1878) by a London solicitor on the "legal tribunals" of Nevada being far from satisfactory and advising the client to have the operating company incorporated under British law.

238. RAL II/51/14B. See Chapter 5, note 178, for details.

239. Feis, *Europe*, 86–87. See also J. Henry Richardson, *British Economic Foreign Policy* (1936; rpt. New York: Garland, 1983), 58–59.

240. Davis, *The English Rothschilds*, 141.

241. G. M. Boissevain, *Money and Banking in the United States* (Amsterdam: J. H. deBussy, 1909), 5.

242. See letter from Lord Rothschild to Paris cousins, March 13, 1907, for example, RAL XI/130A/1.

243. *Nation*, London, 14 (Nov. 29, 1913): 383.

244. On these matters, see D. K. Fieldhouse, *Economics and Empire* (Ithaca, N.Y.: Cornell University Press, 1973); Eugene Staley, *War and the Private Investor* (Garden

City, N.Y.: Doubleday, 1935); and Viner, "International Finance and Balance of Power Diplomacy, 1880–1914," his "Political Aspects," and his "Political Aspects—II," for example.

245. Or perhaps because friendly relations with the United States were seen as important.

246. See William Mackenzie, Dundee, to Earl Granville, Jan. 7, 1881, FO 5/1763, PRO, and other data in this file.

247. For French government protection of investors, see Feis, *Europe*, 118–122.

248. Harry D. White, *French International Accounts, 1880–1913* (1933; rpt. New York: Arno Press, 1978), 280.

249. Viner, "Political Aspects," 144; Edwards, "Government Control of Foreign Investment," 688.

250. An inland revenue report of January 1914 criticized Britishers' avoidance of income tax by accumulating interest abroad and decried the "'retained" income overseas that failed to pay tax in Britain. See Avner Offer, "Empire and Social Reform: British Overseas Investment and Domestic Politics, 1908–1914," *Historical Journal*, 26 (1983): 136.

251. All contemporaries agreed that foreign investment raised interest rates at home, but the effects of higher interest rates brought disagreement. Domestic borrowers believed high interest rates discouraged new investment; lenders (and most economists, 1875–1914) thought high interest rates attracted new investment. Borrowers were the critics.

252. Constantly, in this context, the "patriotism" theme recurred. See, for example, the British Tariff Commission Hearings in 1905: it was "unpatriotic" for British textile manufacturers to be investing abroad.

253. Hobson, *Export of Capital*, xv. A very interesting summary of the debate is in Offer, "Empire and Social Reform," 119–138.

254. Earlier we saw such opinions among Americans. Remember, this was an age when Europeans (though to a lesser extent than Americans) were seeing businesses larger than ever in history.

255. Alfred Marshall, *Principles of Economics*, 4th ed. (London: Macmillan, 1898), 363.

256. Marshall did not make the application to foreign investors (although others did). Likewise, he saw certain advantages accruing to a large firm: "The head of a large business can reserve all his strength for the broadest and most fundamental problems of his trade . . . he need not trouble himself much about details. He can keep his mind fresh and clear for thinking out the most difficult and vital problems of his business; for studying the broader movements of the market, the yet undeveloped result of current events at home *and abroad*; and for contriving how to improve the organization of the internal and external relations of his business" (ibid., my italics).

257. D. C. M. Platt, *Britain's Investment Overseas on the Eve of the First World War* (New York: St. Martin's Press, 1986), 68–70.

258. Not all protectionists, however, condemned foreign investment. See this chapter, note 282.

259. The French, for example, paid particular attention to "securities" issued—domestic as well as foreign. The "anonymous" corporation, with investors as owners of securities rather than of properties, seemed a new phenomenon associated with the *haute banques* and *finance*. See Alfred Neymarck's reports in the *Bulletin de l'Institut International de Statistique*. Neymarck was not a critic of foreign investment; others, who used Neymarck's data, were.

260. See Clarke, *Sovereign and Quasi-Sovereign States*, 9, for the last phrase. His work was published in 1878.

261. On the latter, see comments by E. P. Bouverie to Foreign Office, April 26, 1889, FO 5/2066, PRO.

262. Grodinsky, *Jay Gould*, 323.

263. Ibid., 539–545.

264. Earlier I stated that private information channels made consular service information superfluous. This is not inconsistent with my comments here. All the critics wanted far more depth in information than a consular service ever provided. These people argued that, good as information channels were, they were not good enough.

265. Charles F.Conant to John Sherman, July 14, 1877, U.S. Treasury, *Specie Resumption and Refunding of National Debt*, 46th Cong., 2nd sess., 1880, H. Exec. Doc. 9, 105, described the *Economist* as "unfriendly to all American securities."

266. There was often reason to be dubious. Frequently there was misrepresentation. After the Emma mine fiasco, no Britisher wanted to invest in Utah. Thus in 1898 a Utah mining proposition was floated in London as the "Boston Consolidated Copper and Gold Mining Company, Ltd."! Prospectuses often did not reflect the reality.

267. See, for example, on railway securities, *Economist*, 45 (Jan. 8, 1887): 39, and 47 (June 29, 1889): 829. Interestingly, the *Economist* in certain ways echoed the views of Henry Varnum Poor, editor of *American Railway Journal*, 1849–1862, who had for many years (at least as early as 1852) urged British investors to look at whether Americans were buying a security. See Alfred D. Chandler, *Henry Varnum Poor* (Cambridge, Mass.: Harvard University Press, 1956), 99.

268. This quotation is from the Duke of Marlborough, "Virginia Mines and American Rails," *Fortnightly Review*, n.s., 49 (Jan. 1891): 582, not from the *Economist*, although it could have been from the latter. Poor's advice was to use American advisers (Chandler, *Poor*, 98). The British wondered which ones to trust.

269. *Economist*, 47 (June 29, 1889): 828.

270. Feis, *Europe*, 70.

271. *Economist*, 67 (Dec. 19, 1908): 1170.

272. Conant to Sherman, Oct. 11, 1877, U.S. Treasury, *Specie Resumption*, 167. See also Belmont to Sherman, Nov. 7, 1877, in ibid., 183.

273. U.S. Bureau of the Census, *Historical Statistics of the United States* (Washington, D.C., 1960), 570. By way of comparison with the Great Depression, the 1930 failure rate was 122; 1931, 133; and 1932, 154 per thousand (ibid.). In the forty years between 1940 and 1980, the *highest* failure rate was 64 (1961), and in twenty years it fell below 40 (the nadir was 4 in 1945). See *Economic Report of the President, 1985*, 337.

274. *Northwestern Miller*, 83 (July 27, 1910): 213.

275. Britons had forgotten their own history. "It is singular," wrote D. Morier Evans in 1859, "with what facility new [British] firms are organized after old ones have broken down, and paid, probably, a few shillings in the pound." Quoted in W. J. Reader, *A House in the City* (London: B. T. Batsford, 1979), 20.

276. See the June 29, 1911, article in Lysis [Eugene Letailleur], *Politique et finance d'avant-guerre* (Paris: Payot, 1920), 310.

277. J. Shield Nicholson, "Introductory Essay" to Adam Smith, *Wealth of Nations* (London: T. Nelson, 1901), 26.

278. Ibid., 24–25.

279. Ibid., 26.

280. W. J. Ashley, *The Tariff Problem*, 2nd ed. (London: P. S. King, 1903), 77.

281. Ibid.

282. This was the position of the 1905 Tariff Commission, a private protectionist group that held extensive hearings on plants established abroad by British textile manufacturers. See Chapter 10. Most British protectionists opposed foreign invest-

ment, claiming that the policy of free trade was "driving capital from the country to the detriment of British enterprise and labour." Protectionism would keep capital at home. See Keynes's impatience with those arguments in *New Quarterly*, Feb. 1910, republished in Keynes, *Collected Writings*, XV, 44. Sir Thomas Dewar, in 1911, commenting on the many British companies that had built plants outside the nation, saw this as a reason for protectionism at home. Dewar's comments were made at an annual meeting of A. & F. Pears, Ltd. The soap company was considering a U.S. factory. Dewar did *not* oppose this investment (planned because of the high U.S. duties); indeed, he favored it. He believed, however, that jobs would be lost in Britain; the British, he thought, should also protect their industry. See London *Times*, Oct. 27, 1911.

283. June 28, 1890, letter, quoted in Clements, "The Farmers' Attitude," 154n.

284. J. A. Hobson, *Imperialism* (London: James Nisbet, 1902), 56–69, 82. J. A. Hobson was no relation of C. K. Hobson. Interestingly, in discussing "the financiers," who J. A. Hobson claimed, typically benefited from war, he added, "The policy of these men, it is true, does not necessarily make for war; where war would bring about too great and too permanent a damage to the substantial fabric of industry . . . their influence is cast for peace, as in the dangerous quarrel between Great Britain and the United States regarding Venezuela." (ibid., 66). This is to be compared with data from the Rothschild Archives, cited in Chapter 5, note 178. Fieldhouse, *The Theory of Capitalist Imperialism*, 64–65, shows that the genesis of some of Hobson's views on imperialism lay in his perception of South Africa and the role of "international capitalists" there. See also William Langer, *Diplomacy of Imperialism, 1890–1902*, 2nd ed. (New York: Alfred A. Knopf, 1951), 68–69, 96–97.

285. The notion of "finance capitalists" as economic "parasites" was not original to Hobson. Edward N. Saveth, *American Historians and European Immigrants, 1875–1925* (New York: Columbia University Press, 1948), 71, writes of what Henry Adams learned about " 'parasitic' finance capitalism" from the work of his brother, Brooks Adams, who in 1895 had published in London *The Law of Civilization and Decay*. Offer, "Empire and Social Reform," 128, notes that by 1909 J. A. Hobson's views had changed and that that earlier critic of foreign investment was praising foreign investment as a force for "peace and goodwill between nations" and writing that it was "the most serviceable antidote against war-fevers!"

286. See, for example, Merrill Denison, *Canada's First Bank* (New York: Dodd, Mead, 1967), II, 196.

287. Rudolf Hilferding, *Finance Capital* (1910; English trans.: London: Routledge & Kegan Paul, 1981), 314. This view was not new. See this chapter, note 211, on J. S. Mill.

288. Hilferding, *Finance Capital,* 318.

289. Ibid., 426.

290. Ibid., 365, 427.

291. On the reaction of German socialists, see Laves, *German Governmental Influence,* 11 (quotation), and Feis, *Europe,* 160.

292. Feis, *Europe,* 125. *L'humanité,* a socialist paper, ran regular articles attacking capital exports. See those reprinted in Lysis, *Politique et finance d'avant-guerre* (Paris: Payot, 1920).

293. See comments on those critics by C. K. Hobson, *Export of Capital,* xv.

294. Laves, *German Governmental Influence,* 10–11; Viner, "Political Aspects," 145; and Feis, *Europe,* 160.

295. Lysis, *Contre l'oligarchie financière en France,* 9th ed. (Paris: Aux Bureaux de "La Revue," 1908), 190–191.

296. Émile Becque, *L'internationalisation des capitaux* (Montpellier: Imprimerie Générale du Midi, 1912), 94–99, 173–218. He was critical of both foreign direct and portfolio

investments. Becque was far from alone among Frenchmen in his critique of American investments as "speculative." See, for example, Lysis, *Contre l'oligarchie financière en France*, 144.

297. Feis, *Europe*, 125.

298. Ibid., 125–126, 130.

299. Viner, "Political Aspects," 145. Aristide Briand, Prime Minister of France, in 1909 was expressing anxieties about capital outflow, as was Raymond Poincaré, then Minister of Finance and later (1912–1913) Prime Minister and in 1913 President of the Republic. See Guyot, "The Amount," 36–37. The publicist Lysis lambasted French banks for their role in the export of capital. In 1910 Lysis noted the large number of American railroad bonds being introduced into France. French monies were going to be swallowed up in America as they had been in Russia. See his article in *L'humanité*, June 2, 1910, reprinted in Lysis, *Politique et finance*, 118. Arboux, *Les valeurs, mobilières etrangères* (1913), 234, concluded that the predominant view in France was that foreign securities were bad and should be proscribed.

300. Hans Bauer, *Swiss Bank Corporation, 1872–1972* (Basle: Swiss Bank Corp., 1972). The managing director of Schweizerischer Bankverein countered that there was the economic necessity of Switzerland's taking part in the international exchange of capital and noted that a substantial portion of the securities issued in Switzerland were "bought by our foreign customers."

301. The portion of the negative side of the debate on the European continent that dealt with capital exports, colonies, and international clashes over territory was the one large segment of the overall discussion that bore no relevance to foreign investment *in* the United States.

302. A useful overview of British government attitudes is in Feis, *Europe*, 83–117, and Viner, "Political Aspects," 144–145, 156–158.

303. Feis, *Europe*, 118–188, 55; Guyot, "The Amount," 38; Hobson, *Export of Capital*, 447; Viner, "Political Aspects," 158–165; and Riesser, *German Great Banks*, 532-533.

304. Feis, *Europe*, 69. This was rather a paradox, because the firm had made foreign investments for Bismarck himself.

305. Laves, *German Governmental Influence*, 62–66. The potash affair did involve the German government's support of its own cartel. The latter had a sales subsidiary in the United States, but the role of the German state was not "to protect" that small invest-ment. The decision of the Prussian Minister of Commerce to forbid the listing of the Chicago, Milwaukee and St. Paul shares provoked substantial discussion in Germany (Viner, "Political Aspects—II," 356–357).

306. Also in 1910, the Chicago, Milwaukee and St. Paul had had a large issue in Paris (Lysis, *Politique et finance*, 118).

307. Feis, *Europe*, 123, and Viner, "'Political Aspects—II," 161. Joseph Caillaux (1863–1944) first served as Minister of Finance in the Cabinet of Waldeck-Rousseau in the years 1899–1903. For Caillaux's colorful career, see *New York Times*, Nov. 23, 1944.

308. Nathaniel T. Bacon, "American International Indebtedness," *Yale Review* 9 (Nov. 1900): 273.

309. All the principal secondary sources, from Guyot, "The Amount," 38, to Feis, *Europe*, 125–126, comment on this 1909 exclusion. In another context Feis noted that Creusot, France's greatest maker of steel, was very much involved in the formation of French government policies on "foreign loans" (ibid., 127). Presumably such in-fluence would extend to questions of common stock offerings. Feis also argued that the French government action may have been designed (albeit unsuccessfully) to get lower U.S. tariffs on steel. (ibid., 130). While Guyot, Viner ("Political Aspects," 354), and Feis attribute the government action to pressure from industry groups, Lysis,

Politique et finance, 309, in 1911 indicated that the reason why U.S. Steel Corporation's shares were not listed was that pressure was exerted by the socialist leader Jean Jaurés!

310. There is evidence that a number of Frenchmen did so. Moreover, Lysis, *Contre l'oligarchie financière*, and his *Politique et finance* both make it evident that in the years 1905–1912, particularly, a large number of American securities were newly listed on the *marché officiel* or on the *coulisse*.

311. However, some German reports—the Navy one of 1905, for example—did recognize the differences.

312. T. R. Nevett, *History of British Advertising* (London: Heinemann, 1982), includes material on financial advertising.

313. The stockholders of the firm might (or might not) be told about it.

314. Government-business relations vis-à-vis "loans" and direct investments were clearly quite different.

315. Another route would be to license a U.S. firm to produce behind the tariff wall; often this involved some investment. If it did not, it meant "loss of the market" for the parent, albeit a retention of some income from the former market.

316. See data in FO 5/2043, FO 5/1902, FO 5/1979, PRO, and also in Crapol, *America for Americans*, 107–109.

317. Quoted in Crapol, *America for Americans*, 109 (March 30, 1887, Memo). The federal Alien Property Act (24 U.S. Stats. 476) had become law on March 3, 1887.

318. Memo, April 15, 1889, FO 5/2066, PRO.

319. See *Foreign Relations of the United States, 1911*, 266, 269–270, and statement of Lord Ponsonby (March 12, 1930), quoted in James W. Gantenbein, *Financial Questions in United States Foreign Policy* (New York: Columbia University Press, 1939), 202.

320. In this context I tried to look at the functioning of the Bank of England to see whether its role "on behalf" of the British government affected foreign investment. Clearly its actions as a central bank to prevent large gold outflows did affect investment flows; but its influence appears to have been based on domestic policy requirements and does not appear to have been involved with any particular normative perception of "foreign investment" as "good" or "bad." I have found particularly useful on this Arthur I. Bloomfield, *Monetary Policy under the International Gold Standard, 1880–1914* (1959; rpt. New York: Arno Press, 1978), and Leland B. Yeager, *International Monetary Relations* (New York: Harper & Row, 1966), 258–265. See also Robert Triffin, "National Central Banking and the International Economy," in Lloyd A. Metzler, Robert Triffin, and Gottfried Haberler, *International Monetary Policies* (1947; rpt. New York: Arno Press, 1978), 50, and Lloyd Mints, *A History of Banking Theory in Great Britain and the United States* (Chicago: University of Chicago Press, 1945).

321. Despite Caillaux's 1913 statement quoted above, in June 1911 the publicist Lysis (*Politique et finance*, 310) was, on the one hand, noting that the formidable invasion of American securities presented a great threat to French savings and, on the other hand, condemning the alliance between Caillaux and the great French banks that was allowing the entry of these securities onto the French market!

322. There was an emotional "positive" view that did not relate to foreign investment in the United States, the "imperialist" argument. Thus it was an emotional French Premier Jules Ferry who defended his expansionist policies: colonies were needed for a rich country to place its capital most advantageously. See Viner, "'Political Aspects—II,'" 350.

323. In this chapter, note 231, I indicated U.S. railroadmen's concern about the Canadian government's support of the Canadian Pacific. I do not, however, believe that government assistance made a substantial difference.

Epilogue

1. See Chapter 1, p. 27. I hesitate to translate this into dollars, since I am not certain of a meaningful exchange rate.

2. See Chapter 2, p. 33–34 and note 34; see also Table 3.1.

3. See Chapter 5.

4. This is my own conclusion based on my research on foreign investments and others' research on gross national product, real income per capita, and national wealth.

5. It would entail a complete modern economic history of Britain, for example. I am, moreover, confining myself to near-term effects. It is far beyond the scope of my study to consider whether the less than satisfactory performance of the British economy from 1914 to the present related to that nation's subjects having been in the pre-World War I years heavily involved in international (and particularly American) investments. For the percentage contribution of foreign investment in the United States vis-à-vis total foreign investments of the major capital-exporting countries, see Chapter 5.

6. I went over a list prepared by W. D. Rubinstein, "British Millionaires, 1809–1949," *Bulletin of the Institute of Historical Research*, 47 (1974): 202–223. This sort of evidence is more anecdotal than systematic.

7. There seems no question that nominal long-term *interest rates* on comparable securities (that is, consols versus U.S. federal government paper; British railroads versus American ones) in the United States throughout this entire period were higher than in Europe—albeit the gap narrowed substantially over time. On U.S. railroads, 1870–1913, for example, see Michael Edelstein, *Overseas Investment in the Age of High Imperialism* (New York: Columbia University Press, 1982), 94.

8. *The Nation and the Athenaeum*, 35 (Aug. 9, 1924): 584–586. See also John Maynard Keynes in the London *Times*, Sept. 18, 1921, reprinted in John Maynard Keynes, *Collected Writings*, ed. Elizabeth Johnson (London: Macmillan, 1971), XVII, 274, wherein he conceded that foreign investment might be mutually advantageous to the old and new country in times past, but was not desirable in the 1920s. The *Nation* article echoes some of Nicholson's earlier concerns; see Chapter 16.

9. See Herbert Feis, *Europe: The World's Banker* (1930; rpt. New York: W. W. Norton, 1965), 5–7, on the general views. After World War I, German writers despaired that, whereas the British had sent their capital to "friendly countries," German monies had been invested in enemy nations and lost with the war (F. Lenz, "Wegen und Structure des deutschen Kapitalexports vor 1914," *Weltwirtschaftliches Archiv*, 18 [1922]: 49). Some post-1914 commentators on capital exports took their cue from Lenin's pamphlet *Imperialism* (written in Zurich in the spring of 1916); Lenin, who was greatly influencd by J. A. Hobson's 1902 views and by the ideas of Rudolf Hilferding, linked "finance capital" and capital exports, which served, Lenin believed, to spread capitalism worldwide but also "to a certain extent to arrest development in the countries exporting capital"; capital exports were bad for the home economy, turning it into a "rentier state," one "of parasitic, decaying capitalism" (V. I. Lenin, *Imperialism* [1916, 1920; rpt. New York: International Publishers, 1939], 65, 98, 102). The huge post–World War I literature on imperialism and capital exports offers little assistance (or relevance) in evaluating the *bilateral* benefits and costs to the capital-exporting country *and* to the United States as the capital-importing one. It never deals with America's colonial period or with the losses to the British during the American Revolution. I have scrutinized materials on the capital exports and imperialism to acknowledge an often discussed association. See, for example, D. K. Fieldhouse, *Economics and Empire, 1830–1914* (Ithaca, N.Y.: Cornell University Press, 1973) and his *Theory of Capitalist*

Imperialism (London: Longman, 1967); Alan Hodgart, *The Economics of European Imperialism* (New York: W. W. Norton, 1977); P. J. Cain, *Economic Foundations of British Overseas Expansion, 1815–1914* (London: Macmillan, 1980); and Kenneth E. Boulding and Tapan Mukerjee, eds., *Economic Imperialism: A Book of Readings* (Ann Arbor: University of Michigan Press, 1972). The latter contains articles by D. K. Fieldhouse (1961) and Mark Blaug (1961), which point out that contrary to popular belief and in refutation of the Hobson-Lenin arguments related to "economic imperialism," British and European capital in general went in the pre-1914 years mainly to the "new countries," "the advanced countries," rather than to the backward ones. Blaug argued that "the yield of capital is generally higher in a capital-rich economy than in an underdeveloped one because capital in the advanced country is invested in a complementary fashion in basic industry, transport, and power" (ibid., 109, 146–147). In short, with these few exceptions the immense post–World War I (and post–World War II) literature on capital exports and imperialism fails to illuminate the specific impacts on the home country of its nationals' large investments in the United States. Thus I have not included a discussion of this literature in my text.

10. See Chapter 4 and S. Japhet, *Recollections from My Business Life* (London: privately printed, 1931), 13, 32.

11. Cleona Lewis, *America's Stake in International Investments* (Washington, D.C.: Brookings Institution, 1938), 488, wrote: "The two decades that have elapsed since the United States ceased to be a debtor to other countries have served to dispel some of the illusion surrounding the concept of 'creditor nation' . . . with the coming of depression, and cession of lending, we were confronted with wholesale defaults, moratoria, and standstill agreements. Thus we found that at times the creditor's role was fraught with almost as much difficulty as that of the debtor."

12. Shepard B. Clough and Charles Woolsey Cole, *Economic History of Europe* (Boston: D. C. Heath, 1941), 659–660. Harry D. White, *French International Accounts* (1933; rpt. New York: Arno Press, 1978), chaps. 12 and 13, evaluated the "economic effects of French capital exports" in the prewar years. He believed that—contrary to what contemporaries had assumed—the returns on foreign investment were not, in fact, greater than from domestic ones (p. 274). He explained the bias toward foreign investment as based on higher profits to the issuing houses (the banks) and greater possibilities of tax evasion (p. 283). White concluded that the effects on the French domestic economy were negative: interest rates went up at home (p. 291); capacity to save was reduced (p. 292); income was redistributed, with more accruing to capital to the disadvantage of "wage earners, landowners, and entrepreneurs" (p. 293); French capital abroad, in general, did not lower the cost of imports (pp. 294–295); and worse still, French industry and public works were deprived of capital (pp. 297–299).

13. The pre–World War I theme (from Ricardo and J. S. Mill on) that foreign investment served to offset inevitably "declining returns" to home capital was argued in the post–World War I years only by Marxists; the "inevitably declining return" to capital proved not "inevitable." On the "natural tendency" for the rate of profits to fall and the factors that revesed this trend, see Hodgart, *The Economics of European Imperialism*, 8–9, 16ff.

14. Alec K. Cairncross, *Home and Foreign Investment, 1870–1913* (Cambridge: Cambridge University Press, 1953); "the central portion" of this important book was based on Cairncross' 1935 Cambridge Ph.D. diss. (ibid., xiii). See also Brinley Thomas, *Migration and Economic Growth*, 2nd ed. (Cambridge, Mass.: Harvard University Press, 1973), esp. 97, 108 (1st ed., 1954), and Charles H. Feinstein, "Home and Foreign Investment," Ph.D. diss. University of Cambridge, 1959.

15. Thomas, *Migration and Economic Growth*, 108–109. Thomas and Cairncross—

unlike C. K. Hobson—believed that high home and foreign investment alternated. Fundamental to the difference in view were the effects of higher interest rates (caused by capital outflow): C. K. Hobson thought these caused *more* investment. Cairncross' and Thomas' view seems to have been that although the outflow of capital raised interest rates at home, this made it more costly for home firms to borrow, which accordingly reduced investment.

16. Aside from the examples cited earlier, others especially related to U.S. stakes include J. Fred Rippy, "British Investments in Texas Lands and Livestock," *Southwestern Historical Quarterly,* 57 (Jan. 1955): 338, who concluded that with "few exceptions the profits were small. In many instances, the losses outweighted the gains." Clark C. Spence, *British Investments and the American Mining Frontier, 1860–1901* (Ithaca, N.Y.: Cornell University Press, 1958), 232, quotes the *Anglo-Colorado Mining Guide,* Nov. 28, 1903:

> In modern speculation
>   Your language you must choose.
> It's an "investment" if you win
>   But "gambling" if you lose.

Spence's comment: "When the whole period [1860–1901] is considered, the Englishman who poured his surplus funds into American mines was indeed "gambling.' " Nonetheless, after a very critical analysis, Cairncross, *Home and Foreign Investment,* 235, concluded: "Up until 1914 there was a sufficient coincidence of private profit and social gain in Britain's export of capital . . . Broadly speaking, British foreign investment paid."

17. Rondo E. Cameron, *France and the Economic Development of Europe, 1800–1914* (Princeton, N.J.: Princeton University Press, 1961), 504–505. Nonetheless, François Caron, *An Economic History of Modern France* (New York: Columbia University Press, 1979), 4, writes of the lack of success of "French capitalism" in the late nineteenth and early twentieth centuries in the same passages in which he discusses French capital exports. And Cameron, *France and the Economic Development of Europe,* 504, concluded that "there can be no doubt, in view of the large capital losses through inflation and repudiation after 1914 that France would be better off today if all or most of the exported capital had been invested at home." In the 1960s (and subsequently) there continued to be academic debates on the costs and benefits to creditor nations of international investment. See, for example, John Dunning, "The Costs and Benefits of Foreign Direct Investment to the Investing Country: The U.K. Experience," in his *Studies in International Investment* (London: George Allen & Unwin, 1970), 49–117; Ivor F. Pearce and David C. Rowan, "A Framework for Research into the Real Effects of International Capital Movements" (1966), reprinted in John Dunning, *International Investment* (Harmondsworth: Penguin Books, 1972), 163–197; and Neil Hood and Stephen Young, *The Economics of Multinational Enterprise* (London: Longman, 1979), chap. 7. Most of this theoretical literature, though clearly related to my research, did not deal specifically with pre-1914 investments, much less their costs and benefits vis-à-vis the United States as a host country. Since the general data are extensive (and inconclusive)—as well as tangential to my pre-1914 evaluation—it seemed inappropriate to do more than merely note the existence of such a literature.

18. W. G. Kerr, *Scottish Capital on the American Credit Frontier* (Austin: Texas State Historical Association, 1976), 199–205, writes of the highly successful Scottish mortgage and investment trust companies. Kerr found many more British business successes than had been earlier recognized (ibid., 200). The World Bank, *World Development Report, 1985* (New York: Oxford University Press, 1985), 13, makes the broad statement

that investment abroad in the period 1870–1914 was profitable for investors in Great Britain and continental Europe: "It earned returns that have been calculated to be between 1.6 and 3.9 percentage points higher than returns on domestic investments." The text cites a "background paper" by Albert Fishlow, which has been published as "Lessons from the Past," *International Organization,* 39 (Summer 1985): 383–439. On p. 396 Fishlow cites these same figures for Great Britain alone. The figures are those of Michael Edelstein. They are for all British overseas investments, but U.S. returns figure importantly in the calculations.

19. Michael Edelstein, *Overseas Investment in the Age of High Imperialism: The United Kingdom, 1850–1914* (New York: Columbia University Press, 1982). Edelstein made estimates of the realized price-deflated rate of return, 1870–1913, to first- and second-class equity, preference, and debenture shares that were publicly traded in the United Kingdom. The rate of return included both dividend or interest payments and capital gains (Edelstein assumed the security was purchased in the last week of December and sold a year later). He defined first- and second-class securities as ones that paid dividends or interest regularly and did not go through long periods of heavy price discount. He thus excluded losses through default. He found overseas returns higher than domestic ones. Among these *best* securities, he included the equity shares of ten U.S. railroads (three to nine were actually monitored in any particular year); their return, 1870–1913, averaged 8.41 percent compared with 6.37 percent for all U.K. domestic equity shares studied. Likewise, his research on fifty-one U.S. railroad debentures (between one and thirty-eight in any single year) showed the return to be 6.03 percent compared with 3.21 percent for all U.K. "debenture shares" included in his sample. Clearly, a Britisher buying the "best" U.S. rails did better than his counterpart who invested at home (*Overseas Investment,* 114–127).

Then, on far more tenuous grounds, Edelstein offered "the distinct impression" that even including all overseas defaults and insolvencies (not especially those on U.S. securities), the results would still show that overseas returns exceeded those at home (ibid., 130). Edelstein believed that overseas defaults and insolvencies had been greatly overestimated. His means of testing this proposition has problems. For example, he assumes that U.K.-registered companies operated domestically and that their defaults were domestic ones (ibid., 128, 129). Actually, many U.K.-registered companies did business abroad, and such defaults must be isolated and associated with overseas business. Edelstein is an excellent scholar, and he is well aware that his "'distinct impression" is far from conclusive (ibid., 130).

Albert Fishlow, accepting Edelstein's views on profitability, suggests that "the United States was a positive influence, a 'demonstration effect,' eliciting British investment in other parts of the periphery. American railroads had patently increased the productive capacity and trade of that country and were the implicit model elsewhere" ("'Lessons from the Past," 397). He sees the success of American investment as a benefit to the *home* country, resulting in additional foreign investments.

20. Edelstein, *Overseas Investment,* 65, 73.

21. Cairncross, *Home and Foreign Investment,* 233, wrote, "We gained . . . through a cheapening of [foodstuff] imports." White, *French International Accounts,* 294, saw the cheapening of foodstuffs as a benefit of foreign investment. Edelstein does not even discuss the effects on British agriculture. I think that is wise. There seems to be no question, however, that the fall in agricultural prices that came after America's West was opened gave "an irresistible impetus to the decline of British agriculture." See Charles H. Feinstein, "Home and Foreign Investment." Yet this raised purchasing power in the United Kingdom. The Dutch—also large investors in U.S. railroad securities and assisters in U.S. railroad finance—faced a major depression in the agricul-

tural sector, 1873–1895, caused by cheap U.S. grain imports. See Johan de Vries, *The Netherlands Economy in the Twentieth Century* (Assen: Van Gorcum, 1978), 37.

22. Sidney Pollard, "Capital Exports, 1870–1914: Harmful or Beneficial?" *Economic History Review*, 2nd ser., 38 (Nov. 1985): 489–514.

23. See Chapter 6.

24. See especially Chapters 5, 6, and 13. German and Dutch investors often did well for same reasons as the British.

25. Other exceptions include A. Emil Davies, *Investment Abroad* (1927; rpt. New York: Arno Press, 1977); Eugene Staley, *War and the Private Investor* (Garden City, N.Y.: Doubleday, 1935); plus some very specific literature.

26. Edith Penrose, *The Theory of the Growth of the Firm* (New York: Wiley, 1959), emphasizes expansion based on underutilization of resources. Some British firms, to be sure, failed to meet the challenge. See Geoffrey Jones, "The Performance of British Multinational Enterprise, 1890–1945," in *Multinationals: Theory and History*, ed. Peter Hertner and Geoffrey Jones (Aldershot: Gower, 1986).

27. This statement can be disputed; some claim that profits are never reinvested at home (nonetheless, they are available for that purpose) and that taxes at home are reduced (there is some case to made for this). In net, however, my findings are that the private benefits coincide with the social ones.

28. The major exception is, of course, in the German case, where these interests along with the portfolio ones were lost during World War I. Yet later I will make the point that the loss was less with such investments than with the portfolio ones.

29. The employment effects of foreign direct investments in manufacturing on home economies are far more complex than is suggested here. Studies of the employment effects of multinational enterprise in the 1960s and 1970s are summarized in Hood and Young, *The Economics of Multinational Enterprise*, chap. 7.

30. *And* after World War II.

31. I make this statement on 1875–1914 with hesitation (sharing many of Pollard's concerns), albeit it seems the most generally accepted view. The evidence seems to suggest that returns on U.S. investments—minus defaults and losses—were, in fact, higher than on comparable domestic investments. Here I find myself in basic agreement with Edelstein, my reservations notwithstanding. The comments on Germany by Japhet—as cited above—may be an exaggeration but contain an element of truth. Data on costs and benefits *to the Dutch economy* of their nationals' large investments in the United States are to my knowledge nonexistent (they are not included in Bosch's excellent study of Dutch investment in the United States); there is, however, indication that Dutch investors came out ahead.

The French economy could be the only exception on the net benefits. French investors seemed very gullible in their U.S. investments. For some reasons why, see White, *French International Accounts*, chap. 12. Also in the French case the ratio of multinational-enterprise-type investments to total foreign investments in the United States appears to have been lower than in the case of the other principal capital exporters—and the information channels for all investments were certainly poorer. But if I add France in with *all* the capital exporters, then my overall conclusion would certainly hold (losses in France would be offset by gains of other countries). Moreover, as noted in Chapter 5, foreign investments in the United States represented a far smaller percentage of all French foreign investments worldwide than of British, German, or Dutch foreign investments worldwide.

I have not considered herein the effects of foreign investment in America on the international trade of, on producer versus consumer goods in, on the income distribution in, on emigration from, or on the business cycle in capital-exporting countries.

These matters are very important but well beyond the scope of this study. I also have not included anything on the foreign direct investor as a conduit of technology transfer from the United States to the capital-exporting countries. Such transfers existed with their consequent desirable effects, but their extent was not sufficient to have a material impact on the economic development of the home country of any foreign direct investor.

32. The notes to and the bibliography of this book reveal the numerous works.

33. Although there is no single analysis of the benefits and costs, many authors have offered opinions. Also, there is a sizable literature that deals with benefits and costs of foreign investment to host countires—with no specific applications to pre–1914 foreign investment in the United States. For example, see articles by Ragnar Nurkse, G. D. A. MacDougall, and Murray Kemp in *International Investment*, ed. Dunning, 97–162, and Hood and Young, *The Economics of Multinational Enterprise*, chap. 5.

34. Albro Martin, *James J. Hill* (New York: Oxford University Press, 1976), 440. The foreign investors that Hill attracted did not play a comparably negative role.

35. U.S. Bureau of the Census, *Historical Statistics of the United States, Colonial Times to 1970* (Washington, D.C., 1975), II, 889–890, 864–865. Since 1971, in only two years has America had a positive balance-of-merchandise trade; see *Economic Report of the President, 1985*, 344.

36. Ragnar Nurkse, *Patterns of Trade and Development* (New York: Oxford University Press, 1961), 18.

37. Robert E. Riegel, *The Story of Western Railroads* (Lincoln: University of Nebraska Press, 1926), 283. There is no evidence whatsoever to support the contemporary belief that mortgage lenders had a "preconceived" plan to foreclose. Quite the contrary, lenders wanted income from their mortgages.

38. See Richard A. Brecher and Carlos F. Diaz Alejandro, "Tariffs, Foreign Capital and Immiserizing Growth," *Journal of International Economics*, 7 (Nov. 1977): 317–322; Jagdish N. Bhagwati, Richard A. Brecher, and Tatsuo Hatta, "The Generalized Theory of Transfers and Welfare: Bilateral Transfers in a Multilateral World," *American Economic Review*, 83 (Sept. 1983): 606–618; Richard A. Brecher and Jagdish N. Bhagwati, "Foreign Ownership and the Theory of Trade and Welfare," *Journal of Political Economy*, 89 (June 1981); 497–511; and Richard A. Brecher and Jagdish N. Bhagwati, "Immiserizing Transfers from Abroad," *Journal of International Economics*, 13 (Nov. 1982): 353–364. My colleague Dr. Amitava Dutt was the first to introduce me to this literature. On the U.S. terms of trade, see Lance E. Davis et al., *American Economic Growth* (New York: Harper & Row, 1972), 566.

39. In some cases, to be sure, foreign multinationals participating in this import substitution process acted to restrain the exports of their U.S. affiliates in order to reserve for the parent company, or other foreign affiliates, the markets abroad. If the U.S. affiliate's costs (plus transportation and other costs to reach a foreign market) were lower than those of the parent (or other affiliates), this "restraint of trade" abroad could be considered a "cost" (a penalty) of the foreign direct investment. On the other hand, my research indicates that usually when the parent (or another affiliate of the foreign multinational) handled the foreign trade, and the U.S. affiliate served only the American and possibly nearby foreign markets, the reasons related to least-cost choices rather than to an inefficient cutting back of U.S. exports to benefit other units in a foreign multinational enterprise. (I should also note that similar international restraint-of-trade arrangements could be made under different circumstances with no foreign investment in the United States at all; indeed, such curbs on exports of producers in America were often unrelated to the presence in the United States of foreign multinationals.) In net, foreign direct investments in America seem to have added far more to

U.S. exports than the minor "subtractions" that could be attributable to intraenterprise accords that on occasion accompanied such investment. Moreover, from a "macro" viewpoint, it is evident that any such arrangements by foreign multinationals operating in America did not materially retard the overall growth of U.S. exports of manufactured goods, which, as indicated, rose rapidly in the years 1875–1914.

40. I have weighed the evidence on the dyestuff industry and am convinced that this was not a case of "crowding out" domestic production. Likewise, in rayon production, where a foreign direct investor supplied all American production, I cannot establish a "crowding-out" effect.

41. The figures of Charles Bullock, John H. Williams, and Rufus S. Tucker, "Balance of Trade and the United States," *Review of Economic Statistics*, 1 (July 1919): 227, 231, suggest this. See also summary data in *Survey of Current Business*, July 1954, 14, which was based on Bullock, Williams, and Tucker.

42. This point is made by Fishlow, "Lessons from the Past," 397.

43. In retrospect, it seems extraordinary to find Robert Giffen (a British economist) conceding that America had "a right" to pass this silver legislation. See Hyde Clarke, *Sovereign and Quasi-Sovereign States: Their Debts to Foreign Countries* (London: Effingham Wilson, 1878), 47.

44. On *favoring* protectionism, see, for example, data above on linoleum (Nairn) and cocaine (Merck). German woolen textile makers in the United States also became strong advocates of high tariffs.

45. See William Mackenzie to Earl Granville, Jan. 7, 1881, FO 5/1763, Public Record Office (PRO), London.

46. Ibid.

47. H. Osborne O'Hagan, *Leaves from My Life* (London: John Lane, 1929), I, 296.

48. In Chapter 16 I showed that Europeans in the pre–World War I years debated issues on the relationship of foreign investment and war and peace—and that the U.S. Navy had concerns over foreign investment compromising America's national defense. These issues—not ones that today we typically consider in the context of debtor-nation status—were ones that did prompt much subsequent discussion and can be associated with political sovereignty questions. There was Lenin's view (not in the American context) that capital exports had been the cause of World War I (Lenin, *Imperialism*, 9). After World War I, it would be charged that foreign investment in the United States in 1914 had "created economic suction sufficient to draw us into war." (See, for example, statement by Francis P. Garvan enclosed in James K. Powers, foreign editor of the *Boston Globe*, to Senator David J. Walsh, June 16, 1937, in RG 151, 620 General/1937, National Archives, Washington, D.C. This view was consonant with the Hobson-Lenin notion that foreign investments "cause" international conflict. Francis P. Garvan [1875–1937] had been director of the Bureau of Investigations for the Alien Property Custodian during World War I; see Alien Property Custodian, *Report, 1918–1919*, 156. He became Mitchell Palmer's successor as Alien Property Custodian on March 4, 1919. For biographical data see William Haynes, *American Chemical Industry*, 6 vols. [New York: D. Van Nostrand, 1945–1954], II [1945], 260–263.) If this be true, then political sovereignty was at risk. No concrete evidence, however, substantiates this conclusion, except the legitimate (but not really relevant) assertion that international capital movements created a more integrated interdependent world economy.

National defense may, to be sure, have been temporarily impaired by foreign direct investment (because of the German control over dyestuffs). Foreign dominance in shipping placed the country at great inconvenience after the war broke out. I find, nonetheless, weak and unprovable the contention that the mere presence of foreign investment in the United States by itself acted to propel the country into World War I.

Discussions of Schneider, Krupp, and Vickers and the armaments producers seem of little relevance to foreign investment in the United States. As far as I can ascertain, Schneider had no U.S. investments in 1914; Krupp seems to have had a U.S. representative; and Vickers had interests in submarines, but it is hard to see why such a foreign investment would necessarily thrust America into war. Charles C. Tansill, *America Goes to War* (1938; rpt. Gloucester, Mass.: Peter Smith, 1963), 45, 47n, writes of the connections between Electric Boat and Vickers—after the war began. Neither Tansill nor the Nye Committee—which looked at armament makers and their links with U.S. entry into World War I—knew of Vickers' investment in Electric Boat. Most critics dealt with trade rather than with investment.

The Alien Property Custodian, however, when it confiscated German properties in the United States during World War I, was indeed wont to see the German foreign investment as representing a conspiracy of big banks, aggressive German industry, and the German state to "take over" American industry. I am totally in agreement with the recent conclusions of Thomas R. Kabisch, *Deutsches Kapital in den USA* (Stuttgart: Klett-Cotta, 1982), that the German government's role in promotion of foreign investment in the United States before 1914 was virtually nil and was certainly not a factor propelling the American nation into the war. In sum, contemporary and subsequent concerns notwithstanding, I find it totally inappropriate to include "prospects" of being "sucked" into war as a cost of foreign investment, which is the reason that this long discussion is included in a note rather than in the text.

49. Jacob Viner, "Political Aspects of International Finance," *Journal of Business*, 1 (April 1928): 150 (my italics). The words *economic consideration* and *productive purposes* are very important. From today's vantage point I can, of course, conceive of numerous economic considerations that might militate against the free import of capital for productive purposes—for example, if it caused "immiserizing growth," if it crowded out domestic capital, if it entered in such a manner as to suppress or to introduce substitutes for the output of efficient (or potentially efficient) domestic entrepreneurs, if sufficient export earnings were not generated to acquire foreign exchange to pay for the charges on capital, and so forth. Yet none of these conditions applied in pre–1914 America. My text has not dealt with the impact of foreign capital on income distribution in the United States—an issue often discussed in today's literature on foreign investment in less-developed countries and one that was a matter of concern to contemporaries in pre–1914 America. The first draft of this book had a long section on the subject, but because the evidence was so inadequate, the analysis ended up being totally inconclusive; thus I decided to omit the entire discussion.

50. W. Arthur Lewis, *Growth and Fluctuations, 1870–1913* (London: Allen & Unwin, 1978), 177. Irving B. Kravis has suggested that "internal growth attracted foreign funds more than foreign funds served to set off U.S. economic growth." See "The Role of Exports in Nineteenth Century United States Growth," *Economic Development and Cultural Change*, 20 (April 1972): 404. This is not my conclusion. Rather, my evidence points to a symbiotic relationship whereby growth attracted foreign funds, which in turn "set off" added growth.

51. The G.N.P. in 1914 was $36.4 billion; $7 billion divided by $36.4 billion equals 0.192. If we choose a $7.1 billion figure (see Chapter 5), the results will come to 0.195. This is for comparative purposes only—to show the dimensions of the investment.

Bibliography

Primary Materials: Collections and Companies Consulted

In a number of cases, archivists, librarians, executives, and scholars have mailed me copies of unpublished data or I have borrowed microfilms on interlibrary loan.

Canada

Ottawa. Public Archives. Bank of Montreal. Resolve Books.
———. ———. Baring Brothers & Co. Papers.

England and Scotland

London. Baring Brothers & Co., Ltd. Archives.
———. British Museum. Manuscript Room. Peter Hasenclever Correspondence, Add. Ms. 22679, fs. 38–41.
———. ———. ———. Principio Company Papers, Add. Ms. 29600, fs. 1–46
———. Calico Printers. Data from Anthony Howe.
———. Fine Cotton Spinners' & Doublers' Association. Data from Anthony Howe.
———. Imperial Chemical Industries. Data courtesy of William J. Reader.
———. Lloyds Bank. Data from J. M. L. Booker, Archivist.
———. London School of Economics. Business History Unit. British business history files of Leslie Hannah.
———. ———. ———. Dunlop and the Imperial Bank of Persia. Materials from Geoffrey Jones.
———. Midland Bank. Data from Edwin Green, Archivist.
———. N. M. Rothschild & Sons. Archives.
———. Public Records Office. Foreign Office Records. FO 5/2043 (Reports on the Status of Aliens and Foreign Companies in the United States of America, 1886–1888), FO 5/2066 (Diplomatic Correspondence, Various, 1889), FO 83/110 (Circular Letters), FO 83/111 (British Mercantile Houses in U.S., 1842 [incomplete], 1848), FO 83/115 (French Mercantile Houses in U.S., 1848).
———. Price Waterhouse. Archives.
———. Science Museum Library. S. Pearson & Son Papers.

———. Shell Oil Company. Archives.

———. ———. Library.

———. Unilever PLC. Archives. William Lever Papers.

———. ———. ———. T. J. Lipton, Inc., Papers.

Paisley. Renfrew District Library. J. & P. Coats, Ltd. Text of 150 Year Exhibition. Data from Dr. Stephen Young.

Reading. University of Reading. British business in the United States files of John H. Dunning.

———. ———. Burmah Oil. Materials from T. A. B. Corley.

France

Paris. National Archives. Rothschild Bank Papers.

Germany

Dortmund. Stiftung Westfälisches Wirtschaftsarchiv. Data on Peter Hasenclever.

Munich. Siemens-Museum. Siemens Archives. Data from Harm Schröter.

Stein bei Nürnberg. Faber-Castell. Data from Peter Schafhauser.

Hong Kong

Hong Kong. Hongkong & Shanghai Banking Corporation. Archives. Data from Frank H. H. King and from S. W. Muirhead, Controller Group Archives.

Japan

Tokyo. Mitsui & Co. Archives. Mitsui & Co. *Semi-Annual Reports.* My thanks to Professor Hiroaki Yamazaki for guidance and translations.

Switzerland

Geneva. Lombard, Odier & Cie. Data from Thierry Lombard.

United States

Albany, N.Y. Bureau of Corporations, Department of State. Incorporation data on specific companies.

Ann Arbor, Mich. University of Michigan. William L. Clements Library. Shelburne Papers. Peter Hasenclever, "Thoughts Concerning America" (after 1766).

Baltimore, Md. Maryland Historical Society. Principio Company Papers.

Bay City, Mich. Bay County Library. Edward Salisbury Clark, "An Outline History of the North American Chemical Company of Bay City, Michigan: 1898–1928." Typescript.

Berkeley, Calif. University of California. Bancroft Library. Microfilmed Records from Companies Registration Office (London), Companies Registration Office (Edinburgh), and the Public Records Office on British companies in the United States. 677 Reels.

———. ———. ———. Hongkong and Shanghai Banking Corporation "Signature Book Recording Amounts of Deposit," 1906–1936.

Boston, Mass. Harvard Business School. Baker Library. Kidder, Peabody Papers.

———. ———. ———. Thomas Lamont Papers.

Dearborn, Mich. Ford Motor Company Archives.

Fulton, N.Y. Fulton Public Library. Data on Nestlé's plant from Ellen I. Morin, Librarian.

Hoboken, N.J. Stevens Institute of Technology. Frederick W. Taylor Archives. Michelin Correspondence. File Taylor-France.

Laramie, Wyo. University of Wyoming. Western History Research Center. Western Range Cattle Industry Study. Swan Land and Cattle Company, Ltd. Prospectus, List of Shareholders, etc., Acc. 79.

Long Island City, N.Y. Steinway Company Archives. Data from John Steinway.

Madison, Wis. State Historical Society of Wisconsin. McCormick Collection. Data from Fred Carstensen.

Milltown, N.J. Milltown Public Library. Data on Michelin Tire Company from Dorothy Ji, Director of the Library.

Milwaukee, Wis. Milwaukee County Historical Society. Allis-Chalmers Manuscript Collection. Two typescript histories of Fraser & Chalmers, one by H. Schifflin (1942) and a second not signed, probably prepared in London (1953).

Nashville, Tenn. Vanderbilt University. Data from Franklin Brooks on Edward Tuck.

New York. Allied Chemical (now Allied Signal). Miscellaneous historical data.

———. American Metal Climax (materials from F. Taylor Ostrander).

———. Columbia University Libraries. Graduate School of Business. Marvyn Scudder Financial Records Collection.

———. ———. Special Collections. Belmont Family Papers.

———. ———. ———. James Stillman Papers.

———. ———. ———. Oral History Collection. Walter E. Sachs Reminiscences.

———. Manufacturers Hanover Trust Company. History Center.

———. Moseley, Hallgarten, Estabrook & Weeden Holding Company. "Draft History of Hallgarten & Co." Typescript. From Jon A. Bulkley.

———. New York Historical Society. Erving-King Papers.

———. ———. Linton Wells, "House of Seligman." Microfilm of unpublished typescript.

———. New York Public Library. Manuscript Room. Royal Commission on American Loyalist Claims. 60 volumes of transcripts.

———. ———. ———. Principio Company Records.

———. Western Electric Company. Archives.

Northbrook, Ill. International Minerals and Chemical Corporation. Unofficial, unrevised company history (n.d. 1960). My thanks to Robert Mixter, Director, Public Relations.

Olympia, Wash. State Archives. Data on Moss Bay Iron and Steel Company of America.

Parsippany, N.J. Faber-Castell Corporation. Chronologies.

Pawtucket, R.I. Pawtucket Public Library. Data on J. & P. Coats from Paul Arsenault, Reference Librarian.

South Bend, Ind. Discovery Hall Museum. Studebaker Corporation Papers. Data from Donald F. Davis.

St. Paul, Minn. Minnesota Historical Society. William de la Barre Papers.

———. ———. Northern Pacific Papers.

———. ———. John S. Pillsbury and Family Papers.

Stamford, Conn. American Thread Company. Miscellaneous historical data.

Van Hornesville, N.Y. Owen Young Papers. Data from Mrs. Everett Case on the Marconi organization.

Washington, D.C. Library of Congress. Manuscript Division. Western Range Cattle Industry Study. Acc. 11,092. 75 reels of microfilm.

———. National Archives. Record Groups 40 (Department of Commerce), 59 (Department of State), 122 (Federal Trade Commission and Bureau of Corporations),

131 (Alien Property Custodian), 151 (Bureau of Foreign and Domestic Commerce).

West Orange, N.J. Edison National Historic Site. United States Department of the Interior. Thomas Edison Papers.

Wilmington, Del. Eleutherian Mills Historical Library. Du Pont Papers.

Wilkes-Barre, Pa. Eberhard Faber, Inc. Historical data from Russell H. Williams.

Court Cases

Bayer Company, Inc. v. *United Drug Company.* 272 Fed. Rep. 505 (SDNY 1921).

Clark Thread Company, Appl. v. *Willimantic Linen Company.* 140 U.S. 481 (1891).

Coats et al. v. *Merrick Thread Co. et al.* 36 Fed. Rep. 324 (SDNY 1888).

Hiram Walker & Sons, Ltd. v. *Mikolas et al.* 79 Fed. Rep. 955 (DCMN 1897).

International Harvester Company of America v. *Commonwealth of Kentucky.* 234 U.S. 216 (1914).

J. & P. Coats, Ltd. v. *John Coates Thread Co.* 135 Fed. Rep. 177 (DCMN 1905).

United States v. *Aluminum Company of America.* Eq. No. 85–73 (SDNY 1937–1942). Testimony, exhibits, briefs, and final judgment.

United States v. *American Thread et al.* Final Decree, Equity no. 312 (DCNJ 1914).

United States v. *American Tobacco Company.* 221 U.S. 106 (1911).

Von Faber et al. v. *Faber.* 124 Fed. Rep. 603 (SDNY 1903).

Von Faber-Castell v. *Faber.* 139 Fed. Rep. 257 (CCA2 1905).

Books, Articles, Dissertations, Public Documents

Aalders, Gerald, and Cees Wiebes. "Stockholms Enskilda Bank, German Bosch and IG Farben. A Short History of Cloaking." *Scandanavian Economic History Review,* 33 (1985): 25–50.

Abramovitz, Moses. "The Passing of the Kuznets Cycle." *Economica,* 35 (1968): 349–367.

Abrams, M. A. "The French Copper Syndicate, 1887–1889." *Journal of Economic and Business History,* 4 (1932): 409–428.

Ackerman, Carl W. *George Eastman.* Boston: Houghton Mifflin, 1930.

Adams, Charles Francis. "The Granger Movement." *North American Review,* 120 (1875): 394–424.

Adams, Charles Francis, and Henry Adams. *Chapters of Erie.* 1886. Rpt. Ithaca, N.Y.: Cornell University Press, 1956.

Adams, Donald R., Jr. *Finance and Enterprise in Early America: A Study of Stephen Girard's Bank, 1812–1831.* Philadelphia: University of Pennsylvania, 1978.

Adams, Edward D. *Niagara Power: History of the Niagara Falls Power Company, 1886–1918.* 2 vols. Niagara Falls, N.Y.: Niagara Falls Power Company, 1927.

Adams, Henry. *Letters.* Ed. Worthington Ford. 2 vols. Boston: Houghton Mifflin, 1930, 1938.

Addis, John P. *The Crawshay Dynasty.* Cardiff: University of Wales Press, 1957.

Adler, Cyrus. *Jacob H. Schiff.* 2 vols. Garden City, N.Y.: Doubleday, 1928.

Adler, Dorothy R. *British Investment in American Railways, 1834–1898.* Charlottesville: University Press of Virginia, 1970.

Adler, John H., ed. *Capital Movements and Economic Development.* London: Macmillan, 1967.

Aduddell, Robert M., and Louis P. Cain. "Public Policy toward the Greatest Trust in the World." *Business History Review,* 55 (1981): 217–242.

Aitken, Hugh G. J. *The Continuous Wave: Technology and American Radio, 1900–1932.* Princeton, N.J.: Princeton University Press, 1985.

———. *Syntony and Spark: The Origins of Radio.* New York: John Wiley, 1976.

Albion, Robert G. *The Rise of New York Port, 1815–1860.* Hamden, Conn.: Archon Books, 1961.

Aldcroft, Derek H., ed. *The Development of British Industry and Foreign Competition, 1875–1914.* London: George Allen & Unwin, 1968.

Alderfer, E. G., and H. E. Michl. *Economics of American Industry.* 2nd ed. New York: McGraw-Hill, 1950.

Alford, B. W. E. *W. D. & H. O. Wills.* London: Methuen, 1973.

Allen, William V. "Western Feelings toward the East." *North American Review,* 157 (1896): 588–593.

Allis, Frederick S., Jr., ed. *William Bingham's Maine Lands, 1790–1820.* 2 vols. Boston: Colonial Society of Massachusetts, 1954.

Alt, Lutz. "The Photo-Chemical Industry: Historical Essays in Business Strategy and Internationalization." Ph.D. diss. MIT, 1986.

Alvord, Clarence Walworth. *The Mississippi Valley in British Politics.* 2 vols. 1916. Rpt. New York: Russell & Russell, 1959.

Ambruster, Howard Watson. *Treason's Peace: German Dyes and American Dupes.* New York: Beechhurst Press, 1947.

America's Twelve Master Salesmen. New York: B. C. Forbes, 1952.

Andrews, Charles M. *The Colonial Period of American History.* 4 vols. New Haven: Yale University Press, 1964.

Andrews, E. B. "The Late Copper Syndicate." *Quarterly Journal of Economics,* 3 (1889): 508–516.

Anyon, James T. *Recollections of the Early Days of American Accountancy, 1883–1893.* New York: privately printed, 1925.

Arai, Shinji. *History of the Yokohama Specie Bank* (in Japanese). Vol. 2. Tokyo, 1981.

Arboux, Michel. *Les valeurs mobilières étrangères sur le marché français.* Paris: Recueil Sirey, 1913.

Archer, Gleason L. *History of Radio to 1926.* New York: American Historical Society, 1938.

Armes, Ethel. *The Story of Coal and Iron in Alabama.* 1910. Rpt. New York: Arno Press, 1973.

Armstrong, Christopher, and H. V. Nelles. "A Curious Capital Flow: Canadian Investment in Mexico." *Business History Review,* 58 (1984): 178–203.

Armstrong, Leroy and J. O. Denny. *Financial California.* 1916. Rpt. New York: Arno Press, 1980.

Arndt, Leslie E. *The Bay County Story.* Linwood, Mich. privately printed, 1982.

Arrow, Kenneth J. *The Limits of Organization.* New York: Norton, 1974.

Ashby, N. B. *The Riddle of the Sphinx.* Chicago: Mercantile Publishing, 1892.

Ashley, Sir William. *The Tariff Problem.* 2nd ed. London: P. S. King, 1903.

Ashmead, Edward, *Twenty-Five Years of Mining, 1880–1904.* London: Mining Journal, 1909.

Ashworth, William. *A Short History of the International Economy since 1950.* 3rd ed. London: Longman Group, 1977.

Athearn, R. G. *Westward the Briton: The American Far West, 1865–1900.* New York: Charles Scribner's Sons, 1953.

Atherton, Lewis. *The Cattle Kings.* Bloomington: Indiana University Press, 1961.

Atkins, John Michael. *British Overseas Investment, 1918–1931.* New York: Arno Press, 1977.

Aubert, M. Georges. *La finance Américaine*. Paris: Ernest Flammarion, 1910.

Ayer, Jules. *A Century of Finance, 1804 to 1904: The London House of Rothschild*. London: n.p., 1905.

Babcock, Glenn D. *History of United States Rubber Company*. Bloomington: Bureau of Business Research, Graduate School of Business, Indiana University, 1966.

Bachman, Van Cleaf. *Peltries or Plantations: The Economic Policies of the Dutch West India Company in New Netherland, 1623–1639*. Baltimore: Johns Hopkins University Press, 1969.

Bacon, Nathaniel T. "American International Indebtedness." *Yale Review*, 9 (1900): 265–285.

Bailey, Joseph C. *Seaman A. Knapp*. New York: Columbia University Press, 1945.

Bailey, Thomas A. *A Diplomatic History of the United States*. 6th ed. New York: Appleton-Century-Crofts, 1958.

Bain, Harry Foster, and Thomas Thornton Read. *Ores and Industry in South America*. New York: Harper & Bros., 1934.

Baker, W. J. *A History of the Marconi Company*. London: Methuen, 1970.

Baldy, Edmond. *Les banques d'affaires en France depuis 1900*. Paris: Librairie Générale de Droit & de Jurisprudence, 1922.

Bank of Nova Scotia. *Annual Reports*.

Bank of Nova Scotia. *Bank of Nova Scotia, 1832–1932*. Toronto: privately printed, 1932.

Barclay, R. E. *Ducktown*. Chapel Hill: University of North Carolina Press, 1946.

Bardou, Jean-Pierre, Jean-Jacques Chanaron, Patrick Fridenson, and James M. Laux. *La révolution automobile*. Paris: Albin Michel, 1977.

Baring, Alexander. *My Recollections, 1848–1931*. Santa Barbara, Calif.: Schaver Printing Studio, 1933.

Barker, T. C. *The Glassmakers Pilkington: The Rise of an International Company, 1826–1976*. London: Weidenfeld & Nicolson, 1977.

Baron, Stanley. *Brewed in America: A History of Beer and Ale in the United States*. Boston: Little, Brown, 1962.

Bartlett, Edward Everett. *Edward Dean Adams*. New York: privately printed, 1926.

Bartlett, J. Neville. *Carpeting the Millions: The Growth of Britain's Carpet Industry*. Edinburgh: John Donald Publishers, n.d. [1977?].

Barty-King, Hugh. *Girdle round the Earth*. London: Heinemann, 1979.

Baruch, Bernard. *My Own Story*. London: Odhams Press, 1958.

Baster, A. S. J. *The Imperial Banks*. London: P. S. King, 1929.

———. *The International Banks*. 1935. Rpt. New York: Arno Press, 1977.

Bauer, Hans. *Swiss Bank Corporation, 1872–1972*. Basle: Swiss Bank Corporation, 1972.

Bayles, Richard, ed. *History of Providence County, Rhode Island*. New York: W. W. Preston, 1891.

Bayley, Rafael. *The National Loans of the United States*. 1800. Rpt. New York: Burt Franklin, 1970.

Beaton, Kendall. *Enterprise in Oil*. New York: Appleton-Century-Crofts, 1957.

Beauquis, A. *Histoire économique de la soie*. Paris: H. Dunod et E. Pinat, 1910.

Beaverbrook, Lord. *Politicians and the War*. 1925. Rpt. New York: Archon, 1968.

Becker, William H., and Samuel F. Wells, Jr. *Economics and World Power*. New York: Columbia University Press, 1984.

Becqué, Emile. *L'internationalisation des capitaux*. Montpellier, France: Imprimerie Générale du Midi, 1912.

Beer, John Joseph. *The Emergence of the German Dye Industry*. Urbana: University of Illinois Press, 1959.

Belmont, Perry. *An American Democrat*. 1941. Rpt. New York: AMS Press, 1967.

Bemis, Samuel Flagg. *A Diplomatic History of the United States*. 3rd ed. New York: Henry Holt, 1950.

———. *Jay's Treaty*. Rev. ed. New Haven: Yale University Press, 1962.

Bendikson, L. "Holland. Millions of Dollars in Our Investments." Newspaper Clipping, 1912. New York Public Library.

Bergeron, Louis. *Les capitalistes en France (1780–1914)*. Paris: Gallimard, 1978.

Berle, Adolf A., and Gardiner C. Means. *The Modern Corporation and Private Property*. Rev. ed. New York: Harcourt, Brace & World, 1968.

Bernfeld, Seymour S., with Harold K. Hochschild. "A Short History of American Metal Climax, Inc." In American Metal Climax, Inc., *World Atlas*, pp. 1–16. New York: n.d. (1962).

Berthoff, Rowland Tappan. *British Immigrants in Industrial America, 1790–1950*. Cambridge, Mass.: Harvard University Press, 1953.

Bhagwati, Jagdish N., Richard A. Brecher, and Tatsuo Hatta. "The Generalized Theory of Transfers and Welfare: Bilateral Transfers in a Multilateral World." *American Economic Review*, 83 (1983): 606–618.

Bining, Arthur Cecil. *Pennsylvania Iron Manufacture in the Eighteenth Century*. 2nd ed. Harrisburg: Pennsylvania Historical & Museum Commission, 1973.

Birch, Alan. *The Economic History of the British Iron and Steel Industry, 1784–1879*. London: Frank Cass, 1967.

Birmingham, Stephen. *Our Crowd*. New York: Dell, 1967.

Birnie, Arthur. *An Economic History of the British Isles*. New York: F. S. Crofts, 1940.

Bishop, Charles W. *La France et l'automobile*. Paris: Editions M. Th. Génin, 1971.

Bishop, J. Leander. *A History of American Manufactures from 1608 to 1860*. 3 vols. 1868. Rpt. Philadelphia: Edward Young, 1967.

Black, David. *The King of Fifth Avenue: The Fortunes of August Belmont*. New York: Dial Press, 1981.

Blair, Matthew. *The Paisley Thread Industry and the Men Who Created and Developed It*. Paisley, Scotland: Alexander Gardner, 1907.

Blakey, Arch Fredric. *The Florida Phosphate Industry*. Cambridge, Mass.: Harvard University Press, 1973.

Blodget, Samuel. *Economica: A Statistical Manual for the United States of America*. 1806. Rpt. New York: Augustus M. Kelley, 1964.

Bloomfield, Arthur I. *Monetary Policy under the International Gold Standard, 1880–1914*. New York: Federal Reserve Bank of New York, 1959.

———. *Patterns of Fluctuation in International Investment before 1914*. Princeton, N.J.: Princeton University Press, 1968.

Bloomfield, Gerald. *World Automotive Industry*. North Pomfret, Vt.: David & Charles, 1978.

Blumenthal, Henry. "The California Societies in France, 1849–1855." *Pacific Historical Review*, 35 (1956): 251–260.

———. *A Reappraisal of Franco-American Relations, 1830–1871*. Chapel Hill: University of North Carolina Press, 1959.

Blyth, H. E. *Through the Eye of a Needle: The Story of the English Sewing Cotton Company, 1897–1947*. N.p., n.d. [1947?].

Bogue, Allan G. "The Administrative and Policy Problems of the J. B. Watkins Land Mortgage Company, 1873–1894." *Bulletin of the Business History Society*, 27 (1953): 26–59.

———. "Land Credit for Northern Farmers, 1789–1940." *Agricultural History*, 50 (1976): 68–100.

———. *Money at Interest: The Farm Mortgage on the Middle Border*. Ithaca, N.Y.: Cornell University Press, 1955.

Böhme, Helmut. *Frankfort und Hamburg, Des Deutsches Reiches Silber-und Goldloch und die Allerenglischste Stadt des Kontinents*. Frankfurt: Europäische Verlagsanstalt, 1968.

Boissevain, G. M. *Money and Banking in the United States*. Amsterdam: J. H. de Bussy, 1909.

Bolle, Jacques. *Solvay: L'invention, l'homme, l'entreprise industrielle, 1863–1963*. Brussels: Solvay, 1963.

Bonn, M. J. *The Crumbling of Empire*. London: George Allen & Unwin, 1938.

Bonsor, N. R. P. *North Atlantic Seaway*. Prescot, Lancashire: T. Stephenson, 1955.

Boore, J. Perc. *The Seamless Story: A History of the Seamless Steel Tube Industry in the United States*. Los Angeles: Commonwealth Press, 1951.

Borchard, Edwin, and W. H. Wynne. *State Insolvency and Foreign Bondholders*. 2 vols. 1951. Rpt. New York: Garland, 1983.

Borkin, Joseph. *The Crime and Punishment of I. G. Farben*. New York: Free Press, 1978.

Born, Karl Erich. *International Banking in the 19th and 20th Centuries*. New York: St. Martin's Press, 1983.

[Borsig]. *100 Jahre Borsig, 1837–1937*. Berlin, 1937.

Bosch, K. D. *Nederlandse Beleggingen in De Verenigde Staten*. Amsterdam: Uitgeversmaatschappij Elsevier, 1948.

Boulding, Kenneth E., and Tapan Mukerjee. *Economic Imperialism: A Book of Readings*. Ann Arbor: University of Michigan Press, 1972.

Bouvier, Jean. *Le Crédit Lyonnais de 1863 à 1882*. 2 vols. Paris: S.E.V.P.E.N., 1961.

———. *Le krach de l'Union Générale, 1878–1885*. Paris: Presses Universitaires de France, 1961.

———. *Les Rothschilds*. Paris: Fayard, 1967.

Bovykin, V. I., ed. *Transformation of Bank Structures in the Industrial Period*. Budapest: Akadémiai Kiado, 1982.

Boxer, C. R. *The Dutch Seaborne Empire, 1600–1800*. New York: Knopf, 1970.

Boyer, Charles S. *Early Forges and Furnaces in New Jersey*. Philadelphia: University of Pennsylvania Press, 1963.

Bramsen, Bo, and Kathleen Wain. *The Hambros, 1779–1979*. London: Michael Joseph, 1979.

Branch, Harllee. *Alabama Power Company and the Southern Company*. New York: Newcomen Society, 1967.

Brandfon, Robert L. *Cotton Kingdom of the New South*. Cambridge, Mass.: Harvard University Press, 1967.

Bray, Charles I. "Financing the Western Cattle Man" (1928). Rpt. in *Bankers and Beef*. New York: Arno Press, 1975.

Brayer, Herbert O. "The Influence of British Capital on the Western Range Cattle Industry." *Journal of Economic History, Supplement*, 9 (1949): 85–98.

———. "When Dukes Went West." *Westerners Brand Book*, 4 (1948): 55–76.

———. *William Blackmore*. 2 vols. Denver: Bradford-Robinson, 1949.

Brecher, Richard A., and Jagdish N. Bhagwati. "Foreign Ownership and the Theory of Trade and Welfare." *Journal of Political Economy*, 89 (1981): 497–511.

———. "Immiserizing Transfers from Abroad." *Journal of International Economics*, 13 (1982): 353–364.

Brecher, Richard A., and Carlos F. Diaz Alejandro. "Tariffs, Foreign Capital and Immiserizing Growth." *Journal of International Economics*, 7 (1977): 317–322.

Brewer, H. Peers. "Eastern Money and Western Mortgages in the 1870s." *Business History Review*, 50 (1976): 356–380.

Bridenbaugh, Carl. *Jamestown, 1544–1699.* Oxford: Oxford University Press, 1980.

Bridge, James Howard. *The Inside History of the Carnegie Steel Company.* New York: Aldine, 1903.

Broehl, Wayne G. *John Deere's Company.* New York: Doubleday, 1984.

Brown, John Crosby. *A Hundred Years of Merchant Banking.* New York: privately printed, 1909.

Brown, Michael Barratt. *The Economics of Imperialism.* Harmondsworth: Penguin, 1974.

Bruchey, Stuart. *Colonial Merchants.* New York: Harcourt, Brace & World, 1966.

———. *Robert Oliver: Merchant of Baltimore, 1783–1819.* Baltimore: Johns Hopkins University Press, 1956.

Bryant, Keith L. *Arthur E. Stilwell.* Nashville: Vanderbilt University Press, 1971.

———. *History of the Atchison, Topeka and the Santa Fe.* New York: Macmillan, 1974.

Buck, Solon Justus. *The Granger Movement, 1870–1880.* Cambridge, Mass.: Harvard University Press, 1913.

Buck, Sydney Norman. *The Development of the Organization of Anglo-American Trade, 1800–1850.* New Haven: Yale University Press, 1925.

Buckley, Peter J., and Mark Casson. *The Economic Theory of the Multinational Enterprise.* New York: St. Martin's Press, 1985.

———. *The Future of Multinational Enterprise.* New York: Holmes & Meier, 1976.

Buckley, Peter J., and Brian R. Roberts. *European Direct Investment in the U.S.A. before World War I.* London: Macmillan, 1982.

Buist, Marten G. *At Spes non Fracta: Hope & Co., 1770–1815. Merchant Bankers & Diplomats at Work.* The Hague: Martinus Nijhoff, 1974.

Buley, R. Carlyle. *The Equitable Assurance Society of the United States.* New York: Appleton-Century-Crofts, 1967.

Bullock, Charles, John H. Williams, and Rufus S. Tucker. "Balance of Trade of the United States." *Review of Economic Statistics*, 1 (1919): 213–263.

Bunting, W. H. *Portrait of a Port: Boston, 1852–1914.* Cambridge, Mass.: Harvard University Press, 1971.

Bürgin, Alfred. *Geschichte des Geigy-Unternehmens von 1758 bis 1939.* Basle: J. R. Geigy, 1958.

Burgy, J. Herbert. *The New England Cotton Textile Industry.* Baltimore: Waverly Press, 1932.

Burk, Kathleen. *Britain, America and the Sinews of War, 1914–1918.* Boston: George Allen & Unwin, 1985.

Burnham, T. H., and G. O. Hoskins, *Iron and Steel in Britain, 1870–1930.* London: Allen & Unwin, 1943.

Burns, Duncan. *The Economic History of Steelmaking, 1867–1939.* Cambridge: Cambridge University Press, 1961.

Burr, Anna R. *The Portrait of a Banker: James Stillman.* New York: Duffield, 1927.

Burton, H., and D. C. Corner. *Investment and Unit Trusts in Britain and America.* London: Elek, 1968.

Burton, Harley True. *A History the JA Ranch.* 1927. Rpt. New York: Argonaut Press, 1966.

[Burton, J. C., ed.]. *Arthur Young and the Business He Founded.* New York: privately printed, 1948.

Buss, Dietrich. *Henry Villard: A Study of Transatlantic Investment and Interests, 1870–1895.* New York: Arno Press, 1978.

Byatt, I. C. R. *The British Electrical Industry, 1875–1914.* Oxford: Oxford University Press, 1979.

Cain, P. J. *Economic Foundations of British Overseas Expansion, 1815–1914.* London: Macmillan, 1980.

Cairncross, Sir Alec. "Did Foreign Investments Pay?" *Review of Economic Studies,* 3 (1935): 67–78.

———. "The Early Growth of Messrs. J. & P. Coats." Unfinished, unpublished paper (ca. 1956).

———. *Home and Foreign Investment, 1870–1913.* Cambridge: Cambridge University Press, 1953.

Caldwell, Stephen A. *A Banking History of Louisiana.* Baton Rouge: Louisiana State University Press, 1935.

Callender, Guy S. "The Early Transportation and Banking Enterprises of the States in Relation to the Growth of Corporations." *Quarterly Journal of Economics,* 17 (1902): 111–162.

———. "English Capital and American Resources, 1815–1860." Ph.D. diss., Harvard University, 1897.

Calvert, Albert F. *A History of the Salt Union.* London: Effingham Wilson, 1913.

Cameron, Jenks. *Development of Governmental Forest Control in the United States.* Baltimore: Johns Hopkins University Press, 1928.

Cameron, Rondo. *France and the Economic Development of Europe, 1800–1914.* Princeton, N.J.: Princeton University Press, 1961.

———. "French Foreign Investment, 1850–1880." Ph.D. diss. University of Chicago, 1952.

———, ed. *Banking and Economic Development.* New York: Oxford University Press, 1972.

———, ed. *Banking in the Early Stages of Industrialization.* New York: Oxford University Press, 1967.

Campbell, Edward G. *The Reorganization of the American Railroad System, 1893–1900.* New York: Columbia University Press, 1938.

Canada. Report of Commissioner. Combines Investigation Act. Department of Justice. *Matches.* Ottawa, 1949.

Canovan, Margaret. *Populism.* New York: Harcourt Brace, 1981.

Carey, John L. *The Rise of the Accounting Profession: From Technician to Professional, 1896–1936.* New York: American Institute of Certified Accountants, 1969.

Caron, François. *An Economic History of Modern France.* New York: Columbia University Press, 1979.

Carosso, Vincent P. "A Financial Elite: New York's German-Jewish Investment Bankers." *American Jewish Historical Quarterly,* 56 (1976): 67–88.

———. *Investment Banking in America.* Cambridge, Mass.: Harvard University Press, 1970.

———. *More Than a Century of Investment Banking: The Kidder, Peabody & Co. Story.* New York: McGraw-Hill, 1979.

———. *The Morgans.* Cambridge, Mass.: Harvard University Press, 1987.

———. "The Wall Street Money Trust from Pujo through Medina." *Business History Review,* 47 (1973): 421–437.

Carr, Charles C. *Alcoa.* New York: Rinehart, 1952.

Carr, J. C., and W. Taplin. *History of the British Steel Industry.* Cambridge, Mass.: Harvard University Press, 1962.

Carr, William H. A. *From Three Cents a Week: The Story of Prudential Insurance Co. of America.* Englewood Cliffs, N.J.: Prentice-Hall, 1975.

Carstensen, Fred V. *American Enterprise in Foreign Markets.* Chapel Hill: University of North Carolina Press, 1984.

Carstensen, Vernon, ed. *Farmer Discontent, 1865–1900.* New York: John Wiley, 1974.

———, ed. *The Public Lands.* Madison: University of Wisconsin Press, 1963.

Carswell, John. *The South Sea Bubble.* London: Cresset Press, 1960.

Carter, Alice C. "Dutch Foreign Investments, 1738–1800." *Economica,* n.s., 20 (1953): 322–340.

Carter, George R. *The Tendency toward Industrial Combination.* London: Constable, 1913.

Cartwright, A. P. *The Gold Miners.* Cape Town: Purnell, 1962.

Cassel, Gustav, et al. *Foreign Investments.* Chicago: University of Chicago Press, 1928.

Casson, Mark. *Alternatives to the Multinational Enterprise.* New York: Holmes & Meier, 1979.

———, ed. *The Growth of International Business.* London: George Allen & Unwin, 1983.

———, ed. *Multinationals and World Trade.* London: Allen & Unwin, 1986.

Castronovo, Valerio. *Giovanni Agnelli.* Turin: Einaudi, 1977.

Catterall, R. C. H. *The Second Bank of the United States.* Chicago: University of Chicago Press, 1903.

Caughey, John Walton. *California.* New York: Prentice-Hall, 1940.

Caves, Richard E. *Multinational Enterprise and Economic Analysis.* Cambridge: Cambridge University Press, 1982.

Cecil, Lamar. *Albert Ballin: Business and Politics in Imperial Germany, 1888–1981.* Princeton, N.J.: Princeton University Press, 1967.

Chalmers, Thomas. *100 Years of Guttapercha: R. & J. Dick Ltd.* Glasgow: privately printed, 1947.

Chalmin, Philippe. *Negociants et chargeurs.* Paris: Economica, 1985.

Chamber of Commerce of the United States. *Laws and Practices Affecting the Establishment of Foreign Branches of Banks.* Washington, D.C.: Chamber of Commerce of the United States, 1923.

Chandler, Alfred D., Jr. "Anthracite Coal and the Beginnings of the Industrial Revolution." *Business History Review,* 46 (1972): 141–181.

———. "The Beginnings of "Big Business' in American Industry." *Business History Review,* 33 (1959): 1–31.

———. "The Emergence of Managerial Capitalism." Paper delivered at American Historical Association Meeting, 1983.

———. "Evolution of the Large Industrial Corporation: An Evaluation of the Transaction Cost Approach." *Business and Economic History,* 2nd ser., 11 (1982): 116–134.

———. *Giant Enterprise.* New York: Harcourt Brace, 1964.

———. "The Growth of the Transnational Industrial Firm in the United States and in the United Kingdom: A Comparative Analysis." *Economic History Review,* 2nd ser., 33 (1980): 396–410.

———. *Henry Varnum Poor.* Cambridge, Mass.: Harvard University Press, 1956.

———. "Patterns of American Railroad Finance, 1830–50." *Business History Review,* 28 (1954): 248–263.

———. *Railroads.* New York: Harcourt Brace, 1965.

———. *Strategy and Structure.* Cambridge, Mass.: MIT Press, 1962.

———. *The Visible Hand.* Cambridge, Mass.: Harvard University Press, 1977.

Chandler, Alfred D., Jr., and Herman Daems. *Managerial Hierarchies.* Cambridge, Mass.: Harvard University Press, 1980.

Chandler, Alfred D., Jr., and Stephen Salsbury. *Pierre S. du Pont and the Making of the Modern Corporation*. New York: Harper & Row, 1971.

Chandler, Alfred D., Jr., and Richard Tedlow. *The Coming of Managerial Capitalism*. Homewood, Ill.: Richard D. Irwin, 1985.

Chandler, George. *Four Centuries of Banking*. 2 vols. London: B. T. Batsford, 1964, 1968.

Channon, Derek F. *The Strategy and Structure of British Enterprise*. Boston: Division of Research, Graduate School of Business Administration, Harvard University, 1973.

Chapman, Sidney J. *The History of Trade between the United Kingdom and the United States with Special Reference to the Effects of Tariffs*. London: Swan Sonnenschein, 1899.

Chapman, Stanley D. "British-Based Investment Groups before 1914." *Economic History Review*, 2nd ser., 38 (1985): 230–251.

———. "British Marketing Enterprise: The Changing Roles of Merchants, Manufacturers, and Financiers, 1700–1800." *Business History Review*, 53 (1979): 205–233.

———. "The International Houses: The Continental Contribution to British Commerce, 1800–1860." *Journal of European Economic History*, 6 (1977): 5–48.

———. *The Rise of Merchant Banking*. London: Allen & Unwin, 1984.

Chazal, Philip E. *The Century in Phosphates and Fertilizers: A Sketch of the South Carolina Phosphate Industry*. Charleston, S.C.: Lucas-Richardson, 1904.

Cheape, Charles W. *Moving the Masses: The Evolution of Public Transit*. Cambridge, Mass.: Harvard University Press, 1980.

Checkland, S. G. *The Mines of Tharsis: Roman, French and British Enterprise in Spain*. London: George Allen & Unwin, 1967.

———. *Scottish Banking, 1695–1973*. Glasgow: Collins, 1975.

Cheever, Lawrence O. *The House of Morrell*. Cedar Rapids, Iowa: Torch Press, 1948.

Chester, Edward W. *United States Oil Policy and Diplomacy*. Westport, Conn.: Greenwood Press, 1983.

Choffel, J. *Saint Gobain*. Paris: Plon, 1960.

Cipolla, Carlo M. *Before the Industrial Revolution*. New York: Norton, 1976.

Clapham, J. H. *The Bank of England*. 2 vols. Cambridge: Cambridge University Press, 1966.

———. *Economic Development of France and Germany, 1815–1914*. 4th ed. Cambridge: Cambridge University Press, 1961.

———. *An Economic History of Modern Britain*. Vol. 3. Cambridge: Cambridge University Press, 1968.

———. *The Woolen and Worsted Industries*. London: Methuen, 1907.

Clark, Victor S. *History of Manufactures in the United States*. 3 vols. Washington, D.C.: Carnegie Institution, 1929.

Clarke, Hyde. *Sovereign and Quasi-Sovereign States: Their Debts to Foreign Countries*. London: Effingham Wilson, 1878.

Clay, Sir Henry. *Lord Norman*. London: Macmillan, 1957.

Clay, John. *My Life on the Range* (1924). Rpt. in *Bankers and Beef*. New York: Arno Press, 1975.

Clemen, R. A. *American Livestock and Meat Industry*. New York: Ronald Press, 1923.

Clements, Roger V. "British-Controlled Enterprise in the West between 1870 and 1900 and Some Agrarian Reactions." *Agricultural History*, 27 (1953): 137–141.

———. "British Investment and American Legislative Restrictions in the Trans-Mississippi West, 1880–1900." *Mississippi Valley Historical Review*, 42 (1955): 207–227.

———. "British Investment in the Trans-Mississippi West, 1870–1914, Its Encouragement, and the Metal Mining Interests." *Pacific Historical Review*, 29 (1960): 35–50.

———. "The Farmer's Attitude toward British Investment in American Industry." *Journal of Economic History*, 15 (1955): 151–159.

Clerget, Pierre. *Les industries de la soie en France*. Paris: Libraire Armand Colin, 1925.

Cleveland, Frederick A., and Fred W. Powell. *Railroad Finance*. New York: B. Appleton, 1912.

———. *Railroad Promotion and Capitalization*. New York: Longmans, Green, 1909.

Cleveland, Harold van B., and Thomas F. Huertas. *Citibank, 1812–1970*. Cambridge, Mass.: Harvard University Press, 1985.

Clews, Henry. *Twenty-Eight Years in Wall Street*. New York: Irving, 1888.

Clough, Shepard B., and Charles Woolsey Cole. *Economic History of Europe*. Boston: D. C. Heath, 1941.

Clough, Shepard B., and Richard T. Rapp. *European Economic History*. 3rd ed. New York: McGraw-Hill, 1978.

Coase, Ronald H. "The Nature of the Firm." *Economica*, n.s., 4 (1937): 386–405.

Cobden, Stanley, and Forest G. Hill, eds. *American Economic History*. Philadelphia: Lippincott, 1966.

Cochran, Thomas C. *Frontiers of Change: Early Industrialism in America*. New York: Oxford University Press, 1981.

———. *The Pabst Brewing Co.* New York: New York University Press, 1948.

———. *Railroad Leaders*. Cambridge, Mass.: Harvard University Press, 1953.

Coe, Fred A., Jr. *Burroughs Wellcome Co., 1880–1980*. New York: Newcomen Society, 1980.

Cole, Arthur Harrison. *The American Wool Manufacture*. 2 vols. Cambridge, Mass.: Harvard University Press, 1926.

Coleman, Donald C. *Courtaulds*. 2 vols. Oxford: Oxford University Press, 1969.

Coleman, Peter. *Debtors and Creditors in America, 1607–1900*. Madison: State Historical Society of Wisconsin, 1974.

Collas, Henry. *La Banque de Paris et des Pays-Bas*. Dijon: Imprimerie Barbier, 1908.

Conant, Charles A. "The Economic Basis of Imperialism." *North American Review*, 167 (1898): 326–340.

Condit, Carl W. *The Port of New York*. Chicago: University of Chicago Press, 1980.

Condliffe, J. B. *The Commerce of Nations*. New York: Norton, 1950.

Conybeare, F. A. *Dingle Bank*. Cambridge: W. Heffer, 1925.

Cook, P. Lesley, and Ruth Cohen. *Effects of Mergers*. London: George Allen & Unwin, 1958.

Cooke, Jacob E. *The Reports of Alexander Hamilton*. New York: Harper & Row, 1964.

———. *Tench Cox and the Early Republic*. Chapel Hill: University of North Carolina Press, 1978.

Cope, S. R. "Bird, Savage & Bird of London: Merchants and Bankers, 1782–1803." *Guildhall Studies in London History*, 4 (1981): 202–217.

Copeland, Melvin Thomas. *The Cotton Manufacturing Industry of the United States*. Cambridge, Mass.: Harvard University Press, 1912.

Coram, T. C. "The Role of British Capital in the Development of the United States, 1600–1914." M.Sc. (Soc. Science) thesis, University of Southampton, 1967.

Corey, Lewis. *The House of Morgan*. New York: G. Howard Watt, 1930.

Corina, Maurice. *Trust in Tobacco*. London: Michael Joseph, 1975.

Corley, T. A. B. "From National to Multinational Enterprise: The Beecham Business, 1848–1945." Unpublished paper, 1983.

———. *A History of the Burmah Oil Company, 1886–1924*. London: Heinemann, 1983.

———. *Quaker Enterprise in Biscuits: Huntley & Palmers of Reading, 1822–1972*. London: Hutchinson, 1972.

Corning, Howard. "The First Iron Works in America—1645." Paper read before American Iron and Steel Institute at New York, May 25, 1928. Pamphlet published in New York, 1928.

Corti, Egon Caesar. *The Rise of the House of Rothschild*. New York: Cosmopolitan Book Corp., 1928.

Cotner, Robert C. *James Stephen Hogg*. Austin: University of Texas Press, 1959.

———, ed. *Addresses and State Papers of James Stephen Hogg*. Austin: University of Texas Press, 1951.

Cottrell, P. L. *British Overseas Investment in the Nineteenth Century*. London: Macmillan, 1975.

———. *Industrial Finance, 1830–1914*. London: Methuen, 1980.

———. "Investment Banking in England, 1856–1882: A Case Study of the International Financial Society." Ph.D. diss., University of Hull, 1974.

Council of the Corporation of Foreign Bondholders. *Annual Reports*, 1874–1914.

Court, W. H. B. *British Economic History*. Cambridge: Cambridge University Press, 1965.

Courtney, Leonard H. "On the Finances of the United States of America, 1861–67." *Journal of the Statistical Society of London*, 31 (1868): 164–221.

Cox, Reavis. *Competition in the American Tobacco Industry, 1911–1932*. New York: Columbia University Press, 1933.

Cox, Rowland, ed. *American Trade Mark Cases*. Cincinnati: Robert Clarke, 1871.

Crammond, Edgar. "British Investments Abroad." *Quarterly Review*, 207 (1907): 245–272.

———. "British Investments Abroad." *Quarterly Review*, 215 (1911): 43–67.

———. "The Economic Position of the Allied Powers." *Quarterly Review*, 224 (1915): 193–222.

Crapol, Edward. *America for Americans*. Westport, Conn.: Greenwood Press, 1973.

Crary, Catharine S., ed. *The Price of Loyalty: Tory Writings from the Revolutionary Era*. New York: McGraw-Hill, 1973.

Craven, Wesley Frank. *Dissolution of the Virginia Company*. New York: Oxford University Press, 1932.

———. *The Virginia Company of London, 1606–1624*. Williamsburg: Virginia 350th Anniversary Celebration Corporation, 1957.

Crawford, J. B. *The Credit Mobilier of America*. Boston: C. W. Calkins, 1880.

Crick, W. F., and J. E. Wadsworth. *A Hundred Years of Joint-Stock Banking*. London: Hodder & Stoughton, 1936.

Critchell, James Troubridge, and Joseph Raymond. *A History of the Frozen Meat Trade*. 2nd ed. London: Constable, 1912.

Cross, Ira B. *Financing an Empire: History of Banking in California*. 4 vols. Chicago: S. J. Clarke, 1927.

Crutchley, Geo. W. *John Mackintosh: A Biography*. London: Hodder & Stoughton, 1921.

[Cudahy Packing Co.] *The Cudahy Packing Co*. Chicago: privately printed, 1938.

Curle, J. H. *The Gold Mines of the World*. London: Waterlow, 1902.

Currie, A. W. "British Attitudes toward Investment in North American Railroads." *Business History Review*, 34 (1960): 194–215.

Cyert, Richard, and James G. March. *A Behavioral Theory of the Firm*. Englewood Cliffs, N.J.: Prentice-Hall, 1963.

Däbritz, Walther. *Fünfzig Jahre Metallgesellschaft, 1881–1931*. Frankfurt, privately printed, 1931.

Daems, Herman, and Herman van der Wee. *The Rise of Managerial Capitalism*. Louvain: Lourain University, 1974.

Daggett, Stuart. *Railroad Reorganization*. Boston: Houghton Mifflin, 1908.

Dahl, Albin Joachim. "British Investment in California Mining, 1870–1890." Ph.D. diss., University of California, Berkeley, 1961.

Daniels, John D. *Recent Foreign Direct Manufacturing Investment in the United States.* New York: Praeger, 1971.

Daniels, Joseph. "History of Pig Iron Manufacture on the Pacific Coast." *Washington Quarterly,* 27 (1926): 168–189.

David, Paul A. *Technical Choice, Innovation and Economic Growth.* Cambridge: Cambridge University Press, 1975.

Davies, A. Emil. *Investments Abroad.* 1927. Rpt. New York: Arno Press, 1977.

Davies, Robert Bruce. *Peacefully Working to Conquer the World: Singer Sewing Machines in Foreign Markets.* New York: Arno Press, 1976.

Davis, Charles Thomas. *The Manufacture of Leather.* Philadelphia: H. C. Baird, 1885.

Davis, Donald F. "Studebaker Stumbles into Detroit." *Detroit in Perspective,* 4 (1979): 14–32.

Davis, John. "Alien Landlordism in America." In C. F. Taylor, ed., *The Land Question.* Philadelphia: C. F. Taylor, n.d. (1898?)

Davis, John P. *Corporations.* 1897. Rpt. New York: Capricorn Ed., 1961.

Davis, Joseph S. *Essays in the Earlier History of American Corporations.* 2 vols. Cambridge, Mass.: Harvard University Press, 1917.

Davis, Lance E. "The Investment Market, 1870–1914: The Evolution of a National Money Market." *Journal of Economic History,* 25 (1965): 355–399.

Davis, Lance E., et al. *American Economic Growth.* New York: Harper & Row, 1972.

Davis, Lance E., Jonathan R. T. Hughes, and Duncan C. McDougall. *American Economic History.* Homewood, Ill.: Richard D. Irwin, 1961.

Davis, Lance E., and Robert A. Huttenback. "The Export of British Finance, 1865–1914." In A. N. Porter and R. F. Holland, *Money, Finance and Empire, 1790–1960,* pp. 28–76. London: Frank Cass, 1985.

———. *Mammon and the Pursuit of Empire.* Cambridge: Cambridge University Press, 1986.

———. "The Political Economy of British Imperialism: Measures of Benefits and Support"; "Discussion" by Michael Edelstein. *Journal of Economic History,* 43 (1982): 119–130; 131–132.

Davis, Pearce. *The Development of the American Glass Industry.* Cambridge, Mass.: Harvard University Press, 1949.

Davis, Richard. *The English Rothschilds.* Chapel Hill: University of North Carolina Press, 1983.

Deloitte, Plender, Griffiths & Co. *Deloitte & Co., 1845–1956.* Oxford: privately printed, 1958.

DeMond, C. W. *Price, Waterhouse and Company in America.* New York: Price, Waterhouse, 1957.

de Neuflize et Cie, 1667–1925. Paris: Imprimerie de Vaugirard, 1926.

de Neuflize, Schlumberger et Cie, 1800–1950. Paris, 1950.

Denison, Merrill. *Canada's First Bank: A History of the Bank of Montreal.* 2 vols. New York: Dodd, Mead, 1966, 1967.

———. *Harvest Triumph: The Story of Massey-Harris.* Toronto: Collins, 1949.

DeNovo, John A. "Petroleum and the United States Navy before World War I." *Mississippi Valley Historical Review,* 41 (1955): 641–656.

Depew, Chauncey, ed. *1795–1895: One Hundred Years of American Commerce.* 2 vols. New York: D. O. Haynes, 1895.

Depitre, Edgard. *La mouvement de concentration dans les banques allemandes.* Paris, 1905.

Deterding, Sir Henri. *An International Oilman*. London, New York: Harper & Bros., 1934.

Detjen, David W. *The Germans in Missouri, 1900–1918*. Columbia: University of Missouri Press, 1985.

Devine, T. M., ed. *A Scottish Firm in Virginia, 1767–1777: W. Cunningham & Co.* Edinburgh: Scottish History Society, 1984.

DeVries, Jan. *The Economy of Europe in an Age of Crisis, 1600–1750*. Cambridge: Cambridge University Press, 1976.

De Vries, Johan. *The Netherlands Economy in the Twentieth Century*. Assen: Van Goreum, 1978.

Dewey, Davis R. *Financial History of the United States*. 12th ed. 1934. Rpt. New York: A. M. Kelley, 1968.

Dewing, Arthur S. *Corporate Promotions and Reorganizations*. Cambridge, Mass.: Harvard University Press, 1914.

Diamond, Sigmund, ed. *A Casual View of America: The Home Letters of Salomon de Rothschild, 1859–1861*. London: Cresset Press, 1962.

Dickens, Paul D. "The Transition Period in American International Financing: 1897 to 1914." Ph.D. diss., George Washington University, 1933.

Dickson, P. G. M. *The Sun Insurance Office, 1710–1960*. London: Oxford University Press, 1960.

Donaldson, Frances. *The Marconi Scandal*. London: Rupert Hart-Davis, 1962.

Donaldson, Gordon. *The Scots Overseas*. London: Robert Hale, 1966.

Donaldson, John. *International Economic Relations*. New York: Longmans Green, 1928.

Downard, William L. *Dictionary of the History of American Brewing and Distilling Industries*. Westport, Conn.: Greenwood Press, 1980.

Droulers, Charles. *Le Marquis de Morès, 1858–1896*. Paris: Librairie Plon, 1932.

Du Cros, Sir Arthur. *Wheels of Fortune*. London: Chapman & Hall, 1938.

Dudden, Arthur Power. "Antimonopolism, 1865–1890: The Historical Background and Intellectual Origins of the Antitrust Movement in the United States." Ph.D. diss., University of Michigan, 1950.

Duffus, Roy A., Jr. *The Story of M & T Chemicals, Inc.* New York: Codella Duffus Baker, 1965.

Duguid, Charles. *Story of the Stock Exchange*. London: Grant Richards, 1901.

Dunbar, D. E. *The Tin-Plate Industry*. Boston: Houghton Mifflin, 1915.

Dunlop, Kathleen Edith. "The History of the Dunlop Rubber Co., Ltd. 1888–1939." Ph.D. diss., University of Illinois, Urbana, 1949.

Dunn, William Edward. *Spanish and French Rivalry in the Gulf Region of the United States, 1678–1702: The Beginnings of Texas and Pensacola*. 1917. Rpt. New York: Books for Libraries Press, 1971.

Dunning, John H. "British Investment in U.S. Industry." *Moorgate and Wall Street*, Autumn 1961, pp. 5–23.

———. *International Production and Multinational Enterprise*. London: George Allen & Unwin, 1981.

———. *Studies in International Investment*. London: George Allen & Unwin, 1970.

———. "United States Foreign Investment and the Technology Gap." In Charles P. Kindleberger and Andrew Shonfield, eds., *North American and Western European Economic Policies*, pp. 364–406. London: Macmillan, 1971.

———, ed. *International Investment*. Harmondsworth: Penguin, 1972.

———, ed. *The Multinational Enterprise*. New York: Praeger, 1971.

Dunning, John H., John Stopford, and Klaus Haberick. *World Directory of Multinational Enterprises*. 2 vols. New York: Facts on File, 1980.

Duplan, J. L. *Lettres d'un vieil américain à un français*. Paris: Payot, 1917.

Du Pont, B. G. E. I. *Du Pont de Nemours & Co.: A History, 1802–1902*. New York: privately printed, 1920.

———. *Life of Eleuthère Irénée du Pont, 1799–1802*. Vol. 5. Newark: University of Delaware Press, 1924.

Dutton, William S. *Du Pont*. New York: Charles Scribner's Sons, 1942.

[Earle, Walter K.] *Shearman & Sterling*. [New York]: Shearman & Sterling, 1973.

Eccles, W. J. *France in America*. New York: Harper & Row, 1972.

Eckenrode, H. J., and Pocahontas Wight Edmunds. *E. H. Harriman: The Little Giant of Wall Street*. New York: Greenberg, 1933.

Edelstein, Michael. "The Determinants of U.K. Investment Abroad, 1870–1913: The U.S. Case." *Journal of Economic History*, 34 (1974): 980–1007.

———. "Foreign Investment and Empire, 1860–1914." In Roderick Floud and Donald McCloskey, eds., *The Economic History of Britain since 1700*, II, 70–98. Cambridge: Cambridge University Press, 1981.

———. *Overseas Investment in the Age of High Imperialism*. New York: Columbia University Press, 1982.

———. "Rigidity and Bias in the British Capital Market, 1870–1913." In Donald N. McCloskey, ed., *Essays on a Mature Economy: Britain after 1840*, pp. 83–105. Princeton, N.J.: Princeton University Press, 1971.

Edler, Friederich. *The Dutch Republic and the American Revolution*. Baltimore: Johns Hopkins University Press, 1911.

Edsall, Nicholas C. *Richard Cobden*. Cambridge, Mass.: Harvard University Press, 1986.

Edward, Michael M. *Growth of British Cotton Trade, 1780–1815*. Manchester: Manchester University Press, 1967.

Edwards, George W. *The Evolution of Finance Capitalism*. New York: Longmans, Green, 1938.

Edwards, James Don. *History of Public Accounting in the United States*. University: University of Alabama Press, 1978.

Edwards, Ronald S., and Harry Townsend. *Business Enterprise: Its Growth and Organization*. London: Macmillan, 1961.

Egerton, Hugh Edward, ed. *Mass Violence in America: The Royal Commission on the Losses and Services of American Loyalists, 1783 to 1785*. New York: Arno Press and the New York Times, 1969.

Ehrlich, Cyril. *The Piano*. London: J. M. Dent, 1976.

Eichengreen, Barry. "Mortgage Interest Rates in the Populist Era." *American Economic Review*, 74 (1984): 995–1015.

Elbaum, Bernard, and William Lazonick. *The Decline of the British Economy*. Oxford: Clarendon Press, 1986.

Elliott, Blanche B. *A History of English Advertising*. London: B. T. Batsford, 1962.

Elliott, William Yandell, et al. *International Control in the Non-Ferrous Metals*. 1937. Rpt. New York: Arno Press, 1976.

Ellis, Aytoun. *Heir of Adventure: The Story of Brown, Shipley & Co*. London: Brown, Shipley, 1960.

Emden, Paul H. *Money Powers of Europe in the Nineteenth and Twentieth Centuries*. New York: D. Appleton-Century, 1938.

———. *Quakers in Commerce: A Record of Business Achievement* London: Sampson Low, Marston, 1939.

Engelbourg, Saul. "John Stewart Kennedy and the Scottish American Investment Company." Unpublished paper, October 1986.

Engelbrecht, Helmut Carol, and Frank Cleary Hanighen. *Merchants of Death*. New York: Dodd, Mead, 1934.

English Committee of the Alabama 8 per cent Gold State Bonds of 1870. *Hill Country, Alabama, U.S.A.* London: E. and F. N. Spon, 1878. (British Museum shelf-mark: 10410 cc5.)

Erickson, Charlotte. *American Industry and the European Immigrant, 1860–1885*. Cambridge, Mass.: Harvard University Press, 1957.

———. *British Industrialists: Steel and Hosiery, 1850–1950*. Cambridge: Cambridge University Press, 1959.

Evans, Paul D. *The Holland Land Company*. Buffalo, N.Y.: Buffalo Historical Society, 1924.

———. "Pulteney Purchase." *New York State Historical Association Quarterly Journal*, 3 (1922): 83–104.

Fahey, John. "When the Dutch Owned Spokane." *Pacific Northwest Quarterly*, 72 (1981): 2–10.

Faith, Nicholas. *The Infiltrators*. London: Hamish Hamilton, 1971.

———. *Safety in Numbers*. New York: Viking Press, 1982.

Farnie, D. A. *The English Cotton Industry and the World Market, 1815–1896*. Oxford: Clarendon Press, 1979.

Faust, Albert B. *The German Element in the United States*. 2 vols. Boston: Houghton Mifflin, 1909.

Feinstein, Charles H. "Home and Foreign Investment: Some Aspects of Capital Formation, Finance, and Income in the United Kingdom, 1870–1913." Ph.D. diss., Cambridge University, 1959.

———. "Capital Formation in Great Britain." In Peter Mathias and M. M. Postan, eds., *Cambridge Economic History of Europe*. vol. 7, pt. 1, chap. 2. Cambridge: Cambridge University Press, 1978.

———. *National Income, Expenditure and Output of the United Kingdom, 1855–1965*. Cambridge: Cambridge University Press, 1972.

Feis, Herbert. *Europe: The World's Banker, 1870–1914*. 1930. Rpt. New York: Norton, 1965.

Felix, David. "Alternative Outcomes to the Current LDC Foreign Debt Crisis: Some Lessons from the Past." Department of Economics, Washington University, Working Paper #73, 1984.

Fenn, Charles. *A Compendium of English and Foreign Funds*. 14th ed. London, 1889.

Ferguson, E. James. *The Power of the Purse: A History of American Public Finance, 1776–1790*. Chapel Hill: University of North Carolina Press, 1961.

Ferguson, Edwin E. "The California Alien Land Law and the Fourteenth Amendment." *California Law Review*, 35 (1947): 61–90.

Ferrier, Ronald W. *The History of the British Petroleum Company*. Vol. 1. Cambridge: Cambridge University Press, 1982.

Field, Henry M. *The Story of the Atlantic Telegraph*. New York: Charles Scribner's Sons, 1893.

Fieldhouse, D. K. *Economics and Empire, 1830–1914*. Ithaca, N.Y.: Cornell University Press, 1973.

———. *The Theory of Capitalist Imperialism*. London: Longman, 1967.

———. *Unilever Overseas*. Stanford, Calif.: Hoover Institution Press, 1978.

Firth (Thos.) & John Brown, Ltd. *Souvenir of a Visit to the Atlas and Norfolk Works*. Booklet, Sheffield, 1954. In Nuffield College Library, Oxford University.

Fishlow, Albert. "Lessons from the Past: Capital Markets during the 19th Century and Interwar Period." *International Organization*, 39 (1985): 383–439.

Fisk, Harvey E. *The Inter-Ally Debts*. New York: Bankers Trust, 1924.

Flinn, M. W. *Men of Iron: The Crowleys in the Early Iron Industry*. Edinburgh: University Press, 1962.

Flint, Charles R. *Memories of an Active Life*. New York: G. P. Putnam's Sons, 1923.

Floud, Roderick. *The British Machine Tool Industry, 1850–1914*. Cambridge: Cambridge University Press, 1976.

Floud, Roderick, and Donald McCloskey, eds. *The Economic History of Britain since 1700*. Vol. 2 (1860 to the 1970s). Cambridge: Cambridge University Press, 1981.

Fogel, Robert W. *Railroads and American Economic Growth*. Baltimore: Johns Hopkins University Press, 1964.

Fogel, Robert W., and Stanley L. Engerman, eds. *The Reinterpretation of American Economic History*. New York: Harper & Row, 1971.

Forbes, Bert C. "Investments by Hollanders in America." *Van Norden Magazine*, Oct. 1909, pp. 59–65. On microfiche in New York Public Library.

Forbes, John Douglas. *J. P. Morgan, Jr., 1867–1943*. Charlottesville: University Press of Virginia, 1981.

Forbes, R. J. *A Chronology of Oil*. 2nd ed. N.p.: Bataafse Internationale Petroleum Maatschappij NV and Shell Internationale Petroleum Company, Ltd., 1965.

Forrestal, Dan J. *Faith, Hope, and $5,000: The Story of Monsanto*. New York: Simon & Schuster, 1977.

Forwood, Sir William B. *Recollections of a Busy Life: Being the Reminiscences of a Liverpool Merchant, 1840–1910*. Liverpool: Henry Young, 1910.

Fouraker, Lawrence E., and John M. Stopford. "Organizational Structure and Multi-national Strategy." *Administrative Science Quarterly*, 13 (1968): 47–64.

Foy, Fred C. *Ovens, Chemicals, and Men! Koppers Company, Inc*. New York: Newcomen Society, 1958.

Francis, Anne. *A Guinea a Box*. London: Hale, 1968.

Franko, Lawrence G. *The European Multinationals*. Stamford, Conn.: Greylock, 1976.

Frantz, Joe B. *Gail Borden*. Norman: University of Oklahoma Press, 1951.

Fraser, J. B. "The Emigration of Capital." *Contemporary Review*, 85 (1904): 550–554.

Fraser, W. Hamish. *The Coming of the Mass Market, 1850–1914*. London: Macmillan, 1981.

Freedman, Joseph Robert. "A London Merchant Banker in Anglo-American Trade and Finance, 1835–1850." Ph.D. diss., University of London, 1969.

French, B. F. *History of the Rise and Progress of the Iron Trade of the United States from 1621 to 1857*. 1858. Rpt. Clifton, N.J.: Augustus M. Kelley, 1973.

Frese, Joseph R., and Jacob Judd, eds. *American Industrialization, Economic Expansion, and the Law*. Tarrytown, N.Y.: Sleepy Hollow Press, 1981.

———, eds. *Business Enterprise in Early New York*. Tarrytown, N.Y.: Sleepy Hollow Press, 1980.

———, eds. *An Emerging Independent American Economy, 1815–1875*. Tarrytown, N.Y.: Sleepy Hollow Press, 1980.

Frewen, Moreton. "The Transatlantic Cattle Trade." *Fortnightly Review*, n.s., 49 (1891): 713–724.

Fridenson, Patrick. *Histoire des usines Renault*. Paris: Seuil, 1972.

Friedel, Frank. *America in the Twentieth Century*. New York: Knopf, 1960.

Friedman, Milton, and Ana Jacobson Schwartz. *A Monetary History of the United States, 1867–1960*. Princeton, N.J.: Princeton University Press, 1963.

Frink, Maurice, W. Turrentine Jackson, and Agnes W. Spring. *When Grass Was King.* Boulder: University of Colorado Press, 1956.

Fryer, D. W. *World Economic Development.* New York: McGraw-Hill, 1965.

Fulford, Roger. *Glyn's, 1753–1933.* London: Macmillan, 1953.

Fürstenberg, Hans. *Carl Fürstenberg: Die Lebensgeschichte eines deutschen Bankiers, 1870–1914.* Berlin: Ullstein, 1931.

Galambos, Louis. *Competition and Cooperation.* Baltimore: Johns Hopkins University Press, 1966.

Galenson, David W. "The Rise and Fall of Indentured Servitude in the Americas: An Economic Analysis." *Journal of Economic History,* 44 (1984): 1–26.

Galles, D. L. C. "Bank of Nova Scotia." *Minnesota History,* 42 (1971): 268–276.

Gantenbein, James W. *Financial Questions in U.S. Foreign Policy.* New York: Columbia University Press, 1939.

Garver, John A. *John William Sterling.* New Haven: Yale University Press, 1929.

Gasslander, Olle. *History of Stockholms Enskilda Bank to 1914.* N.p., n.d. [after 1960].

Gates, Paul Wallace. *Frontier Landlords and Pioneer Tenants.* Ithaca, N.Y.: Cornell University Press, 1945.

———. *The Illinois Central Railroad and Its Colonization Work.* Cambridge, Mass.: Harvard University Press, 1934.

Gates, William B. *Michigan Copper and Boston Dollars.* Cambridge, Mass.: Harvard University Press, 1951.

Gatty, Richard. *Portrait of a Merchant Prince: James Morrison, 1789–1857.* Northallerton, Yorkshire: Pepper Arden, n.d. [1977].

Gee, Joshua. *The Trade and Navigation of Great Britain Considered.* London, 1729. Rpt. 1730, 1731, 1738, 1750, 1755, and 1767, and subsequently. I used the 1729 and 1750 editions.

Geist, Walter. *Allis-Chalmers: A Brief History.* New York: Newcomen Society, 1950.

Gérard, Max. *Messieurs Hottinguer, banquiers à Paris.* 2 vols. Paris: Hottinguer, 1968, 1972.

Gerretson, F. C. *History of the Royal Dutch.* 4 vols. Leiden: E. J. Brill, 1953–1957.

Gibb, George Sweet, and Evelyn H. Knowlton. *The Resurgent Years, 1911–1927.* New York: Harper, 1956.

Gibbs (Antony) & Sons, Ltd. *Merchants and Bankers, 1808–1958.* London: Antony Gibbs, 1958.

Gibson, William Marion. *Aliens and the Law.* Chapel Hill: University of North Carolina Press, 1940.

Gignoux, C. J. *Histoire d'une entreprise française.* Paris: Hachette, 1955.

Gilbert, Geoffrey. "Maritime Enterprise in the New Republic." *Business History Review,* 58 (1984): 14–29.

Gilbert, Heather. *Awakening Continent: The Life of Lord Mount Stephen.* Vol. 1: 1829–1891. Aberdeen: Aberdeen University Press, 1965.

———. *The End of the Road: The Life of Lord Mount Stephen.* Vol. 2: 1891–1921. Aberdeen: Aberdeen University Press, 1977.

———. "The Unaccountable Fifth." *Minnesota History,* 43 (1971): 175–177.

Gilbert, J. C. *A History of Investment Trusts in Dundee, 1873–1938.* London: P. S. King, 1939.

Gille, Bertrand. *Histoire de la Maison Rothschild.* 2 vols. Geneva: Librairie Droz, 1965, 1967.

Gilpin, Robert. *U.S. Power and the Multinational Corporation.* New York: Basic Books, 1975.

Gini, Corraco. *Report on Problems of Raw Materials and Food Stuffs.* Geneva: League of Nations, 1921.

Gittins, L. "Innovations in Textile Bleaching in Britain in the Eighteenth Century." *Business History Review,* 53 (1979): 194–204.

Glasgow, George. *The English Investment Trust Companies.* New York: John Wiley, 1931.

———. *Glasgow's Guide to Investment Trust Companies (1935).* London: Eyre & Spottiswoode, 1935.

———. *The Scottish Investment Trust Companies.* London: Eyre & Spottiswoode, 1932.

Glauber, Christian Gottlieb. *Peter Hasenclever.* Landeshut, Schlesien, 1794. I obtained a copy from Stiftung Westfälisches Wirtschaftsarchiv, Dortmund.

Goldbeck, Gustaf. *Kraft für der Welt 1864–1964: Klöckner-Humboldt-Deutz AG.* Düsseldorf: Econ-Verlag, 1964.

Goldsmith, Raymond W. *Comparative National Balance Sheets.* Chicago: University of Chicago Press, 1985.

———. *A Study of Savings in the United States.* Princeton, N.J.: Princeton University Press, 1955.

Goodhart, C. A. E. *The Business of Banking, 1891–1914.* London: Weidenfeld & Nicolson, 1972.

Goodrich, Carter. *Government Promotion of American Canals and Railroads, 1800–1890.* New York: Columbia University Press, 1960.

Goplen, Arnold O. "The Career of Marquis de Mores in the Badlands of North Dakota." *North Dakota History,* 13 (1946): 5–70.

Gorter, Wytze. *United States Shipping Policy.* New York: Harper, 1956.

Goschen, George J. *Essays and Addresses on Economic Questions (1865–1863).* 1905. Rpt. New York: Garland, 1983.

Govan, Thomas P. *Nicholas Biddle.* Chicago: University of Chicago Press, 1959.

Grady, Paul, ed. *Memoirs and Accounting Thoughts of George O. May.* New York: Ronald Press, 1962.

Graham, E. M. "Oligopolistic Imitation and European Direct Investment in the United States." DBA diss., Harvard Business School, 1975.

Graham, Richard. "The Investment Boom in British-Texan Cattle Companies, 1880–1885." *Business History Review,* 34 (1960): 421–445.

Grant, H. Roger. *The Corn Belt Route: A History of the Chicago Great Western Railroad Company.* De Kalb: Northern Illinois University Press, 1984.

Gras, N. S. B., and Henrietta M. Larson. *Casebook in American Business History.* New York: Appleton-Century-Crofts, 1939.

Gray, H. Peter. *Uncle Sam as Host.* Greenwich, Conn.: JAI Press, 1986.

Great Britain. Board of Trade. *Survey of International Cartels and Internal Cartels.* 2 vols. London, 1944, 1946.

———. House of Parliament. Reports of the Assistant Commissioners [Clare Read and Albert Pell], *Agricultural Interests Commission.* August 1880. I used copy on reel 3, Western Range Cattle Industry Study, Library of Congress, Acc. 11,092.

———. Monopolies and Restrictive Practices Commission. *Report on the Supply of Certain Industrial and Medical Gases.* London, 1956.

———. ———. *Report on the Supply of Insulated Electric Wires and Cables.* London, 1952.

———. ———. *Report on the Supply of Linoleum.* London, 1956.

———. Parliamentary Papers. *Report of Commission on Depression of Trade and Industry,* XXI (C.4621) 1886; XXII (C.4715) 1886; XXIII (C.4797) 1886; XXIII (C.4863) 1886.

———. ———. *Report of the American Dollar Securities Committee.* XIII-I (Cd.212) 1919.

Green, George D. *Finance and Economic Development in the Old South.* Stanford, Calif.: Stanford University Press, 1972.

Greenberg, Dolores. *Financiers and Railroads, 1869–1889: A Study of Morton, Bliss & Co.* Newark: University of Delaware Press, 1981.

———. "A Study of Capital Alliances: The St. Paul and Pacific." *Canadian Historical Review,* 47 (1976): 25–39.

———. "Yankee Financiers and the Establishment of Trans-Atlantic Partnerships." *Business History,* 16 (1974): 17–35.

Greene, Evarts, and Richard B. Morris. *Guide to Sources for Early American History in New York City.* New York: Columbia University Press, 1953.

Greever, William S. *The Bonanza West: The Story of Western Mining Rushes, 1848–1900.* Norman: University of Oklahoma Press, 1963.

Gregory, T. E. *The Westminster Bank through a Century.* 2 vols. London: Westminster Bank, 1936.

Gressley, Gene M. *Bankers and Cattlemen.* New York: Knopf, 1966.

———. "Brokers to the British: Francis Smith and Company." *Southwestern Historical Quarterly,* 71 (1967): 7–25.

———. "The French, Belgians and Dutch Come to Salt Creek." *Business History Review,* 44 (1970): 498–519.

Grieve, Robert. *An Illustrated History of Pawtucket.* Pawtucket, R.I.: Pawtucket Gazette & Chronicle, 1897.

Grodinsky, Julius. *Jay Gould.* Philadelphia: University of Pennsylvania Press, 1957.

Grohman, W. Baillie. "Cattle Ranches in the Far West." *Fortnightly Review,* n.s., 28 (1980): 438–457.

Grossmann, Hermann. *Die chemische Industrie in den Vereinigten Staaten und die deutschen handelsbeziehunge.* Leipzig: Verlag von Veit, 1912.

Grunwald, Kurt. " 'Windsor-Cassel'—The Last Court Jew." In *Leo Baeck Institute Year Book XIV,* pp. 119–161. London: Leo Baeck Institute, 1969.

Guéneau, Louis. *Lyon et le commerce des soies.* 1923. Rpt. New York: Burt Franklin, 1973.

Guyot, Yves. "The Amount, Direction and Nature of French Investments." *Annals of the American Academy of Political and Social Science,* 68 (1916): 36–54.

Gwinner, Arthur von. *Lebenserinnerungen.* Frankfurt: Fritz Knapp, 1975.

Gwyn, Julian. "British Government Spending and the North American Colonies, 1740–1775." In Peter Marshall and Glyn Williams, eds. *The British Atlantic Empire before the American Revolution,* pp. 74–84. London: Frank Cass, 1980.

Habakkuk, H. J. *American and British Technology in the Nineteenth Century.* Cambridge: Cambridge University Press, 1962.

Haber, L. F. *The Chemical Industry during the Nineteenth Century: A Study of the Economic Aspect of Applied Chemistry in Europe and North America.* Oxford: Clarendon Press, 1969.

———. *The Chemical Industry, 1900–1930.* Oxford: Clarendon Press, 1971.

Hacker, Louis. *American Capitalism.* Princeton, N.J.: Van Nostrand, 1957.

Haeger, John Denis. *The Investment Frontier: New York Businessmen and the Economic Development of the Old Northwest.* Albany: State University of New York Press, 1981.

Hagedorn, Hermann. *Roosevelt in the Bad Lands.* Boston: Houghton Mifflin, 1921.

Haley, J. Evetts. *Charles Goodnight.* Norman: University of Oklahoma Press, 1949.

———. *The XIT Ranch of Texas and the Early Days of the Llano Estado.* Norman: University of Oklahoma Press, 1953.

Hall, A. R. *The London Capital Market and Australia.* Canberra: Australian National University, 1963.

————, ed. *The Export of Capital from Britain, 1870–1914.* London: Methuen, 1968.

Hammond, Bray. *Banks and Politics in America: From the Revolution to the Civil War.* Princeton, N.J.: Princeton University Press, 1957.

Hammond, J. L., and Barbara Hammond. *The Rise of Modern Industry.* New York: Harcourt, Brace, 1926.

Hammond, John Hays. *Autobiography.* 2 vols. New York: Farrar Rinehart, 1935.

Hammond, John Winthrop. *Men and Volts: The Story of General Electric.* Philadelphia: Lippincott, 1941.

Hannah, Leslie. "Mergers in British Manufacturing Industry, 1880–1918." *Oxford Economic Papers,* 26 (1974): 1–20.

————. *The Rise of the Corporate Economy: The British Experience.* 2nd ed. London: Methuen, 1983.

————, ed. *Management Strategy and Business Development.* London: Macmillan, 1976.

Hannah, Leslie, and J. A. Kay. *Concentration in Modern Industry.* London: Macmillan, 1977.

Hanson, Simon G. *Argentine Meat and the British Market.* London: Oxford University Press, 1937.

Hanson, Walter E. *Peat, Marwick, Mitchell & Co.: 80 Years of Professional Growth.* New York: Newcomen Society, 1978.

Hardenbrook, William Ten Eck. *Financial New York: A History of the Banking and Financial Institutions of the Metropolis.* New York: privately printed, 1897.

Harris, J. R., ed. *Liverpool and Merseyside.* London: Frank Cass, 1969.

Hartley, E. N. *Ironworks on the Saugus.* Norman: University of Oklahoma Press, 1957.

Harvard Business School. Case. "Armour & Co." Mimeo. BH98-1954.

Harvey, Charles E. *Rio Tinto Company, 1873–1954.* Penzance, Cornwall: Alison Hodge, 1981.

Harvey, W. H. *Coin's Financial School.* Chicago: Coin Publishing, 1894.

Hasenclever, Adolf. *Peter Hasenclever aus Remscheid-Ehringhausen.* Gotha: Friedrich Andreas Berthes, 1922.

Hasenclever, Peter. *The Case of Peter Hasenclever.* London, 1774.

Hassbring, Lars. *The International Development of the Swedish Match Company, 1917–1924.* Stockholm: Liber, 1979.

Hauser, Henri. *Germany's Commercial Grip on the World.* New York: Charles Scribner's Sons, 1918.

Hawke, G. R. "The United States Tariff and Industrial Protection in the Late Nineteenth Century." *Economic History Review,* 2nd ser., 28 (1975): 84–99.

Hawley, Ellis. *The Great War and the Search for a Modern Order, 1917–1933.* New York: St. Martin's Press, 1979.

Haynes, Williams. *American Chemical Industry.* 6 vols. New York: Van Nostrand, 1945–1954.

Hedges, James Blaine. *Henry Villard and the Railways of the Northwest.* New Haven: Yale University Press, 1930.

Heer, Jean. *World Events, 1866–1966: The First Hundred Years of Nestlé.* Rivaz, Switzerland, 1966.

Heerding, A. *The History of N. V. Philips' Gloeilampenfabrieken.* Vol. 1. Cambridge: Cambridge University Press, 1985.

Heindel, Richard Heathcote. *The American Impact on Great Britain, 1898–1914.* Philadelphia: University of Pennsylvania Press, 1940.

Helfferich, Karl. *Georg von Siemens.* 3 vols. Berlin: Verlag von Julius Springer, 1923.

————. *Germany's Economic Progress and National Wealth, 1888–1913.* New York: Germanistic Society of American, 1914.

Heller, H. Robert, and Emily Heller. *The Economic and Social Impact of Foreign Investment in Hawaii*. Honolulu: Economic Research Center, University of Hawaii, 1973.

———. *Japanese Investment in the United States: With a Case Study of the Hawaiian Experience*. New York: Praeger, 1974.

Hellmann, Ranier. *The Challenge to U.S. Dominance of the International Corporation*. New York: Dunellen, 1970.

Henderson, W. O. "The American Chamber of Commerce for the Port of Liverpool, 1801–1908." In *Transactions of the Historical Society of Lancashire and Cheshire for the Year 1933*, pp. 1–61. Liverpool, 1935.

Hennart, Jean-François. *A Theory of Multinational Enterprise*. Ann Arbor: University of Michigan Press, 1982.

Henriques, Robert. *Marcus Samuel, First Viscount Bearsted, 1853–1927*. London: Barrie & Rockliff, 1960.

———. *Sir Robert Waley Cohen, 1877–1952*. London: Secker & Warburg, 1966.

Hertner, Peter. "Fallstudien zu deutschen multinationalen Unternehmen vor dem Ersten Weltkrieg." In Norbert Horn and Jürgen Kocka, eds., *Law and the Formation of the Big Enterprises in the 19th and Early 20th Centuries*. Göttingen: Vandenhoeck & Ruprecht, 1979.

———. "German Multinational Enterprise before 1914." Unpublished paper, 1983.

———. "German Multinational Enterprise before 1914: Some Case Studies." In Peter Hertner and Geoffrey Jones, eds., *Multinationals: History and Theory*. Aldershot: Gower, 1985.

Herzen, Alexander. *My Past and Thoughts: The Memoirs of Alexander Herzen*. Berkeley: University of California Press, 1982.

Hessen, Robert. *Steel Titan: The Life of Charles M. Schwab*. New York: Oxford University Press, 1976.

Heuss, Theodor. *Robert Bosch: Leben und Leistung*. Stuttgart: Rainer Wunderlich Verlag, 1946.

Hexner, Ervin. *International Cartels*. Chapel Hill: University of North Carolina Press, 1946.

Hibbert, Christopher. *Edward VII: A Portrait*. London: Allen Lane, 1976.

Hicks, Agnes H. *The Story of the Forestal*. London: Forestal Land, Timber and Railway Company, 1956.

Hicks, John D. *The Populist Revolt*. Minneapolis: University of Minnesota Press, 1931.

Hidy, Muriel E. *George Peabody*. New York: Arno Press, 1978.

Hidy, Ralph W. *The House of Baring in American Trade and Finance*. Cambridge, Mass.: Harvard University Press, 1949.

Hidy, Ralph W., and Muriel E. Hidy. "Anglo-Merchant Bankers and the Railroads of the Old Northwest, 1848–1860." *Business History Review*, 34 (1960): 150–169.

———. *Pioneering in Big Business*. New York: Harper, 1955.

Higham, Charles. *Trading with the Enemy: An Exposé of the Nazi American Money Plot, 1933–1949*. New York: Delacorte, 1983.

Hildebrand, George H. *Borax Pioneer: Francis Marion Smith*. San Diego: Howell-North Books, 1982.

Hildebrand, Karl-Gustaf. *Expansion, Crisis, Reconstruction, 1917–1939*. Stockholm: Liber, 1985.

Hilferding, Rudolf. *Finance Capital*. London: Routledge & Kegan Paul, 1981.

Himmel, Ernst. *Industrielle Kapitalanlagen der Schweiz im Auslande*. Langensalza: Hermann Beyer, 1922.

Hindley, Diana, and Geoffrey Hindley. *Advertising in Victorian England, 1837–1901*. London: Wayland, 1972.

Hines, H. K. *An Illustrated History of the State of Oregon.* Chicago: Lewis, 1893.

Hirst, Francis W. *Monopolies, Trusts and Kartels.* London: Methuen, 1905.

Hobson, C.K. "British Oversea Investments, Their Growth and Importance." *Annals of the American Academy of Political and Social Sciences,* 68 (1916): 23–35.

———. *The Export of Capital.* London: Constable, 1914.

Hobson, J. A. *Imperialism: A Study.* London: James Nisbet, 1902.

Hochheiser, Sheldon. *Rohm and Haas.* Philadelphia: University of Pennsylvania Press, 1986.

Hodgart, Alan. *The Economics of European Imperialism.* New York: Norton, 1977.

Hoffman, Ross J. S. *Great Britain and Germany Trade Rivalry, 1875–1914.* Philadelphia: University of Pennsylvania Press, 1933.

Hoffmann, W. G. *British Industry, 1700–1950.* 2 vols. Oxford: Blackwell, 1955, 1965.

Hogan, Michael J. *Informal Entente: The Private Structure of Cooperation in Anglo-American Economic Diplomacy, 1918–1928.* Columbia: University of Missouri Press, 1977.

Hogan, W. T. *Economic History of the Iron and Steel Industry in the United States.* 5 vols. Lexington, Mass.: Lexington Books, 1971.

Holden, William Curry. *The Spur Ranch.* Boston: Christopher, 1934.

Holdsworth, J. T., and Davis R. Dewey. *The First and Second Banks of the United States.* Washington: 61st Cong., 2nd sess., S. Doc. 571, 1910.

Holland, R. F., and A. N. Porter, eds. *Money, Finance and Empire, 1790–1960.* London: Frank Cass, 1985.

Holländer, Hans. *Geschichte der Schering Aktiengesellschaft.* Berlin: Schering, 1955.

Holmes, George K. "A Decade of Mortgage Lending." *Annals of the American Academy of Political and Social Science,* 4 (1894): 904–918.

Homes, H. A. *Notice of Peter Hasenclever, an Iron Manufacturer of 1764–69.* Albany, N.Y.: Joel Munsell, 1875.

Hood, Neil, and Stephen Young. *The Economics of Multinational Enterprise.* London: Longman, 1979.

Hooker, A. A. *The International Grain Trade.* London: Sir Isaac Pitman, 1939.

Hoover, Herbert. *Memoirs.* Vol. 1. New York: Macmillan, 1952.

Horst, Thomas. *At Home Abroad: A Study of the Domestic and Foreign Operations of the American Food-Processing Industry.* Cambridge: Ballinger, 1974.

Houssiaux, Jacques. *Le pouvoir de monopole.* Paris: Sirey, 1958.

Houston, Tom, and John H. Dunning. *U.K. Industry Abroad.* London: Financial Times, 1976.

Howeth, L. S. *History of Communications-Electronics in the United States Navy.* Washington, D.C.: Government Printing Office, 1963.

Huebner, Solomon S. "Distribution of Stockholders in American Railroads." *Annals of the American Academy of Political and Social Science,* 23 (1903): 475–490.

Hughes, Thomas P. *Networks of Power: Electrification in Western Society, 1880–1930.* Baltimore: Johns Hopkins University Press, 1983.

Huldermann, Bernhard. *Albert Ballin.* London: Cassell, 1922.

Hungerford, Edward. *The Story of the Baltimore and Ohio Railroad, 1827–1927.* 2 vols. New York: G. P. Putnam, 1928.

Hunt, Wallis. *Heirs of Great Adventure: The History of Balfour, Williamson and Company, Ltd.* 2 vols. London: Balfour, Williamson, 1951, 1960.

Hunter, P. V., and J. T. Hazell. *Development of Power Cables.* London: George Newnes, 1956.

Hutchins, John G. B. *American Maritime Industries and Public Policy, 1789–1914.* Cambridge, Mass.: Harvard University Press, 1941.

Huth, Hans, and Wilma J. Pugh. *Talleyrand in America as a Financial Promoter, 1794–96.* New York: Da Capo Press, 1971.

Hyde, Francis Edwin. "British Capital and American Enterprise in the Northwest." *Economic History Review,* 6 (1936): 201–208.

Hymer, Stephen Herbert. *The International Operations of National Firms: A Study of Direct Foreign Investment.* Cambridge, Mass.: MIT Press, 1976.

Imlah, Albert H. "British Balance of Payments and Export of Capital, 1816–1913." *Economic History Review,* 2nd ser., 5 (1952): 208–239.

———. *Economic Elements in the Pax Britannica.* Cambridge, Mass.: Harvard University Press, 1958.

Ince, Clifford H. *The Royal Bank of Canada: A Chronology, 1864–1969* N.p., n.d.

Isaacs, Asher. *International Trade, Tariffs and Commercial Policies.* Chicago: Richard D. Irwin, 1948.

Ise, John. *The United States Oil Policy.* New Haven: Yale University Press, 1926.

Isichei, Elizabeth. *Victorian Quakers.* Oxford: Oxford University Press, 1970.

Iversen, Carl. *Aspects of the Theory of International Capital Movements.* Copenhagen: Levin & Munksgaard, 1936.

Jackson, W. Turrentine. "British Capital in Northwest Mines." *Pacific Northwest Quarterly,* 47 (1956): 75–85.

———. "British Impact on the Utah Mining Industry." *Utah Historical Quarterly,* 31 (1963): 347–375.

———. "British Interests in the Range Cattle Industry." In Maurice Frink, W. Turrentine Jackson, and Agnes Wright Spring, *When Grass was King,* pp. 133–330. Boulder: University of Colorado Press, 1956.

———. *The Enterprising Scot.* Edinburgh: Edinburgh University Press, 1968.

James, F. Cyril. *The Growth of Chicago Banks.* 2 vols. New York: Harper & Bros., 1938.

James, John A. *Money and Capital Markets in Postbellum America.* Princeton, N.J.: Princeton University Press, 1978.

James, Marquis. *Biography of a Business, 1792–1942: Insurance Company of North America.* Indianapolis: Bobbs Merrill, 1942.

Jameson, J. Franklin. *The American Revolution Considered as a Social Movement.* Princeton, N.J.: Princeton University Press, 1967.

Japhet, S. *Recollections from My Business Life.* London: privately printed, 1931.

Jefferys, James B. *Business Organisation in Great Britain, 1856–1914.* New York: Arno Press, 1977.

———. *Retail Trading in Britain, 1850–1950.* Cambridge: Cambridge University Press, 1954.

Jenkins, D. T., and K. G. Ponting. *The British Wool Textile Industry, 1770–1914.* London: Heinemann, 1982.

Jenks, Leland H. "Britain and American Railway Development." *Journal of Economic History,* 11 (1951): 375–388.

———. *The Migration of British Capital to 1875.* New York: Barnes & Noble, 1973.

———. "Railroads as an Economic Force in American Development." *Journal of Economic History,* 4 (1944): 1–20.

Jeremy, David J. *Transatlantic Industrial Revolution: The Diffusion of Textile Technologies between Britain and America, 1790–1830.* Cambridge, Mass.: MIT Press, 1981.

John, A. H. *A Liverpool Merchant House, being the History of Alfred Booth & Co., 1863–1958.* London: George Allen & Unwin, 1959.

Johnson, Arthur M., and Barry Supple. *Boston Capitalists and Western Railroads.* Cambridge, Mass.: Harvard University Press, 1967.

Johnson, Paul. *Consolidated Goldfields*. New York: St. Martin's Press, 1987.

Johnson, Sir William. *Papers of Sir William Johnson*. Albany: The University of the State of New York. Vol. 5, 1923; vol. 6, 1928; vol. 10, 1951; vol. 11, 1953; vol. 12, 1957; and vol. 13, 1962.

Jolly, W. P. *Marconi*. New York: Stein & Day, 1972.

Jones, Alice Hanson. *Wealth of a Nation to Be*. New York: Columbia University Press, 1980.

Jones, Charles A. "Great Capitalists and the Direction of British Overseas Investment in the Late Nineteenth Century: The Case of Argentina." *Business History*, 22 (July 1980): 152-157.

Jones, Edgar. *Accountancy and the British Economy, 1840-1980: The Evolution of Ernst and Whinney*. London: Batsford, 1981.

Jones, Geoffrey. "The Expansion of British Multinational Manufacturing, 1890-1939." In Akio Okochi and Tadakatsu Inoue, eds., *Overseas Business Activities*, pp. 124-153. Tokyo: University of Tokyo Press, 1984.

———. "The Gramophone Company: An Anglo-American Multinational 1899-1931." *Business History Review*, 59 (1985): 76-100.

———. "The Growth and Performance of British Multinational Firms Before 1939: The Case of Dunlop." *Economic History Review*, 2nd ser., 37 (1984): 35-53.

———. "Multinational Chocolate: Cadbury Overseas, 1918-1939." *Business History*, 26 (1984): 59-76.

———. "The Performance of British Multinational Enterprise, 1890-1945." In Peter Hertner and Geoffrey Jones, eds., *Multinationals: Theory and History*, pp. 96-112. Aldershot: Gower, 1985.

———. *The State and the Emergence of the British Oil Industry*. London: Macmillan, 1981.

———, ed. *British Multinationals: Origins, Management and Performance*. Aldershot: Gower, 1986.

Jones, Howard. *To the Webster-Ashburton Treaty: A Study in Anglo-American Relations, 1783-1843*. Chapel Hill: University of North Carolina Press, 1977.

Josephson, Matthew. *Edison*. New York: McGraw-Hill, 1959.

———. *The Robber Barons*. 1934. Rpt. New York: Harcourt, Brace & World, 1962.

Joslin, David. *A Century of Banking in Latin America: The Bank of London & South America Ltd*. London: Oxford University Press, 1963.

Joyner, Fred B. *David Ames Wells*. Cedar Rapids, Iowa: Torch Press, 1939.

Judson, Isabella Field. *Cyrus W. Field: His Life and Work*. New York: Harper & Bros., 1896.

Kabisch, Thomas R. *Deutsches Kapital in den USA*. Stuttgart: Klett-Cotta, 1982.

Katz, Irving. *August Belmont: A Political Biography*. New York: Columbia University Press, 1968.

Kaufmann, Eugène. *La banque en France*. Paris: M. Giard & E. Brière, 1914.

Kawabe, Nobuo. "Japanese Business in the United States before World War II." Ph.D. diss., Ohio State University, 1980.

Keim, Jeannette. *Forty Years of German-American Political Relations*. Philadelphia: William J. Dornan, 1919.

Kelleter, Heinrich. *Geschichte der Familie J. A. Henckels*. Solingen: privately printed, 1924.

Kellett, Richard. *The Merchant Banking Arena*. New York: St. Martin's Press, 1967.

Kennan, George. *E. H. Harriman*. 2 vols. Boston: Houghton Mifflin, 1922.

Kennedy, William P. "Foreign Investment, Trade and Growth, 1870–1913." *Explorations in Economic History*, 11 (1974): 415–444.

———. "Institutional Responses to Economic Growth: Capital Markets in Britain to

1914." In Leslie Hannah, ed. *Management Strategies and Business Development.* London: Macmillan, 1976.

Kenwood, A. G., and A. L. Lougheed. *The Growth of the International Economy.* London: George Allen & Unwin, 1983.

———. *Technological Diffusion and Industrialisation before 1914.* New York: St. Martin's Press, 1982.

Kerr, William G. "Foreign Investments in the United States." In *Dictionary of American History,* vol. 3, pp. 62–67. New York: Charles Scribner's Sons, 1976.

———. *Scottish Capital on the American Credit Frontier.* Austin: Texas State Historical Association, 1976.

Keynes, John Maynard. *Collected Writings.* Vols. 15 and 17. Ed. Elizabeth Johnson. London: Macmillan, 1971, 1977.

———. *The Economic Consequences of the Peace.* New York: Harcourt, Brace & Howe, 1920.

———. "Foreign Investment and National Advantage." *The Nation and the Athenaeum,* 35 (1924): 584–587.

Kindleberger, Charles P. *American Business Abroad.* New Haven: Yale University Press, 1969.

———. *Economic Growth in France and Britain.* 1964. Rpt. New York: Simon & Schuster, 1969.

———. *A Financial History of Western Europe.* London: Allen & Unwin, 1984.

———. *The Formation of Financial Centers.* Princeton, N.J.: International Finance Section, Department of Economics, Princeton University, 1974.

———. *Manias, Panics, and Crashes.* New York: Basic Books, 1978.

———. *Multinational Excursions.* Cambridge, Mass.: MIT Press, 1984.

———, ed. *The International Corporation.* Cambridge, Mass.: MIT Press, 1970.

Kindleberger, Charles P., and David B. Audretsch, eds. *The Multinational Corporation in the 1980s.* Cambridge, Mass.: MIT Press, 1983.

Kingsbury, Susan Myra. *The Records of the Virginia Company of London.* 4 vols. Washington, D.C.: Government Printing Office, 1906–1935.

Kirby, M. W. *The Decline of British Economic Power Since 1870.* London: Allen & Unwin, 1981.

Kirkaldy, A. W. *British Shipping.* London: Kegan Paul, 1914.

Kirkland, Edward C. *Men, Cities and Transportation.* Cambridge, Mass.: Harvard University Press, 1948.

Klebaner, Benjamin J. "State Chartered American Commercial Banks, 1781–1801." *Business History Review,* 53 (1979): 529–538.

Klein, Maury. *History of the Louisville and Nashville Railroad.* New York: Macmillan, 1972.

———. *The Life and Legend of Jay Gould.* Baltimore: Johns Hopkins University Press, 1986.

Knox, John Jay. *A History of Banking.* 1903. Rpt. New York: August Kelley, 1969.

Kouwenhoven, John A. *Partners in Banking.* New York: Doubleday, 1968.

Kranzberg, Melvin, and Carroll W. Pursell. *Technology in Western Civilization.* 2 vols. New York: Oxford University Press, 1967.

Kravis, Irving B. "The Role of Exports in Nineteenth Century United States Growth." *Economic Development and Cultural Change,* 20 (1972): 387–405.

Krooss, Herman E., and Martin R. Blyn. *A History of Financial Intermediaries.* New York: Random House, 1971.

Krooss, Herman E., and Charles Gilbert. *American Business History.* Englewood Cliffs, N.J.: Prentice-Hall, 1972.

Kuhlmann, Charles Byron. *The Development of the Flour-Milling Industry in the United States*. Boston, New York: Houghton Mifflin, 1929.

Kujovich, Mary Yeager. "The Dynamics of Oligopoly in the Meat Packing Industry: An Historical Analysis, 1875–1912." Ph.D. diss., Johns Hopkins University, 1973.

Kuske, Bruno. *100 Jahre Stollwerck Geschichte, 1839–1939*. Cologne: Stollwerck, 1939.

Kuznets, Simon. *Capital in the American Economy*. Princeton, N.J.: Princeton University Press, 1961.

———. "International Differences in Capital Formation and Financing." In National Bureau of Economic Research, *Capital Formation and Economic Growth*, pp. 19–106. Princeton, N.J.: Princeton University Press, 1955.

Kynaston, David. "The Late-Victorian and Edwardian London Stockbroker as Investment Adviser." Unpublished paper, 1982.

Labasse, Jean, and Michel Laferrère. *La région lyonnaise*. 2nd ed. Paris: Presses Universitaires de France, 1966.

Ladas, Stephen P. *The International Protection of Industrial Property*. Cambridge, Mass.: Harvard University Press, 1930.

Laferrère, Michel. *Lyon, ville industrielle*. Paris: Presses Universitaires de France, 1960.

LaFollette, Robert R. "The American Revolutionary Debt and Its Liquidation." Ph.D. diss., George Washington University, 1931.

Lall, Sanjaya, and Siddharthan, N. S. "The Monopolistic Advantages of Multinationals: Lessons from Foreign Investment in the U.S." *Economic Journal*, 92 (1982): 668–683.

Lamb, W. Kaye. *History of the Canadian Pacific Railway*. New York: Macmillan, 1977.

Lamont, Thomas W. *Across World Frontiers*. New York: Harcourt, Brace, 1951.

Landes, David S. *Bankers and Pashas*. 1958. Rpt. New York: Harper Torchbook, 1969.

———. "The Bleichroeder Bank: An Interim Report." In *Leo Baeck Yearbook V*, pp. 201–20. London: Leo Baeck Institute, 1960.

Landmann, Julius. *Leu & Co., 1755–1905*. Zurich: Art Institut Orell Fussli, 1905.

———. *Die schweizerische Volkswirtschaft*. Einsideln: Benziger, 1925.

Lang, Lincoln A. *Ranching with Roosevelt*. Philadelphia: Lippincott, 1926.

Langer, William. *The Diplomacy of Imperialism, 1890–1902*. 2nd ed. New York: Knopf, 1951.

Lanier, H. W. *A Century of Banking in the United States*. New York: George H. Doran, 1922.

Larkin, Manuel. "The Russian Imperial Bank." M.Phil. thesis, University of Chicago, 1910.

Larson, Henrietta. *Jay Cooke*. Cambridge, Mass.: Harvard University Press, 1936.

Larson, John Lauritz. *Bonds of Enterprise*. Boston: Division of Research, Graduate School of Business Administration, Harvard University, 1984.

Laughlin, J. Laurence. *Credit of Nations*. New York: Charles Scribner's Sons, 1918.

Laux, James M. *In First Gear: The French Automobile Industry to 1914*. Montreal: McGill-Queen's University Press, 1976.

Lavender, David. *The Story of Cyprus Mines Corporation*. San Marino, Calif.: Huntington Library, 1962.

Laves, Walter Herman Carl. *German Governmental Influence on Foreign Investments, 1871–1914*. New York: Arno Press, 1977.

Lavington, F. *The English Capital Market*. London: Methuen, 1921.

Leach, Josiah Granville. *History of the Girard National Bank, 1832-1902*. 1902. Rpt. New York: Greenwood Press, 1969.

League of Nations. *Industrialization and Foreign Trade.* 1945. Rpt. New York: Garland, 1983.

———. *Raw Material Problems and Policies.* 1946. Rpt. New York: Garland, 1983.

Lees, Francis A. *Foreign Banking and Investment in the United States.* New York: John Wiley, 1976.

Leighton-Boyce, J. A. S. L. *Smiths the Bankers, 1658–1958.* London: National Provincial Bank, 1958.

Lenfant, J. H. "British Capital Export, 1900–1913." Ph.D. diss., University of London, 1949.

Lenin, V. I. *Imperialism.* 1916. Rpt. New York: International Publishers, 1939.

Lenman, Bruce, and Kathleen Donaldson. "Partners, Incomes, Investment, and Diversification in the Scottish Linen Area, 1850–1921." *Business History,* 13 (1971): 1–18.

Lenz, Friedrich. "Wesen und Struktur des deutschen Kapitalexports vor 1914." *Weltwirtschaftliches Archiv,* 18 (1922): 42–54.

Levy, Hermann. *Monopoly and Competition.* London: Macmillan, 1911.

Lévy-Leboyer, Maurice. *Les banques européennes et l'industrialisation internationale dans la première moitié du XIXe siècle.* Paris: Presses Universitaires de France, 1964.

———. "Hierarchical Structure, Rewards and Incentives in a Large Corporation: The Early Managerial Experience of Saint-Gobain, 1872–1912." In Norbert Horn and Jürgen Kocka, eds., *Law and the Formation of the Big Enterprises in the 19th & Early 20th Century.* Göttingen: Vandenhoeck & Ruprecht, 1979.

———, ed. *La position internationale de la France: Aspects économiques et financiers, XIXe-XXe siècles.* Paris: Éditions de l'École des Hautes Études en Sciences Sociales, 1977.

Lewis, Cleona. *America's Stake in International Investments.* Washington, D.C.: Brookings Institution, 1938.

Lewis, Colin M. *British Railways in Argentina, 1857–1914.* London: Athlone Press, 1983.

Lewis, Lawrence. *A History of the Bank of North America.* Philadelphia: Lippincott, 1882.

Lewis, Ronald L. *Coal, Iron, and Slaves: Industrial Slavery in Maryland and Virginia, 1715–1865.* Westport, Conn.: Greenwood Press, 1979.

Lewis, W. Arthur. *Growth and Fluctuations, 1870–1913.* London: George Allen & Unwin, 1978.

Liebenau, Jonathan. "The Use of American Patents by German and American Industries, 1890–1935." Unpublished paper, 1978.

Liebeschutz, R. "August Belmont and the House of Rothschild." In *Leo Baeck Institute Yearbook XIV.* London: Leo Baeck Institute, 1969.

Liefmann, Robert. *Cartels, Concerns and Trusts.* London 1932. Rpt. New York: Arno Press, 1977.

Lindstrom, Talbot S., and Kevin P. Tighe. *Antitrust Consent Decrees.* 2 vols. Rochester, N.Y.: Lawyers' Cooperative, 1974.

Linen Thread Company, Ltd. *The Faithful Fibre.* Glasgow: Linen Thread Co., 1956.

Lippincott, Isaac. "A Century and a Half of the Fur Trade at St. Louis." *Washington University Studies,* 3 (1916): 205–242.

Lipton, Thomas J. *Leaves from Lipton Logs.* London: Hutchinson, 1931.

Liveing, Edward. *A Century of Insurance: The Commercial Union Assurance Group, 1861–1961.* London: H. F. G. Witherby, 1961.

Livermore, Shaw. *Early American Land Companies.* New York: Commonwealth Fund, 1939.

Lloyd, Ian. *Rolls Royce: The Years of Endeavor.* London: Macmillan, 1978.

Logan, Sheridan. *George F. Baker and His Bank, 1840–1955*. New York: Sheridan A. Logan, 1981.

Lombard, Alex. *Notice sur la position financière actuelle des états de l'Amérique du Nord*. Geneva: Imprimerie de Ch. Gruaz, 1841.

———. *Notes financières et statistiques sur l'état d'Ohio*. Geneva, 1847.

Lysis [Eugene Letailleur]. *Contre l'oligarchie financière en France*. 9th ed. Paris: Aux Bureaux de la Revue, 1908.

———. *Politique et finance d'avant guerre*. Paris: Payot, 1920.

Lytle, Richard H. "The Introduction of Diesel Power in the United States, 1897–1912." *Business History Review*, 42 (1968): 115–148.

MacDonald, James. *Food from the Far West*. London, Edinburgh: William P. Nimmo, 1878.

MacKenzie, Compton. *Realms of Silver*. London: Routledge & Kegan Paul, 1954.

MacKenzie, F. A. *Beaverbrook: An Authentic Biography*. London: Jarrolds, 1931.

Macrosty, Henry W. *The Trust Movement in British Industry*. London: Longmans, Green, 1907.

Madden, John J. *British Investment in the United States, 1860–1880*. Ph.D. diss., Cambridge University, 1958. New York: Garland, 1985.

Madden, John T., Marcus Nadler, and Harry C. Sauvain. *America's Experience as a Creditor Nation*. New York: Prentice-Hall, 1937.

Maddison, Angus. *Phases of Capitalist Development*. New York: Oxford University Press, 1982.

Mahoney, Tom. *The Merchants of Life: An Account of the American Pharmaceutical Industry*. New York: Harper, 1959.

Manchez, Georges. *Sociétés de dépôt, banques d'affaires*. Paris: Librairie Delagrave, 1918.

Mandeville, A. Moreton. *The House of Speyer*. London, 1915.

Marans, J. Eugene, et al., eds. *Foreign Investment in the United States, 1980: Legal Issues and Techniques*. Washington, D.C.: District of Columbia Bar, 1980.

Marcosson, Isaac F. *Anaconda*. New York: Dodd, Mead, 1957.

Markham, Jesse W. *Competition in the Rayon Industry*. Cambridge, Mass.: Harvard University Press, 1952.

Marlborough, Duke of. "Virginia Mines and American Rails." *Fortnightly Review*, n.s., 49 (1891): 570–583, 780–797.

Marlio, Louis. *The Aluminum Cartel*. Washington, D.C.: Brookings Institution, 1947.

Marriner, Sheila, ed. *Business and Businessmen: Studies in Business, Economic and Accounting History*. Liverpool: Liverpool University Press, 1978.

Marshall, A. C., and Herbert Newbould. *The History of Firth's, 1842–1918*. Sheffield: Thos. Firth, 1925.

Marshall, Alfred. *Principles of Economics*. 4th ed. London: Macmillan, 1898.

Marshall, Herbert, Frank A. Southard, and Kenneth W. Taylor. *Canadian-American Industry*. New Haven: Yale University Press, 1936.

Marshall, James l. *Eldridge A. Stuart: Founder of Carnation Co*. Los Angeles: Carnation Co., 1949.

Martin, Albro. *James T. Hill*. New York: Oxford University Press, 1976.

Marwick, W. H. *Economic Developments in Victorian Scotland*. London: George Allen & Unwin, 1936.

Marx, Daniel. *International Shipping Cartels*. Princeton, N.J.: Princeton University Press, 1953.

Mason, Frank R. *American Silk Industry and the Tariff*. Cambridge, Mass.: American Economic Association, 1910.

Masters, Edgar Lee. *Levy Mayer and the New Industrial Era*. New Haven: n.p., 1927.

Mathias, Peter. *The Brewing Industry in England, 1700–1830*. Cambridge: Cambridge University Press, 1959.
———. *The First Industrial Nation, 1700–1914*. London: Methuen, 1969.
———. *Retailing Revolution: A History of Multiple Retailing in the Food Trades*. London: Longmans, Green, 1967.
Mathias, Peter, and M. M. Postan. *The Cambridge Economic History of Europe*. Vol. 7, pt. 1. Cambridge: Cambridge University Press, 1978.
Matthews, P. W., and Anthony Tuke. *History of Barclays Bank, Ltd*. London: Blade, East & Blade, 1926.
May, Earl Chapin. *Principio to Wheeling, 1715–1945*. New York: Harper & Bros., 1945.
Mayer, Josephine, and R. A. East. "An Early Anglo-American Financial Transaction." *Bulletin of the Business Historical Society*, 11 (1937): 88–96.
McClain, David Stanley. "Foreign Direct Investments in the United States: Old Currents, New Waves, and the Theory of Direct Investment." In Charles P. Kindleberger and David B. Audretsch, eds., *The Multinational Corporation in the 1980s*, pp. 278–333. Cambridge, Mass.: MIT Press, 1983.
———. "Foreign Investment in United States Manufacturing and the Theory of Direct Investment." Ph.D. diss., MIT, 1974.
McCloskey, Donald. *Enterprise and Trade in Victorian Britain*. London: Allen & Unwin, 1981.
———. *Essays on a Mature Economy: Britain after 1840*. Princeton, N.J.: Princeton University Press, 1971.
McCusker, John J. "Sources of Investment Capital in the Colonial Philadelphia Shipping Industry." *Journal of Economic History*, 32 (1972): 146–157.
———. *Money and Exchange in Europe and America, 1600–1775*. Chapel Hill: University of North Carolina Press, 1978.
McCusker, John J., and Russell R. Menard. *The Economy of British America, 1607–1789*. Chapel Hill: University of North Carolina Press, 1985.
McDonald, P. B. *A Saga of the Seas: The Story of Cyrus W. Field and the Laying of the First Atlantic Cable*. New York: Wilson-Erickson, 1937.
McFarlane, Larry A. "British Agricultural Investment in the Dakotas, 1877–1953." *Business and Economic History*, 2nd ser., 5 (1976): 112–126.
———. "British Investment and the Land: Nebraska, 1877–1946." *Business History Review*, 57 (1983): 258–272.
———. "British Investment in Mid-Western Farm Mortgages and Land: A Comparison of Iowa and Kansas." *Agricultural History*, 47 (1974): 179–198.
———. "The Missouri Land and Livestock Company, Ltd., of Scotland: Foreign Investment on the Missouri Farming Frontier, 1882–1908." Ph.D. diss., University of Missouri, 1963. Microfilm copy in New York Public Library.
McGovney, Dudley O. "The Anti-Japanese Land Laws of California and Ten Other States." *California Law Review*, 35 (1947): 7–60.
McGrane, Reginald C. *Foreign Bondholders and American State Debts*. New York: Macmillan, 1935.
———. *The Panic of 1837*. Chicago, London: University of Chicago Press, 1924.
McKay, John. "The House of Rothschild (Paris) as a Multinational Industrial Enterprise, 1875–1914." In Alice Teichova et al., *Multinational Enterprise in Historical Perspective*, pp. 74–86. Cambridge: Cambridge University Press, 1986.
Mead, Elwood. *Irrigation Institutions*. New York: Macmillan, 1903.
Meleghy, Gyula. "Die Vermittlerrolle der Banken bei deutschen Investitionen in Nord- und Mittlelamerika bis zum Ersten Weltkrieg." Ph.D. diss., University of Cologne, 1983.

Menzies, W. J. *America as a Field for Investment*. Edinburgh: William Blackwood, 1892.

Metzler, Lloyd A., Robert Triffin, and Gottfried Haberler. *International Monetary Policies*. 1947. Rpt. New York: Arno Press, 1978.

Miall, Stephen. *A History of the British Chemical Industry*. London: Ernest Benn, 1931.

Michalet, Charles Albert, and Michel Delapierre. *The Multinationalization of French Firms*. Chicago: Academy of International Business, 1975.

Michell, Lewis. *The Lives and Times of Cecil John Rhodes, 1853–1902*. 2 vols. New York: Mitchell Kennerley, 1910.

Michener, James A. *Centennial*. New York: Random House, 1974.

Michie, Ranald C. "Crisis and Opportunity: The Formation and Operation of the British Assets Trust, 1897–1914." *Business History*, 25 (1983): 125–147.

————. "The London Stock Exchange and the British Securities Market, 1850–1914." *Economic History Review*, 2nd ser., 38 (1985): 61–82.

————. *Money, Mania and Markets: Investment, Company Formation and the Stock Exchange in Nineteenth Century Scotland*. Edinburgh: John Donald, 1981.

————. "Options, Concessions, Syndicates, and the Provision of Venture Capital, 1880–1913." *Business History*, 23 (1981): 147–164.

Middlemas, Robert Keith. *The Master Builders: Thomas Brassey, Sir John Aird, Lord Cowdray, Sir John Norton-Griffiths*. London: Hutchinson, 1963.

Mikesell, Raymond F., ed. *United States Private and Government Investment Abroad*. Eugene: University of Oregon Press, 1962.

Miles, Robert. *Coffin Nails and Corporate Strategy*. Englewood Cliffs, N.J.: Prentice-Hall, 1981.

Millar, C. C. Hoyar. *Florida, South Carolina and Canadian Phosphates*. London: Eden Fisher, 1892.

Miller, Benjamin L., and Joseph T. Singewald. *The Mineral Deposits of South America*. 1919. Rpt. New York: Arno Press, 1977.

Miller, George H. *Railroads and the Granger Laws*. Madison: University of Wisconsin Press, 1971.

Milward, Alan S. *The Development of the Economies of Continental Europe, 1850–1914*. Cambridge, Mass.: Harvard University Press, 1977.

Minchenton, W. E. *The British Tinplate Industry*. Oxford: Clarendon Press, 1957.

Mints, Lloyd. *A History of Banking Theory in Great Britain and the United States*. Chicago: University of Chicago Press, 1945.

Miquel, René. *Dynastie Michelin*. Paris: La Table Ronde, 1962.

Mitchell, Broadus. *The Rise of Cotton Mills in the South*. Baltimore: Johns Hopkins University Press, 1921.

[Mitsui & Co.]. *The 100 Year History of Mitsui & Co., Ltd., 1876–1976*. Tokyo: Mitsui & Co., 1977.

Montgomery, Robert. *Fifty Years of Accounting*. 1938. Rpt. New York: Arno Press, 1978.

Moody, John. *The Truth about Trusts*. New York: Moody, 1904.

Morgan, Charles. *The House of Macmillan (1843–1943)*. London: Macmillan, 1944.

Morgan, Dan. *Merchants of Grain*. New York: Viking Press, 1979.

Morgan, E. Victor, and W. A. Thomas. *The London Stock Exchange*. New York: St. Martin's Press, 1962.

Morgan, Hal. *Symbols of America*. New York: Penguin, 1987.

Morgan, R. M. *Callender's, 1882–1945*. Prescott, Merseyside: BICC, 1982.

Morison, Samuel Eliot. *The Oxford History of the American People*. New York: Oxford University Press, 1965.

Morley, John. *Life of Richard Cobden*. London: Chapman & Hall, 1883.

Morris, Richard B. *John Jay: The Nation and the Court*. Boston: Boston University Press, 1967.

——. *The Peacemakers: The Great Powers and American Independence*. New York: Harper & Row, 1965.

——, ed. *John Jay: The Making of a Revolutionary: Unpublished Papers, 1745–1780*. New York: Harper & Row, 1975.

Morrison, Fred L., and Kenneth R. Krause. *State and Federal Legal Regulation of Alien and Corporate Land Ownership and Farm Operations*. Economic Research Service, U.S. Department of Agriculture, Agricultural Economic Report no. 284, Washington, D.C., 1975.

Morsell, Henri. "Les rivalités internationales et l'industrie française de l'aluminium." In Maurice Lévy-Leboyer, *La position internationale de la France*, pp. 365–370. Paris: Éditions de l'École des Hautes Études en Sciences Sociales, 1977.

Moss, Scott. *An Economic Theory of Business Strategy*. New York: John Wiley, 1981.

Mothershead, Harmon Ross. *The Swan Land and Cattle Co., Ltd.* Norman: University of Oklahoma Press, 1971.

Mott, Edward H. *Between the Ocean and the Lakes: The Story of the Erie*. New York: John S. Collins, 1901.

Moulton, Harold G. *Japan: An Economic and Financial Appraisal*. Washington, D.C.: Brookings Institution, 1931.

Moulton, Harold G., and Cleona Lewis. *The French Debt Problem*. New York: Macmillan, 1925.

Moulton, Harold G., and Constantine E. McGuire. *Germany's Capacity to Pay: A Study of the Reparation Problem*. New York: McGraw-Hill, 1923.

Muhlstein, Anka. *Baron James: The Rise of the French Rothschilds*. New York: Vendome Press, 1983.

Muir, Augustus. *Nairns of Kirkcaldy. A Short History of the Company (1847–1956)*. Cambridge: W. Heffer, 1956.

Mulhall, Michael G. "British Capital Abroad." *North American Review*, 168 (1899): 499–505.

——. *Dictionary of Statistics*. 4th ed. 1899. Rpt. Detroit: Gale Research, 1969.

Mulholland, James A. *A History of Metals in Colonial America*. University, Ala.: University of Alabama Press, 1981.

Murphy, Mary E. "Sir George Touche, Bart., C.A., 1861–1935: A Memoir." *Business History Review*, 34 (1960): 467–477.

Murray, Andrew J. *Home from the Hill: A Biography of Frederick Huth*. London: Hamish Hamilton, 1971.

Myers, Gustavus. *History of the Great American Fortunes*. New York: Modern Library, 1936.

Myers, Margaret. *The New York Money Market*. New York: Columbia University Press, 1931.

——. *Paris as a Financial Center*. 1936. Rpt. New York: Garland, 1983.

Nash, George. *Herbert Hoover*. New York: Norton, 1983.

Nash, Gerald D. *United States Oil Policy, 1890–1964*. Pittsburgh: University of Pittsburgh Press, 1968.

Nash, Robert. *A Short Inquiry into the Profitable Nature of Our Investments*. 3rd ed. London: Effingham Wilson, 1881.

National Industrial Conference Board. *The International Financial Position of the United States*. New York: National Industrial Conference Board, 1929.

Navin, Thomas R. *Copper Mining and Management*. Tucson: University of Arizona Press, 1978.

————. *The Whitin Machine Works since 1831.* Cambridge, Mass.: Harvard University Press, 1950.

Navin, Thomas R., and Marian V. Sears. "A Study in Merger: Formation of the International Mercantile Marine Company." *Business History Review,* 28 (1954): 291–328.

Naylor, R. T. *History of Business in Canada, 1867–1914.* 2 vols. Toronto: James Lorimer, 1975.

Neill, Edward D. *History of the Virginia Company of London.* Albany, N.Y.: Joel Munsell, 1869.

Nelson, Douglas W. "The Alien Land Law Movement in the Late Nineteenth Century." *Journal of the West,* 9 (1970): 46–59.

Neu, Irene D. "An English Businessman in Sicily, 1806–1861." *Business History Review,* 31 (1957): 355–374.

————. *Erastus Corning: Merchant and Financier, 1794–1872.* Ithaca, N.Y.: Cornell University Press, 1960.

Neuburger, Hugh. *German Banks and German Economic Growth from Unification to World War I.* New York: Arno Press, 1977.

————. "The Industrial Policies of the Kreditbanken, 1880–1914." *Business History Review,* 51 (1977): 190–207.

Neufeld, E. P. *A Global Corporation: A History of the International Development of Massey-Ferguson Ltd.* Toronto: University of Toronto Press, 1969.

Nevett, T. R. *Advertising in Britain.* London: Heinemann, 1982.

Nevins, Allan. *The American States during and after the Revolution, 1775–1789.* 1924. Rpt. New York: Augustus M. Kelley, 1969.

————. *History of the Bank of New York and Trust Company, 1784–1934.* New York: privately printed, 1934.

————. *Study in Power: John D. Rockefeller.* 2 vols. New York: Scribner's, 1953.

Nevins, Allan, and Frank Ernest Hill. *Ford.* 3 vols. New York: Scribner's, 1954–1963.

New Jersey Archives: Documents Relating to the Colonial History of the State of New Jersey, ed. Frederick W. Ricord and William Nelson, ser. 1, vol. 9. Newark: Daily Advertiser Printing House, 1885.

New Jersey Archives: Documents Relating to the Colonial History of the State of New Jersey, ed. William Nelson, ser. 1, vol. 28. Paterson, N.J.: Call Printing and Publishing, 1916.

New Jersey Archives: Documents Relating to the Revolutionary History of the State of New Jersey, ed. William S. Stryker, ser. 2, vol. 1. Trenton: John L. Murphy, 1901.

Newman, Peter C. *Company of Adventurers.* New York: Viking Penguin, 1985.

Neymarck, Alfred. Reports to the Institut International de Statistique. In *Bulletin de l'Institut International de Statistique,* 11–20 (1895–1913).

Nicholas, Stephen J. "British Multinational Investment before 1939" *Journal of European Economic History,* 11 (1982): 605–630.

————. "Agency Contracts, Institutional Modes, and the Transition to Foreign Direct Investment by British Manufacturing Multinationals before 1939." *Journal of Economic History,* 43 (1983): 675–686.

Nicholson, J. Shield. "Introductory Essay." In Adam Smith, *Wealth of Nations.* London: T. Nelson, 1901.

Nimmo, Joseph. "The Range and Ranch Cattle Traffic." U.S. House of Representatives, 48th Cong., 2nd sess., 1885, Exec. Doc. 267.

Nitske, W. R., and C. M. Wilson. *Rudolf Diesel.* Norman: University of Oklahoma Press, 1965.

Noble, H. G. S. *The New York Stock Exchange in the Crisis of 1914*. Garden City, N.Y.: Country Life Press, 1915.

Nolte, Vincent. *Fifty Years in Both Hemispheres or, Reminiscences of the Life of a Former Merchant*. New York: Redfield, 1854.

Nordyke, Lewis. *Cattle Empire*. New York: William Morrow, 1949.

North, Douglass C. *The Economic Growth of the United States, 1790–1860*. Englewood Cliffs, N.J.: Prentice-Hall, 1961.

———. "International Capital Flows and the Development of the American West." *Journal of Economic History*, 18 (1956): 493–505.

———. "International Capital Movements in Historical Perspective." In Raymond F. Mikesell, ed., *U.S. Private and Government Investment Abroad*, pp. 10–43. Eugene: University of Oregon Books, 1962.

———. *Structure and Change in Economic History*. New York: Norton, 1981.

———. "Transaction Costs in History." *Journal of European Economic History*, 14 (1985): 557–576.

———. "The United States Balance of Payments, 1790–1860." In *Trends in the American Economy in the Nineteenth Century*. Studies in Income and Wealth, vol. 24, pp. 573–627. Princeton, N.J.: Princeton University Press, 1960.

North, Douglass C., Terry L. Anderson, and Peter J. Hill. *Growth and Welfare in the American Past: A New Economic History*. 3rd ed. Englewood Cliffs, N.J.: Prentice-Hall, 1983.

Notz, William F. "International Private Agreements." *Journal of Political Economy*, 28 (1920): 658–679.

Notz, William F., and Richard S. Harvey. *American Foreign Trade*. Indianapolis: Bobbs-Merrill, 1921.

Noyes, Alexander Dana. *Thirty Years of American Finance*. 1900. Rpt. New York: Greenwood Press, 1969.

———. *The War Period of American Finance*. New York: G. P. Putnam's Sons, 1926.

Nurkse, Ragnar. *Patterns of Trade and Development*. New York: Oxford University Press, 1961.

Oberholtzer, Ellis Paxson. *Jay Cooke: Financier of the Civil War*. 2 vols. 1907. Rpt. New York: Burt Franklin, 1970.

O'Brien, Denis Patrick, ed. *The Correspondence of Lord Overstone*. 3 vols. Cambridge: Cambridge University Press, 1971.

O'Connor, Harvey. *The Guggenheims*. New York: Covici Friede, 1937.

Offer, Avner. "Empire and Social Reform: British Overseas Investment and Domestic Politics, 1908–1914." *Historical Journal*, 26 (1983): 119–138.

O'Hagan, H. Osborne. *Leaves from My Life*. 2 vols. London: John Lane, 1929.

Okochi, Akio, and Tadakatsu Inoue. *Overseas Business Activities*. Tokyo: University of Tokyo Press, 1960.

Oss, S. F. van. *American Railroads as Investments*. 1893. Rpt. New York: Arno Press, 1977.

Ostrye, Anne T. *Foreign Investment in the American and Canadian West, 1870–1914: An Annotated Bibliography*. Metuchen, N.J.: Scarecrow Press, 1986.

Overton, Richard C. *Burlington West*. Cambridge, Mass.: Harvard University Press, 1941.

Owen, Roger, and Bob Sutcliff, eds. *Studies in the Theory of Imperialism*. London: Longman, 1972.

Oxford Publishing since 1478. London: Oxford University Press, 1966.

Paine, Albert Bigelow. *George Fisher Baker*. New York: G. P. Putnam's Sons, 1938.

Paish, George. "The Export of Capital and the Cost of Living." *Statist Supplement*, 79

(1914): i–viii. In Mira Wilkins, ed., *British Overseas Investments, 1907–1948*. New York: Arno Press, 1977.

——. "Great Britain's Capital Investments in Individual Colonial and Foreign Countries" and "Comments." *Journal of the Royal Statistical Society*, 74, pt. 2 (1911): 167–200. In Mira Wilkins, ed., *British Overseas Investments, 1907–1948*. New York: Arno Press, 1977.

——. "Great Britain's Capital Investments in Other Lands" and "Comments." *Journal of the Royal Statistical Society*, 72, pt. 3 (1909): 465–495. In Mira Wilkins, ed., *British Overseas Investments, 1907–1948*. New York: Arno Press, 1977.

——. "Our New Investments in 1908." *Statist*, 63 (1909): 19–21. In Mira Wilkins, ed., *British Overseas Investments, 1907–1948*. New York: Arno Press, 1977.

——. "Trade Balance of the United States." In U.S. Senate, *National Monetary Commission*. 61st Cong., 2nd sess., 1910, S. Doc. 579.

Palgrave, R. H. Inglis. "An English View of Investments in the United States." *Forum*, 15 (1893): 191–200.

Palyi, M. "Foreign Investment." *Encyclopedia of the Social Sciences*, 6 (1931): 364–378.

Panmure Gordon, H. *The Land of the Almighty Dollar*. London: Frederick Warne, 1892.

Parsons, A. B. *The Porphyry Coppers*. New York: American Institute of Mining and Metallurgical Engineers, 1933.

Passer, Harold C. *The Electrical Manufacturers*. Cambridge, Mass.: Harvard University Press, 1953.

——. "Frank Julian Sprague." In William Miller, ed., *Men in Business*, pp. 212–237. New York: Harper Torchbooks, 1962.

Paterson, Donald G. *British Direct Investment in Canada, 1890–1914*. Toronto: University of Toronto Press, 1976.

——. "The Failure of British Business in Canada, 1890–1914." In Herman Krooss, ed., *Proceedings of the Business History Conference*. Bloomington: School of Business, Indiana University, 1975.

Patterson, Robert T. *Federal Debt Management Policies, 1865–1879*. Durham, N.C.: Duke University Press, 1954.

Paul, Rodman W. *California Gold*. Cambridge, Mass.: Harvard University Press, 1947.

——. *Mining Frontiers of the Far West, 1848–1880*. New York: Holt Rinehart & Winston, 1963.

Pavitt, Keith and L. Soete. "International Differences in Economic Growth and the International Location of Innovations." Unpublished paper, University of Sussex Research Unit, 1981.

Payne, Peter L. *The Early Scottish Limited Companies, 1856–1895*. Edinburgh: Scottish Academic Press, 1980.

——. "The Emergence of the Large-Scale Company in Great Britain, 1870–1914." *Economic History Review*, 2nd ser., 20 (1967): 519–542.

——, ed. *Studies in Scottish Business History*. London: Frank Cass, 1967.

Pearce, W. M. *The Matador Land and Cattle Company*. Norman: University of Oklahoma Press, 1964.

Pearson, Henry G. *Son of New England: James Jackson Storrow, 1864–1926*. Boston: privately printed, 1932.

Pearson, Jim Berry. *The Maxwell Land Grant*. Norman: University of Oklahoma Press, 1961.

Penrose, Edith. *The Theory of the Growth of the Firm*. New York: John Wiley, 1959.

Perine, Edward Ten Boeck. *The Story of the Trust Companies*. New York: G. P. Putnam's Sons, 1916.

Perkins, Edwin J. *The Economy of Colonial America.* New York: Columbia University Press, 1980.

———. *Financing Anglo-American Trade: The House of Brown, 1800–1880.* Cambridge, Mass.: Harvard University Press, 1975.

Perren, Richard. *The Meat Trade in Britain, 1840–1914.* London: Routledge & Kegan Paul, 1978.

Peterson, Walter F. *An Industrial Heritage: Allis-Chalmers Corporation.* Milwaukee: Milwaukee County Historical Society, 1978.

Phelps, C. W. *Foreign Expansion of American Banks.* 1927. Rpt. New York: Arno Press, 1976.

Philip Morris. *Annual Report, 1980.*

Pierce, Bessie L. *A History of Chicago, 1871–1893.* Vol. 3. Chicago: University of Chicago Press, 1957.

Pierce, Harry H. "Anglo-American Investors and Investment in the New York Central Railroad." In Joseph R. Frese and Jacob Judd, eds., *An Emerging Independent American Economy, 1815–1875,* pp. 127–160. Tarrytown, N.Y.: Sleepy Hollow Press, 1980.

———. "Foreign Investment in American Enterprise" and "Comments." In David T. Gilchrist and W. David Lewis, eds., *Economic Change in the Civil War Era,* pp. 41–53, 54–61. Greenville, Del.: Eleutherian Mills–Hagley Foundation, 1965.

———. *Railroads of New York: A Study of Government Aid, 1826–1875.* Cambridge, Mass.: Harvard University Press, 1953.

Pigott, S. C. *Hollins: A Study of Industry, 1784–1949.* Nottingham: William Hollins, 1949.

Pinner, Felix. *Emil Rathenau und das elektrische Zeitalter.* 1918. Rpt. New York: Arno Press, 1977.

Pitkin, Timothy. *A Statistical View of the Commerce of the United States.* 1816. Rpt. New York: Augustus M. Kelley, 1967.

Platt, D. C. M. *Britain's Investment Overseas on the Eve of the First World War.* New York: St. Martin's Press, 1986.

———. "British Portfolio Investment Overseas before 1870: Some Doubts." *Economic History Review,* 2nd ser., 33 (1980): 1–16.

———. *Finance, Trade and Politics in British Foreign Policy, 1815–1914.* London: Oxford University Press, 1968.

———. *Foreign Finance in Continental Europe and the U.S.A., 1850–1870.* London: George Allen & Unwin, 1984.

———. "Foreign Finance in Europe and the Americas, 1815–1875" Typescript, 1981.

———. "The Sixth Great Power in Europe: Baring in High Finance, 1763–1870" Typescript, 1978.

———. "Some Drastic Revisions in the Stock and Direction of British Investment Overseas, 31 Dec. 1913." In R. V. Turrell and T. J. Van Helten, eds., *The City and the Empire,* pp. 11–25. London: University of London, Institute of Commonwealth Studies, 1985.

———, ed. *Business Imperialism, 1830–1840.* Oxford: Clarendon Press, 1977.

Plummer, Alfred. *International Combines in Modern Industry.* Rev. ed. London: Sir Isaac Pitman, 1938.

Pollard, Sidney. "Capital Exports, 1870–1914: Harmful or Beneficial?" *Economic History Review,* 2nd ser., 38 (1985): 489–514.

———. *The Integration of the European Economy since 1815.* London: George Allen & Unwin, 1981.

Porter, A. N., and R. F. Holland, eds. *Money, Finance and Empire, 1790–1960.* London: Frank Cass, 1985.

Powell, Ellis T. *Evolution of the Money Market (1385–1915).* London: Financial News, 1915.

———. *The Mechanism of the City.* London: P. S. King, 1910.

Prais, S. J. *The Evolution of Giant Firms in Britain.* Cambridge: Cambridge University Press, 1976.

Pratt, Edward Ewing. *International Trade in Staple Commodities.* New York: McGraw-Hill, 1928.

Pratt, Sereno S. *The Work of Wall Street.* New York: D. Appleton, 1921.

Presbrey, Frank. *History and Development of Advertising.* 1929. Rpt. New York: Greenwood Press, 1968.

Pressnell, L. S., and John Orbell. *A Guide to the Historical Records of British Banking.* New York: St. Martin's Press, 1985.

Preston, Howard H. *Banking in Iowa.* 1922. Rpt. New York: Arno Press, 1980.

Previts, Gary John and Barbara D. Merino. *A History of Accounting in America.* New York: Ronald Press, 1979.

Price, Jacob M. *Capital and Credit in British Overseas Trade: The View from the Chesapeake, 1700–1776.* Cambridge, Mass.: Harvard University Press, 1980.

———. "The Rise of Glasgow in the Chesapeake Tobacco Trade, 1707–1775." *William and Mary Quarterly,* 9 (1954): 179–200.

———, ed. *Joshua Johnson's Letterbook, 1771–1774.* London: London Record Society, 1979.

Purdy, Helen Throop. *San Francisco.* San Francisco: Paul Elder, 1912.

Pyle, Joseph G. *The Life of James Hill.* 2 vols. Garden City, N.Y.: Doubleday, Page, 1917.

Rabb, Theodore K. *Enterprise and Empire.* Cambridge, Mass.: Harvard University Press, 1967.

Raikes, Thomas. *A Portion of the Journal Kept by Thomas Raikes, Esq., from 1831 to 1847.* 2 vols. New ed. London: Longman, Brown, Green, Longmans & Roberts, 1858.

Randall, Stephen J. "The Development of Canadian Business in Puerto Rico." *Revista/Review InterAmericana,* 7 (1977): 5–20.

Ratchford, B. U. *American State Debts.* Durham, N.C.: Duke University Press, 1941.

Ratcliffe, B. M., ed. *Great Britain and Her World, 1750–1914: Essays in Honor of W. O. Henderson.* Manchester: Manchester University Press, 1975.

Raymond, William J. *American and Foreign Investment Bonds.* Boston: Houghton Mifflin, 1916.

Raynes, Harold E. *A History of British Insurance.* Rev. ed. London: Sir Isaac Pitman, 1950.

Reader, William J. *Bowater: A History.* Cambridge: Cambridge University Press, 1981.

———. *A House in the City: A Study of the City and of the Stock Exchange Based on the Records of Foster and Braithwaite, 1825–1975.* London: B. T. Batsford, 1979.

———. *Imperial Chemical Industries: A History.* Vol. 1. London: Oxford University Press, 1970.

———. *The Weir Group.* London: Weidenfeld & Nicolson, 1971.

Reading, Marquess of. *Rufus Isaacs, First Marquess of Reading.* 2 vols. London: Hutchinson, 1942, 1945.

Reckitt, B. N. *The History of Reckitt and Sons.* London: A. Brown, 1951.

Reddaway, William Brian. *Effects of U.K. Direct Investment Overseas: An Interim Report.* London: Cambridge University Press, 1967.

———. *Effects of U.K. Direct Investment Overseas: Final Report.* London: Cambridge University Press, 1968.

Redlich, Fritz. *The Molding of American Banking*. New York: Johnson Reprint Corp., 1968.

Rees, J. Aubrey. *The Grocery Trade*. 2 vols. London: Duckworth, 1910.

Reich, Cary. *Financier: The Biography of Andre Meyer*. New York: William Morrow, 1983.

Reich, Leonard S. "Research, Patents and the Struggle to Control Radio." *Business History Review*, 51 (1977): 208–235.

Reischauer, Haru Matsukata. *Samurai and Silk*. Cambridge, Mass.: Harvard University Press, 1986.

Remini, Robert V. *Andrew Jackson and the Course of American Freedom, 1822–1832*. New York: Harper & Row, 1981.

Reynolds, Jack. *The Great Paternalist Titus Salt and the Growth of 19th Century Bradford*. New York: St. Martin's Press, 1984.

Richardson, J. Henry. *British Economic Foreign Policy*. New York: Macmillan, 1936.

Rickard, Thomas A. *A History of American Mining*. New York: McGraw-Hill, 1932.

———. *Retrospect*. New York: McGraw-Hill, 1937.

Riegel, Robert Edgar. *The Story of Western Railroads*. Lincoln: University of Nebraska Press, 1926.

Riesser, J. *The German Great Banks and Their Concentration*. 1911. Rpt. New York: Arno Press, 1977.

Riley, James C. *International Government Finance and the Amsterdam Capital Market, 1740–1815*. Cambridge: Cambridge University Press, 1980.

Riley, John J. *A History of the American Soft Drink Industry: Bottled Carbonated Beverages, 1807–1957*. 1958. Rpt. New York: Arno Press, 1972.

Rink, Oliver A. *Holland on the Hudson*. Ithaca, N.Y.: Cornell University Press, 1986.

Ripley, William Z. *Railroads: Finance and Organization*. New York: Longmans, Green, 1915.

Rippy, J. Fred. "British Investments in Texas Lands and Livestock." *The Southwestern Historical Quarterly*, 58 (1955): 331–341.

Robbins, Michael Warren. "The Principio Company: Iron-Making in Colonial Maryland 1720–1781." Ph.D. diss., George Washington University, 1972.

Roberts, Harold D. *Salt Creek Wyoming*. Denver: Midwest Oil Corporation, 1956.

Robertson, Ross M. *The Comptroller and Bank Supervision: A Historical Appraisal*. Washington, D.C.: Office of the Comptroller of the Currency, 1968.

Rogers, T. B. *A Century of Progress, 1831–1931: Cadbury Bournville*. Bournville: Cadbury Bros., 1931.

Rosa, Luigi de. *Emigranti, Capitali e Banche (1896–1906)*. Naples: Edizione del Banco di Napoli, 1980.

Rosenbaum, E., and A. J. Sherman. *M. M. Warburg & Co., 1798–1938: Merchant Bankers of Hamburg*. New York: Holmes & Meier, 1979.

Rose-Troup, Frances. *The Massachusetts Bay Co.* New York: Grafton Press, 1930.

Ross, Victor. *A History of the Canadian Bank of Commerce*. 2 vols. Toronto: Oxford University Press, 1920, 1922.

Rothstein, Morton. "American Wheat and the British Market, 1860–1905." Ph.D. diss., Cornell University, 1960.

———. "A British Firm on the American West Coast, 1869–1914." *Business History Review*, 37 (1963): 392–415.

———. "Multinationals in the Grain Trade, 1850–1914." *Business and Economic History*, 2nd ser., 12 (1983): 85–93.

Rousseau, Jacques. *Histoire mondiale de l'automobile*. Paris: Hachette, 1958.

Rowland, John. *Progress in Power: The Contribution of Charles Merz and His Associates to Sixty Years of Electrical Development, 1899–1959*. London: privately published, 1960.

Royal Institute of International Affairs. *The Problem of International Investment*. 1937. Rpt. London: Cass, 1965.

Rubinstein, W. D. "British Millionaires, 1809–1949." *Bulletin of the Institute of Historical Research*, 47 (1974): 202–223.

———. *Men of Property: The Very Wealthy in Britain since the Industrial Revolution*. New Brunswick, N.J.: Rutgers University Press, 1981.

———. "The Victorian Middle Classes: Wealth, Occupation and Geography." *Economic History Review*, 2nd ser., 30 (1977): 602.

Rugman, Alan M. *Inside the Multinationals: The Economics of Internal Markets*. New York: Columbia University Press, 1981.

Russett, Bruce M. *Community and Contention*. Cambridge, Mass.: MIT Press, 1963.

Sakolski, A. M. *The Great American Land Bubble*. New York: Harper & Bros., 1932.

Salsbury, Stephen. *The State, the Investor and the Railroad*. Cambridge, Mass.: Harvard University Press, 1967.

Salter, Sir Arthur. *Foreign Investments*. Princeton, N.J.: Princeton University Press, 1951.

Sandberg, L. G. *Lancashire in Decline*. Columbus: Ohio State University Press, 1974.

Sanna Randaccio, Francesca. "European Direct Investments in U.S. Manufacturing." B.Litt. diss., Oxford University, 1980.

Sarnoff, David. *Looking Ahead: The Papers of David Sarnoff*. New York: McGraw-Hill, 1968.

Sartorius, A., Freiherrn von Waltershausen. *Das Volkswirtschafliche System der Kapitalanlage im Auslande*. Berlin: Georg Reimer, 1907.

Sasuly, Richard. *I. G. Farben*. New York: Boni & Gaer, 1947.

Satterlee, Herbert L. *The Life of J. Pierpont Morgan*. New York: privately printed, 1937.

Saul, S. B. "The Market and Development of the Mechanical Engineering Industries in Britain, 1860–1914." *Economic History Review*, 2nd ser., 20 (1967): 111–130.

———. *The Myth of the Great Depression*. New York: St. Martin's Press, 1969.

———. *Studies in British Overseas Trade, 1870–1914*. Liverpool: Liverpool University Press, 1960.

Saveth, Edward N. *American Historians and European Immigrants, 1875–1925*. New York: Columbia University Press, 1948.

Sayers, R. S. *The Bank of England, 1891–1944*. 3 vols. Cambridge: Cambridge University Press, 1976.

———. *Lloyds Bank in the History of English Banking*. Oxford: Clarendon Press, 1957.

———, ed. *Banking in Western Europe*. Oxford: Clarendon Press, 1962.

Scharf, J. Thomas. *History of Saint Louis City and County*. 2 vols. Philadelphia: Louis H. Everts, 1883.

Scheiber, Harry N., Harold Vatter, and Harold Underwood Faulkner. *American Economic History*. New York: Harper & Row, 1976.

Scherer, F. M. *Industrial Market Structure and Economic Performance*. Boston: Houghton Mifflin, 1980.

Schiff, Eric. *Industrialization without National Patents*. Princeton, N.J.: Princeton University Press, 1971.

Schneider, Jürgen. "German Investments in the USA (1872–1914)." Paper delivered at 1982 Fuji Conference.

Schooling, William. *Alliance Assurance, 1824–1924*. London: Alliance Assurance, 1924.

Schull, Joseph. *The Century of Sun*. Toronto: Macmillan of Canada, 1971.

Schulze-Gaevernitz, Gerhart von. "Die deutsche Kreditbank." In *Grundriss der Sozialökonomik*. Sec. 5, pt. 2. Tübingen: J. C. B. Mohr, 1915.

Schumpeter, Joseph A. *Business Cycles*. 2 vols. New York: McGraw-Hill, 1939.

———. *Imperialism and Social Classes*. New York: Augustus M. Kelley, 1951.

Schuwer, Philippe. *History of Advertising*. London: Leisure Arts, 1966.

Schwarz, Jordan. *The Speculator: Bernard M. Baruch in Washington, 1917–1965*. Chapel Hill: University of North Carolina Press, 1981.

Scott, J. D. *Siemens Brothers, 1858–1958*. London: Weidenfeld & Nicolson, 1958.

———. *Vickers*. London: Weidenfeld & Nicolson, 1962.

Scott, John, and Michael Hughes. *The Anatomy of Scottish Capital: Scottish Companies and Scottish Capital, 1900–1979*. London: Croom Helm, 1980.

Scott, W. R. *The Constitution and Finance of English, Scottish, and Irish Joint Stock Companies to 1720*. 3 vols. Cambridge: Cambridge University Press, 1912, 1910, 1911.

Scott, William A. *The Repudiation of State Debts*. New York: Thomas Y. Crowell, 1893.

"Scottish Capital Abroad." *Blackwood's Edinburgh Magazine*, 136 (1884): 468–480.

Scranton, Philip. *Proprietary Capitalism*. New York: Cambridge University Press, 1983.

Scrivenor, Harry. *History of the Iron Trade*. London: Longman, 1854.

Sedgwick, M. *Fiat*. London: Batsford, 1974.

Segal, Harvey H., and Matthew Simon. "British Foreign Capital Issues, 1865–1894." *Journal of Economic History*, 21 (1961): 567–581.

Seidenzahl, Fritz. *100 Jahre Deutsche Bank*. Frankfurt: Deutsche Bank, 1970.

Seybert, Adam. *Statistical Annals*. Philadelphia: Thomas Dobson, 1818.

Seyd, Ernest. "The Fall in the Price of Silver, Its Consequences and the Possible Avoidance." *Journal of the Society of the Arts*, 24 (1876): 306–334.

Sherman, John. *Recollections*. 2 vols. Chicago: Werner, 1895.

Sherrard, William Robert. "The Kirkland Steel Mill." *Pacific Northwest Quarterly*, 53 (1962): 129–137.

Shick, Tom W., and Don H. Doyle. "The South Carolina Phosphate Boom and the Stillbirth of the New South, 1867–1920." *South Carolina Historical Magazine*, 86 (1985): 1–31.

Shumway, Harry I. *Famous Leaders*. 4th ser. Boston: L. C. Page, 1936.

Shurtleff, Nathaniel B., ed. *Records of the Governor and Company of the Massachusetts Bay in New England*. Vol. 2. Boston: William White, 1853.

Siemens, Georg. *Carl Friedrich von Siemens*. Freiburg: Karl Alber, 1960.

———. *History of the House of Siemens*. 1957. 2 vols. Rpt. New York: Arno Press, 1977.

Siemens, Werner von. *Inventor and Entrepreneur*. London: Lund Humphries, 1966.

Simmons, Douglas A. *Schweppes*. London: Springwood Books, 1983.

Simon, Matthew. *Cyclical Fluctuations and the International Capital Movements of the United States, 1865–1897*. Ph.D. diss., 1955. New York: Arno Press, 1978.

———. "The Enterprise and Industrial Composition of New British Portfolio Foreign Investment, 1865–1914." *Journal of Development Studies*, 3 (1967): 280–292.

———. "The Pattern of New British Portfolio Foreign Investment, 1865–1914." In A. R. Hall, ed., *The Export of Capital from Britain, 1870–1914*. London: Methuen, 1968.

———. "The United States Balance of Payments, 1861–1900." In *Trends in the American Economy in the Nineteenth Century*. Studies in Income and Wealth, vol. 24, pp. 628–715. Princeton, N.J.: Princeton University Press, 1960.

Simpson, J. Dyer. *1936: Our Centenary Year*. London: Liverpool & London & Globe, 1936.

Smalley, Eugene V. *History of the Northern Pacific Railroad*. 1883. Rpt. New York: Arno Press, 1975.

Smith, Adam. *The Wealth of Nations*. 1776. Rpt. New York: Modern Library, 1937.

Smith, Alice E. *George Smith's Money: A Scottish Investor in America*. Madison: State Historical Society of Wisconsin, 1966.

Smith, Duane A. *Mining America: The Industry and the Environment, 1800–1980*. Lawrence: University Press of Kansas, 1987.

Smith, James. *The Development of Trust Companies in the United States*. New York: Henry Holt, 1928.

Smith, Sydney. *Letters on American Debts*. 2nd ed. London: Longman, Brown, Green & Longmans, 1844.

Smith, Walter Buckingham. *Economic Aspects of the Second Bank of the United States*. 1953. Rpt. New York: Greenwood Press, 1969.

Sobel, Robert. *The Big Board*. New York: Free Press, 1965.

Socolofsky, Homer E. *Landlord William Scully*. Lawrence: Regents Press of Kansas, 1979.

———. "William Scully: Ireland and America, 1840–1900." *Agricultural History*, 48 (1974): 155–175.

Soltow, J. H. "Scottish Traders in Virginia, 1750–1775." *Economic History Review*, 2nd ser., 12 (1959): 83–98.

Soule, George, and Vincent P. Carosso. *American Economic History*. New York: Dryden Press, 1957.

The South in the Building of the Nation. Vols. 5 and 6. Richmond, Va.: Southern Historical Publication Society, 1909.

Soutter, Arthur W. *The American Rolls-Royce*. Providence: Mowbray Company, 1976.

Spackman, William F. *Statistical Tables*. London: Longman, n.d. [1843].

Sparks, Earl Sylvester. *History and Theory of Agricultural Credit in the United States*. New York: Thomas Y. Crowell, 1932.

Speare, Charles F. "Foreign Investments of Nations." *North American Review*, 190 (1909): 82–92.

———. "Selling American Bonds in Europe." *Annals of the American Academy of Political and Social Science*, 30 (1907): 269–291.

Spence, Clark C. "British Investment and Oregon Mining, 1860–1900." *Oregon Historical Society, Portland, Quarterly*, 58 (1957): 101–112.

———"British Investment and the American Mining Frontier, 1860–1914." *New Mexico Historical Review*, 36 (1961): 121–137.

———. *British Investments and the American Mining Frontier, 1860–1901*. Ithaca, N.Y.: Cornell University Press, 1958.

———. *Mining Engineers and the American West: The Lace-Boot Brigade, 1849–1933*. New Haven: Yale University Press, 1970.

———. *The Sinews of American Capitalism*. New York: Hill & Wang, 1964.

Spender, J. A. *Weetman Pearson*. London: Cassell, 1930.

Spotswood, Alexander. *Official Letters*. 2 vols. Richmond: Virginia Historical Society, 1832.

Sprague, Marshall. *Money Mountain: The Story of Cripple Creek Gold*. Boston: Little, Brown, 1953.

Spurr, J. E. *Political and Commercial Geology and the World's Mineral Resources*. New York: McGraw-Hill, 1920.

Stacey, Nicolas A. H. *English Accountancy, 1800–1954*. London: Gee, 1954.

Staley, Eugene W. *Raw Materials in Peace and War*. 1937. Rpt. New York: Arno Press, 1976.

———. *War and the Private Investor*. Garden City, N.Y.: Doubleday, 1935.

Stalson, J. Owen. "The Pioneer in American Life Insurance Marketing." *Bulletin of the Business Historical Society*, 12 (1938): 65–75.

Stanwood, Edward. "Cotton Manufacture." In U.S. Department of Interior, Census

Office, *Report on Manufacturing Industries in the United States.* 11th Census, 1890, pt. 3, pp. 1–236. Washington, D.C., 1895.

Stedman, Edmund C. *The New York Stock Exchange.* 1905. Rpt. New York: Greenwood Press, 1969.

Steen, Herman. *Flour Milling in America.* Minneapolis: T. S. Denison, 1963.

Steiner, Henry J., and Detlev F. Vagts. *Transnational Legal Problems.* Mineola, N.Y.: Foundation Press, 1968.

Stern, Fritz. *Gold and Iron.* New York: Knopf, 1977.

Stern, Siegfried. *The United States in International Banking.* 1951. Rpt. New York: Arno Press, 1976.

Sterns, Worthy P. "The International Indebtedness of the United States in 1789." *Journal of Political Economy,* 5 (1897): 27–53.

Stevens, G. R. *History of the Canadian National.* New York: Macmillan, 1973.

Stevens, John Austin. *Colonial Records of the New York Chamber of Commerce.* 1867. Rpt. New York: Burt Franklin, 1971.

Stevens, Mark. *The Big Eight.* New York: Macmillan, 1981.

Stith, William. *History of Virginia.* 1747. Rpt. Spartanburg, N.C.: Reprint Co., 1965.

Stone, Irving. "British Direct and Portfolio Investment in Latin America." *Journal of Economic History,* 37 (1977): 690–722.

———. "British Long-Term Investment in Latin America, 1865–1913." *Business History Review,* 42 (1968): 311–339.

Stone, William L. *The Life and Times of Sir William Johnson, Bart.* Vols. 1 and 2. Albany: J. Munsell, 1865.

Stopford, John M. "The Origins of British-Based Multinational Manufacturing Enterprises." *Business History Review,* 48 (1974): 303–335.

Storck, John and Walter Dorwin Teague. *Flour for Man's Bread.* Minneapolis: Minnesota Press, 1952.

Stover, John F. *The Railroads of the South, 1865–1900.* Chapel Hill: University of North Carolina Press, 1955.

Strobel, Albrecht. "Aluminium-Industrie-Actien-Gesellschaft Neuhausen (A.I.A.G.) (today: Schweizerische Aluminiumindustrie AG-Alusuisse) and Its Multinational Activity, 1888–1914." Unpublished paper, 1983.

Studenski, Paul, and Herman E. Krooss. *Financial History of the United States.* 2nd ed. New York: McGraw-Hill, 1963.

Sullivan, Charles H. "The Alien Land Laws: A Re-Evaluation." *Temple Law Quarterly,* 36 (1962): 15–53.

Supple, Barry. "A Business Elite: German-Jewish Financiers in Nineteenth Century New York." *Business History Review,* 31 (1957): 143–178.

———. *The Royal Exchange Assurance: A History of British Insurance, 1720–1950.* Cambridge: Cambridge University Press, 1970.

Surrey, N. M. Miller. *The Commerce of Louisiana during the French Regime, 1699–1763.* New York: Columbia University Press, 1916.

Svedberg, Peter. "The Portfolio Direct Composition of Private Foreign Investment in 1914 Revisited." *Economic Journal,* 88 (1978): 763–777.

Swaine, Robert T. *The Cravath Firm and Its Predecessors.* 2 vols. New York: privately printed, 1946, 1948.

Swank, James Moore. *History of the Manufacture of Iron in All Ages.* Philadelphia: American Iron and Steel Association, 1892.

Swift, Louis F. *The Yankee of the Yards.* Chicago: A. W. Shaw, 1927.

Sylla, Richard E. *The American Capital Market, 1846–1914.* New York: Arno Press, 1975.

Tansill, Charles C. *America Goes to War.* 1938. Rpt. Gloucester, Mass.: Peter Smith, 1963.

Tariff Commission. *Report on the Iron and Steel Trades.* Vol. 1. London: P. S. King, 1904.

――――. *Report on the Textile Trades.* Vol. 2. London: P. S. King, 1905.

Taussig, F. W. *The Tariff History of the United States.* 8th rev. ed. New York: Capricorn, 1964.

Taylor, A. J. P. *Beaverbrook.* New York: Simon & Schuster, 1972.

Taylor, C. F., ed. *The Land Question from Various Points of View.* Philadelphia: C. F. Taylor, 1898.

Taylor, Graham D., and Patricia E. Sudnik. *DuPont and the International Chemical Industry.* Boston: Twayne, 1984.

Taylor, James. *Ellermans: A Wealth of Shipping.* London: Wilton House Gentry, 1976.

Taylor, James Karr. "Escheats under Statutes Disqualifying Aliens from Holding Property." Masters' thesis, Faculty of Law, Columbia University, 1935.

Taylor, Virginia H. *Franco-Texan Land Company.* Austin: University of Texas Press, 1969.

Teichova, Alice, Maurice Lévy-Leboyer, and Helga Nussbaum. *Multinational Enterprise in Historical Perspective.* Cambridge: Cambridge University Press, 1986.

Temin, Peter. *The Jacksonian Economy.* New York: Norton, 1969.

Thistlethwaite, Frank. *The Anglo-American Connection in the Early Nineteenth Century.* Philadelphia: University of Pennsylvania Press, 1959.

Thomas, A. P. *Woonsocket: Highlights of History, 1800–1976.* East Providence, R.I.: Globe Printing, 1976.

Thomas, Brinley. *International Migration and Economic Development.* Paris: UNESCO, 1961.

――――. *Migration and Economic Growth.* 1st and 2nd eds. London: Cambridge University Press, 1954, 1973.

――――. "Towards an Energy Interpretation of the Industrial Revolution." *Atlantic Economic Journal,* 8 (1980): 1–15.

――――, ed. *Economics of International Migration.* London: Macmillan, 1958.

Thomas, W. A. *The Provincial Exchanges.* London: Cass, 1973.

Thompson, John F., and Norman Beasley. *For the Years to Come: A Story of International Nickel of Canada.* New York: G. P. Putnam's, 1960.

Thomson, H. A., ed. *By Faith and Work: The Autobiography of the 1st Viscount Mackintosh of Halifax.* London: Hutchinson, 1966.

Threlfall, Richard E. *The Story of 100 Years of Phosphorus Making.* Oldbury: Albright & Wilson, 1951.

Thwaites, Reuben Gold. *France in America, 1497–1763.* New York: Harper & Bros., 1905.

Tilley, Nannie May. *The Bright-Tobacco Industry.* Chapel Hill: University of North Carolina, 1948.

Tilly, Richard H. *Financial Institutions and Industrialization in the Rhineland, 1815–1870.* Madison: University of Wisconsin Press, 1966.

――――. "Mergers, External Growth and Finance in the Development of Large Scale Enterprise in Germany, 1880–1913." *Journal of Economic History,* 42 (1982): 629–655.

Tindall, Robert E. *Multinational Enterprise.* Dobbs, Ferry, N.Y.: Oceania, 1975.

Tischendorf, Alfred P. "North Carolina and the British Investor, 1880–1910." *North Carolina Historical Review,* 32 (1955): 512–518.

Tolf, Robert W. *The Russian Rockefellers: The Saga of the Nobel Family.* Stanford, Calif.: Hoover Institution Press, 1976.

Tolley, B. H. "The Liverpool Campaign against the Order in Council and the War of 1812." In J. R. Harris, ed., *Liverpool and Merseyside,* pp. 98–146. London: Frank Cass, 1969.

Tombs, Laurence C. *International Organization in European Air Transport.* New York: Columbia University Press, 1936.

Tosdal, H. R. "The Kartell Movement in the German Potash Industry." *Quarterly Journal of Economics,* 28 (1913): 140–190.

Travis, Norman J., and E. J. Cocks. *The Tincal Trail: A History of Borax.* London: Harrap, 1984.

Travis, Norman J., and Carl L. Randolph. *United States Borax and Chemical Corporation.* New York: Newcomen, 1973.

Trebilcock, Clive. *Phoenix Assurance and the Development of British Insurance.* Vol. 1, *1782–1870.* Cambridge: Cambridge University Press, 1985.

———. *The Vickers Brothers: Armaments and Enterprise, 1854–1914.* London: Europa, 1977.

Trescott, Martha Moore. *The Rise of the American Electrochemicals Industry, 1880–1910.* Westport, Conn.: Greenwood Press, 1981.

Trevelyan, Raleigh. *Princes under the Volcano.* London: Macmillan, 1972.

Trotter, Alexander. *Observations on the Financial Position and Credit of Such of the States of the North American Union as Have Contracted Public Debts.* London: Longman, Orme, Brown, Green and Longmans, 1839.

Trottman, Nelson. *The History of the Union Pacific.* New York: Ronald Press, 1923.

Trump, Edward N. "Looking Back at 50 Years in the Ammonia-Soda Alkali Industry." *Chemical and Metallurgical Engineering,* 40 (1933): 126–129.

Truptil, R. J. *British Banks and the London Money Market.* London: Jonathan Cape, 1936.

Tugendhat, Christopher. *The Multinationals.* London: Eyre & Spottiswoode, 1971.

Turner, Graham. *Business in Britain.* Boston: Little, Brown, 1969.

Turrell, R. V., and Jean-Jacques Van Helten. "The Rothschilds, the Exploration Company and Mining Finance." *Business History,* 28 (1986): 181–205.

———, eds. *The City and the Empire.* Collected Seminar Papers no. 35. London: University of London, Institute of Commonwealth Studies, 1985.

Tweedale, Geoffrey. "Sheffield Steel and America." *Business History,* 25 (1983): 225–239.

———. "Sheffield Steel Industry and Its Allied Trades and the American Market, 1850–1913." Ph.D. diss., London School of Economics, 1983.

Tyson, R. E. "Scottish Investment in American Railways: The Case of the City of Glasgow Bank, 1856–1881." In Peter L. Payne, ed., *Studies in Scottish Business History.* London: Frank Cass, 1967.

United Nations. *International Capital Movements during the Inter-War Period.* Lake Success, N.Y.: United Nations, 1949.

U.S. Alien Property Custodian. *Report, 1918–1919.*

U.S. Bureau of the Census. *Historical Statistics of the United States.* Washington, D.C., 1960.

———. *Historical Statistics of the United States, Colonial Times to 1970.* 2 pts. Washington, D.C., 1975.

U.S. Bureau of Corporations. *Report on the Beef Industry.* Washington, D.C., 1905.

U.S. Census Office. *Report on Valuation, Taxation and Public Indebtedness of the United States—10th Census.* Washington, D.C., 1884.

U.S. Commissioner of Patents and Trademarks. *Annual Reports.* Washington, D.C.

U.S. Comptroller of the Currency. *Impact of Foreign Direct Investments: Case Studies in North and South Carolina.* Washington, D.C., 1976.

U.S. Comptroller General of the United States. *Despite Positive Effects, Further Foreign Acquisitions of U.S. Banks Should Be Limited.* Washington, D.C., 1980.

U.S. Congress. *American State Papers on Finance.* Vol. 1. Washington, D.C., 1832.

———. House. *Report from the Secretary of the Treasury on the Condition of State Banks*. 26th Cong., 1st sess., 1840. H. Doc. 172.

———. House. *Report of the Commissioner Sent to Europe to Negotiate a Loan for the Use of the United States*. 27th Cong., 3rd sess., 1843. H. Doc. 197.

———. House. 27th Cong., 3rd sess., 1843. H. Rept. 296.

———. House. 28th Cong., 1st sess., 1844. H. Doc. 15.

———. House. *Report from the Secretary of the Treasury on the Returns of the State Banks from 1841 to 1846*. 29th Cong., 1st sess., 1846. Exec. Doc. 226.

———. House. *Report of the Special Commissioner of Revenue*. 41st Cong., 2nd sess., 1870. Exec. Doc. 27.

———. House. *Gold Panic Investigation*. 41st Cong., 2nd sess., March 1, 1870. H. Rept. 31.

———. House. *Letter from the Secretary of Interior on the Entries of Public Lands by Foreign Companies*. 48th Cong., 1st sess., 1883–84. H. Exec. Doc. 165.

———. House. *Land Titles to Aliens in the United States*. 48th Cong., 2nd sess., Jan. 20, 1885. H. Rept. 2308.

———. House. 48th Cong., 2nd sess., 1885. Exec. Doc. 267. The Nimmo Report (see Nimmo, Joseph).

———. House. *Aliens Owning Lands in the United States*. 49th Cong., 1st sess., April 27, 1886. H. Rept. 1951.

———. House. *Report of the Committee on Public Lands on Ownership of Real Estate in the Territories*. 49th Cong., 1st sess., 1885–86. H. Rept. 3455.

———. House. *Report of the Committee on Mines and Mining to Amend the Alien Land Act*. 50th Cong., 1st sess., 1887–88. H. Rept. 703.

———. House. *Report of Committee on Public Lands on Sale to Aliens of Certain Mineral Lands*. 50th Cong., 1st sess., 1887–88. H. Rept. 3016.

———. House. *Report of the Committee on Mines and Mining to Amend the Alien Land Act*. 51st Cong., 1st sess., 1890. H. Rept. 1140.

———. House. *To Provide for . . . Radium Bearing Ores*. 63rd Cong., 2nd sess., Feb. 3, 1914. H. Rept. 214.

———. House. Committee on Banking and Currency. *Resumption of Specie Payments Hearings*. 45th Cong., 2nd sess., 1878. Misc. H. Doc. 62.

———. House. Committee on Banking and Currency, Subcommittee. *Money Trust Investigation, Hearings*. 62nd Cong., 2nd sess., 1912–1913. The Pujo Committee.

———. House. Committee on Banking and Currency, Subcommittee. *Report of the Committee to Investigate the Concentration of Control of Money and Credit*. 62nd Cong., 3rd sess., 1913. The Pujo Committee Report.

———. House. Committee on Foreign Affairs, Subcommittee on Foreign Economic Policy. *Direct Foreign Investment in the United States, Hearings*. 93rd Cong., 2nd sess., 1974. The Culver Committee.

———. House. Committee on Foreign Affairs, Subcommittee on Foreign Economic Policy. *Direct Foreign Investment in the United States, Report*. 93rd Cong., 2nd sess., 1974. The Culver Committee Report.

———. House. Committee on Government Operations. Subcommittee. *The Adequacy of the Federal Government Response to Foreign Investment in the United States*. 96th Cong., 2nd sess., 1980. The Rosenthal Committee Report.

———. House. Committee on Government Operations. Subcommittee. *The Operations of Federal Agencies in Monitoring, Reporting on, and Analyzing Foreign Investments in the United States*. Pts. 1–5. 95th Cong., 2nd sess., and 96th Cong., 1st sess., 1980. The Rosenthal Committee Hearings.

———. House. Committee on the Judiciary. *The Clayton Act, Hearings.* 63rd Cong., 2nd sess., 1914.

———. House. Committee on the Merchant Marine and Fisheries. *Free Ship Bill, Hearings.* 62nd Cong., 2nd sess., 1912.

———. House. Committee on the Merchant Marine and Fisheries. *Investigation of Shipping Combinations.* 62nd Cong., 1913.

———. House. Committee on the Merchant Marine and Fisheries. *Steamship Agreements and Affiliations in the American Foreign and Domestic Trade.* 63rd Cong., 1914.

———. House. Committee on the Merchant Marine and Fisheries. *Radio Communications, Hearings.* 64th Cong., 2nd sess., 1917.

———. House. Committee on Ways and Means. *Importation and Use of Opium, Hearings.* 61st Cong., 3rd sess., 1910–11.

———. House. Committee on Ways and Means. *Prohibiting the Importation of Opium for the Manufacture of Heroin, Hearings.* 68th Cong., 1st sess., 1924.

———. Senate. *Report of the Secretary of the Treasury.* 33rd Cong., 1st sess., 1854. Exec. Doc. 42.

———. Senate. *Report from the Commission of the General Land Office Concerning Entries of Public Lands by the Estes Park Company and Other Foreign Corporation.* 48th Cong., 1st sess., 1884. Exec. Doc. 181.

———. Senate. *Report of the Committee on Public Lands on Unauthorized Fencing of Public Lands.* 48th Cong., 1st sess., 1884. Exec. Doc. 127.

———. Senate. *Mining Interests of Aliens.* 50th Cong., 2nd sess., 1889. S. Rept. 2690.

———. Senate. *Oil Prospecting in Foreign Countries.* 67th Cong., 1st sess., 1921. S. Doc. 39.

———. Senate. Committee on Agriculture, Nutrition, and Forestry. *Foreign Investment in United States Agricultural Land.* 95th Cong., 2nd sess., 1979. Data collected for the Talmadge Committee.

———. Senate. Committee on Banking, Housing and Urban Affairs, Subcommittee on Financial Institutions. *Foreign Bank Act of 1975, Hearings.* 94th Cong., 2nd sess., 1976. The McIntyre Committee.

———. Senate. Committee on Banking, Housing and Urban Affairs, Subcommittee on International Finance. *Foreign Investment in the United States, Hearings,* 93rd Cong., 2nd sess., 1974. The Stevenson Committee.

———. Senate. Committee on Banking, Housing and Urban Affairs, Subcommittee on Securities. *Foreign Investment Act of 1975,* 94th Cong., 1st sess., 1975. The Williams Committee.

———. Senate. Committee on Commerce, Subcommittee on Foreign Commerce and Tourism. *Foreign Investment in the United States, Hearings.* 93rd Cong., 1st sess., 1973. The Inouye Committee.

———. Senate. Committee on Commerce, Subcommittee on Foreign Commerce and Tourism. *Foreign Investment in the United States, Hearings.* 93rd Cong., 2nd sess., 1974. The Inouye Committee.

———. Senate. Committee on Commerce, Subcommittee on Foreign Commerce and Tourism. *Foreign Investment Review Act of 1974, Hearings.* 93rd Cong., 2nd sess., 1974. The Inouye Committee.

———. Senate. Committee on Commerce, Subcommittee on Foreign Commerce and Tourism. *Foreign Investment Legislation, Hearings.* 94th Cong., 1st sess., 1975. The Inouye Committee.

———. Senate. Committee on Finance. *Sale of Foreign Bonds, Hearings.* 72nd Cong., 1st sess., 1931–32.

————. Senate. Committee on the Judiciary. *Alleged Dye Monopoly, Hearings.* 67th Cong., 1922.

————. Senate. Committee on Patents. *Patents Hearings.* 77th Cong., 2nd sess., 1942.

————. Senate. Committee on Patents. *Salvarsan, Hearings.* 65th Cong., 1st sess., 1917.

————. Senate. National Monetary Commission. *Digest of State Banking Statutes.* 61st Cong., 2nd sess., 1910. S. Doc. 353.

————. Senate. National Monetary Commission. *State Banking before the Civil War.* By Davis R. Dewey. 61st Cong., 2nd sess., 1910.

————. Senate. National Monetary Commission. *Trade Balance of the United States.* By George Paish. 61st Cong., 2nd sess., 1910. S. Doc. 579.

————. Senate. Special Committee Investigating the Munitions Industry. *Hearings,* pts. 1–40. 73rd and 74th Cong., 1934–1936. The Nye Committee.

————. Senate. Special Committee Investigating the Munitions Industry. *Munitions Industry.* Report no. 944, pts. 1–6. 74th Cong., 1st and 2nd sess., 1935–36. The Nye Committee Report.

U.S. Department of Agriculture. Economic, Statistics, and Cooperatives Service. *Foreign Ownership of U.S. Agricultural Land.* Agricultural Economic Report no. 447. Washington, D.C., 1980.

————. *Monitoring Foreign Ownership of U.S. Real Estate.* 3 vols. Washington, D.C., 1979.

————. *Yearbook, 1914.* Washington, D.C., 1915.

U.S. Department of Commerce. *Long Term Economic Growth, 1860–1965.* Washington, D.C., 1966.

————. *Foreign Direct Investment in the United States, Interim Report to Congress.* 2 vols. Washington, D.C., 1975.

————. *Foreign Direct Investment in the United States.* 9 vols. Washington, D.C., 1976.

————. Bureau of Foreign and Domestic Commerce. *British Investment Trusts.* Trade Information Bulletin no. 88. Washington, D.C., 1923.

————. Bureau of Foreign and Domestic Commerce. *The German Dyestuff Industries.* Misc. ser. 126. Washington, D.C., 1924.

————. Bureau of Foreign and Domestic Commerce. *Foreign Investments in the United States.* Washington, D.C., 1937.

————. Bureau of International Commerce. Office of International Investment. "List of Foreign Firms with Some Interest/Control in American Manufacturing and Petroleum Companies." Unpublished, July 1971.

U.S. Department of the Navy. *Annual Reports of Director of Communication.*

————. *Annual Reports of the Secretary.* 1913, 1914.

U.S. Department of State. *Foreign Relations of the United States.*

U.S. Department of the Treasury. *Annual Reports.* 1850–1914.

————. *Specie Resumption and Refunding of National Debt. Official Correspondence, Aug. 24, 1876 to Oct. 18, 1879.* 46th Cong., 2nd sess., 1880. H. Exec. Doc. 9.

————. *Summary of Federal Laws Bearing on Foreign Investment in the United States.* Washington, D.C., 1975.

————. *Taxation of Foreign Investment in U.S. Real Estate.* Washington, D.C., 1979. Thomas Horst Study.

————. Bureau of Statistics. *Commerce and Navigation of the United States.* Washington, D.C., 1878–1890.

U.S. Federal Energy Administration. Office of International Energy Affairs. *Report to Congress on Foreign Ownership, Control, and Influence on Domestic Energy Sources and Supply.* Washington, D.C., 1974.

U.S. Federal Trade Commission. *Report on Cooperation in American Export Trade.* 2 vols. Washington, D.C., 1916.
———. *Report on Foreign Ownership in the Petroleum Industry.* Washington, D.C., 1923.
———. *Report on Milk and Milk Products, 1914–1918.* Washington, D.C., 1921.
———. *Report on the Meatpacking Industry.* Summary and pt. 1. Washington, D.C., 1919.
———. *Report on the Radio Industry.* Washington, D.C., 1924.
———. *Report on the Petroleum Industry of Wyoming.* Washington, D.C., 1921.
U.S. General Accounting Office. "Emerging Concerns over Foreign Investment in the United States." Unpublished Staff Paper, 1975.
U.S. Industrial Commission. *Reports.* 19 vols. Washington, D.C., 1900–1902.
U.S. Securities and Exchange Commission. *Investment Trusts in Great Britain.* 76th Cong., 1st sess., 1939.
U.S. Tariff Commission. *Report on Dyes and Related Coal Tar Chemicals, 1918.* Rev. ed. Printed for use of Ways and Means Committee. Washington, D.C., 1918.
U.S. Temporary National Economic Committee. *Investigation of Concentration of Economic Power, Hearings* 76th Cong., 3rd sess., pt. 25 (Cartels), 1940.
———. *Investigation of the Concentration of Economic Power, Regulation of Economic Activity in Foreign Countries.* Monograph no. 29. 76th Cong., 3rd sess., 1940.
United States Borax & Chemical Corporation. *The Story of Borax.* Los Angeles: United States Borax & Chemical Corp., 1979.
Vagts, Detlev F. "The Corporate Alien: Definitional Questions in Federal Restraints on Foreign Enterprise." *Harvard Law Review,* 74 (1961): 1489–1551.
Vaizey, John. *The Brewing Industry, 1886–1951.* London: Sir Isaac Pitman, 1960.
Vale, Vivian. *The American Peril: Challenge to Britain on the North Atlantic, 1901–04.* Manchester, University Press, 1984.
Van der Haas, H. *The Enterprise in Transition: An Analysis of European and American Practice.* London: Tavistock, 1967.
Van der Zee, Jacob. *The British In Iowa.* Iowa City: State Historical Society of Iowa, 1922.
Van Winter, Pieter J. *American Finance and Dutch Investment, 1780–1805.* 2 vols. New York: Arno Press, 1977.
Veenendaal, Augustus J., Jr. "The Kansas City Southern Railway and the Dutch Connection." *Business History Review,* 61 (1987): 291–316.
———. "Railroads, Oil and Dutchmen." *Chronicles of Oklahoma,* 63 (1985): 4–27.
Vernon, Raymond. *Big Business and the State.* Cambridge, Mass.: Harvard University Press, 1974.
———. "The Location of Economic Activity." In John Dunning, ed., *Economic Analysis and the Multinational Enterprise.* London: George Allen & Unwin, 1974.
———. "The Product Cycle Hypothesis in a New International Environment." *Oxford Bulletin of Economics and Statistics,* 41, (1979): 255–267.
———. *Storm over the Multinationals.* Cambridge, Mass.: Harvard University Press, 1977.
Vila, Adis M. "Legal Aspects of Foreign Direct Investments in the United States." *International Lawyer,* 16 (1982): 1–49.
Villard, Henry. *Memoirs of Henry Villard.* 2 vols. Boston: Houghton Mifflin, 1904.
Viner, Jacob. *Canada's Balance of International Indebtedness, 1900–1913.* Cambridge, Mass.: Harvard University Press, 1924.
———. "International Finance and Balance of Power Diplomacy, 1880–1914." *Southwestern Political and Social Science Quarterly,* 9 (1929): 407–451.
———. "Political Aspects of International Finance." *Journal of Business,* 1 (1928): 141–173.

———. "Political Aspects of International Finance, II." *Journal of Business*, 1 (1928): 324–363.

———. *Studies in the Theory of International Trade*. 1937. Rpt. Clifton, N.J.: Augustus M. Kelley, 1975.

Waldmann, Raymond T. *Direct Investment and Development in the United States*. Washington, D.C.: Transnational Investments, 1979.

Walker, James. *Epic of American Industry*. New York: Harper & Bros., 1949.

Wall, Bennett H., and George S. Gibb. *Teagle of Jersey Standard*. New Orleans: Tulane University, 1974.

Wall, Joseph Frazier. *Andrew Carnegie*. New York: Oxford University Press, 1970.

Wallace, Benjamin B., and Lynn Ramsay Edminster. *International Control of Raw Materials*. Washington, D.C., Brookings Institution, 1930.

Wallace, Don, Jr., ed. *International Control of Investment*. New York: Praeger, 1974.

Wallace, Donald H. *Market Control in the Aluminum Industry*. Cambridge, Mass.: Harvard University Press, 1937.

Wallich, Hermann, and Paul Wallich. *Zwei Generationen im deutschen Bankwesen, 1833–1914*. Frankfurt: Fritz Knapp, 1978.

Walton, Gary M., and James F. Shepherd. *The Economic Rise of Early America*. Cambridge, Mass.: Cambridge University Press, 1979.

Warren, Charles. *Bankruptcy and American History*. Cambridge, Mass.: Harvard University Press, 1935.

Waugh, Alec. *The Lipton Story*. Garden City, N.Y.: Doubleday, 1950.

Webster, Daniel. *Works*. Vols. 3 and 4. 8th ed. Boston: H. G. Brown, 1854.

Webster, Norman E. *The American Association of Public Accountants*. New York: Arno Press, 1978.

Wechsberg, Joseph. *The Merchant Bankers*. Boston: Little, Brown, 1976.

Weir, Ronald B. *History of the Scottish-American Investment Co., Limited, 1873–1973*. Edinburgh: Scottish-American Investment Co., 1973.

Wells, F. A. *Hollins and Viyella*. Newton Abbot: David & Charles, 1968.

Wells, Linton. "House of Seligman." Microfilm of unpublished typescript, 1931. New York Historical Society, New York.

Welsh, Donald H. "Pierre Wibaux: Bad Lands Rancher." Ph.D. diss., University of Missouri, 1955.

Werking, Richard Hume. *The Master Architects: Building the United States Foreign Service, 1890–1913*. Lexington: University of Kentucky Press, 1977.

Westerman, J. C. *The Netherlands and the United States*. The Hague: Martinus Nijhoff, 1935.

Westphall, Victor. *Public Domain in New Mexico, 1854–1891*. Albuquerque: University of New Mexico Press, 1965.

White, Gerald T. *Formative Years in the Far West: A History of Standard Oil of California and Predecessors through 1919*. New York: Appleton-Century-Crofts, 1962.

White, Harry Dexter. *The French International Accounts, 1880–1913*. 1933. Rpt. New York: Arno Press, 1978.

Whitely, William G. [mistake for Henry Whitely, corrected in third article]. "The Principio Company" *Pennsylvania Magazine of History and Biography*, 11 (1887): 63–68, 190–198, 288–295.

Wilgus, William J. *The Railway Interrelations of the United States and Canada*. New Haven: Yale University Press, 1937.

Wilkins, Mira. "American-Japanese Direct Foreign Investment Relationships, 1930–1952." *Business History Review*, 56 (1982): 497–518.

———. "Crosscurrents: American Investments in Europe, European Investments in the United States." *Business and Economic History*, 2nd ser., 6 (1977): 22–35.

———. *The Emergence of Multinational Enterprise: American Business Abroad from the Colonial Era to 1914*. Cambridge, Mass.: Harvard University Press, 1970.

———. "European Multinationals in the United States: 1875–1914." In Alice Teichova et al., eds., *Multinational Enterprise in Historical Perspective*, pp. 55–64. Cambridge: Cambridge University Press, 1986.

———. *Foreign Enterprise in Florida*. Gainesville: University Presses of Florida, 1979.

———. "The Free Standing Company, 1870–1914." *Economic History Review*, 2nd ser., 41 (1988): 259–282.

———. "The History of European Multinational Enterprise: A New Look." *Journal of European Economic History*, 15 (1986): 483–510.

———. "The Internationalization of the Corporation—The Case of Oil." In K. E. Lindgren, H. H. Mason, and B. L. J. Gordon, eds., *The Corporation and Australian Society*, pp. 276–290. Sydney: Law Book Co., 1974.

———. "Japanese Multinational Enterprise before 1914." *Business History Review*, 60 (1986): 199–231.

———. *The Maturing of Multinational Enterprise: American Business Abroad from 1914 to 1970*. Cambridge, Mass.: Harvard University Press, 1974.

———. "Modern European Economic History and the Multinationals." *Journal of European Economic History*, 6 (1977): 575–595.

———. "Multinational Automobile Enterprises and Regulations: An Historical Overview." In Douglas Ginsburg and William J. Abernathy, eds., *Government, Technology, and the Future of the Automobile*, pp. 221–258. New York: McGraw-Hill, 1978.

———. "The Role of Private Business in the International Diffusion of Technology." *Journal of Economic History*, 34 (1974): 166–188.

———, ed. *British Overseas Investments, 1907–1948*. New York: Arno Press, 1977.

———, ed. *European Foreign Investments, as Seen by the Department of Commerce*. New York: Arno Press, 1977.

———, ed. *Foreign Investment in the United States*. New York: Arno Press, 1977.

Wilkins, Mira, and Frank Ernest Hill. *American Business Abroad: Ford on Six Continents*. Detroit: Wayne State University Press, 1964.

Williams, Benjamin H. *Economic Foreign Policy of the United States*. New York: McGraw-Hill, 1929.

Williams, D. M. "Liverpool Merchants and the Cotton Trade, 1820–1850." In J. R. Harris, ed., *Liverpool and Merseyside*, pp. 182–211. London: Frank Cass, 1969.

Williams, Iolo A. *The Firm of Cadbury, 1831–1931*. London: Constable, 1931.

Williamson, Harold F., ed. *Evolution of International Management Structures*. Newark: University of Delaware Press, 1975.

———, ed. *The Growth of the American Economy*. 2nd ed. Englewood Cliffs, N.J.: Prentice-Hall, 1951.

Williamson, Harold F., et al. *The American Petroleum Industry, 1899–1959*. Evanston, Ill.: Northwestern University Press, 1963.

Williamson, Harold F., and Arnold R. Daum. *The American Petroleum Industry, 1859–1899*. Evanston, Ill.: Northwestern University Press, 1959.

Williamson, Jeffrey G. *American Growth and the Balance of Payments, 1820–1913*. Chapel Hill: University of North Carolina Press, 1964.

———. *Late Nineteenth Century American Development*. Cambridge: Cambridge University Press, 1974.

Williamson, John G. *Karl Helfferich, 1872–1924*. Princeton, N.J.: Princeton University Press, 1971.

Williamson, Oliver E. *Corporate Control and Business Behavior*. Englewood Cliffs, N.J.: Prentice-Hall, 1970.

———. *The Economic Institutions of Capitalism*. New York: Free Press, 1985.

———. *Markets and Hierarchies: Analysis and Antitrust Implications: A Study in the Economics of Internal Organization*. New York: Free Press, 1975.

———. "Microanalytic Business History." *Business and Economic History*, 2nd ser., 11 (1982): 106–115.

———. "The Modern Corporation: Origins, Evolution, Attributes." *Journal of Economic Literature*, 19 (1981): 1537–68.

Willis, H. Parker, and Jules I. Bogen. *Investment Banking*. 1936. Rpt. New York: Arno Press, 1975.

Willson, Beckles. *The Life of Lord Strathcona and Mount Royal*. 2 vols. Boston: Houghton Mifflin, 1915.

Wilmot, John Eardley. *Historical View of the Commission for Enquiring into the Losses, Services, and Claims of the American Loyalists, at the Close of the War between Great Britain and Her Colonies in 1783*. London: J. Nichols, Son, & Bentley, 1815.

Wilson, Charles. *Anglo-Dutch Commerce and Finance in the Eighteenth Century*. Cambridge: Cambridge University Press, 1941.

———. *The History of Unilever*. 3 vols. New York: Frederick A. Praeger, 1968.

Wilson, J. S. G. *French Banking Structure and Credit Policy*. Cambridge, Mass.: Harvard University Press, 1957.

Wilson, Ross. *Scotch: The Formative Years*. London: Constable, 1970.

Wiman, Erastus. "British Capital and American Industries." *North American Review*, 150 (1890): 220–234.

Winston, W. E., and R. W. Columb. "How the Louisiana Purchase Was Financed." *Louisiana Historical Quarterly*, 12 (1929): 189–237.

Wise, T. A. *Peat, Marwick, Mitchell & Co.: 85 Years*. N.p.: Peat, Marwick, Mitchell, 1982.

Wolvekamp-Baxter, Brenda M. "New Mexico, 1883: The Maxwell Grant and the Cimarron Country in the Letters of Albert Verwey." *New Mexico Historical Review*, 54 (1979): 125–147.

Woodruff, William. *Impact of Western Man*. New York: St. Martin's Press, 1967.

Woodward, C. Vann. *Origins of the New South, 1877–1933*. Baton Rouge: Lousiana State University Press, 1951.

World Bank. *World Development Report 1985* (*International Capital and Economic Development*). New York: Oxford University Press, 1985.

World's Columbian Exposition. *Guide to the Exhibits of the American Wool Manufacturers*. Chicago, 1893.

Woytinsky, W. S., and E. S. Woytinsky. *World Commerce and Government*. New York: Twentieth Century Fund, 1955.

Wray, William D. *Mitsubishi and the N.Y.K., 1870–1914: Business Strategy and the Japanese Shipping Industry*. Cambridge, Mass.: Harvard University Press, 1984.

Wrenn, John H. *John Dos Passos*. New York: Twayne, 1961.

Wright, Benj. C. *Banking in California, 1849–1910*. San Francisco: H. S. Crocker, 1910.

Wright, Helena E. *The Merrimack Valley Textile Museum: A Guide to Manuscript Collections*. New York: Garland, 1983.

Wright, Ivan. *Farm Mortgage Financing*. New York: McGraw-Hill, 1923.

Wyckoff, William C. *American Silk Manufacture*. New York: Silk Association of America, 1887.

———. *Silk Goods of America*. 2nd ed. New York: Silk Association of America, 1880.

———. *Silk Manufacture in the United States.* New York, 1883.

Yeager, Leland B. *International Monetary Relations.* New York: Harper & Row, 1966.

Yeager, Mary. *Competition and Regulation: The Development of Oligopoly in the Meatpacking Industry.* Greenwich, Conn.: JAI Press, 1981.

Yokohama Specie Bank. *The History of the Yokohama Specie Bank.* Tokyo, 1920. In Japanese.

Young, Alexander K. *The Sogo Shosha: Japan's Multinational Trading Company.* Boulder, Colo.: Westview Press, 1979.

Young, James Harvey. *The Medical Messiahs.* Princeton, N.J.: Princeton University Press, 1967.

———. *Toadstool Millionaires.* Princeton, N.J.: Princeton University Press, 1961.

Yui, Tsunehiko, and Keiichiro Nakagawa. *Business History of Shipping.* Tokyo: University of Tokyo Press, 1985.

Zartman, Lester W., ed. *Yale Readings in Insurance: Fire Insurance.* New Haven: Yale University Press, 1909.

———. *Yale Readings in Insurance: Life Insurance.* New Haven: Yale University Press, 1909.

Zimmerman, W. D. "Live Cattle Export Trade between the United States and Great Britain, 1868–1885." *Agricultural History,* 36 (1962): 46–52.

Zimmermann, Erich W. *World Resources and Industries.* New York: Harper & Bros., 1933.

Newspapers, Journals, Directories, Bulletins, Encyclopedias

Advertising Age
American Cutler
American Iron and Steel Association Bulletin
American Silk Goods Directory
Annalist
Annals of the American Academy of Political and Social Science
Arthur Young Journal
Bankers' Magazine, London
Banker's Magazine, New York (title varies)
Best's Insurance Reports (Casualty and Miscellaneous)
Best's Insurance Reports (Fire and Marine)
Best's Insurance Reports (Life)
Blackwood'ʲ Edinburgh Magazine
Bradstreet's
Buffalo City Directories
Bulletin de l'Institut International de Statistique
Bulletin of the National Association of Wool Manufacturers
Burdett's Official Intelligence
Burke's Peerage and Baronetage
Business History
Business History Review
Cigarette World and Tobacco News
Commercial and Financial Chronicle
Contemporary Review
Dictionary of American Biography
Dictionary of Business Biography
Dictionary of National Biography
Directory of Directors

Directory of Foreign Firms Operating in the United States, 1971
Economist
Encyclopedia of the Social Sciences
Encyclopedia of World History
Engineering and Mining Journal
Federal Reserve Bulletin
Financial News
Financial Times
Fortnightly Review
Harper Encyclopedia of the Modern World
Hunt's Merchant Magazine
Insurance Yearbook
International Encyclopedia of the Social Sciences
Investment Bankers' Association Annual Reports
Investors' Review
Issues Advertised in the Times
Journal of Economic History
Journal of the Royal Society
Journal of the Society of the Arts
Mineral Industry
Mining Journal
Mining Manual
Mining World
Moody's Industrial Manual (title varies)
Moody's Manual of Public Utilities (title varies)
Moody's Manual of Railroads (title varies)
Nation, London
Nation, New York
National Cyclopedia of American Biography
New York State Superintendent of Banking, Annual Reports
New York State Superintendent of Banking, Annual Reports Relative to Foreign Mortgage,
        Loan, Investment, and Trust Companies
New York Times
Niles' National Register
Niles' Weekly Register
North American Review
Northwestern Miller
Oil and Petroleum Manual
Saturday Evening Post
Sears, Roebuck Catalogues
Silk Association of America Annual Reports
Statist
Stock Exchange Official Intelligence
Stock Exchange Year Book
Survey of Current Business
Times, London
Wall Street Journal
Who's Who in America
Who Was Who in America

Index